Preface

The stepwise refinement method postulates a system construction route that starts with some relatively high-level specification, goes through a number of provably correct development steps, each of which replaces some declarative, non-executable (or merely inefficient) aspects of the specification by imperative executable constructs, and ends with an (efficiently) executable program.

In the past decade, this paradigm has generated an extremely active research area. The proceedings of this workshop are intended to survey the state of the art in this area, both from the theoretical and from the practical side. The following topics were discussed:

Models: What are the features of a specification that may change during refinement and what features should be maintained? Trace based refinement concentrates on the sequences of system actions. Yet others maintain that the ability to make certain choices during computations should be maintained during refinement. Then again, maybe such decisions should follow from the interactions that are possible between systems. Other important topics are independence and interface refinement. Refinement notions for distributed systems should express that parts of such systems act independently and concurrently from each other.

Also, during development not only a system's control changes but also a system's interface, e.g., an event may become a signal on a serial port. This is an extremely important topic that is only now starting to be addressed by researchers.

Formalisms: What constitutes a good formalism to specify systems and their development? Much of the theoretical research has used various artificial programming languages. But, also the use of various forms of transition systems or automata has been proposed, and is becoming increasingly popular for specifying complicated systems. In that case, should one specify system behavior by giving the concrete automata that generate it or should one give such automata in a more abstract way, e.g. by specifying the possible transitions by assertional means. Other viable options are the use of temporal logic and of algebraic specifications as formalisms.

Correctness: How is a program-development step verified? The answer is to a large extent determined by the formalism that is used and the refinement notion that is adopted. Much theoretical work has concentrated on equational axiomatizations of refinement notions, thus giving rise to calculi on program terms. Using automata engenders the use of simulation relations with which to prove refinement; a method which may come closer to the operational intuitions of an implementor. Temporal logic-like formalisms need first order proof systems, while (equational) algebraic specifications make use of rewrite systems or theorem provers.

The material presented in this volume was prepared after the workshop took place by the lecturers, their co-authors, and some of the observers — in this way the results of the discussions during the workshop could be reflected in the proceedings. We are proud that we had such an excellent group of lecturers and we believe that this volume represents rather completely the state of the research in this field at the moment. We are very grateful to the lecturers and the other participants for making the workshop a scientific and social success. We wish to thank R. Gerth, A. Pnueli, R. van Glabbeek, E.-R. Olderog, C. Courcoubetis, and L. Lamport for their help in suggesting speakers and in defining the format of this workshop.

Judging by the number of Dutch authors in the present volume and the quality of their contributions, in our own opinion this volume demonstrates that the extra funding by the Dutch Government of computer science in the Netherlands in general, and of the field of concurrency in particular, is bearing fruit. We gratefully acknowledge the financial support from our funding agency, the Netherlands National Facility for Informatics (NFI).

We thank the Eindhoven University of Technology for the technical organisation of the workshop and its financial support. We want to extend our special thanks to E. van Thiel-Niekoop and A. Smulders for their organisational assistance, and to Ron Koymans and Kees Huizing for taking the burden of the local organisation upon their shoulders at late notice.

We believe that it is no coincidence that the participants were boarded in Hotel de Plasmolen and Hotel de Molenhoek; the Dutch word "molen" means mill, one of mankind's earliest refinement devices.

March 1990

The editors

J.W. de Bakker
W.P. de Roever
G. Rozenberg

The REX project

The REX — **R**esearch and **E**ducation in **C**oncurrent **S**ystems — project investigates syntactic, semantic and proof-theoretic aspects of concurrency. In addition, its objectives are the education of young researchers and, in general, the dissemination of scientific results relating to these themes. REX is a collaborative effort of the Leiden University (G. Rozenberg), the Centre for Mathematics and Computer Science in Amsterdam (J.W. de Bakker), and the Eindhoven University of Technology (W.P. de Roever), representing the areas of syntax, semantics and proof theory, respectively. The project is supported by the Netherlands National Facility for Informatics (NFI); its expected duration is four years starting in 1988. In the years 1984-1988, the same groups worked together in the Netherlands National Concurrency Project (LPC), supported by the Netherlands Foundation for the Advancement of Pure Research (ZWO). The research activities of the REX project include, more specifically:

1. Three subprojects devoted to the themes:
   - syntax of concurrent systems: a graph oriented framework for structures and processes
   - process theory and the semantics of parallel logic programming languages
   - high-level specification and refinement of real-time distributed systems.
2. Collaboration with visiting professors and post-doctoral researchers, in particular focused on the research themes mentioned above. In 1989/1990 these visitors include Dr. E.-R. Olderog (Kiel), Dr. W. Penczek (Warsaw), and Prof. P.S. Thiagarajan (Madras).
3. Workshops and Schools. In 1988 we organised a school/workshop on "Linear Time, Branching Time and Partial Order in Logics and Models for Concurrency"; its proceedings appeared as Lecture Notes in Computer Science, Vol. 354, Springer, 1989. The workshop on "Stepwise Refinement of Distributed Systems" in 1989 is the second in a series of such events. For 1990, we plan a work shop on "Foundations of Object-oriented Languages" (FOOL).

The educational activities of REX include regular "concurrency days". A concurrency day may consist of tutorial introductions to selected topics, and of presentations of research results to a non-specialist audience. Often, experts from abroad are invited to contribute to these days. In addition, visiting professors are asked to present lecture series concerning recent developments in their fields of specialization. Clearly, the school/workshops have the additional important function of providing their participants with an intensive introduction to new areas.

Finally, we mention another aspect of the REX project. We are continuing the regular contacts with other European projects in the area of concurrency built up during the LPC years. In particular, this applies to the French C^3 – Cooperation, Communication, Concurrency – program, to the British Computer Society – the Formal Aspects of Computer Science group – and to groups within the Gesellschaft für Mathematik und Datenverarbeitung (GMD) in Bonn.

We would like to conclude this brief presentation of the future of the REX project by inviting everyone who is interested in more information concerning REX (possibility of visits, plans for workshops, other forms of exchanges, etc.) to write to one of the project leaders.

J.W. de Bakker
W.P. de Roever
G. Rozenberg

List of participants

Ralph Back, Åbo Akademi

Jaco de Bakker, C.W.I.

Howard Barringer, Manchester Univ.

Frank de Boer, C.W.I.

Ed Brinksma, Twente Univ.

Manfred Broy, Passau Univ.

Tineke de Bunje, Philips Res. Labs.

Jos Coenen, T.U. Eindhoven

Costas Courcoubetis, Crete Univ.

Werner Damm, Oldenburg Univ.

Eduard Diepstraten, T.U. Eindhoven

Hans-Dieter Ehrich, T.U. Braunschweig

Hartmut Ehrig, T.U. Berlin

Rob Gerth, T.U. Eindhoven

Rob van Glabbeek, C.W.I.

Ursula Goltz, G.M.D.

He Jifeng, Oxford Univ.

Wim Hesselink, Groningen Univ.

Hendrik Jan Hoogeboom, Leiden Univ.

Jozef Hooman, T.U. Eindhoven

Kees Huizing, T.U. Eindhoven

Bernhard Josko, Oldenburg Univ.

Bengt Jonsson, Swed. Inst. CS

Joost Kok, Utrecht Univ.

Ron Koymans, T.U. Eindhoven

Ruurd Kuiper, T.U. Eindhoven

Bob Kurshan, AT&T Bell Labs.

Simon Lam, Texas Univ.

Leslie Lamport, Dig. Res. Center

Kim Larsen, Aalborg Univ.

Nancy Lynch, M.I.T.

Michael Merritt, AT&T Bell Labs.

Carroll Morgan, Oxford Univ.

Tobias Nipkow, Cambridge Univ.

Ernst-Rüdiger Olderog, Chr. Albrecht Univ.

Paritosh Pandya, Tata Inst.

Amir Pnueli, Weizmann Inst.

Lucia Pomello, Milan Univ.

Wolfgang Reisig, T.U. Munich

Willem Paul de Roever, T.U. Eindhoven

Marly Roncken, Philips Res. Labs.

Grzegorz Rozenberg, Leiden Univ.

Udaya Shankar, Maryland Univ.

Joseph Sifakis, IMAG

Frank Stomp, Nijmegen Univ.

Jeannette Wing, C.M.U.

Ping Zhou, T.U. Eindhoven

Job Zwiers, Philips Res.Labs.

Contents

Preface iii

About the REX project v

List of participants vii

Invited lecture **1**

M. Abadi, L. Lamport
Composing Specifications 1

Technical Contributions **42**

R.J.R. Back, J. von Wright
Refinement Calculus, Part I: Sequential Nondeterministic Programs 42

R.J.R. Back
Refinement Calculus, Part II: Parallel and Reactive Programs 67

H. Barringer, M. Fisher, D. Gabbay, G. Gough, R. Owens
METATEM: A Framework for Programming in Temporal Logic 94

E. Brinksma
Constraint-Oriented Specification in a Constructive Formal Description Technique 130

M. Broy
Functional Specification of Time Sensitive Communicating Systems 153

W. Damm, G. Döhmen, V. Gerstner, B. Josko
Modular Verification of Petri Nets: The Temporal Logic Approach 180

E. Diepstraten, R. Kuiper
Abadi & Lamport and Stark: towards a Proof Theory for Stuttering, Dense Domains and Refinement Mappings 208

H.-D. Ehrich, A. Sernadas
Algebraic Implementation of Objects over Objects 239

R. van Glabbeek, U. Goltz
Refinement of Actions in Causality Based Models 267

M. Große-Rhode, H. Ehrig
Transformation of Combined Data Type and Process Specifications Using Projection Algebras 301

He Jifeng
Various Simulations and Refinements 340

B. Jonsson
On Decomposing and Refining Specifications of Distributed Systems 361

B. Josko
Verifying the Correctness of AADL Modules Using Model Checking 386

J.N. Kok
Specialization in Logic Programming: from Horn Clause Logic to Prolog and Concurrent Prolog . . . 401

R.P. Kurshan
Analysis of Discrete Event Coordination . . . 414

S.S. Lam, A.U. Shankar
Refinement and Projection of Relational Specifications . . . 454

K.G. Larsen
Compositional Theories Based on an Operational Semantics of Contexts . 487

N.A. Lynch
Multivalued Possibilities Mappings . . . 519

M. Merritt
Completeness Theorems for Automata . . . 544

T. Nipkow
Formal Verification of Data Type Refinement — Theory and Practice . . . 561

E.-R. Olderog
From Trace Specifications to Process Terms . . . 592

P.K. Pandya
Some Comments on the Assumption-Commitment Framework for Compositional Verification of Distributed Programs . . . 622

L. Pomello
Refinement of Concurrent Systems Based on Local State Transformations . 641

A.U. Shankar, S.S. Lam
Construction of Network Protocols by Stepwise Refinement . . . 669

F.A. Stomp
A Derivation of a Broadcasting Protocol Using Sequentially Phased Reasoning . . . 696

J.M. Wing
Verifying Atomic Data Types . . . 731

J. Zwiers
Predicates, Predicate Transformers and Refinement . . . 759

R. Gerth
Foundations of Compositional Program Refinement — Safety Properties . 777

Composing Specifications

Martín Abadi Leslie Lamport

Digital Equipment Corporation
130 Lytton Avenue
Palo Alto, California 94301, USA

Abstract

A rigorous modular specification method requires a proof rule asserting that if each component behaves correctly in isolation, then it behaves correctly in concert with other components. Such a rule is subtle if a component need behave correctly only when its environment does, since each component is part of the others' environments. We examine the precise distinction between a system and its environment, and provide the requisite proof rule when modules are specified with safety and liveness properties.

Contents

1 **Introduction** **3**
- 1.1 States versus Actions . . . 3
- 1.2 System versus Environment . . . 4
- 1.3 Specifying the Environment . . . 5
- 1.4 Composition and Proof . . . 6
- 1.5 Semantics versus Logic . . . 6

2 **The Semantic Model** **7**

3 **Realizability** **10**
- 3.1 Safety Properties . . . 11
- 3.2 Realizability of Arbitrary Properties . . . 11
  - 3.2.1 Definitions . . . 11
  - 3.2.2 Consequences of the Definitions . . . 13
  - 3.2.3 Some Results about Realizability . . . 14

4 **The Form of a Specification** **15**
- 4.1 The Form of a Complete Program . . . 15
  - 4.1.1 The Parts of a Complete Program . . . 15
  - 4.1.2 The Progress Property . . . 16
- 4.2 The Form of a Partial Program . . . 18
  - 4.2.1 The Parts of a Partial Program . . . 18
  - 4.2.2 Hiding the Internal State . . . 21
- 4.3 The Normal Form of a Specification . . . 23
- 4.4 An Overly Normal Form . . . 25

5 **Composing Specifications** **26**
- 5.1 The Composition of Specifications . . . 26
  - 5.1.1 Assumptions about the States . . . 27
  - 5.1.2 Assumptions about the Agents . . . 28
- 5.2 Implementing One Specification by Another . . . 29
  - 5.2.1 Definition . . . 29
  - 5.2.2 Proving That One Specification Implements Another . . . 30
- 5.3 The Main Theorem . . . 32
  - 5.3.1 Deriving a Theorem from Necessity . . . 32
  - 5.3.2 The Hypotheses of the Theorem . . . 35
  - 5.3.3 The Hypotheses of the Proof Rule . . . 36

6 **Concluding Remarks** **37**

References **38**

1 Introduction

The transition-axiom method specifies concurrent systems by a combination of abstract programs and temporal logic [Lam89]. It permits a hierarchical approach in which the composition of lower-level specifications is proved to implement a higher-level specification. The method for proving that one specification implements another was discussed in [AL88]. Here, we examine how specifications are composed. Although we are interested primarily in the transition-axiom method, our results can be applied to several other specification methods as well [LS84a, LT87].

Attempts at modular reasoning about composite specifications must provide an answer to the following fundamental question. Assume that each component i behaves correctly when its environment satisfies an assumption E_i, and that the correct behavior of the other components implies that assumption E_i is satisfied. Under what conditions can we conclude that all the components behave correctly in the composite system? This question was answered by Misra and Chandy [MC81] with a proof rule for specifications of safety properties of processes communicating by means of CSP primitives. Pnueli [Pnu84], considering a different class of programs, gave a more general proof rule that handled liveness properties with an explicit induction step. (Pnueli also had a general rule that did not require induction, but it did not permit the separation of component requirements from environment assumptions.) By examining the precise distinction between a system and its environment, we develop a simple proof rule (without induction) that handles arbitrary properties, providing what we believe to be a completely satisfactory answer to the question.

1.1 States versus Actions

The popular approaches to specification are based on either states or actions. In a state-based approach, an execution of a system is viewed as a sequence of states, where a state is an assignment of values to some set of components. An action-based approach views an execution as a sequence of actions. These different approaches are, in some sense, equivalent. An action can be modeled as a state change, and a state can be modeled as an equivalence class of sequences of actions. However, the two approaches have traditionally taken very different formal directions. State-based approaches are often rooted in logic, a specification being a formula in some logical system. Action-based approaches have tended to use algebra, a specification being an object that is manipulated algebraically [Mil80].

State-based and action-based approaches also tend to differ in practice. To specify keyboard input using an action-based approach, the typing of a single character might be represented as a single action. In our state-based approach, it would be represented by two separate state changes: the key is first depressed and then released. An action-based representation often appears simpler—pressing a key is one action instead of two state changes. But this simplicity can be deceptive. A specification in which typing a character is a single action does not provide for the real situation in which a second key is depressed before the first is released. We have no reason to expect actions to be simpler than states for accurately describing real systems. We have found that a state-based approach forces a close examination of how the real system is represented in the model, helping to avoid oversimplification. On the other hand, there are circumstances in which oversimplified models are useful.

We adopt a state-based approach and use the term "action" informally to mean a state change.

1.2 System versus Environment

We view a specification as a formal description of the interface between the system and its environment. A state completely describes the state of the interface at some instant.

It is necessary to distinguish actions performed by the system from ones performed by the environment. For example, consider the specification of a clock circuit whose output is an increasing sequence of values; the circuit does not change the clock value until the environment has acknowledged reading it. The specification might include state components *clock* and *ack*, with a correct behavior consisting of a sequence of actions that alternately increment *clock* and complement *ack*.

Now, consider an "anti-clock", which is a circuit that assumes its environment (the rest of the circuit) provides a clock. The anti-clock issues acknowledgements and expects the environment to change the clock. The clock and anti-clock both display the same sequence of states—that is, the same sequence of *clock* and *ack* values—but they are obviously different systems. To distinguish them, we must specify not only what state changes may occur, but also which state changes are performed by the system and which by the environment.

An action-based formalism could simply partition the actions into system and environment actions. Formalisms based on joint system/environment actions require more subtle distinctions, such as between "internal" and "external" nondeterminism, or between the $\sqcap$ and $\Box$ operators of CSP [Hoa85].

In a state-based formalism, the easiest way to distinguish system actions from environment actions is to partition the state components into input and output components and require that the values of an input and an output component cannot both change at once. We can then declare that changes to output components are performed by the system and changes to input components are performed by the environment.

This method of partitioning the state components is not as general as we would like. For example, we might want to specify an individual assignment statement $x := x + 1$ as a system whose environment is the rest of the program. Since x can be modified by other parts of the program, it is both an input and an output component for this system. In general, we want to allow module boundaries to be orthogonal to process boundaries, so modules need not communicate only by means of simple input and output variables.

Instead of partitioning state components, we assume that each state change is performed by some "agent" and partition the set of agents into environment agents and system agents. A system execution is modeled as a *behavior*, which is a sequence of alternating states and agents, each agent being responsible for the change into the next state.

1.3 Specifying the Environment

Systems are usually not meant to work properly in arbitrary environments. For example, a self-timed circuit may display bizarre electrical behavior if its environment does not obey the correct signaling protocol. A component of a larger system need not behave properly in any environment, just in the one provided by the rest of the system.

A specification should assert that the system behaves properly if the environment fulfills its requirements. We write such a specification in the form $E \Rightarrow M$, where M describes the proper functioning of the system and E describes the assumptions made about the environment.

It is important to distinguish assumptions made about the environment from constraints placed on it. The environment cannot be constrained or controlled by the system. The system cannot prevent the user from depressing two keys at the same time. A specification may assume that the user does not press two keys at once, meaning that the system will behave properly only if he doesn't. A specification that requires the user not to press two keys at once cannot be implemented unless the system can control what the user does with his fingers. This distinction between assumption and requirement is central to our results and is addressed formally in Section 3.

1.4 Composition and Proof

In a modular specification method, one proves that the composition of lower-level systems implements a higher-level one. Section 5.2 explains how the method described in [AL88] can be used to prove that a specification of the form $E \Rightarrow M$ implements a higher-level specification of the same form.

In our approach, composition is conjunction, so the composition of systems with specifications $E_1 \Rightarrow M_1$ and $E_2 \Rightarrow M_2$ satisfies $(E_1 \Rightarrow M_1) \wedge (E_2 \Rightarrow M_2)$. To prove that this composition implements a specification $E \Rightarrow M$, we first show that it satisfies the specification $E \Rightarrow M_1 \wedge M_2$ and then use the method described in [AL88] to prove that $E \Rightarrow M_1 \wedge M_2$ implements $E \Rightarrow M$.

Theorem 2 of Section 5.3 enables us to conclude that if $E \wedge M_2$ satisfies the environment assumption E_1, and $E \wedge M_1$ satisfies the environment assumption E_2, then the composition of $E_1 \Rightarrow M_1$ and $E_2 \Rightarrow M_2$ satisfies $E \Rightarrow M_1 \wedge M_2$. This rule looks suspiciously like circular reasoning. For example, suppose that the environment assumption E is identically true, and that $E_1 = M_2$ and $E_2 = M_1$. The theorem makes the apparently absurd assertion that from $M_1 \Rightarrow M_2$ and $M_2 \Rightarrow M_1$ we can conclude $M_1 \wedge M_2$. Yet, under rather weak hypotheses, this absurd deduction rule is valid.

The major hypothesis of Theorem 2 is that the environment assumptions are safety properties. Section 4 discusses the logical form of a specification and culminates in Theorem 1, which asserts that a specification can be rewritten to satisfy this hypothesis.

1.5 Semantics versus Logic

In the transition-axiom method, a specification is a logical formula that describes a set of behaviors. Instead of stating our results for the particular temporal logic on which transition axioms are based, we take a more general semantic view in which a specification *is* a set of behaviors. The relation between logic and semantics is indicated by the following list of logical formulas and their corresponding semantic objects. The symbols P and Q denote formulas (logical view) and their corresponding sets of behaviors (semantic view), and Υ denotes the set of all behaviors.

Logic	Semantics	Logic	Semantics
$\neg P$	$\Upsilon - P$	$\models P$	$P = \Upsilon$
$P \wedge Q$	$P \cap Q$	$\models P \Rightarrow Q$	$P \subseteq Q$
$P \Rightarrow Q$	$(\Upsilon - P) \cup Q$		

Our semantic model is described in the following section.

2 The Semantic Model

We now define the semantic concepts on which our results are based. Most of these concepts have appeared before, so they are described only briefly; the reader can consult the cited sources for more complete discussions.

States

A *state* is an element of a nonempty set **S** of states. Except where stated otherwise, we assume that **S** is fixed. A *state predicate*, sometimes called an **S**-*predicate*, is a subset of the set **S** of states.

We think of an element of **S** as representing the state, at some instant, of the relevant universe—that is, of the interfaces of all the systems under consideration. A specification should describe only what is externally visible, so elements of **S** represent only the state of the interfaces and not of any internal mechanisms.

Agents

We assume a nonempty set **A** of *agents.* If μ is a set of agents, then $\neg\mu$ denotes the set $\mathbf{A} - \mu$ of agents. An *agent set* is a subset of **A** such that neither μ nor $\neg\mu$ is empty.

We think of the elements of **A** as the entities responsible for changing the state. A specification describes what it means for a set of agents μ to form a correctly operating system—in other words, what it means for a behavior to be correct when the agents in μ are considered to form the system and the agents in $\neg\mu$ are considered to form the environment. Specifications in which μ or $\neg\mu$ is empty turn out to be anomalous for uninteresting technical reasons, so we unobtrusively rule out that case by assuming μ to be an "agent set" rather than a set of agents.

In describing a system, the particular agent that performs an action is not important; what matters is whether the agent belongs to the system or the environment. Thus, if dealing with a single specification, one could assume just two agents, a system agent and an environment agent, as was done by Barringer, Kuiper, and Pnueli in [BKP86] and by us in [ALW89]. However, for composing specifications, one needs more general sets of agents, as introduced in [Lam83a] (where agents were called "actions").

It may help the reader to think of the agents as elementary circuit components or individual machine-language instructions. However, the actual identity of the individual agents never matters.

Behaviors

A *behavior prefix* is a sequence

$$s_0 \xrightarrow{\alpha_1} s_1 \xrightarrow{\alpha_2} s_2 \xrightarrow{\alpha_3} \dots \tag{1}$$

where each s_i is a state and each α_i is an agent (an element of $\mathbf{A}$), and the sequence is either infinite or else ends in a state s_m for some $m \geq 0$. A *behavior* is an infinite behavior prefix. If σ is the behavior prefix (1), then $\mathbf{s}_i(\sigma)$ denotes s_i and $\mathbf{a}_i(\sigma)$ denotes α_i. For a behavior σ, we let $\sigma|_m$ denote the finite prefix of σ ending with the mth state $\mathbf{s}_m(\sigma)$, for $m \geq 0$. We sometimes use the term $\mathbf{S}$-behavior to indicate that the states in the behavior are elements of $\mathbf{S}$.

A behavior represents a possible complete history of the relevant universe, starting at some appropriate time. As usual in state-based approaches, we adopt an interleaving semantics, in which the evolution of the universe is broken into atomic actions (state changes), and concurrent actions are considered to happen in some arbitrary order. A step $s_{i-1} \xrightarrow{\alpha_i} s_i$ of a behavior denotes an action in which agent α_i changes the state of the universe from s_{i-1} to s_i. Steps in our formalism correspond to the actions of action-based formalisms.

Stuttering-Equivalence

If μ is any set of agents, then a *μ-stuttering step* is a sequence $s \xrightarrow{\alpha} s$ with $\alpha \in \mu$. If σ is a behavior prefix, then $\natural_\mu \sigma$ is defined to be the behavior prefix obtained from σ by replacing every maximal (finite or infinite) sequence $s \xrightarrow{\alpha_1} s \xrightarrow{\alpha_2} s \dots$ of μ-stuttering steps with the single state s. Two behavior prefixes σ and τ are said to be *μ-stuttering-equivalent*, written $\sigma \simeq_\mu \tau$, iff (if and only if) $\natural_\mu \sigma = \natural_\mu \tau$. When μ equals $\mathbf{A}$, we write $\sigma \simeq \tau$ instead of $\sigma \simeq_{\mathbf{A}} \tau$ and *stuttering-equivalent* instead of $\mathbf{A}$-*stuttering-equivalent*. If σ is a finite behavior prefix, then $\widehat{\sigma}$ is defined to be some arbitrary behavior such that $\widehat{\sigma} \simeq \sigma$ and $\widehat{\sigma}|_m = \sigma$ for some m. (The precise choice of $\widehat{\sigma}$, which involves choosing which agents perform the infinite number of stuttering steps that must be added to σ, does not matter.)

A state describes the state of the entire relevant universe, and a stuttering step does not change the state, so a stuttering step has no observable effect. Therefore, two behaviors that are stuttering-equivalent should be indistinguishable. A useful way to think about stuttering is to imagine that a state in $\mathbf{S}$ describes only the observable parts of the universe, and that there are also unobservable, internal state components of the various objects that make up the universe. A stuttering step represents a step in which some object changes only its internal state. As explained in [Lam83b] and [Lam89], considering stuttering-equivalent behaviors to be equivalent allows the hierarchical decomposition of specifications by refining the grain of atomicity.

If σ is a finite behavior prefix, then $\widehat{\sigma}$ is obtained from σ by adding an infinite number of stuttering steps. The behavior $\widehat{\sigma}$ represents a history of the universe in which all externally observable activity ceased after a finite number of steps. (For example, a computer that has halted continues to take stuttering steps because its internal clock keeps ticking.)

Properties

A *property* P is a set of behaviors that is closed under stuttering-equivalence, meaning that for any behaviors σ and τ, if $\sigma \simeq \tau$ then $\sigma \in P$ iff $\tau \in P$. We sometimes call P an **S**-property to indicate that it is a set of **S**-behaviors. A state predicate I is considered to be the property such that $\sigma \in I$ iff $\mathbf{s}_0(\sigma) \in I$. For properties P and Q, we define $P \Rightarrow Q$ to be the property $(\neg P) \cup Q$, where $\neg$ denotes complementation in the set of all behaviors. In formulas, $\Rightarrow$ has lower precedence than $\cap$, so $P \cap Q \Rightarrow R$ denotes $(P \cap Q) \Rightarrow R$.

A property P is a *safety* property iff it satisfies the following condition: a behavior σ is in P iff $\widehat{\sigma|_m} \in P$ for all $m \geq 0$. A property P is a *liveness* property iff every finite behavior prefix is a prefix of a behavior in P. Letting safety properties be closed sets defines a topology on the set of behaviors in which liveness properties are dense sets [AS85]. By a standard result of topology, this implies that every property is the conjunction of a safety property and a liveness property. The closure of a property P in this topology, written $\overline{P}$, is the smallest safety property containing P.

Property P is a safety property iff every behavior not in P has a finite prefix that is not in P. Hence, a safety property is one that is finitely refutable. For any state predicate I, the property I depends only on the initial state, so it is a safety property. A property P is a liveness property iff every finite behavior prefix can be completed to a behavior in P. Hence, a liveness property is one that is never finitely refutable. Alpern and Schneider [AS85] discussed these definitions in more detail.

The specification of a system is the property consisting of all behaviors (histories of the relevant universe) in which the system is considered to perform correctly.

μ-Abstractness

If μ is a set of agents, then two behaviors σ and τ are *μ-equivalent* iff, for all $i \geq 0$:

- $\mathbf{s}_i(\sigma) = \mathbf{s}_i(\tau)$
- $\mathbf{a}_{i+1}(\sigma) \in \mu$ iff $\mathbf{a}_{i+1}(\tau) \in \mu$.

A set P of behaviors is *μ-abstract* iff, for any behaviors σ and τ that are μ-equivalent, $\sigma \in P$ iff $\tau \in P$.

Two behaviors are μ-equivalent iff they would be the same if we replaced every agent in μ by a single agent ν, and every agent not in μ by a single agent ϵ. A reasonable specification of a system does not describe which agent performs an action, only whether the action is performed by a system or an environment agent. Thus, if μ is the set of system agents, then the specification should not distinguish between μ-equivalent behaviors, so it should be a μ-abstract property.

3 Realizability

A specification of a system is a property P consisting of all behaviors in which the system behaves correctly. A system satisfies this specification iff every possible behavior of any universe containing the system is an element of P.

Whether a behavior is allowed by the specification may depend upon the environment's actions as well as the system's actions. This dependence upon what the environment does is unavoidable, since the system cannot be expected to perform in a prescribed fashion if the environment does not behave correctly. However, the ability to specify the environment as well as the system gives us the ability to write specifications that constrain what the environment is allowed to do. Such a specification requires the system to control (or predict) what the environment will do; it is unimplementable because the environment is precisely the part of the universe that the system *cannot* control.

A specification should assert that the system performs properly if the environment does; it should not assert that the environment performs properly. For example, assume that the environment is supposed to increment some state component x. A specification (property) P asserting that the environment must increment x would not be implementable because given any system, there is a possible universe containing the system whose behavior is not in P—namely one in which the environment never increments x. Hence, no system can satisfy the specification P. A specification of the system should allow all behaviors in which the environment never increments x.

A specification that is unimplementable because it constrains the environment's actions is called *unrealizable.* (A specification may be unimplementable for other reasons that do not concern us here—for example, because it requires the system to compute a noncomputable function.) We now define precisely what realizability means, and explore some of its implications for specifications. The definitions are almost identical to the ones in [AL88].

3.1 Safety Properties

A safety property is finitely refutable, so if a behavior does not satisfy the property, then we can tell who took the step that violated it. More precisely, if P is a safety property and a behavior σ is not in P, then there is some number $m \geq 0$ such that $\widehat{\sigma|_m}$ is not in P. If m is the smallest such number, then we can say that P was violated by the agent that performed the mth step of σ, assuming $m > 0$. A safety property is defined to constrain only the system iff the property can be violated only by system agents.

We now formalize this definition. For any property P and behavior σ, let $V(P, \sigma)$ equal the smallest nonnegative integer m such that $\widehat{\sigma|_m}$ is not in P. (We leave $V(P, \sigma)$ undefined if there is no such m.) If μ is an agent set, then a safety property P *constrains at most* μ iff for all behaviors σ, if $\sigma \notin P$ then $V(P, \sigma) > 0$ and $\mathbf{a}_{V(P,\sigma)}(\sigma) \in \mu$.

3.2 Realizability of Arbitrary Properties

3.2.1 Definitions

To understand the general concept of realizability, it helps to think of a behavior as the outcome of a two-person infinite game played by the system and the environment. The environment chooses the initial state, and then the environment and the system alternate moves to produce the behavior, with the environment taking the first move. An environment move consists of adding any finite number (possibly zero) of steps performed by environment agents; a system move consists of doing nothing or adding one step performed by a system agent. (A similar class of games was studied by Morton Davis [Dav64].) The system wins the game iff the resulting behavior prefix satisfies the specification or is finite. (If the system decides to stop, it is the environment's responsibility to keep adding steps.) A specification is said to be *realizable* iff the system has a winning strategy—that is, iff the system can always win no matter what moves the environment makes.

A specification is realizable if it has enough behaviors so that the system can win even if the environment plays as well as it can. A specification may also contain behaviors that are outcomes of games in which the environment had a chance to win but played badly and lost. A correct implementation can never allow such behaviors to occur because it can't count on the environment playing badly. The *realizable part* of a specification is defined to consist only of those behaviors in which the environment never had a chance to win. An implementation that satisfies the specification can produce only behaviors in the realizable part. Hence, two specifications have the same implementations iff they have the same realizable parts. Two such specifications are said to be *equirealizable.* We can replace a specification with an equirealizable one without changing the class of real systems that are being specified.

The formal definitions of these concepts is based on the definition of a strategy, which is a rule by which the system determines its next move. More precisely, a strategy is a partial function that determines the system's next step as a function of the behavior up to that point. It suffices to consider deterministic strategies, since the set of behaviors that result from a nondeterministic strategy is the union of the sets of behaviors produced by some set of deterministic strategies. In the following definitions, μ is an arbitrary agent set.

- A *μ-strategy* f is a partial function from the set of finite behavior prefixes to $\mu \times \mathbf{S}$. (Intuitively, $f(\sigma) = (\alpha, s)$ means that, if the system gets to move after play has produced σ, then it adds the step $\xrightarrow{\alpha} s$. If $f(\sigma)$ is undefined, then the system chooses not to move.)

- A *μ-outcome* of a μ-strategy f is a behavior σ such that for all $m > 0$, if $\mathbf{a}_m(\sigma) \in \mu$ then $f(\sigma|_{m-1}) = (\mathbf{a}_m(\sigma), \mathbf{s}_m(\sigma))$. A μ-outcome σ is *fair* iff $\mathbf{a}_{m+1}(\sigma) \in \mu$ or $\sigma|_m$ is not in the domain of f for infinitely many values of m. (A μ-outcome of f is one in which all the μ-moves were produced by the strategy f. It is fair iff it could have been obtained by giving the system an infinite number of chances to move.)

- If f is a μ-strategy, then $\mathcal{O}_\mu(f)$ is the set of all fair μ-outcomes of f.

- The *μ-realizable* part of a property P, denoted $\mathcal{R}_\mu(P)$, is the union of all sets $\mathcal{O}_\mu(f)$ such that f is a μ-strategy and $\mathcal{O}_\mu(f) \subseteq P$. (Intuitively, $\mathcal{R}_\mu(P)$ is the set of fair outcomes that can be produced by correct implementations of P.)

- A property P is *μ-realizable* iff $\mathcal{R}_\mu(P)$ is nonempty. (A μ-realizable property is one that has a correct implementation.)
- Properties P and Q are *μ-equirealizable* iff $\mathcal{R}_\mu(P) = \mathcal{R}_\mu(Q)$. (Equirealizable properties have the same correct implementations.)
- A property P is *μ-receptive* iff $\mathcal{R}_\mu(P) = P$. (A μ-receptive property includes only behaviors that can be produced by correct implementations.)

To our knowledge, Dill was the first to study receptiveness [Dil88]. In [ALW89], a concept of realizability was defined in which $\mathcal{O}_\mu(f)$ included all outcomes, rather than just fair ones. By eliminating unfair outcomes, we are preventing the environment from ending the game by taking an infinite number of steps in a single move. Allowing such an infinite move, in which the environment prevents the system from ever taking another step, would produce a game that does not correspond to the kind of autonomous system that we are concerned with here. Our concept of realizability is similar but not identical to fair realizability as defined in [ALW89]. The difference between these two concepts is described below.

3.2.2 Consequences of the Definitions

The set $\mathcal{O}_\mu(f)$ is not in general a property; it can contain a behavior σ and not contain a behavior σ' that is stuttering-equivalent to σ. Moreover, since the strategy f chooses specific agents, the set $\mathcal{O}_\mu(f)$ is not μ-abstract. However, we have:

Proposition 1 *For every agent set μ and property P, the set $\mathcal{R}_\mu(P)$ is a property. If P is μ-abstract then $\mathcal{R}_\mu(P)$ is μ-abstract.*

The proof of this and our other results will appear in a forthcoming report.

Our definition allows strategies to depend upon the presence or absence of stuttering. In other words, if f is a μ-strategy, then $f(\sigma)$ and $f(\tau)$ can be different for two stuttering-equivalent prefixes σ and τ. This seems to contradict our assertion that stuttering-equivalent behaviors should be indistinguishable. If we think of a stuttering step as representing an externally unobservable step of some object, then the system should certainly not be able to detect stuttering actions performed by the environment. Define f to be *invariant under $\neg\mu$-stuttering* iff $\sigma \simeq_{\neg\mu} \tau$ implies $f(\sigma) = f(\tau)$, for all behavior prefixes σ and τ. It would be more natural to add to the definition of a μ-strategy f the requirement that f be invariant under $\neg\mu$-stuttering. The following proposition shows that adding this requirement to the definition of a μ-strategy would not change the definition of $\mathcal{R}_\mu(P)$. Hence, there is no need to complicate the definition in this way.

Proposition 2 *For any agent set μ, any μ-strategy f, and any behavior σ in $\mathcal{O}_\mu(f)$, there exists a behavior σ' that is stuttering-equivalent to σ and a μ-strategy f' that is invariant under $\neg\mu$-stuttering such that $\sigma' \in \mathcal{O}_\mu(f')$ and every behavior in $\mathcal{O}_\mu(f')$ is stuttering-equivalent to a behavior in $\mathcal{O}_\mu(f)$.*

Although it makes no difference whether or not we require a μ-strategy to be invariant under $\neg\mu$-stuttering, requiring it to be invariant under all stuttering, as in the definition of "fair realizability" of [ALW89], would change our definitions. For example, consider the property P consisting of all behaviors containing infinitely many nonstuttering steps. With the definitions used here, P equals its μ-realizable part. With the definition in [ALW89], the "fairly μ-realizable" part of P would consist of all behaviors containing infinitely many nonstuttering μ-steps.

System stuttering steps represent ones in which the system changes only its internal state, so allowing a μ-strategy to depend upon μ-stuttering steps is equivalent to allowing the strategy to depend upon the system's internal state. More precisely, suppose that the state includes some "variable" that the property P does not depend on. Then adding the requirement that a μ-strategy be invariant under stuttering does not change the definition of $\mathcal{R}_\mu(P)$. (This is proved by showing that if a μ-strategy f is invariant under $\neg\mu$-stuttering, then one can modify f to obtain an "equivalent" strategy f' that is invariant under all stuttering by letting f' take a step that changes only the extra variable whenever f takes a stuttering step.) By allowing a strategy to depend upon stuttering steps, we obviate the need to rely upon internal state for our definitions.

3.2.3 Some Results about Realizability

We now give some results about realizability. The first asserts that the realizable part of a property is receptive.

Proposition 3 *For any property P and agent set μ, $\mathcal{R}_\mu(\mathcal{R}_\mu(P)) = \mathcal{R}_\mu(P)$.*

The next result provides a useful representation of the realizable part of a property.

Proposition 4 *For any property P and agent set μ, $\mathcal{R}_\mu(P) = \overline{\mathcal{R}_\mu(P)} \cap P$.*

The next result indicates that "constrains at most" and receptiveness are essentially the same for safety properties.

Proposition 5 *For any nonempty safety property P and any agent set μ, property P constrains at most μ iff P is μ-receptive.*

Proposition 3 asserts that the μ-realizable part $\mathcal{R}_\mu(P)$ of a property P is μ-receptive. Hence, Proposition 5 implies that, if $\mathcal{R}_\mu(P)$ is a nonempty safety property, then it constrains at most μ. The following result generalizes this to the case when $\mathcal{R}_\mu(P)$ is not a safety property.

Proposition 6 *For any agent set μ and μ-realizable property P, $\overline{\mathcal{R}_\mu(P)}$ constrains at most μ.*

4 The Form of a Specification

We now consider the formal structure of a specification. Before considering general specifications, we first examine a particular class of specifications—programs. A program is a specification that is sufficiently detailed so a system that satisfies it can be generated automatically. Typically, a system satisfying the specification is generated by compiling the program and executing the resulting code on a computer.

4.1 The Form of a Complete Program

We start by considering complete programs. In formal models of complete programs, there are no environment actions, only system actions. Input occurs through initial values of variables or by executing a nondeterministic *input* statement in the program. (An *input* statement is nondeterministic because the program text and the behavior of the program up to that point do not determine the input value.) Thus, a complete program is a specification in which every agent in $\mathbf{A}$ is a system agent. Since we want the specification to be $\mathbf{A}$-abstract, it does not matter what agents perform the steps of a behavior, so we can ignore the agents and consider a behavior to be a sequence of states.

4.1.1 The Parts of a Complete Program

A complete program is defined by four things:

set of states A state provides an "instantaneous picture" of the execution status of the program. It is determined by such things as the values of variables, the loci of control of processes, and the messages in transit—the details depending upon the programming language.

initial predicate The initial predicate I is a state predicate that specifies the set of valid starting states of the program. Recall that the predicate I (a set of states) is interpreted as the property consisting of all behaviors whose starting state is in I.

next-state relation The next-state relation $\mathcal{N}$ is a set of pairs of states that describes the state transitions allowed by the program, where $(s,t) \in \mathcal{N}$ iff executing one step of the program starting in state s can produce state t. It is described explicitly by the program text and the assumptions about what actions are considered to be atomic. The next-state relation $\mathcal{N}$ determines a property $\mathcal{TA}(\mathcal{N})$, defined by $\sigma \in \mathcal{TA}(\mathcal{N})$ iff $\mathbf{s}_i(\sigma) = \mathbf{s}_{i+1}(\sigma)$ or $(\mathbf{s}_i(\sigma), \mathbf{s}_{i+1}(\sigma)) \in \mathcal{N}$, for all $i \geq 0$. In other words, $\mathcal{TA}(\mathcal{N})$ is the set of all behaviors in which each nonstuttering step is allowed by the next-state relation $\mathcal{N}$.

progress property The next-state relation specifies what state changes *may* occur, but it does not require that any state changes actually do occur. The progress property L specifies what must occur. A common type of progress property is one asserting that if some state change is allowed by the next-state relation, then some state change must occur.

Formally, the program is the property $I \cap \mathcal{TA}(\mathcal{N}) \cap L$. Note that I and $\mathcal{TA}(\mathcal{N})$, and hence $I \cap \mathcal{TA}(\mathcal{N})$, are safety properties.

All assertional methods of reasoning about concurrent programs are based on a description of the program in terms of a set of states, an initial predicate, and a next-state relation. By now, these methods should be familiar enough that there is no need for us to discuss those parts of the program. Progress properties are less well understood and merit further consideration.

4.1.2 The Progress Property

Assertional methods that deal with liveness properties need some way of specifying the program's progress property. The requirement that the program be executable in practice constrains the type of progress property that can be allowed. The initial state and the computer instructions executed by a program are derived from the program's code, which specifies the next-state relation.

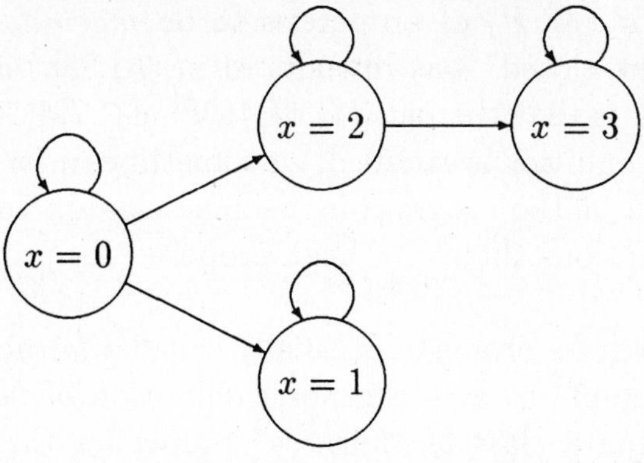

Figure 1: A simple next-state relation.

The progress property should constrain the eventual scheduling of instructions, but not which instructions are executed. For the program to be executable in practice, the state transitions that it may perform must be determined by the initial state and the next-state relation alone; they must not be constrained by the progress property.

As an example, consider the simple next-state relation pictured in Figure 1, where the program state consists of the value of the single variable x. Assume that the initial predicate asserts that x equals 0. The property $\Diamond x = 3$, which asserts that $x = 3$ holds at some time during execution, is a liveness property. However, for the program to satisfy this property, it must not make the state transition from $x = 0$ to $x = 1$ allowed by the next-state relation. Thus, if $\Diamond x = 3$ were the program's progress property, a compiler would have to deduce that the transition from $x = 0$ to $x = 1$, which is permitted by the next-state relation, must not occur.

The condition that the progress property L does not further constrain the initial state or the next-state relation is expressed formally by the following conditions, which are all equivalent.

- For every finite behavior prefix ρ with $\widehat{\rho}$ in $I \cap \mathcal{TA}(\mathcal{N})$, there exists a behavior σ in $I \cap \mathcal{TA}(\mathcal{N}) \cap L$ such that ρ is a prefix of σ.

- $I \cap \mathcal{TA}(\mathcal{N}) \;=\; \overline{I \cap \mathcal{TA}(\mathcal{N}) \cap L}$

- If S is any safety property, then $I \cap \mathcal{TA}(\mathcal{N}) \cap L \subseteq S$ iff $I \cap \mathcal{TA}(\mathcal{N}) \subseteq S$.

The last condition asserts that the safety properties satisfied by the program are completely determined by the initial predicate and the next-state relation; the progress property does not add any safety properties.

We define a pair (M, P) of properties to be *machine-closed* iff $M = \overline{P}$. (The term "machine-closed" was introduced in [AL88].) Our condition on a progress property L is that the pair $(I \cap \mathcal{TA}(\mathcal{N}), I \cap \mathcal{TA}(\mathcal{N}) \cap L)$ be machine-closed. When this condition is satisfied, we sometimes informally write that the progress property L or the program is machine-closed. To our knowledge, all the progress assumptions that have been proposed for programs are machine-closed.

A program's progress property is usually called a fairness condition. There have been few attempts to give a general definition of fairness. Manna and Pnueli [MP87] define a class of "fairness" properties that is independent of any next-state relation, but they provide no justification for their terminology. Apt, Francez, and Katz [AFK88] discuss three "fairness criteria"; one of them is machine-closure, which they call "feasibility".

Most of the progress properties that have been proposed can be stated as fairness conditions on program actions—for example, the condition that certain state transitions cannot be enabled forever without occurring. These progress properties are not all considered to be fairness properties. In particular, the property asserting that the entire program never stops if some step can be executed is machine-closed, but multiprocess programs satisfying only this progress assumption are generally called unfair. We believe that machine-closure provides the proper definition of a progress property, and that the distinction between fairness properties and progress properties is probably language-dependent and not fundamental.

4.2 The Form of a Partial Program

A partial program is part of a larger program. It may be a single process in a CSP program, or a single assignment statement in a Pascal program. It should be possible to implement the partial program independently of the rest of the program, which constitutes its environment. Such an implementation might be very inefficient—as, for example, if each assignment statement of a Pascal program were compiled independently without knowing the types of the variables—but it should be possible. Actions may be taken either by the partial program or by the rest of the program, which constitutes the partial program's environment.

4.2.1 The Parts of a Partial Program

The following modifications of the parts that define a program are needed to handle partial programs.

set of states The complete state cannot be determined from the text of the partial program. For example, there is no way of knowing what variables are introduced in other parts of the complete program. There are two ways to define the set of states **S** for a partial program.

- **S** is the set of states defined by the complete program. Since the complete program is not known, **S** is not known, so the meaning of the partial program depends upon a fixed but unknown set of states.
- **S** includes all possible program variables and other state components. The meaning of the partial program is defined in terms of a known set of states, but it is a very "large" set of states, since it must accommodate all possible complete programs.

Both approaches lead to equivalent formalisms. Here, we find the first assumption most convenient, and we take **S** to be the unknown set of states of the larger program. The partial program modifies only those components of the state explicitly mentioned; the environment can modify any part of the state.

agent set We use agents to distinguish the actions performed by the partial program from the ones performed by its environment. Program steps are taken by agents in μ, environment steps by agents in $\neg\mu$. We don't care which agents in μ or in $\neg\mu$ take the steps, so it suffices to distinguish only μ steps and $\neg\mu$ steps.

initial predicate In our "realization game", the environment chooses the initial state. The initial condition must therefore become part of the environment specification, so it disappears from the program.

next-state relation The next-state relation $\mathcal{N}$ now constrains only the state transitions performed by the program, not the ones performed by the environment. It describes the property $\mathcal{TA}_\mu(\mathcal{N})$, defined by $\sigma \in \mathcal{TA}(\mathcal{N})$ iff $\mathbf{a}_{i+1}(\sigma) \in \mu$ implies $\mathrm{s}_i(\sigma) = \mathrm{s}_{i+1}(\sigma)$ or $(\mathrm{s}_i(\sigma), \mathrm{s}_{i+1}(\sigma)) \in \mathcal{N}$, for all $i \geq 0$. The next-state relation must be defined in such a way that any part of the state not explicitly mentioned is left unchanged.

This leaves the question of what is the appropriate modification to the machine-closure condition for progress properties. Recall that machine-closure was derived from the requirement that a complete program be implementable in practice. Ignoring the initial predicate, machine-closure asserts that any finite execution satisfying the next-state relation can be completed to an execution satisfying the next-state relation and the progress property. We similarly require that the partial program be implementable in practice, except now we have the additional requirement that it be implementable without knowing its environment. In other words, the implementation must work regardless of what the environment does. We therefore require that given any finite behavior prefix in which the program's actions satisfy the next-state relation, there is a strategy that the program can play from that point on and "win"—that is, produce a behavior satisfying the next-state relation and the progress property.

The formal expression of this condition is statement (a) in the following proposition, when $\mathcal{TA}_\mu(\mathcal{N})$ is substituted for P. Statement (b) is a slightly weaker form of (a) that is sometimes useful, and (c) is a formulation in terms of topology and realization.

Proposition 7 *For any agent set μ, safety property M, and arbitrary property L, the following three conditions are equivalent:*

(a) For every finite behavior ρ such that $\widehat{\rho} \in M$, there exist a μ-strategy f with $\mathcal{O}_\mu(f) \subseteq M \cap L$ and a behavior $\sigma \in \mathcal{O}_\mu(f)$ with ρ a prefix of σ.

(b) For every finite behavior ρ such that $\widehat{\rho} \in M$, there exist a μ-strategy f with $\mathcal{O}_\mu(f) \subseteq M \cap L$ and a behavior $\sigma \in \mathcal{O}_\mu(f)$ with ρ stuttering-equivalent to a prefix of σ.

(c) The pair $(M, M \cap L)$ is machine-closed, and $M \cap L$ is μ-receptive.

We define a pair of properties (M, P) to be *μ-machine-realizable* iff it is machine-closed and P is μ-receptive. The generalization to partial programs of the machine-closure condition on a progress property L is that the pair $(\mathcal{TA}_\mu(\mathcal{N}), \mathcal{TA}_\mu(\mathcal{N}) \cap L)$ be μ-machine-realizable, where $\mathcal{N}$ is the program's next-state relation. In this case, we say informally that L is machine-realizable.

To illustrate the difference between progress properties of partial and complete programs, let $L_{\mathcal{A}}$ be the property asserting that if some program action $\mathcal{A}$ is infinitely often enabled, then that action must occur infinitely often. More formally, let $\mathcal{A}$ be a subset of the next-state relation $\mathcal{N}$, define $\mathcal{A}$ to be enabled in a state s iff there exists a state t with $(s, t) \in \mathcal{A}$, and define $L_{\mathcal{A}}$ to be the property such that $\sigma \in L$ iff either $\mathcal{A}$ is enabled in state $\mathbf{s}_i(\sigma)$ for only finitely many values of i, or else $(\mathbf{s}_i(\sigma), \mathbf{s}_{i+1}(\sigma)) \in \mathcal{A}$ for infinitely many values of i. The property $L_{\mathcal{A}}$ is the usual *strong fairness* requirement for action $\mathcal{A}$. Strong fairness is a reasonable progress property for a complete program, since it is machine-closed.

Now, suppose that $L_{\mathcal{A}}$ is the progress property of a partial program. When playing the "realization game", the environment can play infinitely many moves in which it adds two states—one in which $\mathcal{A}$ is enabled followed by one in which it is not enabled. (Such environment moves are "legal" because the partial program's safety property $\mathcal{TA}_{\mu}(\mathcal{N})$ allows any steps by the environment.) The program never has a chance to take an $\mathcal{A}$ step because it never gets to play a move when $\mathcal{A}$ is enabled. Thus, the resulting outcome does not satisfy the property $L_{\mathcal{A}}$, so $L_{\mathcal{A}}$ is not a machine-realizable progress property. In fact, it is not even realizable. This losing outcome corresponds to a physical situation in which the environment changes the state so fast that $\mathcal{A}$ never stays enabled long enough for the program to react in time to perform an $\mathcal{A}$ action.

To obtain a machine-realizable progress property, let $\mathcal{N}'$ be a next-state relation asserting that $\mathcal{A}$ is never disabled. Formally, $(s, t) \in \mathcal{N}'$ iff $\mathcal{A}$ is not enabled in s or is enabled in t. The property $\mathcal{TA}_{\neg\mu}(\mathcal{N}')$ asserts that the environment never disables $\mathcal{A}$. The progress property $\mathcal{TA}_{\neg\mu}(\mathcal{N}') \Rightarrow L_{\mathcal{A}}$ is machine-realizable. In the realization game, the environment loses if it ever disables $\mathcal{A}$, since doing so ensures that $\mathcal{TA}_{\neg\mu}(\mathcal{N}')$ will be false, making $\mathcal{TA}_{\neg\mu}(\mathcal{N}') \Rightarrow L_{\mathcal{A}}$ true. The program can therefore always win the game by taking an $\mathcal{A}$ step whenever it gets to move with $\mathcal{A}$ enabled.

4.2.2 Hiding the Internal State

Another important concept introduced when considering partial programs is *hiding*. Variables and other state components that are local to the partial program should be hidden—meaning that they are modified only by the program and do not conflict with similarly-named components in the environment. In our approach, hiding is effected by existential quantification over state components.

Existential Quantification Existential quantification is defined formally as follows. Let $\mathbf{X}$ denote a set of values, let $\Pi_{\mathbf{S}}$ and $\Pi_{\mathbf{X}}$ denote the projection functions from $\mathbf{S} \times \mathbf{X}$ to $\mathbf{S}$ and $\mathbf{X}$, respectively, and let $\mathbf{x}$ be an abbreviation for $\Pi_{\mathbf{X}}$. We extend $\Pi_{\mathbf{S}}$ to a mapping from $\mathbf{S} \times \mathbf{X}$-behaviors to $\mathbf{S}$-behaviors by letting $\Pi_{\mathbf{S}}(\sigma)$ be the behavior such that, $\mathbf{a}_i(\Pi_{\mathbf{S}}(\sigma)) = \mathbf{a}_i(\sigma)$ and $\mathbf{s}_i(\Pi_{\mathbf{S}}(\sigma)) = \Pi_{\mathbf{S}}(\mathbf{s}_i(\sigma))$ for all i. For any $\mathbf{S} \times \mathbf{X}$-property P, we define $\exists \mathbf{x} : P$ to be the $\mathbf{S}$-property such that σ is in $\exists \mathbf{x} : P$ iff there exists an $\mathbf{S} \times \mathbf{X}$-behavior σ' in P with $\Pi_{\mathbf{S}}(\sigma') \simeq \sigma$.

Intuitively, $\mathbf{S} \times \mathbf{X}$ is a set of states in which $\mathbf{S}$ is the externally observable component and $\mathbf{X}$ is the component internal to the program. The property $\exists \mathbf{x} : P$ is obtained from P by hiding the $\mathbf{x}$-component. We use the notation "$\exists \mathbf{x}$" for this hiding operator because it obeys the logical rules of existential quantification when properties are expressed as formulas in an appropriate logic.

Hiding with Existential Quantification Let $\mathcal{N}$ be the next-state relation of the program and L its progress property. When there is an internal state component, $\mathcal{N}$ is a set of pairs of elements of $\mathbf{S} \times \mathbf{X}$—in other words, a subset of $(\mathbf{S} \times \mathbf{X}) \times (\mathbf{S} \times \mathbf{X})$—and L is an $\mathbf{S} \times \mathbf{X}$-property. Formally, the program is the property $\exists \mathbf{x} : P \cap \mathcal{TA}_\mu(\mathcal{N}) \cap L$, where P is the $\mathbf{S} \times \mathbf{X}$-property asserting that the $\mathbf{x}$-component of the state has the correct initial value and is not changed by the environment. The correct initial value of the state's $\mathbf{x}$-component is specified by an initial $\mathbf{S} \times \mathbf{X}$-predicate $I_\mathbf{x}$. (Remember that the initial value of the $\mathbf{S}$-component is described by the environment specification.) The assertion that the environment leaves the $\mathbf{x}$-component unchanged is $\mathcal{TA}_{\neg\mu}(\mathcal{U}_\mathbf{x})$, where $\mathcal{U}_\mathbf{x}$ is the next-state relation consisting of all pairs $((s, x), (s', x'))$ such that $x = x'$. The program is then the property

$$\exists \mathbf{x} : I_\mathbf{x} \cap \mathcal{TA}_{\neg\mu}(\mathcal{U}_\mathbf{x}) \cap \mathcal{TA}_\mu(\mathcal{N}) \cap L \tag{2}$$

Since we want the program to be machine-realizable, it is natural to ask under what conditions the specification (2) is machine-realizable. Machine-realizability is defined for a pair of properties (M, P), where M is the program's safety property and P is the complete specification, which in this case equals (2). We expect the safety property M to be

$$\exists \mathbf{x} : I_\mathbf{x} \cap \mathcal{TA}_{\neg\mu}(\mathcal{U}_\mathbf{x}) \cap \mathcal{TA}_\mu(\mathcal{N}) \tag{3}$$

This is not always a safety property, but it turns out to be a safety property for ordinary specifications written in a "reasonable" way—meaning that the next-state relation is not using the internal state component $\mathbf{x}$ to encode progress properties. For the precise condition under which (3) is a safety property, see Proposition 2 of [AL88]. A sufficient condition for (M, P) to be μ-machine-realizable is given by the following result.

Proposition 8 *Let μ be an agent set, let $\mathbf{x}$ be the projection function from $\mathbf{S} \times \mathbf{X}$ to $\mathbf{X}$, and let $I_\mathbf{x}$ be an $\mathbf{S} \times \mathbf{X}$-predicate, $\mathcal{N}$ a next-state relation on $\mathbf{S} \times \mathbf{X}$, and L an $\mathbf{S} \times \mathbf{X}$-property. Let M equal (3) and let P equal (2). Assume that:*

(a) *For all* $s \in \mathbf{S}$ *there exists* $x \in \mathbf{X}$ *such that* $(s, x) \in I_{\mathbf{X}}$.

(b) *The pair* $(I_{\mathbf{X}} \cap \mathcal{TA}_{\neg\mu}(\mathcal{U}_{\mathbf{X}}) \Rightarrow \mathcal{TA}_{\mu}(\mathcal{N}),\ I_{\mathbf{X}} \cap \mathcal{TA}_{\neg\mu}(\mathcal{U}_{\mathbf{X}}) \Rightarrow \mathcal{TA}_{\mu}(\mathcal{N}) \cap L)$ *is* μ*-machine-realizable.*

(c) M *is a safety property.*

Then (M, P) *is* μ*-machine-realizable.*

4.3 The Normal Form of a Specification

As we have already indicated, a specification should assert that the system operates properly if the environment does. Such a specification should therefore be a property of the form $E \Rightarrow M$, where E is the property that is true iff the environment behaves properly, and M is the property that is true iff the system behaves properly. In the transition-axiom approach [Lam83a, Lam89], E and M are written as abstract partial programs, using next-state relations and progress properties. Since the environment makes the first move in our realizability game, the initial predicate must be included with E; the abstract program M has no initial predicate—except on its internal, hidden state. (Intuitively, we are assuming that the system has control of the initial values only of its internal state, not of the externally visible state.) We therefore write our specification in the canonical form

$$I \cap E_S \cap E_L \;\Rightarrow\; M_S \cap M_L \tag{4}$$

where I is an initial predicate, E_S is a safety property constraining only $\neg\mu$, and M_S is a safety property constraining only μ.

If the system property M were written as an executable program, then we would expect the pair $(M_S, M_S \cap M_L)$ to be machine-realizable. However, M is an abstract program that is meant to specify *what* the system is allowed to do, not *how* it does it. Requiring the abstract program to be executable in practice—that is, capable of being transformed into executable code by a real compiler—is too restrictive, leading to overly complex and overly specific specifications. It is not clear whether requiring the abstract program to be executable in principle—that is, to be machine-realizable—is too restrictive. If $(M_S,\ M_S \cap M_L)$ is not machine-realizable, then it allows behaviors that cannot be achieved by any implementation. Most of the practical specifications we have seen are machine-realizable. But allowing unimplementable behaviors causes no harm, as long as implementable behaviors are also allowed—that is, as long as the specification is realizable. Allowing some unimplementable behaviors may yield a simpler specification. For example, the simplicity of the specification of a serializable database in [Lam89] results from its not being machine-closed, hence not machine-realizable. We have too little experience writing practical specifications to know if this example is an anomaly or if others will arise. We therefore do not assume machine-realizability of the pair $(M_S, M_S \cap M_L)$.

The situation is different for the environment property E. Progress assumptions about the environment seem to be unusual. A specification usually requires that the system eventually do something after the environment has taken some action, but rarely does it assume that the environment must take that action. Thus, E_L is almost always identically true, and the pair (E_S, E_S) is $\neg\mu$-machine-realizable if E_S constrains only $\neg\mu$, which it will in a transition-axiom specification where it has the form $\mathcal{TA}_{\neg\mu}(\mathcal{N})$.

Even if a specification does include a nontrivial progress assumption E_L about the environment, we believe that it is reasonable to require the pair $(E_S, E_S \cap E_L)$ to be $\neg\mu$-machine-realizable. The intent of the specification $E \Rightarrow M$ is that the system should win the specification game by making M true, not by making E false. The machine-realizability condition means that the system can never win by forcing E to be false. A specification in which $(E_S, E_S \cap E_L)$ is not $\neg\mu$-machine-realizable is probably incorrect, in the sense that it does not capture the intent of its author.

Once we assume that the environment assumption should be machine-realizable, there is no need for an environment progress assumption. The following result shows that the property E_L can be incorporated into the system's progress property.

Theorem 1 *If I is an initial predicate, $(E_S, E_S \cap E_L)$ is $\neg\mu$-machine-realizable, and M_S is a safety property, then*

$$I \cap E_S \cap E_L \;\Rightarrow\; M_S \cap M_L$$

and

$$I \cap E_S \;\Rightarrow\; M_S \cap (E_L \Rightarrow M_L)$$

are μ-equirealizable.

The abstract programs describing the system and the environment may contain hidden, internal state components, in which case the specification involves existential quantification. We now show that Theorem 1 can still be applied.

Existential quantification in the environment's description is handled with Proposition 8. Suppose the environment description E has the form

$$I \cap \exists \mathbf{x} : (I_{\mathbf{x}} \cap \mathcal{TA}_{\mu}(\mathcal{U}_{\mathbf{x}}) \cap \mathcal{TA}_{\neg\mu}(\mathcal{N}) \cap L)$$

(Since this is a specification of the environment rather than the system, we have interchanged μ and $\neg\mu$ and added the initial predicate I to (2).) We can apply Theorem 1, substituting $\exists \mathbf{x} : I_{\mathbf{x}} \cap \mathcal{TA}_{\mu}(\mathcal{U}_{\mathbf{x}}) \cap \mathcal{TA}_{\neg\mu}(\mathcal{N})$ for E_S and $\exists \mathbf{x} : I_{\mathbf{x}} \cap \mathcal{TA}_{\mu}(\mathcal{U}_{\mathbf{x}}) \cap \mathcal{TA}_{\neg\mu}(\mathcal{N}) \cap L$ for E_L, using Proposition 8 to prove that (E_S, E_L) is $\neg\mu$-machine-realizable—assuming, of course, that the hypotheses of the proposition are satisfied.

Existential quantification in the system's description M is handled by the following generalization of Theorem 1, which follows easily from the theorem.

Corollary *Let μ be any agent set, let $\mathbf{x}$ be the projection function from $\mathbf{S}\times\mathbf{X}$ to $\mathbf{X}$, let I be an initial $\mathbf{S}$-predicate, let $(E_S,\ E_S \cap E_L)$ be a $\neg\mu$-machine-realizable pair of $\mathbf{S}$-properties, and let M_S and M_L be $\mathbf{S}\times\mathbf{X}$-properties such that $\exists \mathbf{x} : M_S$ is a safety property. Then*

$$I \cap E_S \cap E_L \;\Rightarrow\; \exists \mathbf{x} : M_S \cap M_L$$

and

$$I \cap E_S \;\Rightarrow\; \exists \mathbf{x} : M_S \cap (E_L \Rightarrow M_L)$$

are μ-equirealizable.

4.4 An Overly Normal Form

Theorem 1 permits us to take a specification of the form (4) and move the environment's progress property to the right of the implication. But, can we always write the specification in the form (4) in the first place? The answer is that not only can we, but we don't even need the left-hand side of the implication. Propositions 4 and 6 imply that the realizable part of any property P can be written as $M_S \cap M_L$, where M_S is a safety property that constrains only μ. (Just take M_S to be $\overline{\mathcal{R}_{\mu}(P)}$ and M_L to be P.) In fact, we can choose the pair $(M_S,\ M_S \cap M_L)$ to be μ-machine-realizable. (The μ-machine-realizability of $(\overline{\mathcal{R}_{\mu}(P)},\ P)$ follows from Propositions 3 and 4.)

We can go still further in finding a representation of the realizable part of any property. It can be shown that any safety property that constrains at most μ can be written in the form

$$\exists \mathbf{x} : I_{\mathbf{x}} \cap \mathcal{TA}_{\neg\mu}(\mathcal{U}_{\mathbf{x}}) \cap \mathcal{TA}_{\mu}(\mathcal{N})$$

for some initial predicate $I_{\mathbf{x}}$ satisfying hypothesis (a) of Proposition 8 and some next-state relation $\mathcal{N}$. (This result is a simple generalization of Proposition 3 of [AL88]). Thus, the μ-realizable part of any property P can be written in the form $\exists \mathbf{x} : M_S \cap M_L$, where M_S has the form $I_{\mathbf{x}} \cap \mathcal{TA}_{\neg\mu}(\mathcal{U}_{\mathbf{x}}) \cap \mathcal{TA}_{\mu}(\mathcal{N})$ and the pair $(\exists \mathbf{x} : M_S, \exists \mathbf{x} : M_S \cap M_L)$ is μ-machine-realizable.

The ability to write a specification in this form seems to imply that there is no need to write an explicit assumption about the environment. Why write a specification of the form $E \Rightarrow M$ when we can simply write M? The answer lies in the practical matter of what the specification looks like. If we eliminate the explicit environment assumption, then that assumption appears implicitly in the property M describing the system. Instead of M describing only the behavior of the system when the environment behaves correctly, M must also allow arbitrary behavior when the environment behaves incorrectly. Eliminating E makes M too complicated, and it is not a practical alternative to writing specifications in the form $E \Rightarrow M$.

To be useful, a specification must be understandable. Theorems that assert the existence of a specification in a certain form are of no practical interest because they prove only that the specification exists, not that it is understandable. On the other hand, a result like Theorem 1 that provides a simple way to rewrite existing specifications can be of practical interest because the rewritten specification will be understandable if the original one is.

5 Composing Specifications

Our main result is a rule for proving that the composition of two specifications implements a third specification. Before stating the result, we must explain how specifications are composed and what it means for the composition to implement a third specification.

5.1 The Composition of Specifications

Suppose we have two component systems, as shown schematically in Figure 2, where the "wires" *inp*, *mid*, and *out* denote state components and μ_1 and μ_2 are the systems' agent sets. Let S_1 and S_2 be the specifications of the two systems. What is the specification of the composition of the two systems, drawn in Figure 3? Each S_i is the property consisting of all histories of the universe (behaviors) in which component i functions correctly. A history of the universe is one in which both components function correctly iff it is in both S_1 and S_2. Thus, the specification of the composition of the two systems is

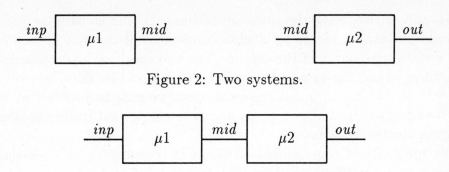

Figure 2: Two systems.

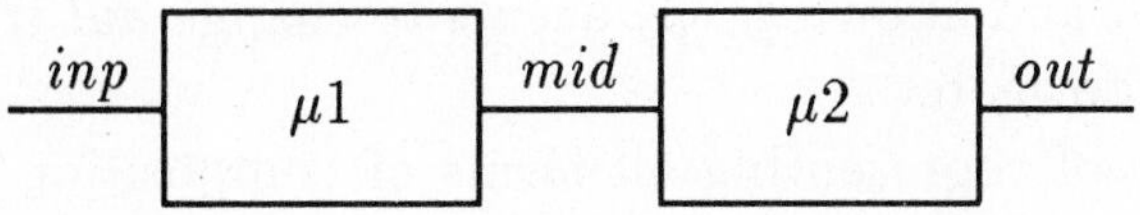

Figure 3: The composition of two systems.

simply $S_1 \cap S_2$. This simple semantics of composition as intersection rests on some assumptions that we now discuss.

5.1.1 Assumptions about the States

In combining the two systems of Figure 2 into the single system of Figure 3, we combined the two "wires" labeled *mid* into a single "wire". When two specifications are written as logical formulas, a state-component variable like *mid* that appears in both formulas is considered to represent the same state component. In some situations, this use of names to identify state components in the two systems is natural—for example, if the "systems" are the assignment statements $mid := inp+1$ and $out := 2*mid$. In other situations, there may be no connection between the names used in the two specifications, so renaming is necessary. For example, if the systems are circuits, component 1's wire labeled *mid* in Figure 2 might have been labeled *out*, and component 2's wire labeled *mid* might have been labeled *inp*. In that case, the specification of the system in Figure 3 would be $S_1|^{out}_{mid} \cap S_2|^{inp}_{mid}$, where $S_1|^{out}_{mid}$ is obtained by substituting *mid* for *out* in the formula for S_1.

It is this kind of renaming that allows us to make do with the single operator $\cap$ for composing properties instead of having a multitude of different composition operators. For example, two programming-language statements can be combined by parallel composition or by sequential composition (";"). Simple intersection of their specifications provides parallel composition; sequential composition is obtained by first renaming components of their control states in such a way that control is at the end of one statement iff it is at the beginning of the other, then taking the intersection of the resulting specifications.

Even with the proper choice of state-component names, we can write the composition as the intersection $S_1 \cap S_2$ only if S_1 and S_2 are both **S**-properties—

that is, only if they have the same set of states **S**. But looking at Figure 2, we would not expect *out* to be a state component of the first system or *inp* to be a state component of the second. The two specifications might have to be modified to use the same set of states. This would be done by expanding S_1's state to include an *out* component, modifying S_1 to prohibit μ_1 agents from changing *out*, and allowing $\neg\mu_1$ agents to change *out* freely—making the analogous change to S_2 too.

The simplicity of representing all forms of composition as intersection is therefore somewhat illusory. We need renaming and state expansion as well. (By adopting the approach mentioned in Section 4.2.1 of having a single universal set of states, state expansion can be avoided at the expense of additional renaming.) Moreover, we might want some state components of the composed system to be hidden—for example, the component *mid* in Figure 3. This requires the use of existential quantification, as described in Section 4.2.2. Still, we feel that the ability to reduce composition to the well-understood operation of intersection—or, in the corresponding logical view, to conjunction—is a significant benefit of our approach.

5.1.2 Assumptions about the Agents

In drawing Figure 3, we have made a subtle assumption about the agent sets μ_1 and μ_2. Suppose we want to compose two copies of the first component without renaming, so the *inp* state components of the two copies would be identified (the two *inp* "wires" would be connected), as would the *mid* state components. The discussion so far might lead one to write the resulting specification as $S_1 \cap S_1$. But this is obviously wrong, since $S_1 \cap S_1$ equals S_1. Simple intersection of S_1 with itself yields a specification of the same system, not of the composition of two separate copies of the system.

A property S specifies what it means for a particular agent set μ to perform correctly. Making a separate copy of S means replacing μ by a different agent set. Let $S|^{\mu}_{\mu_i}$ denote the property obtained by substituting μ_i for μ in the formula describing S. The property $S|^{\mu}_{\mu_1} \cap S|^{\mu}_{\mu_2}$ specifies a system in which the agent sets μ_1 and μ_2 each behave like the agent set μ in the specification S—in other words, a system in which each μ_i is a separate copy of the original system μ.

By drawing separate, nonoverlapping boxes for μ_1 and μ_2 in Figure 3, we have tacitly assumed that the agent sets μ_1 and μ_2 are disjoint. As we have seen in the extreme case when S_1 equals S_2, the intersection $S_1 \cap S_2$ does not represent the expected composition of separate systems unless $\mu_1 \cap \mu_2$ is the empty set of agents.

5.2 Implementing One Specification by Another

5.2.1 Definition

A system's specification S describes the set of all behaviors in which the system is considered to behave correctly. For a system specified by S' to satisfy specification S, every behavior it allows must be in S. Thus, the system specified by S' satisfies the specification S if $S' \subseteq S$. Eliminating the phrase "the system specified by", we say that specification S' implements S if $S' \subseteq S$.

While sufficient, the condition $S' \subseteq S$ is stronger than strictly necessary for S' to implement S. We view S' as a prescription for building an implementation, and we say that S' implements S iff every real system built according to the specification S' satisfies S. It is not necessary for every behavior in S' to be in S, just for every behavior that can be generated by a real implementation of S' to be in S. The set of behaviors that can be generated by a real implementation of S' is included in the realizable part of S', so we define S' implements S to mean $\mathcal{R}_\mu(S') \subseteq S$.

We expect "implements" to be transitive, meaning that if S'' implements S', and S' implements S, then S'' implements S. Proving transitivity requires showing that $\mathcal{R}_\mu(S'') \subseteq S'$ and $\mathcal{R}_\mu(S') \subseteq S$ imply $\mathcal{R}_\mu(S'') \subseteq S$. This implication is valid because, by Proposition 3, $\mathcal{R}_\mu(S'') \subseteq S'$ iff $\mathcal{R}_\mu(S'') \subseteq \mathcal{R}_\mu(S')$.

We now return to the composition of systems. Let S_1 and S_2 be specifications of systems with agent sets μ_1 and μ_2, respectively. Any real implementation that satisfies S_i will satisfy $\mathcal{R}_{\mu_i}(S_i)$, so combining an implementation of S_1 with an implementation of S_2 produces a system whose set of behaviors is contained in $\mathcal{R}_{\mu_1}(S_1) \cap \mathcal{R}_{\mu_2}(S_2)$. Thus, to prove that the composition of a system specified by S_1 and one specified by S_2 implements a specification S, it suffices to prove

$$\mathcal{R}_{\mu_1}(S_1) \cap \mathcal{R}_{\mu_2}(S_2) \subseteq S \qquad (5)$$

If (5) holds, then the following proposition allows us to infer the stronger result $\mathcal{R}_{\mu_1}(S_1) \cap \mathcal{R}_{\mu_2}(S_2) \subseteq \mathcal{R}_{\mu_1 \cup \mu_2}(S)$.

Proposition 9 *For any disjoint pair of agent sets μ_1 and μ_2, and any properties P_1 and P_2, the property $\mathcal{R}_{\mu_1}(P_1) \cap \mathcal{R}_{\mu_2}(P_2)$ is $\mu_1 \cup \mu_2$-receptive.*

Proposition 9 also implies that $\mathcal{R}_{\mu_1}(S_1) \cap \mathcal{R}_{\mu_2}(S_2) \subseteq \mathcal{R}_{\mu_1 \cup \mu_2}(S_1 \cap S_2)$. This in turn implies that condition (5) is weaker than $\mathcal{R}_{\mu_1 \cup \mu_2}(S_1 \cap S_2) \subseteq \mathcal{R}_{\mu_1 \cup \mu_2}(S)$, which is what we would have to prove to show that $S_1 \cap S_2$ implements S.

5.2.2 Proving That One Specification Implements Another

We now comment briefly on how one can prove in practice that a specification S' of the form $E' \Rightarrow M'$ implements a specification S of the form $E \Rightarrow M$. If S' is not μ-receptive (equal to its realizable part), then deriving an explicit formula for $\mathcal{R}_\mu(S')$ is likely to be very difficult. (If it were easy, then we would have written $\mathcal{R}_\mu(S')$ instead of S' in the first place.) Therefore, unless we can apply some general theorem—like Theorem 2 of Section 5.3 below—to prove that S' implements S, we will have to prove that $S' \subseteq S$.

Specification S' has environment assumption E', while S has environment assumption E. If the system specified by S' is to satisfy the specification S, it must do so assuming only that the environment satisfies E. Therefore, E' must be equal to or weaker than E—that is, we must have $E \subseteq E'$. Since $E \subseteq E'$ implies $(E' \Rightarrow M') \subseteq (E \Rightarrow M')$, if the implementation satisfies $E' \Rightarrow M'$ then it also satisfies $E \Rightarrow M'$. Therefore, it suffices to prove $E \Rightarrow M \subseteq E \Rightarrow M'$.

By elementary set theory, $(E \Rightarrow M') \subseteq (E \Rightarrow M)$ is equivalent to $E \cap M' \subseteq E \cap M$. (This equivalence was pointed out to us by Amir Pnueli.) Whereas $E \Rightarrow M$ consists of all behaviors in which the system behaves correctly in the face of arbitrary environment behavior, $E \cap M$ consists of only those behaviors in which both the environment and system behave correctly. In the transition-axiom approach, E is an abstract partial program describing the environment and M is an abstract partial program describing the system, so $E \cap M$ defines the program obtained by composing these two partial programs. Similarly, $E \cap M'$ describes a program. Therefore, proving $E \cap M' \subseteq E \cap M$ requires proving that one program implements another.

Proving that one program implements another is a problem that has been addressed extensively in earlier work. The basic transition-axiom approach is described in [Lam89], and a formal basis along with a completeness result can be found in [AL88]. We briefly sketch this approach.

The specification $E \cap M$ can be written in the form

$$\exists \mathbf{x} : I \cap \mathcal{TA}_{\neg\mu}(\mathcal{N}_E) \cap \mathcal{TA}_\mu(\mathcal{N}_M) \cap L$$

where I is an initial predicate, $\mathcal{N}_E$ and $\mathcal{N}_M$ are next-state relations describing the environment and system actions, respectively, and L is a progress property—all with set of states $\mathbf{S} \times \mathbf{X}$. (Here, $\mathbf{X}$ includes the internal state components of both the environment and the system.) We can write I as a logical formula on the state variables, $\mathcal{N}_E$ and $\mathcal{N}_M$ as relations between old and new state values, and L as a formula in some temporal logic. Similarly, $E \cap M'$ can be written in the form $\exists \mathbf{y} : I' \cap \mathcal{TA}_{\neg\mu}(\mathcal{N}'_E) \cap \mathcal{TA}_\mu(\mathcal{N}'_M) \cap L'$, with a set of internal states $\mathbf{Y}$. Moreover, $\mathcal{N}_E$ and $\mathcal{N}'_E$ will be essentially the same relations, depending only on the externally visible state and the environment's internal state components, which are are common to $\mathbf{X}$ and $\mathbf{Y}$. To prove that $E \cap M'$ implements $E \cap M$, we construct a *refinement mapping* f from $\mathbf{S} \times \mathbf{Y}$ to $\mathbf{S} \times \mathbf{X}$ that satisfies the following four conditions.

1. *f preserves the externally visible* **S***-component.* In other words, for all $(s, y) \in \mathbf{S} \times \mathbf{Y}$, there is some $x \in \mathbf{X}$ such that $f(s, y) = (s, x)$.

   In practice, a set of states is defined by a collection of state components. Let $e_1, \ldots, e_m$ denote the components defining $\mathbf{S}$, so an element s of $\mathbf{S}$ is an m-tuple $(e_1(s), \ldots, e_m(s))$; let $x_1, \ldots, x_n$ and $y_1, \ldots, y_p$ denote the similar components defining $\mathbf{X}$ and $\mathbf{Y}$. To specify the refinement mapping f, one must define functions $f_1, \ldots, f_n$ such that $f(s, y) = (s, (f_1(s, y), \ldots, f_n(s, y)))$. The f_j can be described by formulas having the components e_i and y_k as free variables. For example, the formula $e_1 + 4y_2$ denotes the function g such that $g(s, y) = e_1(s) + 4y_2(y)$.

2. *f takes initial states to initial states.* The formal condition is $f(I') \subseteq I$.

   To explain what this condition means in practice, we first make the following definition. For any formula H with free variables $e_1, \ldots, e_m$ and $x_1, \ldots, x_n$, define $f^*(H)$ to be the formula obtained by substituting f_j for x_j, for $j = 1, \ldots, n$. This defines $f^*(H)$ to be a formula with free variables $e_1, \ldots, e_m$ and $y_1, \ldots, y_p$. Translating the semantic condition $f(I') \subseteq I$ into the logical framework of formulas gives the condition $\models I' \Rightarrow f^*(I)$, which is a formula "about" the implementation. In most cases, this condition is easy to check.

3. *f maps $\mathcal{N}'_M$ steps into $\mathcal{N}_M$ steps or stuttering steps.* Formally, we require that if (s, y) is any state reachable from a state in I' by a sequence of $\mathcal{N}'_E$ and $\mathcal{N}'_M$ steps, then $((s, y), (t, z)) \in \mathcal{N}'_M$ implies $(f(s, y), f(t, z)) \in \mathcal{N}_M$ or $f(s, y) = f(t, z)$.

   In practice, verifying this condition involves finding an $\mathbf{S} \times \mathbf{Y}$-predicate P such that $I \subseteq P$ and P is left invariant by $\mathcal{N}'_E$ and $\mathcal{N}'_M$, meaning that $(s, y) \in P$ and $((s, y), (t, z)) \in \mathcal{N}'_E \cup \mathcal{N}'_M$ imply $(t, z) \in P$. One then proves $old.P \wedge \mathcal{N}'_M \Rightarrow f^*(\mathcal{N}_M)$, where $old.P$ is the formula asserting that P is true in the first state of a step. Finding an invariant P and proving its invariance is exactly what one does in a proof by the Owicki-Gries method [LS84b, OG76], so the method for proving this condition generalizes the standard method for proving invariance properties of concurrent programs.

4. *f maps behaviors that satisfy $I' \cap \mathcal{TA}_{\neg\mu}(\mathcal{N}'_E) \cap \mathcal{TA}_{\mu}(\mathcal{N}'_M) \cap L'$ into behaviors that satisfy L.* The formal condition is $f(I' \cap \mathcal{TA}_{\neg\mu}(\mathcal{N}'_E) \cap \mathcal{TA}_{\mu}(\mathcal{N}'_M) \cap L') \subseteq L$.

   Translated into the logical framework, the formula to be verified becomes $I' \wedge \mathcal{TA}_{\neg\mu}(\mathcal{N}'_E) \wedge \mathcal{TA}_{\mu}(\mathcal{N}'_M) \wedge L' \Rightarrow f^*(L)$. This formula asserts that the abstract program described by $I' \wedge \mathcal{TA}_{\neg\mu}(\mathcal{N}'_E) \wedge \mathcal{TA}_{\mu}(\mathcal{N}'_M) \wedge L'$ satisfies the property $f^*(L)$, which is generally a liveness property. Thus, verification of this condition is tantamount to proving that a program satisfies a liveness property, which can be done with the method of [OL82] when L and L' are expressed as temporal logic formulas.

Condition 3 is weaker in two ways than the corresponding condition R3 in the definition of a refinement mapping in [AL88]. First, condition 3 applies only to μ steps, while condition R3 applies to all steps. The weaker condition is sufficient because $\neg\mu$ steps, which are taken by the environment, are essentially the same in both $E \cap M'$ and $E \cap M$. (The formalism of [AL88] did not include agents and made no distinction between system and environment steps.) Second, condition 3 applies only to steps taken from a reachable state, while R3 applies to steps taken from any state. The weaker condition was not needed in [AL88], where history variables were used to eliminate unreachable states.

Theorem 2 of [AL88] asserts the existence of a refinement mapping under certain reasonable assumptions about the specifications, providing a completeness theorem for the proof method. In general, obtaining the refinement mapping may require adding two auxiliary variables to the lower-level specification: a history variable used to record past actions, and a prophecy variable used to predict future ones. Our limited experience indicates that prophecy variables are almost never needed and, with condition 3 rather than R3, history variables are seldom needed. Although our experience with this method for verifying concurrent systems is limited, refinement mappings are essentially abstraction functions of the kind that have been used for years to prove that one data type implements another [Hoa72], so we have good reason to believe that these mappings can be constructed in practice.

5.3 The Main Theorem

5.3.1 Deriving a Theorem from Necessity

Having discussed composition and implementation, we come to the problem of proving that the composition of two component specifications S_1 and S_2

implements a specification S, which means proving $\mathcal{R}_{\mu_1}(S_1) \cap \mathcal{R}_{\mu_2}(S_2) \subseteq S$. One might attempt to do this with the refinement-mapping method of Section 5.2.2. Since we cannot expect to construct the realizable part of a specification, we would have to prove the stronger result that $S_1 \cap S_2$ implements S. However, our specifications have the form "environment assumption implies system correctness", so S equals $E \Rightarrow M$ and each S_i equals $E_i \Rightarrow M_i$. The refinement-mapping method proves that a specification of the form $E \Rightarrow M'$ implements $E \Rightarrow M$, but $S_1 \cap S_2$ is not in this form. So, a new technique is needed.

We split the proof that the composition of S_1 and S_2 implements S into two steps: first finding a property M' so that the composition implements $E \Rightarrow M'$, and then using a refinement mapping to prove that $E \Rightarrow M'$ implements S. By transitivity of "implements", we can infer that the composition of S_1 and S_2 implements S. Since M_i asserts that component i behaves properly, the obvious choice of M' is $M_1 \cap M_2$, which asserts that both components behave properly. Thus, for the first step, we have to prove

$$\mathcal{R}_{\mu_1}(E_1 \Rightarrow M_1) \cap \mathcal{R}_{\mu_2}(E_2 \Rightarrow M_2) \subseteq E \Rightarrow M_1 \cap M_2 \tag{6}$$

We now consider under what hypotheses we can expect (6) to be true—in other words, what proof rule we can write with (6) as its conclusion. To simplify the discussion, we drop the $\mathcal{R}$'s by assuming for now that all the specifications are receptive.

Formula (6) asserts that if the two components satisfy their specifications, then the composition satisfies $E \Rightarrow M_1 \cap M_2$. Satisfying $E \Rightarrow M_1 \cap M_2$ means that if the environment satisfies assumption E, then each component i satisfies M_i. What must we assume to ensure that the first component satisfies M_1? The specification $E_1 \Rightarrow M_1$ asserts that component 1 satisfies M_1 if its environment satisfies E_1. But in the composite system, the environment of component 1 consists of the environment of the composite system together with component 2. We assume that the composite system's environment satisfies E, and component 2 should satisfy M_2, so the environment of component 1 in the composite system satisfies $E \cap M_2$. Therefore, the hypothesis we want asserts that $E \cap M_2$ implies E_1, which is written formally as

$$E \cap M_2 \subseteq E_1 \tag{7}$$

Similarly, to deduce that the second component satisfies M_2, we need the hypothesis

$$E \cap M_1 \subseteq E_2 \tag{8}$$

The nicest possible proof rule has these as the only hypotheses:

$$\frac{E \cap M_2 \subseteq E_1, \qquad E \cap M_1 \subseteq E_2}{(E_1 \Rightarrow M_1) \cap (E_2 \Rightarrow M_2) \subseteq E \Rightarrow M_1 \cap M_2} \tag{9}$$

If we view (9) as a rule of inference for arbitrary properties E, E_1, E_2, M_1, and M_2, we find that it is invalid. For example, suppose $E_1 = E_2 = M_1 = M_2 = P$ for some property P. Both hypotheses then reduce to the tautology $E \cap P \subseteq P$, and the conclusion reduces to $E \subseteq P$, so (9) allows us to deduce that E is a subset of P for completely arbitrary properties E and P. To understand exactly why the rule is invalid, assume that the three properties E, $E_1 \Rightarrow M_1$, and $E_2 \Rightarrow M_2$ hold. The first hypothesis then asserts that if component 2 satisfies M_2, then E_1 holds, so we can conclude that component 1 satisfies M_1. The second hypothesis asserts that if component 1 satisfies M_1, then E_2 holds, so we can conclude that component 2 satisfies M_2. In a classic example of circular reasoning, the rule then concludes that component 1 satisfies M_1 and component 2 satisfies M_2.

Proof rule (9) is invalid for arbitrary properties, and our examination of what it means gives us no reason to expect it to be valid for our specifications. Yet remarkably, it is valid for the specifications that we write—assuming that the properties $(E_1 \Rightarrow M_1)$ and $(E_2 \Rightarrow M_2)$ are receptive. If they aren't, we simply replace them by their realizable parts. Having done that, we can then strengthen the rule by applying Proposition 9 to replace $E \Rightarrow M_1 \cap M_2$ with its realizable part.

We now state the precise theorem. Its hypotheses are discussed later.

Theorem 2 *If μ_1, μ_2, and $\mu_1 \cup \mu_2$ are agent sets and E, E_1, E_2, M_1, and M_2 are properties such that:*

1. *$E = I \cap P$, $E_1 = I_1 \cap P_1$, and $E_2 = I_2 \cap P_2$, where*
   (a) *I, I_1, and I_2 are initial predicates.*
   (b) *P, P_1, and P_2 are safety properties that constrain at most $\neg(\mu_1 \cup \mu_2)$, $\neg\mu_1$, and $\neg\mu_2$, respectively.*
2. *$\overline{M_1}$ and $\overline{M_2}$ constrain at most μ_1 and μ_2, respectively.*
3. *M_1 and M_2 are μ_1- and μ_2-abstract properties, respectively.*
4. *$\mu_1 \cap \mu_2 = \emptyset$.*

Then the rule of inference

$$\frac{E \cap M_2 \subseteq E_1, \qquad E \cap M_1 \subseteq E_2}{\mathcal{R}_{\mu_1}(E_1 \Rightarrow M_1) \cap \mathcal{R}_{\mu_2}(E_2 \Rightarrow M_2) \ \subseteq \ \mathcal{R}_{\mu_1 \cup \mu_2}(E \Rightarrow M_1 \cap M_2)}$$

is sound.

The theorem handles the composition of two systems. It has an obvious generalization to the composition of n systems. For $n = 3$, the rule of inference is

$$\frac{E \cap M_2 \cap M_3 \subseteq E_1, \quad E \cap M_1 \cap M_3 \subseteq E_2, \quad E \cap M_1 \cap M_2 \subseteq E_3}{\begin{array}{c}\mathcal{R}_{\mu_1}(E_1 \Rightarrow M_1) \cap \mathcal{R}_{\mu_2}(E_2 \Rightarrow M_2) \cap \mathcal{R}_{\mu_3}(E_3 \Rightarrow M_3) \\ \subseteq \ \mathcal{R}_{\mu_1 \cup \mu_2 \cup \mu_3}(E \Rightarrow M_1 \cap M_2 \cap M_3)\end{array}}$$

The general result can be derived from the theorem by using Proposition 9.

5.3.2 The Hypotheses of the Theorem

We now discuss the four hypotheses of the theorem.

1. Any safety property E' can be written as $I' \cap P'$, where I' is an initial predicate and P' is a safety property that constrains at most ν for some set of agents ν. If E' specifies the environment of a system with agent set μ, then ν should equal $\neg\mu$. Therefore, Hypothesis 1 will be satisfied if the environment assumptions E, E_1, and E_2 are safety properties. Theorem 1 allows us to rewrite a specification so its environment assumption is a safety property.

   Observe that a system implemented by components with agent sets μ_1 and μ_2 should have $\mu_1 \cup \mu_2$ as its agent set. But, the higher-level specification $E \Rightarrow M$ may have been written in terms of an agent set μ rather than $\mu_1 \cup \mu_2$. In this case, we must perform a renaming operation, substituting $\mu_1 \cup \mu_2$ for μ, before applying the theorem.

2. In the transition-axiom approach, each M_i has the form

   $$\exists \mathbf{x} : I_{\mathbf{x}} \cap \mathcal{TA}_{\neg\mu}(\mathcal{U}_{\mathbf{x}}) \cap \mathcal{TA}_{\mu}(\mathcal{N}) \cap L$$

   and we expect $\overline{M_i}$ to equal $\exists \mathbf{x} : I_{\mathbf{x}} \cap \mathcal{TA}_{\neg\mu_i}(\mathcal{U}_{\mathbf{x}}) \cap \mathcal{TA}_{\mu_i}(\mathcal{N})$, in which case Hypothesis 2 is satisfied.

3. If we write M_i directly, either as an abstract program or by any sort of logical formula, individual agents cannot be mentioned. The only reference to agents is through the symbol "μ_i", so there is no way to write M_i without making it μ_i-abstract.

4. As we mentioned in Section 5.1.2, this hypothesis means that the two components are distinct. They need be distinct only at the current level of abstraction; their implementations could contain common parts. For example, the two components might specify distinct program procedures, while their implementations both invoke a common subprocedure. We can consider the subprocedure to be executed by different agents depending upon which procedure invoked it. Alternatively, we can generalize our notion of implementation to allow renaming of agents. In practice, this hypothesis seems to be a petty nuisance of the formalism, not a real concern.

5.3.3 The Hypotheses of the Proof Rule

We now consider how to verify the hypotheses of the proof rules. Since the two hypotheses are symmetric, we look at only the first one: $E \cap M_2 \subseteq E_1$. This hypothesis asserts that the environment of the composite system together with component 2 implements the environment of component 1.

Hypothesis 1 of the theorem asserts that E and E_1 are safety properties. Property M_2 may include a progress condition. However, a progress condition should not help in proving a safety property. If we can prove E_1 assuming E and M_2, then we should be able to prove E_1 assuming E and only the safety part $\overline{M_2}$ of M_2. In fact, an important step in the proof of Theorem 2 states that, under the hypotheses of the theorem, $E \cap M_2 \subseteq E_1$ and $E \cap \overline{M_2} \subseteq E_1$ are equivalent.

In the transition-axiom approach, the properties E, M_2, and E_1 are written as abstract programs. If the program M_2 is machine-closed, then simply removing its progress property gives the program $\overline{M_2}$. Proving $E \cap \overline{M_2} \subseteq E_1$ means proving that the abstract program obtained by combining the programs E and $\overline{M_2}$ implements the program E_1. In general, this proof can be done with a refinement mapping. Since there is no liveness property, condition 4 of the definition of a refinement mapping in Section 5.2.2 becomes vacuous.

To see more concretely how this proof works, consider the example of Figures 2 and 3. The fact that we can connect the *inp* and *mid* wires of component 1 to different components means that the environment assumptions about these wires must be independent. Therefore, E_1 can be written as $E_1^{inp} \cap E_1^{mid}$, where E_1^{inp} is the assumption about how the environment changes *inp*, and E_1^{mid} is the assumption about how the environment changes *mid*. Similarly, we expect E_2 to equal $E_2^{mid} \cap E_2^{out}$. The environment condition E for the composed system should equal $E_1^{inp} \cap E_2^{out} \cap I^{mid} \cap \mathcal{TA}_{\neg(\mu_1 \cup \mu_2)}(\mathcal{U}_{mid})$, where the last conjunct asserts that only components 1 and 2 can change *mid*, and I^{mid} is the initial condition for that wire.

The formula $E \cap \overline{M_2} \subseteq E_1$ is then

$$E_1^{inp} \cap E_2^{out} \cap I^{mid} \cap \mathcal{TA}_{\neg(\mu_1 \cup \mu_2)}(\mathcal{U}_{mid}) \cap \overline{M_2} \subseteq E_1^{inp} \cap E_1^{mid}$$

This formula is implied by the following condition.

$$E_2^{out} \cap I^{mid} \cap \mathcal{TA}_{\neg(\mu_1 \cup \mu_2)}(\mathcal{U}_{mid}) \cap \overline{M_2} \subseteq E_1^{mid} \tag{10}$$

Neglecting internal state components, $\overline{M_2}$ will have the form $\mathcal{TA}_{\mu_2}(\mathcal{N}_M)$ and E_1^{mid} will have the form $I^{mid} \cap \mathcal{TA}_{\neg\mu_1}(\mathcal{N}_E^{mid})$, where $\mathcal{N}_E^{mid}$ restricts only changes to *mid*. Thus, (10) is equivalent to

$$E_2^{out} \cap I^{mid} \cap \mathcal{TA}_{\neg(\mu_1 \cup \mu_2)}(\mathcal{U}_{mid}) \cap \mathcal{TA}_{\mu_2}(\mathcal{N}_M) \subseteq \mathcal{TA}_{\neg\mu_1}(\mathcal{N}_E^{mid}) \tag{11}$$

The formula $\mathcal{TA}_{\neg\mu_1}(\mathcal{N}_E^{mid})$ asserts that any $\neg\mu_1$ step either leaves *mid* unchanged or changes it according to $\mathcal{N}_E^{mid}$. Any $\neg\mu_1$ agent is either in μ_2 or in $\neg(\mu_1 \cup \mu_2)$. Since $\mathcal{TA}_{\neg(\mu_1 \cup \mu_2)}(\mathcal{U}_{mid})$ guarantees that no $\neg(\mu_1 \cup \mu_2)$ agent changes *mid*, to prove (11) it suffices to prove

$$E_2^{out} \cap I^{mid} \cap \mathcal{TA}_{\mu_2}(\mathcal{N}_M) \subseteq \mathcal{TA}_{\mu_2}(\mathcal{N}_E^{mid}) \tag{12}$$

Property E_2^{out} will have the form $I^{out} \cap \mathcal{TA}_{\neg\mu_2}(\mathcal{N}_E^{out})$, where $\mathcal{N}_E^{out}$ restricts only changes to *out*. We can therefore rewrite (12) as

$$I^{mid} \cap I^{out} \cap \mathcal{TA}_{\neg\mu_2}(\mathcal{N}_E^{out}) \cap \mathcal{TA}_{\mu_2}(\mathcal{N}_M) \subseteq \mathcal{TA}_{\mu_2}(\mathcal{N}_E^{mid}) \tag{13}$$

Formula (13) asserts that, in an environment specified by initial predicate $I^{mid} \cap I^{out}$ and next-state relation $\mathcal{N}_E^{out}$, the partial program defined by the next-state relation $\mathcal{N}_M$ implements the partial program defined by the next-state relation $\mathcal{N}_E^{mid}$. In other words, if the environment assumption about *out* and the initial condition for *mid* hold, then component 2 satisfies the assumption that component 1 makes about how its environment changes *mid*. Relating the pieces I^{mid}, I^{out}, $\mathcal{N}_E^{out}$, $\mathcal{N}_M$, and $\mathcal{N}_E^{mid}$ of condition (13) to the parts of Figure 3 reveals how reasonable the condition is. Since (13) asserts that one program implements another, it can be proved with a refinement mapping.

6 Concluding Remarks

We have approached the problem of composing specifications from a purely semantic point of view. A formal specification method will use a language and logic based on this semantics. Our Theorem 2 will appear as a proof rule in the logic. We have touched lightly on logical issues in our discussion, mentioning what form some logical formulas might take. Some concluding remarks about language and logic are in order.

The semantic form of our specifications suggests the general style of a specification language. Safety properties are expressed by describing a next-state relation, and progress properties are expressed either directly in some form of temporal logic, or with fairness conditions that can be translated into temporal logic.

There are obvious desiderata for a specification language: it should be expressive, readable, concise, fully abstract, etc. There are also more precise attributes that the specification logic must have. Clearly, we want all the sets of behaviors expressed to be properties, meaning that they are closed under stuttering-equivalence. Another simple attribute of a logic is *explicitness*, meaning that whether or not a behavior satisfies a formula F depends only on the values assumed during the behavior by the state components that are free variables of F. Explicitness is necessary if existential quantification is to have its expected meaning, but it poses a surprisingly serious constraint on how specifications are written. For example, consider a formula F that specifies the assignment statement $x := x + 1$. If this formula is to assert that executing the assignment statement does not change y, then explicitness requires that y (and every other variable that is not changed) be free variables of F. A practical language must allow one to write the formula F so that y is a free variable of F even though it does not actually appear.

Closure under stuttering-equivalence and explicitness may seem esoteric to readers accustomed to popular, simple semantics of programs. In a typical semantics, the formula specifying a program is satisfied only by behaviors in which each step corresponds to the execution of a program action—for example, this is the natural way to write a semantics using the "next-time" temporal operator. However, composition cannot be conjunction in such a semantics. For example, consider two completely noninteracting programs, with separate sets of variables, described by formulas F and G. A behavior of their composition is obtained by interleaving actions from the two programs. But such an interleaved behavior does not satisfy F, since it contains steps that do not represent actions of that program, nor does it satisfy G. Thus, the composition of the two programs is not described by the formula $F \wedge G$. Closure under stuttering-equivalence and explicitness are needed for composition to be conjunction even in the trivial case of noninteracting programs.

References

[AFK88] Krzysztof R. Apt, Nissim Francez, and Shmuel Katz. Appraising fairness in languages for distributed programming. *Distributed Computing*, 2:226–241, 1988.

[AL88] Martín Abadi and Leslie Lamport. The existence of refinement mappings. Research Report 29, Digital Systems Research Center, 1988. To appear in *Theoretical Computer Science.* A preliminary version appeared in *Proceedings of the Third Annual Symposium on Logic In Computer Science*, pages 165-177, Edinburgh, Scotland, July 1988, IEEE Computer Society.

[ALW89] Martín Abadi, Leslie Lamport, and Pierre Wolper. Realizable and unrealizable program specifications. In G. Ausiello, M. Dezani-Ciancaglini, and S. Ronchi Della Rocca, editors, *Automata, Languages and Programming*, Lecture Notes in Computer Science, 372, pages 1–17. Springer-Verlag, July 1989.

[AS85] Bowen Alpern and Fred B. Schneider. Defining liveness. *Information Processing Letters*, 21(4):181–185, October 1985.

[BKP86] Howard Barringer, Ruurd Kuiper, and Amir Pnueli. A really abstract concurrent model and its temporal logic. In *Thirteenth Annual ACM Symposium on Principles of Programming Languages*, pages 173–183. ACM, January 1986.

[Dav64] Morton Davis. Infinite games of perfect information. In M. Dresher, L. S. Shapley, and A. W. Tucker, editors, *Advances in game theory*, volume 52 of *Annals of Mathematics Studies*, pages 85–101. Princeton University Press, Princeton, New Jersey, 1964.

[Dil88] David L. Dill. *Trace Theory for Automatic Hierarchical Verification of Speed-Independent Circuits.* PhD thesis, Carnegie Mellon University, February 1988.

[Hoa72] C. A. R. Hoare. Proof of correctness of data representations. *Acta Informatica*, 1:271–281, 1972.

[Hoa85] C. A. R. Hoare. *Communicating Sequential Processes.* Series in Computer Science. Prentice-Hall International, London, 1985.

[Lam83a] Leslie Lamport. Specifying concurrent program modules. *ACM Transactions on Programming Languages and Systems*, 5(2):190–222, April 1983.

[Lam83b] Leslie Lamport. What good is temporal logic? In R. E. A. Mason, editor, *Information Processing 83: Proceedings of the IFIP 9th World Congress*, pages 657–668, Paris, September 1983. IFIP, North Holland.

[Lam89] Leslie Lamport. A simple approach to specifying concurrent systems. *Communications of the ACM*, 32(1):32–45, January 1989.

[LS84a] S. S. Lam and A. U. Shankar. Protocol verification via projections. *IEEE Transactions on Software Engineering*, SE-10(4):325–342, July 1984.

[LS84b] Leslie Lamport and Fred B. Schneider. The "Hoare logic" of CSP, and all that. *ACM Transactions on Programming Languages and Systems*, 6(2):281–296, April 1984.

[LT87] Nancy Lynch and Mark Tuttle. Hierarchical correctness proofs for distributed algorithms. In *Proceedings of the Sixth Symposium on the Principles of Distributed Computing*, pages 137–151. ACM, August 1987.

[MC81] Jayadev Misra and K. Mani Chandy. Proofs of networks of processes. *IEEE Transactions on Software Engineering*, SE-7(4):417–426, July 1981.

[Mil80] R. Milner. *A Calculus of Communicating Systems.* Springer-Verlag, Berlin, Heidelberg, New York, 1980.

[MP87] Zohar Manna and Amir Pnueli. A hierarchy of temporal properties. Technical Report STAN-CS-87-1186, Department of Computer Science, Stanford University, October 1987.

[OG76] Susan Owicki and David Gries. Verifying properties of parallel programs: An axiomatic approach. *Communications of the ACM*, 19(5):279–284, May 1976.

[OL82] Susan Owicki and Leslie Lamport. Proving liveness properties of concurrent programs. *ACM Transactions on Programming Languages and Systems*, 4(3):455–495, July 1982.

[Pnu84] Amir Pnueli. In transition from global to modular temporal reasoning about programs. In Krzysztof R. Apt, editor, *Logics and Models of Concurrent Systems*, NATO ASI Series, pages 123–144. Springer-Verlag, October 1984.

Refinement Calculus, Part I: Sequential Nondeterministic Programs

R.J.R. Back
Åbo Akademi University, Department of Computer Science
Lemminkäinengatan 14, SF-20520 Åbo, Finland

J. von Wright
Swedish School of Economics and Business Education
Biblioteksgatan 16, SF-65100 Vasa,Finland

Abstract A lattice theoretic framework for the calculus of program refinement is presented. Specifications and program statements are combined into a single (infinitary) language of commands which permits miraculous, angelic and demonic statements to be used in the description of program behavior. The weakest precondition calculus is extended to cover this larger class of statements and a game-theoretic interpretation is given for these constructs. The language is complete, in the sense that every monotonic predicate transformer can be expressed in it. The usual program constructs can be defined as derived notions in this language. The notion of inverse statements is defined and its use in formalizing the notion of data refinement is shown.

Key words Stepwise refinement, weakest preconditions, angelic nondeterminism, demonic nondeterminism, miraculous statements, data refinement, inverse statements, total correctness, lattices, specification methods.

Contents

1. Introduction
   1.1 A lattice-theoretic basis
   1.2 Overview of the paper

2. Predicates and predicate transformers
   2.1 Lattices
   2.2 States and state spaces
   2.3 Predicate lattice
   2.4 Operations on predicates
   2.5 Predicate transformer lattices

3. A command language
   3.1 The command language
   3.2 Commands as predicate transformers
   3.3 Completeness of command language
   3.4 Sublanguages of $\mathcal{C}$

3.5 Subcommand replacement
3.6 Refinements in the command languages

4. Specification and program constructs
4.1 Assert commands and guards
4.2 Update commands
4.3 Nondeterministic variable introduction
4.4 Conditional composition
4.5 Recursion and iteration
4.6 Blocks with local variables
4.7 Assignment commands

5. Inverse commands and data refinement
5.1 Inverse commands
5.2 A characterization of refinement
5.3 Data refinement
5.4 Abstraction and representation commands

6. Conclusions and related work

1 Introduction

Stepwise refinement is one of the main methods for systematic construction of sequential programs: an originally high level program specification is transformed by a sequence of correctness preserving refinements into an executable and efficient program. The origins of this method are in the writings of Dijkstra and Wirth [18,37] and in the program transformation approach of Gerhart [21] and Burstall and Darlington [15].

The stepwise refinement approach was formalized by Back [1,2] in a *refinement calculus* , using the weakest precondition technique of Dijkstra [19] as a basis. The central notion in this calculus is a relation of refinement between program statements: Statement S is said to be *(correctly) refined* by statement S', denoted $S \leq S'$, if

$$\forall P, Q : P\langle S \rangle Q \Rightarrow P\langle S' \rangle Q.$$

Here $P\langle S \rangle Q$ stands for total correctness of S with respect to precondition P and postcondition Q. An equivalent characterization in terms of weakest preconditions is

$$\forall R : \mathrm{wp}(S, R) \Rightarrow \mathrm{wp}(S', R).$$

The refinement relation is reflexive and transitive. Hence, if we can prove that $S_0 \leq S_1 \leq \ldots \leq S_{n-1} \leq S_n$, then $S_0 \leq S_n$. This models the successive refinement steps in program development. S_0 is the initial high level specification statement and S_n is the final executable program derived through the intermediate program versions $S_1, \ldots, S_{n-1}$. Each refinement step preserves the correctness of the previous step. Hence the final program preserves the correctness of the original specification. Specifications are treated as generalized statements and may include higher level, not necessary computable notions.

The refinement relation is monotonic with respect to the sequential statement constructors. This means that if T is a statement where S occurs as a substatement, $T = T(S)$, then

$$S \leq S' \Rightarrow T(S) \leq T(S').$$

In other words, we may replace a substatement by its refinement in any program context. This justifies the top-down method of program constructions that is very important in stepwise refinement.

The refinement calculus was used to formalize different aspects of the stepwise refinement method, such as the use of specifications as program statements, procedural abstraction, refinement of data representations in programs, use of context information in refining program components and proving correctness of program transformation rules.

The notion of correctness preserving program refinements need not be restricted to total correctness. Back [3] studies the notion of correct refinement in general, for different classes of correctness properties to be preserved by the refinement steps.

The foundations of the refinement calculus is further developed by Back in [5]. In [4] the calculus is used to give a simple formalization of procedures and to derive proof rules for procedures, in [6] to handle data abstraction in general. Back and Sere extend the applicability of the refinement calculus to the stepwise refinement of parallel algorithms in [7,8]. In [12,11] we further develop the mathematical foundations of the refinement calculus, in a simple and very general lattice-theoretic framework.

The refinement calculus has attracted renewed interest lately also by other researchers. Morgan has together with Gardiner studied both procedural and data refinement [30,29,33] along somewhat similar lines as in [4,6], as well as the use of types in the refinement calculus [32]. Morris [34] is largely a reinvention of the refinement calculus, but does present a more elegant treatment of predicate transformers and unbounded nondeterminism than [2]. He also treats data refinement [35], as do Chen and Udding [16], along similar lines as [29].

An important contribution of this recent work has been to permit miraculous program statements, which were not included in the original refinement calculus. Miracles were originally proposed for program construction by Nelson [36], although miraculous statements were studied semantically already by de Bakker [17]. The use of miracles simplifies the theory, and were also employed by Back [7] in the extension of the refinement calculus to parallel programs.More algebraic approaches to program construction, but in a similar spirit, are described by Hoare and others in [28] and by Hesselink [26].

Our purpose here is to present an overview of the refinement calculus for sequential and parallel programs. We focus on the basic kernel of the calculus, referring to other publications for applications and for detailed proofs of the results presented. The presentation has been divided into two parts. Part I presents the basic lattice-theoretic framework for sequential and nondeterministic programs, providing a unified treatment of ordinary and miraculous statements, as well as permitting both demonic and angelic nondeterminism in statements. Part II shows how to combine the action system framework with the refinement calculus for sequential programs, in particular the method of data refinement, to get a simple and general framework for the stepwise refinement of parallel and reactive programs.

1.1 A lattice-theoretic basis

The original weakest precondition calculus of Dijkstra [19] identified the meaning of a program statement with its weakest precondition predicate transformer. Dijkstra's also introduced a number of "healthiness conditions" to characterize those predicate transformers that could be considered as meanings of programs. These required that predicate transformers for executable program statements to be strict (satisfy the "Law of Excluded Miracle"), monotonic, conjunctive and continuous.

The main idea of the refinement calculus [2] was to generalize the notion of executable programs to also include program specifications, which can be understood as executable in an idealized sense, even if they need not be executable by a machine. This makes it possible to treat program specifications and executable program statements in the same way, and combine them in a single framework.

Treating specifications as programs has the consequences for the healthiness conditions. Introducing weakest preconditions for *specification statements* [2] implies that the continuity restriction has to be dropped. This is because unbounded nondeterminism, even if it is not realizable by a machine, is a reasonable property of a specification and unbounded nondeterminism violates the continuity assumption. The *miraculous statements* [17,36,34,30,7] do not satisfy the Law of Excluded miracle, but are well motivated in program specifications. The *angelic statements* [6] are disjunctive but not conjunctive, but turn out to be very useful in data refinements with non-functional data abstractions.

Thus, in going from an executable programming language to a language which also treats specifications as executable entities, most of the original healthiness conditions have been questioned. The driving force has been to gain expressive power and to develop more powerful calculi for program development. A specification language is in this sense truly more general than a programming language, for which all the original healthiness conditions are well motivated.

The only healthiness criteria that has gone unquestioned is the monotonicity requirement. Morris [34] noted that the monotonic predicate transformers form a lattice, with the partial order corresponding to the refinement ordering of statements. Lattice-like operators on statements have been considered by Gardiner and Morgan [20] and by Hoare and others [28]. We have carried this lattice-theoretic approach further in [12,11], with the purpose of providing a simple and unified framework in which to incorporate the above extensions .

1.2 Overview of the paper

This paper gives an overview of our work on the foundations of the refinement calculus, reported in [12,11,9,13,10]. We do not give proofs of the results here as they can be found in these references. Our main purpose is to present the refinement calculus in a lattice-theoretic framework. We describe a simple lattice-based language in which all monotonic predicate transformers can be expressed. This language permits unbounded nondeterminism, nontermination and miracles as well as demonic and angelic nondeterminism. The refinement relation coincides with the lattice ordering. We show how ordinary program constructs can be defined in this language. The main tools for program development are described, on which e.g., data and procedural refinement can be based.

The lattice of monotonic predicate transformers is described in section 2. A language of *commands* is described in section 3. This language is a generalization and also a simplification of the original guarded commands language of Dijkstra, hence the name. The only constructors in this language are the lattice operators meet and join, together with functional composition. In section 4 we define ordinary program constructs, such as assignments, conditional composition, recursion and blocks with local variables, in terms of the more basic constructs of the command language. In section 5 we introduce the concept of *inverse commands* and show how these can be used in data refinement.

2 Predicates and predicate transformers

2.1 Lattices

We assume the concepts of partial orders and lattices (complete, distributive and boolean lattices) are familiar, as presented in e.g. [14,22], as well as the weakest precondition technique of Dijkstra [19]. The ordering of a partial order K is denoted $\leq_K$ (the subscript is usually dropped, if it is clear from the context which ordering is intended).

Assume that K and L are partial orders. We write $[K \to L]$ for the set of all monotonic functions from K to L. This set is a partial order, when ordered by

$$f \leq g \quad \stackrel{\text{def}}{=} \quad \forall x \in K.(f(x) \leq g(x)).$$

This is called the *pointwise extended* partial order.

If L is a (complete) lattice, then $[K \to L]$ is also a (complete) lattice for this partial ordering.

The partial order K is said to be *discrete*, if $a \leq_K a'$ holds if and only if $a = a'$. The set $[K \to L]$ will then consist of all functions from K to L.

2.2 States and state spaces

Let *var* be a countable set of *program variables.* Elements of *var* will be denoted x, y, z and lists of (distinct) program variables u, v, w. Subsets of *var* will also be denoted u, v and w, and we will usually not distinguish between a list of distinct variables and the set of these variables, using the same name ambiguously for both notions. The specific interpretation will be pointed out when necessary, but in most cases the context will make clear which interpretation is intended. We assume that there is some unique ordering of all variables, so that each set of variables u denotes a unique list of variables u. Superposition uv of two variable lists u and v denotes the union $u \cup v$ with the implicit assumption that $u \cap v = \emptyset$.

We assume that every variable x is associated with a nonempty set D_x of values. Values are typically denoted $c, c', \ldots$ and lists of values $d, d', \ldots$.

Let $v \subseteq var$. A *state on* v is a (total) function mapping every x in v to some value in D_x. We assume that there are no undefined values. The set of all states on v is called the *state space on* v and is denoted Σ_v. Typical states on v are denoted $\sigma_v, \sigma'_v, \ldots$. We often drop the subscript when the *variable environment* v of the state space is clear from the context. The state space Σ_v is discrete. To avoid degenerate cases we assume that Σ_v contains at least two elements, i.e.,. that there is some $x \in v$ such that D_x contains at least two elements.

2.3 Predicate lattice

Let

$$Bool = \{ff, tt\}$$

be the set of truth values for a two-valued logic. We define the ordering

$$a \leq b \stackrel{\text{def}}{=} a = ff \text{ or } b = tt.$$

of *Bool* (the *implication ordering*). *Bool* is a complete lattice with this ordering.

A *predicate on* v is a total function from Σ_v to *Bool*. The *predicate space over* v is

$$Pred_v = [\Sigma_v \to Bool],$$

with typical elements P,Q and R. An element P of $Pred_v$ is called a *predicate on* v. Pointwise extension of the partial order on *Bool*,

$$P \leq Q \stackrel{\text{def}}{=} \forall \sigma \in \Sigma_v.(P(\sigma) \leq Q(\sigma))$$

makes $Pred_v$ a complete boolean lattice. The meet and join operators on $Pred_v$ are denoted $\wedge$ and $\vee$. We have that $P \leq Q$ corresponds to $P \Rightarrow Q$, while meet and join correspond to logical conjunction and disjunction of predicates.

The bottom element of $Pred_v$ is the predicate $false_v$ which maps every state σ_v to ff. The top element is the predicate $true_v$ that maps every state to tt.

2.4 Operations on predicates

Substitutions A *(semantic) substitution* in Σ_v is defined in the following way: $\sigma[c/x]$ is the state which differs from σ only in that it assigns the value c to the variable x.

Substitutions in Σ_v are extended to $Pred_v$ in the usual way. The predicate $P[d/v]$ is defined by

$$P[d/v](\sigma) \quad = \quad P(\sigma[d/v])$$

We say that a *predicate* P *depends on the variable* x if there exist values c_1 and c_2 such that $P[c_1/x] \neq P[c_2/x]$. The set of variables that the predicate P depends on is denoted vP.

Qualified meets and joins Assume that v is a list of distinct variables and that $\{Q_d\}$ is a set of predicates indexed by the set of all lists of values from D of the same length as v. We use the following notations for *qualified meets* (and the corresponding notations for joins): $\bigwedge_{d:P[d/v]} Q_d$ (or simply $\bigwedge_{d:P} Q$) means taking the meet over all lists d of elements from D such that $P[d/v] = true$. Thus

$$\bigwedge_{d:P[d/v]} Q_d \stackrel{\text{def}}{=} \bigwedge(d : P[d/v] = true : Q_d)$$

$$\bigvee_{d:P[d/v]} Q_d \stackrel{\text{def}}{=} \bigvee(d : P[d/v] = true : Q_d)$$

Then $\bigwedge_{d:true} Q_d$ is the same as $\bigwedge_d Q_d$, the meet over all lists d of appropriate length, and $\bigvee_{d:true} Q_d$ is the same as $\bigvee_d Q_d$. The length of the list d is assumed to be clear from the context.

Quantification We define *quantified predicates* as follows:

$$\forall v.P \stackrel{\text{def}}{=} \bigwedge_d P[d/v]$$

$$\exists v.P \stackrel{\text{def}}{=} \bigvee_d P[d/v]$$

with d ranging over all lists of values of the same length as v.

Given these definitions, we can treat predicates much in the same way as we treat ordinary first-order formulas.

Moving between predicate spaces Let v and w be subsets of var with $v \subseteq w$. If σ is a state on w, we define the *restriction of σ to v*, denoted $\sigma \downarrow v$, by

$$(\sigma \downarrow v)(x) = \sigma(x)$$

for all variables x in v.

If Q is a predicate on v, we define its *generalization* (its upward projection) to w, denoted $Q \uparrow w$ by

$$(Q \uparrow w)(\sigma) = Q(\sigma \downarrow v) \tag{1}$$

for all states σ over w. Intuitively speaking, $Q \uparrow w$ is the same predicate as Q, viewed in the enlarged variable environment.

Conversely, if Q is a predicate over w, we define its *restriction* (its downward projection) to v, denoted $Q \downarrow v$, by the following:

$$(Q \downarrow v)(\sigma) = tt \text{ iff } (\forall u.Q)(\sigma') = tt \text{ for all } \sigma' \text{ such that } \sigma' \downarrow v = \sigma \tag{2}$$

where $u = w - v$. Intuitively speaking, $Q \downarrow w$ is the same predicate as $\forall u.Q$, viewed in the restricted variable environment.

We write $Q : v$ to show that Q is a predicate in $Pred_v$. If $v \subseteq w$, we can consider Q as a predicate in $Pred_w$ without explicitly writing $Q \uparrow w$. Thus v is the *minimal type* of Q. A simple typing algorithm computes a unique minimal result type for any predicate formula, when the minimal types of its predicate symbols are given. From now on we assume this algorithm is at work. Thus we write Q instead of $Q \uparrow w$ and $\forall u'.Q$ instead of $Q \downarrow u$, when $Q : v$ and $uu' = v \subseteq w$.

2.5 Predicate transformer lattices

We now define *predicate transformers* as total functions from one predicate lattice to another. Let v and w be arbitrary subsets of *var*. We write $Mtran_{v \to w}$ for the set of all *monotonic* predicate transformers from $Pred_w$ to $Pred_v$,

$$Mtran_{v \to w} = [Pred_w \to Pred_v]$$

(note the reversed order of v and w). The pointwise extended partial order from $Pred_v$,

$$t \leq t' \stackrel{\text{def}}{=} \forall P \in Pred_w.(t(P) \leq t'(P)).$$

makes $Mtran_{v \to w}$ a complete lattice. This ordering is the *refinement ordering* introduced in Back[1,2] and later also used in Morris[34] and by Gardiner and Morgan [20] .

A predicate transformer t in $Mtran_{v \to w}$ is said to have *arity* $v \to w$, written $t : v \to w$. We are going to identify such a predicate transformer with a command executed with initial state in Σ_v and intended to terminate in a state in Σ_w, hence the reverse ordering in the arities.

The top element $magic_{v \to w}$ maps every predicate in $Pred_w$ to $true_v$. It is the unit element of lattice meet: $magic \wedge t = t \wedge magic = t$. The bottom element $abort_{v \to w}$ maps every predicate in $Pred_w$ to $false_v$, and is the unit element of lattice join, $abort \vee t = t \vee abort = t$.

The functional composition of two predicate transformers $t : u \to v$ and $t' : v \to w$ is called their *sequential composition*, denoted $t; t'$. It is a predicate transformer with arity $u \to w$, defined by $(t; t')(P) = t(t'(P))$. The sequential composition of two predicate transformers is defined only when their arities match.

We often work with predicate transformers on some specific predicate lattice $Pred_v$. The lattice $Mtran_{v \to v}$ (abbreviated $Mtran_v$) is a complete lattice which is also closed under sequential composition. The element *skip* is the identity predicate transformer, which maps every predicate to itself. It is the unit element of sequential composition: $skip; t = t; skip = t$.

3 A command language

3.1 The command language

We will now define a small language for specifying computations. The language will be powerful enough so that both program specifications and executable statements can be expressed within it.

Syntax The *commands* are defined by the following syntax:

$$
\begin{array}{rcll}
S & ::= & \langle u = d \rangle & (\textit{strict test}) \\
 & | & \langle u \approx d \rangle & (\textit{miraculous test}) \\
 & | & \langle +u := d \rangle & (\textit{variable introduction}) \\
 & | & \langle -u \rangle & (\textit{variable elimination}) \\
 & | & S_1; S_2 & (\textit{sequential composition}) \\
 & | & \bigwedge_{i \in I} S_i & (\textit{demonic choice}) \\
 & | & \bigvee_{i \in I} S_i & (\textit{angelic choice})
\end{array}
$$

Here S and S_i are commands for all i and I is an index set (I could also be infinite), u is a list of distinct variables and d a list of values of the same length as u.

Note that we permit the use of values $d \in D_x$ as such in commands. Alternatively, we can assume that there is a name (a *constant symbol*) for each value d in D_x.

The language of commands is *infinitary*, as we permit the meets and joins to be taken also over infinite sets of commands.

Operational meaning The meaning of a command is described with respect to a final condition Q that it is intended to establish. The *strict test* $\langle u = d \rangle$ will leave the state unchanged if the variables u have corresponding values d, otherwise it fails. It thus succeeds if Q was true initially and in addition $u = d$, but fails otherwise. The *miraculous test* $\langle u \approx d \rangle$ also leaves the state unchanged if $u = d$, but succeeds (miraculously) otherwise. It thus succeeds to establish Q if either Q holds initially or if $u \neq d$ (the success is said to be *miraculous* when $u \neq d$, because the command will succeed in establishing *any* Q desired, even *false*).

The *variable introduction* $\langle +u := d \rangle$ adds the variables u to the state space, assigning them the values d. The old variables keep their values. The command succeeds to establish condition Q, if $Q[d/v]$ holds before execution of the command. The *variable elimination* command $\langle -u \rangle$ simply deletes the variables u from the state space. It succeeds to establish Q if Q holds before execution of the command.

The execution of a compound command S is described as a game between two parties, the *demon* and the *angel*. The demon chooses a command S_i to be executed in a demonic choice $\bigwedge_{i \in I} S_i$, while the angel chooses a command S_i to be executed in an angelic choice$\bigvee_{i \in I} S_i$. Sequential composition $S_1; S_2$ is executed in the usual way, i.e., S_1 is executed first, and then S_2.

Assume that S is executed in the initial state σ_0 and that the desired condition to be established is Q. The angel tries to reach a state where Q holds, whereas the demon tries to prevent this. S is considered to (be guaranteed to) succeed in establishing Q if and only if the angel has a *winning strategy*, i.e.,. no matter what choices the demon makes, the angel can force the execution into a final state where Q holds.

Note that there are no looping constructs, so execution must always finish after a finite number of moves. Because of the infinite meets and joins, the number of moves needed need not, however, be bounded.

Arities Let v and w be sets of program variables. We write $S : v \to w$ to denote that command S has *arity* $v \to w$. The arity of a command is established by the following rules:

$$
\begin{array}{lll}
\langle u = d \rangle : v \to v & \text{if} & u \subseteq v \\
\langle u \approx d \rangle : v \to v & \text{if} & u \subseteq v \\
\langle +u := d \rangle : v \to uv & & \\
\langle -u \rangle : uv \to v & & \\
S_1; S_2 : v \to w & \text{if} & S_1 : v \to v' \text{ and } S_2 : v' \to w \text{ for some } v' \\
\bigwedge_{i \in I} S_i : v \to w & \text{if} & S_i : v \to w \text{ for each } \; i \in I \\
\bigvee_{i \in I} S_i : v \to w & \text{if} & S_i : v \to w \text{ for each } i \in I
\end{array}
$$

We write $\mathcal{C}_{v \to w}$ for the set of all commands of arity $v \to w$. A command is *well-formed* if it can be assigned an arity by the above rules. The union of all well-formed commands is denoted $\mathcal{C}$.

In the operational interpretation, $S : v \to w$ means that we can interpret S as a command with initial state in Σ_v and final state in Σ_w.

Note that we may associate different arities with the same command. There is, however, always a minimal arity $v \to w$, where v and w are as small as possible, only containing those variables that have to be there by the rules.

3.2 Commands as predicate transformers

A command $S : v \to w$ denotes a predicate transformer t_S in $Mtran_{v \to w}$. For any predicate $Q \in Pred_w$, $t_S(Q) \in Pred_v$ is the predicate that holds for exactly those initial states in Σ_v for which S is guaranteed to succeed in establishing Q. This is, in essence, the *weakest precondition* semantics of [19], extended to the larger set of program constructs considered here.

The meaning of a command $S : v \rightarrow w$ is defined as follows, for any $Q \in \mathit{Pred}_w$:

$$
\begin{aligned}
\langle u = d\rangle(Q) &= (u = d) \wedge Q \\
\langle u \approx d\rangle(Q) &= (u = d) \Rightarrow Q \\
\langle +u := d\rangle(Q) &= Q[d/u] \\
\langle -u\rangle(Q) &= Q \\
(S_1; S_2)(Q) &= S_1(S_2(Q)) \\
(\bigwedge_{i \in I} S_i)(Q) &= \bigwedge_{i \in I} S_i(Q) \\
(\bigvee_{i \in I} S_i)(Q) &= \bigvee_{i \in I} S_i(Q)
\end{aligned}
$$

We permit empty variable lists in the primitive commands, with the convention that $\langle \epsilon = \epsilon\rangle = \langle \epsilon \approx \epsilon\rangle = \langle +\epsilon := \epsilon\rangle = \langle -\epsilon\rangle = \mathit{skip}$, where ϵ is the empty list.

These definitions encode the informal operational meaning of commands described above. The compound commands are just the basic operations in function lattices, i.e.,. demonic choice is lattice meet, angelic choice is lattice join and sequential composition is functional composition. The fact that each command denotes a monotonic predicate transformer is established by the following theorem.

THEOREM 1 *Each command $S : v \rightarrow w$ determines a predicate transformer in $\mathit{Mtran}_{v \rightarrow w}$.*

The partial order on $\mathit{Mtran}_{v \rightarrow w}$ determines a *refinement relation* on the set of commands of arity $v \rightarrow w$; we say that S *is refined by* S' if $S \leq S'$.

3.3 Completeness of command language

The above shows that each command corresponds to a monotonic predicate transformer. conversely, it turns out that every monotonic predicate transformer can be constructed as a command.

THEOREM 2 *Let v and w be arbitrary subsets of var and let t be an arbitrary predicate transformer in $\mathit{Mtran}_{v \rightarrow w}$. Then there exists a command $S : v' \rightarrow v'$ and commands $\langle +u := d\rangle : v \rightarrow v'$ and $\langle -u'\rangle : v' \rightarrow w$ such that*

$$
t = \langle +u := d\rangle; S; \langle -u'\rangle
$$

(We choose $v' = v \cup w$, $u = w - v$ and $u' = v - w$ in the theorem.) This, together with the previous result, shows that the language $\mathcal{C}$ is complete in a very strong sense.

COROLLARY 1 (COMPLETENESS OF COMMAND LANGUAGE) *The (monotonic) predicate transformers in $\mathit{Mtran}_{v \rightarrow w}$ are exactly those that can be constructed as commands in $\mathcal{C}_{v \rightarrow w}$.*

Thus, the set of commands $\mathcal{C}_{v \rightarrow w}$ is a complete lattice for any $v, w \subseteq \mathit{var}$. This means that we are free to use all lattice operations on commands (as is also permitted by the syntax of commands) and also that all properties of complete lattices hold for commands. We can therefore reason conveniently about properties of commands without explicitly referring to their weakest precondition interpretation.

Note that $\mathcal{C}$ as a whole is not a lattice, as meets and joins are not defined for all pairs of commands but only for those with the same arity. Also, sequential composition is defined only when arities match.

Note also that the completeness of the command language is bought at a certain price: we have to permit infinitary constructs in our language, so a command need not necessarily have a finite syntactic representation.

3.4 Sublanguages of $\mathcal{C}$

The command language introduces a number of new features into the weakest precondition approach which are not present in the original guarded command language of [19]. We will here characterize these features in somewhat more detail and identify a number of sublanguages of $\mathcal{C}$ based on these features.

Dijkstra originally proposed five healthiness conditions that every statement language would have to satisfy. Of these, only the monotonicity condition is satisfied by all commands in $\mathcal{C}$, and, by the completeness result above, turns out to be the defining characteristics for the predicate transformers generated by the command language.

Each of the new features added to the language breaks one or more of the original healthiness conditions formulated by Dijkstra in [19]. The fact that we permit arbitrary meets means that the assumption of bounded nondeterminism is not satisfied, the miraculous commands violate the "Law of Excluded Miracles" and the angelic choice violates the conjunctivity condition.

Let us make the following definitions, for any $S \in \mathcal{C}$:

($\bot$) S is *non-miraculous* (*strict with respect to false*) if $S(\mathit{false}) = \mathit{false}$.

($\top$) S is *always terminating* (*strict with respect to true*) if $S(\mathit{true}) = \mathit{true}$.

($\wedge$) S is *conjunctive* if $S(\bigwedge_{i\in I} Q_i) = \bigwedge_{i\in I} S(Q_i)$ for all nonempty sets of predicates $\{Q_i\}_{i\in I}$.

($\vee$) S is *disjunctive* if $S(\bigvee_{i\in I} Q_i) = \bigvee_{i\in I} S(Q_i)$ for all nonempty sets of predicates $\{Q_i\}_{i\in I}$.

We call $S(\mathit{false})$ the *domain of miracles* and $S(\mathit{true})$ the *domain of termination* of S. A command that is both conjunctive and disjunctive is called *deterministic*.

These four properties are independent of each other. Thus there are 16 different ways of combining them. Indexing $\mathcal{C}$ with some of the symbols for these properties denotes a sublanguage where all commands are required to have the properties in question. Thus, for example, $\mathcal{C}_{\vee}^{\top}$ is the set of all always terminating disjunctive commands. The guarded commands of Dijkstra belong to the language $\mathcal{C}_{\wedge}^{\bot}$, i.e., all non-miraculous conjunctive commands. The language $\mathcal{C}_{\wedge\vee}^{\bot\top}$, the most restrictive of these all, consists of all non-miraculous and always terminating deterministic commands. The different sublanguages are analyzed in more detail in [9].

There is a duality between the commands in $\mathcal{C}$ which we define as follows. For any command S we define its *dual* command S° by

$$S^\circ(Q) \stackrel{\text{def}}{=} \neg S(\neg Q)$$

The duality operator is defined and investigated in more detail in [12]. We have that $(S^\circ)^\circ = S$. The duality operator will change both strictness and the kind of nondeterminism, so that e.g. $(\mathcal{C}_{\wedge}^{\bot})^\circ = \mathcal{C}_{\vee}^{\top}$.

The basic commands are to a large extent dual to each other or self-duals. We have that

$$\begin{aligned}
\langle u = d\rangle^\circ &= \langle u \approx d\rangle \\
\langle +u := d\rangle^\circ &= \langle +u := d\rangle \\
\langle -u\rangle^\circ &= \langle -u\rangle \\
(S_1; S_2)^\circ &= S_1^\circ; S_2^\circ \\
\left(\bigwedge_{i\in I} S_i\right)^\circ &= \bigvee_{i\in I} S_i^\circ
\end{aligned}$$

This shows how duality interchanges the possibility for non-termination with the possibility of miracles, as well as interchanging demonic and angelic nondeterminism.

3.5 Subcommand replacement

Let $\mathcal{C}_1 = \mathcal{C}_{v \to w}$ and $\mathcal{C}_2 = \mathcal{C}_{v' \to w'}$ be two command lattices of specific arities. Then the set of *command constructors* from $\mathcal{C}_1$ to $\mathcal{C}_2$,

$$[\mathcal{C}_1 \to \mathcal{C}_2]$$

is a complete lattice, with the pointwise ordering

$$T \leq T' \stackrel{\text{def}}{=} \forall S \in \mathcal{C}_2.(T(S) \leq T'(S)).$$

We can have higher order order command constructors by iterating the functional space constructor, e.g. $[\mathcal{C}_1 \to [\mathcal{C}_2 \to \mathcal{C}_3]]$ and $[[\mathcal{C}_1 \to \mathcal{C}_2] \to \mathcal{C}_3]$. These are all complete lattices with the pointwise ordering. Command constructors of more than two arguments are modelled by currying, so that e.g. $[\mathcal{C}_1 \times \mathcal{C}_2 \to \mathcal{C}_3]$ stands for $[\mathcal{C}_1 \to [\mathcal{C}_2 \to \mathcal{C}_3]]$.

A *command constructor on* $\mathcal{C}$ is any command constructor that has been built out of the basic commands and the basic constructors (sequential composition, meet and join) in $\mathcal{C}$ using only lambda abstraction and application (we assume that typed lambda calculus is used, so that the arities are well defined). Thus e.g.

$$\lambda X : \mathcal{C}_{v \to w}. \bigvee_d (\langle u = d\rangle; X; \langle +u' := d\rangle)$$

is an element of $[\mathcal{C}_{v \to w} \to \mathcal{C}_{v' \to w'}]$ if the body of the lambda expression has arity $v' \to w'$ when X is assumed to have arity $v \to w$.

The basic constructors are all monotonic, as shown by the following lemma.

LEMMA 1 *Let $S_i \leq S_i'$ for every i. Then*

$$S_1; S_2 \leq S_1'; S_2', \quad \bigwedge_{i \in I} S_i \leq \bigwedge_{i \in I} S_i' \quad \text{and} \quad \bigvee_{i \in I} S_i \leq \bigvee_{i \in I} S_i'$$

This established the following central result.

THEOREM 3 (MONOTONICITY OF CONSTRUCTORS) *All command constructors on $\mathcal{C}$ are monotonic.*

Monotonicity means that any function $f : \mathcal{C}_1 \to \mathcal{C}_2$ that we can construct out of the basic commands and constructors in $\mathcal{C}$ using only lambda abstraction and application will be an element of $[\mathcal{C}_1 \to \mathcal{C}_2]$.

An important consequence of this is that we may always replace a subpart of a command with its refinement; the resulting command will be a refinement of the original command.

THEOREM 4 (SUBCOMMAND REPLACEMENT) *Let $T(S)$ be any command with a command S as a component. Then*

$$S \leq S' \Rightarrow T(S) \leq T(S').$$

This result permits the top-down development of programs.

It should be noted that the duality operator is not permitted as a constructor of the language. In fact, dualization is antimonotonic with respect to subcommand replacement:

$$S_1 \leq S_2 \Rightarrow S_2^\circ \leq S_1^\circ.$$

3.6 Refinements in the command languages

Traditionally, a demonic and non-miraculous command S has been defined to be *totally correct* with respect to precondition P and postcondition Q, denoted $P[S]Q$, if P implies the weakest precondition for S to establish Q. We extend this definition to the whole of $\mathcal{C}$ by

$$P[S]Q \stackrel{\text{def}}{=} P \leq S(Q).$$

A straightforward consequence of this definition and of the definition of refinement is the following.

LEMMA 2 *Let S and S' be any commands in $C_{v \to w}$. Then $S \leq S'$ if and only if*

$$\forall P \in Pred_v, Q \in Pred_w . (P[S]Q \Rightarrow P[S']Q).$$

The refinement relation thus captures the notion of preserving total correctness: S' will satisfy every total correctness specification that S satisfies (and maybe some others too).

In the traditional context of non-miraculous and demonic commands, a refinement $S \leq S'$ holds if S' decreases the domain of nontermination or decreases the nondeterminism of S (or both). When permitting miracles and angelic nondeterminism, this has to be extended.

We first state the following result.

THEOREM 5 *Let u be an arbitrary list of variables, d a list of values of the same length as v, and let $\{S_i\}_{i \in I}$ be a family of commands in C. Then*

(a) $abort \leq \langle u = d \rangle \leq skip$,

(b) $skip \leq \langle u \approx d \rangle \leq magic$,

(c) $\bigwedge_{i \in I} S_i \leq \bigwedge_{i \in I'} S_i$ *when* $I' \subseteq I$,

(d) $\bigvee_{i \in I} S_i \leq \bigvee_{i \in I'} S_i$ *when* $I \subseteq I'$.

Case (a) shows how to decrease the domain of nontermination and case (b) how to increase the domain of miracles. Case (c) shows how to decrease the demonic nondeterminism and case (d) how to increase the angelic nondeterminism.

The command constructors (meet, join and sequential composition) are all monotonic with respect to refinement, by the subcommand replacement property. This means that any refinement of the above kind to a subcomponent of S yields a refinement of S itself. In general, a command S is refined by a command S' if

1. S' decreases the domain of nontermination of S, or
2. S' increases the domain of miracles of S, or
3. S' decreases the demonic nondeterminism of S, or
4. S' increases the angelic nondeterminism of S.

If $S \leq S'$, this is equivalent by the lattice properties of commands to $S \wedge S' = S$ and $S \vee S' = S'$. Hence, in a certain (trivial) way, each refinement corresponds to either decreasing demonic nondeterminism or increasing angelic nondeterminism.

4 Specification and program constructs

The command language constructs are quite low level, and not as such very usable in program derivations. We will show in this section how to define more useful *derived* constructs in the command language. The new constructs will be defined as abbreviations for certain compound commands in C. We can compute the weakest precondition predicate transformer directly for the derived construct by using the definition of commands. The derived constructs can therefore be used as such in calculations, without the need to refer to their explicit definition in terms of more primitive commands.

The derived constructs provide us with very powerful tools for describing computations. Not all of these constructs are necessary computable. For instance, all input-output specifications can be expressed directly by derived constructs. We will also have recursion, loops and blocks with local variables. The language can also be extended with (possibly recursive) procedures and parameters, as shown in [4], although we will not treat this aspect of the language here. Ordinary program statements, such as the *guarded commands* in [19] can be expressed as commands. These form a very restricted sublanguage of $\mathcal{C}$.

We assume below that there is a language for defining predicates, such as the usual first-order predicate calculus with equality, and that each predicate expression P is associated with an arity v, denoted $P : v$, with the meaning that P can be interpreted as a predicate in $Pred_v$. In particular, this means that the predicate does not depend on any variables not in v, i.e.,. that $vP \subseteq v$.

4.1 Assert commands and guards

Let P be an arbitrary predicate formula and let $v = vP$. Then we define the *assert command* $\{P\}$ and its dual, the *guard command* $P \rightarrow$ by

$$\begin{aligned} \{P\} &\stackrel{\text{def}}{=} \bigvee_{d:P} \langle v = d \rangle \\ P \rightarrow &\stackrel{\text{def}}{=} \bigwedge_{d:P} \langle v \approx d \rangle \end{aligned}$$

(the guard command has been introduced in [25]). Computing the predicate transformers gives

$$\begin{aligned} \{P\}(Q) &= P \wedge Q \\ (P \rightarrow)(Q) &= P \Rightarrow Q \end{aligned}$$

As special cases, we have

$$\begin{array}{ll} \{\mathit{false}\} = \mathit{abort} & \{\mathit{true}\} = \mathit{skip} \\ (\mathit{false} \rightarrow) = \mathit{magic} & (\mathit{true} \rightarrow) = \mathit{skip} \end{array}$$

The *guarded command* $P \rightarrow S$ can be considered to be an abbreviation for the composition $(P \rightarrow); S$. Thus,

$$(P \rightarrow S)(Q) = P \Rightarrow S(Q)$$

which corresponds to the definitions given in [36,30,7]. Note that the dual of $P \rightarrow$ is $\{P\}$, and that we have the similar abbreviation $\{P\}S$, so

$$(\{P\}S)(Q) = P \wedge S(Q)$$

4.2 Update commands

The update commands permit an arbitrary postcondition to be established directly, if possible, by assigning suitable values to the program variables. These commands permit us to model input-output specifications in a convenient fashion. In the definitions we will make use of the *value assignment command* $\langle u := d \rangle$, defined as $\langle u := d \rangle = \langle -u \rangle; \langle +u := d \rangle$.

Demonic update The *demonic update command* $\langle \wedge u.P \rangle$ is defined as follows:

$$\langle \wedge u.P \rangle \stackrel{\text{def}}{=} (\bigwedge_d \langle u := d \rangle); P \rightarrow$$

The predicate transformer for this command can be computed from the definition. It is

$$\langle \wedge u.P \rangle(Q) = \forall u.(P \Rightarrow Q).$$

It is a possibly miraculous and always terminating demonic choice command. It will nondeterministically assigns suitable values to the variables u to establish the condition P. If this is not possible, the command succeeds miraculously.

Angelic update The *angelic update command* $\langle \vee u.P\rangle$ is constructed in the dual way. We define

$$\langle \vee u.P\rangle \stackrel{\text{def}}{=} (\bigvee_d \langle u := d\rangle);\ \{P\}$$

The angelic update command thus determines the predicate transformer

$$\langle \vee u.P\rangle(Q) = \exists u.(P \wedge Q).$$

It is a non-miraculous but possibly nonterminating angelic choice command. It will choose some value for the variable u that establishes the condition P, if this is possible. If it is not possible, the command aborts.

The demonic and angelic update commands are each others duals,

$$\langle \wedge u.P\rangle^\circ = \langle \vee u.P\rangle.$$

We note that the update commands can be described in the following simple way:

$$\begin{aligned} \langle \wedge u.P\rangle &= \langle \wedge u.true\rangle;\ P \rightarrow \\ \langle \vee u.P\rangle &= \langle \vee u.true\rangle;\ \{P\} \end{aligned}$$

Both of these can be interpreted as assigning arbitrary values to u and then forcing them to backtrack if the values do not establish P. A similar idea is used in [36] when defining the ordinary assignment statement.

4.3 Nondeterministic variable introduction

We define two nondeterministic variable introduction commands,

$$\begin{aligned} \langle \wedge + u\rangle &\stackrel{\text{def}}{=} \bigwedge_d \langle +u := d\rangle \\ \langle \vee + u\rangle &\stackrel{\text{def}}{=} \bigvee_d \langle +u := d\rangle \end{aligned}$$

The command $\langle \wedge + u\rangle$ introduces the variables u assigning arbitrary (demonically chosen) values to them. Dually, $\langle \vee + u\rangle$ introduces the variables u assigning angelically chosen values to them. Thus $\langle \vee + u\rangle$ and $\langle \wedge + u\rangle$ are duals and they determine the following predicate transformers:

$$\begin{aligned} \langle \wedge + u\rangle(Q) &= \forall u.Q \\ \langle \vee + u\rangle(Q) &= \exists u.Q \end{aligned}$$

4.4 Conditional composition

The usual *(demonic) conditional composition* is defined as

$$\textbf{if } b_1 \rightarrow S_1 [\!] b_2 \rightarrow S_2 \textbf{ fi} \stackrel{\text{def}}{=} \{b_1 \vee b_2\};\ ((b_1 \rightarrow S_1) \wedge (b_2 \rightarrow S_2))$$

We can also define an *angelic conditional composition*, by

$$\textbf{if } b_1 \rightarrow S_1 \Diamond b_2 \rightarrow S_2 \textbf{ fi} \stackrel{\text{def}}{=} \{b_1\}S_1 \vee \{b_2\}S_2$$

When executed in a state where both b_1 and b_2 holds, it makes an angelic choice between S_1 and S_2. In all other states it acts like the ordinary conditional composition.

When there is only one alternative, the two conditional compositions coincide, so we define

$$\textbf{if } b \rightarrow S \textbf{ fi} \stackrel{\text{def}}{=} \{b\};\ S$$

The conditional composition can be defined as a program constructor in S_1 and S_2, by

$$cond_{b_1,b_2} = \lambda S_1, S_2.(\{b_1 \vee b_2\}; ((b_1 \rightarrow S_1) \wedge (b_2 \rightarrow S_2))).$$

Thus, the conditional composition is monotonic in the bodies of the conditionals, i.e.,

$$S_1 \leq S_1' \text{ and } S_2 \leq S_2' \quad \Rightarrow \quad \textbf{if}\, b_1 \rightarrow S_1 \| b_2 \rightarrow S_2 \textbf{ fi} \leq \textbf{ if}\, b_1 \rightarrow S_1' \| b_2 \rightarrow S_2' \textbf{ fi}$$

However, we cannot define the conditional composition as a constructor in terms of the guarded commands $b_1 \rightarrow S_1$ and $b_2 \rightarrow S_2$, because the initial assert command needs to refer to the guards of these commands (so the definition would not be compositional). The subcommand replacement property also does not hold for the replacement of these, i.e., **if** $S_1 \| S_2$ **fi** $\leq$ **if** $S_1' \| S_2'$ **fi** need not hold even if $S_1 \leq S_1'$ and $S_2 \leq S_2'$.

4.5 Recursion and iteration

Let X be a command variable of arity $v \rightarrow w$, and let $T(X) : v \rightarrow w$ be a command constructed out of X together with the basic commands and constructors of $\mathcal{C}$. Then $\lambda X.T(X)$ is an element in $[\mathcal{C}_{v\rightarrow w} \rightarrow \mathcal{C}_{v\rightarrow w}]$. As this is a monotonic function on a complete lattice, the least fixed point of this function exists in $\mathcal{C}_{v\rightarrow w}$. We let the *recursive composition*

$$\mu X.T(X)$$

denote this least fixpoint.

This definition is generalized by an inductive argument to the case when the expression $T(X)$ itself contains recursive composition.

The greatest fixpoint $\nu X.T(X)$ of $\lambda X.T(X)$ also exists. It is the dual of the least fixed point: we have that

$$(\mu X.T(X))^\circ = \nu X.T^\circ(X)$$

where we define $T^\circ(S) = (T(S^\circ))^\circ$ for every command S.

Note that there is no need to introduce recursion as a basic constructor into the command language, as $\mu X.T(X)$ is just used as an abbreviation for a command that already exists. This is one of the main payoffs from permitting the infinite meets and joins in our command language.

The subcommand replacement property holds for the recursive construct. This follows from the fact that the fixpoint operator is monotonic:

$$\lambda X.T(X) \leq \lambda X.T'(X) \;\Rightarrow\; \mu X.T(X) \leq \mu X.T'(X).$$

The *iteration command* is defined in the usual way with recursion,

$$\textbf{do}\ b \rightarrow S\ \textbf{od} \quad = \quad \mu X.\ \textbf{if}\, b \rightarrow S; X \ \|\ \neg b \rightarrow \textit{skip}\ \textbf{fi}.$$

The iteration command with many alternatives is as usual treated as an abbreviation,

$$\begin{aligned} &\textbf{do}\ b_1 \rightarrow S_1 \ \|\ \ldots \ \|\ b_n \rightarrow S_n\ \textbf{od} \\ \stackrel{\text{def}}{=}\ &\mu X.\ \textbf{if}\, b_1 \rightarrow S_1; X \ \|\ \ldots \ \|\ b_n \rightarrow S_n; X \ \|\ \neg(b_1 \vee \ldots \vee b_n) \rightarrow \textit{skip}\ \textbf{fi}. \end{aligned}$$

As the iteration command is defined in terms of the conditional command, it will be monotonic in the bodies of the alternatives (but not in the guarded commands themselves). In other words, we have

$$S \leq S' \Rightarrow \textbf{do}\ b \rightarrow S\ \textbf{od} \leq \textbf{do}\ b \rightarrow S'\ \textbf{od}.$$

4.6 Blocks with local variables

We define the ordinary block construct as

$$|[\ \mathbf{var}\ u;\ S\ ]| \stackrel{\text{def}}{=} \langle\wedge + u\rangle;\ S;\ \langle -u\rangle$$

The arity of the block is $v \to w$, if the arity of the command S is $uv \to uw$ (note that we do not permit redeclaration of variables).

The predicate transformer for the block construct is then

$$|[\ \mathbf{var}\ u;\ S\ ]|(Q) = \forall u.S(Q)$$

The subcommand replacement property holds directly for the block:

$$S \leq S' \quad \Rightarrow \quad |[\ \mathbf{var}\ u;\ S\ ]| \leq |[\ \mathbf{var}\ u;\ S'\ ]|$$

Logical variables A block with the *logical constant* u [33,31] can be defined as

$$|[\ \mathbf{con}\ \ u;\ S\ ]| \stackrel{\text{def}}{=} \langle\vee + u\rangle;\ S';\ \langle -u\rangle$$

The subcommand replacement property holds also for this construct:

$$S \leq S' \quad \Rightarrow \quad |[\ \mathbf{con}\ \ u;\ S\ ]| \leq |[\ \mathbf{con}\ \ u;\ S'\ ]|.$$

4.7 Assignment commands

The update commands defined above are not real update commands, in the sense that the new values of the variables being updated do not depend on the old values of the variables. We can, however, easily define real update commands (*assignments*) by combining update commands with the block command.

Nondeterministic assignments The *demonic miraculous assignment* $\langle\wedge u :\approx u'.Q\rangle$ is defined as

$$\langle\wedge u :\approx u'.P\rangle \stackrel{\text{def}}{=} |[\ \mathbf{var}\ u';\ \langle\wedge u'.P\rangle;\ \langle\wedge u.u = u'\rangle\ ]|.$$

Here P may refer to the variables u and to u', the latter standing for the new values of u. In this way we indicate how the new values of u are to be related to the old values of u.

This command will demonically assign some value u' to u such that P becomes satisfied, if there exists such a value. Otherwise it will succeed miraculously. The predicate transformer for it is

$$\langle\wedge u :\approx u'.P\rangle(Q) = \forall u'.(P \Rightarrow Q[u'/u]).$$

Similarly, the *angelic strict assignment* $\langle\vee u := u'.Q\rangle$ is defined as

$$\langle\vee u := u'.P\rangle \stackrel{\text{def}}{=} |[\ \mathbf{var}\ u';\ \langle\vee u'.P\rangle;\ \langle\vee u.u = u'\rangle\ ]|.$$

This command will angelically assign some value u' to u such that P becomes satisfied, if there exists such a value. Otherwise it will fail. The predicate transformer for it is

$$\langle\vee u := u'.P\rangle(Q) = \exists u'.(P \wedge Q[u'/u]).$$

This command is the dual of the previous command.

The *demonic strict assignment* of [2] is defined as

$$\langle\wedge u := u'.P\rangle \stackrel{\text{def}}{=} \langle\vee u := u'.P\rangle;\ \mathit{magic} \wedge\ \langle\wedge u :\approx u'.P\rangle$$

The command behaves as the demonic miraculous assignment command, except that it fails if there is no value v' that satisfies P. The predicate transformer for it is

$$\langle \wedge u := u'.P\rangle(Q) = \exists u'.P \wedge \forall u'.(P \Rightarrow Q[u'/u]).$$

Dually we can define the *angelic miraculous assignment command* as

$$\langle \vee u :\approx u'.P\rangle \stackrel{\text{def}}{=} \langle \wedge u :\approx u'.P\rangle; \textit{abort} \vee \langle \vee u := u'.P\rangle$$

This behaves as the angelic strict assignment command, except that it will succeed miraculously if there is no value u' that satisfies the required conditions. The predicate transformer for it is

$$\langle \vee u :\approx u'.P\rangle(Q) = \exists u'.P \Rightarrow \exists u'.(P \wedge Q[u'/u]).$$

We take the demonic nondeterministic execution as the default, when we omit the explicit indication of the kind of nondeterminism intended: we write $u :\approx u'.Q$ for $\langle \wedge u :\approx u'.Q\rangle$ and $u := u'.Q$ for $\langle \wedge u := u'.Q\rangle$.

Multiple assignment commands The multiple assignment command is defined using e.g. the demonic strict assignment:

$$u := e \quad \stackrel{\text{def}}{=} \quad u := u'.(u' = e)$$

determining the ordinary predicate transformer

$$(u := e)(Q) \quad = \quad Q[e/u]$$

We will assume in the sequel that all expressions are total. However, assignments with expressions that are not total are automatically accommodated into this framework. If $def(e)$ is a predicate which holds exactly in those states where the expression e is defined, then the definition gives

$$(u := e)(Q) \quad = \quad def(e) \wedge Q[e/u]$$

Alternatively, we could choose to use the miraculous multiple assignment, defined as

$$u :\approx e \quad \stackrel{\text{def}}{=} \quad u :\approx u'.(u' = e)$$

with

$$(u :\approx e)(Q) \quad = \quad def(e) \Rightarrow Q[e/u]$$

Let us look at the example assignment $x := x \div y$. If $y \neq 0$ then both $x := x \div y$ and $x :\approx x \div y$ assign the value $x \div y$ to x. However, if $y = 0$ then $x := x \div y$ aborts while $x :\approx x \div y$ succeeds miraculously. The idea of a miraculous multiple assignment was introduced in [32] as an aid in type checking.

5 Inverse commands and data refinement

5.1 Inverse commands

A *true inverse* of a command $S \in C$ is a command S^{-1} that satisfies

$$S^{-1}; S = \textit{skip} = S; S^{-1}.$$

A true inverse of S exists if and only if S is bijective. The set of bijective commands form a subset of $C^{\perp\top}_{\wedge\vee}$. This is a very restrictive class of commands, making the usefulness of this notion of true inverses rather limited.

We can generalize the notion of an inverse command as follows. The *inverse* of command $S : v \to w$ is a command $S^{-1} : w \to v$ that satisfies

(i) $skip_v \leq S; S^{-1}$ and

(ii) $S^{-1}; S \leq skip_w$.

Let S be a command in $\mathcal{C}$. We show in [10] the following result.

THEOREM 6 *Let S be a command in $\mathcal{C}$. The following properties then hold:*

(i) *S^{-1} is unique if it exists.*

(ii) *S^{-1} exists if and only if $S \in \mathcal{C}_\wedge^\top$.*

(iii) *$S^{-1} \in \mathcal{C}_\vee^\perp$ if it exists.*

Thus the inverse command is defined only for conjunctive and always terminating commands and is then unique.

In [9] it is shown how different sublanguages of $\mathcal{C}$ are constructed using suitable subsets of the basic commands and constructors of $\mathcal{C}$. In particular, we have the following result for $\mathcal{C}_\wedge^\top$:

LEMMA 3 *Every conjunctive and always terminating command can be constructed using the primitive commands $\langle u \approx d\rangle$, $\langle +u := d\rangle$, $\langle -u\rangle$ and the constructors ; and $\wedge$.*

The inverse command of any conjunctive and always terminating command can be computed using the following rules:

$$\begin{aligned}
\langle u \approx d\rangle^{-1} &= \langle u = d\rangle \\
\langle +u := d\rangle^{-1} &= \langle u = d\rangle; \langle -u\rangle \\
\langle -u\rangle^{-1} &= \langle \vee + u\rangle \\
(S_1; S_2)^{-1} &= S_2^{-1}; S_1^{-1} \\
(\bigwedge S_i)^{-1} &= \bigvee S_i^{-1}
\end{aligned}$$

As special cases, we have

$$\begin{aligned}
magic^{-1} &= abort \\
(P \rightarrow)^{-1} &= \{P\} \\
\langle u := d\rangle^{-1} &= \langle u = d\rangle; \langle \vee u.true\rangle
\end{aligned}$$

We note that the inverse command construct is antimonotonic with respect to subcommand replacement:

$$S_1 \leq S_2 \Rightarrow S_2^{-1} \leq S_1^{-1}.$$

5.2 A characterization of refinement

For general conjunctive commands $S \in \mathcal{C}_\wedge$ there need not always be any S' such that $skip \leq S; S'$ is satisfied. This is because *skip* always terminates, while $S; S'$ does not terminate if S does not terminate. However, we can get around the nontermination of S if we weaken the requirement as follows. We say that $S^- \in \mathcal{C}_\vee^\perp$ is a *generalized inverse* of S, if

$$S^-; S \leq skip \quad \text{and} \quad \{S(true)\} \leq S; S^-.$$

This does not define S^- uniquely. However, we can show that a kind of compositionality does exist for generalized inverses also, making it possible to compute a generalized inverse of an arbitrary conjunctive command. Thus, if S_i^- is a generalized inverse of S_i for each i, then

$$\begin{aligned}
\langle u = d\rangle &\quad \text{is a generalized inverse of} \quad \langle u = d\rangle \\
S_2^-; S_1^- &\quad \text{is a generalized inverse of} \quad S_1; S_2 \\
\bigvee S_i^- &\quad \text{is a generalized inverse of} \quad \bigwedge S_i
\end{aligned}$$

For conjunctive and always terminating commands the generalized inverse command is unique and coincides with the ordinary inverse.

We can use generalized inverses to get a characterization of refinement between conjunctive commands in the weakest precondition calculus.

THEOREM 7 *Let $S : u \to v$ and $S' : u \to v$ be conjunctive commands. Then $S \leq S'$ if and only if*

$$S(true) \wedge (u = u_0)[S']S^{-}(u = u_0)$$

where u_0 is a list of fresh variables of the same length as u and S^{-} is any generalized inverse of S.

This gives us a bridge between the refinement calculus and the weakest precondition calculus. We can establish any refinement between conjunctive commands by proving the corresponding total correctness assertion in the weakest precondition calculus, and, conversely, any refinement between commands corresponds to a specific total correctness assertion. This characterization is essentially the same as in [5], except that the inverse command here plays the role of the strongest postconditions.

5.3 Data refinement

Encoding and decoding Consider two commands, $S : uv \to uv$ and $S' : u'v \to u'v$. We want to model the intuitive idea that $S' : u'v \to u'v$ is constructed from S by changing the way in which the program state is represented, from a representation in terms of uv (the *abstract state space*) to a representation in terms of $u'v$ (the *concrete state space*).

The basic idea is to introduce an *encoding* command $E : uv \to u'v$ that computes the representation $\sigma' \in \Sigma_{u'v}$ of each state $\sigma \in \Sigma_{uv}$. We require that $E \in \mathcal{C}_{\wedge}^{\top}$, i.e., it is always terminating and demonic (but it may be miraculous) . The inverse of E is the *decoding* command $E^{-1} : u'v \to uv$.

We say that command S is *refined* by S' *through the encoding* E *and decoding* F, denoted $S \leq_{E,F} S'$, if

$$S \leq E; S'; F^{-1}.$$

When $F = E$, we say that command S is *refined* by S' *through the encoding* E, denoted $S \leq_E S'$.

Data refinement with encoding and decoding Because our language permits subcommands with different arities to coexist in a command, we can work with different representations of the data in different parts of a program. Thus, we might start with a command

$$S = \ldots S_1 \ldots S_2 \ldots,$$

We can then replace the subcommand S_1 by an encoding $E; S_1'; E^{-1}$. If $S_1 \leq E; S_1'; E^{-1}$, then we have that

$$S' = \ldots E; S_1'; E^{-1} \ldots S_2 \ldots$$

is a refinement of the original command, by the subcommand replacement property. The command S' contains two different subcomponents, one (S_2) working on the original data representation and the other (S_1') working on a data new representation.

The monotonicity of subcommand replacement permits us to replace subcommands by their encodings at will. However, the result of this is that we introduce encoding and decoding commands, which need to be removed if we do not want to actually execute them. The following lemma shows how to remove these.

LEMMA 4 *Let E, F and G be encoding commands.*

(i) *If $S_1 \leq_{E,F} S_1'$ and $S_2 \leq_{F,G} S_2'$, then $S_1; S_2 \leq_{E,G} S_1'; S_2'$*

(ii) *If $S_i \leq_{E,F} S_i'$ for each i, then $\bigwedge S_i \leq_{E,F} \bigwedge S_i'$.*

(iii) *If* $S_i \leq_{E,F} S_i'$ *for each* i, *then* $\bigvee S_i \leq_{E,F} \bigvee S_i'$.

These properties follow directly from the properties of the inverse commands. Thus, for (i) we have e.g. that

$$S_1;\, S_2 \leq E;\, S_1';\, F^{-1};\, F;\, S_2';\, G^{-1} \leq E;\, S_1';\, S_2';\, G^{-1},$$

because $F^{-1}; F \leq \mathit{skip}$.

The method for data refinement should now be clear. We start with some command S, and show how the individual pieces S_i of S can be refined by encoding to $E_i;\, S_i';\, F_i^{-1}$, possibly using different encodings and decodings in different parts of the program. Then we combine these pieces by the above rules, so that intermediate encodings are removed. We are then left with an initial encoding E and a final decoding F^{-1}, such that $S \leq E;\, S';\, F^{-1}$ for some command S'.

Manipulating encodings and decodings The encoding and decoding commands are just special kinds of commands, so we may combine them in the same way as we combine other commands. Thus we may e.g. take the sequential composition of two encodings, $E;\, F$, to describe the successive applications of encoding E and encoding F. The inverse of this is calculated by the rule for inverse commands; it is $F^{-1};\, E^{-1}$.

We may also refine encodings and decodings themselves. Consider e.g. the following situation. Our intention has been to refine the sequential composition $S_1;\, S_2$. We have derived $S_1 \leq E;\, S_1';\, F^{-1}$ and $S_2 \leq G;\, S_2';\, H^{-1}$. Thus we

$$S_1;\, S_2 \leq E;\, S_1';\, F^{-1};\, G;\, S_2';\, H^{-1}.$$

The problem is that the decoding and the encoding do not match. We can, however, still remove the intermediate encoding, if we can prove that

$$F^{-1};\, G \leq \mathit{skip}$$

If this is not the case, then we can instead decide that a real, actually executed change of data representation is called for. In that case, we prove that

$$F^{-1};\, G \leq S_{12}$$

for some command S_{12}. This command will change the data representation in a suitable way. We then have that

$$S_1;\, S_2 \leq E;\, S_1';\, S_{12};\, S_2';\, H^{-1}.$$

Data refinement with indifferent commands The command S is said to be *indifferent* with respect to the encoding command E if S does not refer to any variables that E refers to. In this case S is invariant under the encoding E, as the following lemma shows.

LEMMA 5 *If* S *is indifferent with respect to the encoding command* E, *then*

$$S \leq_E S$$

In particular, the unit elements in the command language are invariant under encoding:

$$\begin{aligned} \mathit{abort} &\leq_E \mathit{abort} \\ \mathit{skip} &\leq_E \mathit{skip} \\ \mathit{magic} &\leq_E \mathit{magic} \end{aligned}$$

Data refinement with derived commands We now extend the data refinement rules for the basic constructors given above to data refinements of derived commands. We will treat conditional composition, recursion/iteration and blocks here, and assignments in the next subsection.

We have the following result for the derived commands.

LEMMA 6 *Let E and F be encoding commands. Then*

(i) If $S_1 \leq_{E,F} S_1'$ and $S_2 \leq_{E,F} S_1'$, then

$$\mathbf{if}\, b_1 \rightarrow S_1 \| b_2 \rightarrow S_2 \,\mathbf{fi} \leq_{E,F} \mathbf{if}\, b_1' \rightarrow S_1' \| b_2' \rightarrow S_2' \,\mathbf{fi}$$

provided $\neg b_1 \leq E(\neg b_1')$, $\neg b_2 \leq E(\neg b_2')$ and $b_1 \vee b_2 \leq E(b_1' \vee b_2')$

(ii) If $T(E; S; F^{-1}) \leq_{E,F} T'(S)$ for all commands S then

$$\mu X.T(X) \leq_{E,F} \mu X.T'(X)$$

(iii) If $S \leq_E S'$ then

$$\mathbf{do}\ b \rightarrow S\ \mathbf{od} \leq_E \mathbf{do}\ b' \rightarrow S'\ \mathbf{od}$$

provided $b \leq E(b')$ and $\neg b \leq E(\neg b')$

(iv) If E is the encoding command $\langle \wedge + u' \rangle; \langle -u \rangle$ then

$$|[\ \mathbf{var}\ u;\ E;\ S;\ E^{-1}\ ]| \leq |[\ \mathbf{var}\ u';\ S\ ]|$$

This shows that we may use the technique of data refinement freely also with the derived constructs.

5.4 Abstraction and representation commands

The idea of data refinement was first introduced by Hoare in [27]. He proposed that one uses an *abstraction function* f to determine the abstract state $(u, v) = f(u', v)$ that a concrete state $u'v$ represents. The abstraction function need not be defined for every concrete state, but only for those that satisfy some *data invariant* $I(u', v)$.

This makes the abstract state functionally dependent on the concrete state, i.e.,. for each concrete state there is at most one abstract state that it represents. The other way the dependence need not be functional, i.e., there may be more than one concrete state that represents a certain abstract state.

The idea of an abstraction function and a data invariant can be generalized to an arbitrary *abstraction relation* $R(v, u, u')$ that is to hold between abstract and concrete data spaces. No functional dependence is assumed.

We can easily see that the use of explicit abstraction relations is a special case of the idea of making data refinements by encoding and decoding commands. We may choose as the encoding command

$$\alpha = \langle \wedge + u' \rangle; \langle \wedge u'.R \rangle; \langle -u \rangle$$

abbreviated $\alpha = \langle \wedge + u' - u.R \rangle$. This command first adds the concrete variables u' to the state, then assigns them values so that the abstraction relation $R(v, u, u')$ is established, and finally removes the abstract variables u from the state. The command is demonic and always terminating. If there is no way of establishing the abstraction relation, then the command succeeds miraculously.

Computing the inverse of α gives

$$\alpha^{-1} = \langle \vee + u \rangle; \langle \vee u.R \rangle; \langle -u' \rangle$$

abbreviated $\alpha^{-1} = \langle \vee + u - u'.R \rangle$. Thus, the inverse command introduces the abstract variables and assigns them values so that the abstraction relation is satisfied, and then removes the concrete variables from the state space. This command is angelic and non-miraculous. It fails to terminate if there is no way of establishing the abstraction relation by assigning suitable values to the abstract variables.

Computing the weakest precondition transformers for these commands gives

$$\begin{aligned} \alpha(Q) &= \forall u'.(R \Rightarrow Q) \\ \alpha^{-1}(Q) &= \exists u.(R \wedge Q) \end{aligned}$$

The condition

$$S \leq \alpha;\, S';\, \alpha^{-1}$$

then becomes the following. For any Q, we must have that

$$\begin{aligned} S(Q) &\leq (\alpha;\, S';\, \alpha^{-1})(Q) \\ &= \alpha(S'(\alpha^{-1}(Q))) \\ &= \forall u'.(R \Rightarrow S'(\exists u.(R \wedge Q))) \end{aligned}$$

Hence, the data refinement holds if and only if for any $Q(u,v)$,

$$\forall u'.[R(v,u,u') \wedge S(Q(u,v)) \Rightarrow S'(\exists u.(R(v,u,u') \wedge Q(u,v)))].$$

Data refinement of specification statements We will finally apply the characterization theorem to show how to implement a specification commands such as a demonic nondeterministic assignment using encoding with α. We assume that v is the list of variables that are both in the abstract and the concrete state space. By the characterization theorem and using the fact that $\alpha = \langle \wedge + u' - u.R \rangle$, we get that $S \leq_\alpha S'$ if and only if

$$S(true) \wedge u,v = u_0, v_0 \wedge R\ [S']\ \exists u.(R \wedge S^-(u,v = u_0, v_0)).$$

For the special case of $S = (u, v := u', v'.P)$, the rules for computing the generalized inverses give us that

$$\begin{aligned} S true &= \exists u', v'.P \\ S^-(u, v = u_0, v_0) &= P[u_0, v_0, u, v / u, v, u', v']. \end{aligned}$$

This gives us in fact a proof rule for showing that a specification statement is correctly data refined by a concrete statement.

6 Conclusions and related work

We have defined a language of commands that permits both miracles and angelic nondeterminism, in addition to the more traditional features of nontermination and demonic nondeterminism. The language is very simple and semantically complete. On the other hand, it is infinitary, meaning that not every command has a finite syntactic representation. All traditional program constructs can be defined in this language. The idea of accepting miraculous statements originates with Nelson[36] (where they are interpreted as failures, requiring backtracking). Miracles were applied to program development by Morgan for sequential programs [30,29] and by Back for parallel programs [7].

A nonconjunctive operator on statements is introduced by Gardiner and Morgan in [20], but its properties are not investigated more closely. Back[6] defines a disjunctive data abstraction statement and interprets it as being angelic. We extend this approach here, accepting angelic commands as first-class citizens and permitting demonic and angelic commands to be mixed in command constructions.

The concept of the dual of a predicate transformers is not new, it has been defined previously by Guerreiro[24]. However, we consider duals of commands to be commands in their own right.

Permitting both miracles and angelic nondeterminism makes this possible, and the game-theoretic interpretation of commands gives a reasonable intuitive understanding of statements where these different kinds of language features are intermixed.

Inversion of statements has been discussed previously by Dijkstra[19] and by Gries[23]. Since they consider only non-miraculous and demonic statements, their inverses are more restricted than ours. We generalize the concept of inverse so that every terminating demonic command has a unique inverse, which is angelic and possibly nonterminating. We have generalized the concept further, so that every demonic command has a generalized inverse (not necessarily unique). The generalized inverse is used to give a first-order characterization of the refinement relation, playing the same role as the strongest postconditions in Back[5].

Recent work on refinement of programs in the weakest precondition-tradition has to a great extent concentrated on data refinement. Most authors have defined a data refinement relation which is distinct from the ordinary (algorithmic) refinement relation (Morgan[29], Morris[35], Chen and Udding[16]). We find it preferable not to introduce a separate data refinement relation, instead algorithmic refinement and data refinement are carried out within the framework of one common refinement relation. This approach was originally proposed for functional data abstraction in Back[2] and generalized to relational data abstraction in Back[6]. Here we have generalized this even further, permitting any conjunctive and total statements as a data abstractions.

Acknowledgements

The work reported here was supported by the FINSOFT III program sponsored by the Technology Development Centre of Finland. We would like to thank Orna Grumberg, Nissim Francez, Viking Högnäs, Schmuel Katz, Joost Kok, Reino Kurki-Suonio, Carroll Morgan, Kaisa Sere and John Tucker for helpful discussions on the topics treated here.

References

[1] R. J. R. Back. *On the Correctness of Refinement Steps in Program Development.* PhD thesis, Department of Computer Science, University of Helsinki, Helsinki, 1978. Report A–1978–4.

[2] R. J. R. Back. *Correctness Preserving Program Refinements: Proof Theory and Applications*, volume 131 of *Mathematical Center Tracts.* Mathematical Centre, Amsterdam, 1980.

[3] R. J. R. Back. On correct refinement of programs. *J. Computer and Systems Sciences*, 23(1):49 – 68, August 1981.

[4] R. J. R. Back. Procedural abstraction in the refinement calculus. Reports on computer science and mathematics 55, Åbo Akademi, 1987.

[5] R. J. R. Back. A calculus of refinements for program derivations. *Acta Informatica*, 25:593–624, 1988.

[6] R. J. R. Back. Changing data representation in the refinement calculus. In *21st Hawaii International Conference on System Sciences*, January 1989. Also available as Åbo Akademi reports on computer science and mathematics no. 68, 1988.

[7] R. J. R. Back. Refining atomicity in parallel algorithms. In *PARLE Conference on Parallel Architectures and Languages Europe*, volume 366 of *Lecture Notes in Computer Science*, Eindhoven, the Netherlands, June 1989. Springer Verlag. Also available as Åbo Akademi reports on computer science and mathematics no. 57, 1988.

[8] R. J. R. Back and K. Sere. Refinement of action systems. In *Mathematics of Program Construction*, volume 375 of *Lecture Notes in Computer Science*, Groningen, The Netherlands, June 1989. Springer–Verlag.

[9] R. J. R. Back and J. von Wright. Combining angels, demons and miracles in program specifications. Reports on computer science and mathematics 86, Åbo Akademi, 1989.

[10] R. J. R. Back and J. von Wright. Command lattices, variable environments and data refinement. Reports on computer science and mathematics (in preparation), Åbo Akademi, 1989.

[11] R. J. R. Back and J. von Wright. Duality in specification languages: a lattice-theoretical approach. Reports on computer science and mathematics 77, Åbo Akademi, 1989. To appear in Acta Informatica.

[12] R. J. R. Back and J. von Wright. A lattice-theoretical basis for a specification language. In *Mathematics of Program Construction*, volume 375 of *Lecture Notes in Computer Science*, Groningen, The Netherlands, June 1989. Springer–Verlag.

[13] R. J. R. Back and J. von Wright. Statement inversion and strongest postcondition. Reports on computer science and mathematics (in preparation), Åbo Akademi, 1989.

[14] G. Birkhoff. *Lattice Theory.* American Mathematical Society, Providence, 1961.

[15] R. M. Burstall and J. Darlington. Some transformations for developing recursive programs. *J. ACM*, 24(1):44–67, 1977.

[16] W. Chen and J. T. Udding. Towards a calculus of data refinement. In *Mathematics of Program Construction*, volume 375 of *Lecture Notes in Computer Science*, Groningen, The Netherlands, June 1989. Springer–Verlag.

[17] J. W. de Bakker. *Mathematical Theory of Program Correctness.* Prentice-Hall, 1980.

[18] E. W. Dijkstra. Notes on structured programming. In E. D. Dahl, O.J. and C. Hoare, editors, *Structured Programming.* Academic Press, 1971.

[19] E. W. Dijkstra. *A Discipline of Programming.* Prentice–Hall International, 1976.

[20] P. Gardiner and C. C. Morgan. Data refinement of predicate transformers. Manuscript (to appear in Theoretical Computer Science), 1988.

[21] S. L. Gerhart. Correctness preserving program transformations. In *Proc. 2nd ACM Conference of Principles of Programming Languages*, pages 54–66, 1975.

[22] G. Grätzer. *General Lattice Theory.* Birkhäuser Verlag, Basel, 1978.

[23] D. Gries. *The Science of Programming.* Springer–Verlag, New York, 1981.

[24] P. Guerreiro. Another characterization of weakest preconditions. In *Lecture Notes in Computer Science 137.* Springer–Verlag, 1982.

[25] W. H. Hesselink. An algebraic calculus of commands. Report CS 8808, Department of Mathematics and Computer Science, University of Groningen, 1988.

[26] W. H. Hesselink. Command algebras, recursion and program transformation. Report CS 8812, Department of Mathematics and Computer Science, University of Groningen, 1988.

[27] C. A. R. Hoare. Proofs of correctness of data representation. *Acta Informatica*, 1(4):271–281, 1972.

[28] C. A. R. Hoare, I. J. Hayes, J. He, C. C. Morgan, A. W. Roscoe, J. W. Sanders, I. H. Sorensen, J. Spivey, and A. Sufrin. Laws of programming. *Communications of the ACM*, 30(8):672–686, August 1987.

[29] C. C. Morgan. Data refinement by miracles. *Information Processing Letters*, 26:243–246, January 1988.

[30] C. C. Morgan. The specification statement. *ACM Transactions on Programming Languages and Systems*, 10(3):403–419, July 1988.

[31] C. C. Morgan. Programming from specifications. Manuscript, 1989.

[32] C. C. Morgan. Types and invariants in the refinement calculus. In *Mathematics of Program Construction*, volume 375 of *Lecture Notes in Computer Science*, Groningen, The Netherlands, June 1989. Springer–Verlag.

[33] C. C. Morgan and P. Gardiner. Data refinement by calculation. Technical report, Programming Research Group, Oxford University, 1988.

[34] J. M. Morris. A theoretical basis for stepwise refinement and the programming calculus. *Science of Computer Programming*, 9:287–306, 1987.

[35] J. M. Morris. Laws of data refinement. *Acta Informatica*, 26:287–308, 1989.

[36] G. Nelson. A generalization of Dijkstra's calculus. Tech. Rep 16, Digital Systems Research Center, Palo Alto, Calif., April 1987.

[37] N. Wirth. Program development by stepwise refinement. *Communications of the ACM*, 14:221–227, 1971.

Refinement Calculus, Part II: Parallel and Reactive Programs

R.J.R. Back

Åbo Akademi University, Department ofComputer Science

Lemminkäinengatan 14, SF-20520 Åbo, Finland

Abstract It is shown how to apply the refinement calculus to stepwise refinement of both parallel programs and reactive programs. The approach is based on using the action systems model to describe parallel and reactive systems. Action systems are sequential programs which can be implemented in a parallel fashion. Hence the refinement calculus for sequential programs carries over to the parallel programs expressed in this framework. Refinement of reactive programs can be expressed and proved in the refinement calculus by using the methods of data refinement from the sequential refinement calculus.

Key words Stepwise refinement, weakest preconditions, total correctness, parallel programs, reactive programs, refinement mappings, parallel composition, hiding, stuttering, action systems, fairness, simulation.

Contents

1. Introduction

2. Parallel programs as action systems
   2.1 Action system
   2.2 Parallel execution of action systems
   2.3 Fairness in action system executions
   2.4 Stepwise refinement of parallel programs

3. Refinement of action systems
   3.1 Iteration statements
   3.2 Data refinement
   3.3 Action systems
   3.4 Refinement with fairness constraints

4. Reactive programs as action systems
   4.1 Parallel composition and hiding
   4.2 Refinement of reactive components
   4.3 Permitting stuttering
   4.4 Example: Correctness of parallel execution model
   4.5 Refinement in context

5. Refinement of reactive systems
 5.1 Simulation refinement
 5.2 Preserving temporal properties

6. Example derivation
 6.1 Refinement by transformations
 6.2 Refining a reactive component

7. Concluding remarks

1 Introduction

In part I of this overview we have presented a lattice-theoretic framework for the refinement calculus. In this second part we apply this to the stepwise refinement of parallel and reactive programs. We will base our approach on the action system model for parallel programs.

The *action system* formalism for parallel and distributed computations was introduced by Back and Kurki-Suonio in [5] and is further developed in [8,7]. The behavior of parallel and distributed programs is described in terms of the actions that processes in the system carry out in co–operating with each other. Several actions can be executed in parallel, as long as the actions do not have any variables in common. The actions are *atomic*: if an action is chosen for execution, it is executed to completion without any interference from the other actions in the system.

Atomicity guarantees that a parallel execution of an action system gives the same results as a sequential and nondeterministic execution. We can therefore describe a parallel action system as a sequential statement in the language of commands. This allows us to use the sequential refinement calculus for stepwise refinement of action systems. We can start our derivation from a more or less sequential algorithm and successively increase the degree of parallelism in it, while preserving the correctness of the algorithm.

The refinement calculus is based on the assumption that the notion of correctness we want to preserve is total correctness. This is appropriate for *parallel algorithms*, i.e., programs that differ from sequential algorithms only in that they are executed in parallel, by co-operation of many processes. They are intended to terminate, and only the final results are of interest. Parallelism is introduced by merging action systems and refining the atomicity of actions. This approach to stepwise refinement of parallel algorithms has been put forward by Back and Sere [3,12].

In this paper we will concentrate on showing how the stepwise refinement method for action systems can be extended to also cover the stepwise refinement of reactive systems. Our starting point is the approach to refining reactive programs by refinement mappings put forward by Lamport in [25] and further developed by Abadi and Lamport [1], Stark [33,34], Jonsson [21], Lynch and Tuttle [27] and Lam and Shankar [24]. We will show that refinement of reactive systems can be seen as a special case of the general method for data refinement described in part I of this paper.

The action system approach is describe in more detail in Section 2. Action systems will be just a special kind of block statements, consisting of an initialization and a loop. In Section 3 we show how to apply the general refinement theory to the specific case of refining action systems, with and without data refinement. In Section 4 we show how to describe reactive systems in this framework, and introduce operators for reactive composition. The notion of *simulation refinement* between reactive components is introduced based on data refinement, and we give a general method for refining reactive components of action systems. In Section 5 we study the notion of simulation refinement more closely and show that it can be used as such for refining reactive systems. Finally, in Section 6 we give an example derivation of a parallel program, showing both how to derive parallel algorithms and how to refine reactive components of parallel algorithms.

2 Parallel programs as action systems

We will below show that a subset of the command language of part I of this paper can be used for describing both parallel and reactive systems. As a consequence, the theory of program refinement can be carried over directly to this class of programs.

2.1 Action system

An *action system* is a statement in the command language of the form

$$\mathcal{A} = |[\ \mathbf{var}\ x;\ S_0;\ \mathbf{do}\ A_1\ [\!]\ \ldots\ [\!]\ A_m\ \mathbf{od}\ ]| : z.$$

Here x are the *local variables* of $\mathcal{A}$, z are the *global variables* of $\mathcal{A}$, S_0 is the *initialization statement* and $A_1, \ldots, A_m$ are the *actions* (or *guarded commands*) of $\mathcal{A}$. Each action is of the form

$$A_i = g_i \rightarrow S_i,$$

where g_i is the *guard* of the action and S_i is the *statement* (or *body*) of the action. We denote the *guard* of action A_i by $g(A_i)$ and the *statement* of it by $s(A_i)$, so $A_i = g(A_i) \rightarrow s(A_i)$. We use the shorter forms gA_i and sA_i for these whenever it is unambiguous.

The local and global variables are assumed to be distinct, i.e., $x \cap z = \emptyset$ (no redeclaration of variables is thus permitted). Each variable may be associated with an explicit type. The *state variables* y consists of the local and global variables, $y = x \cup z$. The set of (free) state variables in action A_i is denoted $v(A_i)$ (an action can also have variables declared in local blocks, which are then bound).

An action system provides a global description of the system behavior. The state variables determine the state space of the system. The initialization statement establishes an initial state of the system by assigning suitable values to these variables. The actions determine what can happen in the system during an execution. The execution terminates when no action is enabled anymore.

An action system can be seen as a syntactic description of a *transition system*. However, we are here proposing action systems as a specification and programming language for parallel systems rather than as a way of modelling the semantics of parallel programs, for which purpose transition systems are usually employed. The action system formalism is quite general: The body of an action may be an arbitrary, possibly nondeterministic statement, it need not terminate and the nondeterminism may be unbounded.

We will in the sequel assume that each action A in an action system satisfies the following two conditions:

(a) The body of A is *strict*, i.e., $sA(false) = false$.

(b) The body of A is *conjunctive*, i.e., $sA(\bigwedge_i Q_i) = \bigwedge_i sA(Q_i)$ for any set $\{Q_i\}$ of predicates.

This rules out angelic and miraculous statements for action bodies. The first assumption can be done without loss of generality. If sA is not strict, then we can write A in the equivalent form $g' \rightarrow S'$, where $g' = gA \wedge \neg sA(false)$ and $S' = \{\neg sA(false)\}$, where S' is strict. The second assumption is, however, fundamental and is a real restriction on the language of action systems.

$$
\begin{array}{ll}
|[\ x.1,\ldots,x.n := X.1,\ldots,X.n; & \\
\quad \mathbf{do}\ x.1 > x.2 \rightarrow x.1, x.2 := x.2, x.1 & \text{(Ex.1)} \\
\quad \vdots & \\
\quad [\!]\ x.(n-1) > x.n \rightarrow x.(n-1), x.n := x.n, x.(n-1) & \text{(Ex.(n-1))} \\
\quad \mathbf{od} & \\
]|\ : x.1,\ldots,x.n \in \mathit{integer} &
\end{array}
$$

Figure 1: Exchange sorting

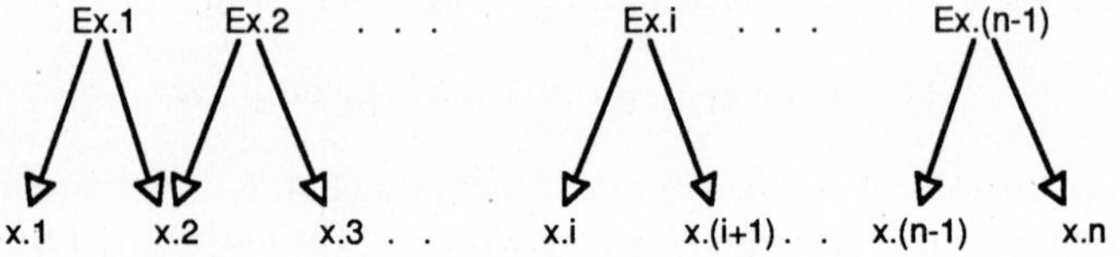

Figure 2: Sorting program actions and variables

Example Figure 1 shows an example of a simple sorting program (exchange sort) described as an action system. This program will sort n integers $X.1,\ldots,X.n$ in ascending order. The initialization statement assigns the initial values $X.1,\ldots,X.n$ to the local variables $x.1,\ldots,x.n$, while the $n-1$ sorting actions exchange neighboring values if they are out of order. The program terminates in a state where the array x is a permutation of the original array X and $x.i \leq x.(i+1)$ for $i = 1,\ldots,n-1$. All variables are global in this simple example. Figure 2 shows the *access relation* of the system, i.e., the way in which the actions access the state variables.

Notation The symbol $[\!]$ is the same as meet on commands. Hence $A = A_1 \ [\!]\ \ldots\ [\!]\ A_m = A_1 \wedge \ldots \wedge A_m$ is a command in itself. It can be written as a single action,

$$A_1 \ [\!]\ \ldots\ [\!]\ A_m = \bigvee_{i=1}^{m} gA_i \rightarrow \mathbf{if}\, A_1 \ [\!]\ \ldots\ [\!]\ A_m\ \mathbf{fi}$$

We write $gA = \bigvee_i gA_i$ and $sA = \mathbf{if}\, A_1 \ [\!]\ \ldots\ [\!]\ A_m\ \mathbf{fi}$. This permits us to consider the whole action system A as consisting of a single action A, i.e., $\mathcal{A} = |[\ \mathbf{var}\ x;\ S_0;\ \mathbf{do}\ A\ \mathbf{od}\ ]| : z$. Note also that $vA = \bigcup_i vA_i$.

When S_0 is $x := x0$, where $x0$ is a list of initial values for the variables x, we write $\mathbf{var}\ x := x0$ for $\mathbf{var}\ x;\ x := x0$.

2.2 Parallel execution of action systems

The definition of action systems above presumes a sequential nondeterministic execution model. Action systems may, however, also be executed in parallel. Consider again the action system $\mathcal{A}$,

$$\mathcal{A} = |[\ \mathbf{var}\ x;\ S_0;\ \mathbf{do}\ A_1 \ [\!]\ \ldots\ [\!]\ A_m\ \mathbf{od}\ ]| : z.$$

Let

$$\mathcal{P} = \{p_1,\ldots,p_r\}$$

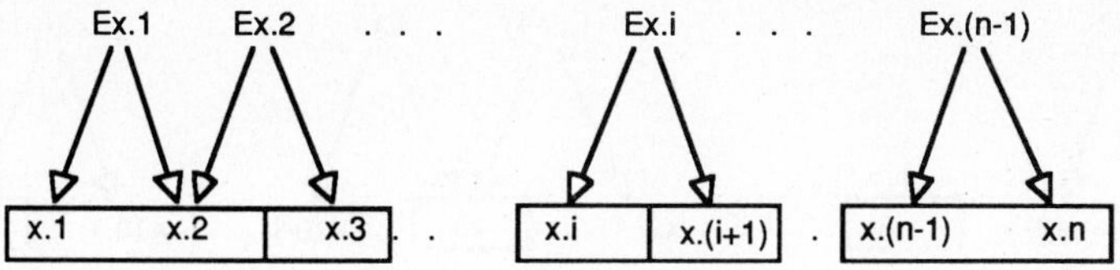

Figure 3: Distributed sorting

be a partitioning of the state variables $y = x \cup z$, i.e.,

(i) $\emptyset \neq p_i \subseteq y$ for each i,

(ii) $p_i \cap p_j = \emptyset$ whenever $i \neq j$ and

(iii) $y = \cup\mathcal{P}$.

We refer to each p_i as a *process*. Intuitively, we identify a process with the set of state variables located at the process. We will refer to the pair $(\mathcal{A}, \mathcal{P})$ as a *partitioned action system.*

The action A is said to *involve* process p if $vA \cap p \neq \emptyset$, i.e., if A accesses some variable in p. Let us denote by pA the set of processes involved in A for a given partitioning $\mathcal{P}$, so $pA = \{p \in \mathcal{P} | vA \cap p \neq \emptyset\}$.

An action A that involves only one process p is said to be *private* to p. If A involves two or more processes, it is said to be *shared* between these. Two actions A_i and A_j are said to be *independent*, if $pA_i \cap pA_j = \emptyset$. The actions are *competing* if they are not independent.

A *parallel execution* of an action system is any execution where only independent actions are executed in parallel. As independent actions do not have any processes in common, they can also have no state variables in common. Hence, the effect of executing two independent actions in parallel is the same as executing them sequentially, in either order. The enabledness of two independent actions is also not affected by the order in which they are executed. This means that a parallel execution cannot produce any results that cannot be produced by a sequential execution (we will show this formally in Section 4.4). Different partitionings of the state variables will induce different parallel executions for the action system.

Distributed action systems We can view a partitioned action system as a *distributed system*, with each variable being local to some process. A shared action corresponds to a generalized handshake, executed jointly by all the processes involved in it. The processes must be synchronized for execution of such an action. Shared actions also provide communication between processes: a variable in one process may be updated in a way that depends on variables in other processes involved in the shared action. This model generalizes the conventional synchronous message passing models for distributed systems such as CSP[18].

As an example, consider the sorting program where the variables are partitioned into the sets $\{x.1, x.2\}, \{x.3\}, \{x.4\}, \ldots, \{x.(n-2)\}, \{x.(n-1), x.n\}$ (Figure 3). Then the action $Ex.1$ is private to the first process and action $Ex.(n-1)$ is private to the last process. All other actions are shared between two neighboring processes and require a synchronizing handshake for execution.

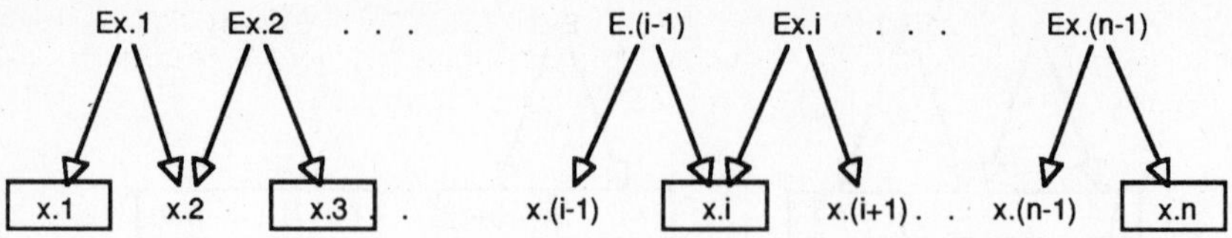

Figure 4: Shared variable sorting

Shared variable model We can also view a partitioned action system as a *concurrent system* with shared variables. Some processes are then considered as (passive) protected regions of shared variables. The variables in such a region may only be accessed under mutual exclusion. The other processes are active, communicating with each other by executing actions that access the shared regions.

As an example, we might consider a partitioning where each variable $x.i$ forms its own partition. We could take every even numbered variable to be a shared variable and every odd numbered variable to be an active process (see Figure 4, where the active processes are boxed in). Then process $\{x.i\}$, i an odd number, uses the two actions $Ex.(i-1)$ and $Ex.i$ to communicate with its neighboring processes, via the shared variables $x.(i-1)$ and $x.(i+1)$. The variable $x.i$ is internal to this active process. As long as the shared variables are accessed under mutual exclusion, any parallel execution will sort the array of x values. No explicit synchronization is needed between the actions here, mutual exclusion of the shared variable regions is sufficient.

Partitioning is thus sufficient to describe different kinds of parallel execution models. The way in which these models are implemented may of course be very different depending on the view taken. A distributed implementation requires that the synchronizing handshake is implemented, while a shared variable implementation requires some locking mechanism. However, from a logical point of view, these models are isomorphic.

We will not go deeper into the subject of how to implement the action systems in a parallel fashion. Distributed implementations of action systems are described by Back and Kurki-Suonio [5] for two-process actions in CSP with output guards. Efficient implementations of so-called *decentralized action systems* on broadcasting networks are presented in [4,7]. Implementations of action systems on point-to-point networks are described by Eklund [15,13] and Bagrodia [13]. In a forthcoming paper written jointly with Sere [11] we show how to implement action systems in Occam [20] (which does not permit output guards).

2.3 Fairness in action system executions

Action systems in the form presented above do not have any kind of fairness conditions or liveness assumptions built into them. However, we can encode a fairness constraint into an action system by explicitly scheduling actions with the unbounded nondeterministic assignment statement. This can e.g. be used to enforce *action fairness* in executions [6,16,7], i.e. that the individual actions in the action system are selected in a fair manner. The method of encoding fairness was proposed by Apt and Olderog [2].

We will not go very deeply into the issue of how to encode fairness into action system here, as this has been treated elsewhere. However, we show by an example how to ensure fairness for a specific action in an action system. Let $\mathcal{A}$ be the action system

$$\mathcal{A} = |[\ \textbf{var}\ x;\ S_0;\ \textbf{do}\ B\ \|\ A_1\ \|\ \ldots\ \|\ A_m\ \textbf{od}\ ]| : z.$$

We want the execution to treat action B in a fair manner: if B is enabled continuously from some point on (or infinitely often), then B must be executed infinitely often (*weak fairness* respectively *strong fairness*). The action system $\mathcal{A}^F$ encodes this fairness constraint,

$$\mathcal{A}^F = |[\ \textbf{var}\ x, cB;\ S_0;\ cB := c.(c > 0);\ \textbf{do}\ B^F\ \|\ A_1^F\ \|\ \ldots\ \|\ A_m^F\ \textbf{od}\ ]| : z.$$

Here cB is an integer variable used to eventually force the execution of action B, and

$$\begin{aligned} B^F &= gB \rightarrow sB;\ cB := c.(c > 0) \\ A_i^F &= gA_i \wedge \neg(gB \wedge cB \leq 0) \rightarrow \textit{update}\ cB;\ sA_i. \end{aligned}$$

The definition of *update* cB depends on the kind of fairness one requires. For weak fairness we define it by

$$\textit{update}\ cB = \ \textbf{if}\, gB \rightarrow cB := c.(c < cB)\ \|\ \neg gB \rightarrow cB := c.(c > 0)\ \textbf{fi}$$

and for strong fairness by

$$\textit{update}\ cB = \ \textbf{if}\, gB \rightarrow cB := c.(c < cB)\ \|\ \neg gB \rightarrow \textit{skip}\ \textbf{fi}$$

The *fair termination* of an action system $\mathcal{A}$ is also expressible within this framework: It is sufficient to prove termination for the corresponding action system where the appropriate fairness requirements have been encoded.

2.4 Stepwise refinement of parallel programs

The action system approach makes stepwise refinement of parallel programs simple and convenient. Parallel programs are just special kinds of sequential statements, so one can apply the refinement calculus as such to the stepwise refinement of parallel programs. The basic framework need not be extended with new program constructs in order to handle parallel execution and communication. Stepwise refinement of both sequential and parallel programs can thus be carried out within a single unifying framework.

The action system approach permits the design of the logical behavior of a system to be separated from the issue of how the system is to be implemented. The latter is seen as a design decision that does affect the way in which the action system is built, but is not reflected in the logical behavior of the system. The decision whether the action system is to be executed in a sequential, shared variable or distributed fashion can be postponed to a later stage, when the logical behavior of the action system has been designed. Also the specific way in which the system is partitioned into processes can be determined at a later stage, and possibly only for the last program version. We can experiment with different ways of partitioning variables into processes to see which gives the best performance or can be implemented in the most efficient way on the available hardware.

Stepwise refinement would typically start with a specification of the intended behavior of the system, possibly given in the form of a sequential statement. The goal is to construct a partitioned action system that satisfies some efficiency or implementation criteria. Often one has a specific target architecture in mind, so that the partitioning of some of the variables or actions is already determined (the partitioning of the global variables into processes could e.g. already be determined by the problem formulation). The required parallel action system is constructed by small refinement steps leading up to an action system satisfying the stated requirements.

A method for stepwise refinement of action systems in a temporal logic framework, based on the idea of *superposition*, was first put forward in Back and Kurki-Suonio [5] (now also published in [9]). Refining action systems in the refinement calculus was first described Back and Sere in [10,3,12,32]. The emphasize in these works is on the refinement of parallel programs preserving their input - output behavior.

We will in the sequel consider in more detail the specific properties that action systems have, in order to build a theory of stepwise refinement of parallel programs. We will specifically concentrate on the refinement of reactive action systems, referring to the above sources for the work on refining parallel algorithms preserving input-output behavior.

3 Refinement of action systems

We will in this section apply the general theory or program refinement that was presented in part I to action system refinement. We will first consider refinement of actions and iteration statements as such. We then generalize this to data refinement of actions and iteration statements. Finally, we give general rules for proving refinement between action systems.

3.1 Iteration statements

Actions Let us first consider under what conditions an action is refined by another action. We have the following result.

LEMMA 1 *Let A and A' be two actions. Then $A \leq A'$ if and only if*

(i) $sA \leq A'$ *and*

(ii) $\neg gA \leq \neg gA'$.

Note that we use $\leq$ for the implication ordering, so condition (ii) is equivalent to $\neg gA \Rightarrow \neg gA'$. An equivalent formulations for these conditions is

(i) $\{gA'\}; sA \leq sA'$ and

(ii) $gA' \leq gA$.

In other words, action A is refined by action A' if and only if the following two conditions hold: (i) whenever A' is enabled, the body of A is refined by the body of A' and (ii) A is enabled whenever A' is enabled .

Iteration statements Let us next consider refinement between iteration statements. Let

$$\begin{aligned} DO &= \textbf{do } A_1 \,[\!]\, \ldots \,[\!]\, A_m \textbf{ od} : y \text{ and} \\ DO' &= \textbf{do } A'_1 \,[\!]\, \ldots \,[\!]\, A'_k \textbf{ od} : y. \end{aligned}$$

Let $A = A_1 \,[\!]\, \ldots \,[\!]\, A_m$ and $A' = A'_1 \,[\!]\, \ldots \,[\!]\, A'_k$. We have the following result.

LEMMA 2 *$DO \leq DO'$ if*

(i) $A \leq A'$ *and*

(ii) $gA \leq gA'$

An equivalent formulation is

LEMMA 3 *$DO \le DO'$ if*

(i) $sA \le A'_j$, *for* $i = 1, \ldots, k$, *and*

(ii) $gA \equiv gA'$

Thus the exit conditions must be exactly the same in the refining and the refined loop.

Condition (i) can be difficult to prove directly in terms of the definition of refinement. The characterization theorem (of part I) permits us, however, to express it as a total correctness assertion.

LEMMA 4 *$DO \le DO'$ if the following two conditions hold:*

(i) *Let sA_i^- be some generalized inverse of sA_i, for $i = 1, \ldots, m$. Then*

$$sA(true) \wedge gA'_j \wedge y = y_0 \; [sA'_j] \; \bigvee_{i=1}^{m} sA_i^-(gA_i \wedge y = y_0)$$

must hold for $j = 1, \ldots, k$.

(ii) $gA \equiv gA'$

We have here used the fact that $\bigvee sA_i^-; \{gA_i\}$ is a generalized inverse of **if**A **fi**. The generalized inverses can be rather simply calculated for action bodies without loops or recursion, so this is quite a useful method for establishing refinement between loops.

3.2 Data refinement

When making a refinement of an action system we usually also need to change local variables. This means that we have to make a data refinement. We show here how to apply the method for data refinement described in part I to data refinement of actions and loops.

Actions Let us first consider data refinement of actions. We have the following result.

LEMMA 5 *Let $A : y$ and $A' : y'$ be actions and let $E : y \to y'$ be an encoding statement. Then $A \le_E A'$ if and only if*

(i) $sA \le_E A'$ *and*

(ii) $\neg gA \le E(\neg gA')$

Let us consider the special case when the encoding is given in terms of an abstraction relation $R(u, u', v)$, where $y = u, v$ and $y' = u', v$. In this case we have

$$E = \langle \wedge + u' - u.R(u, u', v) \rangle.$$

The characterization theorem gives us the following result.

LEMMA 6 *Let $A : y$ and $A' : y'$ be actions and let $E = \langle \wedge + u' - u.R(u, u', v) \rangle$ be an encoding. Then $A \le_E A'$ if and only if*

(i) $sA(true) \wedge R \wedge gA' \wedge y = y_0 \; [sA'] \; \exists u.(R \wedge sA^-(gA \wedge y = y_0))$

(ii) $R \wedge gA' \Rightarrow gA$

The conjunct $sA(true)$ is not needed in the assumption if A is *total*, i.e., if $A(true)$ holds (which is equivalent to $gA \Rightarrow sA(true)$).

Iteration statements We now generalize the result for refinement of iteration statements to data refinement of these. Let $E : y \rightarrow y'$ be an encoding and let

$$\begin{aligned} DO &= \textbf{do } A_1 \parallel \ldots \parallel A_m \textbf{ od} : y \text{ and} \\ DO' &= \textbf{do } A_1' \parallel \ldots \parallel A_k' \textbf{ od} : y'. \end{aligned}$$

As before, let $A = A_1 \parallel \ldots \parallel A_m$ and $A' = A_1' \parallel \ldots \parallel A_k'$. We have the following result.

LEMMA 7 *$DO \leq_E DO'$ if*

(i) *$A \leq_E A'$ and*

(ii) *$gA \leq E(gA')$*

An equivalent formulation is

LEMMA 8 *$DO \leq_E DO'$ if*

(i) *$sA \leq_E A_j'$ for $i = 1, \ldots, k$ and*

(ii) *$gA \leq E(gA')$ and $\neg gA \leq E(\neg gA')$*

Using the characterization theorem and assuming that the encoding is given by a relation, we then get the following proof rule for data refinement of iteration statements.

LEMMA 9 *Let $E = \langle \wedge + u' - u.R(u, u', v) \rangle$, where $y = u, v$ and $y' = u', v$. Then $DO \leq_E DO'$ if the following two conditions hold:*

(i) *Let sA_i^- be some generalized inverse of sA_i for $i = 1, \ldots, m$. Then*

$$sA(true) \wedge R \wedge gA_j' \wedge y = y_0 \; [sA_j'] \; \exists u.(R \wedge \bigvee_{i=1}^{m} sA_i^-(gA_i \wedge y = y_0))$$

must hold for $j = 1, \ldots, k$.

(ii) *$R \Rightarrow (gA \equiv gA')$*

3.3 Action systems

We now put all this together. Let us consider the action systems

$$\begin{aligned} \mathcal{A} &= |[\textbf{ var } x;\ S_0;\ \textbf{do } A_1 \parallel \ldots \parallel A_m \textbf{ od }]| : z \\ \mathcal{A}' &= |[\textbf{ var } x';\ S_0';\ \textbf{do } A_1' \parallel \ldots \parallel A_k' \textbf{ od }]| : z. \end{aligned}$$

We want to prove that $\mathcal{A} \leq \mathcal{A}'$. It is sufficient to show that there is an encoding $E : x \rightarrow x'$ such that the initialization and iteration of the first action system is data refined by respectively the initialization and the iteration in the second action system. Hence, we have the following result.

THEOREM 1 *$\mathcal{A} \leq \mathcal{A}'$ if there exists an encoding $E : x \rightarrow x'$ such that*

(i) *$\langle \wedge + x \rangle;\ S_0 \leq \langle \wedge + x' \rangle;\ S_0';\ E^{-1}$,*

(ii) *$A \leq_E A'$ and*

(iii) *$gA \leq E(gA')$.*

Using the characterization theorem and assuming that the encoding is given by an abstraction relation, this gives us the following proof rule.

COROLLARY 1 *Let $x = u, v$ and $x' = u', v$. Assume that the initialization statements are of the form $S_0 = (u, v := u_0, v_0)$ and $S_0' = (u', v := u_0', v_0)$. Then $\mathcal{A} \leq_E \mathcal{A}'$ if there exists a relation $R(u, u', v)$ such that the following conditions hold:*

(i) $R(u_0, u_0', v_0)$.

(ii) *Let sA_i^- be some generalized inverse of sA_i for $i = 1, \ldots, m$. Then*

$$sA(true) \wedge R \wedge gA_j' \wedge u, v, z = u_0, v_0, z_0 \; [sA_j'] \; \exists u.(R \wedge \bigvee_{i=1}^{m} sA_i^-(gA_i \wedge u, v, z = u_0, v_0, z_0))$$

must hold for $j = 1, \ldots, k$.

(iii) $R \Rightarrow (gA \equiv gA')$.

3.4 Refinement with fairness constraints

As indicated in the previous section, the requirement that some actions must be treated fairly in every execution can be coded into an action system. Thus, given a specification statement S, we can give a fair action system $\mathcal{A}^F$ as an implementation of it. The refinement $S \leq \mathcal{A}^F$ is established in the usual way. A later refinement $\mathcal{A}'$ might remove these fairness constraints, by introducing explicit scheduling among the actions, without using the unbounded nondeterministic assignment statement. The additional variables introduced to enforce fairness can be removed by data refinement. Alternatively, the action system may be refined into a form where the fairness requirements are guaranteed by the intended parallel implementation of the system. See [7] for a detailed discussion of these issues.

Proving properties of an action system $\mathcal{A}$ without fairness assumptions is conservative, in the sense that any total correctness property that holds for this action system must also hold for any action system derived from this by imposing fairness constraints. Fairness constraints can only narrow down the set of possible final states, but cannot introduce any new finite or infinite computations.

On the other hand, there might be properties that hold for every fair execution of an action system but which do not hold for the unfair executions. To prove these will require that the fairness constraints are explicitly coded into the action system.

4 Reactive programs as action systems

A refinement $\mathcal{A} \leq \mathcal{A}'$ will guarantee that the total correctness of action system $\mathcal{A}$ is preserved by $\mathcal{A}'$. This means that the latter will satisfy any total correctness specification that the former satisfies. However, it will not guarantee that the behavior of $\mathcal{A}'$ during execution will be the same as the behavior of $\mathcal{A}$. Hence, the input-output correctness of parallel programs is preserved, but not necessary their *reactive behavior*, i.e. the way in which they react with their environment during the execution. We will here show how to extend the refinement calculus so that also this aspect of program correctness can be preserved by refinement steps.

For simplicity, we assume in the sequel that all initializations are just assignments of initial values.

4.1 Parallel composition and hiding

Parallel composition Given two action systems $\mathcal{A}$ and $\mathcal{B}$,

$$\begin{aligned} \mathcal{A} &= |[\; \textbf{var}\; x := x0;\; \textbf{do}\; A_1 \;[\!]\; \ldots \;[\!]\; A_m \;\textbf{od}\;]| : z \\ \mathcal{B} &= |[\; \textbf{var}\; y := y0;\; \textbf{do}\; B_1 \;[\!]\; \ldots \;[\!]\; B_k \;\textbf{od}\;]| : u, \end{aligned}$$

we define their *parallel composition* $\mathcal{A} \parallel \mathcal{B} : z \cup u$ to be

$$\mathcal{A} \parallel \mathcal{B} = |[\ \textbf{var}\ x, y := x0, y0;\ \textbf{do}\ A_1 \mathbin{[\!]} \ldots \mathbin{[\!]} A_m \mathbin{[\!]} B_1 \mathbin{[\!]} \ldots \mathbin{[\!]} B_k\ \textbf{od}\ ]| : z \cup u$$

This is the same as the union operator in UNITY [14], except that we also keep track of which variables are local and which are global (UNITY only has global variables. For simplicity, we assume that $x \cap y = \emptyset$. If this is not the case, we first need to rename local variables in the action systems so that the condition becomes fulfilled, before the parallel composition is formed.

Note that while the local variables are *distinct*, the global variables are *shared*, i.e., a variable that occurs in both z and u is considered to be the same. This explains the use of union to determine the global variables of the parallel composition.

Renaming We can always use substitution to *rename* the global variables of action systems. Thus if $\mathcal{A}$ is an action system on the global variables z, then $\mathcal{A}[z'/z]$ is an action system on the global variables z' (a list of distinct variables), which we get by replacing each occurrence of a variable in z by the corresponding variable in z', changing local (bound) variables if necessary to avoid capture of global variables.

Hiding Given an action system $\mathcal{A} : z$ of the form above, where $z = z_1, z_2$, we can *hide* some of its variables by making them local. This is achieved by the block construct,

$$\mathcal{A}' = |[\ \textbf{var}\ z_1 := z_1 0;\ \mathcal{A}\ ]| : z_2.$$

Hiding the variables z_1 thus makes them inaccessible from other actions outside $\mathcal{A}'$ in a parallel composition.

Given an action system

$$\mathcal{C} = |[\ \textbf{var}\ v := v0;\ \textbf{do}\ C_1 \mathbin{[\!]} \ldots \mathbin{[\!]} C_n\ \textbf{od}\ ]| : z,$$

we can *decompose* it into smaller action systems by parallel composition and hiding. Let $A = \{A_1, \ldots, A_m\}$ and $B = \{B_1, \ldots, B_k\}$ be a partitioning of the actions in C (we deliberately use the symbol A for both the set of actions $\{A_1, \ldots, A_m\}$ and the action $A_1 \mathbin{[\!]} \ldots \mathbin{[\!]} A_m$; which one is intended should be clear from the context). Let

$$\begin{aligned} x &= vA - vB - z \\ y &= vB - vA - z \\ w &= vA \cap vB - z \end{aligned}$$

We can then write $\mathcal{C}$ as

$$\mathcal{C} = |[\ \textbf{var}\ w := w0;\ \mathcal{A} \parallel \mathcal{B}\ ]| : z,$$

where

$$\begin{aligned} \mathcal{A} &= |[\ \textbf{var}\ x := x0;\ \textbf{do}\ A\ \textbf{od}\ ]| : z, w \\ \mathcal{B} &= |[\ \textbf{var}\ y := y0;\ \textbf{do}\ B\ \textbf{od}\ ]| : z, w \end{aligned}$$

The main advantage of using blocks with local variables is that it permits us to clearly state which variables are used by which actions. The difference, as compared to the process algebra framework ([29]) is that communication is by shared variables rather than by shared actions. Hence, hiding really means hiding variables, to prevent access to them, rather than hiding actions.

4.2 Refinement of reactive components

Consider the action system

$$\mathcal{C} = |[\textbf{ var } v := v0; \textbf{ do } C_1 \, [\!] \, \ldots \, [\!] \, C_n \textbf{ od }]| : z.$$

Assume that we want to refine $\mathcal{C}$ to another action system $\mathcal{C}'$ by replacing some actions $A_1, \ldots, A_m$ in $\mathcal{C}$ by some other actions $A'_1, \ldots, A'_r$, possibly also changing some local variables.

Our first step is then to decompose $\mathcal{C}$ into

$$\mathcal{C} = |[\textbf{ var } w := w0; \mathcal{A} \parallel \mathcal{B}]|,$$

as described above. Here $\mathcal{A}$ collects the actions $A_1, \ldots, A_m$ to be replaced and hides the variables that are only accessed by these actions. The component $\mathcal{A}$ is again an action system. It is reactive, as the total system behavior (and final result) is determined by how $\mathcal{A}$ reacts with the other component $\mathcal{B}$ during execution.

We want to find conditions under which the replacement of the old actions by new actions in $\mathcal{C}$ is permitted also in a reactive context. In other words, we want to find conditions under which

$$\mathcal{C} = |[\textbf{ var } w := w0; \mathcal{A} \parallel \mathcal{B}]| \leq |[\textbf{ var } w := w0; \mathcal{A}' \parallel \mathcal{B}]| = \mathcal{C}',$$

for an action system $\mathcal{A}'$.

It turns out that the method of data refinement is in fact sufficient for this purpose. We will say that action system $\mathcal{A} : z$ is *strongly simulation refined* by action system $\mathcal{A}' : z$, denoted $\mathcal{A} \preceq_s \mathcal{A}'$, if the conditions of Theorem 1 are satisfied, i.e., if there exists an encoding statement $E : x \rightarrow x'$ from the local variables x of $\mathcal{A}$ to the local variables x' of $\mathcal{A}'$ such that the following three conditions are satisfied:

(i) $\langle \wedge + x \rangle; S_0 \leq \langle \wedge + x' \rangle; S'_0; E^{-1}$,

(ii) $A \leq_E A'$ and

(iii) $gA \leq E(gA')$.

THEOREM 2 (REFINEMENT OF REACTIVE COMPONENTS) *Let $\mathcal{A}$ and $\mathcal{A}'$ be two action systems. Then $\mathcal{A} \preceq_s \mathcal{A}'$ implies that*

$$|[\textbf{ var } w := w0; \mathcal{A} \parallel \mathcal{B}]| \leq |[\textbf{ var } w := w0; \mathcal{A}' \parallel \mathcal{B}]|$$

for any choice of w, $w0$ and $\mathcal{B}$.

This result follows directly from the fact that the data refinement $\mathcal{A} \preceq_s \mathcal{A}'$ is achieved by an encoding statement on the local variables of $\mathcal{A}$ and $\mathcal{A}'$ only. Hence, for each action $B_i \in \mathcal{B}$ we have $B_i \leq_E B_i$, i.e., B_i is invariant under the encoding E, as E and B_i do not have any variables in common.

4.3 Permitting stuttering

The above result shows that data refinement is sufficient to permit replacement of a reactive component of an action system by another, so that the total correctness of the whole action system is preserved. However, this relation is more restrictive than what is often needed. The problem is that it requires a one to one correspondence between the actions executed by $\mathcal{A}$ and by $\mathcal{A}'$. Even though an action execution in $\mathcal{A}'$ need not always correspond to an execution of the same action in $\mathcal{A}$, it must always correspond to some action execution of $\mathcal{A}$. In practice, however, executing a simple action in $\mathcal{A}$ will often correspond to executing a sequence of two or more actions in $\mathcal{A}'$, so that the one to one correspondence is not maintained.

Following Lamport [26,1], this problem can be overcome by permitting *stuttering actions* in $\mathcal{A}'$, i.e., actions which do not correspond to any state change in $\mathcal{A}$. The way we will handle this problem is actually quite simple. We note that for any execution of the action system $\mathcal{A}$,

$$\mathcal{A} = |[\textbf{ var } x := x0; \textbf{ do } A \textbf{ od }]| : z,$$

the meaning of $\mathcal{A}$ is unchanged (i.e., the weakest precondition transformer is the same) if we permit a finite number of *skip* actions (stutterings) to be inserted into the execution. Moreover, the behavior of $\mathcal{A}$ in any reactive context is also unchanged if we add stutterings. The only restriction is that we may not add an infinite sequence of successive stutterings.

The action system $\mathcal{A}^+$ is derived from $\mathcal{A}$ by permitting any finite amount of consequtive stuttering (but it does not permit infinite stuttering):

$$\mathcal{A}^+ = |[\textbf{ var } x, h := x0, ?; \textbf{ do } gA \rightarrow sA; h :=? \; [\!] \; h > 0 \rightarrow h := h'.(h' < h) \textbf{ od }]| : z.$$

We assume that h ranges over a well-founded set with least element 0. The statement **var** $x, h := x0, ?$ is an abbreviation for the statement **var** x, h; $x := x0$; $h :=?$ while $h :=?$ in turn is an abbreviation for the statement $h := h.true$.

LEMMA 10 *Let $\mathcal{A}$ and $\mathcal{A}^+$ be defined as above. Then*

$$|[\textbf{ var } w := w0; \mathcal{A} \parallel \mathcal{B}]| = |[\textbf{ var } w := w0; \mathcal{A}^+ \parallel \mathcal{B}]|$$

for any choice of w, $w0$ and $\mathcal{B}$.

We will say that the action system $\mathcal{A}$ is *(weakly) simulation refined* by action system $\mathcal{A}'$, denoted $\mathcal{A} \preceq \mathcal{A}'$, if $\mathcal{A}^+ \preceq_s \mathcal{A}'$.

Simulation refinement is stronger than ordinary (total correctness) refinement, i.e., we always have that $\mathcal{A} \preceq \mathcal{A}' \Rightarrow \mathcal{A} \leq \mathcal{A}'$.

The following result now follows directly from Theorem 2, in combination with the lemma above (we also need the transitivity of simulation relation proved in Theorem 6).

THEOREM 3 (REFINEMENT OF REACTIVE COMPONENTS WITH STUTTERING) *Let $\mathcal{A}$ and $\mathcal{A}'$ be two action systems. Then $\mathcal{A} \preceq \mathcal{A}'$ implies that*

$$|[\textbf{ var } w := w0; \mathcal{A} \parallel \mathcal{B}]| \leq |[\textbf{ var } w := w0; \mathcal{A}' \parallel \mathcal{B}]|,$$

for any choice of w, $w0$ and $\mathcal{B}$.

Proof rule for refinement with stuttering Let us check more carefully what the conditions for refinement are in the presence of stuttering. Let

$$A^+ = (gA \rightarrow sA; h :=? \; [\!] \; h > 0 \rightarrow h := h'.(h' < h)).$$

Let the local variables of $\mathcal{A}$ be $x = u, v$ and the local variables of $\mathcal{A}'$ be $x' = u', v$. We assume that the encoding is given in terms of an abstraction relation $R(u, h, u', v)$, which now also has h as an (abstract variable) argument. We then have that $\mathcal{A} \preceq \mathcal{A}'$ if and only if

(i) $\exists h. R(u0, h, u'0, v0)$,

(ii) $sA^+ \leq_E A'_j$ for each $j = 1, \ldots, k$, and

(iii) $R(u, h, u', v) \Rightarrow (gA' \equiv (gA \vee h > 0))$.

In condition (ii), we have

$$sA^+ = \textbf{if } gA \rightarrow sA;\ h :=?\ \|\ h > 0 \rightarrow h := h'.(h' < h) \textbf{ fi}.$$

Computing the second condition using the characterization theorem then gives us the following proof rule.

THEOREM 4 *Let $\mathcal{A}$ and $\mathcal{A}'$ be two action systems with local variables $x = u, v$ and $x' = u', v$ respectively. Then $\mathcal{A} \preceq \mathcal{A}'$ if there exists a relation $R(u, h, u', v)$ such that the following conditions hold:*

(i) $\exists h.R(u0, h, u'0, v0)$,

(ii) *Let sA_i^- be some generalized inverse of sA_i, for $i = 1, \ldots, m$. Then*

$$x, h, z = x0, h0, z_0 \wedge (gA \Rightarrow sA(true)) \wedge R(u, h, u', v) \wedge gA'_j$$
$$[sA'_j]$$
$$\exists u, h.(R(u, h, u', v) \wedge (sA^-(gA \wedge x = x0) \vee (h < h0 \wedge x, z = x0, z_0))$$

must hold for every $j = 1, \ldots, k$.

(iii) $R(u, h, u', v) \Rightarrow (gA' \equiv (gA \vee h > 0))$.

This provides us with a general method for proving the correctness of refinement in reactive contexts.

The way that we have presented the proof rule here only shows that $\mathcal{C}(\mathcal{A}) \leq \mathcal{C}(\mathcal{A}')$ holds if $\mathcal{A} \preceq \mathcal{A}'$ holds, i.e., we get a total correctness refinement of the whole program when making a simulation refinement of its component. We show in Section 5.2 that in fact $\mathcal{C}(\mathcal{A}) \preceq \mathcal{C}(\mathcal{A}')$ will also hold, so that our approach gives a general method for refinement of reactive programs.

4.4 Example: Correctness of parallel execution model

We will exemplify simulation refinement of action systems by showing that parallel execution of action systems is correct for any partitioning of the state variables.

Let $\mathcal{A}$ be the action system

$$\mathcal{A} = |[\textbf{ var } x;\ S_0;\ \textbf{do } A_1\ \|\ \ldots\ \|\ A_m \textbf{ od }]| : z$$

and let $\mathcal{P} = \{p_1, \ldots, p_k\}$ be a partitioning of the state variables $y = x \cup z$. Let $\mathcal{A}^{\mathcal{P}}$ be the action system

$$\mathcal{A}_{\mathcal{P}} = |[\textbf{ var } x, res;\ S_0;\ res := \emptyset;\ \textbf{do } A_1^{\mathcal{P}}\ \|\ \ldots\ \|\ A_m^{\mathcal{P}}\ \|\ R_{p_1}\ \|\ \ldots\ \|\ R_{p_k} \textbf{ od }]| : z.$$

Here *res* is a variable that records the processes that are presently involved in the execution of some action, and

$$\begin{aligned} A_i^{\mathcal{P}} &= gA_i \wedge (pA_i \cap res = \emptyset) \rightarrow res := res \cup pA_i;\ sA_i \\ R_p &= p \in res \rightarrow res := res - \{p\}. \end{aligned}$$

The action system $\mathcal{A}^{\mathcal{P}}$ models the parallel execution of actions in $\mathcal{A}$ for the partitioning $\mathcal{P}$. It guarantees that two actions that involve the same process cannot be executing at the same time, one must release the process before the other can begin. The *handshake actions* $A_i^{\mathcal{P}}$ synchronize the processes for execution of an action, while the *release actions* R_p release the processes one-by-one from the actions (there is no end-synchronization). This model for parallel execution is studied in a temporal logic framework in Back and Kurki-Suonio [6,7].

The following result now states that executing an action system in parallel is a correct refinement of a sequential execution of the same action system, for any partitioning of the state variables.

THEOREM 5 *$\mathcal{A} \leq \mathcal{A}^{\mathcal{P}}$ for any partitioning $\mathcal{P}$ of $\mathcal{A}$.*

Proof We need to show that $\mathcal{A}^+$ is data refined by $\mathcal{A}^{\mathcal{P}}$ for a suitable relation R. We note that data refinement here only consists in adding the single variable *res*. We choose

$$R(h, res) \stackrel{\text{def}}{=} (h = \#res),$$

where $\#res$ is the size of the set *res*.

We need to prove that conditions (i) – (iii) of Theorem 1 hold. The first condition requires that $\exists h.(h = \#\emptyset)$. This is evidently true.

We have to show condition (ii) for each $A_i^{\mathcal{P}}$ and for each R_p. In the first case, the condition follows from the fact that

$$\begin{gathered} x, z = x0, z_0 \wedge gA_i \\ [res := res \cup pA_i;\ sA_i] \\ \exists h.(h = \#res \wedge sA_i^{-}(gA_i \wedge x, z = x0, z_0)) \end{gathered}$$

for every $i = 1, \ldots, m$, where sA_i^{-} is some generalized inverse of sA_i. In the second case, the condition follows from the fact that

$$\begin{gathered} x, h, z = x0, h0, z_0 \wedge (h = \#res) \wedge p \in res \\ [res := res - \{p\}] \\ 0 \leq \#res < h0 \wedge x, z = x0, z_0 \end{gathered}$$

for every $j = 1, \ldots, k$.

The last condition requires us to show that

$$\bigvee_{i=1}^{m} (gA_i \wedge (pA_i \cap res = \emptyset)) \vee \bigvee_{j=1}^{k} p_j \in res \quad \Longleftrightarrow \quad 0 < h \vee \bigvee_{i=1}^{m} gA_i.$$

This is easily proved by case analysis. □

4.5 Refinement in context

Consider again the refinement

$$\mathcal{C} = |[\ \textbf{var}\ w := w0;\ \mathcal{A} \parallel \mathcal{B}\ ]| \leq |[\ \textbf{var}\ w := w0;\ \mathcal{A}' \parallel \mathcal{B}\ ]| = \mathcal{C}'. \tag{1}$$

This is established if we can prove that $\mathcal{A} \preceq \mathcal{A}'$. This in turn implies that $\mathcal{A}$ can be replaced by $\mathcal{A}'$ in any context, which is a very strong requirement. The fact that we are only interested in replacing $\mathcal{A}$ with $\mathcal{A}'$ in the specific context of $\mathcal{B}$ is not taken into account. Hence, it is quite possible that (1) holds even if $\mathcal{A} \preceq \mathcal{A}'$ does not hold. Thus, we need a method for taking the context into account when establishing program refinements.

The problem here is that in making the refinement $\mathcal{A} : wz \preceq \mathcal{A}' : wz$ we may not make any assumptions about how the values of w and z may be changed by the environment. The abstraction relation may only relate the local states of $\mathcal{A}$ and $\mathcal{A}'$ to each other, i.e., it must be of the form $R(x, x')$.

The simple solution to this is to make a data refinement of the whole $\mathcal{C}$, i.e., to establish directly $\mathcal{C} \preceq \mathcal{C}'$, which then implies $\mathcal{C} \leq \mathcal{C}'$. This permits us to include the variables w also in the abstraction relation. This approach is, however, in most cases too cumbersome: it does not take into account that only a part of the actions in $\mathcal{C}$ actually influence $\mathcal{A}$. However, we can base a more refined method for replacement in context on this basic idea.

The idea is to add to $\mathcal{A}$ those actions from the environment $\mathcal{B}$ that are important to determine the context of $\mathcal{A}$, but no others. At the same time, we add the environment variables through which the behavior of $\mathcal{A}$ is influenced. We do this by partitioning the actions in $\mathcal{B}$ into two sets, the *interface actions* B^i and the *environment actions* B^e. The interface actions capture those aspects of the environment that are of importance for the refinement of the actions that we are interested in. We then decompose $\mathcal{C}$ as

$$\mathcal{C} = |[\ \textbf{var}\ v := v0;\ \mathcal{C}_1 \parallel \mathcal{C}_2\ ]|$$

where

$$\begin{aligned} \mathcal{C}_1 &= |[\ \textbf{var}\ u := u0;\ \textbf{do}\ A \,[\!]\, B^i\ \textbf{od}\ ]| \\ \mathcal{C}_2 &= |[\ \textbf{var}\ y := y0;\ \textbf{do}\ B^e\ \textbf{od}\ ]|. \end{aligned}$$

Here u are the variables shared by $\mathcal{A}$ and $\mathcal{B}^i$ but not by others, y are the variables of $\mathcal{B}^e$ that are not accessed by other actions and v are the variables that are shared by $\mathcal{C}_1$ and $\mathcal{C}_2$. Notice that $x \subseteq u$, but u may also contain variables from w or variables local to $\mathcal{B}$. Hence, more variables may be local in $\mathcal{C}_1$ than in $\mathcal{A}$.

We then establish the refinement

$$\mathcal{C}_1 \preceq \mathcal{C}_1'.$$

This is less restrictive than proving $\mathcal{A} \preceq \mathcal{A}'$, but more restrictive than proving $\mathcal{C} \preceq \mathcal{C}'$. This refinement gives us

$$\begin{aligned} \mathcal{C} &= |[\ \textbf{var}\ w := w0;\ \mathcal{A} \parallel \mathcal{B}\ ]| \\ &= |[\ \textbf{var}\ v := v0;\ \mathcal{C}_1 \parallel \mathcal{C}_2\ ]| \\ &\leq |[\ \textbf{var}\ v := v0;\ \mathcal{C}_1' \parallel \mathcal{C}_2\ ]| \\ &= |[\ \textbf{var}\ w' := w'0;\ \mathcal{A}' \parallel \mathcal{B}'\ ]| \\ &= \mathcal{C}'. \end{aligned}$$

Here

$$\mathcal{B}' = |[\ \textbf{var}\ y' := y'0;\ \textbf{do}\ B^{i'} \,[\!]\, B^e\ \textbf{od}\ ]|.$$

Thus the interface actions and interface variables may also change in the refinement, to adjust for changes in the target action system $\mathcal{A}$.

This method essentially constructs an envelope or *interface* $\mathcal{C}_1$ for $\mathcal{A}$, and refines $\mathcal{A}$ together with this envelope. For an arbitrary action system, one may need to first transform it into a form where the target actions (the actions to be replaced), the environment action and the interface actions are clearly separated before doing the actual refinement in context.

5 Refinement of reactive systems

We have shown above that simulation refinement $\preceq$ can be used as such for refinement of reactive systems. We will here take a closer look at the properties of this relation.

5.1 Simulation refinement

The simulation refinement relation has the basic properties required of a refinement relation, i.e., reflexivity, transitivity and monotonicity.

THEOREM 6 *Let $\mathcal{A}, \mathcal{A}', \mathcal{A}'', \mathcal{B}, \mathcal{B}'$ be action systems, w and z' lists of distinct variables and $w0$ a list of initial values. Then the following properties hold:*

(i) $\mathcal{A} \preceq \mathcal{A}$.

(ii) $\mathcal{A} \preceq \mathcal{A}' \preceq \mathcal{A}'' \Rightarrow \mathcal{A} \preceq \mathcal{A}''$.

(iii) *If $\mathcal{A} \preceq \mathcal{A}'$ and $\mathcal{B} \preceq \mathcal{B}'$ then*

(a) $\mathcal{A} \parallel \mathcal{B} \preceq \mathcal{A}' \parallel \mathcal{B}'$,

(b) $\mathcal{A}[z'/z] \preceq \mathcal{A}'[z'/z]$ *and*

(c) $|[\ \mathbf{var}\ w := w0;\ \mathcal{A}\ ]| \preceq |[\ \mathbf{var}\ w := w0;\ \mathcal{A}'\ ]|$.

This means that we can do stepwise refinement directly in terms of simulation refinement. Starting from some action system $\mathcal{A}_0$ that serves as the initial specification, we can construct a sequence of action system refinements

$$\mathcal{A}_0 \preceq \mathcal{A}_1 \preceq \ldots \preceq \mathcal{A}_n,$$

until we reach a reactive system $\mathcal{A}_n$ that is considered adequate. The correctness of each step can be established in the refinement calculus, and thus ultimately in the weakest precondition calculus. Thus, the theory of total correctness, originally only intended for establishing input–output correctness, turns out to be adequate also for the refinement of reactive systems.

Simulation refinement relation is monotonic with respect to parallel composition, renaming and hiding. This implies that we may replace any *reactive component* $\mathcal{A}$ of a reactive system $\mathcal{C}[\mathcal{A}]$ with its simulation refinement $\mathcal{A}'$. In other words, we always have that

$$\mathcal{A} \preceq \mathcal{A}' \Rightarrow \mathcal{C}[\mathcal{A}] \preceq \mathcal{C}[\mathcal{A}'].$$

A reactive component is here a component built out of action systems using parallel composition, renaming and hiding. For non-reactive components, we can use the ordinary refinement relation and data refinement of statements.) In this way the refinement calculus provides a uniform framework in which to establish correctness of refinement for both reactive and non-reactive (input-output) systems.

5.2 Preserving temporal properties

Let us also look a little closer on the semantic interpretation of simulation refinement for action systems. Let $\mathcal{A} : z$ and $\mathcal{A}' : z$ be two action systems. We write $\mathcal{A}(\sigma)$ for the set of all possible complete execution sequences of $\mathcal{A}$ that start from initial state σ. A *complete* execution sequence is here defined as an execution sequence of $\mathcal{A}$ that does not lead to abortion. A complete execution sequence may thus be either finite or infinite. We include $\perp$ in $\mathcal{A}(\sigma)$ if there is an incomplete execution sequence from σ.

Let us further denote by $\mathcal{A}_z(\sigma)$ the set of execution sequences that result from $\mathcal{A}(\sigma)$ by only showing the values of the program variables z (the *z-projection* of $\mathcal{A}(\sigma)$) and removing any finite stuttering from the resulting execution sequences (we call these the *z-visible execution sequences*). We have the following result.

LEMMA 11 *If $\mathcal{A} \preceq \mathcal{A}'$, then for each σ,*

$$\text{either } \mathcal{A}'_z(\sigma) \subseteq \mathcal{A}_z(\sigma) \text{ or } \bot \in \mathcal{A}(\sigma).$$

In other words, if $\mathcal{A}(\sigma)$ cannot lead to abortion, then any z-visible execution sequence of $\mathcal{A}'(\sigma)$ is a possible z-visible execution sequence of $\mathcal{A}(\sigma)$ (and hence also complete).

Let $\phi : z$ be a temporal logic formula (on the variables z). Let us write $s \models \phi$ if ϕ holds for execution sequence s and $\mathcal{A}(\sigma) \models \phi$ if $s \models \phi$ for every execution sequence s in $\mathcal{A}(\sigma)$. We postulate that $\bot \not\models \phi$, for any ϕ. The formula ϕ is said to be *insensitive to stuttering* if $s \models \phi \iff s' \models \phi$ holds whenever s and s' are equivalent up to stuttering.

The previous lemma now implies that simulation refinement preserves all (linear) temporal logic properties, in the following sense.

LEMMA 12 *If $\mathcal{A} : z \preceq \mathcal{A}' : z$, then*

$$\mathcal{A}(\sigma) \models \phi \Rightarrow \mathcal{A}'(\sigma) \models \phi$$

for any $\phi : z$ that is insensitive to stuttering and for any initial state σ.

Combining this with the monotonicity property of simulation refinement then gives us the following general result.

THEOREM 7 *Let $\mathcal{C}[\mathcal{A}] : v$ be any action system where $\mathcal{A} : z$ is a reactive component. If $\mathcal{A} \preceq \mathcal{A}'$, then*

$$\mathcal{C}[\mathcal{A}](\sigma) \models \phi \Rightarrow \mathcal{C}[\mathcal{A}'](\sigma) \models \phi$$

for any $\phi : v$ that is insensitive to stuttering and for any initial state σ.

Thus, we may replace $\mathcal{A}$ by $\mathcal{A}'$ in any context $\mathcal{C}[\cdot]$ without loosing any temporal properties.

6 Example derivation

We will exemplify the method for stepwise refinement of action systems by the following simple problem. Let X_i, $i = 1, \ldots, n$, be a sequence of (real) numbers, $n \geq 0$. We want to compute $\sum_{1=1}^{n} X_i^2$ in a parallel fashion.

6.1 Refinement by transformations

We will first derive a solution in which the squaring of the vector elements is done in parallel with summing of the squares. The two tasks will be performed in a pipelined fashion, using an intermediate buffer for communication. The refinement steps can be justified using the transformation rules in [12]. We omit these justifications for lack of space. In the second subsection we then show how to implement the buffer in a way which permits parallel insertion and removal from the buffer.

The global variables are assumed to be $X \in$ *sequence of real*, $n \in$ *integer* and $s \in$ *real*. The initial specification is as follows

S0: $s := \sum_{1=1}^{n} X_i^2$

We split the computation into two parts, squaring and summing.

S1: $|[$ **var** $M \in$ *sequence of real*;
$M := \langle X_i^2 : i = 1, \ldots, n \rangle$;
$s := \sum M$;
$]|$

We then implement squaring and summing by loops. We have indicated concatenation of sequences by $H \cdot H$, and $\langle y \rangle \cdot M := M$ stands for taking the head and the tail of M.

S2: $|[$ **var** $M \in$ *sequence of real*; $i \in$ *integer*; $y \in$ *real*;
$M := \langle\rangle$; $i := 1$; $s := 0$;
do $i \leq n \rightarrow M := M \cdot \langle X_i^2 \rangle$; $i := i + 1$ **od**;
do $M \neq \langle\rangle \rightarrow \langle y \rangle \cdot M := M$; $s := s + y$ **od**
$]|$

The two loops are then merged. The justification for this refinement step is the rule for loop merge described in [12]. Basically, the two loops can be merged because the second loop does not interfere with the computation of the first loop, even if their execution is interleaved.

S3: $|[$ **var** $M \in$ *sequence of real*; $i \in$ *integer*; $y \in$ *real*;
$M := \langle\rangle$; $i := 1$; $s := 0$;
do $i \leq n \rightarrow M := M \cdot \langle X_i^2 \rangle$; $i := i + 1$ (square)
$\|$ $M \neq \langle\rangle \rightarrow \langle y \rangle \cdot M := M$; $s := s + y$ (sum)
od
$]|$

The squaring and summing actions can now be done interleaved, but they cannot be done in parallel, as they access a common variable (M). We therefore split the squaring action into a proper squaring action and an action for inserting the next square into the buffer M. Similarly we split the summation action into an action for removing the next square from the buffer and a proper summation action. The required scheduling is achieved by the boolean variables *prod* and *cons*.

S4: $|[$ **var** $M \in$ *sequence of real*; $y, x \in$ *real*; $i \in$ *integer*;
prod, *cons* $\in$ *boolean*;
$M := \langle\rangle$; $i := 1$; $s := 0$, *prod* := *false*; *cons* := *true*;
do $i \leq n \wedge \neg$*prod* $\rightarrow x := X_i^2$; $i := i + 1$; *prod* := *true* (square')
$\|$ *prod* $\rightarrow M := M \cdot \langle x \rangle$; *prod* := *false* (insert)
$\|$ $M \neq \langle\rangle \wedge$ *cons* $\rightarrow \langle y \rangle \cdot M := M$; *cons* := *false* (remove)
$\|$ $\neg$*cons* $\rightarrow s := s + y$; *cons* := *true* (sum')
od
$]|$

The access relation for $S4$ is shown in Figure 5. We see that the summing and the squaring action can now proceed in parallel, as they do not have any common variables. The insertion and removal from the buffer do, however, still exclude each other, as both access M.

Finally, we will change the unbounded buffer into a bounded one, by only allowing insertions when the length of M is less than 3. This is permitted by the proof rule for iteration, because the exit conditions for the loops in $S4$ and in $S5$ are equivalent.

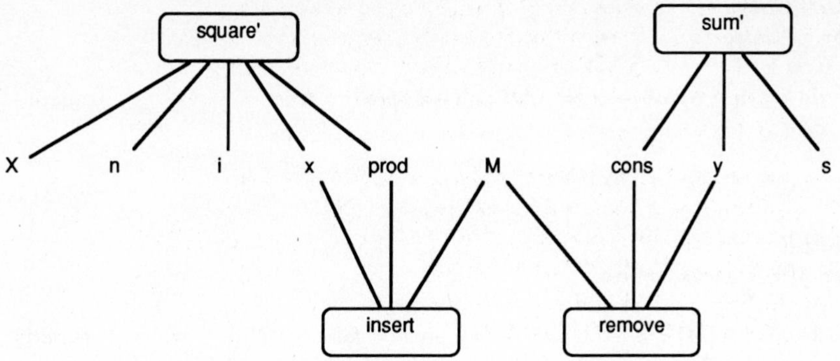

Figure 5: Sum of squares, shared queue

S5: |[**var** $M \in$ *sequence of real*; $y, x \in$ *real*; $i \in$ *integer*;
prod, *cons* $\in$ *boolean*;
$M := \langle\rangle$; $i := 1$; $s := 0$, *prod* := *false*; *cons* := *true*;
do $i \leq n \wedge \neg prod \rightarrow x := X_i^2$; $i := i + 1$; *prod* := *true* (square')
▯ $prod \wedge |M| < 3 \rightarrow M := M \cdot \langle x \rangle$; *prod* := *false* (insert)
▯ $cons \wedge |M| > 0 \rightarrow \langle y \rangle \cdot M := M$; *cons* := *false* (remove)
▯ $\neg cons \rightarrow s := s + y$; *cons* := *true* (sum')
od
]|

6.2 Refining a reactive component

We will exemplify the method for refinement of reactive systems by implementing the buffer in such a way that elements can be inserted into it and removed from it in a parallel fashion. The example was inspired by a similar example treated in UNITY [30].

For this purpose, we will decompose the action system into three parallel components, the *PRODUCER*, the *BUFFER* and the *CONSUMER*. This gives us the following system.

S5: |[**var** $y, x \in$ *real*; *prod*, *cons* $\in$ *boolean*;
prod := *false*; *cons* := *true*;
PRODUCER ‖ *BUFFER* ‖ *CONSUMER*
]|

Here we have

PRODUCER :
$\|[$ **var** $i \in integer$;
  $i := 1$;
  do $i \leq n \wedge \neg prod \rightarrow x := X_i^2;\ i := i+1;\ prod := true$ (square')
  od
$]\|$

BUFFER :
$\|[$ **var** $M \in sequence\ of\ real$;
  $M := \langle\rangle$;
  do $prod \wedge |M| < 3 \rightarrow M := M \cdot \langle x \rangle;\ prod := false$ (insert)
  $[\!]\ M \neq \langle\rangle \wedge cons \rightarrow \langle y \rangle \cdot M := M;\ cons := false$ (remove)
  od
$]\|$

CONSUMER :
$\|[$
  $s := 0$;
  do $\neg cons \rightarrow s := s + y;\ cons := true$ (sum')
  od
$]\|$

We will replace the variable M by three integer variables $q.1$, $q.2$ and $q.3$, to hold the elements of the queue. We assume that there is a distinguished value $\emptyset$ to indicate that no integer is presently stored in the variable. We add internal actions to the buffer that transports the values in the buffer forward from $q.1$ to $q.3$. These will correspond to stuttering actions on the abstract level. This gives us the following refinement of the buffer:

BUFFER' :
$\|[$ **var** $q.1, q.2, q.3 \in real$;
  $q.1, q.2, q.3 := \emptyset, \emptyset, \emptyset$;
  do $prod \wedge q.1 = \emptyset \rightarrow q.1 := x;\ prod := false$ (insert')
  $[\!]\ q.1 \neq \emptyset \wedge q.2 = \emptyset \rightarrow q.1, q.2 := \emptyset, q.1$ (forwardto2)
  $[\!]\ q.2 \neq \emptyset \wedge q.3 = \emptyset \rightarrow q.2, q.3 := \emptyset, q.2$ (forwardto3)
  $[\!]\ cons \wedge q.3 \neq \emptyset \rightarrow y, q.3 := q.3, \emptyset;\ cons := false$ (remove')
  od
$]\|$

Simultaneous insertion and removal is now possible if the variables $q.1$ and $q.3$ are put in different partitions. The access relation is shown in Figure 6, together with a possible partitioning into processes (private processes are shown inside the partitionings, shared outside).

Correctness of refinement step We want to prove that this is a correct refinement, i.e., that $BUFFER \preceq BUFFER'$. To this end, we choose the abstraction relation

$$R(M, h, q.1, q.2, q.3) \stackrel{\text{def}}{=} M = \langle q.3, q.2, q.1 \rangle \wedge h = H(q.3, q.2, q.1).$$

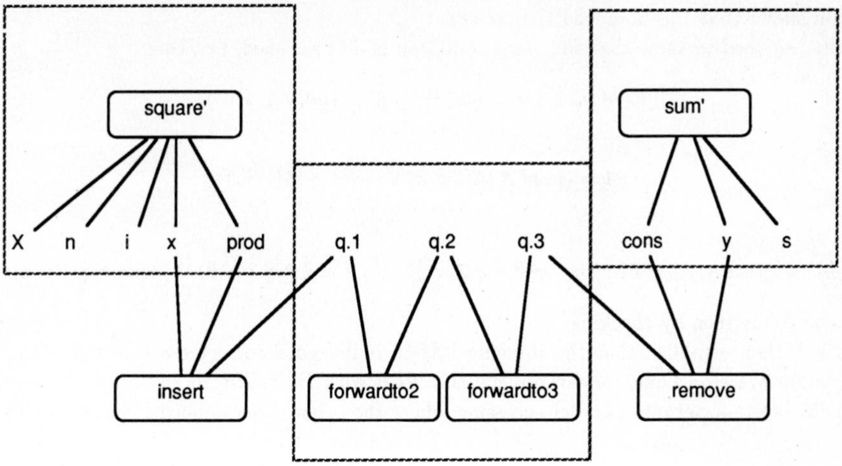

Figure 6: Sum of squares, distributed queue

Here $H(q.3., q.2, q.1)$ is defined to be the number of forward moves that can be made for the values $q.3, q.2, q.1$, and $\langle q.3, q.2, q.1\rangle$ denotes the sequence of nonempty values. E.g. for $q.1 = 12, q.2 = \emptyset, q.3 = 21$ we have $\langle q.3, q.2, q.1\rangle = 21, 12$ and $H(q.3, q.2, q.1) = 1$.

The correctness of the refinement is established by showing that all three conditions in Theorem 3 hold. The first condition requires us to prove that

$$\exists h.R(\langle\rangle, h, \emptyset, \emptyset, \emptyset)$$

This is established by choosing $h = 0$.

Let $z = x, y, prod, cons, M$. The second condition requires us to prove that

$$\begin{array}{c} z, h = z0, h0 \wedge R(M, h, q.1, q.2, q.3) \wedge gB' \\ [sB'] \\ \exists M, h.(R(M, h, q.1, q.2, q.3) \wedge (sA^{-}(gA \wedge z = z0) \vee (h < h0 \wedge z = z0)) \end{array} .$$

for $B' = insert', remove', forwardto2, forwardto3$ and $A = insert \parallel remove$. Here we compute

$$sA^{-}(gA \wedge z = z0)$$

to be

$$\begin{array}{c} (M = M0 \cdot \langle x0\rangle \wedge prod = false \wedge prod0 = true \\ \wedge |M0| < 3 \wedge x = x0 \wedge y = y0 \wedge cons = cons0) \\ \vee \\ (M0 = \langle y\rangle \cdot M \wedge cons = false \wedge cons0 = true \\ \wedge |M0| > 0 \wedge prod = prod0 \wedge x = x0) \end{array}$$

Inspection shows that this is indeed the case.

Finally, we need to show that the third condition is also satisfied, i.e., that

$$R(M, h, q.1, q.2, q.3) \Rightarrow (gA' \equiv (gA \vee h > 0)),$$

where

$$gA = (prod \wedge |M| < 3) \vee (cons \wedge |M| > 0)$$

and

$$gA' = (prod \wedge q.1 = \emptyset) \vee (q.1 \neq \emptyset \wedge q.2 = \emptyset) \vee (q.2 \neq \emptyset \wedge q.3 = \emptyset) \vee (cons \wedge q.3 \neq \emptyset).$$

This is also easily seen by checking.

This will then establish that the implementation is indeed a correct reactive refinement of the original buffer system. Thus, we can replace *BUFFER* with *BUFFER'* in any reactive context, and the resulting system permits parallel accessing where the original one required mutual exclusion.

7 Concluding remarks

We have shown above how to apply the refinement calculus to the stepwise refinement of parallel and reactive systems. The basis for this approach was the action system approach, which permits us to model parallel systems as sequential nondeterministic programs, thus making them suitable targets for the refinement calculus. We have here concentrated in particular on the refinement of reactive systems. In essence, we have shown that the methods for data refinement developed in part I of this paper are sufficient for expressing the requirements for refinement of reactive systems. The approach was applied to the derivation of a small example system, to illustrate how it works in practice.

The action system approach bears a number of similarities to the UNITY approach by Chandy and Misra [14]. UNITY programs are similar to action systems, although their actions are restricted to conditional, deterministic assignment statements. Also, the fairness assumptions are hardwired into the system. The approach to refinement of UNITY programs is different from ours: the specification of the program is refined instead of refining the program text as we do here. The logic used is a variant of temporal logic, whereas we base our reasoning in this paper on the weakest precondition calculus.

The framework built by Manna and Pnueli [28,31], using transition systems for modelling the execution of parallel and reactive programs, is quite close to the action system approach. In fact, one of the original inspirations to using action systems was to be able to use temporal logic directly to reason about execution of parallel programs, rather than to introduce a confusing transformation from some ordinary programming language to a transition system representation. The action systems are more general than transition systems are usually taken to be, as the bodies can be arbitrary, possibly nonterminating statements. However, the main difference is that we propose the action system formalism as a programming language. This makes it possible to reason directly about action systems either in temporal logic or in the weakest precondition calculus, making program derivations and proofs more syntactic in nature.

A difference in our approach, as compared to the approach by Abadi and Lamport [1] is that we do not have explicit liveness conditions for action systems. We also do not make any implicit fairness assumptions for the action systems. Different notions of fairness in action systems are studied in detail by Back and Kurki-Suonio [7], in a temporal logic framework. Here we have been content with the fact that fairness constraints can be encoded in the action system, if so desired. The encoding can, however, be quite cumbersome, so more specialized rules for refinement of action systems with implicit fairness constraints would be needed. A suitable framework for this could be the way in which fairness is modelled Francez [16], as fairness of choice in guarded iteration statements. We leave this as an issue for further research.

One of the main result of the study above is that refinement of reactive systems can be proved in the refinement calculus directly (and thus in the weakest precondition calculus). It seems that the more powerful temporal logic framework is not needed for proving correctness of reactive refinements. On the other hand, one could argue that temporal logic is necessary (or at least convenient) for specifying the behavior of the required reactive system. The starting point of a reactive refinement would have to be a specification in e.g., temporal logic or in UNITY, even if the successive refinement steps only work on action systems and rely solely on simulation refinement and the refinement calculus. In particular, the liveness constraints are often convenient to express in temporal logic.

Although the above position is reasonable, one can also argue for a more operational specification as the starting point of a derivation. The behavior of a reactive system is an operational notion, and automata theoretic approaches have been found quite useful in giving detailed specifications for such systems, e.g., Milner's CCS[29] and Hoare's CSP [19]. A disadvantage of such specifications is that they do not handle variables and more complicated states too well. Taking a high-level action system directly as the specification of a reactive system combines the advantages of the automata theoretic approach and the temporal logic approach: it has a simple operational interpretation but one can still reason about the properties of states variables. Liveness conditions can be expressed by action fairness assumptions. Work on applying this approach to the specification of large reactive systems has been carried out by Kurki-Suonio [23,22], combining the action system formalism, Harel's state charts [17] and object oriented programming concepts.

We have not touched upon the completeness of the simulation refinement method here. A completeness result is proved by Abadi and Lamport [1], under the condition that one may add history and prophecy variables to the specification of a reactive system. The additional assumptions that are made for this completeness result rule out the use of unboundedly nondeterministic assignment statements, which we again need to model stuttering and fairness. Hence, the completeness result by Abadi and Lamport do not carry over directly to our approach. Their framework also differs from ours in that they postulate an explicit liveness requirement of the transition system. We leave this issue also to further study.

Acknowledgements

The work reported here was supported by the FINSOFT III program sponsored by the Technology Development Centre of Finland. I would like to thank Bengt Jonsson, Reino Kurki-Suonio, Leslie Lamport, Carroll Morgan and Amir Pnueli for helpful discussions on the topics treated here and Joakim von Wright for useful comments on the preliminary version of this paper.

References

[1] M. Abadi and L. Lamport. The existence of refinement mappings. In *Proc. 3rd IEEE Symp. on LICS*, Edinburgh, 1988.

[2] K. R. Apt and E.-R. Olderog. Proof rules dealing with fairness. *Science of Computer Programming*, 3:65–100, 1983.

[3] R. J. R. Back. Refining atomicity in parallel algorithms. In *PARLE Conference on Parallel Architectures and Languages Europe*, volume 366 of *Lecture Notes in Computer Science*, Eind-

hoven, the Netherlands, June 1989. Springer Verlag. Also available as Åbo Akademi reports on computer science and mathematics no. 57, 1988.

[4] R. J. R. Back, E. Hartikainen, and R. Kurki-Suonio. Multi-process handshaking on broadcasting networks. Reports on computer science and mathematics 42, Åbo Akademi, 1985.

[5] R. J. R. Back and R. Kurki-Suonio. Decentralization of process nets with centralized control. In *2nd ACM SIGACT-SIGOPS Symp. on Principles of Distributed Computing*, pages 131–142. ACM, 1983.

[6] R. J. R. Back and R. Kurki-Suonio. Co-operation in distributed systems using symmetric multiprocess handshaking. Reports on computer science and mathematics 34, Åbo Akademi, 1984.

[7] R. J. R. Back and R. Kurki-Suonio. Distributed co-operation with action systems. *ACM Transactions on Programming Languages and Systems*, 10:513–554, October 1988. Previous version in Åbo Akademi reports on computer science and mathematics no. 34, 1984.

[8] R. J. R. Back and R. Kurki-Suonio. Serializability in distributed systems with handshaking. In *International Colloquium on Automata, Languages and Programming*, volume 317 of *Lecture Notes in Computer Science*, 1988. Previous version in CMU-CS-85-109, Carnegie-Mellon University 1985.

[9] R. J. R. Back and R. Kurki-Suonio. Decentralization of process nets with centralized control. *Distributed Computing*, 3(2):73–87, 1989. Appeared previously in *2nd ACM SIGACT-SIGOPS Symp. on Principles of Distributed Computing 1983.*

[10] R. J. R. Back and K. Sere. An exercise in deriving parallel algorithms: Gaussian elimination. Reports on computer science and mathematics 65, Åbo Akademi, 1988.

[11] R. J. R. Back and K. Sere. An implementation of action systems in occam. (in preparation), 1989.

[12] R. J. R. Back and K. Sere. Refinement of action systems. In *Mathematics of Program Construction*, volume 375 of *Lecture Notes in Computer Science*, Groningen, The Netherlands, June 1989. Springer–Verlag.

[13] R. Bagrodia. *An environment for the design and performance analysis of distributed systems.* PhD thesis, The University of Texas at Austin, Austin, Texas, 1987.

[14] K. Chandy and J. Misra. *Parallel Program Design: A Foundation.* Addison–Wesley, 1988.

[15] P. Eklund. Synchronizing multiple processes in common handshakes. Reports on computer science and mathematics 39, Åbo Akademi, 1985.

[16] N. Francez. *Fairness.* Springer-Verlag, 1986.

[17] D. Harel. Statecharts: a visual formalism for complex systems. *Science of Computer Programming*, 8(3):231–274, 1987.

[18] C. A. R. Hoare. Communicating sequential processes. *Communications of the ACM*, 21(8):666–677, August 1978.

[19] C. A. R. Hoare. *Communicating Sequential Processes.* Prentice-Hall, 1985.

[20] INMOS Ltd. *occam Programming Manual.* Prentice–Hall International, 1984.

[21] B. Jonsson. *Compositional Verification of Distributed Systems.* PhD thesis, Dept. of Computer Systems, Uppsala University, Uppsala, 1987. Available as report DoCS 87/09.

[22] R. Kurki-Suonio and H.-M. Järvinen. Action system approach to the specification and design of distributed systems. In *Proc. 5th International Workshop on Software Specification and Design*, volume 14(3) of *ACM Software Engineering Notes*, pages 34–40, 1989.

[23] R. Kurki-Suonio and T. Kankaanpää. On the design of reactive systems. *BIT*, 28(3):581–604, 1988.

[24] S. S. Lam and A. U. Shankar. A relational notation for state transition systems. Technical Report TR-88-21, Dept. of Computer Sciences, University of Texas at Austin, 1988.

[25] L. Lamport. Reasoning about nonatomic operations. In *Proc. 10th ACM Conference on Principles of Programming Languages*, pages 28–37, 1983.

[26] L. Lamport. A simple approach to specifying concurrent systems. *Communications of the ACM*, 32(1):32–45, January 1989.

[27] N. A. Lynch and M. R. Tuttle. Hierarchical correctness proofs for distributed algorithms. In *Proc. 6th ACM Symp. on Principles of Distributed Computing*, pages 137–151, 1987.

[28] Z. Manna and A. Pnueli. How to cook a temporal proof system for your pet language. In *Proc. 10th ACM Symp. on Principles of Programming Languages*, pages 141–154, 1983.

[29] R. Milner. *A Calculus of Communicating Systems*, volume 92 of *Lecture Notes of Computer Science.* Springer Verlag, 1980.

[30] J. Misra. Specifications of concurrently accessed data. In J. van de Snepscheut, editor, *Mathematics of Program Construction*, volume 375 of *Lecture Notes in Computer Science*, Groningen, The Netherlands, June 1989. Springer–Verlag.

[31] A. Pnueli. Applications of temporal logic to the specification and verification of reactive systems: A survey of current trends. In de Bakker, de Roever, and Rozenberg, editors, *Current Trends in Concurrency*, volume 224 of *Lecture Notes in Computer Science*, pages 510–584. Springer Verlag, 1986.

[32] K. Sere. Stepwise removal of virtual channels in distributed algorithms. In *2nd International Workshop on Distributed Algorithms*, 1987.

[33] E. W. Stark. *Foundations of a Theory of Specification for Distributed Systems.* PhD thesis, Massachussetts Inst. of Technology, 1984. Available as Report No. MIT/LCS/TR-342.

[34] E. W. Stark. Proving entailment between conceptual state specifications. *Theoretical Comput. Sci.*, 56:135–154, 1988.

METATEM:
A Framework for Programming in Temporal Logic *

Howard Barringer[†], Michael Fisher[†], Dov Gabbay[‡],
Graham Gough[†] and Richard Owens[‡]

[†] Department of Computer Science,
University of Manchester,
Oxford Road,
Manchester M13 9PL, UK.
{howard,michael,graham}@uk.ac.man.cs

[‡] Department of Computing,
Imperial College of Science, Technology and Medicine,
180 Queen's Gate,
London SW7 2BZ, UK.
{dg,rpo}@uk.ac.ic.doc

Abstract. In this paper we further develop the methodology of temporal logic as an executable imperative language, presented by Moszkowski [Mos86] and Gabbay [Gab87, Gab89] and present a concrete framework, called METATEM for executing (modal and) temporal logics. Our approach is illustrated by the development of an execution mechanism for a propositional temporal logic and for a restricted first order temporal logic.

Keywords. Modal and Temporal Logics, Reactive Systems, Specification, Verification, Synthesis, Mechanical Verification, Prototyping, Rule-based Systems, Non-procedural Languages, Logic Programming.

Contents

1 Introduction
1.1 Motivation
1.2 The METATEM Approach
1.3 Related Work

*Work supported partially by Alvey under grants PRJ/SE/054 and IKBS/170 and by ESPRIT under Basic Research Action 3096 (SPEC).

2 Propositional METATEM and its Execution
2.1 A Propositional Linear-time Temporal Logic
2.2 METATEM Programs and Execution
2.3 Examples
2.4 An Interpreter for Propositional METATEM

3 METATEM Interpreter Strategies
3.1 Choosing a disjunct
3.2 Binding strategies
3.3 Loop-checking
3.4 Propositional METATEM Interpreter Correctness

4 Towards a First-order METATEM
4.1 Syntax and Semantics of FML
4.2 Executing First-Order METATEM
4.3 Meta-programming in METATEM

5 A General Framework
5.1 γ two sorted predicate logic

A Proofs of Theorems

B Automata-Theoretic aspects of METATEM execution

1 Introduction

The purpose of this paper is twofold:

1. to re-emphasise and further develop the methodology of temporal logic as an executable imperative language, presented by Moszkowski [Mos86] and Gabbay [Gab87, Gab89]

2. to present a concrete framework, called METATEM for executing (modal and) temporal logics, illustrated by the development of an execution mechanism for a propositional temporal logic and then for restricted first order temporal logic.

The main import of this paper is the latter, and it is developed within the more general framework of the former. This methodology can serve as the natural meeting ground for the declarative and imperative approaches in computing, namely *imperative logic*.

We have structured this presentation on METATEM as follows. Section 1 outlines the METATEM approach and compares it to other work on the execution of temporal logics. Section 2 illustrates this approach by the introduction of a propositional temporal logic for METATEM. An execution mechanism for this form of METATEM is described and an outline given for an interpreter. Section 3 expands the description of the interpreter and discusses some of the issues raised in the its design. Section 4 introduces a limited first order temporal logic and describes its execution mechanism. Section 5 concludes the paper by discussing a general framework in which the METATEM approach to executing temporal logic resides.

1.1 Motivation

We distinguish two views of logic, the declarative and the imperative. The declarative view is the traditional one, and it manifests itself both syntactically and semantically. Syntactically a logical system is taken as being characterised by its set of theorems. It is not important how these theorems are generated. Two different algorithmic systems generating the same set of theorems are considered as producing the same logic. Semantically a logic is considered as a set of formulae valid in all models. The model $\mathcal{M}$ is a static semantic object. We evaluate a formula φ in a model and, if the result of the evaluation is positive (notation $\mathcal{M} \models \varphi$), the formula is valid. Thus the logic obtained is the set of all valid formulae in some class $\mathcal{K}$ of models.

In contrast to the above, the imperative view regards a logic syntactically as a dynamically generated set of theorems. Different generating systems may be considered as different logics. The way the theorems are generated are an integral part of the logic. From the semantic viewpoint, a logical formula is not *evaluated* in a model but performs *actions* on a model to get a *new* model. Formulae are accepted as valid according to what they do to models. For example we may take φ to be valid in $\mathcal{M}$ if $\varphi(\mathcal{M}) = \mathcal{M}$. (i.e. $\mathcal{M}$ is a fixed-point of φ.)

Applications of logic in computer science have mainly concentrated on the exploitation of its declarative features. Logic is taken as a language for describing properties of models. The formula φ is evaluated in a model $\mathcal{M}$. If φ holds in $\mathcal{M}$ (evaluation successful) then $\mathcal{M}$ has property φ. This view of logic is, for example, most suitably and most successfully exploited in the areas of databases and in program specification and verification. One can present the database as a deductive logical theory and query it using logical formulae. The logical evaluation process corresponds to the computational querying process. In program verification, for example, one can describe in logic the properties of the programs to be studied. The description plays the rôle of a model $\mathcal{M}$. One can now describe one's specification as a logical formula φ, and the query whether φ holds in $\mathcal{M}$ (denoted $\mathcal{M} \vdash \varphi$) amounts to verifying that the program satisfies the specification. These methodologies rely solely on the declarative nature of logic.

Logic programming as a discipline is also declarative. In fact it advertises itself as such. It is most successful in areas where the declarative component is dominant, for example deductive databases. Its procedural features are not imperative (in our sense) but computational. In the course of evaluating whether $\mathcal{M} \vdash \varphi$, a procedural reading of $\mathcal{M}$ and φ is used. φ does not imperatively act on $\mathcal{M}$, the declarative logical features are used to guide a procedure, that of taking steps for finding whether φ is true. What does not happen is that $\mathcal{M}$ and φ are read imperatively, resulting in some action. In logic programming such actions (e.g. assert) are obtained by side-effects and special non-logical imperative predicates and are considered undesirable. There is certainly no conceptual framework within logic programming for allowing only those actions which have logical meaning.

Some researchers have come close to touching upon the imperative reading of logic. Belnap [Bel77] and the later so-called data semantics school regard a formula φ as generating an action on a model $\mathcal{M}$, and changing it. In logic programming and deductive databases the handling of integrity constraints borders on the use of logic imperatively. Integrity constraints have to be maintained. Thus one can either reject an update or do some corrections. Maintaining integrity constraints is a form of executing logic, but it is logically ad-hoc and has to do with the local problem at hand. Truth maintenance is another form. In fact, under a suitable interpretation, one may view any resolution mechanism as model building which is a form of execution. In temporal logic, model construction can be interpreted as execution. Generating the model, i.e. finding the truth values of the atomic predicates in the various moments of time, can be taken as a sequence of execution.

As the need for the imperative executable features of logic is widespread in computer science, it is not surprising that various researchers have touched upon it in the course of their activity. However there has been no conceptual methodological recognition of the imperative paradigm in the community, nor has there been a systematic attempt to develop and bring this paradigm forward as a new and powerful logical approach in computing.

The area where the need for the imperative approach is most obvious and pressing is temporal logic. In general terms, a temporal model can be viewed as a progression of ordinary models. The ordinary models are what is true at each moment of time. The imperative view of logic on the other hand also involves step by step progression in virtual "time", involving both the syntactic generation of theorems and the semantic actions of a temporal formula on the temporal model. Can the two intuitive progressions, the semantic time and the action (transaction) time, be taken as the same? In the case of temporal logic the answer is yes. We can act upon the models in the same time order as their chronological time. This means acting on earlier models first. In fact intuitively a future logical statement can be read (as we shall see) both declaratively and imperatively. Declaratively it describes what should be true, and imperatively it describes the actions to be taken to ensure that it becomes true. Since the chronology of the action sequence and the model sequence are the same, we can virtually *create* the future model by our actions. The logic USF, defined by Gabbay [Gab89], was the first attempt at promoting the imperative view as a methodology, with a proposal for its use as a language for controlling processes.

1.2 The METATEM Approach

Work in the field of logic programming has demonstrated the utility of systems within which a single statement can be given both declarative and procedural readings. However, adapting existing systems to handle time dependent data and reasoning has proved to be difficult, since attempts to do so have involved simulating time rather than incorporating it at the heart of the system. Our approach is to place temporal considerations at the centre of the execution model, while maintaining the advantages of both declarative and procedural readings. A consequence of this is a more powerful expressive framework which incorporates Horn clause logic as a subset. Consider a temporal sentence of the form:

antecedent about the past $\Rightarrow$ consequent about the present and future

this can, in general, be interpreted as if the "antecedent (about the past)" is true then **do** the "consequent (about the present and future)". Adopting this imperative reading, in fact, yields us with an execution mechanism for temporal logics. We take this as the basis of the METATEM approach. The name METATEM, in fact, captures two key aspects of our developing framework:

- the use of TEMporal logic as a vehicle for specification and modelling, via direct execution of the logic, of reactive systems;
- the direct embodiment of META-level reasoning and execution, in particular, identifying metalanguage and language as one and the same, providing a highly reflective system.

This paper focusses on the former point. Generally, the behaviour of a reactive component is given by specifying the interactions that occur between that component and the context, or environment, in which it is placed. In particular, a distinction needs to be made between actions made by the component and those made by the environment. In METATEM, we perpetuate such distinctions. The behaviour of a reactive component is described by a collection of temporal rules, in the form mentioned above. The occurrence, or otherwise, of an action is denoted by the truth, or falsity, of a proposition. The mechanism by which propositions are linked to actual action occurrences is not an issue here and is left to the reader's intuition. However, the temporal logics presented in Sections 2.1 and 4 do distinguish between component and environment propositions.

1.3 Related Work

The study of temporal and modal logics in the formal development of reactive systems has, in the main, been concentrated on techniques for specification and verification. The study of synthesis from temporal logic based specification, e.g. [MW84] and more recently [PR89a, PR89b], and, alternatively, the direct execution of temporal and modal logic, e.g. [Mos86] has not been so widespread, despite there being some fascinating starts.

Currently, the most developed implementation of an executable temporal logic is that of Moszkowski and Hale. Moszkowski [Mos86] has implemented a subset of a temporal logic, known as Tempura, based on interval models [MM84]. In fact, that particular interval temporal logic was first introduced for describing hardware [Mos83] and has now been put to the test with some examples of hardware simulation within Tempura [Hal87]. However, although Tempura is, in the computational sense, expressive enough, Tempura is limited in the sense of logic programming as in Prolog. Concurrent with the development of Moszkowski's work, Tang [Zhi83] defined and implemented a low-level temporal (sequential) programming system XYZ/E. His logic is based upon a linear, discrete, future-time temporal logic. Recent developments in that area have been developments of the logic (to obtain XYZ/D) to handle limited forms of distributed programming. Again, the drawback of this work, from the declarative and logic programming perspective, is the very traditional low-level state machine style. Steps towards the development of richer and more expressive executable subsets have since occurred. In particular, Gabbay [Gab87, Gab89] who describes general execution models, Abadi et al. [AM85, AM86, Aba87b, Aba87a, Bau89] who investigate temporal resolution mechanisms, Sakuragawa [Sak86] for a similar resolution-based "Temporal Prolog" and Hattori et al. [HNNT86] describe a modal logic based programming language for real-time process control, RACCO, based on Temporal Prolog.

2 Propositional METATEM and its Execution

In this section we illustrate the general principles outlined in Section 1 by the development of an execution mechanism for a propositional linear temporal logic.

2.1 A Propositional Linear-time Temporal Logic

We introduce a basic *linear* and *discrete* propositional temporal logic, PML (propositional METATEM logic). The language is obtained by augmenting classical propositional logic with *temporal* operators. The reader who is familiar with such standard temporal logics may prefer to skip the next two subsections and proceed to Section 2.2 where our execution approach is outlined.

The logic is presented in the usual way: Section 2.1.1 introduces the syntactic elements; Section 2.1.2 introduces the semantics.

2.1.1 Syntax

The basic symbols of the logic are depicted in Figure 1. We assume an alphabet of proposition symbols $\mathcal{A}_P$

Proposition Symbols

$a, b \ldots \in \mathcal{A}_E$

$x, y \ldots \in \mathcal{A}_C$

Note: $\mathcal{A}_P = \mathcal{A}_E \cup \mathcal{A}_C$ and $\mathcal{A}_E \cap \mathcal{A}_C = \emptyset$

Classical Propositional Connectives

true **false**

$\neg \quad \wedge \quad \vee \quad \Rightarrow \quad \Leftrightarrow$

Temporal Connectives

unary	$\bigcirc$	next
	$\bullet$	last
	$\square$	always in future
	$\blacksquare$	always in past
	$\lozenge$	sometime in future
	$\blacklozenge$	sometime in past
binary	$\mathcal{W}$	unless
	$\mathcal{Z}$	zince
	$\mathcal{U}$	until
	$\mathcal{S}$	since

Figure 1: Basic Symbols

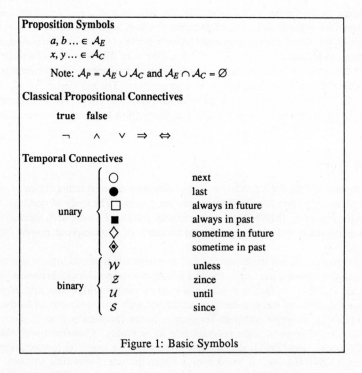

which is the union of two disjoint sets $\mathcal{A}_C$ and $\mathcal{A}_E$ of propositions controlled, respectively, by the component and by the environment. A standard collection of propositional connectives together with a collection of temporal connectives complete the basic symbols. $\bigcirc$, $\square$ and $\Diamond$ are unary *future*-time connectives; $\mathcal{W}$ and $\mathcal{U}$ are binary *future*-time connectives; $\bullet$, $\blacksquare$ and $\blacklozenge$ are unary *past*-time connectives; $\mathcal{Z}$ and $\mathcal{S}$ are binary *past*-time connectives.

The formulae of this propositional temporal logic are constructed inductively in the normal way. Figure 2 summarises the definition. Thus, propositions p from $\mathcal{A}_P$ are formulae, then given formulae φ and

- A proposition p drawn from $\mathcal{A}_P$ is a formula.
- If φ and ψ are formulae, then so are
  - **true** **false**
  - $\neg\varphi$ $\varphi \wedge \psi$ $\varphi \vee \psi$ $\varphi \Rightarrow \psi$ $\varphi \Leftrightarrow \psi$
  - $\bigcirc\varphi$ $\square\varphi$ $\Diamond\varphi$
  - $\bullet\varphi$ $\blacksquare\varphi$ $\blacklozenge\varphi$
  - $\varphi\mathcal{W}\psi$ $\varphi\mathcal{U}\psi$
  - $\varphi\,\mathcal{Z}\,\psi$ $\varphi\mathcal{S}\,\psi$
- If φ is a formula, then so is (φ).

Figure 2: Formula Definitions

ψ, so are the propositional combinations **true**, **false**, $\neg\varphi$, $\varphi \wedge \psi$, $\varphi \vee \psi$, $\varphi \Rightarrow \psi$ and $\varphi \Leftrightarrow \psi$, and the temporal combinations, $\bigcirc\varphi$, $\square\varphi$, $\Diamond\varphi$, $\bullet\varphi$, $\blacksquare\varphi$, $\blacklozenge\varphi$, $\varphi\mathcal{W}\psi$, $\varphi\mathcal{U}\psi$, $\varphi\,\mathcal{Z}\,\psi$ and $\varphi\mathcal{S}\psi$. The binding of the propositional connectives is assumed prioritized in the order given, i.e. (highest) $\neg$, $\wedge$, $\vee$, $\Rightarrow$, $\Leftrightarrow$ (lowest). The unary temporal connectives, i.e. $\bigcirc$, $\square$ and $\Diamond$, have binding equal to negation, i.e. $\neg$. The binary temporal connectives have binding in between $\neg$ and $\wedge$. However, as usual, to change the effect of binding, bracketing of formulae is allowed; so, given formula φ, then (φ) is also a formula.

The syntactic class of well-formed formulae defined in Figure 2 is referred to as *Wff*. It is also useful to define the subclasses $\mathit{Wff}_<$, $\mathit{Wff}_=$, $\mathit{Wff}_\geq$, covering, respectively, strict past time formulae, present time formula and non-strict future time formulae.

$\mathit{Wff}_=$ is the set which includes the propositions p from $\mathcal{A}_P$ and is closed under the propositional connectives.

$\mathit{Wff}_<$ is the set which includes the formulae $\bullet\phi$, $\blacksquare\phi$, $\blacklozenge\phi$, $\phi\mathcal{S}\,\psi$ and $\phi\,\mathcal{Z}\,\psi$, where ϕ and ψ are in $\mathit{Wff}_\leq$, and is closed under unary and binary propositional connectives. $\mathit{Wff}_\leq$ includes the set of propositions and is closed under the propositional and past-time temporal connectives.

$\mathit{Wff}_\geq$ is the set which includes $\mathit{Wff}_=$ and is closed under the propositional and future-time temporal connectives.

2.1.2 Semantics

Model structures (σ, i) are used to provide an interpretation for the temporal formulae. Figure 3 summarises the structure. The σ component provides an interpretation for the atomic propositions of the language. Given some moment in time, represented by a natural number, j, $\sigma(j)$ is a set of propositions drawn from the alphabet $\mathcal{A}_P$ and denotes all those propositions that are to be taken true at that moment. σ is total with respect to $\mathbf{N}$. The i component of the model gives the index which is to represent the current moment, i.e. *now*, in the model (referred to as the *reference point* of the model). Clearly, indices greater than i represent future moments and indices less than i represent past moments.

Model $\mathcal{M}$ is a structure (σ, i)

$$\sigma, i \in (\mathbf{N} \rightarrow 2^{\mathcal{A}_P}) \times \mathbf{N}$$

σ provides an interpretation for the propositions. Often, σ is treated as a *state* sequence

$$s_0 \quad s_1 \quad s_2 \quad s_3 \quad \ldots$$

Here, state s_j denotes a set of propositions given true by σ at j

i represents the current moment in time

Figure 3: Model Structure

The model is *linear* because for every moment j there is exactly one future, i.e. given by the points $j+1, j+2$, etc. The model is *discrete*: it is based on the natural numbers. Furthermore, as the mapping is assumed total over the naturals, time is infinite in the future and finite, or bounded, in the past. Because of the linearity and discreteness properties, the σ mapping can be conveniently represented by a sequence of *states*, e.g. $s_0, s_1, s_2, s_3, \ldots$.

A relation $\models$ is defined inductively over the structure of formulae and provides an interpretation for temporal formulae in the given model structures. Figure 4 provides its definition. Clearly, **true** is true in any model $\mathcal{M}$ and **false** is true in no model.

For propositions $p \in \mathcal{A}_P$, p is true in the model if and only if p is true in the current moment, i.e. is in the set $\sigma(i)$. The interpretations of the propositional connectives are defined in the obvious way.

The truth of a next time formula, e.g. $\bigcirc\varphi$, in the model (σ, i) is given by the truth of the formula φ in the successor model of (σ, i) , i.e. by the truth in the model $(\sigma, i+1)$.

The formula $\Box\varphi$, read as "always φ", is true for a model (σ, i) if and only if the formula φ is true in all the future (including the current) models of (σ, i), i.e. the models $(\sigma, i+k)$ for every $k \in \mathbf{N}$. Thus, if $\Box p$ is true for some model, then p will be true now and in every future moment of that model.

The diamond formula $\Diamond\varphi$, read as "eventually φ", is true in (σ, i) if and only if φ is true for the model σ, j with reference point, j, now or later than i $(j \geq i)$.

The strong until formula $\varphi\mathcal{U}\psi$ is true in model (σ, i) if and only if (i) ψ is true eventually in that model, say with reference point $i+k$, and (ii) the formula φ is true for all the models $(\sigma, i+j)$ where the reference points $i+j$ ranges up to but not including the reference point for which ψ is true. Note that the $\varphi\mathcal{U}\psi$ is true in any model for which ψ is true, i.e. $\psi \Rightarrow \varphi\mathcal{U}\psi$ is true for every model.

The past time temporal operators are defined to be strict past time versions of their future time counterparts, i.e. the past does not include the present moment. Since the model structure allows easy backwards as well as forwards reasoning the interpretations given should be self evident. However, it is worth discussing the beginning of time. What interpretation should be given to the $\bullet$ operator. We have given $\bullet$ a weak interpretation, i.e. for any formula φ, $\bullet\varphi$ is true at the beginning of time. Hence the $\bullet$false can be used to determine the beginning of time. One can define a strong (existential) last time operator $\odot$ such that $\odot\varphi$ is false at the beginning of time for any φ. Then, of course, notice the duality between the two last time operators, i.e. $\odot\varphi \Leftrightarrow \neg\bullet\neg\varphi$.

Definition 2.1 *A formula φ is said to be* satisfied *by a model $\mathcal{M} = (\sigma, i)$ if and only if $\sigma, i \models \varphi$.*

(Alternatively, $\sigma, i \models \varphi$ can be read as φ is true in the model (σ, i).)
The definition of validity is as in classical logic.

Definition 2.2 *A formula φ is said to be* valid, $\models \varphi$, *if and only if it is true for all models $\mathcal{M}$ ($\mathcal{M} \models \varphi$).*

Theorem 2.1 *PML is decidable.*

Propositions

$$\sigma, i \models p \quad \text{iff} \quad p \in \sigma(i)$$

Propositional Connectives

$\sigma, i \models$ **true**

$\sigma, i \models \neg\varphi \quad$ iff $\quad$ not $\sigma, i \models \varphi$

$\sigma, i \models \varphi \wedge \psi \quad$ iff $\quad \sigma, i \models \varphi$ and $\sigma, i \models \psi$

etc.

Temporal Connectives

$\sigma, i \models \bigcirc\varphi \quad$ iff $\quad \sigma, i+1 \models \varphi$

$\sigma, i \models \Box\varphi \quad$ iff $\quad$ for all $k \in \mathbf{N}$ $\sigma, i+k \models \varphi$

$\sigma, i \models \Diamond\varphi \quad$ iff $\quad$ for some $k \in \mathbf{N}$ $\sigma, i+k \models \varphi$

$\sigma, i \models \varphi\mathcal{U}\psi \quad$ iff $\quad$ for some $k \in \mathbf{N}$
$\sigma, i+k \models \psi$ and
for all $j \in 0..k-1$, $\sigma, i+j \models \varphi$

$\sigma, i \models \varphi\mathcal{W}\psi \quad$ iff $\quad \sigma, i \models \varphi\mathcal{U}\psi$ or $\sigma, i \models \Box\varphi$

$\sigma, i \models \bullet\varphi \quad$ iff $\quad$ if $i > 0$ then $\sigma, i-1 \models \varphi$

$\sigma, i \models \blacksquare\varphi \quad$ iff $\quad$ for all $k \in 1..i$ $\sigma, i-k \models \varphi$

$\sigma, i \models \diamondsuit\varphi \quad$ iff $\quad$ for some $k \in 1..i$ $\sigma, i-k \models \varphi$

$\sigma, i \models \varphi\mathcal{S}\psi \quad$ iff $\quad$ for some $k \in 1..i$
$\sigma, i-k \models \psi$ and
for all $j \in 1..k-1$, $\sigma, i-j \models \varphi$

$\sigma, i \models \varphi\mathcal{Z}\psi \quad$ iff $\quad \sigma, i \models \varphi\mathcal{S}\psi$ or $\sigma, i \models \blacksquare\varphi$

Figure 4: Interpretation in Model Structure

Proof See [Gou84], for example. This is an important result. It means that algorithms can be constructed to determine the validity, or otherwise, of any given PML formula.

2.2 METATEM Programs and Execution

A METATEM program for controlling a reactive process is presented as a collection of temporal rules. The rules apply universally in time and determine how the process progresses from one moment to the next. A temporal rule is given in the following clausal form

$$\text{past time antecedent} \Rightarrow \text{future time consequent.}$$

This is not an unnatural rule form and occurs in some guise in most programming languages. For example, in imperative programming languages it corresponds to the conditional statement. In declarative logic programming, we have the Horn clause rule form of Prolog and other similar languages. In METATEM, the "past time antecedent" is a temporal formula referring strictly to the past, i.e. it is in $Wff_<$; the "future time consequent" is a temporal formula referring to the present and future, i.e. it is in $Wff_\geq$. Although we can adopt a declarative interpretation of the rules, for programming and execution purposes we take an imperative reading following the natural way we ourselves tend to behave and operate, namely,

on the basis of the past **do** the future.

Given a program consisting of a set of rules R_i, this imperative reading results in the construction of a model for the formula $\Box \bigwedge_i R_i$, which we refer to as the program formula. The execution of a METATEM program proceeds, informally, in the following manner. Given some initial history of execution:

1. determine which rules currently apply, i.e. find those rules whose past time antecedents evaluate to true in the current history;

2. "jointly execute" the consequents of the applicable rules together with any commitments carried forward from previous times — this will result in the current state being completed and the construction of a set of commitments to be carried into the future;

3. repeat the execution process for the next moment in the context of the new commitments and the new history resulting from 2 above.

The "joint execution" of step 2 above relies upon a separation result for non-strict future-time temporal formulae, i.e. of the syntactic class $Wff_\geq$. Given a formula ψ in $Wff_\geq$, it can be written in a logically equivalent form as

$$\bigvee_{i=1}^{n} f_i$$

where each f_i is either of the form $\varphi_i \wedge \bigcirc \psi_i$ or of the form φ_i where each φ_i is a conjunction of literals[1], i.e. a present time formula from $Wff_=$, and ψ_i is a future (non-strict) time formula, i.e. in $Wff_\geq$. Thus φ_i can be used to build the current state, and recursive application of the execute mechanism on ψ_i (with the program rules) will construct the future states.

It is worth mentioning that although the METATEM program rule form of "past implies future" is a syntactic restriction on *Wff*, it is not a semantic restriction. A Separation Theorem (see [Gab89] for proof details) establishes that arbitrary temporal formulae, of class *Wff*, can be written in the form

$$\Box(\bigwedge_{i=1}^{n}(\xi_i \Rightarrow \psi_i))$$

where ξ_i are strict past time formulae, i.e. in $Wff_<$, and ψ_i are non-strict future time formulae, i.e. in $Wff_\geq$[2].

[1] A literal is either a proposition or its negation.

[2] The future time formulae are restricted so that they contain no environment propositions.

2.3 Examples

To demonstrate the execution process we offer two simple examples. The first is a resource manager, the second is the ubiquitous "dining philosophers".

2.3.1 A Resource Manager

Consider a resource being shared between several (distributed) processes, for example a database lock. We require a "resource manager" that satisfies the constraints given in Figure 5.

1. If the resource is requested by a process then it must eventually be allocated to that process.
2. If the resource is not requested then it should not be allocated.
3. At any one time, the resource should be allocated to at most one process.

Figure 5: Resource Manager Constraints

To simplify the exposition of the execution process, we restrict the example to just two processes. Let us use propositions r_1 and r_2 to name the occurrence of a request for the resource from process 1 and process 2 respectively. Similarly, let propositions a_1 and a_2 name appropriate resource allocations. It is important to note that the difference between propositions r_i and a_i. The request propositions are those controlled by the environment of the resource manager, whereas the allocation propositions are under direct control of the resource manager and can not be effected by the environment. Writing the given informal specification in the desired rule form, i.e. "pure past formula implies present and future formula", results in the rules of Figure 6.

$$\odot r_1 \Rightarrow \Diamond a_1 \qquad (1)$$

$$\odot r_2 \Rightarrow \Diamond a_2 \qquad (2)$$

$$\neg r_1 \; \mathcal{Z} \; (a_1 \wedge \neg r_1) \Rightarrow \neg a_1 \qquad (3)$$

$$\neg r_2 \; \mathcal{Z} \; (a_2 \wedge \neg r_2) \Rightarrow \neg a_2 \qquad (4)$$

$$\bullet\, \mathbf{true} \Rightarrow (\neg a_1 \vee \neg a_2) \qquad (5)$$

Figure 6: Temporal Rules for Resource Manager

We take the "state" as consisting of the four propositions r_1, r_2, a_1 and a_2. Given particular settings for the environment propositions, i.e. r_1 and r_2, the execution will determine appropriate values for the allocation propositions. Figure 7 gives the first seven steps of a typical trace.

Step 0. The environment has requested the resource for process 1. To see how the current state is completed, we must find which rules from Figure 6 apply. Clearly rules 1 and 2 do not apply; we are currently at the beginning of time and hence $\odot \phi$, for any ϕ, is false. The other rules do apply and require that both a_1 and a_2 are made false. No extra commitments are to be carried forward. Execution proceeds to the next time step.

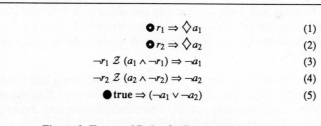

Requests		*Allocations*		*Time*	*Commitments*
r_1	r_2	a_1	a_2	*Step*	
y	n	n	n	0	
n	n	y	n	1	
y	y	n	n	2	
n	n	y	n	3	$\Diamond a_2$
y	n	n	y	4	
n	y	y	n	5	
n	n	n	y	6	

Figure 7: Sample Execution of Resource Manager

Step 1. First, there are no new requests from the environment. However, in examining which rules apply, we note that hypothesis of rule 1 is true (there was a request in the previous moment), hence we must "execute" $\Diamond a_1$. Also, rule 4 and rule 5 applies, in fact, the latter rule applies at every step because its hypothesis is always true. To execute $\Diamond a_1$, we execute $a_1 \vee (\neg a_1 \wedge \bigcirc\Diamond a_1)$. We have a choice; however, our mechanism will prioritise such disjunctions and attempt to execute them in a left to right order. One reason for this is that to satisfy an eventuality such as $\Diamond\phi$, we must eventually (in some future time step) satisfy ϕ; [3] so we try to satisfy it immediately. If we fail then we must carry forward the commitment to satisfy $\Diamond\phi$. Here we can make a_1 true. Rule 4 requires that a_2 is false, leaving rule 5 satisfied.

Step 2. The environment makes a request for both process 1 and process 2. The hypotheses of rules 1 and 2 are false, whereas those of rules 3 and 4 are true. So a_1 and a_2 are made false. No commitments are carried forward.

Step 3. No new requests from the environment, but there are two outstanding requests, i.e. both rule 1 and 2 apply. However, rule 5 requires that only one allocation may be made at any one time. The execution mechanism "chose" to postpone allocation to process 2. Thus, the eventuality from rule 1 is satisfied, but the eventuality for rule 2 is postponed, shown in the figure by carrying a commitment $\Diamond a_2$.

Step 4. A further request from the environment occurs, however, of interest here is the fact that $\Diamond a_2$ must be satisfied in addition to the commitments from the applicable rules. Note that this time, rule 4 does not apply as there is an outstanding request. Fortunately, the execution mechanism has no need to further postpone allocation to process 2 and a_2 is made true.

Steps 5 – 6 Similar to before.

2.3.2 Dining Philosophers

Our second example illustrates a rather simple solution to the dining philosophers problem. First, consider, if you can, a dining philosopher, Philosopher$_A$, alone in a closed environment. What is it that we wish to express about this philosopher? Basically that he never goes hungry, i.e. that he eats sufficiently often. So in our abstraction we use the proposition eaten$_A$ to denote that Philosopher$_A$ has just eaten. Hence a rather high level description of the behaviour of this chap might be given by the temporal logic formula

$$\Box\Diamond \text{eaten}_A.$$

[3] This particular choice of execution is described in more detail in section 3.1.2

However, since we know that he will eventually be rather more sociable and want to dine with colleagues, we'll give him a couple of forks and get him used not to using his fingers. In order to have eaten, we pretend that he needs to have possessed a fork in his left hand and one in his right hand for at least two moments; we denote possession of forks in left and right hands by the propositions fork_{AL} and fork_{AR}, respectively. Thus we should add to the above the formula

$$\Box(\mathrm{eaten}_A \Rightarrow \odot(\odot(\mathrm{fork}_{AL} \wedge \mathrm{fork}_{AR}) \wedge (\mathrm{fork}_{AL} \wedge \mathrm{fork}_{AR}))).$$

Writing this as a METATEM process in rule form, we get the following

$$\bullet\,\mathbf{true} \Rightarrow \Diamond\mathrm{eaten}_A$$

$$\neg\odot(\odot(\mathrm{fork}_{AL} \wedge \mathrm{fork}_{AR}) \wedge (\mathrm{fork}_{AL} \wedge \mathrm{fork}_{AR})) \Rightarrow \neg\mathrm{eaten}_A$$

which we will refer to as the $\mathrm{Philosopher}_A$ program. Let us execute, i.e. run, not kill, $\mathrm{Philosopher}_A$. Remember that he is alone in his own closed world, with, therefore, everything under his own control. The interpretation process in fact will produce a run of $\mathrm{Philosopher}_A$ that has him eating infinitely often, that is if it were given enough time. Although he doesn't necessarily eat continuously, one possible execution trace will satisfy the temporal formula $\Diamond\Box\mathrm{eaten}_A$. For example, all moments have fork_{AL} and fork_{AR} true, but the first two moments have eaten_A false. The first few steps of a trace produced by a prototype METATEM interpreter [Fis88] are given in Figure 8. In the first step, the interpreter sets fork_{AL} true but fork_{AR} false. Since both forks have not been held by the philosopher for the last two moments, eaten_A must be made false and the satisfaction of $\Diamond\mathrm{eaten}_A$ must be postponed. A commitment to satisfy $\Diamond\mathrm{eaten}_A$ is carried forward to step 1. The birthdate of the commitment tags the formula. The next two steps have fork_{AL} and fork_{AR} set true, but again postponement of satisfaction of $\Diamond\mathrm{eaten}_A$ has to occur. These new commitments are absorbed into the commitment to satisfy $\Diamond\mathrm{eaten}_A$ from step 0. In step 3 the philosopher can eat, therefore no commitment is carried forward. In step 4, we have a repeat of the situation from step 0. It is more interesting to create a process with two, or more, philosophers. In such a situation,

Propositions			*Time*	*Commitments*
fork_{AL}	fork_{AR}	eaten_A	*Step*	
y	n	n	0	$\Diamond\mathrm{eaten}_A(0)$
y	y	n	1	$\Diamond\mathrm{eaten}_A(0)$
y	y	n	2	$\Diamond\mathrm{eaten}_A(0)$
n	n	y	3	
y	n	n	4	$\Diamond\mathrm{eaten}_A(4)$
y	y	n	5	$\Diamond\mathrm{eaten}_A(4)$
y	y	n	6	$\Diamond\mathrm{eaten}_A(4)$
n	n	y	7	
y	n	n	8	$\Diamond\mathrm{eaten}_A(8)$

Figure 8: Sample Trace of Single Philosopher

the philosophers need to share forks, i.e. there should only be two real forks for two philosophers, three forks for three philosophers, etc. Consider just two philosophers. Assuming fork_{BL} and fork_{BR} are the propositions indicating that $\mathrm{Philosopher}_B$ has left and right forks, the following interfacing constraint needs to be placed.

$$\Box(\neg(\mathrm{fork}_{AL} \wedge \mathrm{fork}_{BR}) \wedge \neg(\mathrm{fork}_{AR} \wedge \mathrm{fork}_{BL}))$$

In rule form we thus have:

$$\bullet\,\mathbf{true} \Rightarrow \Diamond \text{eaten}_A$$
$$\neg \circledbullet(\circledbullet(\text{fork}_{AL} \wedge \text{fork}_{AR}) \wedge (\text{fork}_{AL} \wedge \text{fork}_{AR})) \Rightarrow \neg\text{eaten}_A$$
$$\bullet\,\mathbf{true} \Rightarrow \Diamond \text{eaten}_B$$
$$\neg \circledbullet(\circledbullet(\text{fork}_{BL} \wedge \text{fork}_{BR}) \wedge (\text{fork}_{BL} \wedge \text{fork}_{BR})) \Rightarrow \neg\text{eaten}_B$$
$$\bullet\,\mathbf{true} \Rightarrow \neg(\text{fork}_{AL} \wedge \text{fork}_{BR})$$
$$\bullet\,\mathbf{true} \Rightarrow \neg(\text{fork}_{AR} \wedge \text{fork}_{BL})$$

If we now consider execution of this set of rules, we should observe that both philosophers do eventually eat. Imagine the following potentially disastrous execution, e.g. Figure 9, from Philosopher$_A$'s point of view. The interpreter decides to allocate both forks to Philosopher$_B$ forever, i.e. it attempts to maintain $\neg\text{fork}_{AL}$,

Propositions						*Time*	*Commitments*
fork_{AL}	fork_{AR}	eaten_A	fork_{BL}	fork_{BR}	eaten_B	*Step*	
n	n	n	y	y	n	0	$\Diamond\text{eaten}_A(0)$, $\Diamond\text{eaten}_B(0)$
n	n	n	y	y	n	1	$\Diamond\text{eaten}_A(0)$, $\Diamond\text{eaten}_B(0)$
n	n	n	y	y	y	2	$\Diamond\text{eaten}_A(0)$
n	n	n	y	y	y	3	$\Diamond\text{eaten}_A(0)$
n	n	n	y	y	y	4	$\Diamond\text{eaten}_A(0)$
n	n	n	y	y	y	5	$\Diamond\text{eaten}_A(0)$
n	n	n	y	y	y	6	$\Diamond\text{eaten}_A(0)$

Figure 9: Bad Trace for Two Philosophers

$\neg\text{fork}_{AR}$, fork_{BL} and fork_{BR} true. Thus the interpreter is not forced to make eaten_B false and hence will always be able to satisfy the constraint $\Diamond\text{eaten}_B$. However, the interpreter is forced to make eaten_A false, because the appropriate fork propositions are not true, and hence the satisfaction of $\Diamond\text{eaten}_A$ is continually postponed. Eventually the loop checking mechanism of the interpreter recognises this potential continual postponement of $\Diamond\text{eaten}_A$ since step 0 and backtracks to make a different choice. This loop checking mechanism will eventually cause both forks to be "allocated" to Philosopher$_A$. So the disaster, in fact, does not occur and both philosophers eat infinitely often.

Figure 10 gives part of a trace that can be obtained with the METATEM interpreter for this example.

2.4 An Interpreter for Propositional METATEM

Figure 11 contains, in a Prolog-like notation, a basic interpreter for propositional METATEM. A predicate **execute** is defined which takes three arguments: **rules**, a list of the program rules; **commitments**, a list of commitments that need to be satisfied; and **history**, a sequence of states to be regarded as the history so far.

Below we give a brief description of each of the predicates used in the interpreter. A more detailed description of aspects relating to the predicates **choose** and **build-new-state** is given in Section 3.

- **check-past(rules, history, constraints)**
  This predicate, when satisfied, has the effect of first determining the activated rules from **rules**, i.e. those rules that have past-time antecedents satisfied on **history**. The variable **constraints** is

Propositions						*Time*	*Commitments*
fork_{AL}	fork_{AR}	eaten_A	fork_{BL}	fork_{BR}	eaten_B	*Step*	
y	n	n	n	n	n	0	$\Diamond\text{eaten}_A(0)$, $\Diamond\text{eaten}_B(0)$
y	y	n	n	n	n	1	$\Diamond\text{eaten}_A(0)$, $\Diamond\text{eaten}_B(0)$
y	y	n	n	n	n	2	$\Diamond\text{eaten}_A(0)$, $\Diamond\text{eaten}_B(0)$
n	n	y	y	y	n	3	$\Diamond\text{eaten}_B(0)$
n	n	n	y	y	n	4	$\Diamond\text{eaten}_A(4)$, $\Diamond\text{eaten}_B(0)$
y	y	n	n	n	y	5	$\Diamond\text{eaten}_A(4)$
y	y	n	n	n	n	6	$\Diamond\text{eaten}_A(4)$, $\Diamond\text{eaten}_B(6)$
n	n	y	y	y	n	7	$\Diamond\text{eaten}_B(6)$
n	n	n	y	y	n	8	$\Diamond\text{eaten}_A(8)$, $\Diamond\text{eaten}_B(6)$

Figure 10: Sample Trace of Two Philosophers

```
execute([],[],history) :- true.

execute(rules,commitments,history) :-
        check-past(rules, history, constraints),
        rewrite(constraints, commitments, exec-form),
        choose(exec-form, rules, current-constraints, new-commitments),
        build-new-state(history, current-constraints, new-history),
        execute(rules, new-commitments, new-history).
```

Figure 11: A basic interpreter for METATEM.

then bound to a list of the future parts of the activated rules. Thus, **constraints** contains all new commitments to be satisfied in any future execution.

- **rewrite(constraints, commitments, exec-form)**
  The rewrite predicate has the effect of rewriting the conjunction of all the formulae in **constraints** and those from **commitments** as a formula in standard form. This formula is bound to **exec-form** and represents the formula to be executed in the current state.

  The standard form adopted is one of

$$\textbf{true}, \quad \text{or} \quad \textbf{false}, \quad \text{or} \quad \bigvee_{i=1}^{n\geq 1} f_i$$

where each f_i is either of the form

$$\bigwedge_{j=1}^{m_i\geq 0} \lambda_{ij} \wedge \bigcirc \varphi_i$$

or

$$\bigwedge_{j=1}^{m_i\geq 1} \lambda_{ij}$$

and where λ_{ij} is a literal and $\varphi_i \in Wff_{\geq}$.

Note that all the future time temporal connectives for PML can be translated into disjunctions of present and next-time formulae. For example, the following rewrite rules are sound

$$\begin{aligned}
a\mathcal{U}b &\longrightarrow b \vee (a \wedge \neg b \wedge \bigcirc a\mathcal{U}b)\\
a\mathcal{W}b &\longrightarrow b \vee (a \wedge \neg b \wedge \bigcirc a\mathcal{W}b)\\
\Box a &\longrightarrow a \wedge \bigcirc \Box a\\
\Diamond a &\longrightarrow a \vee (\neg a \wedge \bigcirc \Diamond a)
\end{aligned}$$

Furthermore, we use rewrite rules such as

$$\begin{aligned}
\bigcirc a \wedge \bigcirc b &\longrightarrow \bigcirc(a \wedge b)\\
\bigcirc a \vee \bigcirc b &\longrightarrow \bigcirc(a \vee b)
\end{aligned}$$

to ensure that each disjunct of the standard form contains at most one next-time formula.

As an example, consider the resource controller described above, where the rules (2), (3), and (5) are the ones whose past-time parts are satisfied on the current history. The list bound to **constraints** is, therefore,

$$[\Diamond a_2,\ \neg a_1,\ \neg a_1 \vee \neg a_2]$$

Now, assuming that the **commitments** carried over from the previous state is the list

$$[\Diamond a_1]$$

then the formulae from both lists are conjoined to form

$$\Diamond a_2 \wedge \neg a_1 \wedge (\neg a_1 \vee \neg a_2) \wedge \Diamond a_1$$

and then rewritten in the standard form as

$$(\neg a_1 \wedge a_2 \wedge \bigcirc \Diamond a_1) \vee (\neg a_1 \wedge \neg a_2 \wedge \bigcirc(\Diamond a_2 \wedge \Diamond a_1)).$$

This resulting formula is bound to **exec-form**.

- **choose(exec-form, rules, current-constraints, new-commitments)**
  The predicate **choose** has the effect of picking a disjunct to execute from **exec-form** and binding propositional constraints to **current-constraints** and next-state commitments to **new-commitments** (with the principal $\bigcirc$ stripped off). Clearly, several different strategies could be adopted for picking a disjunct, some of which are described in Section 3. Continuing the example above, if we assume that the disjunct containing the fewest temporal subformulae is chosen, this gives

  $$\neg a_1 \wedge a_2 \wedge \bigcirc\Diamond a_1$$

  current-constraints is the list $[\neg a_1, a_2]$ together with bindings for any other unbound propositions[4], and **new-commitments** is

  $$[\Diamond a_1]$$

  So, if the only component propositions are a_1 and a_2, **current-constraints** is simply

  $$[\neg a_1, a_2].$$

  This gives the propositional interpretation for the new state.

- **build-new-state(history, current-constraints, new-history)**
  The effect of this predicate is to build a new state by binding propositions in accordance with **current-constraints**. A loop-checking mechanism is invoked to ensure that the state about to be constructed does not perpetuate a situation where eventualities (such as $\Diamond\varphi$) are continually postponed[5]. If such postponement is detected, **build-new-state** fails and backtracking to a previous choice point occurs.

  If backtracking does not occur, the values of appropriate environment propositions are recorded and the new state generated is then appended to **history** to form **new-history**.

3 METATEM Interpreter Strategies

The predicate **choose** is the heart of the interpretation process. Its effect is to take the currently executable formula and the current program rules, and to choose a disjunct from the formula to execute, constructing the current constraints and the future continuation for that execution. The choices for this predicate are categorised as follows:

- Choosing a disjunct to execute.
  Given the executable formula in standard form, the disjunct to be executed can be chosen in several ways; for example,

  1. by non-deterministic choice,
  2. by using an ordering on the disjuncts, or,
  3. by choosing a disjunct that is most likely to lead to a successful execution.

- Binding strategies for variables.
  Once a particular disjunct has been chosen for execution, the bindings for the propositions constrained by that disjunct are determined. However, the choice of bindings for other propositions remains. The choice for these bindings can be made

  1. non-deterministically
  2. by choosing a binding that is most likely to lead to a successful execution, or,
  3. by delaying bindings until they are needed.

The following two subsections described these choice mechanisms in more detail.

---

[4]Though other strategies can be used, e.g. see Section 3, we will assume for the moment that random values in $\{true, false\}$ are given to these other propositions.

[5]This *loop-checking* mechanism is briefly described in Section 3.3.

3.1 Choosing a disjunct

3.1.1 Non-deterministic choice of disjunct

Making a non-deterministic choice of disjunct to execute can be problematic; the interpreter could possibly delay the satisfaction of eventualities indefinitely. Consider, for example, the execution of $\Diamond p$. This can be rewritten as

$$p \vee (\neg p \wedge \bigcirc \Diamond p)$$

If we make a non-deterministic choice then it is possible to always choose the second disjunct, i.e. $\neg p \wedge \bigcirc \Diamond p$, making p false in every state, thus delaying indefinitely the time when p becomes true. Although a loop-checking mechanism, see Section 3.3, would eventually detect such a situation, it is desirable that excessive backtracking be avoided by use of an alternative choice mechanism.

3.1.2 Selection by order

The disjuncts of the executable formula can be ordered, then the predicate **choose** may select disjuncts following that ordering. There are several ways to obtain such an ordering, two of which are described below.

- Disjuncts are ordered by the number of eventualities which they contain, and then by the number of propositions which they leave unbound. However, consider the execution of the following set of rules:

$$\begin{array}{l} \bullet\,\textbf{false} \Rightarrow \Diamond a \\ \bullet\,\textbf{true} \Rightarrow \Diamond b \wedge \Diamond c \\ \bullet\,\textbf{true} \Rightarrow (\neg a \wedge b \wedge c) \vee (\neg b \wedge \neg c) \end{array}$$

  which expands, in the first state, to

$$\begin{array}{l} (\neg a \wedge b \wedge c \wedge \bigcirc \Diamond a) \quad \vee \\ (a \wedge \neg b \wedge \neg c \wedge \bigcirc(\Diamond b \wedge \Diamond c)) \quad \vee \\ (\neg a \wedge \neg b \wedge \neg c \wedge \bigcirc(\Diamond a \wedge \Diamond b \wedge \Diamond c)) \end{array}$$

  The ordering described would thus cause the left-most disjunct to be selected postponing the satisfaction of $\Diamond a$. However, in all subsequent states, the above would then remain the executable formula. In this case, the execution of a would again be delayed indefinitely.

- To avoid such possibilities, we introduce a further ordering on disjuncts to be applied after the above ordering has been carried out and then only on disjuncts containing postponed eventualities. This further ordering orders the disjuncts so that those that contain the oldest eventualities appear last in the ordering. For example, using this strategy on the above formula, the executable formula in the first state could be, as above,

$$\begin{array}{l} (\neg a \wedge b \wedge c \wedge \bigcirc \Diamond a) \quad \vee \\ (a \wedge \neg b \wedge \neg c \wedge \bigcirc(\Diamond b \wedge \Diamond c)) \quad \vee \\ (\neg a \wedge \neg b \wedge \neg c \wedge \bigcirc(\Diamond a \wedge \Diamond b \wedge \Diamond c)) \end{array}$$

  If the leftmost disjunct were chosen, then in the next state, because the $\Diamond a$ eventuality remained unsatisfied, the executable formula would be

$$\begin{array}{ll} (a \wedge \neg b \wedge \neg c \wedge \bigcirc(\Diamond b \wedge \Diamond c)) \quad \vee & (1) \\ (\neg a \wedge \neg b \wedge \neg c \wedge \bigcirc(\Diamond a \wedge \Diamond b \wedge \Diamond c)) \quad \vee & (2) \\ (\neg a \wedge b \wedge c \wedge \bigcirc \Diamond a) & (3) \end{array}$$

and the a would be executed. Note that the eventuality $\Diamond a$ has been present since the previous state, state 1, while both $\Diamond b$ and $\Diamond c$ were generated in state 2. Thus the oldest postponed eventuality in disjunct 1 is from state 2, while the oldest postponed eventualities in disjuncts 2 and 3 are from state 1.

The executable formula for the third state would then be

$$(\neg a \wedge b \wedge c) \vee (\neg b \wedge \neg c \wedge \bigcirc(\Diamond b \wedge \Diamond c))$$

and choosing the left-most disjunct satisfies the remaining eventualities immediately.

Thus, by always ordering the disjuncts such that all satisfying subformulae for the longest outstanding eventuality occur in the leftmost disjuncts, or equivalently that the oldest postponed eventuality occurs in the rightmost disjunct, we are guaranteed to avoid the delay of eventualities described above.

Though this strategy is inefficient in particular cases, it is simple and forms a useful starting point from which to develop more sophisticated heuristics.

3.1.3 Choice directed by future satisfiability

An alternative approach is to attempt to eliminate disjuncts that can not lead to a successful execution. In the case of PML, the satisfiability of a chosen disjunct, which is a future-time formula, can be determined. If no disjunct is satisfiable, then there is no possible execution path from this state; otherwise, there may be some execution path that can be followed[6].

Suppose the following program is to be executed

$$\bullet \textbf{false} \Rightarrow \Diamond a \wedge \bigcirc \Box \neg a \wedge \Diamond \neg a.$$

In the first state, the executable formula is

$$(\neg a \wedge \bigcirc(\Diamond a \wedge \Box \neg a)) \vee (a \wedge \bigcirc(\Diamond \neg a \wedge \Box \neg a))$$

The previous choice strategy would result in an attempt to execute the first disjunct. However, a satisfiability check would eliminate this disjunct from consideration.

There are two major problems with this approach. The first is that when using more general versions of METATEM (e.g. first order) satisfiability is not decidable. The other is that satisfiability in PML is PSPACE-complete, which has obvious implications for the speed of the execution process.

3.2 Binding strategies

When a disjunct has been chosen for execution, it may not fully determine the values of all propositions in the current state, in which case, bindings for the unconstrained propositions must be found.

As in Section 3.1, the choice of binding can be made using non-deterministic or satisfiability directed strategies. Unfortunately, these binding strategies suffer the same problems as their choice strategy counterparts, for example excessive backtracking. One way to avoid some of these problems is to delay the binding of propositions until their values are neeeded.

3.2.1 Delayed binding

Consider the following set of rules:

$$\begin{aligned} \odot\odot\odot p &\Rightarrow \Box \neg a_1 \\ \odot r_1 &\Rightarrow \Diamond a_1 \end{aligned}$$

[6]Note that when the formula is satisfiable, the model constructed can be used to help the interpreter find an executable path.

If all propositions are bound at each computation step then an arbitrary value is chosen for p. Suppose p is set to true in the first state and that the environment keeps r_1 false until the third state. In the fourth state, the premise of the first rule is true and henceforth a_1 must be false. However, the interpreter also has to satisfy $\Diamond a_1$. After several more steps the fact that an unsatisfiable loop has been generated is detected and execution fails causing a backtrack to state 1 where p was set. p is then set to false in the first state and when the r_1 occurs again, it can be satisfied[7].

By delaying the binding of p in the first state until it is needed, much of this backtracking can be avoided. The binding of p can be delayed until the fourth state when the value of p in the first state is required. In the fourth state, the commitments can be examined and a suitable value for p in state 1 chosen; in the above scenario p would be retrospectively set to false in state 1.

One problem with this approach is that propositions may be unbound for an indeterminate length of time. However, the values of such propositions may be required by the environment.

3.3 Loop-checking

The disjunctive nature of formulae involving eventualities, e.g., $\Diamond \varphi$, $\varphi \mathcal{U} \psi$, will often lead to postponement of their satisfaction. If the formula being executed contains an unsatisfiable eventuality then this continual postponement can be seen as a loop. The problem that then arises is how to detect such loops and then to distinguish between genuine loops that are due to unsatisfiable eventualities and apparent loops that have satisfiable extensions.

For example, if the formula to be executed were

$$\Diamond a \wedge \Box \neg a$$

which expands to

$$\neg a \wedge \bigcirc(\Diamond a \wedge \Box \neg a)$$

then the eventuality $\Diamond a$ would be continuously postponed, as the formula is not satisfiable. In the example below, the eventuality $\Diamond q$ is postponed but only for a finite time. Indeed, it can only be satisfied int the fifth state when q can be set to true.

$$\bullet\bullet\bullet\bullet p \Rightarrow \neg q$$
$$\bullet \textbf{false} \Rightarrow \neg p \wedge \bigcirc \Box p \wedge \Diamond q$$

Using the above execution mechanism there is a bound, within which any satisfiable eventuality must be satisfied. This bound, which depends on the size of the formula, enables us to distinguish between real and apparent loops. Thus the loop-checking mechanism causes the execution to fail and backtrack if an eventuality has been outstanding for more than the fixed number of states.

A coarse bound can be given by the number of different states that appear in the semantic tableau for the program formula, f. This bound is $2^{5|f|}$ where $|f|$ is the length of the formula f [LP85]. (Note that such a bound can not be established where arbitrary environment interaction occurs.) It can be shown that the execution mechanism described in Section 3.4 satisfies any satisfiable eventuality within such a fixed number of states.

3.4 Propositional METATEM Interpreter Correctness

Using the choice strategy based on ordering by eventuality age (described in Section 3.1.2) and the loop-checking mechanism described above defines an execution function, *execute*, for PML without environment propositions. This function takes a METATEM program and returns the model constructed during execution (unless the execution fails in which case an empty model is returned). We can then establish the following:

[7]Note that the satisfiability directed choice of binding described above would not help the choice of the binding for p as no matter what p is bound to initially, in state 4 the formula to be executed is still satisfiable. In this case it is only when an r_1 occurs that satisfiability is potentially lost.

Theorem 3.1 *Let P be a program consisting of a set of program rules $\{R_i \mid i \in I\}$, each of the form $\xi_i \Rightarrow \psi_i$ where $\xi_i \in Wff_<$ and $\psi_i \in Wff_\geq$. If the program formula, f, defined as $\Box \bigwedge_{i \in I} R_i$ is satisfiable then execute($\bigwedge_{i \in I} R_i$, **true**, []) will generate a model for f.*

Theorem 3.2 *Let P be a program consisting of a set of program rules $\{R_i \mid i \in I\}$, each of the form $\xi_i \Rightarrow \psi_i$ where $\xi_i \in Wff_<$ and $\psi_i \in Wff_\geq$. If execute($\bigwedge_{i \in I} R_i$, **true**, []) does not fail, then the program formula f, defined as $\Box \bigwedge_{i \in I} R_i$ is satisfiable and* execute *generates a model for f.*

Outline proofs of these results are given in Appendix A.

4 Towards a First-order METATEM

In this section we consider a subset of first-order temporal logic, called FML, that can be executed in a similar manner to PML. Program rules are again written in the 'past implies future' form

$$\xi(\bar{x}) \Rightarrow \psi(\bar{x}, \bar{y})$$

where $\bar{x}$ and $\bar{y}$ represent tuples of variables, implicitly quantified as follows.

$$\forall \bar{x}.\ \exists \bar{y}.\ \xi(\bar{x}) \Rightarrow \psi(\bar{x}, \bar{y})$$

In FML the set of predicates is partitioned into component and environment predicates and, as in propositional METATEM, environment literals are not allowed in the future-time part of FML clauses.

Before describing an execution mechanism for FML, we will outline the syntax and semantics of FML.

4.1 Syntax and Semantics of FML

4.1.1 Syntax

The language FML consists of the following symbols

- A countable set, $\mathcal{A}_P$, of *predicate symbols*, each with an associated non-negative integer, its *arity*; predicate symbols of arity 0 are called *proposition symbols*. The set $\mathcal{A}_P$ is the disjoint union of the sets $\mathcal{A}_{PC}$ and $\mathcal{A}_{PE}$, of *component* and *environment* predicate symbols.
- A countable set, $\mathcal{A}_F$, of *function symbols*, each with an associated arity; function symbols of arity 0 are called *constant symbols*.
- A infix binary predicate symbol =.
- A countable set, $\mathcal{A}_V$, of *variable symbols*. The set $\mathcal{A}_V$ consists of the disjoint union of the sets $\mathcal{A}_{V\exists}$ and $\mathcal{A}_{V\forall}$, of *existential* and *universal* variables.
- Quantifiers $\exists$, $\forall$.
- A set of propositional and temporal connectives, as in PML.

A *term* is defined by

- a variable symbol is a term,
- if f is a function symbol of arity n, and $t_1, t_2, \ldots t_n$ are terms then $f(t_1, t_2, \ldots t_n)$ is a term.

Denote by $\mathcal{G}$ the set of *ground terms*, i.e. terms containing no occurrences of variables. A *binding* is then a partial function $\alpha : \mathcal{A}_V \rightarrow \mathcal{G}$.
A function η which applies bindings, α, to terms is now defined.

- If $x \in \mathcal{A}_V$ is in the domain of α, then $\eta(\alpha, x) = \alpha(x)$.
- If $x \in \mathcal{A}_V$ is not in the domain of α, then $\eta(\alpha, x) = x$.
- If f is an n-ary function symbol and $t_1, t_2, \ldots t_n$ are terms, then

$$\eta(\alpha, f(t_1, t_2, \ldots t_n)) = f(\eta(\alpha, t_1), \eta(\alpha, t_2), \ldots \eta(\alpha, t_n)).$$

An *atomic formula* is defined to be an application of a predicate to term arguments, i.e. if p is a predicate symbol of arity n, and $t_1, t_2, \ldots t_n$ are terms then $p(t_1, t_2, \ldots t_n)$ is an atomic formula A *grounded atomic formula* is an atomic formula containing no occurrences of variables.
We also assume the existence of a countable set, $\mathcal{A}_T$, of atoms, which is a subset of the set of all grounded atomic formulae. The existence of this set enables us to restrict the domains of individual predicate and function symbols and also to implicitly restrict quantification; for example, if p is a predicate symbol then, in the expression $\forall x.p(x)$, x ranges only over those ground terms t for which $p(t) \in \mathcal{A}_T$.
The *well formed formulae* of the language are now defined by

- If φ is an atomic formula such that, for some binding α, $\eta(\alpha, \varphi) \in \mathcal{A}_T$, then φ is a well-formed formula.
- If t_1, t_2 are terms, then $t_1 = t_2$ is a well-formed formula.
- Well-formed formulae are constructed from other formulae by application of propositional and temporal connectives as in PML.
- If $x \in \mathcal{A}_{V\forall}$ and φ is a well-formed formula, then $\forall x.\varphi$ is a well-formed formulae.
- If $y \in \mathcal{A}_{V\exists}$ and φ is a well-formed formula, then $\exists y.\varphi$ is a well-formed formulae.

The definition of the function η is extended in the obvious way over well-formed formulae.

4.1.2 Semantics

Well-formed formulae of FML are interpreted over model structures of the form (σ, α, i) where

$$\sigma : \mathbf{N} \rightarrow 2^{\mathcal{A}_T}, \quad \alpha \text{ is a binding, and } i \in \mathbf{N}$$

The satisfaction relation $\models$ of PML is extended over model structures and well-formed formulae of FML as follows

$(\sigma, \alpha, i) \models \varphi$	only if $\eta(\alpha, \varphi)$ is a well-formed formula containing no free variables
$(\sigma, \alpha, i) \models p(t_1, t_2, \ldots t_n)$	iff $p(\eta(\alpha, t_1), \eta(\alpha, t_2), \ldots \eta(\alpha, t_n)) \in \sigma(i)$
$(\sigma, \alpha, i) \models t_1 = t_2$	iff $\eta(\alpha, t_1) = \eta(\alpha, t_2)$
$(\sigma, \alpha, i) \models \forall x.\varphi$	iff for *all* $\gamma \in \mathcal{G}$, such that $\eta(\alpha \dagger [x \mapsto \gamma], \varphi)$ is a well-formed formula[8], $(\sigma, \alpha \dagger [x \mapsto \gamma], i) \models \varphi$
$(\sigma, \alpha, i) \models \exists y.\varphi$	iff for *some* $\gamma \in \mathcal{G}$, such that $\eta(\alpha \dagger [y \mapsto \gamma], \varphi)$ is a well-formed formula, $(\sigma, \alpha \dagger [y \mapsto \gamma], i) \models \varphi$

Note that the above semantics imply a *rigid* interpretation of variables, i.e. the binding of a variable name is fixed over time.

[8]Here $\alpha \dagger [x \mapsto \gamma]$ denotes the binding obtained by overwriting α with the binding $[x \mapsto \gamma]$.

4.2 Executing First-Order METATEM

The execution mechanism for FML proceeds in a similar manner to that of PML, see Figure 12 for an outline interpreter in Prolog-like notation. As with the execution of PML, a predicate **execute** is defined which takes, as arguments, a list of the program rules, a list of commitments that need to be satisfied, and a sequence of states to be regarded as the history so far. We use in our specification rules of the form

$$\xi(x_1, \ldots, x_m) \Rightarrow \psi(x_1, \ldots, x_m, y_1, \ldots, y_n)$$

where the variables of ξ appear in ψ. These variables are interpreted universally and the extra variables y_i are interpreted existentially. ξ is a past formula, and ψ is a present or future formula. Note that this is in contrast to the Logic Programming convention where the additional variables in the antecedent are read existentially. Thus when we query the past with $\xi(x_1, \ldots, x_m)$ as a query, we must find all instantiations t_i of x_i for which $\xi(x_1, \ldots, x_m)$ is true and execute $\psi(t_0, \ldots, t_m, y)$ by finding at least one $f_j(t_1, \ldots, t_m)$, for each j, for which $\psi(t_1, \ldots, t_m, f_1(t_1, \ldots, t_m), \ldots, f_n(t_1, \ldots, t_m))$ is true.

Before outlining the predicates used in the FML interpreter, we give its formal derivation.

4.2.1 Derivation of Execution Mechanism for FML

Assume the following is given in the context of the above definition of FML.

1. A set of program rules, R_i, $i \in I$, each of the form

   $$\forall \overline{x_i}.\ \exists \overline{y_i}.\ \xi_i(\overline{x_i}) \Rightarrow \psi_i(\overline{x_i}, \overline{y_i})$$

   where

$\overline{x_i}$	is a tuple of distinct universal variables,
$\overline{y_i}$	is a tuple of distinct existential variables,
$\xi_i(\overline{x_i})$	is a pure past time formula dependent on $\overline{x_i}$,
$\psi_i(\overline{x_i}, \overline{y_i})$	is a future time formula dependent on $\overline{x_i}$ and $\overline{y_i}$.

2. A future time formula C, known as the commitment formula.

3. A finite prefix, or history sequence of states, σ_h, each state being a subset of the atoms defining FML.

4. An infinite state sequence continuation, σ.

Let $\mathcal{M}(\alpha)$ denote the model structure $(\sigma_h{}^\frown\sigma, \alpha, |\sigma_h|)$. We now derive conditions that establish

$$\mathcal{M}([]) \models \Box \bigwedge_{i \in I} R_i \wedge C \tag{6}$$

First note that we can expand $\Box$ in 6 to give

$$\mathcal{M}([]) \models \bigwedge_{i \in I} \forall \overline{x_i}\, \exists \overline{y_i}\ \xi_i(\overline{x_i}) \Rightarrow \psi_i(\overline{x_i}, \overline{y_i}) \wedge C \wedge \bigcirc \Box \bigwedge_{i \in I} R_i \tag{7}$$

By appropriate renaming, the variables in each tuple $\overline{x_i}$ can be made unique. Without any loss in generality we assume this is the case, i.e. letting $vars = \{x \mid x \in \textbf{elems}\ \overline{x_i}, i \in I\}$, $|vars| = \Sigma_{i \in I}\textbf{len}\ \overline{x_i}$. The universal quantifiers in 7 can be thus be moved outwards over the conjunction. Independently, the existential quantifiers can be moved inwards; each $\xi_i(\overline{x_i})$ formula is independent of $\overline{y_i}$. The following, therefore, needs to be satisfied.

$$\mathcal{M}([]) \models \forall \overline{x_{i,i \in I}}.\ \bigwedge_{i \in I} \xi_i(\overline{x_i}) \Rightarrow \exists \overline{y_i}.\ \psi_i(\overline{x_i}, \overline{y_i}) \wedge C \wedge \bigcirc \Box \bigwedge_{i \in I} R_i \tag{8}$$

By the definition of the semantics of universal quantification, for 8 to hold, the formula

$$\bigwedge_{i\in I} \xi_i(\overline{x_i}) \Rightarrow \exists\overline{y_i}.\ \psi_i(\overline{x_i},\overline{y_i})$$

must be true for all bindings giving assignments to the variables in the tuples $\overline{x_i}$. As $\xi_i(\overline{x_i})$ is a pure past time formula, bindings for $\overline{x_i}$ can be determined from the history sequence σ_h.
Define J to be largest subset of I and B the largest set of bindings α each with domain $\bigcup_{j\in J}$ **elems** $\overline{x_j}$ such that for all state sequence extensions σ

$$\text{for all } \alpha \in B,\ \mathcal{M}(\alpha) \models \bigwedge_{j\in J} \xi_j(\overline{x_j}) \tag{9}$$

In effect, the set J defines the set of rules which are activated in this state and B gives the set of bindings that apply. Thus to satisfy 8 we need now just satisfy 10 below.

$$\text{for all } \alpha \in B,\ \mathcal{M}(\alpha) \models \bigwedge_{j\in J} \exists\overline{y_j}.\ \psi_j(\overline{x_j},\overline{y_j}) \wedge C \wedge \bigcirc\Box\bigwedge_{i\in I} R_i \tag{10}$$

At this stage, we apply the substitution function η, defined in Section 4.1.2 to remove the universal variable references. That is to say, 10 is semantically equivalent to 11 below.

$$\mathcal{M}([]) \models \bigwedge_{\alpha\in B} \eta(\alpha, \bigwedge_{j\in J} \exists\overline{y_j}.\ \psi_j(\overline{x_j},\overline{y_j}) \wedge C \wedge \bigcirc\Box\bigwedge_{i\in I} R_i) \tag{11}$$

Since $C \wedge \bigcirc\Box\bigwedge_{i\in I} R_i$ have no free variables, the formula can be moved out of scope of η; 11 leads to 12.

$$\mathcal{M}([]) \models \bigwedge_{\alpha\in B} \eta(\alpha, \bigwedge_{j\in J} \exists\overline{y_j}.\ \psi_j(\overline{x_j},\overline{y_j})) \wedge C \wedge \bigcirc\Box\bigwedge_{i\in I} R_i \tag{12}$$

By definition, η distributes over conjunctions, thus 13 is obtained.

$$\mathcal{M}([]) \models \bigwedge_{j\in J}\bigwedge_{\alpha\in B} \eta(\alpha, \exists\overline{y_j}.\ \psi_j(\overline{x_j},\overline{y_j})) \wedge C \wedge \bigcirc\Box\bigwedge_{i\in I} R_i \tag{13}$$

For each distinct $\alpha \in B$ choose a distinct k from K and let $G_{jk}(\overline{y_j})$ denote the formula resulting from the substitution given by $\eta(\alpha, \psi_j(\overline{x_j},\overline{y_j}))$. This leads to 14.

$$\mathcal{M}([]) \models \bigwedge_{j\in J}\bigwedge_{k\in K} \exists\overline{y_j}.\ G_{jk}(\overline{y_j}) \wedge C \wedge \bigcirc\Box\bigwedge_{i\in I} R_i \tag{14}$$

By renaming the variables in the tuples $\overline{y_j}$ to be unique across the k conjuncts, the existential quantification can be moved outwards over the conjunctions. Let $\overline{z_{jk}}$ denote the tuples of distinct variables. Furthermore, since C is independent of the variables in the tuples $\overline{z_{jk}}$, it can be moved into the quantifiers scope.

$$\mathcal{M}([]) \models (\exists\overline{z_{jk}}_{\,j\in J,k\in K}.\ \bigwedge_{j\in J}\bigwedge_{k\in K} G_{jk}(\overline{z_{jk}}) \wedge C) \wedge \bigcirc\Box\bigwedge_{i\in I} R_i \tag{15}$$

Consider now the subformula $\bigwedge_{j\in J}\bigwedge_{k\in K} G_{jk}(\overline{z_{jk}}) \wedge C$. This is a future time formula and can be rewritten in a standard form which separates out present and strict future subformulae. For 15 to be satisfied, this form may be **true**, or a disjunction $\bigvee_{l\in L} f_l(\overline{u_l})$ where

$$\bigcup_{l\in L} \textbf{elems}\ \overline{u_l} = \bigcup_{j\in J}\bigcup_{k\in K} \textbf{elems}\ \overline{z_{jk}}$$

and each $f_l(\overline{u_l})$ is of either the form

$\Lambda_l(\overline{u_l})$	a conjunction of literals
$\Lambda_l(\overline{v_l}) \wedge \bigcirc C_l(\overline{w_l})$	where **elems** $\overline{v_l} \cup$ **elems** $\overline{w_l}$ = **elems** $\overline{u_l}$
$\bigcirc C_l(\overline{u_l})$	

where $C_l(\ldots)$ is a future time formula. Assuming that the separated form is not **true**, the existential quantifiers $\exists \overline{z_{jk}}_{j\in J, k\in K}$ can now be moved inwards over the disjunction, giving 16.

$$\mathcal{M}([]) \models (\bigvee_{l\in L} \exists \overline{u_l} . f_l(\overline{u_l})) \wedge \bigcirc \square \bigwedge_{i\in I} R_i \tag{16}$$

For 16 to be satisfied, one of the disjuncts must be true. Without loss of generality, let this disjunct have index l. A binding α_l, for sake of argument, must also exist for the variables contained in the tuple $\overline{u_l}$. Thus 16 reduces to satisfying the following.

$$\mathcal{M}([]) \models \eta(\alpha_l, f_l(\overline{u_l})) \wedge \bigcirc \square \bigwedge_{i\in I} R_i \tag{17}$$

By writing f_l in its general separated form, and letting Λ'_l denote $\eta(\alpha_l, \Lambda_l(\overline{v_l}))$ and C'_l denote $\eta(\alpha_l, C_l(\overline{w_l}))$, the following is obtained

$$\mathcal{M}([]) \models \Lambda'_l \wedge \bigcirc C'_l \wedge \bigcirc \square \bigwedge_{i\in I} R_i \tag{18}$$

For this to be satisfied, the propositional part Λ'_l must be true in the current state (i.e. the first state of σ). Assume that this is the case. Now, by letting $\mathcal{M}([])'$ denote the model structure $(\sigma_h \hat{} [\mathbf{hd}\ \sigma] \hat{} \mathbf{tl}\ \sigma, [], |\sigma_h|+1)$, it is clear that the following must be satisfied.

$$\mathcal{M}([])' \models \square \bigwedge_{i\in I} R_i \wedge C'_l \tag{19}$$

This is precisely the form with which we started. Hence we have derived a recursive mechanism which will construct models in a stepwise fashion.

Using this derivation, an execution mechanism for FML can be defined, see Figure 12 for an outline interpreter in Prolog-like notation. An explanation of the predicates used in the interpreter follows,

```
execute([],[],history) :- true.

execute(rules,commitments, history) :-
        check-past(rules, history, constraints, bindings),
        rewrite(constraints, commitments, bindings, exec-form),
        choose(exec-form, rules, current-constraints, new-commitments),
        build-new-state(history, current-constraints, new-history),
        execute(rules, new-commitments, new-history).
```

Figure 12: A basic interpreter for First-Order METATEM.

emphasising the connection with the derivation given above.

- **check-past(rules, history, constraints, bindings)**
  As in PML, this predicate, when satisfied, has the effect of determining the activated rules from **rules**, i.e. those rules that have past-time antecedents satisfied on **history**, for particular bindings of variables. The variable **constraints** is then bound to a list of the future parts of the activated rules, and a list of bindings that apply to the universal variables in **constraints** is bound to **bindings**[9]. This process of generating the universal bindings corresponds to the transformation from formula 8 and 10 in the derivation.

[9]Note that, as all universal variable bindings have been added to **bindings**, the only variables that appear in **constraints** and have no binding are existentially quantified.

- **rewrite(constraints, commitments, bindings, exec-form)**
  The **bindings** are used to expand the formulae in **constraints** (as in 11 to 16), which are then conjoined with those from **commitments** and rewritten into a formula in the standard form. This corresponds to the formula to be executed in the current state, given as the disjunction in 16, and is bound to **exec-form**.

- **choose(exec-form, rules, current-constraints, new-commitments)**
  The predicate **choose** has the effect of picking a disjunct to execute from **exec-form** and binding propositional constraints to **current-constraints** and next-state commitments to **new-commitments** (with the principal $\bigcirc$ stripped off). At this stage, not only are the bindings for unbound atoms chosen, but bindings are also chosen for any unbound existential variables. This procedure corresponds to the transformation from 16 to 18 in the derivation.

  Once a disjunct and binding has been chosen, the current state is fully constrained.

- **build-new-state(history, current-constraints, new-history)**
  This predicate has the same effect in the the case of FML as it did in PML: a new state is built in accordance with **current-constraints** and enviroment values are recorded. The formula represented by **current-constraints** is equivalent to Λ'_l in formula 18 of the derivation.

  Note that a loop-checking mechanism is again invoked at this point. If backtracking does not occur, the new state generated is appended to **history** to form **new-history**.

4.2.2 Example

As an example of the use of first-order METATEM, consider extending the resource controller given earlier to a greater number of processes. We could achieve this by having, as we do in the earlier rules, a different proposition for each request or allocation for each process, i.e.,

$$r_1, r_2, \ldots, r_n \quad \text{and} \quad a_1, a_2, \ldots, a_n$$

However, this is tedious, difficult to extend and clutters the program rules. We can represent the resource controller in first-order METATEM using the rules given in Figure 13.

$$\bullet R(x) \Rightarrow \Diamond A(x) \quad (1)$$

$$\neg R(x)\ \mathcal{Z}\ (A(x) \wedge \neg R(x)) \Rightarrow \neg A(x) \quad (2)$$

$$\bullet (A(x_1) \wedge A(x_2)) \Rightarrow (x_1 = x_2) \quad (3)$$

Figure 13: First-order METATEM rules for a Resource Manager

In this example, x, x_1, and x_2 are universal variables, R is an environment predicate, A is a component predicate, and a, b, and c are ground terms. The set of atoms includes $R(a)$, $R(b)$, $R(c)$, $A(a)$, $A(b)$, and $A(c)$. A sample run of this resource controller is given in Figure 14.

The convention used in the example is that atoms that are not explicitly mentioned in the state are assumed to be false. Thus, $R(c)$ and $A(b)$ are false in state 0. Below, a more detailed description of the steps involved in the execution of the resource controller will be given. The states referred to are those outlined in the execution trace in Figure 14.

In the initial state (state 0), the environment sets $R(a)$ and $R(b)$ to be true and, by default, sets $R(t)$ to false for other terms t where $R(t) \in$ Atoms. As there is no previous state, the antecedent of rule 2 in the program rules is trivially satisfied for all x. Thus, $A(t)$ is set to false for other terms, t, where $A(t) \in$ Atoms. As the executable formula generated refers only to the current state, no commitments are carried forward.

Environment	*Component*	*State*	*Commitments*
$R(a)$, $R(b)$		0	
$R(c)$	$A(a)$, $A(b)$	1	
In the process of building state 2, the execution mechanism finds inconsistencies such as $a = b$ and $b = a$. Consequently, the construction of state 2 is aborted and the execution backtracks to the choice point in state 1.			
$R(c)$	$A(a)$	1	$\Diamond A(b)$
	$A(b)$	2	$\Diamond A(c)$
	$A(c)$	3	

Figure 14: Sample Execution of Resource Manager

In state 1, the environment sets $R(c)$ to be true, but sets $R(t)$ to be false for all other appropriate terms t. The antecedent of rule 3 is again unsatisfied as there was no binding of x for which $A(x)$ was true in the previous state. Also, the antecedent of rule 2 is unsatisfied for a and b (as $R(a)$ and $R(b)$ occurred in the last state), but is satisfied for all other bindings of x. This generates a commitment to make $A(t)$ false for all terms t, except a and b, where $A(t) \in$ Atoms.

During the construction of state 2 an inconsistency is found as the antecedent fo rule 3 is satisfied for $x_1 = a$ and $x_2 = b$ giving a commitment to make $a = b$ true (similarly with $x_1 = b$ and $x_2 = a$). As these is no way to make this true and as there are no choices that avoid trying to make it true, the execution mechanism backtracks to a choice point that occurred during the construction of state 1. The only choice made in state 1 was to execute the disjunct that set both $A(a)$ and $A(b)$ to be true. A different disjunct is then chosen that sets $A(a)$ to be true, $A(b)$ to be false and generates the commitment $\Diamond A(b)$. Thus $A(a)$ is set to true in state 1.

During the construction of state 2, no inconsistency is found as the antecedent of rule 3 is satisfied only for $x_1 = a$ and $x_2 = a$ and making $a = a$ true is not difficult. The environment sets $R(t)$ to be false for all terms t where $R(t) \in$ Atoms and the rules generate $\Diamond A(c)$, to execute along with the commitment $\Diamond A(b)$. At this stage, the disjunct that set both $A(b)$ and $A(c)$ to be true could have been chosen; if it had, backtracking would have occurred during the construction of state 3. We chose to show the execution of one of the satisfiable disjuncts and so $A(b)$ is set to true while $A(t)$ is set to false for all other appropriate terms t. This generates a commitment to satisfy $\Diamond A(c)$.

In state 4, the environment sets $R(t)$ to be false for all terms t where $R(t) \in$ Atoms and the rules generate the constraint that $A(t)$ must be false for all t except c. As there is commitment of $\Diamond A(c)$, carried over from the previous state, $A(c)$ is here set to true and no commitments are carried forward.

4.3 Meta-programming in METATEM

A further aspect of METATEM is its meta-programming capability. We will here only provide a flavour of this and, as a first example, will consider the outline of a simple meta-interpreter for METATEM given in Figure 15. This has been defined by three rules in the appropriate form. The first rule defines the initial state; the second rule defines an execution step of the interpreter; and finally, the third rule defines the execution to be infinite. The definition of the computation step (rule 2) is similar in form to the interpreter given in Section 2.4. However, the major difference is that the execution state, previously an argument of the execute predicate, is now implicit in the meta-interpreter execution.

One unusual aspect of this meta-interpreter is that the (conceptually) infinite tower of such interpreters are all running in step and in the same logical time. They are all running in step because the $\bullet$ operator in rule 2 forces each meta-interpreter to be in step with the interpreter on which it is being executed. They

(1) $\bullet$**false** $\Rightarrow$ input(rules) $\wedge$
check-past(rules, satisfied-rules) $\wedge$
rewrite(satisfied-rules, [ ], exec-form) $\wedge$
choose(exec-form, current-constraints, new-commitments) $\wedge$
apply(current-constraints) $\wedge$
to-execute(rules, new-commitments)

(2) $\odot$ to-execute(rules, commitments) $\Rightarrow$ check-past(rules, satisfied-rules) $\wedge$
rewrite(satisfied-rules, commitments, exec-form) $\wedge$
choose(exec-form, current-constraints, new-commitments) $\wedge$
apply(current-constraints) $\wedge$
to-execute(rules, new-commitments)

(3) $\bullet$**false** $\Rightarrow$ $\square$tick

Figure 15: A basic meta-interpreter for METATEM—M_1

all run in the same logical time because, in the first execution state, rule 1 has the effect of reading in the new program rules (i.e. a new meta-interpreter) and executing them. Thus all the meta-interpreters begin execution from the same state!

Suppose now we wished to provide a METATEM interpreter that allows the dynamic modification of program rules. This would require producing a new meta-interpreter, say M_2, which has as its computation step the following rule.

$\odot$ to-execute(rules, commitments) $\Rightarrow$ input-new-rules(rules, new-rules) $\wedge$
check-past(new-rules, satisfied-rules) $\wedge$
rewrite(satisfied-rules, commitments, exec-form) $\wedge$
choose(exec-form, current-constraints, new-commitments) $\wedge$
apply(current-constraints) $\wedge$
to-execute(new-rules, new-commitments)

The rules of M_2 are then used as the program rules for M_1, thus providing a new top level interpreter. Note that M_2 is in fact just another meta-interpreter, given that it too can run on top of an infinite tower of M_2's. This mechanism can also be used to change the future commitments between execution steps.

5 A General Framework

The METATEM approach can be considered as a special case of a more general computational problem involving quantifiers in Herbrand universes. To explain what we mean, consider the following example. We are given a database with the following items of data:

(1) $Bad(O)$ "Oliver is bad"

(2) $\forall x[Bad(x) \Rightarrow Bad(S(x))]$ "Any son of a bad person is also bad"

(3) $\exists x Tall(x)$ "Someone is tall"

our query is

(4) $\exists x[Tall(x) \wedge Bad(x)]$ "Is there someone both tall and bad?"

The answer to this query is negative. It does not follow from the database in first order classical logic. If we try to use a Horn Clause procedural computation we get:

Data

(1) $Bad(O)$

(2) $Bad(x) \Rightarrow Bad(S(x))$

(3) $Tall(c)$

Query

(4) $Tall(x) \wedge Bad(x)$

The c is a Skolem constant. The query will fail or loop.

Suppose we add the *extra assumption* 5 to the database, where:

> (5) The existential quantifiers involved (i.e. the $\exists x$ in (3)) refer to the Herbrand universe generated by the function symbol $S(x)$.

This means that the constant c must be an element of the set $\{O, S(O), S^2(O), \ldots\}$. In this case, the query should succeed. There does exist an x which is both tall and bad. How can we logically put this extra input (5) into the database? Are we doomed to reasoning in such cases in the meta-language only?

The answer is that temporal logic does it for us. Let the "flow of time" be the set

$$\{O, S(O), S^2(O), \ldots\}$$

i.e. Oliver and his descendants are considered to be points of time. We let $S^m(O) < S^n(O)$ iff $m < n$.

We can read $Tall(x)$ (respectively $Bad(x)$) to mean *Tall* (respectively *Bad*) is true at "time" x. The data and query now become

Data

(1*)	Bad	*Bad* is true at time O, which is "now"
(2*)	$\Box(Bad \Rightarrow \bigcirc Bad)$	Always if *Bad* is true then *Bad* is also true next
(3*)	$\Diamond Tall$	Sometime *Tall* is true

Query

(4*) $\Diamond(Tall \wedge Bad)$

We see that $\Diamond$ is read exactly as we want it and the simple database (1), (2), (3), (5) is properly logically represented by (1*), (2*), (3*).

We can now see what is the general framework involved. First we are dealing with first order logic with function symbols. Second we are dealing with special quantifiers, which we call *γ-quantifiers* (γ for "generated" universe quantifiers). These quantifiers have the form $\exists_{\{f_i\}}$, $\forall_{\{f_i\}}$, where $\exists_{\{f_i\}}A(x)$, is true iff there exists an element y generated in the Herbrand universe of the function symbols $\{f_i\}$, such that $A(y)$ is true. $\forall_{\{f_i\}}A(x)$ reads for all y in the Herbrand universe of the function symbols $\{f_i\}$, $A(y)$ is true.

The data and query can now be written in the new γ-quantifiers language as follows:

Data

(1**) $Bad(O)$

(2**) $\forall_{\{O,S\}}Bad(x)$

(3**) $\exists_{\{O,S\}}Tall(x)$

Query

(4**) $\exists_{\{O,S\}}(Tall(x) \wedge Bad(x))$

Our METATEM interpreter is nothing more than a model generating method for first order logic with γ-quantifiers for unary Skolem functions. We now give formal definitions.

Definition 5.1 *A* γ-first order logic with unary functions *consists of the following.*

1. *A first order language with variables* $\{x_i\}$*, predicates* P_i*, a stock of unary functions* $\{f_i\}$*, a stock of 0-functions (constants)* $\{c_i\}$ *and the usual classical connectives.*
2. *A stock of* γ*-quantifiers* $\exists_\Gamma$ *and* $\forall_\Gamma$*, indexed by* finite *sets* $\Gamma = \{f_i, c_j\}$ *of unary functions and constants. We assume that each such* Γ *contains at least one constant* c_1.
3. *Well-formed formulae are defined in the usual way*

Definition 5.2 *Given a set* Γ *as in definition 5.1,* the Herbrand universe generated by Γ, *denoted by* H_Γ*, is the smallest set containing the constants of* Γ *which is closed under the application of the functions of* Γ*, i.e. satisfying*

$$\text{if } c_i \in \Gamma \text{ then } c_i \in H_\Gamma \text{ and,}$$

$$\text{if } x \in H_\Gamma \text{ and } f \in \Gamma \text{ then } f(x) \in H_\Gamma.$$

Definition 5.3 *For any* Γ*, the binary relation* N_Γ *on the Herbrand universe,* H_Γ*, is defined by*

$$t_1 N_\Gamma t_2 \text{ iff } t_2 = f(t_1)$$

where $f \in \Gamma$ *is a unary function symbol. Define* $<_\Gamma$ *as the transitive closure of* N_Γ.

Notice that if $\Gamma \subseteq \Gamma'$ *then* $<_\Gamma \subseteq <_{\Gamma'}$*. For example,* $x < f(x) < ff(x)$.

Definition 5.4 *A* γ-structure *for a* γ*-first order logic has the form* (D, h, R)*, where D is the domain* $(D \neq \emptyset)$*, h is an assignment and R is a transitive relation on D, satisfying the following conditions:*

1. *if x is a constant* $c \in \Gamma$ *then* $h(c) \in D$*,*
2. *if f is a unary function symbol then* $h(f)$ *is a unary function on D such that for all* $d \in D$*,* $d R h(f)(d)$ *holds,*
3. *h is a* Herbrand assignment, *i.e. the following hold for any* $c, d, f, g \in \Gamma$*:*
   (a) *if* $c \neq d$ *then* $h(c) \neq h(d)$
   (b) *if* $f \neq g$ *then* $\forall x \in D(h(f)(x) \neq h(g)(x))$
   (c) *if* $x \neq y$ *then* $h(f)(x) \neq h(f)(y)$

The definition of truth in such a model is the same as in the classical case, with the following clauses added for the γ-quantifiers.

$$h \models \forall_\Gamma A(x) \quad \text{iff} \quad \text{for all } x \in H_\Gamma, h \models A(x)$$
$$h \models \exists_\Gamma A(x) \quad \text{iff} \quad \text{for some } x \in H_\Gamma, h \models A(x)$$

For example, consider a language with one constant O and two function symbols f_1 and f_2. Thus $\Gamma = \{O, f_1, f_2\}$. The Herbrand universe H_Γ is $\{O, f_1(O), f_2(O), f_1f_2(O), f_2f_1(O), \ldots\}$. The natural ordering on the Herbrand universe is $<$ $(<_{\{O,f_1,f_2\}})$. $(H_\Gamma, <_\Gamma)$ can be viewed as a binary temporal tree. The quantifier $\exists_\Gamma$ corresponds to $\Diamond$.

Definition 5.5 *(*Γ*-specification)*
Let there be given a first order γ*-quantifier language. A database is said to be a* Γ*-specification database if it contains clauses of the form* $\forall_\Gamma x_i[A(x_i) \to B(x_i)]$ *where A is a formula with free variables* x_i*. The quantifiers in A all have the form* γ*-quantifiers restricted to be* $< x_i$*. The quantifiers of B are of the form*

$$Q_\Gamma(x, y) = \exists_\Gamma y > x_i \forall_\Gamma u(x_i < u < y)$$

$A(x_i)$ *corresponds to querying the past and* $B(x_i)$ *corresponds to specifying the future.*

We are now ready to explain the general framework in which the METATEM interpreter resides. METATEM is a method for generating Herbrand γ-models for γ-specification first order databases.

Example — Linear Time Temporal Logic Thus, the PML interpreter described above is an interpreter for a language $\Gamma = \{O, S\}$, with one constant and one unary function. It utilises specific properties of this Γ (flow of time).

Example — Branching Time Temporal Logic There exist temporal logics such as CTL [CES86] that contain connectives of the form $\overline{\Diamond}$, which operate on the Herbrand universe of a set Γ of functions and have semantics:

$\overline{\Diamond}A$ is true at t iff for all paths π through t, there exists an x such that $x > t$ and $x \in \pi$ and A is true at x.

Thus for example, if $\Gamma = \{f_1, \ldots, f_k\}$, $\overline{\Diamond}A$ is true at t iff for every path π with $t \in \pi$, there exists an $x \in H_\Gamma \cap \pi$, $t <_\Gamma x$, in which A is true. In CTL, this operator is represented by the pair AF.

Since H_Γ is a Herbrand universe, there is a finite set, S_A, of points in which A is true such that

$$\forall x \exists y.\, x \leq y \wedge y \in H_A.$$

Let $\mathbf{Fin}_A$ be the connective saying that A is true at a finite number of points of the Herbrand universe. Then $\overline{\Diamond}$ is essentially inter-definable using **Fin** as follows:

Definition 5.6 *Let Γ be a set of unary functions and c a constant. A path π in H_Γ is a sequence (t_i) such that $t_i N_\Gamma t_{i+1}$*[10]*. Consider the following connectives ($[A]_t$ reads A is true at t):*

$$[\Diamond_\Gamma A]_t = 1 \textit{ iff } \exists x \in H_\Gamma.\, t <_\Gamma x \wedge [A]_x = 1$$

$$[\blacklozenge_\Gamma A]_t = 1 \textit{ iff } \exists x \in H_\Gamma.\, x <_\Gamma t \wedge [A]_x = 1$$

$$[\overline{\Diamond}_\Gamma A]_t = 1 \textit{ iff } \forall \pi.\, (\pi \textit{ is a path in } H_\Gamma \wedge t \in \pi) \Rightarrow (\exists x.\, x \in \pi \wedge t <_\Gamma x \wedge [A]_x = 1)$$

$$[\mathbf{Fin}_\Gamma A]_t = 1 \textit{ iff the set of x such that } t <_\Gamma x \textit{ and } [A]_x = 1 \textit{ is finite}$$

Let $\square = \neg\Diamond\neg$, $\blacksquare = \neg\blacklozenge\neg$ and $\overline{\square} = \neg\overline{\Diamond}\neg$.

Proposition 5.1 *For Γ finite, we have:*

$$(k \wedge \blacksquare_\Gamma \neg k \wedge \square_\Gamma \neg k) \Rightarrow (\overline{\Diamond}_\Gamma A \Leftrightarrow \square_\Gamma \Diamond_\Gamma \blacklozenge_\Gamma (A \wedge \blacklozenge_\Gamma k) \wedge \mathbf{Fin}\Diamond_\Gamma (A \wedge \blacksquare_\Gamma (\blacklozenge_\Gamma k \Rightarrow \neg A)))$$

Proof: The above says that if k is true exactly at the point t that $\overline{\Diamond}_\Gamma A$ is equivalent to saying that

1. every point has a higher point somewhere in whose past, after the point at which k is true, A is true and
2. the set of points above t in which A first becomes true is finite.

Clearly there is equivalence over the Herbrand universe H_Γ.

Thus the general framework for our temporal language is model building for the quantifiers $\forall_\Gamma$, $\exists_\Gamma$, and **Fin**.

Definition 5.7 *The execution predicate for $\overline{\Diamond}$ and $\Diamond$ are as follows:*

1.

$$\mathbf{exec}(\overline{\Diamond}_\Gamma A) = \bigwedge_{i=1}^{m} \mathbf{exec}(\bigcirc_i A \vee \bigcirc_i \overline{\Diamond}_\Gamma A)$$

[10]Note that set membership, $\in$, is extended in the obvious way to sequence membership.

2.

$$\mathbf{exec}(\overline{\Diamond}_\Gamma A) = \bigvee_{i=1}^{m} \mathbf{exec}(\bigcirc_i A \vee \bigcirc_i \overline{\Diamond}_\Gamma A)$$

where $\Gamma = \{c, f_1, \ldots, f_m\}$ *and* $\bigcirc_i A$ *is true at t iff A true at* $f_i(t)$.

Note that proposition 5.1 depends on the fact that Γ is finite. If we have an infinite number of successor functions, the connective $\overline{\Diamond}$ is independent. We can regard $\overline{\Diamond}$ as a special second order quantifier on the Herbrand universe.

5.1 γ two sorted predicate logic

We are now ready to extend the γ-quantifier approach to predicate logic. The extension is simple. We imagine many sorted predicates $P(t, x_i, \ldots, x_n)$ defined over two domains. t ranges over a Herbrand universe H_Γ and $x_i, \ldots, x_n$ range over an ordinary set D. The language contains the usual connectives and the two sets of quantifiers — $\forall x$ and $\exists x$ for the $\{x\}$ sort and $\forall_\Gamma t$ and $\exists_\Gamma t$ for the t sort. This language defined the γ-predicate logic. It corresponds to ordinary temporal predicate logic.

Definition 5.8 *A γ two sorted predicate logic consists of the following:*

1. *A two sorted language with variables $\{t_i\}$ for the first sort and $\{x_i\}$ for the second sort, predicates of the form $P(t, x_i, \ldots, x_n)$ where $n \geq 0$ and t is the one sort of variable and the x_i are the other sort, a stock of unary functions and a stock of constants c_i for generating the terms of the first sort.*

2. *A stock of Γ quantifiers for the first sort (as in definition 5.1) and the usual quantifiers $\forall$ and $\exists$ for the second sort.*

3. *well-formed formulas are defined as usual for the two-sorted predicate logic.*

4. *A γ two sorted structure has the form (D, h, R, g, U), where U is the universe of the $\{x_i\}$ sort, (D, h, R) is as in definition 5.4 and g is an assignment function, assigning for each $n+1$ predicate symbol P and each $t \in D$ a subset $g(t, P) \subseteq D^n$.*

The definition of truth in such a model is the same as the classical one on $\forall x$, $\exists x$ and the γ-definition and conditions (of 5.6) on the $\forall_\Gamma t$, $\exists_\Gamma t$.

A Proofs of Theorems

Here we present outline proofs for Theorems 3.1 and 3.2. First we establish the following Lemmas.

Lemma A.1 *Given a set of rules $\{R_i \mid i \in I\}$, each of the form $\xi_i \Rightarrow \psi_i$ where $\xi_i \in Wff_<$ and $\psi_i \in Wff_\geq$, together with a commitment C ($\in Wff_\geq$), and a finite history state sequence σ_h,*

if *execute*$(\bigwedge_{i \in I} R_i, C, \sigma_h)$ *fails* **then** *there is no extension σ such that $\sigma_h\hat{}\sigma, |\sigma_h| \models (\Box \bigwedge_{i \in I} R_i) \wedge C$*

Outline Proof We use computation induction.
First note that *execute* calls *check-past* to reduce the formula to be executed, namely

$$\Pi: \qquad (\Box \bigwedge_{i \in I} R_i) \wedge C$$

to the formula

$$\Pi': \qquad (\bigwedge_{j \in J} \psi_j) \wedge C \wedge \bigcirc(\Box \bigwedge_{i \in I} R_i)$$

where

$$R_i \;=\; \xi_i \Rightarrow \psi_i \quad \text{and} \quad J \;=\; \{i \mid \exists\sigma.\sigma_h\hat{}\sigma, |\sigma_h| \models \xi_i{}^{11},\ i \in I\}$$

such that

$$\exists\sigma.\sigma_h\hat{}\sigma, |\sigma_h| \models \Pi \quad \text{iff} \quad \exists\sigma.\sigma_h\hat{}\sigma, |\sigma_h| \models \Pi'$$

The variable *satisfied-rules* of *check-past*, in fact returns the formula $\bigwedge_{j\in J}\psi_j$.
Next *execute* uses *rewrite* to reduce Π' to a logically equivalent form, separating out the present,

$$\Pi'': \qquad (\bigvee_{k\in K} G_k) \wedge \bigcirc\Box(\bigwedge_{i\in I} R_i)$$

where

$K \neq \emptyset$: each G_k is either of the form $\varphi_k \wedge \bigcirc\psi_k$ or of the form φ_k, where $\varphi_k \in Wff_=$ is propositionally consistent and $\psi_k \in Wff_\geq$,

$K = \emptyset$: Π'' is **false**.

In the case of K being empty, *rewrite*(...) fails, causing failure of *execute*($\bigwedge_{i\in I} R_i, C, \sigma_h$). Clearly there is no extension to σ_h that will be a model for **false**.
In the case of K being non-empty, *choose*(...) will fail, causing subsequent failure of

$$execute(\bigwedge_{i\in I} R_i, C, \sigma_h)$$

if for every $k \in K$ either

1. for every state s, total wrt the proposition alphabet, satisfying φ_k, the recursive call of *execute* on the history extended by state s fails, i.e. *execute*($\bigwedge_{i\in I} R_i, \psi_k, \sigma_h\hat{}[s]$) fails, or

2. ψ_k contains an unsatisfiable eventuality with respect to the history σ_h and rules R_i.
   As mentioned previously this critical condition can be detected in a number of ways. The prototype [Fis88] uses a loop check mechanism described in Section 3.3.

Again, these are precisely the cases when there is no extension to σ_h that will yield a model for Π. Note that 1 above is the computation induction step.

Lemma A.2 *Given a set of rules* $\{R_i \mid i \in I\}$, *each of the form* $\xi_i \Rightarrow \psi_i$ *where* $\xi_i \in Wff_<$ *and* $\psi_i \in Wff_\geq$, *together with a commitment* C ($\in Wff_\geq$), *and a finite history state sequence* σ_h,

> **if** *execute*($\bigwedge_{i\in I} R_i, C, \sigma_h$) *does not fail*
>
> **then** *its infinite* (ω) *execution will generate an infinite* (ω) *extension to* σ_h.

Outline Proof Consider an infinite, non-failing, run of *execute*($\bigwedge_{i\in I} R_i, C_0, \sigma_h$). The run can viewed as an exploration of the following computation tree.

The computation starts at node 0 with a call of *execute*($\bigwedge_{i\in I} R_i, C_0, \sigma_h$). Each, actual, node in the computation tree is generated by some recursive call of *execute*. At each node, *execute* has a finite number of potential ways to recurse, each way corresponding to execution of one of the disjuncts from the formula to be executed at that point. Some recursive calls of *execute* may fail and backtracking to an earlier choice point, i.e. node, occurs. Consider node j. The shaded, finite, tree branching from the left of node j corresponds to n_j first level recursive calls of *execute* , each of which failed and caused a backtrack to node j. The unshaded tree branching to the right of node j represents potential unexplored computation tree. The branching at any node j in this tree is finite and matches with the number of choices that exists from the expansion of the formula to be executed at that node into the disjunctive form $\bigvee_i^{n_j} f_{j_i}$ (cf. Section 2.4). By

[11] Remember that ξ_i is a pure past time formula and only depends on the real history, σ_h

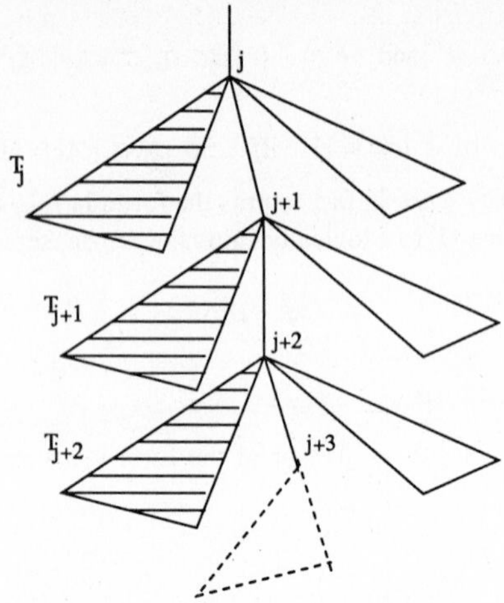

Figure 16: Partial Computation Tree

ensuring that *execute* never explores any branch from a node more than once, an infinite (ω), backtracking, run of *execute* explores the tree to an infinite (ω) depth. Consider an ω-sequence of nodes "visited" by *execute* during its backtracking, but infinite, run. For example,

$$\ldots, j, \underbrace{\ldots\ldots}_{T_j}, j+1, \underbrace{\ldots\ldots}_{T_{j+1}}, j+2, \underbrace{\ldots\ldots}_{T_{j+2}}, j+3, \underbrace{\ldots\ldots}_{T_{j+3}} \ldots$$

The subsequences denoted by T_j, etc, correspond to nodes constructed during failing calls of *execute* from node j, i.e. the shaded trees, T_j in Figure 16. Of interest is the projection of nodes $j, j+1, \ldots$. Each recursive call of *execute*, say to node $j+1$ from node j, extends the previous history argument σ_j by one state s_j. The ω-extension implicitly generated by *execute* is defined as the sequence of states $s_0, \ldots, s_j, s_{j+1}, \ldots$.

Lemma A.3 *Given a set of rules $\{R_i \mid i \in I\}$, each of the form $\xi_i \Rightarrow \psi_i$ where $\xi_i \in Wff_<$ and $\psi_i \in Wff_\geq$, together with a commitment C ($\in Wff_\geq$), and a finite history state sequence σ_h,*

if *execute*$(\bigwedge_{i\in I} R_i, C, \sigma_h)$ *does not fail*

then *there is an extension σ generated by execute such that* $\sigma_h\hat{}\sigma, |\sigma_h| \models \Box(\bigwedge_{i\in I}) \wedge C$

Outline Proof If the computation of *execute* does not fail then, by Lemma A.2 it will recurse infinitely generating an infinite extension to σ_h, namely the sequence $\sigma = s_0, s_1, s_2, \ldots$, where the states s_i, etc, are, in fact, total with respect to the proposition alphabet. It is easy to see that, by the construction process applied by *execute* (*build-new-state*), the extension σ will yield a model in the cases that the commitment argument of *execute* never contains a $\Diamond$-formula. We argue that a model is also obtained in the case that the commitment contains a $\Diamond$-formula. If such $\Diamond$-formula is never satisfied, then by definition it will be continually postponed for satisfaction in some future moment, i.e. will always be carried forward in the commitment argument. Since the number of possible distinct states is finite, repetition must occur and hence a loop carrying an unsatisfied $\Diamond$-formula will be detected and failure of *execute* will occur. But *execute* does not fail, therefore, the extension it produces must also satisfy all $\Diamond$-formulae that may occur.

The proof of Theorem 3.1 and 3.2 is now trivial.

Theorem 3.1 Let P be a program consisting of a set of program rules $\{R_i \mid i \in I\}$, each of the form $\xi_i \Rightarrow \psi_i$ where $\xi_i \in Wff_<$ and $\psi_i \in Wff_\geq$. If the program formula, f, defined as $\Box \bigwedge_{i \in I} R_i$ is satisfiable then *execute*($\bigwedge_{i \in I} R_i$, **true**, []) will generate a model for f.

Proof First note that if $\Box \bigwedge_{i \in I} R_i$ is satisfiable, then is some extension σ to the empty sequence, [], such that $[]\hat{}\sigma, 0 \models (\Box \bigwedge_{i \in I} R_i) \wedge \mathbf{true}$. Therefore by Lemma A.1, *execute*($\bigwedge_{i \in I} R_i$, **true**, []) does not fail. By Lemma A.3, as *execute* does not fail, it will generate an infinite extension σ such that $[]\hat{}\sigma, 0 \models (\Box \bigwedge_{i \in I} R_i) \wedge$ **true**, i.e. $\sigma, 0 \models (\Box \bigwedge_{i \in I} R_i)$

Theorem 3.2 Let P be a program consisting of a set of program rules $\{R_i \mid i \in I\}$, each of the form $\xi_i \Rightarrow \psi_i$ where $\xi_i \in Wff_<$ and $\psi_i \in Wff_\geq$. If *execute*($\bigwedge_{i \in I} R_i$, **true**, []) does not fail, then the program formula f, defined as $\Box \bigwedge_{i \in I} R_i$ is satisfiable and *execute* generates a model for f.

Proof Follows directly from Lemma A.3.

B Automata-Theoretic aspects of METATEM execution

If METATEM programs contain no references to environment variables then we can view the execution mechanism as tracing out a subtree of a semantic tableau associated with the program rules. This special construction is driven by the future formulae of the rules, the past formulae only being evaluated at existing nodes, with further nodes being introduced without gaps.

Thus, if the program consists of a set of METATEM rules $R_1, \ldots, R_n$ then the associated tableau is that for the program formula

$$\Box \bigwedge_{i=1}^{n} R_i$$

If we construct a Hintikka Graph[12] for such a formula (the graph will be finite due to the finite model property exhibited by this PML) we can then describe an infinite tree representing all the paths through this graph. Even if we assume that the graph construction filters out all propositionally inconsistent and next-time inconsistent sequences, some of the paths through the infinite tree may still be inconsistent. This is because eventualities (i.e., commitments generated by $\Diamond$ and $\mathcal{U}$ formulae) may be generated but never satisfied on certain branches. In the tableau method for temporal logic, the Hintikka Graph is usually 'marked' in such a way that no such sequences can be generated as models[13]. We can see this as pruning of the infinite tree, removing all paths that contain continually unsatisfied eventualities. This tree can be seen as the 'satisfiable subtree' of the original tree in which no checks for inconsistencies have been carried out.

The execution mechanism proceeds by exploring a portion of the tree that can be generated from a Hintikka Graph in an attempt to follow an infinite branch of the satisfied subtree described above. Though unsatisfiable branches may be followed for a finite number of states, the invocation of the loop-checking mechanism will force the execution mechanism to backtrack down such branches and explore different branches. Eventually, the execution mechanism will follow an infinite branch of the satisfied subtree. Once it has chosen such a path it will never backtrack past the choice point again. Though a branch that goes from the satisfied subtree back out into the unsatisfiable part of the original tree can be followed for a finite number of states, backtracking will eventually occur and exploration of the satisfied subtree will continue.

The soundness of the execution mechanism is given in such a way in Theorem 3.1.

Thus, METATEM programs can be 'compiled' into automata, i.e, those automata generated from Hintikka Graphs. A similar approach to the 'compilation' of METATEM program rules into automata is that of the synthesis of programs from reactive system specifications described by Pnueli and Rosner [PR89b]. As part

[12]For an overview of the tableau method in propositional temporal logics, see Gough [Gou84] and Wolper [Wol85] and for an automata-theoretic view of this process, see [VW86].

[13]A Hintikka graph marked in this way is equivalent to a Büchi automaton.

of their work on the synthesis of reactive modules they synthesize, for finite systems with no environment interaction, Streett tree automata that are similar to the automata described above.

References

[Aba87a] M. Abadi.
Temporal-Logic Theorem Proving.
PhD thesis, Department of Computer Science, Stanford University, March 1987.

[Aba87b] M. Abadi.
The Power of Temporal Proofs.
In *Proc. Symp. on Logic in Computer Science*, pages 123–130, Ithaca, June 1987.

[AM85] M. Abadi and Z. Manna.
Non-clausal Temporal Deduction.
Lecture Notes in Computer Science, 193:1–15, June 1985.

[AM86] M. Abadi and Z. Manna.
A Timely Resolution.
In *Proc. Symp. on Logic in Computer Science*, pages 176–186, Boston, June 1986.

[Bau89] M. Baudinet.
Temporal Logic Programming is Complete and Expressive.
In *Proceedings of ACM Symposium on Principles of Programming Languages*, Austin, Texas, January 1989.

[Bel77] N. D. Belnap.
A Useful Four-Valued Logic.
In J. M. Dunn and G. Epstein, editors, *Modern Uses of Multiple-Values Logic*, pages 5–37. D. Reidel Publishing Company, 1977.

[CES86] E.M. Clarke, E.A. Emerson, and A.P. Sistla.
Automatic Verification of Finite-State Concurrent Systems Using Temporal Logic specifications.
ACM Transactions on Programming Languages and Systems, 8(2):244–263, January 1986.

[Fis88] M. D. Fisher.
Implementing a Prototype METATEM Interpreter.
Temple Group Report, Department of Computer Science, University of Manchester, November 1988.

[Gab87] D. Gabbay.
Modal and Temporal Logic Programming.
In A. Galton, editor, *Temporal Logics and their Applications.* Academic Press, London, December 1987.

[Gab89] D. Gabbay.
Declarative Past and Imperative Future: Executable Temporal Logic for Interactive Systems.
In B. Banieqbal, H. Barringer, and A. Pnueli, editors, *Proceedings of Colloquium on Temporal Logic in Specification, Altrincham, 1987*, pages 402–450. Springer-Verlag, 1989.
LNCS Volume 398.

[Gou84] G. D. Gough.
Decision procedures for Temporal Logic.
Master's thesis, Department of Computer Science, University of Manchester, October 1984.

[Hal87] R. Hale.
Temporal Logic Programming.

In A. Galton, editor, *Temporal Logics and their Applications*, chapter 3, pages 91–119. Academic Press, London, December 1987.

[HNNT86] T. Hattori, R. Nakajima, N. Niide, and K. Takenaka. RACCO: A Modal-Logic Programming Language for Writing Models of Real-time Process-Control Systems. Technical report, Research Institute for Mathematical Sciences, Kyoto University, November 1986.

[LP85] O. Lichtenstein and A. Pnueli. Checking that Finite State Concurrent Programs Satisfy their Linear Specification. In *Proceedings of the Twelfth ACM Symposium on the Principles of Programming Languages*, pages 97–107, New Orleans, Louisiana, January 1985.

[MM84] B. Moszkowski and Z. Manna. Reasoning in Interval Temporal Logic. In *AMC/NSF/ONR Workshop on Logics of Programs*, pages 371–383, Berlin, 1984. Volume 164, LNCS, Springer-Verlag.

[Mos83] B. Moszkowski. *Resoning about Digital Circuits.* PhD thesis, Department of Computer Science, Stanford University, July 1983.

[Mos86] B. Moszkowski. *Executing Temporal Logic Programs.* Cambridge University Press, Cambridge, England, 1986.

[MW84] Z. Manna and P. Wolper. Synthesis of Communicating Processes from Temporal Logic Specifications. *ACM Transactions on Programming Languages and Systems*, 6(1):68–93, January 1984.

[PR89a] A. Pnueli and R. Rosner. On the Synthesis of a Reactive Module. In *Proceedings of the 16th ACM Symposium on the Principles of Programming Languages*, pages 179–190, 1989.

[PR89b] A. Pnueli and R. Rosner. On the Synthesis of an Asynchronous Reactive Module. In *Proceedings of the 16th International Colloquium on Automata, Languages and Programs*, 1989.

[Sak86] T. Sakuragawa. Temporal Prolog. Technical report, Research Institute for Mathematical Sciences, Kyoto University, 1986. to appear in *Computer Software*.

[VW86] M.Y. Vardi and P. Wolper. Automata-Theoretic Techniques for Modal Logics of Programs. *Journal of Computer and System Science*, 32(2):182–21, April 1986.

[Wol85] Pierre Wolper. The Tableau Method for Temporal Logic: An overview. *Logique et Analyse*, 110–111:119–136, June-Sept 1985.

[Zhi83] Tang Zhisong. Toward a Unified Logic Basis for Programming Languages. In R. E. A. Mason, editor, *Information Processing 83*, pages 425–429, Amsterdam, 1983. IFIP, Elsevier Science Publishers B.V. (North Holland).

Constraint-oriented specification in a constructive formal description technique†

Ed Brinksma
Tele-Informatics Group
Department of Computer Science, University of Twente
PO Box 217, 9700 AE Enschede, The Netherlands
e-mail: mcvax!utinu1!infed

ABSTRACT. Constraint-oriented specification is a style that can be used in some process algebraic formalisms to 'implement' the power of a logical conjunction. Although this type of conjunction is usually limited to properties of traces, and therefore to the safety aspects of a specification, it turns out to be an extremely useful tool in realistic applications, where it is used to carry out successive steps of logical refinement in specifications. In this paper we explain this specification style and give examples of its use in the specification language LOTOS. We then proceed with a proposal for a sophistication of the forms of parallel composition and abstraction (hiding) that are used to improve the large scale applicability of this style of specification. We give an example of their use, and discuss some other, related uses of the new operators.

Key words: conjunction, constraint-oriented specification, formal specification, LOTOS, multi-way synchronization, parallel composition, process algebra, refinement, specification styles, synchronization by association.

CONTENTS

0 Introduction
1 Logical refinement
2 Parallel composition as conjunction
3 Refining the constraint-oriented style
4 Synchronization by association
5 Conclusion

---

† This work was supported in part by the CEC under ESPRIT project 2304 (LOTOSPHERE) and the Dutch Ministry of Education and Sciences under project P2601-85 "OSI Conformance Testing".

0 Introduction

In this paper we want to take a closer look at a particular aspect of process algebraic languages as formal description techniques, viz. the problem of *logical refinement* of specifications. By this we understand the capacity to add new constraints to existing specifications. It is our goal to show that simple ideas on the definition of parallel composition and synchronization can be of great practical consequence if they are incorporated in a well-designed language and complemented with appropriate specification methods.

In the methodology of specification languages an important role is played by the choice of different specification *styles*; in [Vi] Vissers four different styles of specification are distinguished and analysed, each of them connected to a particular method and objective. Following the terminology in [Vi], it is the *constraint-oriented* specification *style* on which we focus in this paper. It is based on the effects of *multi-way synchronization*, which has been incorporated in the combinators for parallel composition of languages like CIRCAL [M], CSP [Ho2], and, via the latter, LOTOS [BoBr,LOT].

The objective of this paper is twofold: first, we want to explain the basic ideas behind constraint-oriented specification, and explain their practical importance; second, we propose a sophistication of the relevant process algebraic combinators that enables a cleaner exploitation the constraint-oriented style in large scale applications. In fact, as we will point out, the new combinators also allow a constraint-oriented treatment of dynamic interconnection problems, which increases greatly the simplicity and modularity of their solutions. Finally, we draw some conclusions on the merits and limitations of constraint-oriented specification in (constructive) process algebraic specification techniques.

In the paper we will use a notational variant of LOTOS as the linguistic vehicle for our examples. This is natural as the problems that we want to discuss arise from experience with large scale applications that require a specification formalism that can represent complicated data structures and operations on them in addition to the dynamic process behaviour. LOTOS is a specification language standardized by ISO (IS 8807) [LOT] for the formal description of standards related to protocol systems, or, more precisely open distributed systems [OSI]. Its design was strongly influenced by the process algebraic theories of CCS [Mi1] and CSP [Ho2], together with the abstract data type formalism ACT ONE [EM] for the representation of data aspects. The first large scale LOTOS application using of the constraint-oriented style can be found in [To]; since then many LOTOS specifications of OSI standards containing important constraint-oriented fragments have been produced, see [EVD]. The ideas presented in this paper are mostly based on the work on Extended LOTOS, which is reported in [Bri].

1 Logical refinement

A particular point in favour of logical specification formalisms is that they allow a rather uncomplicated treatment of a particular notion of *refinement*. It is a naturally occurring situation, as part of a design process or as a result of maintenance, that an existing specification (theory) T_1 is changed to a new specification T_2. T_2 is a (logical) refinement of T_1 is it is upward compatible with T_1, or in a more logical vein, if

$$\forall \varphi \in T_1 \; T_2 \vdash \varphi \tag{1.1}$$

This notion of refinement coincides with the $\subseteq$-ordering on the deductive closures of T_1 and T_2, i.e. T_2 refines T_1 iff $\{\varphi \mid T_1 \vdash \varphi\} \subseteq \{\varphi \mid T_2 \vdash \varphi\}$. For many practical purposes a useful notion of refinement is already obtained by replacing it by the stronger condition

$$T_1 \subseteq T_2 \tag{1.2}$$

In this case one is only allowed to *add* new requirements to the already existing ones, i.e. allow the logical conjunction of new constraints. This more restricted notion of refinement is of interest in the specification phase itself because it corresponds to a natural way to approach a specification problem: to move from the simple to the more complicated, to expand and combine specifications of parts of a system into specifications of the whole.

Remark 1.1

The above explication of logical refinement is given from the *syntactic* point of view, i.e. in terms of an axiomatic derivation relation $\vdash$. It is also possible, and in some cases preferable (e.g. when an axiomatic characterization is lacking), to formulate it in terms of the *semantic* relation $\models$ expressing logical consequence.

[*End of remark*]

In this paper we discuss the ways in which this refinement strategy can be adapted and used for non-logical specification techniques, viz. process algebras and in particular LOTOS. The comparison of logical and behavioural approaches to specification and verification has been a topic of a quite number of papers and presentations, see e.g. [La,Pn,Si]. Below, we mention two particular points in favour of behavioural formalisms for specification that we found to be of considerable importance in large scale applications (mainly OSI protocol systems).

Due to a high level of abstraction logical specifications usually lack information concerning the architectural structure of the system under specification, so that this is often reflected only by informal elements of a specification, e.g. names of identifiers, grouping of formulae, etc. For large specifications architectural information is a valuable key to their interpretation. Combinators such as sequential, choice, and parallel composition (and more application generated ones such as disruption composition, see [BoBr]), allow a semantically and technically meaningful decomposition of large specifications into the specifications of system parts. This turns out to be of great practical value for controlling the complexity of specifications.

Behavioural formalisms typically have a constructive nature allowing for simulation and prototyping, which are important tools in the design of complex systems. This feature, of course, goes hand in hand with an incapability of expressing important nonconstructive properties directly, such as liveness and fairness aspects. This drawback is often compensated by the advantages when the complexity of the system defies a complete mathematical treatment of its correctness, leaving experimentation by simulation as a valuable, though perhaps less satisfactory means of gaining confidence in what has been specified. Also, specifications usually result from a formalization of informal requirements of a system enduser. In many cases a confrontation with the formal specification itself is inadequate to verify whether the informal intentions have been represented correctly, as endusers generally cannot be assumed to have a sufficient knowledge of the formalism at hand. In such cases prototypes can be valuable alternatives.

Not surprisingly research is conducted to see how logical and constructive methods may be combined to allow smooth transitions between logical and behavioural specifications, thus hopefully combining the advantages of both approaches, see e.g. [GSi,Ho1,Zw]. As we already explained, our goal is more modest: to study specification styles that in a restricted way mimic the effect of logical refinement in process algebraic specification languages. Although clearly limited, this approach has the (shortterm) advantage that the method may be used on the basis of a language definition, which makes it attractive for industrial application (cf. [EVD]).

2 Parallel composition as conjunction

The main LOTOS composition operators for dynamic process behaviour are based on the set of combinators whose SOS-style semantics is contained in table 1 (we have made some simplifications). For the moment we restrict ourselves to the basic case, i.e. without data structures and value passing; thus we are dealing with a simple process algebraic calculus over an unspecified alphabet of actions L. The combinators for parallel composition and hiding (abstraction) have not been included in table 1, but are defined separately elsewhere. Table 2 contains the definitions of some notations.

The definition of a parallel composition as contained in table 3 is a slightly simplified version of the parallel composition of [LOT] (provisions for successful termination have been left out), and can be seen as a generalization of the parallel composition in [Ho2]. Processes are forced to synchronize on actions in the index set $A \subseteq L$, and must interleave with respect to the other actions. It is important to note that that synchronization takes place on the basis of identical actions (cf. the complementary offers in CCS [Mi1]) and that the result of synchronization of an action $a \in A$ is again a. This feature is sometimes referred to as *multi-way synchronization* as it allows the synchronization of an arbitrary finite number of processes on a given $a \in A$. Conversely, this means that each process in such a parallel composition can be used to express a *constraint* on the occurrences of actions $a \in A$. The synchronization in parallel composition of such constraining processes thus results in the combination of their constraints, or, more precisely, their conjunction.

inaction **stop**	no rules
action-prefix $a;B \;\; (a \in L \cup \{\tau\})$	$a;B \;-a\!\to\; B$
selection $\Sigma\{B_i \mid i \in I\}$	$\dfrac{B_i \;-a\!\to\; B_i'}{\Sigma\{B_i \mid i \in I\} \;-a\!\to\; B_i'} \; (i \in I)$
fixpoint $\mathrm{fix}_i \langle X_i \rangle_{i \in I}.\langle B_i \rangle_{i \in I}$	$\dfrac{B_i\{\mathrm{fix}_i \langle X_i \rangle_{i \in I}.\langle B_i \rangle_{i \in I} / X_i \mid i \in I\} \;-a\!\to\; B'}{\mathrm{fix}_i \langle X_i \rangle_{i \in I}.\langle B_i \rangle_{i \in I} \;-a\!\to\; B'} \; (i \in I)$
relabelling $B[S] \;\; (S{:}L \to L)$	$\dfrac{B \;-a\!\to\; B'}{B[S] \;-S(a)\!\to\; B'[S]}$
disruption $B_1[{>}B_2$	$\dfrac{B_1 \;-a\!\to\; B_1'}{B_1[{>}B_2 \;-a\!\to\; B_1'[{>}B_2}$ $\dfrac{B_2 \;-a\!\to\; B_2'}{B_1[{>}B_2 \;-a\!\to\; B_2'}$

table 1: *some LOTOS-like combinators*

Notation	**Meaning**
$B{-}a_1..a_n{\to}C$	$\exists B_i (1 \le i \le n)\; B{=}B_0{-}a_1{\to}B_1{-}a_2{\to}\ldots{-}a_n{\to}B_n{=}C$
$B{=}\varepsilon{\Rightarrow}C$	$B \equiv C$ or $\exists n \ge 1\; B{-}\tau^n{\to}C$
$B{=}a{\Rightarrow}C$	$\exists B_1, B_2\; B{=}\varepsilon{\Rightarrow}B_1{-}a{\to}B_2{=}\varepsilon{\Rightarrow}C$
$B{=}a_1..a_n{\Rightarrow}C$	$\exists B_i (1 \le i \le n)\; B{=}B_0{=}a_1{\Rightarrow}B_1{=}a_2{\Rightarrow}\ldots{=}a_n{\Rightarrow}B_n{=}C$
$B{=}a_1..a_n{\Rightarrow}$	$\exists C\; B{=}a_1..a_n{\Rightarrow}C$
$Tr(B)$	$\{\sigma \in L^* \mid B{=}\sigma{\Rightarrow}\}$
$\sigma \lceil A$	restriction of $\sigma \in L^*$ to $A \subseteq L$
$V \lceil A$	$\{\sigma \lceil A \mid \sigma \in V\}$
$B \;\mathbf{sat}_A\; P$	$\forall \sigma \in Tr(B)\; P(\sigma \lceil A)$ (P a property of traces)

table 2: *some notation*

concurrency

$B_1|_A B_2$ $(A \subseteq L)$

$$\frac{B_1 \text{-}a\rightarrow B_1'}{B_1|_A B_2 \text{-}a\rightarrow B_1'|_A B_2} \quad (a \notin A)$$

$$\frac{B_2 \text{-}a\rightarrow B_2'}{B_1|_A B_2 \text{-}a\rightarrow B_1|_A B_2'} \quad (a \notin A)$$

$$\frac{B_1 \text{-}a\rightarrow B_1' \quad B_2 \text{-}a\rightarrow B_2'}{B_1|_A B_2 \text{-}a\rightarrow B_1'|_A B_2'} \quad (a \in A)$$

abstraction

B/A $(A \subseteq L)$

$$\frac{B \text{-}a\rightarrow B'}{B/A \text{-}a\rightarrow B'/A} \quad (a \notin A)$$

$$\frac{B \text{-}a\rightarrow B'}{B/A \text{-}\tau\rightarrow B'/A} \quad (a \in A)$$

table 3: *LOTOS parallel composition and abstraction*

It is not hard to prove that for the parallel combinator defined in table 3 the following property holds:

Lemma 2.1

For all behaviour expressions B_1, B_2 and all $A \subseteq L$

$$Tr(B_1|_A B_2) \lceil A = Tr(B_1) \lceil A \cap Tr(B_2) \lceil A \quad (2.1)$$

Proof

Using the inference rules for $|_A$ it is not hard to check that:

1) for all $\sigma \in Tr(B_1|_A B_2)$ there exist $\sigma_1 \in Tr(B_1)$ and $\sigma_2 \in Tr(B_2)$ with $\sigma \lceil A = \sigma_1 \lceil A = \sigma_2 \lceil A$ (induction on the length of σ);
2) for all $\sigma_1 \in Tr(B_1)$ and $\sigma_2 \in Tr(B_2)$ with $\sigma_1 \lceil A = \sigma_2 \lceil A$ there exists a $\sigma \in Tr(B_1|_A B_2)$ with $\sigma \lceil A = \sigma_1 \lceil A = \sigma_2 \lceil A$ (induction on the sum of the lengths of σ_1 and σ_2).

■

Corollary 2.2

For all behaviour expressions B_1, B_2, all $A \subseteq L$, and all trace properties P, Q

$$\text{if } B_1 \textbf{ sat}_A\, P \text{ and } B_2 \textbf{ sat}_A\, Q \text{ then } B_1|_A B_2 \textbf{ sat}_A\, P \wedge Q \quad (2.2)$$

Proof

For all $\sigma \in Tr(B_1|_A B_2)$ we have $\sigma \lceil A \in Tr(B_1) \lceil A \cap Tr(B_2) \lceil A$ and thus $P(\sigma \lceil A) \wedge Q(\sigma \lceil A)$.

■

In special cases we can in fact obtain a useful result that is even stronger.

Lemma 2.3

Let $L(.)$ be a *sorting*, i.e. a mapping that assigns to each behaviour expression B a set $L(B) \subseteq L$ such that $Tr(B) \subseteq L(B)^*$ (such sortings can be obtained by a standard inductive definition over the structure of B, see e.g. [Mil]). If $L(B_1) \cap L(B_2) \subseteq A$ then

$$\text{If } B_1 \ \mathbf{sat}_{L(B1)}\ P \text{ and } B_2 \ \mathbf{sat}_{L(B2)}\ Q \text{ then } B_1|_A B_2 \ \mathbf{sat}_{L(B1)}\ P \text{ and } B_1|_A B_2 \ \mathbf{sat}_{L(B2)}\ Q \tag{2.3}$$

Proof

With induction on the length of σ one can easily check that $Tr(B_1|_A B_2) \lceil L(B_i) \subseteq Tr(B_i)$ $(i=1,2)$. It follows that for all $\sigma \in Tr(B_1|_A B_2)$ $\sigma \lceil L(B_i) \in Tr(B_i)$ and thus $P(\sigma \lceil L(B_1))$ and $Q(\sigma \lceil L(B_2))$. (2.3) implies (2.2) in the case that $A = L(B_1) \cap L(B_2)$.

■

Using (2.2) and (2.3) we can refine the trace properties of specifications by applying appropriate forms of the parallel composition operator $|_A$. We illustrate this with the following example in Basic LOTOS [BoBr].

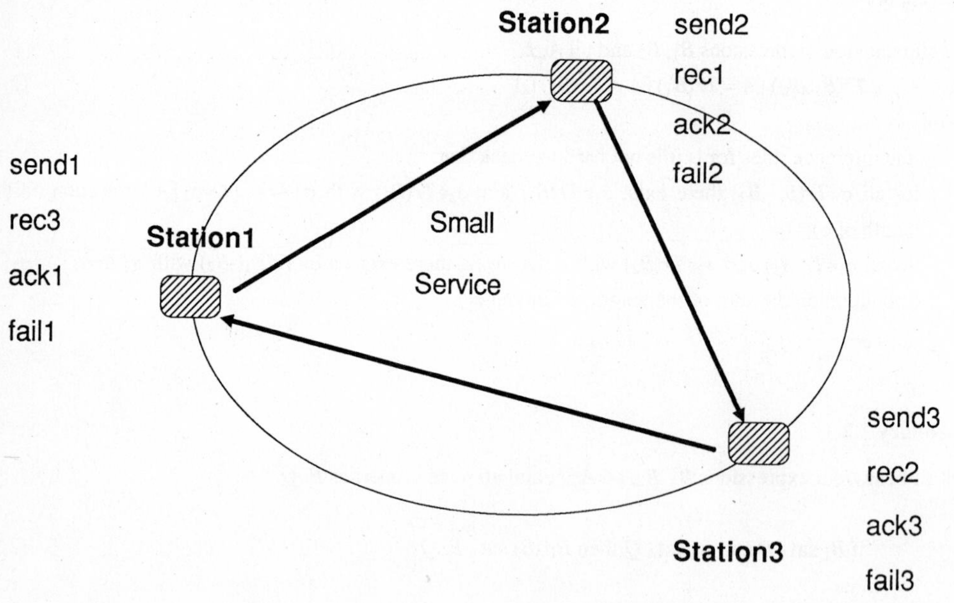

figure 1: *layout of a simple communication service*

Example 2.1

We want to specify the very simple communication service whose layout is depicted in figure 1. The system consists of three local stations that are interconnected in a ring fashion by a medium. The medium can forward messages from one station to the next, one at a time. This message transfer is medium confirmed, i.e. if a message is received by a station the medium provides an acknowledgement to the sending station. The medium may also fail to deliver a message; in this case the medium reports the failure to the sending station. Each station can only do one thing at a time, i.e. it can only receive when it is not busy sending, including the waiting for a confirmation.

Figure 2 contains a specification of the system. The interpretation of the main elements of the concrete syntax is as follows (for details we refer the reader to [BoBr,LOT]):

- the process definitions correspond to applications of the fixpoint operator (in this case to the process variables *Simple_Service*, *Medium*, and *Station*); the processes are parameterized by the action names occurring in their defining behaviour expressions: the meaning of applied instances of such processes is obtained by applying the corresponding relabelling operator (mapping the formal action names to the actual action names); thus the application $P[a,b]$ of the process definition **process** $P[c,d]:=B$ **endproc** is interpreted as (fix $P.B)[a/c,b/d]$;
- ||| and || are the concrete syntactic representations of the $|_{\emptyset}$-operator and the $|_{L}$-operator, with synchronization on no and on all actions, respectively;
- [] is the binary form of Σ, i.e. $B_1[]B_2 =_{df} \Sigma\{B_1,B_2\}$;
- **i** is the LOTOS representation of the internal or silent action τ, see [Mi1].

---

process *Simple_Service*
    [*send1,send2,send3,rec1,rec2,rec3,ack1,ack2,ack3,fail1,fail2,fail3*]
:= (*Medium*[*send1,rec2,ack1,fail1*]
    ||| *Medium*[*send2,rec3,ack2,fail2*]
    ||| *Medium*[*send3,rec1,ack3,fail3*])
    ||
    (*Station*[*send1,rec1,ack1,fail1*]
    ||| *Station*[*send2,rec2,ack2,fail2*]
    ||| *Station*[*send3,rec3,ack3,fail3*])
where
    process *Medium*[*send,rec,ack,fail*]
    := *send*
        ;   (*rec* ; *ack* ; *Medium*[*send,rec,ack,fail*]
            [] **i** ; *fail* ; *Medium*[*send,rec,ack,fail*])
    endproc (* *Medium* *)

```
process Station[send,rec,ack,fail]
:=  (   send
        ;   (   ack ; Station[send,rec,ack,fail]
            []  fail ; Station[send,rec,ack,fail] )
    []  rec ; Station[send,rec,ack,fail])
endproc (* Station *)
endproc (* Simple_Service *)
```

figure 2: *a LOTOS specification of the simple communication service*

[*End of example*]

Although simple, the structure of the specification of example 2.1 is representative of those of larger LOTOS service specifications (see [EVD]). The independent (=interleaving) composition of the three *Station* processes constitute the *local* constraints of the service, that of the *Medium* processes the *end-to-end* constraints. The concurrent composition of these two groups with synchronization on all system actions consequently specifies the behaviour of a system satisfying each of the constraints. For example, let L be the set of all actions occurring in *Simple_Service* and $L_i =_{df} \{send_i, rec_i, ack_i, fail_i\}$, then

$$Station[send_i, rec_i, ack_i, fail_i]\ \mathbf{sat}_{L_i}\ SendOrRec_i(\sigma) \tag{2.4}$$

for i=1,2,3, where $SendOrRec_i(\sigma)$ is defined as $\forall j (0 \leq j < \sigma \rightarrow \neg(\sigma_j = send_i \wedge \sigma_{j+1} = rec_i))$, formally expressing the property that in σ a $send_i$ action is never immediately followed by a rec_i action. Then using (2.3) if follows that

$$Stations\ \mathbf{sat}_{L_i}\ SendOrRec_i(\sigma) \tag{2.5}$$

where *Stations* is the interleaving composition of the local constraints, i.e. the three *Station* processes

```
Stations =df
    (   Station[send1,rec1,ack1,fail1]
    |||  Station[send2,rec2,ack2,fail2]
    |||  Station[send3,rec3,ack3,fail3] )
```

From (2.5) it follows that

$$Stations\ \mathbf{sat}_{L}\ SendOrRec_i(\sigma \lceil L_i) \tag{2.6}$$

and therefore by (2.2) we have

$$Simple\_Service\ \mathbf{sat}_{L}\ SendOrRec_i(\sigma \lceil L_i) \tag{2.7}$$

In other words: the sending procedure at station i is never interrupted by the receipt of a message.

It is interesting to note that the structure of such proofs is quite independent of the formalism that is adopted for the description of trace properties; it is only required that restrictions to subsequences can be expressed. In fact, it is a point of (process algebraic) specification that the behaviour expressions themselves are the statements of properties. If the requirements of the system under specification are of a mostly constructive nature this can lead to quite concise specifications.

On the basis of the above example one can already see how one may further refine the specification, e.g. one could specify that the stations will only send in ascending order of index (modulo 3) by synchronization with the process

process *Circulate*[*send*1,*send*2,*send*3]
:= *send*1 ; *send*2 ; *send*3 ; *Circulate*[*send*1,*send*2,*send*3]
endproc

with the LOTOS parallel composition corresponding to $|_{\{send1,send2,send3\}}$. The logical modularity of the specification also makes it easy to adapt the specification to other changes, e.g. a system with four stations and four media.

The reader should bear in mind that the conjunctivity that is implied by (2.2) and (2.3) only applies to *safety* properties (i.e. 'nothing bad will happen'); it is inadequate to deal with *liveness* properties (i.e. 'something good will happen'). We can see this as follows: by definition B **sat**$_A$ P implies B' **sat**$_A$ P if $Tr(B')\subseteq Tr(B)$, in particular **stop sat**$_A$ P for all satisfiable trace properties P. Thus the liveness aspects of a constraint-oriented specification must be checked by analysing its deadlock properties. This, in fact, corresponds to checking the logical consistency of the constraints that are expressed by the argument processes. An analoguous checking for consistency is required in logical specifications to prevent that specification theories are refined by inconsistent theories (which refines all theories).

In the case of our example it is not very hard to show that the *Simple_Service* is live in the sense that its environment can always execute a next action. Each *Station* has two states, viz. its initial state and a state in which it is waiting for an acknowledgement or a failure. It is easily checked that in its initial state a *Station* can always perform a *send* action on its outgoing medium. Thus the critical case is when all three stations are simultaneously in their waiting states. In this case one of the three *Medium* processes will eventually fail by executing the internal step **i**, and subsequently reporting failure, thus returning one *Station* to its initial state. The internal step **i** can be seen as an abstract representation of an internal mechanism of the *Medium* process, e.g. the expiration of a timer.

Note that it is not possible to write such specifications like in figure 2 with the aid of CCS combinators, because in CCS each synchronization is always combined with an abstraction. In the past this observation led to the inclusion of the $|_A$-type parallel composition in LOTOS in favour of the previously used CCS-style concurrent composition. In LOTOS, apart from the two special, but frequent cases where $A=\varnothing$ and $A=L$ (represented by ||| and ||, respectively), there is also the concrete indexed operator |[A]| that corresponds to $|_A$ in our notation, to deal with those cases in which synchronization is required on a nonempty subset of L.

To end this section we give another small example of constraint-oriented specification, but now in the presence of value-communication between the processes.

Example 2.2

The example we give is that of a bounded bag that consists of a process specifying the bag-like behaviour and another process that specifies that at each point in time the contents of the bag cannot exceed n elements. Note that the latter process is independent in the sense that it could also be combined with e.g. FIFO- or LIFO-type processes to obtain bounded versions of those. This shows the potential for modular specification using constraining processes. The specification is given relative to some external description of data types defining sorts *elem* and *nat* and some operations.

The new LOTOS features that are used here are:

- parameterization of processes by data values: both formal and actual parameters are written in parentheses following the action parameters (between square brackets) of a process;
- substructured actions: actions in LOTOS consist of a *synchronization label* and zero or more value *communication attributes*. Syntactically, this is done using the frequently used ?/! notation for communication. Conceptually, an action is now of the form a_v with a a synchronization label and v a value. For example:

  $a?x{:}s;B(x) \quad =_{df} \quad \Sigma\{a_v;B(v) \mid v \in Domain(s)\}$; and

  $a!v;B(v) \quad =_{df} \quad a_v;B$

  where *Domain*(*s*) denotes the set of objects, the *data carrier*, that is the interpretation of the sort name *s*
- guarded commands:

  $[P] \rightarrow B \quad =_{df} \quad B$ if P holds

  $=_{df}$ **stop** otherwise

```
process Bounded_Bag[input,output](n:nat)
:=   (    Bag[input,output]
     ||   Bound[input,output](n) )
where
     process Bag[input,output]
     :=   input?x:elem
          ;    (    Bag[input,output]
               |||  output!x ; stop )
     endproc (* Bag *)
```

```
process Bound[input,output](n:nat)
:=  (    output?x:elem ; Bound[input,output](n+1)
    []   [n>1] → input?x:elem ; Bound[input,output](n-1) )
endproc (* Bound *)
endproc (* Bounded_Bag *)
```

figure 3: *a LOTOS specification of a bounded bag*

[*End of example*]

3 Refining the constraint-oriented style

So far we have explained the mechanism of constraint-oriented specification on the basis of well-known properties of parallel composition with multi-way synchronization, and gave some indication of its usefulness. In this section we discuss some drawbacks of this specification style in the context of complicated interprocess communication, and present a 'refined' form of parallel composition to overcome these problems. First, we illustrate the the nature of the complications with, again, an example.

Example 3.1

This example deals with some elements of a local interface in an open distributed systems, such as a *s*ervice *a*ccess *p*oint (SAP, see [OSI]). At such interfaces information exchanges take place in the form of *interaction primitives*. These can be seen as the exchange of special data structures at an address local to the given SAP. Such local addresses are usually determined in the first interaction primitive that is executed in a series of related primitive interactions (e.g. all those related to a particular connection), and remains constant throughout the subsequent interactions of the series. In LOTOS this is conveniently modelled by associating two attributes with a synchronization label representing the access point: one for representing the address and one for the data structure related to the primitive.

To help the interpretation of the LOTOS text we give an example of the meaning of multi-attributed actions in LOTOS:

- $a?x{:}s?y{:}t;B(x,y) \;=_{df}\; \Sigma\{a_{v,w};B(v,w) \mid v\in Domain(s), w\in Domain(t)\}$
- $a!v?y{:}t;B(y) \;=_{df}\; \Sigma\{a_{v,w};B(w) \mid w\in Domain(t)\}$

```
process Local_Interface[sap]
:=  Primitives[sap] || Address[sap]
where
    process Primitives[sap]
    :=  sap?ad:Address_type?pr:Primitive_type ; Primitives[sap]
    endproc (* Primitives *)
```

```
process Address[sap]
:=    sap?ad:Address_type?pr:Primitive_type ; Constant_Address[sap](ad)
where
      process Constant_Address[sap](ca:Address_type)
      :=    sap!ca?pr:Primitive_type ; Constant_Address[sap](ca)
      endproc (* Constant_Address *)
endproc (* Address *)
endproc (* Local_Interface *)
```

figure 4: *a LOTOS specification of a local interface*

[*End of example*]

If we analyse example 3.1 we see that the process *Address* constrains the behaviour of *Local_Interface* so that the address that is selected in the first interaction is used in all subsequent interactions. Thus *Address* only affects the values of one attribute of the interaction primitives, viz. the local address. Nevertheless, as synchronization between actions in a parallel composition is on an 'all or nothing' basis, each action of *Address* must also specify the other attribute, concerning the data structure of the primitive, whose values are irrelevant for the purpose of *Address*. Therefore, *Address* specifies a vacuous constraint on the value of the second attribute by always synchronizing on all possible values. This problem is, in fact, also present in example 2.2: the process *Bound* does not need information on the actual values that are being put in or taken out of the bag, but only that *something* is being put in or taken out.

Although this may not be immediately apparent from the small examples given here, the effects of this lack of separation of concerns can be quite desastrous for the specification of large systems with a complicated interaction structure (i.e. many action attributes, e.g. the OSI Transport Protocol [TP,ISO]):

- the duplication of all the attributes of an action to all constraining processes makes the size of a specification increase rapidly with the number of attributes: a rough estimate is that the specification size is proportional to the square of the number of attributes of the main types of interaction, on the basis that both the number of constraining processes is directly proportional to the number of attributes (one for each attribute), and also their size (length increases linearly with the number of attributes);
- the presence of locally irrelevant information in the specification makes it less clear;
- the need to specify locally irrelevant information makes the specification less modular, complicating the independent development of parts of a specification.

The solution that we propose is to add different synchronization labels to each attribute of an action, thus creating the possibility of synchronization with attributes instead of actions. This implies that actions are structures of the form $\{a(1)_{v(1)},\ldots,a(n)_{v(n)}\}$ with $a(1),\ldots,a(n)$ different synchronization labels and $v(1),\ldots,v(n)$ values (we can introduce 'empty' values to allow the occurrence of bare synchronization labels in actions). The empty set $\varnothing$ corresponds nicely with the internal action τ. We use the variable $\mu,\mu_1,\mu_2,\ldots$ to range over the universe of set-structured actions that we denote with *Act*; henceforth we use L to denote the universe of elements of the set-structured actions.

concurrency		
$B_1|_A B_2$ $(A \subseteq L)$	$\dfrac{B_1 -\mu\rightarrow B_1'}{B_1|_A B_2 -\mu\rightarrow B_1'|_A B_2}$	$(\mu \cap A = \varnothing)$
	$\dfrac{B_1 -\mu\rightarrow B_2'}{B_1|_A B_2 -\mu\rightarrow B_1|_A B_2'}$	$(\mu \cap A = \varnothing)$
	$\dfrac{B_1 -\mu_1\rightarrow B_1' \quad B_1 -\mu_2\rightarrow B_2'}{B_1|_A B_2 -\mu_1\cup\mu_2\rightarrow B_1'|_A B_2'}$	$(\mu_1\cap\mu_2 = \mu_1\cap A = \mu_2\cap A)$
abstraction		
B/A $(A \subseteq L)$	$\dfrac{B -\mu\rightarrow B'}{B/A -(\mu\text{-}A)\rightarrow B'/A}$	

Table 4: *refined parallel composition and abstraction*

The new parallel composition defined in table 4 allows, by the first two rules, the argument processes to move independently with respect to actions that are not subject to synchronization. The third rule of parallel composition is quite sophisticated: to processes can only synchronize on two actions μ_1, μ_2 if their intersections with the synchronization set A are identical and $\mu_1 \cap \mu_1 \subseteq A$. The latter condition is necessary to ensure that the resulting action $\mu_1 \cup \mu_1$ does not contain more than one element with the same synchronization label. Such actions do not make sense in our interpretation, where one could say that synchronization labels represent *synchronization obligations* with respect to their associated attributes. Note that the third rule of parallel composition also allows the *coincidence* of independent actions, i.e. if $\mu_1 \cap \mu_1 = \varnothing$. Since we have introduced a notion of coincidence by substructuring actions into sets, it is natural not to exclude the coincidence of independent actions. Moreover, we will need the property to allow an elegant use of the new parallel oprerator, as we will indicate below. An operator very close to ours is defined in CIRCAL [M], although there the motivation to study set structured actions seems to be different, viz. to introduce a notion of coincidence, which from our point of view, as we just indicated, is a derived feature.

To study the counterparts of properties (2.2) and (2.3) in the new setting we must extend the usual definition of restriction of traces. We define for $A \subseteq L$

$$\mu_1\mu_2\ldots\mu_n \lceil A =_{df} (\mu_1 \lceil A)(\mu_2 \lceil A)\ldots(\mu_n \lceil A) \tag{3.1}$$

where we identify $\varnothing$ with the empty string $\varepsilon = \varepsilon \lceil A$. With this definition we obtain

Lemma 3.2

For all behaviour expressions B_1, B_2, and all $A \subseteq L$

$$Tr(B_1 |_A B_2) \lceil A \subseteq Tr(B_1) \lceil A \cap Tr(B_1) \lceil A \tag{3.2}$$

Proof

Analoguous to 2.1 1). The proof of the analogy of 2.1. 2) fails due to the deadlocks that can occur in $B_1 |_A B_2$ with actions μ_1, μ_2 with $\mu_1 \cap \mu_2 \not\subseteq A$, even if $\mu_1 \cap A = \mu_2 \cap A$.

■

In (3.2) equality is obtained if $L(B_1) \cap L(B_2) \subseteq A$, where the notion of sorting is extended such that $L(B)$ contains the *elements* (in L) that occur in the actions of traces in $Tr(B)$.

Lemma 3.3

If $L(B_1) \cap L(B_2) \subseteq A$ then

$$Tr(B_1 |_A B_2) \lceil A = Tr(B_1) \lceil A \cap Tr(B_1) \lceil A \tag{3.3}$$

Proof

The assumption that $L(B_1) \cap L(B_2) \subseteq A$ reduces the condition on the third derivation rule of $|_A$ (in table 4) to $\mu_1 \cap A = \mu_2 \cap A$, thus making the proof is analoguous to that of 2.1 2).

■

In either case we retain property (2.2) in the new interpretation of the symbols; in the case that $L(B_1) \cap L(B_2) \subseteq A$ also (2.3) remains valid (for details see [Bri]).

On the basis of our refined form of actions and parallel compositions, we would now like to structure specifications of interactions involving the attribute synchronization labels $a_1, \ldots, a_n$ according to the following format:

(...(*Main_Structure*$[a_1, \ldots, a_n]$
$|_{\{a_1\}}$ *Constraint*$[a_1]$)
...
$|_{\{a_n\}}$ *Constraint*$[a_n]$)

Here, we parameterize processes on the basis of the synchronization labels: by $|_{\{a\}}$ we mean $|_{\{av \mid v \in D\}}$ for some suitable domain of values D.

The above schema relies heavily on the repeated application of parallel composition with *different* synchronization sets. Such compositions in general do not enjoy the property of associativity, as the following example shows:

$$
\begin{array}{ll}
 & (\{a\};\textbf{stop}\,||\,\{a\};\textbf{stop})\,|||\,\{a\};\textbf{stop} \\
\sim & \{a\};\textbf{stop}\,|||\,\{a\};\textbf{stop} \\
\sim & \{a\};\{a\};\textbf{stop}
\end{array}
$$

whereas

$$
\begin{array}{ll}
 & \{a\};\textbf{stop}\,||\,(\{a\};\textbf{stop})\,|||\,\{a\};\textbf{stop}) \\
\sim & \{a\};\textbf{stop}\,||\,\{a\};\{a\};\textbf{stop} \\
\sim & \{a\};\textbf{stop}
\end{array}
$$

where $\sim$ is strong (bisimulation) equivalence [Mi2].

This lack of associativity could make the writing such specifications cumbersome. Fortunately, we have the following property applies.

Lemma 3.4

Let B_1, B_2 and B_3 be behaviour expressions, and $L(.)$ be a sorting then

$$B_1|_{L(B1)\cap(L(B2)\cup L(B3))}(B_2|_{(L(B2)\cap L(B3))}B_3)\sim(B_1|_{(L(B1)\cap L(B2))}B_2)|_{((L(B1)\cup L(B2))\cap L(B3))}B_3 \tag{3.4}$$

Proof

See [Bri].

■

This result allows us to define an auxiliary operator (like || in CSP, • in CIRCAL)

$$B_1||B_2 =_{df} B_1|_{L(B1)\cap L(B2)}B_2$$

which is associative. This operator, however, is context dependent (it depends on the label sortings of its arguments) and the price for the associativity is a complication in the formulation laws. Consider, for example

$$
\begin{array}{ll}
 & \{a\};\{b\};\textbf{stop}\ ||\ \{a\};\{a\};\textbf{stop} \\
\sim & \{a\};\{b\};\textbf{stop}\ |_{\{a\}}\ \{a\};\{a\};\textbf{stop} \\
\sim & \{a\};(\{b\};\textbf{stop}\ |_{\{a\}}\ \{a\};\textbf{stop}) \\
\sim & \{a\};\{b\};\textbf{stop}
\end{array}
$$

which is *not* strong equivalent with

$$\{a\};(\{b\};\textbf{stop} \parallel \{a\};\textbf{stop}) \qquad \sim \qquad \{a\};(\{b\};\textbf{stop} \mid_{\varnothing} \{a\};\textbf{stop})$$

The usual solutions are either to treat || as a macro-definition that must be rewritten to its defining expression before applying laws to it, or to work with *alphabets* of behaviour expressions that are preserved by subexpressions, as in CSP or CIRCAL, instead of sortings, see [Ho2,M].

Our schema now becomes:

$$
\begin{array}{ll}
 & \mathit{Main\_Structure}[a_1,\ldots,a_n] \\
\parallel & \mathit{Constraint}[a_1]\,) \\
\ldots & \\
\parallel & \mathit{Constraint}[a_n]\,)
\end{array}
$$

Remark

It is interesting to observe that || can only be associative if the coincidence of independent actions is allowed. This can be seen from the example:

$$\{a\};\textbf{stop}\parallel\{b\};\textbf{stop}\parallel\{a,b\};\textbf{stop}$$

Associating to the right we see that this expression is strong equivalent to $\{a,b\}$;**stop**; associating to the left we see that this is only possible if $\{a\}$;**stop**||$\{b\}$;**stop** has $\{a,b\}$ as an initial action.
[*End of remark*]

Example 3.2 (3.1 revisited)

We now apply our solution to the *Local_Interface* example, using, using angular brackets to group labelled attributes into action denotations. Some example interpretations of these concrete syntactic structures are:

- $\langle a?x{:}s, b?y{:}t\rangle;B(x,y) =_{df} \Sigma\{\{a_v,b_w\};B(v,w) \mid v\in Domain(s), w\in Domain(t)\}$
- $\langle a!v, b?y{:}t\rangle;B(y) \quad =_{df} \Sigma\{\{a_v,b_w\};B(w) \mid w\in Domain(t)\}$

---

process *Local_Interface[address,prim]*
:= *Primitives[address,prim]* || *Address[address]*
where
  process *Primitives[address,prim]*
  := *<address?ad:Address_type,prim?pr:Primitive_type>* ; *Primitives[address,prim]*
  endproc (* *Primitives* *)

```
        process Address[address]
        :=      <address?ad:Address_type> ; Constant_Address[address](ad)
        where
                process Constant_Address[address](ca:Address_type)
                :=      <address!ca> ; Constant_Address[address](ca)
                endproc (* Constant_Address *)
        endproc (* Address *)
endproc (* Local_Interface *)
```

figure 5: *modified specification of Local_Interface*

In Extended LOTOS [Bri], instead of writing $a?x{:}s$ for some synchronization label a and for some sort s, a variable x can be declared by simply writing $a?x$. In that language sorts are assigned to synchronization labels, and the sort of a is assigned to x. This reduces the complexity of the representation of action attributes.

[*End of example*]

4 Synchronization by association

Having refined the structure of actions and adapted the definitions of the parallel and hiding combinators accordingly, we now have at our disposal a quite flexible language that can help to improve the structure of specifications not only in the case constraint-oriented specification of interactions with many attributes. It turns out that the modular structure of the specifications many systems can be improved considerably by the simultaneous availability of a set of synchronization labels. In particular problems related to the interconnection of processes can sometimes be solved elegantly by a proper use of a combination of constraining processes and abstraction.

The essential construction that we wish to explain here is that of *synchronization by association*. In the 'single label per action' paradigm synchronization between actions is carried out on the basis of static information, e.g. complementary label names (CCS), identical label names (CSP,LOTOS), communication axioms (ACP, see [BK]). In the 'multiple label per action' situation we can synchronize two independent actions by a third action that 'associates' their labels. For example, in

$$F[a,b] \| G[c,d] \| \{b,c\}\omega$$

the process $\{b,c\}\omega$ (infinite sequence of $\{b,c\}$-actions) synchronizes actions of $F[a,b]$ containing a b label with actions of $G[c,d]$ containing a c label. This means that the synchronization obligations between processes can be made dependent of the behaviour of other processes, i.e. made dynamic. This synchronization can include value communication; for example, replacing $\{b,c\}\omega$ in the above example with

$$\text{fix } X.\Sigma\{\{b_v,c_v\};X \mid v\in Domain(s)\}$$

enables the communication of values v of a given sort s between F and G. Note that, interestingly enough, no information is required regarding the *direction* of the communication. It is only stipulated that the values associated with b and c should be the same in each instance of synchronization.

We give an example of a dynamic interconnection structure of processes in the next example.

Example 4.1

Let $f{:}elem\rightarrow elem$ and $g{:}elem\rightarrow elem$ be two total functions, and *Apply_f* and *Apply_g* two processes applying f and g to their input values, respectively, yielding the results as their output values. The process *Compose_and_Switch* composes *Apply_f* and *Apply_g* to calculate $f\circ g$ or $g\circ f$, switching between the two modes whenever the action <*switch*> is executed.

In this example we use the LOTOS feature of *selection predicates*, i.e. predicates that may be used qualify the allowed values of action attributes. We give an example of the interpretation of this feature:

$$\langle a?x{:}s,b?y{:}t :: P(x,y)\rangle \,;\, B(x,y)$$
$$=_{df}\ \Sigma\{\{a_v,b_w\};B(v,w) \mid v\in Domain(s)\wedge w\in Domain(t)\wedge P(v,w)\}$$

```
process Compose_and_Switch[input,output,switch]
:=    hide in_g,out_g,in_f,out_f
      in    (     Apply_g[in_g,out_g]
            ||    Apply_f[in_f,out_f]
            ||    Assoc_and_Switch[input,output,in_g,out_g,in_f,out_f,switch] )
where
      process Apply_g[in_g,out_g]
      :=    <in_g?x:elem> ; <out_g!g(x)> ; Apply_g[in_g,out_g]
      endproc (* Apply_g *)
      process Apply_f[in_f,out_f]
      :=    <in_f?x:elem> ; <out_f!f(x)> ; Apply_f[in_f,out_f]
      endproc (* Apply_f *)
      process Assoc_and_Switch[input,output,in_g,out_g,in_f,out_f,switch]
      :=    (     (     Assoc[input,in_g]
                  |||   Assoc[out_g,in_f]
                  |||   Assoc[out_f,output] )
            [>    <switch> ; Assoc_and_Switch[input,output,in_f,out_f,in_g,out_g,switch] )
      where
```

```
        process Assoc[inp,outp]
        :=    <inp?x:elem,outp?y:elem :: x=y> ; Assoc[inp,outp]
        endproc (* Assoc *)
    endproc (* Assoc_and_Switch *)
endproc (* Compose_and_Switch *)
```

figure 6: *dynamic process interconnection*

[*End of example*]

The example 4.1 shows some of the flexibility that is available to represent interconnection structures; in [Bri] an application of this feature to CIM-architectures [Bi] is given. In the next example we show how a constraint-oriented approach can be applied to a typical feature of the architecture of open systems.

Example 4.2

Consider an interface where interactions take place that have two attributes: a local address and data. Suppose we have at our disposal specifications of two processes *F* an *G* that can synchronize with the data attribute, constraining its possible values and possibly processing these values. The interface is such that *F* should synchronize with the data attribute if predicate *P* is true for the local address attribute, and *G* should synchronize with it otherwise. This problem is a simplified version of a part of the specification of the OSI Transport Protocol, see [ISO,TP].

First, we give a specification in the case that only one synchronization label is available. The label of the interaction at the interface is denoted by *ip*; *out_F* and *out_G* represent possible other labels of the *F* and *G* processes, respectively.

```
(     ( F'[ip,out_F] ||| NoConstraints_F[ip] )
||    ( G'[ip,out_G] ||| NoConstraints_G[ip] ) )
where
    process F'[ip,out_F]
    :=    (* F with every action at in_F extended with an attribute ?ad:Address_type and
             selection predicate P(ad) *)
    endproc (* F' *)
    process G'[ip,out_G]
    :=    (* G with every action at in_G extended with an attribute ?ad:Address_type and
             selection predicate ¬P(ad) *)
    endproc (* F' *)
    process NoConstraints_F[ip]
    :=    <ip?ad:Address_type?x:data :: ¬P(ad)> ; NoConstraints_F[ip]
    endproc (* NoConstraints_F *)
```

```
process NoConstraints_G[ip]
:=    <ip?ad:Address_type?x:data :: P(ad)> ; NoConstraints_G[ip]
endproc (* NoConstraints_G *)
```

figure 7: *the 'single synchronization label' solution*

We analyse the problems of the above specification as follows:

1) The original specifications of *F* and *G* cannot be used, but must be extended with the new interface attribute concerning the local address. This extension can only be obtained by rewriting the available specifications, and affects the modularity of the specification (if multiple labels are permitted this extension can be obtained by associating with a new label that has both attributes, and hiding the former label).

2) By itself *F'* would constrain the interactions at the interface also in the case that *P*(*ad*) does *not* hold for the local address *ad*, viz. by blocking them. Since such interactions should be constrained only by *G'*, the behaviour of *F'* must be compensated by putting it in parallel with a process *NoConstraints_F* that implements a vacuous constraint in the case that ¬*P*(*ad*) holds; there is a symmetric problem with respect to *G'*. This solution reduces the clarity of the specification by introducing vacuous constraints, at the same time increasing its length and complexity.

Using the full flexibility of the new action structure and combinators we specify the relation between *F*,*G* and the interface as a separate constraint on the composition of *F* and *G*. This solution requires the temporary use of the additional labels *in_F* and *in_G*, thus creating a larger 'virtual' interface, which is reduced to the intended interface by the subsequent application of an abstraction on those labels.

```
hide in_F, in_G
in   (    F[in_F,out_F]
     ||   G[in_G,out_G]
     ||   Virtual_Interface[ip,in_F,in_G] )
where
    process Virtual_Interface[ip,in_F,in_G]
    :=   (    <ip?ad:Address_type?x:data, in_F?y:data :: P(ad)∧x=y>
              ; Virtual_Interface[ip,in_F,in_G]
         []   <ip?ad:Address_type?x:data, in_G?y:data :: ¬P(ad)∧x=y>
              ; Virtual_Interface[ip,in_F,in_G] )
    endproc (* Virtual_Interface *)
```

figure 8: *the 'virtual interface' solution*

[*End of example*]

5 Conclusion

In this paper we have explained the concept of constraint-oriented specification based on the use of combinators for parallel composition that implement multi-way synchronization, and illustrated its applicability with a number of small examples. We have indicated the limitations of this style for specifications that have to deal with complicated communication interfaces between processes. The main problem is an improper separation of concerns with respect to the different attributes of such interfaces.

To overcome this complication we have proposed a generalization of the structure of action and the related combinators for parallel composition and hiding (abstraction), close to those suggested in [M]. We have shown, in further examples, how separation of concerns with respect to interface attributes can be achieved, and moreover, that the new formalism is powerful enough to express complicated, dynamic process interconnections and interdependencies by separate processes that constrain the behaviour of the component processes. A complete language design based on these principles can be found in [Bri].

If we try to put our approach into perspective we can observe that the (enhanced) constraint-oriented style is a useful, albeit restricted way of introducing a notion of logical refinement into a constructive specification formalism. It does not suffice to cure such specification techniques of all their problems, e.g. specification of non-constructive properties like starvation-freedom, but this is to some extent offset by the practical importance of constructivity. In the light of the existing efforts to combine logical and process algebraic techniques our proposals can be seen as suggestions for process algebraic formalisms that can be applied to realistic problems, and at the same time prepare the ground for the use of integrated techniques at a later stage. Such integrations are of great methodological value, even if the willingness to apply mixed formalisms in a practical environment does not seem (yet?) very great.

In the process algebraic context our proposal provides new evidence for the practical use for formalisms with substructured actions, which curiously enough is completely based on considerations of specification style, and not on misgivings about nature of parallel composition in the simpler approaches.

Topics for further research related to our work are:

- the further development of specification styles, and process algebraic formalisms supporting them, that produce good results for given specification problems and objectives;
- the study of the refinement/implementation problem as a transformation between such styles; in this case refinement is not viewed as the addition of information, but its reorganisation, cf. the transformation of the constraint-oriented style to the resource- or state-oriented style in [Vi].

Acknowledgements

The methodological advantages of parallel composition with multi-way synchronization were pointed out to me by Alastair Tocher and Carroll Morgan several years ago. My ideas for the refinement of the constraint-oriented approach have been significantly influenced by many discussions with Juan Quemada, Giuseppe Scollo and Chris Vissers.

References

[BoBr] T.Bolognesi, E.Brinksma, Introduction to the ISO Specification Language LOTOS, Computer Networks and ISDN Systems, vol. 14, nr. 1 (1987) 25-59.

[BiB] F.P.M.Biemans, P.Blonk, On the Formal Specification and Verification of CIM Architectures Using LOTOS, Computers in Industry 7 (1986), 491-504.

[BK] J.A.Bergstra, J.W.Klop, Algebra of Communicating Processes with Abstraction, TCS 37 (1985) 77-121.

[Bri] E.Brinksma, On the design of Extended LOTOS, doctoral dissertation, University of Twente, 1988.

[EVD] P.H.J.van Eijk, C.A.Vissers, M.Diaz (eds.), The Formal Description Technique LOTOS, Results of the ESPRIT/SEDOS project, (North-Holland, Amsterdam).

[EM] H. Ehrig, B. Mahr, Fundamentals of Algebraic Specification I (Springer-Verlag, Berlin) 1985.

[GSi] S.Graf, J.Sifakis, An Expressive Logic for a Process Algebra with Silent Actions, RT Cesar nr. 4, Laboratoire de Génie Informatique de Grenoble, December 1986.

[Ho1] C.A.R. Hoare, Programs are predicates, Phil. Trans. R. Soc. Lond. A 312, 475-489 (1984).

[Ho2] C.A.R. Hoare, Communicating Sequential Processes, (Prentice-Hall International) 1985.

[OSI] ISO, IS7498, Information Processing Systems - Open Systems Interconnection - Basic Reference Model (1984).

[ISO] ISO, IS8073, Information Processing Systems - Open Systems Interconnection - Connection Oriented Transport Protocol Specification (1985).

[La] L. Lamport, What good is temporal logic?, in: R.E.A. Mason (ed.), Information Processing 83, (North-Holland) 1983, 657-668.

[LOT] ISO, DIS 8807, Information Processing Systems, Open Systems Interconnection, LOTOS - A Formal Description Technique Based on the Temporal Ordering of Observational Behaviour (September 1987).

[TP] ISO, ISO/IEC JTC1/SC6 N4871, Formal description of ISO 8073 in LOTOS (working draft).

[M] G.J.Milne, CIRCAL and the Representation of Communication, Concurrency, and Time, ACM TOPLAS, Vol.7, No.2, April 1985, 270-298.

[Mi1] R. Milner, A Calculus of Communicating Systems, LNCS 92, (Springer-Verlag, Berlin) 1980.

[Mi2] R. Milner, Communication and Concurrency, (Prentice-Hall International) 1989.

[Pn] A. Pnueli, Specification and development of reactive systems, in: H.-J. Kugler (ed.), Information Processing 86, (North-Holland) 1986, 845-858.

[Si] J. Sifakis, A Response to Amir Pnueli's Specification and development of reactive systems, in: H.-J. Kugler (ed.), Information Processing 86, (North-Holland) 1986, 1183-1187.

[To] A.J. Tocher, OSI Transport Service: A Constraint-Oriented Specification in LOTOS (Draft 1), ESPRIT/SEDOS/C1/ WP/21/IK, ICL, Kidsgrove, GB, July 1986.

[Vi] C.A. Vissers G. Scollo, M. van Sinderen, Architecture and Specification Style in Formal Descriptions of Distributed Systems, in: S. Aggarwal, K. Sabnani (eds.), Protocol Specification, testing, and verification, VIII, (North-Holland) 1988, 189-204.

[Zw] J. Zwiers, Predicates, Predicate Transformers and Refinement, this volume.

Functional Specification
of
Time Sensitive Communicating Systems

Manfred Broy
Institut für Informatik, Technische Universität München
Postfach 20 24 20, D-8000 München, FRG

Abstract

A formalism for the functional specification of time sensitive communicating systems and their components is outlined. The specification method is modular w.r.t. sequential composition, parallel composition, and communication feedback. Nondeterminism is included by underspecification. The application of the specification method to timed communicating functions is demonstrated. The relationship between nondeterminism and timed systems is investigated. Forms of reasoning are considered. The alternating bit protocol is used as a running example.

1. Introduction

In a functional specification of a component being part of a distributed system, called an *agent* in the following, interaction and communication have to be considered essential. The behavior of system components can be understood by mappings that relate the input received from the environment to output sent to the environment (cf. [Kahn, MacQueen 77], [Broy 85]). Formally this can be modelled by prefix monotonic functions mapping histories of input communications onto histories of output communications.

Prefix monotonicity reflects a basic property of communicating systems: if we have observed a finite sequence of output for a corresponding finite sequence of input, then if we observe additional input (thus the old input sequence is a prefix of the extended one) we may just observe additional output (thus the old output sequence is a prefix of the extended one). Prefix monotonicity provides a notion of causality between input and output. It models the stepwise consumption of input and production of output and guarantees the existence of least fixpoints, which is mandatory for giving meaning to communication feedback loops.

A specification of a system component is understood as a predicate that characterizes the component's behavior. Technically it describes a class of prefix monotonic functions. For every input x and every choice of a function f from this class a system behavior with output f(x) is obtained.

Agents the behaviors of which depend on the timing of the input messages can be modelled by the same concepts by introducing particular time messages. An interesting question that we also want to discuss in the following concerns the relationship between models of communicating systems including explicit time and abstractions from time by the concept of nondeterminism.

Nondeterminism generally brings a number of complications for the semantic treatment. Nevertheless, since nondeterminism is an important methodological concept, it should be incorporated into a specification formalism. The reasons are as follows:

- the abstraction from certain operationally relevant details (such as time, storage etc.) keeps the specification more manageable,
- leaving open certain properties in specifications that are not relevant or should be determined only later in the design process allows to avoid overspecification.

Accordingly also nondeterministic specifications of systems with time dependent behavior are of interest.

Nondeterminism of systems is easily incorporated into functional specifications by underspecification: there may be several functions that meet the predicate specifying an agent and any of them can be chosen for generating system behaviors. However, for particular agents the behavior cannot be modelled simply by a set of prefix monotonic functions. Examples are nonstrict merge or system components that produce output until there is input on one of its input lines. For those agents certain behaviors should only be chosen for input histories with certain properties. In particular there may exist conflicts between real time oriented choice conditions and the requirement of monotonicity. These conflicts can be solved by either introducing an explicit notion of time into the used model or by considering so-called *input choice specifications*. Input choice specifications allow to express liveness properties of agents that depend on certain real time properties of input histories. For such agents the nondeterministic choice of a behavior function may depend on the timing of the specific input. Input choice specifications try to handle even such time dependent agents by nondeterminism without including necessarily time notions into the semantic model.

The presented approach is powerful enough to deal with the specification of properties that are considered especially difficult such as fairness or responsiveness in the absence of input. The particular formal model for specification has been chosen carefully for avoiding anomalies (such as the one described in [Brock, Ackermann 81]).

2. Basic Structures

Given a set M of messages a stream over M is a finite or infinite sequence of elements from M. The set of streams is denoted by M^{ω} where we define

$$M^{\omega} =_{df} M^* \cup M^{\infty}$$

We use the pseudo element $\perp$ to represent the result of diverging computations. We add this element to M and write $M^{\perp}$ for $M \cup \{\perp\}$.

By & the function

$.\&. : M^{\perp} \times M^{\omega} \to M^{\omega}$

is denoted that adds an element from $M^{\perp}$ as first element to a stream, by ^ we denote concatenation. Let ft and rt stand for the functions that when applied to a stream yield its first element or the stream without the first element resp. By ε we represent the empty ("undefined") stream and by ‹a› we denote the one-element stream containing just the element a. This is expressed by the following equations:

$\perp \& s = \varepsilon,$ $\qquad$ $rt.\varepsilon = \varepsilon,$

$ft(x \& s) = x,$ $\qquad$ $x \neq \perp \Rightarrow rt(x \& s) = s,$

$\varepsilon\hat{\ }s = s = s\hat{\ }\varepsilon,$ $\qquad$ $x \neq \perp \Rightarrow (x \& s)\hat{\ }r = x \& (s\hat{\ }r).$

For avoiding brackets we often write function application by f.x instead of f(x).

The set M^{ω} is partially ordered by the prefix ordering ⊑ on sequences (and equipped with ⊑ forms a domain) defined by:

$s \sqsubseteq r \equiv_{df} \exists u \in M^{\omega}: s\hat{\ }u = r.$

The functions ft, rt, & are prefix continuous. The concatenation function ^ is not even prefix monotonic.

A *stream processing function* is a prefix continuous mapping on streams. We denote the function space of (n,m)-ary prefix continuous stream processing functions by:

$[(M^{\omega})^n \to (M^{\omega})^m]$

The prefix ordering ⊑ induces an ordering on tuples of streams and on this function space, too.

For composing stream processing functions we may use the three classical forms of composition namely sequential and parallel composition and feedback. Let g be a (n,m)-ary function and h be a (n',m')-ary stream processing function.

We denote *parallel composition* of g and h by g||h. g||h is a (n+n',m+m')-ary stream processing function. We define for $x \in (M^{\omega})^n$, $z \in (M^{\omega})^{n'}$

$(g\|h).(x,z) = (g.x, h.z)$

Let m = n'; we denote *sequential composition* by g∘h. g∘h is a (n,m')-ary stream processing function. We define for $x \in (M^{\omega})^n$:

$(g\circ h).x = h.g.x$

We define the feedback operator μ^k for a (n+k,m)-ary stream processing function f where m ≥ k. $\mu^k f$ is a (n,m)-ary stream processing function derived from f by k feedback loops. This can be visualized by a diagram:

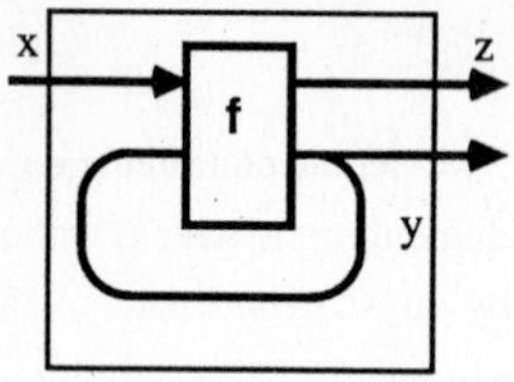

We define for $x \in (M^{\omega})^n$

$$(\mu^k f).x = \mathbf{fix}\ \lambda\ z, y{:}\ f(x, y)$$

where $z \in (M^{\omega})^{m-k}$, $y \in (M^{\omega})^k$. By **fix** we denote the least fixpoint operator. We write μf for $\mu^1 f$.

3. System Specification

An agent with n input lines and m output lines accepts n streams as input and produces m streams as output. It is called *(n,m)-ary agent.* An agent specification describes the behavior of an agent.

For a deterministic agent its behavior is represented by a stream processing function. For a simple nondeterministic agent its behavior is specified by a *class* of stream processing functions. Several instances of an agent may occur in a system. In every instance one function is chosen from that class for determining some output. An agent specification thus can be represented by a predicate

$$Q: [(M^{\omega})^n \rightarrow (M^{\omega})^m] \rightarrow \mathbb{B}$$

where $\mathbb{B} = \{\mathbb{1}, \mathbb{0}\}$ represents the set of truth values.

We give the definitions of the combining forms for system specifications. Let Q and Q' be specifications for (n, m)-ary and (n',m')-ary agents resp. We define:

$$(Q \| Q').f \equiv_{df} \exists\ g, h{:}\ Q.g \wedge Q'.h \wedge f = g \| h,$$

$$(Q \circ Q').f \equiv_{df} \exists\ g, h{:}\ Q.g \wedge Q'.h \wedge f = g \circ h,$$

$$(\mu^k Q).f \equiv_{df} \exists\ g{:}\ Q.g \wedge f = \mu^k g.$$

A decomposition of specifications into safety and liveness properties as suggested in [Lamport 83] and [Schneider 87] may help in the understanding of an agent's behavior. It can be explained as follows:

- *safety properties* correspond to finite observations. A finite observation for an input x consists of some finite output which is an approximation for some possibly infinite totally correct output produced for input x.

- *liveness properties* correspond to additional infinite observations.

Since a specification of an agent should provide enough information about its safety properties to determine the safety properties of systems in which the agent is used we do not specify a simple input/output relation, but a set of prefix continuous (and thus monotonic) functions. This will be demonstrated by an example below. Each of the functions specifies information about system behaviors in the sense of possible courses of computation.

For an agent specification Q and some input $x \in (M^{\omega})^n$ an output $y \in (M^{\omega})^m$ is called *totally correct*, if there exists a stream processing function f such that

$$Q.f \wedge f.x = y$$

Partial correctness corresponds to safety properties. For an input x partial correctness corresponds to observations restricted to finite prefixes of the output streams, but it includes observations of maximal output to approximations (prefixes) of x. For modelling this we introduce the notion of output finite function. We define a function f to be *output finite*, if its output always is a tuple of finite streams, i.e. if

$$f: (M^{\omega})^n \rightarrow (M^*)^m$$

A prefix monotonic function f is called *partially correct* for the specification Q, if for all input elements x and all prefix monotonic output finite functions $h \sqsubseteq f$ we have:

$$\exists\, g: Q.g \wedge h \sqsubseteq_x g$$

where $h \sqsubseteq_x f$ is specified by

$$h \sqsubseteq_x f \quad \equiv_{df} \forall\, z: z \sqsubseteq x \Rightarrow h.z \sqsubseteq f.z$$

Similarly we write $h =_x f$ for $h \sqsubseteq_x f \wedge f \sqsubseteq_x h$. According to this definition if for a function f which is partially correct for Q we have f.x = y where y is infinite, this does not imply that there exists a function g with Q.g and g.x = y. It does only indicate that for all finite prefixes y' of y there exist a function g with Q.g and $y' \sqsubseteq g.x$. By this definition we can be sure that the following property of compositionality holds: if f is partially correct w.r.t. Q, then $\mu^k f$ is partially correct w.r.t $\mu^k Q$.

There are two reasons why we work with sets of functions rather than set-valued functions or relations when modelling nondeterminism in communicating systems:

- we can use the classical functional calculus for proving properties of specifications,
- for determining the meaning of feedback loops least fixpoints have to be considered, which cannot be characterized uniquely in the framework of set-valued functions or relations.

We illustrate the second remark by an example.

Example: *Agent specification with identical input/output relations*

We consider two (1,1)-ary agents. Let the continuous stream processing functions

$$g, h, i, j: [\{1\}^{\omega} \rightarrow \{1\}^{\omega}]$$

be specified (for all $x, y \in \{1\}^{\omega}$) by the following equations

$$g.\varepsilon = h.\varepsilon = 1\&\varepsilon, \qquad i.\varepsilon = j.\varepsilon = \varepsilon,$$

$$y = 1\&\varepsilon \Rightarrow g.y = j.y = 1\&y \wedge h.y = i.y = y,$$

$y = 1\&1\&x \Rightarrow g.y = h.y = i.y = j.y = 1\&1\&\varepsilon$.

We define the specifying predicates Q1 and Q2 by

$Q1.f \equiv (f = g \vee f = i)$,

$Q2.f \equiv (f = h \vee f = j)$.

Obviously for every input the sets of totally correct output of Q1 and Q2 coincide. The behaviors μQ1 and μQ2 for the agent specifications Q1 and Q2 under feedback are given by the least fixpoints z of functions f with Q1.f and Q2.f resp. The least fixpoint of the functions i and j is ε. The least fixpoints of g is 1&1&ε. The least fixpoints of h is 1&ε. So μQ1 is distinct from μQ2. ◊

For explaining the adequacy of the given approach let us for a moment refer to operational considerations: for an agent specification Q given some input x every finite prefix y of f.x for some function f with Q.f represents some approximation for the totally correct output f.x. y can be seen as the output produced for the input x after a certain finite amount of computation time. It corresponds to a "finite observation". If we "wait long enough" then the output should be increased eventually as long as "more" output is guaranteed by all functions f with Q.f and $y \sqsubseteq f.x$.

4. The Alternating Bit Protocol

For illustrating the proposed specification techniques we use the alternating bit protocol. The alternating bit protocol can be graphically represented by the following diagram:

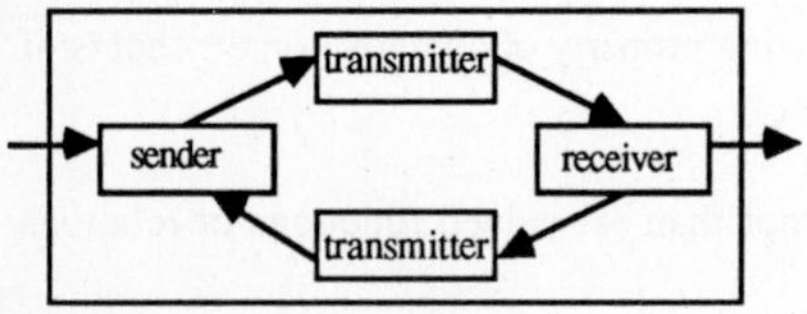

From this diagram the number of input lines and output lines for the involved agents are obvious. The diagram represents the following composed specification

$AB = \mu(CS \circ CT \circ CR \circ (ID \parallel CT)) \circ CP$

where CP specifies the projection function

$CP.f \equiv \forall\ x, y: f(x, y) = x$

and ID specifies the identity function

$ID.f \equiv \forall\ x: f.x = x$

The function that is to be realized by the alternating bit protocol is simply the identity.

We may specify the agent receiver by specification CR:

$CR.f \equiv \forall\ x: f.x = h(x, 1)$

where $\forall\ x, b, a: h(\varepsilon, b) = (\varepsilon, \varepsilon) \wedge$

$$h(\langle a,b\rangle \& x, b) = (a \& r, b \& y) \quad \textbf{where } (r, y) = h(x, \neg b) \land$$
$$h(\langle a,\neg b\rangle \& x, b) = (r, \neg b \& y) \quad \textbf{where } (r, y) = h(x, b)$$

Note that the receiver and hence also the function h in the specification above yield pairs of result streams (r, y) where r is the output of the system and y is the stream of alternating bits that is produced as feedback to the sender.

For a specification technique it is essential that we can specify also the behavior of highly (unbounded) nondeterministic components for representing the behavior of physical devices. As an illustration for such components we specify the transmitter. We give a specification by the predicate CT:

$$CT.f \equiv \forall x: \exists s \in \mathbb{B}^{\omega}: f.x = h(x, s) \land \#(1©s) = \infty$$
$$\textbf{where } \forall x, b: h(x, 1\&s) = ft.x \;\&\; h(rt.x, s) \land h(x, 0\&s) = h(rt.x, s)$$

Here #s denotes the number of elements in stream s and a©s denotes the substream of s containing only the element a. Similarly we write M©s for denoting the substream of s built by the elements of set M.
A further example for a specification is the sender. The sender should send its current message again and again as long as there is no (correct) feedback from the receiver. However, there is a clear conflict between the prefix monotonicity and the intended behavior: if there is no feedback the message should be repeated infinitely often, if there is correct feedback the message should be sent no longer (i.e. only finitely often after all). We may try to give a specification CS for the sender as follows:

$$CS.f \equiv (Q.1).f \quad \textbf{where} \quad \forall f, b: (Q.b).f \equiv \forall x, y, a, m:$$
$$(\#(b©y) = 0 \Rightarrow f(a\&x, y) = \langle a,b\rangle^{\infty}) \land$$
$$\exists n, g: (Q.\neg b).g \land n < \infty \land f(a\&x, (\neg b)^{m}\hat{}\langle b\rangle\hat{}y) = \langle a,b\rangle^{n+m+1}\hat{}g(x, y)$$

By d^n we denote the stream consisting of n elements of d. From CS.f we may conclude

$$f(a\&a'\&x, \varepsilon) = \langle a, 1\rangle^{\infty},$$

$$\#(\langle a',0\rangle©f(a\&a'\&x, 1\&y)) \geq 1.$$

Therefore there does not exist a prefix monotonic function that fulfils the predicate CS. So we have either to introduce explicit time considerations (see below) or to consider the specification either as contradictory w.r.t. monotonicity or we have to give up the requirement of monotonicity which makes it difficult to ensure the existence of least fixpoints. Least fixpoints, however, are badly needed to give meaning to feedback loops such as the one occurring in the alternating bit protocol.

For solving this tradeoff we switch to real time models and later to so-called input choice specifications of the form introduced in the following sections.

5. Agents with Time Dependent Behavior

For many applications of communicating systems the timing of the input history is essential: the behavior of a communicating agent may critically depend on information about the relative or absolute timing of received messages. Such a situation can be formally modelled by introducing a notion of time explicitly into a semantic model. We work with a fairly simple model of time by using a special element $\surd$ called "tick" or "timeout" for representing the situation that no message has arrived at some input line (or no message has been produced at some output line) within a certain time interval. The fact that no actual message has arrived within such an interval of time can be seen as the specific information represented by $\surd$.

A *timed stream* is an element from the set

$$(M \cup \{\surd\})^{\omega}$$

It represents the communication over a channel with additional time information about the time that it takes between the transmission of two messages on some input or output line. A *timed (n, m)-ary stream processing function* f is of the following functionality :

$$f: ((M \cup \{\surd\})^{\omega})^n \to ((M \cup \{\surd\})^{\omega})^m$$

In principle timed streams and timed stream processing function can be specified by the same techniques as introduced and used for streams without time information above.

Example: *Specification of a time sensitive function*

A time sensitive stream processing function f that produces some input message as output only if the input is repeated within a certain amount of time can be specified by the following equations (let $x \in (M \cup \{\surd\})^{\omega}$, $a, b \in M$, $a \neq b$):

$$f.\varepsilon = \varepsilon,$$

$$f(\surd \mathbin{\&} x) = \surd \mathbin{\&} f.x,$$

$$f(a \mathbin{\&} a \mathbin{\&} x) = \surd \mathbin{\&} a \mathbin{\&} f.x,$$

$$f(a \mathbin{\&} \surd \mathbin{\&} a \mathbin{\&} x) = \surd \mathbin{\&} \surd \mathbin{\&} a \mathbin{\&} f.x,$$

$$f(a \mathbin{\&} b \mathbin{\&} x) = \surd \mathbin{\&} \surd \mathbin{\&} f.x,$$

$$f(a \mathbin{\&} \surd \mathbin{\&} b \mathbin{\&} x) = \surd \mathbin{\&} \surd \mathbin{\&} \surd \mathbin{\&} f.x,$$

$$f(a \mathbin{\&} \surd \mathbin{\&} \surd \mathbin{\&} x) = \surd \mathbin{\&} \surd \mathbin{\&} \surd \mathbin{\&} f.x.$$

Note that we have $\#f.x = x$ for all input streams x. ◊

From every timed stream $s \in (M \cup \{\surd\})^{\omega}$ we may derive its time information free stream of actual messages by M©s. Note that an infinite timed stream $s \in (M \cup \{\surd\})^{\omega}$ provides a complete timing information about the communication history on a channel.

A timed partial stream $s \in (M \cup \{\surd\})^{\omega}$ of length n provides incomplete information about the communication history on a channel just representing the behavior on the channels in the first n time intervals. In contrast to this a nontimed partial stream $s \in M^{\omega}$ of length n represents more ambiguous information. It may correspond to the complete information about the communication history on an input channel where after all only a finite number of messages is sent (i.e. it is the abstraction from an infinite timed stream s' by s = M©s') or it may just represent the behavior on the channels in the first n+k time intervals (i.e. it is the abstraction from a finite timed stream s' of length n+k by s = M©s'). The identification of these two essentially different situations into one when abstracting away time information is the reason for the problems with monotonicity (and continuity) in the sender example above. The sender should behave differently on a finite timed stream (which of course contains only a finite number of messages) of acknowledgement feedbacks without the expected bit (where it should send only a "sufficient" number of messages) in contrast to its behavior on an infinite timed stream without the expected bit (where it should send an infinite number of messages).

If an infinite timed stream s contains only a finite number of proper messages, i.e. if

$$\#(M©s) < \infty,$$

then after a finite prefix the stream s consists of an infinite stream of $\surd$. However, there is a remarkable difference between s and M©s (and also between s and every finite stream $s' \in (M \cup \{\surd\})^{\omega}$ with M©s' = M©s). The stream s is a total element w.r.t. prefix ordering, while M©s (and similarly s') is a partial element.

Note that there does not exist a prefix continuous function end_of_transmission with

$$\text{end\_of\_transmission.s} = \text{true} \qquad \text{if } s = \surd^{\infty}$$

However, we may define functions that for instance repeat a message as often as there is no new actual message. Such a repeater f_m starting with message m can be defined on timed streams as follows (for $x \in M$):

$$f_m(\surd \mathbin{\&} s) = m \mathbin{\&} f_m(s),$$

$$f_m(x \mathbin{\&} s) = x \mathbin{\&} f_x(s).$$

Of course there is no way to define a monotonic function g_m in analogy to the repeater on the level of nontimed streams such that

$$f_m(s) = g_m(M©s).$$

This simple observation throws some light on the difference between modelling systems with timed or with nontimed streams. In an infinite stream s including ticks with $\#(M©s) < \infty$ (i.e. s is the representation of the partial stream M©s with full time information) we cannot test (by monotonic predicates) whether the stream M©s is empty, but we can test again and again whether a stream is not continued by actual messages and according to this react to this situation by producing more and more output. We get this way a weak test for the availability of further input on timed streams which does not exist (by a monotonic predicate) for the nontimed partial stream M©s.

The behavior of a timed agent with n input lines and m output lines can be specified by a predicate over the space of timed stream processing functions. A nontimed agent may be obtained as an abstraction from a timed agent. If the timing information for the input streams does not influence the actual messages in the output streams but only their timing, then an agent is called *time insensitive*. A more formal definition of time insensitivity is given later.

The use of time notions in specifications may make specifications more difficult, since we have to deal with all kinds of time considerations, but it may also make the specification of certain agents more simple, since using the explicit notion of time may allow to express certain liveness aspects more directly.

Example: *Timed specifications for the alternating bit example*

Assuming time information in the input streams the sender specification of the alternating bit example above for instance is rather simple. We give such a specification by the predicate TCS for the sender:

TCS.f ≡ (Q.1).f **where**

$\forall$ f, b: (Q.b).f ≡ $\forall$ x, y, a: f(a & x, ε) = ‹a,b› & ε ∧

f(a & x, √ & y) = ‹a,b› & f(a & x, y) ∧

f(a & x, ¬b & y) = ‹a,b› & f(a & x, y) ∧

f(a & x, b & y) = ‹a,b› & g(x, y) **where** (Q.¬b).g

In contrast to the time free specification above there do not arise problems with monotonicity here. Of course, we may also give more nondeterministic versions of the sender (repeating a message an arbitrary number of times on nonpositive feedback).

For being able to use such a specification for the alternating bit protocol we need to have of course also time depending specifications for the transmitter and the receiver. We may specify the agent receiver by the timed agent specification TCR:

TCR.f ≡ $\forall$ x: f.x = h(x, 1)

where $\forall$ x, b, a: h(ε, b) = (ε, ε),

h(√ & x, b) = (√ & r, √ & y) **where** (r, y) = h(x, b),

h(‹a,b› & x, b) = (a&r, b&y) **where** (r, y) = h(x, ¬b),

h(‹a,¬b› & x, b) = (r, ¬b&y) **where** (r, y) = h(x, b).

We give a timed specification for the transmitter by the predicate TCT:

TCT.f ≡ $\forall$ x: ∃ s ∈ $\mathbb{B}^{\omega}$: f.x = h(x, s) ∧ #(1©s) = ∞

where $\forall$ x, b: h(x, 1&s) = ft.x & h(rt.x, s) ∧ h(x, 0&s) = √ & h(rt.x, s)

The specifications of the timed agents given here are rather simple and straightforward. ◊

In the next section we study the abstraction from time for agents with time dependent behavior.

6. Properties of Agents with Time Dependent Behavior: Abstracting from Time

In principle the message √ can be used like any other message. However, looking at timed systems we may assume additional properties that are characteristic for timing. We may assume that for every agent it takes some time until arriving input messages lead to certain output messages. This can be modelled by time ticks in the output streams.

According to this assumption for every output stream its first k elements are determined by the first k element of the input streams. A timed stream processing function is called *pulse driven,* if we have (for all i, $1 \leq i \leq m$, $x \in ((M \cup \{\surd\})^{\omega})^n)$:

$$\#(f.x).i \geq \min \{\#x.j\colon 1 \leq j \leq n\}$$

This formula expresses that for each output channel at least the first k output elements are determined by the first k input elements. The function f is called *fully pulse driven* with delay k if (for all i, $1 \leq i \leq m$)

$$\#(f.x).i = \min \{\#x.j\colon 1 \leq j \leq n\}+k$$

We may even ask for the time that it takes until messages received at input lines show effects at output lines. The most remarkable observations, however, can be stated as follows

(a) (Fully) pulse driven agents produce infinite output streams on infinite input streams.

(b) The streams that are components of least fixpoints of fully pulse driven functions with delay $k > 0$ are infinite.

(c) Parallel and sequential composition of (fully) pulse driven agents as well as feedback leads to (fully) pulse driven agents.

Observation (b) allows to conclude that fixpoints of fully pulse driven functions with delay $k > 0$ are unique. Observation (a) shows that for (fully) pulse driven functions every input history with a complete timing is mapped onto an output history with a complete timing.

Studying communicating systems by abstracting away time information is an important issue. Therefore it is useful to classify those timed functions and timed agents that do not use timing information in an essential way.

In general the behavior of communicating systems may depend on timing. The order in which messages are received on different input lines may influence the behavior of systems. Nevertheless for some agents this timing is not relevant for the produced actual messages or it influences the produced actual messages not in an essential way: this can be modelled by nondeterminism. Some other situations cannot be mapped so simply onto nondeterminism. The resp. agents are called *time critical.*

A timed stream processing function f is called *time insensitive*, if the time information does not influence the produced message streams at all, i.e. if

$$M©x = M©x' \Rightarrow M©f.x = M©f.x'$$

Here we write for $x \in (S^{\omega})^n$ simply $M©x$ instead of $(M©x_1, ..., M©x_n)$.

A time insensitive timed stream processing function f determines uniquely a nontimed stream processing function g by

$$g(M©x) = M©f.x$$

Moreover g is prefix monotonic and continuous, if f is so. This is immediately seen by the fact that $M^{\omega} \subseteq (M \cup \{\surd\})^{\omega}$, and, since $M©x = x$ for $x, y \in M^{\omega}$ with $x \sqsubseteq y$ we have:

$$g.x = M©f.x \sqsubseteq M©f.y = g.y$$

Here we used the fact that λ x: M©x is prefix monotonic.

For a time insensitive function abstracting away time does not introduce any nondeterminism. We obtain a uniquely determined function on nontimed pure message streams.

Functions specified by the predicate TCR characterize timed functions that are time insensitive and their time abstractions coincide with the functions specified by CR given for nontimed functions above.

Given a (n, m)-ary timed agent specification Q the relation

$$W: (M^{\omega})^n \times (M^{\omega})^m \rightarrow \mathbb{B}$$

defined by

$$W(x, y) \equiv \exists\, x' \in ((M \cup \{\surd\})^{\omega})^n, f: Q.f \wedge x = M©x' \wedge y = M©f.x',$$

is called *time free input/output relation.*

For keeping specifications abstract we would like to be able to abstract away time aspects in specifications. This is certainly not reasonable for arbitrary timed agents or stream processing functions. However, for certain agents it is possible.

Of course we require some properties for the abstraction mapping. These requirements are classical:

(a) the abstraction allows to deduce the time free input/output relation,

(b) the abstraction is *modular* w.r.t. parallel and sequential composition as well as w.r.t. feedback.

The requirement (b) essentially means that the abstraction function is to be a homomorphism w.r.t. the compositional forms. We define a time abstraction function Φ for timed stream processing functions f by

$$(\Phi.f).x =_{df} M©f.x$$

provided f fulfils the requirements for time insensitive functions. From Φ.f we may deduce the time free input/output relation. Φ is modular, i.e. we have

$$\Phi(h \parallel g) = \Phi.h \parallel \Phi.g,$$

$$\Phi(h \circ g) = \Phi.h \circ \Phi.g,$$

$$\Phi(\mu^k f) = \mu^k\, \Phi.f.$$

as long as f, h, g are time insensitive. The proof is straightforward.

If a stream processing function is not time insensitive, then abstracting away time can be seen as introducing forms of nondeterminism.

Given a timed function f, a nontimed function g is called a *time abstraction for f,* if

$$\forall\, x \in M^{\omega}: \exists\, y \in (M \cup \{\surd\})^{\omega}: x = M©y \wedge \forall\, z: z \sqsubseteq y \Rightarrow g(M©z) = M©f.z.$$

A timed function f is called *weakly time insensitive*, if for every input $y \in (M \cup \{\surd\})^{\omega}$ there exists a prefix continuous time abstraction g for f such that:

$$g(M©y) = M©f.y$$

Then abstracting from time we may represent the behavior (apart from timing aspects) of a weakly time insensitive function by its set of time abstractions. For a time insensitive function all its time abstractions coincide.

Example: *Weakly time insensitive functions*

Let us consider a function that reproduces its input messages provided there is "sufficient time" between two messages:

$$f: (M \cup \{\surd\})^{\omega} \rightarrow (M \cup \{\surd\})^{\omega}$$

is specified by (let $x \in M$, i.e. $x \neq \surd$, $y \in M \cup \{\surd\}$):

$$f.\varepsilon = \varepsilon,$$

$$f.y \ \& \ \varepsilon = \langle\surd\rangle,$$

$$f(x \ \& \ y \ \& \ s) = \surd \ \& \ x \ \& \ f.s.$$

f is not time insensitive, since

$$M©f(x \ \& \ \surd \ \& \ x \ \& \ \surd \ \& \ \varepsilon) = x \ \& \ x \ \& \ \varepsilon \neq x \ \& \ \varepsilon = M©f(x \ \& \ x \ \& \ \varepsilon)$$

Nevertheless f is weakly time insensitive. All time abstractions for f are functions that fulfil the transmitter specification. ◊

The transmitter specification TCT defines functions that are weakly time insensitive. The sender specification TCS by the timed agent above is not weakly time insensitive. Since the input of an infinite stream $\surd^{\infty}$ of ticks leads to an infinite output of messages ‹a,b›, there is no monotonic time abstraction for the timed functions specified by TCS.

In a weakly time insensitive function the output may depend on the timing of the input, but only in a very weak ("nondeterministic") form. In particular, the function f must not react to infinite streams of time ticks by an infinite number of actual messages (but with different messages as reaction to proper messages), since this would generally be in conflict to the monotonicity requirement.

A further example for a timed function that is not weakly time insensitive is the repeater f_m. We have

$$f_m(\surd^{\infty}) = m^{\infty}$$

and (for $a \in M$):

$$f_m(\surd^n \hat{} \langle a\rangle \hat{} \surd^{\infty}) = (m^n)\hat{}(a^{\infty})$$

which contradicts the required monotonicity for time abstractions.

Our notion of time insensitivity can be extended to the case of nondeterministic timed agents. A nondeterministic timed agent is represented by a specification T standing for a predicate on timed stream processing functions. A nontimed agent specified by the predicate Q on nontimed stream processing functions is called *time abstraction* for T and we denote Q by Φ.T, if for every nontimed input x for Q every nontimed behavior shown by Q is a reflection of a timed behavior of T:

$$\forall x, g: Q.g \Rightarrow \exists f, y: T.f \wedge x = M©y \wedge \forall z: z \sqsubseteq y \Rightarrow g(M©z) = M©f.z.$$

This generalizes the notion of time insensitivity to timed agents. A timed agent is called *weakly time sensitive,* if for every timed input y to T all behaviors generated are mirrored by Q:

$$\forall y, f: T.f \Rightarrow \exists g: Q.g \wedge \forall z: z \sqsubseteq y \Rightarrow g(M©z) = M©f.z.$$

However, even for not weakly time insensitive agents we may look for a nondeterministic modelling under certain assumptions.

7. Input Choice Specifications

For certain agents such as the sender in the example of the alternating bit protocol the choice of the (function generating its) behavior may depend on the timing of the input. This can be represented at the level of nondeterminism by an input choice specification.

Formally an *input choice specification* of an (n,m)-ary agent is given by a predicate

$$R: [(M^{\omega})^n \rightarrow (M^{\omega})^m] \times (M^{\omega})^n \rightarrow \mathbb{B}$$

The proposition R(f, x) specifies the behavior of an agent. It is supposed to express that f is a partially correct stream processing function w.r.t. the specified agent i.e. f specifies certain safety properties. Moreover for the input x the output f.x is even totally correct output, i.e. correct w.r.t. liveness conditions. In other words R(f, x) is supposed to stand for the following two logical statements

- f is a function that is safe (fulfils the safety requirements),
- the output f.x is live (fulfils the liveness requirements) for input and the behavior specified by f.

For a programming language to write programs satisfying such specifications cf. [Broy 86] and [Broy 87a]. For a logical calculus for relating the programs written in this language to input choice specifications see [Broy 87b].

Seen as a time abstraction of an agent T specifying a set of timed functions g we may understand R(f, x) as the logical statement "f is partially correct w.r.t. some function g with T.g and f.x is totally correct", i.e.

$$\forall y \in ((M \cup \{\surd\})^{\omega})^n: \exists g: T.g \wedge (\forall z: z \sqsubseteq y \Rightarrow f(M©z) \sqsubseteq M©g.z) \wedge$$

$$(\#y = \infty \wedge M©y = x \Rightarrow f.x = M©g.y)$$

This way input choice specifications provide a concept for a very particular abstraction from time.

For composing input choice specifications of system components we may again use the three classical concepts of sequential and parallel composition and feedback. For input choice specifications R and R' we define the compositional forms as follows:

$$(R\|R').(f, (x, z)) \equiv \exists\, g, h: R(g, x) \wedge R'(h, z) \wedge f = g\|h,$$

$$(R \circ R').(f, x) \equiv \exists\, g, h: R(g, x) \wedge R'(h, g.x) \wedge f = g \circ h,$$

$$(\mu^k R).(f, x) \equiv \exists\, y, z, g: R(g, (x,y)) \wedge (z, y) = f.x \wedge f = \mu^k g.$$

We again write μR for $\mu^1 R$.

For an input choice specification R and an input $x \in (M^\omega)^n$ an output $y \in (M^\omega)^m$ is called *totally correct*, if there exists a stream processing function f such that

$$R(f, x) \wedge f.x = y$$

A function f is called *partially correct* for the specification R, if for all input elements x and all prefix monotonic output finite functions $h \sqsubseteq f$ we have:

$$\exists\, g: R(g, x) \wedge h \sqsubseteq_x g$$

We call two specifications R and R' *relationally equivalent*, if for every input x the sets of totally correct output for R and R' coincide. We then write

$$R \sim R'.$$

Unfortunately the equivalence relation ~ is not a congruence.

Example: *The equivalence ~ is not a congruence.*

We consider two (1,1)–ary agents. Let the continuous stream processing functions

$$f, g, h: [\mathbb{B}^\omega \to \mathbb{B}^\omega]$$

be defined (for all $x \in \mathbb{B}^\omega$) by the following equations

$$f.x = 1\&1\&\varepsilon, \qquad g.\varepsilon = 1\&\varepsilon, \qquad h.\varepsilon = \varepsilon,$$

$$g(1\&x) = h(1\&x) = 1\&0\&\varepsilon,$$

$$g(0\&x) = h(0\&x) = 1\&0\&\varepsilon.$$

We define the specifying predicates R1 and R2 by

$$R1(q, x) \equiv (q = f \vee (x \neq \varepsilon \wedge q = g))$$

$$R2(q, x) \equiv (q = f \vee (x \neq \varepsilon \wedge q = h))$$

If we consider feedback $\mu R1$ and $\mu R2$ for the agents R1 and R2 we define its meaning by the least fixpoints z of functions q with R(q, z). The least fixpoints of f and g are $1\&1\&\varepsilon$ and $1\&0\&\varepsilon$ resp. and fulfil R1. The least fixpoint of f also fulfils R2. So R1 exhibits two behaviors under feedback while R2 exhibits only one, since the least fixpoint of h is ε which is ruled out since it does not satisfy the input choice condition. ◊

The example in particular shows that relationally equivalent agents may lead under feedback to agents that are not relationally equivalent.

This trivial example shows further aspects of safety properties. If we give a partial input x (in our example ε) to an agent and we observe some finite output y, which of course has to be an approximation for some totally correct output, then this may indicate that some particular decisions have been taken inside the agent (in the sense of nondeterministic choices). If we observe in our example the output $1\&\varepsilon$ for the input ε, then agent R1 still may be free to choose between f and g, while R2 certainly has already chosen f. Partial output may indicate that certain choices have taken place. This is relevant for determining the behavior of agents within feedback loops. Note that the chosen examples correspond directly to the example provided in [Brock, Ackermann 81].

Instead of using the concept of input choice specifications we may specify the behavior of an agent also by a predicate

$$C: ((M^{\omega})^n \to (M^{\omega})^m) \to \mathbb{B}$$

that defines a class of *possibly nonmonotonic* functions, and relate C to an input choice specification

$$R: [(M^{\omega})^n \to (M^{\omega})^m] \times (M^{\omega})^n \to \mathbb{B}$$

by the following formula

$$R(f, x) \equiv \forall\, h \in [(M^{\omega})^n \to (M^*)^m]: h \sqsubseteq f \Rightarrow \exists\, g: C.g \wedge h \sqsubseteq g \wedge g.x = f.x$$

Such a specification C that implicitly defines an input choice specification is called *extensional.* By an extensional specification we specify a set of not necessarily continuous or monotonic functions. As an example for an extensional specification consider the sender specification CS.

A special case of an extensional specification characterizes a set of continuous functions. Such a specification is called *free choice*. The set may contain exactly one element. Then the specification is called *deterministic*. However, not every input choice agent specification can be derived by the formula above from an extensional specification. An example is found by R1 or R2 above.

The sequential and parallel composition of extensional specifications follows the schemes for free choice specifications as given in section 3. For the feedback operator we need a more sophisticated definition.

We define the feedback operator for extensional specifications by:

$$(\mu^k C).f \equiv \exists\, h: C.h \wedge \forall\, x, y, z: h(x, y) = (z,y) \Rightarrow f.x = (z,y) \wedge$$
$$\exists\, g \in [(M^{\omega})^n \to (M^*)^m]: f.x = (\mu^k g).x \wedge g \sqsubseteq_{(x,y)} h$$

Unfortunately if we compose two agents the behavior of which can be described by extensional specifications we do not necessarily get an agent which can be described by an extensional specification.

8. Safety and Liveness

The concept of input choice specification is closely related to the notion of safety and liveness. An input choice specification

$$R: [(M^{\omega})^n \to (M^{\omega})^m] \times (M^{\omega})^n \to \mathbb{B}$$

may be decomposed into safety and liveness properties.

Partial correctness or safety properties of communicating systems indicate which communications may occur as output. The predicate

$$S: [(M^{\omega})^n \to (M^{\omega})^m] \to \mathbb{B}$$

is called the *safety predicate* for the specification R, if a function f is partially correct w.r.t. R iff S.f.

According to our definition of partial correctness if f is lub of a chain of functions fulfilling S, then S.f. The safety predicate is downward closed and closed w.r.t. lubs of chains of functions.

Note that S specifies more than just a relation between input and output: as examplified in section 3 additional information about the causality between input, output and nondeterministic choice is provided by S, too.

For the specification R the predicate

$$L: [(M^{\omega})^n \to (M^{\omega})^m] \times (M^{\omega})^n \to \mathbb{B}$$

is called the *liveness predicate* for R if

$$L(f, x) \equiv (S.f \Rightarrow R(f, x))$$

The liveness predicate indicates for a partially correct function, if for some input history enough output is provided. Obviously an input choice specification R can be reconstructed from its safety and its liveness predicates.

9. Abstracting from Time (continued)

Even for timed agents that are not weakly time insensitive we may find ways to abstract away the timing information and still represent their behavior sufficiently. For making this more precise we first introduce the notion of finite time transformation.

A *finite time transformation* is a continuous function

$$t: (M \cup \{\surd\})^{\omega} \to (M \cup \{\surd\})^{\omega}$$

that causes only finite timeshifts, i.e. we require

(i) $M©t.x = M©x$,

(ii) $\#(\surd©x) = \infty \Leftrightarrow \#(\surd©t.x) = \infty$.

We write FTT.t if a function t fulfils the requirements (i) and (ii). Finite time transformations allow to formalize the concept of independent timing (or speed). This is often used informally when it is stated that "nothing is assumed about the relative speed of two units running in parallel".

An (n,m)-ary timed agent specification T is called *timing stable,* if for all finite time transformations $t_1, \ldots, t_n$

$$T.f \Rightarrow T((t_1 \parallel \ldots \parallel t_n) \circ f)$$

Otherwise the agent specification is called *time critical.*
Having time information available it is rather simple to specify certain behaviors. For instance using timed agents it is rather simple to specify timed nondeterministic "strict" fair merge:

$$\text{TNFM.f} \equiv_{df} \forall\, x, y{:}\ \exists\, r, t{:}\ \text{FTT.t} \wedge f(x, y) = t.\text{scd}(x, y, r) \wedge \#(\mathbb{1}©r) = \infty \wedge \#(\mathbb{0}©r) = \infty$$

$$\textbf{where } \forall\, x, y, r{:}\quad \text{scd}(x, y, \mathbb{1}\&r) = \text{ft}.x \,\&\, \text{scd}(\text{rt}.x, y, r) \wedge$$
$$\text{scd}(x, y, \mathbb{0}\&r) = \text{ft}.y \,\&\, \text{scd}(x, \text{rt}.y, r)$$

The agent specified by TNFM is timing stable. The timing influences the output in a nondeterministic way, but time shifts do not essentially change the behavior.

However, this agent behaves differently on finite timed streams and infinite timed streams. If the input on both of the input lines is infinite, then all the input on both lines is guaranteed to appear as output. This is not true for finite input. This indicates that the specification TFNM is not weakly time insensitive. Otherwise there would exist a nontimed function g such that(for certain i and j):

$$g(M©(\surd^{i}\hat{\ }\langle 1\rangle\hat{\ }\surd^{\infty}), M©(\surd^{j}\hat{\ }\langle 2\rangle\hat{\ }\surd^{\infty})) = \langle 1\rangle\hat{\ }\langle 2\rangle,$$

and

$$g(\varepsilon, M©(\surd^{j}\hat{\ }\langle 2\rangle\hat{\ }\surd^{\infty})) = \langle 2\rangle.$$

This, however, is in conflict with our monotonicity assumptions for g.

When considering abstractions from time the difference between fully timed agents and their time abstractions becomes crucial, if timed agents behave essentially differently on timed partial i.e. finite streams s and timed total i.e. infinite streams t with M©s = M©t. A special problem arises in particular for completely timed streams s and r (i.e. $\#s = \#r = \infty$) where $M©s \sqsubseteq M©r$. Without assuming $s \sqsubseteq r$ we cannot assume for timed stream processing functions f any particular relationship between f.s and f.r and therefore nothing specific can be said in general about the relationship between M©f.s and M©f.r.

From $M©s \sqsubseteq M©r$ we may only conclude that there exists a finite time transformation t such that for some finite stream v we have

$$v \sqsubseteq t.s \wedge v \sqsubseteq r \wedge M©v = M©s.$$

An abstraction from time can be obtained also for certain not weakly time sensitive agents by input choice specifications as follows. Let T be a specifying predicate for a timed agent with n input lines and m output lines. We define the input choice specification R specifying an abstraction from T without time as follows:

$$R(f, x) \equiv_{df} \exists h, y: T.h \wedge (\forall z: f.M©z \sqsubseteq M©h.z) \wedge (M©y = x \Rightarrow f.x = M©h.y)$$

We denote R by Φ.T. A timed agent specification T is called *nearly time insensitive*, if there exists a nontimed input choice specification R such that every computation in T is reflected by R and vice versa. Formally this is expressed by (let R = Φ.T be defined as above for T):

$$T.f \Rightarrow \forall x: \exists g: R(g, M©x) \wedge g(M©x) = M©f.x \wedge \forall z: z \sqsubseteq x \Rightarrow g(M©z) \sqsubseteq M©f.z$$

The agent specified be TNFM is nearly time insensitive. This also means that the associated input choice specification fulfils the requirements that will be given for input choice specifications below.

Again we have for nearly time insensitive input choice specifications R, Q that they are modular, i.e.

$$\Phi(R \parallel Q) = \Phi.R \parallel \Phi.Q,$$

$$\Phi(R \circ Q) = \Phi.R \circ \Phi.Q,$$

$$\Phi(\mu^k R) = \mu^k \, \Phi.R.$$

Sketch of proof: For parallel composition the proof is straightforward. For sequential composition we have to prove that the assertion that there exist g, h, such that:

$$R.g \wedge Q.h \wedge (\forall z: f.M©z \sqsubseteq M©h.g.z) \wedge (M©y = x \Rightarrow f.x = M©h.g.y)$$

is equivalent to the assertion that there exist g', h', g'', h''such that :

$$f = g''{\circ}h'' \wedge \quad R.g' \wedge (\forall z: g''.M©z \sqsubseteq M©g'.z) \wedge (M©y = x \Rightarrow g''.x = M©g'.y) \wedge$$

$$Q.h' \wedge (\forall z: h''.M©z \sqsubseteq M©h'.z) \wedge (M©y = g.x \Rightarrow h''.x = M©h'.y)$$

We essentially have to prove that we may obtain the functions g'' and h'' in the second formula by Φ.g and Φ.h in the first formula. Since R and Q are nearly time insensitive every behavior with output h.g.x for input x can be reflected by functions g'' and h'' with the properties mentioned in the second formula and vice versa.

For feedback we have to prove that there exist g such that:

$$R.g \wedge (\forall z: f.M©z \sqsubseteq M©\mu^k g.z) \wedge (M©x' = x \Rightarrow f.x = M©\mu^k g.x')$$

is equivalent to the assertion that there exist g', g'', x'', y', z' such that:

$$f = \mu^k g'' \wedge R.g' \wedge (\forall z: g''.M©z \sqsubseteq M©g'.z) \wedge \mu^k g'.x' = (z', y') \wedge$$

$$(M©x' = x \Rightarrow g''(x, M©y') = M©g'(x', y')).$$

We essentially have to prove that we may obtain the function g'' in the second formula by Φ.g in the first formula. Since R is nearly time insensitive every timed behavior g can be reflected by nontimed functions g'' with the properties mentioned in the second formula and vice versa. ◊

Φ therefore provides a time abstraction for nearly time insensitive input choice specifications.

10. Proper Specifications and Least Fixpoints

As in every powerful specification mechanism it is possible to write inconsistent input choice specifications. But apart from consistency there are additional properties we want to assume for an input choice specification. Given an input choice specification

$$R: [(M^{\omega})^n \to (M^{\omega})^m] \times (M^{\omega})^n \to \mathbb{B}$$

we want to analyse in the following some properties that should be required for it.

An input choice specification R is called *consistent*, if

$$\forall x: \exists f: R(f, x)$$

From the viewpoint of a time abstraction consistency just means that for a nearly time insensitive agent T from which R is the time abstraction there is at least a timed stream-processing function f with T.f. So the definition coincides with in classical notion of consistency.

We are especially interested in the question under which conditions an input choice specification (with n = m) has a least fixpoint, i.e. if for an input choice specification R we have:

$$\exists f: R(f, \textbf{fix } f)$$

Operationally one may think about a computation of an agent specified by the input choice specification R as follows: the agent gets step by step input and produces step by step output. The input can be modelled by a chain $\{x.i: i \in \mathbb{N}\}$ of finite elements, the corresponding output is also modelled by a chain $\{y.i: i \in \mathbb{N}\}$ of finite elements. Every time the agent gets additional input, which can be modelled by going from x.i to x.i+1, it may add messages to its output by going from y.i to y.i+1. However, the strategy has to be chosen carefully such that the stepwise produced output is large enough, such that the least upper bound of $\{y.i: i \in \mathbb{N}\}$ is totally correct, but it has to be small enough, such that the output produced so far is still partially correct for any possible additional input.

We write

$$f =|_{(x,y)} g$$

if

$$\forall x', y': x' \sqsubseteq x \wedge y' \sqsubseteq y \Rightarrow (y' \sqsubseteq f.x' \Leftrightarrow y' \sqsubseteq g.x').$$

An input choice specification R is called *weakly continuous,* if there exists a function

$$apx: (M^{\omega})^n \times (M^{\omega})^m \times \mathbb{N} \to (M^{\omega})^m$$

that allows for some input x and some safety correct output y to produce a chain $\{apx(x, y, i): i \in \mathbb{N}\}$ of approximations the least upper bound y' we have $y \sqsubseteq y'$ and for every i we have that if we increase the input x to x' (i.e. $x \sqsubseteq x'$) then apx(x, y, i) is safe output for x'. More formally we require for apx with following properties:

$apx(x, y, i) \sqsubseteq y$,

$R(f, x) \wedge apx(x, f.x, i) \sqsubseteq y \Rightarrow apx(x, f.x, i) = apx(x, y, i)$,

$x \sqsubseteq x' \wedge y \sqsubseteq y' \wedge i \leq i' \Rightarrow apx(x, y, i) \sqsubseteq apx(x', y', i')$,

such that for all chains $\{x.i: i \in \mathbb{N}\} \subseteq (M^{\omega})^n$ and for all continuous functions f:

(1) lub $\{apx(x.i, f.x.i, i): i \in \mathbb{N}\} = f.lub \{x.i: i \in \mathbb{N}\}$.

(2) For all x, z and i we have

$$R(f, x) \wedge x \sqsubseteq z \Rightarrow \exists\, g: R(g, z) \wedge f =|_{(x,\ apx(x,\ f.x,\ i))}\ g$$

(3) For every set $\{f.i: i \in \mathbb{N}\}$ where for all i:

(a) $f.i =|_{(x.i,\ apx(x.i,\ (f.i).x.i,\ i))}\ f.i{+}1$

(b) $R(f.i, x.i)$

there exists a continuous function f' such that for all i:

(a) $f.i =|_{(x.i,\ apx(x.i,\ (f.i).x.i,\ i))}\ f'$

(b) $R(f', \text{lub}\ \{x.i: i \in \mathbb{N}\})$.

Intuitively speaking the function apx gives for every input x and every output f.x produced so far for x and every i an approximation apx(x, f.x, i) such that for every continuation of the input stream x the approximation is safe and can be continued to a live output. With increasing i the approximation converges to a live output for x.

A stream z is called *least fixpoint* of an input choice specification if there exists a function f with z = **fix** f i.e. z is least fixpoint of f and R(f, z).

By the assumptions above we may prove the existence of least fixpoints. An agent specification is called *proper*, if it is consistent and weakly continuous.

Theorem: A proper input choice specification has a least fixpoint.

Proof: We define chains of tuples of streams $\{x.i: i \in \mathbb{N}\}$ and functions $\{f.i: i \in \mathbb{N}\}$ such that

$x.0 = \varepsilon^n$
f.0 is arbitrary such that R(f.0, x.0).

f.0 does exist according to consistency of R. Given x.i, f.i we define

$x.i{+}1 =_{df} apx(x.i, (f.i).x.i, i)$
f.i+1 arbitrary, such that $R(f.i{+}1, x.i{+}1) \wedge f.i =|_{(x.i,\ apx(x,\ (f.i).x.i,\ i))}\ f.i{+}1$

Again such a function f.i+1 always exists since R is weakly continuous. According to weak continuity there exists a continuous function f such that

- $x.i{+}1 = apx(x.i, f.x.i, i)$,

- R(f, lub {x.i: i ∈ ℕ}).

By our assumption we obtain

f. lub{x.i: i ∈ ℕ} =

lub {apx(x.i, f.x.i, i): i ∈ ℕ} =

lub {apx(x.i, (f.i).x.i, i): i ∈ ℕ} =

lub {x.i+1: i ∈ ℕ} ◊

The existence of least fixpoints is essential for proofs that rely on fixpoint arguments. An example is the alternating bit protocol again.

What is also important is the invariance of the properties used in the theorem above.

Theorem: The sequential and parallel composition and feedback applied to proper agents yields proper agents.

Proof: For sequential and parallel composition the proof of the theorem is rather straigth-forward. Therefore we concentrate only on feedback. Let R be a proper specification. According to the theory on the existence of least fixpoints $\mu^k R$ is consistent. Weak continuity follows from the continuity of the fixpoint operator. ◊

The properness of agents replaces the classical monotonicity and continuity requirements for functions.

11. Correctness Proof of the Alternating Bit Protocol

Coming back to the alternating bit protocol for proving the correctness of the transmission, it suffices to prove

AB.f ≡ ∀ x: ∃ g: AB.g ∧ f.x = ft.x & g.rt.x

This specification AB is only fulfilled by the identity function. According to the definition of sequential and parallel composition we obtain for input a&x by the original specification of the alternating bit protocol:

t = fs(a&x, v)	**where** CS.fs
u = f.t	**where** CT.f
(r, y) = fr.u	**where** CR.fr
v = g.y	**where** CT.g

Since the assumption #(1©v) = 0 leads to a contradiction (then we have t = ‹a,1›$^\infty$ by CS, thus u = ‹a,1›$^\infty$ by CT, thus y = 1^∞ by CR, thus v = 1^∞ by CT) we have #©(1,v) > 0. We obtain r = a&r' by CR where

t' = fs'(x, v')	**where** CS.fs'
u' = f'.t'	**where** CT.f'
(r', y') = fr'.u'	**where** CR.fr'
v' = g'.y'	**where** CT.g'

and for some i, k, m, n:

$t = \langle a, 1\rangle^n \& t'$,

$u = \langle a, 1\rangle^m \& u'$,

$y = 1^k \& y'$,

$v = 1^i \& v'$.

Induction gives r' = x.

12. Full Abstractness

The three combining forms of sequential and parallel composition as well as feedback define contexts for agent specifications. We are interested in a relation $\approx$ on input choice agent specifications such that (remember that $\sim$ denotes relational equivalence):

$$R1 \approx R2 \Rightarrow R1 \sim R2$$

and moreover $\approx$ forms a congruence w.r.t. the combining forms

$$R1 \approx R2 \Rightarrow R \| R1 \approx R \| R2 \wedge R1 \| R \approx R2 \| R$$

$$R1 \approx R2 \Rightarrow R \circ R1 \approx R \circ R2 \wedge R1 \circ R' \approx R2 \circ R'$$

$$R1 \approx R2 \Rightarrow \mu^k R1 \approx \mu^k R2$$

A relation $\approx$ with such properties is called *compositional.*

The concept for the specification of distributed system components has been carefully chosen to be compositional. However, our specifications carry too much information, in general. In this section we answer the question under which circumstances two logically distinct input choice specifications are equivalent in all contexts. This leads to the concept of full abstractness. A compositional relation is called *fully abstract,* if there is no weaker compositional relation (cf. [Kok 87], [Jonsson 88]).

For defining a fully abstract relation we introduce the notion of computation. A pair of chains $(\{x.i: i \in \mathbb{N}\}, \{y.i: i \in \mathbb{N}\})$ is called a *computation* for an input choice specification R, if there exists a function f with

$$R(f, \text{lub } \{x.i: i \in \mathbb{N}\}),$$

$$\forall i \in \mathbb{N}: y.i \sqsubseteq f.x.i,$$

$$f.\text{lub } \{x.i: i \in \mathbb{N}\} = \text{lub } \{y.i: i \in \mathbb{N}\}.$$

We define a relation $\approx$ on input choice specifications as follows:

$R \approx R'$ iff the sets of computations of R and R' coincide.

Now we prove that the relation $\approx$ is fully abstract.

Theorem: The relation $\approx$ is fully abstract.

Proof: We start by proving that the relation cannot be weakened without loosing compositionality: R and R' are not relational equivalent for some context, if they have different sets of computations: Assume there is a function

$$f: [(M^{\omega})^n \rightarrow (M^{\omega})^m]$$

and a chain $\{x.i: i \in \mathbb{N}\}$ with $x.0 = (\varepsilon)^n$ and

$$R(f, \text{lub } \{x.i: i \in \mathbb{N}\})$$

and there does not exist a function f' with

$$f.\text{lub } \{x.i: i \in \mathbb{N}\} = f'.\text{lub } \{x.i: i \in \mathbb{N}\}$$

and $f.x.i \sqsubseteq f'.x.i$ for all $i \in \mathbb{N}$ and $R'(f', \text{lub } \{x.i: i \in \mathbb{N}\})$. W.l.o.g. we may assume $n = m$ (add dummy arguments or dummy results) and that either $f(x.i) \neq f(x.i+1)$ for all i or there exists an index j with $f(x.i) \neq f(x.i+1)$ for all $i < j$ and $f(x.i) = f(x.i+1)$ for all $i \geq j$.

We define a specification R" for (m, n)-ary functions g by

$$R''(g, y) = \forall z: g.z = \text{lub } \{x.i: f.x.i \sqsubseteq z\}$$

We consider the least fixpoint y of f∘g where R"(g, f.y). This corresponds to an element of $\mu^n(R \circ R'')$. We show that y is not totally correct w.r.t. $\mu^n(R' \circ R'')$. We define the chain $\{z.i: i \in \mathbb{N}\}$ by

$$z.0 = (\varepsilon)^n$$
$$z.i+1 = g.f.z.i$$

We prove that $\text{lub } \{z.i: i \in \mathbb{N}\} = \text{lub } \{x.i: i \in \mathbb{N}\}$. If there exists an index j with $f(x.i) \neq f(x.i+1)$ for all $i < j$ and $f.x.i = f.x.(i+1)$ for all $i \geq j$, then this is obvious; otherwise for all $k \in \mathbb{N}$: $x.k = z.k+1$:

$$z.k+1 =$$
$$g.f.x.k =$$
$$\text{lub } \{x.i: f.x.i \sqsubseteq f.x.k\} =$$
$$x.k$$

Thus the lubs of $\{z.i: i \in \mathbb{N}\}$ and of $\{x.i: i \in \mathbb{N}\}$ coincide (and $y = \text{lub } \{z.i: i \in \mathbb{N}\}$).

For every function f' with not $f.x.k \sqsubseteq f'.x.k$ for some k we obtain for the chain z'.i defined by

$$z'.0 = (\varepsilon)^n$$
$$z'.i+1 = g.f'.z.i$$

the equation

$$z'.i = z.k \text{ for all } i \geq \min \{j: \neg(f.x.j \sqsubseteq f'.x.j)\}$$

since with $k = \min \{j: \neg(f.x.j \sqsubseteq f'.x.j)\}$ we obtain

$$z'.k+1 =$$
$$g.f'.x.k =$$
$$\text{lub } \{x.i: f.x.i \sqsubseteq f'.x.k\} =$$

z'.k

Thus y cannot be a behavior of $\mu^n(R' \circ R'')$. This concludes the first part of the proof. Next we prove that the relation $\approx$ is a congruence, i.e. it is invariant under our compositional forms. For every continuous operator

$$\tau: [(M^\omega)^n \to (M^\omega)^m] \times (M^\omega)^{n'} \to [(M^\omega)^{n'} \to (M^\omega)^{m'}] \times (M^\omega)^n$$

we have if $R \approx R'$, then $Q \approx Q'$ where

$$Q(f,x) = \exists\ f', x': R(f', x') \wedge (f, x') = \tau(f', x)$$

(and in analogy Q' is defined based on R'). Since parallel and sequential composition and feedback operator correspond to such continuous operators, the condition is invariant under the considered compositional forms. ◊

Based on this theorem we may prove equivalences of the form $R \approx R'$ for given specifications R and R'. Moreover we may derive a fully abstract model. Note that $R \approx R'$ if R and R' are relational equivalent and the set of partially correct functions for R and R' coincide.

13. Timed Agents Revisited

The inclusion of explicit time considerations into the specification of communicating systems leads to a tradeoff. Certain properties are easier and more explicitly expressible, however, the detailed consideration of timing may lead to problems with overspecification. This tradeoff can be partly solved, if we can use techniques that allow us to specify parts of a system with explicit timing and other parts without explicit timing. For doing so, however, we need interfaces between those timed and nontimed parts of system specifications. The interfaces can be again provided by appropriately specified agents. Basically we need agents that filter out time informations as well as agents that (re-)introduce time information. The first is simple. The later is more difficult.

A function

$$t: M^\omega \to (M \cup \{\surd\})^\omega$$

is called *complete timing function,* if

(i) $M©t.x = x$,

(ii) $\#t.x = \infty$.

Of course a timing function t is not prefix monotonic as can be seen by the fact that all images of t are maximal. Consider for instance the following equations

$$t.\varepsilon = \surd^\infty \text{ and } t.\langle a\rangle = \surd^n \mathbin{\hat{}} \langle a\rangle \mathbin{\hat{}} \surd^\infty.$$

Complete timing functions are not monotonic. Nevertheless we may give an input choice specification T for complete timing functions

$$T(f, x) \equiv_{df} (\forall z \in M^{\omega}: M©f.z \sqsubseteq z) \wedge \#f.x = \infty \wedge M©f.x = x.$$

The input choice specification T fulfils all the requirements necessary for guaranteeing the existence of least fixpoints. This shows that by the technique of input choice specification we may combine timed and nontimed models of communicating systems.

We may now specify the sender by:

$$CS = (ID \parallel T) \circ TCS \circ (\lambda x: M©x)$$

where we include complete time information in the stream of acknowledgements and later filter out the time information again.

14. Conclusion

Functional techniques comprising fixpoint theory with concepts like monotonicity and continuity together with logical techniques can be seen as the backbone of formal methods for program construction. When considering communicating systems a straightforward application of such techniques seems difficult. This is due to the very particular abstractions by information hiding (such as hiding time information) and the nondeterminism introduced thereby. Fortunately these difficulties can be mastered by a careful choice of the specification formalism. This way a relatively simple and powerful formal framework for the functional treatment of communicating systems is obtained.

For many applications time aspects are important. According to the principle of abstraction computing scientists are interested in techniques that allow to talk about timing wherever this seems appropriate and to avoid time consideration wherever possible. A rigorous formal foundation for time sensitive communicating systems therefore is of high importance.

Acknowledgement

Discussions with Leslie Lamport have motivated part of this work. I am grateful to Frank Dederichs, Thomas Streicher, and Rainer Weber for helpful remarks on draft versions of this paper.

References

[Brock, Ackermann 81]

J.D. Brock, W.B. Ackermann: Scenarios: A model of nondeterminate computation. In: J. Diaz, I. Ramos (eds): Lecture Notes in Computer Science 107, Springer 1981, 225-259

[Broy 83]

M. Broy: Applicative real time programming. Information Processing 83, IFIP World Congress, Paris 1983, North Holland Publ. Company 1983, 259-264

[Broy 85]

M. Broy: Specification and top down design of distributed systems (invited talk). In: H. Ehrig et al. (eds.): Formal Methods and Software Development. Lecture Notes in Computer Science 186, Springer 1985, 4-28, Revised version in JCSS 34:2/3, 1987, 236-264

[Broy 86]

M. Broy: A theory for nondeterminism, parallelism, communication and concurrency. Habilitation, Fakultät für Mathematik und Informatik der Technischen Universität München, 1982, Revised version in: Theoretical Computer Science 45 (1986) 1-61

[Broy 87a]

M. Broy: Semantics of finite or infinite networks of communicating agents. Distributed Computing 2 (1987), 13-31

[Broy 87b]

M. Broy: Predicative specification for functional programs describing communicating networks. Information Processing Letters 25 (1987) 93-101

[Dybier, Sander 88]

P. Dybier, H. Sander: A functional programming approach to the specification and verification of concurrent systems. Chalmers University of Technology and University of Göteborg, Department of Computer Sciences 1988

[Jonsson 88]

B. Jonsson: A fully abstract trace model for dataflow networks. Swedish Institute of Computer Science. SICS Research Report 88016

[Kahn, MacQueen 77]

G. Kahn and D. MacQueen, Coroutines and networks of processes, Proc. IFIP World Congress 1977, 993-998

[Kok 87]

J.N. Kok: A fully abstract semantics for data flow networks. Proc. PARLE, Lecture Notes in Computer Science 259, Berlin-Heidelberg-New York: Springer 1987, 214-219

[Lamport 83]

L. Lamport: Specifying concurrent program modules. ACM Toplas 5:2, April 1983, 190-222

[Park 80]

D. Park: On the semantics of fair parallelism. In: D. Björner (ed.): Abstract Software Specification. Lecture Notes in Computer Science 86, Berlin-Heidelberg-New York: Springer 1980, 504-526

[Schneider 87]

F.B. Schneider: Decomposing properties into safety and liveness using predicate logic. Cornell University, Department of Computer Science, Technical Report 87-874, October 1987

Modular Verification of Petri Nets

The Temporal Logic Approach

Werner Damm
Gert Döhmen
Volker Gerstner
Bernhard Josko

FB 10, University of Oldenburg
D – 2900 Oldenburg, Fed. Rep. of Germany

Abstract. "How does reactive behaviour decompose? What can be done to encourage stepwise refinement of the behavioural aspects of a system? How can one cope with the intricacy, that the behaviour of a complex reactive system presents??" These questions, posed in [HP85] and informally discussed there in the setting of statecharts, are taken up in this paper using a particular class of Petri-Nets as models for **open reactive systems**. It presents an assumption/commitment style temporal logic [Pn85] for specifying the behaviour of such systems, an automatic proof method for verifying the correctness of an implementation of such a specification in terms of the considered class of Petri-Nets based on modelchecking of MCTL formula (discussed in a companion paper [Jo89]), and presents a proof-method for infering the behaviour of a compound reactive system from the behaviour of its constituents.

Key words: Petri nets, temporal logic, specification, verification, modular system design, computer architecture,

Contents

1 Introduction

2 The definition of AADL nets

3 A temporal logic for the specification of AADL nets

4 A net semantics for the specification logic

5 Verification of AADL nets

1 Introduction

For a theoretical computer scientist it is a disturbing fact, that electical engineers seemingly have "solved" the problem of modular design of reactive systems. Every (correctly designed ...) printed circuit board provides new evidence of their skill to realise a complex global functional specification by a parallel combination of open reactive systems (there called **chips**), asynchronously communicating over ports (there called **pins**) according to a statically determined communication structure (given by the printed circuit board). If EE - people can, why can‘t we?

This paper is about cheating. It is based on extensive case-studies in the design of parallel computing systems, trying to find out exactly what ingredients allowed the engineers to cope with the complexities of such designs. What has evolved and is presented in this paper can indeed be viewed as a natural, indeed canonical extension of the approach taken at the PCB-level to higher levels of the design of distributed system, where **causality** rather than absolut timing is relevant.

To be as widely applicable as possible, we cast the description of this approach in the language of Petri-net based system-design. Indeed, it is natural to view a Petri-Net[1] as a model for an open reactive system. By analogy to the PCB-level, let us postulate in the class of nets to be considered a designation of **ports** which intuitively represent the **"pins"** of our module. Internally, the reception (the sending) of a message through an in(out)port p will correspond to the firing of one transition in a set comm(p) of transitions associated with port p . In this paper we restrict ourselves to **synchronuous** communication of modules over ports. We emphasize that the same approach can be chosen to handle the in fact easier case of asynchronous communication through ports.

Much as only the signal flow through pins is observable in PCB-design, we postulate sending and reception of messages to be **observable events** of such a module, represented by the proposition **at**(p)[2]. As messages flow into the module through inports (which is now an observable event), messages will eventually be produced on outports (possibly in reaction of incoming tokens). The net will maintain some relationship between such observable events; it is exactly this relationship which we take as **observable behaviour** of a module.

The decision to consider synchronuous communication entails, that we have to be able to observe not only the actual transmission of a message, but as well the **willingness** of a module to engage in communication. Informally, a module is willing to communicate over port p (abbreviated **before**(p)) iff the preset of one of the transitions associated with p is marked. A crucial point concerns the willingness of the - at the time of the design of the module - **unknown** communication partner to engage in communication. How much can we say **locally** about the behaviour of the module, without knowing with whom and when a synchronisation will occur? For reasons motivated below, it is sufficient to associate with each port a "new" unique place labeled **enabled**(p). Intuitively, this place is marked iff the environment is willing to engage in synchronuous communication through port p . Clearly this place has an empty preset as long as we consider a module in isolation: no **local** transition will mark this place. We include this place in the preset of any transition belonging to p , thus a transition associated with synchronuous communication over port p may only fire, if **both**

---

[1]for reasons to be motivated below, we restrict ourselves to one-safe nets.

[2]the distinction between sending and reception of messages follows from the fact, that ports are directed.

the environment and the module itself are willing to engage in communication. While considering a module in isolation, we need a nonstandard adaption of the firing rule with respect to the enable-places in order to model the fact, that the environment can at any time withdraw its willingness to engage in a communication[3]: at any time an oracle will tell us, whether a place labeled **enabled**(p) is currently marked or not. Once we know the communication-partner, a suitable operator on nets modelling parallel execution of modules will ensure, that **enabled**(p) corresponds to **before**(p'), where p' is the partner port for this synchronuous communication. Finally, we also consider completion of a communciation action to be observable, by including a predicate **after**(p). Note that observable events will in general only be **partially** ordered.

Having motivated "the right" notion of observability, we are ready to address the issue of the proper **specification** method. A key issue to be learned from the engineers is that of **modularity**: in PCB design, the specification of a compound circuit can be (automatically!) infered from the specification of its components. As an instance of this process, timing verification propagates set-up and pulse-width constraints on incoming pins backwards following the "topology" of the circuit. Note that this exploits the fact, that such constraints on the usage of pins are **explicity visible** in the data-sheets; this suggests to use an **assumption/commitment style logic** [MC 81] , [Pn 85] as specification language. It also exploits the fact, that all constraints (in a "reasonable" design) can either be validated after a finite number of propagation steps or induce constraints on the user of the constructed board, i.e. to the "outside world", an observation which will be picked up later in connection with verification methods.

PCB designers use **timing diagrams** both as a characterization of their basic building blocks as well as for the constructed systems. Such timing diagrams depict **causal dependencies between observable events**. As pointed out above, they can be viewed as an assumption/commitment type specification logic: a memory-board specification will only guarantee proper storage of data at its data-pins, if the "user" promises to keep the data- and address-lines stable until some acknowledge signal indicates, that subsequent changes won't effect the memory-read operation. Whereas absolute timings do play a role in PCB design and are thus present in data-sheets, only causal dependencies of observable events will matter at higher design-levels. We can still borrow the idea of timing diagrams in the specification of causal dependencies between observable events. Fig. 1 below exemplifies the use of timing diagrams in the specification of a module of some communication protocol.

Rows in the timing-diagram are labeled by observable events. The particular module considered in the example has one inport in and two outports remote_out and local_out . The truth of one of the atomic propositions over time is depicted through the attached waveforms, high "voltage" representing

---

[3]think e.g. of input-guards

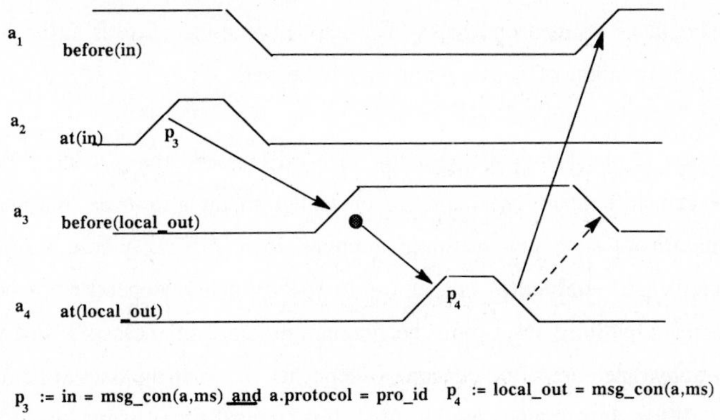

Fig. 1 A sample timing diagram

the fact that the proposition is currently true. Two forms of causal dependencies between observable events are shown in the diagram:

- a **weak arrow** (represented with dashed line) between events e and e' indicates that e' may only occur after e has occured;
- a **strong arrow** between events e and e' implies that e' will eventually occur if e has occured in addition to guaranteeing e ---> e' .

People familiar with timing diagrams will easily be able to understand such specifications. For the purpose of this paper, however, it is more important to observe, that such a timing diagram can indeed be viewed as defining a set of formulae in an assumption/commitment style temporal logic MCTL [Jo87]. The translation of the timing diagram into this logic is discussed in section 4 of this paper. In this introduction we continue our discussion on the basis of this timing - diagram. Note that - apart from the distinction between weak and strong arrows - another graphical element - a shaded circle at the orign of an arrow - is used to indicate **assumptions on the environment**, while "normal" arrows represent **commitments of the module**. Thus in the example, the module promises to be willing to communicate over inport in , while the environment has to guarantee, that eventually a message will be send through outport remote_out after having observed the willingness of the module to engage in a communication through this port. In order to be able to succintly express standard assumptions on the environment regarding synchronuous communication we interpret a strong constraint-arrow from

before(p) to **at**(p) for a **synchronuous** outport p as meaning "**enabled**(p) is infinitely often **true**". If indeed the environment observes this constraint, then, by combining the arrows, we immediately infer that the module will be willing to engage in a communication over inport in after having received a message. It should be pointed out that asynchronous communication is easier to handle in the sense that no special intepretation of constraint-arrows is needed.

Yet another aspect of the timing-diagram has to be discussed, also shedding light on the notion of message left vague until now. The language presented so far allows as to state specifications in an assumption/commitment style **propositional** temporal logic MCTL, whose atomic propositions **at**(p), **before**(p), **after**(p), and **enabled**(p) only allow to specify causal dependencies between reception and sending of messages **without** inspecting the internal structure of messages. For protocol applications, the actual data transmitted are of no concern, except that we want the data to be transmitted unchanged to the receiver. What **does** matter, are "header" bits, typically consisting of address information and control bits for the protocol. In the example shown in Fig.1, we have annotated certain events by first-order predicates handling this kind of control-information. We demand that these predicates are "syntactically abstract" in a stronger sense than used in [Pn86] : free variables occuring in predicates must either be ports or logical variables; no location - or control variables are allowed. Coming back to Fig. 1, the module will only guarantee, that it will be willing to communicate over local_out after having received a message whose addressee is local to this processor-node. Also note that it is indeed guaranteed, that the message will pass the module without being changed; here we used the usal trick of freezing the transmitted value in auxiliary variables.

While clearly in general such predicates are beyond the scope of propositional temporal reasoning, in certain simple cases, as the one used in the example, such predicates can be "encoded" into the implementation-module (by inventing new places and embedding them properly in the net) and then be checked through automatic verification tools. In [Wo86] it is shown, that a large class of non-finite state systems, there called **data-independent** programs, yield to propositional specification methods. Data-independence can be syntactically checked for a given net, by observing that the only operations performed on messsage contents are reading from ports to variables, writing from variables to ports, and copying between variables. In setting up our approach, our strive has been to stretch the applicability of automatic verification tools to the limit, even at the cost of using only such approximate (but safe) information, and to use first- order reasoning only when such methods fail and a deeper anylsis is considered mandatory. As a consequence, we use **unstructured** tokens at the net-level, leading to purely propositional reasoning at the schematic level. To capture the first order aspects in its full generality, we consider nets whose transitions are labeled by **state transformations** operating on a state-space of a module. Predicates can then be entered as labels of places; if such a place is in the postset of a transition t , it will only become marked if the associated predicate is true in the state resulting from firing this transition (see [DD89]). In this paper we will only discuss verification methods operating on the **uninterpreted** (schematic) level, entailing that the result of evaluating such a predicate will be **guessed**.

The particular class of nets used in this paper is introduced in chapter 2. It also fixes the form of parallel composition of modules considered in this paper through the definition of an operator on the class of nets. We restrict ourselves to **static** process generation, where a process is an incarnation of a module. As mentioned above, processes communicate over ports according to an again statically determined communication structure: much as in OCCAM [Occam], links (i.p,i'p') specify the connection of port p of process i with port p' of process i'. Again we prefer a graphical representation as user-interface in a form indicated in Fig.2. It shows the parallel composition of three processes comm_prim, mux, and I_process , together defining a module called protocol . The figure indicates as well shared storage used in the communication between these processes, a feature omitted in this paper but heavily exploited in the application of the presented theory in architecture design [DD88].

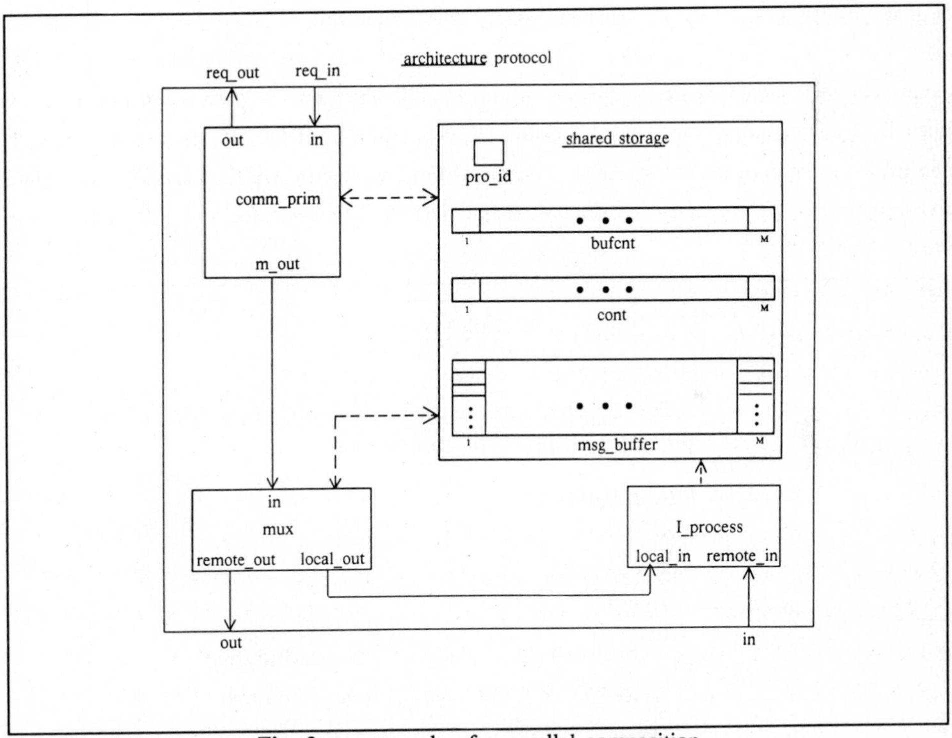

Fig. 2 an example of a parallel composition of modules

Based on such a specification-style, two major verifcation steps can be identified. **Service verification** considers one module in isolation and proves the consistency of the specification of the module given in MCTL against the implementation given by a Petri-Net. Proving a formula (assm , comm) in a net essentailly amounts to establishing the commitment for all pathes in the case graph of the net which meet the assumptions on the environment. Section 3 gives the precise construction of a model in the sense of MCTL out of the given net. The employed modelchecking procedure is linear in the size of the model and the length of the commitment, but exponential in the size of assm ; it is discussed in the companion paper [Jo 89]. **Horizontal verification** uses a proof-rule for the parallel composition of modules. This rule checks the mutual satisfaction of assumptions and propagates the resulting combined behaviour. A crucial point in this proof-rule is the existence of a well-founded ordering on the set of assumptions inhibiting circular reasoning. This rule is presented in section 5.

Though formulated in terms of specification and verification of Petri-nets, the methods presented in this paper are applicable to a broad class of parallel implementation languages. The major restriction imposed by the framework concerns process generation: the number of processes has to be statically determined. For any such language whose semantics can be formalized using nets whose transitions are labeled by state-transformations we can apply the specification and verification methods using the translation to nets defined by the semantics as an intermediate step.

Examples of such languages are modular extensions of CSP which refer to ports rather than to process-names in their input/output commands [Occam] , [JG80] , [Ko 87] , [DDG89]. Fig.3 shows an example of an implementation of the timing-diagram shown as Fig.1 written in AADL, a specification language aiming particularly at computer architecture design [DD88]. The net associated with this module is shown in section 2.

```
architecture multiplexer
 sync inport in : msg;
 synch outport remote_out , local_out : msg;
 storage protocol_id : nodeno
 implementation
  rep
   in ? msg_con(a,ms) ->
     case a.node of
       protocol_id : local_out ! msg_con(a,ms);
       otherwise remote_out ! msg_con(a,ms)
     esac
  per
 end /* architecture multiplexer */
```

Fig. 3 : an AADL implementation module

A net-based semantics for such a language (see e.g. [DGM 88] , [Re 84] , [DD89]) provides us with the link to our setting. Viewing such modules as open reactive systems, it is natural (and standard) to consider reception and sending of messages through ports to be observable. Temporal logic has been used to synthesize synchronisation skeletons for CSP-like programs [EC 83] , [Wo82] , [MW84] as well as to specify and verify such systems [NGO 85]. In [HO83] history variables are used to specify the behaviour of such systems.

While research on compositional proof methods using temporal logic is comparatively young, several papers have already appeared addressing compositional proof-methods for reactive system based on temporal logic [BK83] , [BKP84] , [Pn85] , [Pn86] . We view our main contribution in the introduction of a compositional assumption/commitment style proof system with two innovative features of mayor practical relevance:

- the verification of a module in isolation can be carried out by modelchecking with complexity which in typical examples is drastically lower than the exponential complexity of linear time logic;

- our specification language allows a pure top-down design style by refraining from the use of location - or control variables and refering only to ports. This is a prerequisite for a compositional hierarchic design. In particular, replacing a module by a lower level implementation observing the same specification will preserve all properties allready established in horizontal verification.

The results presented in this paper were achieved in the context of the COMDES project, developing a COMputer architecture DEsign System including tools for multi-level simulation and verification of computer architectures from operating system interfaces down to chip level. The verification methods have been implemented in C on SUN-workstations. The project has been funded both through ESPRIT within project 415 and the German Science Foundation under contract Da 206.

2 The definition of AADL nets

In this section we define the class of Petri nets used within this paper. We call these nets **AADL-nets** because they have been designed with regard to their use as semantics of AADL. Apart from this they will also be used within CAD-tools for the simulation and verification of AADL-specifications. AADL-nets are one-safe condition-event systems syntactically enriched by ports, special arcs and some auxiliary components. The special arcs can be implemented in conventional Petri nets. We start by explaining the main differences to standard condition/event nets.

The class of nets we consider should be able to serve as model for deifing semantics of paralle impertive languages. To this end, we will assume, that a state space underlying the net is defined by some external specification mechanism. In derivatives of CSP, this is canonically derived from the declaration of variables. Similarly, we asume that trasnitions of a net correspond to atomic statements of such a language and hence are labeled by state transformations (or continuations in a set CONT). Places will represent both the control flow as well as semaphores (necessary when modelling shared varaible parallelism as well as conditons on the underlying state space (e.g. evaluated in alternative or await statements). To simplify the presentation,we will assume that all plaes are labeled by predicates on the state space; places modelling control-flow or seamphores would then be labeld by **true**.

As indicated in the introduction, we view an AADL-net N as an open reactive system communicating with its environment through a designated set of ports Ports(N). Internally messages are received through such a port p by firing one out of a set of a associated transitions. This asscoiation will be defined using a function $comm_N$ which together with a transition indicates whether the port is an **outport** and - for **inports** - a pattern used to match the incoming message. To model the willingness of the environment to communicate synchronously over port p , we assume for each port the existence of a designated place labeled **enabled**(p). We require that the preset of a transition associated with p contains this designated place. The set of all enable places of net N will be denoted EN (where we assume that the related net is clear from the context). We recall that not only the reception or sending of messages is observable, but also the willingness of a module to engage in communication as well as the completion of a transmission. These propositions are internally representable through the preset and postset of interface transitions. We denote this set of **interface places** by IF. Note that EN is a subset of IF.

In AADL-nets we distinguish two classes of arcs which point from places to transitions: enabling-arcs and consuming-arcs.

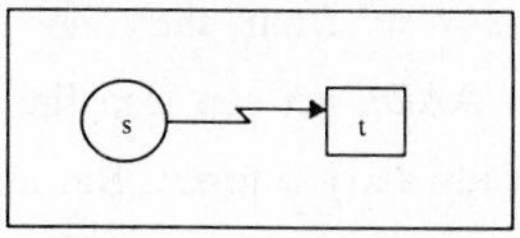

Fig. 4 enabling arc

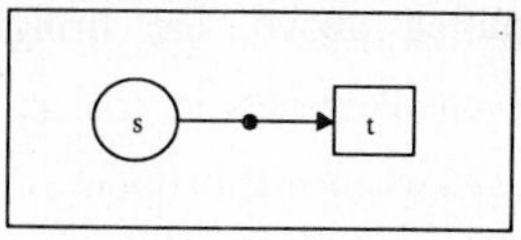

Fig. 5 consuming arc

The firing rule is extended to such arcs as follows : all places connected by an enabling-arc with a specific transition have to carry a token in order to allow the firing of that transition. Firing such a transition will **not** remove the token from a place (unless the place is also connected via a consuming-arc - to be discussed below - to this transition).

In fact **removal** of tokens is only done via consuming-arcs. Places which are exclusively connected by a consuming-arc to a transition need not carry a token in order to allow the firing of that transition. But they may carry a token which is then removed by the firing of that transition.

Combining the two different arcs (both pointing from one specific place to one specific transition) will constitute the normal Petri-net arc who's firing necessitates the presence of a token in the place and which removes this token upon it's firing.

We have only one type of arcs pointing from transitions to places, called delivering arcs. Such an arc will be called conditional if it points to a place labeled with a non-trivial predicate (i.e. a predicate different from <u>true</u>).

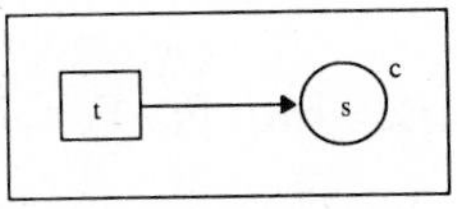

Fig. 6 delivering-arc

Intuitively a conditional arc will only allow a token to be passed to its place if the condition of the place is satisfied in the current state. Since this property cannot be decided on the schematic-level, we introduce a firing-rule for conditional arcs, which "guesses" whether the condition is satisfied. In Fig. 7 we have only written down one possible situation for the firing of t in which we assumed that c_5 is satisfied whereas c_7 is not. (Note that it is not relevant whether c_6 is <u>true</u> or not!)

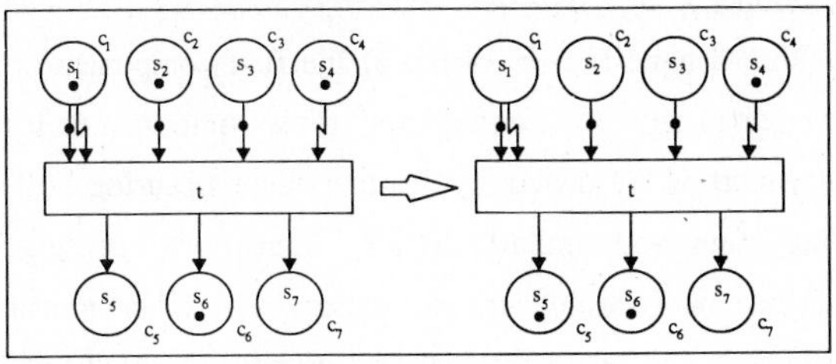

Fig. 7 firing rule

As examplified above, the firing-rule for AADL-nets differs also from the one of normal condition/event Petri-nets in contact situations. A transition in an AADL-net can also fire in contact situations, i.e. when one or more of the places in the postset already carry a token. But also in such situations the firing-rule will guarantee the property of one-saveness because it does not put a second token on such a place. This seemingly strange decision stems from the pragmatics associated with places in AADL-nets : they are associated with certain conditions on the underlying state-space. In the context of the net-semantics of AADL, a contact situation would merely represent the fact, that the execution of an AADL action makes a condition true which was already valid in the state prior to the execution of this action. The construction of AADL nets will guarantee that contact-situations only arise for a subclass of all places called trigger-places (see below).

Given a reachable marking M we use the standard notation M [Z> M' to denote that the marking M' is reached from the marking M by firing a set of transitions Z. M [∅> M holds by definition. As indicated in the introduction, we have to include a nonstandard tratmnet of enable places in order to model the fact, that the environmnet may at any time indicate and withdraw its willingness to engage in a communication through some given port. To this end the above firing relation is extended by allowing in one step to arbitrarily mark or unmark any number of enable places.

Definition (AADL-nets)

We define an AADL-net as a structure

$$N = (Ports , S, T, comm , EN , F_{enb} , F_{cons} , F_{del}, \Gamma, \pi, M_0, s_0, s_e)$$

where

ports — is a designated set of port-names

S and T — are nonempty finite sets with $S \cap T = \emptyset$ (they represent the places and transitions of the AADL-net).

comm — We associate with each net N its communication capabilities by $comm_N$ where $comm : Ports \rightarrow \mathcal{P} (T \times (Patterns \cup out))$

where Patterns is some set of patterns used in pattern matching reception of messages.

Within a tuple $(t,x) \in comm(p)$ the first component t represents a transition for port p and x is either "out" for an outport p or it represents the pattern for an inport p. We denote by T_{out} transitions occuring in the image of comm with "tag" out, and similarly by T_{in} transitions occuring in the image of comm with some (possibly trivial) pattern. All other transitions in T are called **internal**. The set of internal transitions is denoted by T_{int}.

$EN \subseteq IF \subseteq S$ where IF is defined as the union of all pre- and postsets of transitions occuring in the image of comm . The places in EN represent enabling conditions. IF represents the interface places.

$F_{enb} \subseteq S \times T$ and $F_{cons} \subseteq S \times T$

represent the enabling- and consuming-arcs. We require that enable places in EN are exclusively connected to a single transition in $T_{in} \cup T_{out}$ with an enabling arc.

$F_{del} \subseteq T \times S$ represent the delivering-arcs

$\Gamma : T \rightarrow CONT$

where CONT is the set of transformations on the underlying state-space. The exact structure of CONT is is not relevant to this paper.

$\pi : Tri \rightarrow PRED$

where PRED is the set of quantifier-free first-order formulas in some signature determined by the modeled porgramming language. For a place $s \in EN$ $\pi(s) =$ **enabled**(port) where port is the unique port associated with some transition with s in its pre_{enb} set.

$s_0, s_e \in S$ are the unique entry/exit places (modelling contol-flow) of the net

$M_0 \in S$ represents the initial marking. We assume that $\{ s_0 \} \subseteq M_0$.
We denote the set of all AADL nets by $\mathcal{N}$.

As usual in petri net theory for a transition t preset(t) (postset(t)) denotes the set of places connected to t by an arc from the place to t (from t to the place). With $pre_{enb}(t)$ we denote the set of places connected by an enabling arc to t.

We now define the operator formalising parallel composition of modules. In this paper we suppose that such modules can communicate over linked ports in a synchronous way. In the application of the presented theory to AADL we consider as well asynchronous communication and communication using shared memory. To model synchronous communication in AADL-nets we introduce for each pair of transitions which read and write on linked ports a new transition originating from the glueing of the two original transitions. Thus such a combined transition can only fire when all places in charge for the firing of both transitions carry a token.

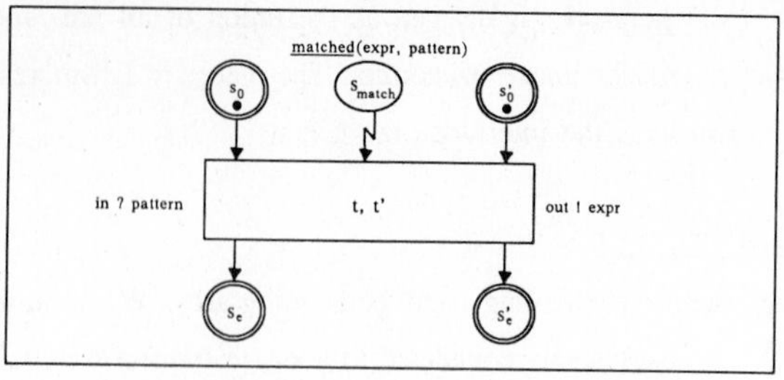

Fig. 8 Joined transition for input/output

We assume that the semantics of the parallel programming language will generate for transitions representing the sending of an expression expr a place labeled with a predicate **matched**(expr,dummy). Moreover, this place is connected via an enabling arc to the out-transition. Recall that the function comm will provide the actual pattern to be substituted for the second dummy argument of this predicate. For readers interested in the underlying state-space we note that the "local" state transformations associated with input and output commands will be "merged" when defining the net operator corresponding to a parallel composition of modules.

We define an auxiliary function SYNCH which constitutes the set of combined transitions and an auxiliary function ADAPT which performes the connection of arcs to these combined transitions. Another auxiliary function named MATCH will be used to substitute the dummy entry within the formula attached to the pattern-matching place in the preset of an output-transition with the appropriate pattern. This pattern will be taken from the $comm_N$ function of the glued input-transition.

Definition (glueing of transitions for linked input/output ports)

Let $N_i \in \mathcal{N}$ for $1 \leq i \leq n$ and let T be the union of all transitions in the N_i's. Let link be a set of tuples (outport, inport) representing the connection of ports.

Each combined transition (representing a synchronous communication) will be denoted as a tuple (t, t') of an output-transition t and an input-transition t' in the set SYNCH (...). The transitions have to write resp. read on ports which are connected according to the link specification. This can be evaluated by looking at the $comm_N$ function of the appropriate nets where the ports are defined.

$$\begin{aligned} SYNCH(N_1,...,N_n,link) = \{(t,t') \,/\, t,t' \in T \wedge \exists\, (port, port') \in link :\\ port \in Ports(N_i) \wedge port' \in Ports(N_j)\\ \wedge\, (t, out) \in comm_{Ni}(port) \wedge \exists\, pattern : (t', pattern) \in comm_{Nj}(port')\} \end{aligned}$$

Let F be a set of arcs $F \subseteq S \times T \cup T \times S$ where S, T are disjoint sets (of places resp. transitions)

and let SYNCH denote a set of combined transitions, i.e. tuples (t, t') with $t, t' \in T$.
ADAPT(F, SYNCH) denotes a new relation where an arc pointing to or from a transition occurring in a tuple $(t, t') \in$ SYNCH has been substituted by an arc pointing to or from that new tuple. Thus

$$\mathrm{ADAPT}(F, \mathrm{SYNCH}) \subseteq (S \times (T \cup (T \times T))) \cup ((T \cup (T \times T)) \times S) \text{ with}$$
$$\mathrm{ADAPT}(F, \mathrm{SYNCH}) = F \setminus \{(a, b) \mid \exists (x, y) \in \mathrm{SYNCH} : x = a \vee y = a \vee x = b \vee y = b\}$$
$$\cup \{(a, b) \mid a = (x, y) \in \mathrm{SYNCH} \wedge ((x, b) \in F \vee (y, b) \in F)$$
$$\vee\ b = (x, y) \in \mathrm{SYNCH} \wedge ((a, x) \in F \vee (a, y) \in F)\}.$$

Let F, SYNCH as in the definition before and let $\pi : S \to \mathrm{PRED}$.
We define a function MATCH(...) : $S \to \mathrm{PRED}$ where the dummy entries occurring in formulae has been substituted by the concrete pattern when the attached output-transition is combined with an input-transition. The pattern will be taken from the value of the comm_N function applied to the inport of the respective input-transition.

$$\mathrm{MATCH}(\pi, \mathrm{SYNCH}, F)(s) = \begin{cases} \mathrm{matched(expr, pattern)} & \text{for } \exists\, t,t' : (s,t) \in F \wedge (t,t') \in \mathrm{SYNCH} \\ & \wedge\ \pi(s) = \mathrm{matched(expr, dummy)} \\ & \wedge\ \exists\, \mathrm{port} \in \mathrm{Ports}(N) : (t', \mathrm{pattern}) \in \mathrm{comm}_N(\mathrm{port}) \\ \pi(s) & \text{otherwise} \end{cases}$$

[]

Definition (net operator for AADL modules)

The operator COMB_n combines n AADL-nets to a net representing their parallel execution.

$$\mathrm{COMB}_n \quad : N \times \ldots \times N \times \mathrm{link} \to N$$

link denotes the set of all possible linkings of ports where a linking is represented by a set of tuples (outport, inport).

Let for $i \in \{1,..,n\}$ the nets $N_i = (\mathrm{Ports}^i, S^i, T^i, \mathrm{comm}^i, EN^i, F_{enb}{}^i, F_{cons}{}^i, F_{del}{}^i, \Gamma^i, \pi^i, M_0{}^i, s_0{}^i, s_e{}^i)$ be given where the Ports^i, S^i, and T^i are pairwise disjoint.

We define the net

$$\mathrm{COMB}_n (N_1,\ldots,N_n, L) = (\mathrm{Ports}', S', T', \mathrm{comm}', EN', F'_{enb}, F'_{cons}, F'_{del}, \Gamma', \pi', M'_0, s'_0, s'_e)$$

where the net-components are given by:

$\text{Ports}' = \bigcup_{1\le j\le n} \text{Ports}^j \setminus \{\ p \mid \exists\ p' \text{ with } (p,p') \in L \text{ or } (p',p) \in L\ \}$

$S' = \bigcup_{1\le j\le n} S^j \setminus \{s \mid \exists\ i\text{: } s \in EN^i \wedge \exists\ (t,t') \in \text{SYNCH}(N_1,\dots,N_n, L)\text{: } s \in \text{pre}_{enb}(t) \cup \text{pre}_{enb}(t')\}$

$T' = \bigcup_{1\le j\le n} T^j \setminus \{t \ /\ \exists\ (x,y) \in \text{SYNCH}(N_1,\dots,N_n, L) : x = t \vee y = t\}$

$\cup\ \text{SYNCH}(N_1,\dots,N_n, L)$

$\text{comm}' = \bigcup_{1\le j\le n} \text{comm}^j \setminus \text{Ports}'$

$EN' = \bigcup_{1\le j\le n} EN^j \cap S'$

$F'_{enb} = \text{ADAPT}(\bigcup_{1\le j\le n} F_{enb}^j, \text{SYNCH}(N_1,\dots,N_n, L))$

$F'_{cons} = \text{ADAPT}(\bigcup_{1\le j\le n} F_{cons}^j, \text{SYNCH}(N_1,\dots,N_n, L))$

$F'_{del} = \text{ADAPT}(\bigcup_{1\le j\le n} F_{del}^j, \text{SYNCH}(N_1,\dots,N_n, L))$

$$\Gamma'(t) = \begin{cases} \Gamma^i(t) \text{ for } t \in T^i \\ \Gamma^i(y)(\Theta) \text{ for } t = (x, y) \in \text{SYNCH}(N_1,\dots,N_n, L) \\ id_{CONT} \text{ otherwise} \end{cases}$$

Where Θ is the mapping which substitutes pattern-variables by their corresponding (sub)expressions according to the pattern-matching.

$\pi' = \text{MATCH}(\bigcup_{1\le j\le n} \pi^j, \text{SYNCH}(N_1,\dots,N_n, L), F'_{enb})$

$M'_0 = \bigcup_{1\le j\le n} M_0^j$ []

We now briefly indicate the translation from AADL to AADL-nets using the example of Fig.3 (see [DD89] for a complete treatment).

For the semantics we assume, that the set of places is split into the following disjoint classes:

- so called **control places** in the set **Con** will represent the flow of control as dictated by the AADL control specification;
- **semaphore places** in the set **Sem** will be generated between concurrently executed actions which share resources;
- **trigger places** in the set **Tri** represent conditions on the underlying state-space, which in the context of the semantics of AADL are evaluated in an await-command, causing non-procedural activation of its body. These places are labeled by the condition which they represent.

Control-places and semaphore-places are always connected via combined arcs to transitions.

The compilation of AADL - implementation modules is done in a compositional way by using net operators for the syntactic operators of AADL. Fig.9 shows the net resulting from translating the module Multiplexer of Fig.3.

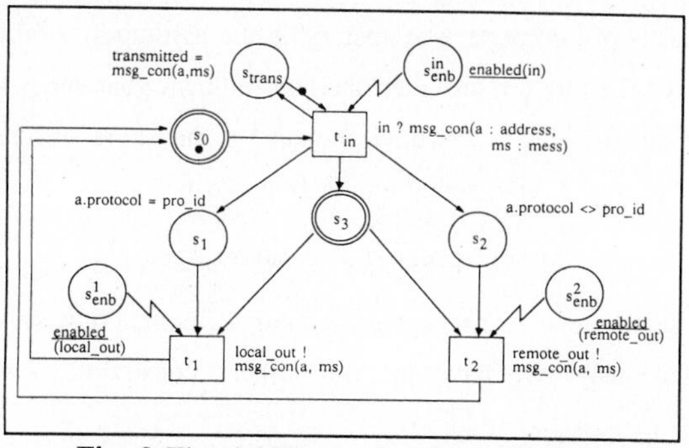

Fig. 9 The AADL net for the multiplexer

Control places are represented by double circles. The implicit control flow of actions which is specified in the implementation part (for example a sequence of actions) is represented by such control places. In the example above the control place s_0 is the entry place of the net. It is linked with a 'normal' arc to the transition t_{in}. This transition represents the input command 'in ? ...' in the implementation part of the multiplexer. Each transition reflects an action or an input or output command. Essentially this petri net is a translation from the case-command of the implementation part of the multiplexer. If a message is received (s_3 is set) and the receiving process resides on the same processor (a.protocol = pro_id, s_1 is set) it delivers the messages via port 'local_out' (t_1 fires), otherwise (s_2 and s_3 are set) it delivers the message via port 'remote_out' (t_2 fires).

3 A temporal logic for the specification of AADL nets

Specifications of AADL nets will be given by temporal logic formulae. There exist many kinds of temporal logics: linear time TL (e.g. PTL, QPTL), branching time TL (e.g. CTL, CTL*), interval TL. These logics differ in the underlying computation model and in their expressive power. To choose an appropriate logic we have to consider two important aspects: its expressive power and the existance of efficient verification algorithms (e.g. model checking algorithm). For most logics the model checking problem is NP-hard [EH85], one exception is the branching time temporal logic CTL, for which a linear model checking algorithm exists (cf. [CES83]), hence this logic is widely used in verification tools. But this logic is only suitable for closed systems, its expressiveness is too weak for specifying open systems. As we are interested in modular design techniques we need a specification language for reactive components. Hence we will use an extension of the logic CTL, called MCTL, which allows modular specification and which has an acceptable model checking algorithm (cf. [Jo87], [Jo89]).
As a module interacts with other modules, its behaviour depends on the reactions of the environment.

Therefore the behaviour of a module may only be guaranteed provided the environment reacts correctly. Hence a module specification will include some assumptions on the correct behaviour of the environment. To distinguish the assumptions on the environment and the commitment of a module, a module specification consists of two parts, one specifying the assumptions on the environment and one specifying the behaviour of the module provided the environment guarantees the given constraints. As a module can offer different services to the environment we may have different constraints according to the offered services. Thus an AADL specification is given by

$$(\mathrm{assm}_1,\mathrm{spec}_1) \wedge \ldots \wedge (\mathrm{assm}_n,\mathrm{spec}_n)$$

As we will interpret these formulae w.r.t. a step semantics (interleaving semantics allowing a set of actions to occur simultaneously) we have to add fairness constraints. Thus the general form of specifications are

$$(\mathrm{fc},\mathrm{assm}_1,\mathrm{spec}_1) \wedge \ldots \wedge (\mathrm{fc},\mathrm{assm}_n,\mathrm{spec}_n)$$

To be more formally, we assume that *ATOMS* is a (finite) set of atomic propositions with typical elements a, a_i, ... In the context of AADL *ATOMS* includes for every port p the atomic propositions **at**(p), **before**(p), **after**(p), and **enabled**(p); furthermore we need for every transition t the atomic propositions **enb**(t) and **exc**(t) to express the fairness constraints. The set of boolean expressions will be denoted by *BExpr* and its elements are denoted by b, ...

Commitments, denoted by *spec*, are state formulae (CTL formulae) given by the following rules:

$$\begin{aligned} spec \;::=\; & b \mid spec \wedge spec \mid spec \vee spec \mid \\ & \forall\,[\, spec\ \mathbf{until}\ spec \,] \mid \forall\,[\, spec\ \mathbf{unless}\ spec \,] \mid \\ & \forall[]\, spec \mid \forall\Diamond\, spec \end{aligned}$$

and assumptions are restricted PTL formulae given by

$$assm \;::=\; [\,]\,(b \rightarrow uf) \mid uf \mid assm \wedge assm$$

where *uf* is an iterated until/unless-formula defined by

$$uf \;::=\; b \mid [\, b\ \mathbf{until}\ uf \,] \mid [\, b\ \mathbf{unless}\ uf \,] \quad .$$

The syntax of fairness constraints is given by

$$fc \;::=\; [\,]\Diamond\, b \mid \Diamond[\,]\, b \mid fc \wedge fc \mid fc \vee fc \quad .$$

Assumptions and fairness constraints are given by path formulae, which restrict the paths relevant for a ∀-quantifier in a commitment. As we use only ∀-quantified formulae the ∀-quantifers can be omitted.

4 A net semantics for the specification logic

Usually the semantics of temporal logic formulae is given with respect to Kripke-structures (models, state/transition-graphs) consisting of a set of states, a binary transition relation on the set of states and a labelling function, assigning to every state a set of atomic propositions. As we are dealing with modules the transitions may depend on some inputs; hence we will label the transitions with conditions on the inputs. Therefore a model is given by

$\mathcal{M} = (\Sigma,\sigma^0,IN,OUT,R,\beta)$, where

Σ	is a set of states
σ^0	is the initial state
IN	is a set of input propositions (input signals)
OUT	is a set of internal and output propositions with $IN \cap OUT = \emptyset$
R	is the transition relation, consisting of triples (σ, b, σ'), where b is a satisfiable boolean expression on the inputs IN, which determines the condition under which a transition from state σ to state σ' can occur.
β	is an assignment of internal and output propositions to states. $a \in \beta(\sigma)$ means that the atomic proposition a is true in state σ.

Note: The notion of transition in the context of models is different from the notion of transition in Petri nets. Both notions express progress in a system, in a Petri net a transition is the execution of a single atomic action, whereas in a model a transition defines a step of the systems, which may be compared with the firing of a set of transitions in a petri net.

Computations are reflected by paths in the transition system. An (infinite) sequence of pairs $(\sigma_i,in_i) \in \Sigma \times IN$ is a path iff for every $i \in N$ there is a boolean expression b_i with in_i **sat** b_i and $(\sigma_i, b_i, \sigma_{i+1}) \in R$.

For a Petri net a transition system is given by its case graph: The states are given by the marking sets and the transition relation is given by the reachability relation M [Z> M'. However, using this case graph, too much information is lost. E.g. in the case graph there is no information of the transitions which have fired, hence there is no way to express that conflicts have to be solved in a fair way. Furthermore, we should be able to talk about the communications to other modules, thus we have to refer to the points where these communications occur. For these reasons we will use an extended case graph where the (Petri net) transitons are included.

In order to define the validity of formulae with respect to a net, we will associate an appropriate model to the given AADL-net and then interpret the formulae with respect to this model.

4.1 Translation of nets into models

The computations in a net are determined by the relation M [Z> M' (marking M' is obtained from the marking M by firing the transitions Z). If M [Z> M' holds, then M $\rightarrow$ M' is an arc in the usual case graph. As we have to reflect the firing transitions in our model, M [Z> M' will be modelled by two transitions M $\rightarrow$ M$\cup$Z $\rightarrow$ M', where the "intermediate state" M$\cup$Z contains the information of the firing transitions. Another possibility to reflect the firing transition would be to label the arc M $\rightarrow$ M' with the transition set Z. But in that case we can not distinguish e.g. the fact that a module is ready to communicate with another module (**before**(p) is true for some port p) and the fact that the communication take place (**at**(p) is true). Hence we will use "intermediate states". The marking of enabled-places is determined by the environment, hence these are modelled by inputs. Given an AADL-net $N = (Ports,S,T,comm,EN,F_{enb},F_{cons},F_{del},\Gamma,\pi,M_0,s_0,s_e)$ we define a model $\mathcal{M}_N = (\Sigma_N,\sigma^0_N,IN_N,OUT_N,R_N,\beta_N)$ by

Σ_N := $2^{\{ s \mid s \in S \setminus EN\}} \cup T$

σ^0_N := $M_0 \setminus EN$

IN_N := { **enabled**(p) | $\exists s \in EN$ with **enabled**(p) $\in \pi(s)$ }

OUT_N := { $\pi(s)$ | $s \in IF \setminus EN$ } $\cup$ {**at**(p), **before**(p), **after**(p) | $p \in Ports(N)$ }
$\cup$ {**enb**(t), **exc**(t) | $t \in T$ }

R_N := { (M, be(B), M$\cup$Z), (M$\cup$Z, **true**, M') | $M \subseteq S \setminus EN$, $B \subseteq EN$,
$Z \subseteq \{t \in T \mid$ t is enabled in $(M \cup B)\}$, and $M \cup B$ [Z>M' }

For a set $B \subseteq EN$, be(B) denotes the boolean expression $\bigwedge_{s \in B} \pi(s)$

β(M):

$M \subseteq S \setminus EN$:

β(M) is the least set with

- { $\pi(s)$ | $s \in IF \cap M$ } $\subseteq \beta(M)$
- { **enb**(t) | $(M,b,M') \in R$ and $t \in M'$) } $\subseteq \beta(M)$
- { **before**(port) | $\exists t \in T$: (t, .) $\in comm_N$(port) and $(pre_{enb}(t) \cap S \setminus EN) \subseteq M$ } $\subseteq \beta(M)$
- { **after**(port) | $\exists t \in T$: (t, .) $\in comm_N$(port) and $(post_{del}(t) \cap CON) \subseteq M$ } $\subseteq \beta(M)$

M$\cup$Z, where $M \subseteq S \setminus EN$ and $Z \subseteq T$:

$\beta(M \cup Z)$ is the least set with

- { $\pi(s)$ | $s \in IF \cap M$ } $\subseteq \beta(M \cup Z)$
- { **exc**(t) | $t \in Z$ } $\subseteq \beta(M \cup Z)$
- { **at**(port) | $\exists t \in Z$: (t, .) $\in comm_N$(port) } $\subseteq \beta(M \cup Z)$
- { **enb**(t) | **enb**(t) $\in \beta(M) \setminus Z$ } $\subseteq \beta(M \cup Z)$
- { **before**(port) | $\exists t \in T \setminus Z$: (t,.) $\in comm_N$(port) and $(pre_{enb}(t) \cap S \setminus EN) \subseteq M$ } $\subseteq \beta(M \cup Z)$
- { **after**(port) | $\exists t \in T \setminus Z$: (t,.) $\in comm_N$(port) and $(post_{del}(t) \cap CON) \subseteq M$ }

$\subseteq \beta(M \cup Z)$

and

$$fc_N \quad := \quad \bigwedge_{t \in T} \left([]\Diamond\ \mathbf{enb}(t) \wedge \mathbf{env}(t) \;\rightarrow\; []\Diamond\ \mathbf{exc}(t) \right) \qquad \text{where}$$

$$\mathbf{env}(t) := \begin{cases} \mathbf{true} & \text{if } pre(t) \cap EN = \emptyset \\ \mathbf{enabeled}(p) & \text{if there is some } s \in pre(t) \cap EN \text{ with } \pi(s) = \mathbf{enabeled}(p) \end{cases}$$

This model $\mathcal{M}_N$ together with the fairness constraint fc_N defines a step semantics for the AADL-net N. As the size of the model $\mathcal{M}_N$ is exponential in the size of the given net N, minimization techniques are important in the context of design and verification tools. The model may be reduced by considering only the observable behaviour of the net given by the marking of the interface places and the communication transitions. Furthermore, the "intermediate states", which represent the firing transitions, may be introduced only if necessary, i.e. if there are some conflicts which have to be mentioned or if there some communication transitions. Fig. 9 shows such an optimized model of the AADL-net for the multiplexer.

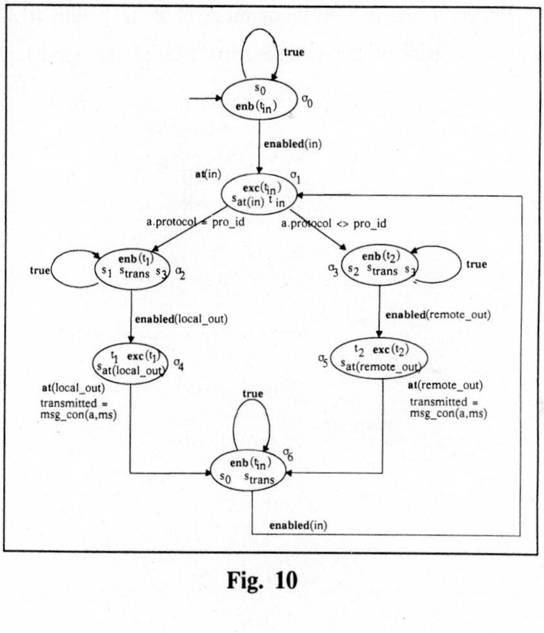

Fig. 10

4.2 Semantics w.r.t. models

In this section we will briefly describe the interpretation of MCTL formulae w.r.t. models. We assume that the reader is familiar with temporal logics and its semantics definition. Fairness constraints *fc* and assumptions *assm* are interpreted w.r.t. paths as usually, i.e. an assumption $[](b_1 \rightarrow \Diamond b_2)$ is true along a path p=((σ_i,in_i) | i∈N) iff for all i with (σ_i,in_i) ⊨ b_1 there is some j>i with (σ_j,in_j) ⊨ b_2. A specification *(fc, assm, spec)* of a module is then interpreted inductivley on the structure of *spec* similarily to the interpretation in CTL but with the restriction that a path quantifier is restricted to those paths which satisfy the given assumptions and fairness constraints. Assume that a model $\mathcal{M}$ = (Σ,σ^0,IN,OUT,R,β) is given. Then the validity of a formula *(fc,assm,spec)* is defined with respect to a state σ and an input set in ⊆ IN in the following way:

(1) Construct the (infinite) computation tree of $\mathcal{M}$ with root (σ, in)
(The computation tree is obtained from $\mathcal{M}$ by unravelling the transition graph starting at state σ with inputs in.)

(2) Mark those paths in the tree starting at (σ,in) which satisfy the given assumptions *assm* and fairness constraints *fc*.

(3) Interpret *spec* as in CTL but with the restriction that only the marked paths are considered when evaluating a path quantifier ∀

E.g. the formula *(fc, assm, ∀[b_1 **unless** b_2])* is true w.r.t. a state σ and inputs in iff for all paths p=((σ_i,in_i) | i∈N) starting at (σ,in) and satisfying the fairness constraint *fc* and the assumption *assm* it holds that either for all integer i (σ_i,in_i) ⊨ b_1 or there is some j with (σ_j,in_j) ⊨ b_2 and for all i<j (σ_j,in_j) ⊨ b_1. Fig. 10 shows a part of the computation tree of the model given in Fig. 9 with the initial state as root.

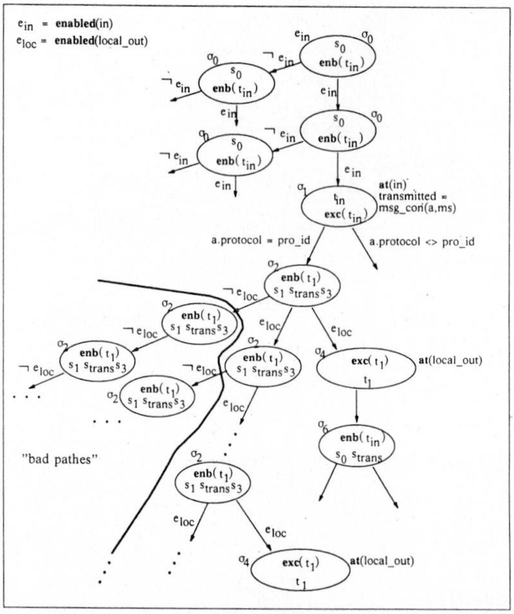

Fig. 11

A detailed definition of the semantics can be found in [Jo89].

The interpretation of a formulae *(assm, spec)* w.r.t. an AADL-net N =

$(Ports,S,T,comm,EN,F_{enb},F_{cons},F_{del},\Gamma,\pi,M_0,s_0,s_e)$ is defined by:

$$N \models (assm,spec) \quad \text{iff} \quad \mathcal{M}_N, \sigma_N^0, \{\pi(s) \mid s \in M_0 \cap EN\} \models (fc_N,assm,spec)$$

5 Verification of AADL nets

As an AADL net is an implementation of a specification given by a temporal logic formula, we have to prove that this implementation is correct. As we use modular design techniques, verifying that a net satisfies its specification should be done in a modular way, too. Hence we will define some proof rules which allow to derive the correctness of a net, which is given as a composition of subnets using the net operator COMB, from thc correctness of its subnets. If the net is basic, i.e. it is not a combination of submodules, the correctness proof will be done by model checking. While the model checking procedure is described in [Jo89] we will discuss the composition in this chapter.
Roughly spoken the composition of subnets will satisfy the conjunction of the specifications of the subnets. The specification for the composition should be a consequnece of this conjunction. But this conjunction contains some references to internal ports, i.e. ports linked together in the composition. As these ports are not visible outsides the specification have not to mention these ports. Hence they have to be eliminated.
The correctness of COMB(N_1, ..., N_n, L) w.r.t. a specification *(assm, spec)* may be derived from the correctness of the submodules N_i w.r.t. their specifications *($assm_i$, $spec_i$)* in the following way:

(1) Prove the correct interaction of the submodules, i.e. prove that a module communicating with another module satisfies the assumed constraints.

(2) Due to (1) only assumptions on the environment are left. Let $assm_E$ be the conjunctions of all assumptions made on the environment by some subnet. Then we can conclude the validity of $(assm_E, spec_1 \wedge ... \wedge spec_n)$ for the composition.

(3) Prove that *(assm, spec)* is a consequence of $(assm_E, spec_1 \wedge ... \wedge spec_n)$

Step (1) is necessary as the composition have only to deal with ports visible outsides, hence assumptions dealing with internal ports have to be eleminated. When verifying the constraints one module assumes on another, we have to be careful to avoid cyclic reasoning. If we prove $assm_1$ in N_1 using $assm_2$ and prove $assm_2$ in N_2 using $assm_1$, nothing is proved for the composition of N_1 and N_2. Hence we demand a well founded ordering on the assumptions and only those assumptions which are less than a considered assumption *assm* may be used to prove the validity of *assm* in the corresponding module.
In addition, when proving that an assumption is guaranteed in a module we have to translate the path formula *assm* into a state formula br(*assm*). According to our restriction in the syntax of assumptions this can be done straightforwardly. (Note that in general PTL and CTL are incomparable [EH83].) The translation, denoted by br, is done by prefixing every temporal operator with the path-quantifier $\forall$. E.g.

$br([](b_1 \rightarrow [b_2 \textbf{ until } b_2])) = \forall[](b_1 \rightarrow \forall[b_2 \textbf{ until } b_2])$. Due to our convention that the path quantifiers $\forall$ may be omitted, there is no syntactical translation necessary, the formula have only to be evaluated in the branching time setting.

Fact

(1) Assume that *assm* is an assumption without an **unless**-operator, then:
$(\sigma_0, in_0) \models (fc, assm', br(assm))$ iff for all path p starting at (σ_0, in_0) it holds: p $\models fc \wedge assm'$ implies p $\models fc \wedge assm$.

(2) If *assm* contains an **unless**-operator we have:
if $(\sigma_0, in_0) \models (fc, assm', br(assm))$ then for all path p starting at (σ_0, in_0) it holds: p $\models fc \wedge assm'$ implies p $\models fc \wedge assm$.

The formulae can talk about ports using the atomic propositions **at**(port), **before**(port), **after**(port), and **enabled**(port). When modules are composed together the ports are linked according to the given set L of outport - inport pairs. These links induce some equivalences between propositions related to ports. If $port_1$ of module N_i is linked together with $port_2$ of module N_j, then the propositions **enabled**($port_2$) and **before**($port_1$) are equivalent, furthermore **at**($port_1$) is equivalent to **at**($port_2$). Hence these equivalences may be used in the correctness proof by adding the formula

$$\textbf{link}(L) := \bigwedge_{\substack{(p,p')\in L \\ \vee\ (p',p)\in L}} \forall[](\ (\textbf{before}(p) \leftrightarrow \textbf{enabled}(p')) \wedge (\textbf{at}(p) \leftrightarrow \textbf{at}(p'))\ )$$

Instead of these equivalences we may use substitutions, this will be done in the constraint verification. When an assumption $assm_l$, module N_i assumes on module N_j, is proved in N_j, the propositions **enabled**($port_1$) will be replaced by **before**($port_2$), **before**($port_1$) will be replaced by **enabled**($port_2$), and **at**($port_1$) will be replaced by **at**($port_2$). This substitution will be denoted by $[L_{ij}]$.
As we want to be able to substitute a submodule by another submodule satisfying the same temporal specification, we do not want to loose the correctness of the composed object, hence the proof rules have to deal with composition of specifications instead of nets.
Putting all these consideration into account we can formulate the composition rule. For simplicity we further assume that every assumption is a conjunction of subassumptions where every subassumption is related only to the communication with one other module. This can be done w.o.l.g. as if we have an assumption dealing with several other modules, first these modules may be composed together using proof rules and then they are handled as one module.

Proof Rule I (Composition Rule):

Assume that we have interface specifications $ispec_1$, ..., $ispec_n$ together with sets of ports $Port_1$, ..., $Port_n$, and assume that L is a set of links between these ports. (W.l.o.g. we assume that the sets of ports are disjoint.). Furthermore, let $Port_{ij} \subseteq Port_i$ denote those ports which are linked to ports of $Port_j$. $Port_{iE}$ denotes the ports to the environment.

$ispec_i = (assm_{i,1}, spec_{i,1})$ **and** ... **and** $(assm_{i,k(i)}, spec_{i,k(i)})$

$assm_{i,j} = assm^1_{i,j} \wedge ... \wedge assm^n_{i,j} \wedge assm^E_{i,j}$, where $assm^r_{i,j}$ is an assumption on the r-th component where only ports concerning that module are mentioned, i.e. only atomic propositions refering to a port $p \in Port_{ir}$ are allowed.

- $(\{assm^j_{i,r} \mid 1 \le i,j \le n,\ 1 \le r \le k(i)\}, <)$ is a well-founded ordering
- for all i, $1 \le i \le n$: $N_i \models ispec_i$
- for all i, $1 \le i \le n$, for all j, $1 \le j \le n$ and for all r, $1 \le r \le k(j)$:

$$ispec_i \models \Big(\bigwedge_{\substack{1 \le h \le n,\ 1 \le t \le k(i) \\ assm^h_{i,t} < assm^i_{j,r}}} assm^h_{i,t}\ ,\quad br(assm^i_{j,r}[L_{ij}]) \Big)$$

- $\models \bigwedge_{\substack{1 \le i \le n \\ 1 \le j \le k(i)}} spec_{i,j} \wedge \mathbf{link}(L) \rightarrow spec$

$$COMB_n(N_1, ..., N_n, L) \models \Big(\bigwedge_{\substack{1 \le i \le n \\ 1 \le j \le k(i)}} assm^E_{i,j}\ ,\quad spec \Big)$$

As in AADL nets there is some relationship between the atomic propositions **at**(p), **before**(p), and **after**(p), the universal validity of the consequence $\bigwedge spec_{i,j} \wedge \mathbf{link}(L) \rightarrow spec$ may be restricted to fair models of a theory describing the relationship between **at**(p), **after**(p) and **before**(p). We have not yet worked out the appropriate description of this theory. Such a theory should contain the following properties:

- **at**(p) $\rightarrow$ [**at**(p) **until after**(p)]
- **at**(p) $\rightarrow$ **previously before**(p)
- **after**(p) $\rightarrow$ **previously at**(p)

Observe, that in our models the propositions **at**(p), **before**(p) and **after**(p) are not exclusive, as these are propositions on ports and not on transitions, and there can be several transitions dealing with port p.

Furthermore,if the ports p and p' are linked together, we could add

$\forall\Box$ (**at**(p) $\rightarrow \forall\Diamond$ (**after**(p) **and after**(p')))

to the formula **link**(L).

The composition rule is the main rule in the proof system. In addition rules for weakening specifications may be used.

Proof Rule II (Consequence Rule):

$$\frac{N \models (assm,\ spec), \qquad \models (assm,\ spec) \rightarrow (assm',\ spec')}{N \models (assm',\ spec')}$$

In practice a weaker form of this consequence rule is sufficient, where *assm'* implies the validity of *assm* and *spec'* can be derived from *spec*.

Proof Rule IIa (Consequence Rule):

$$\frac{N \models (assm,\ spec), \qquad \models assm' \rightarrow assm, \qquad \models spec \rightarrow spec'}{N \models (assm',\ spec')}$$

The given proof rules are sound, but they do not necessarily define a complete proof system.
We will demonstrate the application of the proof rules by showing that the composition of the multiplexer and the I-process has the property "Whenever a message is received from the environment the commponent will eventually be ready to receive another message".

$ispec_M$ is given by the conjunction of the following specifications:

$ispec_{M,1}$:= (, ∀[](**at**(in) ∧ local → ∀◊**before**(local_out)))

$ispec_{M,2}$:= (, ∀[](**before**(local_out) → ∀[**before**(local_out) **unless** **at**(local_out)]))

$ispec_{M,3}$:= (, ∀[](**at**(local_out) → ∀◊**before**(in)))

$ispec_{M,4}$:= ([]◊ **enabled**(local_out), ∀[](**before**(local_out) → ∀◊**at**(local_out)))

$ispec_{M,5}$:= (, ∀[](**at**(in) ∧ remote → ∀◊**before**(remote_out)))

$ispec_{M,6}$:= (, ∀[](**before**(remote_out) → ∀[**before**(remote_out) **unless** **at**(remote_out)]))

$ispec_{M,7}$:= (, ∀[](**at**(remote_out) → ∀◊**before**(in)))

$ispec_{M,8}$:= ([]◊ **enabled**(remote_out), ∀[](**before**(remote_out) → ∀◊**at**(remote_out)))

...

Fig. 12

The specifications of the multiplexer and the I-process are given in Fig. 11 resp. in Fig. 12. There is only one link between these two components: local_out is linked with local_in, i.e.

L := { (local_out, local_in) }

The specification we want to prove for the composition COMB(multiplexer,I-process,L) is:

spec := ∀[](**at**(in) ∧ local → ∀◊ **before**(in))

The proof proceeds as follows:

$ispec_I$ is given by the conjunction of the following specifications:

$ispec_{I,1}$:= (, ∀[] ∀◊**before**(local_in))

$ispec_{I,2}$:= ([](**enabled**(local_in) → [**enabled**(local_in) **unless** **at**(local_in)]),
∀[](**before**(local_in) ∧ **enabled**(local_in) → ∀◊ **at**(local_in)))

$ispec_{I,3}$:= (, ∀[] ∀◊**before**(remote_in))

$ispec_{I,4}$:= ([](**enabled**(remote_in) → [**enabled**(remote_in) **unless** **at**(remote_in)]),
∀[](**before**(remote_in) ∧ **enabled**(remote_in) → ∀◊ **at**(remote_in)))

...

Fig. 13

According to the proof rule I we have to verify that the constraints are derivable from the specifications of the modules. Here now ordering on the assumptions are necessary, because the assumptions can be proved without using any other assumption:

(1) $ispec_{I,1}$ ⊨ (,br([]◊ **enabled**(local_out)[**enabled**(local_out)/**before**(local_in)]))

(2) $ispec_{M,2}$ ⊨ (,br([](**enabled**(local_in) → [**enabled**(local_in) **unless** **at**(local_in)])
[**enabled**(local_in), **at**(local_in) / **before**(local_out), **at**(local_out)]))

Now our specification *spec* is a consequence of the commitments of $ispec_{M,1}$, ..., $ispec_{M,4}$, $ispec_{I,1}$, and $ispec_{I,2}$ and the equivalences **link**(L). This can be seen by the following steps:

(3)	assume that: **at**(in) ∧ local	
(4)	**before**(local_out)	by the commitment of $ispec_{M,1}$
(5)	**at**(local_out)	by the commitment of $ispec_{M,4}$
(6)	**before**(in)	by the commitment of $ispec_{M,3}$

Conclusion

While providing mayor innovative features in assumption/commitment style compositional proof-methods, many aspects have just been touched upon and demand further investigation. As three major topics currently under investigation we mention a characterization of the equivalence on AADL nets defined by MCTL formula in terms of an equivalence based on observable places, an investigation of the expressiveness of timing diagrams, and the development of a Hoare style proof system for AADL-nets.

References

[BK83] H.Barringer, R.Kuiper : A Temporal Logic Specification Method Supporting Hierarchical Development, University of Manchester, 1983

[BKP84] H.Barringer, R.Kuiper, A.Pnueli : Now You May Compose Temporal Logic Specifications, Proc. 16th ACM Symposium on Theory of Computing, 1984, 51-63

[CES83] E.M. Clarke, E.A. Emerson, A.P. Sistla: Automatic verification of finite-state concurrent systems using temporal logic specifications: a practical approach. Tenth ACM Symposium on principles of Programming Languages (1983)

[DD88] W.Damm, G.Döhmen: Specifying Distributed Computer Architectures in AADL, Parallel Computing, Vol 9, 1988, 193-211

[DD89] W.Damm, G.Döhmen : AADL: a Net-Based Specification Method for Computer Architecture Design, in: Languages for Parallel Architectures: Design, Semantics, and Implementation Models", edt. J.de Bakker, Wiley & Sons, 1989

[DDG89] W.Damm, G.Döhmen, V.Gerstner, J.Helbig, B.Josko, F.Korf, T.Peikenkamp: AADL Language Document, University of Oldenburg, FRG, 1989

[DGM 88] P.Degano, R.Gorrieri, S.Machetti : An excercise in concurrency: a CSP process as a Condition/Event system, Advances on Petri-Nets 1988, edt G.Rozenberg, Lecture Notes in Computer science 340, Springer Verlag, 1988, 83-105

[EC 83] E.A.Emerson, E.M.Clarke: Using branching time temporal logic to synthesisze synchronization skeletons, Science of Computer Programming, Vol 2, 1982, 241-266

[EH83] E.A. Emerson, J.Y. Halpern: Sometimes and not never revisited: On branching time versus linear time. 10th ACM Symposium on Principles of programming Languages. 1983

[EH85] E.A. Emerson, J.Y. Halpern: Decision procedures and expressiveness in the temporal logic of branching time. Journal of Computer and System Science 30 (1985), pp. 1-24

[HO83] B.Hailpern, S.Owicki : Modular Verification of Computer Communication Protocols, IEEE Trans. on Communication, Vol COM-31, 1983,56-68

[HP85] D.Harel, A.Pnueli: On the Development of Reactive Systems, Nato ASI Series, Vol. F13, Logics and Models of Concurrent Systems, edt. K.Apt, Springer Verlag, 1985

[JG80] M.Jazayeri, C.Ghezzi, D.Hoffman,. D.Middleton, M.Smotherman: Design and Implemantation of a Language for Communicating Sequential Processes, IEEE Proc. 9th Int.Conf. on Parallel Processes, Harbor Spring, Michigan, USA, 1980

[Jo87] B. Josko: Modelchecking of CTL formulae under liveness assumptions. Proceedings ICALP 87. Lecture Notes in Computer Science 267 (1987), 280-289

[Jo89] B. Josko: Verifying the correctness of AADL-modules using model checking. Proceedings REX-Workshop on Stepwise refinement of Distributed systems: models, formalisms, correctness

[Ko 87] F. Korf : M-CSP - eine modulare Sprache mit Prozeßkommunikation und ihre Implemntierung, Master Thesis, RWTH Aachen, 1987

[MC 81] J.Misra, K.M. Chandy : Proofs of Networks of Processes, IEEE Trans. Software Enginering. 7, 1981, 417-426

[MW84] Z.Manna,P.Wolper: Synthesis of Communicating Processes from Temporal Logic Specifications, ACM Toplas 6, 1984, 68-93

[NGO 85] V.Nguyen, D.Gries, S.Owicki : A Model and Temporal Proof System for Network of Proceses, 12 POPL, 1985, 121-131

[Occam] OCCAM Programming Manual, INMOS Ltd, Whitefriars, Lewins Mead, Bristol, England

[Pn85] A.Pnueli : In transition from Global to Modular Temporal Reasoning about Programs, in: Logics and Models of Concurrent Systems, edt. K.R.Apt, Springer Verlag, 1985, 123-144

[Pn86] A.Pnueli, Applications of Temporal Logic to the Specification and Verification of Reactive Systems: a Survey of Current Trends, in: Current Trends in Concurrency, edts. J.W.de Bakker, W.-P. de Roever, G.Rozenberg, Lecture NOtes in Computer Science 224, Springer Verlag, 1986, 510-584

[Re 84] W.Reisig : Partial Order Semantics versus Interleaving Semantics of CSP-like languages and its Impact on Fairness, Lecture Notes in Computer Science 172, Springer Verlag, 1984, 403-413

[Wo82] S.P.Wolper : Specification and Synthesis of Communicating Processes using an extended Temporal Logic, POPL 82, 1982, 20-33

[Wo86] P.Wolper : Expressing INteresting Properties of Programs in Propositional Temporal Logic, 13th POPL, 1986, 184-193

ABADI & LAMPORT and STARK: towards a proof theory for stuttering, dense domains and refinement mappings
(Extended Abstract)

Eduard Diepstraten*, Ruurd Kuiper†
Eindhoven University of Technology
P.O. Box 513
5600 MB Eindhoven, The Netherlands

Abstract

Crucial in proving refinement between specifications (of concurrent programs) is the role of ghost variables. On one hand they enhance expressivity. On the other hand they introduce stuttering and, in the case of refinement mappings, lead to the non-existence of such mappings.

Semantically, the these problems are solved satisfactorily in the work of Abadi & Lamport [AL88]. Syntactically, however, their solutions have no obvious prooftheoretic counterpart. By formulating Abadi & Lamport's concepts within Stark's formalism for dense Linear Time Temporal Logic [Sta88] a step in this direction is made.

Keywords: Temporal logic, ghost variables, stuttering, refinement mappings, simulation relations, history and prophecy variables.

Contents

1 Desired abstraction level of descriptions
- 1.1 Behaviour
- 1.2 Satisfaction and refinement

2 Models
- 2.1 Sequences
- 2.2 Histories

3 Description languages
- 3.1 $\mathcal{L}(\mathcal{U})$ as a sequence logic
- 3.2 $\mathcal{L}(\mathcal{U})$ as a history logic

4 About expressivity
- 4.1 Models for the enhanced logics

---

*Supported by the Netherlands Organisation for Scientific Research (NWO) under grant NF 62-519: Refinement and Education in Concurrent Systems (REX). E-mail address: wsined@win.tue.nl .

†Supported partially by ESPRIT project no. 3096 "SPEC: Formal Methods and Tools for the Development of Distributed and Real Time Systems". E-mail address: wsinruur@win.tue.nl .

4.2 Problems in the enhanced logics
4.3 Can we still express refinement in a simple way?

5 Problems at the proof system level
5.1 Proving refinement via construction
5.2 Splitting safety and liveness
5.3 Stuttering problems again

6 Stronger proof rules

A Safety specifications
A.1 Relation between these approaches
A.2 Stark-specifications

B Counterexamples from [AL88]
B.1 Lack of historical information
B.2 Nondeterministic choices made too late
B.3 Lack of stutter steps

C AL-specifications in $\mathcal{L}_G(\mathcal{U},')$

D Proof rules of Abadi & Lamport
D.1 Refinement mappings
D.2 Addition of auxiliary (i.e. ghost) variables

Introduction

The new element in this paper is formulation of Lamport's Transition Axiom Method [Lam89] in a restriction of Stark's formalism for dense LTL. In this context two approaches are discussed: one based on Manna & Pnueli's discrete linear time temporal logic (LTL) [MP82], the other on dense LTL as developed in Stark's work on refinement [Sta88] and the work of Barringer et al. on fully abstract models for LTL [BKP86]. Technically speaking, we trace the causes of stuttering in mainly the discrete framework, more specifically the use of ghost variables to enhance the expressive power of these logics.

A rigorous framework is developed to describe various approaches to the so-called "stuttering problem". This problem is the following one:

1. The use of ghost variables in a specification enforces the existence of stutter steps (steps which leave the observable component of the state invariant).

2. An implementation (specification) that intuitively satisfies this specification may enforce less stuttering (stutter steps).

3. With obvious notions of satisfaction and refinement such an implementation will not formally satisfy the specification (because of lack of a sufficient amount of stutter steps).

4. In the context of refinement, the stuttering problem is: find a semantics and proof theory in which the above intuitive implementation indeed refines the original specification.

Upon closer analysis a second problem arises, due to the usage of so-called refinement mappings to link the values of observable and ghost variables at different levels. Namely, if at a lower level less information is present in the state than at the higher level, such mappings don't exist and neither do relations between these two levels.

Historically, the latter is solved by introducing extra ghost variables in the implementation: so called history variables (recording the history of a computation) and prophecy variables (determinizing future nondeterminism in a computation).

At the semantic level, the stuttering problem in discrete LTL is solved level by adding artificially extra stutter steps in the implementation. However, this seems to have no obvious syntactic counterpart. A more elegant solution is to use dense LTL instead. This reduces the semantical problems to so-called initial stuttering only, and even that problem can be solved, namely by adding an extra primitive predicate to the logic.

Unfortunately, this solution at the semantic level does not take away the need for prophecy variables to deal with stuttering at the proof system level. Therefore we conclude our paper with the formulation of Abadi & Lamport's proof rules for a concrete specification language, namely a dense linear time temporal logic that is developed from Stark's.

The paper is organized as follows, in two parts. The first topic is, with the benefit of hindsight, to evaluate and compare the approaches of Abadi & Lamport and of Stark. In Section 1 the scene is set by arguing the desired level of abstractness of descriptions. Section 2 contains corresponding models, and Section 3 languages to describe these models. Sections 4 and 5 concern the heart of the matter: the problem of stuttering, and an assessment of various solutions.

The second topic looks ahead rather than back. In Section 6 we attempt to evaluate consequences of placing the comprehensive approach to auxiliary variables presented in [AL88] in the concrete setting of a dense time temporal logic specification language.

1 Desired abstraction level of descriptions

Formalisms to describe the concrete behaviour of systems always abstract away some detail. In most cases, the abstraction level depends partly on a reasoned choice of which features of systems are important to reason about and partly on what can be described elegantly by available formalisms.

The aim of this section is to determine what features should be described when focussing on refinement of concurrent systems; we defend our choice by giving an intuition that is inspired by Abadi & Lamport, Barringer, Kuiper & Pnueli, and Stark, the designers of the formalisms discussed in [AL88,BKP86,Lam89,Sta88].

We define a basic model of behaviour that is based on this intuition, and a notion of refinement in terms of this model. Whether there are formalisms available that can describe elegantly the properties that are important to us is a question that is dealt with in Sections 2, 3 and 4.

1.1 Behaviour

The aspect of systems that we want to model and that we define by specifications is their *observable* behaviour. To define this notion we answer the following three questions:

- What do we observe when we take a momentary look at (a snapshot of) a system, i.e. what is visible at one point in time during one execution of a system?
- What do we observe when we watch a system continuously, i.e. what is visible in terms of observations throughout a whole execution?
- What is the behaviour of a system, i.e. what should be known about all possible executions?

The answer to the first question is straightforward. What can be observed momentarily is the *state* of the system; more precisely the values of an a priori chosen set of observable *variables.*

At first sight, the second question isn't very difficult to answer either, when one thinks of a watcher as someone who does observations continually. One assumes that this watcher is attentive enough, in that he notices all state changes during the execution.

The use of *state sequences* as a model of executions is based on this intuition. But what to think of observers that are too attentive, in that they do observations when nothing has changed yet, or at least no *observable* has changed? Their observations correspond to *stuttering sequences*, i.e. sequences that contain repeated states.

Lamport's methods [Lam85,Lam89,AL88] use state sequences as model of executions; his intuition with respect to stuttering is reflected by the following quotations (comments are put in parentheses):

> We use an abstract logic instead of reasoning directly about the underlying model (namely sequences of states) because the logic does not let us talk about irrelevant properties of the model (especially "stuttering"). [Lam83b]
>
> (...) the number of steps in a Pascal implementation is not a meaningful concept when one gives an abstract, high level specification (...). [Lam83b]
>
> Temporal logics should allow "stuttering" actions, so an atomic operation is represented by a finite sequences of actions, only the last one having any effect. [Lam85, p. 77]
>
> It is the inability to distinguish stuttering that makes it easy to talk about a lower-level program implementing a higher-level one. [Lam85, p. 103]

From the above we conclude that Lamport does not want to specify stutter steps, though they are visible within the model he uses.

Others use dense time models, in which an execution is modeled by a state-valued function of the set of non-negative reals. Using dense time is based on the intuition that state changes happen only now and then, so that in between two consecutive changes there are uncountable moments at which *nothing* happens. Consequently, it is impossible to count or talk about stutter steps.

> The reason for making these nonstandard definitions (namely of a model based on dense time) is to obtain a temporal logic whose sentences are incapable of distinguishing between (executions that are equal modulo) occurrences of "null events", in which no changes are made to the values of variables. [Sta88]

> At the qualitative level that we want to analyze concurrent programs, the following two program segments should be considered equivalent:
>
> P_1 :: $x := 1$; $x := x$; $x := 2$, and
> P_2 :: $x := 1$; $x := x$; $x := x$; $x := 2$ [BKP86].

According to our intuition, consecutive identical observations during one execution should be identified; only changes are observable, and not the lengths of periods in which the values of the observables are constant. Therefore, we choose to define a model in which there is no stuttering: a record is a sequence in which consecutive observations are *different*.

Finally, we define the behaviour of a system as the set of all its possible executions. A system can have more than one execution due to non-determinism of both its environment and the system itself. We conclude with the following formalization:

Definition 1.

state: a mapping $s \in \mathrm{Obs} \to \mathrm{Val}$ *giving values in* Val *to the observable variables* (Obs)*;*

record: a sequence $\sigma = s_0, s_1, \ldots$ *of states such that for all* $i \geq 0$, $s_i \neq s_{i+1}$*;*

behaviour: a set of records. □

1.2 Satisfaction and refinement

As was indicated above, specifications define an observable behaviour. When does a system satisfy a specification?

The intuitive idea behind satisfaction is, that an implementation may choose between the possibilities allowed by a specification. We do not want to force something like a minimum amount of non-determinism (which makes sense, for example, when specifying a random number generator). Therefore, we define satisfaction to hold if all executions of the system are allowed by the specification. This explains the use of inclusion in Definition 3.

Definition 2. *For a system* P, $[\![P]\!]$ *denotes the set of records corresponding to the executions that can be performed by* P*. For a specification* S, $[\![S]\!]$ *denotes the set of records allowed by* S*.* □

Please note that behaviour can be viewed as generated by an existing system, but can equally well be viewed as desired of a yet to be constructed one.

Definition 3. *A system P* **satisfies** *a specification S (denoted by P* **sat** *S) if $[\![P]\!] \subseteq [\![S]\!]$.* □

Finally, we define the notion of refinement between two specifications.

The same intuition as for satisfaction between a system and a specification underlies the notion for refinement between two specifications: some specification non-determinism may be resolved. In the model this is again reflected by set inclusion between the behaviours defined by the specifications.

Definition 4. *Specification S_1* **refines** *specification S_2 (denoted by $S_1 \sqsubseteq S_2$) if $[\![S_1]\!] \subseteq [\![S_2]\!]$.* □

2 Models

In the preceding section, we chose records as the most intuitive model of executions of programs. Unfortunately, for the record model no description language is readily available. However, for two other, closely related, models languages *do* exist.

Firstly, we discuss a model based upon infinite sequences of states. Sequences can be viewed as functions from a discrete domain, usually the natural numbers. Secondly, we present a model based on histories. Histories are (in this paper) functions from a dense domain, in our case the set of non-negative reals.

Both sequences and histories provide a way to encode the more intuitive records. However, the presence of more structure makes it possible to express *more* properties than can be expressed by records. As we argued that a record describes all relevant properties of the behaviour, we do not want specifications that describe these extra properties. We discuss and compare several attempts at solving this problem.

2.1 Sequences

If we compare the properties of sequences with those of records, we observe that a sequence can contain successive occurrences of the *same* state, and is always infinite. The first phenomenon is called *stuttering.* This problem was first observed by Lamport in [Lam83a].

Definition 5. *A V-state sequence is an infinite sequence $\sigma = s_0, s_1, \ldots$ where the s_i are V-states. The set of V-state sequences is denoted by $\Sigma(V)$.* □

Definition 6. *We denote the* **sequence-semantics** *of a specification S by $[\![S]\!]^s$.* □

To obtain the record that is represented by a sequence, a collapse-operator is used that removes all stuttering (cf. [AL88]):

Definition 7 (collapse). *Let $\sigma \in \Sigma(V)$ be a sequence, $\sigma = s_0, s_1, \ldots$. Then $\natural\sigma$ is the* **record** *$s'_0, s'_1, \ldots$ (i.e. $s_i \neq s_{i+1}$ for all i!) such that there exists an increasing sequence of natural numbers $n_0, n_1, \ldots$ such that*

$$(\forall i, j : 0 \leq i \wedge n_i \leq j < n_{i+1} : s_j = s'_i)$$

If Σ is a set of sequences, then $\natural\Sigma = \{\natural\sigma \mid \sigma \in \Sigma\}$. □

Definition 8 (equivalence modulo stuttering). *Let $\sigma, \tau \in \Sigma(V)$ be sequences. Then*

$$\sigma \simeq \tau \stackrel{\text{def}}{=} \natural\sigma = \natural\tau \;. \;\square$$

$\sigma \simeq \tau$ expresses that σ and τ correspond to the same record.

In Section 1, refinement was defined as $S_1 \sqsubseteq S_2 \stackrel{\text{def}}{=} [\![S_1]\!] \subseteq [\![S_2]\!]$. The definition of refinement in the sequence framework should correspond to the intuitive notion; thus, be such that $S_1 \sqsubseteq_s S_2 \iff \natural[\![S_1]\!]^s \subseteq \natural[\![S_2]\!]^s$. This can be achieved by introducing a closure Γ (cf. [AL88]):

Definition 9. *Let Σ be a set of sequences. Then $\Gamma(\Sigma) = \bigcup_{\sigma\in\Sigma}\{\tau \mid \sigma \simeq \tau\}$.* □

Definition 10. $S_1 \sqsubseteq_s S_2 \stackrel{\text{def}}{=} [\![S_1]\!]^s \subseteq \Gamma([\![S_2]\!]^s)$. □

The effect of the introduction of Γ in these definitions is that all possible stutter-variants are added to the right hand side (that is enough, because of the asymmetry of "$\subseteq$").

2.2 Histories

Histories are mappings into states; the difference with sequences is that the domain is *dense* instead of discrete. To rule out the possibility of infinitely many changes in finite time, we demand a finite variability constraint (cf. [BKP86]).

Definition 11 (history). *A V-history is a function x from $\mathcal{R}^+$, the set of non-negative reals, to V-states such that for all $0 \leq t$, there exists an $\epsilon > 0$ such that $x(t') = x(t)$, for all $t' \in \mathcal{R}^+$ such that $t - \epsilon < t' < t$, and $x(t'') = x(t + \epsilon)$ for all $t < t'' < t + \epsilon$.* □

Definition 12. *The set of all V-histories is denoted by $\mathcal{H}(V)$.* □

Definition 13. *We denote the* history-semantics *of a specification S by $[\![S]\!]^h$.* □

One can prove (cf. [Sta88]) that a history x determines a (maybe infinite) sequence of time-instants $\tau = t_0, t_1, \ldots$ such that:

- $t_0 = 0$.
- For all $i \geq 0$ and all t such that $t_i < t < t_{i+1}$, $x(t) = x(t_{i+1})$: the state $x(t)$ is constant in all left open intervals $(t_i, t_{i+1}]$.
- For all $i > 0$, $x(t_i) \neq x(t_{i+1})$. We say that the state changes at moment t_i.
- If τ is a finite sequence of length $N + 1$, then for all $t > t_N$, $x(t) = x(t_N)$.

- If τ is an infinite sequence, then $\lim_{i\to\infty} t_i = \infty$.

Remark. From the existence of this sequence follows the finite variability constraint of [BKP86]. □

Definition 14. *Let h be a history, and let $\tau = t_0, t_1, \ldots$ be the sequence of time-instants satisfying the above mentioned conditions. Then $\natural h = u_0, u_1, \ldots$, the record that corresponds to h, is defined by:*

$$u_n = h(t_n) \quad , \text{if } h(t_0) \neq h(t_1);$$
$$u_n = h(t_{n+1}) \quad , \text{if } h(t_0) = h(t_1). \ \square$$

When we compare histories with sequences, we see two differences. Firstly, between any two state changes in a history there are infinitely many moments at which the state does *not* change; therefore it is not possible to *count* stuttering steps like in the sequence case. But still we can have "timing" variants: histories that record the same states, but do not always have state changes at the same points in time.

Like in the case of sequences, we define an equivalence relation that holds between histories that represent the same record, and a closure operator to define refinement.

Definition 15. *Let x and y be V-histories. Then $x \simeq y \stackrel{\text{def}}{=} \natural x = \natural y$.* □

Definition 16. *Let H be a set of histories. Then $\mathrm{T}(H) = \bigcup_{h\in H}\{h' \mid h \simeq h'\}$.* □

Definition 17. $S_1 \sqsubseteq_h S_2 \stackrel{\text{def}}{=} [\![S_1]\!]^h \subseteq \mathrm{T}([\![S_2]\!]^h)$. □

3 Description languages

In this section temporal logics are given for the models introduced in the preceding section. A very convenient property of these logics is that they don't contain specifications that distinguish between different representations of the same record. That is, the discrete linear time temporal logic introduced for sequences is insensitive to stuttering, and the history logic introduced for histories is insensitive to both stuttering and timing variants.

Common features

A term is built from variables and function symbols. A formula is built from terms, relation symbols, boolean connectives, quantification and temporal operators. We assume a set G of *freeze* variables that is disjunct from V, the set of observable (program) variables. Boolean connectives are $\wedge$, $\vee$ and $\neg$, as usual. A formula is called *closed* if all occurring freeze variables are bound by a quantifier.

We assume a fixed interpretation for function and relation symbols, and a domain Val for the values of freeze and observable variables.

The logics that are discussed below have the same syntax ($\mathcal{L}(\mathcal{U})$ denotes the language generated by this syntax); of course, the interpretation of a formula in the history logic is different from its interpretation in the history logic.

Syntax of $\mathcal{L}(\mathcal{U})$

Terms:

For observable or freeze variables v, v is a term.
For all function symbols f, and terms $t_1, \ldots, t_n$, $f(t_1, \ldots, t_n)$ is a term.

Formulae

For all relation symbols R, and terms $t_1, \ldots, t_n$, $R(t_1, \ldots, t_n)$ is a formula.
For formula φ and *freeze* variable x, $\exists x.\varphi$ and $\forall x.\varphi$ are formulae. For formulae φ and ψ, $\neg\varphi$, $\varphi \vee \psi$ and $\varphi\, \mathcal{U}\, \psi$ are formulae.

3.1 $\mathcal{L}(\mathcal{U})$ as a sequence logic

A sequence model is a tuple $\langle \alpha, \sigma \rangle$, where $\alpha \in G \to \text{Val}$ is an assignment to freeze variables and σ is a V-state sequence. For natural number n and sequence $\sigma = (s_i)_{0 \leq i}$, $\sigma^{(n)}$ is the sequence $(s_i)_{n \leq i}$.

Semantics of terms:

For all freeze variables g, $g(\langle \alpha, \sigma \rangle) = \alpha(g)$.
For all observable variables l, $l(\langle \alpha, \sigma \rangle) = s_0(l)$.
For all function symbols f with interpretation $\bar{f}$, $f(t_1, \ldots, t_n)(\langle \alpha, \sigma \rangle) = \bar{f}(t_1(\langle \alpha, \sigma \rangle), \ldots, t_n(\langle \alpha, \sigma \rangle))$.

Semantics of formulae:

$\langle \alpha, \sigma \rangle \models R(t_1, \ldots, t_n)$ if $\bar{R}$ is the interpretation of R and $\bar{R}(t_1(\langle \alpha, \sigma \rangle), \ldots, t_n(\langle \alpha, \sigma \rangle))$ holds;
$\langle \alpha, \sigma \rangle \models \neg\varphi$ if $\langle \alpha, \sigma \rangle \not\models \varphi$;
$\langle \alpha, \sigma \rangle \models \varphi \vee \psi$ if $\langle \alpha, \sigma \rangle \models \varphi$ or $\langle \alpha, \sigma \rangle \models \psi$;
$\langle \alpha, \sigma \rangle \models \exists x.\varphi$ if there exists an assignment α' differing from α only in the value assigned to x such that $\langle \alpha', \sigma \rangle \models \varphi$;
$\langle \alpha, \sigma \rangle \models \varphi\, \mathcal{U}\, \psi$ if there exists an $n \geq 0$ such that $\langle \alpha, \sigma^{(n)} \rangle \models \psi$, and for all i in $\{0, 1, \ldots, n-1\}$, $\langle \alpha, \sigma^{(i)} \rangle \models \varphi$.

Remark. If φ is closed, then the validity of φ does not depend on the values assigned to freeze variables: if there exists a assignment α such that $\langle \alpha, \sigma \rangle \models \varphi$, then $\langle \beta, \sigma \rangle \models \varphi$ holds for any β. Therefore, we omit α, and write $\sigma \models \varphi$. □

Definition 18. *If V is the set of observable variables and φ is a closed formula, then $[\![\varphi]\!]^s$, the sequence-semantics of φ is defined by:*

$$[\![\varphi]\!]^s = \{\sigma \in \Sigma(V) \mid \sigma \models \varphi\} \,. \square$$

In Section 2.1 we argued that in a sequence semantics, refinement does not correspond with inclusion: it corresponds with a more complicated relation involving the closure operator Γ. The above logic, however, has the comfortable property that it cannot distinguish between stutter equivalent sequences (which represent the same record). Therefore, the semantics of a specification is closed under stuttering, and we do not need to introduce strange operators like $\natural$ (collapse) and Γ (stutter-closure).

Proposition 1. *For any specification φ in the language $\mathcal{L}(\mathcal{U})$, $[\![\varphi]\!]^s = \Gamma([\![\varphi]\!]^s)$.*

Proof. By induction on the structure of formulae. The only interesting case is the until-operator. Suppose that $\sigma \simeq \tau$ and that $\sigma \models \varphi\, \mathcal{U}\, \psi$. By the semantics of $\mathcal{U}$, there exist a valuation α and $n \geq 0$ such that $\langle \alpha, \sigma^{(n)} \rangle \models \psi$ and for all $i < n$, $\langle \alpha, \sigma^{(i)} \rangle \models \varphi$. By the induction hypothesis, and the definition of $\simeq$ there exists an $m \geq 0$ such that $\langle \alpha, \tau^{(m)} \rangle \models \psi$ and for all $i < m$, $\langle \alpha, \tau^{(i)} \rangle \models \varphi$. Hence, $\langle \alpha, \tau \rangle \models \varphi\, \mathcal{U}\, \psi$. □

Corollary 2. *For any $\varphi \in \mathcal{L}(\mathcal{U})$, $\varphi_1 \sqsubseteq_s \varphi_2 \iff [\![\varphi_1]\!]^s \subseteq [\![\varphi_2]\!]^s$.*

3.2 $\mathcal{L}(\mathcal{U})$ as a history logic

A history model is a tuple $\langle \alpha, h \rangle$, where $\alpha \in G \to \mathrm{Val}$ is an assignment to freeze variables and h is a V-history. For $\tau \in \mathcal{R}^+$ and history h, $h^{(\tau)}$ is the history $\lambda t.h(t + \tau)$.

Semantics of terms:

For all freeze variables g, $g(\langle \alpha, h \rangle) = \alpha(g)$.
For all observable variables l, $l(\langle \alpha, h \rangle) = h(0)(l)$.
For all function symbols f with interpretation $\bar{f}$, $f(t_1, \ldots, t_n)(\langle \alpha, h \rangle) = \bar{f}(t_1(\langle \alpha, h \rangle), \ldots, t_n(\langle \alpha, h \rangle))$.

Formulae:

$\langle \alpha, h \rangle \models R(t_1, \ldots, t_n)$ if $\bar{R}$ is the interpretation of R and $\bar{R}(t_1(\langle \alpha, h \rangle), \ldots, t_n(\langle \alpha, h \rangle))$ holds;
$\langle \alpha, h \rangle \models \neg\varphi$ if $\langle \alpha, h \rangle \not\models \varphi$;
$\langle \alpha, h \rangle \models \varphi \vee \psi$ if $\langle \alpha, h \rangle \models \varphi$ or $\langle \alpha, h \rangle \models \psi$;

$\langle \alpha, h \rangle \models \exists x.\varphi$ if there exists an assignment α' differing from α only in the value assigned to x such that $\langle \alpha', h \rangle \models \varphi$;

$\langle \alpha, h \rangle \models \varphi \,\mathcal{U}\, \psi$ if there exists an $t \in \mathcal{R}^+$ such that $\langle \alpha, h^{(t)} \rangle \models \psi$, and for all $\tau \in [0, t)$, $\langle \alpha, h^{(\tau)} \rangle \models \varphi$.

Like above, the truth of a closed formula does not depend on α; thus, we write $h \models \varphi$ instead of $\langle \alpha, h \rangle \models \varphi$.

Definition 19. *If V is the set of observable variables and φ is a closed formula, then $[\![\varphi]\!]^h$, the history-semantics of φ is defined by:*

$$[\![\varphi]\!]^h = \{h \in \mathcal{H}(V) \mid h \models \varphi\} \; . \; \square$$

Like the sequence logic defined above, this logic cannot distinguish between representations of the same record:

Proposition 3. *For any specification φ in the language $\mathcal{L}(\mathcal{U})$, $[\![\varphi]\!]^s = \Gamma([\![\varphi]\!]^s)$.*

Corollary 4. *For any $\varphi \in \mathcal{L}(\mathcal{U})$, $\varphi_1 \sqsubseteq_h \varphi_2 \iff [\![\varphi_1]\!]^h \subseteq [\![\varphi_2]\!]^h$.*

Remark. Apart from the operators defined above, we can also define the following derived operators (in both languages):

$$\varphi \wedge \psi \equiv \neg(\neg\varphi \vee \neg\psi)$$
$$\varphi \Rightarrow \psi \equiv \neg\varphi \vee \psi$$
$$\Diamond\varphi \equiv \text{true}\,\mathcal{U}\,\varphi$$
$$\Box\varphi \equiv \neg\Diamond\neg\varphi$$

$\square$

Consider again Corollaries 2 and 4. Due to the fact that refinement corresponds to inclusion, we can formulate the refinement relation within the logic, in a very simple way: $\varphi_1 \sqsubseteq \varphi_2$ if and only if $\varphi_1 \Rightarrow \varphi_2$. The significance of this fact is the following: if we have a complete proof system for our logic, then we can always prove refinement.

4 About expressivity

Unfortunately, $\mathcal{L}(\mathcal{U})$ is not expressive enough. There are relevant properties, especially safety properties (see for a definition [AS85]) that cannot be specified or can only be specified in a difficult way. And we want to be able to express safety properties because of their specific proof theory (that differs from the proof theory for liveness properties). This is discussed further in Section 5 and Appendix A.

Below, we discuss enhancements in order to increase the expressive power. Our argument here is twofold: on the one hand, these extensions are convenient, as they enable one to specify any possible safety property using transition systems. On the other hand, they have the disadvantage that they enable one to express properties one *doesn't* want to specify, in the sense that some formulae in the enhanced logics distinguish between (sequence or history) representatives of the same record.

Specification of allowed transitions

Traditionally, safety properties are specified by means of transition systems. A transition system is a specification that specifies (a) initial states and (b) allowed state transitions. To express allowed state transitions, we need to refer to two consecutive states.

For the sequence case this can be achieved by introducing a next-state operator $\bigcirc$ (as defined, for example, in [MP82]), or Lamport's **allowed changes**-operator as defined in [Lam83a]. However, the semantics of the latter appears to be rather complicated. The following clause extends the sequence logic $\mathcal{L}(\mathcal{U})$ to $\mathcal{L}(\mathcal{U},\bigcirc)$:

> If v is an observable variable, then $\bigcirc v$ is a term; $\bigcirc v(\langle\alpha,\sigma\rangle) = s_1(v)$. If φ is a formula, then $\bigcirc\varphi$ is a formula. Semantics: $\langle\alpha,\sigma\rangle \models \bigcirc\varphi$ if $\langle\alpha,\sigma^{(1)}\rangle \models \varphi$.

For histories, we introduce an operator that refers to what can be viewed intuitively as the state "immediately after" the present state. This is a compilation of Stark's idea to distinguish between *before* and *after* states. The history logic $\mathcal{L}(\mathcal{U})$ is extended to $\mathcal{L}(\mathcal{U},')$ with:

> If v is an observable variable, then v' is a term; $v'(\langle\alpha,h\rangle) = \lim_{t\downarrow 0} h(t)$.

Definition and existence of the limit are obvious because of the finite variability requirement: by Definition 11 h is constant for a nonnull period of time after any moment t. Note that the values of v and v' differ if and only if v changes at the beginning of h.

Using ghost variables

One would expect that a specification of a system with V as the set of observable variables is an assertion about these variables only. However, practice turns out to be different. Some safety properties cannot even be specified in $\mathcal{L}(\mathcal{U},\bigcirc)$ or $\mathcal{L}(\mathcal{U},')$. One solution would be to add extra operators to these logics. Objections are, that doing so may make the logic harder to understand. Also, the need of expressing new properties might call for new operators again and again.

The solution that we are interested in is to use ghost variables, such as location variables and counters. The intuition is that we describe a V-behaviour indirectly, namely by describing a $(V \cup A)$-behaviour, where A is a set of ghost variables, disjunct from both V and G, the set of freeze variables. The V-behaviour defined by such a specification is the V-part of the defined $(V \cup A)$-behaviour. Intuitively, one has to project away the A-part.

Example. Suppose that we want to specify the following behaviour: we have a variable x that is initially zero, and that is incremented by one continually until it has reached a value that is higher than all previous values; at that moment it is reset to zero, after which the process of incrementing restarts. So the consecutive values of x are $0, 1, 0, 1, 2, 0, 1, 2, 3, 0, \ldots$.

We can specify this behaviour as follows. Let y be a ghost variable. The idea is to record in y the highest value of x in the past.

In the sequence logic, this is characterized by the formula

$$x=0 \wedge y=0 \wedge \Box((x > y \Rightarrow \bigcirc x=0 \wedge \bigcirc y=x) \;\wedge\; (x \leq y \Rightarrow \bigcirc x=x+1 \wedge \bigcirc y=y))$$

The equivalent in the history logic is:

$$x=0 \wedge y=0 \wedge$$
$$\Box((x=x' \wedge y=y') \;\vee\; ((x > y \Rightarrow x'=0 \wedge y'=x) \;\wedge\; (x \leq y \Rightarrow x'=x+1 \wedge y'=y)))$$

The x-parts of the $\{x, y\}$-behaviours that are described by these formulae correspond to the behaviour that we were trying to specify. $\Box$

Ghost variables turn out to be a powerful mechanism. Abadi & Lamport have proved that *every* safety property is the observable semantics of some state machine [AL88, Proposition 3]; thus, transition systems and ghost variables are sufficient to define safety properties.

$\mathcal{L}_G(\mathcal{U}, \bigcirc)$ and $\mathcal{L}_G(\mathcal{U}, ')$ denote the enhancements with ghost variables of $\mathcal{L}(\mathcal{U}, \bigcirc)$ and $\mathcal{L}(\mathcal{U}, ')$, respectively.

4.1 Models for the enhanced logics

The semantics of the next-operators was defined in terms of the models of Section 2. To define the semantics of a specification that contains ghost variables we have to use a slightly different model.

The semantics of a specification is now not a set of V-state sequences (or histories), but of $(V \cup A)$-state sequences (or histories). Of course, the intuitive semantics is still a set of V-records. Two questions arise: given a sequence (or history) semantics, what is the corresponding record semantics, and how should refinement be defined?

Sequences

To obtain records from $(V \cup A)$-state sequences, we first project away the part of the states that describes the values of ghost variables; after that the collapse operator $\natural$ is used to remove stuttering. Note that this order is obligatory, as projection may cause extra stuttering; see also Section 4.2.

Definition 20 (projection). *Let s be a $(V \cup A)$-state. $\Pi_V(s)$ is the unique V-state that assigns to all elements v of V the value $s(v)$. For $\sigma = (s_i)_{0 \leq i} \in \Sigma(V \cup A)$, $\Pi_V(\sigma) = (\Pi_V(s_i))_{0 \leq i}$.* $\Box$

Like in Section 2.1, refinement are defined in correspondence to the intuitive notion of Section 1.

Definition 21. $S_1 \sqsubseteq_s S_2 \stackrel{\text{def}}{=} \Pi_V([\![S_1]\!]^s) \subseteq \Gamma(\Pi_V([\![S]\!]^s))$. □

Histories

To obtain a V-history from a $(V \cup A)$-history, we extend projection to histories. On the resulting V-history we apply the construction of Section 2 to obtain the corresponding V-record.

Definition 22. *Let h be a $(V \cup A)$-history. Then $\Pi_V(h)$, the projection of h on V is the unique V-history such that, for all $t \in \mathcal{R}^+$ and all $v \in V$, $\Pi_V(h)(t)(v) = h(t)(v)$.* □

Definition 23. $S_1 \sqsubseteq_h S_2 \stackrel{\text{def}}{=} \Pi_V([\![S_1]\!]^h) \subseteq \mathcal{T}(\Pi_V([\![S_2]\!]^h))$. □

4.2 Problems in the enhanced logics

In Section 3 we argued that refinement corresponds to inclusion if our specification language cannot distinguish between representations of the same record.

The additions proposed in this section, however, *can* make this distinction. Examples are given below. As a consequence, refinement corresponds to a more difficult relation; efforts are made to keep those as simple as possible.

Problems caused by $\bigcirc$

The presence of $\bigcirc$ makes it possible to count stuttering steps. For example, let $\varphi \equiv x=2 \wedge \bigcirc \Box(x=3)$, and let $\psi \equiv x=2 \wedge \bigcirc(x=2) \wedge \bigcirc \bigcirc \Box(x=3)$. Though both formulae specify the same behaviour, there is no sequence that is allowed by both. There are unique $\{x\}$-state sequences σ and τ such that $\sigma \models \varphi$ and $\tau \models \psi$. Though $\sigma \simeq \tau$, neither $\sigma \models \psi$ nor $\tau \models \varphi$.

Problems caused by $'$

The possibility to refer to the after-value of variables allows one to distinguish between histories that represent the same record: we can force a state change at time 0.

Example. Let $\varphi \equiv x \neq x'$. Let h be a $\{x\}$-history such that $h \models \varphi$. Define h' as h preceded by a short interval in which nothing happens: for all $0 \leq t < 1$, $h'(t) = h(0)$, and for all $t \geq 1$, $h'(t) = h(t-1)$. Then h and h' represent the same record, though $h' \not\models \varphi$. □

Problems caused by ghost variables

Here a problem arises because projection can cause extra stuttering: the projection of two different $(V \cup A)$-states on V may be equal. If a sequence has two consecutive states that differ only in the values assigned to ghost variables, then the projection of that sequence on the observable part contains stuttering. A similar observation holds for histories: projection can reduce the number of state changes. In particular, the projection of a initially non-stuttering history can be initially stuttering.

As a consequence, the projection of a set of sequences (or histories) that is closed with respect to $\simeq$ may *not* be closed. Therefore, refinement doesn't correspond to inclusion after projection (but we would like things to be that simple).

It should be noticed that this fact is completely independent of the properties of $\bigcirc$ and $'$; this is made clear in the following examples:

Example. Let $\varphi \equiv (x=0 \wedge y=0)\ \mathcal{U}\ ((x=0 \wedge y=1)\ \mathcal{U}\ \Box(x=1 \wedge y=1))$, where y is a ghost variable. Then $\Pi_x([\![\varphi]\!]^s)$ does not contain the x-state sequence $\langle 0, 1, 1, \ldots \rangle$, though this sequence corresponds exactly to what we want to specify. $\Box$

Example. We can use the same φ as an example for history specifications: take $\varphi \equiv (x=0 \wedge y= 0)\ \mathcal{U}\ ((x=0 \wedge y=1)\ \mathcal{U}\ \Box(x=1 \wedge y=1))$, where y is a ghost variable. Then $\Pi_x([\![\varphi]\!]^h)$ does not contain the x-state history h, defined by

$$h(0)(x) = 0$$
$$h(t)(x) = 1 \quad \text{for all } t > 0$$

though it corresponds exactly to what we want to specify. $\Box$

4.3 Can we still express refinement in a simple way?

Our aim is to be able to derive $S_1 \sqsubseteq S_2$ whenever that is valid. For that sake, it is convenient if we can express refinement *within* the logic. Because of the addition of $\bigcirc$, $'$ and ghost variables, we cannot express refinement as an implication. For the moment, we cannot express it at all, because we can neither express projection, nor stutter-closure!

So the question arises what can be done about this. A solution is to add constructs to the logic that correspond to projection and closure. But is it possible to do that in an acceptable, simple way?

Fortunately, there exists a good solution for projection: existential quantification over ghost variables (as introduced in [BKP86]). Intuitively, this allows one to choose the values of ghost variables throughout an execution freely. As an abbreviation, we write $\exists A$, where A is a set of ghost variables, by which quantification over all elements of A is meant. Semantics:

$\sigma \models \exists A.\varphi$ if there exists a τ such that $\Pi_V(\tau) = \Pi_V(\sigma)$ and $\tau \models \varphi$.

$h \models \exists A.\varphi$ if there exists a h' such that $\Pi_V(h') = \Pi_V(h)$ and $h' \models \varphi$.

So τ and h' differ from σ and h, respectively, only in the values assigned to ghost variables.

Proposition 5. *If* $\exists A.\varphi_1 \Rightarrow \exists A.\varphi_2$, *then* $\varphi_1 \sqsubseteq \varphi_2$. *This holds for both the sequence and the history logic.*

Proof. We only prove the sequence case (the history case is analogous). Suppose $\exists A.\varphi_1 \Rightarrow \exists A.\varphi_2$, i.e. for all $\sigma \in \Sigma(V)$ and all $\alpha : G \to \text{Val}$, $\sigma \models \exists A.\varphi_1 \Rightarrow \exists A.\varphi_2$. We have to prove: $\varphi_1 \sqsubseteq_s \varphi_2$, i.e. $\Pi_V([\![\varphi_1]\!]^s) \subseteq \Gamma(\Pi_V([\![\varphi_2]\!]^s))$.

Let $\sigma \in ([\![\varphi_1]\!]^s)$. Then $\sigma \models \varphi_1$. By the semantics of $\exists A$, this implies $\Pi_V(\sigma) \models \exists A.\varphi_1$, and thus $\Pi_V(\sigma) \models \exists A.\varphi_2$. This proves $\Pi_V([\![\varphi_1]\!]^s) \subseteq \Pi_V([\![\varphi_2]\!]^s)$, which immediately implies the demonstrandum because Γ is a closure (thus $\Sigma \subseteq \Gamma(\Sigma)$, for all sets Σ). □

We still have to solve the stuttering problem. There seems to be no nice way to hide stuttering within the logic.

Reconsider the examples given in Section 4.2. The trouble is caused by specifications that force or disallow a state change at time 0. So, the history logic $\mathcal{L}_G(\mathcal{U},')$ suffers from the fact that it can express too much about the *start* of an execution. Fortunately, this is the only bad thing about $\mathcal{L}_G(\mathcal{U},')$. This is stated more formally below.

Definition 24. *A history h is called* initially stuttering *if there exists a $\delta > 0$ such that for all $\epsilon < \delta$, $h(0) = h(\epsilon)$. IS(V) denotes the set of all initially stuttering V-histories.* □

Definition 25 (the predicate **is**). *To express initial stuttering within $\mathcal{L}(\mathcal{U},')$ we add a primitive predicate* **is**. *Semantics: $h \models$* **is** *iff $h(0) = lim_{t \downarrow 0} h(t)$.* □

Remark. The predicate **is** corresponds to a conjunct of terms $(v = v')$, for all variables. □

Definition 26. *For $h_1, h_2 \in \mathcal{H}(V)$, $h_1 \sim h_2$ if and only if there exists a monotonously increasing bijection $f : \mathcal{R}^+ \to \mathcal{R}^+$ such that $h_2 = h_1 \circ f$.* □

Property 6. *If $h_1 \sim h_2$, then $h_1 \simeq h_2$, and h_1 is initially stuttering if and only if h_2 is.*

Property 7. *If $h_1 \simeq h_2$, and h_1 is initially stuttering if and only if h_2 is, then $h_1 \sim h_2$.*

Theorem 8. *For all $\varphi \in \mathcal{L}(\mathcal{U},')$, and all (not necessarily initially stuttering) histories h_1 and h_2 such that $h_1 \sim h_2$, $h_1 \models \varphi \iff h_2 \models \varphi$.*

Proof. Given in [Die89]. Omitted from this abstract. □

We return to the problem of initial stuttering. What we would like to have, is equivalence instead of implication in Proposition 5. The examples of Section 4.2 show that this equivalence does not hold in general. On the other hand, from Theorem 8 one feels that it holds "almost".

Let, in the following argument, φ_i $(i = 1, 2, 3, 4)$ be specifications of V-behaviours using ghost variables in A_i.

Compare the semantics of the formulae $\varphi_i \sqsubseteq_h \varphi_j$ and $\exists_{A_i}.\varphi_i \Rightarrow \exists_{A_j}.\varphi_j$. The semantics of $\varphi_i \sqsubseteq_h \varphi_j$ is: $\Pi_V([\![\varphi_i]\!]^h) \subseteq \mathcal{T}(\Pi_V([\![\varphi_j]\!]^h))$, and that of $\exists_{A_i}.\varphi_i \Rightarrow \exists_{A_j}.\varphi_j$ is $\Pi_V([\![\varphi_i]\!]^h) \subseteq \mathcal{T}(\Pi_V([\![\varphi_j]\!]^h))$. The only (subtle) difference is the application of closure T in the semantics of the first formula.

For the sake of brevity, we abbreviate $\Pi_V([\![\varphi_i]\!]^h)$ to P_i. Assume $\varphi_1 \sqsubseteq \varphi_j$, i.e. $P_1 \subseteq T(P_j)$; under what conditions does $P_1 \subseteq P_j$ hold $(j = 2, 3, 4)$?

The problems can be illustrated with the following example specifications:

$$\begin{array}{llr}
\varphi_1 & \stackrel{\text{def}}{=} (x = 0)\,\mathcal{U}\,\Box(x = 1); & A_1 = \emptyset; \\
\varphi_2 & \stackrel{\text{def}}{=} \varphi_1 \wedge (x \neq x'); & A_2 = \emptyset; \\
\varphi_3 & \stackrel{\text{def}}{=} \varphi_1 \wedge (x = x'); & A_3 = \emptyset; \\
\varphi_4 & \stackrel{\text{def}}{=} (x = 0 \;\wedge\; a = 0)\,\mathcal{U}\,((x = 0 \;\wedge\; a = 1)\,\mathcal{U}\,(x = 1 \;\wedge\; a = 1)); & A_4 = \{a\}.
\end{array}$$

The equivalence in Proposition 5 does hot hold if:

- there exist histories $h \in P_1 \setminus P_j$ such that h is initially stuttering. Example: take $j = 2$. Two solutions are possible. Firstly, if we require that φ_j is not sensitive to initial stuttering (i.e. does not distinguish between $\simeq$-equivalent histories) then $\exists_{A_j}.\varphi_j$ always allows initially stuttering, and such h do not exist. Secondly, one could require specifications to be of the form $\psi \wedge \mathbf{is}$; by Property 7 and Theorem 8, this is sufficient.

- there exist histories $h \in P_1 \setminus P_j$ such that h is *not* initially stuttering. Example: take $j = 3, 4$. Though φ_3, like φ_2, may be considered as an unnatural specification, φ_4 is completely reasonable. So, the problem is that φ_1 allows initially not stuttering histories. Two observations can be made.

  Firstly, if we require that both φ_i and φ_j are insensitive to initial stuttering, then $P_i \subseteq \mathcal{T}(P_j)$ if and only if $P_i \cap \mathrm{IS}(V) \subseteq P_j \cap \mathrm{IS}(V)$ (by Property 7 and Theorem 8); thus, it is sufficient to check $\exists_{A_i}.\varphi_i \Rightarrow \exists_{A_j}.\varphi_j$ only for initially stuttering histories.

  Secondly, one can require that φ_1 has the form $\varphi \wedge \mathbf{is}$ as well.

We conclude our arguments with the following theorems:

Theorem 9. *For all specifications* φ_1, φ_2,

$$\mathbf{is} \wedge \varphi_1 \sqsubseteq_h \mathbf{is} \wedge \varphi_2 \iff \exists A_1.\mathbf{is} \wedge \varphi_1 \Rightarrow \exists A_2.\mathbf{is} \wedge \varphi_2$$

where A_i *is the set of ghost variables occurring in* φ_i, $i = 1, 2$.

Theorem 10. *For all specifications* φ_1, φ_2 *that are insensitive to initial stuttering,*

$$\varphi_1 \sqsubseteq_h \varphi_2 \iff \mathbf{is} \wedge \exists A_1.\varphi_1 \Rightarrow \mathbf{is} \wedge \exists A_2.\varphi_2$$

where A_i *is the set of ghost variables occurring in* φ_i, $i = 1, 2$.

Proof. Omitted. □

So now we can conclude that in the history logic $\mathcal{L}_G(\mathcal{U},')$ it is possible to express refinement!

5 Problems at the proof system level

Now that we have discussed the notion of refinement, it is time to think about methods to prove refinement. Below we analyze Lamport's refinement mappings, as discussed in [Lam89] and defined formally in [AL88], and Stark's simulation relations [Sta88]. To clarify these special instruments also more general ones are assessed.

For the sake of brevity (and without loss of generality), let $\varphi_1(x, a)$ and $\varphi_2(x, b)$ be specifications of $\{x\}$-behaviours: x is the observable variable; a and b are ghost variables.

A first attempt to prove $\varphi_1(x, a) \sqsubseteq \varphi_2(x, b)$ is to prove implication.[1] If $\varphi_1(x, a) \Rightarrow \varphi_2(x, b)$ is valid, then, given a proof system for the logic, it can be proven. But as argued in Section 4, implication does not generally hold if refinement holds.

A second attempt is to prove

$$\exists a.\varphi_1(x, a) \Rightarrow \exists b.\varphi_2(x, b) \,. \qquad (*)$$

In the preceding section it was shown that, in the sequence interpretation, this is still stronger than refinement (because of stuttering), but at this moment we ignore that.

5.1 Proving refinement via construction

General proof scheme

Proving $\exists a.\varphi_1(x, a) \Rightarrow \exists b.\varphi_2(x, b)$ is equivalent to proving $\varphi_1(x, a) \Rightarrow \exists b.\varphi_2(x, b)$, as $a \notin \mathrm{fv}(\varphi_2(x, b))$. Below, proof methods are discussed that are based upon the following scheme: given that $\varphi_1(x, a)$ holds, is it possible to construct a b such that $\varphi_2(x, b)$ holds?

Proposition 11. *If there exists a mapping f such that $\varphi_1(x, a) \wedge \Box(f(x, a) = b) \Rightarrow \varphi_2(x, b)$, then $\varphi_1(x, a) \sqsubseteq \varphi_2(x, b)$.*

Proposition 12. *If there exists a relation R such that $\varphi_1(x, a) \wedge \Box R(x, a, b) \Rightarrow \varphi_2(x, b)$, and for all values X, A of x and a, respectively, there exists a value B of b such that $R(X, A, B)$ holds, then $\varphi_1(x, a) \sqsubseteq \varphi_2(x, b)$.*

The extra constraint is necessary, because otherwise $R \equiv$ false would do (which would destroy the soundness of the rule).

As mappings are a special case of relations, one would expect that relations offer more possibilities to prove refinement than mappings. The following theorem asert that this is not the case. The intuitive reason for this is that in Proposition 12, it is required that *all* choices for b satisfy $\varphi_2(x, b)$.

[1] In this section, subscripts to $\sqsubseteq$ are omitted when the argument holds for both $\sqsubseteq_s$ and $\sqsubseteq_h$.

Theorem 13. *Mappings and relations are equally strong.*

Proof. Let R be a relation such that $\varphi_1(x,a) \wedge \Box R(x,a,b) \Rightarrow \varphi_2(x,b)$. Define f such, that $R(p,q,f(p,q))$ holds for all p and q. This is possible by the choice axiom and the fact that for all p and q, there exists a r such that $R(p,q,r)$. Then $\varphi_1(x,a) \wedge \Box(f(x,a)=b) \Rightarrow \varphi_2(x,b)$, because $\Box(f(x,a)=b) \Rightarrow \Box R(x,a,b)$.

On the other hand, let f be a mapping: $\varphi_1(x,a) \wedge \Box(f(x,a)=b) \Rightarrow \varphi_2(x,b)$. Define relation R by $R(p,q,r) \equiv f(p,q)=r$. Then R is a relation such that for all values X, A of x and a, respectively there exists a value B of b such that $R(X,A,B)$ holds. $\Box$

Proof of Propositions 11 and 12. Because of Proposition 13, we only need to prove one of these propositions.

Let R be a relation satisfying the conditions stated in Proposition 12. Then $\varphi_1(x,a) \Rightarrow \exists b.\Box R(x,a,b)$. This can be proved as follows. Let $\sigma = s_0, s_1(x,a), \ldots$ be a $\{x,a\}$-sequence such that $\langle\alpha,\sigma\rangle \models \varphi_1(x,a)$ (for all α). Define $\{x,a,b\}$-sequence $\tau = t_0, t_1(x,a), \ldots$ by

$$\begin{aligned} t_i(x) &= s_i(x) \\ t_i(a) &= s_i(a) \\ t_i(b) &= \text{“some } B \text{ such that } R(s_i(x), s_i(a), B) \text{ holds”} \end{aligned}$$

for all $i \geq 0$. Then $\langle\alpha,\tau\rangle \models \varphi_1(x,a) \wedge \Box R(x,a,b)$; thus, by the first condition on R, $\langle\alpha,\tau\rangle \models \varphi_2(x,b)$. Because $\Pi_{\{x,a\}}(\tau) = \sigma$, this implies $\langle\alpha,\sigma\rangle \models \exists b.\varphi_2(x,b)$. By Proposition 5, $\varphi_1(x,a) \sqsubseteq \varphi_2(x,b)$. $\Box$

5.2 Splitting safety and liveness

Both Lamport and Stark make a distinction between safety and liveness properties, and base their proof schemes on this distinctions. The reason for this is that the way safety properties are proved is essentially different from proving liveness properties. We don't discuss this choice, but for the rest of this paper we assume that specifications $\varphi(x,a)$ are Stark-specifications (see Appendix A), that is they consist of a safety part $\mu(x,a)$, conjuncted with an additional term $\lambda(x,a)$ that is intended to describe liveness properties. $\mu(x,a)$ has the form $\gamma(x,a) \wedge \Box\tau(x,a,x',a')$, where γ describes initial states and τ allowed state transitions. See Appendix A for more details. In the discussion below, p, p', q and q' denote values (i.e. elements of Val) of x, x', a and a', respectively.

Lamport's refinement mappings

Definition 27 (refinement mappings). *A* refinement mapping *from $\varphi_1(x,a)$ to $\varphi_2(x,b)$ is a mapping f such that:*

1. $\gamma_1(p,q) \Rightarrow \gamma_2(p,f(p,q))$ *for all p and q;*
2. $\tau_1(p,q,p',q') \Rightarrow \tau_2(p,f(p,q),p',f(p',q'))$ *for all p, p',q and q';*

3. $\mu_1(x,a) \wedge \lambda_1(x,a) \wedge \Box(b = f(x,a)) \Rightarrow \lambda_2(x,b)$. □

Lemma 14 ([AL88]). *If f is a refinement mapping from $\varphi_1(x,a)$ to $\varphi_2(x,b)$, then*

$$\mu_1(x,a) \wedge \Box(b = f(x,a)) \Rightarrow \mu_2(x,b) \ .$$

Proof. Directly from (1) and (2). □

Proposition 15. *If f is a refinement mapping from $\varphi_1(x,a)$ to $\varphi_2(x,b)$, then $\varphi_1(x,a) \sqsubseteq \varphi_2(x,b)$.*

Proof. Assume $\varphi_1(x,a)$, i.e. $\mu_1(x,a) \wedge \lambda_1(x,a)$ and $\Box(b = f(x,a))$. From Lemma 14 follows $\mu_2(x,b)$, and from (3) in Definition 27 follows $\lambda_2(x,b)$; hence $\varphi_2(x,b)$. Thus, f is a mapping that proves refinement like in Proposition 11. □

The immediate consequence of this proof is that the existence of a refinement mapping implies the existence of a mapping in the sense of Section 5.1. Hence, splitting safety and liveness does not lead to a stronger proof rule based on refinement mappings.

Unfortunately, the approaches discussed above are not powerful enough. This has already been illustrated by examples in [AL88]; see also Appendix B. Part of the problem is that $\varphi_1(x,a) \Rightarrow \exists b.\varphi_2(x,b)$ may hold though no relation (nor mapping) can be found.

Example. Define $\varphi_1(x,a)$ as $x = 0 \wedge \Box(x = a \wedge (\bigcirc x = x \vee \bigcirc x = (x+1) \ \mathbf{mod}\ 2))$ and $\varphi_2(x,b)$ as $x{=}0 \wedge b{=}0 \wedge \Box((\bigcirc x{=}x \wedge \bigcirc b{=}b) \vee (\bigcirc x{=}(x+1)\ \mathbf{mod}\ 2 \wedge \bigcirc b{=}(b+1)\ \mathbf{mod}\ 3))$.

The behaviour specified by $\varphi_1(x,a)$ and $\varphi_2(x,b)$ can be characterized by the following table:

x	0	1	0	1	0	1	...
a	0	1	0	1	0	1	...
b	0	1	2	0	1	2	...

Suppose there exists a relation R. By the above constraint on relations, $R(p,q,r)$ must hold for all p,q,r such that $p{=}q \in \{0,1\}$ and $r \in \{0,1,2\}$. Then $\varphi_1(x,a) \wedge \Box R(x,a,b)$ does *not* imply $\varphi_2(x,b)$: R is to weak to conclude $\varphi_2(x,b)$. For example, the following behaviour is not allowed by $\varphi_2(x,b)$:

x	0	1	0	1	0	1	...
a	0	1	0	1	0	1	...
b	0	2	2	0	2	2	...

□

Though the split of specifications into safety and liveness parts adds no extra strength to refinement mappings, it does enable a stronger rule based on relations:

Stark's simulation relations

Definition 28 (simulation relations). *A* simulation relation *from* $\varphi_1(x, a)$ *to* $\varphi_2(x, b)$ *is a relation* $R(p, q, r)$ *such that:*

1. *For all* p, q *such that* $\gamma_1(p, q)$, *there exists an* r *such that* $R(p, q, r)$ *and* $\gamma_2(p, r)$ *hold.*
2. *For all* p, q, r, p' *and* q' *such that* $\tau_1(p, q, p', q')$ *and* $R(p, q, r)$ *hold, there exists an* r' *such that* $\tau_2(p, r, p', r')$ *and* $R(p', q', r')$ *hold.* □

Lemma 16. *If* R *is a simulation relation from* $\varphi_1(x, a)$ *to* $\varphi_2(x, b)$, *then*

$$\mu_1(x, a) \Rightarrow \exists b. [\Box R(x, a, b) \wedge \mu_2(x, b)] \ .$$

Proof. Like the proof of Theorem 5.5 in [Sta88]. Omitted. □

Proposition 17. *If* R *is a simulation relation from* $\varphi_1(x, a)$ *to* $\varphi_2(x, b)$ *such that*

$$\mu_1(x, a) \wedge \lambda_1(x, a) \wedge \mu_2(x, b) \wedge \Box R(x, a, b) \Rightarrow \lambda_2(x, b) \qquad (^{**})$$

then $\varphi_1(x, a) \sqsubseteq_h \varphi_2(x, b)$.

Proof. Let $\sigma \in \Sigma(\{x, a\})$ be such that $\sigma \models \varphi_1(x, a)$. Then $\Pi_x(\sigma) \models \exists a. \varphi_1(x, a)$. By Proposition 5, it is enough to prove $\Pi_x(\sigma) \models \exists b. \varphi_2(x, b)$ for all such σ.

Define τ such that $\Pi_{\{x,a\}}(\tau) = \sigma$ and $\tau \models \Box R(x, a, b) \wedge \mu_2(x, b)$. This is possible because of Lemma 16. Then $\tau \models \mu_1(x, a) \wedge \lambda_1(x, a) \wedge \mu_2(x, b) \wedge \Box R(x, a, b)$, and thus, because (**) holds, $\tau \models \lambda_2(x, b)$. Therefore, $\Pi_x(\sigma) = \Pi_x(\tau) \models \exists b. \varphi_2(x, b)$. Q.e.d. □

Theorem 18. *If there exists a refinement mapping from* $\varphi_1(x, a)$ *to* $\varphi_2(x, b)$, *then refinement can also be proved via a simulation relation.*

Proof. Let f be such a refinement mapping. From conditions 1–2 of Definition 27 follows:

$$\mu_1(x, a) \wedge \Box(b = f(x, a)) \Rightarrow \mu_2(x, b)$$

and that is equivalent to

$$\mu_1(x, a) \Rightarrow \exists b. [\Box(b = f(x, a)) \wedge \mu_2(x, b)]$$

Define simulation relation $R(x, a, b) \equiv (b = f(x, a))$. Together with condition 3 and Proposition 17 this proves $\varphi_1(x.a) \sqsubseteq_h \varphi_2(x, b)$. □

As a consequence, Stark's simulation relations are at least as strong as the proof methods discussed above (including refinement mappings). The following proves that they are even stronger.

Proof of refinement in the above example.

Define $R(p,q,r,s)$ by

true if $p=r$ and $q=s$

true if $p \neq r$ and $s=(r+1) \bmod 3$

false otherwise

Then R is a simulation relation from $\varphi_1(x,a)$ to $\varphi_2(x,b)$, and as $\lambda_1(x,a) = \lambda_2(x,b) =$ **true**, $\varphi_1(x,a) \sqsubseteq_h \varphi_2(x,b)$. □

Thus, Stark's simulation relations allow one to prove refinement in cases where Lamport's refinement mappings don't. The intuitive reason for this is that in the case of simulation relations, it is only required that there is *one* correct choice for b, whereas in Proposition 12, it was required that *all* choices were correct.

In Section 6 it is shown that simulation relations can be used to prove refinement if there is a lack of history information at the lower level (see the first example in Appendix B). However, they fail in the other two examples of Appendix B.

5.3 Stuttering problems again

The third example of Appendix B shows that when two specifications specify the same behaviour, but differ in the amount of invisible steps, then there need not exist a refinement mapping. So the refinement mapping technique cannot cope with stuttering. The same holds for the simulation relation technique.

Note, that in the sequence interpretation, (*) does not hold in general when φ_1 and φ_2 specify the same behaviour (see Section 4). As a consequence, the proof techniques discussed above are not applicable. Therefore, the question arises how refinement can be proven in cases like this.

A partial solution has been proposed by Abadi & Lamport [AL88]: add extra ghost variables c and d to $\varphi_1(x,a)$, giving a still equivalent specification $\varphi_3(x,a,c,d)$, such that there *is* a refinement mapping from $\varphi_3(x,a,c,d)$ to $\varphi_2(x,b)$.

Soundness is guaranteed by requiring a lot of constraints on the addition of ghost variables. However, these constraints are in terms of semantics rather than syntax.

In the next section we attempt to formulate their results at a more syntactic level, namely in the context of the specification language $\mathcal{L}_G(\mathcal{U},')$.

6 Stronger proof rules

As pointed out by the authors, the exposition in [AL88] is purely semantic. Whether their theory can be expressed in any temporal specification language is left as an open question.

This section is an attempt to reformulate that theory within $\mathcal{L}_G(\mathcal{U},')$. In Appendix C, it is demonstrated how this dense time language can be used as an alternative to the discrete time based specifications of [AL88]. There we prove that the intuitive semantics of Abadi & Lamport's specifications on the one hand, and of Stark's specifications on the other hand, coincide. Moreover we argue there that Abadi & Lamport's notion of refinement coincides with Stark's, the one we also use. The soundness of the proof rules implied by Propositions 19, 20 and 21 can be derived from the validity of the theory of Abadi & Lamport.

As was argued in Section 5, refinement mappings need not always exist. To prove refinement in these cases, we need extra proof rules. The extra rules presented in [AL88] (listed in Appendix D) prescribe under what conditions one can add auxiliary variables to a specification, the result being an *equivalent* specification from which a refinement mapping *can* be found.

The conditions of [AL88] have been transliterated for specifications formulated in $\mathcal{L}_G(\mathcal{U},')$ in such a way that the transliterated conditions imply the original ones. Like in Section 5, all specifications φ are assumed to be a conjunction of a safety part μ and a liveness part λ, as described in detail in Appendix A.

For the sake of simplicity, we only describe how one auxiliary variable (a) can be added to a specification $\varphi_1(x)$ that describes only one observable variable (x), thus resulting in a specification $\varphi_2(x,a)$. In the propositions below, p, p', q and q' denote values (i.e. elements of Val) of x,x', a and a', respectively. The role of ρ is similar to that of Stark's simulation relations (and in the case of history variables, it *is* a simulation relation); in the original formulations this is done by defining a set of "allowed combinations" (denoted by Σ^h and Σ^p in Appendix D).

Proposition 19 (Addition of a history variable a). *If ρ is a binary relation such that the following conditions hold:*

1. *For all p and q such that $\rho(p,q)$: $\gamma_2(p,q) \Rightarrow \gamma_1(p)$.*
2. *For all p satisfying $\gamma_1(p)$ there is a q such that $\rho(p,q)$ and $\gamma_2(p,q)$.*
3. *For all p and p', q and q' such that $\tau_2(p,q,p',q')$ and $\rho(p,q)$ and $\rho(p',q')$ hold, $\tau_1(p,p')$ holds.*
4. *For all p, p', and q such that $\tau_1(p,p')$ and $\rho(p,q)$ hold there is a q' such that $\tau_2(p,q,p',q')$ and $\rho(p',q')$ hold.*
5. $\Box\rho(x,a) \Rightarrow (\lambda_1(x) \equiv \lambda_2(x,a))$

then $\varphi_1(x)$ and $\varphi_2(x,a)$ refine each other.

Proof. The above conditions imply Abadi & Lamport's conditions H1 to H5 (see Appendix D). □

Alternative proof. By means of Proposition 16. Use simulations ρ^+ to prove $\varphi_1(x) \sqsubseteq_h \varphi_2(x,a)$, and ρ^- to prove $\varphi_2(x,a) \sqsubseteq_h \varphi_1(x)$, where ρ^+ and ρ^- are defined by:

- $\rho^+(p,q,r) \stackrel{\text{def}}{=} \rho(p,r)$
- $\rho^-(p,q,r) \stackrel{\text{def}}{=} \rho(p,q)$

Details omitted. □

Observe that we can prove the equivalence of a specification with and without history variable by means of simulation relations; hence, when using simulation relations instead of refinement mappings, history variables are not necessary to prove refinement.

The restrictions that prescribe how prophecy variables can be added without changing the semantics of the specification are less straightforward. In the case of adding history variables it is clear that the state machine is altered in such a way that for each computation of the old machine there exists a computation of the new machine with the same observable part. The value of the history variable can be constructed step by step.

This is different when prophecy variables are added, due to the fact that the value of a prophecy variable depends on the future part of the computation. Therefore, its values are constructed backwards. Because the computations of a transition system are constructed in a forward direction, more complicated constraints are necessary to ensure soundness.

Proposition 20 (Addition of a simple prophecy variable a). *If ρ is a binary relation such that the following conditions hold:*

1. *For all p and q such that $\rho(p,q)$: $\gamma_2(p,q) \equiv \gamma_1(p)$.*
2. *For all p and p', q and q' such that $\tau_2(p,q,p',q')$ and $\rho(p,q)$ and $\rho(p',q')$ hold, $\tau_1(p,p')$ holds.*
3. *For all p, p', and q' such that $\tau_1(p,p')$ and $\rho(p',q')$ hold there is a q such that $\tau_2(p,q,p',q')$ and $\rho(p',q')$ hold.*
4. $\Box\rho(x,a) \Rightarrow (\lambda_1(x) \equiv \lambda_2(x,a))$
5. *For all p there exists a P-state q such that $\rho(p,q)$ holds.*
6. *The set $\{q \mid \rho(p,q)\}$ is finite.*

then $\varphi_1(x)$ and $\varphi_2(x,a)$ are equivalent.

The above prophecy variables can encode future choices. The prophecy variables defined below can encode stuttering as well. Intuitively, they guess the numbering of stuttering steps before the next observable step.

Proposition 21 (Prophecy variables that add stuttering). *If ρ is a binary relation such that the following conditions hold:*

1. *For all p and q such that* $\rho(p,q)$: $\gamma_2(p,q) \Rightarrow \gamma_1(p)$.
2. *For all p and q such that* $\rho(p,q)$ *and* $\gamma_1(p)$, *there exist* $q_0,\ldots,q_n$ *such that* $\gamma_2(p,q_0)$, $q_n = q$ *and, for all* $0 \le i < n$, $\rho(p,q_i)$ *and* $\tau_2(p,q_i,p,q_{i+1})$.
3. *For all p and* p', *q and* q' *such that* $\tau_2(p,q,p',q')$ *and* $\rho(p,q)$ *and* $\rho(p',q')$ *hold,* $\tau_1(p,p')$ *holds.*
4. *For all p,* p', *and* q' *such that* $\tau_1(p,p')$ *and* $\rho(p',q')$ *hold there exist P-states* $q,q_0,\ldots,q_n = q$ *such that* $\rho(p,q)$ *and, for all* $0 \le i < n$, $\rho(p',q_i)$ *and* $\tau_2(p',q_i,p',q_{i+1})$ *hold.*
5. $\Box\rho(x,a) \;\Rightarrow\; (\lambda_1(x) \equiv \lambda_2(x,a))$
6. *For all p there exists a q such that* $\rho(p,q)$ *holds.*
7. *The set* $\{q \mid \rho(p,q)\}$ *is finite.*

then $\varphi_1(x)$ *and* $\varphi_2(x,a)$ *are equivalent.*

The proof rules implied by these propositions can be used to prove refinement in the counterexamples listed in Appendix B.

Conclusions

Both Abadi & Lamport's and Stark's notions of refinement correspond to an intuitive notion: record refinement. Because there is no description language available for records, sequence logics like discrete LTL, and history logics (like Stark's) are used.

We have shown that it is easier to find an appropriate logic based on a dense time model, i.e. a logic that is insensitive to differences w.r.t. the numbers of stutter steps. Still, for both discrete and dense time models it is necessary to add information to the states when refinement is proved using refinement mappings or simulation relations. Partial solutions to this problem have been proposed by Abadi & Lamport, namely history and prophecy variables.

The contribution of this paper is a more syntactic formulation of their theory and a comparison with the theory developed by Stark. Another way to a proof theory for refinement might be a further axiomatization of the dense time logic $\mathcal{L}_G(\mathcal{U},')$ (including the primitive predicate **is**).

Acknowledgement

We thank Willem-Paul de Roever for scrutinizing this text and his many suggestions w.r.t. the presentation.

References

[AL88] M. Abadi and L. Lamport. The existence of refinement mappings. In *Third annual symposium on Logic in Computer Science*, pages 165–175. IEEE, July 1988.

[AS85] B. Alpern and F.B. Schneider. Defining liveness. *Information Processing Letters*, 21:181–185, 1985.

[BKP86] H. Barringer, R. Kuiper, and A. Pnueli. A really abstract concurrent model and its temporal logic. In *13th Annual ACM Symposium on Principles of Programming Languages*, pages 173–183, 1986.

[Die89] E.C.M. Diepstraten. Specifying observable behavior using temporal logic and auxiliary variables. Master's thesis, Eindhoven University of Technology, July 1989.

[Lam83a] L. Lamport. Specifying concurrent progam modules. *ACM Transactions on Programming Languages and Systems*, 5(2):190–222, September 1983.

[Lam83b] L. Lamport. What good is temporal logic. In R.E.A. Manson, editor, *Information Processing 83: Proceedings of the IFIP 9th World Congress*, pages 657–668. IFIP, Elsevier Science Publishers, North Holland, September 1983.

[Lam85] L. Lamport. An axiomatic semantics of concurrent programming languages. In K.R. Apt, editor, *NATO ASI Series, vol. F13: Logics and Models of Concurrent Systems*, pages 77–122. Springer-Verlag, January 1985.

[Lam89] L. Lamport. A simple approach to specifying concurrent systems. *Communications of the ACM*, 32(1):32–45, January 1989.

[MP82] Z. Manna and A. Pnueli. Verification of concurrent programs: The temporal framework. In Academic Press, editor, *The Correctness Problem in Computer Science*, chapter 5, pages 215–273. International Lecture Series in Computer Science, London, 1982.

[Sta88] E.W. Stark. Proving entailment between conceptual state specifications. *Theoretical Computer Science*, 56:135–154, 1988.

A Safety specifications

Safety properties are specified by means of transition systems. A transition system consists of an initial state relation and a transition (or next state) relation. A computation of a transition system is such that its initial state satisfies the initial state relation, and that two successive state satisfy the transition relation. A transition relation does not specify liveness or fairness properties.

Stark's machines

Like in Sections 5 and 6, we only consider specifications that have one observable (x) and one ghost variable (a). Like in Section 3, Val is the domain of values of variables.

Definition 29. *A Stark-machine is a specification* $\mu(x,a) \stackrel{\text{def}}{=} \gamma(x,a) \wedge \Box\tau(x,a,x',a')$, *where*

1. γ *is a relation on* $\mathrm{Val} \times \mathrm{Val}$ *defining initial states.*
2. τ *is a relation on* $\mathrm{Val} \times \mathrm{Val} \times \mathrm{Val} \times \mathrm{Val}$ *such that* $\tau(p,q,p,q)$ *holds for all* p,q.

$\square$

Thus, $\Box\tau(x,a,x',a')$ defines allowed transitions between $\{x,a\}$-states. Using an irreflexive transition relation makes no sense, as no history can violate the finite variability constraint. Example: let $\tau(p,q,r,s) \equiv (r = p+1)$, then there is no history h such that $h \models \Box\tau(x,a,x',a')$.

Property 22. *Stark-machines are insensitive to initial stuttering.*

Abadi & Lamport's state machines

These machines are ordinary state automata. Lamport's states consist of an external and an internal part. The external part describes the values of observable variables, the internal part describes those of unobservable ones, i.e. ghost variables.

For the sake of simplicity, we fix a set Σ_E of external states and a set Σ_I of internal states, and define $\Sigma = \Sigma_E \times \Sigma_I$.

Definition 30. *A state machine is a tuple $M = (F, N)$, where*

1. *$F \subset \Sigma$, called the initial state relation.*
2. *$N \subseteq \Sigma \times \Sigma$, called the next state relation.*

□

The semantics of a state machine is a stutter-closed set of (infinite) state sequences, i.e. a subset of Σ^ω:

Definition 31. $[\![M]\!]^s = \{\sigma = s_0, s_1, \ldots \mid s_0 \in F \wedge (s_i = s_{i+1} \vee (s_i, s_{i+1}) \in N)\}$ □

Observation: requiring N to be reflexive would have simplified this definition and the proof rules given in Appendix D.

Property 23. $\Gamma([\![M]\!]^s) = [\![M]\!]^s$

A.1 Relation between these approaches

Stark's machines and state machines look very similar. Below, we give concrete form to this similarity.

Definition 32. *Let μ be a Stark-machine, and let M be a state machine. We say that μ and M correspond to each other if $\natural[\![\mu]\!]^h = \natural[\![M]\!]^s$; i.e. when both machines have the same intuitive semantics.* □

Proposition 24. *For each state machine M, there exists a Stark-machine μ that corresponds to M; on the other hand, for each Stark-machine μ there exists a state machine M that corresponds to μ.*

Proof. We associate Σ_E, the set of external states, with the possible values of the observable variable x, and Σ_I with the values of ghost variable a.
The relation between F and γ is simple: given γ, define $F = \{s \in \Sigma \mid \gamma(s)\}$; given F, define $\gamma(p,q) \equiv (p,q) \in F$.
Given τ, define $N = \{(s,t) \in \Sigma \times \Sigma \mid \tau(s,t)\}$; Given N, define $\tau(p,q,r,s) \equiv (p = r \wedge q = s) \vee ((p,q),(r,s)) \in N$.
Now it is easy to see that $\natural[\![\mu]\!]^h = \natural[\![M]\!]^s$. □

A.2 Stark-specifications

Definition 33. *A Stark-specification $\varphi(x,a)$ is a conjunct $\mu(x,a) \wedge \lambda(x,a)$, where $\mu(x,a)$ is a Stark-machine and $\lambda(x,a)$ is an element of $\mathcal{L}(\mathcal{U},')$ that is insensitive to initial stuttering (e.g. a formula that does not contain the "$'$"-operator is insensitive).* □

Property 25. *Stark-specifications are insensitive to initial stuttering.*

B Counterexamples from [AL88]

In [AL88], examples are given of pairs of specifications such that the first specification refines the second, though no refinement mapping can be found. Below we give formal specifications in $\mathcal{L}_G(\mathcal{U},')$ that correspond to these examples, and indicate how refinement can be proved using the proof rules of Section 6.

B.1 Lack of historical information

Specification φ_1 specifies that x records the value of a one-bit clock. Specification φ_2 specifies that x records the value of the low order bit of a three-bit clock (y). Hence, y is not a function of x.

$$\varphi_1 \stackrel{\text{def}}{=} x=0 \wedge \Box(x'=x \vee x'=(x+1) \ \mathbf{mod}\ 2)$$

$$\varphi_2 \stackrel{\text{def}}{=} x=0 \wedge y=0 \wedge \Box((x' \neq x \vee y' \neq y) \Rightarrow (x'=y \ \mathbf{mod}\ 2 \wedge y' = (y+1) \ \mathbf{mod}\ 8))$$

Refinement can be proved using Proposition 19, and relation ρ_1, defined by:

$$\rho_1(p,q) \equiv (p \in \{0,1\}) \wedge (q \in \{0,1,2\})$$

B.2 Nondeterministic choices made too late

The following specifications both specify that ten arbitrary numbers between 1 and 10 are written to a display (represented by the observable variable d); additionally, the second specification enforces that these numbers are chosen (that is, assigned to the ghost variables $x(1),\ldots,x(10)$) before the first one is displayed (that is, concatenated to d).

$$\begin{aligned}\varphi_1 \stackrel{\text{def}}{=}\ & d = \langle\rangle \wedge i = 10 \wedge \\ & \Box((d' = d \wedge i' = i) \vee (i > 0 \wedge \exists_{n\in\{1,\ldots,10\}}[d' = d \oplus \langle n \rangle \wedge i' = i-1]))\end{aligned}$$

$$\begin{aligned}\varphi_2 \stackrel{\text{def}}{=}\ & d = \langle\rangle \wedge i = 10 \wedge \forall_{j\in\{1,\ldots,10\}}[x(j) \in \{1,\ldots,10\}] \wedge \\ & \Box((d' = d \wedge i' = i) \vee (i > 0 \wedge d' = d \oplus \langle x(i) \rangle \wedge i' = i-1))\end{aligned}$$

Refinement can be proved using Proposition 20, and relation ρ_2, defined by:

$$\rho_2(p, q_1, \ldots, q_10) \equiv (|p| \leq 10) \wedge \forall_{i\in\{1,\ldots,10\}}[q_i \in \{1,\ldots,10\}]$$

B.3 Lack of stutter steps

Both specifications below specify a clock of which the minutes counter is observable. But while the seconds counter of φ_1 is incremented by 10 at a time, the one of φ_2 is incremented by one at a time. Therefore, the second specification enforces more stutter steps, so that no refinement mapping exists.

$$\varphi_1 \stackrel{\text{def}}{=} m = 0 \wedge s = 0 \wedge \Box(m' = s \ \mathbf{div}\ 60 \wedge (s' = s \vee s' = s + 10))$$

$$\varphi_2 \stackrel{\text{def}}{=} m = 0 \wedge s = 0 \wedge \Box(m' = s \ \mathbf{div}\ 60 \wedge (s' = s \vee s' = s + 1))$$

Refinement can be proved using Proposition 21, and relation ρ_3, defined by:

$$\rho_3(p,q,r) \equiv 10 * (r \ \mathbf{div}\ 10) = q$$

(p corresponds to the value of m, q to the value of s in φ_1, and r to the value of s in φ_2).

C AL-specifications in $\mathcal{L}_G(\mathcal{U},')$

Specifications in [AL88] have the following form:

Definition 34. *An AL-specification is a tuple $S = (\Sigma, \Sigma_E, \Sigma_I, M, L)$ where*

- *Σ_E is a set of so-called external states.*
- *Σ_I is a set of so-called internal states.*
- $\Sigma \subseteq \Sigma_E \times \Sigma_I$
- *M is a state machine as defined in Appendix A.*
- *$L \subseteq \Sigma^\omega$ is a stutter-closed set of infinite sequences over Σ. L is called the supplementary property of S.* □

The intention of Abadi and Lamport is to specify safety properties by means of transition systems (i.e. by F and N). L is used to specify additional properties, especially liveness properties.

The semantics of AL-specification S is defined by:

Definition 35. $[\![S]\!]^{AL} = \Gamma(\Pi_E([\![M]\!]^{AL} \cap L))$, *where for state* s, $\Pi_E(s)$ *is the observable part of* s. □

Abadi & Lamport's notion of refinement is defined by:

Definition 36. *For AL-specification* S_1 *and* S_2, $S_1 \sqsubseteq_{AL} S_2 \stackrel{\text{def}}{=} [\![S_1]\!]^{AL} \subseteq [\![S_2]\!]^{AL}$. □

Property 26. $S_1 \sqsubseteq_{AL} S_2 \iff \natural[\![S_1]\!]^{AL} \subseteq \natural[\![S_2]\!]^{AL}$.

Corollary 27. *AL-refinement = record refinement = history refinement.*

Thus, $\sqsubseteq_{AL}$ corresponds completely with the intuitive notion of record refinement given in Section 1. Together with the observation in Appendix A that state machines correspond to Stark-machines, this suggest that it might be possible to formulate AL-specifications in $\mathcal{L}_G(\mathcal{U},')$, and to apply the proof rules of [AL88] to this temporal logic.

As L is a completely arbitrary (though stutter-closed) set of state sequences, it need not have a syntactic counterpart λ such that $\natural[\![\lambda]\!]^h = \natural L$. But for any $\lambda \in \mathcal{L}(\mathcal{U},')$ there exists a corresponding L: define $L = \{\sigma \mid \natural\sigma \in \natural[\![\lambda]\!]^h\}$.

From the argument below we conclude that $\mathcal{L}_G(\mathcal{U},')$ is a suitable syntactic alternative to AL-specifications. The fact that Abadi & Lamport's notion of refinement is equivalent to the history notion (as defined in Section 4) legitimates the application of the new proof rules in [AL88] to specifications formulated in $\mathcal{L}_G(\mathcal{U},')$.

Proposition 28. *Each Stark-specification has a corresponding AL-specification.*

Proof. Let $\varphi(x,a)$ be a Stark-specification; $\varphi(x,a) \equiv \mu(x,a) \wedge \lambda(x,a)$ as in Appendix A. Define AL-specification $S = (\Sigma, \Sigma_E, \Sigma_I, M, L)$ by

- $\Sigma_E = \Sigma_I =$ Val, the domain of values of variables;
- $\Sigma = \Sigma_E \times \Sigma_I$;
- M as the state machine corresponding to μ, as in Appendix A;
- $L = \{\sigma \mid \natural\sigma \in \natural[\![\lambda]\!]^h\}$.

We want to prove:

$$\natural[\![S]\!]^{AL} = \natural(\Pi_x([\![\varphi(x,a)]\!]^h))$$

Proof of "$\subseteq$": Let $\sigma \in [\![S]\!]^{AL}$. Define τ such that $\sigma \simeq \Pi_E(\tau)$ and $\tau \in [\![M]\!]^{AL} \cap L$ (this is possible). Then $\natural\sigma = \natural(\Pi_E(\tau))$. Next, let $g, h \in \mathcal{H}\{x,a\}$ be such that $\natural g = \natural\tau = \natural h$, $g \models \mu(x,a)$ and $h \models \lambda(x,a)$. Then $g \simeq h$, and therefore $h \models \lambda(x,a)$. This leads to $\Pi_x(h) \in [\![\varphi(x,a)]\!]^h$. Finally, $\natural\Pi_x(h) = \natural\sigma$ holds because for initially stuttering h, $\natural\Pi_x(h) = \Pi_x(\natural(h))$.

Proof of "$\supseteq$": Let $h \in [\![\varphi(x,a)]\!]^h$. We have to prove: there exists $\sigma \in [\![S]\!]^{AL}$ such that $\natural\Pi_x(h) = \natural\sigma$. Because of the definitions of M and L above, and because $h \models \mu(x,a) \wedge \lambda(x,a)$, there exists a $\tau \in \Sigma^\omega$ such that $\natural\tau = \natural h$ and $\tau \in [\![M]\!]^s \cap L$. By Definition 35, $\Pi_E(\tau) \in [\![S]\!]^{AL}$; moreover, $\natural\Pi_E(\tau) = \natural\Pi_x(h)$. □

The fact that Abadi & Lamport's notion of refinement is equivalent to Stark's (the one we also use) legitimates the application of the new proof rules in [AL88] to Stark-specifications, i.e. AL-specifications formulated in $\mathcal{L}_G(\mathcal{U},')$.

D Proof rules of Abadi & Lamport

D.1 Refinement mappings

If there is a *refinement mapping* from specification $S_1 = (\Sigma_1, F_1, N_1, L_1)$ to specification $S_2 = (\Sigma_2, F_2, N_2, L_2)$, i.e. a mapping f such that:

R1. for all $s \in \Sigma_1 : \Pi_E(f(s)) = \Pi_E(s)$;

R2. $f(F_1) \subseteq F_2$;

R3. if $(s,t) \in N_1$ then $f(s), f(t) \in N_2$ or $f(s) = f(t)$;

R4. $f([\![S_1]\!]^s) \subseteq L_2$.

D.2 Addition of auxiliary (i.e. ghost) variables

For the sake of simplicity we formulate how variables may be added to the specification $S = (\Sigma, F, N, L)$, where Σ is a set of V-states.

Addition of a history variable

If specification $S^h = (\Sigma^h, F^h, N^h, L^h)$ is obtained from the specification S by adding a history variable h, i.e. if the following conditions hold:

H1. $\Sigma^h \subseteq \Sigma \times \Sigma_H$, for some set $\{h\}$-states Σ_H;

H2. $\Pi_V(F^h) = F$;

H3. if $((s,t),(s',t')) \in N^h$ then $(s,s') \in N$ or $s = s'$;

H4. if $(s,s') \in N$ and $(s,t) \in \Sigma^h$ then there exists $t' \in \Sigma_H$ such that $((s,t),(s',t')) \in N^h$;

H5. $L^h = \Pi_V^{-1}(L)$;

then S^h and S are equivalent.

Addition of a simple prophecy variable

If specification $S^p = (\Sigma^p, F^p, N^p, L^p)$ is obtained from the specification S by adding a simple prophecy variable p, i.e. if the following conditions hold:

P1. $\Sigma^p \subseteq \Sigma \times \Sigma_P$, for some set $\{p\}$-states Σ_P;

P2'. $F^p = \Pi_V^{-1}(F)$;

P3. if $((s,t),(s',t')) \in N^p$ then $(s,s') \in N$ or $s = s'$;

P4'. if $(s,s') \in N$ and $(s',t') \in \Sigma^p$ then there exists $t \in \Sigma_P$ such that $((s,t),(s',t')) \in N^p$;

P5. $L^p = \Pi_V^{-1}(L)$;

P6. for all $s \in \Sigma$, the set $\Pi_V^{-1}(s)$ is finite and nonempty;

then S^p and S are equivalent.

Addition of a prophecy variable that adds stuttering

If specification $S^p = (\Sigma^p, F^p, N^p, L^p)$ is obtained from the specification S by adding a prophecy variable p that adds stuttering, i.e. if the following conditions hold:

P1. $\Sigma^p \subseteq \Sigma \times \Sigma_P$, for some set $\{p\}$-states Σ_P;

P2a. $\Pi_V(F^p) \subseteq F$;

P2b. for all $(s,t) \in \Pi_V^{-1}(F)$ there exist $t_0, \ldots, t_n = t$ such that $(s,t_0) \in F^p$, and for $0 \leq i < n$, $((s,p_i),(s,p_{i+1})) \in N^p$;

P3. if $((s,t),(s',t')) \in N^p$ then $(s,s') \in N$ or $s = s'$;

P4. if $(s,s') \in N$ and $(s',t') \in \Sigma^p$ then there exist $t, t'_0, \ldots, t'_n = t' \in \Sigma_P$ such that $((s,t),(s',t'_0)) \in N^p$and, for $0 \leq i < n$, $((s',p'_i),(s',p'_{i+1})) \in N^p$;

P5. $L^p = \Pi_V^{-1}(L)$;

P6. for all $s \in \Sigma$, the set $\Pi_V^{-1}(s)$ is finite and nonempty;

then S^p and S are equivalent.

Algebraic Implementation of Objects over Objects

H.-D. Ehrich

Abteilung Datenbanken, Technische Universität Braunschweig, Postfach 3329, D-3300 Braunschweig, FRG

A. Sernadas

Departamento de Matematica, Instituto Superior Técnico, 1096 Lisboa Codex, PORTUGAL

Abstract - *This paper gives semantic foundations of (correct) implementation as a relationship between an "abstract" object and a community of "base" objects. In our aproach, an object is an "observed process". Objects and object morphisms constitute a category* ***OB*** *in which colimits reflect object aggregation and interaction between objects. Our concept of implementation allows for composition, i.e. by composing any number of (correct) implementation steps, a (correct) entire implementation is obtained. We study two specific kinds of implementation, extension and encapsulation, in more detail and investigate their close relationship to object morphisms. Our main technical result is a normal form theorem saying that any regular implementation, i.e. one composed of any number of extensions and encapsulations, in any order, can be done in just two steps: first an extension, and then an encapsulation.*

Key words - *object-oriented systems ; objects ; object morphisms ; processes ; process morphisms ; semantic fundamentals ; algebraic implementation ; reification ; refinement ; extension ; encapsulation.*

CONTENTS

1. Introduction
2. Motivation
3. Objects
   3.1 Processes
   3.2 Observations
   3.3 Object Communities
4. Implementation
   4.1 Concept
   4.2 Extension
   4.3 Encapsulation
   4.4 Normal Form
5. Concluding Remarks
References

1. Introduction

Computing systems are built in layers. Each layer offers an interface with a collection of services to its upper neighbors, and it makes these services operational by programming them on top of the interfaces offered by the lower neighbors. Between an end user interface and the switching circuitry inside a computer, there are usually many layers, both hardware and software. It is of vital importance, both for correctness and efficiency, to understand clearly and thoroughly what happens inside each layer, and what happens when moving up and down across layers.

When speaking of implementation intuitively, we sometimes mean the activity of establishing a new layer on top of existing ones, and sometimes we mean the result of this activity, i.e. the new layer itself. In any case, the notion of implementation refers to a relationship between layers.

This paper gives mathematical foundations of (correct) implementation as a relationship between layers, based on an object-oriented model of layer.

Typically, each layer shows the following concepts: *data* with operations, *variables* with the capability of storing data values, and *actions* changing the contents of variables. While one or the other of these concepts might be missing, the main difference is in the level of abstraction. Bits, switching gates, flipflops, and digital signals is an example of a rather low-level layer, whereas, say, relational algebra, databases, and database transactions constitute a somewhat higher level.

Among the many approaches to model aspects of structure and behaviour of computing layers in a rigorous mathematical setting, there are three complementary theories which have found wide attention: the algebraic theory of *abstract data types* dealing with data and operations, the theory of *state machines* dealing with states (of variables) changed by actions, and the theory of *processes* dealing with actions (or "events") happening in time in some controlled way, in sequence or concurrently.

We favor an object-oriented approach for modeling layers. The concept of an *object* in the sense of object-oriented programming incorporates data, variables (or "attributes" or "slots"), and actions (or "methods" or "events"). Moreover, objects can communicate with each other, e.g. by means of messages. This supports viewing a computing system (one layer) as a *community of interacting objects*.

The object concept is not new. Its origins trace back to the class concept in SIMULA (DMN67), and the module concept of Parnas (Pa72), but it developed and became popular only much later, with the advent of Smalltalk (GR83). Object-orientation has been proposed as a programming paradigm by itself (HB77, He77), and this idea has found wide acceptance by now.

In contrast to its practical impact for quite a while (Lo85, DD86, SW87, Di88), mathematical foundation of object-orientation in all its aspects is still feeble. An interesting early contribution is (Go75), but only recently the issue has found wider interest (Am86, GM87, AR89). In a series of papers (SSE87, ESS88, ESS89, ESS90, SEC89), we contributed to a model of objects, object types, and aggregation of concurrent, interacting objects. The three complementary theories mentioned above are reflected in various degrees: an object is considered to be an "observed process" where the observation is done via attributes, each one capable of holding values from an arbitrary abstract data type. In defining a category of objects and object morphisms, we take benefit from algebraic data type theory also in a different, and more interesting respect. As in the algebraic data type case, colimits play an essential role.

In this paper, we investigate (correct) implementation as a relationship between an "abstract" object "built on top" of a community of (possibly interacting) "base" objects. Again, we capitalize in some analogies with algebraic data types, taking benefit especially from work in (Eh81, Li82).

In section 2, we give motivating background for our object, object morphism, and implemetation concepts. In section 3, we develop the theory of objects in more detail, showing how object interaction and object aggregation can be uniformly handled in categorial terms, and in section 4 we present our theory of implementing objects over objects. Extensions and encapsulations are introduced as special cases of implementations, and their close relationship to object morphisms is clarified. Our main technical result is a normal form theorem saying that any regular implementation, i.e. one composed of any number of extensions and encapsulations, in any order, can be done in just two steps: first an extension, and then an encapsulation.

We make moderate use of a few category-theoretic notions. The reader may find it helpful to consult the first chapters of (Go79) where all relevant notions are defined and explained, or any other textbook on category theory.

2. Motivation

We explain the intuitive background of our object model and the relevant relationships between objects. Then we outline the idea of what we mean by an implementation of an "abstract" object over a given community of "base" objects.

Example 2.1: A very simple example of an object is a natural variable nvar , i.e. a variable for natural numbers. We recognize the following ingredients:

data: the natural numbers (with their operations)

attribute: val, the current value

events: open, bringing the variable into existence,
close, bringing the variable out of existence, and
asg(n), for each $n \in \mathbb{N}$, assigning value n to the variable. □

Example 2.2: A slightly more elaborate example of an object is an (infinite) array of integers, indexed by natural numbers. More precisely, we have

data: the natural numbers and the integers,

attributes: conts(n), for each $n \in \mathbb{N}$, the current value of the n-th component,

events: create, bringing the array into existence,
destroy, bringing the array out of existence, and
set(n, i), for each $n \in \mathbb{N}$ and each $i \in \mathbb{Z}$, assigning value i to the n-th component. □

Example 2.3: An interesting example of an object is a stack of integers with the following ingredients:

data: the integers,

attribute: top, the value of the topmost element,

events: new, bringing the stack into existence,
drop, bringing the stack out of existence,

push(i), for each $i \in \mathbb{Z}$, putting element i on top of the stack, and
pop, taking the topmost element away. □

Knowing about the data, attributes and events of an object does by no means provide a sufficiently complete picture of what an object is. We need to know more than its static structure, we need to know its *dynamic behavior*. The behavior of an object is specified by answering two questions:

(1) How can events happen in time ?

(2) Which values are assumed by the attributes ?

Question 1 refers to viewing the event part of an object as a *process* rather than just a set of events. It is essential to know about nvar, for instance, that open has to be the first event before nvar is ready to do anything else, and that close, if it ever happens, is the last event after which nvar is not ready to do anything, etc. For stack, as another example, we would perhaps like to impose that we cannot pop the empty stack, i.e. that in any permissable sequence of stack events starting with new, we would insist to have at least as many push's as pop's, etc. These are typical *safety* conditions.

It is essential, however, that we can also handle *active* objects, not only passive ones. Typically, active objects have to satisfy *liveness* conditions. As an example, for a user program operating on a stack, we might want to impose that it may not leave the stack as garbage behind, i.e. it has to drop the stack eventually once it exists.

Therefore, we need a process model which can deal with both safety and liveness.

There are plenty of process models around, and it is not clear which one is better or even the best of all for our purposes. In order to facilitate developing ideas, we adopt, for the moment being, the simplest interleaving model incorporating safety and liveness and allowing for infinite behaviour: our *life cycle* model says that a process is a set of streams, i.e. finite or infinite sequences, over a given alphabet of events (SEC89 treats the finite case). The alphabet may be infinite, as suggested by the examples above. It is true that we do not capture full concurrency and internal nondeterminism this way, but we are prepared to substitute a more powerful process model later on. In this sense, we consider our theory as being parameterized with respect to the process model.

Processes as sets of life cycles do not have to be prefix closed! For instance, consider a stack user program which has to drop the stack eventually once it exists. After performing the trace <new;push(1);push(1);pop;push(2)> of stack events (disregarding non-stack events), the program still has to do something with the stack, whereas after <new;push(1);pop;drop>, we have a "complete life cycle" of stack events so that the program may terminate. In fact, viewing a process as a set of *complete* life cycles and not insisting in prefix closure is the way liveness is expressed in our model.

Processes do not tell everything about an object. For fully capturing its behavior, we have to answer the second question posed above.

The values assumed by the attributes depend, of course, on what happened before. For instance, after a trace, i.e. a finite sequence of events ending with asg(10), the current value of nvar should be 10. The case of stack is more complicated: the current value of top may depend on an arbitrarily long trace of events before the point of observation.

Our model is to let *observations*, i.e. sets of attribute-value pairs, be functionally dependent on traces of events: after each trace, the observation is uniquely determined. We allow, however, for "non-deterministic" observations in that there may be any number of attribute-value pairs with the *same* attribute. This way, one attribute may have any number of values, including none at all. The intuition is that an empty observation expresses that the value is not known, and more than one value expresses that it is one of these, but it is unknown which one. The case that the attribute value is a *set* of values is different: this is captured by *one* attribute-value pair where the value is a set of elements, i.e. an instance of the data type of sets of these elements. Our notion of observation is an abstraction and generalization of that of a "record" or "tuple".

In short, we view objects as "observed processes", as made precise in section 3.1.

Objects in isolation do not tell everything about the structure and behaviour of a computing system. Typically, we have *object communities* where there are many objects around, passive ones like those in the examples above, or active ones like programs or transactions. These objects interact with each other, and they are put together to form aggregate objects in a variety of intricate ways. Therefore, it is essential to study *relationships* between objects. Our basic concept for this is that of an *object morphism*, general enough for including

- *specializations* like roadster $\hookrightarrow$ car
- *parts* like engine $\longrightarrow$ car
- *links* like owner $\longrightarrow$ car

Moreover, our theory can deal with *shared parts* in a satisfactory way, including *event sharing* as the basis for (synchronous and symmetric) communication between objects. In fact, interaction and aggregation are treated in the uniform mathematical framework of colimits in the category of objects. More detailed motivation will be given in sections 3.2 and 3.3, respectively.

The central subject of this paper, implementation (or "reification" or "refinement"), is a very peculiar relationship between objects that goes beyond morphisms as oulined above. The general idea of implementing an "abstract" object over a community of "base" objects is to

- translate abstract event streams to base streams, and
- translate base observations back to abstract observations .

This way, the behavior of an abstract object is *simulated* via the base: after an abstract trace τ, we "calculate" the abstract observation (which we do not have directly) in the following way: we translate τ to base trace τ', look at the base observation y' after τ', and translate y' back to the abstract level, yielding abstract observation y. Of course, y should be the "correct" abstract observation after τ, as laid down in some abstract specification.

Example 2.4: A well known implementation of an integer stack over an integer array indexed by natural numbers, together with a natural variable as top pointer, would evaluate the top value of the stack trace

<new;push(2);push(1);pop>

as follows (cf. examples 2.1 to 2.3). Translating to base traces event by event (for details see example 4.4), we would obtain, say,

<create;open;asg(0)><set(0,2);asg(1)><set(1,1);asg(2)><asg(1)> .

At the end of this trace, we have 1 as the natural variable's value, so that the top value of the stack is in the 1-component of the array, and we have 2 as this component's value. From this, we easily obtain 2 as the current top value of the stack. □

We give more detailed motivation for our approach to implementation in section 4.1.

Since implementations in general are rather complex relationships between objects, the question naturally arises whether we can "tame" the concept so that the inter-object relationships become managable. The latter are harder to deal with than intra-object structure and behaviour. If possible, the inter-object relationships should be (close to) morphisms.

Extensions and encapsulations are two kinds of implementation which are well-behaved in this respect. Extensions capture the idea that - within one object - everything is "defined upon" a proper part, and encapsulation captures the idea to establish an "interface" to an object, abstracting some of the items and hiding the rest. More detailed motivation is given in sections 4.2 and 4.3, respectively.

3. Objects

Objects are observed processes. We first present our (preliminary) life cycle model of processes and process morphisms. Then we extend processes to objects by adding observations, and process morphisms are accordinly extented to object morphisms. In the resulting category ***OB*** of objects, we investigate the existence of colimits and show how colimits are used to deal with communities of interacting objects, and with aggregation of objects into complex objects.

3.1 Processes

In the life cycle process model, a process consists of an alphabet X of events and a set of life cycles over X. Let X^* be the set of finite sequences over X, and let X^ω be the set of ω-sequences over X. By X^σ we denote the set of *streams* over X, defined by $X^\sigma = X^* \cup X^\omega$.

Definition 3.1: A *process* $P=(X,\Lambda)$ consists of a set X of *events* and a set $\Lambda \subseteq X^\sigma$ of *life cycles* such that $\varepsilon \in \Lambda$.

The empty life cycle expresses that the process does not do anything, no events happen. The reason why we impose that each process has the potential of remaining inactive is motivated by the examples in section 2: before the first event (and after the last one if it ever happens), an object "does not exist". It is brought into and out of existence by means of events. And each object should have the potential of remaining nonexistent. The deeper reason for that comes from object *types* (which we do not deal with in this paper, cf. ESS90): an object type provides a large, possibly infinite supply of object instances, and many of these will never be activated.

Referring to examples 2.1 to 2.3, we give the processes underlying objects nvar, array and stack.

Example 3.2: Let $P_{nvar}=(X_{nvar},\Lambda_{nvar})$ be the following process.

$$X_{nvar} = \{ \text{open} , \text{close} \} \cup X_{asg} \qquad \text{where } X_{asg} = \{ asg(n) \mid n \in \mathbb{N} \} .$$

$$\Lambda_{nvar} = \{\text{open}\}X^*_{asg}\{\text{close}\} ,$$

i.e. the variable must eventually terminate with a close event, after finitely many assignments. □

Example 3.3: Let $P_{array}=(X_{array},\Lambda_{array})$ be the following process.

$$X_{array} = \{ \text{create} , \text{destroy} \} \cup X_{set} \qquad \text{where} \quad X_{set} = \{ \text{set}(n,i) \mid n \in \mathbb{N} \wedge i \in \mathbb{Z} \} .$$

$$\Lambda_{array} = \{\text{create}\}X^*_{set}\{\text{destroy}\} \cup \{\text{create}\}X^{\omega}_{set} ,$$

i.e. the array can accept infinitely many assignments without ever being terminated by a destroy event. □

Example 3.4: Let $P_{stack}=(X_{stack},\Lambda_{stack})$ be the following process.

$$X_{stack} = \{ \text{new} , \text{drop} \} \cup X_{pp} \qquad \text{where} \quad X_{pp} = \{ \text{pop} \} \cup \{ \text{push}(i) \mid i \in \mathbb{Z} \} .$$

$$\Lambda_{stack} = \{\text{new}\}L1\{\text{drop}\} \cup \{\text{new}\}L2 ,$$

where $L1 \subseteq X^*_{pp}$ is the set of all finite sequences of pop's and push's with the property that each prefix contains at most as many pop as push events, and $L2 \subseteq X^{\omega}_{pp}$ is the set of all ω-sequences where the same holds for each finite prefix. □

As pointed out in section 2, it is important to study relationships between objects, and, in the first place, between processes. The simplest relationship is that of being a *subprocess*, by which we mean a process over a subset of all events where a certain relationship holds between the life cycle sets. For intuition, we look at examples 3.2 to 3.4, respectively.

Example 3.5: Let $P'_{nvar}=(X'_{nvar},\Lambda'_{nvar})$ be defined by the restriction "only values up to 1000 can be assigned, and the variable need not terminate":

$$X'_{nvar} = \{ \text{open} , \text{close} \} \cup X'_{asg} \qquad \text{where} \quad X'_{asg} = \{ \text{asg}(n) \mid n \in \mathbb{N} \wedge n \leq 1000 \}$$

$$\Lambda'_{nvar} = \{\text{open}\}X'^*_{asg}\{\text{close}\} \cup \{\text{open}\}X'^{\omega}_{asg}$$

□

Example 3.6: Let $P'_{array}=(X'_{array},\Lambda'_{array})$ be defined by the following idea: "values can only be assigned to components up to 1000":

$$X'_{array} = \{ \text{create} , \text{destroy} \} \cup X'_{set} \qquad \text{where} \quad X'_{set} = \{ \text{set}(n,i) \mid n \in \mathbb{N} \wedge i \in \mathbb{Z} \wedge n \leq 1000 \}$$

$$\Lambda'_{array} = \{\text{create}\}X'^*_{set}\{\text{destroy}\} \cup \{\text{create}\}X'^{\omega}_{set}$$

□

Example 3.7: Let $P'_{stack}=(X'_{stack},\Lambda'_{stack})$ be a (strange) stack which cannot be pushed, but popped arbitrarily often:

$$X'_{stack} = \{ \text{new} , \text{drop} \} \cup X'_{pp} \qquad \text{where} \quad X'_{pp} = \{ \text{pop} \}$$

$$\Lambda'_{stack} = \{\text{new}\}X'^*_{pp}\{\text{drop}\} \cup \{\text{new}\}X'^{\omega}_{pp}$$

□

The relationships between the life cycle sets of the corresponding examples 3.5 and 3.2 as well as 3.6 and 3.3 are established by projection, defined as follows.

Definition 3.8: Let $X' \subseteq X$. The *projection of a stream* $\lambda \in X^{\sigma}$ *to* X', $\lambda \downarrow X'$, is defined recursively by

$$\varepsilon \downarrow X' = \varepsilon$$

$$x\rho \downarrow X' = \begin{cases} x(\rho \downarrow X') & \text{if } x \in X' \\ \rho \downarrow X' & \text{otherwise} \end{cases}$$

for each $\rho \in X^{\sigma}$. The *projection of a stream set* $\Lambda \subseteq X^{\sigma}$ *to* X' is given by

$$\Lambda \downarrow X' = \{ \lambda \downarrow X' \mid \lambda \in \Lambda \} .$$

In the examples given above, we obtain only valid life cycles by restriction, i.e.

$$\Lambda_{nvar} \downarrow X'_{nvar} \subset \Lambda'_{nvar} \quad \text{and}$$
$$\Lambda_{array} \downarrow X'_{array} = \Lambda'_{array}$$

As for the stack examples, neither is $\Lambda_{stack} \downarrow X'_{stack}$ a subset of Λ'_{stack} nor the other way round, both sets are incomparable. Intuitively, we would not accept P'_{stack} as a subprocess of P_{stack}, because the life cycle sets are largely unrelated. On the other side, we easily accept P'_{array} as a subprocess of P_{array}, because the former behaves "like" the latter, albeit in a restricted way. The question is whether we should accept P'_{nvar} as a "subvariable" of P_{nvar}: we have a subset of events, but the life cycle set is larger than that obtained by projecting Λ_{nvar} to X'_{nvar}. Our decision is to accept this situation as a subprocess relationship, too: the subprocess "contains" the behavior of the superprocess, but may allow for "more freedom". This decision is justified by the results described in section 3.3 below.

Summing up, we consider $P'=(X',\Lambda')$ to be a subprocess of $P=(X,\Lambda)$ iff $X' \subseteq X$ and $\Lambda \downarrow X' \subseteq \Lambda'$.

It is straightforward to generalize from inclusions to injective mappings among event alphabets, obtaining injective process morphisms. For the results in section 3.3, however, we have to cope with arbitrary mappings between event alphabets, also noninjective ones, and it is by no means straightforward how to generalize the above ideas to that case. The following version is different from that in (ESS89, ESS90), but it leads to nicer results about colimits and their usefulness for describing parallel composition, as presented in section 3.3.

Let X be an alphabet of events, and let X′ be a finite subset of X. By a *permutation* of X′ we mean a trace $\pi \in X'^*$ containing each event in X′ exactly once. Thus, the length of π coincides with the cardinality of X′. Let

$$perm(X') = \{ \pi \in X'^* \mid \pi \text{ is a permutation of } X' \} .$$

For $X'=\emptyset$, we define $perm(\emptyset)=\{\varepsilon\}$.

Let X_1 and X_2 be event alphabets, and let $h: X_1 \longrightarrow X_2$ be a mapping. In what follows, we assume that $h^{-1}(e)$ is finite for each $e \in X_2$. h gives rise to a mapping $\bar{h}$ in the reverse direction.

Definition 3.9: For h as given above, $\bar{h}$ is defined as follows

(1) For an event $e \in X_2$: $\quad \bar{h}(e) = perm(h^{-1}(e))$.

(2) For a stream $e_1 e_2 \ldots \in X_2^{\sigma}$: $\quad \bar{h}(e_1 e_2 \ldots) = \bar{h}(e_1)\bar{h}(e_2)\ldots$,
where juxtaposition denotes concatenation of trace sets.

(3) For a stream set $\Lambda \subseteq X_2^{\sigma}$: $\quad \bar{h}(\Lambda) = \bigcup_{\lambda \in \Lambda} \bar{h}(\lambda)$.

Proposition 3.10: If $h: X_1 \hookrightarrow X_2$ is an inclusion, then we have for each $e \in X_2, \lambda \in X_2^{\sigma}$ and $\Lambda \subseteq X_2^{\sigma}$:

$$\bar{h}(e) = \begin{cases} \{e\} & \text{if } e \in X_1 \\ \{\varepsilon\} & \text{otherwise} \end{cases} ,$$

$$\bar{h}(\lambda) = \lambda \downarrow X_1 ,$$

$$\bar{h}(\Lambda) = \Lambda \downarrow X_1 .$$

Definition 3.11: Let $P_1=(X_1,\Lambda_1)$ and $P_2=(X_2,\Lambda_2)$ be processes. A *process morphism* $h: P_1 \longrightarrow P_2$ is a mapping $h: X_1 \longrightarrow X_2$ satisfying the following *life cycle inheritance* condition:

$$\forall \lambda_2 \in \Lambda_2 \; \exists \lambda_1 \in \Lambda_1 : \; \lambda_1 \in \bar{h}(\lambda_2)$$

The life cycle inheritance condition is illustrated by the following diagram which commutes if we interpret $*$ as "pick the right one".

Refinement of Actions in Causality Based Models [1]

Rob van Glabbeek
Centre for Mathematics and Computer Science
P.O. Box 4079, 1009 AB Amsterdam, The Netherlands

Ursula Goltz
Gesellschaft für Mathematik und Datenverarbeitung
Postfach 1240, D-5205 Sankt Augustin 1, Federal Republic of Germany

Abstract

We consider an operator for refinement of actions to be used in the design of concurrent systems. Actions on a given level of abstraction are replaced by more complicated processes on a lower level. This is done in such a way that the behaviour of the refined system may be inferred compositionally from the behaviour of the original system and from the behaviour of the processes substituted for actions. We define this refinement operation for causality based models like event structures and Petri nets. For Petri nets, we relate it to other approaches for refining transitions.

Keywords Concurrency, action refinement, Petri nets, event structures

Contents

Abstract

Introduction

1 Refinement of actions in prime event structures

2 Refinement of actions in flow event structures

3 Configuration structures and refinement of actions

4 Refinement of transitions in Petri nets

Related work

References

[1]Contributed in part to Esprit Basic Research Action 3148 (DEMON).

Introduction

In this paper we consider the design of concurrent systems in the framework of approaches where the basic building blocks are the actions which may occur in a system. By an action we understand here any activity which is considered as a conceptual entity on a chosen level of abstraction. This allows to design systems in a top–down style, changing the level of abstraction by interpreting actions on a higher level by more complicated processes on a lower level. We refer to such a step in the design of a system as *refinement of actions.* An action could be refined by the sequential execution of several subactions, or by activities happening independently in parallel. One could also implement an action by a set of alternatives, of which only one should be taken.

0.1 Example

Consider the design of a sender, repeatedly reading data and sending them to a certain receiver. A first description of this system is given by the Petri net shown below. An introduction to Petri nets and the way they model concurrent systems can be found in [Reisig a]; the refinement mechanism used in this example will be treated formally in Section 4.

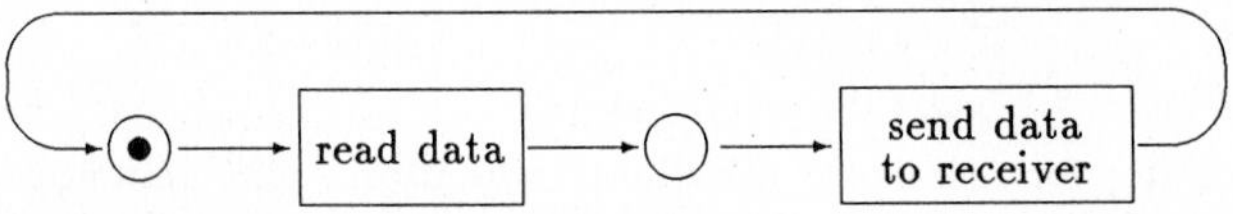

On a slightly less abstract description level the action "send data to receiver" might turn out to consist of two parts "prepare sending" and "carry out sending", to be executed sequentially. This corresponds to the following refined Petri net.

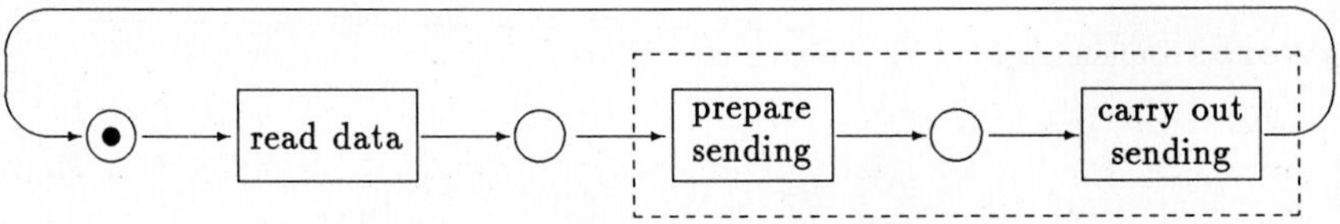

Refinement by a sequential process

Then the action "prepare sending" may be decomposed in two independent activities "prepare data for transmission" and "get permission to send", to be executed on different processors:

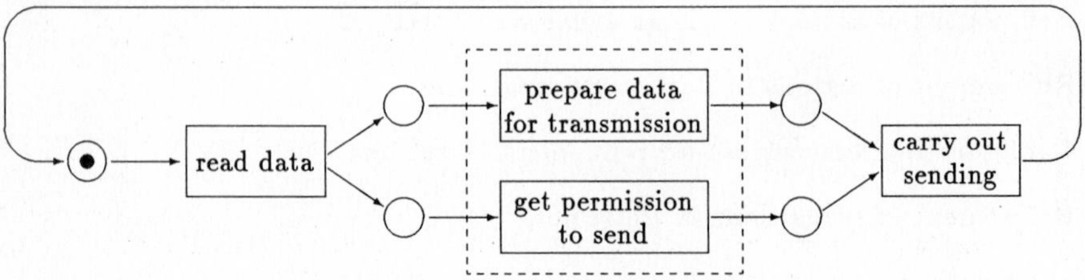

Refinement by a parallel process

Furthermore it may turn out that there are two alternative channels for sending messages. Each time the sender should choose one of them to send a message, perhaps depending on which one is available at the moment.

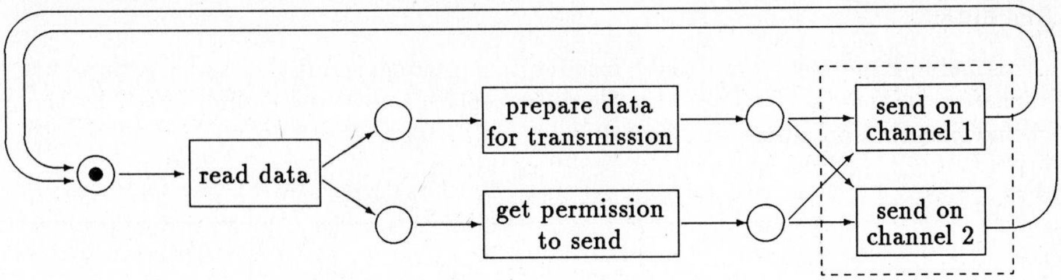

Refinement by alternative actions

On an even more concrete level of abstraction, channel 2 may happen to be rather unreliable, and getting a message at the other end requires the use of a communication protocol. On the other hand, channel 1 may be found to be reliable, and does not need such a precaution.

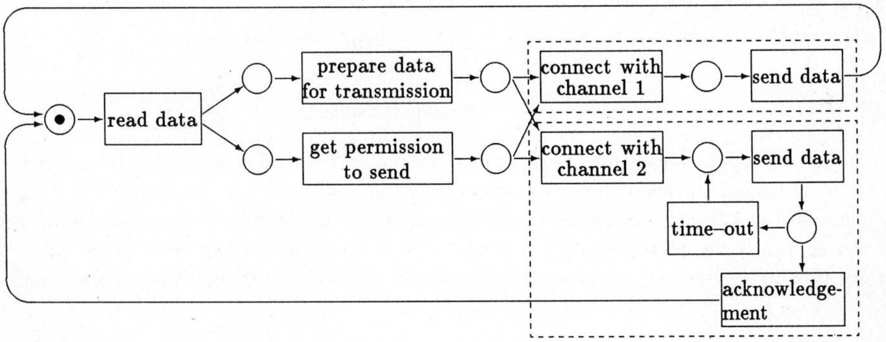

Refinement by an infinite process

Here we see that it may happen that the process we have substituted for the action "send on channel 2" does not terminate. It may happen that the attempt of sending data always fails and this prevents the system of reaching its initial state again.

Our aim is to define an operator for refinement of actions, taking as arguments a system description on a given level of abstraction and an interpretation of (some of) the actions on this level by more complicated processes on a lower level, and yielding a system description on the lower level. This should be done in such a way that the behaviour of the refined system may be inferred compositionally from the behaviour of the original system and from the behaviour of the processes substituted for actions.

As illustrated above, we want to allow to substitute rather general kinds of behaviours for actions. We even allow the refinement of an action by an infinite behaviour. This contradicts a common assumption that an action takes only a finite amount of time. It means that when regarding a sequential composition $a; b$ we can not be sure that b occurs under all circumstances; it can only occur if the action a really terminates.

There is one type of refinement that we do not want to allow, namely to "forget" actions by replacing them with the empty process.

0.2 Example

Continuing Example 0.1 we could imagine that getting permission to send turns out to be unnecessary and can be skipped. Hence we replace the corresponding action by the empty behaviour, thus obtaining

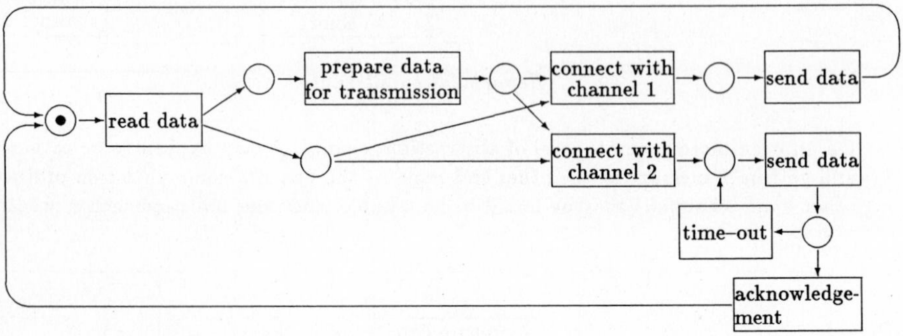

Forgetful refinement

Even though this operation seems natural when applied as in the above example, it may cause drastic changes in the possible behaviours of a system. It may happen that executing a certain action a prevents another action from happening. This property should be preserved under refinement of a. However, if a is completely removed, it cannot prevent anything any more, which can remove a deadlock possibility from the system. For this reason "forgetful" refinements will not be considered here.

0.3 Example

Consider the Petri net

$N =$ 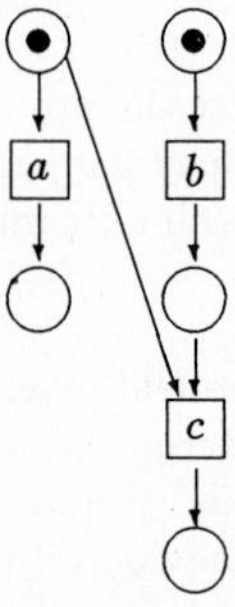

and the net obtained when refining a by the empty behaviour:

$N' =$ 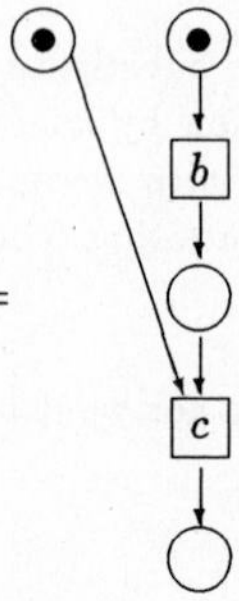

.

In the first net it is possible to execute a and b, and by this reach a state where no further action is possible. If we try to deduce the behaviour after refinement from the behaviour of N, we would expect that the refined system may reach a state, by executing b, where no more action is possible. However, this is not the case for N'. After b, it is always possible to execute c in N'.

In order to define a suitable refinement operator, one first has to select a model for the description of concurrent systems. The models of concurrency found in the literature can roughly be distinguished in two kinds: those in which the independent execution of two processes is modelled by specifying the possible interleavings of their (atomic) actions, and those in which the causal relations between the actions of a system are represented explicitly. The interleaving based models were devised to describe systems built from actions that are assumed to be instantaneous or indivisible. Nevertheless, one might be tempted to use them also for the description of systems built from actions that may have a duration or structure. However, the following example shows that it is not possible to define the desired compositional refinement operator on such models of concurrency without imposing some restrictions (as already observed in [Pratt] and [CDP]).

0.4 Example

The systems $P = a \parallel b$, executing the actions a and b independently, and $Q = a;b + b;a$, executing either the sequence ab or the sequence ba, cannot be distinguished in interleaving models; they are represented by the same tree in the model of synchronisation trees [Milner].

tree (P) = tree (Q) = 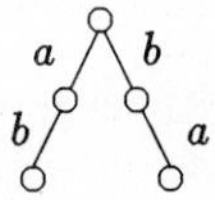

After refining a into the sequential compositon of a_1 and a_2, thereby obtaining the systems

$$P' = (a_1; a_2) \parallel b \quad \text{and} \quad Q' = (a_1; a_2); b + b; (a_1; a_2),$$

their tree representations are different:

tree (P') = 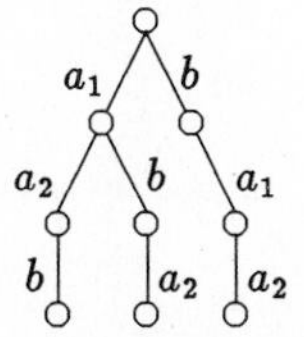

, tree (Q') = 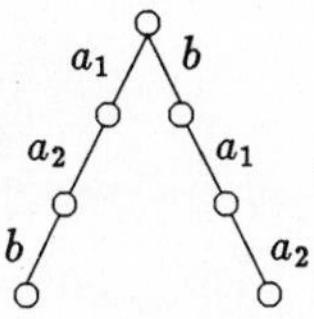

.

The two systems are even non–equivalent, according to any reasonable semantic equivalence, since only P' can perform the sequence of actions a_1ba_2. Hence, in the model of synchronisation trees the semantic representation of the refined systems is not derivable from the semantic representation of the original systems. The same holds for other interleaving models.

There are still ways left to define a compositional refinement operator on interleaving based models. First of all one could restrict the kind of refinements that are allowed in such a way that situations as in Example 0.4 cannot occur. Of course this would exclude the possibility of refining a in $a_1; a_2$ in either P or Q (or both). Although we consider this to be an interesting option, in this paper we choose to allow rather general refinements, including at least the one of Example 0.4. Furthermore, some approaches have been proposed which are based on a concept of "atomic" actions; refining an atomic action would then result in an "atomic" process that cannot be "interupted" by other activities (the refinement of P in Example 0.4 would not have the execution a_1ba_2). We will comment on these approaches in the concluding section. In this paper we choose not to assume action atomicity in any way, and to allow the parallel or independent execution of actions. Hence interleaving based models are unsuited for our approach. On the other hand we will show that the desired compositional refinement operator *can* be defined on causality based models of concurrency without imposing such restrictions. We will do this for semantic models like Petri nets and event structures. Since these models are being used as a semantics of languages like CCS, we hope that this will lead also to extending these languages by a mechanism for refinement.

0.5 Example

The systems $P = a \parallel b$ and $Q = a;b + b;a$ from Example 0.4 may be represented by the (labelled) Petri nets

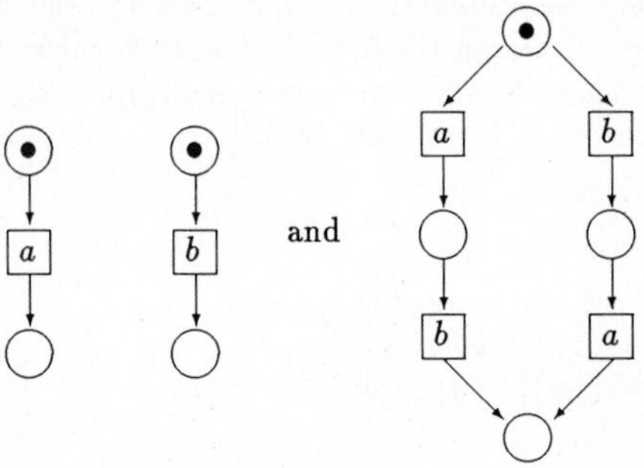

The Petri net representations of the refined systems P' and Q', where a is replaced by the sequence $a_1 a_2$, are then derivable by transition refinement from the nets for the original systems. We obtain

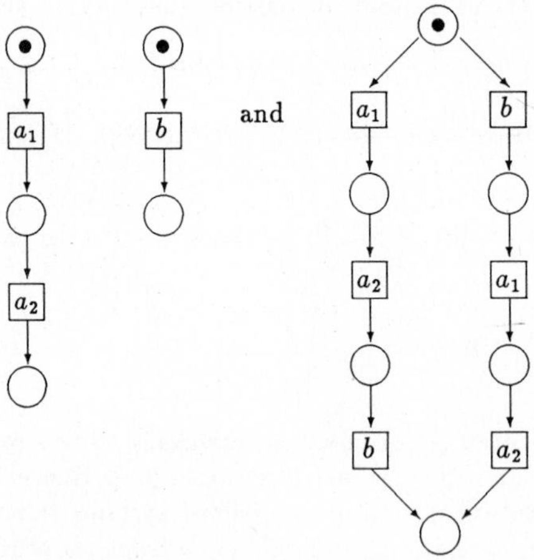

We will use two kinds of semantic models. Both of them are based on the idea of [Petri] to model causalities in concurrent systems explicitly and thereby also representing independence of activities. Additionally, the models we use represent the choice structure of systems; they show where decisions between alternative behaviours are taken.

We will not distinguish external and internal actions here; we do not consider abstraction by hiding of actions.

The more basic model, in particular when being concerned more with actions than with states, are *event structures.* We will consider three types of event structures here: *prime event structures* with a binary conflict relation [NPW], *flow event structures,* which are particularly suited as a semantic model of CCS [BC], and, as a more abstract and general model, *configuration structures* (*families of configurations* [Winskel]), where a system is represented by its subsets of events which determine possible executions.

The models considered so far are usually not applied to model systems directly, but rather as the underlying semantics of system description languages like CCS. One of the reasons for this is that infinite behaviours can only be represented by infinite structures (with an infinite set of events). So, finally, we will consider Petri nets as a framework which is directly applicable in the design process. Event structures may be derived from Petri nets as a particularly simple case, but Petri nets are more powerful. For example, infinite behaviours may be represented as finite net structures together with the "token game". However, causality is then no longer a basic notion but has to be derived. Petri nets with their appealing graphical representation are being used extensively for the — more or less formal — representation of systems and — mostly less formal — during the design process. A disciplined way for developing net models systematically by refinement is therefore very important.

We start in Section 1 by recalling the basic notions for prime event structures and a result from [GG], showing how to refine actions by finite, conflict–free behaviours. We show that, for refining actions with more general behaviours, it is convenient to use more expressive models. In Section 2, we introduce flow event structures and show how to refine actions also by (possibly infinite) behaviours with conflicts. We show that, as for prime event structure refinement, the behaviour of a refined flow event structure may be deduced compositionally. In Section 3, we introduce configuration structures and a refinement operation for them. We show that the more "syntactic" constructions in the previous sections are consistent with this general notion. Finally, we give an overview on the work on refinement in Petri nets, and we suggest a rather general notion of refinement of transitions which is still modular with respect to behaviour. Related work is discussed in the concluding section.

1 Refinement of actions in prime event structures

In this section, we will recall definitions and results from our previous paper [GG]. There we have shown how to refine actions in the most simple form of event structures, prime event structures with a binary conflict relation [NPW]. Here, this is supposed to serve as an introduction to the concepts and as a motivation to move to more general structures because of the limitations of this approach.

We consider systems that are capable of performing actions from a given set *Act* of action names.

1.1 Definition

A *(labelled) prime event structure (over an alphabet Act)* is a 4–tuple $\mathcal{E} = (E, \leq, \#, l)$ where

- E is a set of *events,*
- $\leq\ \subseteq E \times E$ is a partial order (the *causality relation*) satisfying the *principle of finite causes:*

$$\forall e \in E : \{d \in E | d \leq e\} \text{ is finite},$$

- $\# \subseteq E \times E$ is an irreflexive, symmetric relation (the *conflict relation*) satisfying the *principle of conflict heredity:*

$$\forall d, e, f \in E : d \leq e \wedge d \# f \Rightarrow e \# f,$$

- $l : E \rightarrow Act$ is a *labelling function.*

The components of a prime event structure $\mathcal{E}$ will be denoted by $E_{\mathcal{E}}, \leq_{\mathcal{E}}, \#_{\mathcal{E}}$ and $l_{\mathcal{E}}$. If clear from the context, the index $\mathcal{E}$ will be omitted. As usual, we write $d < e$ for $d \leq e \wedge d \neq e$, etc.

A prime event structure represents a concurrent system in the following way: action names $a \in Act$ represent actions the system might perform, an event $e \in E$ labelled with a represents an occurrence of a during a possible run of the system, $d < e$ means that d is a prerequisite for e and $d\#e$ means that d and e cannot happen both in the same run.

Causal independence *(concurrency)* of events is expressed by the derived relation $co \subseteq E \times E$: $d \; co \; e$ iff $\neg(d < e \vee e < d \vee d\#e)$. By definition, $<, >, \#$ and co form a partition of $E \times E$.

Throughout the paper, we assume a fixed set Act of action names as labelling set. Let $\mathbf{E}_{prime}$ denote the domain of prime event structures labelled over Act.

A prime event structure $\mathcal{E}$ is *finite* if $E_{\mathcal{E}}$ is finite; $\mathcal{E}$ is *conflict–free* if $\#_{\mathcal{E}} = \emptyset$.
O denotes the empty event structure $(\emptyset, \emptyset, \emptyset, \emptyset)$.

For $X \subseteq E_{\mathcal{E}}$, the *restriction of $\mathcal{E}$ to X* is defined as

$$\mathcal{E}\lceil X = (X, \; \leq \cap (X \times X), \; \# \cap (X \times X), \; l\lceil X).$$

Two prime event structures $\mathcal{E}$ and $\mathcal{F}$ are *isomorphic* ($\mathcal{E} \cong \mathcal{F}$) iff there exists a bijection between their sets of events preserving $\leq, \#$ and labelling. Generally, we will not distinguish isomorphic event structures.

Isomorphism classes of conflict–free event structures are called *pomsets* [Pratt]. Pomsets generated by certain subsets of events may be considered as possible "executions" of the system represented by the event structure. The partial order between action occurrences then represents causal dependencies in the execution. Subsets of events representing executions (called *configurations*) have to be conflict–free; furthermore they must be left–closed with respect to $\leq$ (all prerequisites for any event occurring in the "execution" must also occur). It is assumed that in a finite period only finitely many actions are performed. We will consider only finite executions when describing the behaviour of systems. So, unlike [Winskel], we require configurations to be finite. We will comment on this point in Section 3.

1.2 Definition

i. A subset $X \subseteq E$ of events in a prime event structure $\mathcal{E}$ is *left–closed* in $\mathcal{E}$ iff, for all $d, e \in E$, $e \in X \wedge d \leq e \Rightarrow d \in X$.
   X is *conflict–free in* $\mathcal{E}$ iff $\mathcal{E}\lceil X$ is conflict–free.

ii. A subset $X \subseteq E$ will be called a *(finite) configuration* of a prime event structure $\mathcal{E}$ iff X is finite, left–closed and conflict–free in $\mathcal{E}$. $Conf\,(\mathcal{E})$ denotes the set of all configurations of $\mathcal{E}$. A configuration $X \in Conf\,(\mathcal{E})$ is called *complete* iff $\forall d \in E : d \notin X \Rightarrow \exists e \in X$ with $d\#e$.

Configurations may be considered as possible states of the system; they determine the remaining behaviour of the system as being the set of all events which have not yet occurred and are not excluded because of conflicts. Note that a configuration X is complete iff it is maximal, i.e. $X \subseteq Y \in Conf\,(\mathcal{E})$ implies $X = Y$.

1.3 Example

The system $a \parallel b + a; b$, executing either a and b independently or a and b sequentially, may be represented by the prime event structure

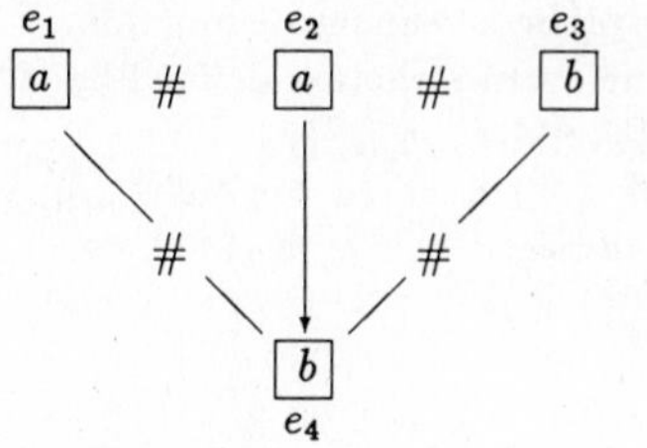

where the causality relation is represented by arcs.

The configurations of $\mathcal{E}$ are

$$\emptyset, \{e_1\}, \{e_2\}, \{e_3\}, \{e_1, e_3\}, \{e_2, e_4\},$$

corresponding to the pomsets

$$\emptyset,\ a,\ b,\ \begin{smallmatrix} a \\ b \end{smallmatrix} \text{ and } a \longrightarrow b.$$

$\begin{smallmatrix} a \\ b \end{smallmatrix}$ and $a \longrightarrow b$ correspond to complete configurations.

We will now define a refinement operation substituting actions by finite, conflict-free, non-empty event structures. As discussed in the introduction, we will not allow forgetful refinements replacing actions by the empty event structure. We will later explain why we have to restrict to finite and conflict-free refinements of actions.

A refinement function will be a function *ref* specifiying, for each action a, an event structure $ref(a)$ which is to be substituted for a. Interesting refinements (and also the refinements in our examples) will mostly refine only certain actions, hence replace most actions by themselves. However, for uniformity (and for simplicity in proofs) we consider all actions to be refined.

Given an event structure $\mathcal{E}$ and a refinement function *ref*, we construct the refined event structure $ref(\mathcal{E})$ as follows. Each event e labelled by a is replaced by a disjoint copy, $\mathcal{E}_e$, of $ref(a)$. The causality and conflict structure is inherited from $\mathcal{E}$: every event which was causally before e will be causally before all events of $\mathcal{E}_e$, all events which causally followed e will causally follow all the events of $\mathcal{E}_e$, and all events in conflict with e will be in conflict with all the events of $\mathcal{E}_e$.

Graphically, the idea may be sketched as follows (in this picture we omit arcs derivable by transitivity and inherited conflicts).

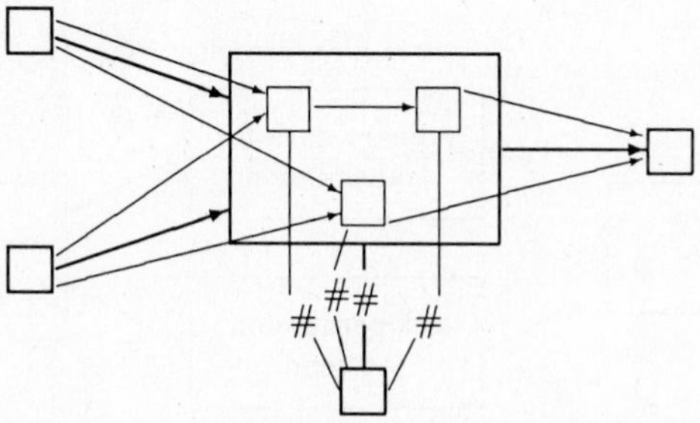

1.4 Definition

(i) A function $ref: Act \to \boldsymbol{E}_{prime} - \{O\}$ is called a *refinement function (for prime event structures)* if $\forall a \in Act : ref(a)$ is finite and conflict-free.

(ii) Let $\mathcal{E} \in \boldsymbol{E}_{prime}$ and let ref be a refinement function.
Then $ref(\mathcal{E})$ is the prime event structure defined by
- $E_{ref(\mathcal{E})} = \{(e, e') | e \in E_{\mathcal{E}}, e' \in E_{ref(l_{\mathcal{E}}(e))}\}$,
- $(d, d') \leq_{ref(\mathcal{E})} (e, e')$ iff $d <_{\mathcal{E}} e$ or $(d = e \wedge d' \leq_{ref(l_{\mathcal{E}}(d))} e')$,
- $(d, d') \#_{ref(\mathcal{E})} (e, e')$ iff $d \#_{\mathcal{E}} e$,
- $l_{ref(\mathcal{E})}(e, e') = l_{ref(l_{\mathcal{E}}(e))}(e')$.

We show that refinement is a well-defined operation on prime event structures, even when isomorphic prime event structures are identified.

1.5 Proposition

(i) If $\mathcal{E} \in \boldsymbol{E}_{prime}$ and ref is a refinement function then $ref(\mathcal{E})$ is a prime event structure indeed.

(ii) If $\mathcal{E} \in \boldsymbol{E}_{prime}$ and ref, ref' are refinement functions with $ref(a) \cong ref'(a)$ for all $a \in Act$ then $ref(\mathcal{E}) \cong ref'(\mathcal{E})$.

(iii) If $\mathcal{E}, \mathcal{F} \in \boldsymbol{E}_{prime}$ and ref is a refinement function then $ref(\mathcal{E}) \cong ref(\mathcal{F})$.

Proof Straightforward. ■

1.6 Example

We consider a simplified version of the sender (Example 0.1) from the introduction. We assume that the sender reads and sends only once. We may carry out the first two steps of the design in terms of prime event structures as follows.

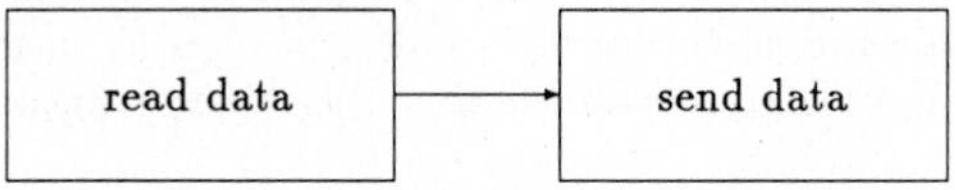

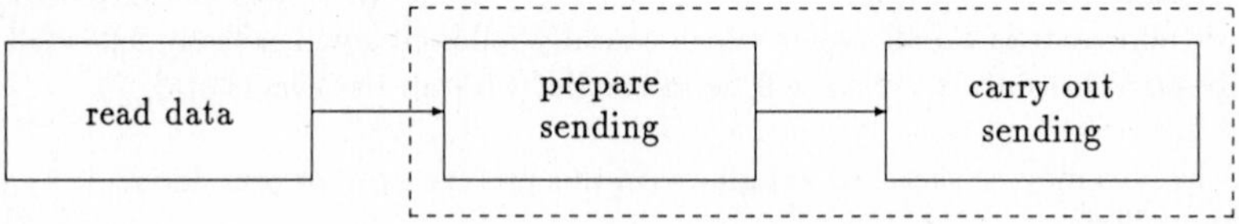

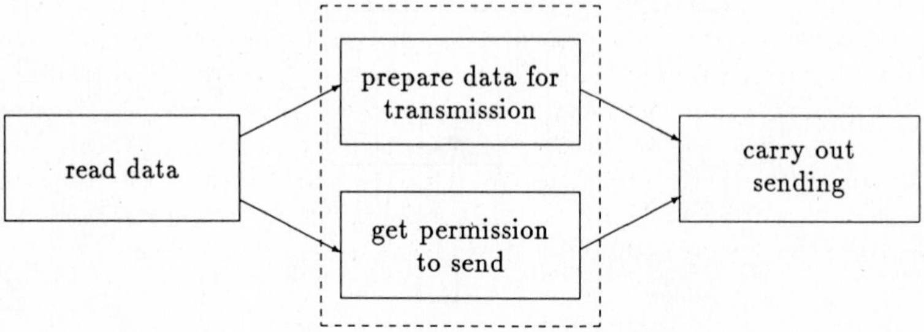

The next refinement step would require a refinement of an action by conflicting behaviours. This is not possible in our framework up to now.

The reason that we can only refine actions by conflict–free event structures is the axiom of conflict heredity and the notion of configuration in prime event structures. They imply that any event will always occur with a unique history (in terms of its causal predecessors) [Winskel].

Now consider e.g. $\mathcal{E} = \overset{a}{\underset{b}{\downarrow}}$. Replacing a by $c\#d$ would require to duplicate the event labelled by b in some way, since b should then occur either caused by c or by d. Since this would lead to a complicated definition, we will consider more general forms of event structures that do not require duplication in Section 2 and 3.

The restriction to refinement of actions by finite event structures is necessary to ensure that the resulting event structure will obey the axiom of finite causes. In the more general models we will consider later, we will not assume this axiom, and this will allow also refinements by infinite behaviours as discussed in the introduction.

Finally, we show how the behaviour of the refined event structure $ref(\mathcal{E})$ is determined by the behaviour of $\mathcal{E}$ and by the behaviour of the event structures which are substituted for actions.

1.7 Proposition

Let $\mathcal{E} \in \boldsymbol{E}_{prime}$, let ref be a refinement function.

We call $\tilde{X}$ a *refinement of configuration* $X \in Conf(\mathcal{E})$ *by* ref iff

- $\tilde{X} = \bigcup_{e \in X} \{e\} \times X_e$ where $\forall e \in X : X_e \in Conf(ref(l_{\mathcal{E}}(e))) - \{\emptyset\}$,

- $e \in busy(\tilde{X}) \Longrightarrow e$ maximal in X with respect to $\leq_{\mathcal{E}}$
  where $busy(\tilde{X}) := \{e \in X \mid X_e \text{ not complete}\}$.

Then $Conf(ref(\mathcal{E})) = \{\tilde{X} \mid \tilde{X}$ is a refinement of a configuration $X \in Conf(\mathcal{E})\}$.

Proof [GG] or as a special case of Proposition 2.8. ■

Hence the configurations of $ref(\mathcal{E})$ are exactly those configurations which are refinements of configurations of $\mathcal{E}$. A refinement of a configuration X of $\mathcal{E}$ is obtained by replacing each event e in X by a non–empty configuration X_e of $ref(l_{\mathcal{E}}(e))$. Events which are causally necessary for other events in X may only be replaced by complete configurations.

2 Refinement of actions in flow event structures

In the previous section, we have indicated that for refining actions by event structures with conflicts more general models than prime event structures are appropriate. In [BC] a form of event structures, called *flow event structures*, is suggested which is particularly suited for giving semantics to languages like CCS. Flow event structures are more general than prime events in the following sense: they do not assume conflict heredity and the axiom of finite causes, they allow inconsistent (self–conflicting) events and the causality relation is not required to be transitive and may even contain (syntactic) cycles. This makes it very easy to define operations like parallel composition and restriction, and we will show here that they are also well suited to deal with refinement of actions.

2.1 Definition

A *(labelled) flow event structure (over an alphabet Act)* is a 4–tuple $\mathcal{E} = (E, \prec, \#, l)$ where

- E is a set of *events*,
- $\prec \subseteq E \times E$ is an irreflexive relation, the *flow relation*,
- $\# \subseteq E \times E$ is a symmetric relation, the *conflict relation*,
- $l : E \longrightarrow Act$ is the *labelling function*.

Let $\mathbb{E}$ denote the domain of flow event structures labelled over *Act*. The components of $\mathcal{E} \in \mathbb{E}$ will be denoted by $E_\mathcal{E}, \prec_\mathcal{E}, \#_\mathcal{E}$ and $l_\mathcal{E}$. The index $\mathcal{E}$ will be omitted if clear from the context. $\mathcal{E}$ is *conflict-free* if $\#_\mathcal{E} = \emptyset$. For $X \subseteq E_\mathcal{E}$, $\mathcal{E}\lceil X = (X, \prec_\mathcal{E}\lceil X, \#_\mathcal{E}\lceil X, l_\mathcal{E}\lceil X)$ is the *restriction of $\mathcal{E}$ to X*.

Two flow event structures $\mathcal{E}$ and $\mathcal{F}$ are *isomorphic* ($\mathcal{E} \cong \mathcal{F}$) iff there exists a bijection between their sets of events preserving $\prec, \#$ and labelling.

The interpretation of the conflict and the flow relation is formalised by defining configurations of flow event structures. Configurations must be conflict free; in particular, self-conflicting events will never occur in any configuration. $d \prec e$ will mean that d is a *possible immediate cause* for e. For an event to occur it is necessary that a *complete* non–conflicting set of its causes has occurred. Here a set of causes is complete if for any cause which is not contained there is a conflicting event which is contained. Finally, no cycles with respect to causal dependence may occur.

2.2 Definition Let $\mathcal{E} \in \mathbb{E}$.

(i) $X \subseteq E$ is *left–closed in $\mathcal{E}$ up to conflicts* iff $\forall d, e \in E$: if $e \in X, d \prec e$ and $d \notin X$ then there exists an $f \in X$ with $f \prec e$ and $d\#f$.
$X \subseteq E$ is *conflict–free* iff $\mathcal{E} \lceil X$ is conflict–free.

(ii) $X \subseteq E$ is a *(finite) configuration* of $\mathcal{E}$ iff X is finite, left–closed up to conflicts and conflict–free and does not contain a causality cycle: $\leq_X := (\prec \cap (X \times X))^\star$ is an ordering.
A configuration X is called *maximal* iff $X \subseteq Y \in Conf(\mathcal{E})$ implies $X = Y$.
A configuration X is called *complete* iff $\forall d \in E : d \notin X \Rightarrow \exists e \in X$ with $d\#e$.
$Conf(\mathcal{E})$ denotes the set of all configurations of $\mathcal{E}$.

The causal dependence between action occurrences in a configuration may again, as for prime event structures, be represented by a pomset; for $X \in Conf(\mathcal{E})$, we take the isomorphism class of $(X, \leq_X, l_\mathcal{E}\lceil X)$.

2.3 Example

The system $((a + b) \parallel c); d$ may be represented by the flow event structure

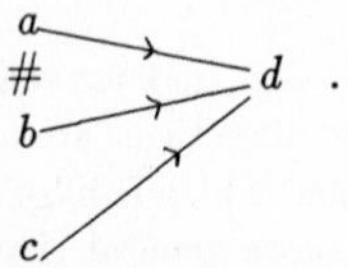

(in graphical representations we omit names of events and represent $\prec$ by arcs of the form $\longrightarrow$).

The pomsets 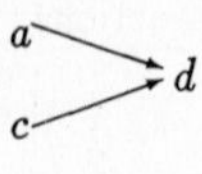

and 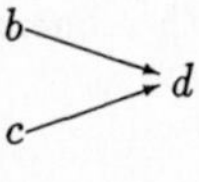

correspond to complete configurations.

Note that prime event structures are special flow event structures defining $d \prec e$ iff $d < e$; the definition of configuration then coincides.

However, in contrast to prime event structures, not all *maximal* configurations are complete. Partly this is due to the fact that, in flow event structures, syntactic and semantic conflict not necessarily coincide, (two events are in *semantic conflict* if there is no configuration containing them both). Flow event structures where syntactic and semantic conflict coincide are called *faithful* in [Boudol b]. However, also in faithful flow event structures maximal configurations are not necessarly complete, either due to inconsistent events, but also in flow event structures without inconsistent events, as shown by the following example.

2.4 Example

Let $\mathcal{E}$ =

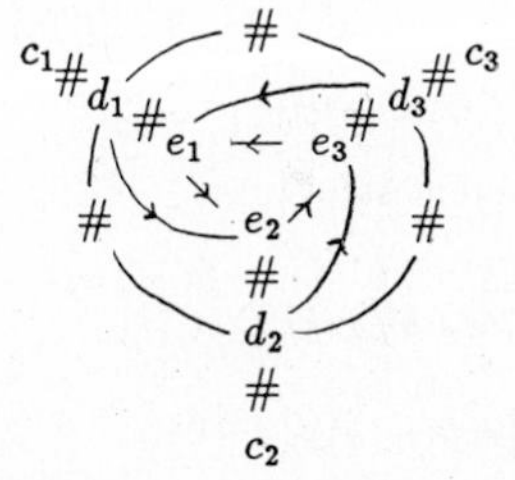

The configuration $\{c_1, c_2, c_3\}$ is maximal but not complete.

Maximal but incomplete configurations may be interpreted as deadlocking behaviours. Assume that a semantic sequential composition is defined for flow event structures by putting all events in the first component in $\prec$–relation with the events of the second component. Any incomplete maximal configuration of the first component would then disable the second component. Thus, in flow event structures, deadlock and termination may be distinguished.

2.5 Definition

A flow event structure $\mathcal{E}$ is *deadlock–free* iff every maximal configuration of $\mathcal{E}$ is complete.

Refinement of actions in flow event structures may now be defined as follows. We assume a refinement function $ref : Act \longrightarrow \mathbb{E} - \{O\}$ (where O denotes the empty flow event structure) and replace each event labelled by a by a disjoint copy of $ref(a)$. The conflict and causality structure will just be inherited.

Hence, we may replace actions also by behaviours with conflicts and by infinite behaviours.

2.6 Definition

(i) A function $ref : Act \longrightarrow \mathbb{E} - \{O\}$ is called a *refinement function (for flow event structures)*.

(ii) Let $\mathcal{E} \in \mathbb{E}$ and let ref be a refinement function.
Then the *refinement of $\mathcal{E}$ by ref*, $ref(\mathcal{E})$, is the flow event structure defined by
- $E_{ref(\mathcal{E})} = \{(e, e') | e \in E_{\mathcal{E}}, e' \in E_{ref(l_{\mathcal{E}}(e))}\}$,
- $(d, d') \prec_{ref(\mathcal{E})} (e, e')$ iff $d \prec e$ or $(d = e \wedge d' \prec_{ref(l_{\mathcal{E}}(d))} e')$,
- $(d, d') \#_{ref(\mathcal{E})} (e, e')$ iff $d \#_{\mathcal{E}} e$ or $(d = e \wedge d' \#_{ref(l_{\mathcal{E}}(d))} e')$,
- $l_{ref(\mathcal{E})}(e, e') = l_{ref(l_{\mathcal{E}}(e))}(e')$.

As for prime event structures, we verify that $ref(\mathcal{E})$ is well-defined, even when isomorphic flow event structures are identified.

2.7 Proposition

(i) If $\mathcal{E} \in \boldsymbol{E}$ and *ref* is a refinement function then $ref(\mathcal{E})$ is a flow event structure indeed.

(ii) If $\mathcal{E} \in \boldsymbol{E}$ and *ref*, *ref'* are refinement functions with $ref(a) \cong ref'(a)$ for all $a \in Act$ then $ref(\mathcal{E}) \cong ref'(\mathcal{E})$.

(iii) If $\mathcal{E}, \mathcal{F} \in \boldsymbol{E}$ and *ref* is a refinement function then $ref(\mathcal{E}) \cong ref(\mathcal{F})$.

Proof Straightforward. ■

Finally, we show that, analogously to prime event structures, the behaviour of a refined flow event structure $ref(\mathcal{E})$ may be deduced compositionally from the behaviour of $\mathcal{E}$ and the behaviour of the refinements of actions.

2.8 Proposition

Let $\mathcal{E} \in \boldsymbol{E}$, let *ref* be a refinement function for flow event structures.

We call $\tilde{X}$ a *refinement of configuration* $X \in Conf(\mathcal{E})$ *by ref* iff

- $\tilde{X} = \bigcup_{e \in X} \{e\} \times X_e$ where $\forall e \in X : X_e \in Conf(ref(l_\mathcal{E}(e))) - \{\emptyset\}$,

- $e \in busy(\tilde{X}) \Longrightarrow e$ maximal in X with respect to $\leq_X$ where $busy(\tilde{X}) := \{e \in X \mid X_e \text{ not complete}\}$.

Then $Conf(ref(\mathcal{E})) = \{\tilde{X} \mid \tilde{X}$ is a refinement of a configuration $X \in Conf(\mathcal{E})\}$.

Proof

"$\subseteq$" Let $\tilde{X} \in Conf(ref(\mathcal{E}))$.

First we show that $X := pr_1(\tilde{X}) \in Conf(\mathcal{E})$.
X is finite since $\tilde{X}$ is finite.

X is left-closed in $\mathcal{E}$ up to conflicts:
Let $e \in X, d \in E_\mathcal{E}$ with $d \prec_\mathcal{E} e$ and $d \notin X$.
We have to show that there exists an $f \in X$ with $f \prec_\mathcal{E} e$ and $f \#_\mathcal{E} d$.
Since $e \in X$ there must be some $(e, e') \in \tilde{X}$.
There exists $(d, d') \in E_{ref(\mathcal{E})}, (d, d') \notin \tilde{X}$ since $ref(d) \neq O$ and $d \notin X$.
Furthermore $(d, d') \prec_{ref(\mathcal{E})} (e, e')$ since $d \prec_\mathcal{E} e$.
So $\exists (f, f') \in \tilde{X}$ with $(f, f') \prec_{ref(\mathcal{E})} (e, e')$ and $(f, f') \#_{ref(\mathcal{E})} (d, d')$.
$f \neq d$ since $f \in X, d \notin X \Longrightarrow f \#_\mathcal{E} d$.
If $f \neq e$ we have $f \prec_\mathcal{E} e$ and we are done.
Assume $f = e$ then $(d, d') \prec_{ref(\mathcal{E})} (f, f')$.
Then there exists $(g, g') \in \tilde{X}$ with $(g, g') \prec_{ref(\mathcal{E})} (f, f') = (e, f')$ and $(g, g') \#_{ref(\mathcal{E})} (d, d')$.
$g \#_\mathcal{E} d$ since $g \neq d$. Furthermore $g \in X$.
If $g \neq f = e$ then $g \prec_\mathcal{E} e$ and we are done. Since $\tilde{X}$ is finite, we will find (by repeating this), after finitely many steps, $(\tilde{f}, \tilde{f}') \in \tilde{X}$ with $\tilde{f} \#_\mathcal{E} d$ and $\tilde{f} \prec_\mathcal{E} e$. Hence X is left-closed up to conflicts.

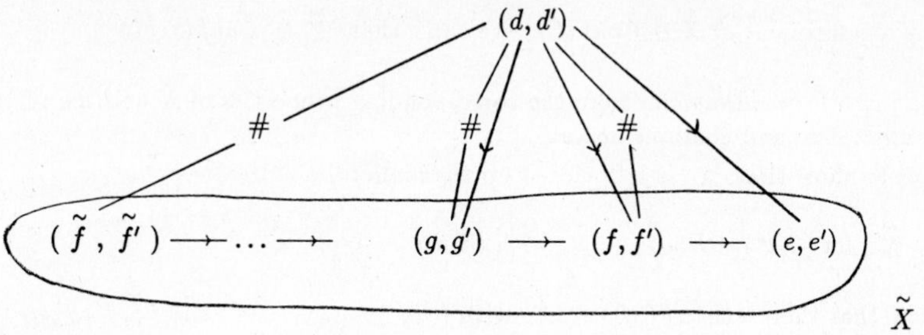

X is conflict–free:
Assume $d, e \in X$ with $d \#_{\mathcal{E}} e$.
Then there exist $(d,d'),(e,e') \in \tilde{X}, (d,d')\#_{ref(\mathcal{E})}(e,e')$.
This is a contradiction since $\tilde{X}$ is conflict–free.

Finally we have to show that X does not contain a causality–cycle. Assume $d, e \in X, d \neq e, d \leq_X e$ and $e \leq_X d$ (where $\leq_X$ is derived from $\prec_{\mathcal{E}}$). It is straightforward to verify that this implies $\exists (d,d'),(e,e') \in \tilde{X}$ with $(d,d') \neq (e,e')$, $(d,d') \leq_{\tilde{X}} (e,e')$ and $(e,e') \leq_{\tilde{X}} (d,d')$. This is in contradiction with the cyclefreeness of $\tilde{X}$.

Hence $X = pr_1(\tilde{X}) \in Conf(\mathcal{E})$. We will show that $\tilde{X}$ is a refinement of X.
Let $e \in X$ and $X_e := \{e' \mid (e,e') \in \tilde{X}\}$. By construction $X_e \neq \emptyset$.
Let $\mathcal{E}_e := ref(l_{\mathcal{E}}(e))$. We want to show that $X_e \in Conf(\mathcal{E}_e)$.

Obviously $X_e \subseteq E_{\mathcal{E}_e}$.
X_e is finite, conflict–free and cycle–free since $\tilde{X}$ is finite, conflict–free and cycle-free. So it only remains to be shown that X_e is left–closed up to conflicts.

Let $d' \in \mathcal{E}_e, d' \prec_{\mathcal{E}_e} e' \in X_e, d' \notin X_e$.
Then $(e,d') \in E_{ref(\mathcal{E})}, (e,d') \prec_{ref(\mathcal{E})} (e,e') \in \tilde{X}$ and $(e,d') \notin \tilde{X}$.
So there exists $(f,f') \in \tilde{X}$ with $(f,f') \prec_{ref(\mathcal{E})} (e,e')$ and $(f,f')\#_{ref(\mathcal{E})}(e,d')$.
$f, e \in X \Longrightarrow \neg(f \#_{\mathcal{E}} e) \Longrightarrow f = e \wedge f' \#_{\mathcal{E}_e} d' \Longrightarrow f' \in X_e$ and $f' \prec_{\mathcal{E}_e} e'$.
Hence $X_e \in Conf(\mathcal{E}_e)$.

From what we have shown by now it follows that
$\tilde{X} = \bigcup_{e \in X} \{e\} \times X_e$ with $X \in Conf(\mathcal{E})$ and, for all $e \in X$, $X_e \in Conf(ref(l_{\mathcal{E}}(e))) - \{\emptyset\}$.

Now let $e \in busy(\tilde{X})$. We have to show that e is maximal in X whith respect to $\leq_X$.

Suppose e is not maximal in X. Then there exists $f \in X$ with $e \prec_{\mathcal{E}} f$, and there exists $(f,f') \in \tilde{X}$.
Since X_e is not complete there exists $d' \in E_{\mathcal{E}_e} - X_e$ with

$$(*) \forall e' \in X_e : \neg(d' \#_{\mathcal{E}_e} e').$$

We have $(e,d') \prec_{ref(\mathcal{E})} (f,f')$, $(e,d') \notin \tilde{X}$.
Since $\tilde{X}$ is a configuration, there then exists $(g,g') \in \tilde{X}$ with $(g,g') \prec_{ref(\mathcal{E})} (f,f')$ and $(g,g')\#_{ref(\mathcal{E})}(e,d')$
Since $g, e \in X$, we have $\neg(g \#_{\mathcal{E}} e)$.
Hence $g = e$ and $g' \in X_e$, $g' \#_{\mathcal{E}_e} d'$.
However this contradicts $(*)$.

"$\supseteq$" Let $\tilde{X}$ be a refinement of $X \in Conf(\mathcal{E})$. We show that $\tilde{X} \in Conf(ref(\mathcal{E}))$.

It follows in a straightforward manner from the corresponding properties of X and the X_e's that $\tilde{X}$ is finite and conflict–free and contains no causality cycles.
Hence it suffices to show that $\tilde{X}$ is left–closed up to conflicts.

So let $(e, e') \in \tilde{X}$, let $(d, d') \in E_{ref(\mathcal{E})} - \tilde{X}$ with $(d, d') \prec_{ref(\mathcal{E})} (e, e')$.

We have to show that there exists $(f, f') \in \tilde{X}$ with $(f, f') \prec_{ref(\mathcal{E})} (e, e')$ and $(f, f')\#_{ref(\mathcal{E})}(d, d')$.

First assume $d = e$. Then this follows immediately from the corresponding property of X_e.

Now let $d \neq e$.
If $d \notin X$ then the requirement follows from the corresponding property of X.
So we now consider the remaining case that $d \neq e$ and $d \in X$. Then $d' \notin X_d$.
Since $d \neq e$ we have $d \prec_{\mathcal{E}} e$, hence d is not maximal in X.
Then X_d must be complete.
So $d' \notin X_d$ implies $\exists f' \in X_d$ with $f' \#_{ref(l_{\mathcal{E}}(d))} d'$.
Hence $(d, f') \in \tilde{X}$, $(d, f') \prec_{ref(\mathcal{E})} (e, e')$ and $(d, f')\#_{ref(\mathcal{E})}(d, d')$. ■

We end this section with a lemma that will be useful later on.

2.9 Lemma Let $\mathcal{E} \in \mathbb{E}$, $X \in Conf(\mathcal{E})$ and $busy \subseteq X$.

Then $\forall e \in busy : e$ maximal in X with respect to $\leq_X$
$\iff \forall Y \subseteq busy : X - Y \in Conf(\mathcal{E})$.

Proof
" $\Longrightarrow$ " Let $\mathcal{E} \in \mathbb{E}$, $X \in Conf(\mathcal{E})$, $Y \subseteq X$ and $\forall e \in Y : e$ maximal in X w.r.t. $\leq_X$. It suffices to prove that $X - Y \in Conf(\mathcal{E})$. $X - Y$ is finite and conflict-free and does not contain causality cycles since X has these properties.
It remains to be shown that $X - Y$ is left-closed up to conflicts.
Suppose $e \in X - Y$, $d \prec_{\mathcal{E}} e$ and $d \notin X - Y$. If $d \in Y$ then d would be maximal in X w.r.t. $\leq_X$, contradicting $d \prec_{\mathcal{E}} e$. Thus $d \notin X$. Hence there is an $f \in X$ with $f \prec_{\mathcal{E}} e$ and $d \#_{\mathcal{E}} f$. Since $f \prec_{\mathcal{E}} e$, f is not maximal in X w.r.t. $\leq_X$, so $f \in X - Y$, which had to be proven.

" $\Longleftarrow$ " Let $\mathcal{E} \in \mathbb{E}$, $X \in Conf(\mathcal{E})$, $d \in X$ and $X - \{d\} \in Conf(e)$. It suffices to proof that d is maximal w.r.t. $\leq_X$.
Suppose it is not, then $\exists e \in X$ with $d \prec_{\mathcal{E}} e$. Since $X - \{d\} \in Conf(\mathcal{E})$, there exists an $f \in X - \{d\}$ with $f \prec_{\mathcal{E}} e$ and $d \#_{\mathcal{E}} f$, contradicting the conflict-freeness of X. ■

This means that, in Proposition 2.8, the condition "$e \in busy(\tilde{X}) \Longrightarrow e$ maximal in X w.r.t. $\leq_X$" can be replaced by "for all $Y \subseteq busy(\tilde{X})$, $X - Y \in Conf(\mathcal{E})$".

3 Configuration structures and refinement of actions

In the previous section we have shown that flow event structures may be used for refinement of actions, even when substituting actions by behaviours with conflicts or by infinite behaviours. However, the refinement operation we have defined depends on the particular "syntax" of flow event structures. In this section, our aim is to define a refinement operation for a very general model of concurrent systems, such that refinement operations for particular representations, as flow event structures, are obtained as a special case.

We will consider a model where a system is represented by its set of configurations. As in the previous sections, occurrences of actions are represented by *events* labelled by the corresponding action names. A *configuration* is a set of events representing a state of the system where exactly its elements have happened. We only consider finite configurations here. Following ideas of [Winskel] we represent a system by a family of configurations satisfying certain consistency requirements.

3.1 Definition

A *(labelled) configuration structure (over an alphabet Act)* is a pair $\mathcal{C} = (C, l)$ where C is a family of finite sets (*configurations*) such that
- $\emptyset \in C$,
- $X, Y, Z \in C,\ X \cup Y \subseteq Z \Longrightarrow X \cup Y \in C$,
- $X \in C \wedge d, e \in X, d \neq e \Longrightarrow \exists Y \in C$ with $Y \subseteq X$ and $(d \in Y \Longleftrightarrow e \notin Y)$,

and $l : \bigcup_{X \in C} X \rightarrow Act$ is a *labelling function.*

The requirements for a family of sets of events to form a configuration structure may be explained as follows. The initial state of a system is the state where no action has been performed yet. Hence $\emptyset$ is always a configuration. Now, if two configurations X, Y are contained in a third configuration Z then $X \cup Y$ is consistent or *conflict-free*; e.g. all its elements can happen together in one run. Since both X and Y represent already possible runs, it should then also be possible to execute just the events in X and Y, hence $X \cup Y$ should be a configuration. If we consider two distinct events occurring in some run, then there must be an intermediate state where already one of them has occurred whereas the other has not yet occurred (coincidence can not be enforced). This is guaranteed by the third requirement.

Finally, a remark on our requirement that configurations should be finite. As usual, we assume that in a finite period only finitely many actions may be performed. Now the requirement says that we only consider states that are reachable in a finite period of time. [Winskel] allows configurations to be infinite, thus representing also those states which can be reached in an infinite period of time. However, his infinite configurations are completely determined by the finite ones. Hence configuration structures as defined here are equally expressive as Winskel's families of configurations.

Convention We will denote the components of a configuration structure $\mathcal{C}$ by $C_\mathcal{C}$ and $l_\mathcal{C}$ respectively. By abuse of language, $C_\mathcal{C}$ will also be denoted by $\mathcal{C}$. Furthermore the set $E_\mathcal{C}$ of events of $\mathcal{C}$ is defined by $E_\mathcal{C} = \bigcup_{X \in \mathcal{C}} X$.

Let $\mathbb{C}$ denote the domain of configuration structures labelled over *Act*.

3.2 Example

We consider the example refered to as a "parallel switch" in [Winskel].

We have two actions 0 and 1 interpreted as closing switch 0 and closing switch 1, respectively, in an electric circuit. As soon as at least one of the switches is closed, a bulb lights up; this is represented as an action b.

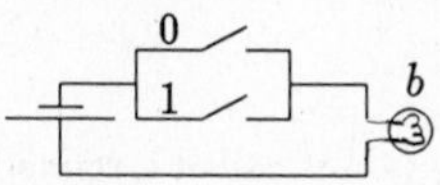

This may be represented by the following configuration structure (with a unique correspondence between actions and events):

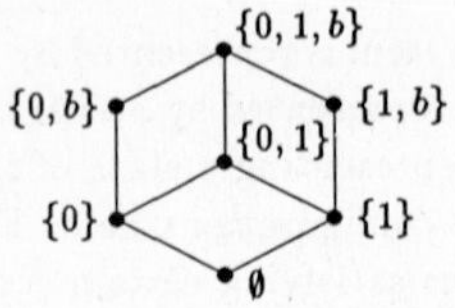

The b–event may occur here without a unique "causal history"; in the configuration $\{0,1,b\}$ it is not clear whether b is caused by 0 or by 1.

Usually, the names of events are not important; hence we will not distinguish configuration structures which are isomophic in the sense that they only differ with respect to names of events.

3.3 Definition

A configuration structure isomorphism between two configuration structures $\mathcal{C}, \mathcal{D} \in \mathbb{C}$ is a bijective mapping $f : E_{\mathcal{C}} \longrightarrow E_{\mathcal{D}}$ such that
- $X \in \mathcal{C} \Longleftrightarrow f(X) \in \mathcal{D}$ for $X \subseteq E_{\mathcal{C}}$,
- and $l_{\mathcal{D}}(f(e)) = l_{\mathcal{C}}(e)$ for $e \in E_{\mathcal{C}}$.

$\mathcal{C}$ and $\mathcal{D}$ are *isomorphic* — notation $\mathcal{C} \cong \mathcal{D}$ — if there exists a configuration structure isomorphism between them.

In configuration structures, completeness and maximality of configurations coincide. Deadlock and termination may not be distinguished.

3.4 Definition

A configuration X of a configuration structure $\mathcal{C}$ is called *complete* iff there is no $Y \neq X$ in $\mathcal{C}$ containing X.

We may now associate a configuration structure with each flow event structure (and via this also with each prime event structure).

3.5 Definition Let $\mathcal{E} \in \mathbb{E}$.

The configuration structure of $\mathcal{E}$, $\mathcal{C}(\mathcal{E})$, is defined as $\mathcal{C}(\mathcal{E}) = (\mathit{Conf}(\mathcal{E}),\ l_{\mathcal{E}} \lceil \bigcup_{X \in \mathit{Conf}(\mathcal{E})} X)$.

There is no unique corresponence in general: different flow event structures may have the same configuration structure (but not vice versa). In particular, the distiction between deadlock and termination is lost.

Next, we define refinement of actions for configuration structures. A refinement will be specified by a function *ref* specifying for each action a a configuration structure $\mathit{ref}(a)$ which is to be substituted for a. Again we only consider non–forgetful refinements here, hence $\mathit{ref}(a) \neq O$ for all $a \in \mathit{Act}$ where O denotes the empty configuration structure with $C_O = \{\emptyset\}$. Apart from this restriction, we may replace an action by any configuration structure.

3.6 Definition

(i) A function $\mathit{ref} : \mathit{Act} \longrightarrow \mathbb{C} - \{O\}$ is called a *refinement function (for configuration structures).*

(ii) Let $\mathcal{C}$ be a configuration structure and let *ref* be a refinement function.
We call $\tilde{X}$ a *refinement of a configuration* $X \in \mathcal{C}$ *by ref* iff
- $\tilde{X} = \bigcup_{e \in X} \{e\} \times X_e$ where $\forall e \in X : X_e \in ref(l_{\mathcal{C}}(e)) - \{\emptyset\}$,
- for all $Y \subseteq busy(\tilde{X})$, $X - Y \in \mathcal{C}$, where $busy(\tilde{X}) = \{e \in X | X_e \text{ not complete}\}$.

The *refinement of* $\mathcal{C}$ *by ref* is defined as $ref(\mathcal{C}) = (C_{ref(\mathcal{C})}, l_{ref(\mathcal{C})})$ with

$$C_{ref(\mathcal{C})} := \{ \tilde{X} \mid \tilde{X} \text{ is a refinement of some } X \in \mathcal{C} \text{ by } ref\}$$

and

$$l_{ref(\mathcal{C})}(e, e') = l_{ref(l_{\mathcal{C}}(e))}(e') \text{ for all } (e, e') \in \bigcup_{\tilde{X} \in C_{ref(\mathcal{C})}} \tilde{X}.$$

Intuitively, this definition may be explained as follows.

The configuration structure $ref(\mathcal{C})$ is obtained by taking all possible refinements of configurations of $\mathcal{C}$. A refinement of a configuration X of $\mathcal{C}$ is obtained by replacing each event e in X by a non–empty configuration X_e of $ref(l_{\mathcal{C}}(e))$. Events which are causally necessary for other events in X may only be replaced by complete configurations, hence it must be possible to take any subset of "uncompleted" or busy events out of X, again obtaining a configuration.

Next we show that refinement is a well–defined operation on configuration structures, even when isomorphic configuration structures are identified.

3.7 Proposition

(i) If $\mathcal{C} \in \mathbb{C}$ and *ref* is a refinement function then also $ref(\mathcal{C})$ is a configuration structure.

(ii) If $\mathcal{C} \in \mathbb{C}$ and *ref*, *ref'* are refinement functions with $ref(a) \cong ref'(a)$ for all $a \in Act$ then $ref(\mathcal{C}) \cong ref'(\mathcal{C})$.

(iii) If $\mathcal{C}, \mathcal{D} \in \mathbb{C}$, *ref* is a refinement function and $\mathcal{C} \cong \mathcal{D}$ then $ref(\mathcal{C}) \cong ref(\mathcal{D})$.

Proof (i) cumbersome and omitted here, (ii) and (iii) straightforward. ■

Finally, we want to show that the easier syntactic refinement operation for flow event structures defined in section 2 is consistent with the refinement operation for configuration structures. However, since the distinction between deadlock and termination is lost in configuration structures, this is only true for deadlock–free refinements.

3.8 Theorem

Let $\mathcal{E} \in \mathbb{E}$, let *ref* be a refinement function for flow event structures with $\forall a \in Act : ref(a)$ deadlock-free.

Then $\mathcal{C}(ref(\mathcal{E})) = ref'(\mathcal{C}(\mathcal{E}))$
where $ref'(a) = \mathcal{C}(ref(a))$ for all $a \in Act$.

Proof

It has to be shown that $C_{\mathcal{C}(ref(\mathcal{E}))} = C_{ref'(\mathcal{C}(\mathcal{E}))}$ and $l_{\mathcal{C}(ref(\mathcal{E}))} = l_{ref'(\mathcal{C}(\mathcal{E}))}$.
The first requirement translates to

$$Conf(ref(\mathcal{E})) = \{ \tilde{X} \mid \tilde{X} \text{ is refinement of some } X \in Conf(\mathcal{E}) \text{ by } ref'\}.$$

From Proposition 2.8 we know

$$Conf(ref(\mathcal{E})) = \{ \tilde{X} \mid \tilde{X} \text{ is a refinement of some } X \in Conf(\mathcal{E}) \text{ by } ref\}.$$

So it suffices to establish that a refinement by *ref'* is the same as a refinement by *ref*. This follows immediately from Proposition 2.8 and Lemma 2.9 in combination with Definition 3.6, provided that for $a \in Act$: X is a complete configuration of $ref(a)$ iff X is complete in $ref'(a) = \mathcal{C}(ref(a))$. This is the case if *ref* is deadlock-free.

The second requirement is straightforward. ■

4 Refinement of transitions in Petri nets

We start by giving some basic definitions and notations for Petri nets; for explanations and concepts we refer to introductory texts on nets, e.g. [Reisig a].

For simplicity we assume that there is a one to one correspondence between the transitions in the net and the actions that the system modelled by the net can perform; we do not consider nets with labelled transitions. However, we will show later that our approach can easily be extended to this case.

4.1 Definition $N = (S, T, F)$ is called a *net structure* iff

- S is a set (of *places*),
- T is a set (of *transitions*), $S \cap T = \emptyset$,
- $F \subseteq (S \times T) \cup (T \times S)$ such that
  $\forall t \in T : \exists s, s'$ with sFt and tFs' (transitions have non–empty pre– and postsets)
  and $\forall s \in S : sFt \Longrightarrow \neg\ tFs$ (no self–loops).

The restrictions we have made here — non–empty pre– and postsets of transitions and no self–loops — will be needed for our refinement construction.

Two nets $N = (S, T, F)$ and $N' = (S', T', F')$ are *isomorphic* — notation $N \cong N'$ — if $T = T'$ and there exists a bijective mapping $f : S \longrightarrow S'$ satisfying $sFt \Longleftrightarrow f(s)F't$ and $tFs \Longleftrightarrow tF'f(s)$.

Generally, we will not distinguish isomorphic net structures.

As usual, we introduce the following notations.
For $x \in S \cup T$, let ${}^\bullet x := \{y \in S \cup T | yFx\}$ (*preset of* x), $x^\bullet := \{y \in S \cup T | xFy\}$ (*postset of* x).
Let ${}^\circ N := \{x \in S \cup T | {}^\bullet x = \emptyset\}$ (*initial places of* N), $N^\circ := \{x \in S \cup T | x^\bullet = \emptyset\}$ (*final places of* N).
Note that ${}^\circ N, N^\circ \subseteq S$.

The components of a net N will be denoted by S_N, T_N, F_N (the index is omitted when clear from the context). We will sometimes use the characteristic mapping of F as a function $F : (S \times T) \cup (T \times S) \longrightarrow \{0, 1\}$.

A concurrent system may be modelled by a net structure where the places carry tokens, indicating the state of the system. The dynamic behaviour of the system is derived by the so called firing rule.

We assume that all places have unbounded capacities; any mapping $M : S_N \longrightarrow \mathbb{N}$ will be called a *marking* of the net N. However, we will restrict our considerations to one–safe nets here. We will illustrate later why refinement in non–one–safe nets may lead to problems.

4.2 Definition

(N, M_o) is called a P/T–system or a *marked net* iff N is a net structure and $M_o : S \longrightarrow \mathbb{N}$ (*initial marking*).

By abuse of notation, we will use N both for (N, M_o) (when M_o is clear from the context) and for the underlying net structure.

4.3 Definition Let (N, M_o) be a marked net, let $M, M' : S \longrightarrow \mathbb{N}$, let $t \in T$.

(i) t is *enabled by* M iff $\forall s \in {}^\bullet t : M(s) > 0$.

(ii) M' is reached from M by firing t ($M[t > M'$) iff
t is enabled by M and
$\forall s \in S : M'(s) = M(s) - F(s,t) + F(t,s)$.

The *marking class* $[N, M_o>$ of a marked net (N, M_o) is then defined as the set of all markings reachable from M_o by finitely many transition firings. A marked net is *one–safe* if $\forall M \in [N, M_o>$, $\forall s \in S : M(s) \leq 1$. In one–safe nets, we may use set notations for markings: $M \subseteq S$ is the marking where exactly the places in M carry a token.

Whenever refering to a marked net in the following, we assume it to be one–safe.

A conceptual framework for refinement in Petri nets are *net morphisms* [GS]. A net morphism is a mapping between the elements of two net structures such that the distinction between places and transitions is observed to some extent. It is possible to map, for example, a place to a transition, but only if this place is surrounded by transitions with the same image.

4.4 Definition Let $N = (S, T, F)$, $N' = (S', T', F')$ be net structures.

(i) A mapping $f : S \cup T \longrightarrow S' \cup T'$ is called a *net morphism* iff
$\forall x, y \in S \cup T$ with $f(x) \neq f(y)$ and $(x, y) \in F : [(f(x), f(y)) \in F'$ and $x \in S \Leftrightarrow f(x) \in S']$.

(ii) A net morphism $f : S \cup T \longrightarrow S' \cup T'$ is called a *quotient* iff f is surjective and
$(x', y') \in F' \Longrightarrow \exists (x, y) \in F$ with $f(x) = x', f(y) = y'$ (surjectivity also with respect to arcs).

A quotient can be thought of as a factorisation. The net is partitioned such that sorts are preserved: each subset of elements forming a class in this partition must have a boarder consisting just of places or just of transitions and is then considered as one place or one transition, respectively. A quotient N_1 of a net N_2 is considered as an *abstraction* of N_2 [Reisig b]. Conversely, N_2 is then called a *refinement* of N_1. In this framework, transitions as well as places may be refined.

However, behavioural aspects are not taken precisely into account and this may lead to problems.

4.5 Example

Consider

$N_1 =$ 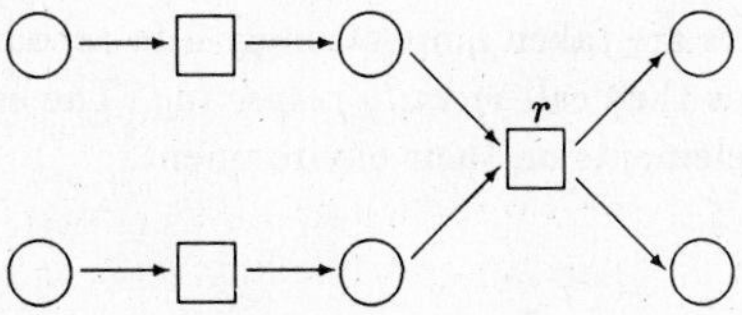

.

The net N_1 is an abstraction of

N_2 =

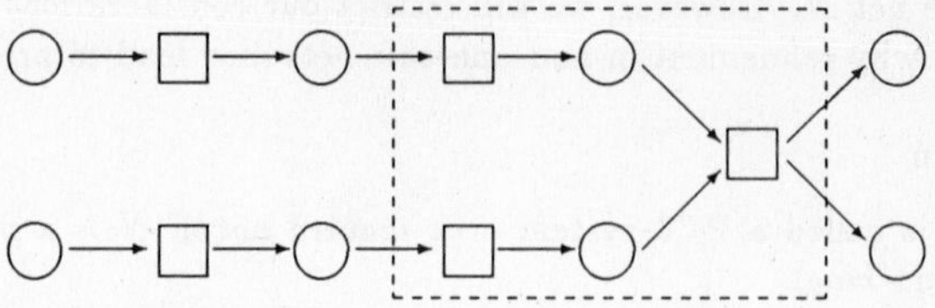

by the quotient mapping all elements inside the broken line to r (and otherwise the identity). Conversely, N_2 is considered as a refinement of N_1.

However, consider the slightly enlarged system

N_1' =

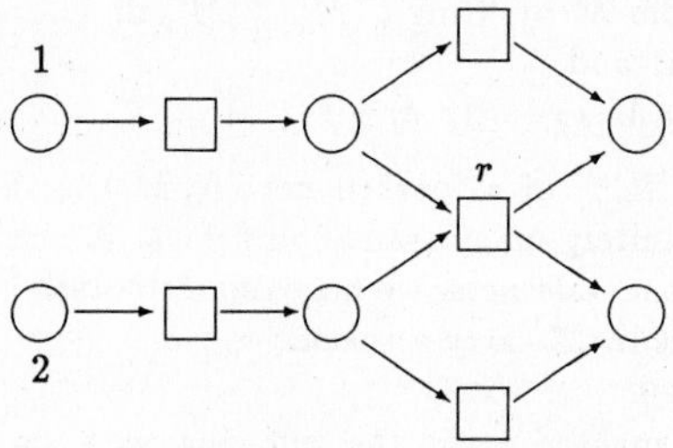

and

N_2' =

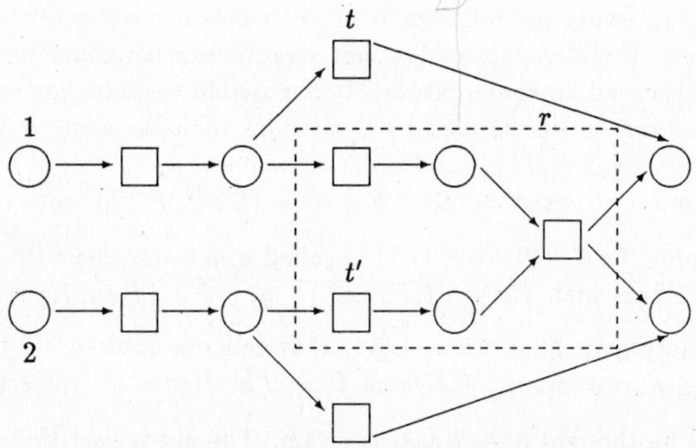

Again, N_1' is a quotient of N_2', hence N_2' may be considered as a refinement of N_1'.

Assuming that places 1 and 2 are initially marked, we find that the net N_1' is deadlock–free in the sense that it is possible to fire transitions until the two final places are both marked. However, even though the part of N_2' corresponding to r is also deadlock-free (namely N_2 is deadlock–free), N_2' may reach a deadlock situation by firing t and t'.

This shows that the notion of a net morphism or quotient is in general not strong enough to reason about the behaviour of refinements in a compositional way. An attempt to restrict it in such a way that behavioural aspects are taken more strongly into account has been made in [DM]. They identify a subclass of morphisms they call *vicinity respecting.* The essential idea is that those net morphisms respect the impact of elements on their environment.

4.6 Definition

A net morphism $f : N \longrightarrow N'$ is said to be *vicinity respecting* iff $\forall x \in S \cup T$:

- $f(^{\odot}x) = \{f(x)\} \vee f(^{\odot}x) = {}^{\odot}f(x)$, and
- $f(x^{\odot}) = \{f(x)\} \vee f(x^{\odot}) = f(x)^{\odot}$,

where $^{\odot}x := \{x\} \cup {}^{\bullet}x$, $x^{\odot} := \{x\} \cup x^{\bullet}$, respectively.

The morphisms considered in Example 4.5 are not vicinity respecting. We will discuss later to what extent this notion does indeed characterise the refinements we are interested in.

In order to avoid confusion, we have to mention here another notion of morphism suggested for Petri nets [Winskel]. This notion is particularly tailored to take behavioural aspects into account, however it does not allow to contract for example a line of two transitions into one transition. So it is not suited for treating refinement. More recent approaches in the categorical framework [MM, Korczyński] have not yet been evaluated under this aspect.

For the case of refining transitions, which we are interested in here, also more constructive approaches are being considered explaining how to replace a transition in a net by a "refinement net". The problem is to specify how to connect the "refinement net" to the environment of the refined transition, and to investigate what restrictions on refinement nets are then necessary for a sensible refinement operation.

One possibility is to require a one to one correspondence between "input/output-places" of the refinement net and the surrounding places of the refined transition. In [Vogler a], a construction for this case is proposed, and it is shown that it is then necessary to impose certain restrictions on refinement nets, in particular disallowing initial concurrency (otherwise a situation as in Example 4.5 might occur).

Most constructions for refining transitions are based on distinguishing initial and final transitions in a refinement net and connecting them to the preset and postset, respectively, of the refined transition ([Valette] and subsequently [SM, Vogler b, BDKP]).

In these approaches, the main idea is that a transition may only be replaced by a net behaving like a transition with respect to its effect on the environment:

- it cannot move without being activated by the environment,
- it has the same possible behaviours whenever it is activated,
- it may not deadlock,
- it consumes and produces tokens in a coincident manner.

The final condition ensures that the problematic situation explained in Example 4.5 may not occur. [Valette] and others ensure this property by allowing only refinements for transitions with at most one initial and at most one final transition. [Vogler b] generalises this by allowing several initial transitions which must be in conflict (and, symmetrically, the same for final transitions). This means that we may not have initial or final concurrency in refinement nets.

The other requirements are usually ensured by extending the net which is supposed to be substituted for a transition by a new place supplying a token to the initial transition(s) and receiving a token from the final transition(s) and then analysing the behaviour of this net.

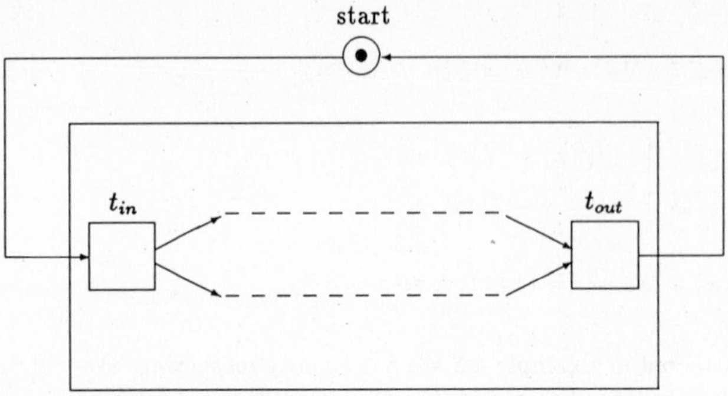

The interesting problem discussed in Example 4.5 was to refine a transition by some behaviour exhibiting initial concurrency. Symmetrically, we also want to allow refinements with final concurrency. This may not be handled in these approaches ([Vogler a] excludes only initial concurrency). A possibility to get rid of this restriction which has not yet been persued further is to restrict the environment of transitions which are refined.

Here we propose a construction which generalises the approach of [Valette] and [Vogler b] for the class of one–safe nets without self–loops, and which offers the possibility of refining transitions also with initial and final concurrency. This will be achieved by extending these approaches by specifying explicitly which initial transitions should be concurrent or in conflict (additionally to constraints already imposed by the internal structure of the refinement net). For this, we extend the refinement net with initial places in the preset of initial transitions. Similarly, we add end places specifying the relationsship between final transitions. Clearly, in the refinement net, initial places have no ingoing arcs and final places have no outgoing arcs. When analysing the behaviour of a refinement net, we assume that all initial places (and no final places) carry tokens. As in [Valette], we allow that also other places in a refinement net carry initial tokens. The approach of [Valette] and [Vogler b] may be seen as a special case of our approach by splitting the start–place considered above into two places: one initial and one final place. Since we will require as [Valette] that a refinement net has the same possible behaviour whenever it is activated, it is reasonable to assume that the initial places are just those places without ingoing arcs and the final places just those without outgoing arcs. The initial and final places will then be used in the embedding construction to ensure that causal dependencies are preserved by the refenement operation.

4.7 Example

Consider again the net N_1' of Example 4.5.

N_1' =

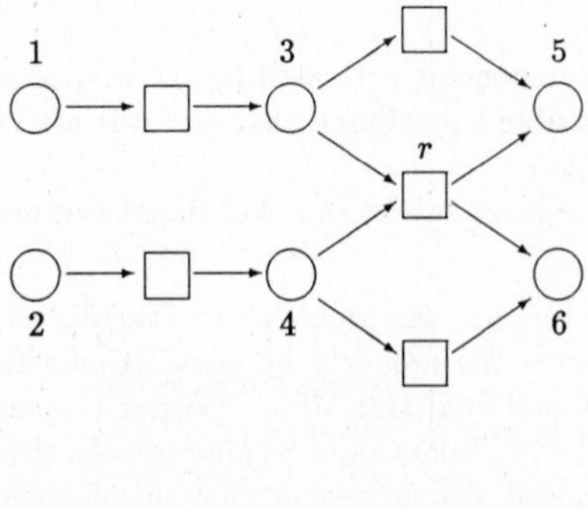

We tried to refine r by two concurrent transitions followed by another transition which causally depends on both of them. This refinement of r may be represented as

R =

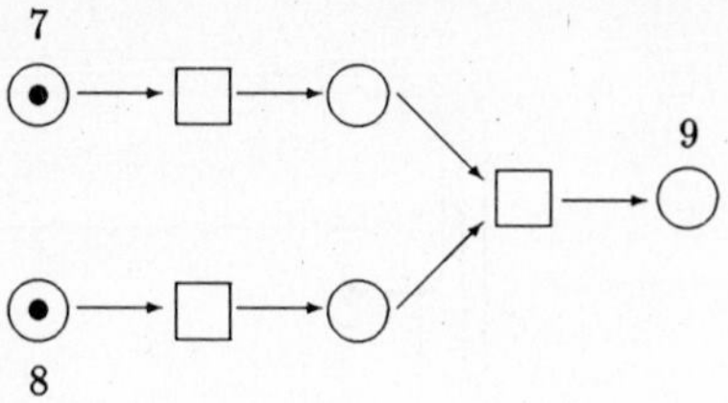

Places 7 and 8 are initial places, place 9 is the final place.

Now R is inserted into N_1' for the transition r by taking the cartesian product of the preplaces of r with the initial places of R and of the postplaces of r with the final places of R. We obtain

N_2'' =

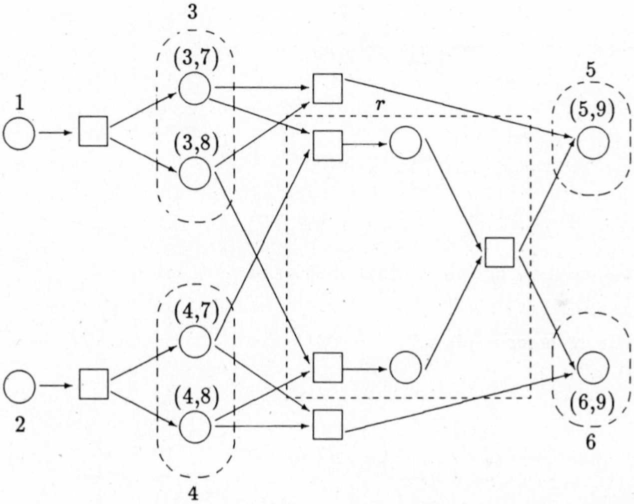

N_2'' is a again a quotient of N_1', however the mapping between places is no longer the identity. We see that, even though tokens are not removed coincidently by the refinement of r, we have ensured that either both transitions in the refinement of r will fire or none of them, hence N_2'' will not deadlock. This has been achieved by preserving precisely the conflict and causality structure.

In contrast to the approaches similar to [Valette], we do allow to refine transitions by deadlocking behaviours (where we use the word deadlock in the usual intuitive meaning rather than in the net theoretic sense). The reason is that we do not expect that the properties of the original net, like deadlock-freeness, are preserved by refinement. We only require that the properties of the resulting net are derivable in a compositional way. Whether or not a net to be inserted deadlocks is specified by its behaviour with respect to its final places. A refinement net *deadlocks* if it may reach a situation where no transition may fire but not all its final places are marked. This may be explained by putting the refinement net in a context by connecting its final and its initial places by a transition.

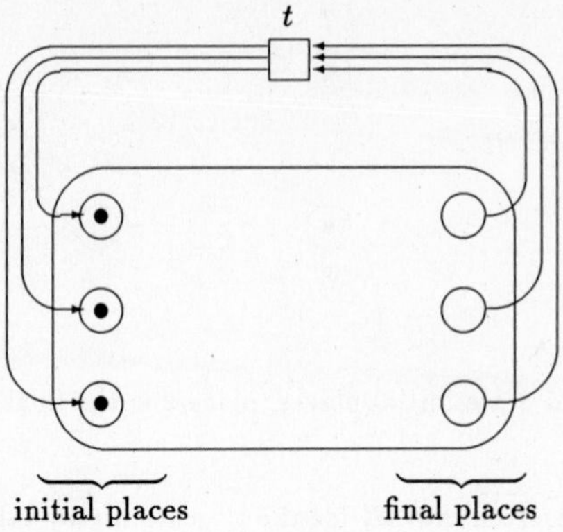

The refinement net deadlocks iff t may not occur.

4.8 Example

Let N =

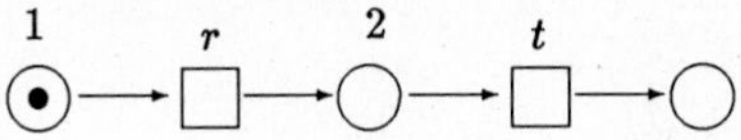

Let R =

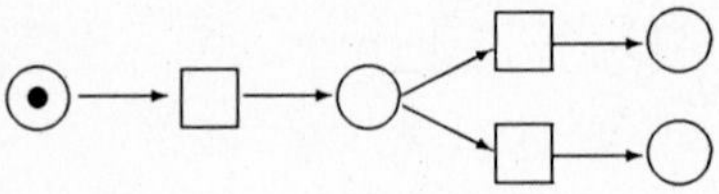

R will deadlock since not all its final places can get a token.

When replacing R for r, we get

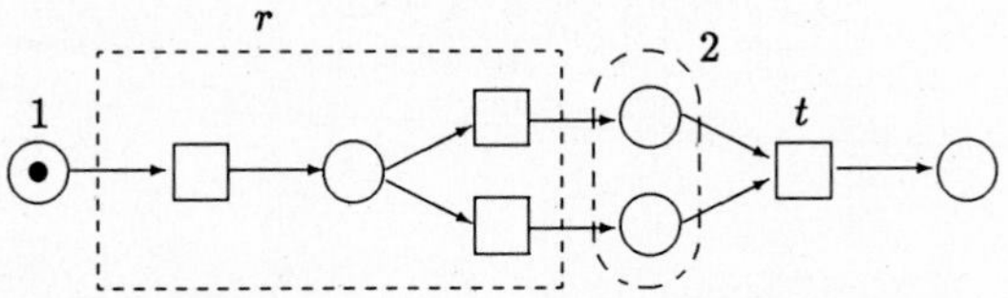

where t will never occur.

However, replacing r by

R' =

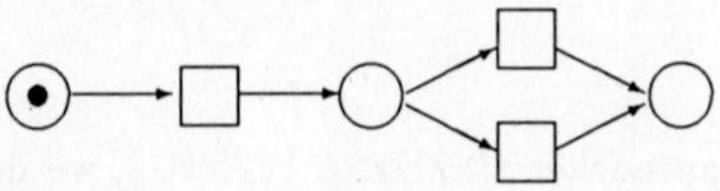

gives

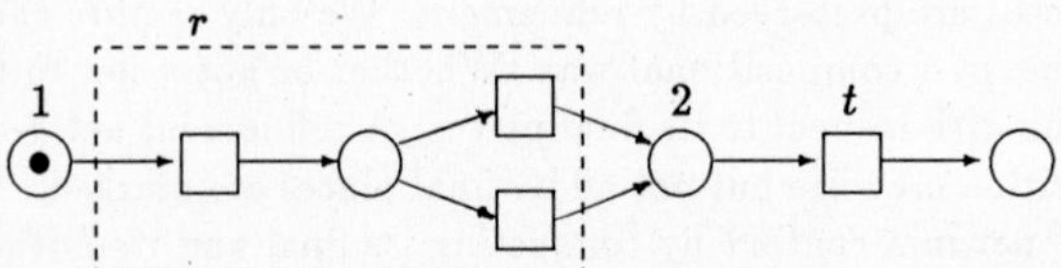

where t will occur.

The next example shows that it is not possible to consider places which have ingoing arcs as initial places of a refinement net.

4.9 Example

Let $N =$ 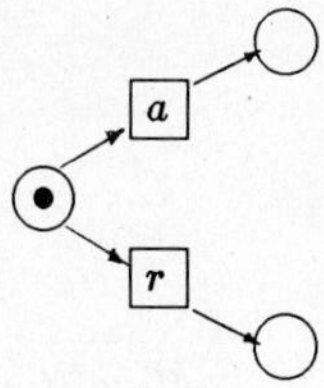

and

consider the net

$R =$ 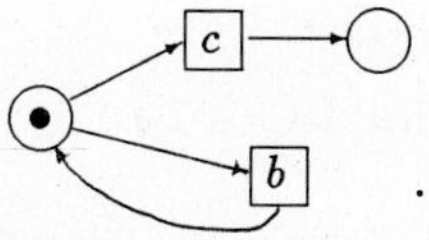

.

If we would replace R for r, we would obtain

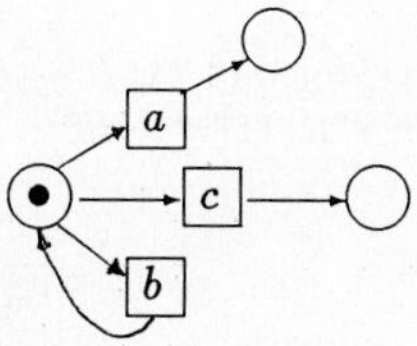

which has not the expected behaviour, since once the refined r has been chosen, no a should be possible any more.

This problem can be solved by using labelled nets and unfolding R into

$R' =$ 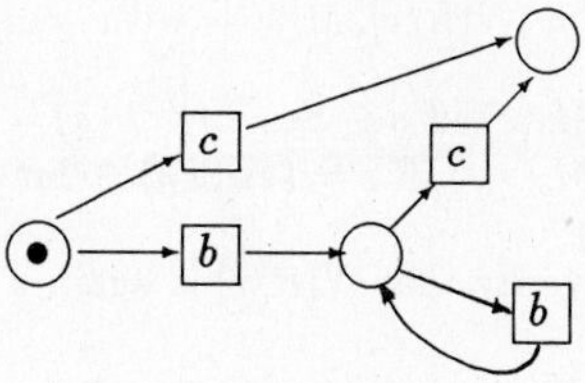

Inserting R' into N yields

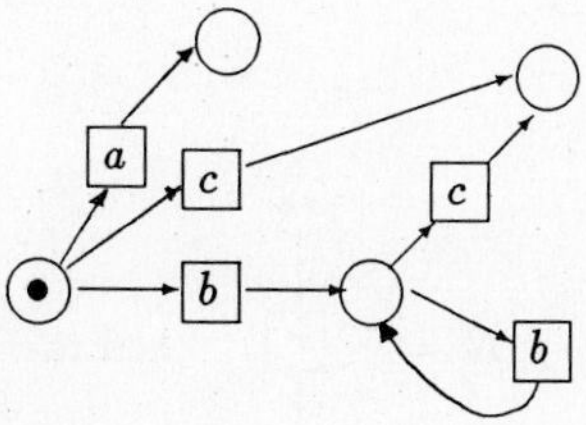

which has indeed the expected behaviour.

Next, we will define our construction formally and, in particular, describe formally the requirements on nets which may be inserted for transitions. We will then relate our construction to the notion of vicinity respecting net morphisms and to our approach for refinement in event structures.

4.10 Definition

(N, M_o) with $N = (S, T, F)$ is a *refinement net* iff

- ${}^oN \neq \emptyset$ and $N^o \neq \emptyset$,
- ${}^oN \subseteq M_o$ and $N^o \cap M_o = \emptyset$,
- no $t \in T$ is enabled by $M_o - {}^oN$,
- for any $M \in [N, M_o\rangle$ with $N^o \subseteq M$ we have $M - N^o = M_o - {}^oN$, (N will exhibit identical behaviour when reactivated).

4.11 Definition

Let (N, M_o) be a marked net, let $r \in T_N$.

Let (R, M_o^R) be a refinement net, w.l.o.g. $T_N \cap T_R = \emptyset, S_N \cap S_R = \emptyset$.
Then $N[R/r] := (S, T, F)$ is defined by

$$S := (S_N - ({}^\bullet r \cup r^\bullet)) \cup (S_R - ({}^oR \cup R^o)) \cup \mathit{Int}$$
$$\text{where } \mathit{Int} := ({}^\bullet r \times {}^oR) \cup (r^\bullet \times R^o),$$

$$T := (T_N - \{r\}) \cup T_R,$$

$$\begin{aligned} F := {} & (F_N \cup F_R)\lceil(S \times T \cup T \times S) \\ & \cup\{((s_N, s_R), t) | (s_N, s_R) \in \mathit{Int}, \\ & \qquad (t \in T_N \setminus \{r\} \wedge (s_N, t) \in F_N) \ \vee (t \in T_R \wedge (s_R, t) \in F_R)\} \\ & \cup\{(t, (s_N, s_R)) | (s_N, s_R) \in \mathit{Int}, \\ & \qquad (t \in T_N \setminus \{r\} \wedge (t, s_N) \in F_N) \ \vee (t \in T_R \wedge (t, s_R) \in F_R)\} \end{aligned}$$

and $(N, M_o)[R/r] = (N[R/r], M_o^{[R/r]})$ with

$$M_o^{[R/r]}(s) = M_o(s) \text{ iff } s \in S_N, \ M_o^{[R/r]}(s) = M_o^R(s) \text{ iff } s \in S_R,$$
$$M_o^{[R/r]}(s) = M_o(s_N) \text{ iff } s = (s_N, s_R) \in \mathit{Int}.$$

It is straightforward to verify that $N[R/r]$ is again a one-safe net.

The following example illustrates why we restrict ourselves to one–safe nets (a similar example is given in [BDKP]).

4.12 Example

Consider the net $N =$ 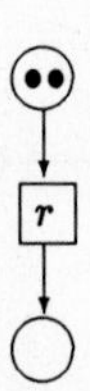

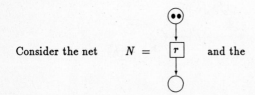

and the

refinement

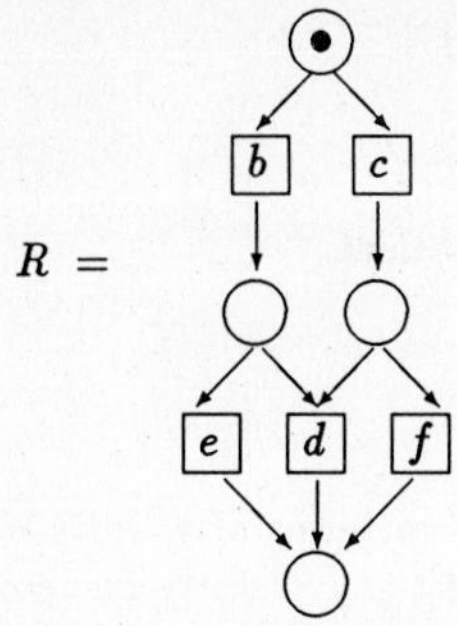

for r .

When replacing r by R, we would obtain

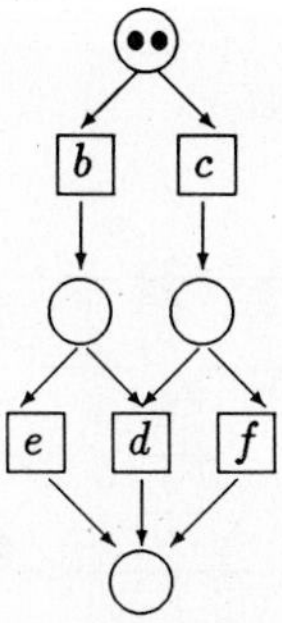

However, this net has not the expected behaviour, since the two independent occurrences of the refined r–transition may now cooperate and execute d. As remarked in [Valette], this problem can only occur if in N the refined transition can be "two-enabled".

Next we show that the order in which transitions are replaced does not matter. In particular, this means (at least for finite nets) that we can extend our approach to non–injective labellings of transitions by action names by refining all transitions labelled by the same action one by one by disjoint copies of the corresponding refinement net.

4.13 Proposition

Let (N, M_o) be a marked net, $r_1, r_2 \in T_N$, $r_1 \neq r_2$, and let R_1, R_2 be refinement nets.

Then $N_1 = ((N, M_o)[R_1/r_1])[R_2/r_2]$ is isomorphic to $N_2 = ((N, M_o)[R_2/r_2])[R_1/r_1]$.

Proof Straightforward. ■

We now show that, for any refinement $N[R/r]$, there exists a canonical vicinity respecting net morphism from $N[R/r]$ to N.

4.14 Proposition

Let (N, M_o) be a marked net, let $r \in T_N$, let R be a refinement net.

Then $f : N[R/r] \longrightarrow N$ with

$$f(x) = \begin{cases} x & \text{iff} \quad x \in (S_N - ({}^{\bullet}r \cup r^{\bullet})) \cup (T_N - \{r\}), \\ r & \text{iff} \quad x \in (S_R - ({}^{\circ}R \cup R^{\circ})) \cup T_R, \\ s_N & \text{iff} \quad x = (s_N, s_R) \in Int \end{cases}$$

is a vicinity respecting morphism, in particular a quotient.

Proof Straightforward ■

We have shown that our construction may be understood in terms of vicinity respecting quotients. However, one could now pose the converse question. May any vicinity respecting quotient which refines only transitions, that is never maps a transition to a place, be generated by our construction? The answer is no, as shown in the following example. However, we would not consider the morphism in this example as a sensible transition refinement.

4.15 Example

Consider

$N_1 =$

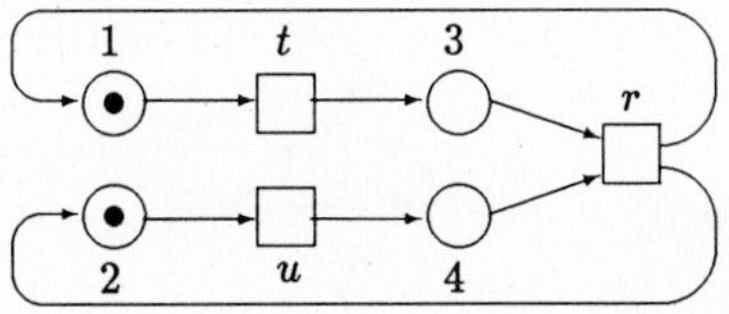

and

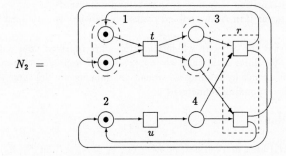

$N_2 =$

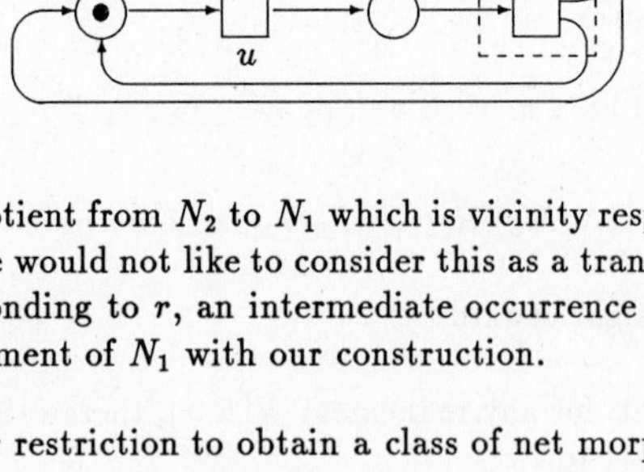

The broken lines in N_2 indicate a quotient from N_2 to N_1 which is vicinity respecting and maps no transition to a place. However, we would not like to consider this as a transition refinement. To execute both transitions corresponding to r, an intermediate occurrence of u is necessary. N_2 may not be generated as a refinement of N_1 with our construction.

An interesting problem is to find a further restriction to obtain a class of net morphisms characterising refinement.

Finally, we would like to show that the construction for refinement of transitions we have presented is consistent with the refinement operation on event structures. This would mean in particular, that this construction for nets indeed preserves precisely the conflict– and causality structure. We will show this for the special case of *occurrence nets*, nets with acyclic flow relation and only forward branched places. These nets correspond directly to prime event structures as defined in Section 1.

As refinement nets, we will consider special (finite) occurrence nets, called *causal nets*, with only unbranched places. Causal nets correspond to conflict–free prime event structures. This yields precisely the class of refinements which we have considered in Section 1.

4.16 Definition

(i) A net structure N is an *occurrence net* iff

- the transitive closure of F is irreflexive,
- $\forall s \in S_N : |{}^\bullet s| \leq 1$,
- $\#_N$ is irreflexive, where for $x, y \in S_N \cup T_N$,
  $x \#_N y \iff \exists t, t' \in T_N$ with $t \neq t'$, ${}^\bullet t \cap {}^\bullet t' \neq \emptyset$, $tF^* x$ and $t'F^* y$,
- $\forall t \in T_N : \{t' \in T_N \mid t'F^* t\}$ finite (axiom of finite causes).

(ii) A net structure N is a *causal net* iff N is an occurrence net and $\forall s \in S_N : |s^\bullet| \leq 1$.

4.17 Definition Let N be an occurrence net.

The *(prime) event structure of* $N, Ev(N)$, is defined as
$Ev(N) := (T_N, F^* \lceil T_N, \#_N, id_{T_N})$.

It is straightforward to verify that $Ev(N)$ is indeed a prime event structure [Winskel].

Using these notions, we may now show the consistency of transition refinement in this class of nets with prime event structure refinement as defined in Section 1.

4.18 Theorem

Let N be an occurrence net, let $r \in T_N$; let R be a finite causal net.

Then $Ev(N[R/r]) \cong ref(Ev(N))$ where $ref(r) := Ev(R)$,
$ref(t) := (\{t\}, \{(t,t)\}, \emptyset, \{(t,t)\})$ for $t \neq r$
(identical refinement).

Proof Omitted. ■

More general consistency results, by unfolding marked nets or associating configuration structures with marked nets and relating with our refinement notion in Section 3, have to be left for further research.

Related work

In this paper we defined a compositional refinement operator on three kinds of event structures and on Petri nets. Our operator on nets can be regarded as a generalisation of the refinement operators of [Valette, SM, BDKP] and [Vogler b] (although we use a less general kind of nets), and we have compared it with the notions of net morphism [Reisig b] and vicinity respecting quotients [DM]. The operator on *prime* event structures was introduced in [GG]. It has been defined on sets of pomsets – a linear time variant of the model of prime event structures – in [Gischer] and on process graphs modelling only sequential processes in [GW].

In principle there are two ways to treat "syntactic" action refinement in system description languages like CCS. One of them is to use the CCS–actions for modelling the refinable actions of this paper. In the absence of communication (or synchronisation) refinement can simply be defined as syntactic substitution of an action by a process expression. This approach has been taken in [AH] and [NEL], and has also been mentioned in [CDP]. In the presence of communication defining such a refinement operator is much more difficult. A first proposal, for the simple case of an operator only splitting actions in two parts to be executed sequentially, can be found in [GV].

An alternative is to use the actions of CCS for modelling "atomic" or instantaneous actions that cannot be refined, and representing our refinable actions by means of variables or *parameters*. This approach requires a general sequential composition operator and has been carried out in [BT] in the setting of ACP. In particular [BT] shows that there is no problem in defining a refinement operator while working in interleaving semantics: atomic actions a, b cannot be refined, so the equation $a \parallel b = a;b + b;a$ is harmless; parameters x, y can be refined, but there is no equation $x \parallel y = x;y + y;x$. Of course the refinement operator, ordinary substitution, is defined in the language (that still contains all information about causal dependence) and not in the associated interleaving model (which would be impossible according to Example 0.4).

A completely different approach is taken in [GMM] and [Boudol a]. There all actions are assumed to be "atomic", and this property should be preserved if they are refined. In [Boudol a] even two kinds of atomicity are proposed, corresponding with two kinds of refinement. In [GMM] this kind of refinement is carried out in an interleaving based model, as mentioned in the introduction.

Refinement in more concrete programming languages is treated in [Gribomont].

It is often argued that a concurrent system should not be represented just by a Petri net or an event structure, but rather by an equivalence class of such objects. Action refinement is only well-defined on a quotient domain induced by a semantic equivalence if this equivalence is a congruence for refinement, i.e. if $P = Q \Longrightarrow \mathit{ref}(P) = \mathit{ref}(Q)$. The search for suitable equivalences has been reported e.g. in [CDP, GG, van Glabbeek, Vogler b, AH, NEL, BDKP and GW].

Acknowledgements

We would like to thank Ilaria Castellani, Wolfgang Reisig and Walter Vogler for many helpful discussions and suggestions. Special thanks also to Ingrid Filter and Gertrud Jacobs for their careful and patient preparation of the manuscript, and to Thomas Lang for his help in proofreading.

References

[AH] L. Aceto, M. Hennessy: *Towards Action-Refinement in Process Algebras*, in: Proc. LICS'89, Asilomar, California, IEEE Computer Society Press, Washington, pp 138–145, 1989

[BT] J.A. Bergstra, J.V. Tucker: *Top-down Design and the Algebra of Communicating Processes*, Science of Computer Programming 5, pp 171–199, 1985

[BDKP] E. Best, R. Devillers, A. Kiehn, L. Pomello: *Fully Concurrent Bisimulation*, unpublished, 1989

[Boudol a] G. Boudol: *Atomic Actions (Note)*, Bulletin of the EATCS 38, pp 136–144, 1989

[Boudol b] G. Boudol: *Computations of Distributed Systems, Part 1: Flow Event structures and Flow Nets*, report INRIA Sophia Antipolis, to appear

[BC] G. Boudol, I. Castellani: *Permutation of Transitions: An Event Structure Semantics for CCS and SCCS*, in: Linear Time, Branching Time and Partial Order in Logics and Models for Concurrency, LNCS 354, Springer–Verlag, pp 411–427, 1989

[CDP] L. Castellano, G. De Michelis, L. Pomello: *Concurrency vs Interleaving: An Instructive Example*, Bulletin of the EATCS 31, pp 12–15, 1987

[DM] J. Desel, A. Merceron: *Vicinity Respecting Net Morphisms*, in: Advances in Petri Nets 89, LNCS, Springer-Verlag, to appear

[GS] H.J. Genrich, E. Stankiewicy-Wiechno: *A Dictionary of some Basic Notions of Net Theory*, in: Net Theory and Applications, LNCS 84, Springer-Verlag, pp 519–535, 1979

[Gischer] J.L. Gischer: *The Equational Theory of Pomsets*, Theoretical Computer Science 61, pp 199–224, 1988

[van Glabbeek] R.J. van Glabbeek: *The Refinement Theorem for ST-Bisimulation Semantics*, Report, Centrum voor Wiskunde en Informatica, Amsterdam 1990; to appear in: Proceedings IFIP Working Conference Programming Concepts and Methodes, Israel at sea Gallilee 1990

[GG] R.J. van Glabbeek, U. Goltz: *Equivalence Notions for Concurrent Systems and Refinement of Actions*, Arbeitspapiere der GMD 366, February 1989, Extended Abstract in Proc. MFCS 89, LNCS 379, Springer–Verlag, pp 237–248, 1989

[GV] R.J. van Glabbeek, F.W. Vaandrager: *Petri Net Models for Algebraic Theories of Concurrency*, Proc. PARLE, Vol. II, LNCS 259, Springer–Verlag, pp 224–242, 1987

[GW] R.J. van Glabbeek, W.P. Weijland: *Refinement in Branching Time Semantics*, Report CS-R8922, Centrum voor Wiskunde en Informatica, Amsterdam 1989; in: J.W. de Bakker, 25 jaar semantiek, liber amicorum, Centrum voor Wiskunde en Informatica, Amsterdam 1989, pp 247–252; and in: Proceedings AMAST Conference, Iowa City, USA, 1989, pp 197–201

[GMM] R. Gorrieri, S.Marchetti, U. Montanari: *A^2CCS: A Simple Extension of CCS for Handling Atomic Actions* in: Proc. CAAP'88, LNCS 299, Springer-Verlag, 1988

[Gribomont] E.P. Gribomont: *Stepwise Refinement and Concurrency: A Small Exercise*, in: Mathematics of Program Construction, LNCS 375, Springer–Verlag, pp 219–238, 1989

[Korczyński] W. Korczyński: *An Algebraic Characterization of Concurrent Systems*, Fundamenta Informaticae, Vol.11, No. 2, pp 171–194, 1988

[Milner] R. Milner: *A Calculus of Communicating Systems*, LNCS 92, Springer–Verlag, 1980

[MM] J. Meseger, U. Montanari: *Petri Nets are Monoids*, in: Proc. LICS '88, Edinburgh, 1988

[NEL] M. Nielsen, U. Engberg, K.S. Larsen: *Fully Abstract Models for a Process Language with Refinement*, in Linear Time, Branching Time and Partial Order in Logics and Models for Concurrency, LNCS 354, Springer-Verlag, pp 523–548, 1989

[NPW] M. Nielsen, G.D. Plotkin, G. Winskel: *Petri Nets, Event Structures and Domains, Part I*, Theoretical Computer Science, Vol. 13, No. 1, pp 85–108, 1981

[Petri] C.A. Petri: *Non-Sequential Processes*, Interner Bericht 77–05, GMD, Institut für Informationssystemforschung, 1977

[Pratt] V.R. Pratt: *Modelling Concurrency with Partial Orders*, International Journal of Parallel Programming, Vol. 15, No. 1, pp 33–71, 1986

[Reisig a] W. Reisig: *Petri Nets*, EATCS Monographs on Theoretical Computer Science 4, Springer–Verlag, 1985

[Reisig b] W. Reisig: *Petri Nets in Software Engineering*, in: Petri Nets: Applications and Relationships to other Models of Concurrency, LNCS 255, Springer–Verlag, pp 63–96, 1987

[SM] I. Suzuki, T. Murata: *A Method for Stepwise Refinement and Abstraction of Petri Nets*, Journal of Computer and System Sciences, Vol. 27, No. 1, pp 51–76, 1983

[Valette] R. Valette: *Analysis of Petri Nets by Stepwise Refinements*, Journal of Computer and System Sciences, Vol. 18, pp 35–46, 1979

[Vogler a] W. Vogler: *Behaviour Preserving Refinements of Petri Nets*, in: Proc. 12th Int. Workshop on Graph Theoretic Concepts in Computer Science, LNCS 246, Springer–Verlag, pp 82–93, 1987

[Vogler b] W. Vogler: *Failure Semantics Based on Interval Semiwords is a Congruence for Refinement*, in Proc. STACS'90, LNCS, Springer-Verlag, to appear

[Winskel] G. Winskel: *Event Structures*, in: Petri Nets: Applications and Relationships to Other Models of Concurrency, LNCS 255, Springer–Verlag, pp 325–392, 1987

TRANSFORMATION OF COMBINED DATA TYPE AND PROCESS SPECIFICATIONS USING PROJECTION ALGEBRAS

M.Große-Rhode , H.Ehrig

TU Berlin, Fachbereich Informatik (20), Sekr. FR 6-1
Franklinstr. 28/29, D-1000 Berlin 10

Abstract : The concept of projection specifications was recently introduced as a purely algebraic approach to the specification of continuous algebras in the framework of metric spaces. It allows to combine data type- and process specifications within one formalism. Parameterized projection specifications, corresponding to usual algebraic parameterized specifications, carry over compositionality to combined data type and process specifications. The parameter part may contain data types as well as process types. Transformation concepts for algebraic specifications are shown to apply also to projection specifications; i.e. extension and refinement, and different notions of implementation can be generalized to projection specifications.

Keywords : Projection Specification, Projection Algebra (Continuous Algebra), Parameterized Projection Specification, Horizontal and Vertical Operations, Refinement, R-Implementation.

Contents

1 Introduction
2 Review of Projection Spaces, Specifications and Algebras
3 Parameterized Projection Specifications and Actualization
4 Refinement of Projection Specifications
5 R-Implementations
6 Projection Specification and Induced Refinement of Petri Net Processes
7 Conclusion and Open Problems

1 Introduction

This paper mainly contains two parts: one is the algebraic specification of combined data- and process types, the other one is the transformation of such specifications. In the first part we review projection specifications as introduced in /EPBRDG88/ and /Gro89/. The main new ideas are transformation concepts for projection specifications which are presented in the second part of this paper.

For the specification of abstract data types algebraic specification with initial algebra semantics is a widely accepted approach, which allows formal correctness proofs and an abstract representation of a system with formal semantics. A variety of structuring mechanisms for algebraic specifications, including parameterized and modular algebraic specifications, as well as systems and tools to support the supply of algebraic specifications in software development have been developed (see /COMPASS89/).
For the specification of processes, however, the problem how to specify infinite objects occurs. They cannot be denoted by finite terms, thus a notion of limits has to be added to (or better included into) the specification. Besides the ordered algebra approach (see /TW86/,/MD86/) there is another main approach using metric spaces as base sets for the algebras, uniformly continuous functions as operations and Banach´s Fixed Point Theorem for recursive equation systems (see /BK83/,/BK86/,/BZ82a,b/). In 1987 at the ADT-workshop in Gullane "projection spaces" were introduced (see /EPBRDG88/), which can be interpreted as an algebraic version of (ultra) metric spaces providing a convenient mean for algebraic specifications of process algebras. Instead of an external metric projections are specified that induce a metric. The specification of the projections is a part of the whole specification so that its semantics can be constructed in one step, without additional definition of a metric etc.. Thus all the advantages of algebraic specifications, especially parameterization, carry over to projection specifications very naturally. The definition of discrete projections - which induce the discrete metric on a base set - makes it possible to write projection specifications for data types, too; i.e. there is no formal distinction between data types and process types. In this way combined data type and process algebras can be specified within one projection specification. The categorical definition of the semantics of a projection specification as initial algebra in a suitable category (resp. a free functor) implies that projection specifications are compatible with algebraic specifications, such that there is no need for a further integration mechanism.

Transformations of specifications are most important for all kinds of development steps within software development. Taking a very general point of view a transformation of specification is any kind of construction or relation between specifications. A correct transformation should also be compatible with the semantics of the corresponding specification in a well-defined way.
This general view includes "horizontal" as well as "vertical" development steps within software development, where "horizontal" means to build up structured specifications from smaller components and "vertical" means a step from a more abstract (resp. less detailed) level to a more concrete (resp. more detailed) level of specifications. Some authors prefer to speak of transformations only in the sense of vertical development steps, while the horizontal steps are discusses in connection with horizontal structuring or modularization concepts.

In this paper both horizontal and vertical transformations are considered. Actualization of a parameterized projection specification is a horizontal operation to put specifications together, i.e. construct larger specifications from generic and actual components. As vertical operations on projection specifications refinement and R-implementation (= implementation with a restriction construction) are introduced. A refinement allows to define new sorts and operations, and renaming and identification in the abstract specification. In an R-implementation the implementing specification in addition may contain "junk", i.e. data items which are needed to define the implementing data type but do not represent an abstract data item.

To support a classification of projection specifications let us now briefly introduce three alternative approaches to combined data type and process specification. Process algebra, an algebraic specification technique for communicating processes developed by J.Bergstra and J.W.Klop (see /BK86/) mainly influenced our appraoch. It belongs to the CCS family (see /Mil80/), as well as the process specification formalism LOTOS (see /ISODIS86/), which uses the specification language ACT ONE for the specification of the data type part. High level nets are a different approach, a further development of Petri nets combining algebraic data type specification with concurrent processes modeled by Petri nets.

Process Algebra (cf./BK83/,/BK86): Process algebra is an axiomatic theory for concurrent systems developed by Bergstra/Klop and deBakker/Zucker (/BZ82a,b/). It is based on Milners CCS (Calculus for Communicating Systems, /Mil80/) and uses the theorems derived from the CCS model as axioms, thus reversing the appraoch. This axiomatic approach is much more amenable to a mathematical analysis.
The complete specification of the algebra of communicating processes ACP can be developed in several steps.
First a basic process algebra BPA is specified by a given set of atomic actions and two binary operations: "·" (sequential composition) and "+" (alternative composition). Models for BPA are constructed as projective limit of a finite initial model of the specification, which contains all infinite processes that can be approximated by finite ones, or as graph models modulo bisimulation. The projective limit models are derived from topological investigations of concurrent systems (see /BZ82a,b/), using metrical spaces and their completion.
Next further operations are specified, such as parallel composition, which is modeled as arbitrary interleaving using an auxiliary operation "left merge". It is shown that these operations enrich the initial infinite models indicated above.
Furhtermore a hiding operator is introduced which, however, is only defined for finite processes. To extend it to infinite processes "fair abstraction" is introduced, formalized as deduction rule for process expressions. Thus for process algebras with hiding another kind of semantics is needed.
Besides the projective limit models there are other interesting models, such as the algebra of recursively definable processes, most of which are submodels of the projective limit models.
Of course process algebra is open for further extensions concerning the set of operations as well as the model level.

LOTOS : LOTOS (Language Of Temporal Ordering Specification) is a formal description technique developed within ISO for the description of OSI protocols and services. LOTOS is strongly guided by architectural principles of distributed systems, which is reflected in the four basic language design choices

- the interaction concept,
- the temporal ordering principle,
- process abstraction, and
- the use of abstract data types.

The interaction concept replaces the traditional input/output concepts by arbitrary common activities of two or more processes. This allows to model also arbitrary forms of synchronization and non deterministic generation of information.
The temporal ordering principle is used to define the externally observable behaviour of a process by the temporal ordering of its interaction with its environment. This allows a process specification independent of internal organization and implementation. LOTOS provides a set of temporal order operators that allow to combine and structure behaviour expressions, and a set of transformation rules which relate expressions with the same observable behaviour.
Process abstraction allows to define formal processes with formal interaction points and formal parameters. This genericity together with the possibility of recursive process instantiations provides a powerful specification structuring principle.
The use of abstract data types allows, for instance, to represent a set of connection endpoint identifiers in a completely abstract way, rather than by way of particular concrete data structure. The LOTOS approach is based on equational specification of data types with initial algebra semantics as given in the specification language ACT ONE (see /EFH83/,/EM85/).

High Level Nets (see /Vau86/,/Jen86/,/Hum89/): High level nets are a further development of Petri nets which inherit the main features for the specification of concurrent systems from the Petri net approach, add further structuring mechanisms and use algebraic specifications for the specification of token, transitions and the firing relation. Usual Petri nets (resp. place/transition nets) define the basic notions for the specification of processes in concurrent systems. *Distribution* and consecutive execution of actions (i.e. *dependency*) is specified by the underlying graph of a Petri net. The definition of the token game of a Petri net includes a notion of *indeterminism*, corresponding to the indeterministic choice of one set of transitions which is ready to fire. Furthermore *concurrency* in a Petri net can be defined as orthogonal relation to sequential dependency.
High level nets extend the Petri net approach w.r.t. the specification of token, transitions and firing conditions. First token and transitions may have different colours, making it possible to unite similar parts of a net. The transitions may be guarded by certain additional conditions, which makes the representation of the firing relation more compact. Both, the colours of token and transitions, and the guards are specified by an algebraic specification, i.e. there are terms for token and transitions (resp. sorts for their colours) and equations for the guards. To integrate the possibilities offered by algebraic specifications for the static aspects of a concurrent system and the features of Petri nets for the specification of their dynamic aspects, the underlying graph of a Petri net is specified by a net scheme. The net scheme Ω (of the graph) and the algebraic specification SPEC (of the colours and the guards) define an abstract high level net which can be instantiated by any SPEC-algebra to obtain a concrete high level net.
Another way how to integrate Petri nets and algebraic specifications is indicated in section 6 of this paper, where Petri net processes are specified by a projection specification.

Other interesting approaches to the specification of concurrency, which are currently under investigation in the COMPASS project, are e.g.:

- Consider processes to be just special data types as algebraic transition systems, the specification of a concurrent system being parameterized on specifications describing the interactions of component processes (the SMoLCS approach /AMRW85/,/AR87/).
- Combine abstract data types with denotational techniques based on stream processing functions (see /Bro87/).

The specification and development problem has been considered by Broy in various papers (/Bro85/, /Bro86/,/Bro87/) and by Kaplan and Pnueli (/KP87/). In general it seems useful to combine classical abstract data type specification with other techniques (like temporal logic), in order to have property-oriented specifications of dynamic temporal behaviours.

To finish the introduction we give an overview over the paper.
In section 2 projection specifications are reviewed. First projection spaces are defined which form the basis for the definition of a semantics, then projection specifications and the construction of their semantics is discussed.
In section 3 parameterized projection specifications and projection parameter passing are studied, and the relation with algebraic parameterized specifications is pointed out.
Two vertical transformations of parameterized projection specifications are discussed in sections 4 and 5, refinement and R-implementation (implementation with restriction).
In addition to the process algebra specifications, which are used as a running example throughout the paper, in section 6 a projection specification of the token game of a Petri net is presented, which indicates another possible combination of Petri nets and algebraic specifications. This example specification is then refined to illustrate the concepts of section 4.

Concerning algebraic specifications we refer to /EM85/. Projection specifications were introduced in /EPBRDG88/ and /Gro89/ The restriction construction for algebraic specification is introduced in /BEP87/, the corresponding construction for projection specifications is treated in /Dim89/. In this paper proofs from other papers are not repeated, on the other hand we tried to keep the paper self contained. Full proofs concerning projection specifications can be found in /Gro88/ and /Dim89/.

For fruitful discussions about transformation concepts we are grateful to the members of the COMPASS group at the TU Berlin, concerning the projection specification part we would like to thank C.Dimitrovici for his support.

2 Review of Projection Spaces, Specifications and Algebras

In this section we review the basic notions of projection specifications as given in /EPBRDG88/ and /Gro89/.
We start this section with one of the process algebra models which initiated our concept of projection spaces.

2.1 Motivation for Projection Spaces :

In the process algebra approach a model for infinite processes is constructed in two consecutive steps : First finite action trees are specified, including the set of atomic actions and the basic operations "sequential composition" and "indeterministic choice". This can be done by a usual algebraic specification. On the initial algebra BPA (Basic Process Algebra) of (finite) trees modulo bisimulation a metric is defined via a binary projection operation $p:\mathbf{N}_1 x BPA \rightarrow BPA$ (where $\mathbf{N}_1$ denotes the natural numbers starting with 1). The n´th projection cuts a tree to depth n, i.e. the projection p(n,t) of t is the given tree t, cut to depth n. An infinite tree (process) then can be uniquely defined as the limit of a sequence of finite trees $(t_n)_{n\geq 1}$ with $p(n,t_{n+1})=t_n$ $(n\geq 1)$.

The projection induces a metric "dist" on BPA by

$$dist(a,b)=2^{-min\{n\in \mathbf{N}_1:p(n,a)\neq p(n,b)\}} \quad \text{if } \{n\in \mathbf{N}_1:p(n,a)\neq p(n,b)\}\neq\emptyset, \text{ and}$$

$$dist(a,b)=0 \quad \text{if } \forall n\in \mathbf{N}_1\ p(n,a)=p(n,b)$$

The metrical completion of BPA w.r.t. the metric "dist", including the limits and the extension of the operations to infinite processes, then serves as model for finite and infinite processes. □

From this example we derived in /Gro89/ the definition of projection spaces and projection compatible functions. The specification of the projections instead of the metric seems more suitable for algebraic specification purposes and does not reduce the expressivness of continuous algebras based on metrics.

2.2 Definition (Projection Space, Projection Compatible Function) :

(1) A projection space (A,p) is a set A together with a function $p:\mathbf{N}_1 xA\rightarrow A$, satisfying $\forall n,m\in \mathbf{N}_1\ p(n,\_)\circ p(m,\_)=p(min(n,m),\_)$.

(2) Given projection spaces (A,p) and (B,q) a function $f:(A,p)\rightarrow(B,q)$ is called projection compatible, if $\forall n\in \mathbf{N}_1\ q(n,\_)\circ f=q(n,\_)\circ f\circ p(n,\_)$. □

Since we do not require a separation axiom

(like $(\forall n\in \mathbf{N}_1\ p(n,a)=p(n,b)) \rightarrow a=b$, $(a,b\in A)$) ,

the "dist"-function corresponding to a projection now is only a pseudo ultra metric, i.e. there may be different elements which have distance 0. In fact separation will later be implied by a standard constuction for the semantics (see 2.9, 2.11 and 2.15).

Recall that a metric is a function $d:AxA\rightarrow \mathbf{R}^{\geq 0}$ (the non negative real numbers) satisfying (for all $a,b\in A$)

(1) $d(a,b) = d(b,a)$

(2) $d(a,b) \leq d(a,c)+d(c,b)$ for all $c\in A$

(3) $d(a,b)=0 \Leftrightarrow a=b$.

If (2) can be replaced by the sharper inequality

(2´) $d(a,b) \leq max\{d(a,c),d(c,b)\}$

d is called an ultra metric. If only conditions (1) and (2) [resp. (2´)] are satisfied d is called a pseudo [ultra] metric.

2.3 Remarks :

(1) The "dist" function given in example 2.1. above defines for each projection space (A,p) a corresponding pseudo ultra metric space $(A,dist_p)$ with the same underlying topology. Vice versa for a given pseudo ultra metric space (A,d) a projection $p:\mathbf{N}_1 xA \rightarrow A$ can be defined which induces the same topology on A as d does.
The topology induced by a projection $p:\mathbf{N}_1 xA \rightarrow A$ on A is the topology generated by the sets $X \subseteq A$ with $x \in X \Rightarrow \exists n \forall k \geq n \ \ p(k,x) \in X$.

(2) Projection compatible functions correspond to non expansive functions w.r.t. the induced (pseudo ultra) metric and form a (proper) subclass of the uniformly continuous functions, i.e. functions satisfying

$$\forall n \in \mathbf{N}_1 \ \exists m \in \mathbf{N}_1 \ q(n,\_) \circ f = q(n,\_) \circ f \circ p(m,\_) .$$

Projection compatible functions guarantee the existence of initial algebras (which do not necessarily exist in a category with uniformly continuous functions as morphisms).

(3) Projection spaces and projection compatible functions form a category PRO_c which is complete, cocomplete, cartesian closed and a topos. The notions can also be interpreted topologically, as spaces with a topology induced by a metric and (a subclass of) continuous functions. □

It can be shown that PRO_c is equivalent to a category of pseudo ultra-metric spaces with nonexpansive functions as morphisms.

Now we want to introduce **projection specifications.**The idea of projection specifications is that the sorts incorporating processes in the specification are enriched by non-discrete projection operations, while for the data sorts discrete projections are added. Thus a projection specification is a specification which includes a selected projection operation for each sort and therefore must also contain a specification of $\mathbf{N}_1$. Completion (w.r.t. the induced metric) of the initial algebra then leaves the data sorts invariant, while the process sorts are enlarged by infinite processes, which are limits of the given finite processes. Here (in-)finiteness is defined relative to the projections. The completion is done by standard construction leading to an initial complete separated projection algebra as semantics of the projection specification.
Syntactically projection specifications differ from usual algebraic specifications only by the requirement, that there has to be a selected projection operation symbol for each sort. It is equivalent to define projections as a family of unary operations $(p_n)_{n \geq 1}$, $p_n:A \rightarrow A$, or as one operation $p:\mathbf{N}_1 xA \rightarrow A$. The latter version, which we have chosen, yields finite signatures and makes calculations in the index explicit, i.e. dependencies between p(n,_) and p(n+1,_), which are likely to occur, are expressed in the specification. The disadvantage is, that each projection specification must contain a nat1-part that must be invariant under all constructions of specifications (extension, parameterization, renaming etc.) and must always be interpreted by $\mathbf{N}_1$, i.e. an (algebraic) initiality constraint is needed (see /EM89/).
To make this nat1-part a projection specification **pnat1** a projection p-nat1 is added which defines a discrete metric on the natural numbers. In this case also the projection p-nat1 is called discrete.

pnat1 =

<u>sorts</u> nat1

<u>opns</u> 1: $\rightarrow$ nat1

succ: nat1 $\rightarrow$ nat1

min, p-nat1: nat1 nat1 $\rightarrow$ nat1

<u>eqns</u> <u>for all</u> m,n <u>in</u> nat1 :

min(n,1)=1

min(1,n)=1

min(succ(n),succ(m))=succ(min(n,m))

p-nat1(m,n)=n

Next projection specifications and constrained projection specifications are defined. The constraints correspond to the requirements of a projection algebra (see definition 2.7): Each base set together with its projection is a projection space and the operations are projection compatible.

<u>2.4 Definition</u> (Projection Specification) :
A <u>projection specification</u> PS=(S,OP,E) is an algebraic specification with :
(i) PS is a conservative extension of **pnat1** ,
i.e. $(T_{PS})_{\mathbf{pnat1}} \cong T_{\mathbf{pnat1}}$, where T_{SPEC} denotes the initial algebra, SPEC$\in$ {PS,**pnat1**},
(ii) for each sort $s \in S$ there is a selected operation symbol p-s:nat1 s$\rightarrow$s $\in$ OP .

<u>2.5 Remark</u> :
<u>Projection constraints</u> C_{PS} for a given projection specification PS=(S,OP,E) can be defined by $C_{PS}=C1 \cup C2 \cup C3$, where

$C1_s : \forall n,m \in \text{nat1}\ \forall x \in s\quad \text{p-s}(n,\text{p-s}(m,x))=\text{p-s}(\min(n,m),x)$

$C1=\bigcup_{s \in S}\{C1_s\}$

$C2_N : \forall k \in \text{nat1}\ \forall x1 \in s1 \ldots \forall xn \in sn$

$\text{p-s}(k,N(x1,\ldots,xn)) = \text{p-s}(k,N(\text{p-s1}(k,x1),\ldots,\text{p-sn}(k,xn)))$

$C2=\bigcup_{N \in OP}\{C2_N\}$

C3={INIT **pnat1**} (algebraic constraint) .

This allows to define a <u>constrained projection specification CPS</u> as a projection specification PS=(S,OP,E) together with the corresponding projection constraints C_{PS} , i.e. CPS=(S,OP,E,C_{PS}), leading to a projection specification with constraints in the sense of /EM89/. □

<u>2.6 Example</u> : probpa0 is a **pro**jection specification of the **b**asic **p**rocess **a**lgebra BPA (**0** indicates that it is only a preliminary version), given in /BK86/.

probpa0 = **pnat1** +

<u>sorts</u> action, proc

<u>opns</u>	a1,...,an	:	→ action	{elementary actions}
	c	: action	→ proc	{coercion}
	+,·	: proc proc	→ proc	{choice,sequence}
	p-action	: nat1 action	→ action	{projection of sort action}
	p-proc	: nat1 proc	→ proc	{projection of sort proc}

<u>eqns</u> <u>for all</u> x,y ,z <u>in</u> proc :

x+x=x (idempotent)
x+y=y+x (commutative)
(x+y)+z=x+(y+z) (associative)
(x·y)·z=x·(y·z) (associative)
(x+y)·z=x·z+y·z (left distributive)

<u>for all</u> n <u>in</u> nat1; <u>for all</u> a <u>in</u> action :
p-action(n,a)=a

<u>for all</u> n <u>in</u> nat1; <u>for all</u> a <u>in</u> action; <u>for all</u> x, y <u>in</u> proc :
p-proc(n,c(a))=c(a)
p-proc(1,c(a)·x)=c(a)
p-proc(succ(n),c(a)·x)=c(a)·p-proc(n,x)
p-proc(n,x+y)=p-proc(n,x)+p-proc(n,y)

The projection "p-action" is discrete, thus "action" is considered as a data type. Its semantics coincides with the usual initial algebra semantics, i.e. there are no additional infinite elements (see next section). In contrast the projection "p-proc" is not discrete. In the semantics infinite processes are included as limits of sequences $(p_n)_{n\geq 1}$ with $\text{p-proc}(n,p_{n+1})\equiv p_n$ $(n\in \text{nat1})$. □

The next step is to introduce **projection algebras**. The class of models for a projection specification is defined to be the class of all projection algebras, i.e. algebras with projection spaces as base sets and projection compatible operations. As indicated in remark 2.3 projection algebras can also be interpreted as continuous algebras. The projections are specified as operations, but also interpreted as to define the metrics on the base sets.

<u>2.7 Definition</u> **(Category of Projection-PS-Algebras Cat(CPS)) :**
Given a projection specification PS=(S,OP,E)

(1) a <u>projection-PS-algebra</u> is an algebra $A=((A_s)_{s\in S},(N_A)_{N\in OP})$ of the specification PS with

(i) $(A_s,\text{p-s}_A)$ is a projection space for all $s\in S$,

(ii) the operations N_A are projection compatible, i.e.

$\forall N{:}s1...sn\to s\ \ \forall k\geq 1\ \ \forall a1\in A_{s1}\ ...\ \forall an\in A_{sn}$

$\text{p-s}_A(k,N_A(a1,...,an)) = \text{p-s}_A(k,N_A(\text{p-s1}_A(k,a1),...,\text{p-sn}_A(k,an)))$;

(iii) $A_{\mathbf{pnat1}}\cong \mathbf{N}_1$;

(2) a <u>projection-PS-homomorphism</u> is a homomorphism $f{:}A\to B$ of projection-PS-algebras such that f_{nat1} is an isomorphism;

(3) Cat(CPS) is the category of projection-PS-algebras with projection-PS-homomorphisms. □

The interpretation of the constraints C_{PS} in remark 2.5 makes sure that a PS-algebra is a projection PS-algebra if and only if it satisfies the projection constraints C_{PS} (see /Gro88/, /Gro89/ for more detail).

To define the semantics of a projection specification the initial algebra of the specification (denoting finite processes) must be completed to obtain the infinite processes, and separated to obtain ultra metric spaces as domains. Completeness and separation for projection algebras are defined as follows.

2.8 Definition (Completeness,Separation) :
Given a projection specification PS a projection-PS-algebra A is

(1) complete , if for each $s \in S$ and each sequence $(a_n)_{n\geq 1}$ in A_s with
$\forall n \exists m \forall k,j \ p\text{-}s_A(n,a_{m+k})=p\text{-}s_A(n,a_{m+j})$
there is an $a \in A_s$ with
$\forall n \exists m \forall k \ p\text{-}s_A(n,a_{m+k})=p\text{-}s_A(n,a)$;

(2) separated , if for all $a,b \in A_s$
$(\forall n \in \mathbf{N}_1 \ p\text{-}s_A(n,a)=p\text{-}s_A(n,b)) \rightarrow a=b$.

Here $p\text{-}s_A$ denotes the projection in A of sort A_s. □

Completeness of a projection algebra corresponds to the usual completeness of metric spaces (algebras) w.r.t. Cauchy sequences. It guarantees that each Cauchy sequence (equivalently each projective sequence, i.e. a sequence $(a_n)_{n\geq 1}$ with $p(n,a_{n+1})=a_n$ $(n\geq 1)$) of processes converges to an (infinite) process . Conversly each element can be approximated by finite elements. Separation corresponds to the approximation induction principle : Each infinite process is uniquely determined by its finite approximations (projections) (see /BK86/). If a projection is discrete, i.e. $p\text{-}s_A(n,x)=x$ for all n and x, then the corresponding base set A_s of each algebra $A \in Cat(CPS)$ is always complete and separated, i.e. completion and separation leave this sort invariant.

A procedure which simultaneously completes and separates a projection algebra is the following standard construction, which can be extended to a functor $SC:Cat(CPS) \rightarrow Cat_{C,S}(CPS)$, the full subcategory of complete and separated projection algebras.

2.9 Definition (Standard Construction) :
Given a projection specification PS=(S,OP,E) and a projection-PS-algebra $A=((A_s)_{s\in S},(N_A)_{N\in OP})$ the standard construction $A^\infty=((A_s^\infty)_{s\in S},(N_A^\infty)_{N\in OP})$ is defined by

$$A_s^\infty = \{(a_n)_{n\geq 1} : \forall n \in \mathbf{N}_1 \ p\text{-}s_A(n,a_{n+1})=a_n\}$$

$$N_A^\infty((a1_n)_{n\geq 1},\ldots,(ak_n)_{n\geq 1}) = (p\text{-}s_A(n,N(a1_n,\ldots,ak_n)))_{n\geq 1} \ .$$

Further for projection-PS-homomorphisms $h:A\rightarrow B$ define $h^\infty:A^\infty\rightarrow B^\infty$ by $h_s^\infty((a_n)_{n\geq1})=((h_s(a_n))_{n\geq1})$ $(s\in S)$. □

2.10 Fact **(Standard Construction Functor) :**
The functor $SC:Cat(CPS)\rightarrow Cat_{C,S}(CPS)$, defined on algebras by $SC(A):=A^\infty$ and on homomorphisms by $SC(h):=h^\infty$, is a left adjoint for the inclusion of complete separated projection algebras and -homomorphisms $Incl:Cat_{C,S}(CPS)\rightarrow Cat(CPS)$, and $SC\circ Incl\cong ID_{Cat_{C,S}(CPS)}$.

Proof Idea : To show that SC is well defined amounts to some straightforward computations. The universal homomorphism $u_A:A\rightarrow SC(A)$ is given by

$$u_{A,s}(a) = (p\text{-}s_A(n,a))_{n\geq1}$$

A homomorphism $h:A\rightarrow B$, $B\in Cat_{C,S}(CPS)$ factors (uniquely) through u_A by $\underline{h}:SC(A)\rightarrow B$, $\underline{h}_s((a_n)_{n\geq1})=\lim_{n\rightarrow\infty}h_s(a_n)$. The limit exists since B is complete and $(a_n)_{n\geq1}$ is a Cauchy sequence. u_A is injective iff A is separated, and u_A is surjective iff A is complete. (see /Gro88/ for more detail) □

To fill the gap between PS-algebras (for a given projection specification PS), which need not be projection algebras, and complete separated projection algebras, the models of projection specifications, we still need to transform PS-algebras into projection-PS-algebras. Concerning the projection constraints C1 and C2 (projection space axiom and projection compatibility of the operations), which are equations w.r.t. PS, this can be done by a free functor $Constr:Cat(PS)\rightarrow Cat(PS+C1+C2)$ (called projection constraints functor). Concerning initiality of the **pnat1**-reduct of a PS-algebra we must reduce the construction to PS-algebras which already satisfy this constraint. Fortunately, by definition of a projection specification, an initial PS-algebra always has an initial **pnat1**-reduct.

2.11 Definition **(Projection Semantics Functor PSEM) :**
Given a projection specification PS, let $Cat_i(PS)$ denote the subcategory of the category of PS-algebras and PS-homomorphisms Cat(PS) (PS considered as algebraic specification) with

objects : PS-algebras with initial **pnat1**-reduct

morphisms : PS-algebra homomorphisms h with $h_{\mathbf{pnat1}}$ is an isomorphism.

The projection semantics functor $PSEM:Cat_i(PS)\rightarrow Cat_{C,S}(CPS)$ is defined as the composition of the projection constraints functor $Constr:Cat_i(PS)\rightarrow Cat(CPS)$ (restricted to $Cat_i(PS)$) and the standard construction functor $SC:Cat(CPS)\rightarrow Cat_{C,S}(CPS)$, i.e.

$$PSEM = SC\circ Constr .$$ □

2.12 Remark :
PSEM is a left adjoint for the inclusion functor $I:Cat_{C,S}(CPS)\rightarrow Cat_i(PS)$, since the functors Constr and SC are left adjoints for their respective inclusion functors. Furthermore

$$PSEM\circ I \cong ID_{Cat_{C,S}(CPS)} .$$ □

<u>2.13 Remark</u> :
The projection semantics functor is used to prove the existence of initial algebras in $Cat_{C,S}$(CPS), which define the semantics of the projection specification PS. If all projections in PS are discrete, then the (projection) semantics of PS coincides with the algebraic semantics of PS considered as algebraic specification. □

<u>2.14 Definition</u> (Semantics of a Projection Specification CT_{PS}) :
The <u>semantics</u> of a projection specification PS is the (class of) initial algebra(s) in the category of complete separated projection-PS-algebras $Cat_{C,S}$(CPS). An initial algebra is denoted by CT_{PS} . □

<u>2.15 Remark</u> :
Since PSEM is a left adjoint and the initial algebra T_{PS} in Cat(PS) has an initial **pnat1**-reduct, $CT_{PS} \cong PSEM(T_{PS})$. □

<u>2.16 Example</u> :
The semantics of the projection specification **probpa0** is isomorphic to the algebra of infinite trees, with edges labeled by actions modulo bisimulation. Since specification and definition of the semantics in this case coincide with the constructions given in the papers about process algebra (see /BK86/), we do not explicit the construction here. □

3 Parameterized Projection Specifications and Actualization

In this section we extend the theory of parameterized specifications as given in /EM85/ for equational specifications to the case of projection specifications as introduced in the previous section.
Parameterization is a powerful mechanism for algebraic specifications, making it possible to structure specifications allowing compositionality and reusability of the parts. A parameterized algebraic specification is a pair (FSPEC,TSPEC) of algebraic specifications : the formal specification FSPEC and the target specification TSPEC. Its semantics is the (equivalence class of) free functor(s) F:Cat(FSPEC)→Cat(TSPEC) (see /EM85/). This can similarly be defined for projection specifications; the free functor of the subcategories of complete separated projection algebras is the composition of this free functor and the projection semantics functor PSEM.

<u>3.1 Definition</u> (Parameterized Projection Specification) :
(1) A <u>parameterized projection specification</u> (FPS,TPS) is a pair of projection specifications FPS,TPS with FPS⊆TPS; i.e. a parameterized specification where formal- and target specification are projection specifications.

(2) The <u>semantics</u> of a parameterized projection specification (FPS,TPS) is the class of <u>projection free functors</u> PF:$Cat_{C,S}$(CFPS)→$Cat_{C,S}$(CTPS) given by PF=PSEM∘F∘I, where

I:$Cat_{C,S}$(CFPS)→Cat_i(FPS)	is the inclusion functor (see 2.12)
F:Cat_i(FPS)→Cat_i(TPS)	is the restriction of a free functor
PSEM:Cat_i(TPS)→$Cat_{C,S}$(CTPS)	is the projection semantics functor (see 2.11)

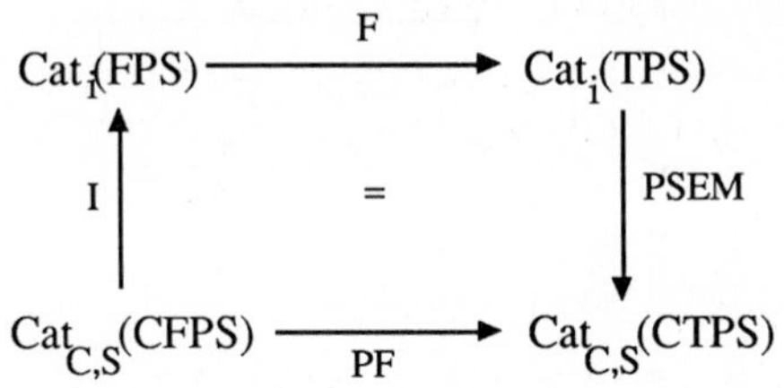

□

<u>3.2 Remark</u> :
A free functor F always exists (see /EM85/) and its restriction to algebras with initial **pnat1**-part is well defined. Thus also the projection free functor PF always exists.
By definition the projection free functor PF:$Cat_{C,S}$(CFPS)→$Cat_{C,S}$(CTPS) is a left adjoint for the forgetful functor V:$Cat_{C,S}$(CTPS)→Cat(FPS), restricted to the subcategory of complete separated projection algebras. Since completeness and separation are properties of sorts (together with their projections), the projection constraints are preserved by the forgetful functor, and V preseves the initial **pnat1**-reduct, the restriction of V:$Cat_{C,S}$(CTPS)→Cat(FPS) is V:$Cat_{C,S}$(CTPS)→$Cat_{C,S}$(CFPS). Thus PF is free w.r.t. V, and the projection semantics of parameterized projection specifications is compatible with the semantics of parameterized algebraic specifications. □

<u>3.3 Example</u> : probpa(action)=(action,probpa)
The following example takes the "action part" of the projection specification **probpa0** given in example 4.2 as formal part, whence the processes become parameterized processes. A problem arises here, if the projection p-action of actions is not discrete, i.e. also processes or other infinite objects are allowed as actions. The coercion c:action→proc then is not projection compatible, unless the projection p-proc of processes is adopted to this more general case: The n´th projection of a process x now cuts x and all actions in x to length n.

action = **pnat1** +
    <u>sorts</u> action
    <u>opns</u> p-action:nat1 action → action

probpa = **action** +
    <u>sorts</u> proc
    <u>opns</u> c : action → proc
        +,· : proc proc → proc
        p-proc : nat1 proc → proc
        cut : nat1 nat1 proc → proc
        { cut(n,m,x) cuts the process x to length m and each action in x to length n }

<u>eqns</u> <u>for all</u> x,y,z <u>in</u> proc :
x+x=x
x+y=y+x
(x+y)+z=x+(y+z)
(x·y)·z=x·(y·z)
(x+y)·z=x·z+y·z
<u>for all</u> n,m <u>in</u> nat1; <u>for all</u> a <u>in</u> action; <u>for all</u> x, y <u>in</u> proc :
p-proc(n,x)=cut(n,n,x)
cut(n,m,c(a))=c(p-action(n,a))
cut(n,1,c(a)·x)=c(p-action(n,a))
cut(n,succ(m),c(a)·x)=c(p-action(n,a))·cut(n,m,x)
cut(n,m,x+y)=cut(n,m,x)+cut(n,m,y)

This example also indicates how data types with process subtypes and coercion, e.g. lists of processes, can be specified.

To define the semantics note that all operations in the target specification are projection compatible and p-proc satisfies the projection space axiom. Thus $PF_{\mathbf{probpa}}(A) = SC \circ F_{\mathbf{probpa}}(A)$.
Now $F_{\mathbf{probpa}}(A)$ constructs finite trees, like $T_{\mathbf{probpa}}$, but the edges are labeled by elements of the algebra A. Since all trees in $F_{\mathbf{probpa}}(A)$ are finite w.r.t. the projection p-$proc_{F_{\mathbf{probpa}}(A)}$, $F_{\mathbf{probpa}}(A)$ is separated and $PF_{\mathbf{probpa}}(A)$ only adjoins the infinite trees as limits of sequences $(t_n)_{n\geq 1}$ with p-$proc_{F_{\mathbf{probpa}}(A)}(n,t_{n+1})=t_n$. □

Actualization of parameterized projection specifications is given similar to the equational case by standard and paramterized parameter passing. The actualization of the formal part of a parameterized projection specification is expressed by a projection specification morphism, that ensures that the **pnat1**-part is actualized by **pnat1**.

<u>3.4 Definition (Projection Specification Morphism)</u> :
Given projection specifications PS=(S,OP,E), PS´=(S´,OP´,E´) a <u>projection specification morphism</u> h:PS→PS´ is a specification morphism with

(i) $h|\mathbf{pnat1}=id_{\mathbf{pnat1}}$
(ii) h(s)=nat1 implies s=nat1 , for all s∈S
(iii) for each projection operation symbol p-s:nat1 s→s ∈ OP , h(p-s):nat1 h(s)→h(s) is the projection operation symbol of sort h(s) in OP´. □

Since standard parameter passing is a special case of parameterized parameter passing, where the formal part of the actual parameter is empty (i.e. FPS´=∅ in the definition below) we immediately define the general case.

3.5 Definition (Parameterized Projection Parameter Passing) :
Given parameterized projection specifications (FPS,TPS), (FPS´,TPS1´) and a projection specification morphism h:FPS→TPS´ parameterized projection parameter passing is defined as follows:
(1) Syntax : the syntax of parameterized projection parameter passing is given by the following pushout diagram, where (FPS´,TPS2) is the (parameterized projection) value specification :

$$\begin{array}{ccccc} & & FPS & \xrightarrow{\;i\;} & TPS \\ & & h\downarrow & (PO) & \downarrow h1 \\ FPS' & \xrightarrow[i']{} & TPS' & \xrightarrow[i1]{} & TPS2 \end{array}$$

(2) Semantics : the semantics of parameterized projection parameter passing is the triple of the semantics of the three components :
- $PF:Cat_{C,S}(CFPS) \to Cat_{C,S}(CTPS)$,
- $PF':Cat_{C,S}(CFPS') \to Cat_{C,S}(CTPS')$ and
- $PF *_h PF':Cat_{C,S}(CFPS') \to Cat_{C,S}(CTPS2)$, where $PF *_h PF' = PSEM2 \circ (F *_h F') \circ I'$ is

the projection free functor induced by the free functor $F *_h F':Cat(FPS') \to Cat(TPS2)$.
(3) Correctness : parameterized projection parameter passing is correct, if
(i) $V_{i1} \circ (PF *_h PF') \cong PF'$ (naturally) (actual parameter protection)
(ii) $V_{h1} \circ (PF *_h PF') \cong PF \circ V_h \circ PF'$ (naturally) (passing compatibility) . □

For the discussion of the semantics of projection parameter passing amalgamation, persistency and extension of persistent functors are the central notions.
The *amalgamation lemma* states how the category of the value projection specification can be represented in terms of the given parameterized projection specification and the actual projection specification. A *persistent projection specification* always preserves the actual parameter and the corresponding projection free functor can be *extended* to the projection free functor of the value projection specification.
In order to formulate amalgamation in the case of complete separated projection algebras in 3.7 we review the amalgamation lemma for algebraic specifications /EM85/ 8.11.

3.6 Amalgamation Lemma :
Given a (simple) parameter passing diagram

$$\begin{array}{ccc} SPEC & \xrightarrow{\;i\;} & SPEC1 \\ h\downarrow & (PO) & \downarrow h1 \\ SPEC' & \xrightarrow[i1]{} & SPEC2 \end{array}$$

the value specification SPEC2 has the representation

$Cat(SPEC2)=Cat(SPEC') +_{Cat(SPEC)} Cat(SPEC1)$, i.e.

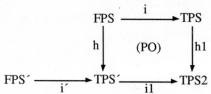

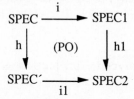

(1) each Cat(SPEC2)-algebra A2 has a unique representation $A2=A'+_A A1$, where
- $A'=V_{i1}(A2)\in Cat(SPEC')$,
- $A1=V_{h1}(A2)\in Cat(SPEC1)$ and
- $A=V_h(A')=V_i(A1)\in Cat(SPEC)$.

Vice versa given $A'\in Cat(SPEC')$, $A1\in Cat(SPEC1)$ and $A=V_h(A')=V_i(A1)\in Cat(SPEC)$, then $A2=A'+_A A1$ is the unique Cat(SPEC2)-algebra satisfying $V_{i1}(A2)=A'$ and $V_{h1}(A2)=A1$.

(2) the same representation holds for Cat(SPEC2)-morphisms.

(3) Given $A2\in Cat(SPEC2)$ $A2\cong A'+_A A1$ if and only if $V_{i1}(A2)\cong A'$ and $V_{h1}(A2)\cong A1$.

(4) the same equivalence holds for Cat(SPEC2)-morphisms. □

Since forgetful functors preserve completeness, separation and the projection constraints (see remark 3.2), a similar representation of the corresponding subcategories holds:

3.7 Fact (Amalgamation Lemma for Projection Specifications) :
Given a projection parameter passing diagram 3.5(1), we have

$$Cat_{C,S}(CTPS2)=Cat_{C,S}(CTPS')+_{Cat_{C,S}(CFPS)}Cat_{C,S}(CTPS) .$$ □

Persistency of a parameterized (projection) specification ensures that the actual parameter of the (projection) parameter passing is respected by the semantics of the value (projection) specification. Persistency of a projection free functor is defined like persistency of other free functors. Note, however, that persistency of the projection free functor and persistency of the free functor of the underlying algebraic specification are in general not equivalent (see remark 3.10).

3.8 Definition (Persistency) :
A parameterized projection specification (FPS,TPS) is called persistent, if the projection free functor $PF:Cat_{C,S}(CFPS)\rightarrow Cat_{C,S}(CTPS)$ is persistent w.r.t. the forgetful functor $V:Cat_{C,S}(CTPS)\rightarrow Cat_{C,S}(CFPS)$; i.e. $V\circ PF \cong ID_{Cat_{C,S}(CFPS)}$ (naturally). □

Similar to the case of algebraic specifications, each persistent projection free functor can be replaced by a naturallly isomorphic strongly persistent projection free functor.

A projection parameter passing diagram 3.5(1) induces a free functor $F'':Cat(TPS')\rightarrow Cat(TPS2)$. If the free functor $F:Cat(FPS)\rightarrow Cat(TPS)$ is strongly persistent, then F'' is the extension of F via h ($F''=Ext(F,h)$), i.e. $F''(A1')=A1'+_A F(A)$, with $A=V_h(A1')$, for $A1'\in Cat(TPS')$.

A similar representation of the induced projection free functor $PF'':Cat_{C,S}(CTPS')\rightarrow Cat_{C,S}(CTPS2)$ can be given :

3.9 Fact (Extension Lemma for Projection Specifications) :
Given a projection parameter passing diagram 3.5(1) and a strongly persistent functor $PF:Cat_{C,S}(CFPS) \to Cat_{C,S}(CTPS)$ there is a strongly persistent functor $Ext(PF,h):Cat_{C,S}(CTPS') \to Cat_{C,S}(CTPS2)$ given by the amalgamated sums

$$Ext(PF,h)(A1') = A1' +_A PF(A), \text{ with } A = V_h(A1') \qquad (A1' \in Cat_{C,S}(CTPS')),$$
$$Ext(PF,h)(f1') = f1' +_f PF(f), \text{ with } f = V_h(f1') \qquad (f1' \in Cat_{C,S}(CTPS')).$$

Ext(PF,h) is uniquely determined by the equations

$$V_{i1} \circ Ext(PF,h) = ID_{Cat_{C,S}(CTPS')} \text{ and } V_{h1} \circ Ext(PF,h) = PF \circ V_h .$$

If in addition PF is a left adjoint to the forgetful functor $V_i:Cat_{C,S}(CTPS) \to Cat_{C,S}(CFPS)$, then Ext(PF,h) is a left adjoint to the forgetful functor $V_{i1}:Cat_{C,S}(CTPS2) \to Cat_{C,S}(CTPS')$.

Proof : The assertion follows directly from fact 3.7 (amalgamation) and the extension lemma for algebraic specifications (EM85, 8.15). □

The following remark has been initiated by a further investigation of our examples and corresponding correctness proofs. It has not been presented in other papers yet.

3.10 Remark :
Syntax and semantics of projection specifications and projection parameter passing are defined w.r.t. the underlying algebraic specifications. The following definition characterises cases in which the properties of the corresponding free functors carry over to the projection free functors (see the "fact" below).

Definition (h-Security) :
Given projection specifications PS=(S,OP,E), PS´=(S´,OP´,E´) and a projection specification morphism $h:PS \to PS'$, PS´ is called <u>h-secure</u> if all operations from OP´-h(OP) are projection compatible; i.e.

$$\forall N':s1'...sn' \to s' \in OP'-h(OP)$$
$$E' \vdash p\text{-}s'(k,N'(x1,...,xn)) = p\text{-}s'(k,N'(p\text{-}s1'(k,x1),...,p\text{-}sn'(k,xn)))$$

A parameterized projection specification (FPS,TPS) (resp. the free functor $F:Cat(FPS) \to Cat(TPS)$) is called <u>secure</u>, if TPS is secure w.r.t. the inclusion $in:FPS \to TPS$.

Fact : Let (FPSi,TPSi) (i=0,1) be parameterized projection specifications, $F0:Cat(FPS0) \to Cat(TPS0)$ be the free functor of (FPS0,TPS0) considered as algebraic specification and the projection specification TPS2 be given by the parameter passing diagram

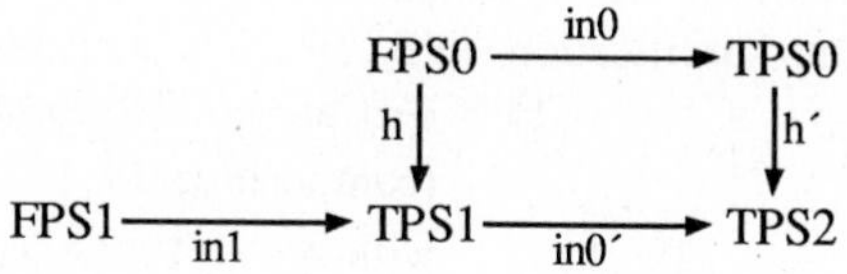

(1) <u>Amalgamation</u>
If (FPS0,TPS0) is secure, TPS1 is h-secure and $A2 \in Cat_I(TPS2)$ has the representation $A2=A1+_A A0$
then $PSEM2(A2)=PSEM1(A1)+_{PSEM(A)}PSEM0(A0)$
where PSEMi is the corresponding projection semantics functor.
(2) <u>Persistency</u>
If (FPS0,TPS0) is secure and F0 is persistent, then also the corresponding projection free functor $PF0:Cat_{C,S}(CFPS0) \rightarrow Cat_{C,S}(CTPS0)$ is persistent.
(3) <u>Extension</u>
If (FPS0,TPS0) is secure, TPS1 is h-secure and F0 is strongly persistent, then the extended projection free functor Ext(PF0,h) is persistent and has the representation $Ext(PF0,h)=PSEM2 \circ Ext(F0,h) \circ I1$, where I1 denotes the inclusion of complete separated TPS1-projection algebras.

Proof : In /Gro88/ it is shown that h-security implies compatibility of forgetful functor and projection semantics functor, i.e. given $h:PS \rightarrow PS'$ such that PS´ is h-secure we have $PSEM \circ V_h = V_h \circ PSEM'$.

(1) TPS2 is in0´-secure and h´-secure, since $OP(TPS2)=in0'(OP(TPS1)) \cup h'(OP(TPS0))$, TPS1 is h-secure and TPS0 is in0-secure. Thus

$$V_{in0'} \circ PSEM2(A2) = PSEM1 \circ V_{in0'}(A2) = PSEM1(A1)$$
$$V_{h'} \circ PSEM2(A2) = PSEM1 \circ V_{h'}(A2) = PSEM0(A0)$$
$$V_h \circ PSEM1(A1) = PSEM \circ V_h(A1) = PSEM(A) = PSEM \circ V_{in0}(A1) = V_{in0} \circ PSEM1(A1) \ .$$

(2) $V_{in0} \circ PF0 = V_{in0} \circ PSEM0 \circ F0 \circ I = PSEM \circ V_{in0} \circ F0 \circ I = PSEM \circ I \cong ID_{Cat_{C,S}(CFPS0)}$

(3) Using fact 3.9 (extension) the following equations prove the assertion:

$$V_{in0'} \circ PSEM2 \circ Ext(F0,h) \circ I1 = PSEM1 \circ V_{in0'} \circ Ext(F0,h) \circ I1 = PSEM1 \circ I1 \cong ID_{Cat_{C,S}(CTPS1)}$$
$$V_{h'} \circ PSEM2 \circ Ext(F0,h) \circ I1 = PSEM0 \circ V_{h'} \circ Ext(F0,h) \circ I1 = PSEM0 \circ F0 \circ V_h \circ I1 =$$
$$= PSEM0 \circ F0 \circ I \circ V_h = PF0 \circ V_h$$ □

Using amalgamation and extension lemma we can show that persistent parameterized projection specifications are correct w.r.t. projection parameter passing.

<u>3.11 Theorem</u> (Correct Parameterized Projection Parameter Passing) :
Given persistent parameterized projection specifications (FPS,TFPS), (FPS´,TPS´) and a projection parameter passing morphism $h:FPS \rightarrow TPS'$ we have
(1) The parameterized projection value specification (FPS´,TPS2) is persistent.
(2) The projection free functor $PF *_h PF':Cat_{C,S}(CFPS') \rightarrow Cat_{C,S}(CTPS2)$ of (FPS´,TPS2) is given by $PF *_h PF' \cong Ext(PF,h) \circ PF'$ (compositionality)
i.e. $(PF *_h PF')(A') \cong PF'(A')+_A PF(A)$ with $A=V_h \circ PF'(A')$
and $(PF *_h PF')(f') \cong PF'(f')+_f PF(f)$ with $f=V_h \circ PF'(f')$
where PF, PF´ are the projection free functors of (FPS,TPS) and (FPS´,TPS´) respectively.
(3) Parameterized projection parameter passing is correct.

Proof : We may assume that the projection free functors PF and PF′ are strongly persistent. By fact 3.9 (extension) $Ext(PF,h):Cat_{C,S}(CPS')\rightarrow Cat_{C,S}(CTPS2)$ is a persistent (projection) free functor, thus $Ext(PF,h)\circ PF' \cong PF *_h PF'$(naturally) and (FPS′,TPS2) is persistent.
Lastly $V_{h1}\circ(PF*_h PF')\cong V_{i1}\circ Ext(PF,h)\circ PF' \cong PF'$, since Ext(PF,h) is persistent, and $V_{h1}\circ(PF*_h PF')\cong V_{h1}\circ Ext(PF,h)\circ PF' = PF\circ V_i \circ PF'$, by fact 3.9 (extension), showing correctness of the parameterized projection parameter passing. □

To finish this section we consider external correctness of a parameterized projection specification which is defined as compatibility of the projection free functor with a given model functor.

3.12 Definition **(External Correctness) :**
Given
(1) a parameterized projection specification (FPS,TPS) with its semantics (projection free functor) $PF:Cat_{C,S}(CFPS)\rightarrow Cat_{C,S}(CTPS)$,
(2) a parameterized model projection specification (MFPS,MTPS) with projection specification morphisms $j_F:MFPS\rightarrow FPS$, $j_T:MTPS\rightarrow TPS$ such that $i\circ j_F = j_T\circ m$, where $i:FPS\rightarrow TPS$ and $m:MFPS\rightarrow MTPS$ are the inclusions,
(3) a model functor $PM:Cat_{C,S}(CMFPS)\rightarrow Cat_{C,S}(CMTPS)$,
then
(4) (FPS,TPS) is called <u>(externally) correct</u> w.r.t. PM, if $PM\circ V_{jF}\cong V_{jT}\circ PF$ (naturally), i.e. the following diagram commutes up to isomorphism :

$$\begin{array}{ccc} Cat_{C,S}(CMFPS) & \xrightarrow{PM} & Cat_{C,S}(CMTPS) \\ \uparrow V_{jF} & & \uparrow V_{jT} \\ Cat_{C,S}(CFPS) & \xrightarrow{PF} & Cat_{C,S}(CTPS) \end{array}$$

□

Using the amalgamation lemma for projection specifications 3.7 and correctness of persistent parameterized projection specifications we obtain the following compositionality theorem, which is an extension of the corresponding induced correctness theorem for algebraic specifications given in /EM85/ : Actualization with externally correct parameterized projection specifications results in an externally correct parameterized projection specification.

3.13 Theorem **(Induced Correctness of Value Specifications) :**
Given
(1) a persistent parameterized projection specification (FPS,TPS) which is correct w.r.t. a strongly persistent model functor $PM:Cat_{C,S}(CMFPS)\rightarrow Cat_{C,S}(CMTPS)$, related by morphisms $j_F:MFPS\rightarrow FPS$ and $j_T:MTPS\rightarrow TPS$;

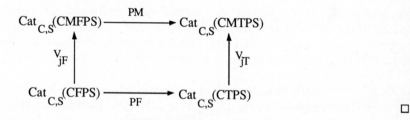

(2) a persistent parameterized projection specification (FPS′,TPS′) which is correct w.r.t. a strongly persistent model functor $PM':Cat_{C,S}(CMFPS') \rightarrow Cat_{C,S}(CMTPS')$, related by morphisms $j_{F'}:MFPS' \rightarrow FPS$ and $j_{T'}:MTPS' \rightarrow TPS'$;

(3) a projection parameter passing morphism $h:FPS \rightarrow TPS'$ which is compatible with the model projection specifications MFPS and MTPS′, i.e. there is a projection specification morphism $k:MFPS \rightarrow MTPS'$ with $j_{jT'} \circ k = h \circ j_{jF}$;

then we have

(4) the value projection specification (FPS′,TPS2) is correct w.r.t. the model functor $PM *_k PM':Cat_{C,S}(CMFPS') \rightarrow Cat_{C,S}(CMTPS2)$ given by the amamlgamated sums

(5) $PM *_k PM'(A') = PM'(A') +_A PM(A)$, with $A = V_k \circ PM'(A')$,

where MTPS2 is the value specification in the projection parameter passing diagram

$$
\begin{array}{ccccc}
 & & MFPS & \xrightarrow{m} & MTPS \\
 & & \downarrow k & (PO) & \downarrow k1 \\
MFPS' & \xrightarrow{m'} & MTPS' & \xrightarrow{m1} & MTPS2
\end{array}
$$

□

4 Refinement of Projection Specifications

This section introduces refinement as a vertical transformation of parameterized projection specifications. We will first discuss horizontal and vertical transformations and their compatibility properties in general. This includes an overview over this and the next section, where R-implementation is introduced as another vertical operation.

In the previous section actualization of parameterized projection specifications has been introduced as an operation on specifications to build large specifications from smaller ones. At the end of this section extension of parameterized projection specification will be introduced, which is also frequently used to build specifications for different applications from smaller basic versions. Both operations can be subsumed under the general notion of horizontal operation, which denotes an operation which is used to combine small specifications to larger ones (for a more detailed discussion see /KHGB87/, /Ehr89/).

In contrast vertical operations on specifications are used to develop more concrete versions for abstract specifications. This and the next section of this paper are devoted to two vertical operations on parameterized projection specifications : refinement and (one version of) implementation.

In our approach vertical operations are considered as relations between specifications. So the accent is laid on what a correct vertical development step is, syntactically and semantically, rather than how to construct a refinement or an implementation.

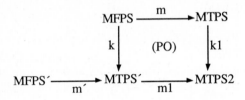

The distinction between horizontal and vertical operations need not necessarily be as sharp as indicated here and may altogether depend on the constructs a language or framework offers. Furthermore an operation can be interpreted as a relation between arguments and result as well as as procedure which produces the result out of its arguments. In this paper, however, we use the definition and distinction indicated above which, in our opinion, matches the requirements stated in software engeneering.

Generally we demand of a class of vertical operations to be closed under composition; i.e. for instance two consecutive refinements or implementations can be interpreted as one (composed) refinement or implementation respectively. From the application point of view this requirement seems sensible, since if SPEC2 implements SPEC1 and SPEC1 implements SPEC0, then SPEC2 should also be an implementation of SPEC0. If furthermore a vertical operation is reflexive (i.e. SPEC refines or implements itself) this opens the possibility to treat vertical development categorically, which in general makes a thorough investigation of formal semantics much easier. (We will not pursue this direction extensively in this paper, but see e.g. /GB80/, /Ehr89/).

As a second requirement on vertical operations we impose compatibility with horizontal operations, i.e. vertical development should preserve the horizontal structure of the specification. In our case this means: given parameterized projection specifications PPSi=(FPSi,TPSi) (i=0,1) such that the target specification TPS1 of the actual parameter PPS1 matches the requirements of the formal specification FPS0, further given vertical transformations fi:PPSi→PPSi´ (i=0,1) such that TPS1´ still matches FPS0´, then there should be an induced vertical transformation of the actualized specifications f0∗f1:PPS0∗PPS1→PPS0´∗PPS1´. If f0 and f1 are correct then also the induced vertical operation f0∗f1 should be correct.

Both directions should be compatible, i.e. the composition of two vertical development steps induced by a horizontal operation should be the same as the vertical operation induced by the composition.

In the dicussion of refinement and implementation in the following two sections we will refer to these three points as

- **vertical composition**	(transitivity and reflexivity)
- **horizontal composition**	(refinement/implementation induced by actualization resp. any horizontal operation)
- **2-dimensional compatibility**	(composition of induced vertical operations = vertical operation induced by the composition).

A refinement will in general consist in additional operations with some equations, or even additional sorts, which can be described by inclusion morphisms. But there is no need to restrict oneself to inclusion morphisms on the syntactical level. The semantical correctness condition (defining coherent refinements) excludes refinements which change the semantics of a specification; a case which can also occur using inclusions only.

4.1 Definition (Refinement) :

A refinement f:PPS0→PPS1 consists of a pair $f=(f_F,f_T)$ of projection specification morphisms such that the following diagram commutes:

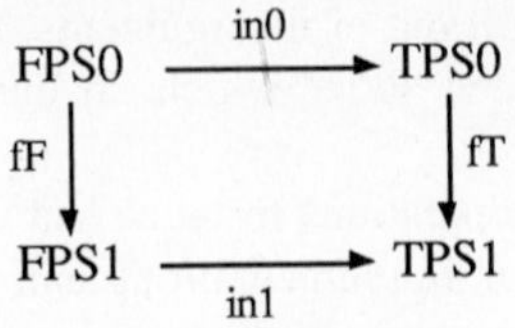

A refinement is called <u>coherent</u> (or <u>correct</u>) if the semantical functors PF0 and PF1 of PPS0 and PPS1 are compatible w.r.t. the forgetful functors V_{fF} and V_{fT} corresponding to the components f_F and f_T of the refinement f. This means that the following diagram commutes (up to isomorphism):

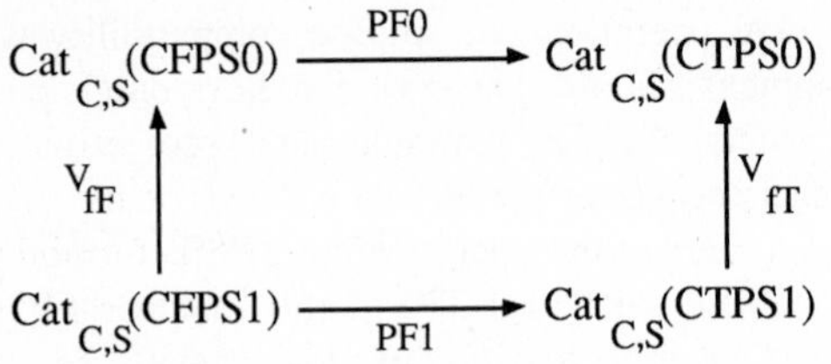

□

As an example we refine the parameterized projection speciifation probpa (action) of the basic process algebra (with arbitrary actions) given in 3.3. by parallelism and communication. As in the original Process Algebra parallelism is modeled by arbitrary interleaving, using the auxiliary operation "left merge". Communication between processes is induced by atomic communication between actions, which in our case is a formal operation (on the formal action part). Communication is a complete function which results in deadlock if the two actions cannot communicate.

<u>4.2 Example</u> : propa(action) = (action-with-comm,propa)
Next we refine the specification of the basic process algebra **probpa(action)** given in 3.3 by parallel execution of processes and communication, leading to a parameterized projection specification **propa(action-with-comm)** of the process algebra PA (see /BK86/).
Parallelism is modelled by arbitrary interleaving; for communication a formal communication function on the action sort is needed, gluing atomic actions to communication actions. Then parallel execution of two processes with communication starts with either the first action of one of the processes of with the communication of both. The deadlock δ specifies unsuccessful communication between actions and processes.

action-with-comm = **action** +

<u>opns</u> δ: → action {deadlock}
| : action action → action {communication function}

<u>eqns</u> <u>for all</u> a,b,c <u>in</u> action :

$\delta | a = \delta$

$a | b = b | a$

$(a | b) | c = a | (b | c)$

propa = **action-with-comm** + **probpa** +

<u>opns</u> $|, ||, |L$: proc proc $\rightarrow$proc {communication, merge, left merge}

<u>eqns</u> <u>for all</u> a,b <u>in</u> action; <u>for all</u> x,y,z <u>in</u> proc :

$\delta + x = x$

$\delta x = \delta$

$c(a)|c(b) = c(a|b)$

$(c(a)x)|c(b) = c(a|b)x$

$(c(a)x)|(c(b)y) = c(a|b)(x||y)$

$(x+y)|z = (x|z)+(y|z)$

$x|y = y|x$

$(x|y)|z = x|(y|z)$

$x||y = x|Ly + y|Lx + x|y$

$c(a)||Lx = c(a)x$

$c(a)x|Ly = c(a)(x||y)$

$(x+y)|Lz = (x|Lz)+(y|Lz)$

In /BK86/ it is shown that the underlying parameterized algebraic specifications with inclusions form a correct refinement, i.e $V_{h2} \circ F_{f2} \cong F_{f1} \circ V_{h1}$ (see theorem 2.1 (Normal Forms) and remarks in BK86).

$$\begin{array}{ccc} F0 = \textbf{action} & \xrightarrow{f1} & \textbf{probpa} = T0 \\ \downarrow h1 & & \downarrow h2 \\ F1 = \textbf{action-with-comm} & \xrightarrow[f2]{} & \textbf{propa} = T1 \end{array}$$

Projection compatibility of $|, ||$ and $|L$ can easily be shown by induction. Thus, using remark 3.10 T1 is h2-secure and $PSEM_{T0} \circ V_{h2} \cong V_{h1} \circ PSEM_{T1}$, i.e. $V_{h2} \circ PF_{f2} \cong PF_{f1} \circ V_{h1}$, what was to be shown. □

Transitivity and reflexivity of refinement follow directly from the definition.

<u>4.3 Fact</u> (Vertical Composition) :
The composition of two refinements $f:PPS0 \rightarrow PPS1$ and $g:PPS1 \rightarrow PPS2$, given by the composition of the respective components $(g_F \circ f_F, g_T \circ f_T)$, is a refinement $g \circ f:PPS0 \rightarrow PPS2$. Furthermore $id_{PPS}=(id_{FPS}, id_{TPS}):PPS \rightarrow PPS$ is the identical refinement satisfying $id_{PPS} \circ f = f \circ id_{PPS} = f$ for all refinements f of PPS.
Thus refinement defines a category **REF(PPS)** whose objects are parameterized projection specifications and whose morphisms are refinements.
If the refinements f and g are coherent, then also their composition is coherent, since $V_{gX \circ fX} = V_{fX} \circ V_{gX}$ (for X=F,T). Thus **REF(PPS)** has a subcategory of coherent refinements with the same class of objects and coherent refinements as morphisms. □

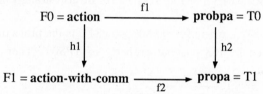

As indicated above a refinement of parameterized projection specifications induces a refinement of the corresponding actualization, provided that the refinements of formal and actual parameter are compatible. If only the projection parameter passing morphism of the actualization which is to be refined is given there need not exist a projection parameter passing morphism between the refined formal parameter specification and the refined actual target specification.

4.4 Fact (Compatibility with Actualization) :
Given
(1) parameterized projection specifications PPSi=(FPSi,TPSi), PPSi´=(FPSi´,TPSi´) (i=0,1)
(2) refinements f:PPS0→PPS1, f´:PPS0´→PPS1´
(3) projection specification morphisms hi:FPSi→TPSi´ (i=0,1) which are compatible with the refinements, i.e. $h1 \circ f_F = f_{T'} \circ h0$

there is an induced refinement of the value specification of the actualized parameterized projection specifications
(4) $f*_{(h0,h1)}f'$:$PPS0*_{h0}PPS0' \rightarrow PPS1*_{h1}PPS1'$.

If the parameterized projection specifications PPSi, PPSi´ are strongly persistent and the refinements f and f´ are coherent, then the induced refinement $f*_{(h0,h1)}f'$ is also coherent. (Recall that in this case $PPS0*_{h0}PPS0'$ and $PPS1*_{h1}PPS1'$ are also strongly persistent.)

Proof : Let $f*_{(h0,h1)}f'=(f_{F'},f_{T''})$, where $f_{T''}$:TPS0´´→TPS1´´ is the projection specification morphism uniquely defined by the pushout property of TPS0´´. Then $f*_{(h0,h1)}f'$ is a refinement.

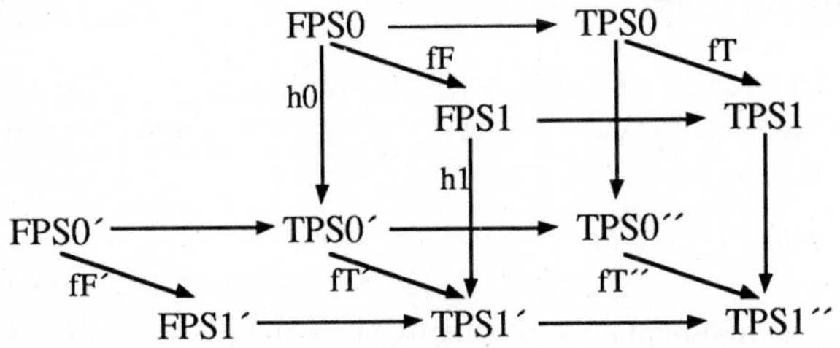

The second part of the theorem, stating correctness of the induced refinement, is a renaming (reinterpretation) of the "induced correctness"-theorem 3.13, where "a persistent parameterized projection specification which is correct w.r.t. a strongly persistent model functor" corresponds to "a coherent refinement", and the induced model functor $PM*_kPM'$ corresponds to the semantics of the actualization $PF0*_{h0}PF0'$=Ext(PF0,h0)∘PF0´. □

In 4.3 and 4.4 above the two dimensions of composition of refinements have been defined: vertical composition of successive refinements f:PPS0→PPS1 and g:PPS1→PPS2, and horizontal composition w.r.t. horizontal operations, i.e. a refinement of an actualization induced by (compatible) refinements of the ingoing parameterized specifications.
Thus there may be two ways to define a refinement between actualized parameterized projection specifications $PPS0*_{h0}PPS0'$ and $PPS2*_{h2}PPS2'$. First it may be the vertical composition via an intermediate actualized parameterized projection specification $PPS1*_{h1}PPS1'$ (see the left side of the diagram below). Secondly it could be the refinement

induced by the actualization of the twice refined components $f1 \circ f0: PPS0 \to PPS1 \to PPS2$ and $f1' \circ f0': PPS0' \to PPS1' \to PPS2'$ (see the right side of the diagram).
The following theorem shows that both ways in fact define the same refinement.

4.5 Fact (2-dimensional Compatibility) :
Given

(1) parameterized projection specifications $PPSi=(FPSi,TPSi)$, $PPSi'=(FPSi',TPSi')$ $(i=0,1,2)$

(2) refinements $fj:PPSj \to PPS(j+1)$, $fj':PPSj' \to PPS(j+1)'$ $(j=0,1)$

(3) compatible projection parameter passing morphisms $hi:FPSi \to TPSi'$ $(i=0,1,2)$ (i.e. $h(j+1) \circ f_{jF} = f_{jT'} \circ hj$)

we have the following 2-dimensional compatibility between refinement and actualization

(4) $(f1 \circ f0) *_{(h0,h2)} (f1' \circ f0') = (f1 *_{(h1,h2)} f1') \circ (f0 *_{(h0,h1)} f0')$.

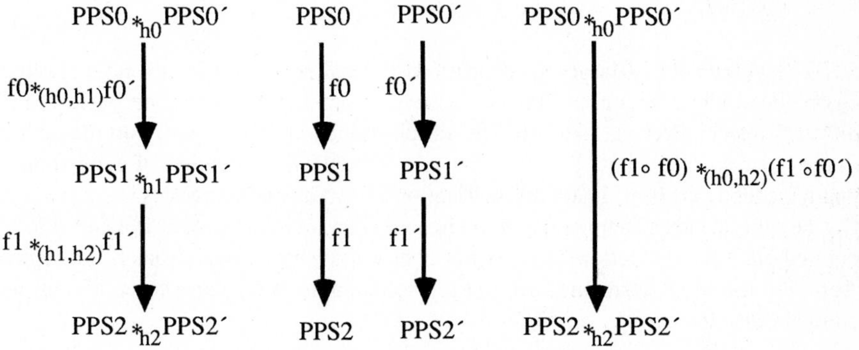

Proof :
(Concerning the notations see also the diagram on the next page.)
$[(f1 *_{(h1,h2)} f1') \circ (f0 *_{(h0,h1)} f0')]_F$ by definition consists of the composition $f1_{F'} \circ f0_{F'}$.
$[(f1 *_{(h1,h2)} f1') \circ (f0 *_{(h0,h1)} f0')]_T$ is defined by the pushout property of $TPS0''$, i.e. $[(f1 *_{(h1,h2)} f1') \circ (f0 *_{(h0,h1)} f0')]_T = f1_{T''} \circ f0_{T''}$.
Thus $(f1 \circ f0) *_{(h0,h2)} (f1' \circ f0') = (f1_{F'} \circ f0_{F'}, f1_{T''} \circ f0_{T''}) = (f1_{F'}, f1_{T''}) \circ (f0_{F'}, f0_{T''}) =$
$= (f1 *_{(h1,h2)} f1') \circ (f0 *_{(h0,h1)} f0')$.

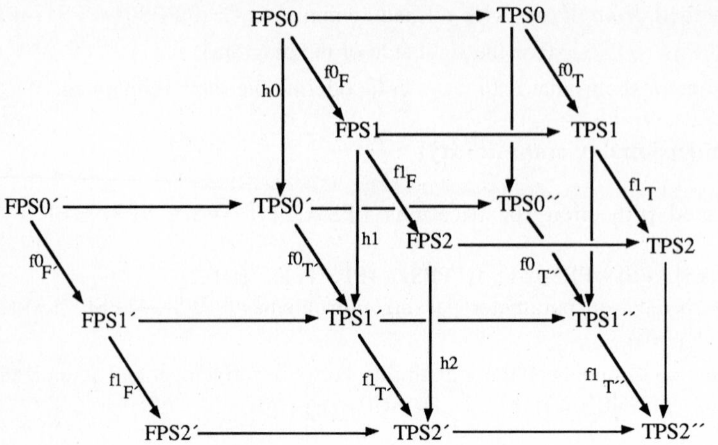

□

In the development of larger specifications extension plays a centrs role. Having defined a basic constructive specification one or several extensions adapt the basic specification to different needs, offering additional operations which act consistently on the data constructed in the basic specification. The problem of a semantical foundation of extension, however, is that the added part itself is not a specification and so has no semantics.
On the other hand refinement (with inclusions) can be reinterpreted as extension. (As already pointed out : the distinction between horizontal and vertical operations is conceptual.)
Applying the same correctnes criteria to extension as to refinement we obtain the following compatibility theorem :

<u>4.6 Theorem</u> (Compatibility with Extension) :
Given persistent parameterized projection specifications PPSi (i=0,1,2), a coherent refinement f:PPS0→PPS1 and a coherent extension e:PPS0→PPS2, there are an induced coherent refinement f´:PPS2→PPS3 and an induced coherent extension e´:PPS1→PPS3 with a persistent parameterized projection specification PPS3.

<u>Proof</u> : Let PPS3, f´ and e´ be given by the following pushout diagram in REF(PPS) (which can be constructed componentwise).

$$\begin{array}{ccc} PPS0 & \xrightarrow{e} & PPS2 \\ f \downarrow & (PO) & \downarrow f' \\ PPS1 & \xrightarrow[e']{} & PPS2 \end{array}$$

The extension lemma 3.9 shows that the amalgamated functor PF3 $=PF1+_{PF0}PF2$ is persistent and that f´ and e´ are coherent. □

5 R-Implementations

According to our general assumption about vertical operations implementation is considered as relation between parameterized projection specifications. Corresponding to different requirements, how close the implementation shall meet the abstract specification, there are different versions of implementation. E.g. the implementation may have multiple representations of one abstract data item or may produce data which represent no abstract data at all. The semantics of the implementation must of course be compatible with the semantics of the abstract specification, i.e. there must be a (sensible) semantical construction relating the semantics of abstract specification and implementation.
Refinement of parameterized projection specifications, as introduced in the previous section, may serve as a simple version of implementation. It does not include, however, any semantical deviation of the implementation w.r.t. the abstract specification. In this section we introduce an implementation which allows additional data in the implementing specification. A restriction construction, which removes these additional data, relates the semantics of the implementation and the abstract specification. It is defined analogously to the restriction construction for algebraic specifications (see e.g. /BEP87/).
This section starts with the definitions of the restriction construction for projection specifications and R-implementation (= implementation with restriction). Then R-implementation is discussed along the line indicated in section 4 for vertical operations; i.e. vertical and horizontal composition, and 2-dimensional compatibility are shown to hold for R-implementation.

The restriction construction for projection specifications is the transcription of the corrseponding restriction construction for algebraic specifications and analogously extends to an endofunctor.

5.1 Definition (Projection Restriction Functor) :
Given projection specifications PS0, PS1, a projection specification morphism $h{:}PS0 \rightarrow PS1$ and the corresponding forgetful functor $V_h{:}Cat_{C,S}(CPS1) \rightarrow Cat_{C,S}(CPS0)$, the projection restriction functor $PRestr_h{:}Cat_{C,S}(CPS1) \rightarrow Cat_{C,S}(CPS1)$ is defined by:

$$PRestr_h(A1) = \bigcap\{A \in Cat_{C,S}(CPS1) \mid A \text{ is a subalgebra of } A1 \ \& \ V_h(A1)=V_h(A)\}$$
$$PRestr_h(f1) = f1|PRestr_h(A1)\ .$$

A proof of the welldefinedness of $PRestr_h(f1)$ for the corresponding restriction functor $Restr_h{:}Cat(SPEC1) \rightarrow Cat(SPEC1)$ based on algebraic specifications is given in /BEP87/. Since it only uses the properties of restriction functors listed in fact 5.2 below, which hold for both restriction functors, the proof holds for the projection restriction functor, too. □

Next we state some basic facts of a restriction functor. Part (1) could also serve as set of axioms for an abstract definition of a restriction functor.

5.2 Fact (Restriction) :
Using the notation as in 5.1 we have

(1) (a) $PRestr_h \circ PRestr_h = PRestr_h$

(b) $V_h \circ PRestr_h = V_h$

(c) $PRestr_{g \circ h} \circ PRestr_h = PRestr_{g \circ h}$ (for all composable pairs of projection specification morphisms g,h)

(2) $PRestr_h \cong PSEM1 \circ Restr_h \circ I1$,

where $PSEM1{:}Cat_i(PS1) \rightarrow Cat_{C,S}(CPS1)$ is the projection semantics functor corresponding to PS1 and $I1{:}Cat_{C,S}(CPS1) \rightarrow Cat_i(PS1)$ is the inclusion.

Proof : (1) follows directly from the definition of restriction.

(2) $PSEM1 \circ Restr_h(A1) =$

$= PSEM1(\bigcap\{A \mid A \text{ is a PS1-subalgebra of } A1 \ \& \ V_h(A1)=V_h(A)\}) =$

$= \bigcap\{PSEM1(A) \mid A \text{ is a PS1-subalgebra of } A1 \ \& \ V_h(A1)=V_h(A)\} \cong$

(since each subalgebra A is a separated projection algebra and $Cat_{C,S}(CPS1)$ is closed under intersections)

$\cong \bigcap\{A' \mid A' \text{ is a complete separated projection subalgebra of } A1 \ \& \ V_h(A1)=V_h(A)\} =$

(since $A' \cong PSEM1(A')$)

$= PRestr_h(A1)$

$PSEM1 \circ Restr_h(f1{:}A1 \rightarrow B1) = PSEM1(f1{:}Restr_h(A1) \rightarrow Restr_h(B1)) =$

$= PSEM1(f1){:}PSEM1 \circ Restr_h(A1) \rightarrow PSEM1 \circ Restr_h(B1)) \cong$

$\cong PSEM1(f1){:}PRestr_h(A1) \rightarrow PRestr_h(B1)) \cong f1{:}PRestr_h(A1) \rightarrow PRestr_h(B1))$ □

Syntactically R-implementation of parameterized projection specifications is defined by a pair of projection specification morphisms, like refinement. On the semantical level, however, we have to take into account the restriction of data representing implementations to items generated by the specification which is to be implemented.

5.3 Definition (R-Implementation) :
An R-implementation $f{:}PPS0 \rightarrow PPS1$ consists of a pair $f=(f_F,f_T)$ of projection specification morphisms such that the following diagram commutes:

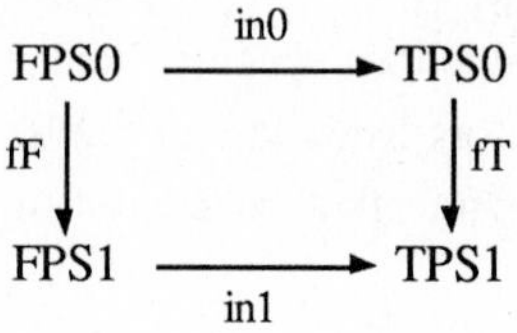

An R-implementation is called correct if $PF0 \circ V_{fF} \cong PRestr_{in0} \circ V_{fT} \circ PF1$

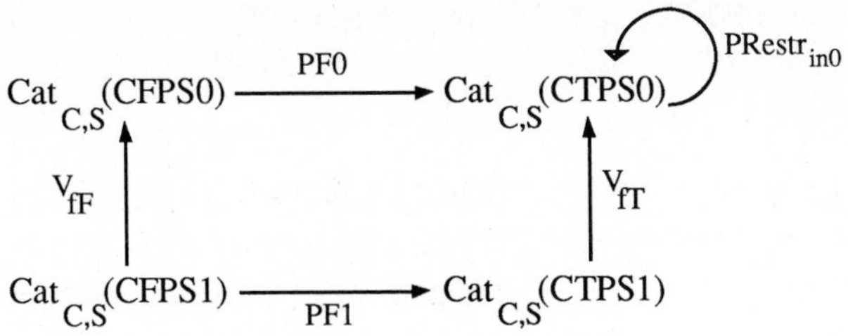

where PFi (i=0,1) are projection free functors, V_{fX} (X=F,T) are forgetful functors and $PRestr_{in0}$ is the projection restriction functor. □

5.4 Example :
In /EKMP82/ and /EKP80/ examples for R-implementations of abstract data type specifications are worked out, e.g. an R-implementation of sets by hash tables. These examples are formulated as two step implementations there, a synthesis step followed by restriction. The synthesis, however, can be subsumed under the implementing specification, such that the notations used in /EKMP82/ and /EKP80/ fit into the framework used in this paper.
According to fact 5.9 below, given a parameterized process specification PPS and a projection specification morphism h for the actualization of its formal data type part, an R-implementation of the actual data type specification SPEC (considered as projection specification with discrete projections) induces an R-implementation of the actualized projection specification PS = $PPS*_h SPEC$.
An example of an R-implementation of a process type will be worked out for subsequent papers. □

5.5 Remark (Vertical Composition) :
Since syntactically R-implementation is defined like refinement, R-implementations are also transitive and reflexive. Thus **REF(PPS)** can (on the syntactical level) also be interpreted as **R-IMPL(PPS)**, the category of parameterized projection specifications with R-implemenations as morphisms.

The following theorem states that vertical composition preserves correctness, i.e. the composition of correct R-implementations is itself a correct R-implementation.

5.6 Theorem (Correct Vertical Composition) :
Given correct R-implementations f:PPS0→PPS1 and g:PPS1→PPS2, their composition is a correct R-implementation g∘f:PPS0→PPS2.

Proof : We have to show that $PF0 \circ V_{gF \circ fF} = PRestr_{in0} \circ V_{gT \circ fT} \circ PF2$.

$PF0 \circ V_{gF \circ fF} = PF0 \circ V_{fF} \circ V_{gF} =$

$PRestr_{in0} \circ V_{fT} \circ PF1 \circ V_{gF} =$	(since f is correct)
$PRestr_{in0} \circ V_{fT} \circ PRestr_{in1} \circ V_{gT} \circ PF2 =$	(since g is correct)
$PRestr_{in0} \circ V_{fT} \circ V_{gT} \circ PF2 =$	(by part (3) of the restriction lemma below)
$PRestr_{in0} \circ V_{gT \circ fT} \circ PF2$	□

5.7 Restriction Lemma :
Given projection specifications PSi (i=0,1,2,3) and projection specification morphisms fj,gj (j=1,2), such that diagram (1) commutes

$$\begin{array}{ccc} PS0 & \xrightarrow{f1} & PS1 \\ {\scriptstyle f2}\downarrow & (1) & \downarrow{\scriptstyle g1} \\ PS2 & \xrightarrow[g2]{} & PS3 \end{array}$$

we have

(1) $PRestr_{f2} \circ V_{g2} \subseteq V_{g2} \circ PRestr_{g1}$
(2) $V_{f2} \circ PRestr_{f2} \circ V_{g2} = V_{f2} \circ V_{g2} \circ PRestr_{g1}$
(3) $PRestr_{f2} \circ V_{g2} = PRestr_{f2} \circ V_{g2} \circ PRestr_{g1}$
(4) If (1) is a pushout diagram, then $PRestr_{g1}(A2+_{A0}A1) = PRestr_{f2}(A2)+_{A0}A1$

A proof for the case of algebraic specifications, which carries over to projection specifications directly, is given in /EM89/. Thus we do not give an explicit proof here. □

For compatiblity with the restriction construction we need (strongly) conservative functors, i.e. functors preserving injective homomorphisms. Persistency alone is not enough to make a free functor commute with the corresponding restriction functor. But like persistency conservativity carries over to the extended functor (via a pushout diagram). These facts are proved in /BEP87/ for algebraic free- and restriction functors, and in /Dim89/ for projection free functors.

5.8 Lemma (Conservativity) :
A (stongly) persistent functor F is called (strongly) conservative, if it preserves monomorphisms, i.e. f mono ⇒ F(f) mono.
(1) Given projection specifications and projection specification morphisms s:PS→PS1, i:PS1→PS2; if the projection free functor $PF_i:Cat_{C,S}(CPS1) \to Cat_{C,S}(CPS2)$ is strongly conservative it commutes with projection restriction, i.e. $PRestr_{i \circ s} PF_i = PF_i \circ PRestr_s$.

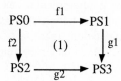

(2) Given a pushout diagram in the category of projection specifications

$$
\begin{array}{ccc}
PS0 & \xrightarrow{\ i1\ } & PS1 \\
{\scriptstyle h1}\big\downarrow & (PO) & \big\downarrow{\scriptstyle h2} \\
PS2 & \xrightarrow[\ i2\ ]{} & PS3
\end{array}
$$

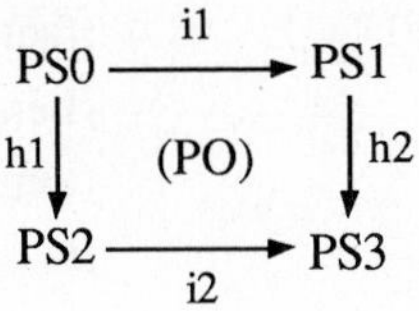

such that the projection free functor $PF_{i1}:Cat_{C,S}(CPS0)\to Cat_{C,S}(CPS1)$ is strongly conservative, the extended projection free functor $Ext(PF,h1):Cat_{C,S}(CPS2)\to Cat_{C,S}(CPS3)$ is also strongly conservative. $\qquad\square$

5.9 Fact (Compatibility with Actualization) :

Given

(1) strongly conservative parameterized projection specifications $PPSi=(FPSi,TPSi)$, and strongly persistent parameterized projection specifications $PPSi´=(FPSi´,TPSi´)$ (i=0,1)

(2) correct R-implementations $f:PPS0\to PPS1$, $f´:PPS0´\to PPS1´$

(3) projection specification morphisms $hi:FPSi\to TPSi´$ (i=0,1) which are compatible with the R-implementations, i.e. $h1\circ f_F=f_T\circ h0$

the induced R-implementation

(4) $f*_{(h0,h1)}f´:PPS0*_{h0}PPS0´\to PPS1*_{h1}PPS1´$

given by

(5) $f*_{(h0,h1)}f´=(f_{F´},f_{T´´})$,

where $f_{T´´}:TPS0´´\to TPS1´´$ is the projection specification morphism uniquely defined by the pushout property of $TPS0´´$, the target projection specification of $PPS0*_{h0}PPS0´$

is correct.

Proof : We have to show the equation $PRestr_{in0*}\circ V_{fT´´}\circ PF1´´\circ PF1´ = PF0´´\circ PF1´\circ V_{fF´}$.

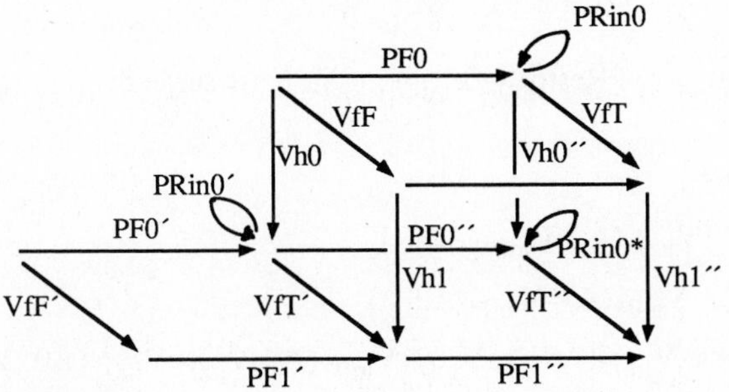

where $in0* = in0´´\circ in0´$.

Using the amalgamation lemma this is equivalent to

(1) $V_{h0´´}\circ(PRestr_{in0*}\circ V_{fT´´}\circ PF1´´\circ PF1´) = V_{h0´´}\circ(PF0´´\circ PF1´\circ V_{fF´})$ and

(2) $V_{in0´´}\circ(PRestr_{in0*}\circ V_{fT´´}\circ PF1´´\circ PF1´) = V_{in0´´}\circ(PF0´´\circ PF1´\circ V_{fF´})$.

ad (1)

$V_{h0''}\circ PRestr_{in0*}\circ V_{fT''}\circ PF1''\circ PF1' =$

$= V_{h0''}\circ PRestr_{in0*}\circ PRestr_{in0''}\circ V_{fT''}\circ PF1''\circ PF1' =$ (fact 5.2.1)

$= V_{h0''}\circ PRestr_{in0*}\circ PF0''\circ V_{fT'}\circ PF1' =$ (Lemma 1)

$= V_{h0''}\circ PF0''\circ PRestr_{in0'}\circ V_{fT'}\circ PF1' =$ (Lemma 5.8)

$= V_{h0''}\circ PF0''\circ PF1'\circ V_{fF'}$ (f´ correct)

ad(2)

$V_{in0''}\circ PRestr_{in0*}\circ V_{fT''}\circ PF1''\circ PF1' =$

$= PRestr_{in0'}\circ V_{in0''}\circ V_{fT''}\circ PF1''\circ PF1' =$ (Lemma 2)

$= PRestr_{in0'}\circ V_{fT'}\circ V_{in1''}\circ PF1''\circ PF1' =$

$= PRestr_{in0'}\circ V_{fT'}\circ PF1' =$ (PF1´´ persistent)

$= V_{in0''}\circ PF0''\circ PRestr_{in0'}\circ V_{fT'}\circ PF1' =$ (PF0´´ persistent)

$= V_{in0''}\circ PF0''\circ PF0'\circ V_{fF'}$ (f´ correct)

<u>Lemma 1</u> : $PRestr_{in0''}\circ V_{fT''}\circ PF1'' = PF0''\circ V_{fT'}$

<u>Proof of lemma 1</u> : (by amalgamation lemma)

$V_{h0''}\circ PRestr_{in0''}\circ V_{fT''}\circ PF1'' =$

$= PRestr_{in0}\circ V_{h0''}\circ V_{fT''}\circ PF1'' =$ (restriction lemma 5.7.4)

$= PRestr_{in0}\circ V_{fT}\circ V_{h1''}\circ PF1'' =$

$= PRestr_{in0}\circ V_{fT}\circ PF1\circ V_{h1} =$ (extension lemma)

$= PF0\circ V_{fF}\circ V_{h1} =$ (f correct)

$= PF0\circ V_{h0}\circ V_{fT'} =$

$= V_{h0''}\circ PF0''\circ V_{fT'}$ (extension lemma)

$V_{in0''}\circ PRestr_{in0''}\circ V_{fT''}\circ PF1'' =$

$= V_{in0''}\circ V_{fT''}\circ PF1'' =$ (5.2.1)

$= V_{fT'}\circ V_{in1''}\circ PF1'' =$

$= V_{fT'} = V_{in0''}\circ PF0''\circ V_{fT'}$

<u>Lemma 2</u> : $V_{in0''}\circ PRestr_{in0*} = PRestr_{in0'}\circ V_{in0''}$, if $V_{in0''}$ is surjective.

<u>Proof of lemma 2</u> :

$V_{in0''}\circ PRestr_{in0*}(A0'') =$

$= V_{in0''}(\bigcap\{A \mid A\subseteq A0'' , V_{in0*}(A)=V_{in0*}(A0'')\}$

$= \bigcap\{V_{in0''}(A) \mid A\subseteq A0'' , V_{in0*}(A)=V_{in0*}(A0'')\}$

$= \bigcap\{V_{in0''}(A) \mid V_{in0''}(A)\subseteq V_{in0''}(A0'') , V_{in0'}\circ V_{in0''}(A)=V_{in0'}\circ V_{in0''}(A0'')\}$ (∗)

$= \bigcap\{B \mid B\subseteq V_{in0''}(A0'') , V_{in0'}(B)=V_{in0'}\circ V_{in0''}(A0'')\}$ (∗∗)

$= PRestr_{in0'}\circ V_{in0''}(A0'')$

(∗) If $V_{in0''}(A)\subseteq V_{in0''}(A0'')$ then $A\cap A0''\subseteq A0''$ and $V_{in0''}(A\cap A0'')=V_{in0''}(A0'')$.

(∗∗) Since $V_{in0''}$ is surjective.

$V_{in0''} \circ PRestr_{in0*}$ (f0'':A0''→B0'') =
= $V_{in0''}$(f0'':$PRestr_{in0*}$ (A0'')→$PRestr_{in0*}$ (B0'') =
= $V_{in0''}$(f0''):$V_{in0''} \circ PRestr_{in0*}$ (A0'')→$V_{in0''} \circ PRestr_{in0*}$ (B0'') =
= $V_{in0''}$(f0''):$PRestr_{in0'} \circ V_{in0''}$ (A0'')→$PRestr_{in0'} \circ V_{in0''}$ (B0'') =
= $PRestr_{in0'} \circ V_{in0''}$(f0'':A0''→B0'') □

<u>5.10 Remark</u> :
2-dimensional compatibility is a synatctical property, thus holds for R-implementations as well as for refinements, as shown already in fact 4.5. □

6 Projection Specification and Induced Refinement of Petri Net Processes

In this section we outline a projection specification of the token game of a Petri net as an infinite process. The specification of the Petri net itself is not given here, since it is a usual (static) data type. Adding discrete projections for each sort turns an algebraic specification of Petri nets into a projection specification with the same semantics. (An example is given in /Gro88/.) Furthermore the token game specification can be applied to Petri nets of different types, thus the subspecification **petri-net** could also be used as a formal parameter. A suitable set of operations which are needed for the token game must be included in the parameter (like "select-active-and-independent-transitions" or "change-markings-conform-the-firing-of-transitions"), but the firing condition itself or the special structure of the net and the labels are variable.
For the specification of the token game we use the notions of parallelism and concurrency expressed in the Petri net itself. Thus for the process specification we only need sequential composition (_·_) and indeterministic choice (_+_) as operations, as in the **probpa(action)** specification given in 3.3. It will be extended by an empty process to make the recursive definitions possible which are needed in the token game specification (see **probpa**$_\varepsilon$**(action)** below).
One action of the token game is specified as a set of independent and active transitions S, i.e. the occurence of a set of transitions as an action in the process "token game" is interpreted as its firing. This coincides with the usual interpretation of the labels in action trees. The specification **petri-net** must contain the specification of an operation FIRE(S,PN), which maps a Petri net PN and a set of transitions S on a Petri net with same underlying graph and the new marking which results from firing all transitions $t \in S$. The transitions themselves can be specified as a formal sort with arbitrary projection.

The token game TG of a Petri net PN with set of transitions T now is given by the following recursive equation :

$$TG(PN)=\Sigma_{\{S \subseteq T: S \text{ independent and active}\}} S \cdot TG(FIRE(S,PN)) .$$

This means :

(1) First all sets of active and independent transitions are collected; this determines the domain (the index) of the choice operator Σ.

(2) Then a set of processes is constructed (recursively) by : fire a set of transitions, then start the tokengame with the new marking, for all sets of transitions given by step (1).

(3) The choice operator chooses one of the processes out of the set consructed in step (2).

Thus an operation FIRESETS is needed in the specification **petri-net** which collects all subsets of the set of transitions which are independent and active, i.e. ready to fire. The part S·TG(FIRE(S,PN)) of the recursive equation above is specified by a binary operation PREFIX, mapping a powerset of transitions POST and a Petri net PN on the set of processes {ST·TG(FIRE(ST,PN)) : ST∈POST}.

The choice operator Σ can be defined recursively over **probpa**$_\varepsilon$**(action)**. To make **probpa**$_\varepsilon$**(action)** a consistent extension we must replace the distributivity equation in **probpa(action)** (x+y)z=xz+yz by a set of equations which guarantee that neither x nor y are empty; i.e. enumerate all cases " a, aw, aw+w´ " for x and y. The semantics of **probpa(action)** is thereby not changed.

The example is given in an ACT ONE like syntax (see /EM85/,/EFH83/). The complete specification is given in /Gro88/.

<u>act text</u>

token-game = **set(data)** actualized by **pn-action** +

    <u>opns</u>   token-game : petri-net → proc
            prefix : poset-of-trans petri-net → set-of-procs
            sigma : set-of-procs → proc

    <u>eqns</u>   <u>for all</u> pn <u>in</u> petri-net :
            token-game(pn) = sigma(prefix(firesets(pn),pn))

            <u>for all</u> st <u>in</u> set-of-trans; <u>for all</u> post <u>in</u> poset-of-trans;<u>for all</u> pn <u>in</u> petri-net :
            prefix(empty-poset-of-trans,pn) = empty-set-of-procs
            prefix(insert-set-of-trans(st,post),pn) =
                        insert-proc(st·token-game(fire(st,pn)),prefix(post,pn))

            <u>for all</u> p <u>in</u> proc; <u>for all</u> sp <u>in</u> set-of-procs :
            sigma(empty-set-of-procs) = ε
            sigma(insert-proc(p,sp)) = p+sigma(sp)

pn-action = **probpa**$_\varepsilon$**(action)**

    <u>actualized by</u> **petri-net** <u>using</u>
            <u>sortnames</u> set-of-trans <u>for</u> action
            <u>opnames</u> p-set-of-trans <u>for</u> p-action

probpa$_\varepsilon$(action) = **probpa(action)** +

<u>opns</u> $\varepsilon \to$ proc

<u>eqns</u> <u>for all</u> x <u>in</u> proc; <u>for all</u> a,b <u>in</u> action; <u>for all</u> n <u>in</u> nat1 :

$\varepsilon \cdot x = x$

$x \cdot \varepsilon = x$

$x + \varepsilon = x$

p-proc(n,ε) = ε

<u>uses from library</u> **petri-net** , **probpa(action)** , **set(data)**

<u>end of text</u>

The token game specification is based on the extension **probpa$_\varepsilon$(action)** of the **probpa(action)** specification. In 4.2 we have refined **probpa(action)** by parallel composition and communication, called **propa(action-with-comm)**. Fact 4.6 states that there is a (uniquely determined) parameterized projection specification **propa$_\varepsilon$(action)** which refines **probpa$_\varepsilon$(action)** and extends **propa(action)**. Since refinement is compatible with actualization (see 4.4) and reflexive (each specification refines itself coherently, see 4.3), the refinement **probpa$_\varepsilon$(action)$\to$propa$_\varepsilon$(action)** induces a refinement **token-game $\to$token-game1**.
In this specification it is possible to give an equivalent specification of a token game, using parallel composition and communication. As atomic actions of "token-game-1" (TG1) we take the firing of one transition, in contrast with a set of transitions as in TG specified above. Communication between the firing of two transitions t1 and t2 then corresponds to the set $\{t1\} \cup \{t2\}$, i.e. the formal communication function | is actualized by union (of finite sets). Thus in addition to the atomic actions (= singleton sets of transitions) we have all finite sets of transitions as communication actions.
Since TG1 distinguishes between single transitions and sets of transitions two new operators are needed: in step (2) DISPOSE places a powerset of processes at disposal, where only single transitions occur as first action of a process. in step (3) the operator ΣP chooses one of the sets of processes and executes its processes in parallel, where the single transitions are collected to sets again.
Thus TG1 (token game 1) is given by the recursive equations

TG1(PN) = ΣP(DISPOSE($\{S \subseteq T$: S independent and active$\}$,PN))
DISPOSE(POST,PN) = $\{\{\{s\} \cdot$TG1(FIRE($\{s\}$,PN)) : $s \in S\}$: $S \in$ POST$\}$

That means:
(1) all sets of active and independent transitions are collected by FIRESETS as before;
(2) DISPOSE produces the set of all processes $\{s\} \cdot$TG1(FIRE($\{s\}$,PN)) , $s \in S$, for all given sets of transitions $S \in$ POST.
Since the argument of DISPOSE is a power set of transitions, its result is a power set of processes, where each single process starts with the firing of one transition.
(3) ΣP chooses one of the sets of processes offered by DISPOSE and executes all of the processes in this set in parallel.

TG1 coincides with TG, if communication between two sets of transitions is actualized by their union, which corresponds to the usual interpretation of concurrency in Petri nets. A formal proof of the equivalence of token-game and token-game1, however, will not be given here.

act text

token-game1 = **poset(data)** actualized by **pn-par-action** +

```
    opns   token-game1 : petri-net                 → proc
           dispose     : poset-of-trans petrinet   → poset-of-trans
           sigma-p     : poset-of-procs            → proc
           par         : set-of-procs              → proc

    eqns   for all pn in petri-net :
           token-game1(pn) = sigma-p(dispose(firesets(pn),pn))

           for all t in transition; for all st in set-of-trans; for all post in poset-of-trans;
           for all pn in petri-net :
           dispose(empty-poset-of-trans,pn) = empty-poset-of-procs
           dispose(insert-set-of-trans(empty-set-of-trans,post),pn) = dispose(post,pn)
           dispose(insert-set-of-trans(insert-trans(t,st),post),pn) =
              = insert-set-of-procs
                  (insert-proc( singleton(t)·token-game1(fire(singleton(t),pn)),
                                dispose(insert-set-of-trans(st,post),pn)),
                   dispose(post,pn))

           for all sp in set-of-procs; for all posp in poset-of-procs :
           sigma-p(empty-poset-of-procs) = ε
           sigma-p(insert-set-of-procs(sp,posp)) = par(sp)+sigma-p(posp)

           for all p in proc; for all sp in set-of-procs :
           par(empty-set-of-procs) = ε
           par(insert-proc(p,sp)) = p||par(sp)
```

...

end of text

7 Conclusion and Open Problems

In this paper we have reviewed projection specifications as a purely algebraic approach to the specification of concurrent systems. The metric algebra approach could be formulated categorically and combined with equational algebraic specifications, leading to combined data

type and process specifications.
The constructions and proofs for the transformations of parameterized projection specifications as given in sections 3 - 5 could be carried over from the corresponding notions for algebraic parameterized specifications quite directly. (So that we did not present the transcripted proofs here.) In both cases there are some central notions and relation between them, which imply all results concerning compositionality, correctness and compatibility. On the syntactical level pushouts are needed, on the semantical level free functors for the definition of a semantics, and persistency, amalgamation, extension of persistent functors and restriction for the semantical constructions.
Since this internal structure is independent of algebraic- or projection specifications a general setting for transformation concepts is suggested, which offers the (compositionality-, correctness- etc.) results to different specification formalisms.
Such a general framework is specification logic, a categorical formulation of syntax and semantics of a specification formalism (see /EPO89/). Specification logics correspond to theory presentations in the sense of institutions. A projection specification logic will be presented in a subsequent paper.
A specification logic could also offer a framework for a new definition of a semantics of recursive processes. In /Gro88/, /Gro89/ a fixed point theorem for projection spaces has been introduced to define the semantics of recursively defined parameterized processes. The next step would be to define the semantics of a projection specification to consist of recursively definable processes only, such that each single process has a finite specification. In the classical completion approach, which leads to uncountable models, this is in general not the case. This topic will be worked out for later presentation.
In this paper transformation has been considered as a relation between specifications. But also transformation concepts could be formulated for single processes. E.g. term rewriting defines transformations. Note, however, that infinite processes are not specified by infinite terms, but by (infinite) sequences of (finite) terms. Moreover one could specify a transformation relation between processes (e.g. implementation or bisimulation), but due to the topological approach this relation cannot be specified as a boolean valued operation (it would not be projection compatible). The topological approach of properties as open sets (see /Smy88/ should be further investigated to clear this topic.

References

/AMRW85/ E.Astesiano, G.F.Mascari, G.Reggio, M.Wirsing : On the Parameterized Algebraic Specification of Concurrent Systems, Proc. CAAP85 - TAPSOFT Conference, Springer LNCS 185, 1985

/AR87/ E.Astesiano, G.Reggio : An Outline of the SMoLCS Methodology, Mathematical Models for the Semantics of Parallelism, Springer LNCS 280, 1987

/BEP87/ E.K.Blum, H.Ehrig, F.Parisi-Presicce : Algebraic Specification of Modules and Their Basic Interconnections, in JCCS Vol.34, No.2/3, pp.293-339, 1987

/BG80/ R.M.Burstall, J.A.Goguen : CAT, a System for the Structured Elaboration of Correct Programs from Structured Specifications, unpublished draft, University of Edinburgh / SRI International, March 1980

/BK83/ J.A.Bergstra, J.W.Klop : The Algebra of Recursively Defined Processes and the Algebra of Regular Processes, Report IW 235/83, Math. Centrum, Amsterdam 1983

/BK86/ J.A.Bergstra, J.W.Klop: Algebra of Communicating Processes, in: CWI Monographs I Series, Proceedings of the CWI Symposium Mathematics and Computer Science, North-Holland, p. 89-138, Amsterdam 1986

/Bro85/ M.Broy : Specification and Top Down Design of Distributed Systems, Proc. of TAPSOFT, Joint Concerence of Theory and Practice of Software Development, Berlin, Springer LNCS 185, 1985

/Bro86/ M.Broy : A Theory for Nondeterminism, Parallelism, Communication and Concurrency, Habilitation, Fakultät für Mathematik und Informatik der Technischen Universität München,1982, revised version in Theoretical Computer Science 45, pp 1-61, 1986

/Bro87/ M.Broy : Algebraic and Functional Specification of a Serializable Database Interface, Technical Report, Universität Passau, MIP-8718, 1987

/BZ82a/ J.W.DeBakker, J.I.Zucker : Denotational Semantics of Concurrency Proc. 14th. ACM Symp. on Theory of Computing, p.153-158, 1982

/BZ82b/ J.W.DeBakker, J.I.Zucker : Processes and the Denotational Semantics of Concurrency, Information and Control, Vol.54, No.1/2, p.70-120, 1982

/COMPASS89/ COMPASS Working Group: A Comprehenisve Approach to System Specification and Development, B.Krieg Brückner (ed.), Technical Report No 6/89, Universität Bremen 1989

/DEGR87/ C.Dimitrovici, H.Ehrig, M.Große-Rhode, C.Rieckhoff : Projektionsräume und Projektionsalgebren: Eine Algebraisierung von ultrametrischen Räumen , Technical Report No. 87-7, TU Berlin, 1987

/Dim89/ C.Dimitrovici : Projection Module Specifications and Their Basic Interconnections, Technical Report No. 89-5, TU Berlin 1989

/EFH83/ H.Ehrig,W.Fey,H.Hansen : ACT ONE: An Algebraic Specification Language with Two Levels of Semantics, TUB Bericht Nr.83-01

/Ehr89/ H.Ehrig : Concepts and Compatibility Requirements for Implementations and Transformations of Specifications, Algebraic Specification Column Part 6, EATCS Bulletin 38, April 1989

/EKMP82/ H.Ehrig, H.J.Kreowski, B.Mahr, P.Padawitz : Algebraic Implementation of Abstract Data Types, Theor. Comp. Science 20, pp.209-263, 1982

/EKP80/ H.Ehrig, H.J.Kreowski, P.Padawitz : Algebraic Implementation of Abstract Data Types: Concept, Syntax, Semantics and Correctness. Proc. ICALP 80, Springer LNCS 85 , pp. 142-156, 1980

/EM85/ H.Ehrig, B.Mahr : Fundamentals of Algebraic Specifications 1 : Equations and Initial Semantics , Springer Verlag , Berlin-Heidelberg-NewYork-Tokyo 1985

/EM89/ H.Ehrig, B.Mahr : Fundamentals of Algebraic Specifications 2 : Modules and Constraints, Springer Verlag , Berlin-Heidelberg-NewYork-Tokyo 1989

/EPBRDG88/ H.Ehrig, F.Parisi-Presicce, P.Boehm, C.Rieckhoff, C.Dimitrovici, M.Große-Rhode : Algebraic Data Type and Process Specifications Based on Projection Spaces , Springer LNCS 332, p.23-43, 1988

/EPO89/ H.Ehrig, P.Pepper, F.Orejas : On Recent Trends in Algebraic Specification, Invited paper for ICALP´89, Stresa

/Gro88/ M.Große-Rhode : Specification of Projection Algebras , Diploma Thesis, TU Berlin, 1988

/Gro89/ M.Große-Rhode : Parameterized Data Type and Process Specifications Using Projection Algebras, in: Categorical Methods in Computer Science with Aspects from Topology, H.Ehrig, M.Herrlich, H.J.Kreowski G.Preuß (eds.), Springer LNCS 393, 1989

/HE88/ H.Herrlich, H.Ehrig : The Construct PRO of Projection Spaces: Its Internal Structure, in: Categorical Methods in Computer Science with Aspects from Topology, H.Ehrig, M.Herrlich, H.J.Kreowski G.Preuß (eds.), Springer LNCS 393, 1989

/HS73/ H.Herrlich, G.E.Strecker : Category Theory, Allyn and Bacon, Boston 1973

/Hum87/ U.Hummert : High Level Netze, Technical Report No. 87-10, TU Berlin 1987

/Hum89/ U.Hummert : Algebraische Theorie von High Level Netzen, Dissertation, TU Berlin, 1989

/ISODIS86/ ISO-DIS 8807, ISO/TC97/SC21/WG1-FDT/SC-C, "LOTOS, a formal description technique based on the temporal ordering of observational behaviour", December 1986

/Jen86/ K.Jensen : Coloured Petri Nets, Advances in Petri Nets, Springer LNCS 255, 1986

/KHGB87/ B.Krieg-Brückner, B.Hoffmann, H.Ganzinger, M.Broy, R.Wilhelm, U.Möncke, B.Weisgerber, A.McGettrick, I.G. Campbell, G.Winterstein : PROgram development by SPECification and TRAnsformation. In: M.W.Roger (ed.): Results and Achievements, Proc. ESPRIT Conf. 86, North Holland (1987) 301-312

/KP87/ S.Kaplan, A.Pnueli : Specification and Implementation of Concurently Accessed Data Structures: An Abstract Data Type Approach, Proc. Symp. on Theoretical Aspects of Computer Science ´87, Springer LNCS 247, 1987

/MD86/ B.Möller, W.Dosch : On the Algebraic Specification of Domains, in Recent Trends in Data Type Specification (e.d. H.J.Kreowski), Informatik Fachberichte 116, Springer Verlag 1986, 178-195

/Mil80/ R.Milner : CCS, A Calculus of Communicating Systems, Springer LNCS 92, 1980

/Rei85/ Reisig : Petri Nets , Springer Berlin Heidelberg NewYork 1985

/Smy88/ M.Smyth : Quasi-Uniformities: Reconciling Domains and Metric Spaces, Third Workshop on Mathematical Foundations of Programming Language Semantics (Tulane 1987), to appear: Springer LNCS, 1988

/TW86/ A.Tarlecki, M.Wirsing : Continuous abstract data types, Fundamenta Informaticae IX (1986) 95-126, North-Holland

/Vau86/ J.Vautherin : Parallel System Specifications with Coloured Petri Nets and Algebraic Abstract Data Types, 7th European Workshop on Applications and Theory of Petri Nets, Oxford 1986

Various Simulations and Refinements

He Jifeng
Programming Research Group Oxford University
8–11 Keble Road Oxford, OX1 3QD
U.K.

Abstract

In this paper we deal with the problem of specification and design of concurrent programs. The basic notion of refinement is defined in labelled transition system. The concept of simulation is presented and proved to be sound for correctness of implementation. The paper provides a rigorous method for the formal development of communicating processes by integrating the event-based approach (such as CSP [3] and CCS [7]) with the state-based technique (such as Z [10] and VDM [4]). The methodology is illustrated by investigating various kinds of process refinement and their corresponding simulation rules.

Keywords: Labelled Transition System, Refinement, Hiding Refinement, Simulation.

Contents

1 Introduction

2 Simulation on Labelled Transition System

3 Specification of Communicating Processes

4 Refinement of Communicating Processes

5 Hiding Refinement

6 Discussion

1 Introduction

A concurrent program is inherently part of a large environment, with which it interacts in the course of its computation. Therefore a simple input-output function does not seem an adquate model for such a program. The model should need to retain some information about the internal states of a program, so as to be able to express its behaviour in any interacting environment. On the other hand, only those intermediate states should be considered which are related to the *external* behaviour of the program.

Labelled transition systems [6, 9] are generally recognised as an appropriate model for concurrent programs. It provides a very flexible model: by varying the definition of the transition relation one can obtain a whole range of different descriptions of programs. The idea of labels can give information about what went on in the states during the transition (*unobservable actions*) or about the interaction between the system and its environment (*observable actions*). This is useful for specifying distributed systems where the actions may relate to the communications between subsystems.

In the model approach of specification, like VDM [4] and Z [10], a system is specified by constructing an abstract machine which has all the expected properties of the system we want to build. Later in design or implementation phrase, the abstract machine will be developed into a more efficient concrete one with all relevant properties. This technique is known as *refinement.* Because all kinds of environment are regarded as the observer of a concurrent program, the replacement is valid only if the observer decides the concrete system is more controllable than the abstract one.

We would like to be able to refine a system by choosing machine-oriented configurations for the abstract information structure used in the specification. This form of refinement is usually known as *data refinement* and is explained in detail in [4]. The basic idea is to establish a correspondence between the two spaces of configurations, then to check that the behaviour of the implementation adequately *simulates* the behaviour required by the specification under this correspondence. Because we only concern with the preorder defined by refinement between transition systems rather than the equivalence, the correspondence can simple be defined by a (one-way) *simulation* rather than by a bisimulation [8]. In the "classical" formulation of data refinement, the simulation is given as a relation, called *the abstrction relation* between the sets of configurations of the implementation and of the specification. In this paper we will demonstrate that the notion of simulation is powerful enough to handle various refinements on concurrent programs. It will be also shown that simulation can be used both for verification and derivation of implementation against a given specification.

The paper is organised as follows. In section 2 the concept of refinerment of labelled transition system is presented, and the notions of *downward simulation* and *upward simulation* are developed to help the verification of implementation. Section 3 describes communicating processes in the framework of labelled transition system, and integrates CSP [3] with the standard state-based technique. It also investigates the compositionality of the specification technique. Section 4 generalises the definition of simulation in section 2 to cover the deadlock-free property of communicating processes, and examines several examples. In section 5 we deal with internal communications and introduce the concept of the hiding refinement . A corresponding proof method is presented for that case thereafter. The final section devotes to discussion. We illustrate the applicability of simulation by considering a number of concurrent systems: transaction processing system, interactive information system and asynchronous communicating process.

2 Simulation on Labelled Transition System

Definition 2.1 *Labelled Transition System*
A labelled transition system S is a structure

$$S = < \Gamma,\ INIT,\ A,\ \longrightarrow >$$

where

- Γ is a set of *configurations*, ranged over by metavariable γ.
- $INIT$, a subset of Γ, is a set of initial configurations.
- A is a set of *actions*.
- $\longrightarrow \subseteq \Gamma \times A \times \Gamma$ is the *transition relation.*

We interpret a transition $\gamma \xrightarrow{a} \gamma'$ as: S may evolve from configuration γ to configuration γ' via an action a. For a given event a, $\xrightarrow{a}$ can then be regarded as a binary relation on Γ. For any finite sequence $t =< a_1, .., a_n >$ of events of A, the binary relation $\xrightarrow{t}$ is defined

$$\xrightarrow{t} \stackrel{\text{def}}{=} \xrightarrow{a_1}; \ldots\ldots; \xrightarrow{a_n}$$

and $\xrightarrow{\epsilon}$ stands for the identity relation on Γ where ϵ represents the empty sequence.

A transition system ***diverges*** if it may behave like any system whatsoever. It is the least predictable of all systems, the least controllable, and in short the worst. A specific configuration $\perp$ is included in Γ to describe the divergent state with the property that

$$\forall a \in A \bullet (\perp \xrightarrow{a} \perp) \qquad (*)$$

which indicates that once a system enter a divergent state it will never get back to normal again.

According to our definition, a transition system S is a machine starting in one of its intial configurations, and evolving through successive configurations by means of actions. We formalise an execution of a system S as a finite transition sequence

$$\gamma_0 \xrightarrow{a_1} \cdots\cdots \xrightarrow{a_n} \gamma_n$$

where γ_0 is an initial configuration, and all γ_i are configurations. In this case, the sequence of actions $< a_1, .., a_n >$ is called a *trace* of the system S. Here we presume that all actions in A are visible to the environment of the system, thus the user will become aware of the occurrence of all events a_i in the trace. It is clear that any prefix of a trace is also a trace. A *divergence* of S is defined as any trace of the system after which the system behaves chaotically, in other words, if one of the intermediate configuration in the execution is $\perp$. From the property $(*)$ it follows that the divergences of a system are *extention-closed.*

Definition 2.2 *Traces and Divergences*
For a labelled transition system S the sets of traces and divergences are defined

$$\begin{aligned} traces(S) &\stackrel{def}{=} \{t \mid \exists \gamma, \rho \bullet (\gamma \in INIT \wedge \gamma \xrightarrow{t} \rho)\} \\ divergences(S) &\stackrel{def}{=} \{t \mid \exists \gamma \bullet (\gamma \in INIT \wedge \gamma \xrightarrow{t} \perp)\} \end{aligned}$$

For a labelled transition system S, we will use Γ_S, $INIT_S$, A_S and $\rightarrow_S$ instead Γ, $INIT$, A and $\rightarrow$ whenever an explicit reference to S is required.

A labelled transition system is said to a *refinement* of another if the former is more predictable than the latter. Formally the concept of *refinement* can be formalised as follows:

Definition 2.3 *Transition System Refinement*
The transition system T refines S if $A_T = A_S$ and

$$traces(T) \subseteq traces(S) \wedge divergences(T) \subseteq divergences(S)$$

We will use $T \sqsupseteq S$ to denote the above fact.

Theorem 2.1 $\sqsupseteq$ is a *preorder* on labelled transition systems.
Proof: From the fact that $\subseteq$ is a partial order on sets.

Transition systems S and T are said to be *equivalent* if

$$S \sqsupseteq T \wedge T \sqsupseteq S$$

A natural notion of equivalence, ***bisimulation equivalence***, has been proposed by D. Park [8] for transition systems: informally speaking, two systems are said to ***bisimulate*** each other if a full correspondence are to be established between their sets of states, in such a way that from any two corresponding states the two (sub)systems will still (recursively) bisimulate each other. Since this paper only deals with the preorder ***refined-by*** among systems rather than the equivalence relations, the notion of ***one-way simulation*** seems to be simpler than bisimulation for system development.

In the remaining part of this section it is supposed that all transition systems under consideration have the same alphabet A.

Definition 2.4 *Downward Simulation between Labelled Transition Systems*
A binary relation $d : \Gamma_S \times \Gamma_T$ is called a ***downward simulation*** between systems S and T if it satisfies

$$\begin{array}{rcll} INIT_T & \subseteq & d(INIT_S) & \\ d;\xrightarrow{a}_T & \subseteq & \xrightarrow{a}_S;d & \quad for\ all\ a \in A \\ d(\gamma_S, \perp) & \Rightarrow & \gamma_S = \perp & \end{array}$$

where $d(INIT_S)$ stands for the image of the mapping d on the set $INIT_S$.

The first condition of the definition of downward simulation states that each initial configuration of T is corresponding to an initial configuration of S, and the second one says that from any two corresponding configurations the system T will behave like the system S. The final one indicates that T may diverge only if the system S becomes chaotic.

We will use $d : S \geq T$ to denote that d is a downward simulation between labelled transition systems S and T. In the following we want to show that downward simulation is a sound proof method for transition system refinement.

Theorem 2.2 If $d : S \geq T$ then $T \sqsupseteq S$.
Proof: By induction on the length of sequence t we can prove that

$$d;\xrightarrow{t}_T \subseteq \xrightarrow{t}_S;d \qquad (\star)$$

Then we have

$$\begin{array}{r} t \in divergences(T) \;\Rightarrow \\ \{def\ of\ divergences\} \\ \exists\gamma_T \bullet \gamma_T \in INIT_T \wedge \gamma_T \xrightarrow{t}_T \perp \;\Rightarrow \\ \{by\ condition\ 1\ of\ downward\ simulation\} \\ \exists\gamma_S \bullet \gamma_S \in INIT_S \wedge \gamma_S\,(d;\xrightarrow{t}_T) \perp \;\Rightarrow \end{array}$$

$$\{\, by\ condition\ (\star)\,\}$$

$$\exists \gamma_S \bullet \gamma_S \in INIT_S \wedge \gamma_S\,(\xrightarrow{t}_S\,;\, d)\,\bot \quad \Rightarrow$$

$$\{\, by\ condition\ 3\ of\ downward\ simulation\,\}$$

$$\exists \gamma_S \bullet \gamma_S \in INIT_S \wedge \gamma_S\,(\xrightarrow{t}_S)\,\bot \quad \Rightarrow$$

$$\{\, def\ of\ the\ set\ divergences\}$$

$$t \in divergences(S)$$

In a similar way we can prove that $traces(T) \subseteq traces(S)$.

The following theorem shows that composition *preserves* downward simulation. As a result, downward simulation can be used stepwisely in system design.

Theorem 2.3 If $d:\ R \geq S$ and $e:\ S \geq T$, then $d; e:\ R \geq T$.
Proof:

$$INIT_T \quad \subseteq$$

$$\{\, by\ the\ assumption\ e:\ S \geq T\,\}$$

$$e(INIT_S) \quad \subseteq$$

$$\{\, by\ the\ assumption\ d:\ R \geq S\,\}$$

$$e(d(INIT_R)) \quad \subseteq$$

$$\{\, def\ of\ d; e\,\}$$

$$(d; e)(INIT_R)$$

$$(d; e)\,;\, \xrightarrow{a}_T \quad =$$

$$\{\, ;\ is\ associative\,\}$$

$$d;\, (e\,;\, \xrightarrow{a}_T) \quad \subseteq$$

$$\{\, by\ the\ assumption\ e:\ S \geq T\,\}$$

$$d;\, (\xrightarrow{a}_S\,;\, e) \quad \subseteq$$

$$\{\, by\ the\ assumption\ d:\ R \geq S\,\}$$

$$\xrightarrow{a}_R\,;\, (d; e)$$

$$(d; e)(\gamma_R, \bot) \quad \Rightarrow$$

$$\{\, def\ of\ d; e\,\}$$

$$\exists \gamma_S \bullet d(\gamma_R, \gamma_S) \wedge e(\gamma_S, \bot) \quad \Rightarrow$$

$$\{\,by\,the\,assumption\,d:\;R \geq S\,\}$$

$$d(\gamma_R, \bot) \;\Rightarrow$$

$$\{\,by\,the\,assumption\,e:\;S \geq T\,\}$$

$$\gamma_R \;=\; \bot$$

This completes the proof.

The concept of *upward simulation* is dual to that of downward simulation.

Definition 2.5 *Upward Simulation between Labelled Transition Systems*
A binary relation $u : \Gamma_T \times \Gamma_S$ is called a *upward simulation* between systems T and S, denoted by $u : T \leq S$, if it satisfies

$$\begin{array}{rcll} u(INIT_T) & \subseteq & INIT_S & \\ \xrightarrow{a}_T ; u & \subseteq & u ; \xrightarrow{a}_S & \quad for\ all\ a \in A \\ u(\bot, \gamma_S) & \Rightarrow & \gamma_S = \bot & \end{array}$$

In a similar way we can prove that

Theorem 2.4 If $u : T \leq S$ then $T \sqsupseteq S$.

Theorem 2.5 If $u : S \leq R$ and $v : T \leq S$, then $v;u : T \leq R$.

Finally we want to deal with the issue of completeness of simulations for verifying an implementation. As explored in [2], neither downward simulation nor upward simulation is complete. But we can prove that downward simulation and upward simulation together give a complete method for proving labelled transition system refinement in the following sense:

Theorem 2.6 It T refines S, then there are an upward simulation from CT to S, and a downward simulation from CT to T, where CT is a transition system equivalent to T.

3 Specification of Communicating Processes

The object of this section is the specification of communicating processes. It has become widely accepted that it is a good idea to build an abstract mathematical description (*formal specification*) of a system before building the system itself. One good reason for doing so is that it is possible to explore the validity of design choice by reasoning about the description, rather than building the system and only then discovering that we have compromised its usefulness by making a bad decision early in the design process. The labelled transition system will be used to specify the behaviour of communicating processes. It enables us to integrate CSP [3] with state-based approach (such as VDM [4] and Z [10]).

First we examine, as an example, a simple process $bag_{c,d}$ with an input channel c and an output channel d. $bag_{c,d}$ is at all times willing to input message from the channel c, and is also prepared to output any of the messages, which it has received but not delivered yet, to the channel d. Moreover, choice of the message for output is made by the process itself, rather by its environment. We will use $c?m$ to denote the receipt of message m from the input channel c, and $d!m$ the delivery of message m to the output channel d.

Let B be the multiset which contains all the messages the process $bag_{c,d}$ has received but not output yet. It is clear that at the very beginning B is empty, in other words, the *initial state* of the process $bag_{c,d}$ can be described by the predicate:

$$baginit \stackrel{\text{def}}{=} B = \emptyset$$

where $\emptyset$ denotes the empty set.

New message received by the process is inserted into B. Thus the effect of an input event c?m on the process state can be specified by the predicate:

$$bag_{c?m} \stackrel{\text{def}}{=} B' = B \oplus \{m\}$$

where B and B' stand for the state before the occurrence of the input and afterward respectively, and $\oplus$ is the bag addition.

Any message chosen by the process for output will be removed from B. The output event d!m can then be described by

$$bag_{d!m} \stackrel{\text{def}}{=} m \in B \wedge B' = B \ominus \{m\}$$

where $\ominus$ is the bag subtraction.

We define $\alpha(bag_{c,d})$ as the alphabet of the process $bag_{c,d}$, i.e., the set of communications the process can engage in. In summary, the process can be specified by

$$(\alpha(bag_{c,d}),\ BAG,\ baginit,\ \{bag_a \mid a \in \alpha(bag_{c,d})\})$$

where the second component BAG denotes the set of all multisets of messages, and the forth component is a family of predicates each of which specifies the behaviour of a specific communication a.

An non-empty sequence $< a_1, ..., a_n >$ is a trace of $bag_{c,d}$ if

$$\exists B_1, .., B_{n+1} \bullet baginit(B_1) \wedge bag_{a_1}(B_1, B_2) \wedge .. \wedge bag_{a_n}(B_n, B_{n+1})$$

Now it is easy to write down the process $bag_{c,d}$ in CSP notations:

$$\begin{aligned} bag_{c,d} &\stackrel{\text{def}}{=} bag_{c,d}(\emptyset) \\ bag_{c,d}(\emptyset) &\stackrel{\text{def}}{=} c?x \longrightarrow bag_{c,d}(\{x\}) \\ bag_{c,d}(B) &\stackrel{\text{def}}{=} \sqcap_{m \in B}(c?x \rightarrow bag_{c,d}(B \oplus \{x\}) \Box d!m \rightarrow bag_{c,d}(B \ominus \{m\})) \end{aligned}$$

where the first defintion indicates that initially there is no message in store. The second one says that when no message is stored, the process only can engage in the input exent. The third one states that the process can choose any message which it holds for output (thus it is internal), however the choice between input and output is made by the environment.

In general, a non-divergent communicating process P can be described in the framework of labelled transition system as follows:

$$(\alpha(P),\ \Sigma_P,\ Pinit,\ \{P_a \mid a \in \alpha(P)\})$$

where

- $\alpha(P)$ stands for the alphabet of P.
- Σ_P is the set of states, ranged over by the metavariable σ_P .
- *Pinit* is a predicate specifying the initialisation of P.
- The predicate P_a defined on $\Sigma_P \times \Sigma_P$ describes the effect of the execution of the event a on the states.

At the very beginning, P executes *Pinit* silently, and enters one of its initial states. The initialisation of a process is invisible to the external world, and the choice among the initial states is unpredictable. At any state $\sigma_P \in \Sigma_P$, P can then take part in any communication in the set **enabling**(σ_P) defined by:

$$\textbf{enabling}(\sigma_P) \stackrel{\text{def}}{=} \{a \mid \exists \sigma'_P \bullet P_a(\sigma_P, \sigma'_P)\}$$

where the environment decides which of these possible input events will occur, and the process determines which of these output events can happen. Furthermore, state change, after P engages in communication a, is described by the predicate P_a. Additionally, the destination of the transition is decided by the process itself.

In order to describe the *deadlock-free* property of a communicating process, we assume that the status of a channel recently being ready for communication can be detectble by the environment. In general, let X be a set of communications which are offered at the state σ_P by the environment.

If it is possible for P to deadlock when placed in this environment, we say X is a *refusal* of P at the state σ_P. From the definition of **enabling** it is clear that X is a refusal only if

$$(X \cap \textbf{Input} \cap \textbf{enabling}(\sigma_P) = \emptyset) \wedge$$

$$(\textbf{enabling}(\sigma_P) \cap \textbf{Output} = \emptyset \vee \neg(\textbf{enabling}(\sigma_P) \cap \textbf{Output} \subseteq X))$$

where **Input** and **Output** denote the sets of inputs and outputs respectively. In this case a pair (t, X), where t is a trace which leads P to the state σ_P, is called a *failure* of P, and will then be used to describe a computation of P. This concept makes the state-based description of communicating processes more intractable than the ordinary transition system.

The domain of the predicate P_a is defined by

$$\textbf{firing}(P_a)(\sigma_P) \stackrel{\text{def}}{=} \exists \sigma'_P \bullet P_a(\sigma_P, \sigma'_P)$$

which specifies the condition under which P can engage in the event a, and is thus called the *firing condition* of the event a.

For any nonempty sequence $t =< a_1, .., a_n >$ of events, we will use P_t to stand for the composition of predicates $P_{a_1}, .. \ P_{a_n}$:

$$P_t(\sigma, \sigma') \stackrel{\text{def}}{=} \exists s_1, .., s_{n-1} \bullet P_{a_1}(\sigma, s_1) \wedge ... \wedge P_{a_n}(s_{n-1}, \sigma')$$

which describes the change of states caused by the execution of t. Similarly we can define

$$\textbf{firing}(P_t)(\sigma_P) \stackrel{\text{def}}{=} \exists \sigma'_P \bullet P_t(\sigma_P, \sigma'_P)$$

In terms of the above description of a process, a number of useful definition from [3] can be introduced:

$$\begin{aligned} traces(P) &\stackrel{\text{def}}{=} \{t \mid \exists \sigma, \sigma' \bullet Pinit(\sigma) \wedge P_t(\sigma, \sigma')\} \\ failures(P) &\stackrel{\text{def}}{=} \{(t, X) \mid \exists \sigma, \sigma' \bullet Pinit(\sigma) \wedge P_t(\sigma, \sigma') \wedge \\ &\quad (X \cap \textbf{Input} \cap \textbf{enabling}(\sigma') = \emptyset) \wedge \\ &\quad (\textbf{enabling}(\sigma') \cap \textbf{Output} = \emptyset \vee \\ &\quad \neg(\textbf{enabling}(\sigma') \cap \textbf{Output} \subseteq X))\} \end{aligned}$$

We can produce a specification of the system from specifications of its components. Here the CSP interleaving composition $|||$ and parallel compositions $\|$ are investigated, for other CSP operators the reader refers to [2].

The definition of CSP interleaving operator [3] says that each action of the process $R = P|||Q$ is an action of exactly one of its components. If one of the components cannot engage in the action, then it must have been the other one; but if both P and Q could have engaged in the same action, then the choice between them is non-deterministic. The interleaving composition can be formally defined by

Theorem 3.1 Let $R \stackrel{def}{=} P|||Q$, then

$$\begin{aligned} \alpha(R) &\stackrel{\text{def}}{=} \alpha(P)\ (= \alpha(Q)) \\ \Sigma_R &\stackrel{\text{def}}{=} \Sigma_P \times \Sigma_Q \\ Rinit &\stackrel{\text{def}}{=} Pinit \wedge Qinit \\ R_a &\stackrel{\text{def}}{=} P_a \wedge \sigma_Q' = \sigma_Q \ \vee \ Q_a \wedge \sigma_P' = \sigma_P \qquad \textit{for all } a \in \alpha(R) \end{aligned}$$

$P\|Q$ is a process which behaves like P and Q when they operate independently, except all communication in the set $\alpha(P) \cap \alpha(Q)$ must be synchronised. This can be formalised by

Theorem 3.2 Let $S \stackrel{\text{def}}{=} P\|Q$, then

$$\begin{aligned} \alpha(S) &\stackrel{\text{def}}{=} \alpha(P) \cup \alpha(Q) \\ \Sigma_S &\stackrel{\text{def}}{=} \Sigma_P \times \Sigma_Q \\ Sinit &\stackrel{\text{def}}{=} Pinit \wedge Qinit \\ S_a &\stackrel{\text{def}}{=} P_a \wedge \sigma_Q' = \sigma_Q \qquad \textit{if } a \in (\alpha(P) - \alpha(Q)) \\ S_a &\stackrel{\text{def}}{=} Q_a \wedge \sigma_P' = \sigma_P \qquad \textit{if } a \in (\alpha(Q) - \alpha(P)) \\ S_a &\stackrel{\text{def}}{=} P_a \wedge Q_a \qquad\qquad \textit{if } a \in (\alpha(P) \cap \alpha(Q)) \end{aligned}$$

Example 3.1 Specification of the process *dbag* (double-bag) where

$$dbag \stackrel{\text{def}}{=} bag_{c,d}|||bag_{c,d}$$

From theorem 3.1 we have

$$\Sigma_{dbag} \stackrel{\text{def}}{=} BAG \times BAG$$

The pair of metavariables (LB, RB) is used to range over the state space Σ_{dbag}. The initial state of *dbag* is specified by the predicate

$$dbaginit \stackrel{\text{def}}{=} LB = \emptyset \wedge RB = \emptyset$$

The communications $c?m$ and $d!m$ are described by

$$dbag_{c?m} \stackrel{\text{def}}{=} LB' = LB \oplus \{m\} \wedge RB' = RB$$

$$
\begin{aligned}
& \qquad \vee\ LB' = LB \wedge RB' = RB \oplus \{m\} \\
dbag_{d!m} \stackrel{\text{def}}{=} & \quad m \in LB \wedge LB' = LB \ominus \{m\} \wedge RB' = RB \\
& \qquad \vee\ LB' = LB \wedge m \in RB \wedge RB' = RB \ominus \{m\}
\end{aligned}
$$

Example 3.2 Specification of the process *cbag* (chain of bags) where

$$cbag \stackrel{\text{def}}{=} bag_{c,e} \| bag_{e,d}$$

Following theorem 3.2 we obtain

$$
\begin{aligned}
\Sigma_{cbag} & \stackrel{\text{def}}{=} BAG \times BAG \\
cbaginit & \stackrel{\text{def}}{=} LB = \emptyset \wedge RB = \emptyset \\
cbag_{c?m} & \stackrel{\text{def}}{=} LB' = LB \oplus \{m\} \wedge RB' = RB \\
cbag_{d!m} & \stackrel{\text{def}}{=} m \in RB \wedge RB' = RB \ominus \{m\} \wedge LB' = LB \\
cbag_{e!m} & \stackrel{\text{def}}{=} m \in LB \wedge LB' = LB \ominus \{m\} \wedge RB' = RB \oplus \{m\}
\end{aligned}
$$

4 Refinement of Communicating Processes

In this section all processes are assumed to be non-divergent. We say P **refines** Q if $\alpha(P) = \alpha(Q)$ and

$$failures(P) \subseteq failures(Q)$$

We will use $P \sqsupseteq Q$ to denote that P is a refinement of Q. If Q is a specification of a system, then the development process should produce its refinement. The following theorem states that $\sqsupseteq$ is a preorder on processes, consequently the stepwise refinement strategy can be applied in system design.

Theorem 4.1

1. If $P \sqsupseteq Q$ and $Q \sqsupseteq R$ then $P \sqsupseteq R$

2. $P \sqsupseteq P$

Following the approach presented in section 2, we can define *simulations* between communicating processes. Their definitions are more or less the same as their counterpart for labelled transition systems, however they will take into account the deadlock free property of communicating processes.

Definition 4.1 *Downward Simulation between Processes*
A predicate $dn : \Sigma_Q \times \Sigma_P$ is called a *downward simulation* if it satisfies

$$\begin{aligned}
Pinit(\sigma_P) &\Rightarrow \exists \sigma_Q \bullet Qinit(\sigma_Q) \wedge dn(\sigma_Q, \sigma_P) \\
\exists \sigma_P \bullet dn(\sigma_Q, \sigma_P) \wedge P_a(\sigma_P, \rho_P) &\Rightarrow \exists \rho_Q \bullet Q_a(\sigma_Q, \rho_Q) \wedge dn(\rho_Q, \rho_P) \\
& \quad\ for\ all\ a \in \alpha(P) \\
\mathbf{firing}(Q_{c?x})(\sigma_Q) \wedge dn(\sigma_Q, \sigma_P) &\Rightarrow \mathbf{firing}(P_{c?x})(\sigma_P) \\
& \quad\ for\ all\ inputs\ c?x \\
\mathbf{firing}(Q_{d!m})(\sigma_Q) \wedge dn(\sigma_Q, \sigma_P) &\Rightarrow \exists e!n \bullet \mathbf{firing}(P_{e!n})(\sigma_P) \\
& \quad\ for\ all\ inputs\ d!m
\end{aligned}$$

where the first two conditions are the same as those presented for downward simulation between transition systems, and the final two conditions are added to cover the deadlock property of communicating processes. The third one says that P promises to accept any input whatever is agreed by Q. The final condition states that if Q is enable to deliver messages to its users then P must as least be willing to communicate to its output channels.

We will use $dn : Q \geq P$ to denote that dn is a downward simulation between Q and P. The following theorem shows that it is a sound rule for process refinement.

Theorem 4.2 If $dn : Q \geq P$ then $P \sqsupseteq Q$.
Proof: Similar to theorem 2.2.

In the design of a complex system, we are allowed to apply downward simulations in successive steps. The next theorems show how that can work.

Theorem 4.3 If $d_1 : Q \geq P$ and $d_2 : P \geq R$ then

$$\exists \sigma_P \bullet d_1(\sigma_Q, \sigma_P) \wedge d_2(\sigma_P, \sigma_R) : Q \geq R$$

Proof: Similar to theorem 2.3.

Theorem 4.4 If $d_i : Q_i \geq P_i$ for $i = 1, 2$ then

$$\begin{aligned}
d_1 \wedge d_2 &: Q_1 ||| Q_2 \geq P_1 ||| P_2 \\
d_1 \wedge d_2 &: Q_1 || Q_2 \geq P_1 || P_2
\end{aligned}$$

Proof: Routine.

Example 4.1 A refinement of the process $bag_{c,d}$.
Let the process buf be defined by

$$(\alpha(buf), LIST, bufinit, \{buf_{c?x}, buf_{d!m}\})$$

where

$$\begin{aligned} \alpha(buf) &\stackrel{\text{def}}{=} \alpha(bag_{c,d}) \\ LIST &\stackrel{\text{def}}{=} \alpha(buf)^* \\ bufinit &\stackrel{\text{def}}{=} l = \epsilon \\ buf_{c?x} &\stackrel{\text{def}}{=} l' = l \frown < x > \\ buf_{d!m} &\stackrel{\text{def}}{=} l = < m > \frown l' \end{aligned}$$

where for any set U we use U^* to denote the set of all finite sequences of elements of U, and the metavariable l represents an element of the set $LIST$, and ϵ denotes the empty sequence, and $\frown$ the concatenation of sequences. In the following we will use $multiset(l)$ to denote the multiset of elements of l.

Define a predicate $down$ as follows:

$$down(B, l) \stackrel{\text{def}}{=} (B = multiset(l))$$

which says that B and l are related whenever they contain the same messages. Now we are going to show that process buf is a refinement of process $bag_{c,d}$ by demonstrating that the predicate $down$ is really a downward simulation.

$$\begin{aligned} bufinit(l) \;&\Rightarrow \\ \{def\ of\ bufinit\}& \\ l = \epsilon \;&\Rightarrow \\ \{def\ of\ multiset\}& \\ \exists B \bullet B = \emptyset \wedge B = multiset(l) \;&\Rightarrow \\ \{def\ of\ down\, and\, baginit\}& \\ \exists B \bullet baginit(B) \wedge down(B, l)& \end{aligned}$$

$$\begin{aligned} \exists l \bullet down(B,l) \wedge buf_{c?x}(l,l') \;&\Rightarrow \\ \{def\ of\ down\ and\ buf_{c?x}\}& \\ \exists l \bullet B = multiset(l) \wedge l' = l \frown < x > \;&\Rightarrow \\ \{def\ of\ multiset\}& \\ \exists B' \bullet B' = multiset(l') \wedge B' = B \oplus \{x\} \;&\Rightarrow \end{aligned}$$

$$\{def\ of\ bag_{c?x}\}$$
$$\exists B' \bullet bag_{c?x}(B,B') \wedge down(B',l')$$

$$\exists l \bullet down(B,l) \wedge buf_{d!m}(l,l') \Rightarrow$$
$$\{def\ of\ down\ and\ buf_{d!m}\}$$
$$\exists l \bullet B = multiset(l) \wedge l = \langle m \rangle \frown l' \Rightarrow$$
$$\{def\ of\ multiset\}$$
$$\exists B' \bullet B' = multiset(l') \wedge m \in B \wedge B' = B \ominus \{m\} \Rightarrow$$
$$\{def\ of\ bag_{d!m}\}$$
$$\exists B' \bullet bag_{d!m}(B,B') \wedge down(B',l')$$

$$\exists m \bullet \mathbf{firing}(bag_{d!m})(B) \wedge down(B,l) \Rightarrow$$
$$\{def\ of\ down\ and\ bag_{d!m}\}$$
$$\exists m \bullet m \in B \wedge B = multiset(l) \Rightarrow$$
$$\{def\ of\ multiset\}$$
$$l \neq \epsilon \Rightarrow$$
$$\{let\ n = first(l)\ and\ def\ of\ buf_{d!n}\}$$
$$\mathbf{firing}(buf_{d!n})(l)$$

where $first(l)$ stands for the first element of a non-empty sequence l. Combining those results together, we reach the conclusion.

As was already explained in section 2, the concept of upward simulation also provides an effective proof method for process refinement.

Definition 4.2 *Upward Simulation between Processes*
A predicate $up : \Sigma_P \times \Sigma_Q$ is an upward simulation if it satisfies

$$\exists \sigma_P \bullet Pinit(\sigma_P) \wedge up(\sigma_P,\sigma_Q) \Rightarrow Qinit(\sigma_Q)$$
$$\exists \rho_P \bullet up(\rho_P,\rho_Q) \wedge P_a(\sigma_P,\rho_P) \Rightarrow \exists \sigma_Q \bullet Q_a(\sigma_Q,\rho_Q) \wedge up(\sigma_P,\sigma_Q)$$
$$for\ all\ a \in \alpha(P)$$
$$\forall \sigma_P \exists \sigma_Q \forall a \bullet up(\sigma_P,\sigma_Q) \wedge (\mathbf{firing}(Q_a)(\sigma_Q) \Rightarrow \mathbf{firing}(P_a)(\sigma_P))$$

We use $up : P \leq Q$ to denote up is an upward simulation from process P to process Q.

Theorem 4.5 If $up : P \leq Q$ then $P \sqsupseteq Q$.

Theorem 4.6 If $u_1 :\ R \leq P$ and $u_2 :\ P \leq Q$ then

$$\exists \sigma_P \bullet u_1(\sigma_R, \sigma_P) \wedge u_2(\sigma_P, \sigma_Q) : R \leq Q$$

Theorem 4.7 If $u_i :\ P_i \leq Q_i$ for $i = 1, 2$ then

$$\begin{array}{lcl} u_1 \wedge u_2 & : & P_1|||P_2 \leq Q_1|||Q_2 \\ u_1 \wedge u_2 & : & P_1||P_2 \leq Q_1||Q_2 \end{array}$$

Example 4.2 *dbag* is a refinement of $bag_{c,d}$
Define the predicate *up* as follows:

$$up((LB,\ RB),\ B) \stackrel{\text{def}}{=} B\ = LB \oplus RB$$

We can then show that *up* is an upward simulation from *dbag* to $bag_{c,d}$:

$$\begin{array}{rl} dbaginit((LB,\ RB)) \wedge up((LB,\ RB),\ B) & \Rightarrow \\ \{def\ of\ up\} & \\ dbaginit((LB,\ RB)) \wedge B\ =\ LB \oplus RB & \Rightarrow \\ \{def\ of\ dbaginit\} & \\ B = \emptyset \oplus \emptyset & \Rightarrow \\ \{def\ of\ \oplus\} & \\ B = \emptyset & \Rightarrow \\ \{def\ of\ baginit\} & \\ baginit(B) & \end{array}$$

$$\begin{array}{rl} \exists LB',\ RB' \bullet up((LB',\ RB'),\ B') \wedge dbag_{c?x}((LB,\ RB),\ (LB',\ RB')) & \Rightarrow \\ \{\ def\ of\ up\ and\ dbag_{c?x}\ \} & \\ \exists LB',\ RB' \bullet B' = LB' \oplus RB' \wedge & \\ (LB' = LB \oplus \{x\} \wedge\ RB' = RB\ \vee RB' = RB \oplus \{x\} \wedge\ LB' = LB) & \Rightarrow \\ \{\ def\ of\ \oplus\ \} & \\ \exists B \bullet B = LB \oplus RB\ \wedge\ B' = B \oplus \{x\} & \Rightarrow \end{array}$$

$$\{\, def\ of\ bag_{c?x} \,\}$$

$$\exists B \bullet bag_{c?x}(B, B') \wedge up((LB, RB), B)$$

$$\exists LB', RB' \bullet up((LB', RB'), B') \wedge dbag_{d!m}((LB, RB), (LB', RB')) \Rightarrow$$

$$\{\, def\ of\ up\ and\ dbag_{d!m} \,\}$$

$$\exists LB', RB' \bullet B' = LB' \oplus RB' \wedge$$

$$(m \in LB \wedge LB' = LB \ominus \{m\} \wedge RB' = RB \vee$$

$$m \in RB \wedge RB' = RB \ominus \{m\} \wedge LB' = LB) \Rightarrow$$

$$\{\, def\ of\ \oplus\ and \ominus \,\}$$

$$\exists B \bullet B = LB \oplus RB \wedge m \in B \wedge B' = B \ominus \{m\} \Rightarrow$$

$$\{\, def\ of\ bag_{d!m} \,\}$$

$$\exists B \bullet bag_{d!m}(B, B') \wedge up((LB, RB), B)$$

$$\mathbf{firing}(bag_{d!m})(B) \wedge up((LB, RB), B) \Rightarrow$$

$$\{\, def\ of\ up\ and\ bag_{d!m} \,\}$$

$$m \in B \wedge B = LB \oplus RB \Rightarrow$$

$$\{\, def\ of\ \oplus \,\}$$

$$m \in LB \vee m \in RB \Rightarrow$$

$$\{\, def\ of\ dbag_{d!m} \,\}$$

$$\mathbf{firing}(dbag_{d!m})((LB, RB))$$

5 Hiding Refinement

In the previous sections we assume that both specification Q and implementation P have the same alphabet. The design of the process requires us to demonstrate that the computation of the implementation actually simulates that of the specification. In practice, the specification is concerned rather with external behaviour than computational feasibility. One way to make a specification Q more implementable is to add in P some internal events, while taking the alphabet of the process Q as the external event set. The internal events are invisible to the user since they are not included in the specification, and will be hidden later. This section will deal with this case, and provide a proof method for the implementation.

Definition 5.1 *Hiding Refinement*
A process P is a hiding refinement of Q if $\alpha(Q) \subseteq \alpha(P)$ and

$$P \setminus (\alpha(P) - \alpha(Q)) \sqsupseteq Q$$

where $\setminus$ is the CSP hiding operator [3].

As discussed previously the simulation establishes a correspondence between the abstract state space and the concrete state space in such a way that it can be shown that each action of the implementation mimics its counterpart in the specification. It is expected that the user is not informed the existence of those unobservable events, and of course will not be aware of the effect caused by their execution. Therefore, the execution of the hidden events should have nothing to do on the external interface, i.e., the transition of interrnal event will only simulate the identity transition on the abstract state space. Moreover, introducing and hiding of internal events should not lead to divergence [3], as no refinement can be achieved by introducing divergence. It requires that the implementation will never be able to engage in an infinite sequence of internal events. Putting all these requirements together we obtain the definition of downward simulation for the hiding refinement:

Definition 5.2 *Downward Simulation for Hiding Refinement*
A predicate $dn : \Sigma_Q \times \Sigma_P$ is called a *downward simulation* for the hiding refinement with respect to the set of internal events $\alpha(P) - \alpha(Q)$ when

$$\alpha(Q) \subseteq \alpha(P)$$

if it satisfies

$$\begin{aligned}
Pinit(\sigma_P) &\Rightarrow \exists \sigma_Q \bullet Qinit(\sigma_Q) \wedge dn(\sigma_Q, \sigma_P) \\
\exists \sigma_P \bullet dn(\sigma_Q, \sigma_P) \wedge P_a(\sigma_P, \rho_P) &\Rightarrow \exists \rho_Q \bullet Q_a(\sigma_Q, \rho_Q) \wedge dn(\rho_Q, \rho_P) \\
&\quad\ for\ all\ a \in \alpha(Q) \\
\exists \sigma_P \bullet dn(\sigma_Q, \sigma_P) \wedge P_b(\sigma_P, \rho_P) &\Rightarrow dn(\sigma_Q, \rho_P) \\
&\quad\ for\ all\ b \in \alpha(P) - \alpha(Q) \\
\mathbf{firing}(Q_{c?x})(\sigma_Q) \wedge dn(\sigma_Q, \sigma_P) \wedge stable(\sigma_P) &\Rightarrow \mathbf{firing}(P_{c?x})(\sigma_P) \\
&\quad\ for\ all\ inputs\ c?x \\
\mathbf{firing}(Q_{d!m})(\sigma_Q) \wedge dn(\sigma_Q, \sigma_P) \wedge stable(\sigma_P) &\Rightarrow \exists e!n \bullet \mathbf{firing}(P_{e!n})(\sigma_P) \\
&\quad\ for\ all\ outputs\ d!m \\
\forall \sigma_P\, \exists k\, \forall t \bullet (\sharp t \geq k &\Rightarrow \neg \mathbf{firing}(P_t)(\sigma_P))
\end{aligned}$$

where $\sharp t$ denotes the length of the sequence t.

The first two conditions are the same as for the downward simulation between processes. The third one says that the internal event simulates the behaviour of the identity transition on the abstract state space. The predicate $stable(\sigma_P)$ we have introduced in the forth and fifth conditions is defined

$$stable(\sigma_P) \stackrel{\text{def}}{=} \forall b \in (\alpha(P) - \alpha(Q)) \bullet \neg\, \mathbf{firing}(P_b)(\sigma_P)$$

and indicates the set of the so-called ***stable states*** on which only the external communications can be fired. The forth conditions says that if Q is able to accept input then the process P promises to do so on those corresponding stable states. The fifth one deals with the possible external output of P at the stable states. The final one excludes the possibility of an infinite sequence of internal communications in the computation of P.

Downward simulation provides a sound rule for the hiding refinement.

Theorem 5.1 If dn is a downward simulation for hiding refinement, then $P \setminus (\alpha(P) - \alpha(Q)) \sqsupseteq Q$. Proof: Similar to theorem 2.2.

Example 5.1 *cbag* is a hiding refinement of $bag_{c,d}$.
Define

$$dn(B, (LB, RB)) \stackrel{\text{def}}{=} B = LB \oplus RB$$

The proof of dn being a downward simulation for hiding refinement is very close to that in Example 4.1, and is omitted.

6 Discussion

(1). For a communicating process P which may diverge we need to modify our framework by including a specific state $\perp$ into Σ_P. The state $\perp$ is introduced to serve as the divergent state, consequently we require that for all event a in the alphabet of the process P

$$P_a(\perp, \perp)$$

As the result of introducing the divergent state $\perp$, a downward simulation dn should satisfy an extra condition:

$$dn(\sigma_Q, \bot) \;\Rightarrow\; (\sigma_Q = \bot)$$

which says that no state in Σ_Q but the divergent state is related to the divergent state in Σ_P.

Correspondingly, an upward simulation *up* will satisfy the following extra condition:

$$up(\bot, \sigma_Q) \;\Rightarrow\; (\sigma_Q = \bot)$$

For detail see [2, 5].

(2). The same mathematical model has also been pursued in the specification and design of interactive information system [11]. An interactive process is a process driven by a user. The events in which it is prepared to participate include some which are known as *commands*. As each command is accepted, the process moves autonomously from its current state through a succession of one or more states until it is ready to show the user some visible indication of its state, which is does "just after" engaging in one of the events $\triangle$, (pronounced "show"). In addition to this, the process is sometimes prepared to yield the user a result of some kind, which it does "just after" engaging in one of the events ∇ (pronounced "yield").

Thus in order to turn a process specification presented previously into an interactive process specification we need to describe:

- the events which the user can initiate (the *commands*).
- the $\triangle$ events.
- the "view" which is seen after a $\triangle$.
- the ∇ events.
- the result which a ∇ yields when it happens.

In a similar way the concept of simulation is employed in the refinement of interactive procersses. The result is fully explored in [11].

(3). This paper investigates synchronous processes where each communication involves simultaneous participation both of the process and of the environment. If either of them is ready before the other, it must be delayed at least until the other is ready too. Then the communication takes place, and both process and environment may continue independently. For an asynchronous process, all channels are capable of buffering an arbitrary number of messages. Consequently, an output by the environment to the process is never delayed. Conversely, the environment may postpone indefinitely the acceptance of messages, without delaying the internal progress of the process. The model presented in this paper can also be used to describe asynchronous processes. The simulation rules are given in [1]

(4). In a transaction processing system, each transaction with a pair of input $?x$ and output $!y$ is usually specified by a predicate:

$$aop(\sigma, ?x, !y, \sigma')$$

The notation we have explored in this paper can be emplored to tackle the specification and design of this sort of concurrent programs. For example, a transaction system can be expressed in the following way:

$$\begin{array}{rcl} P & \stackrel{\text{def}}{=} & \sqcap_{Pinit(\sigma)} P_\sigma \\ P_\sigma & \stackrel{\text{def}}{=} & \Box_{\exists !y, \rho \bullet aop(\sigma, ?x, !y, \rho)} \\ & & (aop?x \rightarrow \sqcap_{aop(\sigma, ?x, !y, \sigma')} (aop!y \rightarrow P_{\sigma'}) \end{array}$$

The result in that area is reported in [1].

References

[1] He Jifeng. *Specification and Design of the Transaction Processing Systems with Various Interfaces.* Internal Report, Oxford University (1989).

[2] He Jifeng. *Process Refinement.* In "The Theory and Practice of Refinement" J McDermid (eds), Butterworths (1989).

[3] C.A.R. Hoare. *Communicating Sequential Processes.* Prentice Hall International (1985).

[4] C.B. Jones. *Software Development: a Rigorous Approach.* Prentice-Hall International (1980).

[5] M.B. Josephs. *A State-Based Approach to Communicating Processes.* Distributed Computing 3 (1), (1988) 9–18.

[6] R. Keller. *Formal verification of Parallel Programs.* CACM 19 (7), (1976) 371–384.

[7] R. Milner. *Communication and Concurrency.* Prentice Hall International (1989).

[8] D. Park. Concurrency and Automata on Infinite Sequences. LNCS 104, (1981) 167–183.

[9] G. Plotkin. *A Structured Approach to Operational Semantics.* DAINI FN–19, Computer Science Dept. Aarhus University.

[10] J.M. Spivey. *The Z Notation-A Reference Manual.* Prentice-Hall International (1989).

[11] B.A. Sufrin and He Jifeng. *Specification, Analysis and Refinement of Interactive Processes.* in preparation.

On Decomposing and Refining Specifications of Distributed Systems

Bengt Jonsson
Swedish Institute of Computer Science
Box 1263, S-164 28 Kista, Sweden, E-mail: bengt@sics.se
and Dept. of Computer Systems, Uppsala University

Abstract

This paper is concerned with the use of transition systems with fairness constraints for specifying message-passing distributed systems. A distributed system is specified through the sequence of messages that can be sent and received in an execution of the system. We use *fair transition systems* to specify such sequences in analogy with the way finite automata are used as acceptors of finite strings. Safety properties are specified by the set of transitions of the transition system. Liveness properties are specified by the fairness constraints on the executions of the transition system. We consider two verification problems: (1) obtaining the specification of a composed system from specifications of its components, and (2) verifying that one transition system correctly refines (i.e., implements) another. For the second problem, we present existing techniques that reduce the verification problem to classical verification conditions, using a notation with guarded assignment statements. We examine conditions under which the techniques are complete. One results is a variant of a completeness theorem due to Abadi and Lamport [AL88]. Simple examples are included to illustrate the techniques.

Keywords: Fair Transition System, Specification, Verification, Distributed Systems, Fairness, Refinement, Compositionality, Completeness

Contents

1 Introduction
2 Fair Transition Systems and Refinement
3 Composition and I/O-Systems
4 Verifying a Refinement
5 Completeness
6 Related Work

1 Introduction

Distributed computer systems can be specified at many levels of abstraction. For instance, a specification of a computer network can at one level describe an abstract file transfer service, and at another level include a description of a protocol for transmitting data over a physical link. Similarly, correctness proofs can be performed at many levels, where the implementation at one level is a specification at a lower level. This motivates a single language for both specifications and implementations.

This paper is concerned with the use of *fair transition systems* for specifying distributed systems. A fair transition system (fts for short) has a set of labeled transitions and fairness requirements on its executions. For fts:s, we use a notation with guarded multiple assignment statements. Fair transition systems can also be regarded as a programming notation for describing distributed systems. Related notations have been used e.g., as a general model of computing systems by Manna and Pnueli [MP89, Pnu86], in the UNITY notation by Chandy and Misra [CM88], in the action systems used for specification and stepwise development of parallel algorithms by Back and others [BS89, BKS87], and to verify distributed algorithms in our earlier work [Jon87b, Jon87a].

In contrast to sequential programs, which can be adequately specified by a relation between input and output, a distributed system must be specified through its ongoing behavior, which we shall represent by its *traces*. Intuitively, a trace of a system is a sequence of messages that are sent and received during a complete execution of the system. We use fair transition systems to specify sets of traces in analogy with the way finite automata are used as acceptors of finite strings.

An important transformation on specifications is *decomposition*, in which a specification of a system is split into specifications of its components. This operation presupposes that the specification of a composed system can be obtained from the specifications of its components. In our case, it should be possible to obtain the traces of a composed system from the traces of its components. In general, this is not possible for models of message-passing systems such as e.g. CCS [Mil89] and CSP [Hoa85] since traces do not adequately represent potential deadlocks of a system. This problem can be overcome by restricting attention to a class of systems, for which each event of a composed system is "controlled" by at most one of its components. This class, here called I/O-systems (it is similar to the I/O-automata of Lynch and Tuttle [LT87]), cannot arrive at the kind of synchronization deadlocks that occurs in CCS and CSP. I/O-systems are intended to represent distributed systems with asynchronous message-passing, e.g., over a computer network.

The use of fair transition systems to specify sets of traces leads to a notion of *refinement*: a fts $\mathcal{T}_1$ is a correct refinement (implementation) of a fts $\mathcal{T}_2$ if the traces accepted by $\mathcal{T}_1$ is a subset of the traces accepted by $\mathcal{T}_2$. For proving that each trace of $\mathcal{T}_1$ is also a trace of $\mathcal{T}_2$, there exist techniques which reduce the verification problem to a set of classical verification conditions. In these techniques, it must be shown that from an execution of $\mathcal{T}_1$ which accepts a certain trace, an execution of $\mathcal{T}_2$ which accepts the same trace can be constructed step-by-step. This construction can be performed from the beginning of the computation, in which case the main verification effort is to find an establish a simulation relation between the fts:s, or from the end, using a backwards simulation relation. In both cases, liveness properties are established separately, using standard techniques for proving liveness properties of concurrent programs, as in [MP84, MP89].

The above mentioned techniques have in various forms been presented in the literature [Lam83, LT87, AL88, Mer, Jon87a, Jon87b, Sta84, Sta88, LS88]. In this paper, we present the proof techniques in the context of a specific notation, that of guarded multiple assignments, for specifications. In e.g., [Lam83, LT87, AL88, Mer], these techniques are presented in a set-theoretic framework without reference to a specific notation. Stark [Sta88] presents the simulation method using a particular temporal logic as a specification language.

We examine conditions under which the proof techniques are sufficient for proving a refinement. We review and extend completeness results for simulation relations and backwards simulation relations, and a completeness result for combining the two techniques. This last result is a variant of a completeness theorem due to Abadi and Lamport [AL88]; we obtain an alternative way of understanding their result.

In the paper, we include simple examples to illustrate the techniques. More elaborate examples have appeared e.g. in our earlier work [Jon87a, Jon87b].

The rest of the paper is organized as follows: In the next section, we present fair transition systems and the notion of refinement. In Section 3, we consider the composition operation; we present I/O-systems as a special class of fair transition systems and show that specifications of composed I/O-systems can be obtained from specifications of their components. In Section 4, we present methods for establishing a refinement between fair transition systems, using simulation and backwards simulation relations. Section 3 and Section 4 can be read independently of each other. Section 5 contains some completeness results. Section 6 contains comparisons with related work.

2 Fair Transition Systems and Refinement

In this section, we define fair transition systems, (fts for short). We define a notation for fts:s with guarded multiple assignment statements, which is related to e.g., the work by Manna and Pnueli [MP89, Pnu86], Chandy and Misra [CM88], and Back and others [BS89, BKS87]. A difference is that we include communication events as labels on transitions. The labels are intended to represent receptions and transmissions of messages. In the works just cited, a system is characterized by its sequences of states without including labels on transitions.

2.1 Fair Transition Systems

We will use a many-sorted first-order language with variables, constant symbols, function symbols, and predicate symbols. We assume that each variable ranges over an appropriate domain, and that each constant, function, and predicate symbol has a fixed interpretation over the appropriate domains. An *assignment* σ is a mapping from the variables to their domains. We use $\sigma(v)$ to denote the element to which the variable v is mapped by the assignment σ. An assignment can be extended to terms and assertions in the usual way.

We assume a set of *event primitives*, each with a nonnegative arity. This includes the 0-ary event primitive τ. Let X be a set of variables, and let $\mathcal{E}$ be a set of non-τ event primitives. An *action over* $\langle X, \mathcal{E}\rangle$ is a triple of the form

$$\textbf{event } \varepsilon(y_1, \ldots, y_m) \textbf{ when } c \textbf{ do } \langle x_1, \ldots, x_n\rangle := \langle t_1, \ldots, t_n\rangle$$

consisting of (1) an m-ary *event primitive* $\varepsilon \in (\mathcal{E} \cup \tau)$ applied to variables $y_1, \ldots, y_m$ not in X, (2) an *enabling condition* c, which is an assertion, and (3) a multiple assignment statement, which assigns to the tuple $\langle x_1, \ldots, x_n\rangle$ of distinct variables in X the tuple $\langle t_1, \ldots, t_n\rangle$ of terms. We use α to range over actions. For an action α, $ev(\alpha)$ denotes the event primitive of α, and $c(\alpha)$ denotes the enabling condition of α, and $do(\alpha)$ denotes the assignment statement of α. If α is an action of the above form, define $Lvars(\alpha)$ to be the set of free variables of α which are not in X, and define $Ivars(\alpha)$ to be $Ivars(\alpha) \setminus \{y_1, \ldots, y_m\}$. Define $En(\alpha)$ (the action α is enabled) to be $(\exists Lvars(\alpha))[c(\alpha)]$. In the following, we assume that each event primitive ε will occur with the same variables $y_1, \ldots, y_m$ in all actions with the event primitive ε.

As an example, let α be the action **event** $read(y)$ **when** $z < y$ **do** $x := z$ over $\langle \{x\}, \{read\}\rangle$. Here $Ivars(\alpha) = \{z\}$ and $Lvars(\alpha) = \{y, z\}$. The predicate $En(\alpha)$ is $(\exists y, z)[z < y]$. Intuitively, the variables in $Lvars(\alpha)$ are "parameters" of the action α, in the sense that the action can be "instantiated" with values for these variables.

The action **event** τ **when** *true* **do** $\langle\rangle := \langle\rangle$ is called the *stuttering action.*

If α is the action **event** $\varepsilon(y_1,\ldots,y_m)$ **when** c **do** $do(\alpha)$ and φ is an assertion, then $\alpha \wedge \varphi$ is the action **event** $\varepsilon(y_1,\ldots,y_m)$ **when** $c \wedge \varphi$ **do** $do(\alpha)$. A *subaction* of α is an action of form $\alpha \wedge \varphi$ for some assertion φ. If $\mathcal{A}$ and $\mathcal{A}'$ are sets of actions, we say that $\mathcal{A}'$ is an *actionsubset* of $\mathcal{A}$ if each action in $\mathcal{A}'$ is a subaction of some action in $\mathcal{A}$.

Definition 2.1 A *fair transition system* is a tuple $\langle \mathcal{E}, X, \Theta, \mathcal{A}, \mathcal{J}, \mathcal{F}\rangle$, where

$\mathcal{E}$ is a set of event primitives.

X is a set of *state variables,*

Θ is an assertion, the *initial condition,* whose free variables are in X.

$\mathcal{A}$ is a finite set of *actions* over $\langle \mathcal{E}, X\rangle$, which includes the stuttering action,

$\mathcal{J}$ is a collection of sets of actions, called the *justice sets,* each of which is an actionsubset of $\mathcal{A}$,

$\mathcal{F}$ is a collection of sets of actions, called the *fairness sets,* each of which is an actionsubset of $\mathcal{A}$.

□

Let X be a set of variables. A *state over* X is a mapping s from the variables in X to their domains. For an assertion ϕ whose free variables are in X, the state s over X is called a *ϕ-state* if $s(\phi)$ is true.

If $\mathcal{E}$ is a set of event primitives, then an *event* of $\mathcal{E}$ is of the form $\varepsilon(d_1,\ldots,d_m)$, where $\varepsilon \in (\mathcal{E} \cup \{\tau\})$ is an m-ary event primitive, and $d_1,\ldots,d_m$ are in the appropriate domains. A *communication event* of $\mathcal{E}$ is a non-τ event of $\mathcal{E}$. Communication events are intended to represent the reception and transmission of messages. The event τ is the silent event which is associated with (cf. its use in CCS).

Let α be an action of form

$$\textbf{event } \varepsilon(y_1,\ldots,y_m) \textbf{ when } c \textbf{ do } \langle x_1,\ldots,x_n\rangle := \langle t_1,\ldots,t_n\rangle$$

An *α-transition* is a triple $s \xrightarrow{\varepsilon(d_1,\ldots,d_m)} s'$ where s and s' are states over X and $\varepsilon(d_1,\ldots,d_m)$ is an event of $\mathcal{E}$, such that there is an assignment σ for which c is true under σ, and $\sigma(y_i) = d_i$ for $1 \leq i \leq m$, and for all $x \in X$ we have $s(x) = \sigma(x)$ and $s'(x) = \sigma[x_1 \mapsto \sigma(t_1),\ldots,x_n \mapsto \sigma(t_n)](x)$, (i.e., s' is obtained from s by reassigning the value $\sigma(t_i)$ to the variable x_i for $i = 1,\ldots,n$). If α is the stuttering action, then an α-transition, which must be of the form $s \xrightarrow{\tau} s$ for some state s, is called a *stuttering* transition.

If $\mathcal{A}$ is a set of actions, an *$\mathcal{A}$-transition* is an α-transition for some $\alpha \in \mathcal{A}$, and $En(\mathcal{A})$ is the disjunction of $En(\alpha)$ over $\alpha \in \mathcal{A}$. If $\mathcal{T}$ is the fair transition system $\langle \mathcal{E}, X, \Theta, \mathcal{A}, \mathcal{J}, \mathcal{F}\rangle$, then a *(communication) event* of $\mathcal{T}$ is a (communication) event of $\mathcal{E}$. A *state* of $\mathcal{T}$ is a state over X. A *transition* of $\mathcal{T}$ is an $\mathcal{A}$-transition.

Intuitively, a state of a transition system $\mathcal{T}$ assigns values to the state variables of $\mathcal{T}$. The state is changed by performing transitions, which also cause the occurrence of an event. Communication events are intended to represent the transmission or reception of messages. The silen event τ occurs in transitions that are not associated with any message transmission or reception. Note that the variables in $Lvars(\alpha)$ are "parameters" of the action α in the sense that there can be one α-transition for each assignment of values to the variables in $Lvars(\alpha)$. As an example, let α be the action **event** $read(y)$ **when** $z < y$ **do** $x := z$. Given, a certain state (i.e., value of x), and event $read(d)$, there is one α-transition for each value of z which is less than d. Thus an α-transition is of the form $s \xrightarrow{read(d)} s'$ where the value $s'(x)$ of x after the transition is less than d.

The justice and fairness sets exclude certain sequences of transitions. Intuitively, if beyond a certain point a justice set $\mathcal{A}_J$ is continuously enabled, then a $\mathcal{A}_J$-transition must be taken. If beyond a certain point a fairness set $\mathcal{A}_F$ is infinitely often enabled, then an $\mathcal{A}_F$-transition must be taken.

An *execution* of the fair transition system $\mathcal{T} = \langle \mathcal{E}, X, \Theta, \mathcal{A}, \mathcal{J}, \mathcal{F} \rangle$ is a (finite or infinite) sequence of $\mathcal{A}$-transitions

$$s^0 \xrightarrow{e^1} s^1 \xrightarrow{e^2} \cdots \xrightarrow{e^n} s^n \xrightarrow{e^{n+1}} \cdots$$

where s^0 is a Θ-state. A *computation* of $\mathcal{T}$ is an infinite execution which satisfies

Justice: For each justice set $\mathcal{A}_J$ in $\mathcal{J}$, if from some point on, all states of the sequence are $En(\mathcal{A}_J)$-states, then the sequence contains infinitely many occurrences of $\mathcal{A}_J$-transitions.

Fairness: For each fairness set $\mathcal{A}_F$ in $\mathcal{F}$, if infinitely many states of the sequence are $En(\mathcal{A}_F)$-states, then the sequence contains infinitely many occurrences of $\mathcal{A}_F$-transitions.

Intuitively, a computation is an infinite sequence of transitions, which starts in an initial state and satisfies the constraints imposed by the justice and fairness sets. As a technical convenience, we have required that each fair transition system has a stuttering action and require that computations be infinite. This saves us separate treatment of finite and infinite computations in many definitions and proofs. The requirement of infinite computations does not mean that we cannot handle terminating computations: we can consider computations with an infinite suffix of only stuttering transitions to be terminating.

Example 2.2 As an example, we present a fair transition system which can be seen both as a specification and an implementation of an unbounded buffer. The fts has the unary event primitives *in* and *out*. Both event primitives take arguments from a domain of messages. We use the variable v which ranges over messages, and the variable buf which ranges over sequences of messages. We use $\langle\rangle$ to denote the empty sequence, $buf_1 \bullet buf_2$ to denote the concatenation of the sequences buf_1 and buf_2, $tl(buf)$ to denote the sequence buf minus its first element, and $hd(buf)$ to denote the first element of the sequence buf.

Events: $in(v)$, $out(v)$

State Variables: buf

Initialization: $buf = \langle\rangle$

Actions:

	event	when	do
Insert	$in(v)$	*true*	$buf := buf \bullet v$
Remove	$out(v)$	$buf \neq \langle\rangle$ $hd(buf) = v$	$buf := tl(buf)$

Justice: $\{Remove\}$

Figure 1: A fair transition system, specifying a buffer

The fair transition system is shown in Figure 1. It has two actions, which we have named *Insert* and *Remove*. There should also be a stuttering action, whose existence is assumed implicitly. A

state of the transition system is an assignment of a sequence of messages to the variable buf. An *Insert*-transition is of the form $s \xrightarrow{in(d)} s'$ where $s'(buf) = s(buf) \bullet d$, i.e., the message d has been added to buf. A *Remove*-transition is of the form $s \xrightarrow{out(d)} s'$ where $s(buf) = d \bullet s'(buf)$, i.e., the message d has been removed from buf. Note that the free variable v in the *Insert*-action acts as parameters of the action, so that for each value d of v there is a transition in which d is received and added to buf. There is one justice set consisting of the *Remove*-action, which means that if the value of buf is a non-empty sequence, then eventually an event of the form $out(d)$ for some d must occur. This implies that the buffer eventually delivers each message that is received.
□

2.2 Refinement

We intend fair transition systems to specify the observable behavior of a distributed system. We consider this behavior to be given through the sequence of messages, called traces, that are sent and received during a complete execution of the system. When an fts $\mathcal{T}$ is used as a specification, it should specify those traces that are "accepted" by computations of $\mathcal{T}$, in analogy with the way in which finite automata are used as acceptors of finite strings. This leads to a notion of refinement: a fts $\mathcal{T}_1$ is a correct refinement (implementation) of a fts $\mathcal{T}_2$ if the traces accepted by $\mathcal{T}_1$ is a subset of the traces accepted by $\mathcal{T}_2$.

The *trace* of an execution $\mathcal{C}$, denoted *trace*($\mathcal{C}$), is the (finite or infinite) sequence of communication events (i.e., non-τ events) in $\mathcal{C}$. A trace of the fts $\mathcal{T}$ is the trace of a computation of $\mathcal{T}$.

For a sequence q of communication events and a set $\mathcal{E}$ of event primitives, let $q\lceil_{\mathcal{E}}$ denote the projection of the sequence q onto the communication events of $\mathcal{E}$, i.e., the subsequence of q consisting of the non-τ events of $\mathcal{E}$.

Let $\mathcal{T}_i = \langle \mathcal{E}_i, X_i, \Theta_i, \mathcal{A}_i, \mathcal{J}_i, \mathcal{F}_i \rangle$ be fair transition systems for $i = 1, 2$. We say that $\mathcal{T}_1$ *refines* $\mathcal{T}_2$, written $\mathcal{T}_1 \sqsupseteq \mathcal{T}_2$ iff

1. $\mathcal{E}_2 \subseteq \mathcal{E}_1$, and
2. For each trace q_1 of $\mathcal{T}_1$ there is a trace q_2 of $\mathcal{T}_2$ such that $q_2 = q_1\lceil_{\mathcal{E}_2}$.

The refinement relation $\sqsupseteq$ is a reflexive and transitive relation on fair transition systems. Note that the definition of the refinement relation $\sqsupseteq$ has the effect that a fts with event primitives $\mathcal{E}$ only restricts the projection of traces onto communication events of $\mathcal{E}$ rather than the traces themselves. A specification can then ignore "uninteresting" communication events. For instance, the relative ordering of two events e_1 and e_2 can be specified in isolation although the specified system can perform many other events. Furthermore, a specification of a component in a system can be used for the whole system as well, if the traces of the whole systems merely interleave other communication events into the traces of the component.

3 Composition and I/O-Systems

In order to be able to compose and decompose specifications, it must be possible to prove that a composed system satisfies a specification, given that its components satisfy their specifications. Since we specify systems in terms of their traces, this means in our case that it should be possible to obtain the traces of a composed systems from the traces of its components. This is not true for fair transition systems in general: see e.g. [Mil80]. In terms of our framework, a problem is that a justice or fairness set of one component can require that a certain communication event will occur in a computation, whereas the actions of another component disallows the occurrence of this communication event.

To overcome this problem, we shall restrict attention to a class of systems, for which each event of a composed system is "controlled" by at most one of its components. For each system, the communication events are divided into events that are controlled by the system, called output events, and the events that are controlled by its environment, called input events. This class of systems, which we call I/O-systems, are intended to represent distributed systems that communicate via asynchronous message-passing. The term I/O-system was first used by Stark [Sta84]. I/O-systems are similar to I/O-automata [LT87].

3.1 I/O-systems

An *I/O-signature* is a pair (I, O) of disjoint sets of event primitives The set I is called the set of *input event primitives*, and O is called the set of *output event primitives.*

Definition 3.1 An *I/O-system* is a triple $\mathcal{N} = \langle I, O, \mathcal{T}\rangle$, where (I, O) is an I/O-signature, and $\mathcal{T}$ is a fair transition system whose set of event primitives is $(I \cup O)$ which satisfies

1. For each input event primitive ε, the disjunction $\bigvee_{\{\alpha \,:\, \varepsilon = ev(\alpha)\}} (\exists Ivars(\alpha))[c(\alpha)]$ is true, where the disjunction is taken over actions α with event primitive ε.
2. No justice or fairness set contains an action with an input event primitive.

□

Note that the disjunction in Condition 1 has the state variables of $\mathcal{N}$ and the parameter variables of ε as free variables, which are then implicitly universally quantified. In terms of states and transitions, the first condition states that for each input event e (i.e., communication event with an input event primitive) and state s of $\mathcal{N}$, there is a transition $s \xrightarrow{e} s'$ of $\mathcal{N}$ for some state s'.

The intuitive motivation for the first requirement is that since the occurrence of input events are not controlled by the system, they can occur regardless of the state of the system. Therefore there must for each state be a transition which specifies how the state is affected when the input event occurs. The intuitive motivation for the second requirement is that a justice or fairness set $\mathcal{A}$ states that an $\mathcal{A}$-transition must occur under certain conditions. Therefore no $\mathcal{A}$-transition can be labeled by input events, since these are not controlled by the system.

3.2 Parallel Composition

In this subsection, we define an operation that intuitively corresponds to the parallel composition of I/O-systems under the restriction that they must synchronize on common communication events.

Let ε be an event primitive. For $i = 1, \ldots, k$, let α_i be an action

$$\textbf{event } \varepsilon_i(\overline{y}_i) \textbf{ when } c_i \textbf{ do } \overline{x}_i := \overline{t}_i$$

over $\langle X_i, \mathcal{E}_i\rangle$, where $X_i \cap X_j = \emptyset$ for $i \neq j$, and where ε_i is either ε or τ. There should be at least one i for which $\varepsilon_i = \varepsilon$. We assume that the sets $Ivars(\alpha_i)$ and X_j for $i, j = 1, \ldots, k$ are pairwise disjoint (if necessary, variables in the $Ivars(\alpha_i)$:s can be renamed). Now $\alpha_1 \| \cdots \| \alpha_k$ is the action

$$\textbf{event } \varepsilon(\overline{y}) \textbf{ when } c_1 \wedge \cdots \wedge c_k \textbf{ do } \langle \overline{x}_1, \ldots, \overline{x}_k\rangle := \langle \overline{t}_1, \ldots, \overline{t}_k\rangle$$

Definition 3.2 For $i = 1, \ldots, k$, let $\mathcal{T}_i = \langle \mathcal{E}_i, X_i, \Theta_i, \mathcal{A}_i, \mathcal{J}_i, \mathcal{F}_i\rangle$ be fair transition systems over $\mathcal{E}_i$, such that $X_i \cap X_j = \emptyset$ for $i \neq j$ (if necessary, state variables of some $\mathcal{T}_i$:s can be renamed to achieve this). The *composition* of $\mathcal{T}_1, \ldots, \mathcal{T}_k$, denoted $\mathcal{T}_1 \| \ldots \| \mathcal{T}_k$, is the fair transition system $\langle \mathcal{E}, X, \Theta, \mathcal{A}, \mathcal{J}, \mathcal{F}\rangle$, where

$\mathcal{E} = \bigcup_{i=1}^{k} \mathcal{E}_i$,

$X = X_1 \cup \cdots \cup X_k$,

$\Theta = \Theta_1 \wedge \ldots \wedge \Theta_k$,

$\mathcal{A}$ contains

- all actions with event τ in $\mathcal{A}_1, \ldots, \mathcal{A}_k$, and
- all actions of form $\alpha_1 \| \cdots \| \alpha_k$ with non-τ event primitive ε, such that for each $i = 1, \ldots, k$, if $\varepsilon \in \mathcal{E}_i$ then $ev(\alpha_i) = \varepsilon$, otherwise α_i is the stuttering action,

$\mathcal{J} = \pi_1^{-1}(\mathcal{J}_1) \cup \ldots \cup \pi_k^{-1}(\mathcal{J}_k)$, where $\pi_i^{-1}(\mathcal{J}_i)$ is obtained from $\mathcal{J}_i$ by replacing each action of form $\alpha_i \wedge c$ in some justice set of $\mathcal{J}_i$ by the set of actions of form $\alpha \wedge c$ for which α is obtained from α_i,

$\mathcal{F} = \pi_1^{-1}(\mathcal{F}_1) \cup \ldots \cup \pi_k^{-1}(\mathcal{F}_k)$.

□

The above definitions mean that a state s of $\mathcal{T}$ is a mapping from $X = X_1 \cup \cdots \cup X_k$ such that the restriction of s to X_i is a state s_i of $\mathcal{T}_i$. A state of $\mathcal{T}$ is thus a tuple $\langle s_1, \ldots, s_k \rangle$, where s_i is a state of $\mathcal{T}_i$. A transition $\langle s_1, \ldots, s_k \rangle \xrightarrow{e} \langle s'_1, \ldots, s'_k \rangle$ of $\mathcal{T}$ is either (1) a transition with $e = \tau$, such that for some i the transition $s_i \xrightarrow{\tau} s'_i$ is a transition α_i and $s_j = s'_j$ for $j \neq i$, or (2) a transition with $e \neq \tau$ such that $s_i \xrightarrow{e} s'_i$ is a transition of $\mathcal{T}_i$ if e is an event of $\mathcal{T}_i$ and $s_j = s'_j$ otherwise. The justice and fairness sets of $\mathcal{T}$ are intended to be the union of the justice and fairness sets of the components in the sense that a transition $\langle s_1, \ldots, s_k \rangle \xrightarrow{e} \langle s'_1, \ldots, s'_k \rangle$ of $\mathcal{N}$ is a $\mathcal{J}$-transition iff $s_i \xrightarrow{\tau} s'_i$ is a $\mathcal{J}_i$-transition for some i.

We can now define parallel composition on I/O-systems.

Definition 3.3 The I/O-systems $\langle I_1, O_1, \mathcal{T}_1 \rangle, \ldots, \langle I_k, O_k, \mathcal{T}_k \rangle$ are *compatible* if $O_i \cap O_j = \emptyset$ whenever $i \neq j$. If the I/O-systems $\langle I_1, O_1, \mathcal{T}_1 \rangle, \ldots, \langle I_k, O_k, \mathcal{T}_k \rangle$ are compatible, then their *parallel composition* is the I/O-system $\langle I, O, \mathcal{T} \rangle$, where

$$I = \bigcup_{i=1}^{k} I_i - \bigcup_{i=1}^{k} O_i$$

$$O = \bigcup_{i=1}^{k} O_i$$

$$\mathcal{T} = \mathcal{T}_1 \| \ldots \| \mathcal{T}_k.$$

The parallel composition operator is well-defined for I/O-systems:

Proposition 3.4 *If $\mathcal{N}_1, \ldots, \mathcal{N}_k$ are compatible I/O-systems, then their parallel composition is an I/O-system.*

The main theorem of this section is the following, which states that the traces of a composed I/O-system can be obtained from the traces of its components.

Theorem 3.5 *For $i = 1, \ldots, k$, let $\mathcal{N}_i = \langle I_i, O_i, \mathcal{T}_i \rangle$ be compatible I/O-systems, and let $\mathcal{N}$ be their parallel composition $\mathcal{N}_1 \| \ldots \| \mathcal{N}_k$. Let q be a (finite or infinite) sequence of communication events of $\mathcal{N}$. Then q is a trace of $\mathcal{N}$ iff $q\lceil_{(I_i \cup O_i)}$ is a trace of $\mathcal{N}_i$ for each i.*

The theorem intuitively states that the traces of a composed system can be obtained by "merging" the traces of its components while synchronizing on common communication events. Different versions of the theorem have been given in the work by Misra and Chandy [Mis84, Jon85], by Stark [Sta84], by Lynch and Tuttle [LT87], among other works.

Let us define a refinement relation on I/O-systems as follows: If $\mathcal{N}_1 = \langle I_1, O_1, \mathcal{T}_1 \rangle$ and $\mathcal{N}_2 = \langle I_2, O_2, \mathcal{T}_2 \rangle$ are I/O-systems, then $\mathcal{N}_1 \sqsupseteq \mathcal{N}_2$ iff

- $I_2 \subseteq I_1$, and
- $O_2 \subseteq O_1$, and
- $\mathcal{T}_1 \supseteq \mathcal{T}_2$.

From Theorem 3.5 we immediately obtain the result that the specification of a composed system can be obtained from specifications of its components, or more precisely that the parallel composition operator is monotone with respect to the refinement relation on I/O-systems.

Proposition 3.6 *Assume that* $\mathcal{N}'_1, \ldots, \mathcal{N}'_k$ *are compatible I/O-systems, and that* $\mathcal{N}_i \sqsupseteq \mathcal{N}'_i$ *for* $i = 1, \ldots, k$. *Then* $\mathcal{N}_1 \| \ldots \| \mathcal{N}_k \sqsupseteq \mathcal{N}'_1 \| \ldots \| \mathcal{N}'_k$

Example 3.7 The buffer in Example 2.2 is also an I/O-system, viewing *in* as an input event primitive and *out* as an output event primitive. We intend to illustrate the parallel composition of two unbounded buffers. The two buffers are shown in Figure 2. They are identical to the specification in Figure 1, except for renaming of the state variables and an event primitive.

Input Events: $in(v)$
Output Events: $link(v)$
State Variables: buf_1
Initialization: $buf_1 = \langle\rangle$
Actions:

	event	when	do
$Insert_1$	$in(v)$	$true$	$buf_1 := buf_1 \bullet v$
$Remove_1$	$link(v)$	$buf_1 \neq \langle\rangle$ $hd(buf_1) = v$	$buf_1 := tl(buf_1)$

Justice: $\{Remove_1\}$

Input Events: $link(v)$
Output Events: $out(v)$
State Variables: buf_2
Initialization: $buf_2 = \langle\rangle$
Actions:

	event	when	do
$Insert_2$	$link(v)$	$true$	$buf_2 := buf_2 \bullet v$
$Remove_2$	$out(v)$	$buf_2 \neq \langle\rangle$ $hd(buf_2) = v$	$buf_2 := tl(buf_2)$

Justice: $\{Remove_2\}$

Figure 2: Two buffers

The parallel composition of the buffers in Figure 2 is shown in Figure 3.

Input Events: $in(v)$

Output Events: $link(v)$, $out(v)$

State Variables: buf_1 , buf_2 , buf

Initialization: $buf_1 = buf_2 = buf = \langle\rangle$

Actions:

	event	when	do
$Insert_1$	$in(v)$	$true$	$buf_1 := buf_1 \bullet v$
$Remove_1$	$link(v)$	$buf_1 \neq \langle\rangle$ $hd(buf_1) = v$	$\langle buf_1, buf_2 \rangle := \langle tl(buf_1), buf_2 \bullet v \rangle$
$Remove_2$	$out(v)$	$buf_2 \neq \langle\rangle$ $hd(buf_2) = v$	$buf_2 := tl(buf_2)$

Justice: $\{Remove_1\}$, $\{Remove_2\}$

Figure 3: Parallel Composition of Two Buffers

4 Verifying a Refinement

In this section, we consider the problem of verifying the correctness of a refinement between fair transition systems. Recall that to establish $\mathcal{T}_1 \sqsupseteq \mathcal{T}_2$, one must prove that for each trace q_1 of $\mathcal{T}_1$ there is a trace q_2 of $\mathcal{T}_2$ such that $q_1\lceil_{\mathcal{E}_2} = q_2$, where $\mathcal{E}_2$ is the set of event primitives of $\mathcal{T}_2$. In general, such a proof would require reasoning about entire computations, which is rather complex (Sistla [Sis88] has shown that in a related framework this problem is Π^1_2-complete, when the fair transition systems are effectively given). Here we shall look at methods that use reasoning about individual program statements (i.e. actions), in analogy with methods of classical program verification.

A way to reduce the problem of verifying a refinement to properties of program statements is to show that, given a computation $\mathcal{C}_1$ of $\mathcal{T}_1$ with trace q_1, a computation $\mathcal{C}_2$ of $\mathcal{T}_2$ with trace q_2 can be constructed step-by-step. This construction can be performed from the beginning of the computation: the nth transition of $\mathcal{C}_2$ is selected from the information provided by the nth transition of $\mathcal{C}_1$ and the nth states of $\mathcal{C}_1$ and $\mathcal{C}_2$. In order to establish such a construction for all $\mathcal{C}_1$ by reasoning about individual transitions, corresponding states of $\mathcal{C}_1$ and $\mathcal{C}_2$ must be related by a *simulation relation*, which relates the nth states of $\mathcal{C}_1$ and $\mathcal{C}_2$. Such a relationship does not exist in general, but in a large class of cases that is of practical interest. Simulation relations have been used in e.g. [LT87, LS88, Jon87b, Sta88, Ora89]. In this paper, we present the proof technique in the context of a specific notation, that of guarded multiple assignments, for specifications.

Recently, a related proof method has been suggested by Abadi and Lamport [AL88], which works in some cases where there is no simulation relation. Their proof method is a "mirror-image" of the simulation method: instead of showing how $\mathcal{C}_2$ can be constructed by starting from an initial state and working towards the end, the construction starts from the end and works backwards. Of course, there is no "end" of a computation, so instead one works backwards from an arbitrary point of the computation. This proves the existence of an arbitrary finite prefix of $\mathcal{C}_2$. The existence of $\mathcal{C}_2$ is then proven by a separate argument, using König's lemma. Just as in the previous case, we relate the nth states of $\mathcal{C}_1$ and $\mathcal{C}_2$ by a relation, which we shall call *backwards simulation relation* to stress the analogy with the simulation relation. Merritt [Mer] also defines backwards simulation relations, under the name of prophecy mappings.

Both techniques involve showing that the variables of $\mathcal{T}_2$ can be viewed as certain types of auxiliary variables of $\mathcal{T}_1$. In our notation, we carry out auxiliary variable constructions by the operation of *superposition*. In both methods, it must be proven separately that $\mathcal{C}_2$ satisfies the justice and fairness requirements of $\mathcal{T}_2$. This can be done using standard proof techniques for verifying liveness properties of reactive programs, e.g. of Manna and Pnueli [MP84, MP89], using well-founded induction.

Neither of the methods is complete for establishing a refinement between fair transition systems. In section 5 we present some limited completeness results. Abadi and Lamport [AL88] have shown a completeness result for a rather large class of specifications by auxiliary variable constructions. In the context of I/O-automata, Merritt [Mer] has presented analogues to the completeness results of [AL88]. In this section, we present separate (limited) completeness results for simulation relations and backwards simulation relations, and use these to derive a variant of the result in [AL88, Mer].

In the next subsection, we define superpositions. Simulation relations are introduced in Subsection 4.2, and backwards simulation relations are introduced in Subsection 4.3. These sections do not consider fairness requirements. In Subsection 4.4, we consider how to prove justice and fairness requirements. Subsection 4.5 contains examples to illustrate the techniques.

4.1 Superpositions

For $i = 1,2$, let α_i be an action over $\langle X_i, \mathcal{E}_i \rangle$ where X_1 and X_2 are disjoint, and $\mathcal{E}_2 \subseteq \mathcal{E}_1$. A *superposition* of α_2 onto α_1 is an action of form $(\alpha_1 \| \alpha_2) \wedge \varphi$ where φ is an assertion over the variables in X_1, X_2, $Lvars(\alpha_1)$, and $Lvars(\alpha_2)$. Note that the superposition of α_2 onto α_1 is the same as α_1 in the special case where α_2 is a stuttering action and φ is *true*.

For $i = 1,2$, let $\mathcal{T}_i = \langle \mathcal{E}_i, X_i, \Theta_i, \mathcal{A}_i, \mathcal{J}_i, \mathcal{F}_i \rangle$ be fair transition systems such that $\mathcal{E}_2 \subseteq \mathcal{E}_1$ and $X_1 \cap X_2 = \emptyset$. A *superposition* of $\mathcal{T}_2$ on $\mathcal{T}_1$ is a fair transition system $\langle \mathcal{E}_1, X_1 \cup X_2, \Theta_1, \mathcal{A}, \pi_1^{-1}(\mathcal{J}_1), \pi_1^{-1}(\mathcal{F}_1) \rangle$ where each action of $\mathcal{A}$ is a superposition of an action in $\mathcal{A}_2$ onto an action in $\mathcal{A}_1$. If $\mathcal{B}_1$ is an actionsubset of $\mathcal{A}_1$, we let $\pi_1^{-1}(\mathcal{B}_1)$ denote the result of replacing each action of form $\alpha_1 \wedge \varphi$ in $\mathcal{B}_1$ by the set of actions of form $\alpha \wedge \varphi$ such that α is obtained by superposing an action in $\mathcal{A}_2$ onto α_1. This definition is extended to collections of actionsubsets, so that $\pi_1^{-1}(\mathcal{J}_1)$ denotes the result of replacing each action of form $\alpha_1 \wedge \varphi$ in some justice set of $\mathcal{J}_1$ by the set of actions of form $\alpha \wedge \varphi$ such that α is obtained by superposing an action in $\mathcal{A}_2$ onto α_1. The definition of $\pi_1^{-1}(\mathcal{F}_1)$ is analogous. In an analogous way, we define $\pi_2^{-1}(\mathcal{B}_2)$ when $\mathcal{B}_2$ is and actionsubset of $\mathcal{A}_2$.

Intuitively, the idea of a superposition is to let the transitions of $\mathcal{T}_2$ occur synchronized with the transitions of $\mathcal{T}_1$ in order to induce a relation between computations of $\mathcal{T}_2$ and of $\mathcal{T}_1$. Intuitively, the extra assertion φ in the superposition of α_2 onto α_1 states under what conditions an α_2-transition can be synchronized with an α_1-transition. The justice and fairness sets of a superposition of $\mathcal{T}_2$ onto $\mathcal{T}_1$ are intended to be equivalent to those of $\mathcal{T}_1$.

If $\mathcal{T}$ is a superposition of $\mathcal{T}_2$ onto $\mathcal{T}_1$, then each infinite execution $\mathcal{C}$ of $\mathcal{T}$ induces an infinite execution $\pi_i(\mathcal{C})$ of $\mathcal{T}_i$ for $i = 1,2$. The execution $\pi_i(\mathcal{C})$ is obtained by replacing each transition $\langle s_1, s_2 \rangle \xrightarrow{e} \langle s_1', s_2' \rangle$ of $\mathcal{T}$ by the transition $s_i \xrightarrow{e\lceil \mathcal{E}_i} s_i'$ of $\mathcal{T}_i$. Since the fairness and justice sets of $\mathcal{T}$ are equivalent to those of $\mathcal{T}_1$, it follows that $\mathcal{C}$ is a computation of $\mathcal{T}$ iff $\pi_1(\mathcal{C})$ is a computation of $\mathcal{T}_1$. However, $\pi_2(\mathcal{C})$ is in general not a computation of $\mathcal{T}_2$ even though $\mathcal{C}$ is a computation of $\mathcal{T}$, since there is no guarantee that the justice and fairness requirements of $\mathcal{T}_2$ are satisfied in $\mathcal{C}_2$.

4.2 Simulation Relations

For a fair transition system $\mathcal{T}$, and an assertion R over the state variables of $\mathcal{T}$, we say that R is *stable* in $\mathcal{T}$ iff for each action α of $\mathcal{T}$ with $do(\alpha)$ begin $\overline{x} := \overline{t}$, the assertion $(R \wedge c(\alpha)) \implies R[\overline{t}/\overline{x}]$ is true, where $R[\overline{t}/\overline{x}]$ denotes the replacement of the variables in $\overline{x}$ by the corresponding terms in $\overline{t}$. We say that R is *invariant* in $\mathcal{T}$ if R is stable in $\mathcal{T}$ and also implied by the initial condition of $\mathcal{T}$.

Definition 4.1 For $i = 1,2$, let $\mathcal{T}_i = \langle \mathcal{E}_i, X_i, \Theta_i, \mathcal{A}_i, \mathcal{J}_i, \mathcal{F}_i \rangle$ be fair transition systems such that $\mathcal{E}_2 \subseteq \mathcal{E}_1$. Let $\mathcal{T}$ be a superposition of $\mathcal{T}_2$ onto $\mathcal{T}_1$, and let R be an assertion over the state variables of $\mathcal{T}$. The assertion R is called a *simulation relation* if it satisfies

1. $\Theta_1 \implies (\exists X_2)[R \wedge \Theta_2]$
2. For each action α_1 of $\mathcal{T}_1$, the condition

$$(R \wedge c(\alpha_1)) \implies \bigvee_{\left\{\alpha\in\mathcal{A}\,,\,\alpha_2\in\mathcal{A}_2\,:\, \begin{array}{l}\alpha \text{ is a superposition}\\ \text{of } \alpha_2 \text{ onto } \alpha_1\end{array}\right\}} (\exists Ivars(\alpha_2))[do(\alpha)]$$

   is true,

3. R is stable in $\mathcal{T}$.

□

Stated in terms of states and transitions, the conditions imply

1. For each initial state s_1 of $\mathcal{T}_1$, there is an initial state s_2 of $\mathcal{T}_2$, such that $\langle s_1, s_2\rangle$ is an R-state.

2., 3 Whenever $\langle s_1, s_2\rangle$ is an R-state and $s_1 \xrightarrow{e} s_1'$ is a transition of $\mathcal{T}_1$, then there is a transition $\langle s_1, s_2\rangle \xrightarrow{e} \langle s_1', s_2'\rangle$ of $\mathcal{T}$. such that $\langle s_1', s_2'\rangle$ is an R-state. This holds, because second condition gives the existence of the transition $\langle s_1, s_2\rangle \xrightarrow{e} \langle s_1', s_2'\rangle$, and the third condition implies that $\langle s_1', s_2'\rangle$ is an R-state.

Proposition 4.2 *Assume that $\mathcal{T}$ is a superposition of $\mathcal{T}_2$ on $\mathcal{T}_1$, and that the assertion R is a simulation relation. Then for each execution $\mathcal{C}_1$ of $\mathcal{T}_1$ there is a execution $\mathcal{C}$ of $\mathcal{T}$ in which all states are R-states such that $\mathcal{C}_1 = \pi_1(\mathcal{C})$.* □

From Proposition 4.2 it follows that for each execution $\mathcal{C}_1$ of $\mathcal{T}_1$ there is an execution $\mathcal{C}_2$ of $\mathcal{T}_2$ such that $trace(\mathcal{C}_2) = trace(\mathcal{C}_1)\lceil_{\mathcal{E}_2}$: simply choose $\mathcal{C}_2 = \pi_2(\mathcal{C})$, where $\mathcal{C}$ is such that $\mathcal{C}_1 = \pi_1(\mathcal{C})$.

Proof of Proposition 4.2: By induction, we shall establish that for each finite execution $\mathcal{C}_1$ of $\mathcal{T}_1$ that ends in some state s_1, there is a finite execution $\mathcal{C}$ of $\mathcal{T}$ that ends in some state $\langle s_1, s_2\rangle$, for which $\mathcal{C}_1 = \pi_1(\mathcal{C})$. Condition 1 gives this for the base case where $\mathcal{C}_1$ consists of only an initial state of $\mathcal{T}_1$. For the inductive step, we assume that the property is true for $\mathcal{C}_1$ which ends in the state s_1. Assume that $\mathcal{C}_1$ is extended by the transition $s_1 \xrightarrow{e} s_1'$ of $\mathcal{T}_1$. By condition 2, there is a transition $\langle s_1, s_2\rangle \xrightarrow{e} \langle s_1', s_2'\rangle$ of $\mathcal{T}$ which extends $\mathcal{C}$. By the condition that R is stable, the state $\langle s_1', s_2'\rangle$ is an R-state. This completes the inductive step. For infinite executions, the theorem follows by applying the previous argument to successively longer finite prefixes.

□

4.3 Backwards Simulation Relations

In this subsection, we define the backwards analogue of the simulation relation, defined in the previous subsection.

If $\overline{x}$ is a tuple of variables, we denote by $\overline{x}'$ the result of equipping the variables in $\overline{x}$ with primes to obtain fresh variables. In the following, we shall assume that for all actions of $\mathcal{T}$, the tuple $\overline{x}$ of updated variables contains all variables in X (if not, the tuples $\overline{x}$ and $\overline{t}$ in the assignment statement can be "padded" with the missing variables).

Definition 4.3 For $i = 1, 2$, let $\mathcal{T}_i = \langle \mathcal{E}_i, X_i, \Theta_i, \mathcal{A}_i, \mathcal{J}_i, \mathcal{F}_i\rangle$ be fair transition systems such that $\mathcal{E}_2 \subseteq \mathcal{E}_1$. Let $\mathcal{T}$ be a superposition of $\mathcal{T}_2$ onto $\mathcal{T}_1$, and let R be an assertion over the state variables of $\mathcal{T}$. The assertion R is called a *backward simulation relation* if there is an assertion R_1 over the state variables of $\mathcal{T}_1$ which is invariant in $\mathcal{T}_1$ such that

1. $R_1 \implies (\exists X_2)[R]$ is true.

2. For each action α_1 of $\mathcal{T}_1$ with $do(\alpha_1)$ being $\overline{x}_1 := \overline{t}_1$, the condition

$$(R_1 \wedge c(\alpha_1) \wedge R[\overline{t}_1/\overline{x}_1][X_2'/X_2]) \implies \bigvee_{\left\{\begin{array}{l}\alpha \in \mathcal{A}\ ,\ \alpha_2 \in \mathcal{A}_2\ : \\ \alpha \text{ is a superposition} \\ \text{of } \alpha_2 \text{ onto } \alpha_1, \text{ and} \\ do(\alpha_2) = \overline{x}_2 := \overline{t}_2\end{array}\right\}} (\exists Ivars(\alpha_2), \overline{x}_2)[c(\alpha) \wedge (\overline{t}_2 = \overline{x}_2')]$$

   is true. The disjunction is taken over the actions of $\mathcal{T}$ that result from superposing an action α_2 of $\mathcal{T}_2$ with multiple assignment statement $\overline{x}_2 := \overline{t}_2$ of $\mathcal{T}_2$ onto the given action α_1 of $\mathcal{T}_1$.

3. $\neg R$ is stable in $\mathcal{T}_1$,

4. $\Theta_1 \wedge R \implies \Theta_2$

5. For each combination of values of the variables in X_1 such that R_1 is true, there is a finite number of combinations of values of the variables in X_2 such that R is true.

□

The second condition states that if R_1 and the enabling condition c_1 of α_1 holds and the backwards simulation relation R holds after replacing $\overline{x}_1$ by $\overline{t}_1$ and the variables in X_2 by their primed verions X_2', then for one of the actions α obtained by superposing an action α_2 onto α_1 there are values of $Ivars(\alpha_2)$ and of the variables $\overline{x}_2$ of $\mathcal{T}_2$, such that the enabling condition of α is true, and the update $\overline{x}_2 := \overline{t}_2$ of α_2 satisfies $\overline{t}_2 = \overline{x}_2'$.

Stated in terms of states and transitions, the conditions imply

1. For each R_1-state s_1, there is a state s_2 such that $\langle s_1, s_2 \rangle$ is an R-state.

2., 3. Whenever $\langle s_1, s_2 \rangle$ is an R-state and $s_1' \xrightarrow{e} s_1$ is a transition of $\mathcal{T}_1$, then there is a transition $\langle s_1', s_2' \rangle \xrightarrow{e} \langle s_1, s_2 \rangle$ of $\mathcal{T}$ such that $\langle s_1', s_2' \rangle$ is an R-state. This holds, because the second condition gives the existence of the transition $\langle s_1', s_2' \rangle \xrightarrow{e} \langle s_1, s_2 \rangle$ and the third condition implies that $\langle s_1', s_2' \rangle$ is an R-state. Intuitively, conditions 1, 2 and 3 are "time-reversals" of the corresponding conditions for simulation relations.

4. Whenever s_1 is an initial state of $\mathcal{T}_1$, and $\langle s_1, s_2 \rangle$ is an R-state, the state s_2 is an initial state of $\mathcal{T}_2$.

5. For each R_1-state s_1 of $\mathcal{T}_1$ there is at most a finite number of states s_2 of $\mathcal{T}_2$ such that $\langle s_1, s_2 \rangle$ is an R-state.

Proposition 4.4 *Assume that $\mathcal{T}$ is a superposition of $\mathcal{T}_2$ on $\mathcal{T}_1$, and that the assertion R is a backwards simulation relation of $\mathcal{T}$. Then for each execution C_1 of $\mathcal{T}_1$ there is an execution C of $\mathcal{T}$ in which all states are R-states such that $C_1 = \pi_1(C)$.* □

Proof: If s_i are X_i-states for $i = 1, 2$, define $\langle s_1, s_2 \rangle$ to be the state over $(X_1 \cup X_2)$ whose restriction to X_i is s_i for $i = 1, 2$.

Let s_1^f be a reachable state of $\mathcal{T}_1$. By induction, we shall establish that for each finite sequence C_1 of transitions of $\mathcal{T}_1$ that starts in some reachable state s_1 and ends in s_1^f, there is a finite sequence C of transitions of $\mathcal{T}$ that starts in some state $\langle s_1, s_2 \rangle$ and ends in some state $\langle s_1^f, s_2^f \rangle$, such that $C_1 = \pi_1(C)$, and such that $\langle s_1, s_2 \rangle$ is an R-state. The base case follows from condition 1 in the definition of backward simulation relations: given a reachable state s_1^f, it must be an R_1-state, hence there is at least one s_2^f such that $\langle s_1^f, s_2^f \rangle$ is an R-state. For the inductive step, we assume that the property is true for $\mathcal{C}_1$ which starts in the state s_1. By induction, there exists a $\mathcal{C}$ that starts in some state $\langle s_1, s_2 \rangle$ and ends in some state $\langle s_1^f, s_2^f \rangle$, such that $\mathcal{C}_1 = \pi_1(\mathcal{C})$, and such that $\langle s_1, s_2 \rangle$ is an R-state. Assume that $\mathcal{C}_1$ is extended backwards by the transition $s_1' \xrightarrow{e} s_1$ of $\mathcal{T}_1$. By requirement 2, there is a transition $\langle s_1', s_2' \rangle \xrightarrow{e} \langle s_1, s_2 \rangle$ of $\mathcal{T}$, which extends $\mathcal{C}$ backwards. By the requirement that $\neg R$ is stable, the state $\langle s_1', s_2' \rangle$ is an R-state.

Now, if $\mathcal{C}_1$ starts in an initial state of $\mathcal{T}_1$, then by condition 4, the first state of $\mathcal{C}$ is an initial state. This proves the proposition for finite executions.

Next, let $\mathcal{C}_1$ be an infinite execution of $\mathcal{T}_1$. By the preceding argument, there is for each finite prefix $\mathcal{C}_1'$ of $\mathcal{C}_1$ a finite execution $\mathcal{C}'$ of $\mathcal{T}$ such that $\mathcal{C}_1' = \pi_1(\mathcal{C}')$. By condition 5, these executions of $\mathcal{T}$ can be organized into a finitely branching tree with an infinite number of states. By König's lemma, one can extract an infinite execution $\mathcal{C}$ from these finite prefixes such that $\mathcal{C}_1 = \pi_1(\mathcal{C})$. This concludes the proof of the theorem. □

4.4 Proving Justice and Fairness

Given a computation $\mathcal{C}_1$ of $\mathcal{T}_1$, Propositions 4.2 and 4.4 give methods for proving the existence of an execution $\mathcal{C}$ of $\mathcal{T}$ such that $\mathcal{C}_1 = \pi_1(\mathcal{C})$. For establishing a refinement, we must prove that $\pi_2(\mathcal{C})$ is a computation of $\mathcal{T}_2$. It still remains to prove that $\pi_2(\mathcal{C})$ satisfies the requirements imposed by the justice and fairness sets of $\mathcal{T}_2$. That is the purpose of this subsection.

Let $\mathcal{A}$ be an actionsubset of the set of actions of a fair transition system $\mathcal{T}$. Let c, φ, and ψ be assertions over the state variables of $\mathcal{T}$. Say that

$$\varphi \wedge \Box\Diamond c \implies \Diamond(\psi \; ; \; \mathcal{A})$$

holds in $\mathcal{T}$ to mean that in each infinite sequence of transitions of $\mathcal{T}$ which starts in a φ-state, which satisfies the requirements of justice and fairness imposed by the justice and fairness sets of $\mathcal{T}$, and in which infinitely many states satisfy c, there is a later occurrence of a ψ-state or an $\mathcal{A}$-transition. Note that in this definition, it is not required that the first state of the sequence is an initial or even reachable state of $\mathcal{T}$. If c is *true*, we abbreviate the expression to $\varphi \implies \Diamond(\psi \; ; \; \mathcal{A})$. Properties of the above form can be established by standard proof techniques, e.g. variants of those in [MP84, MP89]. We review these techniques later in this subsection.

Theorem 4.5 *For $i = 1, 2$, let $\mathcal{T}_i = \langle \mathcal{E}_i, X_i, \Theta_i, \mathcal{A}_i, \mathcal{J}_i, \mathcal{F}_i \rangle$ be fair transition systems, such that $\mathcal{E}_2 \subseteq \mathcal{E}_1$. If there exists a simulation relation or a backwards simulation relation of a superposition $\mathcal{T}$ of $\mathcal{T}_2$ on $\mathcal{T}_1$ such that $\mathcal{A}$ is the set of actions of $\mathcal{T}$, and*

1. *for each justice set $\mathcal{A}_J$ of $\mathcal{T}_2$, it holds that $(R \wedge En(\mathcal{A}_J)) \implies \Diamond(\neg En(\mathcal{A}_J) \; ; \; \pi_2^{-1}(\mathcal{A}_J))$,*
2. *for each fairness set $\mathcal{A}_F$ of $\mathcal{T}_2$, it holds that $R \wedge \Box\Diamond En(\mathcal{A}_F) \implies \Diamond(false \; ; \; \pi_2^{-1}(\mathcal{A}_F))$,*

then $\mathcal{T}_1 \sqsupseteq \mathcal{T}_2$. □

Proof: By Propositions 4.2 and 4.4 there is for each computation $\mathcal{C}_1$ of $\mathcal{T}_1$ an execution $\mathcal{C}$ of $\mathcal{T}$ in which all states of $\mathcal{C}$ are R-states, such that $\pi_1(\mathcal{C}) = \mathcal{C}_1$, implying that $\pi_2(\mathcal{C})$ is an execution of $\mathcal{T}_2$. It remains to be proven that $\pi_2(\mathcal{C})$ indeed satisfies the justice and fairness requirements of $\mathcal{T}_2$. This is done by proving that each infinite sequence of transitions of $\mathcal{T}$ with only R-states which satisfies the justice and fairness requirements of $\mathcal{T}$ also satisfies the justice and fairness requirements of $\mathcal{T}_2$.

Justice: Assume that $\mathcal{A}_J$ is a justice set of $\mathcal{T}_2$. From condition 1 of the theorem we conclude that each suffix of $\mathcal{C}$, in which all states are $En(\mathcal{A}_J)$-states, must contain a $\pi_2^{-1}(\mathcal{A}_J)$-transition. This implies that each suffix of $\pi_2(\mathcal{C})$, in which all states are $En(\mathcal{A}_J)$-states, must contain a $\mathcal{A}_J$-transition.

Fairness: Assume that $\mathcal{A}_F$ is a fairness set of $\mathcal{T}_2$. From condition 2 of the theorem we conclude that each suffix of $\mathcal{C}$, in which there are infinitely many $En(\mathcal{A}_J)$-states, must contain a $\pi_2^{-1}(\mathcal{A}_J)$-transition. This implies that each suffix of $\pi_2(\mathcal{C})$, in which there are infinitely many $En(\mathcal{A}_J)$-states, must contain a $\mathcal{A}_J$-transition.

□

Formulas of the form

$$\varphi \wedge \Box\Diamond c \implies \Diamond(\psi \,;\, \mathcal{A})$$

cen be proven by variants of standard proof rules for proving liveness properties of concurrent programs, e.g. as in [MP84, MP89]. We now review these rules.

Define

$$\{\varphi\}\ \mathcal{A}\ \{\psi \,;\, \mathcal{A}_1\}$$

to denote that if the first state of an $\mathcal{A}$-transition is a φ-state, then either the transition is an $\mathcal{A}_1$-transition or its second state is a ψ-state. This can be proven by checking that for each action α in $\mathcal{A}$ of form

$$\textbf{event}\ \varepsilon(\overline{y})\ \textbf{when}\ c\ \textbf{do}\ \overline{x} := \overline{t}$$

it holds that $(\varphi \wedge c \wedge \neg c^1 \wedge \cdots \wedge \neg c^l) \implies \psi[\overline{t}/\overline{x}]$, where $c^1, \ldots, c^l$ are the enabling conditions of the actions α_1 in $\mathcal{A}_1$ such that $ev(\alpha_1) = ev(\alpha)$ and $do(\alpha_1) = do(\alpha)$.

Justice rule:
Assume that $\mathcal{A}_J$ is a justice set,

$$\frac{\{\varphi\}\ \mathcal{A}\ \{\varphi \vee \psi \,;\, \mathcal{A}_1\} \qquad \{\varphi\}\ \mathcal{A}_J\ \{\psi \,;\, \mathcal{A}_1\} \qquad \varphi \implies En(\mathcal{A}_J)}{\varphi \wedge \Box\Diamond c \implies \Diamond(\psi \,;\, \mathcal{A}_1)}$$

Fairness rule:
Assume that $\mathcal{A}_F$ is a fairness set,

$$\frac{\{\varphi\}\ \mathcal{A}\ \{\varphi \vee \psi \,;\, \mathcal{A}_1\} \qquad \{\varphi\}\ \mathcal{A}_F\ \{\psi \,;\, \mathcal{A}_1\} \qquad \varphi \wedge \Box\Diamond c \implies \Diamond(En(\mathcal{A}_F) \,;\, \mathcal{A}_1)}{\varphi \wedge \Box\Diamond c \implies \Diamond(\psi \,;\, \mathcal{A}_1)}$$

Infinitely-often rule:

$$\frac{\{\varphi\}\ \mathcal{A}\ \{\varphi \vee \psi \,;\, \mathcal{A}_1\} \qquad \{\varphi\}\ \mathcal{A}\ \{(c \implies \psi) \,;\, \mathcal{A}_1\}}{\varphi \wedge \Box\Diamond c \implies \Diamond(\psi \,;\, \mathcal{A}_1)}$$

Implication rule:

$$\frac{\varphi \implies \psi}{\varphi \wedge \Box\Diamond c \implies \Diamond(\psi \,;\, \mathcal{A}_1)}$$

Chain rule: Assume that W is a set with a well-founded relation $\prec$, and that $\chi(w)$ is an assertion parameterized by $w \in W$.

$$\frac{\varphi \implies \bigvee_{w \in W} \chi(w) \qquad \chi(w) \wedge \Box\Diamond c \implies \Diamond((\exists w' \prec w)[\chi'(w')] \vee \psi] \,;\, \mathcal{A}_1) \quad \text{for each } w \in W}{\varphi \wedge \Box\Diamond c \implies \Diamond(\psi \,;\, \mathcal{A}_1)}$$

Figure 4: Rules for Proving Justice And Fairness Properties. Throughout, $\mathcal{A}$ is the set of actions of the fair transition system under consideration.

Proof rules for formulas of the form $\varphi \wedge \Box\Diamond c \implies \Diamond(\psi\ ;\ \mathcal{A})$ are shown in Figure 4. Throughout, we assume that $\mathcal{A}$ is the set of actions of the fair transition system $\mathcal{T}$ in question. We argue for the soundness of each rule separately.

Justice: To obtain a contradiction, assume that $\mathcal{C}$ is a sequence of $\mathcal{A}$-transitions, which starts in a φ-state and does not contain any ψ-state or $\mathcal{A}_1$-transition. By the first premise, all states of $\mathcal{C}$ are φ-states, whence by the third premise they are also $En(\mathcal{A}_J)$-states. Since $\mathcal{A}_J$ is a justice set, it follows that $\mathcal{C}$ must contain a $\mathcal{A}_J$-transition, which by the second premise leads to a ψ-state or $\mathcal{A}_1$-transition.

Fairness: Assume that $\mathcal{C}$ is a sequence of $\mathcal{A}$-transitions, which starts in a φ-state and does not contain any ψ-state or $\mathcal{A}_1$-transition. By the first premise, all states of $\mathcal{C}$ are φ-states, whence by the third premise $\mathcal{C}$ contains infinitely many $En(\mathcal{A}_F)$-states. Since $\mathcal{A}_F$ is a fairness set, it follows that $\mathcal{C}$ must contain a $\mathcal{A}_F$-transition, which by the second premise leads to a ψ-state or $\mathcal{A}_1$-transition.

Infinitely often: Assume that $\mathcal{C}$ is a suffix of a computation, starting in a φ-state, which does not contain any ψ-state or $\mathcal{A}_1$-transition. By the first premise, all states of $\mathcal{C}$ are φ-states. Hence when a c-state comes, also a ψ-state or $\mathcal{A}_1$-transition must come.

Implication: Obvious.

Chain: Assume that $\mathcal{C}$ is a suffix of a computation, starting in a φ-state, which does not contain any ψ-state or $\mathcal{A}_1$-transition. By the first premise, the first state is a $\chi(w)$-state for some $w \in W$. By the second premise, there is an infinite descending sequence $w = w_0 \succ w_1 \succ w_2 \cdots$ such that each $\chi(w_i)$-state is followed by a $\chi(w_{i+1})$-state in $\mathcal{C}$. This contradicts the assumption that $\prec$ is well-founded.

$\Box$

4.5 Examples

Example 4.6 To illustrate the method of simulation relations, we shall prove that the parallel composition of two buffers, shown in Figure 3, is a correct refinement of the buffer in Figure 1. The superposition in question is shown in Figure 5. In the enabling condition of actions, we have designated the conjuncts that arise from the superposed actions by $\triangleright$.

In order to establish the correctness of the refinement, we must find a simulation relation which relates the state variables of the two transition systems. The simulation relation in question is

$$buf = buf_2 \bullet buf_1$$

We must prove the conditions for it to be a simulation relation.

1. $buf_1 = buf_2 = \langle\rangle \implies (\exists buf)[(buf = buf_2 \bullet buf_1) \wedge (buf = \langle\rangle)]$, which is proven by chosing buf to be the empty sequence $\langle\rangle$.

2. Here, the only nontrivial condition concerns the action $Remove_2$, which yields

$$buf = buf_2 \bullet buf_1 \wedge (buf_2 \neq \langle\rangle \wedge hd(buf_2) = v) \implies (buf \neq \langle\rangle \wedge hd(buf) = v)$$

which is true, since $buf_2 \neq \langle\rangle \wedge hd(buf_2) = v$ implies that $buf_2 \bullet buf_1 \neq \langle\rangle$ and that $hd(buf_2 \bullet buf_1) = v$ for any buf_1.

Events:	$in(v)$, $link(v)$, $out(v)$			
State Variables:	buf_1 , buf_2 , buf			
Initialization:	$buf_1 = buf_2 = buf = \langle\rangle$			
Actions:		**event**	**condition**	**update**
	$Insert_1$	$in(v)$	$true$	$\langle buf_1, buf \rangle := \langle buf_1 \bullet v, buf \bullet v \rangle$
	$Remove_1$	$link(v)$	$buf_1 \neq \langle\rangle$ $hd(buf_1) = v$	$\langle buf_1, buf_2 \rangle := \langle tl(buf_1), buf_2 \bullet v \rangle$
	$Remove_2$	$out(v)$	$buf_2 \neq \langle\rangle$ $hd(buf_2) = v$ $\triangleright\ buf \neq \langle\rangle$ $\triangleright\ hd(buf) = v$	$\langle buf_2, buf \rangle := \langle tl(buf_2), tl(buf) \rangle$
Justice:	$\{Remove_1\}$, $\{Remove_2\}$			

Figure 5: Superposition of buffer onto parallel composition of two buffers

3. Here we must prove that the simulation relation $buf = buf_2 \bullet buf_1$ is stable, i.e., that it is preserved by each action. As an example: for the action $Remove_1$ it must be proven that

$$[buf = buf_2 \bullet buf_1 \ \wedge\ (buf_1 \neq \langle\rangle \ \wedge\ hd(buf_1) = v)] \implies [buf = (buf_2 \bullet v) \bullet tl(buf_1)]$$

This condition is true: the antecedent implies that $buf = buf_2 \bullet (v \bullet tl(buf_1))$, which by associativity of the $\bullet$-operation gives the consequent.

It remains to establish the justice requirement given by the justice set $\{Remove\}$ of the specification in Figure 1. According to Theorem 4.5, this amounts to proving the property

$$(buf = buf_2 \bullet buf_1 \ \wedge\ buf \neq \langle\rangle) \implies \Diamond(buf = \langle\rangle\ ;\ \{Remove_2\})$$

which intuitively states that if buf is not empty, then eventually buf will become empty or a $Remove_2$-transition wil occur (in the statement of the property, we have omitted the conjunct $hd(buf) = v$], since it follows from $buf \neq \langle\rangle$ Using the proof rules, the property can be proven by applying the chain rule to the two premises

$$\begin{array}{l} (R \ \wedge\ buf_1 \neq \langle\rangle) \implies \Diamond((R \ \wedge\ buf_2 \neq \langle\rangle)\ ;\ \{Remove_2\}) \\ R \ \wedge\ buf_2 \neq \langle\rangle \implies \Diamond(buf = \langle\rangle\ ;\ \{Remove_2\}) \end{array}$$

where $R \equiv buf = buf_2 \bullet buf_1$ is the simulation relation. The first premise is established from the Justice rule, using the justice set $\{Remove_1\}$: whenever a $\{Remove_1\}$-action is performed, buf_2 becomes non-empty. The second premise is also established from the Justice rule, using the justice set $\{Remove_2\}$. The first premise of the chain rule: that R implies $buf_1 \neq \langle\rangle \ \vee\ buf_2 \neq \langle\rangle$ is straight-forward.

Example 4.7 In this example, we illustrate the use of backwards simulation relations. We shall consider two specifications of a split node, which receives events of form $in(v)$, where v ranges over messages, and produces events of form $out_A(v)$ and $out_B(v)$, where v is a message. Each received message v is nondeterministically transmitted either onto out_A or onto out_B. We consider the two specifications of the merge node given in Figure 6. The difference between the specifications is that the fts $Split_1$ makes the choice of where to output a message at the transition where the message is output, whereas the fts $Split_2$ makes this choice at the transition where the message is received. While $Split_1$ only has one internal sequence buf for the messages, $Split_2$ has two internal sequences

Transition System $Split_1$
Events: $in(v)$, $out_A(v)$, $out_B(v)$
State Variables: buf
Initialization: $buf = \langle\rangle$
Actions:

	event	condition	update
Insert	$in(v)$	$true$	$buf := buf \bullet v$
$Remove_A$	$out_A(v)$	$buf \neq \langle\rangle$ $hd(buf) = v$	$buf := tl(buf)$
$Remove_B$	$out_B(v)$	$buf \neq \langle\rangle$ $hd(buf) = v$	$buf := tl(buf)$

Justice: $\{Remove_A, Remove_B\}$

Transition System $Split_2$
Events: $in(v)$, $out_A(v)$, $out_B(v)$
State Variables: buf_A , buf_B
Initialization: $buf_A = buf_B = \langle\rangle$
Actions:

	event	condition	update
$Insert_A$	$in(v)$	$true$	$buf_A := buf_A \bullet v$
$Insert_B$	$in(v)$	$true$	$buf_B := buf_B \bullet v$
$Remove_A$	$out_A(v)$	$buf_A \neq \langle\rangle$ $hd(buf_A) = v$	$buf_A := tl(buf_A)$
$Remove_B$	$out_B(v)$	$buf_B \neq \langle\rangle$ $hd(buf_B) = v$	$buf_B := tl(buf_B)$

Justice: $\{Remove_A, Remove_B\}$

Figure 6: Two specifications of split nodes

of messages: the first, buf_A for messages to be transmitted onto out_A, and the second, buf_B, for messages that are to be transmitted onto out_B.

We intend to establish the refinement $Split_1 \sqsupseteq Split_2$. This relation cannot be established by a simulation relation, due to the fact that $Split_2$ makes a nondeterministic choice earlier than $Split_1$. However, it can be done using a backwards simulation relation. The superposition is shown in Figure 7. Note that here we have added extra conditions when superposing actions of $Split_2$ onto actions of $Split_1$; these are the fifth conjuncts in the actions $Remove_A$ and $Remove_B$.

We shall use $buf_1 \| buf_2$ to denotes the set of merges of the sequences buf_1 and buf_2. We use $buf_1 \lfloor buf_2$ to denote the set of "left-merges" of buf_1 and buf_2, i.e., the merges where the first element comes from buf_1. The right-merges $buf_1 \rfloor buf_2$ is defined analogously. The backwards simulation relation is $buf \in buf_A \| buf_B$. sequences buf_1 and buf_2. The invariant of $Split_1$is in this case *true*. We must verify the conditions for a backwards simulation relation.

1. This condition becomes $(\exists buf_A, buf_B)[buf \in buf_A \| buf_B]$, which is true, since for any buf there are sequences buf_A and buf_B that can be merged to obtain buf.

Events: $in(v)$, $out_A(v)$, $out_B(v)$
State Variables: buf , buf_A , buf_B
Initialization: $buf = buf_A = buf_B = \langle\rangle$
Actions:

	event	condition	update
$Insert_A$	$in(v)$	$buf \in buf_A \| buf_B$	$\langle buf, buf_A \rangle := \langle buf \bullet v, buf_A \bullet v \rangle$
$Insert_B$	$in(v)$	$buf \in buf_A \| buf_B$	$\langle buf, buf_B \rangle := \langle buf \bullet v, buf_B \bullet v \rangle$
$Remove_A$	$out(v)$	$buf \neq \langle\rangle$ $hd(buf) = v$ $\rhd\ buf_A \neq \langle\rangle$ $\rhd\ hd(buf_A) = v$ $buf \in buf_A \lfloor buf_B$	$\langle buf, buf_A \rangle := \langle tl(buf), tl(buf_A) \rangle$
$Remove_B$	$out(v)$	$buf \neq \langle\rangle$ $hd(buf) = v$ $\rhd\ buf_B \neq \langle\rangle$ $\rhd\ hd(buf_B) = v$ $buf \in buf_A \rfloor buf_B$	$\langle buf, buf_B \rangle := \langle tl(buf), tl(buf_B) \rangle$

Justice: $\{Remove_A, Remove_B\}$

Figure 7: Superposition of Split Nodes

2. We verify this for the action $Remove_A$. The condition becomes:

$$\begin{bmatrix} & buf \neq \langle\rangle \\ \wedge & hd(buf) = v \\ \wedge & tl(buf) \in buf'_A \| buf'_B \end{bmatrix} \implies (\exists buf_A, buf_B) \begin{bmatrix} & buf_A \neq \langle\rangle \\ \wedge & hd(buf_A) = v \\ \wedge & buf \in buf_A \lfloor buf_B \\ \wedge & tl(buf_A) = buf'_A \\ \wedge & buf_B = buf'_B \end{bmatrix}$$

   which is true if we choose $buf_A = v \bullet buf'_A$ and $buf_B = buf'_B$.

3. It is easy to verify that $\neg(buf \in buf_A \| buf_B)$ is stable, since no transitions are enabled when $\neg(buf \in buf_A \| buf_B)$ holds.

4. The condition becomes $(buf = \langle\rangle \ \wedge \ buf \in buf_A \| buf_B) \implies buf_A = \langle\rangle \ \wedge \ buf_B = \langle\rangle$ which is true.

5. Given a value of buf, there are only a finite number of values of buf_A and buf_B such that $buf \in buf_A \| buf_B$.

To verify the justice requirement $\{Remove_A, Remove_B\}$, one must establish the property

$$[R \ \wedge \ (buf_A \neq \langle\rangle \ \vee \ buf_A \neq \langle\rangle)] \implies \Diamond((buf_A = \langle\rangle \ \wedge \ buf_A = \langle\rangle) \ ; \ \{Remove_A, Remove_B\})$$

where $R \equiv buf \in buf_A \| buf_B$ is the simulation relation. The intuitive reason why this property is true is that when $[R \ \wedge \ (buf_A \neq \langle\rangle \ \vee \ buf_A \neq \langle\rangle)]$ then either $Remove_A$ or $Remove_B$ is enabled, and by justice will be performed.

5 Completeness

The methods of Theorem 4.5 are in general incomplete for establishing the correctness of a refinement. This section contains completeness results for limited classes of systems.

We shall only consider what is termed semantic completeness, without dealing with the problem whether simulation relations etc. can be expressed in the assertion language. We therefore assume that for each relation there is a corresponding assertion in our assertion language. Furthermore, all completeness results for establishing $\mathcal{T}_1 \sqsupseteq \mathcal{T}_2$ will only concern the case when $\mathcal{T}_2$ has no τ-actions, except the stuttering action. In general, we can not obtain completeness when $\mathcal{T}_2$ has τ-actions, since it may then be necessary to relate single transitions of $\mathcal{T}_1$ with sequences of transitions of $\mathcal{T}_2$. This restriction might be relaxed by extending the verification methods, but we shall not consider that issue in this paper.

5.1 Completeness for Simulation Relations

A fair transition system is *deterministic* if (1) it has only one initial state, (2) no transitions with event τ, except stuttering transitions, and (3) for each state s and event e there is at most one transition of form $s \xrightarrow{e} s'$.

Theorem 5.1 *For $i = 1, 2$ let $\mathcal{T}_i = \langle \mathcal{E}_i, X_i, \Theta_i, \mathcal{A}_i, \mathcal{J}_i, \mathcal{F}_i \rangle$ be fair transition systems with $\mathcal{E}_2 \subseteq \mathcal{E}_1$, and let $\mathcal{T}_2$ be deterministic. If $\mathcal{T}_1 \sqsupseteq \mathcal{T}_2$, then there exists a simulation relation R of a superposition $\mathcal{T}$ of $\mathcal{T}_2$ on $\mathcal{T}_1$, such that the conditions in Theorem 4.5 are satisfied.* □

Proof Sketch: The superposition $\mathcal{T}$ is defined as follows: the actions of $\mathcal{T}$ are (1) all actions of $\mathcal{T}_1$, the event primitive of which is not an event primitive of $\mathcal{T}_2$ (these are obtained by superposing the stuttering action of $\mathcal{T}_2$), and (2) all actions of form $\alpha_1 \| \alpha_2$ such that α_1 and α_2 have the same event primitive. Define $\langle s_1, s_2 \rangle$ to be an R-state exactly if for $i = 1, 2$ there are finite executions $\mathcal{C}_i$ of $\mathcal{T}_i$ such that $\mathit{trace}(\mathcal{C}_2) = \mathit{trace}(\mathcal{C}_1)\lceil_{\mathcal{E}_2}$. We shall use the fact that for each finite execution $\mathcal{C}_1$ of $\mathcal{T}_1$ there is exactly one finite execution $\mathcal{C}_2$ of $\mathcal{T}_2$ (modulo stuttering transitions) such that $\mathit{trace}(\mathcal{C}_2) = \mathit{trace}(\mathcal{C}_1)\lceil_{\mathcal{E}_2}$. This follows from the fact that $\mathcal{T}_2$ is deterministic.

We shall prove that R is a simulation relation. Condition 1 of Definition 4.1 follows by choosing $\mathcal{C}_1$ to consist of only an initial state and using the above fact. To prove condition 2, assume that $\langle s_1, s_2 \rangle$ is an R-state, that $s_1 \xrightarrow{e} s_1'$ is an α_1-transition for some action α_1 of $\mathcal{T}_1$. By the definition of R, the states s_i for $i = 1, 2$ are the last states of finite executions $\mathcal{C}_i$ such that $\mathit{trace}(\mathcal{C}_2)$ is $\mathit{trace}(\mathcal{C}_1)\lceil_{\mathcal{E}_2}$. Let $\mathcal{C}_1'$ be $\mathcal{C}_1$ extended by the transition $s_1 \xrightarrow{e} s_1'$. Since $\mathcal{T}_1 \sqsupseteq \mathcal{T}_2$, there must exist a finite execution $\mathcal{C}_2'$ of $\mathcal{T}_2$ with trace $\mathit{trace}(\mathcal{C}_2) \bullet (e\lceil_{\mathcal{E}_2})$. Since $\mathcal{T}_2$ is deterministic, there is only one such computation (modulo insertion of stuttering transitions). Furthermore, $\mathcal{C}_2'$ must extend $\mathcal{C}_2$ by one (possibly stuttering) transition $s_2 \xrightarrow{e'} s_2'$, where $e' = e\lceil_{\mathcal{E}_2}$. It follows that $\langle s_1, s_2 \rangle \xrightarrow{e} \langle s_1', s_2' \rangle$ is a transition of $\mathcal{T}$. Condition 3 follows directly from the definition of R.

To prove the conditions on justice and fairness sets in Theorem 4.5, note that each computation $\mathcal{C}_1$ of $\mathcal{T}_1$ has exactly one corresponding computation $\mathcal{C}$ of $\mathcal{T}$ such that $\pi_1(\mathcal{C}) = \mathcal{C}_1$. Hence $\pi_2(\mathcal{C})$ must satisfy the justice and fairness constraints imposed by the fairness sets of $\mathcal{T}_2$.
□

5.2 Completeness for Backwards Simulation Relations

In this subsection, we prove a completeness result for backwards simulation relations. In the next subsection, we will use this result to obtain a variant of the completeness theorem of Abadi and Lamport [AL88].

A fair transition system is said to be a *forest* if

1. for each state s which is initial there is no transition of form $s' \xrightarrow{e} s$ which leads to s

2. for each reachable state s which is not initial there is at most one transition of form $s' \xrightarrow{e} s$ which leads to s.

Intuitively, if the transition system is displayed as a graph with states as nodes and transitions as edges, then the graph of reachable states will form a forest.

For the next completeness result, we also need two technical restrictions on the fair transition systems. These have been introduced by Abadi and Lamport [AL88].

A fts $\mathcal{T}$ is said to be *finitely invisibly nondeterministic* (*fin* for short) if for each finite sequence q of communication events of $\mathcal{T}$, there are only a finite number of finite executions without stuttering transitions with trace q. A sufficient condition for $\mathcal{T}$ for being fin is that no non-stuttering transition has the event τ, and that for each state s and event e there are only finitely many s' such that $s \xrightarrow{e} s'$ is a transition of $\mathcal{T}$ (this is sometimes referred to as image-finiteness).

A fts $\mathcal{T}$ is said to be *internally continuous* if each infinite execution of $\mathcal{T}$, whose trace is a trace of $\mathcal{T}$, is also a computation of $\mathcal{T}$. Put differently, this means that if $\mathcal{C}$ is an infinite execution, then whether or not $\mathcal{C}$ is a computation depends only on the trace of $\mathcal{C}$.

Theorem 5.2 *For $i = 1,2$ let $\mathcal{T}_i = \langle \mathcal{E}_i, X_i, \Theta_i, \mathcal{A}_i, \mathcal{J}_i, \mathcal{F}_i \rangle$ be fair transition systems with $\mathcal{E}_2 \subseteq \mathcal{E}_1$, such that*

- *$\mathcal{T}_1$ is a forest,*
- *$\mathcal{T}_2$ is fin, internally continuous, and has no τ-transitions, except stuttering ones.*

If $\mathcal{T}_1 \sqsupseteq \mathcal{T}_2$, then there exists a backwards simulation relation R of a superposition $\mathcal{T}$ of $\mathcal{T}_2$ on $\mathcal{T}_1$, such that the conditions in theorem 4.5 are satisfied. □

Proof: Define $\langle s_1, s_2 \rangle$ to be an R-state exactly if for $i = 1,2$ there exists a computation $\mathcal{C}_i$ of $\mathcal{T}_i$ and a finite prefix $\mathcal{C}'_i$ of $\mathcal{C}_i$ such that $trace(\mathcal{C}_2) = trace(\mathcal{C}_1)\lceil_{\mathcal{E}_2}$, and $trace(\mathcal{C}'_2) = trace(\mathcal{C}'_1)\lceil_{\mathcal{E}_2}$, and such that s_i is the last state of $\mathcal{C}'_i$. Let $\langle s'_1, s'_2 \rangle \xrightarrow{e} \langle s_1, s_2 \rangle$ be a transition of $\mathcal{T}$ exactly if $s'_i \xrightarrow{e\lceil_{\mathcal{E}_i}} s_i$ are transitions of $\mathcal{T}_i$ and $\langle s_1, s_2 \rangle$ and $\langle s'_1, s'_2 \rangle$ are R-states.

We must show that R is a backwards simulation relation. Let R_1 characterize the reachable states of $\mathcal{T}_1$. Condition 1 in Definition 4.3 follows from the fact that if s_1 is a reachable state of $\mathcal{T}_1$, then there is a computation $\mathcal{C}_1$ with a prefix $\mathcal{C}'_1$ such that the last state of $\mathcal{C}'_1$ is s_1, whence there must be a corresponding computation of $\mathcal{T}_2$, which contains a state s_2 such that $\langle s_1, s_2 \rangle$ is an R-state. To prove Conditions 2 and 3, assume that $\langle s_1, s_2 \rangle$ is an R-state, and that $s'_1 \xrightarrow{e} s_1$ is a transition of $\mathcal{T}_1$. This means that there are computations $\mathcal{C}_1$, and $\mathcal{C}_2$ and finite prefixes $\mathcal{C}'_i$ of $\mathcal{C}_i$ such that $trace(\mathcal{C}_2) = trace(\mathcal{C}_1)\lceil_{\mathcal{E}_2}$, and $trace(\mathcal{C}'_2) = trace(\mathcal{C}'_1)\lceil_{\mathcal{E}_2}$, and such that s_i is the last state of $\mathcal{C}'_i$. Since $\mathcal{T}_1$ is a forest, the transition $s'_1 \xrightarrow{e} s_1$ must be the last transition of $\mathcal{C}'_1$. The last transition of $\mathcal{C}'_2$ (possibly after adding or deleting a stuttering transition) must be a transition $s'_2 \xrightarrow{e'} s_2$ with the event $e' = e\lceil_{\mathcal{E}_2}$. It also follows that $\langle s'_1, s'_2 \rangle$ is an R-state, whence $\langle s'_1, s'_2 \rangle \xrightarrow{e} \langle s_1, s_2 \rangle$ is a transition of $\mathcal{T}$.

To prove Condition 4, note that if $\langle s_1, s_2 \rangle$ is an R-state and s_1 is an initial state then, since $\mathcal{T}_1$ is a forest, s_1 must be the first state of $\mathcal{C}_1$, in which case the state s_2 must be the first state of a computation and hence initial. Condition 5 follows from the assumption that $\mathcal{T}_1$ is fin.

To prove the conditions on justice and fairness sets in Theorem 4.5, let $\mathcal{C}$ be a computation of $\mathcal{T}$. We have that $\pi_1(\mathcal{C})$ is a computation of $\mathcal{T}_1$. By the above argument, for each prefix $\mathcal{C}'$ of $\mathcal{C}$, we have that $\pi_2(\mathcal{C}')$ is the prefix of a computation of $\mathcal{T}_2$. It follows that $\pi_2(\mathcal{C})$ is in the closure of all computations of $\mathcal{T}_2$ with trace q_2 such that $q_2 = trace(\pi_1(\mathcal{C}))\lceil_{\mathcal{E}_2}$. Since $\mathcal{T}_2$ is internally continuous, it follows that $\pi_2(\mathcal{C})$ is a computation of $\mathcal{T}_2$, and hence the conditions on justice and fairness sets in Theorem 4.5 are satisfied.

□

5.3 A Combined Completeness Result

Using Theorem 5.2, we can now derive a variant of the completeness theorem of Abadi and Lamport [AL88].

Theorem 5.3 *For $i = 1,2$ let $\mathcal{T}_i = \langle \mathcal{E}_i, X_i, \Theta_i, \mathcal{A}_i, \mathcal{J}_i, \mathcal{F}_i \rangle$ be fair transition systems with $\mathcal{E}_2 \subseteq \mathcal{E}_1$. Let $\mathcal{T}_2$ be internally continuous and fin, and have no τ-transitions except stuttering. If $\mathcal{T}_1 \sqsupseteq \mathcal{T}_2$, then there exists a fair transition system $\mathcal{T}_3$ such that $\mathcal{T}_1 \sqsupseteq \mathcal{T}_3$ can be proven using a simulation relation, and $\mathcal{T}_3 \sqsupseteq \mathcal{T}_2$ can be proven using a backwards simulation relation, in both cases using the conditions in Theorem 4.5.* □

Proof: The idea of the proof is to define a fts $\mathcal{T}_3$ which is equivalent to $\mathcal{T}_1$ and is a forest. We can then use Theorem 5.2 to prove the theorem. Each state of $\mathcal{T}_3$ is a pair $\langle s, \mathcal{C} \rangle$, where s is a state of $\mathcal{T}_1$, and $\mathcal{C}$ is a finite partial computation of $\mathcal{T}_1$ whose last state is s. Intuitively, the second component of the state of $\mathcal{T}_3$ is a history variable which records the computation that has been performed so far. The initial states of $\mathcal{T}_3$ are of form $\langle s_0, s_0 \rangle$ where s_0 is an initial state of $\mathcal{T}_1$. The transitions of $\mathcal{T}_3$ are of form $\langle s, \mathcal{C} \rangle \xrightarrow{e} \langle s', \mathcal{C} \xrightarrow{e} s' \rangle$ where $s \xrightarrow{e} s'$ is a transition of $\mathcal{T}_1$. The justice and fairness sets of $\mathcal{T}_3$ are those of $\mathcal{T}$.

We can prove that $\mathcal{T}_1 \sqsupseteq \mathcal{T}_3$ by using a simulation relation. The superposition of $\mathcal{T}_3$ onto $\mathcal{T}_1$ is essentially the same as $\mathcal{T}_3$, and the simulation relation is the conjunction of (1) the identity relation between the state of $\mathcal{T}_1$ and the first component of the state of $\mathcal{T}_3$ and (2) an invariant of $\mathcal{T}_1$ which characterizes the reachable states of $\mathcal{T}_1$. It is easy to check that $\mathcal{T}_3$ is a forest, whence we can use Theorem 5.2 to conclude the proof.
□

This completeness results is a variant of results in [AL88] and [Mer]. Our presentation, using Theorem 5.2 explains why the introduction of history variables that record the past computation is necessary.

Restated in terms of the theorems in this section, the result of [AL88, Mer] states that if $\mathcal{T}_1 \sqsupseteq \mathcal{T}_2$, then there exist fair transition systems $\mathcal{T}_3$ and $\mathcal{T}_4$ such that $\mathcal{T}_1 \sqsupseteq \mathcal{T}_3$ can be proven using a simulation relation, $\mathcal{T}_3 \sqsupseteq \mathcal{T}_4$ can be proven using a backwards simulation relation, and $\mathcal{T}_4 \sqsupseteq \mathcal{T}_2$ can be proven using a simulation relation. In fact, $\mathcal{T}_4 \sqsupseteq \mathcal{T}_2$ can be proven using a refinement mapping (a refinement mapping is a special case of a simulation relation, where for each state s_4 of $\mathcal{T}_4$, there is at most one state of $\mathcal{T}_2$ which is related to s_4). The ftg $\mathcal{T}_4$ is obtained from $\mathcal{T}_2$ by adding a history variable in a similar way as $\mathcal{T}_3$ is obtained from $\mathcal{T}_1$ in the proof of Theorem 5.3.

6 Related Work

Notations for transition systems with fairness properties, that are related to our guarded multiple assignment statements, have been used by e.g. Manna and Pnueli [MP89, Pnu86] as a model of reactive programs, by Chandy and Misra [CM88] in the UNITY notation for describing parallel algorithms, and by Back et al [BS89, BKS87] in the stepwise development of reactive programs. Back et al presents a system of transformation rules on reactive programs. In Chandy and Misra's work, program refinements are carried out using temporal logic as a specification language, generating the UNITY program only as a last refinement step. In contrast, we presents methods for refining the transition systems. It appears that the methods of this paper could be adapted to verify the correctness of refinements between programs expressed in UNITY. This would provide a complement to the refinements on temporal logic specifications performed in [CM88].

Other formalisms for specifying and describing communicating systems in terms of sequences of communication events that can be performed include CCS [Mil80] and CSP [Hoa85]. These works use different criteria for satisfying a specification that do not involve infinite sequences and fairness.

I/O-systems have been studied by Stark [Sta84], in our earlier work [Jon85, Jon87a, Jon87b] which originates from ideas by Misra and Chandy [Mis84], and are similar to the I/O-automata of Lynch and Tuttle [LT87]. A (not very important) difference between I/O-systems and I/O-automata is the kind of fairness properties used. In specifications, Stark and Lynch and Tuttle use temporal logic formulas to specify liveness properties, whereas we retain the use of fairness properties.

Lamport [Lam83] presents a method for establishing refinements by using a mapping between the states of the specifications, instead of a relation. Simulation relations have been used by Stark [Sta84, Sta88], by Lynch and Tuttle [LT87] (there called possibilities mappings), and by Lam and Shankar [LS88]. In [LS88], the specification S_1 is a refinement of the specification S_2 only if the variables of S_2 are a subset of the variables of S_1. In our terminology, this means that a refinement S_1 must show how the specification S_2 is superposed onto S_1.

The completeness result for simulation relations (Theorem 5.1) has appeared in [Sta84] and [Jon87a]. Abadi and Lamport [AL88] have extended the techniques of [Lam83] with auxiliary variable constructions to obtain a more complete verification method. Their addition of history variables is related to the simulation method, and their addition of prophecy variables is related to the backwards simulation method. Merritt [Mer] has presented analogues of the results of Abadi and Lamport for I/O-automata, and studied various products of automata in the proofs.

Finite automata have been used to specify sequences of communication events of finite-state programs, e.g. by Vardi and Wolper [VW86]. In their approach, verification can be automated.

Alpern and Schneider [AS85, AS87] and Manna and Pnueli [MP87] have suggested to specify concurrent programs using predicate automata with various acceptance conditions. The proof methods become generalizations of proof rules [MP89, MP84] for temporal logic formulas.

Acknowledgments

I am grateful to Martin Abadi, Parosh Abdullah, Ralph-Johan Back, Zohar Manna, Ernst-Rüdiger Olderog, Fredrik Orava, Joachim Parrow, Amir Pnueli, Erik Tidén, and Frits Vaandrager for comments and fruitful discussions.

References

[AL88] M. Abadi and L. Lamport. The existence of refinement mappings. In *Proc. 3rd IEEE Symp. on Logic in Computer Science*, Edinburgh, 1988.

[AS85] B. Alpern and F.S. Schneider. Verifying temporal properties without using temporal logic. Technical Report TR 85-723, Cornell University, 1985.

[AS87] B. Alpern and F.S. Schneider. Proving boolean combinations of deterministic properties. In *Proc. 2nd IEEE Symp. on Logic in Computer Science*, 1987.

[BKS87] R.J.R. Back and R. Kurki-Suonio. Distributed co-operation with action systems. Technical Report A. 56, Åbo Akademi, Dept. of Computer Science and Mathematics, 1987.

[BS89] R.J.R. Back and K. Sere. Stepwise refinement of action systems. Technical Report A. 78, Åbo Akademi, Dept. of Computer Science and Mathematics, 1989.

[CM88] K. M. Chandy and J. Misra. *Parallel Program Design: A Foundation.* Addison-Wesley, 1988.

[Hoa85] C.A.R. Hoare. *Communicating Sequential Processes.* Prentice-Hall, 1985.

[Jon85] B. Jonsson. A model and proof system for asynchronous networks. In *Proc. 4:th ACM Symp. on Principles of Distributed Computing*, pages 49–58, Minaki, Canada, 1985.

[Jon87a] B. Jonsson. *Compositional Verification of Distributed Systems.* PhD thesis, Dept. of Computer Systems, Uppsala University, Sweden, Uppsala, Sweden, 1987. Available as report DoCS 87/09.

[Jon87b] B. Jonsson. Modular verification of asynchronous networks. In *Proc. 6th ACM Symp. on Principles of Distributed Computing*, pages 152–166, Vancouver, Canada, 1987.

[Lam83] L. Lamport. Specifying concurrent program modules. *ACM TOPLAS*, 5(2):190–222, 1983.

[LS88] S.S. Lam and A.U. Shankar. A relational notation for state transition systems. Technical Report TR-88-21, Dept. of Computer Sciences, University of Texas at Austin, 1988.

[LT87] N. A. Lynch and M. R. Tuttle. Hierarchical correctness proofs for distributed algorithms. In *Proc. 6th ACM Symp. on Principles of Distributed Computing*, pages 137–151, 1987.

[Mer] M. Merritt. Completeness theorems for automata. In this volume.

[Mil80] R. Milner. *A Calculus of Communicating Systems*, volume 92 of *Lecture Notes of Computer Science.* Springer Verlag, 1980.

[Mil89] R. Milner. *Communication and Concurrency.* Prentice-Hall, 1989.

[Mis84] J. Misra. Reasoning about networks of communicating processes. In *INRIA Advanced Nato Study Institute on Logics and Models for Verification and Specification of Concurrent Systems*, La Colle sur Loupe, France, 1984.

[MP84] Z. Manna and A. Pnueli. Adequate proof principles for invariance and liveness properties of concurrent programs. *Science of Computer Programming*, 4(4):257–289, 1984.

[MP87] Z. Manna and A. Pnueli. Specification and verification of concurrent programs by ∀-Automata. In *Proc.* 14th *ACM Symp. on Principles of Programming Languages*, pages 1–12, 1987.

[MP89] Z. Manna and A. Pnueli. The anchored version of the temporal framework. In de Bakker, de Roever, and Rozenberg, editors, *Linear Time, Branching Time and Partial Order in Logics and Models for Concurrency*, volume 354 of *Lecture Notes in Computer Science*, pages 201–284. Springer Verlag, 1989.

[Ora89] F. Orava. Verifying safety and deadlock properties of networks of asynchronously communicating processes. In *Proc.* 9th *IFIP WG6.1 Symp. on Protocol Specification, Testing, and Verification*, Twente, Holland, 1989.

[Pnu86] A. Pnueli. Applications of temporal logic to the specification and verification of reactive systems: A survey of corrent trends. In de Bakker, de Roever, and Rozenberg, editors, *Current Trends in Concurrency*, volume 224 of *Lecture Notes in Computer Science*, pages 510–584. Springer Verlag, 1986.

[Sis88] A. P. Sistla. On verifying that a concurrent program satisfies a non-deterministic specification. Technical Report TR 88-378.01.1, Computer and Intelligent Systems Lab. GTE Laboratories, May 1988.

[Sta84] E. W. Stark. *Foundations of a Theory of Specification for Distributed Systems.* PhD thesis, Massachussetts Inst. of Technology, 1984. Available as Report No. MIT/LCS/TR-342.

[Sta88] E. W. Stark. Proving entailment between conceptual state specifications. *Theoretical Computer Science*, 56:135–154, 1988.

[VW86] M. Y. Vardi and P. Wolper. An automata-theoretic approach to automatic program verification. In *Proc. IEEE Symp. on Logic in Computer Science*, pages 332–344, June 1986.

Verifying the Correctness of AADL Modules using Model Checking

Bernhard Josko

FB 10, University of Oldenburg
D - 2900 Oldenburg, Fed. Rep. of Germany

Abstract. This paper presents a temporal logic MCTL which is suitable for modular specification and verification of computer architectures. MCTL has the advantage that open systems can be specified and verified; i.e. it allows the specification of properties under some assumptions on the environment. The module concept may help to solve the state explosion problem in the verification of temporal logic specifications. To verify the correctness of an implementation we describe a model checking algoritm for that logic.

Key words: temporal logic, expressiveness, model checking, modular specification, verification, computer architecture.

Contents

1 Introduction
2 The temporal logic MCTL
3 Model checking
3.1 Adding fairness constraints
4 Example
5 Conclusion
6 References

1 Introduction

AADL is a computer architecture description language for developping computer architectures in a hierarchical and modular way [AADL89]. The whole design process - from high level specifications down to low level descriptions - can be done within AADL. The main components are architectures and subarchitectures (modules). The communication between (sub)architectures can be done by shared storage structures or by communication through ports, which may be synchronized or not. Synchronized communication is done in a CSP-style. In AADL the description of an architecture module consists of two main parts: the interface specification and the implementation part. The interface part describes the behaviour visible outside and the second part is an implementation of this specification. As a module communicates with other modules, the behaviour of the module is dependant on the reaction of other modules. Thus the interface specification may contain some constraints on the expected reactions of the environment. Hence interface specifications will be given by pairs (*assm, comm*), where *comm* describes a service (commitment) which will be guaranteed by the module provided the environment will satisfies the assumptions specified by *assm*. As the interface part is the visible description of the module the internal part (implementation part) should satisfy this behaviour. Hence, in a design process the correctness of the implementation has to be verified.

Assumptions and commitments are given by temporal logic formulae. Generally first order temporal logic is necessary to describe the services of a module, but we may seperate the pure communication protocol, which may be described using only propositional temporal logic, from the proper service specification dealing with the computation of data, where first order logic is necessary. For example the exchange of data between asynchronously coupled components can be done using the 4-cycle-signalling scheme, which can easily be expressed in propositional temporal logic, but to specify how the output data is computed from the input data we need first order logic. But in most cases we can seperate the propositional part, describing the pure protocol, and the first order part describing the data transformations. Then the correctness verification can be done in two steps: First verifying the pure protocol using e.g. a modelchecking algorithm and second verifying the correctness of the data transformations using a Hoare calculus. In this paper we will treat only the propositional temporal logic part. Besides verifying the correctness of an implementation part we must be able to derive properties of modules composed from several submodules, hence we need some proof rules to do this. The correctness of a composition of modules may also be verified in the same manner as basic modules will be proved correct. However due to the complexity those modules may have, the associated model may become to large to be verified automatically by model checking (state explosion problem), hence proof rules are an important factor. In this paper we will treat only basic modules and will show how their correctness can be verified using model checking, appropriate proof rules for the composition of modules are described in [DDGJ89].

Fig. 1 gives an example of an AADL module, where the asynchronous exchange of data is described using the 4-cycle-signalling protocol. The interface part consists of the descriptions of the ports to the environment and of the service specifications given in a temporal logic. An architecture module is not characterized by an input/output-relation, but it is a reactive systems, i.e. a system that interacts with the environment (i.e. with other modules). Thus the specification does not only describe the actions of the module, but also specifies the assumed reactions of the environment (cf. the service specification in Fig. 1). As we want to prove the correct behaviour of a subarchitecture without having just designed the concret environment we should be able to prove properties of open systems. ∀n appropriate temporal logic for that purpose is the logic MCTL developped in [Jo87].

To verify that the implementation part satisfies the protocol specified in the interface, we have to construct a model (Kripke structure), representing the implementation, in which the specification formulae can be interpreted. This is done in the following way: The semantics of an AADL-implementation is defined by Petri nets (see [DD90]). Then the case-graph of the Petri net is a Kripke structure associated with the implementation. To be more precise, we use an extented notion of case-graph, where arcs are labelled with input conditions and where some information of the firing transitions are incorporated in order to be able to express fairness constraints. Fairness constraints have to be added as the case graph defines an interleaving semantics (step semantics). Having derived the

```
architecture example
    async inport  data_in : word;
    async inport  req : bit;
    async outport  ack : bit   init 0 ;                                  }
    ...                                                                  }
    :                                                                    }
    service                                                              }
        constraint                                                       }
            req and not ack  →  (req unless req and ack)                 }
            req and ack  →  eventually not req                           } interface
            not req and ack  →  (not req unless not req and not ack)     }
            ...                                                          }
        behaviour                                                        }
            req and not ack  →  eventually ack                           }
            req and ack  →  (ack  unless  not req  and  ack)             }
            not req  and  ack  →  eventually not ack                     }
            not req  and  not ack  →  (not ack  unless  req and not ack) }
            ...                                                          }
    end /* service */                                                    }
    ...                                                                  }
    storage                                                              }
            dat1 : word                                                  }
            ...                                                          }
    behaviour                                                            }
        control                                                          }
            rep                                                          }
                true  →      ...                                         }
                             on req = 1 do skip od;  /* wait for input */}
                             read(data_in,dat1);                         } implementation
                             if  req=1 →     set(ack);                   }
                                             on req=0 do skip od;        }
                                             reset(ack);                 }
                                             ...                         }
                             []                                          }
                                 not(req=1) → skip;                      }
                             fi;                                         }
            per                                                          }
        end /* control */                                                }
    end /* behaviour */                                                  }
end /* architecture example */
```

*In the interface specification we use **req** (resp. **ack**) as an abbreviation for **req** = 1 (resp. **ack** = 1).*

Fig. 1

appropriate model we can check the correctness of the implementation using a model checking algorithm. Fig. 2 gives a model for the module described in Fig. 1, this model is derived from the associated case-graph using some optimization techniques to reduce the size of the model.

In this paper we will describe the temporal logic MCTL and discuss a model checking algorithm for this logic. The procedure will be demonstrated by verifying the commitment "Every request will be acknowledged" in our example.

2 The temporal logic MCTL

The branching time temporal logic CTL has been widely used to specify and verify finite state systems, as this logic has a linear model checking algorithm [CES83]. But to specify open systems the logic CTL is not expressive enough. Therefore the logic CTL* may be used, but this logic has an exponential time complexity. As we are interested in a logic which may be used in practise, we have tried to find a logic of lower complexity, but which can express the desired properties. This has lead to the logic MCTL, which is an extension of CTL.

In MCTL a specification is given by an assumption part and a commitment part. Furthermore, fairness constraints may be added as a third component. Hence a formula of MCTL is given by a tuple

$$(fc,\ assm,\ comm)$$

where *fc* defines the fairness constraints, *assm* describes the expected behaviour of the environment, and *comm* gives the specification of the module.

To be more formally, we assume that *ATOMS* is a (finite) set of atomic propositions with typical elements a, a_i, ... The set of boolean expressions will be denoted by *BExpr* and its elements are denoted by b, ...

Commitments are state formulae (CTL formulae) given by the following rules:

$$\begin{aligned} comm ::= \quad & b \mid comm \wedge comm \mid comm \vee comm \mid \\ & \forall\,[\, comm\ \textbf{until}\ comm \,] \mid \forall\,[\, comm\ \textbf{unless}\ comm \,] \mid \\ & \forall G\ comm \mid \forall F\ comm \mid \\ & \exists\,[\, comm\ \textbf{until}\ comm \,] \mid \exists\,[\, comm\ \textbf{unless}\ comm \,] \mid \\ & \exists G\ comm \mid \exists F\ comm \end{aligned}$$

and assumptions are restricted PTL formulae given by

$$assm \quad ::= \quad [\,]\,(b \rightarrow uf) \mid uf \mid assm \wedge assm$$

where *uf* is an iterated until/unless-formula defined by

$$uf \quad ::= \quad b \mid [\, b\ \textbf{until}\ uf \,] \mid [\, b\ \textbf{unless}\ uf \,]\ .$$

The syntax of fairness constraints is given by

$$fc \quad ::= \quad [\,]\Diamond\, b \mid \Diamond[\,]\, b \mid fc \wedge fc \mid fc \vee fc\ .$$

assm and *fc* are path formulae which restrict the paths relevant for the path quantifiers ∀ and ∃ in a commitment *comm*. In module specifications only ∀-quantified formulae are allowed, the ∃-quantifier is only used in intermediate steps. There are two reasons for the restriction to ∀-quantified formulae in module specifications: First, the specification should not describe that there is *some* computation of the module having a specific behaviour, but it should describe the behaviour of *all* possible computations. Secondly, using ∃-quantification and arbitrary negation can destroy the soundness of proof rules for compostion of modules.

Using only universal quantified commitments the ∀-quantifier may be omitted in module specifications. Furthermore, the G - operator will sometimes be denoted by [] or **always**, and the F-operator is interchangable with ◊ and **eventually**.

A formula (*fc, assm, comm*) of MCTL is interpreted with respect to a Kripke structure which may be represented by a state/transistion-graph. As we deal with modules we use labelled transitions. These labels are propositions on the inputs and specify under which conditions the transition can be applied. Therefore a model is given by

$$M = (S, s^0, IN, OUT, R, \pi)$$

with

S	a set of states
s^0	the initial state
IN	a set of input propositions
OUT	a set of internal and output propositions with $OUT \cap IN = \varnothing$
R	a set of transitions (s, b, s') where $s,s' \in S$ and b is a satisfiable boolean expression on the input propositions
π	an assignment of internal/output propositions to states

Models can be given by graphical representations as it is done in Fig. 2, where an appropriate model for the AADL module of Fig. 1 is given.

$S = \{s_0,...,s_5\}$
$s^0 = s_0$
IN = {req, f1, f2, ...}
OUT = {ack, ...}
R = { (s_0 , **not** req, s_0), (s_0, req **and not** f1, s_0), (s_0, req **and** f1, s_1), (s_1, **true**, s_2),
(s_2, **not** req, s_0), (s_2, req, s_3), (s_3 , req, s_3), (s_3, **not** req **and not** f2, s_3),
(s_3, **not** req **and** f2, s_4), (s_4, **true**, s_5), (s_5, **true**, s_0) }
$\pi(s_0) = \pi(s_1) = \pi(s_2) = \pi(s_5) = \varnothing$
$\pi(s_3) = \pi(s_4) = \{ \text{ack} \}$
fairness constraints: fc = $\Box\Diamond f1 \wedge \Box\Diamond f2$

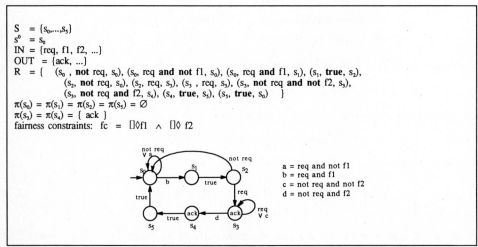

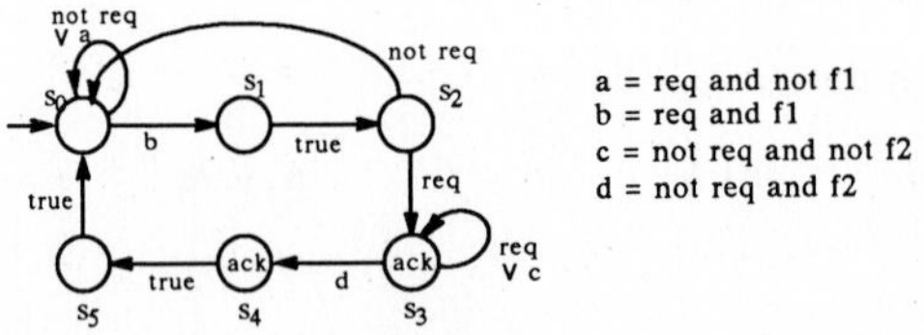

Fig. 2

Given a model $M = (S,s^0,IN,OUT,R,\pi)$, $((s_i,in_i) \mid i \in N)$ is an <u>(infinite) path</u> iff for every $i \in N$ there is a boolean expression b_i with in_i **sat** b_i and $(s_i,b_i,s_{i+1}) \in R$. For a path $p=((s_i,in_i) \mid i \in N)$ p^i denotes the suffix of p starting at (s_i,in_i); i.e. $p^i := ((s_{k+i},in_{k+1}) \mid k \in N)$. The concatenation of a finite path $((s'_0,in'_0),...,(s'_m,in'_m))$ with a path $p = ((s_i,in_i) \mid i \in N)$, denoted by $((s'_0,in'_0),...,(s'_m,in'_m))\cdot p$, is defined if $(s'_m,in'_m)=(s_0,in_0)$ and is then given by $((s''_i,in''_i) \mid i \in N)$, where $(s''_i,in''_i)=(s'_i,in'_i)$ for $i\in \{0,...,m\}$ and $(s''_{i+m},in''_{i+m})=(s_i,in_i)$ for $i\in N$. $(s,in)\cdot p$ will be used as an abbreviation for $((s,in),(s_0,in_0))\cdot p$.

The interpretation of a formula *(fc, assm, comm)* with respect to a model M and a state s ∈ S and inputs in ⊆ IN, denoted by M,s,in ⊨ *(fc,assm,comm)* can be described in the following way:

- Construct the (infinite) computation tree of M with root s (The computation tree is obtained by unravelling the state/transition-graph.)
- Mark those paths in the tree starting at (s,in) which satisfy the given assumptions and fairness constraints.
- Interpret *comm* as in CTL, but with the restriction that only the marked paths are considered (when dealing with path quantifiers)

Fig. 3 gives the computation tree for the model of Fig. 2.

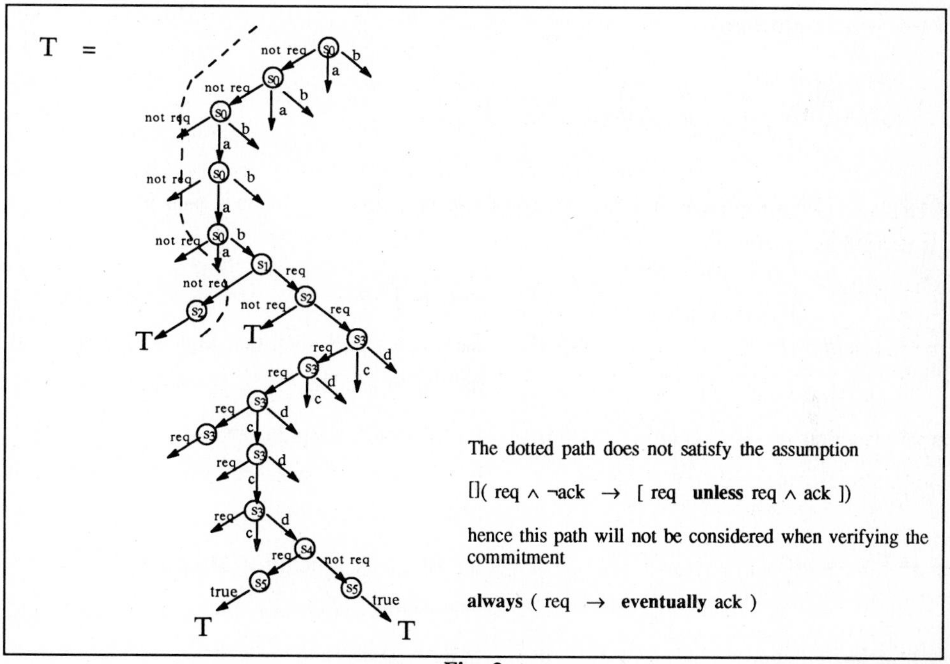
T =
not req
a
b
req
c
d
not req
true
T
The dotted path does not satisfy the assumption
[](req ∧ ¬ack → [req **unless** req ∧ ack])
hence this path will not be considered when verifying the commitment
always (req → **eventually** ack)

Fig. 3

Along a computation path the assumptions on the environment will change, e.g. when the computation reach state s_1 the signal *req* has been set and therefore the environment will guarantee that this signal will not be reset unless the acknowledge signal *ack* has occured. Hence this will be added to the actual assumptions. And when the computation reach a state where the acknowledge signal is set, this added assumption will be removed from the actual assumption list. Given an assumption *assm* describing the actual assumption at state s and given inputs in *update*(*assm*,s,in) will describe the new assumption list relevant for the further computation. If the assumption is given by

$$assm \;=\; \bigwedge_{i=1}^{n} [](b_{i,1} \rightarrow [b_{i,2} \textbf{ until/unless } b_{i,3}]) \;\wedge\; \bigwedge_{i=n+1}^{n+m} [b_{i,2} \textbf{ until/unless } b_{i,3}] \;.$$

the *update*-function is defined by

$$update(assm,s,in) \;=\; \bigwedge_{i=1}^{n} [](b_{i,1} \rightarrow [b_{i,2} \textbf{ until/unless } b_{i,3}]) \;\wedge\; \bigwedge_{i\in J} [b_{i,2} \textbf{ until/unless } b_{i,3}] \;.$$

where the set J is given by

$$J \;:=\; \{i\in\{1,..,n\} \mid s,in \models b_{i,1} \wedge \neg b_{i,3}\} \cup \{i\in\{n+1,...,n+m\} \mid s,in \models \neg b_{i,3}\}.$$

Given a path $p = ((s_i,in_i) \mid i \in N)$ and assumption *assm*, the actual assumption for the path p^i will be denoted by $update_i(p,assm)$ and is given by

$update_0(p,assm) \quad := \quad assm$

$update_{i+1}(p,assm) \quad := \quad update(assm,s_i,in_i)$

The validity of an assumption or a fairness constraint in a structure M on a path $p = ((s_i,in_i) \mid i \in N)$ is defined as usually:

$M,p \models b$	iff	$M,s_0,in_0 \models b$
$M,p \models [b$ ***until*** $uf]$	iff	there is a $j \in N$ such that $M,p^j \models uf$ and for all i, $0 \le i < j$: $M,s_i,in_i \models b$
$M,p \models [b$ ***unless*** $uf]$	iff	for all $j \in N$: $M,s_j,in_j \models b$ or there is a $j \in N$ such that $M,p^j \models uf$ and for all i, $0 \le i < j$: $M,s_i,in_i \models b$
$M,p \models [](b \rightarrow uf)$	iff	for all $i \in N$ it holds: if $M,s_i,in_i \models b$, then $M,p^i \models uf$
$M,p \models assm_1 \wedge assm_2$	iff	$M,p \models assm_1$ and $M,p \models assm_2$
$M,p \models []\Diamond\, b$	iff	there are infinetely many $i \in N$ with $M,s_i,in_i \models b$
$M,p \models \Diamond[]\, b$	iff	there is some $i \in N$ such that for all $j \ge i$: $M,s_j,in_j \models b$
$M,p \models fc_1 \wedge fc_2$	iff	$M,p \models fc_1$ and $M,p \models fc_2$
$M,p \models fc_1 \vee fc_2$	iff	$M,p \models fc_1$ or $M,p \models fc_2$

If the structure M is clear from the context, we will write $p \models assm$ ($p \models fc$) instead of $M,p \models assm$ ($M,p \models fc$). We say that a path $p = ((s_i,in_i) \mid i \in N)$ is assm-good iff $M,p \models assm$

and it is called <u>*(fc,assm)*-good</u> iff $M,p \models assm$ and $M,p \models fc$.

The <u>validity</u> of a formula $(fc,assm,comm) \in$ MCTL in a structure M at some state s_0 with inputs in_0, denoted by $M,s_0,in_0 \models (fc,assm,comm)$, is defined as follows:

$M,s_0,in_0 \models (fc,assm,\ a)$ iff $a \in \pi(s_0) \cup in_0$

$M,s_0,in_0 \models (fc,assm,\ \neg f)$ iff not $M,s_0,in_0 \models (fc,assm,\ f)$

$M,s_0,in_0 \models (fc,assm,\ f_1 \wedge f_2)$ iff $M,s_0,in_0 \models (fc,assm,\ f_1)$ and $M,s_0,in_0 \models (fc,assm,\ f_2)$

$M,s_0,in_0 \models (fc,assm,\ f_1 \vee f_2)$ iff $M,s_0,in_0 \models (fc,assm,\ f_1)$ or $M,s_0,in_0 \models (fc,assm,\ f_2)$

$M,s_0,in_0 \models (fc,assm,\ \forall[f_1 \textbf{ until } f_2])$ iff for all *(assm,fc)*-good paths $p=((s_i,in_i) \mid i \in N)$ there is some $k \geq 0$ with $M,s_k,in_k \models (fc,assm_k,\ f_2)$ and for all j, $0 \leq j < k$: $M,s_j,in_j \models (fc,assm_j,\ f_1)$ where $assm_i$, $i \in N$, is given by $assm_i := update_i(p,assm)$

$M,s_0,in_0 \models (fc,assm,\ \forall[f_1 \textbf{ unless } f_2])$ iff for all *(assm,fc)*-good paths $p=((s_i,in_i) \mid i \in N)$ it holds:
for all $k \in N$: $M,s_k,in_k \models (fc,assm_k,\ f_1)$ or
there is some $k \geq 0$ with $M,s_k,in_k \models (fc,assm_k,\ f_2)$ and for all j, $0 \leq j < k$: $M,s_j,in_j \models (fc,assm_j,\ f_1)$
where $assm_i$, $i \in N$, is given by $assm_i := update_i(p,assm)$

$M,s_0,in_0 \models (fc,assm,\ \forall G\ f)$ iff $M,s_0,in_0 \models (fc,assm,\ \forall[f \textbf{ unless false}])$

$M,s_0,in_0 \models (fc,assm,\ \forall F\ f)$ iff $M,s_0,in_0 \models (fc,assm,\ \forall[\textbf{true until } f])$

$M,s_0,in_0 \models (fc,assm,\ \exists[f_1 \textbf{ until } f_2])$ iff for some *(assm,fc)*-good paths $p=((s_i,in_i) \mid i \in N)$ there is some $k \geq 0$ with $M,s_k,in_k \models (fc,assm_k,\ f_2)$ and for all j, $0 \leq j < k$: $M,s_j,in_j \models (fc,assm_j,\ f_1)$ where $assm_i$, $i \in N$, is given by $assm_i := update_i(p,assm)$

$M,s_0,in_0 \models (fc,assm,\ \exists[f_1 \textbf{ unless } f_2])$ iff for some *(assm,fc)*-good paths $p=((s_i,in_i) \mid i \in N)$ it holds:
for all $k \in N$: $M,s_k,in_k \models (fc,assm_k,\ f_1)$ or
there is some $k \geq 0$ with $M,s_k,in_k \models (fc,assm_k,\ f_2)$ and for all j, $0 \leq j < k$: $M,s_j,in_j \models (fc,assm_j,\ f_1)$
where $assm_i$, $i \in N$, is given by $assm_i := update_i(p,assm)$

$M,s_0,in_0 \models (fc,assm, \exists G\ f)$ iff $M,s_0,in_0 \models (fc,assm, \exists[f\ \textbf{unless false}])$

$M,s_0,in_0 \models (fc,assm, \exists F\ f)$ iff $M,s_0,in_0 \models (fc,assm, \exists[\textbf{true until}\ f])$

If the structure M is clear from the context we will write $s_0,in_0 \models (fc,assm,comm)$ instead of $M,s_0,in_0 \models (fc,assm,comm)$. $(fc,assm,comm)$ is valid in M, denoted by $M \models (fc,assm,comm)$, iff $M,s,in \models (fc,assm,comm)$ for all $s \in S$ and all $in \subseteq IN$, and $(fc,assm,comm)$ is valid, denoted by $\models (fc,assm,comm)$, iff for all models M : $M \models (fc,assm,comm)$.

Comparing the logic MCTL with (F)CTL and CTL*, we can show that MCTL is more expressive than (F)CTL and that CTL* is more expressive than MCTL (cf. [Jo89]).

3 Model checking

In this chapter we will describe the basic ideas underlying the model checking algorithm for the logic MCTL. A model checker is used to prove/disprove the validity of a given formula in a given model (w.r.t. the initial state). Hence, to describe the procedure we assume that a fixed model $M = (S,s^0,IN,OUT,R,\pi)$ and a formula $(fc,assm,comm)$ are given where the initial assumption *assm* has the form

$$assm = \bigwedge_{i=1}^{n} assm_i \qquad \text{with} \quad assm_i = [](b_{i,1} \rightarrow uf_i)\ .$$

In this paper we will discuss the model checking procedure where the subformulae uf_i do not have nested until/unless operators, i.e. they are of the form

$$uf_i = [b_{i,2}\ \textbf{until/unless}\ b_{i,3}].$$

The extension to nested until/unless-formulae is straightforward, but uses a more complex *update*-function.

As the actual assumptions will change along a computation path we have to know in the model checking procedure what the actual assumption is. To get this information we will extend the given model M by adding these informations to the states. To do this we will use an encoding of the actual assumptions. Every actual assumption is the conjunction of the initial assumption and of some of the uf_i-formulae. Such an assumption can be encoded by the set of indices of the included *uf* formulae, i.e. a set $J \subseteq \{1,...,n\}$ encodes the assumption

$$ASSM(J) := assm \wedge \bigwedge_{i \in J} uf_i\ .$$

The *update*-function can be described using this encoding in the following way:

$$update(s,in,J) := (J \setminus \{j \mid s,in \models b_{j,3}\}) \cup \{\ j \in \{1,...,n\} \mid s,in \models b_{j,1} \wedge \neg b_{j,3}\ \}$$

The actual assumptions along a computation path p, $update_i$(p,ASSM(J)), are encoded by $update_i$(p,J), which can be inductively defined by:

$$update_0(p,J) := J$$
$$update_{i+1}(p,J) := update(s_i,in_i,update_i(p,J))$$

As the modelchecker will traverse the model state by state we need some characterizations of the temporal operators using the successor states. Furthermore, the model checker will deal with ∃-quantifiers only, as it is easier to check whether there is some assm-good path satisfying a given specification, than to prove directly that all assm-good paths satisfy the specification. Hence the ∀-quantifier will be substituted by ¬∃¬ in the modelchecker. Then the semantics of the temporal operators can be characterized as follows:

(1) s,in $\models$ $(fc,assm, \exists[f_1$ ***until*** $f_2])$ iff
there is a $(fc,assm)$-good path starting at (s,in) and s,in $\models$ $(fc,assm,f_2)$ or
s,in $\models$ $(fc,assm, f_1)$, and for all $i \in update(s,in,assm)$: s,in $\models b_{i,2}$, and there is a successor state (t,in') of (s,in) with t,in' $\models$ $(fc,update(s,in,assm), \exists[f_1$ ***until*** $f_2])$.

(2) s,in $\models$ $(fc,assm, \forall[f_1$ ***until*** $f_2])$ iff s,in $\models$ $(fc,assm, \neg\exists(\neg[f_1$ ***until*** $f_2]))$
iff s,in $\models$ $(fc,assm, \neg(\exists[\neg f_2$ ***until*** $(\neg f_1 \wedge \neg f_2)] \vee \exists G \neg f_2))$

(3) s,in $\models$ $(fc,assm, \forall[f_1$ ***unless*** $f_2])$ iff s,in $\models$ $(fc,assm, \neg\exists([f_1 \wedge \neg f_2$ ***until*** $\neg f_1 \wedge \neg f_2]))$

(4) s,in $\models$ $(fc,assm, \exists[f_1$ ***unless*** $f_2]l)$ iff s,in $\models$ $(fc,assm, \exists G f_1 \wedge \exists[f_1$ ***until*** $\neg f_2])$

Due to this characterization, one main task in the model checking algorithm is to verify whether there is some assm-good path starting at a state s with inputs in. And another task is the handling of the ∃G-operator.

As we have to trace the actual assumption along a computation path the model checking will be done in an extended model which is given by

Ext(M) := (S', s'^{0}, IN, OUT, R', π') where

S' := {(s,J) | s∈S, J⊆{1,...,n} },

s'^{0} := (s^0,∅)

R' := { ((s,J), in, (s',J')) | there is some c with in **sat** c and (s,c,s')∈R, and J'=$update$(s,in,J), and (s,in $\models b_{i,2} \vee b_{i,3}$ for all i ∈ J∪{ k | s,in $\models b_{k,1}$ })},

π'((s,J)) := π(s).

Using the extended model Ext(M) the existence of an ASSM(J)-good path starting from state s with inputs in can be reduced to the reachability of a strongly connected component satisfying some assumption. Then the construction of the model Ext(M) guarantees that some path leading to the strongly connected component and looping therein forever satisfies the assumption ASSM(J). Let J_W be the subset of {1,..,n}, containing those indices where uf_i contains the weak until operator, i.e. J_W

:= { $k \in \{1,...,n\}$ | uf_k = [$b_{k,2}$ **unless** $b_{k,3}$] }.

Theorem 1

Given a state s_0, an input in_0 and an assumption ASSM(J), then there is a path starting at (s_0,in_0) satisfying ASSM(J) iff there is a transition $((s_0,J),in_0,(s',J')) \in R'$ and there is a strongly connected component C of (S',R') and a state $(t,J') \in C$ such that

(1) for all $i \in J' \setminus J_W$ there is a transition $((s_i,J_i), in_i, (s'_i,J'_i)) \in C$ with $s_i,in_i \models b_{i,3}$.

(2) (t,J') is reachable from (s_0,J) with input in_0.

The strongly connected components of a graph can be found in time linear in the size of the graph (cf. [Ta72]), hence the existence of an ASSM(J)-good path can be checked in time linear in the size of the extended model.

To treat ∃Gf under an assumption ASSM(J) we will consider the submodel of M' consisting of those transitions ((s,J),in,(s',J')) such that (s,in) satisfies (ASSM(J),f).

Theorem 2

M,s,in $\models$ (fc,ASSM(J),∃Gf) iff there exists a (fc,ASSM(J))-good path $p'=((s_i,J_i,in_i) | i \in N)$ in M' with $(s_0,J_0,in_0)=(s,J,in)$ such that $M,s_i,in_i \models$ (fc,ASSM($update_i$(p,J)),f) for all $i \in N$.

As a consequence of Theorem 1 and Theorem 2 we obtain:

Corollary 1

Let $s \in S$, $J \subseteq \{1,...,n\}$ and $f \in CTL$ be given. Define a model M"=(S",s"^{0},IN,OUT,R",π") by

$$S'' := S'$$

$$s''^0 := s'^0$$

$$R'' := \{((s,K), in, (s',K')) \in R' \mid s,in \models (ASSM(K),f) \}$$

$$\pi''((s,J)) := \pi(s).$$

Then:

M,s,in $\models$ (ASSM(J), ∃Gf) iff there is some transition $((s,J),in,(s',J')) \in R''$ and there is a strongly connected component $C \subseteq M''$ and a state $(t,J'') \in C$ such that

(1) for all $i \in J'' \setminus J_W$ there is a transition $((s_i,J_i),in_i,(s'_i,J'_i)) \in C$ with $s_i,in_i \models b_{i,3}$.

(2) in the model M" (t,J") is reachable from (s,J) with input in.

Hence the time complexity for checking the validity of (ASSM(J),∃Gf) is linear in the size of the extended model (provided the validity of (ASSM(K),f) is known for all transitions).

As all other steps in the model checker can be done similarly as in the CTL-modelchecker, checking the validity of *(assm,comm)* can be done linear in the size of the model M, linear in the length of *comm* and exponential in the number of until/unless formulae in *assm* (i.e. linear in the length of *assm*).

3.1 Adding fairness constraints

In [EL85] Emerson and Lei have shown that the fair state problem "Starting from which states does there exist some path along which *fc* holds?" is NP-complete. But if the fairness constraint *fc* is given in a special canonical form the problem can be solved in time which is linear in the size of the model and quadratic in the length of the fairness constraint [EL85]. A fairness constraint is in the canonical form if it is given as

$$\bigvee_{i=1}^{n} \bigwedge_{j=1}^{m} (\Diamond[]\ b_{ij} \vee []\Diamond\ c_{ij}) \ .$$

To check whether there is a (fc,ASSM(J))-good path starting at some state, one has to combine the check for fair paths with the check for ASSM(J)-good paths. If the fairness constraint *fc* is of the simple form

$$fc \quad = \quad \bigwedge_{i=1}^{m} []\Diamond\ c_i$$

we have to add the following condition for the strongly connected components C (cf. Theorem 1 and Corollary 1).

(3) for all $k \in \{1,..,m\}$ there is a transition $((s_k,J_k),\ in_k,\ (s'_k,J'_k)) \in C$ with $s_k,in_k \models c_k$.

4 Example

We will demonstrate the model checking procedure by verifying the commitment that every request of the environment will be acknowledged, i.e. $\forall G(\ (req \wedge \neg ack) \ \rightarrow \ \forall F\ ack)$. For the model checker we have to eleminate the $\forall$-quantifiers which yields the formula

$$\neg\ \exists F\ (\ req \wedge \neg ack \wedge \exists G\ \neg ack\ )$$

First we have to build the extended model Ext(M). In Fig. 4 all possible assumptions are listed, but not all of these actual assumption will occur on a computation path. Some of these assumptions are contradictory. In our example, at every instance only one of the uf-formulae uf_1, uf_2, and uf_3 will be relevant. This fact will reduce the size of the extended model. Ext(M) is shown in Fig. 5, where only the reachable states are given.

The dotted transitions are erased because a path via those transitions will violate some assumption. The next task is to check for every state (s,J) and input in whether there is some (fc, ASSM(J))-good path starting at that state. Hence we have to determine the strongly connected components of the transition graph. In our example we have only one component which is the whole state/transition-graph. It is obvious that all transition can be labelled with ($\exists$F**true**, J). Now let us consider the subformula $\exists G\ \neg ack$. To check which transition can be labelled with this subformula we have to consider the submodel consisting of those states satisfying $\neg$ack. It is shown in Fig. 6. The transitions $((s_5,\{3\}), \neg req, (s_0,\varnothing))$ and $((s_0,\varnothing), \neg req, (s_0,\varnothing))$ can be labelled with $(\exists G\ \neg ack, \{3\})$ resp. $(\exists G\ \neg ack, \varnothing)$. But there is no transition satisfying $\exists G \neg ack$ and req, thus no transition will be labelled with $(req \wedge \neg ack \wedge \exists G \neg ack)$, and thus there is no transition which will be labelled with $\exists F\ (req \wedge \neg ack \wedge \exists G \neg ack\ )$. Hence all transition will be labelled with the negation of this formula. This means that the

The initial assumption is given by

$$
\begin{array}{lcl}
assm & = & [] \, (req \wedge \neg ack \;\; \rightarrow \;\; [req \ \mathbf{unless} \ req \wedge ack]) \\
 & \wedge & [] \, (req \wedge ack \;\; \rightarrow \;\; \Diamond \neg req \ ) \\
 & \wedge & [] \, (\neg req \wedge ack \;\; \rightarrow \;\; [\neg req \ \mathbf{unless} \ \neg req \wedge \neg ack])
\end{array}
$$

If one condition is satisfied the corresponding consequence formula has to be added to the actual assumtions. These are the formulae

$$
\begin{array}{lcl}
uf_1 & = & [req \ \mathbf{unless} \ req \wedge ack]) \\
uf_2 & = & \Diamond \neg \ req \\
uf_3 & = & [\neg req \ \mathbf{unless} \ \neg req \wedge \neg ack])
\end{array}
$$

Hence the actual assumption will be one of the follwing 8 formulae

$assm$

$assm \wedge uf_1$

$assm \wedge uf_2$

$assm \wedge uf_3$

$assm \wedge uf_1 \wedge uf_2$

$assm \wedge uf_1 \wedge uf_3$

$assm \wedge uf_2 \wedge uf_3$

$assm \wedge uf_1 \wedge uf_2 \wedge uf_3$

Fig. 4

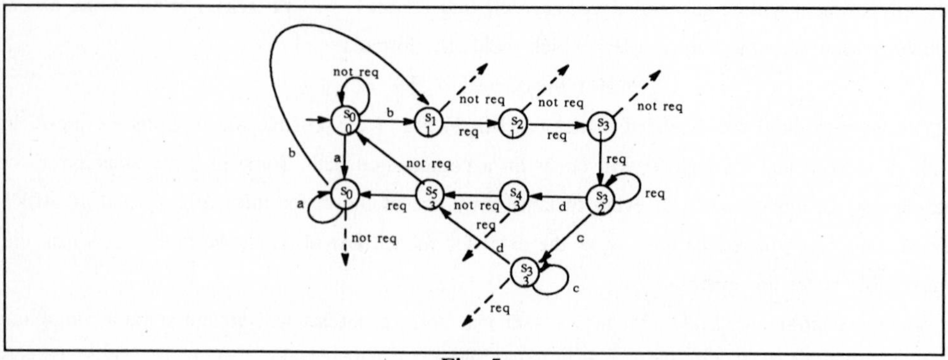

Fig. 5

given commitment is valid especially in state s_0 with all possible inputs.

The submodel for checking ∃G ¬ack:

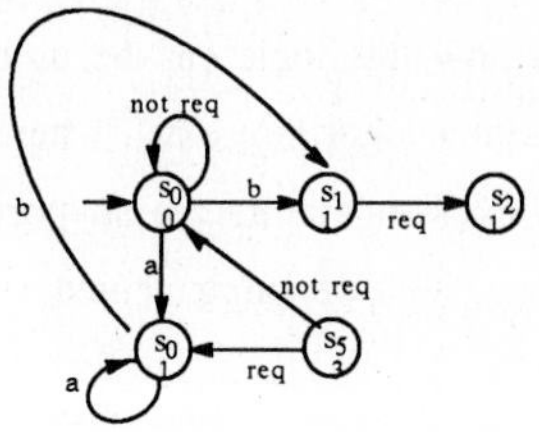

Fig. 6

A run of the implemented modelchecker of the discussed example is shown in Fig. 7.

```
>  mctl example.mod
              *************************************************
              *                                               *
              *        MCTL MODEL CHECKER (version 1.0)       *
              *                                               *
              *            1988           B. Josko            *
              *            University of Oldenburg            *
              *                                               *
              *************************************************

Reading state/transition graph for example
It has 6 states and 11 transitions.

Fairness Constraints: f1.
Fairness Constraints: f2.
Fairness Constraints: .
Assumptions: req & ~ack -> [req u req & ack].
Assumptions: req & ack -> F ~req.
Assumptions: ~req & ack -> [~req u ~req & ~ack].
Assumptions: .

time:  (usr: 16  sys: 6)

|= AG (req & ~ack -> AF ack).

The formula is true for all initial inputs.

time:  (usr: 9  sys: 1)


|= .
End of session.


>
```

Fig. 7

5 Conclusion

In this paper we have given a temporal logic MCTL and we have describe a model checking algorithm for this logic. We have demonstrated how this logic can be used for verification of reactive systems. An implementation of the model checking algorithm exist, where only simple fairness constraints and assumptions without nesting of until/unless-operators are supported. In an ongoing project the model checking algorithm for the full language will be implemented.

6 References

[AADL89] W. Damm, G. Döhmen, B. Josko, F. Korf, T. Peikenkamp: AADL Language Document. Internal report, University of Oldenburg, 1989

[BMP83] M. Ben-Ari, Z. Manna, A. Pnueli: The temporal logic of branching time. Acta Informatica 20, 207-226 (1983)

[CES83] E.M. Clarke, E.A. Emerson, A.P. Sistla: Automatic verification of finite-state concurrent systems using temporal logic specifications: a practical approach. Tenth ACM Symposium on Principles of Programming Languages, 117-126 (1983)

[DD90] W.Damm, G. Döhmen: AADL: A net based specification method for computer architecture design. in: de Bakker (Ed.): Languages for Parallel Architectures: Design, Semantics, and Implementation Models, Wiley & Sons (1990)

[DDGJ89] W. Damm, G. Döhmen, V. Gerstner, B. Josko: Modular verification of Petri nets: The temporal logic approach. REX Workshop on Stepwise Refinement of Distributed Systems: Models, Formalisms, Correctness. 1989

[EH85] E.A. Emerson, J.Y. Halpern: Decision procedures and expressiveness in the temporal logic of branching time. Journal of Computer and System Sciences 30, 1-24 (1985)

[EH86] E.A. Emerson, J.Y. Halpern: "Sometimes" and "not never" revisited: On branching versus linear time temporal logic. Journal of the ACM 33, 151-178 (1986)

[EL85] E.A. Emerson, C.L. Lei: Modalities for model checking: branching time logic strikes back. Technical Report, Dep. of Computer Sciences, University of Texas (1985)

[Jo87] B. Josko: Modelchecking of CTL formulae under liveness assumptions. Proceedings of 14th ICALP-Conference, Lecture Notes in Computer Science 267, 280 - 289 (1987)

[Jo89] B. Josko: Modelchecking of CTL formulae under liveness and safety assumptions. Internal report, University of Oldenburg (1989)

[MP81] Z. Manna, A. Pnueli: Verification of concurrent programs: The temporal framework. in: R,S. Boyer, J.S. Moore (Eds.): The Correctness Problem in Computer Science. Academic Press (1981)

[SC82] A.P. Sistla, E.M. Clarke: The complexity of propositional temporal logic. 14th ACM Symposium on Theory of Computing, 159-167 (1982)

[SC85] A.P. Sistla, E.M. Clarke: The complexity of propositional linear temporal logic. Journal of the ACM 32, 733-749 (1985)

[Ta72] R. Tarjan: Depth-first search and linear graph algorithms. SIAM Journal of Computing 1, 146-160 (1972)

Specialization in Logic Programming: from Horn Clause Logic to Prolog and Concurrent Prolog

Joost N. Kok
Åbo Akademi University
Lemminkäisenkatu 14
SF-20520 Turku
Finland

Abstract

ABSTRACT. A Prolog or a Concurrent Prolog program can be seen as a specialization or refinement of a program in Horn Clause Logic: In addition to the logic component a Prolog or Concurrent Prolog program contains information about the flow of control. In Prolog we have the cut statement and a leftmost depth first search strategy, in Concurrent Prolog we have read-only variables and commits. In this paper we study the flow of control of these languages by giving transition systems for abstract versions of Prolog, Horn Clause Logic and Concurrent Prolog. On the basis of these transition systems we define operational semantics for all three languages. Three basic sets (success set, finite failure set and the infinite failure set or divergence set) can be derived from the operational semantics. A comparison is made between the different sets: for Prolog we show that the success set and the finite failure sets of a Prolog program are smaller than the corresponding sets of a Horn Clause Logic program. The infinite failure sets are incomparable. A similar comparison is made between the success set and the finite failure sets for Horn Clause Logic and Concurrent Prolog. These comparisons give some feeling what happens if we put extra logical information in Horn Clause Logic programs.

Remark: part of the work was carried out in the ESPRIT Basic Research Action Integration.

Key words: Logic programming, operational semantics, Horn Clause Logic, Prolog, Concurrent Prolog, cut operator, backtracking, committed-choice, synchronization mechanisms.

CONTENTS

1 Introduction

2 Prolog

3 Horn Clause Logic

4 Concurrent Prolog

5 Comparison of the basic sets for Prolog, HCL and Concurrent Prolog

6 Conclusions and Future Work

1 Introduction

The ideal way of programming is to start from a specification and to derive in several refinement steps a program that can be executed efficiently. At first sight, logic programming seems to be very suited for this way of programming: the specification equals the program and there are no refinement steps needed. It turns out, however, that the programs we get in this way are not very efficient. Therefore in almost all realistic logic programming languages we have control components like the cut operator of Prolog, the commit operator and the synchronization mechanisms of concurrent logic languages and the different kinds of search strategies. Hence it requires at least one refinement step to go from a specification (a pure logic program) to a program say in Prolog in which we add the control component.

In this paper we look how the addition of control components influences the semantics of logic programs. Also we are interested how certain basis sets are related. The basis sets we consider are

1. the success set: This is the set of instantiations of atoms that (can) successfully terminate (those atoms which associated goal has a finite refutation). We instantiate the atoms with the computed answer substitutions.

2. the finite failure set: the set of atoms for which the execution can end in deadlock (atoms that can fail).

3. the infinite failure set: the set of atoms that can produce infinite computations. (Using a different terminology one might call this set the divergence set.)

These sets are defined in a formal way with the aid of transition systems.

These transition systems are defined for more abstract languages than Prolog, HCL and CP, but they can be seen as a kind of subsets of the abstract languages. In this paper we do not give introductions to the three languages.

The transition systems and the operational semantics that are derived from them focus on the flow of control of the three languages. There are different kinds of semantics that look at other aspects of the languages (for example denotational and declarative semantics). We do not consider them in this paper. One of the advantages of using more abstract languages is that the control aspects become more clear: the logic behind these languages is only used as far it influences the flow of control. In the case of Prolog we consider an extension of the cut operator. In Prolog the range of the cut operator is attached to the choice of a particular clause. We allow, in the abstract language, the choice of the scope of the cut operator. In the language for Concurrent Prolog we introduce a critical section. When a statement is placed in such a section, it behaves like an atomic action. The commit operator of Concurrent Prolog can be seen as a combination of a critical section and the sequential composition.

For the three languages we give transition systems. For Prolog we extend the normal notion of state: due to the backtracking we need to have some mechanism to restore old states. Also we have to keep track in the transition system if we are in a situation in which we execute a cut operator. In this case we have to throw away a certain number of alternatives. For HCL the transition system is relatively easy to give. The only problem is that we should specify a certain kind of fairness for the merge operator. We do this by doing always a step from the left component of a merge and after each step we switch the components. For Concurrent Prolog the transition system has to take care of the critical sections: from a number of steps we derive one step. Another interesting point is the introduction of deadlock rules. Due to the introduction of critical sections we now have the possibility that a statement both can deadlock and succeed. Deadlock is then not a derived notion in the sense that we can derive it from the normal (non deadlocking) transitions.

After giving the three transition systems, we define the three basic sets. In the last section we compare the corresponding sets for (Concurrent) Prolog and Horn Clause Logic.

2 Prolog

In this section we describe the semantics of PROLOG in an operational way. Other examples of such descriptions can be found in [AB87, JM84, DM87, dBdV89]. We use the style of Structured Operational Semantics (SOS) (see [HP79, Plo81]). First an analysis is made about what steps we can do from a configuration. A configuration is a tuple of a state and a statement, a step is the execution of an elementary action. Steps (transitions) relate configurations: if configurations (s_1, σ_1) and (s_2, σ_2) are related then s_1 can perform in state σ_1 an elementary action, changing to state σ_2. The statement s_2 gives the rest of the computation still to be done. Often the transitions are defined with the aid of a transition system: a formal system made up of axioms and rules. In general, the axioms give the transitions for basic statements (the elementary actions) and the rules then show how to derive transitions for more complicated statements.

Our approach has the following distinguishing features (compared with other operational approaches for Prolog): it seperates statements and states and it is defined for a more abstract language than Prolog.

We start by giving the set of statements. The notation $(x \in)X$ introduces the set X with typical element x ranging over X.

Definition 2.1 *Let $(A \in)$ Atom, be the set of atomic formulae. Let $(s \in)$ Stat be the set statements specified by*

$$s ::= A_1 = A_2 \mid A \mid ! \mid s_1; s_2 \mid s_1 \Box s_2 \mid [s_1]$$

We explain later how Prolog can be seen as a subset of this language. We have several kinds of statements, which have the following intuition:

- $A_1 = A_2$ is the atomic action: we have to unify the atoms A_1 and A_2

- A is a kind of procedure call: when we execute it we replace it by a statement
- $s_1; s_2$ is the sequential composition of two statements
- $s_1 \Box s_2$ gives an alternative for s_1: we first try to execute s_1, but when this fails we try s_2
- ! is the cut operator. The range of it is restricted by square brackets (as in $[s_1]$). It throws away all alternatives as long as it does not encounter these square brackets.

Next we introduce the notion of a state $\sigma \in \Sigma$. Basically it consists of the set of substitutions. It is more complicated, because during execution of statement we also have to keep track of previous states: when we backtrack we need to restore old states.

Definition 2.2 $\quad \sigma ::= \theta \in \mathit{Subst} \mid \sigma_1 \Diamond \sigma_2$

The definition of the operational semantics will be based on a transition system. Here, a transition is a tuple in $(\mathit{Stat} \times \Sigma) \times ((\mathit{Stat} \times \Sigma) \cup \{E\})$, written in the notation

$$(s, \sigma) \to (s', \sigma')$$

or

$$(s, \sigma) \to E.$$

Moreover, we are allowed to decorate the arrows with one or more elements from the set

$$\mathit{Label} = \mathit{Subst} \cup \{\delta, !\}$$

The symbol E is called the empty statement and stands for termination.

The procedure call corresponds to the rewriting of an atom in a Prolog goal by using the clauses of the Prolog program. This procedure call has the form of an atom A. Given the present state σ, a function *stm* dependent on A and σ determines the statement by which A should be replaced. As we will see in the next definition, if we tune the transition system towards a Prolog program W, then we pick a particular statement stm_W which

1. gives the scope of the ! operator
2. considers the clauses in a certain order and evaluates the atoms in a goal sequentially from left to right.

As an example, consider the statement A. Assume given a Prolog program of two clauses. The associated statement is then of the form $[s_1 \Box s_2]$, where s_1 corresponds to the first clause and s_2 corresponds to the second clause. The left-choice $s_1 \Box s_2$ is put between square brackets that limit the scope of cuts inside s_1 and s_2. (The left-choice $s_1 \Box s_2$ is like a normal choice, but it tries first the left hand side.) A statement associated to a clause $H \leftarrow A_1, A_2$ is constructed as follows: first unify A with the head of the clause H and compose this sequentially with $A_1; A_2$ (giving the statement $(A = H); A_1; A_2$). In this explanation we did not take into account that A can already be instantiated with a substitution θ: in the statement we should replace $A = H$ by $A\theta = H$.

In this way (by giving the function *stm*) we can use the transition system for giving an operational meaning to a Prolog program. In the next sections we will follow similar procedures for the languages Horn Clause Logic and Concurrent Prolog. This method focuses on the flow of control aspects of the language. There are other kinds of semantics for logic languages that model the logic aspects. For comparative studies for the language HCL we refer to [AvE82, dBKPR89].

Hence the transition system will be parametrized with respect to the function *stm*. We take as elementary actions the unification of atoms. In statements we can use sequential composition, left-choice, a cut operator and a kind of procedure call. We can choose the scope of the cut operator by using square brackets. (In Prolog an implicit choice is made for the scope of the cut.)

Now we introduce stm_W. This function gives the link with PROLOG. If we want to look what steps we can make from an atom A in a goal in a state θ we look at what steps we can make from $stm_W(A,\theta)$. Hence $stm_W(A,\theta)$ can be seen as the procedure body for the procedure call A.

Definition 2.3 *Let* $W = \{C_1,\ldots,C_n\}$ *be a Prolog program. Then the statement* $stm_W(A,\theta)$ *is defined as follows:*

$$stm_W(A,\theta) = [f(A\theta,C_1)\square\cdots\square f(A\theta,C_n)]$$

where

$$f(A, H \leftarrow B_1,\ldots,B_n) = (A = H); B_1;\ldots;B_n$$

Example 2.4 *Consider the following Prolog program* W*:*

$$p(x) \leftarrow !, q(x)$$

$$p(a) \leftarrow$$

Then

$$stm_W(p(x),\{x/b\}) = [p(b) = p(x); !; q(x)\square p(b) = p(a)]$$

We present a formal transition system T which consists of axioms (in one of the forms above) or rules, of the form

$$\frac{(s_1,\sigma_1) \rightarrow (s_1',\sigma_1')}{(s_2,\sigma_2) \rightarrow (s_2',\sigma_2')}$$

in which both (s_1',σ_1') and (s_2',σ_2') can be replaced by E and the arrows can have labels. Transitions which are given as axioms hold by definition. Moreover, a transition which is the consequence of a rule holds whenever it can be established that its premise holds. We give some intuition for the different kind of transitions. The intuitive meaning of a transitions depends on the kind of label(s).

$$(s_1,\sigma_1) \rightarrow (s_1',\sigma_1'):$$

from s_1 we can make a step and after this step we continue with s_1'.

$$(s_1,\sigma_1)\xrightarrow{\theta}(s_1',\sigma_1'):$$

from s_1 we can make a step in which the computation terminates (yielding answer substitution θ). If we want to have more answer substitutions we can continue with s_1' (which sums up the alternatives). This should be contrasted with

$$(s_1,\sigma_1)\xrightarrow{\theta}E$$

where we have the empty statement E on the right hand side: that is termination. Another possibility is deadlock:

$$(s_1,\sigma_1)\xrightarrow{\delta}E$$

we can not make a step from the configuration (s_1, σ_1). If a transition is labeled with δ then we always have the empty statement on the right hand side. We extend the labeling with ! if the present step passes through a cut operator.

After the definition of the axioms and the rules we give some more explanation.

Axioms:

$$(A_1 = A_2, \theta) \xrightarrow{\theta'} E \text{ where } \theta' = mgu(A_1, A_2)\theta$$

$$(A_1 = A_2, \theta) \xrightarrow{\delta} E \text{ if } A_1 \text{ and } A_2 \text{ do not unify}$$

$$(!, \theta) \xrightarrow{\theta!} E$$

Rules:

$$\frac{(s_1, \sigma_1) \xrightarrow{\theta} (s_2, \sigma_2)}{(s_1; s, \sigma_1) \longrightarrow (s \Diamond (s_2; s), \theta \Diamond \sigma_2)}$$
$$(s_1 \Box s, \sigma_1) \xrightarrow{\theta} (s_2 \Diamond s, \sigma_2 \Diamond \sigma_1)$$
$$(A, \sigma_1) \xrightarrow{\theta} (s_2, \sigma_2) \text{ if } s_1 = stm_W(A, \sigma_1) \wedge \sigma_1 \in Subst$$
$$([s_1], \sigma_1) \xrightarrow{\theta} ([s_2], \sigma_2)$$
$$(s_1 \Diamond s, \sigma_1 \Diamond \sigma) \xrightarrow{\theta} (s_2 \Diamond s, \sigma_2 \Diamond \sigma)$$

$$\frac{(s_1, \sigma_1) \xrightarrow{\theta} E}{(s_1; s, \sigma_1) \longrightarrow (s, \theta)}$$
$$(s_1 \Box s, \sigma_1) \xrightarrow{\theta} (s, \sigma_1)$$
$$(A, \sigma) \xrightarrow{\theta} E \text{ if } s_1 = stm_W(A, \sigma) \wedge \sigma \in Subst$$
$$([s_1], \sigma_1) \xrightarrow{\theta} E$$
$$(s_1 \Diamond s, \sigma_1 \Diamond \sigma) \xrightarrow{\theta} (s, \sigma)$$

$$\frac{(s_1, \sigma_1) \xrightarrow{\delta} E}{(s_1; s, \sigma_1) \xrightarrow{\delta} E}$$
$$(s_1 \Box s, \sigma_1) \longrightarrow (s, \sigma_1)$$
$$(A, \sigma) \xrightarrow{\delta} E \text{ if } s_1 = stm_W(A, \sigma) \wedge \sigma \in Subst$$
$$([s_1], \sigma_1) \xrightarrow{\delta} E$$
$$(s_1 \Diamond s, \sigma_1 \Diamond \sigma) \longrightarrow (s, \sigma)$$

$$\frac{(s_1, \sigma_1) \xrightarrow{\theta!} E}{(s_1; s, \sigma_1) \xrightarrow{!} (s, \theta)}$$
$$(s_1 \Box s, \sigma_1) \xrightarrow{\theta!} E$$
$$(A, \sigma) \xrightarrow{\theta!} E \text{ if } s_1 = stm_W(A, \sigma) \wedge \sigma \in Subst$$
$$([s_1], \sigma_1) \xrightarrow{\theta} E$$
$$(s_1 \Diamond s, \sigma_1 \Diamond \sigma) \xrightarrow{\theta!} E$$

$$\frac{(s_1, \sigma_1) \longrightarrow (s_2, \sigma_2)}{(s_1; s, \sigma_1) \longrightarrow (s_2; s, \sigma_2)}$$
$$(s_1 \Box s, \sigma_1) \longrightarrow (s_2 \Diamond s, \sigma_2 \Diamond \sigma_1)$$
$$(A, \sigma_1) \longrightarrow (s_2, \sigma_2) \text{ if } s_1 = stm_W(A, \sigma_1) \wedge \sigma_1 \in Subst$$
$$([s_1], \sigma_1) \longrightarrow ([s_2], \sigma_2)$$
$$(s_1 \Diamond s, \sigma_1 \Diamond \sigma) \longrightarrow (s_2 \Diamond s, \sigma_2 \Diamond \sigma)$$

$$\frac{(s_1,\sigma_1)\xrightarrow{!}(s_2,\sigma_2)}{\begin{array}{l}(s_1;s,\sigma_1)\xrightarrow{!}(s_2;s,\sigma_2)\\(s_1\Box s,\sigma_1)\xrightarrow{!}(s_2,\sigma_2)\\(A,\sigma_1)\xrightarrow{!}(s_2,\sigma_2)\ \textit{if}\ s_1 = stm_W(A,\sigma_1)\wedge\sigma_1\in \textit{Subst}\\([s_1],\sigma_1)\longrightarrow([s_2],\sigma_2)\\(s_1\Diamond s,\sigma_1\Diamond\sigma)\xrightarrow{!}(s_2,\sigma_2)\end{array}}$$

A feature of this transition system is the introduction of the $\Diamond$ operator both in states and statements. It is introduced to have a mechanism to remember states. If we execute the statement $s_1\Box s_2$ in state σ then we look if we can do a step from s_1 (that changes possibly σ say to σ'). If this computation fails at a later stage, then we still have the alternative s_2 left. If we want to backtrack, then we should return to the state σ. In the transition system we indicate that we remember a state by changing $\Box$ to $\Diamond$. If we start with a statement without $\Diamond$ then we always have the same number of $\Diamond$ in the state and the statement.

Next we discuss the cut ! operator. When we execute it, then we label the arrow with a ! in the transition. When we construct transitions for more complicated statements from a transition labeled by !, then we throw alternatives (indicated by $\Box$ and $\Diamond$) away. This goes on till we meet a pair of brackets (the scope delimiters of the cut). At this point we remove the ! label from the transition.

To give some feeling for this transition system, we give the following (rather abstract) example.

Example 2.5 *Assume that a, b, c, d are statements of the form $A_1 = A_2$. First we give a transition sequence from the statement*

$$(a\Box b);(c\Box d)$$

omitting the state components of the configurations and in which we assume that a, b, c, d always succeed. We encounter two kinds of transitions: unlabeled and labeled by a substitution. Here we represent them by $\longrightarrow$ and $\xrightarrow{\theta}$, respectively. This does not imply that all substitutions used in different transitions are the same.

$$(a\Box b);(c\Box d)\longrightarrow$$

$$(c\Box d)\Diamond(b;(c\Box d))\xrightarrow{\theta}$$

$$d\Diamond(b;(c\Box d))\xrightarrow{\theta}$$

$$b;(c\Box d)\longrightarrow$$

$$c\Diamond d\xrightarrow{\theta}$$

$$d\xrightarrow{\theta}$$

$$E$$

Next we consider a transition sequence from

$$(a\Box b);[!\Box d]\longrightarrow$$

$$[!\Box d]\Diamond(b;[!\Box d])\xrightarrow{\theta}$$

$b; [!\Box d] \xrightarrow{\theta}$

$[!\Box d] \xrightarrow{\theta}$

E

We proceed with the definition of the operational semantics $\mathcal{O}$. Let *id* be the identity substitution.

Definition 2.6 *The mapping* $\mathcal{O} : Stat \rightarrow Subst^+ \cup Subst^* \cdot \{\delta, \perp\} \cup Subst^\omega$ *is given by*

$$\mathcal{O}[\![s]\!] = \begin{cases} \theta_1 \cdots \theta_n & \textit{if } (s, id) \cdots \xrightarrow{\theta_1} \cdots \xrightarrow{\theta_n} E \\ \theta_1 \cdots \theta_n \perp & \textit{if } (s, id) \cdots \xrightarrow{\theta_1} \cdots \xrightarrow{\theta_n} \cdots \ (\textit{no more substitutions}) \\ \theta_1 \cdots \delta & \textit{if } (s, id) \cdots \xrightarrow{\theta_1} \cdots \xrightarrow{\delta} E \\ \theta_1 \cdots \theta_n \cdots & \textit{if } (s, id) \cdots \xrightarrow{\theta_1} \cdots \xrightarrow{\theta_n} \cdots (\textit{infinite number of substitutions}) \end{cases}$$

The second and the fourth case of this definition should be understand as follows. In the second case we have an infinite number of transitions, but only a finite number is labeled with a substitution. In the fourth case we have an infinite number of transitions and an infinite number of substitutions.

The next definition gives the three basic sets. This definition is an extension given and explained in [LMP89] of the definition given by [Llo87]. It contains all the atoms that have a finite refutation instantiated with the computed answer substitution. The set *EAtom* is a subset of *Atom* in which we have only atoms of the form $p(\bar{x})$ (that is, besides the predicate symbol only variables).

Definition 2.7 $SS = \{p(\bar{x})\theta : \mathcal{O}[\![p(\bar{x})]\!] = \cdots \theta \cdots \wedge p(\bar{x}) \in EAtom\}$

$FFS = \{A : \mathcal{O}[\![A]\!] = \delta\}$

$IFS = \{A : \mathcal{O}[\![A]\!] = \perp\}$

Note that in the *FFS* and *IFS* case we only take those atoms that go into a finitely failing or infinite computation immediately (not first delivering some answer substitutions).

3 Horn Clause Logic

For Horn Clause Logic we follow a similar path as for Prolog. We define an abstract language and for this language we define a transition system. We show how HCL can be seen as an instance of this language and how to derive the three sets. The main difference with Prolog is that we do not have the cut operator around and its associated brackets. Also we have the freedom to choose our own search strategy (as long as it is fair). In order to indicate this we introduce the $\|$ operator. However, in the transition system we will restrict us to one particular fair search strategy. This restriction does not influence the semantics (cf. the square lemma in [Llo87]). Let $(s \in)$ *Stat* be the set statements specified by

$$s ::= A_1 = A_2 \mid A \mid s_1; s_2 \mid s_1 + s_2 \mid s_1 \parallel s_2$$

Before we give the transition system we introduce the function stm_W for Horn Clause Logic.

Definition 3.1 *Let* $W = \{C_1, \ldots, C_n\}$ *be a HCL program. Then the statement* $stm_W(A, \theta)$ *is defined as follows:*

$$stm_W(A,\theta) = f(A\theta, C_1) + \cdots + f(A\theta, C_n)$$

where

$$f(A, H \leftarrow B_1, \ldots, B_n) = (A = H); B_1 \parallel \ldots \parallel B_n$$

Next we present the transition system:

Axiom:

$$(A_1 = A_2, \theta) \longrightarrow (E, mgu(A_1, A_2)\theta)$$

Rules:

$$\frac{(s,\theta) \longrightarrow (E,\theta')}{\begin{array}{l}(A,\theta) \longrightarrow (E,\theta') \text{ if } s = stm_W(A,\theta)\\ (s; s_1, \theta) \longrightarrow (s_1, \theta')\\ (s + s_1, \theta) \longrightarrow (E, \theta')\\ (s_1 + s, \theta) \longrightarrow (E, \theta')\\ (s \parallel s_1, \theta) \longrightarrow (s_1, \theta')\end{array}}$$

$$\frac{(s,\theta) \longrightarrow (s',\theta')}{\begin{array}{l}(A,\theta) \longrightarrow (s',\theta') \text{ if } s = stm_W(A,\theta)\\ (s; s_1, \theta) \longrightarrow (s'; s_1, \theta')\\ (s + s_1, \theta) \longrightarrow (s', \theta')\\ (s_1 + s, \theta) \longrightarrow (s', \theta')\\ (s \parallel s_1, \theta) \longrightarrow (s_1 \parallel s', \theta')\end{array}}$$

Note that we choose a selection rule by defining the $\parallel$ in a deterministic (but fair) way: when we want to do a step from $s_1 \parallel s_2$ then we first do a step from the left component s_1, say to s_1', and we swap the arguments $s_2 \parallel s_1'$. Hence if we continue with $s_2 \parallel s_1'$ then we will do a step from s_2.

The main differences with the PROLOG transition system are

1. a different function stm_W: there is no cut operator in HCL and hence there are no brackets needed;
2. we have a nondeterministic choice $+$ instead of the deterministic choice $\Box$ (there is no ordering on the clauses in HCL);
3. we do not model backtracking in the transition system: therefore it is not necesary to introduce the $\Diamond$ operator in statements and states;
4. the fair selection rule.

The operational semantics is derived from the transition system:

Definition 3.2 $\quad \mathcal{O}[\![s]\!] = \{\theta : (s, id) \longrightarrow^* (E, \theta)\} \cup \{\bot : (s, id) \longrightarrow \cdots\}$

Note that we only add $\bot$ to $\mathcal{O}[\![s]\!]$ if there is an infinite sequence of transitions from s.

The three basic sets are given in

Definition 3.3 $\quad SS = \{p(\bar{x})\theta : \theta \in \mathcal{O}[\![p(\bar{x})]\!] \wedge p(\bar{x}) \in EAtom\}$

$$FFS = \{A : \mathcal{O}[\![A]\!] = \emptyset\}$$

$$IFS = \{A : \mathcal{O}[\![A]\!] = \{\bot\}\}$$

4 Concurrent Prolog

As a next step we look at a version of the language Concurrent Prolog. Concurrent Prolog is a family of languages, which can be classified according to whether or not certain features in the language are present. For an overview of CP (and also related languages) see [Sha89]. This section is based on [dBK88, dBK89, KK89]. Let ($s \in$) *Stat* be the set statements specified by

$$s ::= A_1 = A_2 \mid A \mid s_1; s_2 \mid s_1 + s_2 \mid s_1 \parallel s_2 \mid \langle s_1 \rangle$$

Compared to the language used for HCL, we have added a *critical section* $\langle s_1 \rangle$ which considers s_1 as an elementary action. In Concurrent Prolog we have a commit operator $|$. In the language above we can express the commit by $s_1|s_2 = \langle s_1 \rangle; s_2$. These critical sections influence the choice operator: when we have a choice $s_1 + s_2$ between two statements we look if statements s_1 and s_2 can do a first step. In case s_i is of the form $\langle s_i' \rangle; s_i''$ ($i = 1, 2$) then the first steps can complicated: we have to look if s_i' terminates or not.

Before we give the transition system we introduce the function stm_W for Concurrent Prolog. This gives us again the link between the abstract language and Concurrent Prolog.

Definition 4.1 *Let $W = \{C_1, \ldots, C_n\}$ be a Concurrent Prolog program. Then the statement $stm_W(A, \theta$ is defined as follows:*

$$stm_W(A, \theta) = f(A\theta, C_1) + \cdots + f(A\theta, C_n)$$

where

$$f(A, H \leftarrow B_1, \ldots, B_n | B_{n+1}, \ldots, B_m) = \langle (A = H); B_1 \parallel \ldots \parallel B_n \rangle; B_{n+1} \parallel \ldots \parallel B_m$$

In Concurrent Prolog there is a special functor ? of arity 1. A term of the form $?(x)$, where x is a variable, is called a read-only variable. A read-only variable can be part of an atom in a conjunctive goal. The atom is not allowed to instantiate the variable with a non-variable term itself: a different atom in the goal should do this. In the transition system we take care of this by defining an extension $mgu_?$ of mgu. It is only defined if the unification of the atoms succeeds and the read-only constraints are satisfied. For more details and the definition we refer to [Sha88, Sar89, Sha89]. Next we present the transition system:

Axiom:

$$(A_1 = A_2, \theta) \longrightarrow (E, mgu_?(A_1, A_2)\theta)$$

Rules:

$$\frac{(s, \theta) \longrightarrow (E, \theta')}{\begin{array}{l} (A, \theta) \longrightarrow (E, \theta') \text{ if } s = stm_W(A, \theta) \\ (s; s_1, \theta) \longrightarrow (s_1, \theta') \\ (s + s_1, \theta) \longrightarrow (E, \theta') \\ (s_1 + s, \theta) \longrightarrow (E, \theta') \\ (s \parallel s_1, \theta) \longrightarrow (s_1, \theta') \end{array}}$$

$$\frac{(s, \theta) \longrightarrow (s', \theta')}{\begin{array}{l} (A, \theta) \longrightarrow (s', \theta') \text{ if } s = stm_W(A, \theta) \\ (s; s_1, \theta) \longrightarrow (s'; s_1, \theta') \\ (s + s_1, \theta) \longrightarrow (s', \theta') \\ (s_1 + s, \theta) \longrightarrow (s', \theta') \\ (s_1 \parallel s, \theta) \longrightarrow (s_1 \parallel s', \theta') \\ (s \parallel s_1, \theta) \longrightarrow (s' \parallel s_1, \theta') \end{array}}$$

Note that the merge is now defined in a nondeterministic way. We extend the transition system with a rule for $\langle s \rangle$. If we can do a finite number of steps from s and terminate, then $\langle s \rangle$ can terminate in one step.

$$\frac{(s,\theta) \longrightarrow^* (E,\theta')}{(\langle s \rangle,\theta) \longrightarrow (E,\theta')}$$

From the transition system as it is now we can derive the success set. It is not possible to derive the finite and infinite failure sets. For the finite failure case we extend the transition system with deadlock rules. It is not possible to derive this information from the previous transitions.

$$(A_1 = A_2,\theta) \longrightarrow (E,\delta) \textit{ if } A_1 \textit{ and } A_2 \textit{ do not unify}$$

$$\frac{(s,\theta) \longrightarrow (E,\delta)}{\begin{array}{l}(A,\theta) \longrightarrow (E,\delta) \textit{ if } s = stm_W(A,\theta)\\ (s;s_1,\theta) \longrightarrow (E,\delta)\end{array}}$$

$$\frac{(s,\theta) \longrightarrow^* (E,\delta)}{(\langle s \rangle,\theta) \longrightarrow (E,\delta)}$$

$$\frac{(s_1,\theta) \longrightarrow (E,\delta) \wedge (s_2,\theta) \longrightarrow (E,\delta)}{\begin{array}{l}(s_1 + s_2,\theta) \longrightarrow (E,\delta)\\ (s_1 \parallel s_2,\theta) \longrightarrow (E,\delta)\end{array}}$$

Note that a statement s can now both deadlock and terminate. Take for example $s = \langle a;b + a;a \rangle$ where a is a unification that always succeeds and b one that always fails. From s we can fail by choosing the left component and succeed by choosing the right component. Both choices are allowed because it is possible to do a first step both of $a;b$ and $a;a$. In the last rule we only have deadlock in a $+$ or $\parallel$ if both arguments can deadlock.

The operational semantics is derived from the transition system:

Definition 4.2 $\quad \mathcal{O}[\![s]\!] = \{\theta : (s,id) \longrightarrow^* (E,\theta)\} \cup \{\delta : (s,id) \longrightarrow^* (E,\delta)\}$

Definition 4.3 $\quad SS = \{p(\bar{x})\theta : \theta \in \mathcal{O}[\![p(\bar{x})]\!] \wedge p(\bar{x}) \in EAtom\}$

$$FFS = \{A : \delta \in \mathcal{O}[\![A]\!]\}$$

We do not give the infinite failure set here. If we want to define it we have to introduce new rules in the transition system and, moreover, there are some problems associated with fairness.

5 Comparison of the basic sets for Prolog, HCL and Concurrent Prolog

We first explain how to derive from a statement used in the section on PROLOG a statement for HCL program. We do this by replacing every cut operator by the atom **true**, removing all the square brackets and replacing $\Box$ by $+$. For a given PROLOG program W we can compare the sets SS, FFS, IFS with the same sets for the derived HCL program W'. For the next definition fix a program W. We call the sets SS, FFS, IFS of W $SS_{PROLOG}, FFS_{PROLOG}, IFS_{PROLOG}$ and the sets SS, FFS, IFS of the derived HCL program $SS_{HCL}, FFS_{HCL}, IFS_{HCL}$. We have the following theorem.

Theorem 5.1 *1.* $SS_{PROLOG} \subseteq SS_{HCL}$

2. $FFS_{PROLOG} \subseteq FFS_{HCL}$

3. IFS_{PROLOG} *is incomparable with* IFS_{HCL}

Given a program in the abstract language for Concurrent Prolog we can derive program in the abstract HCL language by removing all the critical sections.

Theorem 5.2 *1.* $SS_{CONCURRENT\ PROLOG} \subseteq SS_{HCL}$

2. $FFS_{HCL} \subseteq FFS_{CONCURRENT\ PROLOG}$

6 Conclusions and Future Work

We studied the operational semantics of three logic languages by considering more abstract languages. For all three languages we can find in the literature several other semantic models. It would be interesting to see how these models also work on the more abstract level. At the moment there are several ways to derive denotational semantics from transition systems. We currently look if these techniques can be applied in our case. We also consider the possibility to put these abstract languages in a formal refinement calculus.

References

[AB87] B. Arbab and D.M. Berry. Operational and denotational semantics of prolog. *Journal of Logic Programming*, 4:309–330, 1987.

[AvE82] K.R. Apt and M.H. van Emden. Contributions to the theory of logic programming. *JACM*, 29(3):841–862, 1982.

[dBdV89] A. de Bruin and E. de Vink. Continuation semantics for prolog with cut. In J. Diaz and F. Orejas, editors, *Proceedings CAAP 89*, volume 351 of *Lecture Notes in Computer Science*, pages 178–192, 1989.

[dBK88] J.W. de Bakker and J.N. Kok. Uniform abstraction, atomicity and contractions in the comparative semantics of concurrent prolog. In *Proc. Fifth Generation Computer Systems (FGCS 88)*, pages 347–355, Tokyo, Japan, 1988. Extended Abstract, full version available as CWI report CS-8834.

[dBK89] J.W. de Bakker and J.N. Kok. Comparative semantics for concurrent prolog. *Theoretical Computer Sciene*, 1989. To appear.

[dBKPR89] F.S. de Boer, J.N. Kok, C. Palamidessi, and J.J.M.M. Rutten. From failure to success: Comparing a denotational and a declarative semantics for horn clause logic. Technical Report CS-R89.., Centre for Mathematics and Computer Science, Amsterdam, 1989.

[DM87] S.K. Debray and P. Mishra. Denotational and operational semantics for prolog. In M. Wirsing, editor, *Formal Description of Programming Concepts III*, pages 245–269. North-Holland, 1987.

[HP79] M. Hennessy and G.D. Plotkin. Full abstraction for a simple parallel programming language. In J. Becvar, editor, *Proceedings Mathematical Foundations of Computer Science (MFCS 79)*, volume 74 of *Lecture Notes in Computer Science*, pages 108–120. Springer Verlag, 1979.

[JM84] N.D. Jones and A. Mycroft. Stepwise development of operational and denotational semantics for prolog. In *Proceedings International Symposium on Logic Programming (ICLP 84)*, pages 281–288. IEEE, 1984.

[KK89] P. Knijnenburg and J.N. Kok. A compositional semantics for the finite and infinite failures of a language with atomized statements. Technical report, University of Utrecht, 1989. To appear in proceedings CSN 89.

[Llo87] J.W. Lloyd. *Foundations of Logic Programming.* Springer Verlag, 1987. Second edition.

[LMP89] G. Levi, M. Martelli, and C. Palamidesssi. A logic programming semantics scheme. Technical report, Dipartimento di Informatica, Università di Pisa, 1989.

[Plo81] G.D. Plotkin. A structural approach to operational semantics. Technical Report DAIMI FN-19, Aarhus Univ., Comp.Sci.Dept., 1981.

[Sar89] V.A. Saraswat. *Concurrent Constraint Programming Languages.* PhD thesis, Carnegie-Mellon University, 1989.

[Sha88] E.Y. Shapiro. *Concurrent Prolog: Collected Papers*, volume 1-2. MIT press, 1988.

[Sha89] E.Y. Shapiro. The family of concurrent logic programming languages. Technical Report CS 89-09, Department of Applied Mathematics and Computer Science, The Weizmann Institute of Science, Rehovot 76100, Israel, 1989.

Analysis of Discrete Event Coordination

R. P. Kurshan
AT&T Bell Laboratories
Murray Hill, New Jersey 07974

ABSTRACT

A *reduction* is a validity-preserving transformation by which a complex assertion about a complex model may be replaced by a simpler assertion about a simpler model in such a way that the validity of the latter implies the validity of the former. Reductions, in that they are relative to the property to be proved, are significantly more powerful than equivalence and minimization, and are needed to reason about complex coordinating systems. Furthermore, reduction subsumes *refinement*: a model M refines or "implements" a model M' provided M' reduces M relative to all assertions about M which are pullbacks of assertions in M' (so anything proved about M' remains true in the refinement M).

On account of the close relationship between state machines and automata, it is conceptually convenient to reason about reductions of state machine models in the context of formal assertions based in language (automata) theory. However, as a practical matter, state machine models have been felt to have overwhelming drawbacks. First of all, it has been felt that significant hardware and software systems are simply too complex to capture in a meaningful way, through state machine models. Second, even if they could be captured, the complexity of the resulting model has been thought to be too great to analyze: the complexity of the analysis algorithms aside, the size of the resulting state spaces, growing geometrically with the number of system components, has been thought to render analysis intractable in practice. The purpose of this paper is to dispel both of these notions. It is shown how large, complex systems may be modelled accurately in terms of (many) small coordinating component state machines. Second, it is shown how a theory of reduction based upon language homomorphism can render analysis and refinement of such models tractable.

Keywords: *formal verification, reduction, refinement, homomorphism, coordination analysis*

1. Introduction

Continuous-time processes such as asynchronous distributed controllers as well as intrinsically discrete-time distributed processes may coordinate according to discrete events. When such coordination is a significant factor in a system's behavior, its analysis can be extremely difficult in practice: whereas conventional computer programs are serial and deterministic, distributed programs involve branching created by parallelism and non-determinism, resulting in a diversity of possible behaviors which grows geometrically with increasing time.

Formal verification of such processes has been thrust to the forefront by researchers interested in the problem of how to develop control-intensive computer hardware and software so that it works properly. The primary basis for this thrust is the failure of classical methods centered around simulation to cope with increasingly complex coordination problems, brought on by asynchrony and distributed control. It is now standard among theoreticians to analyze such coordination in the context of formal assertions founded in logic, formal language theory and general mathematical reasoning, employing a variety of modelling paradigms such as finite state machines, Petri nets, process algebras, partial orders and so on. Given a modelling paradigm and a formal assertion context such as logic or language theory, a relationship is drawn between the assertion context and the modelling paradigm, in order through formal assertions to draw conclusions about the models. While recent work has spawned a large number of interesting and varied ideas, only a very small number of these truly address the original problem of developing properly functioning programs.

The reason for this seems to be that in order truly to address this problem, one needs a methodology which embraces three objectives simultaneously: formal verification, complexity management and formal refinement, as follows. Formal verification, the basis upon which one determines whether development objectives have been met, has a utility which may be measured by expressiveness (what class of properties can be verified), mitigated by the complexity of the verification methodology. There may be a tradeoff between expressiveness and complexity: the more expressive the formal framework, the more complex and hence less useful the methodology. To address the original problem as a practical matter, one seeks the most expressive framework in which one can deal with verification tractably in a largely algorithmic fashion. As the formal framework in any case introduces a high level of complexity, there must be techniques built into the methodology which can circumvent this complexity; otherwise, the methodology is intractable and the original problem remains unsolved. Finally, to solve the original problem, one needs a methodology to map a design specification to an implementation. Such a mapping, commonly known as a *refinement* mapping, is needed to guarantee that properties verified in a design remain true in an implementation. (Practice has shown that the process of implementation of a design is no less a source of errors than conceptual flaws in the design itself.) These three objectives: verification, complexity management and refinement are like three legs of a stool supporting development of properly functioning hardware and software: less any leg, the support is questionable.

This paper presents a methodology founded in automata theory which encompasses verification, complexity management and refinement. Verification is cast in terms of testing whether the formal language $\mathcal{L}(D)$ of a design specification D is contained in the formal language $\mathcal{L}(T)$ of a "task" T which is to be performed by the design. Complexity management and refinement both are cast in terms of transformations called "reductions". Design specifications D are modelled by state machines, while tasks T are defined by automata.

In order to test whether $\mathcal{L}(D) \subset \mathcal{L}(T)$, one may reduce D, *relative to* T, to a less complex D' with an associated less complex T' such that

$$\mathcal{L}(D') \subset \mathcal{L}(T') \Rightarrow \mathcal{L}(D) \subset \mathcal{L}(T) . \tag{1.1}$$

The reduction of D to D', in that it is relative to the task T to be verified, is significantly more powerful than equivalence and minimization. For example, suppose that T refers only to the parity of outputs $1, \ldots, N$ of D; then, in order to test whether D performs the task T, D may be simplified by abstracting its N output values to 2 values: (*odd* and *even*), although this reduction of D is not equivalent to D and D may be minimal up to equivalence.

The basic concept of "reduction" is as old as mathematics: reduce the amount of effort needed to prove a result by eliminating extraneous or redundant details. To one extent or another, it is used in most actual efforts concerned with the analysis or simulation of real systems. However, it is important to give this basic concept a precise embodiment, whose *validity can be verified algorithmically*. In this paper, the reduction transformation $D \rightarrow D'$ is presented in the form of a formal language *homomorphism*, whose validity can be verified in time linear in the size of components of D, and the number of such components.

It is shown furthermore that refinement is simply inverse reduction, and thus is handled through the same mechanism. In (1.1), if D' is a design, if D is an implementation of D', if T' is a task verified for the design D' and if T is the naturally induced image of T' under the refinement transformation $D' \twoheadrightarrow D$, then the relation (1.1) means that tasks verified for the design remain valid for the implementation. In practice, a design may undergo a succession of refinements, each step refining or "implementing" the "design" of the previous step, consistent with (1.1). By transitivity of such stepwise refinement, (1.1) obtains when D is the ultimate implementation and D' is any design in the refinement hierarchy, verified for any task T' defined at the "level" of D'.

Because of the very large complexity associated with real designs, even defining the reduction homomorphism $D \twoheadrightarrow D'$ directly may well be intractable, simply on account of the size of D. This problem can be circumvented by defining the homomorphism $D \twoheadrightarrow D'$ indirectly in terms of homomorphisms on components of D. If D may be factored as $D = D_1 \otimes \cdots \otimes D_k$ and D' likewise factored as $D' = D'_1 \otimes \cdots \otimes D'_k$, then it is shown that the existence of component homomorphisms $\Phi_i \colon D_i \twoheadrightarrow D'_i$ for $i = 1, \ldots, k$ imply the existence of a product homomorphism

$$\prod_{i=1}^{k} \Phi_i : D \twoheadrightarrow D' . \tag{1.2}$$

Although the size of D grows geometrically with k, the complexity of verifying that each Φ_i has the required properties is only linear in the size of D_i.

In order to carry out a program for the mutual support of formal verification, reduction and refinement as above, it is important to have a close relationship between the formal assertion context used for verification (say, logic or automata theory) and the modelling paradigm used to represent the design specification. Without such a close relationship, methodologies for reduction and refinement may be difficult to discern. Specifically, if the modelling paradigm and the assertion context are not closely related, it may be difficult to relate transformations in the former to transformations in the latter in such a way that an assertion valid for a model transforms to an assertion valid for the transformed model.

As already indicated, this paper adopts the modelling paradigm of finite state machines, using formal assertions founded in automata theory. Finite state machines are bound closely to automata through their respective languages and the similarities of their generators, both given in terms of finite directed graphs. Just how this close relationship affords a tractable theory for reduction and refinement is the subject of this paper. It should be conceded that the regular languages generated by automata are not sufficiently expressive to capture assertions dealing with the correctness of many distributed algorithms, such as those employing recursion and induction. However, verification of such algorithms is problematic in any context, and there is much debate concerning which really have been proved, or even what is a proof [Ba89]. Therefore, there may be some justification to the contention that regular (and ω-regular) assertions encompass the major portion of assertions admitting widely acceptable proofs. If this is the case, it may be futile to adopt a more powerful context for formal assertions, only to find that widely believed proofs (or any proofs at all) are few and far between. On the other hand, automata theory admits certain weak forms of induction [KM89], as well as a context in which to reason about parameterized automata and state machines. This affords a framework in which certain non-regular assertions can be reduced to regular assertions, or at least reasoned about to the extent they may be reasoned about in any other context. While there has been only preliminary thinking in this direction, it may hold a promise for extending automata theory to effectively computable results. In any case, since a Turning machine is an infinite state automaton (with bounded state transitions), all recursively enumerable assertions may be expressed in this context (although not necessarily decided).

In order to facilitate the treatment of state machine models in the context of assertions defined by automata, it has been convenient to alter slightly the standard definitions of both, and present each through a uniform context of enabling transition predicates, non-deterministic outputs (for state machines) and a new acceptance condition (for ω-automata). The enabling transition predicates (Boolean functions of inputs and outputs) combine (through Boolean conjunction, disjunction and negation) to form a Boolean algebra basic to the theory of reduction developed here. State machines are taken to be essentially Moore machines, but unlike Moore machines, the state machines used here are endowed with non-deterministic outputs. This non-determinism is important for several reasons. First of all, it provides a necessary mechanism to introduce uncertainty or variety into a design, allowing designs to be specified as closed systems, containing all "input" and "output" within. (This is basic to the analysis described here.) Nondeterminism also may be used to model incompletely defined response, indeterminate delay and actions whose control is external to the model (and thus unknown, but for their effect). Furthermore, non-determinism affords a "place-keeping" mechanism for refinement: details to be added at a later point in development may be modelled non-deterministically in the high-level design. Finally, non-determinism affords an important reduction mechanism: a deterministic state machine D may be replaced by a non-deterministic state machine D' with fewer states and larger language over the same alphabet; if such a reduced machine D' were shown to have a certain (ω−)regular language property T, then in the sense of (1.1), the original machine would have that property T as well (although the reduced machine and the original machine may by no means be equivalent in any general sense). Such a reduced D' may be obtained by "freeing" a state machine component D_1 of D (*cf.* (1.2)) by replacing D_1 with D_1' where D_1' has a single state from which it non-deterministically outputs all the outputs of D_1. Finally, while a Moore machine with non-deterministic transitions cannot (in general) be determinized, allowing non-deterministic outputs is enough to be able to determinize the transitions of the machine, an important step in many procedures.

The Boolean algebra generated by transition predicates affords a basis for decomposition of state machines. It turns out that a state machine can be represented by a matrix over this Boolean algebra in such a way that decomposition of the state machine into coordinating component machines is represented by the tensor product of the matrices associated with each component machine. This decomposition is essential for verification of reduction and refinement, which must be accomplished component-wise in large systems. Conventional homomorphism of Boolean algebras gives rise to the language homomorphisms used in the theory developed here.

Formal assertions about state machine models are given here in terms of infinitary (ω-regular) automata. Such automata, while generally applied to reasoning about non-terminating processes, apply as well to terminating processes, through concatenation of an infinite tail of "null" symbols to each finite prefix; thus, there is no reason to deal with languages comprised of both (finite) strings and (infinite) sequences together as is commonly done: sequences alone suffice to model both. Like the state machines, the ω-automata used here, the *L-automata* defined over the Boolean algebra L, comprise a slight variation on standard ω-automata. In addition to being defined in terms of the same underlying transition structure and Boolean algebra L as the state machines, they have two acceptance conditions which in an intuitive sense, may be associated, one with "fairness" or "liveness" and the other with "safety" and "eventuality" properties, as they are often understood. While experience [HK90] has indicated the practical utility of this definition with regard to specifying tasks, perhaps more important is that it gives rise to a decomposition technique in which any ω-regular property can be built up from smaller, more easily testable properties.

Classically, given automata Λ and Γ, in order to test whether $\mathcal{L}(\Lambda) \subset \mathcal{L}(\Gamma)$, one first constructs an automaton $\tilde{\Gamma}$ which defines the complementary language $\mathcal{L}(\Gamma)'$, then one constructs an automaton $\Lambda * \tilde{\Gamma}$ satisfying $\mathcal{L}(\Lambda * \tilde{\Gamma}) = \mathcal{L}(\Lambda) \cap \mathcal{L}(\tilde{\Gamma})$ and finally one tests whether $\mathcal{L}(\Lambda * \tilde{\Gamma}) = \emptyset$. This entire procedure is at least as complicated as constructing $\tilde{\Gamma}$, and since Λ may be taken to define all sequences (over the given alphabet), testing language containment is at least as hard as testing whether $\mathcal{L}(\tilde{\Gamma}) = \emptyset$, the so-called "emptiness of complement" problem. This problem is PSPACE-complete in the number of states for non-deterministic Büchi automata [SVW85], while deterministic Büchi automata are strictly less expressive than non-deterministic Büchi automata.

On the other hand, given an ω-regular language $\mathcal{L}$, a finite number of deterministic L-automata $\Gamma_1, \ldots, \Gamma_n$ may be found such that $\mathcal{L} = \bigcap_{i=1}^{n} \mathcal{L}(\Gamma_i)$. (This is not true for Büchi automata.) In order to test $\mathcal{L}(\Lambda) \subset \mathcal{L}$, one tests $\mathcal{L}(\Lambda) \subset \mathcal{L}(\Gamma_i)$ for $i = 1, \ldots, n$. Each test $\mathcal{L}(\Lambda) \subset \mathcal{L}(\Gamma_i)$ may be completed in time linear in the number of edges of Λ and linear in the number of edges of Γ_i [Ku87]. Not only do the several individual tests $\mathcal{L}(\Lambda) \subset \mathcal{L}(\Gamma_i)$, $i = 1, \ldots, n$ defined by the task decomposition $\mathcal{L} = \bigcap_i \mathcal{L}(\Gamma_i)$, provide a test which is more tractable in bounded space than the single test $\mathcal{L}(\Lambda) \subset \mathcal{L}$, but it provides a greater potential for reduction; each test $\mathcal{L}(\Lambda) \subset \mathcal{L}(\Gamma_i)$ may be separately reducible to a test $\mathcal{L}(\Lambda_i') \subset \mathcal{L}(\Gamma_i')$, with each Λ_i' different for different i.

2. Preliminaries

Conventionally, the transition structure of a state machine or automaton is viewed *dynamically* in terms of a "successor" relation on a set of states; this relation defines a "next" state (for deterministic structures) or in general, a set of next states, for each "current" state and "input". I prefer to view a transition structure *statically* as a directed graph whose vertices correspond to states and whose edges are labelled respectively with the set of input values which enable the associated state transition (*cf.* [Ts59]). The labelled graph is defined by its "labelled" adjacency matrix, whose ij-th element is the label on the edge from vertex i to vertex j. We will see that this provides a more convenient notation for combining transition structures than the dynamic definition. Furthermore, it turns out to be natural and useful to impose an algebraic structure on the inputs. Specifically, inputs are manipulated through predicates over input tokens. These predicates, which naturally form a Boolean algebra (a set closed under conjunction, disjunction and negation), provide a succinct means to represent sets of input values. For example, if inputs (say, from two sources) are represented in terms of the respective values of variables x and y, the enabling predicate for a certain transition may be represented syntactically as "$x<y$", denoting the set of all input pairs satisfying that relation. If L is the Boolean algebra of such predicates (semantically, the set of all subsets of inputs), then a transition structure is a square matrix over L. Conversely, for any Boolean algebra L, a square matrix over L may be interpreted as a transition structure for the set of inputs represented by the *atoms* of L (see below).

2.1 Boolean Algebra

Let L be a Boolean algebra, with meet (disjunction, product) $*$, join (conjunction, sum) $+$, complement $\sim$, multiplicative identity 1 and additive identity 0 [Ha74]. A Boolean algebra admits of a partial order $\leq$ defined by $x \leq y$ iff $x * y = x$. If $x \leq y$ and $x \neq y$, write $x < y$. *Atoms* are minimal elements with respect to this order. A Boolean algebra is said to be *atomic* if every non-zero element majorizes an atom. In this case every non-zero element can be expressed as a sum of atoms in a unique way. In this paper, every Boolean algebra L is assumed to be atomic (it is certainly true if L is finite). Let $S(L)$ denote the set of atoms of the Boolean algebra L. For the purposes of this paper, little is lost if one thinks of L as 2^S, the *power field* over S, which is the set of all subsets of a finite set S (the "alphabet") where $1=S$, $0=\varnothing$, $*$ is set intersection, $+$ is set union and $\sim$ is set complementation in S; the atoms of L in this case are the (singleton sets comprised of) the elements of S. A homomorphism of Boolean algebras is a map which is linear with respect to $*$, $+$ and $\sim$ (*i.e.*, $\phi(x*y)=\phi(x)*\phi(y)$, $\phi(x+y)=\phi(x)+\phi(y)$ and $\phi(\sim x)=\sim\phi(x)$). Any homomorphism is order-preserving ($x<y \Rightarrow \phi(x)<\phi(y)$). Every Boolean algebra contains as a subalgebra the trivial Boolean algebra $\mathbb{B}=\{0,1\}$. If $S\subset L$ is a subset of L, $\mathbb{B}[S]$ is defined to be the smallest subalgebra of L containing S. A sum or product indexed over the empty set is 0, 1 respectively.

Suppose $L_1,\ldots,L_k$ are subalgebras of a Boolean algebra L. Define

$$\prod_{i=1}^{k} L_i = \left\{ \sum_{j\in J} x_{ij}*\cdots*x_{kj} \mid x_{ij}\in L_i \text{ for } i=1,\ldots,k,\ j\in J \text{ and } J \text{ is finite}\right\}.$$

It is easily checked that ΠL_i is a subalgebra of L, in fact $\Pi L_i=\mathbb{B}[\cup L_i]$. It is easily seen that $S(\Pi L_i)=\{s_1*\cdots*s_k \mid s_i\in S(L_i),\ 1\le i\le k\}\backslash\{0\}$. Say $L_1,\ldots,L_k$ are *independent* if $0\ne x_i\in L_i$ for $i=1,\ldots,k \Rightarrow x_1*\cdots*x_k\ne 0$. Clearly, $L_1,\ldots,L_k$ are independent if and only if $S(\Pi L_i)=\{s_1*\cdots*s_k \mid s_i\in S(L_i),\ 1\le i\le k\}$. Write $L_1\cdot L_2\cdot\ldots\cdot L_k=\Pi L_i$.

2.2 L-Matrix; Graph

Let L be a Boolean algebra, let V be a non-empty set and let M be a map

$$M: V^2 \to L$$

(where $V^2 = V\times V$ is the Cartesian product). Then M is said to be an *L-matrix* with *state space* $V(M) = V$. The elements of $V(M)$ are said to be *states* or *vertices* of M. An *edge* of an L-matrix M is an element $e\in V(M)^2$ for which $M(e)\ne 0$. ($M(e)$ is the "label" on the edge e.) The set of edges of M is denoted by $E(M)$. If $e=(v,w)\in E(M)$, let $e^- = v$ and $e^+ = w$. If M is an L-matrix and $L\subset L'$ then M is an L'-matrix as well.

An L-matrix provides the transition structure for a state machine or automaton. In automata-theoretic terms, the "alphabet" is the set of atoms $S(L)$ and an "edge label" $M(e)\in L$ of an L-matrix M represents the set of atoms $\lambda=\{s\in S(L) \mid s\le M(e)\}$ which enable the transition along the edge e, since $M(e) = \sum_{s\in\lambda} s$. Since any two distinct atoms $s,t\in S(L)$ satisfy $s*t=0$, M is "deterministic" if for each state v and each "input letter" $s\in S(L)$, $s\le M(v,w)$ for at most one $w\in V(M)$. Likewise, M is "complete" if for each $v\in V(M)$ and each $s\in S(L)$, $s\le M(v,w)$ for *some* $w\in V(M)$. This is recapitulated below.

An L-matrix M is *deterministic* if for all $u, v, w \in V(M)$, $v \neq w \Rightarrow M(u, v) * M(u, w) = 0$. An L-matrix M is *complete* if for all $v \in V(M)$ the sum $\sum_{w \in V(M)} M(v, w) = 1$. If G is an L-matrix and $W \subset V(G)$, then $G|_W$, the *restriction* of G to W, is the L-matrix defined by $V(G|_W) = W$ and $G|_W(e) = G(e)$ for all $e \in W^2$.

A *graph* is a $\mathbb{B}$-matrix. The *graph* of the L-matrix M is the graph $\overline{M}$ with state space $V(\overline{M}) = V(M)$, defined by

$$\overline{M}(e) = \begin{cases} 1 & \text{if } M(e) \neq 0 \\ 0 & \text{otherwise}. \end{cases}$$

A *path* in a graph G of *length* n is an $(n+1)$-tuple $\mathbf{v} = (v_0, \ldots, v_n) \in V(G)^{n+1}$ such that $G(v_i, v_{i+1}) = 1$ for all $0 \leq i < n$; the path $\mathbf{v}$ is a *cycle* if $v_n = v_0$. The path $\mathbf{v}$ is said to be *from* v_0 *to* v_n. The path $\mathbf{v}$ *contains* the edge $(v, w) \in E(G)$ if for some i, $0 \leq i < n$, $v_i = v$ and $v_{i+1} = w$. If $C \subset V(G)$ and each $v_i \in C$, then $\mathbf{v}$ is *in* C. A cycle (v, v) of length 1 is called a *self-loop* (*at* v). A vertex $v \in V(G)$ is *reachable from* $I \subset V(G)$ if for some $v_0 \in I$, there is a path in G from v_0 to v. Any statement about a "path" in a L-matrix M is to be construed as a statement about that path in $\overline{M}$.

Given an L-matrix M, a sequence $\mathbf{x} \in L^\omega$ (a sequence, by definition, is infinite) and a sequence of states $\mathbf{v} \in V(M)^\omega$, say $\mathbf{v}$ is a *run* (*in* M) of $\mathbf{x}$ *from* $v \in V(M)$ provided $v_0 = v$ and $x_i * M(v_i, v_{i+1}) \neq 0$ for all i.

Let G be a graph. A set $C \subset V(G)$ containing more than one element is said to be *strongly connected* provided for each pair of distinct elements $v, w \in C$ there is a path from v to w. A singleton set $\{v\} \subset V(G)$ is *strongly connected* if $(v, v) \in E(G)$. A maximal strongly connected set is called a strongly connected *component* (of G). Clearly, for every graph G, $V(G)$ is uniquely partitioned into strongly connected components and a non-strongly connected set, each vertex of which has no self-loop. (The requirement that a single vertex have a self-loop in order to be strongly connected, at some variance with the customary definition, is important to the theory developed here.)

Let G, H be graphs and let $\Phi: V(G) \rightarrow V(H)$ be a map which satisfies $(v, w) \in E(G) \Rightarrow (\Phi(v), \Phi(w)) \in E(H)$. Then Φ extends to a map

$\Phi: E(G) \twoheadrightarrow E(H)$ and we say Φ is a *homomorphism* from G to H, and write

$$\Phi: G \twoheadrightarrow H.$$

Let M and N be L-matrices. Their *direct sum* is the L-matrix $M \oplus N$ with $V(M \oplus N) = V(M) \cup V(N)$, defined by

$$(M \oplus N)(v, w) = \begin{cases} M(v, w) & \text{if } v, w \in V(M), \\ N(v, w) & \text{if } v, w \in V(N), \\ 0 & \text{otherwise;} \end{cases}$$

their *tensor product* is the L-matrix $M \otimes N$ with $V(M \otimes N) = V(M) \times V(N)$, defined by

$$(M \otimes N)((v, w), (v', w')) = M(v, v') * N(w, w').$$

The direct sum and tensor product can be extended to a commutative, associative sum and an associative product, respectively, of any finite number of L-matrices. If L is complete (*i.e.*, closed under infinite sums and products), the direct sum and tensor product can be extended to infinite sums and products as well.

Lemma: *The tensor product of deterministic L-matrices is deterministic. The tensor product of complete L-matrices is complete.*

Proof: Let $u, v, w \in V(M)$ and $u', v', w' \in V(N)$. Then

$$\begin{aligned} &(M \otimes N)[(v, v'), (w, w')] * (M \otimes N)[(v, v'), (u, u')] \\ &= M(v, w) * N(v', w') * M(v, u) * N(v', u') \\ &= (M(v, w) * M(v, u)) * (N(v', w') * N(v', u')). \end{aligned}$$

If $(w, w') \neq (u, u')$ and M, N are deterministic, then either the left factor or the right factor must be zero, and it follows that $M \otimes N$ is deterministic. If M, N are complete then

$$\sum_{w, w'} (M \otimes N)[(v, v'), (w, w')] = \sum_{w, w'} M(v, w) * N(v', w') = \sum_{w} M(v, w) * \sum_{w'} N(v', w'$$

and it follows that $M \otimes N$ is complete.

Let G, H be graphs. The projection

$$\Pi_G : V(G \otimes H) \to V(G)$$

induces a (not necessarily onto) projection

$$\Pi_G : E(G \otimes H) \to E(G) .$$

If G and H are matrices, Π_G will denote the projection on the underlying graph $\overline{G}$. Given $G_1, G_2, \ldots$, the projections Π_{G_i} may be written as Π_i, for convenience.

3. L-Automata

Finite state automata which accept sequences (rather than strings) define the ω-regular languages. This class of automata is established as a model in logic, topology, game theory and computer science [Bu62, Ra69, Ra72, Ch74, Ku87a, SVW85, etc.]. In computer science, such automata can be used to model non-terminating processes such as communication protocols and integrated hardware systems [AKS83, DC85, Ku85, BC87, KM90, etc.], as well as terminating processes, as already explained. Several different types of such automata have been proposed [Ch74, Sa88], distinguished by the condition under which a "run" of the automaton is accepted. While each type of automaton is well-suited to various applications, none proved well-suited for the reductions described here. A new type of automaton [Ku87] proved better-suited, for reasons described in the introduction.

An *L-automaton* is a 4-tuple

$$\Gamma = (M_\Gamma, I(\Gamma), R(\Gamma), Z(\Gamma))$$

where M_Γ, the *transition matrix* of Γ, is a complete L-matrix, $\emptyset \neq I(\Gamma) \subset V(M_\Gamma)$, the *initial* states of Γ, $R(\Gamma) \subset E(M_\Gamma)$, the *recurring* edges of Γ and $Z(\Gamma) \subset 2^{V(M_\Gamma)}$, the *cycle* sets of Γ, is a (possibly empty) set of non-empty subsets of $V(M_\Gamma)$. Set $V(\Gamma) = V(M_\Gamma)$, $E(\Gamma) = E(M_\Gamma)$ and $\Gamma(v, w) = M_\Gamma(v, w)$ for all $v, w \in V(\Gamma)$. Let $R^-(\Gamma) = \{e^- \mid e \in R(\Gamma)\}$ and $R^+(\Gamma) = \{e^+ \mid e \in R(\Gamma)\}$. Define the *graph* of Γ, $\overline{\Gamma} = \overline{M}_\Gamma$. Let $|\Gamma| = cardV(\Gamma)$.

A sequence of states $\mathbf{v} = (v_0, v_1, \ldots) \in V(\Gamma)^\omega$ is Γ-*cyclic* if for some integer N and some $C \in Z(\Gamma)$, $v_i \in C$ for all $i > N$, while $\mathbf{v}$ is Γ-*recurring* if $\{i \mid (v_i, v_{i+1}) \in R(\Gamma)\}$ is infinite. A sequence of atoms $\mathbf{x} \in S(L)^\omega$ is *accepted* by, or is a *tape* of Γ provided $\mathbf{x}$ has a Γ-cyclic or Γ-recurring run from an initial state.

Such a run is an *accepting* run (of $\mathbf{x}$). The set of tapes of Γ, $\mathcal{L}(\Gamma)$, is defined to be the *language* of (or accepted by) Γ. Two L-automata Γ and Γ' are said to be *equivalent* if $\mathcal{L}(\Gamma) = \mathcal{L}(\Gamma')$. A *chain* of Γ is a pair $(\mathbf{v}, \mathbf{x})$ where $\mathbf{v}$ is an accepting run of a tape $\mathbf{x}$. Let $\mathcal{C}(\Gamma)$ denote the set of chains in Γ.

The L-automaton Γ is said to be *deterministic* if M_Γ is deterministic; if Γ is deterministic and $|I(\Gamma)| = 1$ then Γ is said to be *strongly* deterministic. (Customarily, "deterministic" has been used in the literature to mean what is here called "strongly deterministic"; however, strong determinism often leads to unnecessary restriction, for example, in automata complementation and minimization, where only determinism is required.)

(3.1) **Lemma:** *A tape accepted by a strongly deterministic L-automaton has a unique accepting run.*

Relationships between L-automata and other types of automata are given in [Ku87].

4. L-Process

Evidently, L-automata are not directly suited to define coordinating discrete event systems, as there is no direct way to capture "coordination" of L-automata: they have no outputs, and hence no way to communicate. Instead, a coordinating discrete-event system may be built up from Moore machines, the outputs of each machine providing inputs to various machines. This provides a "data-flow" context [WA85] in which the system is represented by the collection of coordinating machines.

For our purposes here, as already explained in section 1, Moore machines are not quite adequate, on account of their determinism. On the other hand, merely to allow a Moore machine to be non-deterministic is not the answer: a deterministic transition structure is important to be able to compare machines. (Note that a non-deterministic Moore machine may not be determinizable.) Comparison is used to show that one machine abstracts or implements another, for purposes of reduction and refinement. Furthermore, it turns out to be convenient to be able to incorporate fairness constraints directly into the machine definition, rather than through other devices (such as L-automata) which may increase the size of the state space and thus the complexity of verification.

For these reasons, a process is modelled as a Moore-like machine which may at once have non-deterministic outputs and a deterministic transition structure, and incorporate fairness constraints without increasing the size of the state space. Thus, while at each state a Moore machine produces an output as a function of that state, the L-process defined below may produce non-deterministically one of several outputs possible from each state (the set of outputs possible from a state is a function of the state). While the transition structure of an L-process may be deterministic or non-deterministic, it may be determinized through the Rabin-Scott subset construction. Although formally an L-process, like an L-automaton, is defined statically, it has a dynamic interpretation: an L-process recursively "selects" an output allowed from the current state and then "resolves" that selection by changing state along a transition enabled by that selection. This dynamic interpretation is the *selection/resolution* (or *s/r*) model of coordination proposed by B. Gopinath and this author in 1980 [GK80] and illustrated in [AKS83, Ku85] for modelling communication protocols and more general distributed discrete-event systems. More generally, a "system" is comprised of several L-processes, the selections (outputs) of some providing the "inputs" to others. While the dynamic interpretation is convenient conceptually, as with L-automata, a static definition turns out to be more useful for analysis.

Let L be a Boolean algebra. An *L-process* A is a 5-tuple

$$A = (M_A, S_A, I(A), R(A), Z(A))$$

where M_A, $I(A)$, $R(A)$ and $Z(A)$ are as in the definition of L-automaton, except that M_A is not required to be complete; S_A, the *selector* of A, is a function

$$S_A : V(A) \rightarrow 2^L$$

from the states of A to the set of subsets of L, such that for each $v \in V(A)$, the set of *selections* of A *at* v, $S_A(v) \neq \varnothing$, and for all $v, w \in V(A)$,

$$A(v, w) \leq \sum_{x \in S_A(v)} x . \tag{4.1}$$

(The condition (4.1) is explained below.) Let

$$S(A) = \bigcup_{v \in V(A)} S_A(v),$$

the set of selections of A, and set $|A| = card\, V(A)$. Say that an L-process A is *atomic* if each selection $x \in S(A)$ is an atom in the Boolean algebra $\mathbb{B}[S(A)]$ generated by the set of selections of A. Thus, A is atomic iff for any selections $x, y \in S(A)$, $x * y \neq 0 \Leftrightarrow x = y$. An assumption of process atomicity does not compromise expressiveness, and turns out to be fundamental in the analysis of coordination (*cf.* (4.10) below). Therefore, this paper focuses mainly on atomic processes. Fortunately, atomicity is preserved under combining "independent" processes (4.8, below).

A selection $x \in S_A(v)$ enables the state transition (v, w) provided $x * A(v, w) \neq 0$, *i.e.*, provided that x and the transition predicate $A(v, w)$ are jointly satisfiable. The condition (4.1) may be interpreted as meaning that every edge from a state v is enabled by some selection from v (*i.e.*, some $x \in S_A(v)$). (This may be enforced by replacing each edge label $A(v, w)$ by $A(v, w) * \sum_{x \in S_A(v)} x$.) This is a technical assumption needed to relate the "language" of A to the language of a derived L-automaton; clearly, it does not limit the expressiveness of L-processes, as a transition from v enabled by no selection from v is never crossed. Note that a condition equivalent to (4.1) is: for all $v \in V(A)$,

$$\sum_{w \in V(A)} A(v, w) \leq \sum_{x \in S_A(v)} x. \tag{4.2}$$

If in fact equality holds in (4.2) for all v and $0 \notin S(A)$, then A is said to be *lockup-free*. (This is related to completeness for L-automata, if we consider an L-automaton to be an L-process which has the single selection $1 \in L$ from each state.) If A is lockup-free, then for each selection $x \in S_A(v)$, some transition out of v is enabled by x, *i.e.*, $x * A(v,w) \neq 0$ for some $w \in V(A)$. However, equality in (4.2) is stronger than this condition. The problem with this weaker condition is that it is not preserved under products. Since in a strong sense a lockup is a defect in definition, we would like lockup-free components to combine to form a lockup-free system.

Thus far, the transition structure of an L-process has been defined statically and interpreted dynamically. Now, the "behavior" or *language* of an L-process is defined. While sometimes the "language" of a Moore machine is defined to be the set of all its possible productions (output sequences) this in fact is an inadequate definition, in that it masks the essential relationship between input and output. Rather, in dynamic terms, the language of an L-process is defined to be all sequences of input-output pairs, except for those sequences "ruled out" by the "fairness" constraints. More generally, since a "system" may comprise several L-processes, and the inputs of each process are taken from the selections of other processes, it is most suitable to cast the language of a process in terms of the selections of the system.

Let $\mathbf{x} \in S(L)^{\omega}$ (the set of all sequences of atoms of L), and let A be an L-process. A *run* of $\mathbf{x}$ *in* A is a run $\mathbf{v}$ of $\mathbf{x}$ in M_A with $v_0 \in I(A)$. Say $\mathbf{x}$ is a *tape* of A if it admits of a run $\mathbf{v}$ in A which satisfies:

(4.3) for some $N > 0$, $i > N \Rightarrow (v_i, v_{i+1}) \notin R(A)$;

(4.4) for each $C \in Z(A)$ and each $i > 0$ there exists $j > i$ such that $v_j \notin C$.

Such a run $\mathbf{v}$ is said to be an *accepting* run of $\mathbf{x}$. The *language* of A, denoted $\mathcal{L}(A)$, is the set of all tapes of A. Two L-processes A and A' are *equivalent* if $\mathcal{L}(A) = \mathcal{L}(A')$.

A *chain* of an L-process A is a pair $(\mathbf{v}, \mathbf{x})$ where $\mathbf{x} \in \mathcal{L}(A)$ and $\mathbf{v}$ is an accepting run of $\mathbf{x}$ in A. Let $\mathcal{C}(A)$ denote the set of chains of A.

Notice that (4.3) and (4.4) are the negation of the corresponding definitions for an L-automaton. The reason is that $R(A)$ and $Z(A)$ are used in L-processes to define "fairness" constraints: behaviors which are most conveniently and most often expressed negatively (*e.g.*, "A will not forever remain in its 'critical section' states (designated by a cycle set)"). Note, however, that there is no intrinsic notion of "fairness": any ω-regular property may be represented, as shown in (4.5).

An L-process A is said to have *deterministic resolutions* if M_A is deterministic.

(4.5) **Proposition:** *Let L be a Boolean algebra and let $\mathcal{L}$ be an arbitrary ω-regular language over $S(L)$. There exists an L-process A with deterministic resolutions satisfying $\mathcal{L}(A) = \mathcal{L}$.*

Proof: Let $\Lambda_1, \ldots, \Lambda_k$ be strongly deterministic L-automata satisfying $\cap \mathcal{L}(\Lambda_i) = \mathcal{L}'$ [Ku87: Thm. 3; Cor. to Prop. 2]. Define L-processes $P_1, \ldots, P_k$ by $P_i = (M_{\Lambda_i}, \mathbf{1}, I(\Lambda_i), R(\Lambda_i), Z(\Lambda_i))$ where $\mathbf{1}(v) = \{1\}$ for all $v \in V(\Lambda_i)$. By (3.1), $\mathcal{L}(P_i) = \mathcal{L}(\Lambda_i)'$. Set $P = (\bigoplus M_{P_i}, \mathbf{1}, \cup I(P_i), \cup R(P_i), \cup Z(P_i))$. Then $\mathcal{L}(P) = \cup \mathcal{L}(P_i) = \cup \mathcal{L}(\Lambda_i)' = \mathcal{L}$.

In the literature one often finds "process behavior" defined both in terms of (infinite) sequences and (finite) strings. This is an unnecessary complication. If a process models a program which terminates, there is no harm in modelling "termination" as a state in which the process can only self-loop, remaining forever after in that state and selecting thereafter a "null" selection which enables no non-self-loop of any process in the system. On the other hand, if a process terminates on account of a lockup, the view taken here is that this is a defect in the definition: what happens next is undefined. (It is often convenient purposely to introduce lockups in processes which are implemented on a computer, as a practical means to determine if the lockup condition is ever reached, in which case the computer should return an 'error'.)

Given an L-process A, the *reachable subprocess* of A is the L-process A^* defined as the restriction of A to the set of states reachable from $I(A)$. Certainly $\mathcal{L}(A^*) = \mathcal{L}(A)$.

Let A be an L-process. Define the L-automaton $A^{\#}$ as follows: $V(A^{\#}) = V(A) \cup \{\#\}$ where $\#$ is a symbol not in $V(A)$; $I(A^{\#}) = I(A)$; for $v, w \in V(A)$,

$$A^{\#}(v, w) = A(v, w)$$

while

$$A^{\#}(v, \#) = \sum_{x \in S(A) \setminus S_A(v)} x ,$$

$$A^{\#}(\#, \#) = 1, \quad A^{\#}(\#, v) = 0;$$

$R(A^{\#}) = \emptyset$, $Z(A^{\#}) = \{V(A)\}$. Say that an L-process A is *full* if $R(A) = \emptyset$ and $Z(A) = \{\emptyset\}$; if A is full then no runs of the transition matrix of A are "unfair" and $\mathcal{L}(A) = \mathcal{L}(A^{\#})$.

Recall that a regular language C over Σ is said to be *prefix-closed* if for all $x, y \in \Sigma^*$, $xy \in C \Rightarrow x \in C$. The *limit* of a language C is defined to be the ω-language

$$\lim C \equiv \{\mathbf{x} \in \Sigma^\omega \mid \text{for all } i_1 < i_2 < \ldots, \ (x_0, x_1, x_2, \ldots, x_{i_j}) \in C \text{ for all } j\}.$$

(4.6) **Theorem:** *Let L be a Boolean algebra and let $\mathcal{L} \neq \emptyset$ be an ω-regular language over $S(L)$. Then the following are equivalent:*

1. $\mathcal{L} = \mathcal{L}(A^\#)$ *for some (lockup-free) L-process A;*

2. $\mathcal{L} = \lim C$ *for some regular prefix-closed C over $S(L)$.*

Proof: 1. ⇒ 2.: Let C be the (regular) language accepted by the Rabin-Scott acceptor defined by $M = (M_{A^\#}, I(A), V(A))$ (here $V(A)$ is the set of "final" states). If $\mathbf{x} \in \mathcal{L}(A^\#)$ then for all i $x_0 \ldots x_i \in \mathcal{L}(M)$ so $\mathcal{L}(A^\#) \subset \lim C$. If $\mathbf{x} \in \lim C$ then $x_0 \ldots x_{i_j} \in \mathcal{L}(M)$ for $j = 1, 2, \ldots$. Since there is no outgoing edge from the state $\mathbf{x} \in V(M)$, $\mathbf{x} \in \mathcal{L}(A^\#)$. Thus $\mathcal{L} = \mathcal{L}(A^\#) = C$. By construction, C is prefix-closed.

2. ⇒ 1. Let $M = (M, I, F)$ be a deterministic Rabin-Scott acceptor [RS59] with $\mathcal{L}(M) = C$. Since C is prefix-closed, there can be no transition from a state of F' $(\equiv V(M) \backslash F)$ to a state of F. Let A be the full L-process with $V(A) = V(M) \backslash F'$, $M_A = M|_{V(A)}$, $I(A) = I(M) \backslash F'$ and

$$S_A(v) = \{x \in S(L) \mid x * \sum_{w \in F'} M(v, w) = 0\}.$$

Then $\sum_{w \in V(A)} A(v, w) = \Sigma x \ (x \in S(L); w \in V(A); x * M(v, w) \neq 0)$ and since M is deterministic, this sum is equal to $\sum_{x \in S_A(v)} x$. Therefore, A is a lockup-free L-process. Since A is full, $\mathcal{L}(A^\#) = C = \mathcal{L}$.

Given L-processes $A_1, \ldots, A_k$ define their (*tensor*) *product* to be

$$\bigotimes_{i=1}^k A_i = \left(\bigotimes_{i=1}^k M_{A_i}, \ \prod_{i=1}^k S_{A_i}, \ \mathop{\mathbf{X}}_{i=1}^k I(A_i) \ \bigcup_{i=1}^k \Pi_i^{-1} R(A_i), \ \bigcup_{i=1}^k \Pi_i^{-1} Z(A_i) \right)$$

where $\left(\prod_i S_{A_i} \right) (v_1, \ldots, v_k) = \{x_1 * \cdots * x_n \mid x_i \in S_{A_i}(v_i), \ i = 1, \ldots, k\}$.

(4.7) **Lemma:** *If $A_1, \ldots, A_k$ are L-processes, then their product $\otimes A_i$ is an L-process.*

The L-processes $A_1, \ldots, A_k$ are said to be *independent* provided

$$x_i \in S(A_i)\,, \quad (i = 1, \ldots, k) \Rightarrow x_1 * \cdots * x_k \neq 0\,.$$

(4.8) **Proposition:** *If $A_1, \ldots, A_k$ are [atomic and] independent, lockup-free L-processes, then their product $\otimes A_i$ is [respectively, atomic and] lockup-free.*

(4.9) **Proposition:** *Let $A_1, \ldots, A_k$ be independent, lockup-free L-processes. Then.*

$$1. \quad \mathcal{L}\left(\bigotimes_{i=1}^{k} A_i\right) = \bigcap_{i=1}^{k} \mathcal{L}(A_i)\,;$$

$$2. \quad \left(\bigotimes_{i=1}^{k} A_i\right)^{\#} = \bigotimes_{i=1}^{k} A_i^{\#}\,.$$

It follows directly from (4.9.1) that $\mathcal{L}(\otimes A_i^*) = \mathcal{L}((\otimes A_i)^*)$.

The discrete-event coordination in a "system" of atomic, independent, lockup-free L-processes $A_1, \ldots, A_k$ is modelled by the behavior of the product L-process $A = A_1 \otimes \cdots \otimes A_k$. Interpreting this system dynamically, at each time, in each process A_i, a selection x_i possible at the "current" state v_i (*i.e.*, some $x_i \in S_{A_i}(v_i)$) is chosen non-deterministically. The product $x = x_1 * \cdots * x_k$ defines a "current global selection", *i.e.*, a selection of the product A at the state $v = (v_1, \ldots, v_k)$, with $x \in S_A(v)$. At each time, in each process, the current global selection determines a set of possible "next" states, namely those states to which the transition from the current state is enabled by the current global selection. In A_i the transition from state v_i to state w_i is enabled by x iff $x * A_i(v_i, w_i) \neq 0$. Under appropriate conditions, each process separately may be considered to *resolve* the current global selection, by choosing (non-deterministically) one of these possible next states. A system of processes progresses in time by each repeatedly "selecting" and "resolving" (*cf.* Figure 1). This interpretation correctly describes the behavior of the product if $L = \mathbb{B}[S(A)]$, since then by the atomicity assumption on each A_i it follows that for $v = (v_1, \ldots, v_k)$ and $w = (w_1, \ldots, w_k)$,

(4.10) $$x * A_i(v_i, w_i) \neq 0 \text{ for } 1 \leq i \leq k \Leftrightarrow x * A(v, w) \neq 0\,.$$

The assumption that $L = \mathbb{B}[S(A)]$ provides that $S(A)$ includes all the selections of the "system" which determine the transitions of the component processes. If this is the case, then each A_i is a $\mathbb{B}[S(A)]$-process, so one may as well assume that $L = \mathbb{B}[S(A)]$.

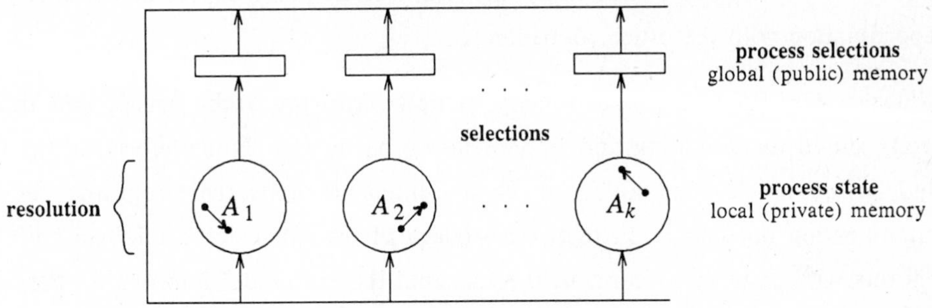

Figure 1
The s/r Model
Each process updates its state by instantaneously resolving the current selection and then (instantaneously) making a new selection from the new state.

Modelling a hardware or software system by a family of coordinating L-processes $A_1, \ldots, A_k$ may be viewed in terms of writing a computer program to implement the functionality of the system, in a programming language in which "process" is a programming primitive. Such a language is intrinsically an automaton data-flow language, in the sense of [WA85], with processes as data nodes, and data-flow determined by the dependency of a process upon the selections of another process. The *S/R* language [JK86], developed explicitly to implement the *s/r* model consistently with (4.10), is an example of such a language.

The modelling discipline imposed by the syntax of the *S/R* language is intrinsically hierarchical in nature, skewed in favor of modelling a system as many small coordinating processes. The simplest processes are ones which play the role of a variable in a conventional program (but rather than being updated through assignment statements, here a "variable" process updates itself as a function of input values). Buffers and other "passive" data structures may be formed as an "array" of such variable processes, *i.e.*, if A_i is a process which models an array element (as a function of the parameter i) then $A = \otimes A_i$ is a process which models the array. The "active" (and typically non-deterministic) portions of an *S/R* program consist of "controller" processes which coordinate the flow of data among the passive data structures. (These controllers correspond to the so-called "state machines" one sometimes finds in conventional programs.) The S/R language lends itself to hierarchical modelling of controller processes as well. Thus, a controller A may be decomposed into several component controllers $A_1, \ldots, A_k$ (with $A = A_1 \otimes \ldots \otimes A_k$), each component controlling some aspect of the data flow, in coordination with the other controllers.

Such a data-flow language directly models hardware architecture, and thus is directly suited to modelling and implementing hardware. Nonetheless, it has been found to be no less suitable for control-intensive software programs such as communication protocols. In fact, on account of the intrinsic parallelism built into programs with distributed control, the fact that the s/r model imposes a "hardware architecture" on S/R programs seems to offer an advantage of modularity and hence clarity over equivalent non-data-flow programs, providing a potential for a dramatic increase in productivity and efficiency [HK90].

The dynamic interpretation of the s/r model may be used to model systems of processes coordinating asynchronously in continuous time by interpreting "at each time" for selecting and resolving consistent with (4.10), as meaning "at each real value of time", this provided state transitions are instantaneous and occurring at discrete points of time. (A necessary requirement for this interpretation is that there be no two adjacent states without self-loops.) This approach is expanded in section 5 below.

An L-process A is said to be *deterministic* if it has deterministic resolutions and for each $v \in V(A)$, $|S_A(v)| = 1$; A is said to be *strongly* deterministic if A is deterministic and $|I(A)| = 1$. Note that a strongly deterministic L-process A is a Moore machine with input alphabet $S(L)$ and output alphabet $S(A)$, and every Moore machine has this form.

(4.11) **Theorem:** Every full L-process is equivalent to a full L-process with deterministic resolutions and unique initial state.

Proof: Use the Rabin-Scott determinization algorithm [RS59].

5. Modelling Asynchrony

Delay may be modelled by a specific "pause" selection with the property that it does not disable the self-loop of any process in the "system". Upon entering a state, a process first selects "pause", causing the process to "self-loop", and conveying "no information" to any other process. By that, it is meant that no process is forced to change state on account of this "pause". At some future point in time, the process selecting "pause" non-deterministically may change its selection to some other value, enabling certain state changes. In this way, if state changes are interpreted as instantaneous events, then they are separated by a non-zero duration defined by such "pause" selections in one or more components; with this interpretation, the system of processes model discrete events occurring asynchronously in continuous time.

In a data-flow model of asynchronous processes, inter-node delays appear as such "pause" delays within particular "channel" processes (whose function may be simply to model such delay). Thus, the delayed asynchronous coordination of two controllers A and B may be modelled through the introduction of a third "channel" process C with the property that all coordination between A and B is via C. This may be realized as follows. At some point in time A changes its selection from a pause selection to a non-pause selection, say x. The (instantaneous) resolution of x in C is a change of state to a new state of C, let us say state "x". From its (new) state x, C may first select a pause selection, (conceptually) for an amount of time equal to the interprocess delay between A and B; the selection of C then changes (non-deterministically) from "pause" to the selection (say) x'. The resolution in B of x' reflects the passage of the "datum x" from A to B. In this case the process C is not part of the "implemented" program, but only a model of (part of) the environment in which the implemented program resides. (For software, C is "implemented" by the operating system interfaces, while for hardware, C may be implemented by wires or other component interface devices.)

When an S/R program is intended to model asynchrony and other continuous-time evolution, the "realizability" of such a program becomes an issue: there may in fact be no continuous-time implementation of a given program. For example, since state transitions are taken to be instantaneous, there can be no continuous-time implementation of a process having two consecutive states without self-loops.

It is important, therefore, to identify a broadly applicable condition which guarantees that an S/R program is realizable.

Given an L-process A with a chain $(\mathbf{v}, \mathbf{x}) \in \mathscr{C}(A)$, a *realization* of $(\mathbf{v}, \mathbf{x})$ is a map

$$\gamma_{\mathbf{v},\mathbf{x}}: [0, \infty[\Rightarrow V(A) \times S(A)$$

with the property that $\gamma_{\mathbf{v},\mathbf{x}}$ is a step-function (piecewise-constant), with i-th step value (v_i, x_i), such that the i-th step has positive measure only if $x_i * A(v_i, v_i) \neq 0$. Say that an L-process A is *realizable* if every chain of A admits of a realization.

A realizable process may be understood to evolve in time as in Figure 2.

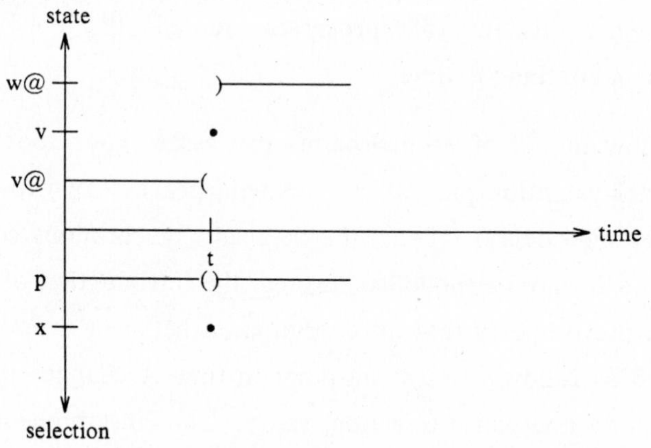

Figure 2
Modelling Continuous Time
A process self-looping in a state v@ *and selecting* p *non-deterministically changes its state at time* t *to state* v, *from which it selects a selection* x ∈ S(v) *and resolves this new selection to a new state* w@, *where it self-loops ...*

(5.1) **Lemma:** *The following are equivalent for an L-process A:*

1. *A is realizable;*
2. *for each chain* $(\mathbf{v}, \mathbf{x})$ *of* A *and each* $i \geq 0$, $x_i * A(v_i, v_i) = 0 \Rightarrow x_{i+1} * A(v_{i+1}, v_{i+1}) \neq 0$;
3. *for each* $v, w \in V(A^*)$, *if* $x \in S_A(v)$, $x * A(v, v) = 0$ *and* $x * A(v, w) \neq 0$ *then* $y * A(w, w) \neq 0$ *for all* $y \in S_A(w)$.

Let A be an L-process. Define $E^1(A) = \{e \in E(A) \mid e^- \neq e^+\}$, the set of non-self-loop edges of A. A set of states $W \subset V(A)$ is said to be *stabilizing* if each selection from each state $w \in W$ enables the self-loop at w, *i.e.*, $x * A(w, \omega) \neq 0$ for each $x \in S_A(w)$, and for each $e \in E^1(A)$, either $e^- \in W$ or $e^+ \in W$. If A admits of a stabilizing set of states, say A is *stable*.

(5.2) **Theorem:** *An L-process is realizable if and only if it is stable.*

For $W \subset V(A)$ define $S_A(W) = \bigcup_{w \in W} S_A(w)$. A family of L-processes $A_1, \ldots, A_k$ is said to be a *stable family* if there are stabilizing sets of states $W_1, \ldots, W_k$ for $A_1, \ldots, A_k$ respectively such that for each $i \neq j$, $1 \leq i, j \leq k$,

(5.3) $\quad p \in S_A(W_i)\,,\ w \in W_j \Rightarrow p * A_j(w, w) \neq 0;$

(5.4) $\quad e \in E^1(A_i)\,,\ f \in E^1(A_j)\,,\ e^- \notin W_i\,,\ f^+ \notin W_j \Rightarrow A_i(e) * A_j(f) = 0.$

(5.5) **Theorem:** *If $A_1, \ldots, A_k$ is a stable family of independent L-processes then $\otimes A_i$ is stable.*

The previous two results give a general means for constructing realizable "systems" (processes whose product is realizable). Indeed, say an L-process A is a "memory" process if A is deterministic, and $V(A)$ is stabilizing (then A in essence "selects its state" and holds the last value "assigned" to it). Say A is an "asynchronous controller" if some set of "pause" states $V^@ \subset V(A)$ is stabilizing, if for some designated "pause" selection p, $S_A(v) = \{p\}$ for all $v \in V^@$ and if the L-matrix derived from M_A by setting $M_A(v@, v@) = 0$ for each $v@ \in V^@$ is deterministic (so A "pauses" for an indeterminant amount of time in state $v@$, selecting the "pause" selection p, thereafter non-deterministically moving to a uniquely designated non-pause state, say v, from which it may make an arbitrary selection and then either move to another "pause" state or self-loop). It is natural and convenient to build asynchronous systems from building blocks comprised of such "memory" processes and "asynchronous controllers". The latter can model delays across asynchronous interfaces, processing-time delays and indeterminacy of actions at higher levels of abstraction. It is likewise natural to model systems consistent with condition (5.3), as no process is expected to branch upon the "pause" (≡ "no information") selection of another process. Condition (5.4) is more problematic, in that it does not arise naturally. However, it does have a natural interpretation: among processes which stop "pausing" at the same time t, each of their respective subsequent "non-pause" selections must be in effect *at* time

t (not one at t and the other in the open interval to the right of t). One way to enforce (5.4) is to choose some $u \in L$ independent of the selections of all the processes in the system, and for each "asynchronous controller" process A, redefine $M_A(v@, v)$ to be $u * M_A(v@, v)$ for each $v@ \in V^@$, $v \notin V^@$ and redefine $M_A(v, w@)$ to be $\sim u * M_A(v, w@)$ for $w@ \in V^@$. This violates (4.10); however, the effect of this violation can be overlooked, since it does not alter the behavior of the component processes. It enforces the requirement that each process which changes its selection "at" time t has the new selection in effect at time t.

6. Verification

As stated in the introduction, "verification" is defined in terms of language properties. Specifically, let A be an L-process. A *task* for A is defined to be a set $\mathcal{T} \subset 2^{S(L)^\omega}$ of ω-languages over $S(L)$. Say A *performs* the task $\mathcal{T}$ provided $\mathcal{L}(A) \in \mathcal{T}$. This definition captures all possible notions of model-checking. For example, if $\mathcal{T}$ represents the branching-time property that a certain state is reachable ("there exists a path from an initial state to the given state"), then $\mathcal{T}$ consists of the set of all subsets of $S(L)^\omega$ which contain at least one sequence admitting a run starting at an initial state and running through the given state. An important class of tasks is the class of ω-regular tasks: a task $\mathcal{T}$ is *ω-regular* provided $\mathcal{T} = 2^{\mathcal{L}}$ for some ω-regular language $\mathcal{L}$. Let $\mathcal{T} = 2^{\mathcal{L}}$ be an ω-regular task for an L-process A. Then A performs $\mathcal{T}$ iff $\mathcal{L}(A) \subset \mathcal{L}$. Since $\mathcal{L}$ is ω-regular, there is an L-automaton T such that $\mathcal{L} = \mathcal{L}(T)$. In such a case we say "T is a task for A" and "A performs T" if $\mathcal{L}(A) \subset \mathcal{L}(T)$. For the remainder of the paper, all tasks are assumed to be ω-regular.

Let A be an L-automaton and let T be a deterministic L-automaton defining a task for A. Then task-performance $\mathcal{L}(A) \subset \mathcal{L}(T)$ may be decided in time linear in $|M_A \otimes M_T| \cdot |S(L)|$ [Ku87]. As an arbitrary ω-regular language $\mathcal{L}$ may be represented as $\mathcal{L} = \bigcap_{i=1}^{n} \mathcal{L}(T_i)$ for deterministic L-automata $T_1, \ldots, T_n$, $\mathcal{L}(A) \subset \mathcal{L}$ can be decided by deciding $\mathcal{L}(A) \subset \mathcal{L}(T_i)$ for $i = 1, \ldots, n$. This is often appropriate in practice, as one often thinks in terms of separate deterministic tasks $T_1, \ldots$ rather than $\mathcal{L}$.

Verification can sometimes be posed as a "controller synthesis" problem [AKS83, RW87]: if $\mathcal{L}(A) \subset \mathcal{L}$ fails, it may nonetheless be the case that for some "controller" L-process C, $\mathcal{L}(A \otimes C) \subset \mathcal{L}$, as $\mathcal{L}(A \otimes C) = \mathcal{L}(A) \cap \mathcal{L}(C)$. A necessary and sufficient condition for the existence of such a controller is that $\mathcal{L}(C) \subset (\mathcal{L}(A) \cap \mathcal{L}) \cup \mathcal{L}(A)'$.

In the course of defining and analyzing a system, one frequently places constraints or "commitments" on the "environment": the source of inputs to the system. Sometimes this has led to confusion due to the potential for circularity concerning "commitments" of the environment to the system and of the system to the environment: for example, "S works if E works; E works if S works" is satisfied if neither work. This potential for confusion can be avoided altogether by providing together with a model of the system, a model of the environment. Then, properties are proved about the closed system comprising the system-environment pair.

An important reduction method may be called "task decomposition". Suppose T is a task for $A = \otimes A_i$ which is "global" in the sense that each component A_i "plays a part" in the performance of T. In this case it may be conceptually difficult to see how to reduce the test $\mathcal{L}(A) \subset \mathcal{L}(T)$. For example, suppose A defines a communication protocol in its environment, as follows. $A = S \otimes SP \otimes CH1 \otimes CH2 \otimes RP \otimes R$ where S and R model respectively the "sending" and "receiving" interfaces of the environment, $CH1$ and $CH2$ model respectively the outgoing and incoming channels between the sender and the receiver, and SP and RP model respectively the "sender protocol" and "receiver protocol" under development, to be verified. Suppose that the channels could lose messages, but the protocols SP and RP work on the basis of sending acknowledgements and retransmissions in case of failures. Let us say the task T is that every message sent by S is eventually received by R, unless there are continual channel failures. The validity of T must depend upon the entire global behavior of the "systems" modelled by A, as messages must flow from S to SP to $CH1$ to RP to R, and in order to handle the case of a failure in $CH1$, acknowledgements must flow from RP to $CH2$ to SP. Therefore, it is unlikely that any significant abstraction of A relative to T could be forthcoming. Nonetheless, in general the task T may be "decomposed" into "subtasks" $T_1, \ldots, T_n$ such that

$\bigcap_{i=1}^{n} \mathcal{L}(T_i) \subset \mathcal{L}(T)$ and $\mathcal{L}(A) \subset \mathcal{L}(T_i)$ for each $i = 1, \ldots, n$, allowing for a reduction of each such test to a test $\mathcal{L}(B_i') \subset \mathcal{L}(T_i')$. In the example, T_1 may be that the sent message arrives from S to SP; to prove this, we may take $B_1' = S \otimes SP \otimes X$ where X is a significant abstraction of $CH1 \otimes CH2 \otimes RP \otimes R$. Likewise, $T_2, \ldots$ may follow the flow of events related to the proper functioning of the protocol.

7. Homomorphism

Homomorphism, the basis of both reduction and refinement, is the means for dealing with large systems. Let L, L' be Boolean algebras, let $\sigma : S(L) \to S(L')$ be an arbitrary map and define the map

(7.0.1) $$\Phi : 2^{S(L)^\omega} \to 2^{S(L')^\omega}$$

of the languages over L to the languages over L' by $\Phi(\mathcal{L}) = \{(\sigma(x_i))_i \mid \mathbf{x} \in \mathcal{L}\}$. Then Φ is said to be a (*language*) *homomorphism* with *support* σ. If $\mathbf{x} \in S(L)^\omega$, define $\Phi(\mathbf{x}) = (\sigma(x_i))_i$. It is shown in section 7.1 that the language homomorphism Φ gives rise to a Boolean algebra homomorphism $F(\Phi) : L' \to L$, and conversely, for any Boolean algebra homomorphism $\phi : L' \to L$ there is a unique language homomorphism (7.0.1) satisfying $F(\Phi) = \phi$. This relationship between a language homomorphism and a Boolean algebra homomorphism is used to generate a language homomorphism which guarantees (1.1) from conditions on the processes and automata. This duality relationship further provides the mechanism for the decomposition (1.2).

First, observe how a language homomorphism can be used to generate a reduction or refinement (1.1). Suppose A is an L-process, T is an L-automaton, A' is an L'-process and T' is an L'-automaton. We seek conditions on their respective languages which will guarantee that

(7.0.2) $$\mathcal{L}(A') \subset \mathcal{L}(T') \Rightarrow \mathcal{L}(A) \subset \mathcal{L}(T).$$

Indeed, suppose a language homomorphism (7.0.1) satisfies

(7.0.3) $$\Phi \mathcal{L}(A) \subset \mathcal{L}(A'),$$

(7.0.4) $$\Phi^{-1} \mathcal{L}(T') \subset \mathcal{L}(T).$$

If $\mathcal{L}(A') \subset \mathcal{L}(T')$ then for any $\mathbf{x} \in \mathcal{L}(A)$, $\Phi(\mathbf{x}) \in \mathcal{L}(A')$ so

$\mathbf{x} \in \Phi^{-1}\Phi(\mathbf{x}) \subset \Phi^{-1}\mathcal{L}(A') \subset \Phi^{-1}\mathcal{L}(T') \subset \mathcal{L}(T)$ and (7.0.2) follows.

7.1 Support

For the remainder of this paper it is assumed that all given Boolean algebras are complete (*i.e.*, infinite products and sums exist [Ha74]). Suppose

$$\phi : L' \to L$$

is a homomorphism of Boolean algebras. For each $x \in L$ define

$$x_\phi = \Pi \{y \in L' \mid x \le \phi(y)\};$$

since L' is complete, $x_\phi \in L'$. The map

$$\hat{\phi} : L \to L'$$

defined by $\hat{\phi}(x) = x_\phi$ is said to be the *support* of ϕ.

(7.1.1) **Proposition:** *For all* $x \in L$, $y \in L'$, $x \le \phi(x_\phi)$, $\phi(y)_\phi \le y$.

Proof: It follows from the Stone representation theorem [Ha74] that for $x \in L$, $\phi(x_\phi) = \Pi\{\phi(y) \mid y \in L', x \le \phi(y)\} \ge x$. For $y \in L'$, $\phi(y)_\phi = \Pi\{y' \in L' \mid \phi(y) \le \phi(y')\} \le y$.

(7.1.2) **Lemma:** $x_\phi = 0$ *iff* $x = 0$.

Proof: Since $0 \le \phi(0)$ $(=0)$, $0_\phi = \Pi\{y \in L' \mid 0 \le \phi(y)\} \le 0$. Conversely, if $x_\phi = 0$ then by (7.1.1) $x \le \phi(x_\phi) = \phi(0) = 0$.

(7.1.3) **Proposition:** $x \in S(L) \Rightarrow x_\phi \in S(L')$.

Proof: Say $x_\phi = y + z$. Then by (7.1.1), $x \le \phi(x_\phi) = y + z$. Since $x \in S(L)$, we may suppose $x \le \phi(y)$; but then $y + z = x_\phi \le y$ from the definition of x_ϕ, so $z \le y$. By (7.1.2), $x_\phi \ne 0$, so it follows that $x_\phi \in S(L')$.

(7.1.4) **Proposition:** $\hat{\phi}(x + x') = \hat{\phi}(x) + \hat{\phi}(x')$ *for all* $x, x' \in L$.

Proof: Since $x \le \phi(x_\phi)$ and $x' \le \phi(x'_\phi)$, $x + x' \le \phi(x_\phi) + \phi(x'_\phi) = \phi(x_\phi + x'_\phi)$ so by the definition of $\hat{\phi}$, $(x + x')_\phi \le x_\phi + x'_\phi$. Conversely, by (7.1.1), $x \le x + x' \le \phi((x + x')_\phi)$ so again by the definition of $\hat{\phi}$, $x_\phi \le (x + x')_\phi$; similarly, $x'_\phi \le (x + x')_\phi$ so $x_\phi + x'_\phi \le (x + x')_\phi$.

(7.1.5) **Corollary:** $x \le x' \Rightarrow x_\phi \le x'_\phi$.

Proof: Set $z = x' * \sim x$. Then, by (7.1.4), $x_\phi \le x_\phi + z_\phi = (x+z)_\phi = x'_\phi$.

(7.1.6) **Theorem:** *The following are equivalent:*

1. ϕ *is* $1-1$ (*i.e., ker* $\phi = 0$);

2. $\hat{\phi}$ *is onto;*

2a. $\hat{\phi} : S(L) \to S(L')$ *is onto;*

3. $\hat{\phi} \circ \phi = id$ (*i.e.,* $\phi(y)_\phi = y$ *for all* $y \in L'$);

4. $1_\phi = 1$.

Proof:
$1 \Rightarrow 3$: Let $z = \phi(y)_\phi$, $z' = y * \sim z$. Then $z * z' = 0$ so since $ker\, \phi = 0$, $\phi(z) * \phi(z') = 0$. By (7.1.1), $\phi(y) \le \phi(\phi(y)_\phi) = \phi(z)$ so $\phi(z) + \phi(z') = \phi(z+z') = \phi(y+z) = \phi(y) + \phi(z) = \phi(z)$ and thus $\phi(z') = 0$. Since $ker\, \phi = 0$, $z' = 0$ so $y \le z = \phi(y)_\phi$. But $\phi(y)_\phi \le y$ by (7.1.1) so $\phi(y)_\phi = y$.

$3 \Rightarrow 2a$: $\hat{\phi} S(L) \subset S(L')$ by (7.1.3); $3 \Rightarrow \hat{\phi}$ is onto.

$2a \Rightarrow 2$: $L' = \mathbb{B}[S(L')]$.

$2 \Rightarrow 1$: If $\phi(y) = 0$ then $\phi(x_\phi) = 0$ for some $x \in L$ (with $x_\phi = y$) by 2., and $x \le \phi(x_\phi) = 0$ so $x = 0$. Thus, by (7.1.2) $y = 0$.

$4 \Leftrightarrow 2a$: If $1_\phi = 1$ then by (7.1.3) and (7.1.4), $\sum_{s' \in S(L')} s' = 1 = 1_\phi = (\sum_{s \in S(L)} s)_\phi = \sum_{s \in S(L)} s_\phi$ so 2a. follows; if 2a. is true then $1 = \Sigma s' = \Sigma s_\phi = (\Sigma s)_\phi = 1_\phi$.

(7.1.7) **Corollary:** *For all* $y \in L'$,

$$(*) \qquad \phi(y) = \sum_{x_\phi \le y} x \ge \sum_{x_\phi = y} x ;$$

if ϕ *is* $1-1$ *then equality holds between the two sums.*

Proof: If $x_\phi \le y$ then $x \le \phi(x_\phi) \le \phi(y)$ so $\sum_{x_\phi \le y} x \le \phi(y)$. On the other hand, $\phi(y)_\phi \le y$ by (7.1.1) so substituting $\phi(y)$ for one of the summands x gives $\sum_{x_\phi \le y} x \ge \phi(y)$ and thus (*) holds. If ϕ is $1-1$ then by (7.1.6) $\hat{\phi}$ is onto; for each

$x \in L$ such that $x_\phi < y$, let $z = y * \sim x_\phi$. Since $\hat{\phi}$ is onto there is some $x' \in L$ such that $x'_\phi = z$. Then, by (7.1.4), $(x+x')_\phi = x_\phi + x'_\phi = y$. It follows that (*) is an equality.

In the main result of this section, it is shown that the conditions of (7.1.3), (7.1.4) and (7.1.7) characterize the homomorphism ϕ. This will enable us to define ϕ from $\hat{\phi}$.

Say that an arbitrary function $f: L \to L'$ is *additively linear* (respectively, *monotone*) if $f(x+y) = f(x)+f(y)$ (respectively, $x \leq y \Rightarrow f(x) \leq f(y)$) for all $x, y \in L$. If f is additively linear, then, as in the proof of (7.1.5), f is monotone.

(7.1.8) **Theorem:** If $f: L \to L'$ is additively linear and $f: S(L) \to S(L')$ then the map $\phi: L' \to L$ defined by

$$\phi(y) = \sum_{f(x) \leq y} x$$

is a homomorphism and for all $0 \neq x \in L'$, $x_\phi = f(x)$.

This theorem gives the functor F described at the beginning of section 7. Its importance lies in the fact that it shows that in order to generate the Boolean algebra homomorphism needed to define a language homomorphism satisfying (7.0.3) and (7.0.4), it is enough to define its support on the set of atoms $S(L)$.

(7.1.9) **Notes:** 1. Without the requirement that $f: S(L) \to S(L')$, it may happen that f is additively linear and yet the map $\phi(y) = \sum_{f(x) \leq y} x$ is not even additively linear (and thus not a homomorphism). Indeed, let $L = \mathbb{B}[x, y]$, $L' = \mathbb{B}[z]$ and define $f: L \to L'$ by $f(x*y) = z$, $f(x * \sim y) = \sim z$, $f(\sim x * y) = f(\sim x * \sim y) = 1$ and extend this to L by linearity, with $f(0) = 0$. Then f is additively linear by construction, but $\phi(1) = 1$ whereas $\phi(z) + \phi(\sim z) = x*y + x* \sim y = x < 1$.

2. In (7.1.8), if $|fS(L)| = 1$ (*i.e.*, if f maps $S(L)$ to a single atom of L') then the hom ϕ satisfies

$$\phi(y) = \begin{cases} 1 & \text{if } f(1) \leq y \\ 0 & \text{otherwise.} \end{cases}$$

However, it could happen that $f(0) = f(1) > 0$. On the other hand, if $|fS(L)| > 1$, say $s, t \in S(L)$ and $f(s) \neq f(t)$, then $f(0) + f(s) = f(0+s) = f(s)$ so

$f(0) \leq f(s)$ and likewise $f(0) \leq f(t)$, so (since $f(s) * f(t) = 0$) $f(0) = 0$.

(7.1.10) **Lemma:** $f(x * x') \leq f(x) * f(x')$.

Proof: Since $x * x' \leq x$ and $x * x' \leq x'$, by the additivity of f, f is monotone and hence $f(x * x') \leq f(x)$, $f(x * x') \leq f(x')$ so $f(x * x') \leq f(x) * f(x')$.

(7.1.11) **Note:** $x \leq \sum_{f(z) \leq f(x)} z$.

(7.1.12) **Lemma:** $f\phi(y) \leq y$, $\phi f(x) \geq x$.

Proof: $f\phi(y) = f \sum_{f(x) \leq y} = \sum_{f(x) \leq y} f(x) \leq y$. $\phi f(x) = \sum_{f(z) \leq f(x)} z \geq x$.

Proof of (7.1.8): Let $y_1, y_2 \in L'$. Then $f(\phi(y_1) + \phi(y_2)) = f\phi(y_1) + f\phi(y_2) \leq y_1 + y_2$ by (7.1.12), so by (7.1.11)

$$\begin{aligned}\phi(y_1) + \phi(y_2) &\leq \sum_{f(x) \leq f(\phi_1(y_1) + \phi_2(y_2))} x \\ &\leq \sum_{f(x) \leq y_1 + y_2} x \\ &= \phi(y_1 + y_2).\end{aligned}$$

If $\phi(y_1) + \phi(y_2) < \phi(y_1 + y_2)$ then there exists an atom $t \in S(L)$ with $t < \phi(y_1 + y_2) * \sim(\phi(y_1) + \phi(y_2))$, and $f(t) \in S(L')$. But $f\phi(y_1 + y_2) \leq y_1 + y_2$ by (7.1.12) so by monotonicity $f(t) \leq f\phi(y_1 + y_2) \leq y_1 + y_2$; since $f(t)$ is an atom, we may as well assume $f(t) \leq y_1$. But then, by the definition of $\phi(y_1)$, $t \leq \phi(y_1)$, a contradiction. Hence ϕ is additively linear. To show that ϕ is multiplicatively linear, observe that by (7.1.10) if $f(x) \leq y_1$ and $f(x') \leq y_2$ then $f(x * x') \leq f(x) * f(x') \leq y_1 * y_2$ while if $f(x) \leq y_1 * y_2$ then $x = x * x$ and $f(x) \leq y_1$, $f(x) \leq y_2$. Hence

$$\phi(y_1 * y_2) = \sum_{f(x) \le y_1 * y_2} x$$

$$= \sum_{\substack{f(x) \le y_1 \\ f(x') \le y_2}} x * x'$$

$$= \left(\sum_{f(x) \le y_1} x \right) * \left(\sum_{f(x') \le y_2} x' \right)$$

$$= \phi(y_1) * \phi(y_2).$$

Next, $1 = f(1) + {\sim}f(1)$ so by (7.1.12) $\phi(1) = \phi f(1) + \phi({\sim}f(1)) \ge 1 + \phi({\sim}f(1)) = 1$. Now, $f\colon S(L) \twoheadrightarrow S(L')$ so by linear additivity of f, $f(x) = 0 \Rightarrow x = 0$, so $\phi({\sim}y) * \phi(y) = \phi({\sim}y * y) = \phi(0) = \sum_{f(x) \le 0} x = 0$, and thus $\phi({\sim}y) \le {\sim}\phi(y)$. Also, $1 = \phi(1) = \phi({\sim}x + x) = \phi({\sim}y) + \phi(y)$. Hence ${\sim}\phi(y) = {\sim}\phi(y) * \phi({\sim}y) = \phi({\sim}y)$. It follows that ϕ is a homomorphism. Finally, for all $x \in L$,

$$x_\phi = \Pi\,\{y \in L' \mid x \le \phi(y)\}$$

$$= \Pi\,\{y \in L' \mid x \le \sum_{f(z) \le y} z\}$$

$$\le f(x) \quad \text{by (7.1.11)}.$$

On the other hand, if $f(x) = 0$ then by (7.1.12) $0 = \phi f(x) \ge x$ so $x = 0$ and $0_\phi = 0 = f(0)$. If $f(x) \ne 0$, write $x = \Sigma s_i$ where $s_i \in S(L)$. Then $f(x) = \Sigma f(s_i)$ and $f(s_i) \in S(L')$ for all i. For any atom $t \le f(x)$ there exists an atom s each that $s \le x$ and $f(s) = t$. To show that $f(x) = x_\phi$ it suffices to show that $t \le x_\phi$. Indeed, if $x \le \sum_{f(z) \le y} y$ then $t = f(s) \le f(x) \le \sum_{f(z) \le y} f(z)$ so for some z, $t \le f(z) \le y$. Thus, $t \le x_\phi$ and it follows that $f(x) \le x_\phi$ so $f(x) = x_\phi$.

(7.1.13) **Lemma:** *$\hat{\phi} \circ \phi = id$ on $\hat{\phi} L$ and $\ker \phi = (L' \setminus \hat{\phi} L) \cup \{0\}$.*

Proof: Let $x \in L$. Then $\phi(x_\phi) \ge \sum_{z_\phi = x_\phi} z$ by (7.1.7). Thus $\hat{\phi} \circ \phi(x_\phi) \ge \hat{\phi}(\Sigma z) = \Sigma z_\phi = x_\phi$. But $\hat{\phi} \circ \phi(x_\phi) \le x_\phi$ by (7.1.1). Therefore,

$\hat{\phi} \circ \phi = id$ on $\hat{\phi} L$, and thus by (7.1.6) $ker\, \phi \cap \hat{\phi} L = \{0\}$. If $y \in L'$ and $\phi(y) \neq 0$ then $s \leq \phi(y)$ for some atom $s \in S(L)$, in which case $s_\phi \leq \phi(y)_\phi \leq y$ by (7.1.1), and so $y \notin L' \backslash \hat{\phi} L$ by (7.1.3).

(7.1.14) **Lemma:** *Suppose $\phi, \psi : L' \twoheadrightarrow L$ are homomorphisms and $\hat{\phi} = \hat{\psi}$ on $S(L)$. Then $\phi = \psi$.*

Proof: If $\hat{\phi} = \hat{\psi}$ on $S(L)$ then by (7.1.4) and (7.1.2), $\hat{\phi} = \hat{\psi}$ and $ker\, \phi = ker\, \psi$ by (7.1.13). Therefore $\phi, \psi : \hat{\phi} L \twoheadrightarrow L$ have 0 kernel so by (7.1.6) for any $y \in \hat{\phi} L$, $\hat{\psi} \circ \psi(y) = y = \hat{\phi} \circ \phi(y) = \hat{\psi} \circ \phi(y)$, and $\hat{\psi}$ is $1-1$ on $\hat{\phi} L$. Therefore, $\psi(y) = \phi(y)$ on $\hat{\phi} L = \hat{\psi} L$. Since by (7.1.13) $ker\, \phi = ker\, \psi = (L' \backslash \hat{\psi} L) \cup \{0\}$, it follows that $\phi = \psi$.

(7.1.15) **Corollary:** *Let $\sigma : S(L) \twoheadrightarrow S(L')$ be an arbitrary map. Then there exists a unique homomorphism $\phi : L' \twoheadrightarrow L$ such that for all $s \in S(L)$, $s_\phi = \sigma(s)$.*

Proof: Define $f : L \twoheadrightarrow L'$ by extending σ linearly to L: set $f(0) = 0$ and for $0 \neq x \in L$, write $x = \Sigma s_i$ for $s_i \in S(L)$, and set $f(x) = \Sigma f(s_i)$. The result follows from (7.1.8) and (7.1.14).

(7.1.16) **Corollary:** *Let $\phi : L' \twoheadrightarrow L$ be a Boolean algebra homomorphism. Then there is a unique language homomorphism $\Phi : 2^{S(L)^\omega} \twoheadrightarrow 2^{S(L')^\omega}$ with support $\hat{\phi}$.*

Suppose $L_1, \ldots, L_k$ are independent subalgebras of L with $L = \Pi L_i$ and $L_1', \ldots, L_k'$ are independent subalgebras of L' with $L' = \Pi L_i'$. If $\sigma_i : S(L_i) \twoheadrightarrow S(L_i')$ are arbitrary maps for $1 \leq i \leq k$, we may define $\sigma : S(L) \twoheadrightarrow S(L')$ by $\sigma(s_1 * \cdots * s_k) = \sigma_1(s_1) * \cdots * \sigma_k(s_k)$, in which case by (7.1.15) there exists a unique homomorphism $\phi : L' \twoheadrightarrow L$ with $\hat{\phi} = \sigma$ on $S(L)$. Conversely, if $\phi_i : L_i' \twoheadrightarrow L_i$ are arbitrary homomorphisms then $\hat{\phi}_i : S(L_i) \twoheadrightarrow S(L_i')$ and by (7.1.15) there is a unique homomorphism $\phi : L' \twoheadrightarrow L$ with $\hat{\phi}(s_1 * \cdots * s_k) = \hat{\phi}_1(s_1) * \cdots * \hat{\phi}_k(s_k)$. Thus, we define the product homomorphism $\prod_{i=1}^{k} \phi_i \equiv \phi : L' \twoheadrightarrow L$. It is this product which will allow us in the next sections to define a homomorphism of a product of L-automata or L-processes in terms of homomorphisms on the components.

7.2 *L*-Automaton Homomorphism

Let Γ be an L-automaton and let Γ' be an L'-automaton. A *homomorphism*

$$\Phi : \Gamma \rightarrow \Gamma'$$

is a pair of maps $\Phi = (\phi, \phi')$ where

$$\phi : \overline{\Gamma} \rightarrow \overline{\Gamma'}$$

is a graph homomorphism satisfying

(7.2.1) $\qquad \phi^{-1} I(\Gamma') \subset I(\Gamma)$

(7.2.2) $\qquad \phi^{-1} R(\Gamma') \subset R(\Gamma)$

(7.2.3) $\qquad C' \in Z(\Gamma') \Rightarrow \phi^{-1}(C') \subset C$ for some $C \in Z(\Gamma)$

and

$$\phi' : L' \rightarrow L$$

is a Boolean algebra homomorphism such that for each $(v, w) \in V(\Gamma)^2$, ϕ and ϕ' jointly satisfy

(7.2.4) $\qquad \Gamma(v, w) \leq \phi' \Gamma'(\phi(v), \phi(w))\,.$

If the containments in (7.2.1-3) are equalities and $Z(\Gamma') = \{\Phi(C) \mid C \in Z(\Gamma)\}$, then Φ is said to be *exact*. We may denote ϕ and ϕ' by Φ.

(7.2.5) **Theorem:** *If* $\Phi : \Gamma \rightarrow \Gamma'$ *is a homomorphism then* $\sum_{\substack{\Phi(r) = \Phi(v) \\ \Phi(s) = \Phi(w)}} \Gamma(r, s)$ $\leq \Phi\Gamma'(\Phi(v), \Phi(w))$, *with equality holding when* Γ' *is deterministic.*

Proof: Inequality is clear. Suppose $\Sigma\Gamma(r, s) < \Phi\Gamma'(\Phi(v), \Phi(w))$. Then some atom $t < \Phi\Gamma'(\Phi(v), \Phi(w))$ satisfies $t * \Sigma\Gamma(r, s) = 0$. Let $\Phi(r_0) = \Phi(v)$, $\Phi(s_0) = \Phi(w)$. Then $t * \Gamma(r_0, s_0) = 0$, so for some $\hat{s}_0 \neq s_0$, $t * \Gamma(r_0, \hat{s}_0) \neq 0$, and $\Phi(\hat{s}_0) \neq \Phi(w)$. Thus $t * \Phi\Gamma'(\Phi(v), \Phi(\hat{s}_0)) \neq 0$ and hence

$$0 \neq (\Phi\Gamma'(\Phi(v), \Phi(w))) * (\Phi\Gamma'(\Phi(v), \Phi(\hat{s}_0))) =$$

$$\Phi(\Gamma'(\Phi(v), \Phi(w)) * \Gamma'(\Phi(v), \Phi(\hat{s}_0)))\,,$$

contrary to the assumption that Γ' is deterministic.

(7.2.6) **Proposition:** *If* $\Phi = (\phi, \phi')$ *and* $\Psi = (\psi, \psi')$ *are homomorphisms,* $\Phi : \Gamma \rightarrow \Gamma'$ *and* $\Psi : \Gamma' \rightarrow \Gamma''$, *then* $\Psi \circ \Phi \equiv (\psi \circ \phi\,,\ \phi' \circ \psi')$ *is a homomorphism* $\Gamma \rightarrow \Gamma''$; *if* Φ *and* Ψ *are exact then so is* $\Psi \circ \Phi$.

(7.2.7) **Lemma:** *Let* $\Phi: \Gamma \to \Gamma'$ *be a homomorphism. If* Γ' *is deterministic then* $\Phi: E(\Gamma) \to E(\Gamma')$ *is onto.*

Proof: Let $v \in V(\Gamma')$. Then there is a path $(v_0, \ldots, v_n)$ in Γ' with $v_0 \in I(\Gamma')$ and $v_n = v$. The proof that Φ is onto follows by induction on n. If $n = 0$, then $v_0 \in \Phi V(\Gamma)$ by the definition of Φ. If $v_0, \ldots, v_{n-1} \in \Phi V(\Gamma)$, let $\hat{v}_{n-1} \in \Phi^{-1}(v_{n-1})$ and let $w_1, \ldots, w_m$ be exactly those states of Γ satisfying $\Gamma(\hat{v}_{n-1}, w_i) \neq 0$. Then $\sum_{i=1}^{m} \Gamma(\hat{v}_{n-1}, w_i) = 1$, and $\Phi \sum_{i=1}^{m} \Gamma'(v_{n-1}, \Phi(w_i)) = \Sigma \Phi\Gamma'(v_{n-1}, \Phi(w_i)) \geq \Sigma\Gamma(\hat{v}_{n-1}, w_i) = 1$ so $\Sigma\Gamma'(v_{n-1}, \Phi(w_i)) = 1$. Since Γ' is deterministic and $\Gamma'(v_{n-1}, v_n) \neq 0$, $v_n = \Phi(w_i)$ for some i, completing the induction step. The same proof thus shows that $\Phi: E(\Gamma) \to E(\Gamma')$ in onto.

Let Γ be an L-automaton, let Γ' be an L'-automaton and let $\Phi: \Gamma \to \Gamma'$ be an exact homomorphism. An L' automaton $\Phi(\Gamma)$, the *image* of Γ under Φ, is defined in terms of $S(L')$ as follows:

$$V(\Phi(\Gamma)) = \Phi(V(\Gamma)),$$

$$(\Phi(\Gamma))(\Phi v, \Phi w) = \sum_{\substack{\Phi(r) = \Phi(v) \\ \Phi(s) = \Phi(w)}} \hat{\Phi}\Gamma(r, s),$$

(where $\hat{\Phi}$ is the support of the Boolean algebra homomorphism $\Phi: L' \to L$),

$$I(\Phi(\Gamma)) = \Phi I(\Gamma),$$

$$R(\Phi(\Gamma)) = \Phi R(\Gamma),$$

$$Z(\Phi(\Gamma)) = \Phi Z(\Gamma)$$

(where $\Phi Z(\Gamma) = \{\Phi(C) \mid C \in Z(\Gamma)\}$.

(7.2.8) **Lemma:** $\Phi(\Gamma)$ *is an* L'*-automaton, and* $\Phi: \Gamma \to \Phi(\Gamma)$ *maps* $E(\Gamma) \to E(\Phi\Gamma)$ *onto.*

Proof: It must be checked that $\Phi(\Gamma)$ is complete. Suppose for some $v \in V(\Gamma)$, $t \in S(L')$ and $t * \sum_{w \in V(\Gamma)} (\Phi\Gamma)(\Phi v, \Phi w) = 0$. Then, by (7.2.4) $0 = \Phi(t) * \sum_w \Phi(\Phi\Gamma)(\Phi v, \Phi w) \geq \Phi(t) * \sum_w \Gamma(v, w)$, contradicting the fact that Γ is complete. To check that $\Phi: E(\Gamma) \to E(\Phi\Gamma)$ is onto, suppose $e \in E(\Phi\Gamma)$ and let t be an atom of L' such that $t * (\Phi\Gamma)(e) \neq 0$. Then for some $v, w \in V(\Gamma)$ with

$(\Phi v, \Phi w) = e$, $\Gamma(v, w) * \Phi(t) \neq 0$, proving that $(v, w) \in E(\Gamma)$.

Note: It is possible for Γ to be deterministic while $\Phi\Gamma$ is not deterministic, as well as for $\Phi\Gamma$ to be deterministic while Γ is not deterministic.

(7.2.9) **Corollary:** *If* $\Phi\colon \Gamma \Rightarrow \Gamma'$ *and* Γ' *is deterministic, then* $\Phi(\Gamma) = \Gamma'$.

Proof: Let t be an atom satisfying $t * \Gamma'(\Phi(v), \Phi(w)) \neq 0$. For some $u \in V(\Gamma)$, $\Gamma(v, u) * \Phi(t) \neq 0$. Then $0 \neq \Gamma(v, u) * \Phi(t) \leq \Phi(\Phi\Gamma)(\Phi v, \Phi u) * \Phi(t)$, so $0 \neq (\Phi\Gamma)(\Phi v, \Phi u) * t$. By the determinism of Γ', $\Phi u = \Phi w$. Thus, $\Phi(\Gamma)(\Phi(v), \Phi(w)) = \Gamma'(\Phi(v), \Phi(w))$. The conclusion follows.

If $\Phi : \Gamma \Rightarrow \Gamma'$ is a homomorphism of the L-automaton Γ to the L'-automaton Γ', then the support $\hat{\Phi}$ of the Boolean algebra homomorphism $\Phi : L' \Rightarrow L$ induces a language homomorphism (7.0.1) which it is natural to call Φ, as well.

(7.2.10) **Theorem:** *If* Γ *is an L-automaton,* Γ' *is an* L'*-automaton and* $\Phi\colon \Gamma \Rightarrow \Gamma'$ *is a homomorphism, then* $\Phi^{-1}\mathcal{L}(\Gamma') \subset \mathcal{L}(\Gamma)$, *with equality holding if* Φ *is exact.*

Proof: Let $\mathbf{c}' = (\mathbf{v}', \mathbf{x}')$ be a chain of Γ', and let $\Phi^{-1}(\mathbf{c}') = \{\mathbf{c} = (\mathbf{v}, \mathbf{x}) \mid \Phi(\mathbf{c}) = \mathbf{c}'\}$ where $\Phi(\mathbf{c}) = ((\Phi(v_i))_i, (\hat{\Phi}(x_i))_i)$. By (7.1.3) and (7.2.1-4) it follows that $\Phi^{-1}(\mathbf{c}') \subset \mathcal{C}(\Gamma)$. Now, $\mathbf{x} \in \mathcal{L}(\Gamma)$ iff $(\mathbf{x}, \mathbf{v}) \in \mathcal{C}(\Gamma)$ for some $\mathbf{v}$, so $\Phi^{-1}\mathcal{L}(\Gamma') \subset \mathcal{L}(\Gamma)$. If Φ is exact, then $\Phi\mathcal{C}(\Gamma) \subset \mathcal{C}(\Gamma')$ and thus $\Phi\mathcal{C}(\Gamma) = \mathcal{C}(\Gamma')$, so $\mathcal{L}(\Gamma) = \Phi^{-1}\mathcal{L}(\Gamma')$.

(7.2.11) **Corollary:** *If* $\Phi : \Gamma \Rightarrow \Gamma'$ *is a homomorphism then* $\mathcal{L}(\Gamma') \subset \Phi\mathcal{L}(\Gamma)$; *if* Φ *is exact,* $\mathcal{L}(\Gamma') = \Phi\mathcal{L}(\Gamma)$.

Let Λ, Γ be L-automata and let Λ', Γ' be L'-automata. Homomorphisms $\Phi : \Lambda \Rightarrow \Lambda'$ and $\Psi : \Gamma \Rightarrow \Gamma'$ are said to be *co-linear* if they agree on L', *i.e.* $\Phi = \Psi : L' \Rightarrow L$.

(7.2.12) **Corollary:** *Let* $\Phi : \Lambda \Rightarrow \Lambda'$ *and* $\Psi : \Gamma \Rightarrow \Gamma'$ *be co-linear homomorphisms. Then*

1. *if* Φ *is exact then* $\mathcal{L}(\Lambda') \subset \mathcal{L}(\Gamma') \Rightarrow \mathcal{L}(\Lambda) \subset \mathcal{L}(\Gamma)$;

2. *if* Ψ *is exact then* $\mathcal{L}(\Lambda) \subset \mathcal{L}(\Gamma) \Rightarrow \mathcal{L}(\Lambda') \subset \mathcal{L}(\Gamma')$.

Proof: If Φ is exact and $\mathcal{L}(\Lambda') \subset \mathcal{L}(\Gamma')$ then $\mathcal{L}(\Lambda) = \Phi^{-1}\mathcal{L}(\Lambda') \subset \Phi^{-1}\mathcal{L}(\Gamma') = \Psi^{-1}\mathcal{L}(\Gamma') \subset \mathcal{L}(\Gamma)$. If Ψ is exact and $\mathcal{L}(\Lambda) \subset \mathcal{L}(\Gamma)$ then $\Phi^{-1}\mathcal{L}(\Lambda') \subset \mathcal{L}(\Lambda) \subset \mathcal{L}(\Gamma)$ so $\mathcal{L}(\Lambda') \subset \Phi\mathcal{L}(\Gamma) = \Psi\mathcal{L}(\Gamma) = \mathcal{L}(\Gamma')$.

7.3 *L*-Process Homomorphism

Process homomorphism is defined in a manner strictly analogous to automaton homomorphism, yielding analogous results. However, because of the difference in acceptance (the cyclic and recurring conditions for automata are negations of the respective conditions (4.3-4) for processes), and on account of the selections in processes, it is necessary to clarify the details.

Let Γ be an L-process and let Γ' be an L'-process. A *homomorphism*

$$\Phi : \Gamma \to \Gamma'$$

is a pair of maps $\Phi = (\phi, \psi')$ as in the definition of automaton homomorphism, satisfying (7.2.1-4). We adopt the same terminology and notational conventions here.

Let A be a lockup-free L-process, A' an L'-process and $\Phi : A \to A'$ a homomorphism. It follows from (4.2), (7.1.13) and the homomorphism condition (7.2.4) that for each $x \in S_A(v)$ there exists an $x' \in S_{A'}(\Phi v)$ such that $\hat{\Phi}(x) \leq x'$. Thus, if $A_1, \ldots, A_k$ are a family of independent, lockup-free L-processes with $L = \mathbb{B}[S(A)]$ for $A = \otimes A_i$, then in view of section (7.1), any homomorphism of A is uniquely defined in terms of maps of the selections of $A_1, \ldots, A_k$. Thus, homomorphisms of A are determined by homomorphisms of $A_1, \ldots, A_k$.

It is easily checked that the corresponding results to (7.2.5-9) hold for L-processes. Analogously, the following hold.

Theorem: *If A is an L-process, A' is an L'-process and $\Phi : A \to A'$ is a homomorphism then $\Phi\mathcal{L}(A) \subset \mathcal{L}(A')$, with equality holding if Φ is exact.*

Theorem: *Let A be an L-process, T an L-automaton, A' an L'-process, T' an L'-automaton and suppose*

$$\Phi : A \to A',$$

$$\Psi : T \to T'$$

are co-linear homomorphisms. Then

1. $\mathcal{L}(A') \subset \mathcal{L}(T') \Rightarrow \mathcal{L}(A) \subset \mathcal{L}(T)$;

2. *if* Φ *and* Ψ *are exact,*

$$\mathcal{L}(A) \subset \mathcal{L}(T) \Rightarrow \mathcal{L}(A') \subset \mathcal{L}(T').$$

8. Conclusions

Homomorphism has been shown to be a tool for reduction and refinement. It was shown how a homomorphism can be defined on a large space (implicitly) through homomorphisms on components. In the development of software and hardware systems, one begins with an abstract, high-level design and formally verifies that design for the performance of a variety of tasks, using reductions to cope with the complexity of this verification. Next, one redefines this design, adding more details. It is verified that this more detailed design is a refinement of the original design, and hence that all tasks whose performance were verified for the high-level design are guaranteed to be performed by the more detailed design as well. This is equivalent to proving that the high-level design is a reduction of the more detailed design, relative to all tasks performed by the high-level design (pulled back to the more detailed design). The more detailed design is verified for the performance of tasks not definable at the high level.

This step-wise refinement and verification continues until all details of the final implementation have been added to the model.

A measure of the success of this methodology may be taken from its application to large system development [HK90], where an order of magnitude saving in development time has been demonstrated, together with the production of an implementation which passing system test on the first trial with zero errors (virtually unknown with conventional development).

REFERENCES

[RS59] M. O. Rabin, D. Scott, "Finite Automata and their Decisions Problems", IBM J. Res. and Dev. **3** (1959) 114-125. (Reprinted in [Mo64] 63-91.)

[Ts59] M. L. Tsetlin, "Non-primitive Circuits" (in Russian) Problemy Kibernetiki **2** (1959).

[Bu62] J. R. Büchi, "On a Decision Method in Restricted Second-Order Arithmetic", Proc. Internat. Cong. on Logic, Methodol. and Philos. of Sci., 1960, 1-11 (Stanford Univ. Press, 1962).

[Ra69] M. O. Rabin, "Decidability of Second-Order Theories and Automata on Infinite Trees", Trans. Amer. Math. Soc. **141** (1969) 1-35.

[Ra72] M. O. Rabin, *Automata on Infinite Objects and Church's Problem.* Amer. Math. Soc., 1972.

[Ch74] Y. Choueka, "Theories of Automata on ω-Tapes: A Simplified Approach", J. Comput. Syst. Sci. **8** (1974), 117-141.

[Ha74] P. Halmos, *Lectures on Boolean Algebras*, Springer-Verlag, N.Y., 1974.

[GK80] B. Gopinath, R. P. Kurshan, "The Selection/Resolution Model of Coordinating Concurrent Processes", internal AT&T report.

[AKS83] S. Aggarwal, R. P. Kurshan, K. K. Sabnani, "A Calculus for Protocol Specification and Validation" in *Protocol Specification, Testing and Verification, III*, North-Holland, 1983, 19-34.

[DC85] D. L. Dill, E. M. Clarke, "Automatic Verification of Asynchronous Circuits Using Temporal Logic", Proc. Chapel Hill Conf. VLSI, Computer Sci. Press (1985) 127-143.

[Ku85] R. P. Kurshan, "Modelling Concurrent Processes", Proc. Symp. Applied Math. **3** (1985) 45-57.

[SVW85] A. P. Sistla, M. Y. Vardi, P. Wolper, "The Complementation Problem for Büchi Automata, with Applications to Temporal Logic", in Proc. 12th Internat. Coll. on Automata, Languages and Programming, *Lect. Notes Comp. Sci.*, 1985, Springer-Verlag.

[WA85] W. W. Wadge, E. A. Ashcroft, *LUCID, The Dataflow Programming Language*, Academic Press, 1985.

[KK86] J. Katzenelson and R. P. Kurshan, "S/R: A Language For Specifying Protocols and Other Coordinating Processes", Proc. 5th Ann. Int'l Phoenix Conf. Comput. Commun., IEEE, 1986, 286-292.

[BC87] M. C. Brown, E. M. Clarke, "SML – A High Level Language for the Design and Verification of Finite State Machines", in *From HDL Descriptions to Guaranteed Correct Circuit Designs* (D. Borrione, ed.) North-Holland (1987) 269-292.

[GK87] I. Gertner, R. P. Kurshan, "Logical Analysis of Digital Circuits", Proc. 8th Intn'l. Conf. Comput. Hardware Description Languages, 1987, 47-67.

[Ku87] R. P. Kurshan, "Reducibility in Analysis of Coordination", LNCIS **103** (1987) Springer Verlag, 19-39.

[Ku87a] R. P. Kurshan, "Complementing Deterministic Büchi Automata in Polynomial Time", J. Comput. Syst. Sci. **35** (1987) 59-71.

[RW87] P. J. Ramadge, W. M. Wonham, "Supervisory Control of a Class of Discrete-Event Processes", SIAM J. Contr. Opt. **25** (1987) 206-230.

[Sa88] S. Safra, "On the Complexity of ω-Automata", 29th FOCS (1988) 319-327.

[Ba89] J. Barwise, "Mathematical Proofs of Computer System Correctness", Notices AMS **36** (1989) 884-851.

[KM89] R. P. Kurshan, K. McMillan, "A Structural Induction Theorem for Processes", Proc. 8th ACM Symp. PODC (1989) 239-247.

[KM90] R. P. Kurshan, K. McMillan, "Analysis of Digital Circuits Through Symbolic Reduction", IEEE Trans. CAD/ICS, to appear.

[HK90] Z. Har'El, R. P. Kurshan, "Software for analytical Development of Communication Protocols", AT&T Tech. J., to appear.

Refinement and Projection of Relational Specifications*

Simon S. Lam

Department of Computer Sciences
The University of Texas at Austin
Austin, Texas 78712

A. Udaya Shankar

Department of Computer Science and
Institute for Advanced Computer Studies,
University of Maryland,
College Park, Maryland 20742

Abstract. A relational specification consists of a state transition system and a set of fairness assumptions. The state transition system is specified using two basic constructs: *state formulas* that respresent sets of states, and *event formulas* that represent sets of state transitions. We present a theory of *refinement* of relational specifications. Several refinement relations between specifications are defined. To illustrate our concepts and methods, three specifications of the alternating-bit protocol are given. We also apply the theory to explain "auxiliary variables." Other applications of the theory to protocol verification, composition, and conversion are discussed. Our approach is compared with the approaches of other authors.

Key words: Specification, refinement, protocols, distributed systems, temporal logic.

CONTENTS

1. Introduction
2. Relational Notation
3. System Specification
4. Proof Rules
5. Distributed Systems
6. Refinement and Projection of Relational Specifications
7. Auxiliary Variables
8. Specification Examples
9. Discussions and Related Work

* The work of Simon S. Lam was supported by National Science Foundation under grant no. NCR-8613338 and by a grant from the Texas Advanced Research Program. The work of A. Udaya Shankar was supported by National Science Foundation under grant no. ECS-8502113 and grant no. NCR-8904590. This paper is an abbreviated version of [Lam & Shankar 88].

1. Introduction

The concepts of *state* and *state transition* are fundamental to many formalisms for the specification and analysis of systems. For example, state-transition models are widely used for the specification of communication protocols in practice [IBM 80, ISO 85, Sabnani 88, West 78]. Most engineers and programmers are familiar with the concepts of state and state tranition and, in fact, many prefer working with these concepts [Piatkowski 86].

During the course of our research on modeling communication network protocols and time-dependent distributed systems, a formalism for specifying them as state transition systems has evolved [Shankar & Lam 84, 87a, 87b, Lam & Shankar 87]. Our formalism has been developed with the hope that protocol engineers will find our notation and the accompanying proof method to be easy to learn because states and state transitions are represented explicitly. But instead of individual states and state transitions, we work with *sets* of states and state transitions; these sets are specified using the language of predicate logic.

Our proof method is based upon a fragment of linear-time temporal logic [Chandy & Misra 88, Lamport 83a, Manna & Pnueli 84, Owicki & Lamport 82, Pnueli 86]. Motivated by examples in communication network protocols, we introduce several extensions to the body of work cited above. First, we introduce a "leads-to" proof rule designed for message-passing networks with unreliable channels. Second, we advocate the approach of stating fairness assumptions explicitly for individual events as part of a specification, noting that for many specifications only *some* events need be fairly scheduled. In general, to facilitate implementation, a specification includes fairness assumptions that are as weak as possible. While this idea is not new (see [Pnueli 86]), our definition of the *allowed behaviors* of a specification differs from Pnueli's definition of *fair computations* in that an allowed behavior may not be "maximal." Our definition is motivated by the specification of program modules to satisfy interfaces [Lynch & Tuttle 87, Lam & Shankar 87].

A *relational specification* consists of a state transition system given in the relational notation together with a set of fairness assumptions. We present a theory of refinement of relational specifications. Let A and B denote specifications. Several relations between A and B are defined. Other authors have defined similar relations between specifications: *A implements B*, *A simulates B*, etc. Every one of these relations is a form of the *subset* relation with the following meaning: every externally visible behavior allowed by A is also allowed by B [Lam & Shankar 84, Lamport 85, Lynch & Tuttle 87]. (There are differences in how behaviors and visible behaviors are defined.) Our definition of *A is a well-formed refinement of B* in this paper is essentially the same.

For many applications, we found the subset relation, as informally defined above, to be too strong to be useful. In refining a specification B to a specification A, it is seldom the case that every progress property of B must be preserved in A. In most cases, only *some* specific progress properties of B are to be preserved. In this paper, we provide a variety of relations between specifications. The *well-formed refinement* relation is the strongest. In our experience, it is seldom used. The *refinement* relation is the weakest. In our experience, it is always used. In [Shankar & Lam 87b], a weaker form of the refinement relation, called *conditional refinement*, is also defined for use in a stepwise refinement heuristic.

In refining a specification B to a specification A, if some state variables in B are replaced by new state variables in A, our approach is to find an "invariant" that specifies the relation between the new and old state variables. The approach of other authors is to find a special mapping from the states of A to the states of B [Abadi & Lamport 88, Lynch & Tuttle 87]. The relation to be found is the *same* in each approach. The approaches differ mainly in how such a relation is represented. (Instead of a special mapping, we use an invariant, auxiliary variables and a projection mapping.) To illustrate our method and to compare it with those of other authors, we present, in Section 8 below, three specifications of the alternating-bit protocol.

Since the specification and proof of communication networks with unreliable channels is an important application domain of ours, we have extended the theory of refinement to include the refinement of messages. Furthermore, for messages represented by a tuple of message fields, the concept of auxiliary variables is extended to include the use of *auxiliary fields* in messages.

2. Relational Notation

We consider state transition systems that are defined by a pair (S,T), where S is a countable set of states and T is a binary relation on S. T is a set of state transitions, each of which is represented by an ordered pair of states. Given (S,T) and an initial condition on the system state, a sequence of states $<s_0, s_1, \cdots>$ is said to be a *path* if s_0 satisfies the initial condition and, for $i \geq 0$, (s_i, s_{i+1}) is in T.

In the relational notation, a state transition system is specified by a set of state variables, $\mathbf{v}=\{v_1, v_2, \cdots\}$, a set of events, $e_1, e_2, \cdots$, and an initial condition, to be defined below. For every state variable, there is a specified domain of allowed values. The system state is represented by the set of values assumed by the state variables. The state space S of the system is the cartesian product of the state variable domains. The binary relation T is defined by the set of events (see below).

Parameters may be used for defining groups of related events, as well as groups of related system properties. Let $\mathbf{w}$ denote a set of parameters, each with a specified domain of allowed values.

Let $\mathbf{v}'$ denote the set of variables $\{v' : v \in \mathbf{v}\}$. In specifying an event, we use $\mathbf{v}$ and $\mathbf{v}'$ to denote, respectively, the system state before and after an event occurrence. Instead of a programming language, the language of predicate logic is used for specifying events. Such a language consists of a set of symbols for variables, constants, functions and predicates, and a set of formulas defined over the symbols [Manna & Waldinger 1985]. We assume that there is a known interpretation that assigns meanings to all of the function symbols and predicate symbols, and values to all of the constant symbols that we use. As a result, the truth value of a formula can be determined if values are assigned to its free variables.

The set of variables in our language is $\mathbf{v} \cup \mathbf{v}' \cup \mathbf{w}$. We will use two kinds of formulas: A formula whose free variables are in $\mathbf{v} \cup \mathbf{w}$ is called a *state formula*. A formula whose free variables are in $\mathbf{v} \cup \mathbf{v}' \cup \mathbf{w}$ is called an *event formula*.

A state formula can be evaluated to be true or false for each system state by adopting this convention: if a parameter occurs free in a state formula, it is assumed to be universally quantified over the parameter domain.

We say that a system state s satisfies a state formula P if and only if (iff) P evaluates to true for s. A state formula P represents the *set* of system states that satisfy P. In particular, the initial condition of the system is specified by a state formula. A system state that satisfies the initial condition is called an *initial state*. In the following, the letters P, Q, R and I are used to denote state formulas.

Events are specified by event formulas. Each event (formula) defines a *set* of system state transitions. (These sets may overlap.) The union of these sets over all events defines the binary relation T of the transition system. Some examples of event definitions are shown below:

$$e_1 \equiv v_1 > 2 \wedge v_2' \in \{1, 2, 5\}$$

$$e_2 \equiv v_1 > v_2 \wedge v_1 + v_2' = 5$$

where " $\equiv$ " denotes "is defined by." In each definition, the event name is given on the left-hand side and the event formula is given on the right-hand side. For convenience, we sometimes use the same symbol to denote the name of an event as well as the event formula that defines it. The context where the symbol appears will determine what it means.

Convention. Given an event formula e, for every state variable v in **v**, if v' is not a free variable of e then each occurrence of the event e does not change the value of v; that is, the conjunct $v'=v$ is implicit in the event formula.

For example, consider a system with two state variables v_1 and v_2. Let e_2 above be an event of the system. Note that v_1' is not a free variable of e_2. By the above convention, the event formula that defines e_2 is in fact $v_1 > v_2 \wedge v_1 + v_2' = 5 \wedge v_1' = v_1$.

If a parameter occurs free in an event definition, then the system has an event defined for each value in the domain of the parameter. For example, consider

$$e_3(m) \equiv v_1 > v_2 \wedge v_1 + v_2' = m$$

where m is a parameter. A parameterized event is a convenient way to specify a group of related events.

We next introduce the notion of the enabling condition of an event. An event (formula) defines a set of ordered pairs (s, s'), where $s \in S$ and $s' \in S$. Let the ordered pairs shown in Figure 1 be those defined by some event. The *enabling condition* of this event is defined by the three states shown inside the shaded area of Figure 1. (A formal definition is given below.)

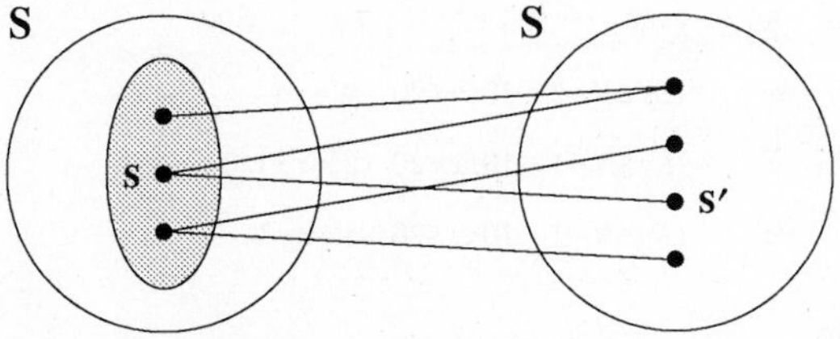

Figure 1. An illustration of an event formula and its enabling condition.

An event can occur only when the system state satisfies the enabling condition of the event. In any system state, more than one event may be enabled. The choice of the next event to occur from the set of enabled events is nondeterministic.[1] When an event occurs, we assume that the state variables of the system are updated in one *atomic* step.

Formally, the enabling condition of an event formula e, to be denoted by $enabled(e)$, is given by

$$enabled(e) \equiv \exists v'[e]$$

which is a state formula. Consider the following event formula as an example:

$$e_4 \equiv v_1 > v_2 \wedge v_1' = 1 \wedge v_2' = 0$$

Suppose the domain of each state variable is the set of natural numbers. We have

$$enabled(e_4) \equiv \exists v_1' \exists v_2' [e_4]$$

which is $v_1 > v_2$, because the expression $\exists v_1' \exists v_2' [v_1' = 1 \wedge v_2' = 0]$ is true.

For readability, we write many event formulas in the following *separable* form:

$$e \equiv guard \wedge action$$

where *guard* is a state formula and *action* is an event formula. We must keep in mind that for *guard* to be logically equivalent to $enabled(e)$, the two conjuncts in the separable form must satisfy the condition:

$$guard \Rightarrow \exists v'[action]$$

Otherwise, part of the enabling condition of e is specified by *action*.

In summary, the relational notation has two basic constructs: state formulas and event formulas. A state formula defines a set of system states. An event formula defines a set of system state transitions.

As an example, consider the following model of an object moving in two-dimensional space. Imagine that the object is an airplane flying from Austin to Dallas. There are two state variables: y is the horizontal distance from Austin along a straight line between the two cities, and z is the altitude of the airplane. The domain of y is $\{0, 1, \cdots, N\}$ such that $y=0$ indicates that the airplane is at Austin airport and $y=N$ indicates that the airplane is at Dallas airport. The domain of z is the set of natural numbers such that $z=0$ indicates that the airplane is on the ground. The initial condition is $y=0 \wedge z=0$, indicating that the airplane is on the ground at Austin airport. The events are defined as follows:

$$TakeOff \equiv y=0 \wedge z=0 \wedge y'=1 \wedge 10 \le z' \le 20$$

$$Landing \equiv y=N-1 \wedge 10 \le z \le 20 \wedge y'=N \wedge z'=0$$

$$Fly \equiv 1 \le y \le N-2 \wedge 10 \le z \le 20 \wedge y'=y+1$$

$$FlyHigher \equiv 1 \le y \le N-1 \wedge 10 \le z < 20 \wedge z'=z+1$$

$$FlyLower \equiv 1 \le y \le N-1 \wedge 10 < z \le 20 \wedge z'=z-1$$

3. System Specification

A system can be specified in many ways, in many notations. In this paper, we consider two related approaches. In the first approach, a system is specified by defining a state space, and giving a set of requirements each of which is an assertion of a desired system property. Two classes of system properties are of interest to us in this paper, namely, safety properties and progress properties. In particular,

[1] The choice is not strictly nondeterministic if the system specification includes fairness assumptions for some events (see Section 3 below).

we will use safety assertions of the form,

P is invariant

and progress assertions of the form,[2]

P *leads-to* Q

where P and Q are state formulas for the state space defined.

In the second approach, a specification consists of a state transition system given in the relational notation.[3] The two approaches are related in the following sense: A specification consisting of a state transition system *implements* a specification consisting of a set of requirements iff all of the requirements are properties of the state transition system.

We use the airplane example in Section 2 to illustrate the two classes of system properties. A safety requirement of the airplane example may be stated as follows: The airplane is in a specified portion of the air space if it is not at one of the airports. This is formalized by the assertion

$y \neq 0 \wedge y \neq N \Rightarrow 10 \leq z \leq 20$ is invariant

Safety properties of a state transition system are determined by its finite paths. The following definitions apply to state transition systems specified in any notation.

Definition. A system state s is *reachable* iff there is a finite path from an initial state to s.

Definition. P is invariant for a state transition system iff every reachable state of the system satisfies P.

If a parameter occurs free in the state formula P, then P is invariant for a state transition system iff, for every allowed value of the parameter, P is invariant for the system.

A progress requirement of the airplane example may be stated as follows: The airplane, initially at Austin, eventually arrives at Dallas. This is formalized by the assertion

$y=0 \wedge z=0$ *leads-to* $y=N \wedge z=0$

Let us first define the meaning of P *leads-to* Q for a sequence of states $\sigma = <s_0, s_1, \cdots>$. The sequence may be finite or infinite.

Definition. P *leads-to* Q for σ iff the following holds: if some state s_i in σ satisfies P then there is a state s_j in σ $(j \geq i)$ that satisfies Q.

Before defining 'P *leads-to* Q for a specification,' we next introduce the concept of fairness and two fairness criteria.

Note that a state transition system specified in the relational notation has the additional concept of named events. In any system state, several events may be enabled. Strict nondeterminism in choosing the event to occur next allows the possibility that some events never occur even though they are enabled continuously (or infinitely often). In the airplane example, for instance, there are many infinite paths that correspond to system executions in which the event *Fly* is continuously enabled but never occurs.

[2] In writing assertions containing *leads-to*, we adopt the convention that its binding power is weaker than any of the logical connectives in state formulas.

[3] and some fairness assumptions. The meaning of fairness is introduced below and can be ignored for now. In general, a specification may consist of a state transition system together with a set of of safety requirements and progress requirements. Such a general approach subsumes both approaches herein. See [Lam & Shankar 87, Shankar & Lam 87b].

Such unfair behavior is undesirable and should be disallowed by the system specification.

One way to disallow certain unfair behaviors is to refine the state transition system specification to include an event scheduler. In the airplane example, for instance, we can keep a count of the number of times *FlyHigher* and *FlyLower* have occurred since the last occurrence of *Fly* or *TakeOff* ; also, *FlyHigher* and *FlyLower* are disabled whenever the count exceeds some threshold value. Such a specification requires an additional state variable and various modifications of event actions. The specification, moreover, leaves little flexibility to system implementors who might have a different, yet better, solution to the event scheduling problem.

Instead of specifying event scheduling explicitly, fairness assumptions can be included as part of a system specification. Different criteria of fairness abound in the literature. The one that we use most often is *weak fairness*, also called *justice* [Manna & Pnueli 1984]. Informally, the meaning of an event having weak fairness is the following: if the event is continuously enabled in a system execution, it eventually occurs. (A more precise definition is given below. The *strong fairness* criterion is also defined below and used in subsequent sections.) For example, the airplane specification satisfies the progress requirement stated above, if the events *TakeOff* , *Fly* and *Landing* are scheduled in such a way that each event has *weak fairness*; the other events in the example do not have to be fairly scheduled.

Generally, to satisfy a given set of progress requirements, only some of the events in a specification need to be fairly scheduled. To facilitate implementation, a specification should include fairness assumptions that are as weak as possible. Very often, fairness assumptions can be weakened by defining a new event to be the disjunction of a set of events already defined, e.g.,

$$e_3 \equiv \exists m \, [e_3(m)]$$

$$e_5 \equiv e_1 \vee e_2$$

and showing that only the new event needs to be fairly scheduled, and not the individual events in the set.

For events defined by a parameterized formula, such as $e_3(m)$, we have to be especially careful. Suppose the domain of m is infinite. In this case, fair scheduling of $e_3(m)$ for every allowed value of m may or may not be a physically meaningful assumption.

At this point, we note that the set of paths is not adequate for defining fairness criteria for events. Specifically, each state transition in a path, say (s_i, s_j), may be due to the occurrence of any of several events. Therefore, the path may correspond to many possible system executions.

To define fairness criteria for events, we represent a system execution by a path in which each transition is labeled by the name of the event whose occurrence caused the transition. We refer to such a labeled path as a *behavior*.

Consider an event e and an infinite behavior β, we define two fairness criteria:

- Event e has *weak fairness* for infinite behavior β iff e either occurs infinitely often or is disabled infinitely often in β. [4]

[4] The following definition is equivalent: Event e has weak fairness for infinite behavior β iff for some state s_k in β and for all $i \geq k$, if state s_i satisfies *enabled(e)* then there is some state s_j in β ($j \geq k$) such that the transition from s_j to s_{j+1} is labeled e.

- Event e has *strong fairness* for infinite behavior β iff the following holds: e occurs infinitely often in β if it is enabled infinitely often in β.

It is easy to see that if β satisfies the strong fairness criterion for event e, then it also satisfies the weak fairness criterion for event e. (The converse does not hold.) The weak and strong fairness criteria are the only ones used in this paper. Thus, when we say that a specification includes a fairness assumption for event e, we mean that event e has either weak fairness or strong fairness.

For a given specification consisting of a state transition system and a set of fairness assumptions, the *allowed behaviors* of the specification are defined as follows: [5]

- A finite behavior of the state transition system is an allowed behavior of the specification iff every event that has a fairness assumption in the specification is disabled in the last state of the behavior.
- An infinite behavior of the state transition system is an allowed behavior of the specification iff every fairness assumption of the specification holds for the behavior.

Definition. P *leads–to* Q for a behavior β iff P *leads–to* Q for the sequence of states in β.

Definition. P *leads–to* Q for a specification iff P *leads–to* Q for every allowed behavior of the specification.

If a parameter occurs free in P or Q, then P *leads–to* Q for a specification iff, for every allowed value of the parameter, P *leads–to* Q for the specification.

In Section 4 below, we present some inference rules for proving the two kinds of assertions introduced above. Before doing that, we digress and discuss the use of *auxiliary variables* in a specification. That is, some of the state variables in **v** may be auxiliary variables, which are needed for specification and verification only, and do not have to be included in an actual implementation (this notion will be made more precise in Section 7). For example, an auxiliary variable may be needed to record the history of certain event occurrences.[6] Informally, a subset of variables in **v** can be considered auxiliary if they do not affect the enabling condition of any event nor do they affect the update of any state variable that is not auxiliary [Owicki & Gries 76]. To state the above condition precisely, let **u** be a proper subset of **v**, and $\mathbf{u}' = \{v' : v \in \mathbf{u}\}$. The state variables in **u** can be considered auxiliary if, for every event e of the system, the following holds:

$$e \Rightarrow \forall \mathbf{u} \exists \mathbf{u}'[e]$$

To see why auxiliary variables do not have to be included in an actual implementation of a specification, suppose there is an observer and it can only see nonauxiliary variables. The above condition ensures that the set of 'observable behaviors' of the specification is the same whether or not auxiliary variables are part of the system state. We will elaborate on this explanation in Section 7 after the theory of refinement and projection has been presented.

---

[5] This definition is motivated by the specification of a program module to satisfy its interfaces; specifically, some interface events may be controlled by the environment and not controllable by the module [Lynch & Tuttle 87, Lam & Shankar 87]. For this reason, an allowed behavior is not necessarily *maximal*, as in [Manna & Pnueli 84].

[6] What we call auxiliary variables here are also known as history variables. Abadi and Lamport [1988] defined another kind of auxiliary variables called prophecy variables.

4. Proof Rules

Consider a specification consisting of a state transition system given in the relational notation and a set of fairness assumptions. Let e denote an arbitrary event and *Initial* denote a state formula specifying the initial condition.

Notation. For an arbitrary state formula Q, we use Q' to denote the formula obtained by replacing every free state variable v in Q by v'.

Invariance rules: For a given specification, P is invariant if one of the following holds:

- $Initial \Rightarrow P$ and, for all e, $P \wedge e \Rightarrow P'$
- for some R, R is invariant and $R \Rightarrow P$

In applying the first invariance rule, if I is invariant for the specification, we can replace $P \wedge e \Rightarrow P'$ in the rule with $I \wedge I' \wedge P \wedge e \Rightarrow P'$. Also, we follow this convention: For p and q being formulas with free variables, $p \Rightarrow q$ is logically valid iff $p \Rightarrow q$ is logically valid for all values of the free variables.

For convenience, if P is invariant for a specification, we refer to the formula P as an *invariant property* of the specification or, simply, an invariant.

Definition: For a given specification in which event e_i has weak fairness, P *leads-to* Q *via* e_i iff

(i) $P \wedge e_i \Rightarrow Q'$,

(ii) for all e, $P \wedge e \Rightarrow P' \vee Q'$, and

(iii) $P \Rightarrow enabled(e_i)$ is invariant.

Definition: For a given specification in which event e_i has strong fairness, P *leads-to* Q *via* e_i iff

(i) $P \wedge e_i \Rightarrow Q'$,

(ii) for all e, $P \wedge e \Rightarrow P' \vee Q'$, and

(iii) P *leads-to* $Q \vee enabled(e_i)$.

If I is invariant for the specification, it can be used to strengthen the antecedent of every logical implication in the above definitions; that is, replace P by $I \wedge I' \wedge P$. Also, if the event formula defining e_i has a free parameter, then P *leads-to* Q *via* e_i holds iff each part of the applicable definition holds for every allowed value of the free parameter.

Leads-to rules: For a given specification, P *leads-to* Q if one of the following holds:

- $P \Rightarrow Q$ is invariant [Implication]
- for some event e_i that has fairness, P *leads-to* Q *via* e_i [Event]
- for some R, P *leads-to* R and R *leads-to* Q [Transitivity]
- $P = \exists m \in M [P(m)]$ and $\forall m \in M : P(m)$ *leads-to* Q [Disjunction]

Note that there are actually two Event rules, one for events that have weak fairness and one for events that have strong fairness, to be referred to as the *weak* and *strong* Event rules, respectively. In the Disjunction rule, m denotes a parameter with domain M; also, m does not occur free in Q. A special case of the Disjunction rule is the following: P *leads-to* Q if P_1 *leads-to* Q, P_2 *leads-to* Q, and $P = P_1 \vee P_2$.

What we have presented above is a fragment of linear-time temporal logic.[7] In the next section, we consider message-passing networks with unreliable channels. An additional leads-to rule is presented there. But before doing so, we state two lemmas that are needed in Section 6. (Proofs of the lemmas can be found in [Lam & Shankar 88].)

Lemma 1: For a given specification, P_0 *leads-to* $(Q \vee P_2)$ if

(i) P_0 *leads-to* $(Q \vee P_1)$, and

(ii) P_1 *leads-to* $(Q \vee P_2)$

Lemma 2: For a given specification, if I is invariant and $P \wedge I$ *leads-to* Q, then P *leads-to* Q.

5. Distributed Systems

The relational notation and proof method introduced above are not dependent on whether a distributed or centralized system is being specified. The relevant assumption we have made is that event actions are atomic; consequently, concurrent actions in different modules of a system are modeled by interleaving them in any order.

We next consider distributed systems that are *message-passing* networks. In particular, the network topology is a directed graph whose nodes are called *entities* and whose arcs are called *channels*. For each channel i, there is a state variable that represents the channel state, given by the sequence of messages travelling along the channel. Errors that can occur to messages travelling along a channel are specified by introducing events whose occurrences can update the channel state.[8] The events of a channel can access (read or update) only the channel state variable and auxiliary state variables of the system.

Each entity in a distributed system is specified by a set of state variables and events. Every nonauxiliary state variable in the set is assumed to be local to the entity; that is, it can only be accessed by events of the entity.[9] Entity events can also access auxiliary state variables of the system, as well as state variables representing channels that are connected to the entity.

For clarity in writing specifications, channel state variables are accessed by entities only via send and receive primitives that are defined for the channels. For example, let $\mathbf{z}_i$ be a state variable

[7] Essentially a derivative of the work in [Manna & Pnueli 84, Pnueli 86]. A proof that the invariance and leads-to rules are sound is straightforward and is omitted. The reader is also referred to [Chandy & Misra 88] for a comprehensive treatment of proof rules.

[8] If a channel is assumed to be error-free, then no event is introduced for the channel and it behaves like a FIFO queue. If messages travelling along a channel can be duplicated and arbitrarily reordered, it might appear that representing the channel state by a bag of messages is more appropriate. It is easy to see, however, that there is no loss of generality in representing the channel state by a sequence of messages.

[9] Actually, a nonauxiliary state variable of one entity can be read by another entity provided that the value read affects the update of auxiliary variables only.

representing channel i that is a channel with unbounded capacity. Let m denote a message. Define

$$Send_i(m) \equiv \mathbf{z}_i' = \mathbf{z}_i @ m$$

$$Rec_i(m) \equiv \mathbf{z}_i = m @ \mathbf{z}_i'$$

where @ denotes the concatenation operator. Note that $Rec_i(m)$ is *false* if $\mathbf{z}_i$ is empty. Primitives for channels with a finite capacity can be similarly defined. Such a primitive is simply an event formula that has m, $\mathbf{z}_i$ and $\mathbf{z}_i'$ as free variables; thus the names $Send_i(m)$ and $Rec_i(m)$ are introduced primarily to improve the readability of events in a system specification.

For a given message m, an event whose occurrence sends message m along a specified channel is called a *send event* of m. An event whose occurrence receives message m from the channel is called a *receive event* of m. If a message symbol m occurs free in a formula that defines a send event or a receive event for the channel, the domain of m is assumed to be known; for notational brevity, it will not be explicitly shown.

To prove that a message-passing network has useful progress properties, we need two assumptions. First, we assume that the system specification includes "adequate" receive events in the following sense:

Receive events assumption: For message m that is sent along channel i, let $\{e_h(m)\}$ denote the set of receive events of m. For every message and every channel, the set of receive events in the specification satisfies

$$m = Head(\mathbf{z}_i) \Rightarrow \exists h\,[enabled(e_h(m))] \text{ is invariant}$$

for the specification, where $\mathbf{z}_i$ is the channel state variable, *Head* is a function whose value is the first element of $\mathbf{z}_i$ if $\mathbf{z}_i$ is not null; otherwise, *Head* returns a null value (that is not an allowed message value).

For distributed systems with unreliable channels that can lose or reorder messages, a second assumption is needed, namely: the unreliable channels have some minimal progress property. (Otherwise, the channels may be so unreliable that they do not really exist.) Such an assumption should be as weak as possible such that it can be satisfied by most physical communication links. The following is adapted from [Hailpern & Owicki 83]:

Channel progress assumption: If messages in a set M are sent infinitely often along a channel, then they are received infinitely often from the channel.

Informally, if messages in set M are sent repeatedly along a channel, one of them is eventually received. The channel progress assumption can be viewed as a fairness assumption. For a system with unreliable channels, an infinite behavior is an allowed behavior of the specification only if the channel progress assumption holds for the behavior.

Before stating another rule for proving leads-to assertions, we define a new *leads-to-via* relation between state formulas. In the following definition, m denotes a message, e_r denotes a receive event of messages in set M for a given channel, and $count(M)$ denotes an auxiliary variable whose value indicates the total number of times messages in M have been sent along the channel since the beginning of system execution.

Definition: For a given specification, P *leads–to* Q *via* M iff

(i) for all e_r, $\forall m \in M\ [P \wedge e_r(m) \Rightarrow Q']$,

(ii) for all e, $P \wedge e \Rightarrow P' \vee Q'$, and

(iii) $P \wedge count(M) \geq k$ *leads–to* $Q \vee count(M) \geq k+1$

Given the channel progress assumption, we have the following leads-to rule (in addition to the ones presented in Section 4).

Leads-to rule: For a given specification, P *leads–to* Q if

- for some M, P *leads–to* Q *via* M [Message]

We next give a few general observations about the use of our notation and proof method for specifying distributed systems.

First, each nonauxiliary state variable in a distributed system, other than channel state variables, is local to some entity and can be accessed by any event of that entity. Suppose we want to refine the entity into a network of entities. To do so, we may have to make some of the nonauxiliary state variables of the entity into auxiliary variables and also introduce new state variables (more on refinement in the next section).

Second, specific applications of our proof rules may be very simple for events that access a small subset of state variables. In applying the first invariance rule, for instance, if none of the free state variables in P is updated by event e then $P \wedge e \Rightarrow P'$ is trivially satisfied. While most events in a distributed system access a small subset of state variables, the above observation is applicable to any system specification. Note that information on the subset of state variables accessed by an event is available from the syntax of the event definition.

Lastly, in applying leads-to rules to prove a progress property, we must be careful to avoid circular reasoning. A good practice is to present the proof as a sequence of leads-to properties: $L_0, L_1, \cdots, L_m$. Suppose L_0 is the desired property. To prove L_i in the sequence by a leads-to rule, or a lemma, that uses another progress property L_j, we require that L_i precedes L_j in the sequence.

6. Refinement and Projection of Relational Specifications

Throughout this section, we consider specifications A and B, each consisting of a state transition system and a set of fairness assumptions. We introduce two relations between A and B: *A is a refinement of B*, and *A is a well-formed refinement of B*. Before defining what they mean, we mention two possible applications for motivation: First, A is the specification of a multifunction communication protocol and B is the specification of a smaller protocol that implements just one of the functions of A [Shankar & Lam 83]. Second, A is the specification of a program module and B is the specification of its user interface.[10]

The refinement relations are useful for composing system specifications, as well as for constructing proofs of system properties, in a hierarchical fashion. (We will elaborate on applications in Section

[10] Actually, a small extension to the theory presented in this section is needed for interfaces; see [Lam & Shankar 87].

9.) In general, we proceed as follows. Suppose B is given or is specified first, and some desirable properties have been proved for B. We would like to derive A from B such that some or all of the desirable properties proved for B are guaranteed, by satisfying certain conditions, to be properties of A. That is, they do not have to be proved again for A.

To define the refinement relation, let V_A and V_B denote the state variable sets of A and B respectively. Specifically, let V_A be the set $\{v_1,v_2, \cdots ,v_n\}$ and V_B the subset $\{v_1,v_2, \cdots ,v_m\}$, where $m \leq n$. That is, in deriving A from B, every state variable in B is kept as a state variable in A with the same name and the same domain of values. (This is not a restriction, as we shall see, because such a state variable can be made into an auxiliary variable in A.) Since V_B is a subset of V_A there is a projection mapping from the states of A to the states of B, defined as follows: those states in A having the same values for $\{v_1,v_2, \cdots ,v_m\}$ are mapped to the same state in B. We further require that every parameter in B is a parameter in A with the same name and same domain of values. Given the above requirements, any state formula, say P, of B is a state formula of A and can be interpreted directly for A without any translation. The interpretation is this one: if state t of B satisfies P then any state of A whose image is t under the projection mapping satisfies P.

For clarity, we assume that A and B have finite sets of state variables and parameters. The domain of a state variable (or parameter) may be countably infinite.

Let $\{a_i\}$ denote the set of events of A, and $\{b_k\}$ the set of events of B. We first provide conditions for an event in specification A to be a refinement of events in specification B. An informal explanation then follows.

Event a_i in A is a refinement of events in B if, for some invariant R_A of A, one of the following holds:

$$R_A \wedge a_i \Rightarrow \exists k\,[b_k] \qquad \text{(event refinement condition)}$$

$$R_A \wedge a_i \Rightarrow v_1'=v_1 \wedge v_2'=v_2 \wedge \cdots \wedge v_m'=v_m \qquad \text{(null image condition)}$$

Very often, a_i is the refinement of a single event in B. In this case, to check that a_i satisfies the event refinement condition, it is sufficient to show that, for some b_k, either $a_i \Rightarrow b_k$ or $R_A \wedge a_i \Rightarrow b_k$.

Informally, the meaning of event a_i being a refinement of events in B is the following: For every state transition defined by a_i that is observable in the state space of B, the same observable state transition is defined in B. More precisely, if a_i can take A from state s_1 to s_2 then there is some event b_k that can take B from state t_1 to t_2, where t_1 and t_2 are the images of s_1 and s_2 respectively under the projection mapping. This condition can be relaxed by introducing an invariant property R_A of A, in which case the condition has to hold only for each (s_1,s_2) pair such that s_1 and s_2 satisfy R_A. Note that the invariant R_A introduced will have to be proved separately to be a property of A.

The null image condition says the following: Event a_i is a refinement of events in B if none of its state transitions are observable in B under the projection mapping, namely, $t_1=t_2$ for all s_1 and s_2 reachable in A such that (s_1,s_2) is defined by a_i. This can be checked very simply by noting that the action of a_i does not update any state variable belonging to V_B.

Suppose specification B is given, and specification A is to be derived from B. The invariant properties needed to guarantee events in A to be refinements of events in B often arise naturally in the following manner. Suppose we want to replace a state variable x in B by two state variables y and z in A; also, x is to become an auxiliary variable in A. To prove $a_i \Rightarrow b_k$, where b_k may contain x as a free variable, a state formula specifying the relation between x, y and z in A must be included as a conjunct of R_A. Note that this relation encodes the same information as the multi-valued possibilities mapping of Lynch and Tuttle [1987]. For the special case of the relation being a function, the function is just like the state functions used by Lamport [1983a]. We provide an example to illustrate this observation.

Example. Let x be a state variable of B. Its domain is the set of natural numbers. The following event is defined in B:

$$b_1 \equiv even(x) \wedge x'=x+1$$

where $even(x)$ is true iff x is an even number. In deriving A from B, suppose we introduce a variable y with domain $\{0,1\}$ to replace x, and the following event is defined:

$$a_1 \equiv y=0 \wedge y'=1 \wedge x'=x+1$$

Event a_1 is a refinement of b_1 given that $y=x \bmod 2$ is invariant for A. Note that x can be made into an auxiliary variable of A so that it does not have to be included in an actual implementation of A.

We next consider the refinement of messages. Let M be a set of messages that can be sent along a channel in B. In deriving A from B, the message set M can be refined as follows: Each message m in M is refined to a nonempty set N_m of messages in A. For two distinct messages i and j in M, we require $N_i \cap N_j = \emptyset$. For message m in B and message n in A, we say that n is a refinement of m, or m is the image of n, if and only if $n \in N_m$. Let N denote the set of messages that can be sent along the same channel in A,

$$N = \bigcup_{m \in M} N_m \cup N_{new}$$

where N_{new} is a set of new messages, if any. Such new messages are not observable in the state space of B and are said to have a *null image* in B. Note that the receive events assumption must be satisfied by specification A for all messages in N.

Example. In B, the message set for some channel consists of the message *ack* only. In A, the message set for the same channel is refined to {*ack*0, *ack*1, *nak*}, such that *ack* is the image of *ack*0 and *ack*1, and the new message *nak* has a null image.

If N is different from M for a channel, then the channel state variables in A and B have different domains for the same channel. The projection mapping from channel states in A to channel states in B is defined as follows [Lam & Shankar 84]: Let $\mathbf{y} = \langle n_1, n_2, \cdots \rangle$ be a sequence of messages representing a channel state in A. The image of the channel state, denoted by $image(\mathbf{y})$, is the sequence obtained by replacing each message in $\mathbf{y}$ by its image in B and deleting null images from the resulting sequence.

Given the above definition of projection mapping for channel states, a state formula of B, say P, can be interpreted for A as before, namely: state s of A satisfies P iff the image of s in B satisfies P. In this case, however, a translation between the message sets N and M is needed to interpret state formulas of B for A.

For a channel with message set N in A and message set M in B, let **y** denote the channel state variable in A, and **x** the channel state variable in B. The send and receive primitives in B are

$$Send(m) \equiv \mathbf{x}'=\mathbf{x}@m \text{ and } Rec(m) \equiv \mathbf{x}=m@\mathbf{x}'$$

The primitives for the same channel in A are

$$Send(n) \equiv \mathbf{y}'=\mathbf{y}@n \text{ and } Rec(n) \equiv \mathbf{y}=n@\mathbf{y}'$$

For send and receive events in A to be refinements of events in B, it is necessary that send and receive primitives in A are refinements of send and receive primitives in B for the same channel. To show that such send and receive primitives satisfy the event refinement condition, let **x** be an auxiliary state variable of A. For every message n in N with a nonnull image m in M, add the conjunct $\mathbf{x}'=\mathbf{x}@m$ to the formula defining $Send(n)$, and the conjunct $\mathbf{x}'=Tail(\mathbf{x})$ to the formula defining $Rec(n)$. It is easy to see that $\mathbf{x}=image(\mathbf{y})$ is an invariant of A, and that this invariant property ensures that the send and receive primitives satisfy the event refinement condition. Note that the relation between **x** and **y** defined by the invariant encodes the same information as the projection mapping defined between channel states in A and channel states in B.

Let $Initial_A$ and $Initial_B$ be state formulas defining the initial conditions of specifications A and B respectively.

Definition: A is a refinement of B if and only if every event in A is a refinement of events in B and $Initial_A \Rightarrow Initial_B$.

We say that B is an image of A under the projection mapping if and only if A is a refinement of B; that is, the relation *image* is the inverse of the relation *refinement* by definition. In some applications, we are first given A, and B is to be derived from A. For example, let A be some multifunction communication protocol. To prove that A has certain desirable properties, the following approach may be taken: Derive from A, single-function protocols that are images of A. Prove that these single-function protocols have the desirable properties, and infer that A has the same properties by the lemmas and theorems presented below.

Recall that P is a state formula of specification B iff every free variable of P is either in V_B or is a parameter.

Theorem 1: Let specification A be a refinement of specification B. If P is invariant for B then P is invariant for A, where P is an arbitrary state formula of B.

Proof: Let R_B denote a state formula that satisfies the first invariance rule for B and $R_B \Rightarrow P$. Let R_A be an invariant of A that makes events of A satisfy the event refinement condition or the null image condition. First, from $Initial_A \Rightarrow Initial_B$ and $Initial_B \Rightarrow R_B$, we have $Initial_A \Rightarrow R_B$. Second, for every event a_i of A that satisfies the event refinement condition, we have

$$\begin{aligned} R_B \wedge R_A \wedge a_i &\Rightarrow R_B \wedge (\exists k\,[b_k]) \\ &\Rightarrow \exists k\,[R_B \wedge b_k] \\ &\Rightarrow R_B{}' \end{aligned}$$

For every event a_i of A that satisfies the null image condition, we have

$$R_B \wedge R_A \wedge a_i \Rightarrow R_B \wedge v_1'=v_1 \wedge v_2'=v_2 \wedge \cdots \wedge v_m'=v_m$$

$$\Rightarrow R_B'$$

Thus, R_B is invariant for A by the first invariance rule. We know that $R_B \Rightarrow P$ holds for A, and the proof is complete by the second invariance rule.

Q.E.D.

For a given specification, the following property

for all event e, $P \wedge e \Rightarrow P' \vee Q'$

is called *P unless Q*, which is a safety property [Chandy & Misra 1988]. If A is a refinement of B, the following lemma says that every *unless* property of B is also an *unless* property of A.

Lemma 3: Let specification A be a refinement of specification B. If P *unless* Q holds for B then P *unless* Q holds for A, where P and Q are arbitrary state formulas of B.

A proof of Lemma 3 is immediate by applying the event refinement and null image conditions. We next consider leads-to properties of B and provide various sufficient conditions for some, or all, of these properties to be properties of A. We first state a useful lemma, which is the PSP theorem in [Chandy & Misra 88].

Lemma 4: For a given specification, if P *unless* Q holds and Q_1 *leads-to* Q_2, then

$P \wedge Q_1$ *leads-to* $Q \vee (P \wedge Q_2)$ for the specification.

A proof of Lemma 4 is given in [Lam & Shankar 88]. (Note that our inference rules and fairness assumptions are different from those of Chandy and Misra [1988].)

Suppose we have proved that P *leads-to* Q for B. The proof may be direct, by an application of the Implication rule or the weak Event rule, or it may consist of a sequence of leads-to properties. We present below various conditions under which we can infer P *leads-to* Q for A, where P and Q are state formulas of B.

First, if the proof is by an application of the Implication rule, we immediately have P *leads-to* Q for A by Theorem 1. Next, consider the weak Event rule. Suppose P *leads-to* Q *via* b_j for B, where b_j has weak fairness. To guarantee that P *leads-to* Q for A, we may apply Lemma 5, 6 or 7, where P and Q are assumed to be known. Or we may apply Lemma 8, where P and Q can be arbitrary state formulas of B. Proofs of these lemmas are given in [Lam & Shankar 88]. In the balance of this section, R_A denotes some invariant of A.

Lemma 5: Let specification A be a refinement of specification B, and b_j an event that has fairness in B. If P *leads-to* Q *via* b_j for B, then P *leads-to* Q for A if there is some event in A, denoted by a_j, that has weak fairness, is a refinement of b_j, and

$R_A \wedge P \Rightarrow Q \vee enabled(a_j)$

The last condition in Lemma 5 can be weakened if event a_j has the following **noninterference property** in A: for all event $a_i, i \neq j$,

$$R_A \wedge enabled(a_j) \wedge a_i \Rightarrow enabled(a_j)'.$$

Lemma 6: Let specification A be a refinement of specification B, and b_j an event that has fairness in B. If P *leads–to* Q *via* b_j for B, then P *leads–to* Q for A if there is some event in A, denoted by a_j, that has weak fairness and the noninterference property, is a refinement of b_j, and

$$R_A \wedge P \text{ leads–to } Q \vee enabled(a_j) \text{ for } A.$$

However, if event a_j has strong fairness in A, the noninterference property is not needed. We have the following result.

Lemma 7: Let specification A be a refinement of specification B, and b_j an event that has fairness in B. If P *leads–to* Q *via* b_j for B, then P *leads–to* Q for A if there is some event in A, denoted by a_j, that has strong fairness, is a refinement of b_j, and

$$R_A \wedge P \text{ leads–to } Q \vee enabled(a_j) \text{ for } A.$$

Now, suppose we want to guarantee that if P *leads–to* Q *via* b_j for B, then P *leads–to* Q for A, for arbitrary state formulas P and Q. We need conditions that do not make use of P or Q.

SWF Condition: For event b_j that has weak fairness in B, an event in A, denoted by a_j, is a well-formed refinement of b_j if

- a_j is a refinement of b_j
- $R_A \wedge enabled(b_j) \Rightarrow enabled(a_j)$, and
- a_j has weak fairness

The conditions in SWF are simple and easy to use. It has been our experience, in specifying communication protocols and concurrency control protocols, that many events can be refined to satisfy SWF. Such an event is said to be a strongly well-formed refinement. But sometimes, SWF cannot be satisfied, or b_j has strong fairness in B. We provide a second condition:

WF Condition: For event b_j that has fairness (weak or strong) in B, an event in A, denoted by a_j, is a well-formed refinement of b_j if

- a_j is a refinement of b_j
- $R_A \wedge enabled(b_j)$ *leads–to* $enabled(a_j)$ for A, and
- either a_j has weak fairness and the noninterference property

  or a_j has strong fairness

Lemma 8: Let specification A be a refinement of specification B, and b_j an event that has weak fairness in B. If P *leads–to* Q *via* b_j for B, then P *leads–to* Q for A if there is some event in A that is a well-formed refinement of b_j.

Note that Lemmas 5-7 are proved for an event b_j that has fairness (weak or strong) in B. Lemma 8 is proved for an event b_j that has weak fairness in B; the more general result for an event b_j that has strong fairness in B is included in Theorem 2 below. For some applications, it is desirable that *every* leads-to property of B is a leads-to property of A. A sufficient condition is the following:

Definition: Specification A is a *well-formed refinement* of specification B (or B is a *well-formed image* of A) if and only if

- A is a refinement of B, and
- for every event b_j that has fairness (weak or strong) in B, there is an event in A that is a well-formed refinement of b_j.

Theorem 2: Let specification A be a well-formed refinement of specification B. If P *leads-to* Q for B then P *leads-to* Q for A, where P and Q are arbitrary state formulas of B.

A proof of Theorem 2 is given in [Lam & Shankar 88]. As an example, let us now consider a refinement of the airplane specification in Section 2. Let the state variables y and z be augmented by a third state variable x, with domain over all integers, so that we will be reasoning about trajectories of the airplane in 3-dimensional space. Initially, $x=0$. Five events, labeled by *, are defined in terms of events of the 2-variable specification as follows:

$$TakeOff^* \equiv TakeOff \wedge x=0 \wedge -10 \le x' \le 10$$

$$Landing^* \equiv Landing \wedge -10 \le x \le 10 \wedge x'=0$$

$$Fly^* \equiv Fly \wedge -10 \le x \le 10$$

$$FlyHigher^* \equiv FlyHigher \wedge -10 \le x \le 10$$

$$FlyLower^* \equiv FlyLower \wedge -10 \le x \le 10$$

It is easy to see that the above events are refinements of corresponding events in the 2-variable specification. Add the following two events:

$$FlyLeft \equiv 1 \le y \le N-1 \wedge 10 \le z \le 20 \wedge -10 < x \le 10 \wedge x'=x-1$$

$$FlyRight \equiv 1 \le y \le N-1 \wedge 10 \le z \le 20 \wedge -10 \le x < 10 \wedge x'=x+1$$

The two new events are also refinements because they are null-image events whose occurrences are not observable in the 2-variable specification. Hence, the new 3-variable specification is a refinement of the 2-variable specification. Like the 2-variable specification, the events *TakeOff**, *Fly** and *Landing** have weak fairness. It is easy to show that each original event and its refinement satisfy the SWF condition given the following invariant requirement:

$$R_A \equiv (y=0 \wedge z=0 \Rightarrow x=0) \wedge (1 \le y \le N-1 \Rightarrow -10 \le x \le 10)$$

The above is easily shown to be an invariant of the 3-variable specification. Thus invariant and progress properties of the 2-variable specification are also properties of the 3-variable specification. Once proved for the 2-variable specification, they do not have to be proved again for the 3-variable specification.

In summary, we have given several conditions to ensure that some or all of the properties of specification B are properties of specification A. Of these conditions, the well-formed refinement relation between two specifications is the strongest. (Its semantics is essentially the same as the *simulation* or *implementation* relation of other authors [Abadi & Lamport 88, Lamport 83b, Lamport 85, Lynch & Tuttle 87].) For some applications, such a condition may be too strong to be useful. For these applications, it may be enough to ensure that only safety properties of B are preserved in A, or safety properties and some *specific* progress properties of B are preserved in A. In this case, only those events that are needed in the proof of the desired progress properties of B have to satisfy the WF or SWF condition. In fact, the weaker conditions in Lemmas 5-7 can be used instead.

In general, the SWF condition should be regarded as a 'shortcut.' For a given event, the SWF condition is checked first. If it is too strong and cannot be easily satisfied, then one of the weaker conditions is used.

In refining the events of B to get events of A, the event refinement and null image conditions are generally easy to satisfy. However, if some state variables in B are replaced by new state variables in A (and made into auxiliary variables in A) then finding an invariant that specifies the relation between the old and new state variables may be nontrivial. This problem is the same as finding a multi-valued possibilities mapping from the states of A to the states of B, as in [Lynch & Tuttle 87].

7. Auxiliary Variables

We can now give a rigorous explanation of auxiliary variables. Consider a specification A consisting of a state transition system and some fairness assumptions. Let the initial condition of A be denoted by $Initial_A$ and its events by $\{a_i\}$. Suppose the set $\mathbf{v}$ of state variables of A is partitioned into two sets, $\mathbf{u}$ and $\mathbf{x}$, such that an observer can only see the state variables in $\mathbf{x}$. In this case, the observable behaviors of A are behaviors of a specification C derived from A as follows: The state variables of C are the ones in $\mathbf{x}$. The initial condition of C is

$$Initial_C \equiv \exists \mathbf{u}[Initial_A]$$

The events of C are defined by

$$c_i \equiv \forall \mathbf{u} \exists \mathbf{u}'[a_i]$$

for every event a_i of A that does not have a null image in the state space of C. Event c_i has a fairness assumption in C if and only if event a_i has the same fairness assumption in A. [11]

Suppose the state variables in $\mathbf{u}$ have been shown to be auxiliary variables of specification A. In Section 3, we assert that auxiliary variables, introduced for specification and verification, do not have to be included in an actual implementation. The meaning of the assertion is this: instead of implementing specification A, we implement specification C which does not have the auxiliary variables in $\mathbf{u}$. (Note that $\mathbf{x}$ may contain other auxiliary variables that are not in $\mathbf{u}$.) We next discuss how properties of C are related to properties of A.

---

[11] Specifically, it is assumed that there is no event of A that has fairness in A and a null image in C. (We cannot think of a reason for having such events.) Given a finite number of such events, this assumption is not necessary. It is made to simplify the proof of Theorem 4 in [Lam & Shankar 88].

By the definition of auxiliary variables, every event a_i of A that does not have a null image in the state space of C satisfies $a_i \Rightarrow c_i$, which is a form of the event refinement condition. Also, we have

$$\begin{aligned} Initial_A &\Rightarrow \exists \mathbf{u}[Initial_A] \\ &= Initial_C \end{aligned}$$

Thus specification C is an image of specification A under the projection mapping. Additionally, we have

$$\begin{aligned} enabled(c_i) &= \exists \mathbf{x}' \forall \mathbf{u} \exists \mathbf{u}' [a_i] \\ &\Rightarrow \forall \mathbf{u} \exists \mathbf{x}' \exists \mathbf{u}' [a_i] \\ &= \forall \mathbf{u} \exists \mathbf{v}' [a_i] \end{aligned}$$

Since variables in **u** do not occur free in $enabled(c_i)$, we have

$$\forall \mathbf{u}(enabled(c_i) \Rightarrow \exists \mathbf{v}'[a_i])$$

which is, by our convention,

$$\begin{aligned} enabled(c_i) &\Rightarrow \exists \mathbf{v}'[a_i] \\ &= enabled(a_i) \end{aligned}$$

Thus, if event a_i has weak fairness, c_i and a_i satisfy the SWF condition. If event a_i has strong fairness, c_i and a_i satisfy the WF condition. And we have the following result:

Corollary 1: Specification C is a well-formed image of specification A.

From Corollary 1 and the results in Section 6, we know that properties of C such as, P is invariant, P *unless* Q and P *leads-to* Q, are also properties of A, where P and Q are arbitrary state formulas of C (that is, variables in **u** do not occur free in P or Q).

Actually, we know more about specification C than what is in Corollary 1. For specifications A and C given above, we have the following results.

Theorem 3: Let p denote an arbitrary state formula of A. If p is invariant for A, then $\exists \mathbf{u}[p]$ is invariant for C.

Corollary 2: P is invariant for C if and only if P is invariant for A, where P is an arbitrary state formula of C.

Theorem 4: P *leads-to* Q for C if and only if P *leads-to* Q for A, where P and Q are arbitrary state formulas of C.

Proofs of the above results are given in [Lam & Shankar 88]. Let p and q denote arbitrary formulas of A. It can be easily shown that if p *unless* q holds for A then $\exists \mathbf{u}[p]$ *unless* $\exists \mathbf{u}[q]$ holds for C. (See Lemma 11 in [Lam & Shankar 88].) However, if p *leads-to* q for A, it does not follow that $\exists \mathbf{u}[p]$ *leads-to* $\exists \mathbf{u}[q]$ for C. (There are counterexamples.)

Auxiliary variables play an important role in our methodology for refining specifications. Let us revisit a scenario considered in Section 6. In the process of refining a specification B, suppose we want to replace a state variable x by two new state variables y and z. In our methodology, we first derive a specification A to be a refinement of B. Specification A has all three state variables x, y and z. The events of A are then refined such that state variable x is an auxiliary variable of A. Lastly, specification C without the auxiliary variable x is derived from A as a well-formed image. A nontrivial example can be found in Section 8 where three specifications of the alternating-bit protocol are given.

We next consider the special case of channel state variables. In modeling communication protocols, the messages that are sent along a channel can be represented by a set of message types [Shankar & Lam 87a]. Each message type is a tuple, for example, $(data, cn)$. Each element of the tuple, called a message field, has a specified domain of allowed values. In the above example, the domain of $data$ is a set of allowed sequences of bits; the domain of cn may be the set $\{0,1\}$. The set of messages represented by a message type is the cartesian product of the domains of its message fields.

In specifying communication protocols, it is sometimes convenient to use *auxiliary message fields*. For example, consider the message type $(data, cn, n)$ where n is a natural number. Think of n as the unbounded sequence number of a message while cn is the corresponding cyclic sequence number that is actually implemented. (Unbounded sequence numbers are needed for specification and proofs.) Since unbounded sequence numbers are not practically implementable, the message field n should be auxiliary in the same sense as an auxiliary variable.

Adding a new field, such as n, to a message type, such as $(data, cn)$, changes the domain of the channel state variable $\mathbf{z}_i$. To ensure that the new field is auxiliary, in the above sense, we can use the following reasoning. Imagine that the channel state variable consists of two variables $\mathbf{z}_i$ and $\mathbf{u}_i$, where $\mathbf{z}_i$ represents the channel state and $\mathbf{u}_i$ represents the sequence of n message fields associated with messages of type $(data, cn)$ in $\mathbf{z}_i$. The message field n is auxiliary iff $\mathbf{u}_i$ is an auxiliary variable of the system specification; informally, $\mathbf{u}_i$ does not affect the enabling condition of any event nor does it affect the update of any nonauxiliary state variable.

8. Specification Examples

To illustrate the various concepts and results presented in this paper, we give three specifications of the alternating-bit protocol, each consisting of a state transition system and a set of fairness assumptions. Specification AB_1 uses state variables and message fields with unbounded domains (i.e., natural numbers). We prove that AB_1 has the desired safety and progress properties of the alternating-bit protocol. (Applications of the leads-to Message rule are illustrated in the proof.) Specification AB_2 is derived by adding binary-valued state variables and message fields to AB_1. We prove that AB_2 is a well-formed refinement of AB_1. Therefore, safety and progress properties proved for AB_1 are also properties of AB_2. Furthermore, we show that those state variables and message fields with unbounded domains are *auxiliary* in AB_2. Specification AB_3 is obtained from AB_2 by deleting the auxiliary state variables and message fields. AB_3 is a well-formed image of AB_2. AB_3 is most suitable for implementation because it is the smallest (i.e., its sender has four states, its receiver has two states, and only modulo-2 sequence numbers are used in its messages).

For all three specifications of the alternating-bit protocol, consider the network configuration in Figure 2, where entity 1 is the sender and entity 2 is the receiver of data blocks. Assume that the channels are lossy; that is, if the channel state variable $\mathbf{z}_i$ is not null, then a loss event is enabled whose occurrence deletes an arbitrary message in $\mathbf{z}_i$. (Recall that the channel progress assumption has to be satisfied.) Initially, both channels are empty.

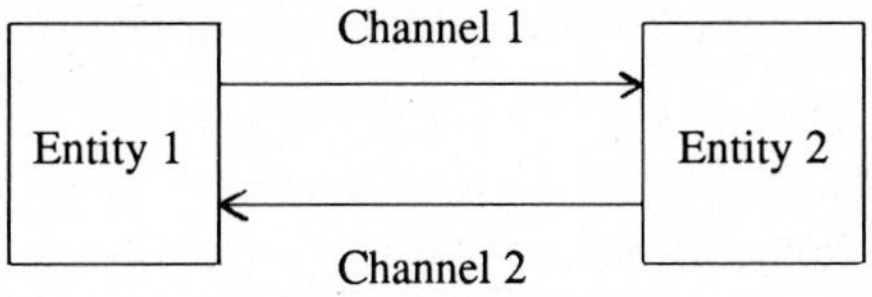

Figure 2. Network topology.

Notation. Let *guard* be a state formula and *action* an event formula such that $guard \Rightarrow enabled(action)$. Let $\mathbf{y}$ be the subset of state variables such that the variables $\{y' : y \in \mathbf{y}\}$ occur free in *action*. Define the event formula

$$guard \rightarrow action \;\equiv\; (guard \wedge action) \vee (\neg guard \wedge \mathbf{y}' = \mathbf{y})$$

Note that if *guard* is false, none of the state variables in $\mathbf{y}$ is updated by the above event formula.

Specification AB_1

Let *DATA* denote the set of data blocks that can be sent in this protocol. Let *natural* denote the set of natural numbers $\{0, 1, \cdots\}$. Entity 1 sends only one type of messages, namely, $(D, data, n)$ where D is a constant denoting the name of the message type, the domain of the message field *data* is *DATA*, and the domain of the message field n is *natural*. Entity 2 sends only one type of messages, namely, (ACK, n) where *ACK* is a constant denoting the name of the message type, and the domain of the message field n is *natural*. Below, we use a Pascal-like notation to define state variables and their domains. We use *empty* to denote a constant not in *DATA*.

- Entity 1 state variables

  produced: sequence of *DATA*, initially null.
  s: *natural*, initially 0.
  sendbuff: $DATA \cup empty$, initially *empty*.

- Entity 1 events

$$Produce(data) \equiv \quad sendbuff{=}empty \wedge produced'{=}produced@data \wedge s'{=}s+1 \wedge sendbuff'{=}data$$

$$SendD \equiv \quad sendbuff{\neq}empty \wedge Send_1(D, sendbuff, s-1)$$

$$RecACK(n) \equiv \quad Rec_2(ACK, n) \wedge ((sendbuff{\neq}empty \wedge s{=}n) \rightarrow sendbuff'{=}empty)$$

- Entity 2 state variables

  consumed: sequence of *DATA*, initially null.
  r: *natural*, initially 0.

- Entity 2 event

$$RecD(data, n) \equiv \quad Rec_1(D, data, n) \wedge Send_2(ACK, r) \wedge (r=n \rightarrow (consumed' = consumed@data \wedge r' = r+1))$$

Note that the events $RecACK(n)$ and $RecD(data, n)$ satisfy the receive events assumption in Section 5. (The enabling condition of $RecACK(n)$ is simply $Head(z_2)=(ACK, n)$.) The desired invariant property of the alternating-bit protocol is I_0 below.

Notation. For a sequence seq, we use $|seq|$ to denote the length of the sequence. For channel state variable z_1, we use $<D, n>$ to denote a sequence of zero or more copies of the $(D, produced(n), n)$ message, where $produced(n)$ is the nth element of *produced* for $n=0,1,\cdots$. For channel state variable z_2, we use $<ACK, n>$ to denote a sequence of zero or more copies of the (ACK, n) message.

Invariant properties:

$I_0 \equiv$ *consumed* is a prefix of *produced*

$$I_1 \equiv |produced| = s \wedge |consumed| = r$$

$$I_2 \equiv (sendbuff=empty \wedge r=s) \vee (sendbuff=produced(s-1) \wedge (r=s \vee r=s-1))$$

$$I_3 \equiv sendbuff=empty \Rightarrow z_1=<D, r-1> \wedge z_2=<ACK, r>$$

$$I_4 \equiv sendbuff \neq empty \wedge s=r+1 \Rightarrow z_1=<D, r-1>@<D, r> \wedge z_2=<ACK, r>$$

$$I_5 \equiv sendbuff \neq empty \wedge s=r \Rightarrow z_1=<D, r-1> \wedge z_2=<ACK, r-1>@<ACK, r>$$

Let $I \equiv I_0 \wedge I_1 \wedge I_2 \wedge I_3 \wedge I_4 \wedge I_5$. It is straightforward to show that I satisfies the first invariance rule. (In applying the rule, keep in mind that the loss event of each channel is in the set of events.)

The desired progress property of the alternating-bit protocol is L_0 below. To prove L_0, five additional leads-to properties are given. For brevity, we use $(D, n-1)$ to denote the message $(D, produced(n-1), n-1)$.

Progress properties:

$$L_0 \equiv sendbuff \neq empty \wedge s=n \text{ leads-to } sendbuff=empty \wedge s=n$$

$$L_1 \equiv sendbuff \neq empty \wedge s=n \wedge r=n-1 \text{ leads-to } sendbuff \neq empty \wedge s=n \wedge r=n$$

$$L_2 \equiv sendbuff \neq empty \wedge s=n \wedge r=n \text{ leads-to } sendbuff=empty \wedge s=n \wedge r=n$$

$$L_3 \equiv \quad sendbuff \neq empty \wedge s=n \wedge r=n-1 \wedge count(D, n-1) \geq k$$
$$leads\text{-}to\ count(D, n-1) \geq k+1 \vee (sendbuff \neq empty \wedge s=n \wedge r=n)$$

$$L_4 \equiv \quad sendbuff \neq empty \wedge s=n \wedge r=n \wedge count(ACK, n) \geq l$$
$$leads\text{-}to\ count(ACK, n) \geq l+1 \vee (sendbuff=empty \wedge s=n \wedge r=n)$$

$$L_5 \equiv \quad sendbuff \neq empty \wedge s=n \wedge r=n \wedge count(ACK, n) \geq l \wedge count(D, n-1) \geq k$$
$$leads\text{-}to\ count(D, n-1) \geq k+1 \vee count(ACK, n) \geq l+1 \vee (sendbuff=empty \wedge s=n \wedge r=n)$$

Proof of L_0:

Assume that *SendD* has weak fairness in specification AB_1.

L_3 holds via event *SendD*.
L_1 holds via message set $\{(D, n-1)\}$, using L_3.

L_5 holds via event *SendD*.
L_4 holds via message set $\{(D, n-1)\}$, using L_5.
L_2 holds via message set $\{(ACK, n)\}$, using L_4.

By Implication, Transitivity and Disjunction rules on L_1 and L_2, we get

$$sendbuff \neq empty \wedge s=n \wedge (r=n \vee r=n-1)\ leads\text{-}to\ sendbuff=empty \wedge s=n$$

L_0 follows from the above property and I_2 by Lemma 2.

Q.E.D.

From the above proof, we see that specification AB_1 requires a fairness assumption for event *SendD* only. The other events do not have to be fairly scheduled. (Of course, the channel progress assumption is needed and it can be viewed as a fairness assumption.)

Specification AB_2

AB_2 is derived from AB_2 by adding binary-valued state variables *cs* and *cr*. The state variables *s* and *r* are made into auxiliary variables. Also, a modulo-2 sequence number field *cn* is added to each message type. The message field *n* is also made auxilary.

- Entity 1 state variables

  produced, *s*, and *sendbuff* as in AB_1.
  cs: {0, 1}, initially 0.

- Entity 1 events

  $Produce^*(data) \equiv \quad Produce(data) \wedge cs'=(cs+1) \bmod 2$

  $SendD^* \equiv \quad sendbuff \neq empty$
  $\wedge Send_1(D, sendbuff, s-1, (cs-1) \bmod 2)$

$RecACK^*(n, cn) \equiv \quad Rec_2(ACK, n, cn)$
$\wedge((sendbuff \neq empty \wedge cs = cn) \rightarrow sendbuff' = empty)$

- Entity 2 state variables

consumed and r as in AB_1.

cr: {0, 1}, initially 0.

- Entity 2 event

$RecD^*(data, n, cn) \equiv Rec_1(D, data, n, cn)$
$\wedge Send_2(ACK, r, cr)$
$\wedge(cr = cn \rightarrow$
$(consumed' = consumed@data \wedge r' = r + 1 \wedge cr' = (cr + 1) \bmod 2))$

Note that the events $RecACK^*$ and $RecD^*$ satisfy the receive events assumption in Section 5. In order for AB_2 to be a well-formed refinement of AB_1, we require that $SendD^*$ has weak fairness.

Proposition: AB_2 is a well-formed refinement of AB_1.

Proof: Event $SendD^*$ is a well-formed refinement of $SendD$ because it satisfies the SWF condition. Since $SendD$ is the only event that has a fairness assumption in AB_1, it is sufficient to prove that the other events in AB_2 satisfy the event refinement condition. (Note that the initial condition of AB_2 implies the initial condition of AB_1.)

Clearly, $Produce^*(data)$ satisfies the event refinement condition because $Produce(data)$ is one of its conjuncts. For $RecACK^*(n, cn)$ to be a refinement of $RecACK(n)$, it is sufficient that the following is invariant:

$$R_0 \equiv \quad Head(\mathbf{z}_2) = (ACK, n, cn) \wedge sendbuff \neq empty \wedge cs = cn \Rightarrow s = n$$

For $RecD^*(data, n, cn)$ to be a refinement of $RecD(data, n)$, it is sufficient that the following is invariant:

$$R_1 \equiv \quad Head(\mathbf{z}_1) = (D, data, n, cn) \wedge cr = cn \Rightarrow r = n$$

Our proof that R_0 and R_1 are invariant for AB_2 is as follows. Define

$$R_2 \equiv \quad cs = s \bmod 2 \wedge cr = r \bmod 2$$
$$R_3 \equiv \quad (D, data, n, cn) \in \mathbf{z}_1 \Rightarrow cn = n \bmod 2$$
$$R_4 \equiv \quad (ACK, n, cn) \in \mathbf{z}_2 \Rightarrow cn = n \bmod 2$$

We first prove the following for AB_2 (proofs are given below):

(1) $R_2 \wedge R_3 \wedge R_4$ is invariant

(2) $I \wedge R_2 \wedge R_3 \wedge R_4 \Rightarrow R_0 \wedge R_1$

Next, we show that (1) and (2) imply that $R_0 \wedge R_1$ is invariant for AB_2, as follows. Let e^* denote an event in AB_2 and e the corresponding event in AB_1.

$$I \wedge R_2 \wedge R_3 \wedge R_4 \wedge e^* \Rightarrow I \wedge R_0 \wedge R_1 \wedge e^* \qquad \text{(from (2))}$$

$$\Rightarrow I \wedge e \qquad \text{(by event refinement condition)}$$

$$\Rightarrow I' \qquad (I \text{ is invariant for } AB_1)$$

Also, the initial condition of AB_2 implies the initial condition of AB_1 which satisfies I. Thus, I is invariant for AB_2 by the first invariance rule. From (2) above, $R_0 \wedge R_1$ is invariant for AB_2 by the second invariance rule.

Note that because of message refinement, the interpretation of I_3, I_4 and I_5 (conjuncts of I) requires a translation from messages in AB_1 to messages in AB_2, using the projection mapping for channel states defined in Section 6. Specifically, given the projection mapping, $<D, n>$ denotes a sequence of zero or more copies of the $(D, produced(n), n, i)$ message, while $<ACK, n>$ denotes a sequence of zero or more copies of the (ACK, n, i) message, where i is a parameter with domain $\{0, 1\}$.

To complete a proof of the proposition, we give proofs of (1) and (2) assumed above.

Proof of (1): Each of the conjuncts in $R_2 \wedge R_3 \wedge R_4$ satisfies the first invariance rule for AB_2, as follows:

The initial condition of AB_2 satisfies R_2.
$R_2 \wedge e \Rightarrow R_2'$ holds for $e = Produce^*(data)$ and $e = RecD^*(data, n, cn)$.
R_2 is not affected by any other event.

The initial condition of AB_2 satisfies R_3.
$R_2 \wedge R_3 \wedge SendD^* \Rightarrow R_3'$.
$R_3 \wedge RecD^*(data, n, cn) \Rightarrow R_3'$.
R_3 is not affected by any other event.

The initial condition of AB_2 satisfies R_4.
$R_2 \wedge R_4 \wedge SendACK^* \Rightarrow R_4'$.
$R_4 \wedge RecACK^*(n, cn) \Rightarrow R_4'$.
R_4 is not affected by any other event.

Proof of (2): Specifically, we prove that $I_2 \wedge I_4 \wedge I_5 \wedge R_2 \wedge R_3 \Rightarrow R_1$ and $I_2 \wedge I_4 \wedge I_5 \wedge R_2 \wedge R_4 \Rightarrow R_0$ hold for specification AB_2. We give below a detailed derivation of the latter; a derivation of the former is similar.

Assume the antecedent of R_0, namely, $Head(z_2) = (ACK, n, cn) \wedge sendbuff \neq empty \wedge cs = cn$. From I_2, I_4, I_5 and R_4, we know that X, Y or Z holds, where

$$X \equiv s = r+1 \wedge Head(z_2) = (ACK, r, r \bmod 2)$$

$$Y \equiv s = r \wedge Head(z_2) = (ACK, r-1, (r-1) \bmod 2)$$

$$Z \equiv s = r \wedge Head(z_2) = (ACK, r, r \bmod 2)$$

From R_2, we have $s \bmod 2 = cn$, which implies $\neg X \wedge \neg Y$. Hence Z holds, which implies $s = r = n$. And the consequent of R_0 holds.

Q.E.D.

Since AB_2 is a well-formed refinement of AB_1, the invariant and progress properties proved above for AB_1 are also properties of AB_2.

Now, consider the state variables s and r, and the message field n in each message type of specification AB_2. They are not practically implementable because their domains are unbounded. It is easy to see that the events of AB_2 satisfy the condition for auxiliary variables for s and r, i.e., their values affect neither the enabling condition nor the updates of the other state variables for each event. To see that the same condition is satisfied for message field n, rewrite the receive events of AB_2 in the following form:

$$RecACKs(cn) \equiv \exists n\ [RecACK^*(n,cn)]$$

$$RecDs(data,cn) \equiv \exists n\ [RecD^*(data,n,cn)]$$

The above receive events satisfy the receive events assumption in Section 5. Note that the safety properties of AB_2 do not depend on how the receive events are represented. Because none of the receive events has a fairness assumption, the progress properties of AB_2 also do not depend on how the receive events are represented. It is now easy to see that the events of AB_2 satisfy the auxiliary variable coditon for the message field n.

Specification AB_3

AB_3 is derived from AB_2 by deleting the auxiliary variables s and r and the auxiliary message field n, in the manner described in Section 7. By Corollary 1, AB_3 is a well-formed image of AB_2.

- Entity 1 state variables

  sendbuff and *cs* as in AB_2.

- Entity 1 events

$$Produce^{**}(data) \equiv \quad sendbuff=empty \wedge cs'=(cs+1) \bmod 2 \wedge sendbuff'=data$$

$$SendD^{**} \equiv \quad sendbuff \neq empty \wedge Send_1(D, sendbuff, (cs-1) \bmod 2)$$

$$RecACK^{**}(cn) \equiv \quad Rec_2(ACK, cn) \wedge ((sendbuff \neq empty \wedge cs=cn) \rightarrow sendbuff'=empty)$$

- Entity 2 state variables

  cr as in AB_2.

- Entity 2 event

$$RecD^{**}(data,cn) \equiv \quad Rec_1(D, data, cn) \wedge Send_2(ACK, cr) \wedge (cr=cn \rightarrow cr'=(cr+1) \bmod 2)$$

Specification AB_3 includes a weak fairness assumption for event *SendD***. Note that the events *RecACK***(*cn*) and *RecD***(*data*,*cn*) satisfy the receives events assumption in Section 5. Invariant and progress properties of AB_3 are inferred from those of AB_2 by applying Theorems 3 and 4 in Section 7.

We first apply Theorem 3. From $\exists s, r, produced, consumed\ [I \wedge R_0 \wedge R_1 \wedge R_2 \wedge R_3 \wedge R_4]$, we infer that the following state formulas are invariant for AB_3:

$$sendbuff = empty \Rightarrow cr = cs$$

$$sendbuff = empty \Rightarrow z_1 = \langle D, cr-1\rangle \wedge z_2 = \langle ACK, cr\rangle$$

$$sendbuff \neq empty \wedge cs = (cr+1) \bmod 2 \Rightarrow z_1 = \langle D, cr-1\rangle @ \langle D, cr\rangle \wedge z_2 = \langle ACK, cr\rangle$$

$$sendbuff \neq empty \wedge cs = cr \Rightarrow z_1 = \langle D, cr-1\rangle \wedge z_2 = \langle ACK, cr-1\rangle @ \langle ACK, cr\rangle$$

where

$\langle D, cr-1\rangle$ denotes a sequence of zero or more copies of the $(D, data, (cr-1) \bmod 2)$ message for some *data* in *DATA*,

$\langle D, cr\rangle$ denotes a sequence of zero or more copies of the $(D, sendbuff, cr)$ message,

$\langle ACK, cr-1\rangle$ denotes a sequence of zero or more copies of the $(ACK, (cr-1) \bmod 2)$ message, and

$\langle ACK, cr\rangle$ denotes a sequence of zero or more copies of the (ACK, cr) message.

The following progress property of AB_1 can be derived from L_0 by applying the Disjunction theorem in [Chandy & Misra 88],

$$sendbuff \neq empty \ \ leads\text{-}to \ \ sendbuff = empty$$

Applying Theorem 4, the above progress property is a property of AB_3.

9. Discussions and Related Work

The basic constructs for specifying systems in the relational notation are *state formulas* and *event formulas*. A state formula defines a set of system states. An event formula defines a set of system state transitions. Additionally, parameters may be used for defining groups of related events, as well as groups of related system properties. We believe that our notation is easy to learn because states and state transitions are represented explicitly. Our objective is to retain much of the intuitive appeal of state-transition models (such as communicating finite state machines), but none of their limitations. Our proof method was also designed to use a minimal amount of notation with the goal that it will be accessible to protocol engineers.

The $\mathbf{v}'$ notation for specifying events as formulas in $\mathbf{v} \cup \mathbf{v}'$ is not unique to our work. The same notational device is used by various other authors [Lamport 83a, Hehner 84, Scheid & Holtsberg 88].

Prototypes of the relational notation and the proof method presented in this paper were described in [Shankar & Lam 84, Shankar & Lam 87a]. Our proof method is based upon a fragment of linear-time temporal logic [Chandy & Misra 88, Lamport 83a, Owicki & Lamport 82, Manna & Pnueli 84, Pnueli 86]. Motivated by examples in communication protocols, we introduced two small extensions to the body of work cited above. First, we defined the *P leads–to Q via M* relation. The resulting leads-to Message rule for unreliable channels is a very useful one for communication protocols.

Second, we advocate the approach of stating fairness assumptions explicitly for individual events as part of a specification, noting that for many systems not all events need be fairly scheduled. This contrasts with the approach of a blanket assumption that all events in a system are fairly scheduled according to some criterion. While this approach is not new (see [Pnueli 86]), our definition of the *allowed behaviors* of a specification differs from the definition of *fair computations* of [Pnueli 86] in that an allowed behavior may not be 'maximal.' Specifically, every fair computation of Pnueli [1986] is an allowed behavior in our model but not vice versa. Our definition of allowed behaviors is motivated by the specification of interfaces of program modules [Lynch & Tuttle 87, Lam & Shankar 87].

We refer to a state transition system given in the relational notation together with a set of fairness assumptions as a *relational specification*. In Section 6, we present a theory of refinement and projection of relational specifications. The theory has been adapted to relational specifications from our earlier work on protocol projections. The relation *A is a well-formed refinement of B*, for two specifications A and B, is by definition the inverse of the relation *B is a well-formed image of A* introduced in [Lam & Shankar 84].

Other authors have defined similar relations between specifications: *A implements B*, *A simulates B*, *A satisfies B*, etc. [Abadi & Lamport 88, Lamport 83b, Lamport 85, Lynch & Tuttle 87]. Informally, the meaning of every one of these relations is the following: every externally visible behavior allowed by A is also allowed by B. (There are some differences in how behaviors and observable behaviors are defined.) Our definition of *A is a well-formed refinement of B* is essentially the same. We differ from the others in how the above definition is applied. First, instead of using it directly, we introduced the relational notation as a specification formalism. In our experience, the event refinement, WF and SWF conditions, expressed in the relational notation, are very convenient to use. Second, if some state variables in B are replaced by new state variables in A, our approach is to find an invariant that specifies the relation between the new and old state variables. The approach of the other authors is to find a mapping from the states of A to the states of B. The relation to be found is the same one in each approach. The approaches differ in how the relation is represented. In [Abadi & Lamport 88], the existence of such mappings is addressed.

For many applications, we found the above relations, *well-formed refinement*, *implements*, etc., to be too strong to be useful. In refining a specification B to A, it is seldom the case that every progress property of B must be preserved in A. In most cases, only *some* specific progress properties of B are to be preserved. Our conditions given in Section 6 are designed for such use. In our theory, the *refinement* relation between two specifications is the weakest. (Only safety properties of B are preserved.) It is always used. The *well-formed refinement* relation is the strongest. It is seldom used.

Chandy and Misra [1988] defined the relation *A is a superposition of B*. In their approach, A is obtained from transforming B by repeated applications of two rules. This approach is attractive because the rules are syntactic and are thus very easy to use. But because the rules are syntactic, the class of specifications that can be derived by applying these rules is much smaller than the class that can be derived as well-formed refinements. Specifically, it is easy to see that if *A is a superposition of B* then *A is a well-formed refinement of B*. The converse does not hold.

While the relational notation and proof method in this paper are applicable to state transition systems in general, their development has been motivated primarily by protocol systems. The ideas and methods in this paper have been applied to the specification and verification of several nontrivial protocols, which are briefly described below.

The first application was the verification of a version of the High-level Data Link Control (HDLC) protocol standard with functions of connection management and full-duplex data transfer. Instead of verifying such a multifunction protocol in its entirety, smaller image protocols were obtained by projection and then verified [Shankar & Lam 83]. Properties of the multifunction protocol were inferred from properties of the image protocols.

Murphy and Shankar demonstrated how a complete transport protocol with functions of connection management and full-duplex data transfer can be composed from protocols specified for the individual functions. Because the multifunction protocol is a refinement of instances of the single-function protocols, safety properties of the single-function protocols are preserved in the multifunction protocol. Proofs of progress properties of the multifunction protocol were obtained in a hierarchical manner [Murphy & Shankar 87, Murphy & Shankar 88].

The well-formed image relation between specifications was also applied to the protocol conversion problem. Suppose a converter (translator) is interposed between two entities, say E_1 and E_2, that implement different communication protocols, say A_1 and A_2, respectively. Whenever, the converter receives an A_1 message sent by entity E_1, it translates the message to an A_2 message which is delivered to E_2. (The converter may delete the message instead of translating it.) Similarly, A_2 messages sent by E_2 are translated into A_1 messages which are delivered to E_1. The well-formed image relation was used to define what it means for a protocol converter to achieve interoperability between E_1 and E_2 [Calvert & Lam 90, Lam 88].

The theory presented in this paper has already been extended in several ways. We mention two of them below.

First, in deriving a specification A from specification B, we found that it is preferable to go through a succession of intermediate specifications, B_1, B_2, $\cdots$. To facilitate such a heuristic search, we defined a weaker form of the refinement relation, called *conditional refinement*. A stepwise refinement heuristic was developed based upon conditional refinement. The heuristic was applied to the specification of sliding window protocols for the transport layer where channels can lose, duplicate, and reorder messages, and the protocols use cyclic sequence numbers [Shankar 86, Shankar & Lam 87b]. It was also applied to the specification of connection management protocols for the transport layer [Murphy & Shankar 87, Murphy & Shankar 88].

Second, an extension to our theory herein is also needed to specify interfaces and implementations of program modules. To get simple conditions for composing modules, we impose a hierarchical relationship between modules that interact via an interface. The theory extension was to define what it means for a program module to *offer an upper interface* to a user, and to *use a lower interface* offered by another program module. It was applied to prove that specifications of two database implementations, based upon a two-phase locking protocol and a multi-version timestamp protocol, satisfy a serializable interface specification [Lam & Shankar 87].

Acknowledgements

This paper is an abbreviated version of [Lam & Shankar 88]. The final presentation of this paper has benefited greatly from the constructive criticisms and diligence of the anonymous referees of *IEEE Transactions on Software Engineering*, who reviewed [Lam & Shankar 88]. We are also grateful to Ken Calvert, Mohamed Gouda, Leslie Lamport, Jayadev Misra, Ambuj Singh, and Thomas Woo for their helpful comments.

REFERENCES

[Abadi & Lamport 88] M. Abadi and L. Lamport, "The Existence of Refinement Mappings," Technical Report, Digitial Systems Research Center, Palo Alto, California, August 1988.

[Calvert & Lam 90] K. L. Calvert and S. S. Lam, "Formal Methods for Protocol Conversion," to appear in *IEEE Journal on Selected Areas in Communications*, January 1990.

[Chandy & Misra 88] K.M. Chandy and J. Misra, *Parallel Program Design: A Foundation*, Addison-Wesley, Reading, MA, 1988.

[Hailpern & Owicki 83] B.T. Hailpern and S. Owicki, "Modular Verification of Computer Communication Protocols," *IEEE Transactions on Communications*, Vol. COM-31, No. 1, January 1983.

[Hehner 84] E.C.R Hehner, "Predicative Programming, Part I and Part II," *Communications of the ACM*, Vol. 27, No. 2, February 1984.

[IBM 80] IBM Corporation, Systems Network Architecture Format and Protocol Reference Manual: Architecture Logic, IBM Form No. SC32-3112-2, 1980.

[ISO 85] ISO/TC97/SC21/WG16-1 N422 Estelle — A Formal Description Technique Based on an Extended State Transition Model, February 1985.

[Lam 88] S. S. Lam, "Protocol Conversion," *IEEE Transactions on Software Engineering*, Vol. 14, No. 3, March 1988.

[Lam & Shankar 84] S. S. Lam and A. U. Shankar, "Protocol Verification via Projections," *IEEE Transactions on Software Engineering*, Vol. SE-10, No. 4, July 1984.

[Lam & Shankar 87] S. S. Lam and A. U. Shankar, "Specifying Implementations to Satisfy Interfaces:

A State Transition System Approach,'' presented at the 26th Lake Arrowhead Workshop on *How will we specify concurrent systems in the year 2000?*, September 1987; full version available as Technical Report TR-88-30, Department of Computer Sciences, University of Texas at Austin, August 1988 (revised June 1989).

[Lam & Shankar 88] S. S. Lam and A. U. Shankar, ''A Relational Notation for State Transition Systems,'' Technical Report TR-88-21, Department of Computer Sciences, The University of Texas at Austin, May 1988 (Second Revision, August 1989).

[Lamport 83a] L. Lamport, ''What Good is Temporal Logic?'' *Proceedings Information Processing 83*, IFIP, 1983.

[Lamport 83b] L. Lamport, ''Specifying Concurrent Program Modules,'' *ACM TOPLAS*, Vol. 5, No. 2, April 1983.

[Lamport 85] L. Lamport, ''What it means for a concurrent program to satisfy a specification: Why no one has specified priority,'' *Proceedings of the 12th ACM Symposium on Principles of Programming Languages*, New Orleans, January 1985.

[Lynch & Tuttle 87] N.A. Lynch and M.R. Tuttle, ''Hierarchical Correctness Proofs for Distributed Algorithms,'' *Proceedings of the ACM Symposium on Principles of Distributed Computing*, Vancouver, B.C., August 1987.

[Manna & Pnueli 84] Z. Manna and A. Pnueli, ''Adequate Proof Principles for Invariance and Liveness Properties of Concurrent Programs,'' *Science of Computer Programming*, Vol. 4, 1984.

[Manna & Waldinger 85] Z. Manna and R. Waldinger, *The Logical Basis for Computer Programming*, Addison-Wesley, Reading, MA, 1985.

[Murphy & Shankar 87] S.L. Murphy and A.U. Shankar, ''A Verified Connection Management Protocol for the Transport Layer,'' *Proceedings ACM SIGCOMM '87 Workshop*, Stowe, Vermont, August 1987.

[Murphy & Shankar 88] S.L. Murphy and A.U. Shankar, ''Service Specification and Protocol Construction for the Transport Layer,'' *Proceedings ACM SIGCOMM '88 Symposium*, Stanford University, August 1988.

[Owicki & Gries 76] S. Owicki and D. Gries, ''Verifying Properties of Parallel Programs: An Axiomatic Approach,'' *Communications of the ACM*, Vol. 19, No. 5, May 1976.

[Owicki & Lamport 82] S. Owicki and L. Lamport, ''Proving Liveness Properties of Concurrent Systems,'' *ACM TOPLAS*, Vol. 4, No. 3, 1982.

[Piatkowski 86] T. F. Piatkowski, ''The State of The Art in Protocol Engineering,'' *Proceedings ACM Sigcomm '86 Symposium*, Stowe, Vermont, 1986.

[Pnueli 86] A. Pnueli, ''Applications of Temporal Logic to the Specification and Verification of Reactive Systems: A Survey of Current Trends,'' in *Current Trends in Concurrency: Overviews and Tutorials*, J.W, deBakker et al. (ed.), LNCS 224, Springer Verlag, 1986.

[Sabnani 88] K. Sabnani, ''An Algorithmic Procedure for Protocol Verification,'' *IEEE Transactions on Communications*, Vol. 36, No. 8, August 1988.

[Scheid & Holtsberg 88] J. Scheid and S. Holtsberg, *Ina Jo Specification Language Reference Manual*, System Development Group, Unisys Corp., Santa Monica, CA, September 1988.

[Shankar 86] A.U. Shankar, ''Verified Data Transfer Protocols with Variable Flow Control,'' *ACM Transactions on Computer Systems*, Vol. 7, No. 3, August 1989; an abbreviated version appears in *Proceedings ACM SIGCOMM '86*, Stowe, Vermont, August 1986.

[Shankar & Lam 83] A.U. Shankar and S.S. Lam, ''An HDLC Protocol Specification and its Verification Using Image Protocols,'' *ACM TOCS*, Vol. 1, No. 4, November 1983.

[Shankar & Lam 84] A.U. Shankar and S.S. Lam, ''Time-dependent communication protocols,'' in *Tutorial: Principles of Communication and Networking Protocols*, S.S. Lam (ed.), IEEE Computer Society, 1984.

[Shankar & Lam 87a] A.U. Shankar and S.S. Lam, ''Time-dependent distributed systems: proving safety, liveness, and real-time properties,'' *Distributed Computing*, Vol. 2, No. 2, 1987.

[Shankar & Lam 87b] A.U. Shankar and S.S. Lam, ''A Stepwise Refinement Heuristic for Protocol Construction,'' Technical Report CS-TR-1812, Department of Computer Science, University of Maryland, March 1987 (revised March 1989).

[West 78] C.H. West, ''A General Technique for Communications Protocol Validation,'' *IBM Journal of Research and Development*, Vol. 22, July 1978.

Compositional Theories based on an Operational Semantics of Contexts

Kim Guldstrand Larsen
Department of Mathematics and Computer Science
Aalborg University Center
9000 Aalborg, DENMARK

Abstract For the verification of large systems in general and parallel systems in particular, it is essential that the proof method used is *compositional* in order to avoid a combinatorial explosion of the verification. That is, the method must allow us to decompose the problem of correctness for a complex system into similar correctness problems for the components of the system.

Compositionality requires a suitable relationship between the constructions available for building systems and the notion of correctness between systems and specifications. In fact, as we show in the paper, compositional proof methods may be classified in a number of ways; in particular classes well–suited for top–down and bottom–up development are identified. The main purpose of this paper is to demonstrate that compositionality in many cases may be achieved though a new *operational understanding of the constructions* (or contexts) used for building systems. The operational model we propose is that of *action transducers*; i.e. a construction is semantically viewed as an object transforming actions of its inner components into actions for the surrounding environment. In particular we demonstrate how to describe the constructions of CCS in this model.

We present three proof methods (*bisimulation*, *relative bisimulation* and *recursive modal logic*), and show that the operational semantics of contexts in all cases leads to compositionality results.

Keywords Process Algebra, Reactive Systems, Compositionality, Classification of Compositionality, Contexts as Transducers, Bisimulation, Relative Bisimulation, Environments, Recursive Modal Logic, Weakest Property Transformer.

Contents

1 Introduction

2 Compositionality

2.1 Hoare Logic

3 Operational Semantics of Contexts

4 Bisimulation Theory

4.1 A simple Scheduler

5 Relativized Theory

5.1 Environments and relative Bisimulation
5.2 The Simple Scheduler
5.3 Combined Environments and Compositionality

6 Logical Theory

6.1 Contexts as Property Transformers
6.2 The Lazy Researcher

7 Concluding Remarks

References

1 Introduction

For the verification of large systems it is essential that the proof method used is *compositional* in order to avoid a combinatorial explosion of the verification. That is, the method must allow us to decompose the problem of correctness for a complex system into similar correctness problems for the components of the system. Dually, it should be possible to reason about the system using only the specifications of its components, and without knowledge as to their implementation.

For sequential systems, there exist well-known compositional methods in which specifications are relations between input and output (e.g. [Hoa69]). However, for many concurrent systems this relational viewpoint is inadequate. Indeed, the purpose of a concurrent system may be entirely different from that of computing a relation: e.g. an operating system is normally considered a rather usefull system, but being non-terminating (ideally) it implements the empty (and useless) relation. Instead, concurrent systems are often best described in terms of their interaction with their environment, in which case we shall call the system *reactive* (following [Pnu85]).

Process algebra [Mil80, Mil89, Hoa78, BK85, Bou85] provides a framework for describing both the spatial and modular structure of reactive systems (or *processes*) and also details of their operational behaviour. Syntactically, processes constitutes a term algebra $\mathcal{P}$, where terms are built by a given set of operators (normally including some operator for parallel composition). Semantically, the operational behaviour of processes are given in terms of a *labelled transition system* [Plo81], $(\mathcal{P}, A, \longrightarrow)$, where $\mathcal{P}$ is the set of processes, A the set of *actions* which processes may perform when interacting with their environment, and $\longrightarrow \subseteq \mathcal{P} \times A \times \mathcal{P}$ the *transition relation* defining the dynamic change of processes as they perform actions.

The *specification* of a reactive system, prescribes formally a number of desired properties of its operational behaviour. The formalisms used for specifying systems may be devided into two main categories: The *logical* approach, allowing specifications to be combined by logical connectives (e.g. conjunction and disjunction); the notion of *refinement* between specifications can be simply understood as logical implication and verification becomes "model–checking". The *behavioural* approach, in which the specification is itself a process (that is, a term of the process algebra) but (somehow) more abstract (or less physical feasible) than the implementation process. In this approach, verification is based on a comparision between the operational behaviours of the specification process and the implementation process.

Given a process algebra $\mathcal{P}$ and a specification formalism $\mathcal{S}$ (i.e. a set of specifications), it is essential — in both the logical and the bahavioural approach — to define the relationship between them. In particular we want to know when a given process P *is correct* with respect to a given specification S. For this, a *satisfaction relation*, $\models \subseteq \mathcal{P} \times \mathcal{S}$, between process terms and specification formulae must be given. Refinements between specifications can now be defined simply as the inclusion between their models; i.e. S_1 refines S_2 (notated $S_1 \Rightarrow S_2$) provided any process P which satisfies S_1 also satisfies S_2. We call the triple, $(\mathcal{P}, \mathcal{S}, \models)$, a *specification theory* (a calculus in [Mil88]). We may also compare the expressive power of two specification theories with common processes algebra. In particular we say that $(\mathcal{P}, \mathcal{S}, \models)$ is *more expressive* than $(\mathcal{P}, \mathcal{S}', \models')$ in case for any specification S' of $\mathcal{S}'$ there exist a specification S in $\mathcal{S}$ such that $P \models S$ if and only if $P \models' S'$ for any process P; i.e. S and S' specifies the same set of processes. (This notion of expressivity is similar to the notion of derivation between process calculi in [Mil88]).

In the present paper we consider three existing specification theories:

> *Bisimulation Theory* in which the specification formalism is the process algebra itself, and the satisfaction relation is that of *bisimilarity* [Par81, Mil83].
>
> *Relativized Theory:* As satisfaction is given in terms of an equivalence, specifications within the Bisimulation Theory tend to be very explicit. In particular — during compositional verification of a complex system — it is not possible to abstract away the behavioural aspects of the components which is irrelevant in the

particular context. In the Relativized Theory — which was developed specifically to allow for such abstractions — a specification consists of a specifying process (as in the Bisimulation Theory) together with information about the behavioural constraints imposed by the context. Satisfaction is given in terms of *relativized bisimilarity*.

Logical Theory in which the specification formalism is a recursive version of the modal logic introduced in [HM85] (the so–called Hennessy–Milner Logic). In [Lar88] it is shown that this recursively extended logic is endeed very expressive; in fact it is shown how to derive all the standard operators from Branching Time Temporal Logic [BAPM83].

We show that all three specification theories are *compositional* in senses (varying in degree) that will be made precise in the next section. In all cases, compositionality is achieved under a very mild assumption about the involved process algebra; namely that all the operations of the algebra can be given a certain *operational semantics*. We shall also see that in the above listing, the theories appears in increasing order with respect to their expressive power.

In the next section, we define precisely the notion of a *compositional specification theory*. In section 3, we propose *action–transducers* as the basic model for an operational semantics of process operations. In particular, we demonstrate how to describe the operations of CCS [Mil80] in this model. In sections 4, 5 and 6 we present the three specification theories above, in each case with a compositionality result and illustration of the resulting theory on examples.

2 Compositionality

In order for a specification theory $(\mathcal{P}, \mathcal{S}, \models)$ to be *compositional*, the operators of the process algebra $\mathcal{P}$ and the presentation of the satisfaction relation $\models$ must be suitable related. In particular, correctness assertions for combined processes — $C(P_1, \ldots, P_n) \models S$, say — must be interreduceable with correctness assertions involving only the component processes — i.e. assertions of the form $P_1 \models S_1, \ldots, P_n \models S_n$ for some subspecifications $S_1, \ldots, S_n$. Hence, we propose proof rules of the following form:

$$\frac{P_1 \models S_1 \cdots\cdots P_n \models S_n}{C(P_1, \ldots, P_n) \models S} \quad \mathcal{R}_C(S_1 \ldots S_n; S) \tag{1}$$

Here C denotes an arbitrary n–ary context of the process algebra (i.e. a derived n–ary operator), and $C(P_1, \ldots, P_n)$ its application to the processes $P_1 \ldots P_n$.

In order for the rule (1) to be *sound*, the subspecifications, $S_1 \ldots S_n$, can not be arbitrary but must be related to the overall specification, S, in a way particular for the context C

involved. In the rule, this relationship is expressed as a side–condition using an $(n+1)$–ary predicate (indexed by the context C), $\mathcal{R}_C$, on specifications. Thus, the requirement of soundness sets a limit as to how weak the predicate $\mathcal{R}_C$ can be. On the other hand, to maximize the usefullness of (1) in establishing properties of composite processes of the form $C(P_1,\ldots,P_n)$, $\mathcal{R}_C$ should be as liberal (i.e. weak) as possible. In particular, whenever $C(P_1,\ldots,P_n) \models S$, we would want this to be infereable from (1); i.e. the rule must be *backwards sound* in the sense that there exist subspecifications, $S_1 \ldots S_n$, such that $P_1 \models S_1,\ldots,P_n \models S_n$, and such that the condition $\mathcal{R}_C(S_1\ldots S_n;S)$ holds. For specification theories fulfilling this requirement, a proof system based on rules of the form (1) will obvioulsy be (relativized) *complete* (relativized with respect to assertions of the form $\mathcal{R}_C(S_1\ldots S_n;S)$). (Our notion of backwards soundness is similar to that of *Elementary Compositional Completeness* in [Zwi89]).

Now, we want our proof rule (1) not only to serve as the basis in a posterior verification of a constructed system, but also to support the actual *development* of the system. In particular we want rules to support both *bottom–up* and *top–down* development.

In *bottom–up* development, a number of component process, $P_1 \ldots P_n$, is assumed to have been already constructed and shown correct with respect to subspecifications, $S_1 \ldots S_n$. We are now considering combining the component processes using some n–ary context C, and therefore want to know what may be concluded about the combined process $C(P_1,\ldots,P_n)$. In order for the rule (1) to support this type of development, the side–condition, $\mathcal{R}_C(S_1\ldots S_n;S)$, should ideally state an explicit *upper bound* (with respect to strength) for the specifications S in terms of the subspecifications, $S_1 \ldots S_n$. Thus, the rule (1) should be of the special form:

$$\frac{P_1 \models S_1 \cdots\cdots P_n \models S_n}{C(P_1,\ldots,P_n) \models S} \qquad \mathcal{S}_C(S_1,\ldots,S_n) \Rightarrow S \tag{2}$$

Here, $\mathcal{S}_C(S_1,\ldots,S_n)$ denotes the strongest specification satisfied by all combined processes $C(P_1,\ldots,P_n)$ with $P_1 \models S_1,\ldots P_n \models S_n$. Clearly, the existence of the rule (2) presumes a certain expressibility of the specification formalism relative to the process algebra.

In *top–down* development we are given the overall specification S of a combined program $C(P_1,\ldots,P_n)$. However, the component processes, $P_1 \ldots P_n$, are to be viewed as black boxes in that they are yet to be constructed. Thus, the question is, what subspecifications the component processes should be required to satisfy. Also — from a development point of view — we would prefer these requirements be as *weak as possible* in order not to restrict unnecessarily the choices of implementations for the components. In order for the rule (1) to support this type of top–down development, the side–condition, $\mathcal{R}_C(S_1\ldots S_n;S)$, should ideally state an explicit *joint, lower bound* (with respect to strength) for the subspecifications, $S_1 \ldots S_n$, in terms of the given overall specification S. Hence, the rule (1) should be of the special form:

$$\frac{P_1 \models S_1 \cdots\cdots P_n \models S_n}{C(P_1,\ldots,P_n) \models S} \qquad S_1 \times \cdots \times S_n \Rightarrow \mathcal{W}_C(S) \tag{3}$$

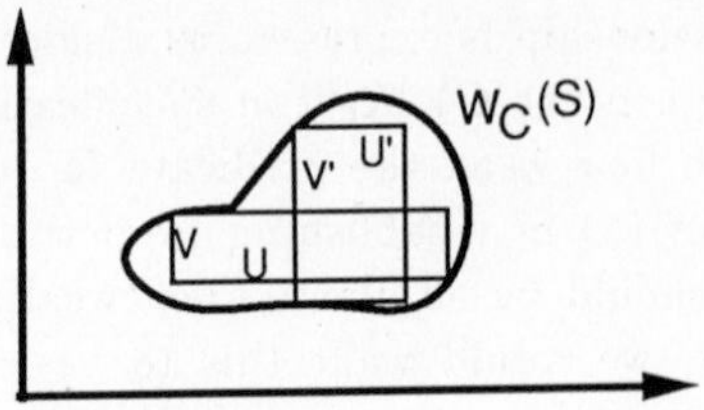

Figure 1: Side–condition of rule (3)

Here, $\mathcal{W}_C(S)$ denotes (semantically) the set of all n–tuples of processes, $(P_1, \ldots, P_n)$, which satisfies S when combined under the context C. $S_1 \times \cdots \times S_n$ denotes (semantically), the set of all n–tuples, $(P_1, \ldots, P_n)$, with process P_i satisfying S_i for all $i = 1..n$. Finally, $\Rightarrow$ is interpreted as set–inclusion in the side–condition.

Figure 1 illustrates the side–condition of (3) (and the problems involved) for the case $n = 2$. Now, $\mathcal{W}_C(S)$ is the *weakest joint* requirement to (the not yet constructed) (P_1, P_2), in order for their combination, $C(P_1, P_2)$, to satisfy S. However, in order to allow the development of P_1 and P_2 to be carried out independently, we (as reflected in the rule (3)) want $\mathcal{W}_C(S)$ to be *decomposed* into requirements of the individual components. However, we can not expect this decomposition to be unique (see figure 1, where $U \times V$ and $U' \times V'$ are two incomparable decomposition of $\mathcal{W}_C(S)$). Obviously, also the existence of rule (3) presumes a certain expressibility of the specification formalism relative to the process algebra.

2.1 Hoare Logic

Here we want to present the Hoare Rules [Hoa69] for the sequential composition in an imperative programming language using compositional proof rules of the type (2) and (3). The Denotational Semantics of the language is supposed to be based on a semantic domain *Store*, being all maps from a given set of variable, *Var*, into the set of natural numbers, *Nat*.

$$Store = Var \longrightarrow Nat$$

Semantically, we view programs in the language as *relations* between stores. Thus, the semantic function, **F**, for programs has the functionality:

$$\mathbf{F} : Prg \longrightarrow 2^{Store \times Store}$$

where *Prg* denotes the syntactic category of programs. The semantics of sequential composition is simply that of relation composition, i.e.:

$$\mathbf{F}[\![P_1; P_2]\!] = \mathbf{F}[\![P_1]\!] \circ \mathbf{F}[\![P_2]\!]$$

where for relations R_1, R_2, $R_1 \circ R_2$ denotes the set of pairs, (p_1, p_3), where $(p_1, p_2) \in R_1$ and $(p_2, p_3) \in R_2$ for some p_2.

A *Hoare–specification* is a pre– and post–condition pair, (A, B), with $A, B \subseteq \mathit{Store}$. Informally, a program P satisfies a Hoare–specification if stores in A are only related to stores in B. Formally [1], we have:

$$P \models (A, B) \;\equiv^{\Delta}\; \forall (s, s') \in \mathbf{F}[\![P]\!].\, s \in A \Rightarrow s' \in B$$

or equivalently

$$P \models (A, B) \;\equiv^{\Delta}\; \mathbf{F}[\![P]\!] \subseteq A \times B \cup A^c \times \mathit{Store}$$

Now, it may be (fairly) easily proven that the ordering (in terms of strength) between Hoare–specifications is characterized by the following:

$$\begin{aligned}&(A, B) \Rightarrow (A', B') \equiv \\ &\qquad A' = \emptyset \text{ or } B' = \mathit{Store} \text{ or } A' \subseteq A \wedge B \subseteq B'\end{aligned}$$

Informally, the third disjunct asserts that, the less a Hoare–specification requires in its pre–condition and the more it guarantees throught its post–condition the stronger it is. This, in fact corresponds to the Rule of Consequence in Hoare Logic, whereas the two first disjuncts reflect the axioms $\{\mathrm{ff}\}P\{B\}$ and $\{A\}P\{\mathrm{tt}\}$

Now, let $\mathrm{wp}(Q, B)$ be the set of stores, s, which is always transformed into stores of B by Q; i.e. $s' \in B$ whenever $(s, s') \in \mathbf{F}[\![Q]\!]$. ($\mathrm{wp}(Q, B)$ is normally called the weakest (liberal) precondition of B under Q [Dij76]). The following properties of wp are easily shown (and completely standard):

$$\begin{aligned} i)&\quad P \models (A, B) \Leftrightarrow A \subseteq \mathrm{wp}(P, B) \\ ii)&\quad P; Q \models (A, B) \Leftrightarrow P \models \big(A, \mathrm{wp}(Q, B)\big) \\ iii)&\quad \mathrm{wp}(P, \mathit{Store}) = \mathit{Store} \\ iv)&\quad \mathrm{wp}(P; Q, B) = \mathrm{wp}\big(P, \mathrm{wp}(Q, B)\big)\end{aligned}$$

Property *ii*) provides the basis for soundness and completeness (i.e. backwards soundness) for the following compositional proof rule:

$$\frac{P \models (A', B')}{P; Q \models (A, B)} \quad (A', B') \Rightarrow \big(A, \mathrm{wp}(Q, B)\big) \tag{4}$$

Also, note that (4) fits the scheme of the generic rule (3) and is thus well–suited for top–down development.

Dually, let $\mathrm{sp}(Q, A)$ denote the set of stores, s, which comes from stores in A; i.e. $(s', s) \in \mathbf{F}[\![Q]\!]$ for some $s' \in A$ (also known as the strongest post–condition of B' under Q [Dij76]). It is trivial to establish the following properties for sp:

$$\begin{aligned} i)&\quad P \models (A, B) \Leftrightarrow \mathrm{sp}(P, A) \subseteq B \\ ii)&\quad P \models (A, B) \Leftrightarrow P; Q \models \big(A, \mathrm{sp}(Q, B)\big) \\ iii)&\quad \mathrm{sp}(P, \emptyset) = \emptyset \\ iv)&\quad \mathrm{sp}(P; Q, A) = \mathrm{sp}\big(Q, \mathrm{sp}(P, A)\big)\end{aligned}$$

---

[1] Our interpretation of $P \models (A, B)$ corresponds to the standard *weak* correctness assertion $\{A\}P\{B\}$ in Hoare Logic, where termination of P is *not* required.

property *ii*) provides the basis for the following (sound and complete) compositional proof rule:

$$\frac{P \models (A', B')}{P; Q \models (A, B)} \quad \big(A', \mathrm{sp}(Q, B')\big) \Rightarrow (A, B) \tag{5}$$

In this case, we note that the rule is an instance of the generic rule (2) well–suited for bottom–up development.

3 Operational Semantics of Contexts

In process algebra, *contexts* (or derived operators) may be represented syntactically as terms with free variables possibly occuring. Thus, for C an n–ary context, $C(P_1, \ldots, P_n)$ denotes the closed term obtained by substituting $P_1 \ldots P_n$ for the (n) free variables occuring in C. However, to facilitate a general investigation of how contexts "transform" specifications, we propose to model the *operational semantics of contexts* in terms of *action–transducers*. [2] That is, a context is semantically viewed as an object which consumes actions provided by its internal processes and in return produces actions for an external observer, thus acting as an interface between the two. Whenever C is an n–ary context we shall use the notation:

$$C \xrightarrow[(a_1 \ldots a_n)]{a} C'$$

to indicate that C may consume the (inner) actions $a_1 \ldots a_n$ and in return produce the (outer) action a while changing into a new context C'.

As an example, consider the parallel operator (context), $|$, of CCS [Mil80]. The standard operational semantics of this (dyadic) operator is given by the inference–rules Par_l, Par_r and Par_c of figure 2. Now, the inference–rule Par_c may be interpreted in the following way: "whenever the inner processes P and Q can produce complementrary actions a and $\hat{a}$, the parallel operator may combine these into the action τ." Note, that the operator after this transition is again a parallel composition. Hence, it seems natural to represent Par_c by the following transduction:

$$| \xrightarrow[(a,\hat{a})]{\tau} |$$

Now, consider the inference–rule Par_l. Obviously, only the inner process P participates in these transitions. Introducing a distinguished *no–action* symbol, 0, to indicate the inactivity of certain inner components, we may represent Par_l by the following transduction:

$$| \xrightarrow[(a,0)]{\tau} |$$

Finally, consider the axiom Act for the (unary) prefixing operator, $a.$. In an initial transition of a process $a.P$, the inner processes P is guarded and hence inaccessible. We may

[2] This idea originates from [Lar86], where a compositional proof method, extending the notion of bisimulation in order to take account of behavioural constraints imposed by contexts, is put forward.

interprete this as: "the prefix operator being able to produce an action without consulting its inner component". However, in contrast to the parallel operator, action prefixing is a *dynamic* operator. In particular, after the initial transition, the prefixing operator will disappear and give an external observer direct access to the inner component P. We model this by the following transductions:

$$a. \underset{0}{\overset{a}{\longrightarrow}} I \qquad I \underset{x}{\overset{x}{\longrightarrow}} I$$

Thus, after the initial transition of $a.P$, P will be "sitting" inside the *identity* context I.

Formally, the *operational semantics* of n–ary contexts over an action set A is described by a labelled transition system of the form:

$$\left(\mathcal{C}, {A_0}^n \times A, \longrightarrow\right)$$

where $\mathcal{C}$ is the set of n–ary contexts, $A_0 = A \cup \{0\}$ with 0 being a distinguished *no-action* symbol ($0 \notin A$), and $\longrightarrow$ is the *transduction relation*. For $\left(C, (\overline{a}, a), C'\right) \in \longrightarrow$, where $\overline{a}$ is a vector $(a_1 \dots a_n) \in {A_0}^n$, we shall use the notation $C \underset{\overline{a}}{\overset{a}{\longrightarrow}} C'$. Note, that ordinary processes may be modelled as 0–ary context systems.

The compositionality results to be presented in the following sections will be based on the assumption that the operators (contexts) of the process algebra may be described as action transducers. Figure 2 shows that CCS meets this assumption. To further indicate the class of process algebras for which our results will apply, consider the following general principle. Assume that an operator (context), C, of the process algebra is described through a number of (derived) inference–rules of the following form: [3]

$$\frac{P_1 \xrightarrow{a_1} {P_1}' \cdots\cdots P_n \xrightarrow{a_n} {P_n}'}{C(P_1 \dots P_n; Q_1 \dots Q_m) \xrightarrow{a} C'({P_1}' \dots {P_n}'; Q_1 \dots Q_m)} \quad \phi(a_1 \dots a_n; a) \tag{6}$$

where ϕ is an $(n+1)$–ary predicate on actions. Then, each such inference–rule will induce a transduction (scheme) of the form:

$$C \underset{(a_1 \dots a_n; 0 \dots 0)}{\overset{a}{\longrightarrow}} C' \qquad \phi(a_1 \dots a_n; a) \tag{7}$$

Dually, for $C(P_1, \dots, P_n)$ a combined process, we want the operational semantics to be expressible in terms of the operational semantics of the component processes, $P_1 \dots P_n$, and the transduction semantics of the context C. Thus, we assume that transitions of combined processes are completely characterized by the following *Uniform Rule*:

$$U \quad \frac{P_1 \xrightarrow{a_1} {P_1}' \cdots\cdots P_n \xrightarrow{a_n} {P_n}' \quad C \underset{(a_1 \dots a_n)}{\overset{a}{\longrightarrow}} C'}{C(P_1, \dots, P_n) \xrightarrow{a} C'({P_1}', \dots, {P_n}')} \tag{8}$$

---

[3]Similar and more general types of inference–rules has been introduced by de Simone [dS85] in order to determine the expressive power of SCCS and MEIJE [Bou85]. Also, in [Blo88] and [Gro89] types of inference–rules are introduced that will ensure bisimulation to be a congruence.

	Inference Rule	Transduction
Act	$a.P \xrightarrow{a} P$	$a. \xrightarrow[0]{a} I$ $I \xrightarrow[x]{x} I$
Sum$_l$	$\dfrac{P \xrightarrow{a} P'}{P + Q \xrightarrow{a} P'}$	$+ \xrightarrow[(a,0)]{a} \Pi^1$ $\Pi^1 \xrightarrow[(x,0)]{x} \Pi^1$
Sum$_r$	$\dfrac{Q \xrightarrow{a} Q'}{P + Q \xrightarrow{a} Q'}$	$+ \xrightarrow[(0,a)]{a} \Pi^2$ $\Pi^2 \xrightarrow[(0,x)]{x} \Pi^2$
Par$_l$	$\dfrac{P \xrightarrow{a} P'}{P \mid Q \xrightarrow{a} P' \mid Q}$	$\mid \xrightarrow[(a,0)]{a} \mid$
Par$_r$	$\dfrac{Q \xrightarrow{a} Q'}{P \mid Q \xrightarrow{a} P \mid Q'}$	$\mid \xrightarrow[(0,a)]{a} \mid$
Par$_c$	$\dfrac{P \xrightarrow{a} P' \quad Q \xrightarrow{\hat{a}} Q'}{P \mid Q \xrightarrow{\tau} P' \mid Q'}$	$\mid \xrightarrow[(a,\hat{a})]{\tau} \mid$
Res	$\dfrac{P \xrightarrow{a} P'}{P\backslash A \xrightarrow{a} P'\backslash A} a, \hat{a} \notin A$	$\backslash A \xrightarrow[a]{a} \backslash A \quad ; a, \hat{a} \notin A$

Figure 2: Operational Semantics of CCS Operations

where we extend the operational semantics of processes such that $P \xrightarrow{0} Q$ if and only if $P = Q$.

Example 3.1 Consider the CCS term a.Nil+b.Nil or in prefix notation $+\big(a.(\text{Nil}), b.(\text{Nil})\big)$. Using the Uniform rule (8) together with the transduction axiom for prefixing and summation (figure 2), the following transition may be infered:

$$\dfrac{\dfrac{\dfrac{-}{\text{Nil} \xrightarrow{0} \text{Nil}} \quad \dfrac{-}{a. \xrightarrow[0]{a} I}}{a.(\text{Nil}) \xrightarrow{a} I(\text{Nil})} \qquad \dfrac{-}{b.(\text{Nil}) \xrightarrow{0} b.(\text{Nil})} \qquad \dfrac{-}{+ \xrightarrow[(a,0)]{a} \Pi^1}}{+\big(a.(\text{Nil}), b.(\text{Nil})\big) \xrightarrow{a} \Pi^1\big(I(\text{Nil}), b.(\text{Nil})\big)}$$

The result of this transition — $\Pi^1\big(I(\text{Nil}), b.(\text{Nil})\big)$ — is clearly behavioural equivalent to the CCS term Nil in accordance with the standard CCS transition $a.\text{Nil} + b.\text{Nil} \xrightarrow{a} \text{Nil}$. □

As an indication of the soundness of the general principle for inducing transductions, we note that the original inference–rules (6) may be derived from the induced tranductions (7) together with the Uniform Rule (8) in the following way:

$$U\dfrac{\dfrac{\vdots}{P_1 \xrightarrow{a_1} P_1'} \cdots \quad \dfrac{-}{Q_1 \xrightarrow{0} Q_1} \cdots \quad \dfrac{-}{C \xrightarrow[(a_1 \ldots, 0 \ldots)]{a} C'}\phi(a_1 \ldots a_n; a)}{C(P_1 \ldots, Q_1 \ldots) \xrightarrow{a} C'(P_1' \ldots, Q_1 \ldots)}$$

Whenever C is an n–ary context and D_i $(i = 1 \ldots n)$ are m_i–ary contexts, we may consider a combined $\sum m_i$–ary context $C(D_1, \ldots, D_n)$, syntactically obtained by substituting $D_1 \ldots D_n$ for the free variables in C (and assuming that the free variables of D_i are mutually disjoint). Note, that a combined process is a combined context with all component contexts having arity 0. Now, the following obvious generalisation of the Uniform Rule (8) describes the transduction semantics of $C(D_1, \ldots, D_n)$ in terms of the behaviour of C and the component contexts, $D_1 \ldots D_n$.

$$G\dfrac{D_1 \xrightarrow[\overline{d_1}]{a_1} D_1' \cdots\cdots D_n \xrightarrow[\overline{d_n}]{a_n} D_n' \quad C \xrightarrow[(a_1 \ldots a_n)]{a} C'}{C(D_1, \ldots, D_n) \xrightarrow[\overline{d_1} \ldots \overline{d_n}]{a} C'(D_1', \ldots, D_n')} \tag{9}$$

where juxtaposition of vectors indicates their concatenation. Also, we have extended the transduction semantics of processes such that $D \xrightarrow[\overline{a}]{0} D'$ if and only if $\overline{a} = \overline{0}$ and $D' = D$. For more general (and categorical) ways of combining contexts and their associated algebraic laws consult [LX89].

Example 3.2 Consider the unary context $(P\,|\,I)\backslash A$, where P is a process and A is a set of (restricted) actions. Then, we may infer the transduction $(P\,|\,I)\backslash A \xrightarrow[a]{a} (P\,|\,I)\backslash A$ (whenever $a, \hat{a} \notin A$) using the Generalised Uniform rule (9):

$$G\frac{\dfrac{P \xrightarrow[a]{0} P \quad I \xrightarrow[a]{a} I \quad | \xrightarrow[(0,a)]{a} |}{(P\,|\,I) \xrightarrow[a]{a} (P\,|\,I)} \qquad \dfrac{-}{\backslash A \xrightarrow[a]{a} \backslash A}a, \hat{a} \notin A}{(P\,|\,I)\backslash A \xrightarrow[a]{a} (P\,|\,I)\backslash A}$$

In fact, it may be shown that the transduction semantics of $(P\,|\,I)\backslash A$ is completely characterized by the following three (derived) inference–rules:

$$i)\quad (P\,|\,I)\backslash A \xrightarrow[a]{a} (P\,|\,I)\backslash A \quad ; a, \hat{a} \notin A$$

$$ii)\quad \frac{P \xrightarrow{a} P'}{(P\,|\,I)\backslash A \xrightarrow[0]{a} (P'|I)\backslash A} \quad a, \hat{a} \notin A$$

$$iii)\quad \frac{P \xrightarrow{\hat{a}} P'}{(P\,|\,I)\backslash A \xrightarrow[a]{\tau} (P'|I)\backslash A}$$

□

4 Bisimulation Theory

Process algebra may itself be used as the specification formalism; i.e. specifications are abstract programs or processes describing the desired behaviour of an implementation. In this case, the satisfaction relation may be based on a comparison between the behaviours of the specification and the implementation.

In recent years a large number of process equivalences and preorders — well–suited for making such comparisons — has been put forward. In this section, we investigate the behavioural specification theory obtained by taking as basis for the satisfaction relation, the well–established notion of *bisimulation* [Par81, Mil83].

Definition 4.1 *Let $(\mathcal{P}, A, \longrightarrow)$ be a labelled transition system. Then a bisimulation $\mathcal{B}$ is a binary relation on $\mathcal{P}$ such that whenever $P\mathcal{B}Q$ the following holds:*

1. *Whenever $P \xrightarrow{a} P'$, then $Q \xrightarrow{a} Q'$ for some Q' with $P'\mathcal{B}Q'$,*
2. *Whenever $Q \xrightarrow{a} Q'$, then $P \xrightarrow{a} P'$ for some P' with $P'\mathcal{B}Q'$*

P and Q are said to be bisimular in case (P, Q) is contained in some bisimulation $\mathcal{B}$. We write $P \sim Q$ in this case.

The specification theory induced by the notion of bisimulaiton enjoys several pleasant properties: the notion of bisimularity is itself a bisimulation (in fact the maximum one) and moreover an equivalence; it admits (consequently) a very elegant proof technique based on fixed point induction [Par81]; it has an alternative modal characterization [HM85]; inequivalent processes can be distinguished by (probabilistic) testing [Abr87, LS89]; and the equivalence of finite–state processes can be automatically decided in polynomial time [KS, PT87]. In fact a fair number of systems has recently emerged that will (among other things) support verification of bisimulation equivalence [CPS88, KS, LMV88, LS87].

However, from a *compositional* point of view, the most important property is that bisimularity is preserved by all *natural* process operators (as stated in the theorem below). In [dS85, Gro89] various restrictions on the inference rules have been imposed in the course of defining the concept of naturality. In this paper *natural* simply means that the operator is *describable as an action transducer.* Thus, according to figure 2, all operators of CCS are natural.

Theorem 4.2 *$C(P_1, \ldots, P_n) \sim C(Q_1, \ldots, Q_n)$ whenever $P_i \sim Q_i$ for all $i = 1 \ldots n$.*

Proof: We show that the relation:

$$\mathcal{B} = \big\{\big(C(P_1 \ldots P_n), C(Q_1 \ldots Q_n)\big) \mid \forall i. P_i \sim Q_i\big\}$$

is a bisimulation. So assume $\big(C(P_1 \ldots P_n), C(Q_1 \ldots Q_n)\big) \in \mathcal{B}$ and assume:

$$C(P_1, \ldots, P_n) \xrightarrow{a} T \tag{10}$$

Using (completeness of) the Uniform Rule (8), this implies:

$$P_1 \xrightarrow{a_1} P_1', \ldots, P_n \xrightarrow{a_n} P_n',\ C \xrightarrow[(a_1 \ldots a_n)]{a} C'$$

for some $a_1 \ldots a_n$, $P_1' \ldots P_n'$ and C' with $T = C'(P_1' \ldots P_n')$. As $P_i \sim Q_i$ for all $i = 1 \ldots n$, there exits $Q_1' \ldots Q_n'$ such that:

$$Q_1 \xrightarrow{a_1} Q_1', \ldots, Q_n \xrightarrow{a_n} Q_n'$$

and with $P_i' \sim Q_i'$ for all $i = 1 \ldots n$. Using once more the Uniform Rule (8) we obtain the following transition matching (10):

$$C(Q_1, \ldots, Q_n) \xrightarrow{a} C'(Q_1', \ldots, Q_n')$$

□

Specification Theory

$$(\mathcal{P}, \mathcal{P}, \sim)$$

Compositional Proof Rule

$$\frac{P_1 \sim S_1 \cdots\cdots P_n \sim S_n}{C(P_1, \ldots, P_n) \sim S} \quad C(S_1, \ldots, S_n) \sim S$$

Ordering

$$S_1 \Rightarrow S_2 \equiv S_1 \sim S_2$$

Figure 3: Bisimulation Theory

It follows immediately from the above theorem, that the (obviously) compositional proof rule of figure 3 is *sound*. Also, the rule clearly fits the general scheme (2) of section 2 suggested for bottom–up development: a constraint on the overall specification S is given in terms of the subspecifications, $S_1 \ldots S_n$. To see that the rule is also *backwards sound* (for completeness), assume $C(P_1, \ldots, P_n) \sim S$. Then by taking $S_i = P_i$ for all $i = 1 \ldots n$, both the hypothesis and the side–condition of the rule will hold trivially.

As the satisfaction relation of the Bisimulation Theory is an equivalence (that of bisimularity) it follows that the ordering between specifications itself degenerates to an equivalence. That is, specifications are either incomparable or equivalent — in particular, the theory does not contain specifications with varying degree of *looseness*.

In the compositional proof rule of figure 3, we see that the side–condition constitutes a problem similar to that of the conclusion. Of course, the hope is that we may find suitable "simple" subspecifications, $S_1 \ldots S_n$, so that the overall effort in establishing the hypothesis and the side–condition of the rule will be significantly smaller than that of establishing the conclusion directly. Now, due to the behavioural constraints which the component processes, $P_1 \ldots P_n$, impose upon each other, only very minor parts of their behaviour need be accessible in the combined system. However, as the satisfaction relation is an equivalence, the subspecifications, $S_1 \ldots S_n$, used in the rule of figure 3 must describe *all* behavioural aspects of the components, including behaviour which is inaccessible. Hence, the subspecifications may be unduely complicated and the amount of labour involved in using the proof rule consequently to high.

In the remainder of this section, we shall illustrate this phenomena through a concrete example. To obtain a specification theory where the subspecifications may be suitable simple, we present in the next section a relativized extension of the Bisimulation Theory, in which specifications may take behavioural constraints into account.

4.1 A Simple Scheduler

We consider a simple scheduler consisting of 3 cyclic cells A, B and C:

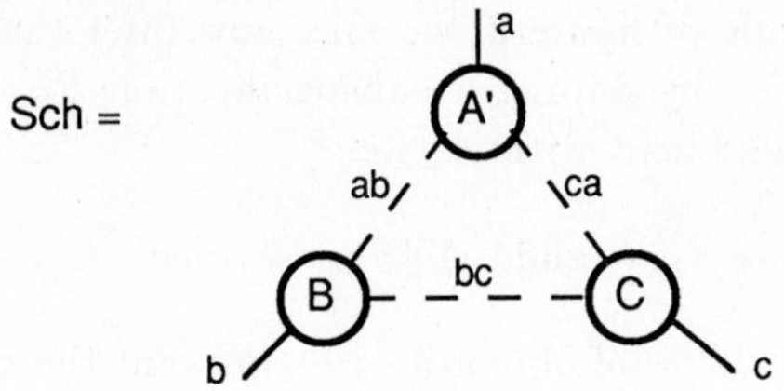

The behaviour of a typical cell X is defined as follows:

$$\begin{aligned} X &\Leftarrow pred.X' \\ X' &\Leftarrow x.X'' \\ X'' &\Leftarrow \overline{succ}.X \end{aligned}$$

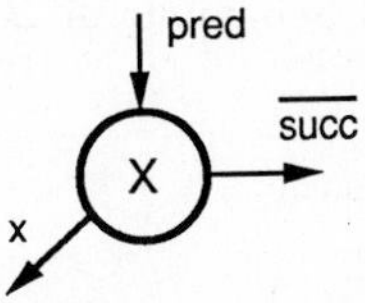

where A, B and C are obtained by suitable renamings. The scheduler *Sch* is then defined as:

$$Sch \Leftarrow (A' \| B \| C)$$

where $P\|Q$ is the restricted composition in CCS, i.e. $P\|Q = (P \mid Q)\backslash A$, where A is the set of common ports (actions) of P and Q. It turns out that $\|$ is associative in our case, since no two ports are identically named.

We want to prove that *Sch* is *bisimular* to the following specification (from which the cyclic behaviour of *Sch* is immediate):

$$Spec \Leftarrow a.\tau.b.\tau.c.\tau.Spec$$

We may prove this fact directly by exhibiting a bisimulation containing the pair (*Spec*, *Sch*). However, in order to demonstrate the limitations of the Bisimulation Theory, we will give a compositional proof based on the proof rule of figure 3. Thus, we decompose *Sch* in the following way:

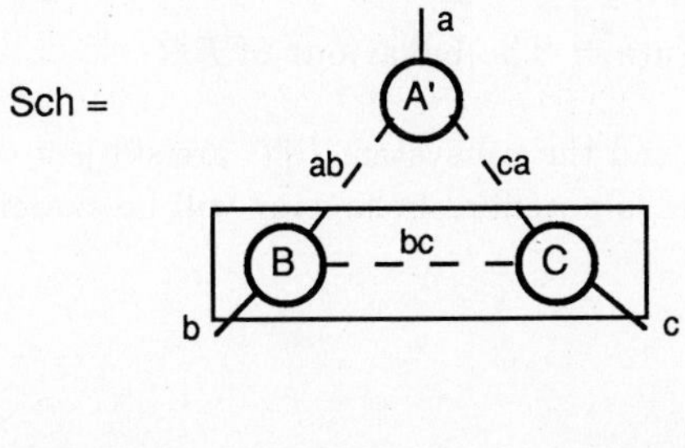

i.e. we view *Sch* as a combined process $C(P)$, where $B \| C$ constitutes the inner process P and $(A' \| I)$ the unary context C. The cell A' and the subsystem $B \| C$ will obviously communicate over the ports ab and ca, and it is intuitively clear that the interaction will consist of a simple alternation of ab and ca, starting with ab.

Using the compositional proof rule of figure 3, we may now infer the desired correctness assertion — $A' \| (B \| C) \sim Spec$ — by finding a subspecification S_{BC} being bisimular to $B \| C$ and entailing *Spec* when combined with A', i.e.:

$$B \| C \sim S_{BC} \quad \text{and} \quad A' \| S_{BC} \sim Spec \tag{11}$$

Obviously — in order to reduce our proof obligations — we want the subspecification S_{BC} to be as simple as possible and a first guess may be:

$$S_{BC} \Leftarrow ab.b.\tau.c.\overline{ca}.S_{BC}$$

However, this subspecification is far too simple for (11) to hold. In fact, no simple subspecification S_{BC}, which will satisfy the equivalences of (11) exists, as may be seen from the display of the full behaviour of $B \| C$ shown in figure 4. As previously mentioned the

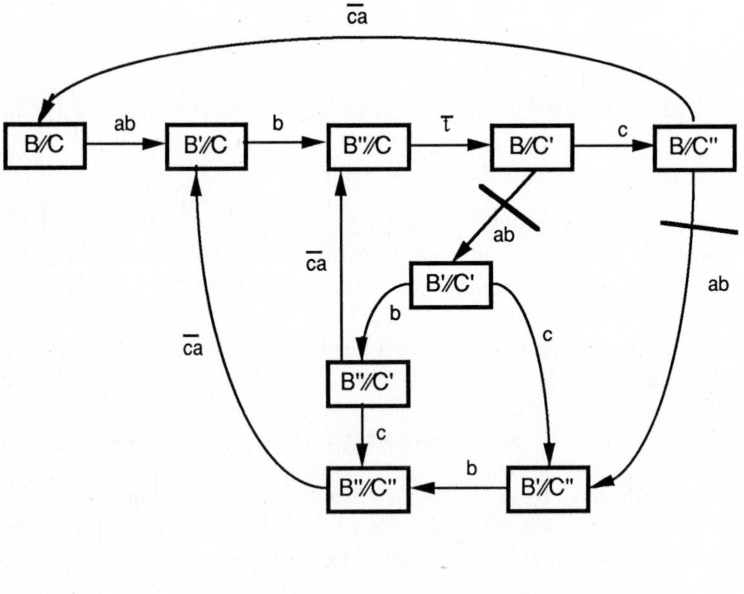

Figure 4: The behaviour of $B \| C$

interactions between the cell A' and the subsystem $B \| C$ are subject to certain restrictions. As a consequence, not all of $B \| C$'s potential behaviour will be exercised. In particular, in an execution of the total system, the overcrossed derivations (marked $\not\longrightarrow$ in figure 4) will never be examined. It follows that approximately 50% of the potential behaviour of $B\|C$ is inaccessible. However, any subspecification satisfying (11) must also cover the inaccessible behaviour, and will therefore be unduly complicated and certainly not intuitive.

5 Relativized Theory

Obviously, the defect of the Bisimulation Theory is that the proof obligations of the compositional proof rule become too difficult since they are in no way allowed to take into consideration — neither explicitely nor implicitely — the behavioural constraints imposed by the subcomponents and the context upon one another.

Reconsidering the simple scheduler from section 4.1, we note that the subcomponent $B\|C$ is placed in a context $(A'\|I)$ with the transducing behaviour (using the derived rules of example 3.2) given in figure 5. It follows that the actions ab and $\overline{ca}$ of any component

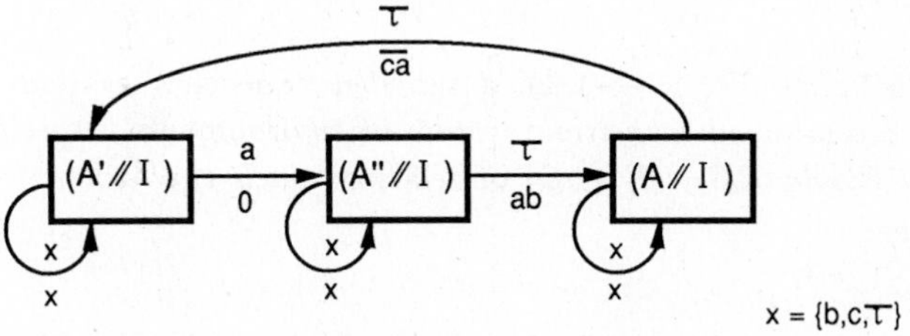

Figure 5: Behaviour of $(A'\|I)$

process inhabiting $(A'\|I)$ must strictly alternate. Intuitively, the behaviour allowed to a component of $(A'\|I)$ may be illustrated by the diagram of figure 6. We now try to relax

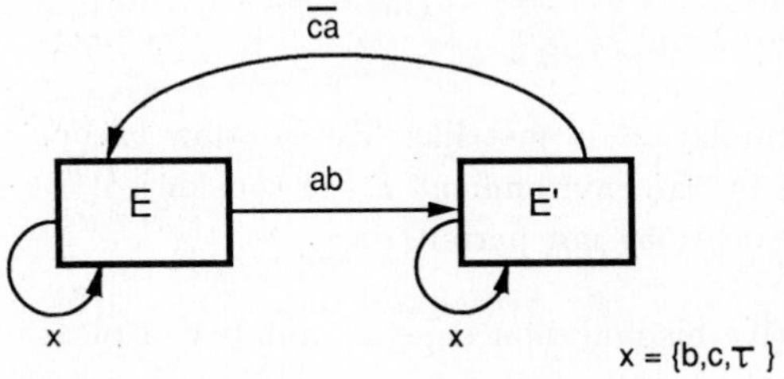

Figure 6: Behaviour allowed by $(A'\|I)$

the compositional proof rule of the Bisimulation Theory so that in the case of the simple scheduler we may use as subspecification an agent, which need not be exactly bisimular to $B\|C$, but is indistinguishable from it under the behavioural constraints expressed by the diagram of figure 6. For this purpose we shall shortly introduce the notion of *relative bisimulation* developed in [Lar86, LM87]. [4]

5.1 Environments and Relative Bisimulation

First, let us proceed by formalising the constraints which a context may impose upon its components. To this end, we will use a new notion of *environments*, which operationally are objects consuming actions produced by their inhabitants. However, an environment's ability to consume actions may be limited, thereby constraining the behaviour of the inhabitant. We describe the consuming behaviour of environments in terms of a labelled transition system $(\mathcal{E}, A, \longrightarrow)$, where $\mathcal{E}$ is the set of environments, A the set of actions and $\longrightarrow$ is the *consumption relation*. For $(E, A, F) \in \longrightarrow$ we shall normally write $E \stackrel{a}{\longrightarrow} F$, which is to be read as: "the environment E is able to consume the action a, and change into the environment F". The diagram in figure 6 may now be interpreted as an environment "projecting out" the consuming behaviour of the context $(A' \| I)$.

We may now formally present the notion of relative bisimulation:

Definition 5.1 *Let $(\mathcal{P}, A, \longrightarrow)$ be a labelled transition system of processes, and let $(\mathcal{E}, A, \longrightarrow)$ be a labelled transition system of environments. A relative bisimulation $\mathcal{RB}$ consists of a family $\mathcal{RB}_E$ $(E \in \mathcal{E})$ of relations such that whenever $(P, Q) \in \mathcal{RB}_E$ and $E \stackrel{a}{\longrightarrow} E'$ then:*

1. *Whenever $P \stackrel{a}{\longrightarrow} P'$, then $Q \stackrel{a}{\longrightarrow} Q'$ for some Q' with $(P', Q') \in \mathcal{RB}_{E'}$,*
2. *Whenever $Q \stackrel{a}{\longrightarrow} Q'$, then $P \stackrel{a}{\longrightarrow} P'$ for some P' with $(P', Q') \in \mathcal{RB}_{E'}$,*

We say that P and Q are bisimular relative to E, and write $P \sim_E Q$, if there exist a relative bisimulation $\mathcal{RB}$ such that $(P, Q) \in \mathcal{RB}_E$.

Thus, relative bisimulation is just like bisimulation except that only those transitions which is permitted by the environment E are considered: we do not care how the agents may perform for transitions not permitted.

The notion of relative bisimulation enjoys a number of pleasant properties: for any given environment E, bisimularity relative to E (i.e. the relation $\sim_E$) is an equivalence weaker than that of bisimularity ($\sim$). In fact, the simpler notion of bisimularity is just relative bisimularity with respect to a universal environment $\mathcal{U}$, which allows any action at any

[4] Note the close analogy to that of *code optimization*, consisting in replacing pieces of code with pieces of more efficient code, while maintaining the meaning of the overall program. Normally, the replacement is only valid under the constraints of the context in which the pieces are "sitting", constraints which will be calculated by som *data flow analyses*

time (i.e. $\mathcal{U} \xrightarrow{a} \mathcal{U}$ for all $a \in A$). The weakest relative bisimulation is that with respect to a completely inactive environment $\mathcal{O}$ (i.e. $\mathcal{O} \not\xrightarrow{a}$ for all $a \in A$), in which case relative bisimularity identifies all processes. A complete characterization of the relative strength of relative bisimularity in terms of the involved environments is given by the notion of *simulation*: [5] for any two environments E and F, $\sim_E$ is weaker than $\sim_F$ if and only if E is simulated by F. We refer the reader to [Lar87] for the non–trivial proof of this simple and useful characterization.

5.2 The Simple Scheduler

Returning to the example of the simple scheduler from section 4.1, we may now formally prove that the subcomponent $B\|C$ is relative bisimular to the (suggested) subspecification S_{BC} under the constraints of the environment E of figure 6.

As illustrated in figure 7, the following relations:

$$\begin{aligned} \mathcal{RB}_E &= \{(S_{BC}, B\|C)\} \\ \mathcal{RB}_{E'} &= \{(S_{B'C}, B'\|C), (S_{B''C}, B''\|C), (S_{BC'}, B\|C'), (S_{BC''}, B\|C'')\} \end{aligned}$$

may be verified to constitute a relative bisimlation. In particular, note that for the pairs $(S_{BC'}, B\|C')$ and $(S_{BC''}, B\|C'')$ of $\mathcal{RB}_{E'}$ the ab–transitions of $B\|C'$ and $B\|C''$ will not be considered as $E' \not\xrightarrow{ab}$.

5.3 Combined Environments and Compositionality

Now, to infer the desired correctness assertion for the total system — $A'\|(B\|C) \sim Spec$ — the following proof obligations seem to remain:

> (1) Prove that the subspecification S_{BC} entails the overall specification *Spec* when combined with A'; i.e. $A'\|S_{BC} \sim Spec$,
>
> (2) Prove that the environment E of figure 6 "contains" the behaviour permitted by the context $(A'\|I)$.

(1) may be proved directly (and easily) using the standard bisimulation technique. For (2), we introduce the notion of a *combined environment* as a dual to that of a combined process. Imagine the execution of a combined process $C(P)$ within some environment E. Now, from the point of view of the internal process, this may alternatively be viewed as an execution of P within a combined environment $E(C)$. But what is the behaviour of

[5] A *simulation* is a relation $\mathcal{S}$ on environments such that whenever $(E, F) \in \mathcal{S}$ and $E \xrightarrow{a} E'$, then $F \xrightarrow{a} F'$ for some F' with $(E', F') \in \mathcal{S}$. We write $E \leq F$ in this case, and say that E is simulated by F.

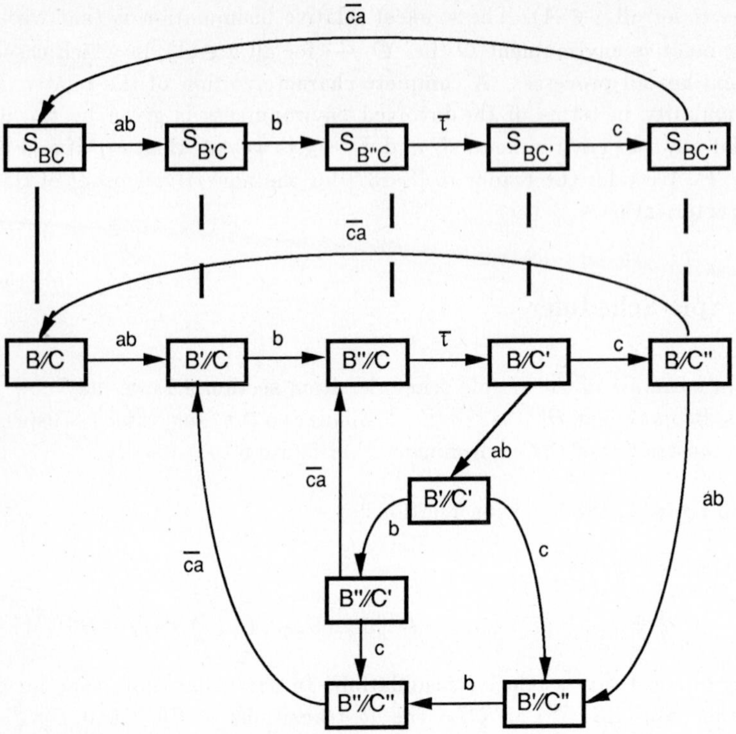

Figure 7: A Relative Bisimulation

the combined environment in terms of the behaviours of the outer environment E and the context C ? Our answer to this is the following inference–rule completely dual to the Uniform Rule (8) for combined processes (here restricted to unary contexts):

$$\frac{C \overset{b}{\underset{a}{\rightarrow}} C' \qquad E \overset{b}{\longrightarrow} E'}{E(C) \overset{a}{\longrightarrow} E'(C')} \tag{12}$$

Based on this notion, the following theorem naturally extends the preservation theorem 4.2 to relative bisimulation:

Theorem 5.2 *Let C be a unary context. Then $C(P) \sim_E C(Q)$ whenever $P \sim_{E(C)} Q$.*

Proof: We show that the family $\mathcal{RB}$ with:

$$\mathcal{RB}_E = \{(C(P), C(Q)) \mid P \sim_{E(C)} Q\}$$

is a relative bisimulation. So assume $\big(C(P), C(Q)\big) \in \mathcal{RB}_E$, $E \xrightarrow{a} E'$ and $C(P) \xrightarrow{a} T$. According to the Uniform Rule (8) for combined processes, $C \underset{b}{\overset{a}{\rightarrow}} C'$ and $P \xrightarrow{b} P'$ for some b, C' and P' with $T = C'(P')$. Now, using the rule (12) for combined environments, we obtain the consumption $E(C) \xrightarrow{b} E'(C')$. As Q is assumed bisimular to P relative to $E(C)$, it follows that $Q \xrightarrow{b} Q'$ for some Q' with $P' \sim_{E'(C')} Q'$. Then, using the Uniform Rule (8), we obtain $C(Q) \xrightarrow{a} C'(Q')$, which clearly is a matching move. □

Thus, relative bisimularity between combined processes may be reduced to relative bisimularity between the component processes with respect to the combined environments.

In the Relativized Specification Theory of figure 8, specifications are given as pairs (S, E), with S being an abstract process describing the desired behaviour of the implementation and E and environment describing the constraints under which the implementation will be used. The satisfaction relation is based on relative bisimularity.

Specification Theory

$$(\mathcal{P}, \mathcal{P} \times \mathcal{E}, \models)$$

$$\text{where } P \models (S, E) \text{ iff } P \sim_E S$$

Compositional Proof Rule

$$\frac{P \models (S', E')}{C(P) \models (S, E)} \quad E(C) \leq E',\; C(S') \models (S, E)$$

Ordering

$$(S_1, E_1) \Rightarrow (S_2, E_2) \text{ if } E_2 \leq E_1 \text{ and } S_1 \models (S_2, E_2)$$

Figure 8: Relativized Theory

To argue for *soundness* of the (obviously) compositional proof rule of figure 8, assume $P \models (S', E')$, $E(C) \leq E'$ and $C(S') \models (S, E)$. Then — since $\sim_{E(C)}$ is weaker that $\sim_{E'}$ — also $P \models (S', E(C))$ and hence, according to theorem 5.2 above, $C(P) \models (C(S'), E)$. As $\sim_E$ is an equivalence, it follows that $C(P) \models (S, E)$.

To see that the rule is also *backwards sound*, assume that $C(P) \models (S, E)$. Then by taking $S' = P$ and $E' = \mathcal{U}$, both the hypothesis and the side–condition of the rule will hold trivially. However, the rule fits neither the scheme for top–down development (3) nor the scheme for bottom–up development (2). Rather it seems to be a mixture, with the part of the side–condition relating the inner and outer *environments* supporting top–down development, and the part relating the subspecification and overall specification suporting bottom–up development.

Clearly, the Relativized Theory is more expressive than the Bisimulation Theory: for any specification S of the Bisimulation Theory, $(S, \mathcal{U})$ gives an equivalent specification in the Relativized Theory.

Finally, the ordering between specifications is easily seen to be (partially) characterized by the simulation ordering on the environment components of specifications.

6 Logical Theory

The specification theories presented in the two previous sections are obviously both behavioural in nature. In this section we investigate a (more expressive) specification theory allowing specifications to be combined logically; i.e. the specification formalism is an extension of Propositional Logic. Also for this theory it turns out that the transductional semantics of contexts leads to compositional proof rules.

As specification formalism we choose an extension of the classical Hennessy–Milner logic [HM85] allowing specifications to be defined recursively. The original Hennessy–Milner logic is a modal propositional logic enabling properties of the observational behaviour of processes to be described; e.g. *whether* a given process can respond to a particular experiment and if so, *how* it responds. Especially, one can express — using the modalities of the logic — what properties *may* and *must* hold of a process after a given experiment.

In [Lar88] it was demonstrated that the recursive extension of Hennessy–Milner logic provides a very expressive specification language; in fact, all the standard operators from Branching Time Temporal Logic [BAPM83] are derivable, allowing *safety* and *liveness* properties of processes to be expressed. In this section we shall see, that the recursive extension of Hennessy–Milner logic also leads to a specification theory more expressive than the Relativized Theory.

The formulae of Hennessy–Milner logic extended with recursion is given by the following abstract syntax:

$$\begin{aligned} F \; ::= \; & \mathsf{tt} \mid X \mid F_1 \wedge F_2 \mid \neg F \mid \langle a \rangle F \mid \\ & \mathsf{letmax}\ \{X_i = F_i\}_{i \in I}\ \mathsf{in}\ F \end{aligned}$$

where I is some index–set, X and X_i belongs to some set of variables, V, and a is an action.

We denote by $\mathcal{L}$ the set of formulae of this logic. In the letmax–construct, $\{X_i = F_i\}_{i \in I}$ is a *declaration* introducing simultaneous recursively specified properties $\{X_i\}_{i \in I}$ with scope being the body F. The concept of free and bound variables are defined as usual; in particular we call a formula *closed* if it contains no free variables and denote by $\mathcal{L}_c$ the set of closed formulae. For reasons of monotonicity, we shall impose the (standard) syntactic restriction, that any free occurrence of a variable X_i in F is under the "scope" of an even number of negations. We shall use the standard notation $F[G/X]$ to describe the substitution of G for all free occurrences of the variable X in F (with bound variables of F being renamed when capturing of free variables of G can occur). Finally, we call a formula *finite* if it is closed and contains no letmax–construct. We denote by $\mathcal{L}_f$ the set of finite formulae (which is identical to the original Hennessy–Milner logic).

A formula of $\mathcal{L}$ is meant to describe a collection of properties that a sought process should have. Thus, the semantic interpretation of a formula F may be taken to be the set of processes enjoying the properties described by F. However, as formulae in general may contain free variables, we define their semantics relative to an *assignment* $\sigma : V \longrightarrow 2^{\mathcal{P}}$ ascribing a set of processes to each variable of V. We use the notation $\sigma\{U_i/X_i\}_{i\in I}$ for the assignment identical to σ except that U_i is returned for the variable X_i for $i \in I$.

Denoting by *Asn* the set of assignments over V, we define the semantic function:

$$\mathsf{F} : \mathcal{L} \longrightarrow Asn \longrightarrow 2^{\mathcal{P}}$$

inductively on the structure of formulae of $\mathcal{L}$ as in figure 9, with $\sigma \in Asn$, and ν being the maximum fixed point operator on assignments (ordered by pointwise set–inclusion).

$$\begin{aligned}
\mathsf{F}[\![\mathsf{tt}]\!]\sigma &= \mathcal{P} \\
\mathsf{F}[\![X]\!]\sigma &= \sigma(X) \\
\mathsf{F}[\![F_1 \wedge F_2]\!]\sigma &= \mathsf{F}[\![F_1]\!]\sigma \cap \mathsf{F}[\![F_2]\!]\sigma \\
\mathsf{F}[\![\neg F]\!]\sigma &= \left(\mathsf{F}[\![F]\!]\sigma\right)^c \\
\mathsf{F}[\![\langle a\rangle F]\!]\sigma &= \{P \in \mathcal{P} \mid \exists P'.P \stackrel{a}{\longrightarrow} P' \wedge P' \in \mathsf{F}[\![F]\!]\sigma\} \\
\mathsf{F}[\![\mathsf{letmax}\ \{X_i = F_i\}_{i\in I}\ \mathsf{in}\ F]\!]\sigma & \\
&= \mathsf{F}[\![F]\!]\left(\nu\rho.\sigma\{\mathsf{F}[\![F_i]\!]\rho/X_i\}_{i\in I}\right)
\end{aligned}$$

Figure 9: Semantic Equations

Now, it is easy to see that the semantics given above is a *denotational* one, in the sense that the semantics of a composite formula is given in terms of the semantics of the component formulae. Moreover, due to the syntactic restriction imposed for recursion, all constructs on formulae induce a *monotonic* operation on the complete lattice $2^{\mathcal{P}}$. Thus, according to classical fixed point theory, the maximum fixed point construct used in the semantics is well–defined.

Obviously, $\mathsf{F}[\![F]\!]\sigma$ only depends on the part of σ which concerns the free variables of F. In particular, if F is closed, σ is immaterial, and we will simply write $\mathsf{F}[\![G]\!]$ for $\mathsf{F}[\![G]\!]\sigma$, where σ could be any assignment.

The logic $\mathcal{L}$ enjoys a number of pleasant properties. The sublogic $\mathcal{L}_f$ was introduced by

Hennessy and Milner [HM85], and shown to characterize bisimulation [6] in the sense that two processes are bisimular if and only if they satisfy the same formulae of $\mathcal{L}_f$:

$$P \sim Q \quad \Leftrightarrow \quad \forall F \in \mathcal{L}_f . P \in \mathsf{F}[\![F]\!] \Leftrightarrow Q \in \mathsf{F}[\![F]\!]$$

In [Lar87], this characterization result is extended to relative bisimulation in the sense that two processes are bisimular ***relative*** to some environment E just in case they satisfy the same formulae of $\mathcal{L}_f$ *which are relevant for* E. Thus, the extended characterization theorem has the form:

$$P \sim_E Q \quad \Leftrightarrow \quad \forall F \in \mathcal{H}(E). P \in \mathsf{F}[\![F]\!] \Leftrightarrow Q \in \mathsf{F}[\![F]\!]$$

where $\mathcal{H}(E) \subseteq \mathcal{L}_f$ is the set of formulae corresponding to properties of processes which can be examined by E. For a definition of $\mathcal{H}(E)$ consult [Lar87].

In fact — using the power of recursion — Skou has shown [Skoar] that the class of processes bisimular to a given process P relative to an environment E may be represented by a single *characteristic* (closed) formula, $F_{P,E}$, in the sense that:

$$Q \sim_E P \quad \Leftrightarrow \quad Q \in \mathsf{F}[\![F_{P,E}]\!]$$

Thus, the logic $\mathcal{L}_c$ will induce a specification theory more expressive than that of the Relativized Theory.

The power of recursion also makes *liveness* and *safety* properties expressible in $\mathcal{L}_c$. We demonstrate this through a few examples, and refer the reader to [Lar88] for further information.

Example 6.1 The property of *divergence*, Div, meaning the presence of an infinite τ–computation, may be expressed by the following recursive formula:

$$\text{Div} \equiv \mathsf{letmax}\ X = \langle\tau\rangle X \ \mathsf{in}\ X$$

The property of *liveness*, Live, in the sense that deadlock will never occur, may be expressed as follows:

$$\text{Live} \equiv \mathsf{letmax}\ X = \langle A\rangle \mathsf{tt} \wedge [A]X \ \mathsf{in}\ X$$

where $\langle A\rangle F$ abbreviates $\bigwedge_{a\in A}\langle a\rangle F$ (assuming that A is finite), and $[A]F$ abbreviates $\neg\langle A\rangle\neg F$. In fact, Live is a safety property expressing that the property $\langle A\rangle\mathsf{tt}$ (meaning can do something initially) holds invariantly. To express the *invariance* of an arbitrary property F, the following scheme may be used:

$$\text{Inv}F \equiv \mathsf{letmax}\ X = F \wedge [A]X \ \mathsf{in}\ X$$

Clearly, Live is an instance of this scheme. The liveness property, that a property F may *possibly* hold (i.e. at some point during some execution), may then be expressed simply as $\neg\text{Inv}\neg F$. □

[6] Actually, the characterization is subject to the technical condition of *image–finiteness* of the process system $(\mathcal{P}, A, \longrightarrow)$; i.e. the set $\{P' \mid P \xrightarrow{a} P'\}$ must be finite for any P and a.

6.1 Contexts as Property Transformers

Let us now consider the logical specification theory

$$(\mathcal{P}, \mathcal{L}_c, \models)$$

where the satisfaction relation is given by the semantics of formulae (figure 9); i.e. $P \models F$ if and only if $P \in \mathsf{F}[\![F]\!]$. Then obviously, as indicated in figure 10, the refinement ordering between specifications becomes set–inclusion between their semantics; i.e. $F \Rightarrow G$ just in case $\mathsf{F}[\![F]\!] \subseteq \mathsf{F}[\![G]\!]$.

Specification Theory

$$(\mathcal{P}, \mathcal{L}_c, \models)$$

where $P \models F$ iff $P \in \mathsf{F}[\![F]\!]$

Compositional Proof Rule

$$\frac{P \models G}{C(P) \models F} \; G \Rightarrow \mathcal{W}(C, F)$$

Ordering

$$F \Rightarrow G \;\equiv\; \mathsf{F}[\![F]\!] \subseteq \mathsf{F}[\![G]\!]$$

Figure 10: Logic Theory

In order to provide a compositional proof rule for this specification theory, we ask the following fundamental question: [7]

> What property must the component process P satisfy, in order that a combined process $C(P)$ satisfies a given property F?

The answer to this question is given in terms of a *property transformer*, $\mathcal{W}$, with the following characteristica:

$$C(P) \models F \;\Leftrightarrow\; P \models \mathcal{W}(C, F) \tag{13}$$

i.e. $\mathcal{W}$ makes correctness assertions for combined processes interreducable with correctness assertions involving only the components. Before stating the formal definition of $\mathcal{W}$ let us first make some informal observations:

[7] In [LX89] this problem is dealt with in more generality, allowing the combined process to have several component processes.

Certainly, we will expect $\mathcal{W}(C, \text{tt}) = \text{tt}$ as $C(P)$ satisfies tt for any process P. Similarly, it can be argued that $\mathcal{W}$ should distribute over the propositional connectives of $\mathcal{L}$.

More interestingly, assume F is of the form $\langle a \rangle H$. According to (13), $\mathcal{W}(C, \langle a \rangle H)$ will express a necessary and sufficient requirement to a process P in order for $C(P)$ to satisfy $\langle a \rangle H$. Thus, for some transduction $C \underset{b}{\overset{a}{\longrightarrow}} C'$ and some transition $P \overset{b}{\longrightarrow} P'$, $C'(P')$ will satisfy H, or equivalently, P' will satisfy $\mathcal{W}(C', H)$. As any a–producing transduction of C will do, we expect P to satisfy $\mathcal{W}(C, \langle a \rangle H)$ if and only if P satisfies $\langle b \rangle \mathcal{W}(C', H)$ for some transduction $C \underset{b}{\overset{a}{\longrightarrow}} C'$.

Finally, consider the case when F is a recursive formula $\mathsf{letmax}\ D\ \mathsf{in}\ G$, where D is some declaration $\{X_i = F_i\}_{i \in I}$. Now, the semantics of F is simply that of G in an assignment σ containing the (recursive) declarations of D. Thus, we expect $\mathcal{W}(C, \mathsf{letmax}\ D\ \mathsf{in}\ G)$ to be essentially $\mathcal{W}(C, G)$, but in an assignment σ^T obtained from σ or stated syntactically:

$$\mathcal{W}(C, \mathsf{letmax}\ D\ \mathsf{in}\ G) = \mathsf{letmax}\ D^T\ \mathsf{in}\ \mathcal{W}(C, G) \tag{14}$$

The question that remains to be answered, is the precise nature of D^T. Now, it turns out that the definition of $\mathcal{W}(C, F)$ will be compositional in the structure of F (which is also confirmed by all our observations so far). Thus, if in (14) X is a free variable of G, $\mathcal{W}(C, G)$ will necessarily contain $\mathcal{W}(C', X)$ as a subformula for some context C'. Assuming that X is declared in D as $X = H$, we will certainly expect the equivalence $\mathcal{W}(C', X) = \mathcal{W}(C', H)$ to hold. Representing $\mathcal{W}(C', X)$ as a new variable $X^{C'}$, this indicates that we should add the equation $X^{C'} = \mathcal{W}(C', H)$ to the transformed declaration D^T. In order to avoid complicated calculations of the precise values for the context C', we suggest that the equation $X^{C'} = \mathcal{W}(C', H)$ is added for *any* context C'.

Following closely the above discussion, we give in figure 11 the formal definition of $\mathcal{W}$ by induction on the structure of formulae. We may now formally state the following main theorem:

Theorem 6.2 *Let C be a unary context, let P be a process, and let F be a closed formula of $\mathcal{L}$. Then*

$$C(P) \models F \;\Leftrightarrow\; P \models \mathcal{W}(C, F)$$

For finite formulae our discussion above may be easily tranformed into a formal proof of this theorem. Due to the lack of space here, we refer the reader to [LX89] for a complete proof.

Now it follows immediately from theorem 6.2, that the compositional proof rule of figure 10 is both sound and backwards sound. Also note, that the proof rule is an instance of the generic rule (3) for top–down development.

$$
\begin{aligned}
\mathcal{W}(C, \mathsf{tt}) &= \mathsf{tt} \\
\mathcal{W}(C, X) &= X^C \\
\mathcal{W}(C, F \wedge G) &= \mathcal{W}(C, F) \wedge \mathcal{W}(C, G) \\
\mathcal{W}(C, \neg F) &= \neg \mathcal{W}(C, F) \\
\mathcal{W}(C, \langle a \rangle F) &= \bigvee_{C \overset{a}{\underset{b}{\longrightarrow}} D} \langle b \rangle \mathcal{W}(D, F) \\
\mathcal{W}(C, \mathsf{letmax}\ D\ \mathsf{in}\ F) &= \mathsf{letmax}\ D^T\ \mathsf{in}\ \mathcal{W}(C, F)
\end{aligned}
$$

where for $D = \{X_i = F_i\}_{i \in I}$ the transformed declaration D^T is $\{X_i^D = \mathcal{W}(D, F_i)\}_{i \in I, D \in \mathcal{C}}$, and $\langle 0 \rangle F$ abbreviates F.

Figure 11: Definition of Property Transformer

6.2 The Lazy Researcher

We consider an extremely simplified office consisting of a machine, *Mac*, and a researcher, *Res*.

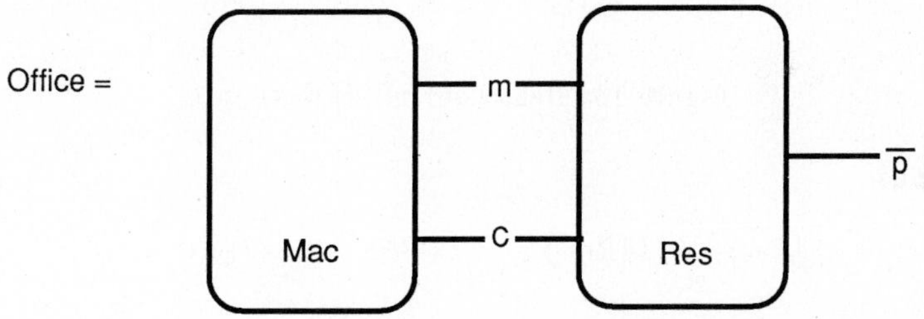

Figure 12: An Office

That is, the office *Office* is defined as the (restricted) parallel composition of *Mac* and *Res*, $(Mac \| Res)$. The (simple–minded) purpose of an office is to provide the surrounding environment with a steady flow of publications $(\overline{p})$. Given the limitations of modern technology, it is the task of the researcher to write these publications. However, in order to publish, the researcher occationally requires a cup of coffee (c) for which (s)he naturally is willing to pay (m).

We now consider a special type of office with a somewhat lazy researcher. In particular, the lazy researcher may always decide to take yet another cup of coffee before finishing a publication (if ever). The behaviour of the researcher *Res* is defined as follows:

$$Res \Leftarrow \overline{m}.c.(\overline{p}.Res + Res)$$

The following interesting question may now be asked:

> What property must the machine *Mac* satisfy, in order that the office *Office* behaves in an orderly manner?

Using the property transformer $\mathcal{W}$ (figure 11) and assuming the notion of well–behavedness to be specified as a formula $F \in \mathcal{L}_c$, the answer to this question is simply $\mathcal{W}((I\|Res), F)$ (as $(I\|Res)$ is the context in which *Mac* will be "sitting").

The transductional behaviour of the context $(I\|Res)$ may be determined by the rules of example 3.2 to that of figure 13, where Res' respectively Res'' abbreviates $c.(\overline{p}.Res + Res)$ respectively $\overline{p}.Res + Res$.

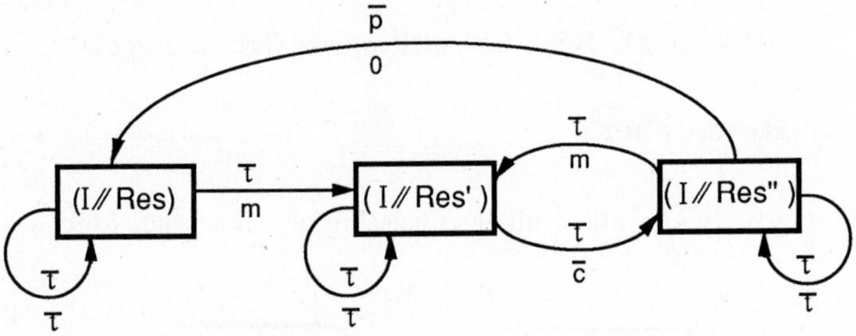

Figure 13: Behaviour of $(I\|Res)$

The transductions

$$(I\|Res) \xrightarrow[m]{\tau} (I\|Res') \qquad (I\|Res'') \xrightarrow[m]{\tau} (I\|Res')$$

will be realized when the machine is willing to accept the money (m) offered by the researcher.

$$(I\|Res') \xrightarrow[\overline{c}]{\tau} (I\|Res'')$$

may take place if the machine can provide the (now coffee craving) researcher with coffee. Finally,

$$(I\|Res'') \xrightarrow[0]{\overline{p}} (I\|Res)$$

indicates that the researcher is capable of emitting a publication without involving the machine.

Now, let the notion of "well–behaved" be specified by the formula $\langle\tau\rangle\langle\tau\rangle\langle\overline{p}\rangle\mathrm{tt}$; i.e. the requirement to *Office* is that a publication is available after two internal computation–steps. Using the property transformer $\mathcal{W}$, the requirement to the machine *Mac* may then be calculated to the following:

$$\begin{aligned}
&\mathcal{W}\big((I\|Res), \langle\tau\rangle\langle\tau\rangle\langle\overline{p}\rangle tt\big)\\
&= \langle m\rangle\mathcal{W}\big((I\|Res'), \langle\tau\rangle\langle\overline{p}\rangle tt\big) \vee \langle\tau\rangle\mathcal{W}\big((I\|Res), \langle\tau\rangle\langle\overline{p}\rangle tt\big)\\
&= \langle m\rangle\big[\langle\tau\rangle\mathcal{W}\big((I\|Res'), \langle\overline{p}\rangle tt\big) \vee \langle\overline{c}\rangle\mathcal{W}\big((I\|Res''), \langle\overline{p}\rangle tt\big)\big] \vee\\
&\quad \langle\tau\rangle\mathcal{W}\big((I\|Res), \langle\tau\rangle\langle\overline{p}\rangle tt\big)\\
&= \langle m\rangle\big(\langle\tau\rangle ff \vee \langle\overline{c}\rangle tt\big) \vee \langle\tau\rangle ff\\
&= \langle m\rangle\langle\overline{c}\rangle tt
\end{aligned}$$

i.e. *Mac* must initially be willing to accept money and immediately thereafter give a cup of coffee.

We now make the following more demanding requirement: the behaviour of *Office* must be free of both deadlock and divergence. Specified as a formula of $\mathcal{L}_c$ this becomes:

$$Office \models \text{Live} \wedge \neg\text{Div}$$

where Live and Div are the abbreviations defined in example 6.1. The requirement to the machine *Mac* then becomes

$$\begin{aligned}
&\mathcal{W}\big((I\|Res), \text{Live} \wedge \neg\text{Div}\big)\\
&= \mathcal{W}\big((I\|Res), \text{Live}\big) \wedge \neg\mathcal{W}\big((I\|Res), \text{Div}\big)
\end{aligned}$$

Using the definition of $\mathcal{W}$ figure 11 together with the semantics of $(I\|Res)$ figure 13, the following may be calculated:

$$\begin{aligned}
&\mathcal{W}\big((I\|Res), \text{Live}\big)\\
&= \mathsf{letmax}\left\{\begin{array}{l} X = (\langle\tau\rangle tt \vee \langle m\rangle tt) \wedge ([\tau]X \wedge [m]X')\\ X' = (\langle\tau\rangle tt \vee \langle\overline{c}\rangle tt) \wedge ([\tau]X' \wedge [\overline{c}]X'')\\ X'' = [\tau]X'' \wedge [m]X' \wedge X \end{array}\right\} \mathsf{in}\ X
\end{aligned} \qquad (15)$$

and

$$\begin{aligned}
&\mathcal{W}\big((I\|Res), \text{Div}\big)\\
&= \mathsf{letmax}\left\{\begin{array}{l} X = \langle\tau\rangle X \vee \langle m\rangle X'\\ X' = \langle\tau\rangle X' \vee \langle\overline{c}\rangle X''\\ X'' = \langle\tau\rangle X'' \vee \langle m\rangle X' \end{array}\right\} \mathsf{in}\ X
\end{aligned} \qquad (16)$$

As $\langle a\rangle tt \wedge [a]F \Rightarrow \langle a\rangle F$, it is easy to see that the equation system in the declaration of (15) implies the corresponding equation system of (16). Hence, fixed point induction yields:

$$\mathcal{W}\big((I\|Res), \text{Live}\big) \Rightarrow \mathcal{W}\big((I\|Res), \text{Div}\big)$$

i.e. any machine ensuring liveness will also create the possibility of divergence. Hence, no matter how advanced the machine is, the resulting office will always fail to have the desired property Live $\wedge$ ¬Div.

7 Concluding Remarks

As the conclusion of this paper, we claim that the operational understanding of contexts as action transducer provides a very useful abstraction when establishing compositional results. Moreover, due to the abstraction, the compositionality results will be valid for most Process Algebras.

In the treatment of the Relativized Theory and the Logical Theory, compositional proof rules are only given for combined systems with a *single* inner component. In [LX89] a generalized treatment may be found for the Logical Theory, allowing combined systems with several components.

Current research (with Liu Xinxin) includes the *synthesis* of solutions to equation systems of the form:

$$C_1(X) \sim P_1 \ldots\ldots C_n(X) \sim P_n$$

Applying the operational semantics of contexts proposed in this paper, this may be dealt with in an elegant and simple manner, and with an implemention being "constructed" as a "side–effect". This work will extend significantly previous work by Shields [Shi] and Parrow [Par89], which only consider a single equation and with strong restictions on the context C (in [Par89] required to be of the form $(Q \mid I)\backslash A$) and the righthand side process P (required to be deterministic in [Par89])

References

[Abr87] S. Abramsky. Observation equivalence as a testing equivalence. *Theoretical Computer Science*, 1987.

[BAPM83] M. Ben-Ari, A. Pnueli, and Z. Manna. The temporal logic of branching time. *Acta Informatica*, 20, 1983.

[BK85] J.A. Bergstra and J.W. Klop. Algebra of communicating processes with abstraction. *Theoretical Computer Science*, 37:77–121, 1985.

[Blo88] Meyer Bloom, Istrail. bisimulation can't be traced. *Proceedings of Principles of Programming Languages*, 1988.

[Bou85] G. Boudol. Calcul de processus et verification. Technical Report 424, INRIA, 1985.

[CPS88] R. Cleaveland, J. Parrow, and B. Steffen. The concurrency workbench. University of Edinburgh, Scotland, 1988.

[Dij76] E.W. Dijkstra. *A Discipline of Programming.* Prentice–Hall, 1976.

[dS85] R. de Simone. Higher–level synchronising devices in MEIJE–CCS. *Theoretical Computer Science*, 37, 1985.

[Gro89] Vaandrager Groote. Structured operational semantics and bisimulation as a congruence. *Lecture Notes in Computer Science*, 1989.

[HM85] M. Hennessy and R. Milner. Algebraic laws for nondeterminism and concurrency. *Journal of the Association for Computing Machinery*, pages 137–161, 1985.

[Hoa69] C.A.R. Hoare. An axiomatic basis for computer programming. *ACM Communications*, 12(10):576–583, 1969.

[Hoa78] C.A.R. Hoare. Communicating sequential processes. *Communications of the ACM*, 21(8), 1978.

[KS] Kannellakis and Smolka. CCS expressions, finite state processes, and three problems of equivalence. To appear in Information and Computation.

[Lar86] K.G. Larsen. *Context–Dependent Bisimulation Between Processes.* PhD thesis, University of Edinburgh, Mayfield Road, Edinburgh, Scotland, 1986.

[Lar87] K.G. Larsen. A context dependent bisimulation between processes. *Theoretical Computer Science*, 1987.

[Lar88] K.G. Larsen. Proof systems for Hennessy–Milner logic with recursion. *Lecture Notes in Computer Science*, 299, 1988. in Proc. of CAAP'88. Full version to appear in Theoretical Computer Science.

[LM87] K.G. Larsen and R. Milner. Verifying a protocol using relativized bisimulation. *Lecture Notes in Computer Science*, 267, 1987. International Colloquium on Algorithms, Languages and Programming.

[LMV88] V. Lecompte, E. Madelaine, and D. Vergamini. Auto: A verfication system for parallel and communicating processes. INRIA, Sophia–Antipolis, 1988.

[LS87] K.G. Larsen and A. Skou. Tau: Theories for parallel systems, their automation and usage. Aalborg University, Denmark, March 1987.

[LS89] K.G. Larsen and A. Skou. Bisimulation through probabilistic testing. *Proceedings of Principles of Programming Languages*, 1989.

[LX89] K.G. Larsen and L. Xinxin. Compositionality through an operational semantics of contexts. Technical Report R 89–13, Aalborg University Center, Denmark, 1989.

[Mil80] R. Milner. *Calculus of Communicating Systems*, volume 92 of *Lecture Notes in Computer Science.* Springer Verlag, 1980.

[Mil83] R. Milner. Calculi for synchrony and asynchrony. *Theoretical Computer Science*, 25, 1983.

[Mil88] R. Milner. Interpreting one concurrent calculus in another. *proceedings of the International Conference on Fifth Generation Computer Systems*, 1988.

[Mil89] R. Milner. *Communication and Concurrency.* Prentice–Hall, 1989.

[Par81] D. Park. Concurrency and automata on infinite sequences. *Lecture Notes in Computer Science*, 104, 1981. in Proc. of 5th GI Conf.

[Par89] J. Parrow. Submodule construction as equation solving in ccs. *Theoretical Computer Science*, 1989. To appear.

[Plo81] G. Plotkin. A structural approach to operational semantics. FN 19, DAIMI, Aarhus University, Denmark, 1981.

[Pnu85] A. Pnueli. Linear and branching structures in the semantics and logics of reactive systems. *Lecture Notes in Computer Science*, 194, 1985. in Proc. of ICALP'87.

[PT87] Paige and Tarjan. Three partition refinement algorithms. *SIAM Journal of Computing*, 16(6), 1987.

[Shi] M.W. Shields. A note on the simple interface equation. Technical report, University of Kent at Canterbury.

[Skoar] A. Skou. *Validation of Concurrent Processes, with emphasis on testing.* PhD thesis, Aalbog University Center, Denmark, to appear.

[Zwi89] J. Zwiers. *Compositionality, Concurrency and Partial Correctness — Proof Theories for Networks of Processes, and Their Relationship*, volume 321 of *Lecture Notes in Computer Science.* Springer Verlag, 1989.

Multivalued Possibilities Mappings *

Nancy A. Lynch
Laboratory for Computer Science
MIT
Cambridge, MA 02139

Abstract: Abstraction mappings are one of the major tools used to construct correctness proofs for concurrent algorithms. Several examples are given of situations in which it is useful to allow the abstraction mappings to be multivalued. The examples involve algorithm optimization, algorithm distribution, and proofs of time bounds.

Keywords: abstraction mapping, mapping, possibilities mapping, safety property, Alternating Bit Protocol, transaction processing, garbage collection, distributed algorithms, time bounds, history variables

Contents

1 Introduction

2 A Formal Framework

3 Algorithm Optimization
- 3.1 Alternating Bit Protocol
  - 3.1.1 Problem Statement
  - 3.1.2 Architecture
  - 3.1.3 Alternating Bit Protocol
  - 3.1.4 Redundant Protocol
  - 3.1.5 Possibilities Mapping Proof
  - 3.1.6 Remarks
- 3.2 Transaction Processing
- 3.3 Garbage Collection
- 3.4 Remarks

4 Distribution

5 Proving Time Bounds
- 5.1 Overview
- 5.2 Formal Model
  - 5.2.1 Timed Automata
  - 5.2.2 The Automaton *time*(A)
  - 5.2.3 Strong Possibilities Mappings

*This work was supported by ONR contract N0014-85-K-0168, by NSF contract CCR-8611442, and by DARPA contract N00014-83-K-0125.

5.3 The Algorithm
5.4 The Performance Automaton
5.5 Proof

6 Conclusions

A Proof

1 Introduction

Abstraction mappings are one of the major tools that my colleagues and I use to construct correctness proofs for concurrent (including distributed) algorithms. In this paper, I will try to make one major point about such mappings: that it is useful to allow them to be *multivalued.* That is, often when one maps a "low-level" algorithm L to a "high-level" algorithm H, one would like to allow *several* states of H to correspond to a *single* state of L. I believe that any useful framework for describing abstraction mappings should include the ability to describe multivalued mappings.

I don't know if this point is especially controversial. I have been using multivalued mappings since I started carrying out such proofs in 1981, and the popular notion of *bisimulation* proposed by Milner [20] also permits multiple values (although bisimulation is a stronger notion than I advocate here, since it requires simulation relationships between L and H in both directions). However, work on *history variables*, tracing its roots to [22], takes pains to avoid the use of multivalued mappings by adding extra information to the state of L, and there are also some recent papers (e.g., [13, 12, 1]) that restrict the notion of mapping to be single-valued.

I will describe some situations in which multivalued abstraction mappings are useful. The examples I consider involve

1. algorithm optimization,

2. distribution, and

3. proving time bounds.

I will illustrate the first of these situations in some detail, using one familiar example (the Alternating Bit Protocol) and two less familiar examples, just touch on the second, and spend the remaining time on the third - it's the newest use I have found and possibly the most interesting.

In my work, abstraction mapping seem most useful for proving safety properties; although I have been involved in some work that proves liveness properties using such mappings (e.g., [17, 27]), these efforts are still somewhat ad hoc. Note that timing properties are more like safety properties than like liveness properties; because of this, mappings are useful for proving timing properties as well. In this paper, I will restrict attention to safety and timing properties.

2 A Formal Framework

To be concrete, I will describe the work in terms of I/O automata [17, 18], since that is what I've actually used. The precise choice of model is not very important for most of what I will discuss here (timing proofs excepted); other state machine models would probably do as well. Here, I will review the definition of an I/O automaton and will give the usual notion of mapping, called a *possibilities mapping*, that I use for defining a correspondence between I/O automata.

Recall that an I/O automaton consists of *states*, *start states*, *actions* classified by a *signature* as *output*, *input* and *internal*, and *steps*, which are (state, action, state) triples. So far, that makes them rather ordinary state machines. There is a fifth component that is not normally relevant to my work involving mappings (but that I will use in the timing example): a *partition* of the output and internal actions into classes indicating which are under the control of the same underlying component in the system being modeled by the automaton. Its main purpose is in describing fair executions of the automaton - executions that allow each component fair turns to continue taking steps. For now, I will ignore this partition.

An *extended step* of an automaton describes a state change that can occur as a result of a finite sequence of actions.

The important behavior of an I/O automaton is normally considered to be its interaction with its environment, in the form of its *behaviors*, i.e., its sequences of input and output actions (more precisely, its fair sequences). Problems to be solved by I/O automata are specified as sets of sequences of such actions, and an automaton is said to *solve* a problem if its (fair) behaviors are a subset of the set of problem sequences.

Let L and H be two I/O automata with the same external action signature (same inputs and outputs). Define a *possibilities mapping* from L to H to be a mapping f from $states(L)$ to the power set of $states(H)$ satisfying the following properties.

1. For every start state s_0 of L, there is a start state u_0 of H such that $u_0 \in f(s_0)$.

2. If s' is a reachable state of L, $u' \in f(s')$ is a reachable state of H and (s', π, s) is a step of L, then there is an extended step (u', γ, u) of H such that:

   (a) $\gamma | ext(H) = \pi | ext(L)$, and

   (b) $u \in f(s)$.

The basic theorem about possibilities mappings is:

Theorem 1 *If there is a possibilities mapping from L to H, then all behaviors of L are also behaviors of H.*

This theorem suggests how a possibilities mapping can be used in proving safety properties (defined here to be nonempty, prefix-closed, limit-closed properties of external action sequences) for an automaton L. For example, a safety property P might be specified as the set of behaviors of an automaton H. Then a possibilities mapping from L to H shows that the behaviors of L all satisfy P. For another example, it might be possible to show that the behaviors of an automaton H all satisfy a safety property P; then a possibilities mapping from L to H shows that the behaviors of L all satisfy P.

Concurrent systems are modeled by compositions of I/O automata, as defined in [17, 18]. In order to be composed, automata must be *strongly compatible*; this means that no action can be an output of more than one component, that input actions of one component are not shared by any other component, and that no action is shared by infinitely many components. The result of such a composition is another I/O automaton.

3 Algorithm Optimization

An important use of a possibilities mapping is to decompose the correctness proof for an "optimized" algorithm L using an "unoptimized" variation H as an intermediate stage. Typically, H would be a simple and redundant algorithm that is easy to understand because it maintains a lot of intuitively meaningful information. The algorithm L would be less redundant, more efficient, and correspondingly more difficult to understand. The behavior of L would be very similar to that of H, but would be determined on the basis of less information. A good way to correspond the two algorithms is via a multivalued mapping from L to H. The mapping "puts back" the information that is lost in "optimizing" H; since there may not be a unique way to do this, the mapping must be multivalued.

In this section, I give three examples. The first is a version of the well-known Alternating Bit Protocol [4], the second an example from database concurrency control, and the third an example from highly available replicated data management.

3.1 Alternating Bit Protocol

I begin with the Alternating Bit Protocol (ABP), mostly because it is simple and should be familiar from other papers on verification. Although the main interest in this example is normally the liveness properties, here I will only consider safety. The key safety property to be proved is, roughly speaking, that the subsequence of messages delivered is a prefix of the subsequence sent.

3.1.1 Problem Statement

More specifically, I define correctness at the external boundary of the ABP component (the data link boundary). The input actions are $SEND(m)$, where $m \in M$, the message alphabet. The output actions are $RECEIVE(m), m \in M$. The correctness property P is the set of sequences β of $SEND$ and $RECEIVE$ actions such that in any prefix β' of β, the sequence of messages received in β' is a prefix of the sequence of messages send in β'.

3.1.2 Architecture

The architecture for an implementation consists of a *sender* automaton, a *receiver* automaton, and two FIFO physical channels, *channel1* and *channel2*. Channel1 has input actions $SEND1(m, b)$ and output actions $RECEIVE1(m, b)$, where $m \in M$ and b is a Boolean. Channel2 has input actions $SEND2(b)$ and output actions $RECEIVE2(b)$, where b is a Boolean. The system is modeled by the composition of these automata, with all actions except $SEND(m)$ and $RECEIVE(m)$ hidden.

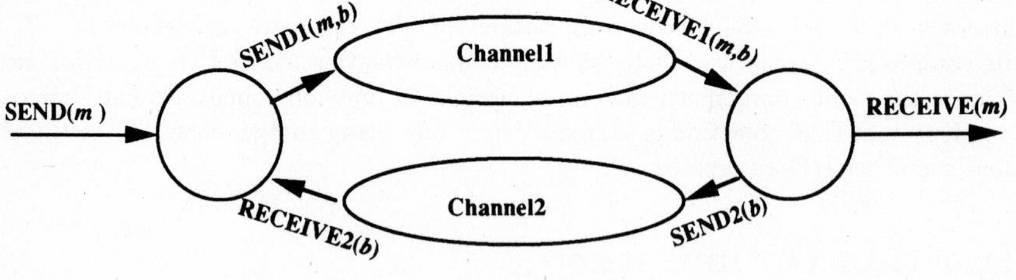

The channels are fairly ordinary FIFO queues, except that the effect of a $SEND1$ or $SEND2$ action might or might not be to put the data at the end of the queue. (The effect of a $RECEIVE1$ or $RECEIVE2$ is always to remove it, however.) More specifically, consider channel1. Its state is a finite queue of pairs (m, b), where $m \in M$ and b is a Boolean. Initially, the queue is empty.

$SEND1(m, b), m \in M, b$ a Boolean
Effect:

Either add (m, b) to the queue or do nothing.

$RECEIVE1(m, b), m \in M, b$ a Boolean
Precondition:
(m, b) is first on the queue.
Effect:
Remove first element from queue.

3.1.3 Alternating Bit Protocol

The ABP uses the following sender. It has inputs $SEND(m), m \in M$ and $RECEIVE2(b), b$ a Boolean, and outputs $SEND1(m, b), m \in M, b$ a Boolean. Its state consists of the following components: QS, (for "sender's queue"), which holds a finite sequence of elements of M, initially empty, and FS (for "sender's flag"), a Boolean, initially 1. The actions are:

$SEND(m), m \in M$
Effect:
Add m to end of QS.

$SEND1(m, b), m \in M, b$ a Boolean
Precondition:
m is first on QS.
$b = FS$
Effect:
None.

$RECEIVE2(b), b$ a Boolean
Effect:
if $b = FS$ then
[remove first element (if any) from QS;
$FS := FS + 1 \bmod 2$]

The corresponding receiver has inputs $RECEIVE1(m, b), m \in M, b$ a Boolean, and outputs $RECEIVE(m), m \in M$ and $SEND2(b), b$ a Boolean. Its state consists of the following components. QR (for "receiver's queue"), which holds a finite sequence of elements of M, initially empty, and FR (for "receiver's flag"), a Boolean, initially 0. The actions are:

$RECEIVE(m), m \in M$
Precondition:
m is first on QR.
Effect:
Remove first element from QR.

$RECEIVE1(m, b), m \in M, b$ a Boolean
Effect:
if $b \neq FR$ then
[add m to end of QR;
$FR := FR + 1 \bmod 2$]

$SEND2(b), b$ a Boolean
Precondition:
$b = FR$
Effect:
None.

3.1.4 Redundant Protocol

To prove the correctness of this protocol, I describe a redundant but much easier to understand variant of the protocol. In this variant, both the sender and receiver keep sequences of messages forever; furthermore, they tag the messages with positive integer sequence numbers and send them with those sequence numbers. The sender continues to send the same message just until it receives an acknowledgement with that message's tag; then it goes on to the next message in sequence. The receiver, on the other hand, keeps acknowledging the last message it has received, just until it gets the next message. It should be easy to prove that this works, using invariant assertions. Then the ABP can be proved to correspond to this protocol via a possibilities mapping, and so is correct as well.

More specifically, the redundant algorithm uses a slight modification of the channels used by the ABP - the only modification is that integer tags, rather than Boolean tags, are used. The redundant algorithm also has the same actions as the ABP (except that tag parameters are now positive integers). Its sender's state consists of the following components. SS (for "sender's sequence"), which holds an array of $(M \cup \perp)$ (where $\perp$ is a special "undefined" indicator, which is not an element of M), indexed by the positive integers, initially identically equal to $\perp$, IS (for "sender's integer"), a positive integer, initially 1, and LS (for "last message sent"), a nonnegative integer, initially 0.

The actions are:

$SEND(m), m \in M$
Effect:
$\quad LS := LS + 1$
$\quad SS(LS) := m$

$SEND1(m, i), m \in M, i$ a positive integer
Precondition:
$\quad SS(i) = m.$
$\quad i = IS$
Effect:
$\quad$ None.

$RECEIVE2(i), i$ a positive integer
Effect:
$\quad$ if $i = IS$ then
$\quad\quad IS := IS + 1$

The corresponding receiver has a state consisting of the following components. SR (for "receiver's sequence"), which holds an array of $(M \cup \perp)$, indexed by the positive integers, initially identically equal to $\perp$, IR (for "receiver's integer"), an integer, initially 0, and LR (for "last message received"), an integer, initially 0. The actions are:

$RECEIVE(m), m \in M$
Precondition:
$\quad m = SR(LR + 1)$
Effect:
$\quad LR := LR + 1.$

$RECEIVE1(m, i), m \in M, i$ a positive integer
Effect:
$\quad$ if $i = IR + 1$ then
$\quad\quad [SR(i) := m;$
$\quad\quad IR := IR + 1]$

$SEND2(i)$, i a positive integer
Precondition:
 $i = IR$
Effect:
 None.

It should be very easy (if I have not made any stupid mistakes) to show that the resulting algorithm correctly delivers messages, i.e., that the messages received are a subsequence of those sent. The actual ABP is somewhat harder to understand because it does not keep all this information explicitly; it removes redundancies. For example, it does not keep the complete sequences forever, but removes elements after they are no longer needed. More interestingly, it does not tag the messages in the channels and on the remaining queues with the integer indices, but only with bits.

For later use, I note here some basic invariants about the behavior of this redundant algorithm. (Call this algorithm H.)

Lemma 2 *The following statements are true about every reachable state of H.*

1. *Consider the sequence consisting of the indices in channel2, followed by IR, followed by the indices in channel1, followed by IS. The indices in this sequence are nondecreasing; furthermore, the difference between the first and last index in this sequence is at most 1.*

2. *If $IS = IR$, then $LS \geq IS$.*

3.1.5 Possibilities Mapping Proof

Now let L denote the ABP. We will show that L is correct by demonstrating a possibilities mapping from L to H. Note that such a mapping needs to be multivalued - it must augment the partial information contained in each of the two queues by filling in all earlier messages, and must fill in the integer values of tags only working from bits.

In particular, we say that a state u of H is in $f(s)$ for state s of L provided that the following conditions hold.

1. $s.QS$ is exactly the sequence of values of $u.SS$ corresponding to indices in the closed interval $[u.IS, u.LS]$.

2. $s.FS = u.IS \bmod 2$.

3. $s.QR$ is exactly the sequence of values of $u.SR$ corresponding to indices in the closed interval $[u.LR + 1, u.IR]$.

4. $s.FR = u.IR \bmod 2$.

5. Channel1 has the same number of messages in s and u. Moreover, for any j, if (m, i) is the jth message in channel1 in u, then $(m, i \bmod 2)$ is the jth message in channel1 in s.

6. Channel2 has the same number of messages in s and u. Moreover, for any j, if i is the jth message in channel2 in u, then $i \bmod 2$ is the jth message in channel2 in s.

Theorem 3 *f above is a possibilities mapping.*

3.1.6 Remarks

Consider the structure of the possibilities mapping f of this example. In going from H to L, unnecessary entries are garbage-collected, and integer tags are condensed to their low-order bits. The multiple values of the mapping f essentially "replace" this information. In this example, the correspondence between L and H can be described in terms of a mapping in the opposite direction - a (single-valued) projection from the state of H to that of L that removes information. Then f maps a state s of L to the set of states of H whose projections are equal to s. While this formulation suffices to describe many interesting examples, it does not always work, as will be seen in some of the subsequent examples in this paper.

Halpern and Zuck [10] outline a way of organizing the proof of the ABP that is similar to the organization I have described; their proofs are presented somewhat differently, however, using a formal theory of knowledge.

3.2 Transaction Processing

With Michael Merritt, Bill Weihl, Alan Fekete and Jim Aspnes [9, 2], I have done some work on describing and proving the correctness of locking- and timestamp-based algorithms for database concurrency control and recovery. Some of this work uses multivalued possibilities mappings in a way that is similar to their use for the ABP. That is, the proofs first show correctness of a simple and inefficient protocol that maintains a lot of extra information, and then shows that some particular protocols of interest implement the inefficient protocol in the formal sense of possibilities mappings.

In this work, the advantage we gain from the mapping strategy is not only the decomposition of the proofs of particular algorithms; we also gain an advantage in generality. The high-level protocol is designed to work for arbitrary data types. The same high-level protocol can be used to prove the correctness of many specific low-level protocols that work (in more efficient ways) for particular data types such as read-write objects. (Halpern and Zuck [10] use mappings informally to get a similar generality for protocols related to the ABP.)

Here, I will just describe what we do for locking; our treatment of timestamps is similar. We develop a locking algorithm for nested transactions; in this model, transactions can have subtransactions, and subtransactions can have further subtransactions, and so on until the leaves of the transaction structure, which actually access data objects. The transaction nesting structure is a forest; we augment it with a dummy "root" transaction representing the "outside world", so that it becomes a tree. Transactions can commit (relative to their parents) or abort, and correctness is defined in terms of serializability among each group of siblings.

Our high-level algorithm allows objects of arbitrary data type. We describe this algorithm using a separate program (automaton) for each data object. The automaton for an object x does all the processing involving x. It receives invocations of accesses to x and decides on the appropriate responses to make. It maintains locks for x, together with any other necessary information such as temporary versions. It receives information about the commit and abort of transactions, in order to help it decide on the appropriate responses (and in order to help it decide when it can discard information and how to manipulate locks).

The complete high-level algorithm can be described as the composition of these object automata with other automata, e.g., automata for transactions and a message system automaton. In [9], we prove the correctness of this composition, with a fairly complicated proof. However, once we have proved this correctness for our high-level algorithm, we have a much easier job for some data-type-specific variants, since we can use possibilities mappings. For example, one very popular kind of locking algorithm is read-write locking. (In [9], we actually handle the slightly different case of read-update locking rather than read-write locking; the difference is that write accesses are constrained only to write the object with a predefined value, whereas update accesses can make arbitrary changes, depending on the object's prior value.) We can describe read-write locking as a similar composition, but with different object automata; in particular, we can use a read-write object automaton for each object x instead of a arbitrary data type object automaton for x. The read-write object automaton for x maintains less information than the corresponding arbitrary data type object automaton, but it can be shown to implement the former in terms of a possibilities mapping.

To be specific, the interface of an object automaton for x consists of input actions $INVOKE(T)$, $INFORM\_COMMIT(T)$, and $INFORM\_ABORT(T)$, and output action $RESPOND(T,v)$. Invocations and responses are for particular accesses to x (T locates the access within the transaction nesting structure); informs are for arbitrary transactions.

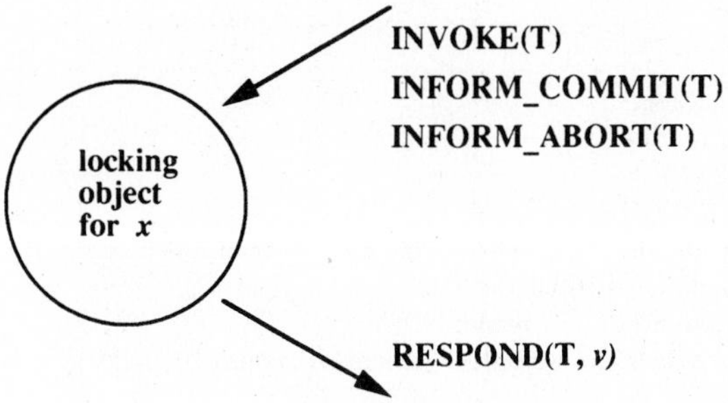

Let H denote the arbitrary data type automaton for x. It maintains "intentions lists", which are sequences of operations (i.e., (access,return value) pairs), for each transaction in the entire nesting structure, initially empty everywhere. The intentions list for T describes all the operations that are known to have occurred at descendants of T, and have committed up to T but not to its parent. It operates as follows. (Note: This is an informal paraphrase of the code in [9].)

$INVOKE(T)$
Effect:
    Record the invocation.

$INFORM\_COMMIT(T)$
Effect:
    intentions(parent(T)) := intentions(parent(T))intentions(T)
    intentions(T) := empty

$INFORM\_ABORT(T)$
Effect:
    intentions(U) := empty for all descendants U of T

$RESPOND(T,v)$
Precondition:
    T has been invoked and not yet responded to.
    (T,v) commutes with every (T',v') in intentions(U), where U is not an ancestor of T.
    total(T)(T,v) is a correct behavior of the underlying serial data object for x.
Effect:
    intentions(T) := intentions(T) (T,v)

Here, operations are said to "commute", roughly speaking, provided that in any situation in which both can be performed, they can be performed in sequence, in either order, and the result is the same in both cases.) Also, total(T) is defined to be the result of concatenating all the intentions lists for ancestors of T, in order from the root down. As I said earlier, our algorithm based on this object has a somewhat complicated proof.

Note that H maintains a good deal of explicit history information in its intentions lists. Now suppose that the underlying serial data object is a read-write object. In this case, we can improve the efficiency of this algorithm by maintaining more condensed, specially-tailored data structures in place of the intentions lists. In particular, we design a read-write object automaton L that keeps sets of read-lockholders and write-lockholders, plus a version of the underlying serial object for each write-lockholder. Initially, the root holds a write-lock, with the start state of the serial object as the associated version. The steps of L are as follows.

$INVOKE(T)$
Effect:
Record the invocation.

$INFORM\_COMMIT(T)$
Effect:
if T is a read-lockholder, then read-lockholders := read-lockholders $\cup\{parent(T)\} - \{T\}$
if T is a write-lockholder, then
[version(parent(T)) := version(T);
write-lockholders := write-lockholders $\cup\{parent(T)\} - \{T\}$]

$INFORM\_ABORT(T)$
Effect:
Remove all locks for descendants of T.

$RESPOND(T, v), T$ a read
Precondition:
T has been invoked and not yet responded to.
All write-lockholders are ancestors of T.
v is the version associated with the least ancestor of T that is a write-lockholder.
Effect:
read-lockholders := read-lockholders $\cup\{T\}$.

$RESPOND(T, v), T$ a write
Precondition:
T has been invoked and not yet responded to.
All read-lockholders and write-lockholders are ancestors of T.
v = "nil"
Effect:
write-lockholders := write-lockholders $\cup\{T\}$
version(T) := v

The correctness of the algorithm using L follows from that of the algorithm using H once we demonstrate a possibilities mapping f from L to H. The mapping says the following (paraphrased): $u \in f(s)$ exactly if

1. u and s record that the same set of transactions has been invoked.
2. u and s record that the same set of transactions has been responded to.
3. s.read-lockholders is exactly the set of transaction names T such that u.intentions(T) contains a read access.
4. s.write-lockholders is exactly the set of transaction names T such that u.intentions(T) contains a write access (together with the root).

5. For every T, evaluating total(T) in u results in the value version(T'), where T' is the least ancestor of T in write-lockholders.

Although a read-write serial object is a special case of an arbitrary data type serial object, note that the read-write object automaton L is not really a special case of the arbitrary data type object automaton: the data structures are different, and f expresses a nontrivial correspondence between the different structures. However, the behaviors of the two objects correspond very closely, as shown by the fact that there is a possibilities mapping between them. Note that the mapping f is multivalued, since the summary version and lock-holder information maintained by the read-write object automaton does not (in general) allow a unique reconstruction of the intentions list information in the arbitrary data type object automaton.

For this example, as for the ABP, the possibilities mapping can be described as the inverse of a projection mapping states of H to states of L, but here that seems like a bit of an accident. For, the read-update objects described in [9] have a similar description and proof, but the mapping used there can associate more than one state of L to a state of H. (This is because the serial object state produced by a sequence of operations might not be uniquely determined.)

Although we have not worked this out, it should be possible to describe optimized variants of our high-level algorithm for other specific data types besides read-write objects and read-update objects. I expect that such optimizations should also be verifiable using possibilities mappings to our high-level objects.

Our treatment of timestamp-based concurrency control algorithms in [2] is analogous to our treatment of locking. Namely, we first present an algorithm for arbitrary data types (based on that of Herlihy [11], but extended to nested transactions); we present this using an automaton for each object. Then we present the specially-tailored algorithm of Reed [23] for read-write objects; correctness of this algorithm is proved using possibilities mappings to the algorithm for arbitrary data types.

3.3 Garbage Collection

With Paul Leach, Liza Martin and Joe Pato at Apollo Computer, I have made use of multivalued possibilities mappings to design and prove correctness of an algorithm for replicated data management. Again, the use involves decomposing the algorithm using a higher-level and less efficient algorithm. I'll just sketch the ideas very roughly and informally here.

The setting we consider involves a replicated data management algorithm in which updates to data objects can be issued at arbitrary nodes. We assume a timestamp mechanism that totally orders all updates produced anywhere in the system. Here I assume for simplicity that all the updates are overwrites. In this setting, nodes exchange information about all the updates that have been generated, so (if the network stays connected), all nodes eventually find out about all updates. (Other transactions, which I will not discuss here, read the data produced by this algorithm and take actions based on it.) We assume that the network is dynamic, i.e., that nodes can be added to and removed from the system during execution. The setting is similar to those considered in [6, 24, 8]. In order to determine whether an incoming update should supersede an already-known update for the same object, a node must maintain some timestamp information for known updates. Because it would be inefficient to keep the complete history of known updates, nodes summarize this history information in a "checkpoint state" that contains summarized values (with associated timestamps) for all objects. But because of the way nodes exchange information about updates, they also maintain some incremental information; the data maintained by each node is thus a combination of a checkpoint state and a log of recent updates. The complete algorithm can be proved correct by standard techniques (basically, the safety properties to be proved say that each node is as up-to-date about the updates originating at each other node as it thinks it is).

Now, the actual system has another complication - we would like to *garbage collect* information about objects whose latest update is an "overwrite(x,nil)", i.e., a "delete(x)". It would be nice not to have to record this update forever (with its associated timestamp). But it is necessary to record it for a while, in order to correctly determine its timestamp ordering with respect to incoming updates of x. We need a criterion that tells us when we may garbage collect such information without affecting the behavior of the algorithm. It is quite nontrivial to determine such a rule, especially in the case we consider, where nodes can be added or removed during computation; e.g., one must ensure that updates issued by newly-added nodes can never get ordered incorrectly with respect to the garbage collected updates.

We have designed an algorithm, L, that includes a local criterion that says when it is safe for a node to garbage collect a delete update. The final algorithm appears to be fairly complicated. It turns out that the best way to understand it is by means of a possibilities mapping from L to the original non-garbage collected algorithm, H. Starting with a state s of L, this possibilities mapping obtains corresponding states of H by adding in information about the missing updates in all possible ways that are consistent with the current remaining state. Of course, there may be many ways to add in such information; thus, the mapping is multivalued. With this correspondence, the correctness proof for the algorithm with garbage collection seems fairly straightforward (although it seemed to us to be quite difficult otherwise).

Note that unlike the two previous examples, this example uses a correspondence that is not expressible as a projection from H to L - here, several L states could also be related to a single H state. That is, given a state of the non-garbage collected algorithm, it is possible to choose the information to garbage collect in many different ways. (Choices of updates to garbage collect are made locally at individual nodes, and asynchronously with respect to the choices made at other nodes.) Thus, in this case, the correspondence is multivalued in both directions.

3.4 Remarks

The idea of decomposing algorithms using unoptimized but simpler variants and possibilities mappings seems to be a very generally useful technique. It is useful for algorithms that perform explicit garbage collection, and also for algorithms such as the ABP, that simply omit unused portions of the simpler information. I think that this idea can be pushed much further in the area of distributed algorithms; many clever and complicated algorithms should have decompositions using simpler variants containing extra information. For example, I wonder whether the many complicated algorithms for implementing atomic registers (e.g., [25, 15]) can be verified in this way. It seems to me that at least Bloom's special-case algorithm [7] should have a nice proof in terms of integer tags rather than bits; perhaps a similar strategy will work for other atomic register algorithms.

Note that all the proofs I have given in this section could be recast in terms of history variables added to the low-level algorithms and single-valued rather than multivalued mappings. Thus, although the proofs in terms of multivalued mappings seem more natural to me, there is no theorem that says that multivalued mappings are necessary.

4 Distribution

Another way that multivalued mappings arise is in describing algorithm *distribution* rather than optimization. In the setting I have in mind, a centralized algorithm H (one not explicitly decomposed into nodes and a message system) is first shown to solve the problem of interest. A related distributed algorithm (one that is described explicitly as the composition of a number of node automata and one or several automata representing the message system) L is then given; we want to show that L is correct by showing that it implements H (that is, that all its behaviors are behaviors of H).

The basic strategy is again to define a mapping f from states of L to sets of states of H. However, in this case it may be helpful to define f in terms of a collection of "component mappings" f_i, one for each component of L. Thus, each node i has an abstraction mapping that maps each of its states to a set of states of H, and likewise the message system M, (or each separate message channel M, if there are several) has a mapping f_M from its states to a set of states of H.

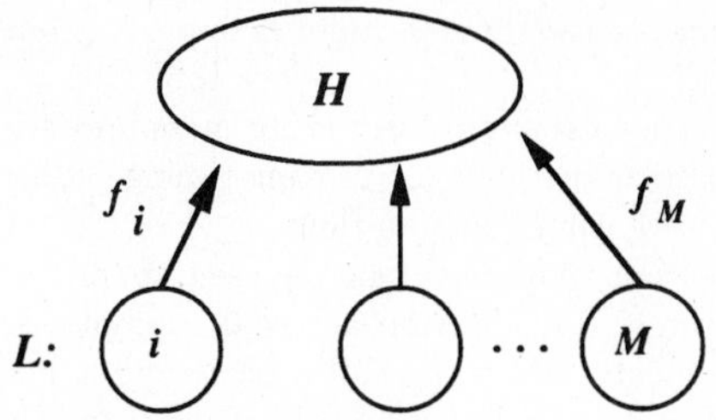

These component mappings have an interesting interpretation - e.g., the mapping f_i for node i describes, in terms of i's state, the "possible states" of the centralized algorithm H, as far as i can tell. Thus, in a sense, this mapping can be thought of as giving the "local knowledge" that i has, of the state of the centralized algorithm.

Under certain conditions ([19, 14]) these component mappings can be "composed" to yield a possibilities mapping from each entire state of L to a set of states of H, representing the "possible states" of H, as far as *any* of the components can tell. Formally, the value of $f(s)$, for a state s of L, is exactly the *intersection* of the values of $f_i(s_i)$, where s_i is component i's state in s. That is, the states that are possible for all the components are just those that are in the intersection of the sets that are possible for all the individual components. In other words, the intersection of the local knowledge of all the components (including the message system) is the global knowledge of the system.

Note that the mapping f might or might not be multivalued, but the individual f_i almost certainly will be. This is because in a typical distributed system, no individual node knows everything about the global state.

This decomposition can sometimes be used to simplify algorithm proofs (at least, it has worked in one substantial case I have tried). This case again arises in transaction processing. In [19], I describe a locking algorithm similar to the read-write locking algorithm I described earlier in this paper, by first giving a centralized description. The algorithm H keeps global information such as the sets of transactions that have been *created*, *committed* and *aborted*, plus certain "version mappings" that keep versions of various objects on behalf of various transactions. In the distributed algorithm, each node keeps part of this information: it knows *some* of the created, committed and aborted transactions, and some of the versions. The mapping f_i for a node i just adds in unspecified other transactions and versions to these sets, in addition to the ones locally known. I prove correctness of H directly, then combine the f_i as described above to get a possibilities mapping f and prove correctness of L using this mapping.

More work is needed to determine how generally useful this proof structure is.

5 Proving Time Bounds

My final example arises in my very recent work (joint with Hagit Attiya) on timing-based algorithms. The idea is to use multivalued mappings for reasoning about upper and lower bounds on time for such algorithms. Although this work is still preliminary, I think that its use of multivalued mappings is quite interesting.

5.1 Overview

So far, abstraction mappings (and assertional reasoning in general) have been used primarily to prove correctness properties of sequential algorithms and synchronous and asynchronous concurrent algorithms. It would also be nice to use these techniques to prove properties of concurrent algorithms whose operation depends on time, e.g., that have a clock that ticks at an approximately predictable rate. Also, the kinds of properties usually proved using mappings are "ordinary" safety properties; it would also be nice to use similar methods for proving timing properties (upper and lower bounds on time) for algorithms that have timing assumptions.

Here, I show how abstraction mappings can be used to prove timing properties of timing-dependent concurrent algorithms. I'll focus on a trivial example, an algorithm consisting of two concurrently-operating components, which we call a *clock* and a *manager*. The clock ticks at an approximately known rate. The manager monitors the clock ticks, and after a certain number have occurred, it issues a *GRANT* (of a resource). It then continues counting ticks; whenever sufficiently many have occurred since the previous *GRANT* event, the manager issues another *GRANT*. We wish to give a careful proof of upper and lower bounds on the amount of time prior to the first *GRANT* event and in between each successive pair of *GRANT* events.

In order to state and prove such results, we need to extend the I/O automaton model to incorporate time in the assumptions and in the conditions to be proved. Fortunately, this has been done for us: Modugno, Merritt and Tuttle [21] define a suitable extension call the *timed automaton* model. In that model, an algorithm with timing assumptions is described as an *I/O automaton* together with a *boundmap* (a construct used to give a formal description of the timing assumptions). This automaton and boundmap generate a set of *timed executions* and a corresponding set of *timed behaviors*. We use timed automata to define the basic assumptions about the underlying system, to describe the algorithm, and to carry out a correctness proof.

In order to carry out an assertional proof about time, we need to reformulate some of the definitions of [21] so that information about time is explicitly included in the algorithm's state. In order to include *assumptions* about time in the state, we use the construction given in [3], of an automaton $time(A)$ for a given timed automaton A. The automaton $time(A)$ is an ordinary I/O automaton (not a timed automaton) whose state includes predictive information describing the first and last times at which various basic events can next occur; this information is derived from the given boundmap. The I/O automaton $time(A)$ is related to the original timed automaton A in that a certain subset of the behaviors of $time(A)$ is exactly equal to the set of timed behaviors of A.

We also require a formal way of describing the timing *requirements* to be proved for our algorithm. In order to do this, we augment A to another I/O automaton B which we call the *performance machine* this time building in predictive information about the first and last times at which certain events of interest (e.g., *GRANT* events) can next occur. Then the problem of showing that the given algorithm satisfies the timing requirements is reduced to that of showing that any behavior of the automaton $time(A)$ is also a behavior of B. *We do this by exhibiting a mapping from* $time(A)$ *to* B. This mapping turns out to be multivalued; in fact, it is in the form of a set of inequalities!

In the remainder of this section, I give more details.

5.2 Formal Model

Here I describe timed automata and the construction of $time(A)$.

5.2.1 Timed Automata

Recall that an I/O automaton consists of *actions*, *states*, *start states*, *steps*, and a fifth component that is a *partition* of the locally controlled (output and internal) actions into equivalence classes. The last is generally used for fairness and liveness, and so I have not used it so far in this paper, but I will need it now. The partition groups actions together that are to be thought of as under the control of the same underlying process.

In [21], the I/O automaton model is augmented to include timing properties as follows. A *timed automaton* is an I/O automaton with an additional component called a *boundmap*. The boundmap associates a closed interval of the nonnegative reals (possibly including infinity, but where the lower bound is not infinity and the upper bound is not 0) with each class in the automaton's partition. This interval represents the range of possible lengths of time between successive times when the given class gets a chance to perform an action. Let $b_\ell(C)$ and $b_u(C)$ denote the lower and upper bounds, respectively, assigned by the boundmap b to class C.

Now I describe how a timed automaton executes. A *timed sequence* is a sequence of alternating states and (action,time) pairs; the times are required to be nondecreasing, and if the sequence is infinite then the times are also required to be unbounded. Such a sequence is said to be a *timed execution* of a timed automaton A provided that the result of removing the time components is an execution of the ordinary I/O automaton underlying A, and the following conditions hold, for each class C of the partition of A and every i.

1. Suppose $b_u(C) \neq \infty$. If some action in C is enabled in a_i and either $i = 0$ or no action in C is enabled in a_{i-1} or π_i is in C, then there exists $j > i$ with $t(j) \leq t(i) + b_u(C)$ such that either π_j is in C or no action of C is enabled in a_j.

2. If some action in C is enabled in a_i and either $i = 0$ or no action in C is enabled in a_{i-1} or π_i is in C, then there does not exist $j > i$ with $t(j) < t(i) + b_\ell(C)$ and π_j in C.

The first condition says that, starting from when an action in C occurs or first gets enabled, within time $b_u(C)$ either some action in C occurs or there is a point at which no such action is enabled. The second condition says that, again starting from when an action in C occurs or first gets enabled, no action in C can occur before time $b_\ell(C)$ has elapsed.

Definitions for composition of timed automata to yield another timed automaton are given in [21]. We model real-time systems as compositions of timed automata.

5.2.2 The Automaton *time*(A)

Given any timed automaton A with boundmap b, we now show how to define the corresponding ordinary I/O automaton *time*(A). This new automaton has the timing restrictions of A built into its state, in the form of predictions about when the next event in each class will occur.

The automaton *time*(A) has actions of the form (π, t), where π is an action of A and t is a nonnegative real number. Each of its states consists of a state of A, augmented with a time called *Ctime* and, for each class C of the partition, two times, *Ftime*(C) and *Ltime*(C). *Ctime*, (the "current time") represents the time of the last preceding event, initially 0. The *Ftime*(C) and *Ltime*(C) components represent, respectively, the first and last times at which an action in class C is scheduled to be performed (assuming it stays enabled). (We use record notation to denote the various components of the state of *time*(A); for instance, *s.automaton_state* denotes the state of A included in state s of *time*(A).) More precisely, each initial state of *time*(A) consists of an initial state s of A, plus $Ctime = 0$, plus values of *Ftime*(C) and *Ltime*(C) with the following properties. If there is an action in C enabled in s, then $s.Ftime(C) = s.Ctime + b_\ell(C)$ and $Ltime(C) = s.Ctime + b_u(C)$. Otherwise, $Ftime(C) = 0$ and $Ltime(C) = \infty$.

Others have proposed building timing information into the state (e.g., [26]); our work differs in the particular choice of information to use - predictive information, giving upper and lower bounds for each automaton class.

The following definitions capture formally what it means for the given timing assumptions to be respected by *time*(A). If (π, t) is an action of *time*(A), then $(s', (\pi, t), s)$ is a step of *time*(A) exactly if the following conditions hold.

1. $(s'.automaton\_state, \pi, s.automaton\_state)$ is a step of A.

2. $s'.Ctime \leq t = s.Ctime$.

3. If π is a locally controlled action of A in class C, then
   (a) $s'.Ftime \leq t \leq s'.Ltime$.
   (b) if some action in C is enabled in $s.automaton\_state$, then $s.Ftime(C) = t + b_\ell(C)$ and $s.Ltime(C) = t + b_u(C)$, and
   (c) if no action in C is enabled in $s.automaton\_state$, then $s.Ftime(C) = 0$ and $s.Ltime(C) = \infty$.

4. For all classes D such that π is not in class D,
   (a) $t \leq s'.Ltime(D)$,
   (b) if some action in D is enabled in $s.automaton\_state$ and some action in D is enabled in $s'.automaton\_state$ then $s.Ftime(D) = s'.Ftime(D)$ and $s.Ltime(D) = s'.Ltime(D)$, and
   (c) if some action in D is enabled in $s.automaton\_state$ and no action in D is enabled in $s'.automaton\_state$ then $s.Ftime(D) = t + b_\ell(D)$ and $s.Ltime(D) = t + b_u(D)$, and
   (d) if no action in D is enabled in $s.automaton\_state$, then $s.Ftime(D) = 0$ and $s.Ltime(D) = \infty$.

Property 3 describes the conditions on the particular class C (if any) containing the action π - basically, that the time for the new action should be in the appropriate interval for the class. New scheduled times are also set for C, in case an action in C is enabled after this step. Property 4 describes conditions involving each other class D. The most interesting is property 4(a), which ensures that the action in C does not occur if D has an action that must be scheduled first.

Now I state how the behaviors of $time(A)$ are related to the timed behaviors of A. Define the *complete executions* of $time(A)$ to be those executions α of $time(A)$ that satisfy one of the following conditions.

1. α is infinite and the time components of the actions in α are unbounded, or

2. α is finite and no locally controlled action of $time(A)$ is enabled in the final state of α.

The *complete schedules* and *complete behaviors* of $time(A)$ are defined to be the schedules and behaviors, respectively, of complete executions of $time(A)$.

The timed executions of a timed automaton A are closely related to the complete executions of the corresponding I/O automaton $time(A)$. In particular, what we use is:

Theorem 4 *The set of timed behaviors of A is the same as the set of complete behaviors of $time(A)$.*

This theorem implies that properties of timed behaviors of a timed automaton A can be proved by proving them about the set of complete behaviors of the corresponding I/O automaton $time(A)$. The latter task is more amenable to treatment using assertional techniques, because of the fact that timing information is built into the state of $time(A)$.

We apply the $time(A)$ construction to the timed automaton A modeling the entire system.

5.2.3 Strong Possibilities Mappings

The work in this section requires a slightly strengthened notion of possibiities mapping - one that preserves the correspondence between *all* actions (internal as well as external). Let L and H be automata with the same actions, and let f be a mapping from states of L to sets of states of H. The mapping f is a *strong possibilities mappings from L to H* provided that the following conditions hold:

1. For every start state s_0 of L, there is a start state u_0 of H such that $u_0 \in f(s_0)$.

2. If s' is a reachable state of A, $u' \in f(s')$ is a reachable state of H, and (s', π, s) is a step of L, then there is a step (u', π, u) of H such that $u \in f(s)$.

The difference between this definition and the ordinary definition for possibilities mappings is in the second condition, where the actions are required to correspond exactly. Now recall that the schedules of an automaton include all its actions.

Lemma 5 *If there is a strong possibilities mapping from L to H, then all schedules of L are also schedules of H.*

5.3 The Algorithm

The algorithm consists of two components, a *clock* and a *manager*. The *clock* has only one action, the output *TICK*, which is always enabled, and has no effect on the clock's state. It can be described as the particular one-state automaton with the following steps.

TICK
Precondition:
  true
Effect:
  none

The boundmap associates the interval $[c_1, c_2]$ with the single class of the partition. This means that successive *TICK* events will occur with intervening times in the given interval.

The manager has input action *TICK*, output action *GRANT* and internal action *ELSE*. The manager waits a particular number k of clock ticks before issuing each *GRANT*, counting from the beginning or from the last preceding *GRANT*. The manager's state has one component: TIMER, holding an integer, initially k.

The manager's algorithm is as follows: (We assume that $k > 0$).

TICK
Effect:
  TIMER := TIMER -1

GRANT
Precondition:
  TIMER ≤ 0
Effect:
  TIMER := k

ELSE
Precondition:
  TIMER > 0
Effect:
  none

Notice that *ELSE* is enabled exactly when *GRANT* is not enabled. The effect of including the *ELSE* action is to ensure that the automaton continues taking steps at its own pace, at approximately regular intervals. Thus, in the situation we are modeling, when the *GRANT* action's precondition becomes satisfied, the action doesn't occur instantly - the action waits until the automaton's next local step occurs. [1]

[1] An alternative situation to model would be an interrupt-driven model in which the action is triggered to occur whenever its precondition becomes true; the action should then occur shortly thereafter; this situation could be modeled by omitting the *ELSE* action. The two automata have slightly different timing properties. In this paper, I only consider the first assumption.

The partition groups the *GRANT* and *ELSE* actions into a single equivalence class, with which the boundmap associates the interval $[0, l]$. We assume that $c_1 > l$. [2] Now we fix L to be the timed automaton which is the composition of the clock and manager.

I now consider the automaton $time(L)$, constructed as described in Section 5.2. In this case, the construction adds the following components to the state of L: *Ctime*, *Ftime*(*TICK*), *Ltime*(*TICK*), *Ftime*(*LOCAL*), and *Ltime*(*LOCAL*). The latter two represent the times for the partition class consisting of *GRANT* and *ELSE*.

Lemma 6 *All complete executions (and therefore all complete schedules) of time(L) are infinite.*

This is essentially because the clock keeps ticking forever. This lemma tells us that for this example we do not have to worry about the case where executions are finite - we can assume that we have infinite executions in which (because of the definition of completeness) the timing component is unbounded.

5.4 The Performance Automaton

We wish to show that all the timed behaviors of L satisfy certain upper and lower bounds on the time for the first *GRANT* and the time between consecutive pairs of *GRANT* events. More precisely, we wish to show the following, for any timed behavior γ of B:

1. There are infinitely many *GRANT* events in γ.
2. If t is the time of the first *GRANT* event in γ, then $k \cdot c_1 \leq t \leq k \cdot c_2 + l$.
3. If t_1 and t_2 are the times of any two consecutive *GRANT* events in γ, then

$$k \cdot c_1 - l \leq t_2 - t_1 \leq k \cdot c_2 + l.$$

We let P denote the set of sequences of $(action, time)$ pairs satisfying the above three conditions. By the earlier characterization, Theorem 4, it suffices to show that all complete behaviors of $time(L)$ are in P.

I have already shown how to describe timing assumptions by building time information into the state. Now I show how to give a similar description for the timing properties to be proved. Thus, we specify P in terms of another I/O automaton, which we call the *performance automaton*. Namely, define a new I/O automaton H by augmenting $time(L)$ with two new components: *Ftime*(*GRANT*) and *Ltime*(*GRANT*). These are designed to represent the first and last times, respectively, that a *GRANT* event might occur. They are maintained as follows.

1. Initially,
   (a) $Ftime(GRANT) = k \cdot c_1$, and
   (b) $Ltime(GRANT) = k \cdot c_2 + l$.
2. For each step $(s', (GRANT, t), s)$ of H,
   (a) $s'.Ftime(GRANT) \leq t \leq s'.Ltime(GRANT)$.
   (b) $s.Ftime(GRANT) = t + k \cdot c_1 - l$ and $s.Ltime(GRANT) = t + k \cdot c_2 + l$.
3. For each step $(s', (\pi, t), s)$ of H, where $\pi = TICK$ or $ELSE$,
   (a) $t \leq s'.Ltime(GRANT)$.
   (b) $s.Ltime(GRANT) = s'.Ltime(GRANT)$ and

[2] Again, a different assumption would change the timing analysis.

(c) $s.Ftime(GRANT) = s'.Ftime(GRANT)$.

In addition, the other components of the state are maintained just as in the definitions of *time*(L).

This automaton simply builds in explicitly the time bounds to be proved. The initial conditions build in the time bounds that are supposed to hold for the first *GRANT*, and condition 2b builds in the time bounds that are supposed to hold for all the subsequent *GRANT* actions. Conditions 2a and 3a ensure that nothing happens strictly after the latest time at which a *GRANT* is supposed to occur. Condition 2a also ensures that the *GRANT* does not occur too soon.

The following lemma gives the relationship we need between the behaviors of H and the condition P. (Note that the behaviors of H and the sequences in P both consist of elements that are pairs, an action of L together with a time.)

Lemma 7 *Let β be an infinite schedule of H in which the time component is unbounded. Then $beh(\beta) \in P$.*

Note that the performance machine H is a somewhat ad hoc description of the particular timing properties to be proved for our particular algorithm. We are currently working on generalizing the treatment of performance machines.

5.5 Proof

Now we sketch how to prove that all timed behaviors of L are in P, as needed. First, we show that all behaviors of *time*(L) are also behaviors of the performance machine H, using a strong possibilities mapping. Namely, we define a mapping f so that a state u of H is in the image set $f(s)$ exactly if the following conditions hold.

1. If $s.TIMER > 0$ then
   (a) $u.Ltime(GRANT) \geq s.Ltime(TICK) + (s.TIMER - 1)c_2 + l$, and
   (b) $u.Ftime(GRANT) \leq s.Ftime(TICK) + (s.TIMER - 1)c_1$.
2. If $s.TIMER = 0$ then
   (a) $u.Ltime(GRANT) \geq s.Ltime(LOCAL)$, and
   (b) $u.Ftime(GRANT) \leq s.Ctime$.

Thus, in this case the mapping takes the form of inequalities giving upper and lower bounds for the time of the next *GRANT* event, in terms of the values of the variables in the state of *time*(L). For example, condition 1a says that (in case the timer is positive), the upper bound that is being proved on the time for the next *GRANT* is any value that is *at least as great* as the latest time for the next *TICK*, plus the number of remaining *TICK* events that will be counted times the maximum time they might take, plus the maximum time for a local step. This makes sense because the quantity on the right-hand side of the inequality is itself an upper bound on the time until the next *GRANT*; if the performance machine designates anything at least as great as this expression as the upper bound to be proved, then it should be possible to prove that the algorithm simulates the performance machine (i.e., that it respects the upper bound described by that machine).

Symmetrically, condition 1b says that (in case the timer is positive) the lower bound that is being proved on the time for the next *GRANT* is any value that is *at most as great* as the earliest time for the next *TICK*, plus the number of remaining ticks that will be counted times the minimum time they might take, (plus the minimum time for a local step, which is 0). This makes sense because the quantity on the right-hand side of the inequality is itself a lower bound on the time until the next *GRANT*; if the performance machine designates anything at most as great as this expression as the lower bound to be proved, then it should be possible to prove that the algorithm simulates the performance machine (i.e., that it respects the lower bound described by that machine).

In case the timer is 0, the upper bound that is being proved on the time for the next *GRANT* is any value that is at least as great as the latest time for the next local step. Again, the quantity on the right-hand side of the inequality is an upper bound on the time until the next *GRANT*, so that if the performance machine designates anything at least that large, it should be possible to prove that the algorithm simulates the performance machine. Also for this case, the lower bound that is being proved is any value that is at most as great as the earliest time for the next local step, which is the current time.

This mapping is obviously multivalued, because it is described in terms of inequalities. The inequalities express the fact that *any* sufficiently large number (with respect to the values of the variables in the state of $time(L)$) should be provable as an upper bound for the time for the next *GRANT*, and any sufficiently small number should be provable as a lower bound. [3] [4] We can now show:

Lemma 8 *The mapping f is a strong possibilities mapping.*

Lemmas 5 and 8 yield the following corollary.

Corollary 9 *All schedules of $time(L)$ are schedules of H.*

Now I can put the pieces together.

Theorem 10 *All timed behaviors of L are in P.*

Proof: Let γ be a timed behavior of L. Then by Theorem 4, γ is a complete behavior of $time(L)$. Let β be a complete schedule of $time(L)$ such that $\gamma = beh(\beta)$. By Lemma 6, β is infinite, and by the definition of completeness for infinite executions, the time components of β are unbounded. Lemma 9 implies that β is also a schedule of H. Since β is an infinite schedule of H in which the time components are unbounded, Lemma 7 implies that $beh(\beta) = \gamma$ is in P. ■

Note that in this case, the possibilities mapping technique yields all the correctness properties we require - including both safety and liveness properties. Certain timing properties are safety properties, e.g., lower bounds, and upper bounds of the form "if time grows sufficiently large, then certain events must occur". These can be proved using possibilities mappings in much the same way as any other safety properties. But when such conditions are combined with the property that all complete executions are infinite and our assumption that the time in infinite timed executions is unbounded (so that "time continues to increase without bound"), they actually imply that the events in question must eventually occur. Thus, liveness properties of the kind that say "certain events must occur" also follow from the mapping technique.

6 Conclusions

In this paper, I have tried to illustrate several situations in which multivalued abstraction mappings are useful in algorithm correctness proofs. Multivalued mappings are useful in cases where one algorithm can be described as an optimized (e.g., garbage collected) version of another algorithm, or where a single high-level algorithm admits several specialized implementations tailored for different

---

[3] If we simply replaced the inequalities with equations, the resulting mapping would not be a possibilities mapping. For example, suppose that a clock tick occurs within less than the maximum c_2. Then the right-hand side expression in 1a would evaluate after the step to an earlier time than before the step. On the other hand, the corresponding step in the performance machine would *not* change the value of $Ltime(GRANT)$; the correspondence thus would not be preserved.

[4] It seems possible to use a single-valued mapping for this example by complicating the definition of the performance machine; however, since the performance machine is serving as the problem specification, that does not seem like a good idea.

situations. They are also useful in relating distributed algorithms to centralized variants, and in proving time bounds.

Work remains to be done in exploiting these techniques further. I believe it will be possible to decompose the proofs of many other complicated concurrent algorithms by expressing the algorithms as optimized versions of simpler algorithms, or as special cases of more general algorithms, or as distributed versions of centralized algorithms. It remains to discover such structure and express it in terms of mappings.

The use of mappings for time analysis is new, and should be tried on more (and larger) examples. It remains to see how this technique combines with other methods for time analysis such as methods based on bounded temporal logic [5] or recurrence equations [16]. I hope I have made the point I have tried to make: that multivalued mappings are sufficiently useful that any useful formal framework incorporating abstraction mappings should permit them to be multivalued.

Acknowledgements:

I would like to thank John Leo for working out the algorithm distribution techniques, and for reading and commenting on an earlier verion of the manuscript.

A Proof

Proof: By induction. For the base, let s be the start state of L and u the start state of H. First, $s.QS$ is empty. Also, $[u.IS, u.LS] = [1,0]$, which implies that $s.QS$ is equal to the appropriate (empty) portion of $u.SS$. Second, $s.FS = 1 = u.IS \, mod\, 2$. Third, $s.QR$ is empty, and $[u.LR+1, u.IR] = [1,0]$, which implies that $s.QR$ is equal to the appropriate portion of $u.SR$. Fourth, $s.FR = 0$ and $u.IR = 0$, which is as needed. Fifth and sixth, both channels are empty.

Now show the inductive step. Suppose (s', π, s) is a step of L and $u' \in f(s')$. We consider cases based on π.

1. $\pi = SEND(m)$

   Choose u to be the unique state such that (u', π, u) is a step of H. We must show that $u \in f(s)$. The only condition that is affected by the step is the first; thus, we must show that $s.QS$ is exactly the sequence of values of $u.SS$ corresponding to indices in the closed interval $[u.IS, u.LS]$. But $s.QS = s'.QSm$. Since $u' \in f(s')$, $s'.QS$ is just the sequence of values from $u'.SS$, from indices $u'.IS$ to $u'.LS$. Since the step of H increases LS by 1 and puts m in the new position, we have the needed equation.

2. $\pi = RECEIVE(m)$

   Since π is enabled in s', m is the first value on $s'.QR$. Since $u' \in f(s')$, $m = u'.SR(u'.LR+1)$, which implies that π is enabled in u'. Now choose u to be the unique state such that (u', π, u) is a step of H. All conditions are unaffected except for the third, that $s.QR$ is exactly the sequence of values of $u.SR$ corresponding to indices in the closed interval $[u.LR + 1, u.IR]$. Now, $s.QR$ is the same as $s'.QR$ with the first element removed. Since $u' \in f(s')$, we have that $s'.QR$ is just the sequence of values from $u'.SR$, from indices $u'.LR + 1$ to $u'.IR$. Since the step of H increases LR by 1, we have the needed equation.

3. $\pi = SEND1(m, b)$

   Since π is enabled in s', $b = s'.FS$ and m is the first element on $s'.QS$. Let i be the integer $u'.IS$. Since $u' \in f(s')$, the first element in $s'.QS$ is the same as the $u'.IS$ entry in $u'.SS$; that is, $u'.SS(i) = m$. It follows that $\bar{\pi} = SEND1(m, i)$ is enabled in u'.

   Now choose u so that $(u', \bar{\pi}, u)$ is a step of H and such that this step puts a message in channel1 exactly if the step (s', π, s) does. We must show that $u \in f(s)$. The only interesting condition is the fifth; that is, we must show that channel1 has the same number of messages in s and u. Moreover, for any j, if (m, k) is the jth message in channel1 in u, then $(m, k \, mod\, 2)$ is the jth message in channel1 in s. The only interesting case is where both steps cause a message to be put into the channel. Then the message value in both cases is m, but the tag is b for algorithm L and i for H. It remains to show that $b = i mod 2$. But $b = s'.FS$ and $i = u'.IS$. Since $u' \in f(s')$, we have $s'.FS = u'.IS mod\, 2$, which implies the result.

4. $\pi = RECEIVE1(m, b)$

   Since π is enabled in s', (m, b) is the first element in channel1 in s'. Since $u' \in f(s')$, (m, i) is the first element in channel1 in u', for some integer i with $b = i mod 2$. Let $\bar{\pi} = RECEIVE1(m, i)$; then $\bar{\pi}$ is enabled in u'. Let u be the unique state such that $(u', \bar{\pi}, u)$ is a step of H. We must show that $u \in f(s)$.

   All conditions except for the third, fourth and fifth are unchanged. It is easy to see that the fifth is preserved, since each of π and $\bar{\pi}$ simply removes the first message from channel1.

   Suppose first that $b = s'.FR$. Then the effects of π imply that the receiver state in s is identical to that in s'. Now, since $u' \in f(s')$, $s'.FR = u'.IR mod\, 2$; since $b = i mod 2$, this case must have $i \neq u'.IR + 1$. Then the effects of $\bar{\pi}$ imply that the receiver state in u is identical to that in u'. It is immediate that the third and fourth conditions hold.

So now suppose that $b \neq s'.FR$. The invariant above for H implies that either $i = u'.IR$ or $i = u'.IR + 1$. Since $b = i \, mod \, 2$ and (since $u' \in f(s')$) $s'.FR = u'.IRmod\, 2$, this case must have $i = u'.IR + 1$. Then $u.IR = u'.IR + 1$ and $s.FR = s'.FR + 1 \, mod \, 2$, preserving the fourth condition. Also, $u.SR$ is the same as $u'.SR$ except that the entry with index $u.IR$ is set equal to m; moreover, $s.QR$ is the same as $s'.QR$ except that m is added to the end. It follows that the third condition is preserved.

5. $\pi = SEND2(b)$

   Since π is enabled in s', $b = s'.FR$. Let i be the integer $u'.IR$. Let $\bar{\pi} = SEND2(i)$; clearly, $\bar{\pi}$ is enabled in u'.

   Now choose u so that $(u', \bar{\pi}, u)$ is a step of H and such that this step puts a message in channel2 exactly if the step (s', π, s) does. We must show that $u \in f(s)$. The only interesting condition is the sixth; that is, we must show that channel2 has the same number of messages in s and u. Moreover, for any j, if k is the jth message in channel2 in u, then $kmod\, 2$ is the jth message in channel2 in s. The only interesting case is where both steps cause a message to be put into the channel. Then the tag is b for algorithm L and i for H. It remains to show that $b = imod\, 2$. But $b = s'.FR$ and $i = u'.IR$. Since $u' \in f(s')$, we have $s'.FR = u'.IRmod\, 2$, which implies the result.

6. $\pi = RECEIVE2(b)$

   Since π is enabled in s', b is the first element in channel2 in s'. Since $u' \in f(s')$, i is the first element in channel2 in u', for some integer i with $b = imod\, 2$. Let $\bar{\pi} = RECEIVE2(i)$; then $\bar{\pi}$ is enabled in u'. Let u be the unique state such that $(u', \bar{\pi}, u)$ is a step of H. We must show that $u \in f(s)$.

   All conditions except for the first, second and sixth are unchanged. It is easy to see that the sixth is preserved, since each of π and $\bar{\pi}$ simply removes the first message from channel2.

   Suppose first that $b \neq s'.FS$. Then the effects of π imply that the sender state in s is identical to that in s'. Now, since $u' \in f(s')$, $s'.FS = u'.IS \, mod \, 2$; since $b = i \, mod \, 2$, this case must have $i \neq u'.IS$. Then the effects of $\bar{\pi}$ imply that the sender state in u is identical to that in u'. It is immediate that the first and second conditions hold for this situation.

   So now suppose that $b = s'.FS$. The invariant above for H implies that either $i = u'.IS - 1$ or $i = u'.IS$. Since $b = i \, mod \, 2$ and (since $u' \in f(s')$) $s'.FS = u'.IS \, mod \, 2$, this case must have $i = u'.IS$. Then $u.IS = u'.IS + 1$ and $s.FS = s'.FS + 1 \, mod \, 2$, preserving the second condition. Also, $u.SS$ is unchanged; moreover, $s.QS$ is the same as same as $s'.QS$ except that the first entry (if any) is removed.

   Now, the invariant for H and the fact that the first entry in channel2 in u' has index $u'.IS$ implies that $u'.IS = u'.IR$. Again by the invariant for H, this implies that $u'.LS \geq u'.IS$. Then the fact that $u' \in f(s')$ implies that $s'.QS$ is nonempty. Therefore, the first entry in $s'.QS$ really is removed by the step. Since $s'.QS$ consists of the entries in $u'.SS$, from indices $u'.IS$ to $u'.LS$, since the first entry in $s'.QS$ is removed to yield $s.QS$ and since $u.IS = u'.IS + 1$, it follows that the first condition is preserved.

■

References

[1] Martin Abadi and Leslie Lamport. The existence of refinement mappings. Digital Equipment Corporation, TR No. 29, August 14,1988.

[2] J. Aspnes, A. Fekete, N. Lynch, M. Merritt, and W. Weihl. A theory of timestamp-based concurrency control for nested transactions. In *Proceedings of 14th International Conference on Very Large Data Bases*, pages 431–444, Los Angeles, CA., August 1988.

[3] H. Attiya and N. Lynch. Time bounds for real-time process control in the presence of timing uncertainty. April 1989. Submitted for publication.

[4] K.A. Bartlett, R.A. Scantlebury, and P.T. Wilkinson. A note on reliable full-duplex transmission over half-duplex links. *Communications of the ACM*, 12, 1969.

[5] Arthur Bernstein and Paul K. Harter, Jr. Proving real-time properties of programs with temporal logic. In *Proceedings of the 8th Annual ACM Symposium on Operating System Principles*, pages 1–11, ACM, 1981.

[6] Andrew D. Birrell, Roy Levin, Roger M. Needham, and Michael D. Schroeder. Grapevine: an exercise in distributed computing. *Communications of the ACM*, 25(4):260–274, April 1982.

[7] B. Bloom. Constructing two-writer atomic registers. In *Proceedings of 6th ACM Symposium on Principles of Distributed Computing*, pages 249–259, Vancouver, British Columbia, Canada, August 1987. Also, to appear in special issue of *IEEE Transactions On Computers on Parallel and Distributed Algorithms.*

[8] A. Demers, D. Greene, C. Hauser, W. Irish, J. Larson, S. Shenker, H. Sturgis, and D. Terry. Epidemic algorithms for replicated database maintenance. In *Proceedings of the 6th Annual ACM Symposium on Principles of Distributed Computing*, pages 1–12, August 1987.

[9] A. Fekete, N. Lynch, M. Merritt, and W. Weihl. Commutativity-based locking for nested transactions. In *Proceedings of 3rd International Workshop on Persistent Object Systems*, pages 113–127, Newcastle, Australia, January 1989. An extended version is available as Technical Memo, MIT/LCS/TM-370, Laboratory for Computer Science, MIT, Cambridge, MA, August 1988.

[10] Joseph Y. Halpern and Lenore D. Zuck. A little knowledge goes a long way: simple knowledge-based derivations and correctness proofs for a family of protocols. In *Proceedings of the 6th Annual ACM Symposium on Principles of Distributed Computing*, pages 269–280, August 1987. A revised version appears as *IBM Research Report RJ 5857*, October, 1987.

[11] Maurice Herlihy. Extending multiversion time-stamping protocols to exploit type information. *IEEE Transactions on Computers*, C-36(4):443–448, April 1987.

[12] Simon S. Lam and A. Udaya Shankar. Protocol verification via projections. *IEEE Transactions on Software Engineering*, SE-10(4):325–342, July 1984.

[13] Leslie Lamport. Specifying concurrent program modules. *ACM Transactions on Programming Languages and Systems*, 5(2):190–222, April 1983.

[14] J. Leo. Personal Communication.

[15] M. Li and P.M.B. Vitanyi. Tape versus stacks and queue: the lower bounds. *Information and Computation*, 78:56–85, 1988.

[16] N. Lynch and K. Goldman. *Distributed Algorithms.* MIT/LCS/RSS 5, Massachusetts Institute of Technology, Laboratory for Computer Science, 1989. Lecture notes for 6.852.

[17] N. Lynch and M. Tuttle. Hierarchical correctness proofs for distributed algorithms. In *Proceedings of the* 6th *Annual ACM Symposium on Principles of Distributed Computing*, pages 137–151, August 1987. Extended version in Technical Report MIT/LCS/TR-387, Lab for Computer Science, Massachusetts Institute of Technology, April 1987.

[18] N. Lynch and M. Tuttle. An introduction to input/output automata. To be published in *Centrum voor Wiskunde en Informatica Quarterly.* Also in Technical Memo, MIT/LCS/TM-373, Lab for Computer Science Massachusettes Institute of Technology, November 1988.

[19] Nancy A. Lynch. Concurrency control for resilient nested transactions. *Advances in Computing Research*, 3:335–373, 1986.

[20] Robin Milner. *A Calculus of Communicating Systems. Lecture Notes in Computer Science 92*, Springer-Verlag, Berlin, 1980.

[21] F. Modugno, M. Merritt, and M. Tuttle. Time constrained automata. November 1988. Unpublished manuscript.

[22] S. Owicki and D. Gries. An axiomatic proof technique for parallel programs. *Acta Informatica*, 6(4):319–340, 1976.

[23] David P. Reed. Implementing atomic actions on decentralized data. *ACM Transactions on Computer Systems*, 1(1):3–23, February 1983.

[24] S.K. Sarin, B.T. Blaustein, and C.W. Kaufman. System architecture for partition-tolerant distributed databases. *IEEE Trans. Comput.*, C-34, December 1985.

[25] R. Schaffer. On the correctness of atomic multi-writer registers. Bachelor's Thesis, June 1988, Massachusetts Institute Technology. Also, Technical Memo MIT/LCS/TM-364.

[26] F. Schneider. Personal Communication.

[27] J.L. Welch, L. Lamport, and N. Lynch. A lattice-structured proof technique applied to a minimum spanning tree algorithm. In *Proceedings of the 7th Annual ACM Symposium on Principles of Distributed Computing*, pages 28–43, Toronto, Canada, August 1988. Expanded version in Technical Memo, MIT/LCS/TM-361, Laboratory for Computer Science, Massachusetts Institute of Technology, Cambridge, MA, June 1988.

Completeness Theorems for Automata

Michael Merritt

AT&T Bell Laboratories
600 Mountain Avenue
Murray Hill, NJ 07922 USA

Abstract. These notes present completeness results for varieties of products, state mappings and auxiliary variable constructions, for a (Mealy) automata-theoretic model of computation that generalizes the I/O automaton model of Lynch and Tuttle [Lyn88, LT87]. Conditions are examined under which these tools suffice to demonstrate that one specification implements another. The major theorem is a restatement of a completeness theorem due to Abadi and Lamport [AL88], translated from their (Moore) state machine model. The multivalued possibilities mappings of Lynch and Tuttle are used in place of the single-valued refinement mappings of Abadi and Lamport. A new kind of state mapping, prophecy mappings, is defined. Prophecy mappings are the time-reversal of possibilities mappings. This definition admits greater modularity in the proofs of Abadi and Lamport's results. Additional results explore properties of products of automata, developing more fully ideas implicit in Abadi and Lamport's work.

Key words. Specification, implementation, completeness, automata, state mappings, products.

Contents

1 Introduction

2 Automata and Specifications
- 2.1 Automata
- 2.2 Specifications

3 Implementation and State Mappings
- 3.1 Possibilities Mappings
- 3.2 Prophecy Mappings
  - 3.2.1 Finite Invisible Nondeterminism
  - 3.2.2 Soundness of Prophecy Mappings

4 Products
- 4.1 Products of Automata and of Specifications
- 4.2 A Completeness Theorem for Products of Specifications
- 4.3 Product of A Specification and an Execution Module

5 Auxiliary Variable Constructions
- 5.1 History Variable Constructions
- 5.2 Prophecy Variable Constructions

6 $(A^hB^p, L_{A^hB^p})$ **as a Prophecy Variable Construction**
6.1 Machine Closure
6.2 Finitely Invisible Nondeterminism
6.3 Internal Continuity
6.4 A Completeness Theorem for Auxiliary Variable Constructions
6.5 Safety Properties

7 **Discussion**
7.1 Relationship to the Results in [AbadiL88]
7.2 Acknowledgement

1 Introduction

These notes were inspired by the paper "The Existence of Refinement Mappings" [AL88], by Martin Abadi and Leslie Lamport, which develops a theory of state machines and proves an intriguing completeness theorem. That paper explores the problem of determining when one specification implements another, and shows that under certain technical restrictions, refinement mappings and two types of auxiliary variable constructions suffice to demonstrate implementation whenever it exists. The results are presented in a state machine model that is an infinite-state version of Moore machines, in which sequences are derived via labels on states.

The material in these notes develops a parallel theory in a corresponding Mealy machine model, in which sequences are derived from labels on state transitions. This model is a slight variation of the I/O automaton model [Lyn88, LT87]. The multivalued possibilities mappings of Lynch and Tuttle are also used in place of the single-valued refinement mappings of Abadi and Lamport. In addition, a new kind of state mapping, prophecy mappings, is defined. Prophecy mappings are the time-reversal of possibilities mappings. This definition admits greater modularity in the proofs of Abadi and Lamport's results.

These notes also develop more fully a theory of products that is suggested by Abadi and Lamport's work, which may provide some additional insight into their completeness theorem. In particular, some of these results may help to clarify the technical motivation for the technical restrictions required by their theorem. (The final section of these notes contains a detailed discussion of the relationship between the results presented here and those of Abadi and Lamport.)

An additional contribution is to provide some basis of comparison between the state machine model used by Abadi and Lamport, and the I/O automaton model of [Lyn88, LT87].

2 Automata and Specifications

Abadi and Lamport define and explore specifications of the form (M, L_M), where M is a state machine and L_M is a predicate over executions of M [AL88]. The executions of M denote sequences via labels on the states of M, and a specification (M, L_M) describes the set of sequences denoted by executions of M that are also in L_M. Because of the notion of implementation they explore, these sequences are defined so as to be closed under stuttering (the introduction or removal of repeated symbols).

These notes explore a similar model, in which specifications are of form (A, L_A), where A is an automaton and L_A is a predicate over executions of A. The executions of A denote sequences via labels on the state transitions of A, and a specification (A, L_A) describes the set of sequences denoted by executions of A that are also in L_A. Because of this difference, the corresponding notion of implementation in this model does not require the specified sequences to be closed under stuttering.

2.1 Automata

The definition of an automaton is a slight simplification of the definition of an I/O automaton [Lyn88, LT87], in that a distinction is made here between internal and external actions (transition labels), but not between input and output actions. [1] An automaton is essentially a (possibly) infinite state Mealy machine, with some additional structure. (E.g. internal, or λ-transitions may be distinguished by different symbols.)

An *action signature* is a pair $sig = (ext, int)$ of disjoint sets of *actions*, or symbols. We define $acts(sig)$ to be the union of its component sets. An action signature specifies the external and internal actions of an automaton.

An *automaton* A consists of four components:

- an action signature $sig(A) = (ext(A), int(A))$
- a set $states(A)$ of *states*,
- a nonempty set $start(A) \subseteq states(A)$ of *start states*, and
- a transition relation $steps(A) \subseteq states(A) \times acts(sig(A)) \times states(A)$

An *execution fragment* of A is a finite sequence $s_0\pi_1 s_1\pi_2 ... \pi_n s_n$ or infinite sequence $s_0\pi_1 s_1\pi_2 ... \pi_n s_n ...$ of alternating states and actions of A such that $(s_i, \pi_{i+1}, s_{i+1}) \in steps(A)$ for every i such that s_{i+1} exists. An execution fragment beginning with a start state is called an *execution*. We denote the set of executions of A by $execs(A)$, and the set of finite executions of A by $finexecs(A)$. A state is said to be *reachable* in A if it is the final state of a finite execution of A.

The *behavior* of an execution fragment α of A is the subsequence of α consisting of external actions of A, and is denoted by $beh(\alpha)$. We say that β is a *behavior* of A if β is the behavior of an execution of A. We denote the set of behaviors of A by $behs(A)$ and the set of finite behaviors of A by $finbehs(A)$.

An *extended step* of an automaton A is a triple of the form (s', γ, s), where s' and s are in $states(A)$, γ is a finite sequence of actions in $acts(A)$, and there is an execution fragment α of A having s' as its first state, s as its last state and $\alpha|acts(A) = \gamma$. (This execution fragment might consist of only a single state, in the case that γ is the empty sequence.)

Similarly, a *move* of an automaton A is a triple of the form (s', β, s), where s' and s are in $states(A)$, β is a finite sequence of actions in $ext(A)$, and there is an execution fragment of A having s' as its first state, s as its last state and β as its behavior. (This execution fragment might consist of only a single state, in the case that β is the empty sequence.)

If β is any sequence and S is a set of actions, we write $\beta|S$ for the subsequence of β consisting of actions in S. If β is any sequence of actions and A is an automaton, we write $\beta|A$ for $\beta|acts(A)$.

For ease of exposition, Abadi and Lamport consider only infinite sequences over a state set $\sum$; finite sequences are extended by stuttering the final symbol forever. Here, we consider finite and infinite sequences of two types: executions, which are alternating state, action sequences (ending in states if finite), and behaviors, which are sequences of just external actions.

Abadi and Lamport mention that state machines define a topology on the properties that are invariant under stuttering, in which the state machines define the closed sets. The closed sets are also characterized as the properties that are invariant under stuttering and limit-closed, and are referred to as *safety* properties. The dense sets are called *liveness* properties. Similarly, automata define a topology on sets of sequences, in which the closed sets are the prefix and limit-closed sets.

Hence, we define $closure(S)$ as the prefix and limit closure of the set of sequences S. We also define $finprefixes(S)$ as the set of finite prefixes of sequences in S.

---

[1] A distinction between input and output actions in [Lyn88, LT87] is crucial in the development of a simple (language-theoretic) semantics for fairness under composition. Such a distinction is perfectly consistent with the results of these notes, but plays no important role in their development.

An *execution module* P is a pair $(sig(P), execs(P))$ where $execs(P)$ is a set of execution fragments having action signature $sig(P)$. Define $start(P)$ to be the set of initial states of sequences in $execs(P)$. We will often use P to denote $execs(P)$. Also, $closure(P)$ denotes the prefix and limit closure of executions in P, and $finprefixes(P)$ denotes the execution fragments that are finite prefixes of executions in $execs(P)$.

Two automata or execution modules A and B are *privacy respecting* if $int(A) \cap acts(B) = int(B) \cap acts(A) = \emptyset$.

2.2 Specifications

A *specification* (A, L_A) is an automaton A together with a predicate L_A on $execs(A)$. Define $execs(A, L_A) = execs(A) \cap L_A$ and $behs(A, L_A) = behs(A, L_A)$. Similarly for $finexecs$ and $finbehs$. (Note that in this notation, we can represent the fairness property for I/O automata in [LT87] by $(A, fairexecs(A))$.)

Also, define $Execs(A, L_A)$ to be the execution module $(sig(A), execs(A, L_A))$.

3 Implementation and State Mappings

One specification (A, L_A) is said to *implement* another, (B, L_B), provided A and B have the same external actions and $behs(A, L_A) \subseteq behs(B, L_B)$.[2]

These notes study proof techniques for establishing that the subset relationship holds between two specifications (A, L_A) and (B, L_B). In particular, they explore two kinds of mappings between (A, L_A) and (B, L_B), either of which suffice to prove implementation. These mappings establish relationships between steps of A and moves of B that suffice to conclude that $behs(A) \subseteq behs(B)$. They thus have the practical advantage of reducing the problem of showing a global relationship between the behaviors of A and B to that of showing more local relationships between components of A and B. (However, they still require that appropriate global conditions be proven for the liveness conditions L_A and L_B.)

The two mappings are called here *possibilities mappings* and *prophecy mappings*. The former are multivalued variants of the refinement mappings studied by Abadi and Lamport [AL88], and are a simple modification to the definition of possibilities mappings studied by Lynch and Tuttle [Lyn88, LT87].

The notion of prophecy mappings is a novel contribution of these notes. However, their use is implicit in the work of Abadi and Lamport, and the definition makes explicit their intuitive notion that prophecy variables are the time-reversal of history variables.

Both types of mappings are proven to be sound techniques for demonstrating implementation. Both proofs involve inductive constructions of an execution α_B of B from a corresponding execution α_A of A. These inductions move in opposite directions: to prove possibilities mappings sound, successive finite prefixes of α_B are constructed to correspond to finite prefixes of α_A, with α_B the limit of the sequence. To prove prophecy mappings sound, an arbitrary finite prefix α'_A of α_A is chosen. Successive finite fragments of the corresponding execution α'_B are constructed to correspond to finite suffixes of α'_A. If α_A is infinite, an additional global condition allows the conclusion (via König's lemma) that the execution α_B exists.

[2]This definition permits trivial implementations, e.g. when $L_A = \emptyset$. Additional restrictions are typically needed to avoid such problems in a fully-developed automata-theoretic specification theory. (For example, the definition of fairness in [Lyn88, LT87] implies that any automaton with an input action has a non-empty set of fair behaviors.) These restrictions vary from theory to theory (sometimes from problem to problem), and generally play no substantive role in proving $behs(A, L_A) \subseteq behs(B, L_B)$.

3.1 Possibilities Mappings

While the work of Abadi and Lamport demonstrates that single-valued refinement mappings provide a (relatively) complete proof technique, there are several reasons for exploring multivalued mappings instead. As we demonstrate in succeeding sections, multivalued mappings can be used in proofs of soundness of product and auxiliary variable constructions, where single-valued mappings do not suffice. This results in more modular proofs.

In addition, multivalued mappings increase the power of the proof techniques employing them. Of the three examples used by Abadi and Lamport to motivate auxiliary variable constructions, two may be resolved instead by admitting multivalued mappings in place of single-valued. Thus, multivalued mappings can admit an alternative to the proof technique of auxiliary variables (in these cases, history variables).

In particular, possibilities mappings generalize refinement mappings in two ways. First, by mapping states of A to sets of states of B, rather than to single states. Second, by mapping steps of A to extended steps of B, instead of a single (possibly stuttering) step of B. Respectively, these extensions allow states of B to contain more information about the history than do those of A, and allow B to take internal steps not required by A.[3]

Suppose A and B are automata and suppose f is a mapping from $states(A)$ to the power set of $states(B)$. That is, if s is a state of A, $f(s)$ is a set of states of B. The mapping f is said to be a *possibilities mapping* from (A, L_A) to (B, L_B) if the following conditions hold. (We use $A \cap B$ as a shorthand for $acts(A) \cap acts(B)$.):

1. For every start state s_0 of A, there is a start state t_0 of B and an extended step (t_0, γ, t) of B such that $t \in f(s_0)$ and $\gamma|(A \cap B)$ is the empty sequence.

2. Let s' be a reachable state of A, $t' \in f(s')$ a reachable state of B, and (s', π, s) a step of A. Then there is an extended step, (t', γ, t), of B such that $\gamma|(A \cap B) = \pi|(A \cap B)$, and $t \in f(s)$.

3. $f(execs(A, L_A)) \subseteq L_B$.[4]

Theorem 1 : Soundness of possibilities mappings
If f is a possibilities mapping from (A, L_A) to (B, L_B), then the following are true.

- *For every execution $\alpha_A \in execs(A, L_B)$ there exists an execution $\alpha_B \in execs(B, L_B)$ such that $\alpha_A|(A \cap B) = \alpha_B|(A \cap B)$.*

- *If A and B are privacy respecting and have the same external signature, then $behs(A, L_A) \subseteq behs(B, L_B)$.*

Proof: It suffices to prove the first item–the second follows immediately.

The proof is an easy inductive construction of α_B from $\alpha_A \in execs(A, L_A)$. The first condition of the definition of possibilities mappings provides a basis, showing that there is an execution of B corresponding to the initial state of α_A. The second condition of the definition of possibilities mappings provides the inductive step, showing that any finite prefix of α_A and corresponding finite execution of B can be extended by another step and extended step, respectively. Then α_B is taken as the limit of the sequences of finite executions of B. The final condition of the definition of possibilities mappings assures that this limit is in L_B. ∎

Lynch and Tuttle define possibilities mappings between two I/O automata A and B: following Abadi and Lamport, we have generalized this definition to specifications by including an extra condition relating the liveness predicates. Hence, the definition of Lynch and Tuttle can be recovered by appending to A and B the trivial liveness predicates *true*. (We use this definition when we speak of a possibilities map between A and B in the proof of soundness of prophecy mappings.)

[3] For a more detailed discussion of the advantages of multivalued mappings, the reader is referred to [Lyn89].

[4] If $\alpha_A \in execs(A, L_A)$, we denote by $f(\alpha_A)$ the set of executions α_B of B that correspond under f to α_A. That is, the sequence of states $s_0, s_1, \ldots$ of α_A must map to a sequence of states $t_0, t_1, \ldots$ of α_B such that $t_i \in f(s_i)$, and for each step $s_{i-1}\pi_i s_i$ of α_A, the corresponding extended step $t_{i-1}\gamma_i t_i$ in α_B must satisfy $\pi_i|(A \cap B) = \gamma_i|(A \cap B)$. The set $f(execs(A, L_A))$ is just the union of $f(\alpha_A)$ for all $\alpha_A \in execs(A, L_A)$.

3.2 Prophecy Mappings

Suppose (A, L_A) and (B, L_B) are specifications, and suppose f is a mapping from *states*(A) to the power set of *states*(B). That is, if s is a state of A, $f(s)$ is a set of states of B. The mapping f is said to be a *prophecy mapping* from (A, L_A) to (B, L_B) if the following conditions hold:

1. If s is a reachable state of A, then $f(s)$ is non-empty.

2. If s is a reachable state of A, (s', π, s) is a step of A and $t \in f(s)$, then there is a state $t' \in f(s')$ and an extended step (t', γ, t) of B such that $\gamma|(A \cap B) = \pi|(A \cap B)$.

3. If $t \in (f(start(A)))$ then there exists $t_0 \in start(B)$ and an extended step (t', γ, t) of B such that $\gamma|(A \cap B)$ is the empty sequence.

4. If s is a reachable state of A, $f(s)$ is finite.

5. $f(execs(A, L_A)) \subseteq L_B$.

Before we can prove the soundness of prophecy mappings as a technique for proving implementation, we require a technical result.

3.2.1 Finite Invisible Nondeterminism

An execution module P is *finitely invisibly nondeterministic* if for all $\beta \in finprefixes(behs(P))$ the set $\{\alpha \in finprefixes(P) : beh(\alpha) = \beta\}$ is finite.

Lemma 2 : Closure and nondeterminism
If a set of executions P is finitely invisibly nondeterministic, then $behs(closure(P))$ $= closure(behs(P))$.

Proof: If $\alpha \in behs(closure(P))$, then $\alpha = beh(\beta)$, for some $\beta \in closure(P)$. Hence, each finite prefix β_i of β is in $finprefixes(P)$. It follows that $beh(\beta_i) \in finprefixes(behs(P))$. For every finite prefix α_j of there is a β_{i_j} such that $\alpha_j = beh(\beta_{i_j})$. Hence, $\alpha_j \in finprefixes(behs(P)) \subseteq closure(behs(P))$, and $\alpha \in closure(behs(P))$.

Now let $\alpha \in closure(behs(P))$. If α is finite, it is a prefix of a behavior $\alpha' \in behs(P)$, with α' $= beh(\beta')$ for some $\beta' \in P$. Then $\alpha = beh(\beta)$ for a prefix β of β', and $\beta \in closure(P)$.

So assume α is infinite. Then all the finite prefixes α_i of α are finite prefixes of sequences in $behs(P)$. As in [AL88], construct a directed graph G, using as nodes the maximal elements of $finprefixes(P)$ corresponding to the finite prefixes of α; $\{\rho \in finprefixes(P) : beh(\rho) = \alpha_i$ for some i and no extension of ρ in $finprefixes(P)$ has behavior $\delta_i\}$. The edges of G go from ρ' to ρ if ρ' is a prefix of ρ containing exactly one less external action. The graph is clearly a forest, rooted at the (by finitely invisible nondeterminism) finite set of start states, and such that all the nodes at the same depth have the same behaviors. By the finite invisible nondeterminism of P, the number of nodes at any depth is finite. Since α has infinite length this tree has infinite depth, and so contains an infinite path by König's lemma [Knu73]. This path is an execution in $closure(P)$. ∎

3.2.2 Soundness of Prophecy Mappings

Theorem 3 : Soundness of prophecy mappings
If f is a prophecy mapping from (A, L_A) to (B, L_B), then the following are true.

- *For every execution $\alpha_A \in execs(A, L_A)$ there exists an execution $\alpha_B \in execs(B, L_B)$ such that $\alpha_A|(A \cap B) = \alpha_B|(A \cap B)$.*

- *If A and B are privacy respecting and have the same external signature, then $behs(A, L_A) \subseteq behs(B, L_B)$.*

Proof: We prove the first item in the lemma–the second follows immediately.

By the condition $f(execs(A, L_A)) \subseteq L_B$, it suffices to argue that for every execution α_A in $execs(A, L_A)$ there exists an execution α_B of B in $f(\alpha_A)$.

Let $\alpha_A = s_0\pi_1 s_1 \ldots$ be an execution in $execs(A, L_A)$. To demonstrate the existence of the corresponding execution α_B of B, we first construct two new specifications, (A_α, L_{A_α}) and (B_α, L_{B_α}). The automaton A_α simply describes the single execution $\alpha_A = s_0\pi_1 s_1 \ldots$ as an automaton:

- $sig(A_\alpha) = (ext(A), int(A))$
- $states(A_\alpha) = (s_i, i) : 0 \leq i \leq |\alpha_A|$
- $start(A_\alpha) = (s_0, 0)$
- $steps(A_\alpha) = (s_{i-1}, \pi_i, s_i) : 0 < i \leq |\alpha_A|$

The set $L_{A\alpha} = \{(s_0, 0), \pi_1, (s_1, 1), \ldots\}$. By a simple induction, $execs(A_\alpha, L_{A_\alpha})$ $= \{(s_0, 0), \pi_1, (s_1, 1), \ldots\}$.

The second specification, (B_α, L_{B_α}), is constructed from α_A using the mapping f:

- $sig(B_\alpha) = (acts(A) \cap acts(B), \{\epsilon\})$, where $\epsilon \notin (acts(A) \cup acts(B))$.
- $states(B_\alpha) = (t, i) : t \in f(s_i), 0 \leq i \leq |\alpha_A|$
- $start(B_\alpha) = (t, 0) : t \in f(s_0)$
- $steps(B_\alpha) = \{((t', i-1), \pi_i, (t, i)) : \pi_i \in acts(B)$ and there is an extended step (t', γ, t) of B such that $\gamma|(A \cap B) = \pi_i\} \cup \{((t', i-1), \epsilon, (t, i)) : \pi_i \notin acts(B)$ and there is an extended step (t', γ, t) of B such that $\gamma|(A \cap B)$ is empty$\}$.

Clearly, projection onto the first state component is a possibilities mapping from B_α to B, and hence $execs(B_\alpha)|(A \cap B) \subseteq execs(B)|(A \cap B)$. Thus, it suffices to show that $\alpha_A|(A \cap B) \in execs(B_\alpha, L_{B_\alpha})|(A \cap B)$.

By an induction on suffixes, for every finite prefix α'_A of α_A, there is a finite execution α'_B of B_α such that $\alpha'_A|(A \cap B) = \alpha'_B|(A \cap B)$.

Finally, by the observation that $execs(B_\alpha)$ is closed and finitely invisibly nondeterministic, Lemma 2 implies that there is an execution α_B of B_α such that $\alpha_A|(A \cap B) = \alpha_B|(A \cap B)$. ∎

4 Products

In the I/O automaton model, collections of automata with distinct output actions may be combined via a restricted composition operator to form more complex automata [Lyn88, LT87]. The proofs in [AL88] implicitly use a similar operation. We define this operation explicitly as the product of two specifications; it is the natural generalization of I/O automata composition, and corresponds to the construction generally used to show that finite state automata are closed under intersection.

The proof of Abadi and Lamport's completeness theorem constructs a product denoted here as $(A^h B^p, L_{A^h B^p})$, which is the product of (A^h, L_{A^h}) and (B^p, L_{B^p}). In turn, (A^h, L_{A^h}) is the product of specification (A, L_A) and the execution module $Execs(A)$ containing all the executions of A. Similarly, the specification (B^p, L_{B^p}) is the product of specification (B, L_B) and the execution module $Execs(B, L_B)$, containing all the executions of (B, L_B).

In the next section, we define two auxiliary variable constructions, history variables and prophecy variables. We demonstrate that (A^h, L_{A^h}) is the result of applying a history variable construction to (A, L_A). However, the product $(A^h B^p, L_{A^h B^p})$ is not in general the result of applying either auxiliary variable construction to (A^h, L_{A^h}). The second section following explores restrictions under which this is the case: in particular, when (A, L_A) is machine closed and (B, L_B) is both finitely invisibly nondeterministic and internally continuous, $(A^h B^p, L_{A^h B^p})$ is the result of applying a prophecy variable construction to (A^h, L_{A^h}).

4.1 Products of Automata and of Specifications

When taking the product of two automata, external actions paired with internal actions become external, and internal actions paired with internal actions stay internal. As the lemmas below demonstrate, the resulting product is closely connected to the intersection operation on sets of sequences.

If A and B are automata, define AB, the *product* of A and B, as follows:

1. $sig(AB) =$
   (a) $(ext(A) \cup ext(B),$
   (b) $int(A) \cup int(B) - (ext(A) \cup ext(B)))$
2. $states(AB) = states(A) \times states(B)$
3. $start(AB) = start(A) \times start(B)$
4. $steps(AB) = ((a', b'), \pi, (a, b))$ such that one of the following holds:
   (a) π is an action of A and B, $(a', \pi, a) \in steps(A)$ and $(b', \pi, b) \in steps(B)$
   (b) π is an action of A but not of B, $(a', \pi, a) \in steps(A)$ and $b' = b$.
   (c) π is an action of B but not of A, $a' = a$ and $(b', \pi, b) \in steps(B)$.

If $\alpha = ((s_0, t_0), \pi_1(s_1, t_1), ...$ is an execution of AB let $\alpha|A$ be the sequence obtained by deleting $\pi_j(s_j, t_j)$ when π_j is not an action of A, and replacing the remaining (s_j, t_j) by s_j. Define $\alpha|B$ similarly.

If (A, L_A) and (B, L_B) are specifications, the *product* of (A, L_A) and $(B; L_B)$ to be (AB, L_{AB}), where AB is the product of A and B and $L_{AB} = \{\alpha \in execs(AB) : \alpha|A \in L_A$ and $\alpha|B \in L_B\}$.

Define the product of two sets of executions P and Q, $P \times Q$, to be the set of execution sequences α over $states(P) \times states(Q)$ and actions $acts(P) \cup acts(Q)$ such that $\alpha|P \in P$ and $\alpha|Q \in Q$.

Proposition 4 : Products of specifications

- $execs(AB) = execs(A) \times execs(B)$
- $execs(AB, L_{AB}) = execs(A, L_A) \times execs(B, L_B)$.
- *The projection operators* $|A$ *and* $|B$ *are possibilities mappings from* (AB, L_{AB}) *to* (A, L_A) *and to* (B, L_B), *respectively.*

4.2 A Completeness Theorem for Products of Specifications

The previous proposition can be seen as a completeness result for products, and by Proposition 4, for possibilities mappings:

Theorem 5 : Completeness of products
Suppose that specifications (A, L_A) *and* (B, L_B) *are privacy respecting and have the same external signature. Then*

- $behs(AB, L_{AB}) = behs(A, L_A) \cap behs(B, L_B)$
- $behs(A, L_A) \subseteq behs(B, L_B)$ *if and only if* $behs(AB, L_{AB}) = behs(A, L_A)$

Thus, whenever (A, L_A) implements (B, L_B), there exists a third specification, (AB, L_{AB}), which is behaviorally equivalent to (A, L_A), and which can be shown to implement (B, L_B) via a possibilities mapping. Moreover, one direction of the equivalence of (AB, L_{AB}) and (A, L_A) is similarly provable using a possibilities mapping. However, showing that (AB, L_{AB}) contains all the behaviors of (A, L_A) remains problematic–in particular, neither possibilities nor prophecy mappings exist in general from (A, L_A) to (AB, L_{AB}). As it stands, this theorem has only transformed the problem of showing $behs(A, L_A) \subseteq behs(B, L_B)$ to that of showing $behs(A, L_A) \subseteq behs(AB, L_{AB})$.

The main theorem of Abadi and Lamport [AL88] shows that under certain restrictions on (A, L_A) and (B, L_B), if (A, L_A) implements (B, L_B) then there exists a third specification which is equivalent to (A, L_A) and can be shown to implement (B, L_B) via a refinement (possibilities) mapping. Strictly speaking then, Theorem 5 can be viewed as a 'stronger' completeness result for refinement mappings than Abadi and Lamport's, which proves the completeness of refinement mappings relative to technical restrictions on (A, L_A) and (B, L_B).

However, this misses the real contribution of Abadi and Lamport's work, which is to show that under their technical restrictions, the third specification they construct is of a particular kind: it is the result of applying two auxiliary variable constructions to (A, L_A). The advantage of this is that the definitions of these constructions include local conditions on steps of A and B. Hence, the global problem of proving $behs(A, L_A) \subseteq behs(B, L_B)$ (or equivalently that $behs(AB, L_{AB}) = behs(A, L_A)$) is reduced to proving some local conditions of A and B, and some simpler global properties of (A, L_A) and (B, L_B).

As we show below, the specification constructed by Abadi and Lamport in the proof of their theorem is also a product, though somewhat more complex than (AB, L_{AB}).

4.3 Product of A Specification and an Execution Module

If (A, L_A) is a specification and S is an execution module define (AS, L_{AS}), the *product* of (A, L_A) and S, as follows:

1. $sig(AS) =$
   (a) $(ext(A) \cup ext(S)$,
   (b) $int(A) \cup int(S) - (ext(A) \cup ext(S)))$.
2. $states(AS) = states(A) \times finprefixes(S)$.
3. $start(AS) = start(A) \times start(S)$.
4. $steps(AS) = ((a', \alpha'), \pi, (a, \alpha))$ such that one of the following holds:
   (a) π is an action of A and S, $(a', \pi, a) \in steps(A)$ and $\alpha' \pi s = \alpha$ for some state s.
   (b) π is an action of A but not of S, $(a', \pi, a) \in steps(A)$ and $\alpha' = \alpha$.
   (c) π is an action of S but not of A, $a' = a$ and $\alpha' \pi s = \alpha$ for some state s.
5. $L_{AS} = \{\alpha \in execs(AS) : \alpha|A \in L_A \text{ and } \alpha|S \in S\}$.[5]

Proposition 6 : Specifications and execution modules

- *(s, α_S) is a reachable step of AS if and only if there exists an execution α_A of A that leaves A in state s and such that $\alpha_A|(acts(A) \cap acts(S)) = \alpha_S|(acts(A) \cap acts(S))$.*
- *$execs(AS)|A = (execs(A) \times closure(execs(S)))|A$.*

[5]We use $\alpha|S$ to as a shorthand for $lim(\alpha|finprefixes(S))$, since $\alpha|S$ is more properly a sequence of prefixes of executions in S.

- $execs(AS)|S = (execs(A) \times closure(execs(S)))|S$.
- $execs(AS, L_{AS})|A = (execs(A, L_A) \times execs(S))|A$.
- $execs(AS, L_{AS})|S = (execs(A, L_A) \times execs(S))|S$.
- *The projection operator* $|A$ *is possibilities mapping from* (AS, L_{AS}) *to* (A, L_A).
- *If* (A, L_A) *and* S *are privacy respecting and have the same external signature, then*
  - $behs(AS) = behs(A) \cap behs(closure(execs(S)))$
  - $behs(AS, L_{AS}) = behs(A, L_A) \cap behs(S)$
  - $behs(A, L_A) \subseteq behs(S)$ *if and only if* $behs(AS, L_{AS}) = behs(A, L_A)$.

Given a specification (A, L_A), we will be particularly interested in the product of (A, L_A) with two particular execution modules: $Execs(A)$, containing all executions of A, and $Execs(A, L_A)$, containing the smaller set of executions of (A, L_A). The slightly different properties of these products are explored next.

Given a specification (A, L_A), define (A^h, L_{A^h}) to be the product of (A, L_A) and $Execs(A)$, the execution module of automaton A.

Proposition 7 : The product (A^h, L_{A^h})

- (s, α) *is a reachable state of* A^h *if and only if* α *is an execution of* A *that leaves* A *in state* s.
- $execs(A^h)|A = execs(A)$
- $execs(A^h, L_{A^h})|A = execs(A, L_A)$
- $behs(A^h) = behs(A)$
- $behs(A^h, L_{A^h}) = behs(A, L_A)$
- $(|A^h)^{-1}$, *the inverse of the projection operator* $|A^h$, *is possibilities mapping from* (A, L_A) *to* (A^h, L_{A^h}).

Given a specification (A, L_A), define (A^p, L_{A^p}) to be the product of (A, L_A) and the execution module $Execs(A, L_A)$.

Proposition 8 : The product (A^p, L_{A^p})

- (s, α) *is a reachable state of* A^p *if and only if*
  α *is an execution of* A *in* $finprefixes(execs(A, L_A))$ *that leaves* A *in state* s.
- $execs(A^p)|A = closure(execs(A, L_A))$
- $execs(A^p, L_{A^p})|A = execs(A, L_A)$
- $behs(A^p) = behs(closure(execs(A, L_A))$
- $behs(A^p, L_{A^p}) = behs(A, L_A)$

Note that $|A^{-1}$ is *not* in general a possibilities map from (A, L_A) to (A^p, L_{A^p}). This is because the automaton component A^p of (A^p, L_A) is restricted only to executions of A with extensions in L_A. This distinguishes the product (A^p, L_{A^p}) from the product (A^h, L_A), in which the executions of the automaton component A^h are essentially unchanged from those of A.

If (A, L_A) and (B, L_B) are specifications then define $(A^h B^p, L_{A^h B^p})$ to be the product of (A^h, L_{A^h}) and (B^p, L_{B^p}).

The product $(A^h B^p, L_{A^h B^p})$ is essentially identical to the specification constructed in the completeness theorem of Abadi and Lamport [AL88].[6]

[6] To be precise, the specification in [AL88] is the product of (A^h, L_{A^h}) and the execution module $Execs(B, L_B)$. The states of this product are thus a triple containing A's current state, the history at A, and the history at B. In

Proposition 9 : The product $(A^hB^p, L_{A^hB^p})$

- *$(s, \alpha_A, t, \alpha_B)$ is a reachable state of A^hB^p if and only if α_A is an execution of A that leaves A in state s, α_B is an execution of B in $finprefixes(execs(B, L_B))$ that leaves B in state t and $\alpha_A|(A \cap B) = \alpha_B|(A \cap B)$.*
- $execs(A^hB^p) = execs(A^h) \times execs(B^p)$
- $execs(A^hB^p)|A = (execs(A) \times closure(execs(B, L_B)))|A$
- $execs(A^hB^p)|B = (execs(A) \times closure(execs(B, L_B)))|B$
- $execs(A^hB^p, L_{A^hB^p})|A = execs(AB, L_{AB})|A$
- $execs(A^hB^p, L_{A^hB^p})|B = execs(AB, L_{AB})|B$
- *The projection operator $|A$ is a possibilities mapping from $(A^hB^p, L_{A^hB^p})$ to (A, L_A).*
- *The projection operator $|B$ is a possibilities mapping from $(A^hB^p, L_{A^hB^p})$ to (B, L_B).*

The previous proposition allows a restatement of the earlier completeness result in terms of a different product:

Theorem 10 : Completeness of $(A^hB^p, L_{A^hB^p})$
Suppose that specifications (A, L_A) and (B, L_B) are privacy respecting and have the same external signature. Then

- $behs(A^hB^p) = behs(A) \cap behs(closure(execs(B, L_B)))$
- $behs(A^hB^p, L_{A^hB^p}) = behs(A, L_A) \cap behs(B, L_B)$
- $behs(A, L_A) \subseteq behs(B, L_B)$ *if and only if* $behs(A^hB^p, L_{A^hB^p}) = behs(A, L_A)$.

5 Auxiliary Variable Constructions

The previous section demonstrates that various product constructions, combined with possibilities mappings, are in a sense complete proof techniques for demonstrating implementation between specifications. However, the correctness of the product construction depends directly on the implementation condition between the specifications–no real progress is made towards proving that this condition exists.

However, Theorem 10 does demonstrate that the problem of proving that (A, L_A) implements (B, L_B) can be reduced to proving that the product $(A^hB^p, L_{A^hB^p})$ is equivalent to (A^h, L_{A^h}) and implements (B^p, L_{B^p}). In addition, possibilities mappings may be used to prove that $(A^hB^p, L_{A^hB^p})$ implements (A^h, L_{A^h}) and (B^p, L_{B^p}). It remains only to prove that (A^h, L_{A^h}) implements $(A^hB^p, L_{A^hB^p})$. In the next section, restrictions on (A, L_A) and (B, L_B) are explored, under which there is a prophecy mapping from $(A^hB^p, L_{A^hB^p})$ to (A^h, L_{A^h}), whenever (A, L_A) implements (B, L_B).

In this section, following Abadi and Lamport, we define two types of auxiliary variable constructions, which can be used to translate one specification into another with equivalent behaviors, but which may be easier to analyze.

History variable constructions are typified by the relationship between (A, L_A) and (A^h, L_{A^h}), in which equivalence follows via a pair of possibilities mappings. Prophecy variable constructions are represented by the relationship between $(A^hB^p, L_{A^hB^p})$ and (A^h, L_{A^h}), under the technical restrictions of the next section, in which equivalence follows by a possibilities mapping in one direction and a prophecy mapping in the other.

effect, the product $(A^hB^p, L_{A^hB^p})$ merely adds an extra component to the states, recording B's current state. Hence, we may use the projection operator $|B$ on the result, and avoid introducing the operator $last(\alpha)$, which is used [AL88] to extract the current state from the state component recording the history at B.

5.1 History Variable Constructions

We say that specification $(A', L_{A'})$ is obtained from specification (A, L_A) by *adding a history variable* if and only if the following conditions are satisfied.

1. $states(A') \subseteq states(A) \times H$ for some state set H.
2. $sig(A') = (ext(A'), int(A'))$, where
   (a) $ext(A) = ext(A')$, and
   (b) $int(A) \subseteq int(A')$.
3. $start(A') \subseteq start(A)|A^{-1}$
4. If (s', h') is a reachable state of A' and $((s', h'), \pi, (s, h)) \in steps(A')$ then $(s', \pi, s) \in steps(A)$ or$\pi \notin acts(A)$ and $s' = s$.
5. For every start state s_0 of A, there is a start state (s_0, h_0) of A'.
6. Let s' be a reachable state of A, (s', h') a reachable state of A', and (s', π, s) a step of A. Then there is a move, $((s', h'), \pi, (s, h))$, of A'.
7. $L_{A'} = \{\alpha \in execs(A') : \alpha|A \in L_A\}$.

(Note that this definition allows A' to take extra stuttering steps that A does not–this is not allowed by Abadi and Lamport, for whom the sixth condition of the definition would be as follows: If $(s', \pi, s) \in steps(A)$ and $(s', h') \in states(A')$ then there exists a $h \in H$ such that $((s', h'), \pi, (s, h)) \in steps(A')$.)

Theorem 11 : Soundness of history variables
If $(A', L_{A'})$ is obtained from (A, L_A) by adding a history variable, then $|A$ is a possibilities mapping from $(A', L_{A'})$ to (A, L_A) and $|A^{-1}$ is a possibilities mapping from (A, L_A) to $(A', L_{A'})$; hence $behs(A', L_{A'}) = behs(A, L_A)$.

Proof: Properties 1 through 4 and 7 of the definition imply directly that $|A$ is a possibilities mapping from A' to A.

Properties 1, 2 and 5 through 7 of the definition imply directly that $|A^{-1}$ is a possibilities mapping from A to A'.

The conclusion $behs(A', L_{A'}) = behs(A, L_A)$ follows by Theorem 1. ∎

Proposition 12 : (A^h, L_{A^h}) is a history variable construction
The specification (A^h, L_{A^h}) is obtained from (A, L_A) by adding a history variable.

Note that in general (A^p, L_A) is *not* obtained from (A, L_A) by adding a history variable. (Consider the case in which L_A is the empty set.)

5.2 Prophecy Variable Constructions

We say that specification $(A', L_{A'})$ is obtained from specification (A, L_A) by *adding a prophecy variable* if and only if the following conditions are satisfied.

1. $states(A') \subseteq states(A) \times P$ for some nonempty state set P.
2. $sig(A') = (ext(A'), int(A'))$, where
   (a) $ext(A) = ext(A')$, and
   (b) $int(A) \subseteq int(A')$.

3. $start(A') \subseteq start(A)|A^{-1}$

4. If (s', p') is a reachable state of A' and $((s', p'), \pi, (s, p)) \in steps(A')$ then $(s', \pi, s) \in steps(A)$ or $\pi \notin acts(A)$ and $s' = s$.

5. If s is a reachable state of A, then the set of reachable states of $s|A^{-1}$ is non-empty.

6. If s is a reachable state of A, (s', π, s) is a step of A and (s, p) is a reachable state of A', then there is a reachable state (s', p') of A' and a move $((s', p'), \pi, (s, p))$ of A'.

7. If (s_0, p) is a reachable state of A' and $s_0 \in start(A)$ then there exists $(s_0, p_0) \in start(A')$ and a move $((s_0, p_0)\gamma(s_0, p))$ of A' such that γ is the empty sequence.

8. For every reachable state s of A, the set of reachable states in $s|A^{-1}$ is finite.

9. $L_{A'} = \{\alpha \in execs(A') : \alpha|A \in L_A\}$

Theorem 13 : Soundness of prophecy variables
If $(A', L_{A'})$ is obtained from (A, L_A) by adding a prophecy variable, then $|A$ is possibilities mapping from $(A', L_{A'})$ to (A, L_A), and $|A^{-1}$ is a prophecy mapping from (A, L_A) to $(A', L_{A'})$, hence $behs(A', L_{A'}) = behs(A, L_A)$.

Proof: Properties 1 through 4 and 9 of the definition imply directly that $|A$ is a possibilities mapping from A' to A.

Properties 1, 2 and 5 through 9 of the definition imply directly that $|A^{-1}$ is a prophecy mapping from A to A'.

The conclusion $behs(A', L_{A'}) = behs(A, L_A)$ follows by Theorems 1 and 3. ∎

6 $(A^h B^p, L_{A^h B^p})$ as a Prophecy Variable Construction

Theorem 10 shows a strong connection between the properties of the product $(A^h B^p, L_{A^h B^p})$ and whether or not $behs(A, L_A) \subseteq behs(B, L_B)$.

While these connections hold in general, the construction of $(A^h B^p, L_{A^h B^p})$ from (A^h, L_{A^h}) and (B^p, L_{B^p}) is not in general a prophecy variable construction. In particular, the fifth, eighth and ninth conditions do not hold:

- If (s, h) is a reachable state of A^h, then the set of reachable states in $A^h B^p$ of the form (s, h, t, p) is non-empty.

- For every reachable state (s, h) of A^h, the set of reachable states in $A^h B^p$ of the form (s, h, t, p) is finite.

- $L_{A^h B^p} = \{\alpha \in execs(A^h B^p) : \alpha|A^h \in L_{A^h}\}$.

The following three subsections explore the restrictions of machine closure of (A, L_A) and the finite invisible nondeterminism and internal continuity of (B, L_B), demonstrating that each of these three assumptions suffices to prove the corresponding missing condition of prophecy variable constructions. Hence, under these restrictions, the construction of $(A^h B^p, L_{A^h B^p})$ from (A^h, L_{A^h}) and (B^p, L_{B^p}) is indeed a prophecy variable construction.

6.1 Machine Closure

Let (A, L_A) be a specification. Then (A, L_A) is *machine closed* if $execs(A) = closure(execs(A, L_A))$.

Note that if L_A is trivial (all sequences) then $execs(A, L_A)$ is machine closed.[7]

The following result shows that the fifth condition of prophecy variable constructions is satisfied by $(A^h B^p, L_{A^h B^p})$ when (A, L_A) is machine-closed and $behs(A, L_A) \subseteq behs(B, L_B)$.

Lemma 14 : Machine closure
If (A, L_A) is machine-closed and $behs(A, L_A) \subseteq behs(B, L_B)$ then for every finite execution α of A there exists an execution β in $finprefixes(execs(B, L_B))$ such that $beh(\alpha) = beh(\beta)$.

Proof: Let $\alpha_A \in finexecs(A)$. By machine-closure, $execs(A) = closure(execs(A, L_A))$. Thus, α_A is a prefix of an execution α'_A in $execs(A, L_A)$. Then there is an execution α'_B in $execs(B, L_B)$ such that $beh(\alpha'_A) = beh(\alpha'_B)$, and hence a prefix α_B of α'_B in $finprefixes(execs(B, L_B))$ such that $beh(\alpha_A) = beh(\alpha_B)$. ∎

6.2 Finitely Invisible Nondeterminism

The following result shows that the eighth condition of prophecy variable constructions is satisfied by $(A^h B^p, L_{A^h B^p})$ when (B, L_B) is finitely invisibly nondeterministic.

Lemma 15 : Finite invisible nondeterminism
If (B, L_B) is finitely invisibly nondeterministic then for every finite execution α of A there are at most finitely many executions β in $finprefixes(execs(B, L_B))$ such that $beh(\alpha) = beh(\beta)$.

Proof: Immediate from the definition of finitely invisible nondeterminism. ∎

6.3 Internal Continuity

A set of executions P is *internally continuous* if $beh(\sigma) \in beh(P)$ and $\sigma \in closure(P)$ implies $\sigma \in P$.

If A is an automaton, $execs(A)$ is internally continuous, since $execs(A) = closure(execs(A))$. However, the corresponding result is not generally true for specifications.[8]

The liveness condition in the definition of prophecy variable constructions is weaker in general than the property $L_{A^h B^p}$ in the product $(A^h B^p, L_{A^h B^p})$. In particular, the liveness condition L_B must not exclude any executions of B that correspond to executions of (A, L_A). The following lemma shows that this property is satisfied when (B, L_B) is internally continuous and $behs(A, L_A) \subseteq behs(B, L_B)$.

Lemma 16 : Internal continuity
If (B, L_B) is internally continuous and $behs(A, L_A) \subseteq behs(B, L_B)$, then $L_{A^h B^p} = \{\alpha \in execs(A^h B^p) : \alpha | A^h \in L_{A^h}\}$.

Proof:
By definition, $L_{A^h B^p} = \{\alpha \in execs(A^h B^p) \text{: } \alpha | A^h \in L_{A^h}\} \cap \{\alpha \in execs(A^h B^p) \text{: } \alpha | B^p \in L_{B^p}\}$. Thus, $L_{A^h B^p} \subseteq \{\alpha \in execs(A^h B^p) \text{: } \alpha | A^h \in L_{A^h}\}$.

So suppose that $\{\alpha \in execs(A^h B^p) : \alpha | A^h \in L_{A^h})\}$. By Proposition 4, $execs(A^h B^p) = execs(A^h) \times execs(B^p)$. It follows from Proposition 7 that $\alpha | A \in execs(A, L_A)$ and by Proposition 8, $\alpha | B \in closure(execs(B, L_B))$. From $\alpha | A \in execs(A, L_A)$ we have $beh(\alpha) \in behs(A, L_A)$, and so by $behs(A, L_A) \subseteq behs(B, L_B)$ we have $beh(\alpha) \in behs(B, L_B)$. Since $beh(\alpha) = beh(\alpha | B)$, by internal continuity $\alpha | B \in execs(B, L_B)$, and so $\alpha | B \in L_B$. Hence $\alpha | B^p \in L_{B^p}$, and $\{\alpha \in execs(A^h B^p) : \alpha | A^h \in L_{A^h}\} \subseteq L_{A^h B^p}$. ∎

---

[7]Note also that in the notation of I/O automata, $(A, fairexecs(A))$ is machine closed.

[8]In particular, it is not always true when the additional liveness condition is the fairness condition for I/O automata.

6.4 A Completeness Theorem for Auxiliary Variable Constructions

Theorem 17 : The Abadi-Lamport completeness theorem
If specifications (A, L_A) and (B, L_B) are privacy respecting and have the same external signature, (B, L_B) is finitely invisibly nondeterministic and internally continuous and (A, L_A) is machine-closed, then $behs(A, L_A) \subseteq behs(B, L_B)$ if and only if $(A^h B^p, L_{A^h B^p})$ is obtained from (A^h, L_{A^h}) by adding a prophecy variable.

Proof: The forward direction follows immediately from Lemmas 14, 15 and 16.
The backward direction is immediate from Theorem 3 and Proposition 9. ∎

6.5 Safety Properties

For completeness, we include in this section the automata-theoretic version of Abadi and Lamport's Theorem 1.

Lemma 18 :
Suppose that B is finitely invisibly nondeterministic, and that for every finite execution α of A there exists an execution β in $execs(B)$ such that $beh(\alpha) = beh(\beta)$. Then $behs(A) \subseteq behs(B)$.

Proof: Let $\alpha \in execs(A)$. By the explicit assumption, for every finite prefix α_i of α there is a set of finite executions β_i in $execs(B)$ such that $beh(\beta_i) = beh(\alpha_i)$. Furthermore, since B is finitely invisibly nondeterministic, the set is also finite.

Let $P = closure(\{\beta_i \in execs(B) : beh(\beta_i) = beh(\alpha_i) \text{ for some } i\})$. Then since P is closed and finitely invisibly nondeterministic, by Lemma 2 $behs(P) = behs(closure(P)) = closure(behs(P))$. Thus, there is an execution β in $execs(B)$ such that $beh(\alpha) = beh(\beta)$, and so $behs(A) \subseteq behs(B)$. ∎

Theorem 19 : Separate safety proofs
If (A, L_A) is machine closed, B is finitely invisibly nondeterministic, and $behs(A, L_A) \subseteq behs(B, L_B)$ then $behs(A) \subseteq behs(B)$.

Proof: Immediate from Lemmas 14 and 18. ∎

7 Discussion

There are three contributions made in these notes. The first is to provide some additional theoretical context for understanding and appreciating the completeness result of Abadi and Lamport [AL88]. The theory elaborated here shows that in general, a close connection exists between the specification $(A^h B^p, L_{A^h B^p})$ constructed by Abadi and Lamport and the intersection of the sets of sequences specified by (A, L_A) and (B, L_B): that, in fact, $behs(A^h B^p, L_{A^h B^p}) = behs(A, L_A) \cap behs(B, L_B)$.

Given this unsurprising result, it is not at all unexpected that $behs(A^h B^p, L_{A^h B^p}) = behs(A, L_A)$ implies $behs(A, L_A) \subseteq behs(B, L_B)$.

Rather, the more interesting contribution of Abadi and Lamport's work is that the construction of $(A^h B^p, L_{A^h B^p})$ can be shown, under the assumption of the machine closure of (A, L_A) and the internal continuity and finite invisible nondeterminism of (B, L_B), to be the result of a history variable construction followed by a prophecy variable construction. The local conditions in the definitions of these constructions provide some significant guidance in constructing an implementation proof. It will be interesting to see whether these techniques can be applied successfully to problems of independent interest.

A second contribution is the explicit definition of *prophecy mappings*, the time-reversal of possibilities mappings. This definition permits somewhat more modular proofs of soundness for history and prophecy variable constructions. In particular, history variables are proven sound via two possibilities mappings, and prophecy mappings via a possibilities mapping and a prophecy mapping. It remains to be seen whether the notion of prophecy mapping will be of independent utility.

A third contribution of these notes is to articulate some aspects of the relationship of the (Moore) state machine model of [AL88] and the (Mealy) automata model. The author hopes that this will contribute to a reasoned discussion of the formal properties one would hope to find in an *ideal* formal model for reasoning about complex computing systems, particularly those constructed of modules with independent loci of control. The presentations here and in [AL88] focus on the notion of what it means for an implementation to satisfy a specification under very general conditions. The work of Chandy and Misra [CM88] and of Lynch and Tuttle [LT87] explore the notion of implementation in restricted versions of the state-machine and automata theory models, respectively. These restrictions are chosen so as to provide an elegant theory of system composition and decomposition that preserves notions of independent control of actions. One is struck in examining this work more by the seeming unity[9] of the emerging theories than by the seemingly superficial differences.

7.1 Relationship to the Results in [AbadiL88]

The most obvious distinction between the material in these notes and the work of Abadi and Lamport is the choice of model. The automaton model used hear is the Mealy-automaton equivalent of the (Moore) state machines used by Abadi and Lamport. All of the results here have corresponding results in the state machine model.

The definitions of possibilities mappings and of auxiliary variables differ in some details from those explored by Abadi and Lamport. Usually, this has involved allowing slightly more general conditions. For example, possibilities mappings are multivalued, while refinement mappings are single-valued. Formally, this makes the completeness theorems explored here somewhat weaker than those in [AL88]. However, the significance of a completeness result should not be overstressed so as to lead to rejection of natural proof-theoretic tools.

The utility of multivalued mappings has been proven in application to problems of independent interest (E.g. in [WLL88, LT87]). In addition, the more general definition has allowed a more modular presentation of these results. For example, the inverse projection operator $(|A^h)^{-1}$ is a possibilities mapping from (A, L_A) to (A^h, L_{A^h}), but because it is multivalued, it is not a refinement mapping. Because of the restriction on refinement mappings, Abadi and Lamport are forced to reprove the soundness of the multivalued version inside of the proof of soundness of history variables.

Many of the results in these notes correspond exactly to results in [AL88]. I have kept Abadi and Lamport's bold-face labels whenever such correspondence (and labels) exist. These correspondences are summarized below:

[9]Forgive the pun.

As numbered here:	In [AL88]:	
Theorem 1	Proposition 1	**Soundness of possibilities mappings**
Lemma 2	Lemma 2	**Closure and nondeterminism**
Theorem 3	(none)	**Soundness of prophecy mappings**
Proposition 4	(none)	**Products of specifications**
Theorem 5	(none)	**Completeness of products**
Proposition 6	(none)	**Specifications and execution modules**
Proposition 7	(none)	**The product** (A^h, L_{A^h})
Proposition 8	(none)	**The product** (A^p, L_{A^p})
Proposition 9	(none)	**The product** $(A^h B^p, L_{A^h B^p})$
Theorem 10	(none)	**Completeness of** $(A^h B^p, L_{A^h B^p})$
Theorem 11	Proposition 4	**Soundness of history variables**
Proposition 12	(none)	(A^h, L_{A^h}) **is a history variable construction**
Theorem 13	Proposition 5	**Soundness of prophecy variables**
Lemma 14	(none)	**Machine closure**
Lemma 15	(none)	**Finite invisible nondeterminism**
Lemma 16	(none)	**Internal continuity**
Theorem 17	Theorem 2	**The Abadi-Lamport completeness theorem**
Theorem 19	Theorem 1	**Separate safety proofs**

7.2 Acknowledgement

The author would like to thank Martín Abadi for helpful discussions and criticism.

References

[AL88] M. Abadi and L Lamport. The existence of refinement mappings. In *Proceedings of the Third Annual Symposium on Logic in Computer Science*, pages 165–175, July 1988. Edinburgh, Scotland. Also available as a Digital Systems Research Center technical report, 130 Lytton Avenue, Palo Alto, CA 94301.

[CM88] K.M. Chandy and J. Misra. *Parallel Program Design: A Foundation.* Addison-Wesley, 1988.

[Knu73] D. E. Knuth. *Fundamental Algorithms. Volume 1 of The Art of Computer Programming.* Addison-Wesley, 1973. Reading, Massachusetts, second edition.

[LT87] N. Lynch and M. Tuttle. Hierarchical correctness proofs for distributed algorithms. In *Proceedings of 6th ACM Symposium on Principles of Distributed Computation*, pages 137–151, August 1987. Expanded version available as Technical Report MIT/LCS/TR-387, Laboratory for Computer Science, Massachusetts Institute Technology, Cambridge, MA., April 1987.

[Lyn88] N. Lynch. I/O automata: A model for discrete event systems. Technical Memo MIT/LCS/TM-351, Massachusetts Institute Technology, Laboratory for Computer Science, March 1988. Also, in 22nd Annual Conference on Information Science and Systems, Princeton University, Princeton, N.J., March 1988.

[Lyn89] N. Lynch. Multivalued possibilities mappings. In *Lecture Notes in Computer Science*, 1989. This volume.

[WLL88] J. Welch, L Lamport, and N. Lynch. A lattice-structured proof of a minimum spanning tree algorithm. In *Proceedings of the Seventh Annual Symposium on Principles of Distributed Computation*, August 1988. Vancouver, BC.

Formal Verification of Data Type Refinement

—

Theory and Practice*

Tobias Nipkow

University of Cambridge
Computer Laboratory
Pembroke Street
Cambridge CB2 3QG
England
tnn@cl.cam.ac.uk

Abstract. This paper develops two theories of data abstraction and refinement: one for applicative types, as they are found in functional programming languages, and one for state-based types found in imperative languages. The former are modelled by algebraic structures, the latter by automata. The automaton-theoretic model covers not just data types but distributed systems in general. Within each theory two examples of data refinement are presented and formally verified with the theorem prover Isabelle. The examples are an abstract specification and two implementations of a memory system, and a mutual exclusion algorithm.

Key words: Abstract Data Types, Data Types, Distributed Processes, Refinement, Implementation, Verification, Theorem Proving.

Contents

1 Introduction

2 The Case Studies

2.1 Extended Guarded Commands

2.2 Simple Memory

2.3 Cache Memory

2.4 Coherent Cache Memory

*Research supported by ESPRIT BRA grant 3245, Logical Frameworks.

3 Isabelle

3.1 Isabelle as a Specification Language

4 General Remarks on Implementations

5 Applicative Data Types

5.1 Nondeterministic Data Types and Their Implementation

5.1.1 Models

5.1.2 Three Implementation Concepts

5.1.3 Homomorphisms

5.1.4 Syntax versus Semantics

5.2 Translation into First Order Logic

5.3 Simple Memory

5.4 Cache Memory

5.5 Coherent Cache Memory

6 State-Based Data Types

6.1 Input/Output Automata

6.2 Simple Memory

6.3 Cache Memory

6.4 Mutual Exclusion

7 Applicative versus State-Based

1 Introduction

The aims of this paper are twofold: to present a theory of data types and their implementation, and to show how the correctness notions supplied by the theory can be verified using a theorem prover. In fact, we discuss two different approaches to abstract data types: an applicative and a state-based one. The emphasis is on correctness notions for data type implementations, i.e. the process of going from some high-level specification of a data type to a lower level implementation. This is also called *data refinement*. The test case for both theories are a specification and two implementations of the data type *memory*. The theorem prover Isabelle is used to verify the correctness of both implementations.

The paper is structured around the two theories of data types that are discussed. Both theories are firmly in the "behavioural" camp. This means that the world of types is divided into two: the "visible" basic types (booleans, integers, characters, ...), and user defined "hidden" abstract types (stacks, queues, buffers, ...). The distinction is that the latter cannot be input to or output of a program. The notion of implementation between data types can now be defined in terms of the visible input/output behaviour of programs that use these types.

The two theories differ in the mathematical model that is used to give meaning to the term data type. There are various ways to characterize the distinction: on the one hand we have applicative, functional, value-oriented, immutable, transformational, or algebraic, on the other hand state-based, imperative, object-oriented, mutable, reactive, or automaton-based. To a large part, the choice of models is dictated by the linguistic framework.

In a pure functional programming language, all data types must be of the first kind: anything is just a value, can be passed around, and can be duplicated at random. There is no distinction between basic and user defined abstract types, apart from input/output restrictions on the latter. Whereas most approaches to algebraic data types assume a deterministic world, i.e. all operations on a data type are functions, this paper develops a theory of nondeterministic data types and their implementations. The underlying mathematical model is a relational generalization of algebras. In order to develop a theory of implementations, we need to say how a data type's behaviour is observed, i.e. what the programs that use it look like. This task is complicated by the presence of nondeterminism and by our desire to design a theory of implementations that is not too dependent on a particular observation language.

The second kind of data type theory, termed state-based above, is associated with imperative programming languages. They permit the definition of, in CLU [21] terminology, "mutable" data types. Objects of these types have internal states that are never passed around outside the object but are changed by side-effect when invoking access functions. This approach is almost the norm in distributed systems, where data types are often identified with processes. Once the step to a distributed system has been made, it is natural if not compulsory to deal with nondeterminism. The obvious model is that of an automaton. The advantage of this model is that it comes with a canonical notion of behaviour: the accepted language or trace set.

We will see that in the end the distinction between the two approaches burns down to the fact that in an applicative system, values can be duplicated (copied), whereas in a state-based system there is only one copy of the state at any time. As a consequence, state-based systems have less observational power, i.e. they make less distinctions. With respect to data refinement it means that implementations in a state-based context may not be implementations in an applicative context.

To fill the theories with life, we go through some case studies of formal verifications using a theorem prover. The basis for these examples are a collection of specifications and implementations of various storage systems found in [20]. Some of the simpler examples are selected and their correctness with respect to our notions of data refinement are shown using the theorem proving system Isabelle.

The outline of the paper is as follows. After a presentation of the three versions of the data type memory in Section 2 and a brief introduction to the theorem prover Isabelle in Section 3, the main body is devoted to the exposition of the two theories of data abstraction sketched above. Section 5 develops a theory of refinement for applicative data types and verifies Lampson's two memory implementations within that theory. Section 6 looks at the verification of distributed systems in general and state-based types in particular. After a brief review of input/output automata and their notion of refinement, the formal correctness proof of a data type (Lampson's cache memory) and a distributed process (mutual exclusion) within this theory is shown. Section 7 concludes the paper with a discussion of the differences between the two theories of data types and their correctness notions.

2 The Case Studies

The examples for our case studies are drawn from a paper by Butler Lampson [20] on the specification of distributed systems. The paper uses an extension of Dijkstra's guarded command language to specify a range of different storage systems. The particular examples we have selected are the specification of the data type *memory* and two implementations using caches. To keep this paper self-contained, we give a brief introduction to Lampson's specification language, followed by the specification of the three memory systems. In sections 5 and 6 we introduce our own formalisms for data type specification and translate his "code" into our notation. The two main points that distinguish his specifications from ours are that in section 5 we view memory as an applicative rather than a state-based type, and in section 6 we are more precise with respect to concurrency and interleaving. We are intentionally vague in this section because it is only meant as an introduction to the problems. Formality is postponed to sections 5 and 6.

2.1 Extended Guarded Commands

Dijkstra's language of guarded commands [7] was extended by Greg Nelson [26] in such a way that it becomes more suitable as a specification language than the original calculus. The major innovation is the introduction of *partial* commands, that is, commands that may fail. The following informal explanation of part of Nelson's calculus is taken from [26].

Command	Operational Meaning
skip	do nothing
$P \rightarrow A$	activate command A if P holds, else fail
$A \boxtimes B$	activate A, else B if A fails
$A; B$	activate A then B
if A **fi**	activate A until it succeeds
do A **od**	activate A until it fails
$x \mid P \rightarrow A$	activate A with a new variable x, initialized such that P holds; if P holds for no value of x, fail

The last command is in fact a combination of the two basic constructs of variable introduction and guards.

The specifications in [20] use three additional language features: grouping into atomic actions, procedures, and data abstraction, neither of which is formally defined. We bypass any questions of atomicity in the initial exposition of the examples. Atomicity becomes important only in the presence of concurrency and the possibility of interference. These issues are resolved when they arise, i.e. in section 6. For similar reasons we rely on the reader's intuition regarding procedures and data abstraction.

2.2 Simple Memory

This is the specification of a simple addressable memory. The data type imports the two types of *addresses* A and *data* D. It exports the two operations *read* and *write* [1]. The *state* of the memory m is a mapping from addresses to data, written $A \overset{m}{\to} D$. It corresponds more to an array than to a function space.

$$\textbf{var } m: A \overset{m}{\to} D$$

$$\begin{array}{lcl} read(a, \textbf{var } d) & = & d := m[a] \\ write(a, d) & = & m[a] := d \end{array}$$

The meaning of this specification is obvious enough. Now we look at two implementations using write-back caches.

2.3 Cache Memory

A first level implementation of the simple memory adds a single cache to the state. Read and write requests are satisfied by the cache if possible, and changes are written back to main memory immediately. The *raison d'être* of a cache is its increased access speed which is achieved at the expense of capacity. As the cache can hold only a small subset of the main memory's address space, it cannot be modelled by a mapping $A \overset{m}{\to} D$. A new element $\bot$, $\bot \notin D$, is used to denote undefinedness. $D_\bot$ is equivalent to $D \cup \{\bot\}$.

$$\begin{array}{ll} \textbf{var} & c: A \overset{m}{\to} D_\bot \\ & m: A \overset{m}{\to} D \end{array}$$

$$\begin{array}{lcl} read(a, \textbf{var } d) & = & load(a); d := m[a] \\ write(a, d) & = & \textbf{if } c[a] = \bot \to flush1 \boxtimes skip \textbf{ fi}; c[a] := d \\ & & \\ load(a) & = & \textbf{if } c[a] = \bot \to flush1; c[a] := m[a] \boxtimes skip \textbf{ fi} \\ flush1 & = & a \mid c[a] \neq \bot \to m[a] := c[a]; c[a] := \bot \end{array}$$

The implementation ensures that the number of addresses at which c is defined remains invariant. For *flush*1 to be total, we have to assume that initially c is defined for least one address. The operations *load* and *flush*1 are auxiliary.

2.4 Coherent Cache Memory

This is a more complex version of the cache memory, suitable for a multiprocessor where each processor has its own write-back cache. The processors are identified by elements from some set P of processor numbers.

$$\begin{array}{ll} \textbf{var} & c: P \overset{m}{\to} A \overset{m}{\to} D_\bot \\ & m: A \overset{m}{\to} D \end{array}$$

[1] The third operation *swap* introduced in [20] has been dropped because it is not sufficiently different from the other two.

$$\begin{array}{lcl}
read(p,a,\mathbf{var}\ d) & = & load(p,a); d := c[p,a] \\
write(p,a,d) & = & \mathbf{if}\ c[p,a] = \bot \rightarrow flush1(p) \boxtimes skip\ \mathbf{fi}; c[p,a] := d; distr(p,a) \\
 & & \\
load(p,a) & = & \mathbf{if}\ c[p,a] = \bot \rightarrow \\
 & & \quad flush1(p); \\
 & & \quad \mathbf{if}\ q \mid c[q,a] \neq \bot \rightarrow c[p,a] := c[q,a] \boxtimes c[p,a] := m[a]\ \mathbf{fi} \\
 & & \boxtimes\ skip\ \mathbf{fi} \\
distr(p,a) & = & \mathbf{do}\ q \mid c[q,a] \neq \bot \wedge c[q,a] \neq c[p,a] \rightarrow c[q,a] := c[p,a]\ \mathbf{od} \\
flush1(p) & = & a \mid c[p,a] \neq \bot \rightarrow m[a] := c[p,a]; c[p,a] := \bot
\end{array}$$

Writing $c[p,a]$ instead of $c[p][a]$ follows the usual convention of indexing multi-dimensional arrays. The formal justification is the isomorphism between $A \overset{m}{\rightarrow} B \overset{m}{\rightarrow} C$ and $A \times B \overset{m}{\rightarrow} C$.

Although it may seem we have changed the interface by adding the parameter p to *read* and *write*, this is not the case. The parameter p has only been introduced on the conceptual level. For each processor p the interface remains as specified in section 2.2. We have simply replaced indexed sets of operations $read_p$ and $write_p$ by a single one.

Note that this specification is still a long way from an implementation. In particular it needs an efficient realization of the auxiliary operation *distr*, which broadcasts a change in one cache to all other caches.

3 Isabelle

Isabelle is a generic theorem prover developed by Larry Paulson at the University of Cambridge. By supplying syntax and inference rules it can be instantiated to support particular logics. Isabelle's style of theorem proving stands in the LCF [34] tradition, i.e. it is interactive and driven by user defined tactics. For an overview of Isabelle see [35]. Isabelle's logical foundation is explored in [36].

All theorems presented in this paper were proved by rewriting related tactics and induction. An anatomy of these tactics can be found in [31]. Their application in the correctness proofs of some sorting algorithms is detailed in [32]. The proofs of the theorems in this paper are in the same style and have been omitted. Only the sequence of lemmas leading up to them is reproduced.

3.1 Isabelle as a Specification Language

In order to use Isabelle for program verification, we identify specifications with logics or extension of logics. Each extension introduces

- a set of new type (constructor) names,
- a set of new (logical or non-logical) constants, and
- a set of axioms and inference rules.

In analogy to OBJ [9] we use the following syntax:

```
Extension = Base1 + ... + Basen + SORTS ... OPS ... RULES ...
```

This means that `Extension` is the extension of the union of the theories `Base1` through `Basen` with the types listed after `SORTS`, the constants after `OPS`, and the inference rules after `RULES`. The syntax of constants is given in mixfix notation. The notation for types follows ML [13] conventions.

This OBJ-like syntax is different from but closely related to the actual syntax used in the definition of Isabelle logics. Apart from some minor matters of surface syntax, the only liberty we have taken is the inclusion of type constructors with arguments, and polymorphic constants. Both are currently not supported by Isabelle, but there are plans for such extensions, along the lines of LCF's [34] and HOL's [11] type system. The actual proofs were conducted in a single-sorted logic. It is only for the sake of presentation that we have introduced many-sortedness and polymorphism.

The starting point for all our specifications is an axiomatization of first-order logic with equality. In addition to the usual logical symbols a conditional, pairs, and triples are defined:

FOLE = SORTS $form,\ (\alpha,\beta)pair,\ (\alpha,\beta,\gamma)triple$

OPS $\_\wedge\_, \_\vee\_, \_\Rightarrow\_, \_\Leftrightarrow\_ : form * form \rightarrow form$

$\_=\_ : \alpha * \alpha \rightarrow form$

$\vdots$

$\mathbf{if}\_\rightarrow\_\boxtimes\_\mathbf{fi} : form * \alpha * \alpha \rightarrow \alpha$

$\langle\_,\_\rangle : \alpha * \beta \rightarrow (\alpha,\beta)pair$

$\langle\_,\_,\_\rangle : \alpha * \beta * \gamma \rightarrow (\alpha,\beta,\gamma)triple$

RULES

$\vdots$

$$C(\mathbf{if}\ P \rightarrow x \boxtimes y\ \mathbf{fi}) \Leftrightarrow (P \Rightarrow C(x)) \wedge (\neg P \Rightarrow C(y))$$

Notice that the polymorphic type of $\mathbf{if}\_\rightarrow\_\boxtimes\_\mathbf{fi}$ allows it to be used for both formulae and expressions. Its defining rule uses the higher order variable C of type $\alpha \rightarrow form$ representing "contexts". Conditionals are only a notational extension of the calculus because they can be removed from any formula containing them.

The decision to use a standard first-order logic is one of convenience. An Isabelle instantiation exists, and logics for total functions are easier to reason in than those for partial functions. However, it means that any extension with partial functions leads to inconsistencies. In the Boyer-Moore system [2] this problem is dealt with by verifying formally that all new functions are total. The consistency of the extensions of `FOLE` presented below has been checked informally only.

4 General Remarks on Implementations

Since the main theme of this volume is refinement, it is appropriate to make some general remarks on this topic before delving into technicalities. We feel that the proper starting point for any treatment of implementations is the following intuition:

Definition 1 A component C implements a component A if and only if the behaviour of a system with component C is also a behaviour of the system with C replaced by A [2].

This defines what we call the *implementation preorder* $C \leq A$.

[2] Read *Abstract* and *Concrete* for A and C.

Although it remains to be fixed what "components", "systems", and "behaviour" are, we think that most computer scientists would agree to this definition [3].

Despite its generality, this definition makes some tacit assumptions by identifying specifications, implementations, and components. If specifications may denote sets of components, we could define that a set of components M implements a set of components N if for all $C \in M$ there is an $A \in N$ such that $C \leq A$ in the sense of Definition 1. However, that forces us to reason about sets rather than single components. In the sequel we stick to our original definition and assume that it suffices to compare individual components. If the specification formalism ensures that the set of components denoted by a specification always has a largest element with respect to the implementation preorder, these elements can be used as representatives in a correctness proof. More precisely, given a set M with greatest component C and a set N with greatest component A, M implements N if and only if $C \leq A$.

The degree to which the observational view has determined the treatment of refinement in the fields of data types and concurrency is markedly different.

In the data type field it is mostly the case that some abstract mathematical notion such as homomorphism is taken as the definition of refinement without any justification in terms of behaviour. A notable exception is the work of Schoett [37,38], who starts from exactly the premises above. For a survey of other approaches to implementations of data types the reader should consult [38] or [29]. Definition 1 can be applied to data types by identifying data types with components and programs with systems. The point is that in contrast to data types, programs come with more or less canonical notions of behaviour in the form of input/output traces. Implementations between data types are now defined in terms of the induced behaviours of programs using the data types.

In the algebra of concurrent processes, the relation $\leq$ is known as a *testing preorder* [6]. Components and systems are both identified with concurrent processes. Since processes come with well-defined notions of behaviour (e.g. in the form of traces), this leads to a notion of *observational equivalence* and *observational congruence* [17]. In automaton-based approaches like [23] or [1], the definition of refinement is based directly on the trace sets generated by the automata.

The two theories studied in this paper are firmly in the behavioural camp.

5 Applicative Data Types

5.1 Nondeterministic Data Types and Their Implementation

This section reviews the theory of nondeterministic data types (for short: data types) established in [27,29,30]. After a brief introduction of the mathematical model we have chosen for data types, we focus on the question of implementation for the rest of the section. In particular we show how the global definition of implementation given in Section 4 can be localized for particular choices of observing systems and behaviours. This means a characterization of refinement as a set-theoretic relationships between models. The important notion is that of a simulation, which is both a

[3] A possible moot point is that the implementation may display only some of the specification's behaviour. Kuiper [19] for example suggests distinguishing *allowed* from *required* nondeterminism. The second kind must be preserved by implementations.

relational generalization of homomorphism and half a bisimulation [33].

All reasoning is on the semantic level of models and thus independent of any particular specification formalism. As discussed in Section 4, specifications and implementations are identified with models. Section 5.1.4 deals with the application to specific formalisms and the step from semantics back to syntax.

5.1.1 Models

The interface to a data type is called its ***signature***. It lists the ***sorts*** and operations exported by the type; sorts are classified as visible or hidden.

Definition 2 *A* signature *is a triple* $\Sigma = (S, V, O)$ *where* S *is a set of* sort *names,* $V \subseteq S$ *the set of* visible *sorts, and* O *a set of* operations. *Each operation* $r \in O$ *is typed as* $r: w \to s$*, where* $w \in S^*$ *and* $s \in S$*.*

In the sequel assume $\Sigma = (S, V, O)$.

Data types are modelled by ***structures***, which almost coincide with ***multi-algebras*** [12] and are closely related to structures in logic [40].

Definition 3 *A* Σ-structure *A consists of*

- *an S-indexed family of sets A_s, $s \in S$, and*
- *a relation $r^A \subseteq A_w \times A_s$ for each operation $r: w \to s$ in O.*

For $r: w \to s$ in O and $a \in A_w$ define $r^A(a) = \{b \in A_s \mid (a, b) \in r^A\}$.

The interpretation of a pair $(a, b) \in r^A$ is that operation r called with argument tuple a *may* return b. If $r^A(a)$ is empty, r is undefined for a, i.e. it diverges.

This model cannot express possible termination or divergence. If $r^A(a)$ is empty, r^A never terminates if applied to a, otherwise it always terminates. To get a finer distinction, we have to extend the model. One can either introduce a special element $\perp$ such that $\perp \in r^A(a)$ means that $r^A(a)$ may diverge, or an explicit *termination set* for each operation, containing the inputs for which termination is guaranteed. Both choices can be found in the literature. In the sequel we work with $\perp$ and require that $r^A(a)$ is always non-empty, i.e. contains at least $\perp$. A structure is now called *total* if $\perp$ does not occur in the range of any of its operations.

5.1.2 Three Implementation Concepts

Having fixed what the components in the sense of Section 4 are, we need a set of observers or systems to exercise the components. It should be a programming language that is general enough to be representative for a wider class of languages and simple enough to be tractable. Ideally, a kind of λ-calculus for applicative nondeterministic computation structures is required. Given such an observation language, one can ask for a characterization of the implementation relation it induces between data types. Alternatively, one can fix some preorder $\sqsubseteq$ between data types and determine requirements on a language semantics which ensure that $C \sqsubseteq A$ implies that C is an implementation of A with respect to any language meeting those requirements. If $\sqsubseteq$ is well chosen those requirements should be the semantic counterpart of the information hiding principle: they should ban all language features which permit access to the representation of an abstract data type. One can then show that particular languages meet these requirements. This is the approach taken in [27,29,30], the technical details of which are only sketched here. It requires a syntactic domain of programs *Prog*, a semantic domain *Sem* with an implementation preorder on it, and a mapping $D[\![.,.]\!]$ which takes a program and a Σ-structure and returns a denotation in *Sem*.

For the time being we do not fix *Sem* completely but assume that it is based on powerdomains [39]. Powerdomains are extensions of domains to powersets. A partial order on a domain D can be extended to a preorder on $\mathcal{P}(D)$ in different ways, two of which give rise to important correctness concepts:

$$M \preceq_1 N \;\Leftrightarrow\; \forall m \in M\; \exists n \in N.\; m \preceq n$$
$$M \preceq_2 N \;\Leftrightarrow\; \forall m \in M\; \exists n \in N.\; n \preceq m$$

The predicates $\preceq_1$ and $\preceq_2$ are the orderings of the so called *Hoare* [16] and *Smyth*[4] [41] powerdomains respectively. We also define $\preceq_0$ to be $\subseteq$. Broy [4] associates the adjectives *loose*, *partial*, and *robust* with the orderings $\preceq_0$, $\preceq_1$ and $\preceq_2$, a terminology we adopt. We assume that *Sem* comes with either of the orderings $\preceq_i$ as the intended notion of refinement between program denotations.

Considering the carriers of a structure as trivially ordered flat domains and the operations as functions returning power sets, the latter can be compared via $\preceq_i$. This in turn extends to structures by defining $A \preceq_i B$ iff $r^A \preceq_i r^B$ for all operations r.

Of the three notions, loose correctness is the strongest. It only allows reduced nondeterminism. Without going into details, let us just mention that partial correctness corresponds to "safety" and robust correctness to "liveness" in the language of distributed systems.

The above correctness notions carry over to data types as follows. We write $C \leq_i A$ if $D[\![p,C]\!] \preceq_i D[\![p,A]\!]$ holds for al programs p. In that case we call C a loose (partial, robust) implementation of A. What we are interested in is to characterize $\leq_i$ without any reference to observing programs, purely as a set-theoretic relation between data types. Our main tools for that purpose are the so called simulations.

Definition 4 *Let C, A be two Σ-structures and let $\sqsubseteq$ be an S-sorted relation $\sqsubseteq_s \subseteq C_s \times A_s$ such that $\sqsubseteq_v$ is the identity for all visible sorts $v \in V$ and $\bot \sqsubseteq \bot$ is the only pair in $\sqsubseteq$ containing $\bot$. For $w \in S^*$ let $\sqsubseteq_w$ be the componentwise extension of $\sqsubseteq_s$.*

$\sqsubseteq$ *is called a* partial simulation *iff for all operations $r : w \to s$ and all a, c and $c' \neq \bot$ we have*

$$c \sqsubseteq_w a \wedge (c,c') \in r^A \;\Rightarrow\; \exists a'.\ (a,a') \in r^A \wedge c' \sqsubseteq_s a'$$

$\sqsubseteq$ *is called a* (loose) simulation *iff for all operations $r : w \to s$ and all a, c and c' we have*

$$c \sqsubseteq_w a \wedge (c,c') \in r^A \;\Rightarrow\; \exists a'.\ (a,a') \in r^A \wedge c' \sqsubseteq_s a'$$

$\sqsubseteq$ *is called a* robust simulation *iff for all operations $r : w \to s$ and all a, c and c' we have*

$$c \sqsubseteq_w a \wedge (a,\bot) \notin r^A \;\Rightarrow\; (c,\bot) \notin r^C \wedge ((c,c') \in r^C \Rightarrow \exists a'.\ (a,a') \in r^A \wedge c' \sqsubseteq_s a')$$

[4]Note that $M \preceq_2 N$ is usually written $N \preceq_2 M$.

We write $C \sqsubseteq_i A$ to indicate that there is a loose ($i = 0$), partial ($i = 1$) or robust ($i = 2$) simulation between C and A. Note that for total structures C and A, all three simulations coincide.

Simulations are generalizations of the correctness notions $\preceq_i$: $C \preceq_i A \Rightarrow C \sqsubseteq_i A$. The weaker relation $\preceq_i$ can only relate structures with identical carriers, whereas $\sqsubseteq_i$ can relate arbitrary structures. This shows that simulations have a twofold task: to relate different carriers and to guarantee the desired correctness notion.

It remains to be seen what simulations have to do with implementations induced by programs. In particular we are interested in the notions of

Soundness : does $C \sqsubseteq_i A$ imply $C \leq_i A$?

Completeness : does $C \leq_i A$ imply $C \sqsubseteq_i A$?

In [29,30] we obtained some rather abstract criteria for soundness based on the decomposition of simulations into simpler relations like homomorphisms and $\preceq$. We showed that $\sqsubseteq_i$ is sound provided that

- D is insensitive to "junk": if B is a substructure of A, i.e. B contains less unreachable elements (junk) than A, then $D[\![p, B]\!] = D[\![p, A]\!]$ should hold.
- D reflects homomorphisms on hidden values accurately: if B is a homomorphic image of A then $D[\![p, B]\!]$ should be a homomorphic image of $D[\![p, A]\!]$.
- D is monotone w.r.t. $\preceq_i$: $B \preceq_i A$ should imply $D[\![p, B]\!] \preceq_i D[\![p, A]\!]$.

The first two requirements of D should be interpreted as the semantic counterpart of the information hiding principle mentioned at the beginning of this section. The third point is a trivial monotonicity requirement which languages with a denotational semantics should satisfy anyway.

In order to show that real toy languages meet these requirements, we look at a particular instantiation for *Prog*, *Sem*, and D. Without going into details (they can be found in [3,27,29,30]), let us just say that the observation language is a first-order applicative stream processing language similar to Broy's AMPL. In particular it features an angelic choice construct. We call this language L and the subset obtained by removing angelic choice L'. The semantic domains are so called *streams* with the *approximation* ordering $\preceq$. It is this ordering $\preceq$ which the $\preceq_i$ extend to powersets of streams. In this particular instance we obtain the following theorem:

Theorem 1 *Loose (partial) simulations are sound criteria for loose (partial) implementations with respect to programs over L.*

Robust simulations are sound criteria for robust implementations with respect to programs over L' but not over L.

The problem with robust implementations is that in case the specified operation diverges for a certain input, the implementation is free to do what it likes: if f^A is a function that always diverges, the function f^C which always returns 1 is a robust implementation. But a program that chooses angelically between 0 and $f(x)$ will always return 0 (and terminate!) if it uses A, whereas it may also return 1 if it uses C.

Completeness results depend very much on the expressive power of the observing programming language. For the particular example of L we have

Theorem 2 *A structure A is called* finitely nondeterministic *iff* $r^A(a)$ *is always finite. For the subclass of finitely nondeterministic structures, loose (partial) simulations are complete criteria for loose (partial) implementations with respect to programs over* L.

The extension to infinite nondeterminism is still open.

This shows that, modulo finite nondeterminism, loose and partial simulations exactly characterize loose and partial implementations with respect to L.

A completeness result for robust simulations holds only for a rather restricted subclass of structures. Details can be found in [29,30].

5.1.3 Homomorphisms

The basic semantic tool for connecting specifications and implementations is a relation, the simulation. An important special case is that of functional simulations, which are easily seen to be homomorphisms. Hoare [14] was one of the first to define data refinement formally using homomorphisms and many authors have since followed him [18,5]. There are two practical reasons for this:

- Functions are in general easier to handle than relations; in particular the existential quantifier in the definition of a simulation disappears. Thus the approach becomes amenable to support from term-rewriting based verification systems like LP [10].
- It is a fact of life that homomorphisms suffice for most of the verification tasks arising in practice.

It is the second point that we want to look at in more detail. To start with, it is not difficult to establish that homomorphisms are not complete, i.e. there are structures $C \sqsubseteq A$, such that there is no homomorphism from C to A. Most examples of this kind are such that there is a third structure B which is behaviourally equivalent[5] to A and a homomorphic image of C. Jones [18] classifies this as an "implementation bias" in the specification. Had B been chosen as the specification instead of A, C could have been shown to be a correct implementation via a homomorphism. Therefore the question is: does every specification have a behaviourally equivalent counterpart which is the homomorphic image of all its implementations. Technically speaking, we are interested in the existence of final objects in a class of behaviourally equivalent structures.

Summarizing the results obtained in [28] we can say that for deterministic specifications such final objects always exist, whereas in general they don't. This means that in a deterministic world homomorphisms suffice because one can always start with a fully abstract, i.e. final, specification. In the presence of nondeterminism one may be forced to work with proper simulations because fully abstract specifications no longer exist.

More precisely, the results are as follows. If we restrict ourselves to partial algebras, i.e. structures where $r^A(a)$ is always a singleton set, fully abstract specifications exist with respect to loose and robust, but not partial implementations. If we consider all structures, fully abstract specifications cease to exist for all notions of implementations discussed in this paper. Only bisimulation equivalence, which is strictly finer than all the above notions, admits fully abstract specifications.

[5] A and B are termed *behaviourally equivalent* if they have the same set of implementations.

Despite the conclusion that simulations are more general, homomorphisms turn out to be sufficient for the correctness proofs in this paper. Using a function $\varphi: C \to A$, correctness of C is depicted in Figure 1: the three solid lines imply the existence of the dashed line completing the square. The corresponding proposition is

$$(c, c') \in r^C \Rightarrow (\varphi(c), \varphi(c')) \in r^A, \tag{1}$$

which is exactly the definition of a homomorphism in [12].

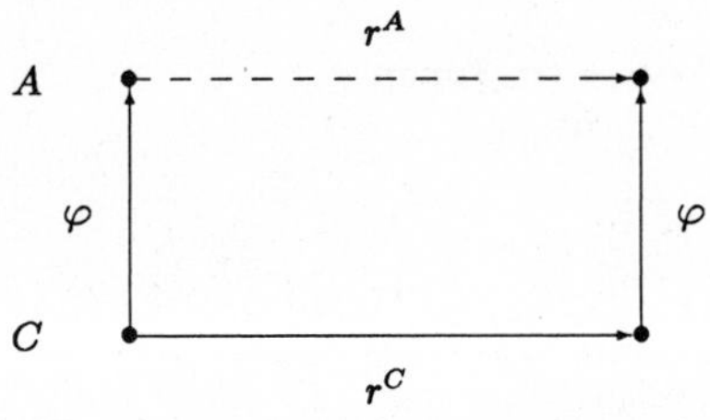

Figure 1: A Homomorphism

5.1.4 Syntax versus Semantics

Having arrived at the actual formula that is the correctness notion in the examples to come, we want to give a brief indication how the results obtained can be applied to particular specification languages. On the one hand there are formalisms like VDM [18], Z [42], or initial or final algebra specifications [8] which associate a canonical model with each specification. Our theory is tailor-made for such formalisms. In fact, defining a notion of implementation for Z has lead to a very similar theory of data refinement [15], although with a state-based view of types.

On the other hand there are formalisms which associate a whole class of models with a specification, e.g. the loose approach to algebraic specifications [8]. Even worse, approaches like [24] come with no model theoretic semantics at all. Nevertheless our theory is still applicable by translating from semantics to syntax. If formal verification is to be supported mechanically, one has to abandon the realm of models in favour of purely syntactic formalisms anyway. In general one is faced with four sets of sentences B, S, I and H, describing the the basic types, the specification, the implementation, and the homomorphism between them. Proving correctness means showing that H does in fact specify a homomorphism:

$$B \cup S \cup I \cup H \vdash \Phi \tag{2}$$

where Φ is (1) above. If S and I are conservative extensions of B with disjoint vocabulary, and H is a conservative extension of $B \cup S \cup I$, there is a simple translation of (2) back into the realm of semantics: from any model of I there is a homomorphism to any other model of S. Thus any model of I implements any model of S, which is certainly sufficient, although in fact stronger than the condition given in Section 4.

This concludes the treatment of the theoretical underpinnings for the actual proofs to come.

5.2 Translation into First Order Logic

The translation of Lampson's specifications in Section 2 into predicate calculus involves both the basic data types, in this case only maps, and the operations of the defined types. For our purposes the following specification of polymorphic maps, called $\xrightarrow{m}$ in Section 2, suffices.

Map = FOLE +

SORTS $(\alpha, \beta)map$

OPS $\_[\_] : (\alpha, \beta)map * \alpha \rightarrow \beta$

$\_[\_/\_] : (\alpha, \beta)map * \beta * \alpha \rightarrow (\alpha, \beta)map$

$\_\backslash\_ : (\alpha, \beta)map * \alpha \rightarrow (\alpha, \beta)map$

$D : (\alpha, \beta)map * \alpha \rightarrow form$

RULES

$$m[b/a][a'] = \textbf{if } a' = a \rightarrow b \boxtimes m[a'] \textbf{ fi}$$
$$a \neq a' \Rightarrow (m\backslash a)[a'] = m[a']$$
$$D(m[b/a], a') \Leftrightarrow a = a' \vee D(m, a')$$
$$D(m\backslash a, a') \Leftrightarrow a \neq a' \wedge D(m, a')$$
$$m = m' \Leftrightarrow \forall a.\ m[a] = m'[a]$$

Instead of returning $\perp$ in case the map is undefined for some argument as in Section 2, we have introduced an explicit definedness predicate D. Notice also that Map has an empty initial model [8] because it lacks constants of type *map*, e.g. the empty map. This is a reflection of the fact that Lampson's memory specifications do not talk about initial states. Of course the correctness theorems we are about to prove remain valid in any extension of the current theory which fixes those details.

Translation of the guarded command text into predicate calculus involves two changes. The specification in Section 2 views the memory as a global variable. In the applicative context of this section, it becomes an additional parameter to each operation which is passed into and out of the operation. Operations are modelled by predicates, which means they are formulae, i.e. constants with result type *form*. The translation of the actual code was guided by Nelson's [26] translation from guarded commands to first-order formulae expressing the relation between pre and post states. In some places the resulting formulae were simplified slightly.

It has to be emphasized that we do not introduce a constant $\perp$, as in Section 5.1, to model nontermination. Instead we stick with the simple model of Definition 3, where divergence of operation r for input c is modelled by $r^C(c) = \{\}$. As a consequence, proposition (1) expresses only partial correctness: if r^C is empty, the proposition always holds. To prove loose correctness, the additional proposition

$$(f(c), a') \in r^A \Rightarrow \exists c'.\ (c, c') \in r^C$$

has to be verified. For simplicity we establish only partial correctness.

5.3 Simple Memory

Lampson's specification of the simple memory translates into

```
SM = Map +
```

$$\texttt{OPS}\ \ read\colon (\alpha,\delta)map * \alpha * (\alpha,\delta)map * \delta \to form$$
$$write\colon (\alpha,\delta)map * \alpha * \delta * (\alpha,\delta)map \to form$$

RULES

$$read(m,a,m',d) \Leftrightarrow m' = m \wedge d = m[a]$$
$$write(m,a,d,m') \Leftrightarrow m' = m[d/a]$$

The operations ***read*** and ***write*** have become predicates relating the memory state before (m) and after (m') the execution and the input and output parameters (a, d). Addresses, data and memory are represented by the type variables α, δ and $(\alpha,\delta)map$ respectively. The polymorphic nature of the specification expresses very clearly that (on an abstract level) memory is independent of the structure of addresses or data.

5.4 Cache Memory

The translation of Lampson's cache memory is fairly straightforward:

```
CM = Map +
```

$$\texttt{SORTS}\ \ (\alpha,\delta)cm \;=\; ((\alpha,\delta)map, (\alpha,\delta)map)pair$$
$$\texttt{OPS}\ \ read'\colon (\alpha,\delta)cm * \alpha * (\alpha,\delta)cm * \delta \to form$$
$$write'\colon (\alpha,\delta)cm * \alpha * \delta * (\alpha,\delta)cm \to form$$
$$load\colon (\alpha,\delta)cm * \alpha * (\alpha,\delta)cm \to form$$
$$flush1\colon (\alpha,\delta)cm * (\alpha,\delta)cm \to form$$

RULES

$$read'(\langle c,m\rangle,a,\langle c',m'\rangle,d) \Leftrightarrow load(\langle c,m\rangle,a,\langle c',m'\rangle) \wedge d = c'[a]$$
$$write'(\langle c,m\rangle,a,d,\langle c',m'\rangle) \Leftrightarrow \textbf{if } D(c,a) \to c' = c[d/a] \wedge m' = m$$
$$\boxtimes\ \exists c''.\ flush1(\langle c,m\rangle,\langle c'',m'\rangle) \wedge c' = c''[d/a]\ \textbf{fi}$$
$$load(\langle c,m\rangle,a,\langle c',m'\rangle) \Leftrightarrow \textbf{if } D(c,a) \to c' = c \wedge m' = m$$
$$\boxtimes\ \exists c''.\ flush1(\langle c,m\rangle,\langle c'',m'\rangle) \wedge c' = c''[m'[a]/a]\ \textbf{fi}$$
$$flush1(\langle c,m\rangle,\langle c',m'\rangle) \Leftrightarrow \exists a.\ D(c,a) \wedge c' = c\backslash a \wedge m' = m[c[a]/a]$$

The interface operations are now called ***read'*** and ***write'*** to distinguish them from those in the specification SM. This is necessary because the correctness requirement (1) talks about both of them at the same time. Correctness is shown by proving that the following function φ is a homomorphism:

```
I1 = SM + CM +
```

$$\texttt{OPS}\ \ \varphi\colon (\alpha,\delta)map * (\alpha,\delta)map \to (\alpha,\delta)map$$

RULES

$$\varphi(c,m)[a] = \textbf{if } D(c,a) \to c[a]\ \boxtimes\ m[a]\ \textbf{fi}$$

Although φ is supposed to produce a mapping, its definition does not actually say what the result mapping is. Instead, it is characterized implicitly by its behaviour w.r.t. application. Because maps are extensional (last axiom in Map), this implicit specification is sufficient.

Correctness, proved in the joint theory `I1`, is immediate for both *read* and *write*:

$$
\begin{aligned}
read'(\langle c,m\rangle,a,\langle c',m'\rangle,d) &\Rightarrow read(\varphi(c,m),a,\varphi(c',m'),d)\\
write'(\langle c,m\rangle,a,d,\langle c',m'\rangle) &\Rightarrow write'(\varphi(c,m),a,d,\varphi(c',m'))
\end{aligned}
$$

5.5 Coherent Cache Memory

The coherent cache memory specification in Section 2.4 translates into

`CCM = Map +`

`SORTS` $(\pi,\alpha,\delta)cache = ((\pi,\alpha)pair,\delta)map$

$(\pi,\alpha,\delta)ccm = ((\pi,\alpha,\delta)cache,(\alpha,\delta)map)pair$

`OPS` $read'\colon (\pi,\alpha,\delta)ccm * \pi * \alpha * (\pi,\alpha,\delta)ccm * \delta \to form$

$write'\colon (\pi,\alpha,\delta)ccm * \pi * \alpha * \delta * (\pi,\alpha,\delta)ccm \to form$

$load, ld\colon (\pi,\alpha,\delta)ccm * \pi * \alpha * (\pi,\alpha,\delta)ccm \to form$

$distr\colon (\pi,\alpha,\delta)cache * \pi * \alpha \to (\pi,\alpha,\delta)cache$

$co : (\pi,\alpha,\delta)cache \to form$

`RULES`

$read'(\langle c,m\rangle,p,a,\langle c',m'\rangle,d) \Leftrightarrow load(\langle c,m\rangle,p,a,\langle c',m'\rangle) \wedge d = c'[\langle p,a\rangle]$

$write'(\langle c,m\rangle,p,a,d,\langle c',m'\rangle) \Leftrightarrow \exists c''.$

$\quad \textbf{if } D(c,\langle p,a\rangle) \to c'' = c \wedge m' = m \boxtimes flush1(\langle c,m\rangle,p,\langle c'',m'\rangle) \textbf{ fi} \wedge$

$\quad c' = distr(c''[d/\langle p,a\rangle],p,a)$

$load(\langle c,m\rangle,p,a,\langle c',m'\rangle) \Leftrightarrow \textbf{if } D(c,\langle p,a\rangle) \to c' = c \wedge m' = m \boxtimes ld(\langle c,m\rangle,p,a,\langle c',m'\rangle) \textbf{ fi}$

$ld(\langle c,m\rangle,p,a,\langle c',m'\rangle) \Leftrightarrow \exists c''.\ flush1(\langle c,m\rangle,p,\langle c'',m'\rangle) \wedge$

$\quad \textbf{if } \forall q.\neg D(c'',\langle q,a\rangle) \to c' = c''[m[a]/\langle p,a\rangle]$

$\quad \boxtimes\, \exists q.\ D(c'',\langle q,a\rangle) \wedge c' = c''[c''[\langle q,a\rangle]/\langle p,a\rangle] \textbf{ fi}$

$flush1(\langle c,m\rangle,p,\langle c',m'\rangle) \Leftrightarrow \exists a.\ D(c,\langle p,a\rangle) \wedge c' = c\backslash\langle p,a\rangle \wedge m' = m[c[\langle p,a\rangle]/a]$

$distr(c,p,a)[\langle q,b\rangle] = \textbf{if } b = a \to c[\langle p,a\rangle] \boxtimes c[\langle q,b\rangle] \textbf{ fi}$

$D(distr(c,p,a),\langle q,b\rangle) \Leftrightarrow D(c,\langle q,b\rangle)$

$co(c) \Leftrightarrow \forall a.\forall p.\forall q.\ D(c,\langle p,a\rangle) \wedge D(c,\langle q,a\rangle) \Rightarrow c[\langle p,a\rangle] = c[\langle q,a\rangle]$

The type variable π is used in places where Lampson's specification talks about the set P of *processors*. Apart from *distr*, `CCM` is a fairly direct translation of Lampson's imperative specification. Because the result (not the computation!) of *distr* is deterministic, *distr* has become a function rather than a relation on caches. It is defined implicitly by its behaviour w.r.t. application and definedness.

The predicate *co* specifies coherence. In order to prove that coherence is an invariant property of this system, we need the following lemmas:

$$
\begin{aligned}
D(c,\langle p,a\rangle) \wedge D(c,\langle q,a\rangle) \wedge co(c) &\Rightarrow c[\langle p,a\rangle] = c[\langle q,a\rangle]\\
co(c) &\Rightarrow co(c\backslash\langle p,a\rangle)\\
(\forall q.\ \neg D(c,\langle q,a\rangle)) \wedge co(c) &\Rightarrow co(c[d/\langle p,a\rangle])\\
D(c,\langle p,a\rangle) \wedge co(c) &\Rightarrow co(c[c[\langle p,a\rangle]/\langle q,a\rangle])\\
co(c) &\Rightarrow co(distr(c[d/\langle p,a\rangle],p,a))
\end{aligned}
$$

Preservation of coherence by *read'* and *write'* can now be proved in a single step.

$$co(c) \wedge read'(\langle c, m\rangle, p, a, \langle c', m'\rangle, d) \Rightarrow co(c') \quad (3)$$
$$co(c) \wedge write'(\langle c, m\rangle, p, a, d, \langle c', m'\rangle) \Rightarrow co(c') \quad (4)$$

Proving partial correctness of CCM w.r.t. SM involves the homomorphism φ:

```
I2 = SM + CCM +
     OPS φ: (π, α, δ)cache * (α, δ)map → (α, δ)map
     RULES
        co(c) ∧ D(c, ⟨p, a⟩) ⇒ φ(c, m)[a] = c[⟨p, a⟩]
        co(c) ∧ (∀p. ¬D(c, ⟨p, a⟩)) ⇒ φ(c, m)[a] = m[a]
```

Notice that removing the assumption $co(c)$ leads to an inconsistency: if both $D(c, \langle p, a\rangle)$ and $D(c, \langle q, a\rangle)$ hold, it would follow that $c[\langle p, a\rangle] = \varphi(c, m)[a] = c[\langle q, a\rangle]$, which is consistent only if $co(c)$ holds.

The following additional lemmas were required before φ could be shown to be a homomorphism.

$$co(c) \wedge co(c[d/\langle p, a\rangle]) \Rightarrow \varphi(c[d/\langle p, a\rangle], m)[b] = \textbf{if } b = a \rightarrow d \boxtimes \varphi(c, m)[b] \textbf{ fi}$$
$$co(c) \wedge b \neq a \Rightarrow \varphi(c, m[d/a])[b] = \varphi(c, m)[b]$$
$$co(c) \wedge b \neq a \Rightarrow \varphi(c \backslash \langle p, a\rangle, m)[b] = \varphi(c, m)[b]$$
$$co(c) \wedge b \neq a \Rightarrow \varphi(distr(c[d/\langle p, a\rangle], p, a), m)[b] = \varphi(c, m)[b]$$

The correctness statements for *read'* and *write'* differ slightly from those for the cache memory because we have to take coherence into account:

$$co(c) \wedge read'(\langle c, m\rangle, p, a, \langle c', m'\rangle, d) \Rightarrow read(\varphi(c, m), a, \varphi(c', m'), d)$$
$$co(c) \wedge write'(\langle c, m\rangle, p, a, d, \langle c', m'\rangle) \Rightarrow write(\varphi(c, m), a, d, \varphi(c', m'))$$

Lemmas (3) and (4) justify assuming $co(c)$. Remember that the free occurrence of p means correctness of *read'* and *write'* is proved for every processor p.

6 State-Based Data Types

The paradigm explored in this section is that of state-based systems. Their canonical model is that of an automaton. The term data type is in fact too narrow to describe the class of systems considered. Automata can model arbitrary algorithms. One of the examples we consider, mutual exclusion, contains very little data but a lot of concurrency and distribution. Thus the term processes is actually more appropriate.

The following subsection introduces a specific model for distributed systems, input/output automata. They were chosen because they cover both the encapsulation and the concurrency aspect and come with a well developed theory of refinement which is very close to the one for applicative data types.

6.1 Input/Output Automata

Input/Output automata were introduced by Lynch and Tuttle [22] for modelling distributed systems. We review only the very basics of the approach. In particular we omit any features dealing with fair computations and restrict ourselves to partial correctness, i.e. safety properties. A complete description of I/O automata can be found in [23].

The interface to an I/O automaton is called an ***action signature*** which is a set Σ partitioned into *input* actions $in(\Sigma)$, *output* actions $out(\Sigma)$, and *internal* actions $int(\Sigma)$. Output and internal actions are locally controlled, whereas input actions may occur at any point. The union of input and output actions is called *external* actions. A collection of action signatures is called ***privacy respecting*** if the internal actions of each of them are disjoint from the actions of all others.

An I/O automaton A consists of

- an action signature $sig(A)$,
- a set of states $states(A)$
- a set of start states $start(A) \subseteq states(A)$, and
- a transition relation $s \xrightarrow{\pi}_A s'$, where $s, s' \in states(A)$ and $\pi \in sig(A)$.

In particular we assume that I/O automata are ***input-enabled***: for every state s and input action π there is a state s' with $s \xrightarrow{\pi}_A s'$. To simplify some of the definitions, we further assume that if $\pi \notin sig(A)$, $s \xrightarrow{\pi}_A s'$ holds iff $s = s'$. This convention extends to the specifications in later sections were such trivial transitions are left implicit.

If $\gamma = \pi_1 \ldots \pi_n \in sig(A)^*$ and $s_i \xrightarrow{\pi_i}_A s_{i+1}$ we write $s_1 \xrightarrow{\gamma}_A s_{n+1}$. Given a sequence γ and some set S, $\gamma|S$ denotes the restriction of γ to S obtained by deleting all elements from γ which are not in S.

Concurrency is modelled by the composition of automata. A countable collection Σ_i, $i \in I$, of action signatures is called ***compatible*** if it is privacy respecting and output signatures are pairwise disjoint. Their ***composition*** $\Sigma = \prod_{i \in I} \Sigma_i$ is defined by

- $in(\Sigma) = \bigcup_{i \in I} in(\Sigma_i) - \bigcup_{i \in I} out(\Sigma_i)$,
- $out(\Sigma) = \bigcup_{i \in I} out(\Sigma_i)$, and
- $int(\Sigma) = \bigcup_{i \in I} int(\Sigma_i)$.

The composition $P = \prod_{i \in I} A_i$ of a countable set of I/O automata A_i, $i \in I$, with compatible action signatures is defined by [6]

- $sig(P) = \prod_{i \in I} \Sigma_i$,
- $states(P) = \prod_{i \in I} states(A_i)$,
- $start(P) = \prod_{i \in I} start(A_i)$, and
- $s \xrightarrow{\pi}_P s'$ iff $s(i) \xrightarrow{\pi}_{A_i} s'(i)$ holds for all $i \in I$.

[6] $states(P)$ and $start(P)$ are defined in terms of the ordinary cartesian product.

The distinction between hidden and visible sorts made in Section 5 is unnecessary for I/O automata because all hidden data is concealed in the state. On the other hand, the distinction between internal and external actions serves exactly the same purpose: internal actions are invisible to the environment, i.e. to automata running in parallel.

Implementations of one I/O automaton by another are defined in terms of traces of external, i.e. visible, actions. A sound proof method for implementations are again simulations, called *possibilities mappings* in [22,23]. Given two I/O automata C and A with the same external actions Σ_e, a relation $\sqsubseteq \subseteq states(C) \times states(A)$ is called an *(I/O automaton) simulation* if

- $\forall c \in start(C)\ \exists a \in start(A).\ c \sqsubseteq a$, and
- $\forall \pi \in sig(C).\ c \sqsubseteq a \wedge c \xrightarrow{\pi}_C c' \Rightarrow \exists \gamma \in sig(A)^*, a'.\ \gamma|\Sigma_e = \pi|\Sigma_e \wedge a \xrightarrow{\gamma}_A a' \wedge c' \sqsubseteq a'$.

Soundness of simulations w.r.t. a trace-based definition of implementation is proved in [22]. However, simulations are not complete, as shown in [25] and Section 7. For a detailed treatment of completeness see Merritt [25].

In the case studies below the situation is somewhat simplified: any state of A is a start state, $\sqsubseteq$ is a total function on reachable states of C, called φ, and A does not have any internal actions. Then φ is a simulation if

$$\forall \pi \in sig(C).\ c \xrightarrow{\pi}_C c' \Rightarrow \varphi(c) \xrightarrow{\pi}_A \varphi(c').$$

This is the usual definition of an automaton homomorphism.

6.2 Simple Memory

The interface of the simple memory changes considerably when going to a state-based model. The reason is that in an applicative context, passing a parameter to an operation and receiving the return value is an atomic action insofar that no interference is possible. In a state-based model, input and output have to be separated because they constitute independent communications. Hence *read* is split into $read_A(a)$, the environment's request for the datum stored at address a, and $read_D(d)$, the memory's response to that request. Thus $read_D(d)$ fulfills two purposes: it returns the requested datum d and tells the environment that the memory is again "enabled", i.e. further requests can be dealt with. Since writing to memory does not produce any output, an explicit acknowledgement is introduced. Hence there are two further actions: $write(a, d)$, which does the obvious thing, and *written*, which tells the environment that the previous *write* action has been completed successfully. Obviously $read_A$ and *write* are input and $read_D$ and *written* output actions of the memory module.

The introduction of explicit acknowledgement actions is symptomatic of the fact that the memory module is not intended to work properly in any arbitrary environment but only if a certain protocol is followed. Acknowledgement actions are means of establishing the required protocol. In our case the protocol requires that the action trace conforms to the following regular expression:

$$((read_A\ read_D)\ |\ (write\ written))^* \qquad (5)$$

This means the memory can only deal with one read or write request at a time. If the environment issues two consecutive read's without waiting for an answer to the first one, the resulting behaviour is not defined. The following specification makes these informal considerations precise.

```
Acts = SORTS (α,δ)action
       OPS read_A : α → (α,δ)action
           read_D : δ → (α,δ)action
           write : α * δ → (α,δ)action
           written : (α,δ)action

SMIO = Map + Acts +
       SORTS (α)cntrl,
             (α,δ)state = ((α)cntrl * (α,δ)map)pair
       OPS id, ack : (α)cntrl
           rd : α → (α)cntrl
           <_,_,_> : (α,δ)state * (α,δ)action * (α,δ)state → form
       RULES
           <⟨id,m⟩, read_A(a), ⟨s',m'⟩> ⇔ s' = rd(a) ∧ m' = m
           <⟨rd(a),m⟩, read_D(d), ⟨s',m'⟩> ⇔ d = m[a] ∧ s' = id ∧ m' = m
           <⟨id,m⟩, write(a,d), ⟨s',m'⟩> ⇔ s' = ack ∧ m' = m[d/a]
           <⟨ack,m⟩, written, ⟨s',m'⟩> ⇔ s' = id ∧ m' = m
```

The state of the I/O automaton is a pair of a control state $(\alpha)cntrl$ and a memory $(\alpha,\delta)map$. The control state enforces the right sequence of events, the memory contains the data. The predicate $<\langle s,m\rangle,\pi,\langle s',m'\rangle>$ is a linear form of $\langle s,m\rangle \xrightarrow{\pi} \langle s',m'\rangle$.

Notice that SMIO specifies the transition relation only partially. For example $<\langle rd(a),m\rangle, read_A(b), \langle s',m'\rangle>$ can be neither proved nor disproved. The reason is that issuing a second request $read_A(b)$, while the automaton has not yet answered $read_A(a)$, violates protocol (5). Thus the specification needs to say nothing about it.

Looking at the specification of *write*, one may wonder why *written* is necessary. The effect of *write* is instantaneous and the automaton could have gone back into the idle state immediately, ready for the next request. The inclusion of *written* was a conscious design decision, anticipating that refinements might take rather longer to carry out a *write*. In that case further requests could interrupt a sequence of internal actions completing the *write*. That is in fact what happens in the next refinement step.

6.3 Cache Memory

The I/O automaton implementation of the cache memory is more complex than Lampson's specification. It consists of two separate automata in charge of the cache and the memory respectively. Figure 2 shows their interconnection. The direction of the arrows indicates whether an action should be considered input or output with respect to a particular automaton. The environment communicates only with the cache. If possible, all read and write requests are satisfied immediately. Only if an address is not in the cache, does the latter communicate with the memory.

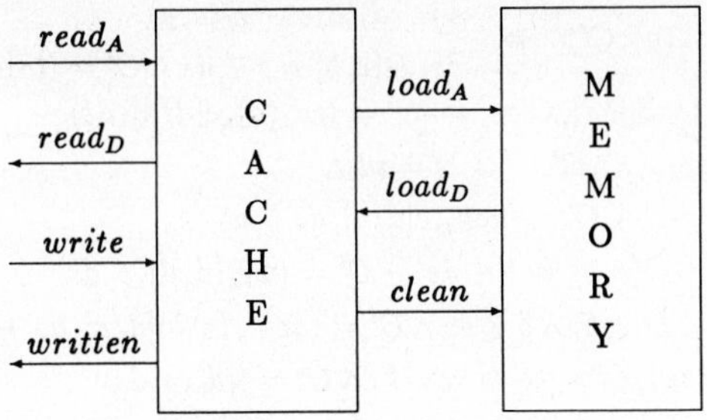

Figure 2: Cache Memory I/O Automaton

Data is loaded into the cache via $load_A/load_D$ and written back via *clean*, all of which are internal actions.

```
CMActs = Acts +
```

$$\begin{aligned} \texttt{OPS}\ & load_A : \alpha \rightarrow (\alpha,\delta)action \\ & load_D : \delta \rightarrow (\alpha,\delta)action \\ & clean : \alpha * \delta \rightarrow (\alpha,\delta)action \end{aligned}$$

In addition we need the following partial specification of sets:

```
Set = FOLE +
```

$$\begin{aligned} & \texttt{SORTS}\ (\alpha)set \\ & \texttt{OPS}\ \_ \in \_ : \alpha * (\alpha)set \rightarrow form \\ & \qquad \_ + \_, \_ - \_ : (\alpha)set * \alpha \rightarrow (\alpha)set \\ & \texttt{RULES} \\ & \qquad x \in (s+y) \ \Leftrightarrow\ x \in s \vee x = y \\ & \qquad x \in (s-y) \ \Leftrightarrow\ x \in s \wedge x \neq y \\ & \qquad s = t \ \Leftrightarrow\ \forall x.\, x \in s \Leftrightarrow x \in t \end{aligned}$$

The last law, known as set extensionality, is only used in the section on mutual exclusion.

An now, the cache automaton:

```
CIO = Map + Set + CMActs +
```

$$\begin{aligned} & \texttt{SORTS}\ (\alpha,\delta)ccntrl, \\ & \qquad (\alpha,\delta)cstate = ((\alpha,\delta)ccntrl, (\alpha,\delta)map, (\alpha)set)triple \\ & \texttt{OPS}\ id_c, ack_c : (\alpha,\delta)ccntrl \\ & \qquad rd_c, ld_c : \alpha \rightarrow (\alpha,\delta)ccntrl \\ & \qquad wr_c : \alpha * \delta \rightarrow (\alpha,\delta)ccntrl \\ & \qquad <\_,\_,\_> : (\alpha,\delta)cstate * (\alpha,\delta)action * (\alpha,\delta)cstate \rightarrow form \\ & \texttt{RULES} \\ & \qquad <\langle s,c,ds\rangle, read_A(a), C'> \ \Leftrightarrow\ s = id_c \wedge C' = \langle rd_c(a), c, ds\rangle \\ & \qquad <\langle s,c,ds\rangle, read_D(d), C'> \ \Leftrightarrow\ \exists a.\ s = rd_c(a) \wedge D(c,a) \wedge d = c[a] \wedge C' = \langle id_c, c, ds\rangle \end{aligned}$$

$$<\langle s,c,ds\rangle, load_A(a), C'> \;\Leftrightarrow\; \begin{array}{l} s = rd_c(a) \wedge \neg D(c,a) \wedge \\ \exists b.\ D(c,b) \wedge b \notin ds \wedge C' = \langle ld(a), c\backslash b, ds\rangle \end{array}$$

$$<\langle ld(a),c,ds\rangle, load_D(d), C'> \;\Leftrightarrow\; C' = \langle rd_c(a), c[d/a], ds\rangle$$

$$\begin{array}{l} <\langle s,c,ds\rangle, write(a,d), C'> \;\Leftrightarrow\; s = id_c \wedge \\ \quad \textbf{if } D(c,a) \rightarrow C' = \langle ack_c, c[d/a], ds + a\rangle \\ \quad \boxtimes \textbf{ if } \forall b.\ D(c,b) \Rightarrow b \in ds \rightarrow C' = \langle wr_c(a,d), c, ds\rangle \\ \quad\quad \boxtimes\ \exists b.\ D(c,b) \wedge b \notin ds \wedge C' = \langle ack_c, (c\backslash b)[d/a], ds + a\rangle \textbf{ fi fi} \end{array}$$

$$<\langle s,c,ds\rangle, written, C'> \;\Leftrightarrow\; s = ack_c \wedge C' = \langle id_c, c, ds\rangle$$

$$\begin{array}{l} <\langle s,c,ds\rangle, clean(a,d), C'> \;\Leftrightarrow\; D(c,a) \wedge d = c[a] \wedge a \in ds \wedge \\ \quad ((s = id_c \wedge C' = \langle id_c, c, ds - a\rangle) \vee \\ \quad ((\exists b.\ s = rd_c(b) \wedge \neg D(c,b)) \wedge (\forall b.\ D(c,b) \Rightarrow b \in ds) \wedge C' = \langle s, c, ds - a\rangle) \vee \\ \quad (\exists b,e.\ s = wr_c(b,e) \wedge C' = \langle ack_c, (c\backslash a)[b/e], ds - a + b\rangle)) \end{array}$$

The state of the cache is a triple: a control state, a cache, and a set of "dirty" addresses. An address is termed dirty if it maps to different data in cache and memory. In that case the cache contains the correct datum which must be written back to memory before the address is overwritten. Keeping track of which cache addresses are dirty reduces communication between memory and cache: clean addresses can be overwritten because they are associated with the right datum in memory.

The transitions under $read_A$, $read_D$ and *written* are straightforward. The $load_A(a)$ action is triggered by $read_A(a)$ in case a is not in the cache. The action $write(a,d)$ can lead to three different responses: if a is in the cache, its contents is overwritten immediately; if it is not in the cache, but there is a clean address b, b is deleted from the cache and (a,d) is added instead. In the worst case, a is not in the cache and all cache addresses are dirty. This prompts the automaton to go into the state $wr_c(a,d)$, which forces a *clean* action. The action $clean(a,d)$ is triggered by the presence of a dirty address a in the cache. It can occur in three circumstances: spontaneously, if the automaton is currently idle, or when trying to read or write a new address while all cache addresses are dirty.

The alert reader will have spotted that `CIO` does not specify an I/O automaton because the transition relation is not input-enabled: the specification of $<\langle s,c,ds\rangle, read_A(a), C'>$ says that the input action $read_A$ can only occur if the automaton is in the idle state. Why did we not write $<\langle id_c,c,ds\rangle, read_A(a), C'>$ instead, just as in `SMIO`, specifying a partial transition relation? Because we would not have arrived at an implementation of `SMIO`. The reason for this is rather subtle. If $read_A$ occurs when the cache is not in state id_c, it may be thrown into an arbitrary state, including one which does not satisfy the invariant relating dirty set, cache, and memory (see `Inv` below). But in those states the cache memory stops to behave like a simple memory: it may for example lose data.

This problem is a symptom of the fact that we try to implement a system that is only supposed to work in certain environments, namely those conforming to the protocol (5). A simple solution is to internalize the environment assumptions by adding the environment as a separate I/O automaton to the original specification. Refinement steps would change the memory but not the environment module. One could then show as a lemma that the cache, which is directly driven by the environment, is always in state id_c when a read request arrives.

The memory automaton is much simpler than the cache and bears a strong resemblance to `SMIO`.

MIO = CMActs +

SORTS $(\alpha)mcntrl$,

$(\alpha,\delta)mstate = ((\alpha)mcntrl, (\alpha,\delta)map)pair$

OPS $id_m : (\alpha)mcntrl$

$ld_m : \alpha \rightarrow (\alpha)mcntrl$

$<\_,\_,\_> : (\alpha,\delta)mstate * (\alpha,\delta)action * (\alpha,\delta)mstate \rightarrow form$

RULES

$$<\langle id_m, m\rangle, load_A(a), m'> \Leftrightarrow m' = \langle ld_m(a), m\rangle$$

$$<\langle s, m\rangle, load_D(d), m'> \Leftrightarrow \exists a.\ s = ld_m(a) \wedge d = m[a] \wedge m' = \langle id_m, m\rangle$$

$$<\langle id_m, m\rangle, clean(a,d), m'> \Leftrightarrow m' = \langle id_m, m[a/d]\rangle$$

In contrast to MIO there is no acknowledgement action corresponding to *written*. At this stage of the development it is not necessary because *clean* happens instantaneously. Further refinement steps may force the addition of such an acknowledgement action, but for the time being we stay with the simpler model.

The complete cache-memory automaton is the composition of CIO and MIO:

CMIO = CIO + MIO +

SORTS $(\alpha,\delta)cmstate = ((\alpha,\delta)cstate, (\alpha,\delta)mstate)pair$

OPS $\ll\_,\_,\_\gg : (\alpha,\delta)cmstate * (\alpha,\delta)action * (\alpha,\delta)cmstate \rightarrow form$

RULES

$$\ll\langle c, m\rangle, \pi, \langle c', m'\rangle\gg \Leftrightarrow <c, \pi, c'> \wedge <m, \pi, m'>$$

In order to prove correctness some further definitions had to be introduced.

Inv = CMIO +

OPS $inv : (\alpha,\delta)cstate * (\alpha,\delta)mstate \rightarrow form$

$con : (\alpha,\delta)map * (\alpha)set * (\alpha,\delta)map \rightarrow form$

$f : (\alpha,\delta)ccntrl \rightarrow (\alpha)mcntrl$

RULES

$$inv(\langle s, c, ds\rangle, \langle t, m\rangle) \Leftrightarrow con(c, ds, m) \wedge (\forall a.\ s = ld_c(a) \Rightarrow \neg D(c,a)) \wedge t = f(s)$$

$$con(c, ds, m) \Leftrightarrow \forall a.\ D(c,a) \wedge a \notin ds \Rightarrow c[a] = m[a]$$

$$f(id_c) = f(rd_c(a)) = f(wr_c(a,d)) = f(ack_c) = id_m,\ f(ld_c(a)) = ld_m(a)$$

The invariant relates the states of the cache and the memory automata and consists of three parts. The most important one, *con*, characterizes clean addresses: if a cache address is not in the dirty set, it is mapped to the same datum by both cache and memory. The second conjunct asserts that the cache automaton is in the load state only if an address isn't in the cache. The last one, $t = f(s)$, asserts that the memory automaton's control state is a particular function of the cache automaton's control state. Start states of CMIO are identified with those meeting the invariant.

The following lemmas show how one of the invariants is preserved under manipulations of the cache and the dirty set.

$$con(c, ds, m) \Rightarrow con(c[d/a], ds + a, m)$$

$$con(c, ds, m) \Rightarrow con(c \backslash a, ds - a, m)$$

$$\begin{aligned} con(c,ds,m) &\Rightarrow con(c\backslash a,ds,m) \\ \neg D(c,a)\wedge con(c,ds,m) &\Rightarrow con(c[m[a]/a],ds,m) \\ D(c,a)\wedge con(c,ds,m) &\Rightarrow con(c,ds-a,m[c[a]/a]) \\ D(c,a)\wedge con(c,ds,m) &\Rightarrow con(c\backslash a,ds-a,m[c[a]/a]) \end{aligned}$$

They enable us to prove that **inv** is in fact invariant:

$$inv(c,m)\wedge \ll\langle c,m\rangle,\pi,\langle c',m'\rangle\gg \;\Rightarrow\; inv(c',m')$$

Finally we come to the homomorphisms mapping concrete to abstract states. Because the state of the simple memory automaton is a pair, two separate functions are specified, one for each component.

Hom = SMIO + Inv +

OPS $\varphi_s : (\alpha,\delta)ccntrl \rightarrow (\alpha)cntrl$

$\varphi_m : (\alpha,\delta)ccntrl * (\alpha,\delta)map * (\alpha,\delta)map \rightarrow (\alpha,\delta)map$

$\varphi : (\alpha,\delta)map * (\alpha,\delta)map \rightarrow (\alpha,\delta)map$

RULES

$\varphi_s(id_c) = id,\ \varphi_s(rd_c(a)) = \varphi_s(ld_c(a)) = rd(a),\ \varphi_s(wr_c(a,d)) = \varphi_s(ack_c) = ack$

$\varphi_m(id_c,c,m) = \varphi_m(rd_c(a),c,m) = \varphi_m(ld_c(a),c,m) = \varphi_m(ack_c,c,m) = \varphi(c,m)$

$\varphi_m(wr_c(a,d),c,m) = \varphi(c[d/a],m)$

$\varphi(c,m)[a] \;=\; \textbf{if } D(c,a)\rightarrow c[a] \boxtimes m[a] \textbf{ fi}$

With the help of two further lemmas

$$\begin{gathered} \varphi(c[d/a],m) = \varphi(c,m)[d/a] \\ con(c,ds,m)\wedge D(c,a)\wedge a\notin ds \;\Rightarrow\; \varphi(c\backslash a,m) = \varphi(c,m) \end{gathered}$$

the main theorem, mapping CMIO to SMIO, can be proved:

$$\begin{aligned} &inv(\langle s,c,ds\rangle,\langle t,m\rangle)\;\wedge\;\ll\langle\langle s,c,ds\rangle,\langle t,m\rangle\rangle,\pi,\langle\langle s',c',ds'\rangle,\langle t',m'\rangle\rangle\gg \\ &\quad\Rightarrow\; <\langle\varphi_s(s),\varphi_m(s,c,m)\rangle,\pi,\langle\varphi_s(s'),\varphi_m(s',c',m')\rangle> \end{aligned}$$

There are two points in the axiomatizations that have been swept under the carpet: equality and exhaustion axioms. More precisely, the specifications also need to state that the actions and states defined are the only ones, and which states and actions are equal or unequal. The former is simply a disjunction, for example $s = id_m \vee \exists a.s = ld_m(a)$ for s of type $(\alpha)mcntrl$. However, stating all possible equalities and inequalities between n constructors requires n^2 axioms, which the reader is spared.

6.4 Mutual Exclusion

A development of coherent caches in the I/O automaton model is considerably more complicated than the applicative version in Section 5.5 because one cannot ignore interference any longer. In fact, it is not even clear in what sense a distributed version of Lampson's original specification implements the simple memory. For those reasons our last example focusses on an archetypical problem in distributed computing: mutual exclusion. Any implementation of the coherent cache memory scheme must contain a solution to this problem because the memory is a centralized resource shared by all processors.

In our formulation of the mutual exclusion problem there are four kinds of actions, indexed by some set ι, the customers to be served: $req(i)$, $do(i)$ and $rel(i)$ indicate the request, the usage and the release of the service by customer i; $grant(i)$ grants the service to customer i.

MutexActs = SORTS $(\iota)action$

OPS $req, grant, do, rel : \iota \rightarrow (\iota)action$

The top level specification defines all legal sequences of these actions. All four actions are output actions of Mutex.

Mutex = Set + MutexActs +

SORTS $(\iota)mcntrl$,

$(\iota)mstate = ((\iota)mcntrl, (\iota)set)pair$

OPS $idle : (\iota)mcntrl$

$active : \iota \rightarrow (\iota)mcntrl$

$<\_,\_,\_> : (\iota)mstate * (\iota)action * (\iota)mstate \rightarrow form$

RULES

$$<\langle a,w\rangle, req(i), \langle a',w'\rangle> \;\Leftrightarrow\; i \notin w \wedge a \neq active(i) \wedge a' = a \wedge w' = w + i$$

$$<\langle a,w\rangle, grant(i), \langle a',w'\rangle> \;\Leftrightarrow\; a = idle \wedge i \in w \wedge a' = active(i) \wedge w' = w - i$$

$$<\langle a,w\rangle, do(i), \langle a',w'\rangle> \;\Leftrightarrow\; a = active(i) \wedge a' = a \wedge w' = w$$

$$<\langle a,w\rangle, rel(i), \langle a',w'\rangle> \;\Leftrightarrow\; a = active(i) \wedge a' = idle \wedge w' = w$$

The state of the automaton consists of a control state which is either idle or records the currently active customer, and a set of waiting customers. The specification is extremely liberal in that either individual processes may get stuck on the waiting list because of an unfair selection strategy, or one customer may grab the service, never to release it again.

The distributed implementation of Mutex involves busy waiting. Each customer i is modelled by the finite state I/O automaton in Figure 3. The up and down arrows indicate output and input actions respectively. In addition to the $req(i)$ action, which just announces the intention of

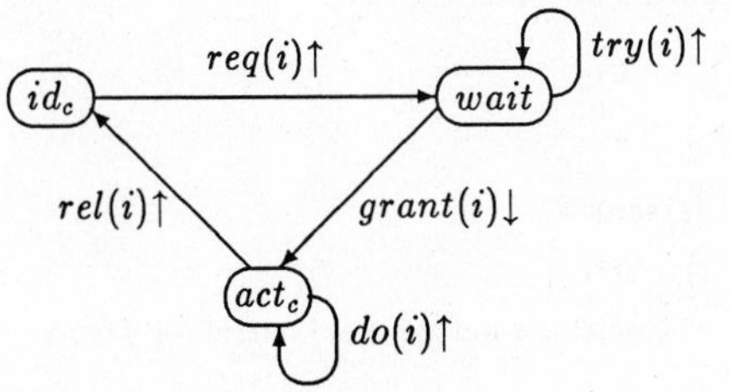

Figure 3: I/O Automaton for Customer i

grabbing the service, there is a new action $try(i)$ which is repeatedly performed until the service is granted.

MutexActs1 = MutexActs + OPS $try : \iota \rightarrow (\iota)action$

The algebraic specification Customers embodies the composition of all customer automata into one. The state is a map from customers to control states.

Customers = MutexActs1 +

SORTS $ccntrl$

OPS $id_c, wait, act_c : ccntrl$

$<\_,\_,\_> : (\iota, ccntrl)map * action * (\iota, ccntrl)map \rightarrow form$

RULES

$$<c, req(i), c'> \ \Leftrightarrow\ c[i] = id_c \wedge c' = c[wait/i]$$
$$<c, try(i), c'> \ \Leftrightarrow\ c[i] = wait \wedge c' = c$$
$$c[i] = wait \ \Rightarrow\ <c, grant(i), c'> \ \Leftrightarrow\ c' = c[act_c/i]$$
$$<c, do(i), c'> \ \Leftrightarrow\ c[i] = act_c \wedge c' = c$$
$$<c, rel(i), c'> \ \Leftrightarrow\ c[i] = act_c \wedge c' = c[id_c/i]$$

The automaton granting access to the service is depicted in Figure 4. The diagram is slightly

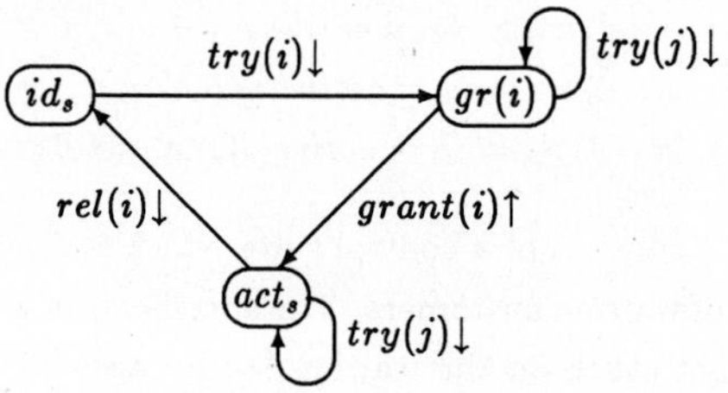

Figure 4: I/O Automaton Granting Access

misleading as there is a state $gr(i)$ for each customer i.

The corresponding algebraic specification is

Service = MutexActs1 +

SORTS $(\iota)scntrl$

OPS $id_s, act_s : (\iota)scntrl$

$gr : \iota \rightarrow (\iota)scntrl$

$<\_,\_,\_> : (\iota)scntrl * action * (\iota)scntrl \rightarrow form$

RULES

$$<id_s, try(i), s'> \ \Leftrightarrow\ s' = gr(i)$$
$$<gr(i), try(j), s'> \ \Leftrightarrow\ s' = gr(i)$$
$$<act_s, try(j), s'> \ \Leftrightarrow\ s' = act_s$$

$$<s, grant(i), s'> \;\Leftrightarrow\; s = gr(i) \wedge s' = act_s$$
$$<act_s, rel(i), s'> \;\Leftrightarrow\; s' = id_s$$
$$<s, req(i), s'> \;\Leftrightarrow\; s' = s$$
$$<s, do(i), s'> \;\Leftrightarrow\; s' = s$$

The complete cache-memory automaton is the composition of `Customers` and `Service`:

```
Mutex1 = Customers + Service +
```
SORTS $(\iota)state = ((\iota, ccntrl)map, (\iota)scntrl)pair$

OPS $\ll\_,\_,\_\gg : (\iota)state * (\iota)action * (\iota)state \rightarrow form$

RULES

$$\ll\langle c, s\rangle, \pi, \langle c', s'\rangle\gg \;\Leftrightarrow\; <c, \pi, c'> \wedge <s, \pi, s'>$$

The correctness of `Mutex1` depends on a number of invariants:

```
Inv = Mutex1 +
```
OPS $inv : (\iota, ccntrl)map * (\iota)scntrl \rightarrow form$

$con : (\iota, ccntrl)map \rightarrow form$

RULES

$$inv(c, s) \;\Leftrightarrow\; con(c) \wedge (\forall i.\; s = gr(i) \Rightarrow c[i] = wait) \wedge (s \neq act_s \Rightarrow \forall i. c[i] \neq act_c)$$
$$con(c) \;\Leftrightarrow\; \forall i, j.\; c[i] = act_c \wedge c[j] = act_c \Rightarrow i = j$$

Consistency (*con*) says that no two customers can be active at any one time. The other two conjuncts of the invariant assert that if the service is about to be granted to customer i, he must be waiting for it, and that no customer can be active if the service isn't.

With the help of the following simple lemmas,

$$con(c) \wedge s \neq act_c \;\Rightarrow\; con(c[s/i])$$
$$(\forall i.\; c[i] \neq act_c) \;\Rightarrow\; con(c[act_c/i])$$
$$con(c) \wedge c[i] = act_c \;\Rightarrow\; c[j] \neq act_c \Leftrightarrow j \neq i$$

invariance of *inv* is readily established:

$$inv(c, s) \wedge \ll\langle c, s\rangle, \pi, \langle c', s'\rangle\gg \;\Rightarrow\; inv(c', s')$$

The need for these invariants becomes apparent during the correctness proof of `Mutex1` based on the two homomorphisms φ_c and φ_w which produce the two components of the abstract state, the control state and the waiting set respectively.

```
Hom = Mutex + Mutex1 +
```
OPS $\varphi_c : (\iota, ccntrl)map \rightarrow (\iota)mcntrl$

$\varphi_w : (\iota, ccntrl)map \rightarrow (\iota)set$

RULES

$$i \in \varphi_w(c) \;\Leftrightarrow\; c[i] = wait$$
$$con(c) \wedge (\forall i. c[i] \neq act_c) \;\Rightarrow\; \varphi_c(c) = idle$$
$$con(c) \wedge c[i] = act_c \;\Rightarrow\; \varphi_c(c) = active(i)$$

The two lemmas

$$con(c) \Rightarrow \varphi_c(c) = active(i) \Leftrightarrow c[i] = act_c$$

$$c[i] \neq act_c \wedge s \neq act_c \wedge con(c) \Rightarrow \varphi_c(c[s/i]) = \varphi_c(c)$$

finally enable us to prove

$$inv(c,s) \wedge \ll\langle c,s\rangle, \pi, \langle c',s'\rangle\gg \Rightarrow <\langle\varphi_s(c),\varphi_w(c)\rangle, \pi, \langle\varphi_s(c'),\varphi_w(c')\rangle>$$

7 Applicative versus State-Based

Whether a data type should be specified as applicative or state-based is a design decision. It is influenced by the anticipated pattern of usage, the environment of the eventual implementation, resource and reliability considerations. Certain implementation languages may not offer any choice, one way or the other. If there is a choice as in CLU or Standard ML, applicative types can cause excessive copying whereas state-based types bring the dangers of changes by side effect with them. Whatever the eventual choice, it must be part of the specification because it affects whether some implementation is correct or not.

A comparison of applicative and state-based formalisms needs a common framework. We use an imperative language where procedures can have side effects. Data type operations are procedures $p(s,\ldots)$, where s is the data type state that may change as a side effect. The other arguments are of visible type. This set up corresponds to the automaton-based formalism of Section 6 *provided* data type states cannot be copied (duplicated). Otherwise we are in the applicative realm of Section 5: the effect of an operation $p(s,\ldots)$ that returns a new hidden value s' can be modelled by $s' := s; p(s',\ldots)$.

As an example we look at the data type of sets with an operation *pick*. The specification A represents sets by lists; $pick(s)$ returns an arbitrary element of s and removes all its occurrences from s, changing s by side effect. The implementation C is identical to A except that it always *pick*s the first element from the list. The only assumption about the other operations is that any permutation of a list that A can generate can be generated by C.

If sets cannot be copied, A and C are behaviourally indistinguishable. If sets can be copied, and s_1 and s_2 are two different copies of the same set, $pick(s_1)$ and $pick(s_2)$ will result in the same elements being picked under interpretation C, but not necessarily so under A. C is still an implementation of A, but not vice versa. A formal demonstration of implementation or non-implementation requires a translation to applicative and automaton-based formalisms which is left to the readers intuition.

In the applicative world, C implements A because the identity relation on lists is a simulation between C and A. A does not implement C because one can easily show that there doesn't exists a simulation in the other direction. In the state-based view, simulations are still a sound implementation criterion (which is why C still implements A) but not a complete one (because there is no simulation between A and C). The issue of completeness is resolved in [15] and [25] by the introduction of the dual of simulation called an "upwards simulation" and a "prophecy mapping" respectively. It can be shown that the relation that pairs two lists iff they contain the same set of elements is an upwards simulation. Thus A also implements C.

A different method of obtaining completeness in the state-based case was studied by Abadi and Lamport [1]. They restrict their simulations to be functions, i.e. homomorphisms, but allow the introduction of auxiliary "history" and "prophecy" variables in the implementation during the correctness proof.

References

[1] M. Abadi, L. Lamport: *The Existence of Refinement Mappings*, Proc. 3rd Symposium Logic in Computer Science (1988), 165-175.

[2] R.S. Boyer, J S. Moore: *A Computational Logic Handbook*, Academic Press (1988).

[3] M. Broy: *A Theory for Nondeterminism, Parallelism, Communication, and Concurrency*, Theoretical Computer Science 45 (1986), 1-61.

[4] M. Broy: *Extensional Behaviour of Concurrent, Nondeterministic, Communicating Systems*, in Control Flow and Data Flow: Concepts of Distributed Programming (M. Broy, ed.), Springer Verlag (1985).

[5] M. Broy, B. Möller, P. Pepper, M. Wirsing: *Algebraic Implementations Preserve Program Correctness*, Science of Computer Programming 7 (1986), 35-53.

[6] R. de Nicola, M.C.B. Hennessy: *Testing Equivalences for Processes*, Proc. 10th ICALP, LNCS 154 (1983), 548-560. Full version in Theoretical Computer Science 34 (1984), 83-133.

[7] E.W. Dijkstra: *A Disciplin of Programming*, Prentice-Hall (1976).

[8] H. Ehrig, B. Mahr: *Fundamentals of Algebraic Specification 1*, EATCS Monograph on Theoretical Computer Science, Springer Verlag (1985).

[9] K. Futatsugi, J.A. Goguen, J.-P. Jouannaud, J. Meseguer: *Principles of OBJ2*, Proc. 12th ACM Symposium on Principles of Programming Languages (1985), 52-66.

[10] S.J. Garland, J.V. Guttag: *An Overview of LP, The Larch Prover*, Proc. 3rd Intl. Conf. Rewriting Techniques and Applications, LNCS 355 (1989), 137-151.

[11] Michael J.C. Gordon: *HOL: A Proof Generating System for Higher-Order Logic*, in: Graham Birtwistle and P.A. Subrahmanyam, editors, VLSI Specification, Verification and Synthesis, Kluwer Academic Publishers (1988), 73-128.

[12] G. Hansoul: *Systemes Relationelles Et Algebres Multiformes*, Ph.D. Thesis, Université de Liege, 1979/80.

[13] R. Harper: *Introduction to Standard ML*, Report ECS-LFCS-86-14, Dept. of Comp. Sci., Univ. of Edinburgh, 1986.

[14] C.A.R. Hoare: *Proof of Correctness of Data Representation*, Acta Informatica 1 (1972), 271-281.

[15] J. He, C.A.R. Hoare, J.W. Sanders: *Data Refinement Refined*, Proc. 1st European Symposium on Programming, LNCS 213 (1986).

[16] M.C.B. Hennessy: *Powerdomains and Nondeterministic Recursive Definitions*, Proc. Intl. Symposium on Programming, LNCS 137 (1982), 178-193.

[17] M. Hennessy, R. Milner: *Algebraic Laws for Nondeterminism and Concurrency*, J. ACM Vol. 32, No. 1, January 1985, 137-161.

[18] C.B. Jones: *Systematic Software Development Using VDM*, Prentice-Hall International (1986).

[19] R. Kuiper: *Enforcing Nondeterminism via Linear Temporal Logic Specifications using Hiding*, Proc. Coll. on Temporal Logic and Specification, Altrincham, 1987, to appear in LNCS.

[20] B. Lampson: *Specifying Distributed Systems*, Proc. 1988 Marktoberdorf Summer School, Springer Verlag.

[21] B. Liskov, R. Atkinson, T. Blum, E. Moss, C. Schaffert, R. Scheifler, A. Snyder: *CLU Reference Manual*, LNCS 114 (1981).

[22] N.A. Lynch, M.R. Tuttle: *Hierarchical Correctness Proofs for Distributed Algorithms*, Proc. 6th ACM Symposium on Principles of Distributed Computing, Vancouver, August 1987, 137-151.

[23] N.A. Lynch, M.R. Tuttle: *An Introduction to Input/Output Automata*, Report MIT/LCS/TM-373, Lab. for Computer Science, MIT (1989), to appear in the CWI Quaterly, September 1989.

[24] T.S.E. Maibaum, Pauolo A.S. Veloso, M.R. Sadler: *A Theory of Abstract Data Types for Program Development: Bridging the Gap?*, Proc. TAPSOFT 1985, LNCS 186, 214-230.

[25] M. Merritt: *Completeness Theorems for Automata*, this volume.

[26] G. Nelson: *A Generalization of Dijkstra's Calculus*, Research Report 16, Digital Equipment Corporation, Systems Research Center, April 1987.

[27] T. Nipkow: *Nondeterministic Data Types: Models and Implementations*, Acta Informatica 22 (1986), 629-661.

[28] T. Nipkow: *Are Homomorphisms Sufficient for Behavioural Implementations of Deterministic and Nondeterministic Data Types?*, Proc. 4th Symposium on Theoretical Aspects of Computer Science, LNCS 247 (1987), 260-271.

[29] T. Nipkow: *Behavioural Implementations Concepts for Nondeterministic Data Types*, Ph.D. Thesis, Tech. Rep. UMCS-87-5-3, Dept. of Comp. Sci., The Univ. of Manchester, 1987.

[30] T. Nipkow: *Observing Nondeterministic Data Types*, Proc. 5th Workshop on Specification of Abstract Data Types (1987), LNCS 332, 170-183.

[31] T. Nipkow: *Equational Reasoning in Isabelle*, Science of Computer Programming 12 (1989), 123-149.

[32] T. Nipkow: *Term Rewriting and Beyond - Theorem Proving in Isabelle*, submitted for publication.

[33] D.M.R. Park: *Concurrency and Automata on Infinite Sequences*, LNCS 104 (1981).

[34] L.C. Paulson: *Logic and Computation*, Cambridge University Press (1987).

[35] L.C. Paulson: *Isabelle: The next 700 Theorem Provers*, in: P. Odifreddi (editor), *Logic and Computer Science*, Academic Press (1989), in press.

[36] L.C. Paulson: *The Foundation of a Generic Theorem Prover*, Journal of Automated Reasoning (1989), in press.

[37] O. Schoett: *Ein Modulkonzept in der Theorie Abstrakter Datentypen*, Report IfI-HH-B-81/81, Universität Hamburg, Fachbereich Informatik, 1981.

[38] O. Schoett: *Data Abstraction and the Correctness of Modular Programming*, Ph.D. Thesis, Tech. Rep. CST-42-87, Dept. of Comp. Sci., Univ. of Edinburgh, 1987.

[39] D.S. Scott, C.A. Gunter: *Semantic Domains*, to appear in Handbook of Theoretical Computer Science, North-Holland.

[40] R.J. Shoenfield: *Mathematical Logic*, Addison-Wesley (1967).

[41] M.B. Smyth: *Powerdomains*, Journal of Computer and System Science 2 (1978), 23-36.

[42] J.M. Spivey: *The Z Notation: A Reference Manual*, Prentice-Hall International (1989).

FROM TRACE SPECIFICATIONS TO PROCESS TERMS

Ernst-Rüdiger Olderog

FB 10 - Informatik, Universität Oldenburg
Ammerländer Heerstr. 114-118
2900 Oldenburg, Fed. Rep. Germany

Vakgroep Programmatuur, Universiteit van Amsterdam
Kruislaan 409, 1098 SJ Amsterdam, The Netherlands

ABSTRACT. We present an approach to the top-down construction of process terms from trace specifications. Process terms are built from operators of CCS, CSP and COSY, and denote labelled Petri nets. Trace specifications are first order formulas of Zwiers' trace logic and denote sets of finite communication sequences. The link between process terms and trace specifications is given by a new notion of process correctness which deals with both safety and liveness properties. The top-down construction proceeds by an application of compositional transformation rules which refine the given trace specification stepwise into a process term satisfying the safety and liveness requirements of the specification.

Key words: Concurrent processes, communication, CCS, CSP, COSY, Petri nets, specification, many-sorted first order logic, trace logic, process correctness, safety, liveness, externally deterministic, modified readiness semantics, top-down construction, transformations, mixed terms, Milner's scheduling problem.

CONTENTS

1. Introduction
2. Trace Logic
3. Process Terms
4. Process Correctness
5. Modified Readiness Semantics
6. Transformations on Mixed Terms
7. Process Construction
8. References

1. INTRODUCTION

In this paper we pesent a simple approach to the top-down construction of concurrent processes from specifications. A process is an object which can interact with its user by communication. In between two subsequent communications the process may engage in internal actions. These are not visible for the user, but as a result of such internal actions the process behaviour may appear nondeterministic to the user. Concurrency arises because there can be more than one user and inside the process more than one active subprocess. For the user(s) of a process its internal structure is irrelevant as long as it exhibits the desired communications behaviour.

In our approach the communication behaviour of a process is defined as a set of finite communication sequences that are possible between user and process. Such sequences are known as *histories* or *traces* [Ho 78]. Since traces are insensitive to intervening internal actions and concurrent process activities, this definiton achieves abstraction from both internal activity and concurrency. Note that our notion of trace differs from the one used by Mazurkiewicz [Ma 77]; there a trace is a certain partial order expressing concurrency.

As a specification language for trace sets we use a *many-sorted first-order predicate logic.* Since its main sort is "trace", it is called *trace logic* and its formulas are called *trace formulas* or *trace specifications.* Informal use of trace logic appears in a number of papers (e.g. [CHo 81, MC 81, Sn 85, Rm 87, WGS 87]). Precise syntax and semantics, however, is given only in [Zw 89]. We shall adopt Zwiers' proposal, but we need only a simplified version of it because we deal here with atomic communications instead of messages sent along channels.

As a description language for processes we use *process terms* built up from operators of CCS, CSP and COSY [Mi 80, Ho 85, LTS 79]. The semantics of process terms is given by labelled Petri nets. This enables us to exhibit all details about the internal process activity and the possible concurrency. We refer here to the operational net semantics of process terms defined and discussed in [Ol 88/89, Ol 89a].

The link between process terms and trace specifications is given by notion of *process correctness.* It is a relationship

P *sat* S

stating when a process term P *satisfies* or is *correct with respect to* a trace specification S. In most papers [CHo 81, MC 81, ZRE 85, Zw 89] trace formulas express only *safety properties* (cf. [OL 82]). In other words, P *sat* S if every trace of P satisfies the formula S. As a consequence, there exists a single process term which satisfies every trace specification with the same alphabet. Such a process term is called a *miracle* after Dijkstra [Di 76].

With miracles the task of *process construction*, i.e. given a trace formula S construct a process term P with P *sat* S, becomes trivial and meaningless. Therefore we shall be more demanding and use trace formulas to express also a simple type of *liveness property* (cf. [OL 82]). Essentially, P *sat* S requires the following:

* Safety: P may only engage in traces satisfying S.
* Liveness: P must engage in every trace satisfying S.

The terminology of "may" and "must" originates from [DH 88] but the details are different here. The liveness condition is due to [OH 86] and related to the idea of Misra and Chandy to use so-called *quiescent* infinite trace specifications to express liveness in the setting of asynchronous communication (see [Jo 87]). It implies that every process P satisfying a trace formula S is divergence free and *externally deterministic.* That is: in every run of the process the user has exactly the same possibilities of communication, no matter which actions the process has pursued internally. Thus in our approach trace formulas can specify only a subset of processes. We are interested in this subset because it has many applications and yields simple compositional transformation rules for process construction.

The concepts of "may" and "must" are clear intuitively, but not helpful for discovering such rules. To simplify this task, we develop a second, more abstract semantics for process terms and trace specifications. It is a *modified* version $\mathfrak{R}^*$ of the *readiness semantics* $\mathfrak{R}$ introduced in [OH 86]. For process terms, $\mathfrak{R}^*$ is defined by filtering out certain informations from the operational net semantics. Among these informations are pairs consisting of a trace and a so-called *ready set* [Ho 81, FLP 84]. Ready sets are used to explain the liveness requirement of process correctness P *sat* S.

In $\mathfrak{R}^*$ process correctness boils down to a *semantic equation* between P and S:

$$P \; sat \; S \quad \text{iff} \quad P \equiv S .$$

Moreover, $\mathfrak{R}^*$ has an equivalent *denotational* definition in the sense of Scott and Strachey [Sc 70, St 77, Ba 80]. This implies that $\mathfrak{R}^*$ is compositional with respect to the process operators and that recursion is dealt with by fixed point techniques. Therefore $\mathfrak{R}^*$ serves well as a stepping stone for developing compositional transformation rules for process construction.

Such a construction is presented as a sequence

$$\begin{array}{rl} S \equiv & Q_1 \\ & \equiv \\ & \vdots \\ & \equiv \\ & Q_n \equiv P \end{array}$$

of semantic equations where Q_1 is the given trace specification and Q_n is the constructed process term P. By the transitivity of $\equiv$, it follows $P \equiv S$ which means P *sat* S. Thus by construction, P satisfies the safety and liveness requirements of S. The terms Q_i in between are *mixed terms*, i.e. syntactic constructs mixing process terms with trace formulas. The idea of mixing programming notation (here represented by process terms) with specification parts (here represented by trace formulas) stems form the work of Dijkstra and Wirth on program development by stepwise refinement [Di 76, Wi 71].

The sequence of equations in the top-down construction is obtained by applying the principle of *transformational programming* as e.g. advocated in the Munich Project CIP [Bau 85, Bau 87]. Thus each equation $Q_i \equiv Q_{i+1}$ is justified by applying a transformation rule on mixed terms. We present a system of such transformation rules based on the modified readiness semantics $\mathfrak{R}^*$. Most rules are extremely simple. For example, parallel composition $P \parallel Q$ of terms P and Q is reflected by the logical conjunction of trace formulas. Only two process operators which can completely restructure the communication behaviour of a process need transformation rules which are difficult to apply. These operators are *hiding* and *renaming with aliasing*.

As an application, we use the transformation rules to construct two different process terms from a trace specification of a scheduling problem due to Milner [Mi 80, Mi 89]. Further applications can be found in [Ol 88/89].

2. TRACE LOGIC

We start from an infinite set Comm of unstructured *communications* with typical elements a, b. By a *communication alphabet* or simply *alphabet* we mean a finite subset of Comm. We let letters A, B range over alphabets. Syntax and semantics of trace logic we adopt from Zwiers [Zw 89]. It is a many-sorted predicate logic with the following sorts:

trace	(finite communication sequences)
nat	(natural numbers)
comm	(communications)
log	(logical values)

Trace logic then consists of sorted expressions built up from sorted constants, variables and operator symbols. For notational convenience, trace formulas count here as expressions of sort *log*.

All communications appear as constants of sort *trace* and *comm*, and all natural numbers $k \geq 0$ appear as constants of sort *nat*. The set Var of variables is partitioned into a set Var:*trace* of variables t of sort *trace* and a set Var:*nat* of variables n of sort *nat*. Among the trace variables there is a *distinguished trace variable* called h; it will be used in the definiton of trace *specification*. For all communication alphabets A and all communications a, b there are unary operator symbols $\cdot\restriction A$ and $\cdot[b/a]$ of sort *trace* —> *trace*. Further on, there are binary operator symbols $\cdot.\cdot$ of sort *trace* × *trace* —> *trace* and $\cdot\,[\,\cdot\,]$ of sort *trace* × *nat* —> *comm*, and a unary operator symbol $|\cdot|$ of sort *trace* —> *nat*. The remaining symbols used in trace logic are all standard.

Definition. The syntax of trace logic is given by a set

$$\text{Exp} = \text{Exp:}\textit{trace} \cup \text{Exp:}\textit{nat} \cup \text{Exp:}\textit{comm} \cup \text{Exp:}\textit{log}$$

of *expressions* ranged over by xe. The constituents of Exp are defined as follows.

(1) The set Exp:*trace* of *trace expressions* consists of all expressions te of the form

$$te ::= \varepsilon \mid a \mid t \mid te_1 . te_2 \mid te\restriction A \mid te[b/a]$$

where every trace variable t in te occurs within a subexpression of the form $te_0\restriction A$.

(2) The set Exp:*nat* of *natural number* consists of the following expressions ne:

$$ne ::= k \mid n \mid ne_1 + ne_2 \mid ne_1 * ne_2 \mid |te|$$

(3) The set Exp:*comm* of *communication expressions* consists of the following expressions ce:

$$ce ::= a \mid te[ne]$$

(4) The set Exp: *log* of *trace formulas* or *logical expressions* consists of the following expressions le:

$$le ::= \textit{true} \mid te_1 \leq te_2 \mid ne_1 \leq ne_2 \mid ce_1 = ce_2$$
$$\mid \neg\, le \mid le_1 \wedge le_2 \mid \exists t.\ le \mid \exists n.\ le \qquad \square$$

Let xe{te/t} denote the result of *substituting* the trace expression te for every free occurrence of the trace variable t in xe. Furthermore, let xe{b/a} denote the result of literally replacing every occurrence of the communication a in xe by b.

The *standard semantics* or *interpretation of trace logic* is introduced along the lines of

Tarski's semantic definition for predicate logic. It is a mapping

$$\mathfrak{I} : \text{Exp} \longrightarrow (\text{Env}_{\mathfrak{I}} \longrightarrow \text{DOM}_{\mathfrak{I}})$$

assigning a value to every expression with the help of so-called *environments*. These are mappings

$$\rho \in \text{Env}_{\mathfrak{I}} = \text{Var} \longrightarrow \text{DOM}_{\mathfrak{I}}$$

assigning values to the free variables in expressions. The semantic domain of $\mathfrak{I}$ is

$$\text{DOM}_{\mathfrak{I}} = \text{Comm}^* \cup \mathbb{N}_0 \cup \text{Comm} \cup \{\perp\} \cup \{\text{true, false}\},$$

and the environments ρ respect sorts, i.e. trace variables t get values in Comm^* and natural number variables n get values in $\mathbb{N}_0$.

Definition. With the above conventions the standard semantics $\mathfrak{I}$ of trace logic is defined as follows.

(1) *Semantics of trace expressions* yielding values in Comm^*:

$\mathfrak{I}[\![\varepsilon]\!](\rho) = \varepsilon$, the empty trace

$\mathfrak{I}[\![a]\!](\rho) = a$

$\mathfrak{I}[\![t]\!](\rho) = \rho(t)$

$\mathfrak{I}[\![te_1 \,.\, te_2]\!](\rho) = \mathfrak{I}[\![te_1]\!](\rho) \cdot_{\mathfrak{I}} \mathfrak{I}[\![te_2]\!](\rho)$, the *concatenation* of the traces

$\mathfrak{I}[\![te\!\upharpoonright\! A]\!](\rho) = \mathfrak{I}[\![te]\!](\rho) \upharpoonright_{\mathfrak{I}} A$, the *projection* onto A, i.e. with all communications outside A removed

$\mathfrak{I}[\![te[b/a]]\!](\rho) = \mathfrak{I}[\![te]\!](\rho)\,\{b/a\}$, i.e. every occurrence of a is *renamed* into b. Brackets [...] denote an unevaluated renaming operator and brackets {...} its evaluation.

(2) *Semantics of natural number expressions* yielding values in $\mathbb{N}_0$:

$\mathfrak{I}[\![k]\!](\rho) = k$ for $k \in \mathbb{N}_0$

$\mathfrak{I}[\![n]\!](\rho) = \rho(n)$

$\mathfrak{I}[\![|te|]\!](\rho) = |\mathfrak{I}[\![te]\!](\rho)|_{\mathfrak{I}}$, the *length* of the trace

Expressions $ne_1 + ne_2$ and $ne_1 * ne_2$ are interpreted as addition and multiplication.

(3) *Semantics of communication expressions* yielding values in $\text{Comm} \cup \{\perp\}$:

$\mathfrak{I}[\![a]\!](\rho) = a$

$\mathfrak{I}[\![te[ne]]\!](\rho) = \mathfrak{I}[\![te]\!](\rho)[\mathfrak{I}[\![ne]\!](\rho)]_{\mathfrak{I}}$, the *selection* of the $\mathfrak{I}[\![ne]\!](\rho)$-th element of the trace $\mathfrak{I}[\![ne]\!](\rho)$ if it exists and $\perp$ otherwise

(4) *Semantics of trace formulas* yielding values in {true, false}:

$\mathfrak{I}[\![\mathit{true}]\!](\rho) = \text{true}$

$\mathfrak{I}[\![te_1 \le te_2]\!](\rho) = (\mathfrak{I}[\![te_1]\!](\rho) \le_{\mathfrak{I}} \mathfrak{I}[\![te_2]\!](\rho))$, the *prefix* relation on Comm^*

$\mathfrak{I}[\![ne_1 \le ne_2]\!](\rho) = (\mathfrak{I}[\![ne_1]\!](\rho) \le_{\mathfrak{I}} \mathfrak{I}[\![ne_2]\!](\rho))$, the standard ordering relation on $\mathbb{N}_0$

$\mathfrak{I}[\![ce_1 = ce_2]\!](\rho) = (\mathfrak{I}[\![ce_1]\!](\rho) =_{\mathfrak{I}} \mathfrak{I}[\![ce_2]\!](\rho))$, the *strong, non-strict equality* on $\text{DOM}_{\mathfrak{I}}$. Thus a value $\perp$, which is possible for a communication expression, does not propagate to the logical level.

Formulas $\neg\, le$, $le_1 \wedge le_2$, $\exists t.le$, $\exists n.\, le$ are interpreted as negation, conjunction and existential quantification over Comm and $\mathbb{N}_0$, respectively.

(5) A trace formula le is called *valid*, abbreviated $\models le$, if $\mathfrak{I}[\![le]\!](\rho) = \text{true}$ for all environments ρ. □

To specify trace sets we use a subset of trace formulas.

Definition. The set Spec of *trace specifications* ranged over by S, T, U consists of all trace formulas where at most the distinguished variables h of sort *trace* is free. □

Thus the logical value $\mathfrak{J}[\![S]\!](\rho)$ of a trace specification S depends only on the trace value $\rho(h)$. We say that a trace $\mathfrak{h} \in Comm^*$ *satisfies* S and write $\mathfrak{h} \models S$ if $\mathfrak{J}[\![S]\!](\rho)$ = true for $\rho(h) = \mathfrak{h}$. Note the following relationship between satisfaction and validity:

$$\mathfrak{h} \models S \quad \text{iff} \quad \models S\{\mathfrak{h}/h\}$$

A trace specification S specifies the set of all traces satisfying S. In fact, wether or not a trace satisfies a trace specification S depends only on the trace value within the *projection alphabet* $\alpha(S)$. This is the smallest set of communications such that h is accessed only via trace projections within $\alpha(S)$. Its definition can be found in [Ol 88/89, Ol 89b]. We also consider the *extended alphabet* $\alpha\alpha(S)$. This is the set of all communications appearing somewhere in S. For example, for

$$S = (lk.h)\upharpoonright\{dn\} \leq (lk.h)\upharpoonright\{up\}$$

we have $\alpha(S) = \{dn, up\}$ and $\alpha\alpha(S) = \{lk, dn, up\}$.

Projection Lemma. Let S be a trace specification. Then

$$\mathfrak{h} \models S \quad \text{iff} \quad \mathfrak{h}\upharpoonright\alpha(S) \models S$$

for all traces $\mathfrak{h} \in Comm^*$. □

Since trace logic includes the standard interpretation of Peano arithmetic, viz. the model $(\mathbb{N}_0, 0, 1, +_{\mathfrak{J}}, *_{\mathfrak{J}}, =_{\mathfrak{J}})$, trace specifications are very expressive.

Expressiveness Theorem. [Zw 89] Let $\mathfrak{T} \subseteq A^*$ be a recursively enumerable set of traces over the alphabet A. Then there exists a trace specification TRACE($\mathfrak{T}$) with projection alphabet $\alpha(TRACE(\mathfrak{T})) = A$ such that

$$\mathfrak{h} \in \mathfrak{T} \quad \text{iff} \quad \mathfrak{h} \models TRACE(\mathfrak{T})$$

for all traces $\mathfrak{h} \in A^*$. The same is true for sets $\mathfrak{T} \subseteq A^*$ whose complement in A^* is recursively enumerable. □

For practical specification, such a general expressiveness result is not very helpful. Then a concise and clear notation is important. We use the following:

* Natural number expressions *counting* the number of communications in a trace:

$$a \# te =_{df} |\, te\upharpoonright\{a\}\, |$$

* Communication expressions *selecting* specific elements of a trace: e.g.

$$\textit{last}\ te =_{df} te[|te|]$$

* Extended syntax for logical expressions: e.g. for $k \geq 3$

$$ne_1 \leq \ldots \leq ne_k =_{df} \bigwedge_{j=1}^{k-1} ne_j \leq ne_{j+1}$$

* *Regular expressions* denoting sets of traces.

3. PROCESS TERMS

Process terms are recursive terms over a certain signature of operator symbols taken from Lauer's COSY [LTS 79, Be 87], Milner's CCS [Mi 80] and Hoare's CSP as in [Ho 85]. More specifically, we take the parallel composition $\|$ from COSY, prefix a., choice + and renaming $[a_1/b_1]$ from CCS, and deadlock *stop* : A , divergence *div* : A, hiding $\setminus B$ and the idea of using communication alphabets to state certain context-sensitive restrictions on process terms from CSP.

To the set Comm of communication we add an element $\tau \in$ Comm yielding the set Act = Comm $\cup \{\tau\}$ of *actions*. The element τ is called *internal* action and the communications are also called *external* actions. We let u,v range over Act. As before let a, b range over Comm and A,B over communication alphabets. The set of *(process) identifiers* is denoted by Idf; it is partitioned into sets Idf:A $\subseteq$ Idf of *identifiers with alphabet* A, one for each communication alphabet A. We let X,Y, Z range over Idf.

Definition. The set Rec of *(recursive) terms*, with typical elements P,Q,R, consists of all terms generated by the following context-free production rules:

P ::=	*stop* : A	(deadlock)
	$\mid$ *div* : A	(divergence)
	$\mid$ a. P	(prefix)
	$\mid$ P + Q	(choice)
	$\mid$ P $\|$ Q	(parallelism)
	$\mid$ $P[b_1/a_1]$	(renaming)
	$\mid$ $P\setminus B$	(hiding)
	$\mid$ X	(identifier)
	$\mid$ $\mu X.P$	(recursion)

□

An occurence of an identifier X in a term P is said to be *bound* if it occurs in P within a subterm of the form μX.Q. Otherwise the occurence is said to be *free.* A term P $\in$ Rec without free occurences of identifiers is called *closed.* $P\{Q/X\}$ denotes the result of *substituting* Q for every free occurence of X in P.

A term P is called *action-guarded* if in every recursive subterm μX.Q of P every free occurence of X in Q occurs within a subterm of the form a.R of Q. E.g. $\mu X.\, a.\, X$ is action-guarded, but $a.\mu X.\, X$ is not.

To every term P we assign a communication alphabet $\alpha(P)$ defined inductively as follows :

$$\begin{aligned}
&\alpha(\mathit{stop}:A) = \alpha(\mathit{div}:A) = A\,,\\
&\alpha(a.P) = \{a\} \cup \alpha(P)\,,\\
&\alpha(P+Q) = \alpha(P \,\|\, Q) = \alpha(P) \cup \alpha(Q)\,,\\
&\alpha(P[b_1/a_1]) = (\alpha(P)-\{a_1\}) \cup \{b_1\},\\
&\alpha(P\setminus B) = \alpha(P) - B,\\
&\alpha(X) = A \text{ if } X \in Idf(A),\\
&\alpha(\mu X.P) = \alpha(X) \cup \alpha(P)\,.
\end{aligned}$$

Thus for every n-ary operator symbol op of Proc there is a set-theoretic operator op_α satisfying $\alpha(op(P_1,\dots,P_n)) = op_\alpha(\alpha(P_1),\dots,\alpha(P_n))$.

Definition. A *process term* is a term $P \in Rec$ which satisfies the following context-sensitive restrictions:

(1) P is action-guarded,
(2) every subterm a.Q of P satisfies $a \in \alpha(Q)$,
(3) every subterm Q+R of P satisfies $\alpha(Q) = \alpha(R)$,
(4) every subterm $\mu X.Q$ of P satisfies $\alpha(X) = \alpha(P)$.

Let Proc denote the set of all process terms and CProc the set of all closed process terms. □

The semantics of process terms is given by Petri nets. We consider here *labelled place/transition nets* with arc weight 1 and place capacity ω [Re 85] but we will mainly work in the subclass of safe Petri nets. We deviate slightly from the standard definition and use the following one which is inspired by [Go 88].

Definition. A *Petri net* or simply *net* is a structure $\mathfrak{N} = (A, Pl, \longrightarrow, M_0)$ where
(1) A is a communication alphabet,
(2) Pl is a possibly infinite set of *places*,
(3) $\longrightarrow \subseteq \mathfrak{P}_{nf}(Pl) \times (A \cup \{\tau\}) \times \mathfrak{P}_{nf}(Pl)$ is the *transition relation*,
(4) $M_0 \in \mathfrak{P}_{nf}(Pl)$ is the *initial marking*. □

Here $\mathfrak{P}_{nf}(Pl)$ denotes the set of all non-empty, finite subsets of Pl. An element (I, u, O) $\in \longrightarrow$ is called a *transition (labelled with the action u)* and will usually be written as

$$I \xrightarrow{u} O .$$

For a transition $t = I \xrightarrow{u} O$ its *preset* or *input* is given by pre(t) = I, its *postset* or *output* by post(t) = O and its action by act(t) = u.

The graphical representation of a net $\mathfrak{N} = (A, Pl, \longrightarrow, M_0)$ is as follows. We draw a rectangular box divided into an upper part displaying the alphabet A and a lower part displaying the remaining components Pl, $\longrightarrow$ and M_0 in the usual way. Thus places $p \in Pl$ are represented as *circles* with the name "p" outside and transitions

$$t = \{ p_1, ..., p_m \} \xrightarrow{u} \{ q_1, ..., q_n \}$$

as *boxes* carrying the label "u" inside and connected via directed arcs to the places in pre(t) and post(t). Since pre(t) and post(t) need not be disjoint, some of the outgoing arcs of u actually point back to places in pre(t) and thus introduce *cycles*. The initial marking is represented by putting a token into the circle of each $p \in M_0$.

As usual the dynamic behaviour of a Petri net is defined by its *token game*; it describes which transitions are concurrently enabled at a given marking and what the result of their concurrent execution is. Though the initial marking of a net is defined to be a set of places, the token game can result in more general markings, viz. multisets. A net $\mathfrak{N}$ is *safe* if in every reachable marking is a set, i.e. each place contains at most one token.

Consider a net $\mathfrak{N} = (A, Pl, \longrightarrow, M_0)$. The set place($\mathfrak{N}$) of *statically reachable places* of $\mathfrak{N}$ is the smallest subset of Pl satisfying

(1) $M \subseteq place(\mathfrak{N})$,

(2) If $I \subseteq place(\mathfrak{N})$ and $I \xrightarrow{u} O$ for some $u \in A \cup \{ \tau \}$ and $O \subseteq Pl$ then also $O \subseteq place(\mathfrak{N})$.

The term "statical" emphasises that, by (2), the set $place(\mathfrak{N})$ is closed under the execution of any transition $t = I \xrightarrow{u} O$ independently of whether t is ever enabled in the token game of $\mathfrak{N}$.

When considering nets, we wish to ignore the identity of places and forget about places that are not statically reachable. We do this by introducing suitable notions of isomorphism and abstract net.

Definition. Two nets $\mathfrak{N}_i = (A_i, Pl_i, \longrightarrow_i, M_{0i})$, $i=1,2$, are *weakly isomorphic*, abbreviated

$$\mathfrak{N}_1 =_{isom} \mathfrak{N}_2,$$

if $A_1 = A_2$ and there exists a bijection $\beta : place(\mathfrak{N}_1) \longrightarrow place(\mathfrak{N}_2)$ such that $\beta(M_{01}) = M_{02}$ and for all $I, O \subseteq place(\mathfrak{N}_1)$ and all $u \in A \cup \{ \tau \}$

$$I \xrightarrow{u}_1 O \quad \text{iff} \quad \beta(I) \xrightarrow{u}_2 \beta(O)$$

where $\beta(M_{01})$, $\beta(I)$, $\beta(O)$ are understood elementwise. The bijection β is called an *weak isomorphism between* $\mathfrak{N}_1$ *and* $\mathfrak{N}_2$. □

Clearly, $=_{isom}$ is an equivalence relation. An *abstract net* is defined as the isomorphism class

$$[\mathfrak{N}]_{=_{isom}} = \{ \mathfrak{N}' \mid \mathfrak{N} =_{isom} \mathfrak{N}' \}$$

of a net $\mathfrak{N}$. It will be written shorter as $[\mathfrak{N}]$. For abstract nets, we use the same graphical representation as for nets; we only have to make sure that all places are statically reachable and eliminate their names. Most concepts for nets can be lifted in a straightforward way to abstract nets. For example, we shall call an abstract net $[\mathfrak{N}]$ safe, if $\mathfrak{N}$ is safe. Let Net denote the set of nets and ANet the set of abstract nets.

Formally, the semantics of process terms is a mapping $\mathfrak{N}[\![\cdot]\!] : CProc \longrightarrow ANet$ which assigns to every proces term $P \in CProc$ an safe abstract net of the form

$$\mathfrak{N}[\![P]\!] = [(\alpha(P), Pl, \longrightarrow , M_0)] .$$

For the definition of the components Pl, $\longrightarrow$ and M_0 we refer to operational net semantics given in [Ol 89a]. Here we have space only for an example.

Example. Consider the process terms $SEM = \mu X. (p_1 . v_1 . X + p_2 . v_2 . X)$ modelling a semaphore and $CYCLE = \mu Y.n.p.b.e.v.Y$ modelling a user cycle with non-critical action n and critical section b.e sheltered by semaphore communications p and v. Applying the renaming operator we generate two copies of CYCLE:

$$CYCLE1 = CYCLE [n_1, p_1, b_1, e_1, v_1 / n,p,b,e,v] ,$$
$$CYCLE2 = CYCLE [n_2, p_2, b_2, e_2, v_2 / n,p,b,e,v] .$$

Applying parallel composition to CYCLE1, SEM and CYCLE2 we obtain the process term

$$MUTEX = CYCLE1 \parallel SEM \parallel CYCLE2$$

modelling the mutual exclusion of the critical sections $b_1 .e_1$ and $b_2 .e_2$. Then $\mathfrak{N}[\![$ MUTEX $]\!]$ is the following abstract net:

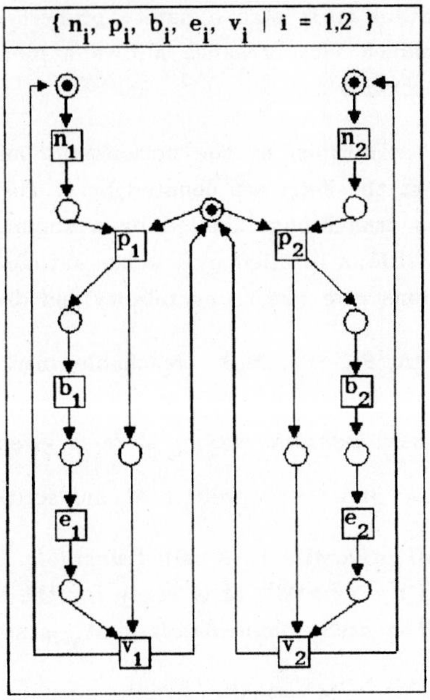

□

4. PROCESS CORRECTNESS

We begin with an informal description. Consider a process term P and a communication trace $\mathfrak{h} = a_1 ... a_n$ over $\alpha(P)$. We say that P *may engage* in $\mathfrak{h}$ if there exists a transition sequence of P where the user is able to communicate $a_1 ... a_n$ in that order. We say that P *must engage* in $\mathfrak{h}$ if the following holds. When started P eventually becomes stable. Then it is possible for the user to communicate a_1. Now P may engage in some internal activity, but eventually it becomes stable again. Then it is ready for the next communication a_2 with the user, etc. for $a_3, ..., a_n$. Also after the last communication a_n the process P eventually becomes stable again. Summarising, in every transition sequence of P the user is able to communicate $a_1, ..., a_n$ in that order after which the process eventually becomes stable. Stability can be viewed as an acknowledgement of P for a successful communication with the user. We say that P is *stable immediately* if initially P cannot engage in any internal action.

Definition. Consider a closed process term P and a trace specification S. Then

$$P \textit{ sat } S$$

if $\alpha(P) = \alpha(S)$ and the following conditions hold:

(1) *Safety.* For every trace $\mathfrak{h} \in \alpha(P)^*$ whenever P may engage in $\mathfrak{h}$ then $\mathfrak{h} \models S$.

(2) *Liveness.* For every trace $\mathfrak{h} \in \alpha(S)^*$ whenever *pref* $\mathfrak{h} \models S$ then P must engage in $\mathfrak{h}$. The notation *pref* $\mathfrak{h} \models S$ means that $\mathfrak{h}$ and all its prefixes satisfy S.

(3) *Stability.* P is stable immediately.

□

The distinction between safety and liveness properties of concurrent processes is due to Lamport (see e.g. [OL 82] and [AS 85]). Note that the notion of safety is different from safeness defined for nets in Section 3: safeness can be viewed as a specific safety property of the token game of a net. Stability is also a safety property, but it is singled out here because its rôle is more technical. Its presence allows a more powerful verification rule for the choice operator in Section 6.

In the following we give formal definitions of the notions of "may" and "must engage" and of initial stability by looking at the Petri net denoted by P. The intuition behind these definitions is as follows. Whereas transitions labelled by a communication occur only if the user participates in them, transitions labelled by τ occur autonomously at an unknown, but positive speed. Thus τ-transitions give rise to unstability and divergence.

Definition. Consider a net $\mathfrak{N} = (A, Pl, \longrightarrow, M_0)$, reachable markings M, M' of $\mathfrak{N}$ and a trace $\mathfrak{h} \in Comm^*$.

(1) *Progess properties.* The set of *next possible actions* at M is given by

$$next(M) = \{u \in Act \mid \exists t \in \longrightarrow : pre(t) \subseteq M \text{ and } act(t) = u\}.$$

M is called *stable* if $\tau \notin next(M)$ otherwise it is called *unstable*. M is *ready* for a communication b if M is stable and $b \in next(M)$. M is ready for the communication set A if M is stable and next(M) = A. $\mathfrak{N}$ is *stable immediately* if M_0 is stable. We write

$$M \overset{\mathfrak{h}}{\Longrightarrow} M'$$

if there exists a finite transition sequence $M \xrightarrow{t_1} M_1 \dots M_{n-1} \xrightarrow{t_n} M_n = M'$ such that $\mathfrak{h} = (act(t_1) \dots act(t_n)) \setminus \tau$, i.e. $\mathfrak{h}$ results from the sequence of actions $act(t_1) \dots act(t_n)$ by deleting all internal actions τ.

(2) *Divergence properties.* $\mathfrak{N}$ *can diverge from* M if there exists an infinite transition sequence

$$M \xrightarrow{t_1} M_1 \xrightarrow{t_2} M_2 \xrightarrow{t_3} \dots$$

such that $\tau = act(t_1) = act(t_2) = act(t_3) = \dots$ $\mathfrak{N}$ *can diverge immediately* if $\mathfrak{N}$ can diverge from M_0. $\mathfrak{N}$ *can diverge after* $\mathfrak{h}$ if there exists a marking M with

$$M_0 \overset{\mathfrak{h}}{\Longrightarrow} M$$

such that $\mathfrak{N}$ can diverge from M. $\mathfrak{N}$ *can diverge only after* $\mathfrak{h}$ if whenever $\mathfrak{N}$ can diverge after some trace $\mathfrak{h}'$ then $\mathfrak{h} \le \mathfrak{h}'$. $\mathfrak{N}$ *can diverge* if there is a reachable marking M of $\mathfrak{N}$ from which $\mathfrak{N}$ can diverge. $\mathfrak{N}$ is *divergence free* if $\mathfrak{N}$ cannot diverge.

(3) *Deadlock properties.* $\mathfrak{N}$ *deadlocks* at M if next(M) = $\emptyset$. $\mathfrak{N}$ *deadlocks immediately* if $\mathfrak{N}$ deadlocks at M_0. $\mathfrak{N}$ *can deadlock after* $\mathfrak{h}$ if there exists a marking M with

$$M_0 \overset{\mathfrak{h}}{\Longrightarrow} M$$

such that $\mathfrak{N}$ deadlocks at M. $\mathfrak{N}$ *can deadlock only after* $\mathfrak{h}$ if whenever $\mathfrak{N}$ can deadlock after some trace $\mathfrak{h}'$ then $\mathfrak{h} \le \mathfrak{h}'$. $\mathfrak{N}$ *can deadlock* if there is a reachable marking M of $\mathfrak{N}$ at which $\mathfrak{N}$ deadlocks. $\mathfrak{N}$ is *deadlock free* if $\mathfrak{N}$ cannot deadlock. □

We now turn to process terms.

Definition. Consider a closed process term P, a representative $\mathfrak{N}_0 = (\alpha(P), Pl, \longrightarrow, M_0)$ of the abstract net $\mathfrak{N}[\![P]\!]$, and a trace $\mathfrak{h} \in Comm^*$.

(1) P is *stable immediately* if $\mathfrak{N}_0$ is so.

(2) P *can diverge (immediately* or *after* $\mathfrak{h}$ or *only after* $\mathfrak{h}$) if $\mathfrak{N}_0$ can do so. P is *divergence free* if $\mathfrak{N}_0$ is so.

(3) P *deadlocks immediately* if $\mathfrak{N}_0$ does so. P *can deadlock (after* $\mathfrak{h}$ or *only after* $\mathfrak{h}$) if $\mathfrak{N}_0$ can do so. P is *deadlock free* if $\mathfrak{N}$ is so.

(4) P *may engage* in $\mathfrak{h}$ if there exists a marking M with $M_0 \overset{\mathfrak{h}}{\Longrightarrow} M$.

(5) P *must engage* in $\mathfrak{h} = a_1 \ldots a_n$ if the process term $P \parallel a_1 \ldots a_n .\ stop\colon \alpha(P)$ is divergence free and can deadlock only after $\mathfrak{h}$. □

Clearly, these definitions are independent of the choice of the representative $\mathfrak{N}_0$. The formalisations of immediate stability and "may engage" capture the above intuitions, but the formalisation of "must engage" requires some explanation. The process term $a_1 \ldots a_n .\ stop\colon \alpha(P)$ models a user wishing to communicate the trace $a_1 \ldots a_n$ to P and stop afterwards. Communication is enforced by making the alphabet of user and process identical. Thus the parallel composition $P \parallel a_1 \ldots a_n .\ stop\colon \alpha(P)$ can behave only as follows: it can engage in some prefix $a_1 \ldots a_k$ of $\mathfrak{h}$ with $0 \le k \le n$ and then either diverge (i.e. never become stable again) or deadlock (i.e. become stable, but unable to engage in any further communication). The user's wish to communicate $\mathfrak{h}$ is realised if and only if $P \parallel a_1 \ldots a_n .\ stop\colon \alpha(P)$ never diverges and if it deadlocks only after $\mathfrak{h}$. A final deadlock is unavoidable because the user wishes to stop. This is how we formalise the notion of "must engage".

The terminology of "may" and "must engage" originates from DeNicola and Hennessy's work on testing of processes [DH 84]. There it is used to define several so-called testing equivalences on processes, among them one for the "may" case and one for the "must" case. Here the definition of "must engage" is stronger than in [DH 84] because we require stability after each communication, also after the last one.

Proposition. Consider a closed process term P and a trace specification S. Then P *sat* S implies the following:

(1) "May" is equivalent to "must", i.e. for every trace $\mathfrak{h}$ the process P may engage in $\mathfrak{h}$ if and only if P must engage in $\mathfrak{h}$.

(2) P is divergence free.

(3) P is externally deterministic. □

Intuitively, a process is externally deterministic if the user cannot detect any nondeterminism by communicating with it. Formally, we define this notion as follows:

Definition. Consider a closed process term P and some representative $\mathfrak{N}_0 = (\alpha(P), Pl, \longrightarrow, M_0)$ of $\mathfrak{N}[\![P]\!]$. Then P is called *externally deterministic* if for all traces $\mathfrak{h} \in Comm^*$ and all markings M_1, M_2 of $\mathfrak{N}_0$ whenever

$$M_0 \overset{\mathfrak{h}}{\Longrightarrow} M_1 \text{ and } M_0 \overset{\mathfrak{h}}{\Longrightarrow} M_2$$

such that M_1 and M_2 are stable then $next(M_1) = next(M_2)$. That is: every communication trace $\mathfrak{h}$ uniquely determines the next stable set of communications. □

Thus trace formulas specify only divergence free and exernally deterministic processes. This is a clear restriction of our approach, but it yields an interesting class of processes with many applications and simplest verification rules (see Sections 6 and 7).

Example. Let us consider the trace specification

$$S = 0 \le up\#h - dn\#h \le 2$$

which is an abbreviation for $dn\#h \le up\#h \le 2+dn\#h$, and examine how a process P satisfying S should behave. Since P *sat* S implies $\alpha(P) = \alpha(S) = \{ up, dn \}$, P should engage only in the communications up and dn. By the safety condition, in every communication trace $\mathfrak{h}$ that P may engage in, the difference of the number of up's and the number of dn's is between 0 and 2. If P has engaged in such a trace $\mathfrak{h}$ and the extension $\mathfrak{h}.dn$ still satisfies S, the liveness condition of P *sat* S requires that after $\mathfrak{h}$ the process P must engage in the communication dn. The same is true for up.

Thus S specifies that P should behave like *2-counter* which can internally store a natural number n with $0 \le n \le 2$. After a communication trace $\mathfrak{h}$; the number stored is $n = up\#\mathfrak{h} - dn\#\mathfrak{h}$. Thus initially, when $\mathfrak{h}$ is empty, n is 0. Communicating up increments n and communicating dn decrements n provided these changes of n do not exceed the bounds 2 and 0.

A process term satisfying S is

$$P = \mu X.\ up.\ \mu Y.\ (\ dn.\ X + up.\ dn.\ Y\ )$$

denoting the following abstract net

$\mathfrak{N}[\![P]\!] =$

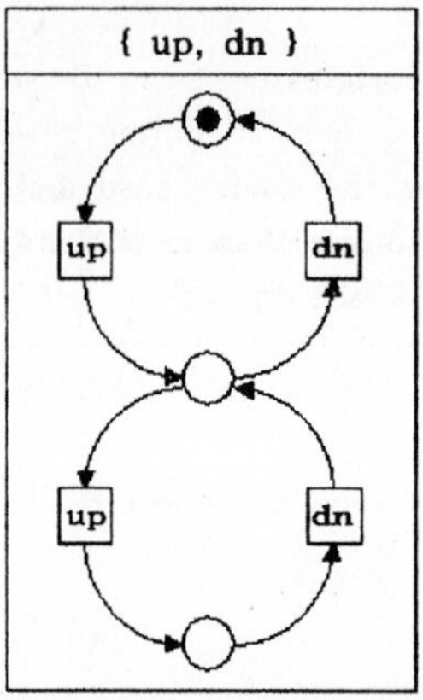

This net is purely sequential, i.e. every reachable marking contains at most one token, and there are no internal actions involved. Another process term satisfying S is

$$Q = ((\ \mu X.\ up.\ dn.\ X\ )\ [\ lk/dn\ ]\ \|\ (\mu X.\ up.\ dn.\ X\ )\ [\ lk/up\ ])\ \backslash lk$$

denoting the following abstract net.

$\mathfrak{N}[\![Q]\!]$ =

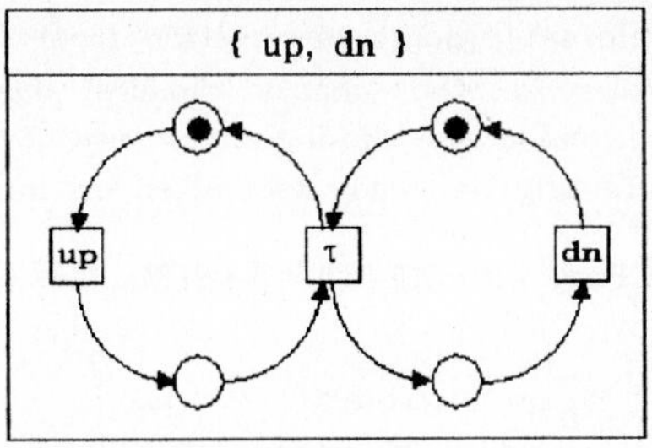

Here, after each up-transition the net has to engage in an internal action τ before it is ready for the corresponding dn-transition. Since τ-actions occur autonomously, readiness for the next dn is guaranteed, as required by the specification S. This leads in fact to a marking where up and dn are concurrently enabled.

The examples of P and Q demonstrate that presence or absence of concurrency or intervening internal activity are treated here as properties of the implementation (process term and net), not of the specification. □

5. MODIFIED READINESS SEMANTICS

The liveness condition of the satisfaction relation P *sat* S is difficult to check when only the net semantics of P is available. To simplify matters, we introduce now a second, more abstract semantics for both process terms and trace specifications. It is a modification of the readiness semantics $\mathfrak{R}$ introduced in [OH 86]. To avoid confusion, we call this modification $\mathfrak{R}^*$. Formally, it is a mapping

$$\mathfrak{R}^* [\![\cdot]\!] : \text{CProc} \cup \text{Spec} \longrightarrow \text{DOM}_{\mathfrak{R}}$$

which assigns to every process term $P \in \text{CProc}$ an element $\mathfrak{R}^*[\![P]\!]$ and to every trace specification $S \in \text{Spec}$ an element $\mathfrak{R}^*[\![S]\!]$ in the readiness domain $\text{DOM}_{\mathfrak{R}}$. This domain consists of pairs (A,Γ) where A is a communication alphabet and Γ is a set of *process informations*. We consider three types of process information:

(1) The element τ indicating initial *unstability*.
(2) *Ready pairs* $(\mathfrak{h}, \mathfrak{F})$ consisting of a trace $\mathfrak{h} \in A^*$ and a *ready set* $\mathfrak{F} \subseteq A$.
(3) *Divergence points* $(\mathfrak{h}, \uparrow)$ consisting of a trace $\mathfrak{h} \in A^*$ and a special symbol ↑ standing for divergence.

The set of these process informations can be expressed as follows:

$$\text{Info}_{\mathfrak{R}}{:}A = \{ \tau \} \cup A^* \times \mathfrak{P}(A) \cup A^* \times \{ \uparrow \}.$$

Define

$$\text{DOM}_{\mathfrak{R}}{:}A = \{ (A,\Gamma) \mid \Gamma \subseteq \text{Info} :A \}.$$

The readiness domain is then given by

$$\text{DOM}_{\mathfrak{R}} = \bigcup \text{DOM}_{\mathfrak{R}}{:}A$$

where the union is taken over all communication alphabets A. We adopt the following notational conventions: letters γ, δ range over $\text{Info}_{\mathfrak{R}}{:}A$, letters Γ, Δ over subsets of $\text{Info}_{\mathfrak{R}}{:}A$ and hence pairs (A, Γ), (B, Δ) over $\text{DOM}_{\mathfrak{R}}$, letters $\mathfrak{F}$, $\mathfrak{G}$ range over ready sets and the letter $\mathfrak{X}$ can either be a ready set or the symbol ↑.

The mapping $\mathfrak{R}^*[\![\cdot]\!]$ retrieves the relevant process information from the operational Petri net semantics and enforces three closures: the "chaotic closure" due to [BHR 84], the "acceptance closure" due to [DH 84], and a new "radiation closure" by which a divergence after a trace $\mathfrak{h}.a$ "radiates up" by affecting the ready sets after the immediate prefix $\mathfrak{h}$.

Definition. For a process term $P \in CProc$ with $\mathfrak{N}[\![P]\!] = [\,(\alpha(P), Pl, \longrightarrow, M_0)\,]$ the *operational readiness semantics* is given by

$$
\begin{aligned}
\mathfrak{R}^*(\mathfrak{N}) = \mathrm{close}(\, A, \; & \{ \quad \tau \quad \mid M_0 \text{ is unstable } \} \\
& \cup \{ (\mathfrak{h}, \mathfrak{F}) \mid \exists \text{ marking } M \text{ of } \mathfrak{N} : \\
& \qquad M_0 \overset{\mathfrak{h}}{\Longrightarrow} M \text{ and } M \text{ is stable and } \mathfrak{F} = \mathrm{next}(M) \} \\
& \cup \{ (\mathfrak{h}, \uparrow) \mid \exists \text{ marking } M \text{ of } \mathfrak{N} : \\
& \qquad M_0 \overset{\mathfrak{h}}{\Longrightarrow} M \text{ and } \mathfrak{N} \text{ can diverge from } M \} \quad)
\end{aligned}
$$

where the *closure operator* close: $DOM_{\mathfrak{R}} \longrightarrow DOM_{\mathfrak{R}}$ is defined as follows:

$$
\begin{aligned}
& \mathrm{close}(A, \Gamma) = \\
& \quad (A, \Gamma \cup \{ (\mathfrak{h}, \mathfrak{G}) \mid \exists\, \mathfrak{F}: \; (\mathfrak{h}, \mathfrak{F}) \in \Gamma \text{ and } \mathfrak{F} \subseteq \mathfrak{G} \subseteq \mathrm{succ}(\mathfrak{h}, \Gamma) \} && \text{"acceptance closure"} \\
& \qquad \cup \{ (\mathfrak{h}', \mathfrak{X}) \mid \exists\, \mathfrak{h} \le \mathfrak{h}' : (\mathfrak{h}, \uparrow) \in \Gamma \text{ and } \mathfrak{h}' \in A^* \\
& \qquad\qquad\qquad \text{and } (\mathfrak{X} \subseteq A \text{ or } \mathfrak{X} = \uparrow) \; \} && \text{"chaotic closure"} \\
& \qquad \cup \{ (\mathfrak{h}, \mathfrak{G}) \mid \exists\, a: \; (\mathfrak{h}.a, \uparrow) \in \Gamma \text{ and } \mathfrak{G} \subseteq \mathrm{succ}(\mathfrak{h}, \Gamma) \; \}\,) && \text{"radiation closure"}
\end{aligned}
$$

Here $\mathrm{succ}(\mathfrak{h}, \Gamma)$ denotes the set of all *successor communications* of $\mathfrak{h}$ in Γ:

$$\mathrm{succ}(\mathfrak{h}, \Gamma) = \{ a \mid \exists\, \mathfrak{G}: (\mathfrak{h}.a, \mathfrak{G}) \in \Gamma \} .$$

For a trace specification $S \in Spec$ the *readiness semantics*

$$
\begin{aligned}
\mathfrak{R}^*[\![S]\!] = (\, \alpha(S), \{ (\mathfrak{h}, \mathfrak{F}) \mid \mathfrak{h} \in \alpha(S)^* \text{ and } & \textit{pref } \mathfrak{h} \models S \\
\text{and } & \mathfrak{F} = \{ a \in \alpha(S) \mid \mathfrak{h}.a \models S \} \} \,)
\end{aligned}
$$

where, as before, *pref* $\mathfrak{h} \models S$ means that $\mathfrak{h}$ and all its prefixes satisfy S. □

The readiness semantics $\mathfrak{R}^*$ is an interleaving semantics because it is insensitive to concurrency. This is demonstrated by the law

$$\mathfrak{R}^*[\![\, a.\, \textit{stop}{:}\{a\} \parallel b.\, \textit{stop}{:}\{b\} \,]\!] \;=\; \mathfrak{R}^*[\![\, a.\, b.\, \textit{stop}{:}\{a, b\} + b.\, a.\, \textit{stop}{:}\{a, b\} \,]\!]$$

which is easily established by retrieving the readiness information from the corresponding nets.

Note that the three closures add ready sets and divergence points to $\mathfrak{R}^*[\![P]\!]$ which are not justified by the token game of $\mathfrak{N}[\![P]\!]$. These additions make the semantics $\mathfrak{R}^*[\![\cdot]\!]$ more abstract so that less process terms can be distinguished under $\mathfrak{R}^*[\![\cdot]\!]$. The resulting level of abstraction is in perfect match with the distinctions that we can make among process terms under the satisfaction relation P *sat* S. Technically speaking, $\mathfrak{R}^*[\![\cdot]\!]$ is *fully abstract* with respect to this relation (see [Ol 88/89, Ol 89b]).

Correctness Theorem. [Ol 88/89] For every closed process term P and trace specification S we have

$$P \textit{ sat } S \quad \text{iff} \quad \mathfrak{R}^*[\![P]\!] = \mathfrak{R}^*[\![S]\!],$$

i.e. in the readiness semantics process correctness reduces to semantics equality. □

The Correctness Theorem simplifies, at least conceptually, the task of proving that a process term P satisfies a trace specification S.

Example. In Section 4 we considered the trace specification $S = 0 \le up\#h - dn\#h \le 2$ and argued informally that the process terms

$$P = \mu X.\ up.\ \mu Y.\ (\ dn.\ X + up.\ dn.\ Y\ )$$

and

$$Q = (\ (\ \mu X.\ up.\ dn.\ X\ )[\ lk/dn\ ]\ \|\ (\ \mu X.\ up.\ dn.\ X\ )[\ lk/up\ ]\ )\ \backslash lk$$

both satisfy S. We can now prove this claim by comparing the readiness semantics of S with that of P and Q:

$$\begin{aligned}\mathfrak{R}^*[\![S]\!] = (\ \{ up, dn \}, \{\ (\mathfrak{h}, \mathfrak{F})\ \mid \forall\ \mathfrak{h}' \le \mathfrak{h}:\ & 0 \le up\#\mathfrak{h}' - dn\#\mathfrak{h}' \le 2 \\ & \text{and } (\text{ if } 0 = up\#\mathfrak{h} - dn\#\mathfrak{h} \text{ then } \mathfrak{F} = \{ up \}\ ) \\ & \text{and } (\text{ if } 0 < up\#\mathfrak{h} - dn\#\mathfrak{h} < 2 \text{ then } \mathfrak{F} = \{ up, dn \}) \\ & \text{and } (\text{ if } up\#\mathfrak{h} - dn\#\mathfrak{h} = 2 \text{ then } \mathfrak{F} = \{ dn \}\ )\ \}\ )\end{aligned}$$

By an exhaustive analysis of the reachable markings of the nets $\mathfrak{N}[\![P]\!]$ and $\mathfrak{N}[\![Q]\!]$ shown in Section 4 we see that $\mathfrak{R}^*[\![P]\!] = \mathfrak{R}^*[\![S]\!] = \mathfrak{R}^*[\![Q]\!]$. Thus indeed P *sat* S and Q *sat* S. □

Above we referred to the obvious way of determining the readiness semantics of a process term P, viz. by analysis of the underlying Petri net $\mathfrak{N}[\![P]\!]$. The drawback of this method is that it is very inflexible: whenever a part of P is exchanged, the analysis of $\mathfrak{N}[\![P]\!]$ has to start again. Instead we would like to reuse the results established for those parts of P which are left unchanged. To this end, we wish to determine the readiness semantics $\mathfrak{R}^*[\![P]\!]$ by induction on the structure of P.

Technically speaking, we provide an alternative, denotational definition $\mathfrak{R}^{**}[\![\cdot]\!]$ of the readiness semantics and show that on closed process terms it coincides with the previous operational definition $\mathfrak{R}^*[\![\cdot]\!]$. In Section 6 this denotational definition will be the basis for developing verification rules for process correctness.

Following the approach of Scott and Strachey [Sc 70, St 77, Ba 80], a semantics of a programming language is called *denotational* if its definition is compositional and employs fixed point techniques when dealing with recursion. These techniques stipulate a certain structure of the composition operators and the semantic domains. We will use here the standard set-up and work with monotonic or (chain-) continuous operators over complete partial orders (cpo's). For the definition and basic properties of these notions we refer to the literature, e.g. [Ba 80]. However, the specific format of our programming language, viz. recursive terms with alphabets as types, requires a few extra details which we explain now.

Definition. The *denotational readiness semantics for process terms* is a mapping

$$\mathfrak{R}^{**} : Proc \longrightarrow (\ Env_{\mathfrak{R}} \longrightarrow DOM_{\mathfrak{R}}\ )$$

which satisfies the following conditions:

(1) The semantic domain $DOM_{\mathfrak{R}}$ is equipped with the following partial ordering $\sqsubseteq$:

$$(A, \Gamma) \sqsubseteq (B, \Delta) \quad \text{if} \quad A = B \text{ and } \Gamma \supseteq \Delta .$$

Intuitively, the reverse set inclusion $\Gamma \supseteq \Delta$ expresses that the process generating Δ is *more controllable*, i.e. *more deterministic* , *less divergent* and *more stable* than the process generating Γ [Ho 85]. For each alphabet $A \subseteq Comm$ the subdomain $DOM_{\mathfrak{R}}:A \subseteq DOM_{\mathfrak{R}}$ is a complete partial order under $\sqsubseteq$.

(2) The set $Env_{\mathfrak{R}}$ of environments consists of mappings $\rho \in Env_{\mathfrak{R}} = Idf \longrightarrow DOM_{\mathfrak{R}}$ which respect alphabets, i.e. $\alpha(X) = A$ implies $\rho(X) \in DOM_{\mathfrak{R}} : A$.

(3) For every n-ary operator symbol op of Proc there exists a corresponding semantic operator

$$op_{\mathfrak{R}} : \underbrace{DOM_{\mathfrak{R}} \times \ldots \times DOM_{\mathfrak{R}}}_{\text{n times}} \longrightarrow DOM_{\mathfrak{R}}$$

defined in [Ol 88/89]. Each of these operators is $\sqsubseteq$-monotonic and satisfies $op_{\mathfrak{R}}(\ (A_1,\Gamma_1)\ ,\ldots,\ (A_n,\Gamma_n)) \in DOM_{\mathfrak{R}} : op_{\alpha}(A_1\ ,\ldots,A_n)$. Here op_{α} is the set-theoretic operator on alphabets that corresponds to op (c.f. Section 3).

(4) The definition of $\mathfrak{R}^{**}$ proceeds inductively and obeys the following principles:

(4.1) *Environment technique.*

$$\mathfrak{R}^{**}[\![X]\!](\rho) = \rho(X)$$

(4.2) *Compositionality.*

$$\mathfrak{R}^{**}[\![op(P_1,\ldots,P_n)]\!](\rho) = op_{\mathfrak{R}}(\mathfrak{R}^{**}[\![P_1]\!](\rho),\ldots,\mathfrak{R}^{**}[\![P_n]\!](\rho))$$

(4.3) *Fixed point technique* .

$$\mathfrak{R}^{**}[\![\mu X.P]\!](\rho) = fix\ \Phi_{P,\rho}$$

Here $fix\ \Phi_{P,\rho}$ denotes the least fixed point of the mapping

$$\Phi_{P,\rho} : DOM_{\mathfrak{R}} : \alpha(X) \longrightarrow DOM_{\mathfrak{R}} : \alpha(X)$$

defined by

$$\Phi_{P,\rho}((A,\Gamma)) = \mathfrak{R}^{**}[\![P]\!](\rho[(A,\Gamma)/X])$$

where $\rho[(A,\Gamma)/X]$ is a modified environment which agrees with ρ, except for the identifier X where its value is (A,Γ). □

By (1)-(3), the inductive definition (4) of $\mathfrak{R}^{**}$ is well-defined and yields a value

$$\mathfrak{R}^{**}[\![P]\!](\rho) \in DOM_{\mathfrak{R}} : \alpha(P)$$

for every process term P. In clause (4.3) we apply Knaster and Tarski's fixed point theorem: if $DOM_{\mathfrak{R}} : A$ is a complete partial order and if all operators $op_{\mathfrak{R}}$ and thus $\Phi_{P,\rho}$ are monotonic then $\Phi_{P,\rho}$ has a least fixed point.

Environments ρ assign values to the free identifiers in process terms, analogously to Tarski's semantic definition for predicate logic in Section 2. Thus for closed process terms the environment parameter ρ of $\mathfrak{R}^{**}$ is not needed. We will therefore write $\mathfrak{R}^{**}[\![P]\!]$ instead of $\mathfrak{R}^{**}[\![P]\!](\rho)$.

Equivalence Theorem. [Ol 88/89] For every closed process term P the operational and denotational readiness semantics coincide:

$$\mathfrak{R}^{*}[\![P]\!] = \mathfrak{R}^{**}[\![P]\!]. \qquad \square$$

As a consequence of the Equivalence Theorem we shall henceforth write $\mathfrak{R}^{*}$ for both the operational and the denotational version of readiness semantics.

6. TRANSFORMATIONS ON MIXED TERMS

We now develop a systematic approach to verification and construction of concurrent processes with respect to our notion of process correctness P *sat* S. *Verification* means: given a process term P and a trace specification S show that P *sat* S. *Construction* means: given a trace specification S find a process term P with P *sat* S. We shall view verification as a special case of construction where the result P is known and only its correctness with respect to S is left to be shown.

Our aim is a top-down construction (and hence verification) starting with a trace specification S describing what the desired communication behaviour is and ending in a process term P describing how this communication behaviour is realised. During the construction we proceed by *stepwise refinement* as advocated by Dijkstra and Wirth [Di 76, Wi 71]. Thus at each step of the construction we replace a part of the specification by a piece of process syntax. Thus at the intermediate steps of the construction we use *mixed terms* (cf. [Ol 85, Ol 86, Ol 88/89]). These are syntactic constructs mixing process terms with trace specifications. An example of a mixed term is

$$a.(\,S \parallel T\,).$$

It describes a process where some parts are already constructed (prefix and parallel composition) whereas other parts are only specified (S and T) and remain to be constructed in future refinement steps.

From now on letters P, Q, R will range over mixed terms whereas letters S, T, U continue to range over the set Spec of trace specifications.

Definition. The set Proc + Spec of *mixed terms* consists of all terms P that are generated by the context-free production rules

P ::=	S	(specification)
	| *stop* : A	(deadlock)
	| *div* : A	(divergence)
	| a. P	(prefix)
	| P + Q	(choice)
	| P || Q	(parallelism)
	| $P\,[a_i / b_i]$	(renaming)
	| $P \setminus B$	(hiding)
	| X	(identifier)
	| $\mu X.\,P$	(recursion)

and that satisfy the context-sensitive restrictions stated in Section 3. Mixed terms without free process identifiers are called *closed*. The set of all closed mixed terms is denoted by CProc + Spec. □

Semantically, mixed terms denote elements of the readiness domain $DOM_{\mathfrak{R}}$. In fact, since trace specifications S have a semantics $\mathfrak{R}^*[\![S]\!] \in DOM_{\mathfrak{R}}$ and since for every operator symbol op of Proc there exists a corresponding semantic operator $op_{\mathfrak{R}}$ on $DOM_{\mathfrak{R}}$, we immediately obtain a denotational readiness semantics

$$\mathfrak{R}^*[\![\cdot]\!] : Proc + Spec \longrightarrow (Env_{\mathfrak{R}} \longrightarrow DOM_{\mathfrak{R}})$$

for mixed terms which is defined as in Section 5. For closed mixed terms the environment parameter ρ of $\mathfrak{R}^*[\![\cdot]\!]$ is not needed. Thus we write $\mathfrak{R}^*[\![P]\!]$ instead of $\mathfrak{R}^*[\![P]\!](\rho)$.

Under the readiness semantics $\mathfrak{R}^*[\![\cdot]\!]$, process terms, trace specifications and mixed terms are treated on equal footing so that they are easy to compare. For $P,Q \in Cproc + Spec$ we write

$$P \equiv Q \quad \text{if} \quad \mathfrak{R}^*[\![P]\!] = \mathfrak{R}^*[\![Q]\!]$$

and call $P \equiv Q$ a *semantic equation* in the readiness semantics.

By the Correctness Theorem, process correctness boils down to a semantic equation, i.e.

$$P \textit{ sat } S \quad \text{iff} \quad P \equiv S$$

for all $P \in CProc$ and $S \in Spec$. Therefore a top-down construction of a process term P from a trace specification S will be presented as a sequence

$$\begin{array}{c} S_1 \equiv Q \\ \equiv \\ \vdots \\ \equiv \\ Q_n \equiv P \end{array}$$

of semantics equations between mixed terms $Q_1, \ldots, Q_n$ where Q_1 is the given trace specification S and Q_n is the constructed process term P. The transitivity of $\equiv$ ensures $P \equiv S$, the desired result.

The sequence of equations is generated by applying the principles of *transformational programming* as e.g. advocated in the Munich Project CIP [Bau 85, Bau 87]. Thus each equation

$$Q_i \equiv Q_{i+1}$$

in the sequence is obtained by applying a *transformation rule* to a subterm of Q_i, usually a trace specification, say S_i. Most of the transformation rules to be introduced below state that under certain conditions a semantic equation of the form

$$S_i \equiv op(S_{i_1}, \ldots, S_{i_n})$$

holds, i.e. the trace specification S_i can be refined into a mixed term consisting of an n-ary process operator op applied to trace specifications $S_{i_1}, \ldots, S_{i_n}$ which are related to S_i by some logical operator. Then Q_{i+1} results from Q_i by replacing the subterm S_i with $op(S_{i_1}, \ldots, S_{i_n})$. Since the underlying readiness semantics is denotational, $S_i \equiv op(S_{i_1}, \ldots, S_{i_n})$ implies $Q_i \equiv Q_{i+1}$. In this way, the original trace specification S is gradually transformed into a process term P.

Transformation rules are theorems about the readiness semantics of mixed terms that can be expressed as deduction rules of the form

$$(\mathfrak{D}) \qquad \frac{\models S_1, \ldots, \models S_m \qquad P_1 \equiv Q_1, \ldots, P_n \equiv Q_n}{P \equiv Q} \quad \text{where} \ldots$$

where m, n ≥ 0 and "..." is a condition on the syntax of the trace specifications $S_1, \ldots, S_m$ and the mixed terms $P_1, Q_1, \ldots, P_n, Q_n, P, Q$. The rule $\mathfrak{D}$ states that if the condition "..." is satisfied, the trace specifications $S_1, \ldots, S_m$ are valid and the semantic equations $P_1 \equiv Q_1, \ldots, P_n \equiv Q_n$ are true then also the semantic equation $P \equiv Q$ holds. If $m=n=0$, the notation simplies to

$$P \equiv Q \quad \text{where} \ldots$$

We say that a deduction rule $\mathfrak{D}$ is *sound* if the theorem denoted by $\mathfrak{D}$ is true.

The condition "..." will always be a simple decidable property, e.g. concerning alphabets. By contrast, the validity of trace specifications is in general not decidable due to the Expressiveness Theorem in Section 2. Thus in general the transformation rules $\mathfrak{D}$ are effectively applicable only *relative to* the logical theory of trace specifications, i.e. the set

$$Th(Spec) = \{ S \in Spec \mid \models S \} .$$

To enhance the readability of transformation rules, we will sometimes deviate from the form $\mathfrak{D}$ above and use equivalent ones. For example, we will often require that certain traces $\mathfrak{h}$ satisfy a trace specification S, but this is of course equivalent to a validity condition:

$$\mathfrak{h} \models S \quad \text{iff} \quad \models S\{\mathfrak{h}/h\} .$$

Depending on the syntactic form of the mixed terms P and Q in the conclusion of $\mathfrak{D}$ we distinguish among several types of transformation rules:

(1) *Equation Rules*: P, Q are arbitrary mixed terms.
(2) *Specification Rules*: P, Q are trace specifications.
(3) *Construction Rules*: P is a mixed term involving one process operator op or one recursion symbol μ and Q is a trace specification.
(4) *Algebraic Rules*: P, Q are mixed terms which both involve certain process operators or recursion symbols.

Some rules of type (1) - (4) will be classified as *derived rules* because they can be deduced from other rules. Their purpose is to organise the presentation of process constructions more clearly. We shall consider here only transformation rules of type (1) - (3); rules of type (4) are not used.

To state the semantic and syntactic conditions of our transformation rules, we need the following notions. The *prefix kernel* of a trace specification S is given by the formula

$$kern(S) =_{df} \forall\, t.\ t \le h \upharpoonright \alpha(S) \longrightarrow S\{ t / h \}$$

Thus kern(S) is a trace specification which denotes the largest prefix closed set of traces satisfying S (cf. [Zw 89]). The set of *initial communications* of a trace specification S is given by

$$\text{init}(S) = \{ a \in \alpha(S) \mid \textit{pref}\ a \models S \}$$

Recall that *pref* a $\models$ S is equivalent to requiring $\varepsilon \models$ S and a $\models$ S.

By definition, every mixed term P is action-guarded. We now introduce a stronger notion of communication-guardedness whereby the guarding communication may not be hidden. The purpose of this notion is a sufficent syntactic condition implying that every recursion in P has a unique fixed point in the readiness semantics. In particular, if this fixed point is given by a trace specification, the recursion is divergence free. This observation gives rise to a corresponding recursion rule. Since uniqueness of fixed points is an undecidable property for the class of terms considered here, no syntactic condition for it will be a necessary one.

Definition. Let A be a set of communications. A mixed term P $\in$ Proc+Spec is called *communication-guarded by A* if for every recursive subterm μX. Q of P every free occurrence of X in Q occurs within a subterm of Q which is of the form a. R with a $\in$ A, but not within a subterm of Q which is of the form R [b/a] or R\a with a $\in$ A and b $\notin$ A. P is called *communication-guarded* if there exists a set A of communications such that P is communication-guarded by A. □

For example, the following terms are all communication-guarded:

$$P_1 = \mu X.\ up.\ \mu Y.\ (\ dn.\ X + up.\ dn.\ Y\ )\ ,$$

$$P_2 = ((\ \mu X.\ up.\ dn.\ X)[\ lk/dn\ ] \parallel 0 \le lk\#h - dn\#h \le 1) \backslash lk\ ,$$

$$P_3 = \mu X.\ up.\ (X[\ lk/dn\ ] \parallel dn.\ (\ dn\#h \le lk\#h\ )) \backslash lk\ .$$

By contrast,

$$Q_1 = \mu X.\ up.\ (X\ [lk/up\ ]) \backslash lk$$

$$Q_2 = \mu X.\ up.\ (X\ [lk/dn\ ] \parallel dn.\ X[\ lk/up\ ]) \backslash lk$$

are action-guarded, but not communication-guarded.

We can now introduce the announced transformation rules for mixed terms.

Definition. In the following transformation rules, letters P, Q, R range over CProc+Spec unless stated otherwise. As usual, letters S, T; X; a, b; A range over Spec, Idf, Comm, and alphabets, respectively.

(1) Equation Rules:

(Reflexivity)

$$P \equiv P$$

(Symmetry)

$$\frac{P \equiv Q}{Q \equiv P}$$

(Transitivity)

$$\frac{P \equiv Q\ ,\ Q \equiv R}{P \equiv R}$$

(Context)

$$\frac{Q \equiv R}{P\{\, Q/X \,\} \equiv P\{\, R/X \,\}}$$ where $P \in$ Proc+Spec and $P\{\, Q/X \,\}, P\{\, R/X \,\} \in$ CProc+Spec

(2) Specification Rules:

(Kernel)

$$S \equiv kern(S)$$

(Logic)

$$\frac{\models S \leftrightarrow T}{S \equiv T}$$ where $\alpha(S) = \alpha(T)$

(3) Construction Rules:

(Deadlock)

$$stop{:}\, A \equiv h \upharpoonright A \le \varepsilon$$

(Prefix)

$$\frac{init(S) = \{\, a \,\}}{a.\, S\{\, a.\, h\, /h \,\} \equiv S}$$

(Choice)

$$\frac{\varepsilon \models S \wedge T\, ,\ init(S \wedge T) = \emptyset}{S + T \equiv S \vee T}$$ where $\alpha(S) = \alpha(T)$

(Parallelism)

$$S \,\|\, T \equiv S \wedge T$$

(Renaming)

- *same traces*:
  $\forall\, \mathfrak{h}' \in \alpha(T)^*$:
  $\mathfrak{h}' \models T$ iff $\exists\, \mathfrak{h} \in \alpha(S)^*$: $\mathfrak{h} \models S$ and $\mathfrak{h}\{\, b_i/a_i \,\} = \mathfrak{h}'$
- *same liveness*:
  $\forall\, \mathfrak{h}_1, \mathfrak{h}_2 \in \alpha(S)^*\ \ \forall\, c \in \alpha(S)$:
  $\mathfrak{h}_1 \models S$ and $\mathfrak{h}_2 \models S$ and $\mathfrak{h}_1\{\, b_i/a_i\} = \mathfrak{h}_2\{\, b_i/a_i\}$
  and $\mathfrak{h}_1.\, c \models S$ imply
  $\exists\, d \in \alpha(S)$: $\mathfrak{h}_2.\, d \models S$ and $c\{\, b_i/a_i\} = d\{\, b_i/a_i\}$

$$S\, [\, b_i/a_i \,] = T$$

where $\alpha(T) = \alpha(S)\{b_i/a_i\}$ and b_i/a_i stands for a renaming $b_1, \ldots, b_n/a_1, \ldots, a_n$ with $n \ge 1$

(Hiding)

- *empty trace*: $\varepsilon \models S$
- *logical implication*: $\models S \longrightarrow T$
- *stability*: $\forall\, b \in B$: $b \models \neg S$
- *divergence freedom*: $\forall\, \mathfrak{h} \in \alpha(S)^*\ \exists\, b_1, \ldots, b_n \in B$:
  $\mathfrak{h}.\, b_1 \ldots b_n \models \neg S$
- *same liveness*: $\forall\, \mathfrak{h} \in \alpha(S)^*\ \forall\, c \in \alpha(T)$:
  $\mathfrak{h} \models S$ and $\forall\, b \in B$: $\mathfrak{h}.\, b \models \neg S$
  and $\mathfrak{h}.\, c \models T$ imply $\mathfrak{h}.\, c \models S$

$$S \backslash B \equiv T$$

where $\alpha(T) = \alpha(S) - B$

(Recursion)

$$\frac{P\ \{\ S/X\ \} \equiv S}{\mu X.\ P \equiv S}$$ where $\mu X.\ P \in$ CProc+Spec is communication-guarded and $\alpha(S) = \alpha(X)$

(Expansion: derived)

$$\frac{\mathrm{init}(S) = \{\ a_1, \dots , a_n\ \}}{\sum_{i=1}^{n} a_i .\ S\ \{\ a_i .\ h\ /\ h\ \} \equiv S}$$ where $a_1, \dots, a_n$ are $n \geq 2$ distinct communications

(Disjoint renaming: derived)

$$S\ [\ b_i/a_i\ ] \equiv S\ \{\ b_i/a_i\ \}$$ where b_i/a_i stands for a renaming $b_1, \dots, b_n/a_1, \dots, a_n$ with $n \geq 1$ and $b_1, \dots, b_n \notin \alpha\alpha(S)$

□

The equation rules are standard for any type of equational reasoning. The kernel rule reflects a property of the process domain, i.e. that the set of traces in which a process may engage in is prefix closed. Hence only the prefix kernel of a trace specification is relevant. The need for such a rule in trace-based reasoning has been observed in [Jo 87, WGS 87, Zw 89]. The logic rule provides the interface between trace logic and equality in the readiness domain.

Of the construction rules those for renaming and hiding are surprisingly complicated. The reason is that renaming and hiding can completely restructure the communication behaviour of a process. In particular, both operators can introduce externally observable nondeterminism and additionally hiding can introduce divergence and initial unstability. Processes with such properties fail to satisfy the liveness conditions of any trace specification. To exclude such failure the rules for renaming and hiding have various semantic premises.

The difficult case of renaming is *aliasing*, i.e. when two originally different communications get the same name. For example, if

$$S \equiv a \# h \leq 1 \wedge b \# h \leq 2$$

then

$$S\ [\ b/a\ ] \equiv b \# h \leq 3$$

but if

$$S \equiv a \# h \leq 1 \vee b \# h \leq 2$$

then $S[\ b/a]$ is externally nondeterministic (it either deadlocks after the first b or accepts a second one) and hence not equivalent to any other trace specification. Fortunately, in most cases we are only interested in renamings $S[\,b_i/a_i]$ without aliasing. Then we can assume that the communications b_i are not in the extended alphabet $\alpha\alpha(\ S\ )$ introduced in Section 2 and apply the extremely simple rule for disjoint renaming. It states that the semantics of $S[\,b_i/a_i]$ is captured by a simple syntactic substitution $S\{\ b_i/a_i\ \}$.

For hiding we have not found a special case that would allow an equally simple treatment. Thus we always have to check all the premises of the hiding rule. In practical applications we found that the first four premises are easily established. Only the premise "same liveness" is more difficult; it is proven by a case analysis for all communications c $\in \alpha(T)$.

The remaining rules are all extremely simple. Parallel composition is just logical conjunction, choice is essentially logical disjunction, prefix is treated by logical substitution, the expansion rule combines prefix with (multiple) choice, and the recursion rule asks for a recursive semantic equation in its premise. Thus when applying the above transformation rules difficulties arise only when they are unavoidable: in the cases of renaming with aliasing and hiding.

We remark that the simple conjunction rule for parallelism was one of our aims when selecting the operators for process terms. That is why we have chosen COSY's version of parallel composition. By contrast, the parallel composition of CCS would be extremely difficult to deal with in our approach because it combines in a single operator the effect of COSY's parallelism, renaming with aliasing (to model *autoconcurrency*, i.e. concurrent communications with the same name) and hiding. Here we follow CSP and treat all these issues separately.

A simple disjunction rule for choice was another aim. It led us to require that processes satisfying a trace specification should be stable initially. Indeed, if S and T would allow processes to have an initial unstability then S + T would exhibit externally observable nondeterminism and hence not satisfy the liveness condition of any other trace specification.

These two examples illustrate how our aim of bringing different views of concurrent processes together influenced certain design decisions in our approach.

Soundness Theorem. [Ol 88/89] The above transformation rules are sound. □

7. PROCESS CONSTRUCTION

In his books on CCS, Milner considers a small scheduling problem [Mi 80, Mi 89]. Specification and implementation are described by CCS terms; the proof that the implementation meets the implementation is purely algebraic, i.e. by application of the algebraic rules of CCS. Interestingly, in [Mi 80] Milner also gives an informal Petri net semantics of his implementation. Milner's example provides a very good illustration for our approach: we start from a trace specification and systematically construct two alternative process term implementations, one of them corresponding to Milner's solution in CCS. For each of the constructed process terms we examine its Petri net semantics. Since we use COSY's parallel operator, our term construction and the resulting Petri net solution turns out to be simpler than Milner's CCS solution.

In trace logic Milner's scheduling problem can be stated as follows:

$$\mathrm{SPEC}_k =_{df} \bigwedge_{i=1}^{k} h\restriction\{a_i, b_i\} \in \mathit{pref}\,(a_i . b_i)^*$$
$$\wedge\; h\restriction\{a_1, \ldots, a_k\} \in \mathit{pref}\,(a_1 \ldots a_k)^*$$

where $k \geq 1$. Thus we use here regular expressions and the prefix operator *pref* to specify a process that can engage in communications $a_1, \ldots, a_k$ and $b_1, \ldots, b_k$. When projected onto $\{a_i, b_i\}$ the process engages in a small cycle $a_i b_i$ and when projected onto $\{a_1, \ldots, a_k\}$ it engages in a large cycle $a_1 \ldots a_k$. There are no further restrictions imposed on the communication behaviour of the process.

For distinct communications $c_1, \ldots, c_n$ consider the trace specifications

$$S =_{df} h\restriction\{c_1, \ldots, c_n\} \in \mathit{pref}\,(c_1, \ldots, c_n)^*$$

and

$$T =_{df} c_n\#h \leq \ldots \leq c_1\#h \leq 1 + c_n\#h.$$

Since $\alpha(S) = \alpha(T)$ and $\models S \longleftrightarrow \mathrm{kern}(T)$, the kernel and logic rule yield

(A) $$S \equiv T.$$

Applying this observation to SPEC_k, we obtain

$$\mathrm{SPEC}_k \equiv \bigwedge_{i=1}^{k} b_i\#h \leq a_i\#h \leq 1 + b_i\#h$$
$$\wedge\; a_k\#h \leq \ldots \leq a_1\#h \leq 1 + a_k\#h.$$

We find regular expressions easier to read, but inequalities between the number of occurrences of certain communications easier to calculate with. We now present two constructions of process terms from SPEC_k.

First construction. Since SPEC_k is given as a conjunction of several conditions, the application of the parallelism rule is straightforward. Define

$$\mathrm{PROC}_i = h\restriction\{a_i, b_i\} \in \mathit{pref}\,(a_i . b_i)^*$$

for $i=1, \ldots, k$ and

$$\mathrm{SCH}_k =_{df} h\restriction\{a_1, \ldots, a_k\} \in \mathit{pref}(a_1 \ldots a_k)^*,$$

standing for "process i" and "scheduler of size k". Then by successive applications of the parallelism rule, we obtain:

(C) $$\mathrm{SPEC}_k \;|||\; \left(\big\|_{i=1}^{k} \mathrm{PROC}_i\right) \| \,\mathrm{SCH}_k$$

Process terms satisfying the specifications PROC_i and SCH_k are easily constructed using the rules for prefix and recursion. We record only the results of these constructions:

(D) $$\mathrm{PROC}_i \;|||\; \mu XX_i . a_i . b_i . XX_i \quad \text{and} \quad \mathrm{SCH}_k \;|||\; \mu YY_k . a_1 \ldots a_k . YY_k$$

where $\alpha(XX_i) = \{a_i, b_i\}$ and $\alpha(YY_k) = \{a_1,\dots,a_k\}$. Combining (C) and (D) completes the first construction:

$$\begin{array}{c} SPEC_k \\ ||| \\ (\overset{k}{\underset{i=1}{||}} PROC_i) \; || \; SCH_k \\ ||| \\ (\overset{k}{\underset{i=1}{||}} \mu XX_i . a_i . b_i . XX_i) \; || \; \mu YY_k . a_1 \dots a_k . YY_k \end{array}$$

For k=3, the constructed process term denotes the following abstract net:

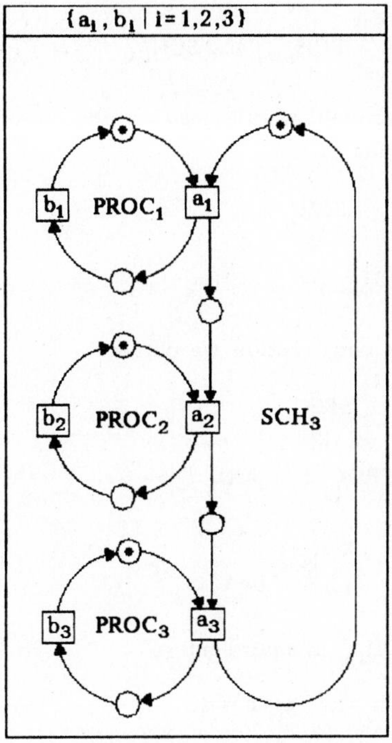

The annotation indicates which cycles in the net implement the specifications $PROC_i$ and SCH_3. Note that a concurrent activation of the transitions labeled by b_i is possible. For arbitrary k, the net has 3k places. The drawback of this implementation is that for each k a new scheduler SCH_k is needed. To overcome this drawback, we present now a process construction corresponding to Milner's original solution.

Second construction. Milner's aim was a *modular* scheduler which for arbitrary problem size could be built as a "ring of elementary identical components" [Mi 80]. This idea can be realised very neathy using transformations on mixed terms. The point is to break down the large cycle $a_1 \dots a_k$ of SCH_k into k+1 cycles of size 2, viz. a_1a_2, a_2a_3, ..., $a_{k-1}a_k$ and a_1a_k.

Formally, this idea is justified by calculations with inequalities based on the representation (A) of cyclic regular expressions. Represent the large cycle $a_1 \dots a_k$ by

$$CYC_k =_{df} a_k \# h \leq \ldots \leq a_1 \# h \leq 1 + a_k \# h$$

and for $1 \leq i < j \leq k$ represent a cycle $a_i a_j$ by

$$SCH_{i,j} =_{df} a_j \# h \leq a_i \# h \leq 1 + a_j \# h.$$

By simple calculations with inequalities, we prove the logical equivalence

(E)
$$\models CYC_k \longleftrightarrow \left(\bigwedge_{i=1}^{k-1} SCH_{i,i+1} \right) \wedge SCH_{1,k} .$$

By (A) above, we have $SCH_k \equiv CYC_k$ and hence by (E), the logic rule yields

$$SCH_k \equiv \left(\bigwedge_{i=1}^{k-1} SCH_{i,i+1} \right) \wedge SCH_{1,k}$$

Thus successive applications of the parallelism rule lead to the following decomposition of the large cycle SCH_k into small cycles $SCH_{i,j}$:

(F)
$$\begin{array}{c} SCH_k \\ ||| \\ \left(\|_{i=1}^{k} SCH_{i,i+1} \right) \| SCH_{1,k} \end{array}$$

Combining (F) with (C) of the previous construction we obtain:

(G)
$$\begin{array}{c} SPEC_k \\ ||| \\ \left(\|_{i=1}^{k} PROC_i \right) \| SCH_k \\ ||| \\ \left(\|_{i=1}^{k} PROC_i \right) \| \left(\|_{i=1}^{k-1} SCH_{i,i+1} \right) \| SCH_{1,k} \end{array}$$

Note that each of the specifications $SCH_{i,j}$ is equivalent to

$$0 \leq a_i \# h - a_j \# h \leq 1.$$

By (A), also each of the specifications $PROC_i$ is equivalent to

$$0 \leq a_i \# h - b_i \# h \leq 1$$

Thus $SCH_{i,j}$ and $PROC_i$ are all renamed copies of a 1-counter specified by

$$S_1 =_{df} 0 \leq up \# h - dn \# h \leq 1.$$

Formally,

(H)
$$\begin{array}{c} PROC_i \\ ||| \\ S_1[a_i, b_i / up, dn] \end{array} \quad \text{and} \quad \begin{array}{c} SCH_{i,j} \\ ||| \\ S_1[a_i, a_j / up, dn] \end{array}$$

by the logic and disjoint renaming rule. By the rules for prefix and recursion,

(I) $$\mu X.up.dn.X \equiv S_1 .$$

Thus combining (G) - (I) we obtain the following process term satisfying $SPEC_k$:

$$(\|_{i=1}^{k} (\mu X.up.dn.X)[a_i,b_i/up,dn])$$
$$\| (\|_{i=1}^{k-1} (\mu X.up.dn.X)[a_i,a_{i+1}/up,dn])$$
$$\| (\mu X.up.dn.X)[a_1,a_k/up,dn]$$

It consists of the parallel composition of 2k copies of the 1-counter. For k=4 this term denotes the following abstract net:

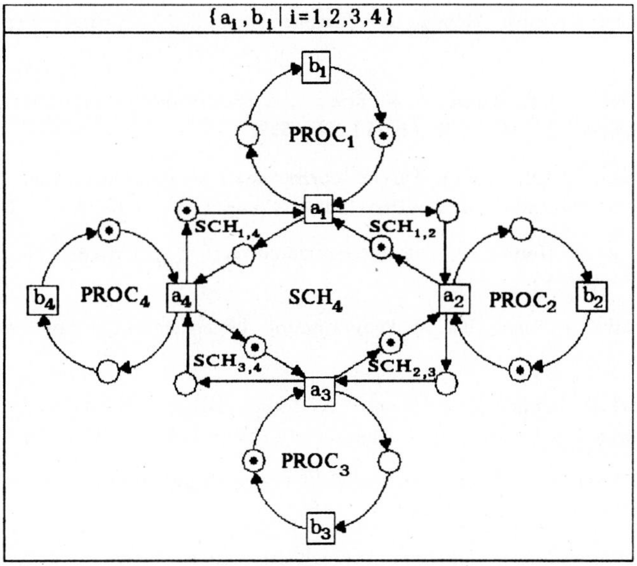

The annotation indicates the cycles that implement the specifications $PROC_i$. The rectangular part in the centre is the implementation of SCH_4 consisting of an appropriate synchronisation of the cycles $SCH_{1,2}$, $SCH_{2,3}$, $SCH_{3,4}$ and $SCH_{1,4}$. Note that the asymmetry in the initial token distribution is due to the cycle $SCH_{1,4}$. For arbitrary k the net has 4k places. (The net given in [Mi 80] needs 5k places.) Since only the part implementing the scheduler SCH_k differs from the previous net implementation, concurrency of the b_i-transitions is still possible. We believe that this is an example where it is fairly difficult to get the net implementation right without the systematic guidance of formulas and terms.

8. REFERENCES

[AS 85] B. Alpern, F.B. Schneider, Defining liveness, Inform. Proc. Letters 21 (1985) 181-185.

[Ba 80] J.W. de Bakker, Mathematical Theory of Program Correctness (Prentice-Hall, London, 1989).

[Bau 85] F.L. Bauer et al., The Munich Project CIP, Vol. I: The Wide Spectrum Language CIP-L, Lecture Notes in Comput. Sci. 183 (Springer-Verlag, 1985).

[Bau 87] F.L. Bauer et al., The Munich Project CIP, Vol. II: The Program Transformation System CIP-S, Lecture Notes in Comput. Sci. 292 (Springer-Verlag, 1987).

[Be 87] E. Best, COSY: its relation to nets and CSP, in: W. Brauer, W. Reisig, G. Rozenberg (Eds.), Petri Nets: Applications and Relationships to Other Models of Concurrency, Lecture Notes in Comput. Sci. 255 (Springer-Verlag, 1987) 416-440.

[BHR 84] S.D. Brookes, C.A.R. Hoare, A.W. Roscoe, A theory of communicating sequential processes, J. ACM 31 (1984) 560-599.

[CHo 81] Z. Chaochen, C.A.R. Hoare, Partial correctness of communicating processes, in: Proc. 2nd Intern. Conf. on Distributed Comput. Systems, Paris, 1981.

[DH 84] R. DeNicola, M. Hennessy, Testing equivalences for processes, Theoret. Comput. Sci. 34 (1984) 83-134.

[Di 76] E.W. Dijkstra, A Discipline of Programming (Prentice-Hall, Englewood Cliffs, NJ, 1976).

[FLP 84] N. Francez, D. Lehmann, A. Pnueli, A linear history semantics for languages for distributed programmming, Theoret. Comput. Sci. 32 (1984) 25-46.

[Go 88] U. Goltz, Über die Darstellung von CCS-Programmen durch Petrinetze, Doctoral Diss., RWTH Aachen, 1988.

[Ho 78] C.A.R. Hoare, Some properties of predicate transformers, J. ACM 25 (1978) 461-480.

[Ho 81] C.A.R. Hoare, A calculus of total correctness for communicating processes, Sci. Comput. Progr. 1 (1981) 44-72.

[Ho 85] C.A.R. Hoare, Communicating Sequential Processes (Prentice-Hall, London, 1985).

[Jo 87] B. Jonsson, Compositional Verification of Distributed Systems, Ph.D. Thesis, Dept. Comput. Sci., Uppsala Univ., 1987.

[LTS 79] P.E. Lauer, P.R. Torrigiani, M.W. Shields, COSY - A system specification language based on paths and processes, Acta Inform. 12 (1979) 109-158.

[Mi 80] R. Milner, A Calculus of Communicating Systems, Lecture Notes in Comput. Sci. 92 (Springer-Verlag, 1980).

[Mz 77] A. Mazurkiewicz, Concurrent program schemes and their interpretations, Tech. Report DAIMI PB-78, Aarhus Univ., 1977.

[Mi 89] R. Milner, Communication and Concurrency (Prentice-Hall, London, 1989).

[MC 81] J. Misra, K.M. Chandy, Proofs of networks of processes, IEEE Trans. Software Eng. 7 (1981) 417-426.

[Ol 88/89] E.-R. Olderog, Nets, Terms and Formulas: Three Views of Concurrent Processes and Their Relationship, Habilitationsschrift, Univ. Kiel, 1988/89.

[Ol 89a] E.-R. Olderog, Strong bisimilarity on nets: a new concept for comparing net semantics, in: J.W. de Bakker, W.P. de Roever, G. Rozenberg (Eds.), Linear Time, Branching Time and Partial Order in Logics and Models of Concurrency, Lecture Notes in Comput. Sci. 354 (Springer-Verlag, 1989) 549-573.

[Ol 89b] E.-R. Olderog, Correctness of concurrent processes, invited paper, in: A. Kreczmar, G. Mirkowska (Eds.), Math. Found. of Comput. Sci. 1989, Lecture Notes in Comput. Sci. 379 (Springer-Verlag, 1989) 107-132.

[OH 86] E.-R. Olderog, C.A.R. Hoare, Specification-oriented semantics for communicating processes, Acta Inform. 23 (1986) 9-66.

[OL 82] S. Owicki, L. Lamport, Proving liveness properties of concurrent programs, ACM TOPLAS 4 (1982) 199-223.

[Re 85] W. Reisig, Petri Nets, An Introduction, EATCS Monographs on Theoret. Comput. Sci. (Springer-Verlag, 1985).

[Rm 87] M. Rem, Trace theory and systolic computation, in: J.W. de Bakker, A.J. Nijman, P.C. Treleaven (Eds.), Proc. PARLE Conf., Eindhoven, Vol. I, Lecture Notes in Comput. Sci. 258, (Springer-Verlag, 1987) 14-33.

[Sc 70] D.S. Scott, Outline of a mathematical theory of computation, Tech. Monograph PRG-2, Progr. Research Group, Oxford Univ., 1970.

[St 77] J.E. Stoy, Denotational Semantics: The Scott-Strachey Approach to Programming Language Theory (MIT Press, Cambridge, Mass., 1977).

[Sn 85] J.L.A. van de Snepscheut, Trace Theory and VLSI Design, Lecture Notes in Comput. Sci. 200 (Springer-Verlag, 1985).

[WGS 87] J. Widom, D. Gries, F.B. Schneider, Completeness and incompleteness of trace-baced network proof systems, in: Proc. 14th ACM Symp. on Principles of Progr. Languages, München, 1987, 27-38.

[Wi 71] N. Wirth, Program development by stepwise refinement, Comm. ACM 14 (1971) 221-227.

[Zw 89] J. Zwiers, Compositionality, Concurrency and Partial Correctness, Lecture Notes in Comput. Sci. 321 (Springer-Verlag, 1989).

[ZRE 85] J. Zwiers, W.P. de Roever, P. van Emde-Boas, Compositionality and concurrent networks, in: W. Brauer (Ed.), Proc. 12th Coll. Automata, Languages and Programming, Lecture Notes in Comput. Sci. 194 (Springer-Verlag, 1985) 509-519.

Some comments on the assumption-commitment framework for compositional verification of distributed programs

Paritosh K. Pandya *
Programming Research Group, Oxford University
8–11 Keble Road, Oxford, OX1 3QD
U.K.

Extended Abstract

Abstract

In this paper we investigate the use of assumption-commitment techniques for compositional proofs of safety and liveness properties of networks of processes. An inductive inference strategy to discharge mutually dependent assumptions is investigated. Some existing proof techniques are justified in terms of this framework.

Keywords: Compositional Verification, Liveness properties, Assumption Commitment Framework, Inductive Inference.

Contents

1 Introduction

2 Executions and their specification

2.1 Execution assertions

3 Assumption-commitment framework

3.1 Mathematical preliminaries

4 Hierarchical Dependence Method

5 Stratified Specification and Inductive Inference

5.1 Misra-Chandy's use of Assumption-Commitment Framework

5.2 Dynamic Ordering

6 Discussion

---

*Supported by SERC, U.K.

1 Introduction

The problem of compositional verification of safety and liveness properties of distributed programs has received much interest. Several techniques have been suggested, and reasonable methods can be said to exist for deriving safety properties. Liveness properties, on the other hand, are believed to be hard to establish compositionally.

In compositional verification properties of a composite object are established from the properties of its components. The properties of the component are established separately, without knowing about the context in which the component occurs [Rov85].

A property β of a process S is called *inviolate* if it is also true of any network containing S. For example, "all messages output by S over channel C are positive" is inviolate. It is very useful to establish inviolate properties for processes (since they hold for the network too). Secondly, there are *composition properties* which are true of any network. Such properties allow us to relate the process behaviours to the behaviour of their network, e.g. "the network terminates when all its processes have terminated". The properties of a network can be derived by taking the conjunction of inviolate process properties along with the composition properties. This paradigm has been applied successfully to safety properties. Keeping within this paradigm, we examine a way of structuring the proofs of network, which often leads to intuitively clearer and simpler proofs for safety and liveness properties. Our method is based on separating assumptions and commitments in the process specification.

First point to note is that in compositional verification, the specification of the process must only specify the part played by the process in the functioning of the network. Thus, the specification of a process must only be in terms of entities locally observable at the process. The next point is that compositionality does not forbid us from tailoring the specification of a component to suit the application in which it is used. This is achieved by including some assumptions about the environment of the component in the specification. Compositionality only requires that the proof that the component meets its specification, is given independently of the other components.

When program designer has some knowledge about the intended environment of a process (as in top-down design), assumptions about the behaviour of the environment enable the designer to give a concise specification of the process which is tailored towards obtaining the desired network behaviour. Such a specification is often easier to prove for the process, and the proof of network composition is also intuitively more appealing. By abandoning assumptions the designer is confined to giving the "strongest" description of the process from which it is harder to establish the network behaviour.

Inclusion of assumptions in the specification of processes of course dictates that we find methods for discharging these assumptions when processes are put together to form a network. Once this is done, the behaviour of the network can be derived from the conjunction of the inviolate safety and liveness properties of the processes along with the composition properties.

In this paper we investigate some strategies which can be used for discharging mutually dependent assumptions by the processes of a network. These strategies have an inductive flavour. Some of the existing proof methods for proving properties of distributed programs [MC81, Sta85] are interpreted in the light of such strategies.

2 Executions and their specification

There are many different models of processes and their networks. Our aim here is to define a general framework relating to these models and then to proceed with the discussion of assumption-commitment style proofs. Hence we do not give any specific model of distributed program; but define a general notion of executions and execution properties which is compatible with many of the existing models.

With each process or network SS we associate $Basis(SS)$ giving the set of observable entities in terms of which the executions of SS are described. The basis is partitioned into

- $StateVar(SS)$ – giving the entities whose value might changes with each step of the execution; for example the program variables and the sequence of values communicated over a channel of SS.
- $ExecVar(SS)$ – giving the entities which record some aspect of the entire execution; for example a boolean variable $\mathbf{finite_i}$ records the finiteness of execution of a process S_i within SS.

Let $BA = SV \cup EV$ be a basis. Let Δ and Σ be the sets of (functions making) assignments of values to the execution variables EV and state variables SV, respectively.

$$EXEC(BA) \stackrel{\text{def}}{=} \Delta \times (\Sigma^* \cup \Sigma^\omega)$$

Thus, an execution (δ, Ψ) consists of an assignment δ of values to the execution variables, and a finite or infinite sequence Ψ of assignments of values to the state variables.

An execution property β over basis BA, denoted by $BA :: \beta$, specifies a subset of executions $EXEC(BA)$. We shall assume an appropriate definition of $(\delta, \Psi) \models \beta$ stating that property β holds for execution (δ, Ψ). Boolean connectives $(\wedge, \vee, \neg, \Rightarrow, \Leftrightarrow)$ of execution properties have the usual definition. For example,

$$(\delta, \Psi) \models \beta_1 \wedge \beta_2 \textbf{ iff } (\delta, \Psi) \models \beta_1 \text{ and } (\delta, \Psi) \models \beta_2$$

The set of executions of SS will be denoted by $\ll SS \gg$, and it must satisfy the condition:

$$\ll SS \gg \subseteq EXEC(Basis(SS))$$

Definition 2.1 Notation SS **sat** β designates that any execution of SS satisfies the execution property β, i.e.

$$SS \textbf{ sat } \beta \stackrel{\text{def}}{=} \forall (\delta, \Psi) \in \ll SS \gg : (\delta, \Psi) \models \beta$$

□

Above definition of S **sat** β gives us the following rules:

$$\frac{SS \textbf{ sat } \beta_1, \quad \beta_1 \Rightarrow \beta_2}{SS \textbf{ sat } \beta_2} \tag{1}$$

$$\frac{SS \textbf{ sat } \beta_1, \quad SS \textbf{ sat } \beta_2}{SS \textbf{ sat } \beta_1 \wedge \beta_2} \tag{2}$$

Not all executions of $EXEC(BA)$ are valid executions of processes and networks. Valid executions can be terms as *computations.* Axioms characterising computations are called computation properties. For example, "number of communications over a channel cannot decrease during execution" is often chosen to be a computation property.

Definition 2.2 An execution property β is called a *computation property* provided

$$SS \textbf{ sat } \beta$$

for any arbitrary process or network SS. □

which (obviously) gives us the following rule:

$$\frac{\beta \text{ is a computation property}}{SS \textbf{ sat } \beta} \tag{3}$$

Networks Consider a network of n processes. Each process as well as the network is identified by a unique index. We shall follow the convention that i'th process of the network has index i and the index of the network is 0. (A more elaborate indexing convention must be used when a network can be a part of other networks. We will disregard this here). Notation $NET[S_i]$ denotes an arbitrary network of n processes containing S_i as one of its process, and NET designates an arbitrary network of n processes. Let the basis of the network be BA and the basis of a process with index i be BA_i. We will continue to use SS to designate either a network or a process.

A semantic model for distributed programs must define the computations of a network, and their relationship to the computations of its processes. In this paper, we shall only consider models satisfying the following requirements:

1. $Basis(S_i) \subseteq Basis(NET[S_i])$. Thus, every observable entity of the process is also observable in the network execution.

2. For every execution $(\delta, \Psi) \in EXEC(BA)$, where BA is the network basis, the model must define a projection function $(\delta, \Psi) \uparrow i$, giving the projection of the execution over the process index i. We require that:

   $$((\delta, \Psi) \uparrow i) \in EXEC(BA_i)$$

3. Given $Basis(S_i) :: \beta$ and $(\delta, \Psi) \in NET$,

   $$(\delta, \Psi) \models \beta \textbf{ iff } \forall i : ((\delta, \Psi) \uparrow i) \models \beta$$

Some remarks about the above restriction are in order. Condition (2) requires that the semantics is formulated such that for every execution over the network basis, we can obtain the corresponding component executions over its process indices. (This may require that the identity of processes participating in a step of execution to be recorded within the execution. A similar requirement has been suggested by Pnueli [Pnu85]). Because of conditions (1) and (2) above, it is meaningful to ask whether a process property holds within a network containing the process. Condition (3) states how the validity of a process property within a network execution is defined.

Note that for a network computation $(\delta, \Psi) \in \ll NET[S_i] \gg$, the above definition does not require that $((\delta, \Psi) \uparrow i) \in \ll S_i \gg$, it suffices for the projection to be an execution over BA_i. One reason for the projection of a network computation not being a process computation is the "interference" between process executions [Owi75]. For example, if two processes S_i, S_j share variables in $NET[S_i, S_j]$, the projection of network computation over i typically includes the effect of the steps of S_j modifying the shared variables. The resulting projection may fail to be a computation of S_i. Another instance of interference is when the projection of a network execution gives rise to an incomplete execution of the process, if the process is "starved" during the network execution.

Definition 2.3 A model of distributed programs is called *projective* if

$$(\delta, \Psi) \in \ll NET[S_i] \gg \quad \Rightarrow \forall i: \ ((\delta, \Psi) \uparrow i) \in \ll S_i \gg \qquad \square$$

There are many different models of distributed programs which fit the framework given above [NGO85, BKP85, Zho85].

Definition 2.4 An execution property β is called *inviolate* provided

$$S_i \textbf{ sat } \beta \quad \Rightarrow NET[S_i] \textbf{ sat } \beta$$

for any arbitrary network $NET[S_i]$ containing S_i. □

Definition 2.5 An execution property γ is called a *composition property* provided

$$NET \textbf{ sat } \gamma$$

for any arbitrary network NET. □

¿From the above definitions, the following rules are obvious.

$$\frac{S_i \textbf{ sat } \beta, \quad \beta \text{ is inviolate}}{NET[S_i] \textbf{ sat } \beta} \tag{4}$$

$$\frac{\gamma \text{ is a composition property}}{NET \textbf{ sat } \gamma} \tag{5}$$

Availability of such rules gives us the following strategy for establishing the properties of a network: Establish inviolate properties for the component processes such that the desired property of the network can be derived from the conjunction of the process properties and composition properties.

This strategy has been widely used in the compositional verification of properties of distributed programs [Hoa81, Sou83, ZBR83, BKP85, NGO85, Zho85, ZRB85, Pan88]. Clearly, the class of inviolate and composition properties differs significantly among different models of distributed programs. For example, some models impose "fairness" conditions on the network executions, thereby enlarging the class of their inviolate properties. Definitions of this section provide only a framework for classifying the execution properties in a given model.

Projective models were defined in Definition 2.3. For examples of such models see [NGO85, Zho85]. Projective models have the following useful property.

Proposition 2.6 If a model of distributed programs is projective then every β over $Basis(S_i)$ is inviolate. □

The proposition follows from the definition of projective models and the restrictions on the network semantics, given earlier.

2.1 Execution assertions

So far, we have not mentioned any specific notation for execution properties. The proof rules in this paper can be applied to execution properties in any assertion language. Temporal logic is a well-studied and comprehensive notation for specifying execution properties. We will use this notation to illustrate the use of our proof rules. All our examples will be for message passing distributed programs.

A *state assertion* over basis BA is a predicate which can be evaluated to be true or false at any point in an execution over the basis BA. Thus,

Definition 2.7 A *state assertion* over basis BA is a first order logic assertion containing free variables from BA. □

A state assertion can be used to specify a set of states. Formulae of linear temporal logic can be used to construct execution assertions from the state assertions. In this paper, we shall make use of this standard notation.

Definition 2.8 An execution assertion is a temporal logic formula formed from operators $\Box$, $\Diamond$, $\mathcal{U}$, **U** and state assertions. $\mathcal{U}$ represents "strong until" whereas **U** represents the "Unless" operator. The reader is referred to [Pnu86] for syntax and semantics of temporal formulae. □

Typically, a *safety* property is designated as $\Box P$ where P is a state assertion. Expressing liveness properties requires the use of other temporal operators.

message passing distributed programs Consider a network of n processes which interact by sending and receiving messages from each other over point-to-point channels. Typical example of a notation for such networks is CSP [Hoa78]. Let **pindex** $= 1..n$, be the set of process indices. Variables i, j will range over **pindex**. For each process S_i its alphabet $B_i = (I_i, O_i, V_i)$ gives the set of input channels, output channels and variables used by the process. For a network of n processes, its alphabet $B = \cup B_i$. We assume that the alphabets B_i of its components are known and that $B_i \cap B_j = \emptyset$ for $i \neq j$ (operations over alphabets are component-wise extensions of the set operations). For an alphabet BB=(I,O,V) the set of its ports is given by $Ports(BB) = I \times \{?\} \cup O \times \{!\}$.

Notation A synchronous communication is represented as tuple $< D.v >$, designating that a value v is communicated over channel D. Asynchronous input and output communications are distinct events, and represented as $< D?v >$ and $< D!v >$, respectively. A port trace $D?$ represents the sequence of values communicated over the port $D?$. Similarly for the port trace $D!$.

Following functions and predicates are available over finite sequences.

$Seq_1 \underline{\propto} Seq_2$	Seq_1 is an initial subsequence of Seq_2
$Seq_1 \propto Seq_2$	$Seq_1 \underline{\propto} Seq_2 \wedge Seq_1 \neq Seq_2$
$\#Seq$	the length of sequence Seq
λ	the empty sequence
$Seq[i]$	the ith element of the sequence Seq
$Seq_1 \frown Seq_2$	the catenation of Seq_1 and Seq_2
dom(seq)	$\{1, .., \#seq\}$

Below we define the basis of processes and their network. By a flag we mean a variable of sort *BOOLEAN*.

Definition 2.9 (process basis) Given a process with alphabet B_i and index i, the set $StateVar(B_i)$ contains

- *trace projections* h_{PS} for all $PS \subseteq Ports(B_i)$. Term h_{PS} designates the sequence of communications over the ports in PS.
- Enabledness flag $en(p)$ for $p \in Ports(B_i)$. Flag $en(D?)$ designates that input port $D?$ is ready for communication. Similarly for enabledness flag $en(D!)$. The enabledness flag $en(*_i)$ designates that the process i is ready to perform an internal action.
- Termination flag u_i designating that the current state is terminal.
- Program variables x,y,$\cdots$ from V_i.

The set $ExecVar(B_i)$ contains the flags

- $\mathbf{finite_i}$ representing that an execution satisfying it is finite.
- $\mathbf{divfree_i}$ representing that an execution satisfying it is divergence-free.

□

Definition 2.10 (network basis) Given a network with alphabet B, the set $StateVar(B)$ contains

- *Trace projections* h_{PS} for all $PS \subseteq Ports(B)$.
- Enabledness flags $en(p)$ for $p \in Ports(B)$. Enabledness flag $en(*_0)$ designates that (some process of) the network is ready to perform an internal action. Flag $en(*_i)$ designates that process i of the network is ready to perform an internal action.
- Termination flag u_0 designating that the current state is a terminal state of the network. Termination flag u_i designates that in the current state process i has terminated.
- Program variables x,y,$\cdots$ from V.

The set $ExecVar(B)$ contains flags

- Flag $\mathbf{finite_0}$ represents that a network execution Ψ satisfying it is finite. A network execution Ψ satisfies formula $\mathbf{finite_i}$ if the corresponding process execution $\Psi \uparrow i$ is finite.
- Flag $\mathbf{divfree_0}$ represents that a network execution Ψ satisfying it is divergence-free. Flag $\mathbf{divfree_i}$ denotes that the corresponding process execution $\Psi \uparrow i$ is divergence-free.

□

It is easy to see that $Basis(B_i) \subset Basis(B)$, as required. Recall that state assertions are formulae of first order logic over the free variables of $Basis(B)$. Execution assertions are temporal formulae formed from these.

With this notation, we can discuss some examples of inviolate and composition properties of message passing distributed programs. Here, we shall not give a specific model for networks of processes, but only list some of the inviolate and composition properties of this desired model.

Example 2.11 (Inviolate properties)

- Let P be a state assertion over B_i. Then, $\Box P$ is inviolate in the sense that $\Box P$ holds for the network $NET[S_i]$ if it holds for S_i.
- $\mathbf{finite_i}$ and $\mathbf{divfree_i}$ are inviolate.

□

Example 2.12 (Composition properties)

1. For a synchronous channel D of a network, a communication can occur only by simultaneous input and output by the sending and the receiving process. Hence at all times the sequence of values received over a synchronous channel is same as the sequence of values sent over it.

   $$\Box(D? = D!)$$

2. For an asynchronous channel E, the sequence of values received is at all times a prefix of the sequence of values sent. The remaining values are in the channel buffer.

   $$\Box(E? \underline{\propto} E!)$$

3. The following property states that the network terminates when all its processes have terminated.

   $$\Box(u_0 \Leftrightarrow u_1 \wedge \cdots \wedge u_n)$$

4. Internal action of any process can be considered as an internal action of the network.

   $$\Box\,(en(*_0) \Leftrightarrow en(*_1) \vee \cdots \vee en(*_n))$$

5. The following property states that a network execution is finite **iff** all the corresponding process executions are finite. Similarly for divergence freedom.

   $$\mathbf{finite_0} \Leftrightarrow \mathbf{finite_1} \wedge \cdots \wedge \mathbf{finite_n}$$
   $$\mathbf{divfree_0} \Leftrightarrow \mathbf{divfree_1} \wedge \cdots \wedge \mathbf{divfree_n}$$

□

In the rest of the paper, $COMP$ shall designate the conjunction of the composition properties.

3 Assumption-commitment framework

Stylistically, there are two approaches to establishing the properties of a network. In the bottom up approach, the specification of a process is developed in isolation. Thus, one comprehensive specification of the process must be developed which allows properties of any network containing the process to be derived. In the top down approach, the specification of a process can be tailored to suit the specific environment by giving a conditional specification of the process relative to some assumptions about the behaviour of the environment.

Assumptions about the behaviour of the environment are useful for establishing properties of processes. Their presence gives rise to conditional specification for a process, conveniently written in the form:

$$\{\alpha\}\ S\ \{\beta\}$$

where α is called the assumption and β is called the commitment.

In this paper, we shall require that the assumptions about the environment of a process are given in terms of its effect on the locally observable entities of the process. Consider the following example.

Example 3.1 Process $FACT$ repeatedly receives an integer over the channel A and outputs the factorial of the received value over channel B.

```
FACT =  while true do
          A?x;
          y:=1;
          while x>0 do y:=y*x; x:=x-1 od;
          B!y
        od
```

Only by making an assumption that no negative integer is received can we ensure that the execution of this process is divergence-free. For this process we can give the following conditional specification.

$$\{\alpha_{fact}\}\ FACT\ \{\beta_{fact}\}$$

where,

$$\alpha_{fact} \stackrel{\text{def}}{=} \Box(\forall\, i \in \mathbf{dom}(A?) :\ A?[i] > 0)$$
$$\beta_{fact} \stackrel{\text{def}}{=} \mathbf{divfree_{fact}} \wedge \Box(\forall\, j \in \mathbf{dom}(B!) :\ B[j] = factorial(A[j]))$$

Divergence-freedom ensures that the process will become ready to output the result within a finite time. □

A conditional specification $\{\alpha\}\ S\ \{\beta\}$ states that for any execution of S satisfying property α the property β holds. Hence, the above specification can be formally interpreted as:

$$\{\alpha\}\ S\ \{\beta\}\ \textbf{iff}\ S\ \textbf{sat}\ (\alpha \Rightarrow \beta) \qquad (6)$$

The main reason for syntactically separating the assumptions and the commitments in the specification is that we would like to investigate special strategies to discharge the assumptions.

¿From the interpretation 6 of the assumption-commitment framework, and using rules 4, 2 we obtain the following rule

$$\frac{\begin{array}{l}\{\alpha_i\}\ S_i\ \{\beta_i\},\\ \alpha_i, \beta_i \text{ are inviolate}\end{array}}{NET\ \mathbf{sat}\ \bigwedge_i (\alpha_i\ \Rightarrow\ \beta_i)} \tag{7}$$

This rule is not very convenient in practise. The assumption α_i refers to the behaviour of the other processes of the network. What we want is a condition, termed **cooperation**, under which we can discharge the process assumptions against the behaviours of the processes in NET, so as to conclude $\{\alpha_{net}\}\ NET\ \{\bigwedge_i\ \beta_i\}$. Here α_{net} is an assumption about the *environment of the network*. Thus, we want a rule of the form:

$$\frac{\begin{array}{l}\{\alpha_i\}\ S_i\ \{\beta_i\},\\ \alpha_i, \beta_i \text{ are inviolate}\\ \mathbf{cooperation}\end{array}}{\{\alpha_{net}\}\ NET\ \{\bigwedge_i \beta_i\}} \tag{8}$$

Some care is required in the formulation of such a rule. A major pitfall is that the rule may become unsound due to circular reasoning. Incorrect assumptions may allow derivation of incorrect commitments which in turn may justify the incorrect assumptions through the **cooperation** condition. Consider the following example.

Example 3.2 Let $Net = (S_1 \| S_2)$ be a closed network. Process S_1 is the environment of S_2 and vice versa. Hence, we might formulate the **cooperation** condition as:

$$\mathbf{cooperation}_e \stackrel{\text{def}}{=} (\beta_2 \Rightarrow \alpha_1) \wedge (\beta_1 \Rightarrow \alpha_2)$$

Unfortunately, this formulation of $\mathbf{cooperation}_e$ leads to unsoundness of rule 8. To see this, select

$$\alpha_1 = \beta_1 = \alpha_2 = \beta_2 \stackrel{\text{def}}{=} false, \quad \alpha_{net} = true$$

It is easy to see that $\mathbf{cooperation}_e$ is satisfied. Hence, using rule 8 we obtain $\{true\}Net\{false\}$. □

The condition under which rule 8 is sound can be stated as follows.

$$\left(\bigwedge_i (\alpha_i\ \Rightarrow\ \beta_i)\ \wedge\ COMP\ \wedge\ \mathbf{cooperation}\ \wedge\ \alpha_{net}\right)\ \Rightarrow\ \bigwedge_i \beta_i \tag{9}$$

Note that rule 8 can be derived from the rules 7, 5 and condition 9, and hence is sound. We omit this obvious proof.

Restated, the main problem is to put additional structure on process assumptions and commitments and to formulate an adequate **cooperation** condition so that condition 9 is satisfied. In the rest of the paper, we shall propose various solutions to the above problem and also try to interpret some of the techniques used in the existing proof methods for distributed programs in the light of the above framework.

3.1 Mathematical preliminaries

Definition 3.3 (Acyclic) *A binary relation* $\sqsubset$ *over set* S *is called* acyclic *provided it is irreflexive and transitive. Let* $\sqsubseteq$ *denote the reflexive closure of* $\sqsubset$*, i.e.*

$$a \sqsubseteq b \ \textbf{iff} \ a \sqsubset b \vee a = b$$

Definition 3.4 (well-order) *Given an acyclic relation* $\sqsubset$ *over* S*, the pair* $(S, \sqsubset)$ *is called a* well-order *provided, every nonempty subset* S' *of* S *has a minimal element w.r.t.* $\sqsubset$.

Theorem 3.5 (Noetherian induction) *Let* $(S, \sqsubset)$ *be a well-order, and* $P(x)$ *be a property of elements of* S*. Then,*

$$(\forall x : (\forall y \sqsubset x : P(y)) \Rightarrow P(x)) \quad \Rightarrow \quad \forall x : P(x)$$

The reader is referred to [LSS84] for a detailed treatment of the above.

4 Hierarchical Dependence Method

In this simple method the processes of NET are assumed to be ordered by an acyclic relation $\sqsubset \subseteq \textbf{pindex} \times \textbf{pindex}$, such that the assumption of a process S_i depends upon the behaviours the processes S_j with $j \sqsubset i$. Note that $(\textbf{pindex}, \sqsubset)$ is a *well-order*, as **pindex** is finite.

$$\textbf{cooperation}_{DP} \stackrel{\text{def}}{=}$$
$$\forall i \in \textbf{pindex} : \left(\left(\bigwedge_{j \sqsubset i} \beta_j \right) \wedge COMP \wedge \alpha_{net} \Rightarrow \alpha_i \right)$$

We prove that condition 9 holds for the above choice of $\textbf{cooperation}_{DP}$. i.e.

$$\textbf{From} \ \bigwedge_i (\alpha_i \Rightarrow \beta_i), \quad COMP, \quad \alpha_{net},$$
$$\forall i \in \textbf{pindex} : \left(\left(\bigwedge_{j \sqsubset i} \beta_j \right) \wedge COMP \wedge \alpha_{net} \Rightarrow \alpha_i \right)$$

$$\textbf{infer} \ \bigwedge_i \beta_i$$

Proof (By Noetherian induction over the well-order $(\textbf{pindex}, \sqsubset)$).
Induction step

1. $\left(\bigwedge_{j \sqsubset i} \beta_j \right)$,by induction hypothesis.
2. α_i , From (1) and premises (2),(3) and (4)
3. β_i from (2) and premise (1)

□

$$\begin{aligned}\delta_i(k) &\stackrel{\text{def}}{=} \Box(\#h_{Ports(S_i)} < k \Rightarrow A_i)\\ \theta_i(k) &\stackrel{\text{def}}{=} \Box(\#h_{ports(S_i)} \le k \Rightarrow C_i)\end{aligned} \tag{10}$$

The cooperation condition can be formulated as

$$\mathbf{cooperation}_{MC} \stackrel{\text{def}}{=} \Box(\bigwedge_i C_i \wedge A_{net} \Rightarrow \bigwedge_i A_i)$$

The reader can easily convince himself that the above stratified specification is equivalent to the Misra-Chandy specification.

Initially, in favour of simplicity, we shall consider a special case where $NET = S_1 \| S_2$ is a closed network, and processes communicate only by synchronous communications. The main advantage (to us) of considering such networks is that the following composition property holds for them.

Lemma 5.1 For a closed network $NET = S_1 \| S_2$,

$$NET\ \mathbf{sat}\ \Box(\#h_{Ports(S_1)} = \#h_{Ports(S_2)} = \#h_{Ports(NET)})$$

□

As we are dealing with closed networks, the network assumption is taken to be *true*. The ordering relation $\sqsubset$ can be selected as follows.

$$(j, m) \sqsubset (i, k)\ \mathbf{iff}\ m < k$$

It is easy to see that this is acyclic. We now prove that

Theorem 5.2

$$\mathbf{cooperation}_{MC} \Rightarrow \mathbf{cooperation}_{IND}$$

□

Its proof is based on the following lemmas.

Lemma 5.3

- $\bigwedge_{l<k} \theta_1(l) \wedge \theta_2(l) \Leftrightarrow \Box(\#h_{Ports(NET)} < k \Rightarrow C_1 \wedge C_2)$
- $\delta_1(k) \wedge \delta_2(k) \Leftrightarrow \Box(\#h_{Ports(NET)} < k \Rightarrow A_1 \wedge A_2)$

Proof Follows from the definitions of θ, δ and lemma 5.1. □

Lemma 5.4

$$\left(\Box(C_1 \wedge C_2 \Rightarrow A_1 \wedge A_2) \wedge (\bigwedge_{l<k} \theta_1(l) \wedge \theta_2(l))\right) \Rightarrow \delta_1(k) \wedge \delta_2(k)$$

Proof The result can be derived easily from lemma 5.3. □

Proof of Theorem 5.2 The proof follows directly from lemma 5.4. □

5.2 Dynamic Ordering

The technique proposed in the last section is too restrictive to allow us to interpret the full generality of the Misra-Chandy network composition rule. The difficulty is in finding beforehand, an ordering relation which will justify the Misra-Chandy rule. The ordering relation (**inddom**, $\sqsubset$) can only be specified in terms of some property of the execution. In such a situation, the ordering relation is not determined statically, but evolves with the execution. We shall call such an ordering relation as *dynamic.* Having a dynamic ordering relation does not affect the soundness of our induction scheme, provided one ensures that any ($\mathbf{inddom}_\Psi, \sqsubset_\Psi$) that arises satisfies the property of being a well-order. We give an example of this in the following interpretation of the Misra-Chandy proof rule.

For each network execution (δ, Ψ) we will define a dynamic ordering relation ($\mathbf{inddom}_\Psi, \sqsubset_\Psi$). The following proposition captures its main properties.

Property 5.5 Let (δ, Ψ) be a network execution. Then,

1. ($\mathbf{inddom}_\Psi, \sqsubset_\Psi$) is a well-order.

2. $\Psi \models \Box\left((\#h_{Ports(S_i)} = k) \Rightarrow (i,k) \in \mathbf{inddom}_\Psi\right)$

3. For all $(i,k) \in \mathbf{inddom}_\Psi$,

$$\Psi \models \Box\left((\#h_{Ports(S_i)} < k) \Rightarrow \bigwedge_j \left(\exists m : ((j,m) \sqsubset_\Psi (i,k)) \wedge \#h_{Ports(S_j)} \leq m\right)\right)$$

□

¿From the above property, we can prove that

Lemma 5.6

$$\bigwedge_{(j,m)\sqsubset_\Psi(i,k)} \theta_j(m) \Rightarrow \Box\left((\#h_{Ports(S_i)} < k) \Rightarrow \bigwedge_l C_l\right)$$

Proof

$$\bigwedge_{(j,m)\sqsubset_\Psi(i,k)} \theta_j(m) \Leftrightarrow \bigwedge_{(j,m)\sqsubset_\Psi(i,k)} \Box(\#h_{Ports(S_j)} \leq m \Rightarrow C_j)$$

Combining this with property 5.5(3) we get,

$$\bigwedge_{(j,m)\sqsubset_\Psi(i,k)} \theta_j(m) \Rightarrow \Box\left((\#h_{Ports(S_i)} < k) \Rightarrow \bigwedge_l C_l\right)$$

□

We now prove the following theorem, which establishes the soundness of the Misra-Chandy proof rule for closed networks (where $A_{net} = true$).

Theorem 5.7

$$\mathbf{cooperation}_{MC} \Rightarrow \mathbf{cooperation}_{IND}$$

Proof We must establish that for all executions

$$\bigwedge_{(j,m)\sqsubset_\Psi(i,k)} \theta_j(m) \wedge \mathbf{cooperation}_{MC} \quad \Rightarrow \quad \Box((\#h_{Ports(S_i)} < k) \Rightarrow A_i)$$

This can be shown as follows.

$$\bigwedge_{(j,m)\sqsubset_\Psi(i,k)} \theta_j(m) \wedge \mathbf{cooperation}_{MC}$$

$$\Rightarrow \quad \Box\left((\#h_{Ports(S_i)} < k) \Rightarrow \bigwedge_l C_l\right) \wedge \mathbf{cooperation}_{MC} \qquad \text{,from lemma 5.6}$$

$$\Rightarrow \quad \Box((\#h_{Ports(S_i)} < k) \Rightarrow A_i) \qquad \text{,from } \mathbf{cooperation}_{MC}$$

□

In the rest of this section, we shall define the dynamic ordering relation $(\mathbf{inddom}_\Psi, \sqsubset_\Psi)$ satisfying property 5.5.

Definition 5.8 Let (δ, Ψ) be a network execution, and $i, j \in$ **pindex**. Then,

1. $Traces(\Psi)$ denotes the set of traces arising in Ψ. Recall that a trace is a finite sequence of communications. Note that $Traces(\Psi)$ is prefix closed.

2. Let $ord(tr, j) \stackrel{\text{def}}{=} (\, j \,,\, \#(tr \uparrow Ports(S_j))\,)$

3. Let $\mathbf{inddom}_{tr} \stackrel{\text{def}}{=} \{ord(tr', j) \mid tr' \underline{\propto} tr\}$.

4. Let $\sqsubset_{tr} \subseteq \mathbf{inddom}_{tr} \times \mathbf{inddom}_{tr}$ such that

$$\sqsubset_\lambda = \emptyset$$

$$\sqsubset_{tr^\frown com} = (\mathbf{inddom}_{tr^\frown com} - \mathbf{inddom}_{tr}) \times \mathbf{inddom}_{tr}$$

5.
$$\mathbf{inddom}_\Psi \stackrel{\text{def}}{=} \bigcup_{tr \in Traces(\Psi)} \mathbf{inddom}_{tr}$$

$$\sqsubset_\Psi \stackrel{\text{def}}{=} \bigcup_{tr \in Traces(\Psi)} \sqsubset_{tr}$$

□

Example 5.9 Consider $S_1 \| S_2$ with $Ports(S_1) = \{A?, B!, C?\}$ and $Ports(S_2) = \{B?, C!, D!\}$. Here, A, B, D are synchronous channels whereas C is an asynchronous channel.
Let $tr = A.3^\frown C!3^\frown B.4$. Then, using definition 5.8 we get

$$\mathbf{inddom}_\lambda = \{(1,0),(2,0)\}$$
$$\mathbf{inddom}_{A.3} = \{(1,1)\} \cup \mathbf{inddom}_\lambda$$
$$\mathbf{inddom}_{A.3^\frown C!3} = \{(2,1)\} \cup \mathbf{inddom}_{A.3}$$
$$\mathbf{inddom}_{A.3^\frown C!3^\frown B.4} = \{(1,2),(2,2)\} \cup \mathbf{inddom}_{A.3^\frown C!3}$$
$$(1,0),(2,0) \sqsubset_{tr} (1,1)$$
$$(1,0),(2,0),(1,1) \sqsubset_{tr} (2,1)$$
$$(1,0),(2,0),(1,1),(2,1) \sqsubset_{tr} (1,2),(2,2)$$

□

The following lemmas characterise main properties of $(\mathbf{inddom}_\Psi, \sqsubset_\Psi)$.

Lemma 5.10 $(\mathbf{inddom}_\Psi, \sqsubset_\Psi)$ is a well-order. □

Lemma 5.11 $(\mathbf{inddom}_\Psi, \sqsubset_\Psi)$ satisfies property 5.5(2). □

Lemma 5.12 $(\mathbf{inddom}_\Psi, \sqsubset_\Psi)$ satisfies property 5.5(3). □

6 Discussion

In this paper, we have attempted to relate the monolithic and conditional specifications of processes. A specification of the form SS **sat** β (see section 2), is called monolithic, whereas a conditional specification (section 3) has the form $\{\alpha\}\ S\ \{\beta\}$. Assumption α gives the condition that the environment of S must guarantee in order to ensure that process S meets its specified behaviour β. Assumption α is formulated in terms of observable entities of the process S.

Formally, a conditional specification can be interpreted as

$$\{\alpha\}\ S\ \{\beta\} \ \textbf{iff}\ \ S\ \textbf{sat}\ (\alpha \Rightarrow \beta)$$

Thus, from the point of view of underlying semantic theory there is no fundamental difference between conditional and monolithic specifications. The difference is perhaps pragmatic.

Hoare has suggested that a process can be identified with its strongest specification [Hoa84]. Such a specification is comprehensive enough to describe the behaviour of the process in any possible environment. A conditional specification of a process is given in presence of some assumptions about the environment of the process, and hence is usually weaker than the strongest specification. When the environment of a process is known, an appropriate conditional specification containing significantly less detail than the strongest process specification can be given, and this is sufficient for establishing the behaviour of the process in the given environment. Such a conditional specification reduces the proof obligations to be met in the verification of the process specification and in combining the specifications of the processes of a network. It can be argued that top-down design of a network of processes naturally gives rise to conditional specification for the processes, whereas bottom-up design is likely to lead to the strongest process specification.

The ability to make assumptions about the environment in the specification is pragmatically attractive. However, combining such specifications of the processes of a network requires us to check that the assumptions made by the processes are "discharged". We have terms this proof obligation as **cooperation**. Assumptions can be made explicitly, as in conditional specification, or implicitly in the monolithic process specification. Syntactic separation of assumptions and commitments enables us to formulate **cooperation** as a *separate* proof obligation. This has the desirable effect of clearly specifying the dependencies between the processes at their interface.

In this paper, we have suggested that an inductive strategy can be used for discharging of mutually dependent assumptions, and proved its soundness. This strategy is formulated as condition $\mathbf{cooperation}_{IND}$ (section 5). By establishing this condition, proof rule 8 enables us to derive the behaviour of a network as as conjunction of the inviolate commitments and the composition properties. Rule 8 can be used for both shared variable and message passing distributed programs. Further, it is independent of the notation used for expressing the execution properties.

Formulation of **cooperation** as a separate proof obligation is particularly attractive when the inductive strategy for proving it can be given in a canonical fashion using some property of the execution. The inductive nature of the $\mathbf{cooperation}_{IND}$ can be left implicit, and a simpler **cooperation** condition can be used in its place. We demonstrated this by interpreting the Misra-Chandy proof rule [MC81] for network composition in terms of of the $\mathbf{cooperation}_{IND}$ condition, thereby establishing its soundness. By leaving implicit the complex pattern of induction (which is not statically determined but in fact evolves dynamically with the execution), the Misra-Chandy rule can considerably reduce the explicit proof obligations to be satisfied during the verification. For an example of this the reader is referred to [ZBR83].

Specifying the properties of a process by making assumptions about the environment is not new. Francez and Pnueli [FP78] suggested this for concurrent programs with shared variables. The rely-guarantee style proof rule for proving correctness of shared variable programs given by Jones [Jon83] is another example. Misra and Chandy [MC81] made use of assumption-commitments to prove safety properties of message passing programs. More recently, Soundararajan [Sou86] has developed a total-correctness proof system for CSP-like programs which also makes use of assumptions to prove the termination of a process. Pandya [Pan88] has used assumptions to establish progress properties of CSP-like processes. Hooman's proof method [Hoo89] for establishing real time properties of distributed programs also uses assumptions and commitments.

Our aim here is to try to provide a general framework in which these diverse uses of conditional specification can be interpreted. Clearly, the current paper is only a start in this direction.

Acknowledgements

The author would like to thank W.P. de Roever for his comments which greatly improved the paper. Chaochen Zhou made numerous suggestions for improving the presentation.

References

[BKP85] H. Barringer, R. Kuiper, A. Pnueli, A compositional temporal approach to CSP-like languages, in Proc. IFIP Working Conf., *The Role of Abstract Models in Information Processing*, Vienna (1985).

[FP78] N. Francez, A. Pnueli, A proof method for cyclic programs, *Acta Informatica* **9** (1978).

[Hoa78] C.A.R. Hoare, Communicating sequential processes, *Comm. ACM* **21**(8) (1978).

[Hoa81] C.A.R. Hoare, A calculus for the total correctness of communicating processes, *Sc. Comp. Progr.* **1**(1,2) (1981).

[Hoa84] C.A.R. Hoare, Programs as Predicates, Philosophical. Transactions of the Royal Society, London, Vol. **A 312**, (1984).

[Hoo89] J. Hooman, Compositional specification and verification of distributed real-time systems, to appear in Proceedings of the Workshop on Real-Time Systems - Theory and Applications, York (U.K.), September (1989).

[Jon83] C.B. Jones, Specification and Design of (Parallel) Programs, in *Information Processing 83* (R.E.A. Mason, ed.,), North-Holland (1983).

[LSS84] J. Loecks, K. Sieber and R.D. Stansifer, The Foundations of Program Verification, John Wiley and Sons (1984).

[MC81] J. Misra, K.M. Chandy, Proofs of networks of processes, *IEEE Trans. SE* **7**(4) (1981).

[NGO85] V. Nguyen, D. Gries, S. Owicki, A model and temporal logic proof system for networks of processes, Proc. *12th ACM Symp. on Princ. of Progr. lang.* (1985).

[Owi75] S. Owicki, Axiomatic proof techniques for parallel programs, Ph.D. Thesis, Cornell University (1975).

[Pan88] P. Pandya, Compositional Verification of Distributed Programs, Ph.D. Thesis, University of Bombay (1988).

[Pnu85] A.Pnueli, "In transition from global to modular temporal reasoning about programs", in *Logics and Models of Concurrent Systems,* (K.R. Apt, ed.), Springer-Verlag (1985).

[Pnu86] A. Pnueli, Application of temporal logic to the specification and verification of reactive system: a survey of current trends, in *Current trends in concurrency,* (J.W. de Bakker, W.P. de Roever and G. Rozenberg, eds.), LNCS **224**, Springer-Verlag (1986).

[Rov85] W.P. de Roever, 'The quest for compositionality - a survey of assertion based proof systems for concurrent programs, Part-I, in *Proc. of the IFIP conference: The role of abstract models in computer science*, (E.J. Neuhold, ed.), North Holland (1985).

[Sta85] E.D. Stark, A Proof Technique for Rely/Guarantee Properties, LNCS **206**, (1985).

[Sou83] N. Soundararajan, Correctness proofs of CSP programs, *Theoret. Comp. Sci.* **24**(2) (1983).

[Sou86] N. Soundararajan, Total correctness of CSP programs, *Acta Informatica* **23** (1986).

[Zho85] Zhou Chaochen, A temporal semantics of CSP, in *Proc. of the First Pan Pacific Computer Conference*, Melbourne (1985).

[ZBR83] J. Zwiers, A. de Bruin, W.P. de Roever, A proof system for partial correctness of dynamic networks of processes, Proc. of the conference on Logics of Programs 1983, LNCS 164 (1984).

[ZRB85] J. Zwiers, W.P. de Roever, P. van Emde Boas, Compositionality and concurrent networks: soundness and completeness of a proof system, Proc. *12th ICALP*, LNCS **194**, Springer-Verlag (1985).

Refinement of Concurrent Systems based on Local State Transformations

Lucia Pomello

Dipartimento di Scienze dell'Informazione

via Moretto da Brescia 9, 20133 Milano, Italy

ABSTRACT

The paper presents a notion of preorder with related equivalence between concurrent systems which supports functional abstraction and refinement. Such abstraction and refinement disregard action names (the action alphabet can be changed) while they require to preserve local state transformations. Since Petri Nets explicitly model both states and state transformations, concurrent systems are considered as modelled by Petri nets, precisely by contact-free Elementary Net systems in which some states are observable (S-labelled systems). The proposed preorder, called State transformation (ST) preorder, is defined on the basis of morphisms between the OLST-algebras associated to the compared systems. OLST-algebras describe the state space of S-labelled systems characterizing system behaviour in terms of observable local state transformations. The paper presents the construction of the unique canonical representative of each ST-equivalence class of S-observable systems, a subclass of S-labelled systems, and discusses ST-preorder and equivalence over S-observable systems in the framework of system development.

Key words: functional abstraction and refinement, observable local/global states, local state transformations, morphisms preserving local state transformations.

CONTENTS

1. Introduction
2. Basic definitions
3. S-labelled systems
4. ST-preorder and ST-equivalence
5. S-observable systems and ST-canonical representatives
6. State observability in system design
7. Conclusions
8. References

1. INTRODUCTION

Concurrent system design by means of stepwise refinement is usually based on abstraction and refinement notions supported by equivalences and preorders.

Equivalence notions can be used for the comparison of system models both at different level of abstraction and at the same one. In the first case they allow one to verify the correctness in the refinement or abstraction process, and then to call one model an implementation, or a specification, of an other one, and to verify an implementation against a specification. In the second case the equivalence of two system models at the same level of abstraction means that the two models are equivalent refinement or abstraction of the same other model and then it is meaningful to compare them with respect to their properties such as for example the degree of concurrency they exhibit or with respect to their performances.

Preorder relations between system models can be useful in the incremental system development in which some system requirements, not satisfied by a first model, are realized in a subsequent one. In this case the latter model, beside incorporating, enriches the first one. A typical application of such a technique is the remodelling of a system by adding to it the facility of error or exception handling.

The approach proposed by Milner for CCS [Mil80] and subsequently exploited for different models of concurrent systems, for example in [Abr87], [DH84], [Hen88], [BHR84], [DDM87], [DDPS85], [Jif89], [Lar89], is based on a notion of abstraction/refinement which allow one to model a system, at a certain level, as the parallel composition of more interacting sequential components, and, at a different level, to remodel each component as the parallel composition of more interacting (sub-) components.

The focus is on the interactions of the considered system component with its environment, where such interactions are modelled as synchronous communications and constitute the interface system/environment. The correctness in the refinement is verified iff the interactions with the environment are preserved. In fact, Observation equivalence [Mil80], as well as the other equivalences introduced on the basis of the same approach, is defined in terms of observable actions and compares concurrent systems from the point of view of the action sequences (or posets) they exhibit to an observer, independently of their internal organization, where the observer plys the role of the environment in which the system is embedded and with whom the system interacts. Moreover Testing equivalence [DH84], [Hen88] and Failure-equivalence [BHR84] are defined on the basis of preorders which can be used in incremental system development as previously mentioned.

All these notions are based on the assumption of atomic action and do not allow one to compare systems

whose actions are defined at different levels of detail. In fact, they compare systems in which the action names are labels belonging to the same alphabet.
On the basis of this last consideration one research line which is under investigation is the study of equivalence notions preserved by the refinement of actions in the composition of more elementary ones. In [CDP87] it is shown, on the basis of a simple example, that Observation equivalence and the other equivalences based on action observation, when defined on the basis of interleaving semantics, are not preserved by action refinements. The problem of equivalence notions preserving action refinements has been investigated also in [BDKP89], [GG89]. In particular in these papers it is shown that a generalization on partial order semantics of Bisimulation [Par81], [Mil80] is preserved by some action refinements.

A different line is the one of considering also an other notion of abstraction, the abstraction from the choice of atomic actions, together with a preorder and an equivalence notion which allows one to compare concurrent systems whose actions are defined at different level of detail, taking into account the state transformation characterizing their behaviour.
It is the generalization to concurrent systems of the notions of functional abstraction and equivalence which have been defined for sequential programs since the '60.

Such proposal has been developed in [DDPS88] and in [PS89a] for concurrent systems modelled by Petri Nets, particularly by the class of contact-free Elementary Net Systems [RT86], [Thi87] in which some cases (global states) are considered as observable (S-labelled systems). Petri Nets, in fact, explicitly model not only events (state transformations) but also states, where global states are represented in terms of local states. This fact allow the introduction of a notion of functional equivalence for concurrent systems modelled by Petri Nets which is defined in terms of observable global state transformation and where the global state structure is considered in terms of the local states of the system components. The result is an equivalence which supports a "modular" functional abstraction and refinement of concurrent systems. In this way, since equivalence notions based on action observation have been defined also for Petri Nets (see for example [Pom 86]), Petri Nets result to provide the designer of concurrent systems with two mechanisms of abstraction/refinement supported by two equivalence notions based on the observation of conditions and events respectively.
In the case of observation of conditions, the interface between the system part under development and its environment is constituted by the observable states.
Exhibited Functionality (EF)-equivalence has been thus introduced on the class of S-labelled systems in [DDPS88]. EF-equivalence requires an isomorphism between the state structures of the compared systems and a correspondence between sequences of observable global state transformations. This notion does not allow the designer to modify the structure of the observable states of the system under

development, in fact, by using such equivalence, the refinement can involve the unobservable parts only.

In order to confront systems at different level of granularity in observable state transformations, a preorder between systems, the State Transformation (ST-) preorder, has been introduced in [PS89a]. Such preorder considers a system less or equal to an other one if each observable state transformation performed by the first one is also performed by the second one, in case in terms of a sequence of more elementary observable state transformations. Moreover, the second system can perform other different observable state transformations. ST-preorder is defined in terms of morphisms between the algebraic structures of observable local states which characterize the S-labelled system behaviour. These algebraic structures are called Observable Local State Transformation algebras.

On the basis of ST-preorder a functional equivalence notion, called State Transformation (ST)-equivalence has been introduced. ST-equivalence fully takes into account the algebraic structure of the system state space by requiring a correspondence between any possible observable local state transformation inside any two equivalent systems. ST-equivalence results stronger than EF-equivalence, but coincides with it in the case of the class of S-observable systems. Informally, S-observable systems are S-labelled systems in which the pre and post sets of each observable state transformation are disjoint.

The class of S-observable systems is of particular interest since when restricted to it EF-equivalence, and then also ST-equivalence, is such that each equivalence class contains a unique (up to isomorphism) EN system minimal w.r.t. the net structure and in which each condition is observable. This system is the canonical representative of the class and can be constructed by a reduction algorithm starting from any element of the class. The proof that two S-observable systems are EF or ST-equivalent can be carried on by reducing them to their canonical representatives and then by verifing if these latter are isomorphic.

This paper presents ST-preorder and ST-equivalence for the refinement of concurrent systems based on local state transformations collecting and working out the results the author has developed together with Fiorella De Cindio, Giorgio De Michelis and Carla Simone in [DDPS88] and in [PS89a].

The paper is organized as follows: section 2 contains some basic definitions of Net Theory; in section 3 we present the class of S-labelled systems, the notion of elementary observable state transformation and the Observable Local State Transformation (OLST-) algebra associated to a S-labelled system. In section 4 we introduce a notion of morphism between OLST-algebras of S-labelled systems on the basis of which ST-preorder and ST-quivalence are defined. In section 5 we give the definition of the class of S-observable systems and show that the OLST-algebra of a S-observable system can be derived from the subalgebra in which only observable global state transformations are considered. Then we show that the isomorphism between such subalgebras is not only necessary but also sufficient to guarantee the isomorphism between OLST-algebras of S-observable systems. Furtheremore we present the construction of the unique canonical representative of each ST-equivalence class of S-observable systems. Section 6 gives some hints on how ST-preorder and ST-equivalence can be used in a combined way in the stepwise development of concurrent systems. Section 7 concludes the paper containing the main lines of the further development of the proposed approach and a brief comparison with related works in the literature.

Before starting with the formal presentation, in order to give the intuition behind the proposed approach, let us consider a very simple example of system refinement based on Local State Transformation.

Let us start considering the atomic state transformation specified by $\{P\}\ \alpha\ \{Q\}$, where P is the predicate $x \geq 0 \wedge y \geq 0$ and Q is $z = 9x^2 - y^2$. In terms of Petri Nets such state transformation can be modelled by the system Σ_1 given in Figure 1, where the places P and Q model the two previous predicates, respectively the pre-condition and the post-condition of α. In the figure the places P and Q are shaded to indicate they model observable states.

The previous state transformation can be equivalently expressed by $\{P_1 \wedge P_2\}\ \alpha\ \{Q\}$ where P_1 is $x \geq 0$ and P_2 is $y \geq 0$ and then modelled by the system Σ_2 given in Figure 1.

The atomic state transformation α can now be refined into the parallel composition of α_1 and α_2 followed by α_3 $((\alpha_1 \parallel \alpha_2); \alpha_3)$ in such a way that the previous state transformation is preserved. We get the system Σ_3 given in Figure 1 in which P_1, P_2 and Q are observable, while R_1 and R_2 are not and where α_1, α_2 and α_3 are respectively the statements $a:=9x^2$, $b:=y^2$ and $z:= ab$. Σ_3 performs the same observable state transformation as Σ_2 does: they both transform the observable state modelled by the validity of the conditions P_1 and P_2 into the observable state modelled by the validity of Q; therefore Σ_2 and Σ_3 are equivalent w.r.t. the observable state transformations.

If now we do not want to consider $((\alpha_1 \parallel \alpha_2); \alpha_3)$ as a single state transformation and, moreover, we want to refine α_1 into the composition of more elementary state transformations, we have first to change the state observability by considering the pre- and post-conditions of α_1 as observable; this is done obtaining the system Σ_4.

To the observable state transformation which transforms $\{P_1 \wedge P_2\}$ into $\{Q\}$ in Σ_3 corresponds now a sequence of observable state transformations in Σ_4, the one transforming $\{P_1 \wedge P_2\}$ into $\{R_1 \wedge P_2\}$ and then $\{R_1 \wedge P_2\}$ into $\{Q\}$. We say that Σ_3 is less than Σ_4 w.r.t. observable state transformations.

Now we can consider the state transformation $\{P_1\}\ \alpha_1\ \{R_1\}$ and refine it into the sequential composition of two more elementary state transformations as is the case in system Σ_5, where α_{11} and α_{12} are respectively the statements $c:=x^2$ and $a:=9c$.

We can say that Σ_4 and Σ_5 are equivalent w.r.t. observable state transformations since they perform correspondent observable state transformations. Furtheremore we can also say that Σ_5 realizes the

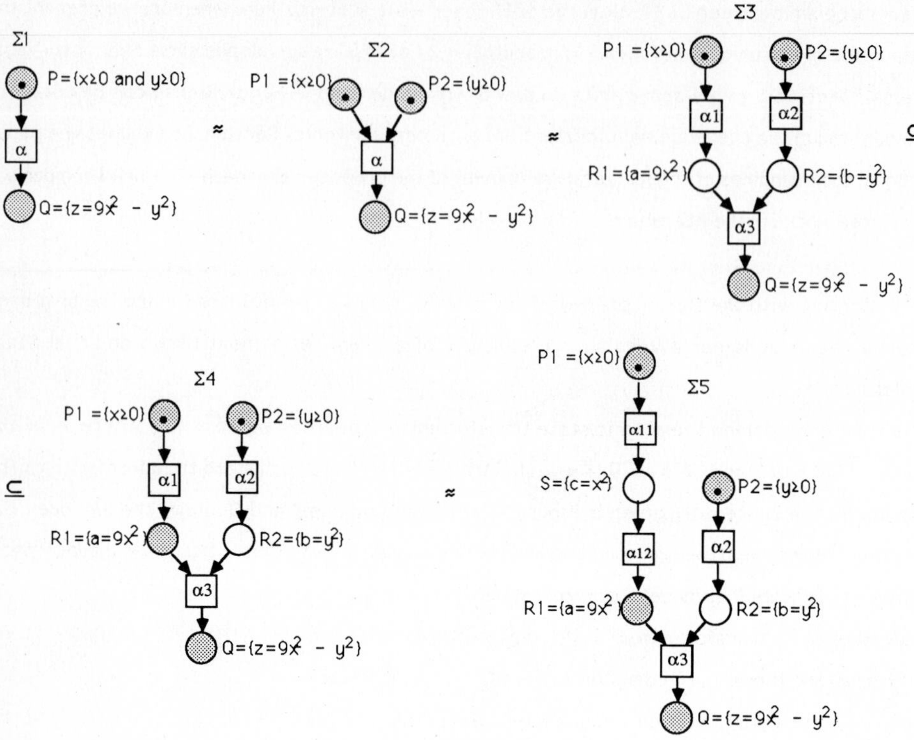

Figure 1

observable state transformation specified by Σ_1 by refining it, since the state transformation performed by Σ_1 is also performed by Σ_5 even if in this last case the transformation is not specified as atomic. Σ_1 is less than Σ_5 w.r.t. observable state transformations.

2. BASIC DEFINITIONS

In the following we give some basic definitions of Net Theory [Bra87], [RT86], [Thi87].

Definition 1 *Net*

A net is a triple N=(S,T,F) such that:

(i) S, T are disjoint sets such that $S \cup T \neq \emptyset$;

(ii) $F \subseteq (S \times T) \cup (T \times S)$ is such that $\underline{dom}(F) \cup \underline{ran}(F) = S \cup T$.

S is the set of S-elements, T is the set of T-elements and F is the flow relation of N.
$X = S \cup T$ is the set of elements of N. S-elements (places) represent local states, conditions or predicates; T-elements (transitions) represent local state transformations, local transitions or predicte transformers. The flow relation models the neighbourhood between local states and local transitions. In diagrams, S-elements are drawn as circles, T-elements as boxes and the flow relation is indicated by appropriate directed arcs.

A "local" form of the flow relation is given associating to each element of a net its pre-set and its post-set: let N be a net and $x \in X$, then

pre-x $= \{y \in X \mid (y,x) \in F\}$ is the pre-set of x and

post-x $= \{y \in X \mid (x,y) \in F\}$ is the post-set of x.

Definition 2 *Structural properties*

Let N=(S,T,F) be a net:

- N is T-restricted iff $T \subseteq dom(F) \cap ran(F)$;
- N is pure iff $\forall x \in X$: pre-x $\cap$ post-x $= \emptyset$;
- N is simple w.r.t. the transitions iff $\forall t_1, t_2 \in T$:
  (pre-t_1 = pre-t_2 and post-t_1 = post-t_2) $\Rightarrow t_1 = t_2$;
- N is simple w.r.t. the places iff $\forall s_1, s_2 \in S$:
  (pre-s_1 = pre-s_2 and post-s_1 = post-s_2) $\Rightarrow s_1 = s_2$;
- N is simple iff $\forall x, y \in X$:
  (pre-x = pre-y and post-x = post-y) $\Rightarrow x = y$.

Definition 3 *Elementary Net system*

An Elementary Net system (EN-system) is a quadruple $\Sigma=(S,T,F, c_{in})$ where N=(S,T,F) is a net called the underlying net of Σ and $c_{in} \subseteq S$ is the initial case (the set of initial local states) of Σ.

The underlying net captures the structure of the system modelled by Σ. The evolution of the behaviour of the system is defined by means of the transition rule which specifies under which conditions a transition can occur, and how the local states are modified by the occurrence of the transitions.

Definition 4 *Transition rule*

Let N=(S,T,F) be a net

- $\forall t \in T, \forall c \subseteq S$, t is enabled in c (c[t>) iff pre-t $\subseteq$ c and post-t $\cap$ c $= \emptyset$;
- if t is enabled in c then the occurrence of t leads the system from c to c' (c[t>c'), where $c' \subseteq S$ is such that c' = (c - pre-t) $\cup$ post-t.

Definition 5 *Set of cases, occurrence sequences*

Let $\Sigma=(S,T,F,c_{in})$ be an EN-system.

- C denotes the set of cases (global states) of Σ and is the least subset of 2^S satisfying:

  1) $c_{in} \in C$;

  2) if $c \in C$, $t \in T$ and $c' \subseteq S$ such that $c[t>c'$ then $c' \in C$.

- Let $w \in T^+$, i.e.: let $w=t_1 t_2 \dots t_n$ with $t_1,\dots,t_n \in T$; then w is an occurrence sequence of Σ iff there exist $c_1, c_2, \dots, c_n \in C$ such that $c_{in}[t_1>c_1[t_2>c_2 \dots [t_n>c_n$.

- A proper subcase c' of a case $c \in C$ ($c' \subset c$) is sometimes called local state.

Definition 6 *Dinamic properties*

Let $\Sigma=(S,T,F,c_{in})$ be an EN-system:

- Σ is contact-free iff $\forall c \in C$, $\forall t \in T$, pre-$t \subseteq c \Rightarrow$ post-$t \cap c = \emptyset$.

- A transition t of Σ is dead iff it is not enabled in any case belonging to C.

Definition 7 *Notations*

Let $\Sigma = (S, T, F; c_{in})$ be an EN system.

For all $w \in T^*$:

- Perm(w) is the set of all permutations of the transitions constituting w.

- F-Perm(w) is the subset of the firable permutations, i.e.,

  F-Perm(w) = $\{ w' \in \text{Perm}(w) \mid \exists\, c,c' \in [c_{in}>$ such that $c[w'>c' \}$

- the post-set of $w \in T^+$ is recursively defined as follows:

  if $w = t$, then $w\bullet = t\bullet$

  if $w = vt$, where $v \in T^+$ and $t \in T$, then $w\bullet = ((v\bullet - \bullet t) \cup t\bullet)$

- the pre-set of $w \in T^+$ is recursively defined as follows:

  if $w = t$, then $\bullet w = \bullet t$;

  if $w = vt$, where $v \in T^+$ and $t \in T$, then $\bullet w = (\bullet v \cup (\bullet t - v\bullet))$

- If $w = \varepsilon$, the empty word over T^*, then $\forall c \in [c_{in}>$, $\forall X \in 2^C-\{\emptyset\}$: $\bullet w = w\bullet = X$.

3. S-LABELLED SYSTEMS

In this paragraph we will present the class of S-labelled systems, the notion of elementary observable state transformation (elementary observable path) and the Observable Local State Transformation-algebra associated to a S-labelled system.

In the following we will consider concurrent systems modelled by contact-free EN systems whose underlying nets are T-restricted and in which some reachable cases are considered as observable, i.e.: modelling global states which the system exhibits to its environment and starting from which the system can interact with the environment. Such systems are called S-labelled systems.

Definition 8 *S-labelled system*

A S-labelled EN-system (S-labelled system) is a couple $\langle\Sigma, C_{oss}\rangle$ (Σ for short) where:

1) $\Sigma=(S,T,F,c_{in})$ is a contact-free EN-system;

2) C_{oss} is a set of reachable cases called set of observable cases (or observable global states) of Σ; C_{oss} is such that $c_{in} \subseteq C_{oss}$.

For each S-labelled system Σ, O denotes the set of observable local states (or observable places) of Σ and is the set of conditions belonging to observable cases, $O = \cup C_{oss}$.

Remark

In [DDPS88] and in [PS89a] S-labelled systems have been equivalently defined giving as basic the notion of observable local states O and as derivative the set of observable cases C_{oss}. A S-labelled system can in fact be equivalently identified by the couple $\langle\Sigma, O\rangle$ where O is the set of observable places (conditions) such that the initial case is contained in O and each observable place belongs to at least a case contained in O.

In the figures S-labelled systems will be drawn representing observable places by shaded circles.

Example 1

Σ_6, given in Figure 2, is not a S-labelled system since place p_2 does not belong to any observable case. Σ_7 and Σ_8, given in Figure 3 and in Figure 4, are example of S-labelled systems.

Once defined how states can be observed, we define when an occurrence sequence can be considered minimal w.r.t. such kind of observation. Intuitively, an occurrence sequence w is an elementary observable state transformation (elementary observable path) iff it is a minimal portion of behaviour leading from an observable case c to an other observable case c' without reaching intermediate observable cases.

For example, the sequence $c[t_1t_2t_3\rangle c'$ of the system Σ_7 given in Figure 3 is an elementary observable path since no other reachable case is observable in Σ_7. The sequence $c[t_4t_5t_6\rangle c'$ of the system Σ_8 given in Figure 4 with $c=\{p_1, p_2\}$ and $c'=\{p_3, p_5\}$ is not an elementary observable path since the observable cases $\{p_3, p_2\}$ and $\{p_1, p_5\}$ can be reached by a subsequence of $t_4t_5t_6$ or by a subsequence

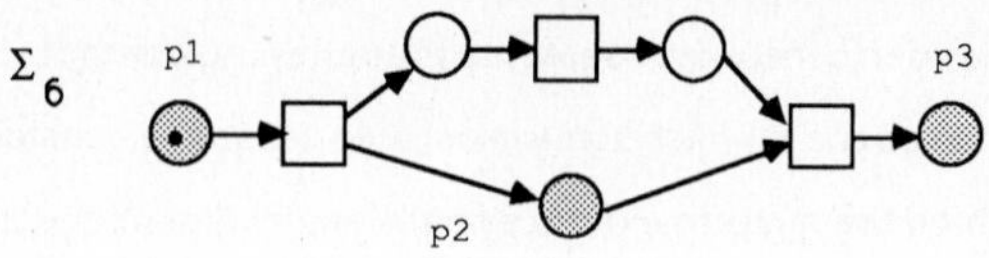

Figure 2

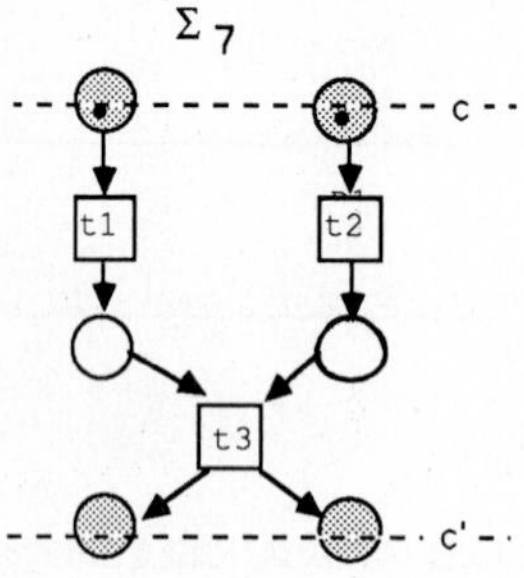

Figure 3

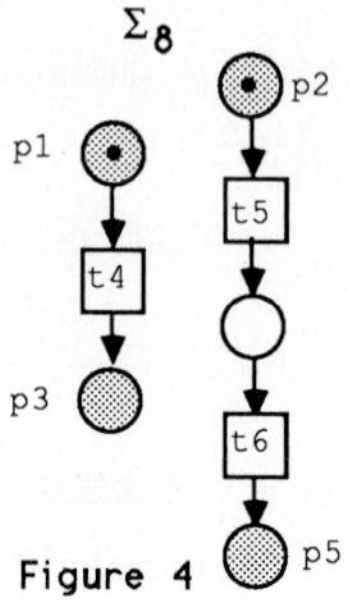

Figure 4

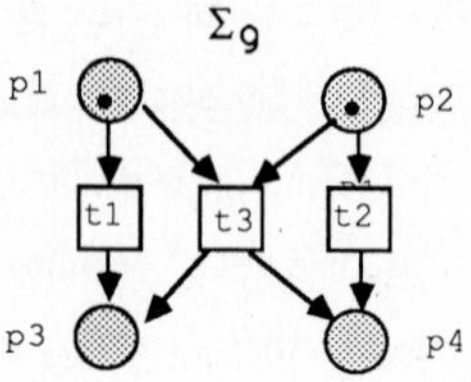

Figure 5

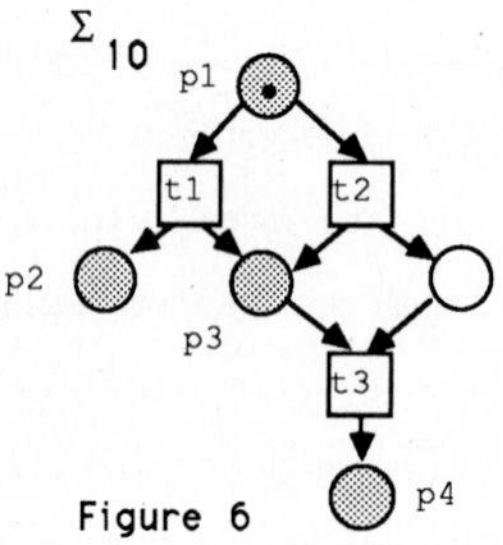

Figure 6

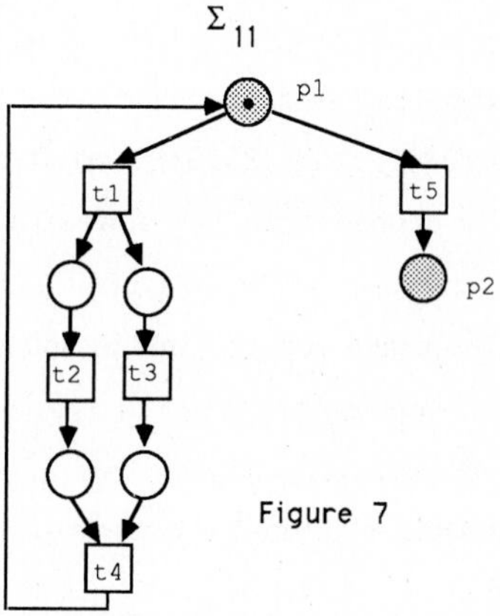

Figure 7

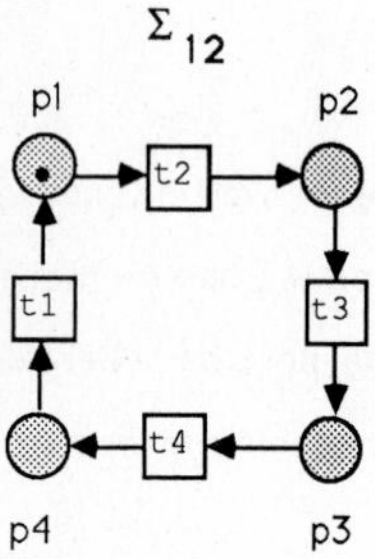

Figure 8

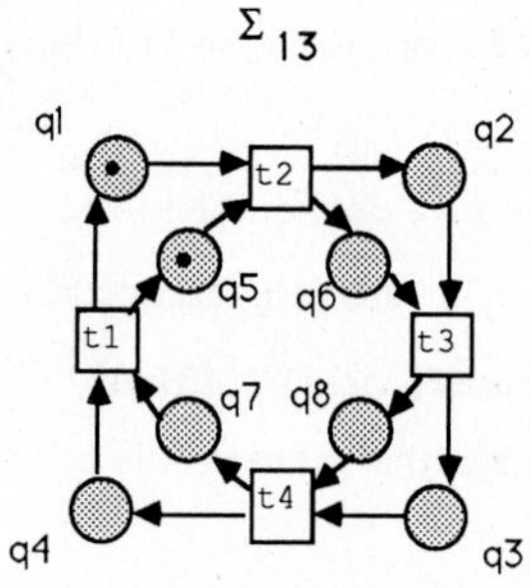

Figure 9

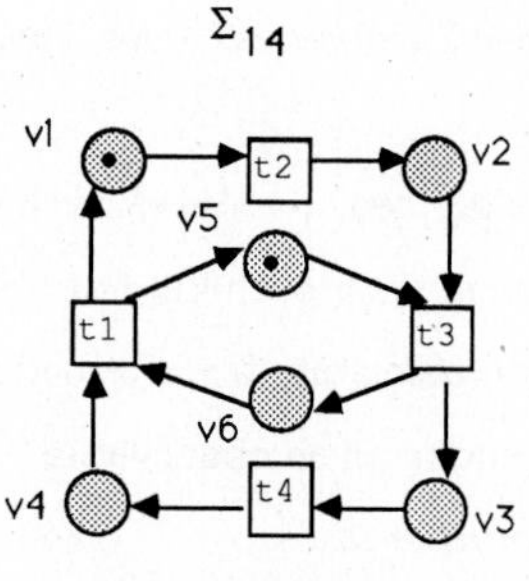

Figure 10

of a permutation of it; or, in other terms, since the S-labelled subsystem generated by the transitions in the sequence $t_4t_5t_6$ does not contain as observable cases only the cases c and c'.
The formal definition of elementary observable path is then given as follows.

Definition 9 *elementary observable path*
Let Σ be a S-labelled system, then $w \in T^*$ is an elementary observable path of Σ iff
$\exists$ c, c'$\in C_{oss}$ such that:
i) c[w>c';
ii) let $\Sigma_w = \langle S_w, T_w; F_w, c_{w0} \rangle$ be the subsystem generated by the transitions occurring in w, with initial case $c_{w0} = c \cap S_w$ and observable cases defined as $C_{ossw} = \{c \in [c_{w0}\rangle \mid \exists\, c' \in C_{oss},\, c \subseteq c'\}$, i.e., C_{ossw} contains the cases c reachable from c_{w0} in Σ_w and contained in observable cases of the system Σ. Then Σ_w is a S-labelled system where $C_{ossw} = \{c \cap S_w, c' \cap S_w\}$ and not $\exists$ w' $\neq \varepsilon$ proper prefix of w''$\in$ F-Perm(w) such that c[w'>c or c[w'>c'.

Let c[(w>>c' denote the occurrence of an elementary observable path and W_Σ denote the set of elementary observable paths of Σ.

Remark
The definition of C_{ossw} is obviously such that Σ_w is a S-labelled system.
The requirement: not $\exists$ w'$\neq \varepsilon$ proper prefix of w''$\in$ F-Perm(w) such that c[w'>c or c[w'>c', makes elementary any path starting and reaching the same observable case without passing through any other observable one (see next example, Figure 7).

Example 2
Let us consider the system Σ_9 in Figure 5.
a) t_1 and t_2 are elementary observable paths.
b) $w=t_1t_2$ is not an elementary observable path since the subnet generated by t_1 and t_2 is a S-labelled system in which $C_{ossw}=\{ \{p_1,p_2\}, \{p_3,p_4\}, \{p_1,p_4\}, \{p_3,p_2\} \} \neq \{ \{p_1,p_2\}, \{p_3,p_4\} \} = \{c \cap S_w, c' \cap S_w\}$.
c) $w=t_3$ is an elementary observable path since the subnet generated by t_3 is such that $C_{ossw}=\{\{p_1,p_2\}, \{p_3,p_4\}\}= \{c \cap S_w, c' \cap S_w\}$.

Let us consider the system Σ_{10} in Figure 6.
t_1 and t_2t_3 are both elementary observable paths. Note that in the second case the case $\{p_3, p_4\}$ does not belong to C_{ossw}, where $w=t_2t_3$.

Let us consider the system Σ_{11} in Figure 7 t_5, $t_1t_2t_3t_4$ are elementary observable paths, while $t_1t_3t_2t_4t_5$ is <u>not</u> since the elementary observable path $t_1t_2t_3t_4$ is a proper prefix of a permutation of it.

In order to intuitively introduce the further ingredients needed for the definitions of ST-preorder and ST-equivalence let us now consider the S-labelled systems Σ_{12}, Σ_{13} and Σ_{14} given respectively in Figure 8, in Figure 9 and in Figure 10.

As well as system Σ_{12}, system Σ_{13} has a cyclic behaviour in which each state transformation is a global one. In fact for example, whenever q_1 holds in Σ_{13} also q_5 holds, and whenever q_1 ceases to hold also q_5 ceases to hold; therefore there is no reason to distinguish q_1 from q_5, as well as q_2 from q_6 and so on. The S-labelled systems Σ_{12} and Σ_{13} can therefore be considered equivalent w.r.t. the state transformations they perform. To this end we have to put into correspondence the case p_1 with the case $\{q_1, q_5\}$, p_2 with $\{q_2, q_6\}$, p_3 with $\{q_3, q_7\}$ and p_4 with $\{q_4, q_8\}$.

The S-labelled system Σ_{14} has a cyclic behaviour in which some state transformations are global while others are local ones; precisely the case $\{v_1, v_5\}$ is transformed into the case $\{v_2,v_5\}$ by means of a local transformation as well as the case $\{v_3, v_6\}$ into the case $\{v_4,v_6\}$; whereas the transformations of $\{v_2,v_5\}$ into $\{v_3, v_6\}$ and of $\{v_4,v_6\}$ into $\{v_1, v_5\}$ are global ones. The system Σ_{14}, with the chosen observability of conditions, cannot be considered equivalent w.r.t. state transformations to the systems Σ_{12} and Σ_{13}.

(Σ_{12} and Σ_{14} would be equivalent with respect to State Transformations if, for example, only the cases $\{p_1\}$ and $\{p_3\}$ of Σ_{12} and $\{v_1, v_5\}$ and $\{v_3, v_6\}$ of Σ_{14} were observable.)

Let us consider the transformation of the case $\{v_1, v_5\}$ into the case $\{v_2,v_5\}$. v_5, the condition into the intersection of the two cases, is not modified by the transformation, it continuously holds before, during and after the transformation occurs; v_1, the condition into the set difference of the first case with the second one, is the precondition which ceases to hold when the transformation occurs, whereas v_2, the condition into the set difference of the second case with the first one, is the condition which starts to hold.

In general, given a state transformation of a S-labelled EN system we have that: the <u>intersection</u> of the two cases yields the set of conditions which hold both before, after and, even if as we will discuss later on not in any case, during the transformation; the <u>set differences</u> of the first case with the second one and, viceversa, of the second with the first one yield respectively the set of conditions which hold before and cease to hold when the transformation occurs, and the set of conditions which do not hold before and start to hold after the transformation occurs.

In order to compare two S-labelled EN systems w.r.t. the state transformations they perform we associate to each of them a relational algebraic structure which defines their state space.

Definition 10 *OLST-algebra*

To each S-labelled EN system Σ it can be associated the algebraic structure $I = \langle C_{oss}, c_{in}, I, \cap, -, \cup;$ $\rightarrow\rangle$ which is called Observable Local State Transformation algebra (OLST-algebra) and where

i) $\langle C_{oss}, c_{in}, I, \cap, -, \cup\rangle$ is the algebra of observable local states (o.l.s.'s) of Σ such that:

a) I is the minimal set containing C_{oss} and closed w.r.t. $\cap$ and $-$.

In the following I_{min} denotes the set of minimal elements of $I-\{\emptyset\}$, where of course x is a minimal o.l.s. of $I-\{\emptyset\}$ if there is no o.l.s. y in $I-\{\emptyset\}$ such that $y \subset x$.

b) $C_{oss} \subseteq I$ is the set of generators of the algebra.

c) c_{in} is the initial case of Σ.

d) $\cap, -, \cup$ are the intersection, difference and union as defined in set theory; while $\cap$ and $-$ are total, $\cup$ is partial and defined as follows:

$$\forall x,y \in I \quad x \cup y \in I \ \text{iff} \ \exists z \in I: x \subseteq z \text{ and } y \subseteq z.$$

ii) $\rightarrow \subseteq I \times I$ is an irreflexive, antisimmetric and not transitive relation which is called local state transformation relation and is defined as follows:

$$\forall x,y \in I \ \ x \rightarrow y \quad \text{iff} \quad \exists w \in W_\Sigma: \bullet w \subseteq x \ \ \text{and} \ \ y = (x - \bullet w) \cup w\bullet$$

Example 3

The OLST-algebras of the S-labelled systems Σ_{12}, Σ_{13} and Σ_{14} respectively given in Figure 8, Figure 9 and Figure 10 are defined by: $I_{12}=\{\{p_1\}, \{p_2\}, \{p_3\}, \{p_4\}\}$; $\rightarrow_{12}= \{\langle \{p_1\}, \{p_2\}\rangle, \langle\{p_2\},\{p_3\}\rangle, \langle\{p_3\},\{p_4\}\rangle, \langle\{p_4\},\{p_1\}\rangle\}$; $I_{13} = \{\{q_1,q_5\}, \{q_2,q_6\}, \{q_3,q_7\}, \{q_4,q_8\}\}$; $\rightarrow_{13} = \{\langle\{q_1,q_5\}, \{q_2,q_6\}\rangle, \langle\{q_2,q_6\}, \{q_3, q_7\}\rangle, \langle\{q_3, q_7\}, \{q_4, q_8\}\rangle, \langle\{q_4, q_8\}, \{q_1, q_5\}\rangle\}$; $I_{14} = \{\{v_1, v_5\}, \{v_2, v_5\}, \{v_3, v_6\}, \{v_4, v_6\}, \{v_1\}, \{v_2\}, \{v_3\}, \{v_4\}, \{v_5\}, \{v_6\}\}$; $\rightarrow_{14} = \{\langle\{v_1,v_5\}, \{v_2,v_5\}\rangle, \langle\{v_2,v_5\}, \{v_3,v_6\}\rangle, \langle\{v_3,v_6\}, \{v_4,v_6\}\rangle, \langle\{v_4,v_6\}, \{v_1,v_5\}\rangle, \langle\{v_1\}, \{v_2\}\rangle, \langle\{v_3\}, \{v_4\}\rangle\}$.

Remarks

- The minimal elements of $I-\{\emptyset\}$ are the minimal o.l.s.'s such that they *all together either hold or do not hold* in each observable case. In order to obtain the minimal elements both intersection and difference are necessary. For example, in the OLST-algebra of the S-labelled system Σ_{14} of Figure 10 the o.l.s. $\{v_5\}$ is obtained as the intersection of $\{v_1,v_5\}$ and $\{v_2,v_5\}$, while the o.l.s. $\{v_1\}$ is obtained as the difference beteween $\{v_1,v_5\}$ and $\{v_2,v_5\}$.
- The relation $\rightarrow$ is consistent with the transition rule, in fact we have that

$$\forall c,c' \in C_{oss}, \quad c \rightarrow c' \quad \text{iff} \quad \exists w \in W_\Sigma: \ c[(w\rangle\rangle c'.$$

In [DDPS88], [PS89a] and [PS89b] the properties of the elementary observable paths and of their pre/post sets, and the properties of the OLST-algebra have been studied. In the following statements we recall the most interesting and useful ones.

Lemma 1 [DDPS88], [PS89a], [PS89b]

Let Σ be a S-labelled system with $I = \langle C_{oss}, c_{in}, I, \cap, ^-, \cup, \rightarrow \rangle$ its OLST-algebra, then

a) for each $w \in W_\Sigma$, the subnet N_w generated by the transitions occurring in w is connected;

b) for each $w \in W_\Sigma$: $\bullet w \in I$ and $w \bullet \in I$;

c) $\forall x \in I \; \exists n \geq 1, \exists y_1, \ldots, y_n \in I_{min}$ such that $x = y_1 \cup \ldots \cup y_n$;

d) $\forall x,y \in I$: $x \rightarrow y$ it holds: $x \in C_{oss} \Leftrightarrow y \in C_{oss}$.

4. ST-PREORDER AND ST-EQUIVALENCE

In this paragraph we present the notions of State Transformation (ST-) preorder and State Transformation (ST-) equivalence on the class of S-labelled systems. To this purpose we introduce a notion of morphism between OLST-algebras of S-labelled systems on the basis of which both preorder and equivalence are defined.

Let us consider the S-labelled systems Σ_{15} and Σ_{16} given respectively in Figure 11 and in Figure 12. In comparing their state transformations we have two possibilities.

a) If we put $\{p_1\}$ into correspondence with $\{q_1\}$ and $\{p_2\}$ with $\{q_2\}$. Then we can say that, in addition to the observable state transformation performed by Σ_{15}, Σ_{16} performs an other observable state transformation, and than that " Σ_{16} is an extension of Σ_{15}" and that Σ_{15} is less than Σ_{16} w.r.t. State Transformation ($\Sigma_{15} \subseteq^{ST} \Sigma_{16}$).

b) If we put $\{p_1\}$ into correspondence with $\{q_1\}$ and $\{p_2\}$ with $\{q_3\}$. Then we can say that Σ_{16} refines the observable state transformation performed by Σ_{15} in a sequence of more elementary observable state transformations, and than that " Σ_{16} is an expansion of Σ_{15}" and again that Σ_{15} is less than Σ_{16} w.r.t. State Transformation ($\Sigma_{15} \subseteq^{ST} \Sigma_{16}$).

Intuitively, a system Σ_1 precedes a system Σ_2 in the preorder iff a) the algebra of o.l.s.'s of Σ_1 is a substructure of the algebra of o.l.s.'s of Σ_2; b) to each observable local state transformation in Σ_1 there is a (sequence of) corresponding local state transformation(s) in Σ_2.

The definition of ST-preorder is therefore based on a notion of morphism between OLST-algebras of S-labelled systems, which is defined by a total, strict and injective function between the observable

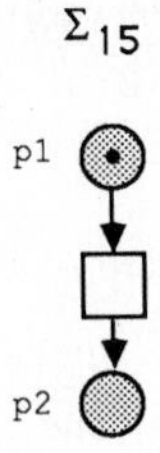

Figure 11

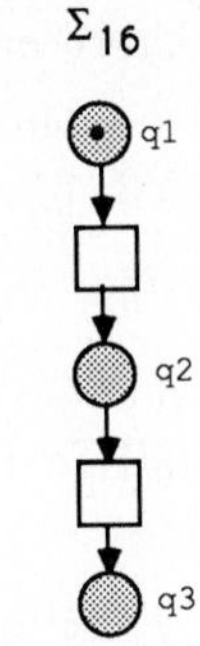

Figure 12

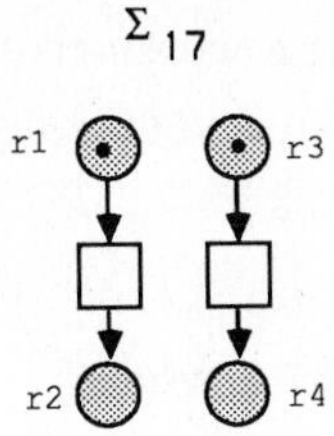

Figure 13

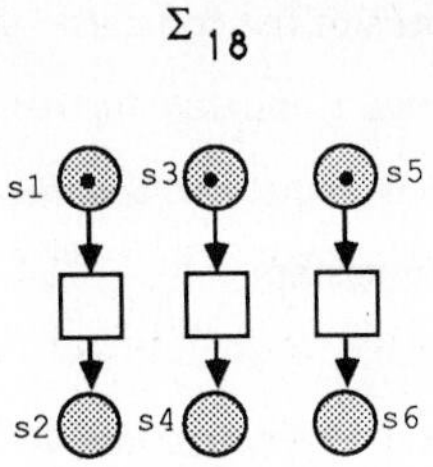

Figure 14

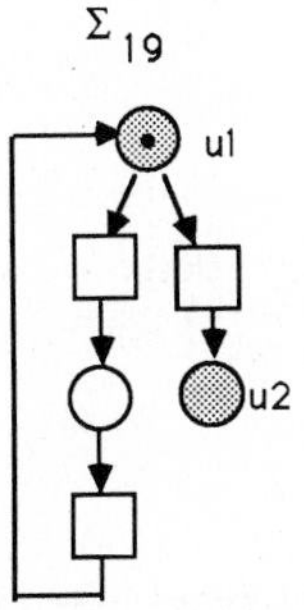

Figure 15

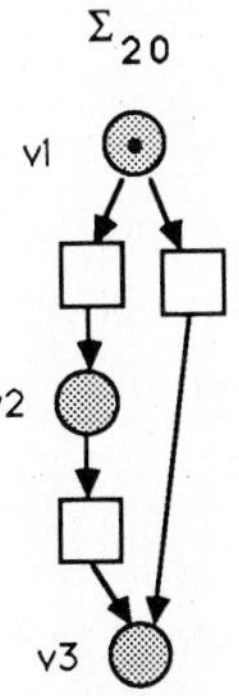

Figure 16

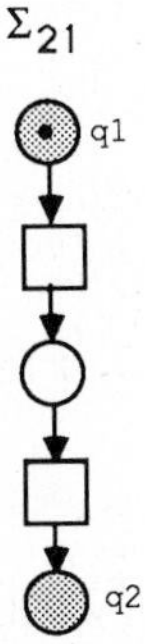

Figure 17

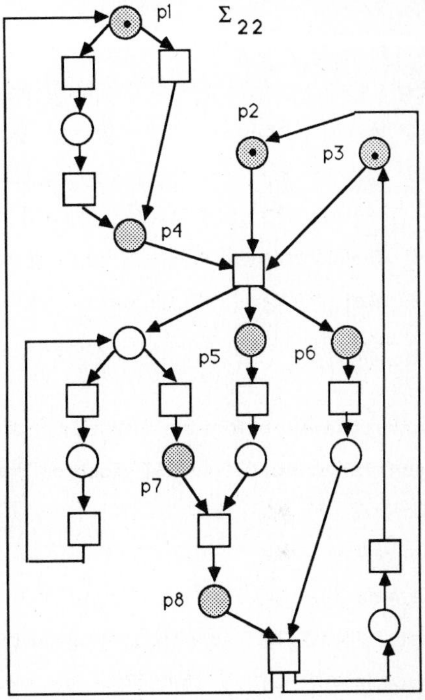

Figure 18

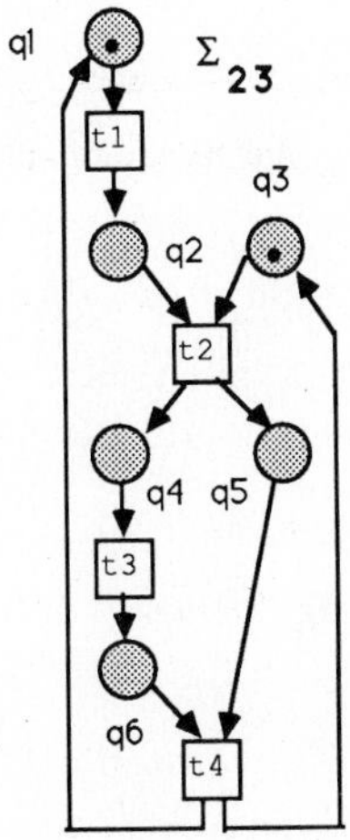

Figure 19

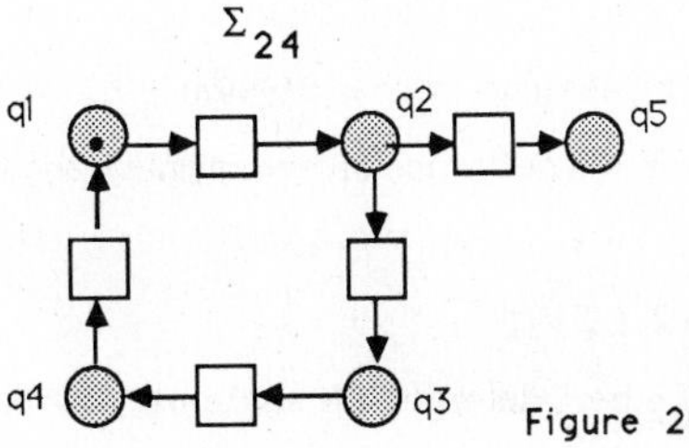

Figure 20

local states of the compared systems which preserves the operation of intersection, difference and, when defined, of union; furtheremore such a function preserves the environment of observable local state transformations and maps the initial case of the first system into a subset of the initial case of the second system.

Definition 11 *morphism between OLST-algebras*

Let Σ_1 and Σ_2 be S-labelled EN systems with $I_1 = \langle C_{oss1}, c_{1in}, I_1, \cap, -, \cup; \rightarrow_1 \rangle$ and $I_2 = \langle C_{oss2}, c_{2in}, I_2, \cap, -, \cup; \rightarrow_2 \rangle$ their OLST-algebras.

- $h: I_1 \dashrightarrow I_2$ is a <u>morphism</u> iff $h: I_1 \dashrightarrow I_2$ is a total <u>injective</u> function such that:

1) $\forall x \in I_1,\ h(x) = \emptyset \Leftrightarrow x = \emptyset$;

2) $h(c_{1in}) \subseteq c_{2in}$;

3) $\forall x,y \in I_1,\ h(x \cap y) = h(x) \cap h(y)$ <u>and</u> $h(x - y) = h(x) - h(y)$;

4) $\forall x,y \in I_1: x \cup y \in I_1,\ h(x \cup y) = h(x) \cup h(y)$;

5) $\forall x,y \in I_1: x \rightarrow_1 y \Rightarrow [\ h(x) \rightarrow_2 h(y)$ <u>or</u>

$\exists n \geq 1,\ \exists i_1, i_2, \ldots, i_n \in (I_2 - h(I_1)):\ h(x) \rightarrow_2 i_1 \rightarrow_2 \ldots i_n \rightarrow_2 h(y)\ ]$.

- The morphism $h: I_1 \dashrightarrow I_2$ is an <u>isomorphism</u> iff $h: I_1 \dashrightarrow I_2$ is a bijection such that:

a) $h(c_{1in}) = c_{2in}$;

b) $\forall x,y \in I_1: x \rightarrow_1 y \Leftrightarrow h(x) \rightarrow_2 h(y)$

In the following before the definition of ST-preorder, we state the most important properties of isomorphisms between OLST-algebras: they preserve both minimal and maximal elements of the algebras.

Lemma 2

Let Σ_1 and Σ_2 be S-labelled systems with $I_1 = \langle C_{oss1}, c_{1in}, I_1, \cap, -, \cup, \rightarrow_1 \rangle$ and $I_2 = \langle C_{oss2}, c_{2in}, I_2, \cap, -, \cup, \rightarrow_2 \rangle$ their algebraic structures and let $h: I_1 \dashrightarrow I_2$ be an isomorphism then: $\forall x \in I_1$

1) $x \in I_{1min} \Leftrightarrow h(x) \in I_{2min}$;

2) $x \in C_{oss1} \Leftrightarrow h(x) \in C_{oss2}$.

Proof

1) is proved by contradiction in [PS89a].

2) follows from the definition of isomorphism and from Lemma 1 point d).

Definition 12 *($\Sigma_1 \subseteq^{ST} \Sigma_2$)*

Let Σ_1 and Σ_2 be S-labelled EN systems with $I_1 = \langle C_{oss1}, c_{1in}, I_1, \cap, -, \cup; \rightarrow_1 \rangle$ and $I_2 = \langle C_{oss2}, c_{2in}, I_2, \cap, -, \cup; \rightarrow_2 \rangle$ their algebraic structures. Then Σ_1 is <u>less or equal</u> than Σ_2 <u>w.r.t.</u>

<u>State Transformation</u> ($\Sigma_1 \subseteq^{ST} \Sigma_2$) iff there is a morphism $h : I_1 \dashrightarrow I_2$.

Remark

The relation $\subseteq^{ST}$ is a preorder over the set of S-labelled systems, it is in fact easy to verify that $\subseteq^{ST}$ is reflexive and transitive.

<u>Examples 4</u>

Let us consider the systems $\Sigma_{15}, \Sigma_{16}, \ldots, \Sigma_{21}$, given respectively in Figure 11, Figure 12, ..., Figure 17, with their related algebraic structures.

a) As previously discussed, $\Sigma_{15} \subseteq^{ST} \Sigma_{16}$ with morphism $h : I_{15} \dashrightarrow I_{16}$ defined by $h(p_1)=q_1$, $h(p_2)=q_2$ in the case in which Σ_{16} is considered an "extension" of Σ_{15}, and morphism $k : I_{15} \dashrightarrow I_{16}$ defined by $k(p_1)=q_1$, $k(p_2)=q_3$ in the case in which Σ_{16} is considered an "expansion" of Σ_{15}.

b) $\Sigma_{15} \subseteq^{ST} \Sigma_{17}$ In fact, considering $I_{15} = \{\{p_1\},\{p_2\}\}$, $\rightarrow_{15} = \{\langle p_1,p_2\rangle\}$ and $I_{17}=\{\{r_1,r_3\},\{r_2,r_4\},\{r_2,r_3\}, \{r_1,r_4\}, \{r_1\},\{r_2\},\{r_3\},\{r_4\}\}$, $\rightarrow_{17}=\langle\{r_1,r_3\},\{r_2,r_3\}\rangle$, $\langle\{r_1,r_4\},\{r_2,r_4\}\rangle$, $\langle\{r_1,r_3\},\{r_1,r_4\}\rangle$, $\langle\{r_2,r_3\},\{r_2,r_4\}\rangle$, $\langle\{r_1\},\{r_2\}\rangle,\langle\{r_3\},\{r_4\}\rangle\}$, there is for example the morphism $h: I_{15} \dashrightarrow I_{17}$ defined by $h(p_1)=r_1$ and $h(p_2)=r_2$.

In this case Σ_{17} is an "extention" of Σ_{15} obtained by adding to this latter a concurrent component.

c) An other example of "extension" by adding a concurrent component is given by the relation $\Sigma_{17} \subseteq^{ST} \Sigma_{18}$. In fact, considering the OLST-algebras I_{17} and I_{18}, there is for example the morphism $h: I_{17} \dashrightarrow I_{18}$ defined by $h(r_1)=s_1$, $h(r_2)=s_2$, $h(r_3)=s_3$ and $h(r_4)=s_4$.

This example together with the previous one (b) justifies the definition of the local state transformation relation $\rightarrow$ which put into relation not only observable cases but also observable local states, i.e.: elements of the algebra of observable local states which are not maximal.

d) An other possible "extension" of Σ_{15} is obtained by adding to this latter an alternative iterative component as is the case in system Σ_{19}. We have in fact $\Sigma_{15} \subseteq^{ST} \Sigma_{19}$ if we consider the morphism h defined by $h(p_1)=u_1$ and $h(p_2)=u_2$.

e) If two S-labelled systems Σ_i and Σ_j are such that $\Sigma_i \subseteq^{ST} \Sigma_j$, then it does not always happen that Σ_j is either an "extension" or an "expantion" of Σ_i, but it can happen that Σ_j is both an "extension" and an "expantion" of Σ_i. This is the case of Σ_{15} and Σ_{20} when the morphism h defined by $h(p_1)=v_1$ and $h(p_2)=v_3$ is considered. In this case $\Sigma_{15} \subseteq^{ST} \Sigma_{20}$ and Σ_{20} is both an "extension" and an "expansion" of Σ_{15}.

f) As previously discussed the S-labelled systems Σ_{12} and Σ_{14} given respectively in Figure 8 and in Figure 10 are <u>not</u> comparable by means of ST-preorder. There is <u>no</u> morphism between the OLST-algebras I_{12} and I_{14} such that $\Sigma_{12} \subseteq^{ST} \Sigma_{14}$ or $\Sigma_{14} \subseteq^{ST} \Sigma_{12}$. <u>not</u>($\Sigma_{12} \subseteq^{ST} \Sigma_{14}$) since any possible total function between I_{12} and I_{14} does not preserve local state transformations. For example, if we consider the function h: I_{12} --> I_{14} defined by $h(p_1)=v_1$, $h(p_2)=v_2$, $h(p_3)=v_3$, $h(p_4)=v_4$, then we have $p_2 \rightarrow_{12} p_3$ but not($h(p_2) \rightarrow_{14} h(p_3)$) and also there are no intermediate states such that $h(p_2) \rightarrow_{12} \ldots \rightarrow_{12} h(p_3)$. Furtheremore not($\Sigma_{14} \subseteq^{ST} \Sigma_{12}$) since there is no injective function h: I_{14} --> I_{12}.

Let us now consider the systems Σ_{15} and Σ_{21} given respectively in Figure 11 and in Figure 17. By means of the isomorphism h : I_{15} --> I_{21} defined by $h(p_1)= q_1$, $h(p_2)= q_2$ we have $\Sigma_{15} \subseteq^{ST} \Sigma_{21}$; by means of k : I_{21} --> I_{15} defined as the inverse of h we have $\Sigma_{21} \subseteq^{ST} \Sigma_{15}$.
We can say that Σ_{15} and Σ_{21} are equivalent with respect to State Transformations (ST-equivalent) and write $\Sigma_{15} \approx^{ST} \Sigma_{21}$.

Before giving the formal definition of ST-equivalence we state the following theorem.

Theorem 1

Let Σ_1 and Σ_2 be S-labelled systems and I_1, I_2 be their algebraic structures.
Then $\Sigma_1 \subseteq^{ST} \Sigma_2$ and $\Sigma_2 \subseteq^{ST} \Sigma_1$ $\Leftrightarrow$ I_1 and I_2 are isomorphic.

Proof

The detailed proof can be found in [PS89a]; it is performed by using the properties of the OLST-algebras as stated in Lemma 1, the fact that morphisms between OLST-algebras are injective and the properties of isomorphisms between OLST-algebras as stated in Lemma 2.

Definition 13 $\Sigma_1 \approx^{ST} \Sigma_2$

Let Σ_1 and Σ_2 be S-labelled systems and I_1, I_2 be their OLST-algebras. Then Σ_1 and Σ_2 are equivalent with respect to State Transformations (ST-equivalent), $\Sigma_1 \approx^{ST} \Sigma_2$, iff $\Sigma_1 \subseteq^{ST} \Sigma_2$ and $\Sigma_2 \subseteq^{ST} \Sigma_1$ or equivalently, iff I_1 and I_2 are isomorphic.

Example 5

Let us consider the S-labelled systems Σ_{22} and Σ_{23} given respectively in Figure 18 and in Figure 19 and whose OLST-algebras are defined by: $c_{in22}=\{p_1, p_2, p_3\}$; $I_{22}= \{ \{p_1, p_2, p_3\}, \{p_4, p_2, p_3\}, \{p_5, p_6, p_7\}, \{p_2, p_3\}, \{p_5, p_7\}, \{p_6, p_8\}, \{p_1\}, \{p_4\}, \{p_6\}, \{p_8\} \}$;
$\rightarrow_{22} = \langle\{p_1\}, \{p_4\}\rangle, \langle\{p_1, p_2, p_3\}, \{p_4, p_2, p_3\}\rangle, \langle\{p_4, p_2, p_3\}, \{p_5, p_6, p_7\}\rangle, \langle\{p_5, p_7\}, \{p_8\}\rangle, \langle\{p_5, p_6, p_7\}, \{p_6, p_8\}\rangle, \langle\{p_6, p_8\}, \{p_1, p_2, p_3\}\rangle$; $c_{in23} = \{q_1, q_3\}$; $I_{23}= \{ \{q_1, q_3\}, \{q_2, q_3\}, \{q_4, q_5\}, \{q_6, q_5\}, \{q_1\}, \{q_2\}, \{q_3\}, \{q_4\}, \{q_5\}, \{q_6\}$; $\rightarrow_{23}= \langle\{q_1\}, \{q_2\}\rangle, \langle\{q_1, q_3\}, \{q_2, q_3\}\rangle, \langle\{q_2, q_3\}, \{q_4, q_5\}\rangle, \langle\{q_4\}, \{q_6\}\rangle, \langle \{q_4, q_5\}, \{q_6, q_5\}\rangle, \langle \{q_6, q_5\}, \{q_1, q_3\}\rangle$.
It is easy to prove that the correspondence defined by $h(p_1) = q_1$, $h(p_2, p_3) = q_3$, $h(p_4) = q_2$, $h(p_5, p_7) = q_4$, $h(p_6) = q_5$, $h(p_8) = q_6$ is an isomorphism between I_{22} and I_{23} and than that Σ_{22} and

Σ_{23} are ST-equivalent ($\Sigma_{22} \approx^{ST} \Sigma_{23}$).

Let us now consider the S-labelled systems Σ_{12} and Σ_{24} given respectively in Figure8 and in Figure 20. It is immediate to verify that $\Sigma_{12} \approx^{ST} \Sigma_{24}$. While the system Σ_{12} has a never ending cyclic behaviour, Σ_{24} can reach the final unobservable case $\{q_5\}$. We can therefore say that ST-equivalence between S-labelled systems does not preserve "deadlock-freeness".

In order to preserve deadlock-freeness without modifying ST-equivalence, we have to consider S-labelled systems not containing reachable unobservable cases in which no state transformation has concession or from which any subsequent state transformation cannot be ever observed. Formally, we have to consider S-labelled systems satisfying the following additional requirement: from any reachable case it is always possible to reach an observable case, i.e.: $\forall c \in C$, $\exists$ c'reachable from c such that: $c' \in C_{OSS}$.

5. S-OBSERVABLE SYSTEMS AND ST-CANONICAL REPRESENTATIVES

We now introduce the subclass of S-labelled system called S-observable systems [DDPS88] which is of particular interest since in this case OLST-algebras and ST-equivalence have the nice properties stated in theorems 2 and 3. Furtheremore we present the construction of the unique canonical representative of each ST-equivalence class of S-observable systems.

S-observable systems are S-labelled systems in which the pre and post sets of each elementary observable path are disjoint.

Definition 14 *S-observable systems*

Let Σ be a S-labelled system, then Σ is S-observable iff $\forall$ $w \in W_\Sigma$ it holds: $\bullet w \cap w \bullet = \emptyset$.

Example 6

The S-labelled systems Σ_{25} and Σ_{26} given in Figure 21 are not S-observable since place p_1 belongs to both $\bullet w$ and $w \bullet$, with w = t1,t2.

On the contrary, the S-labelled-systems Σ_{27}, Σ_{28}, Σ_{29} given in Figure 22, are all S-observable. They show that S-observability requires that places inside loops are either all unobservable (Σ_{27}) or at least two of them are observable (Σ_{28}, Σ_{29}).

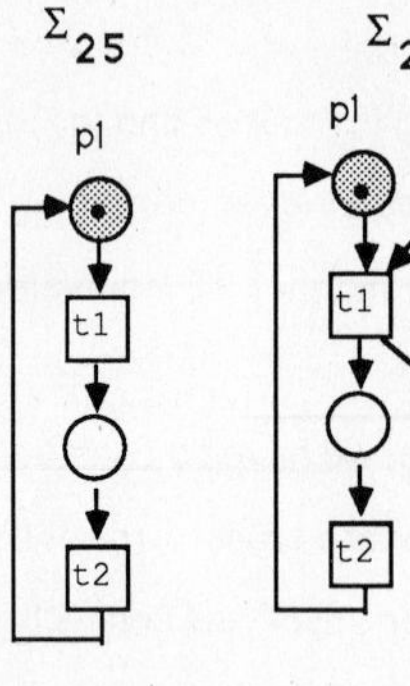

Figure 21

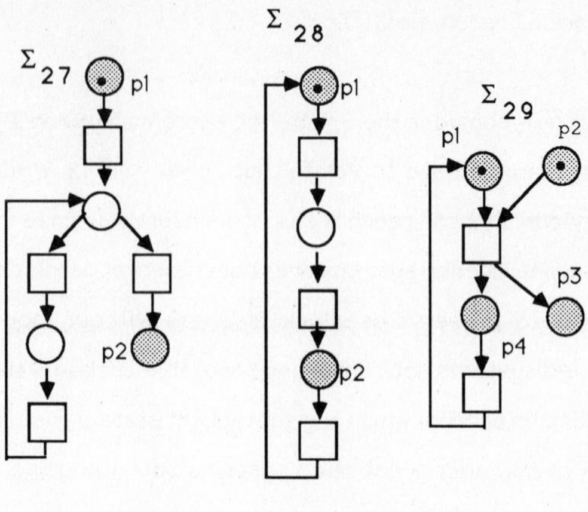

Figure 22

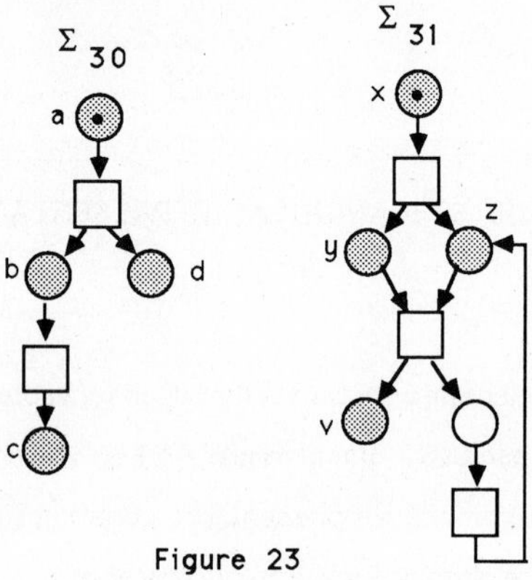

Figure 23

Remark

We can say that S-observable systems are such that:

a) they cannot contain "observable side conditions" on elementary observable paths;

b) empty observable paths are not allowed;

c) for each c, $c' \in C_{OSS}$ and for each $w \in W_\Sigma$ it holds: $c[(w\rangle\rangle c' \Leftrightarrow c - c' = \bullet w$ <u>and</u> $c' - c = w\bullet$.

Furtheremore if a system Σ is S-observable then the observable state transformation relation $\rightarrow$ of its OLST-algebra can be derived from the relation $\rightarrow^c$ which corresponds to $\rightarrow$ restricted to $C_{OSS} \times C_{OSS}$ as it is shown in the following Theorem.

Theorem 2

Let Σ be a S-observable system with OLST-algebra $I = \langle C_{oss}, c_{in}, I, \cap, -, \cup ; \rightarrow \rangle$. Then I can be derived from the subalgebra $I^c = \langle C_{oss}, c_{in}, I, \cap, -, \cup ; \rightarrow^c \rangle$ where $\rightarrow^c \subseteq C_{oss} \times C_{oss}$ and $\rightarrow^c = \rightarrow / Coss \times Coss$

Proof

The proof is performed in two steps.

a) Let us consider I^c and construct the relation $\rightarrow' \subseteq I \times I$ defined by:

$\forall x,y \in I,\ x \rightarrow' y$ iff $\exists\, c, c' \in C_{oss}$: $c \rightarrow^c c'$ <u>and</u>

$[\,(x = c-c'$ <u>and</u> $y = c'-c)$ <u>or</u> $(\exists\, z \subseteq c \cap c'$: $x = (c-c') \cup z$ <u>and</u> $y = (c'-c) \cup z\,)\,]$.

b) We have to prove that the introduced relation $\rightarrow'$ coincides with the relation $\rightarrow$ of the OLST-algebra I. This is done by contradiction and by using the property of S-observable systems as stated in the previous remark point c).

It is to note that the previous construction does not work for S-labelled systems which are no S-observable. For example, if we consider the system Σ_{26} given in Figure 21 we get, by means of the previous construction, $p_2 \rightarrow' p_3$ whereas p_2 and p_3 are not related by the observable state transformation relation $\rightarrow$.

Theorem 3

Let Σ_1 and Σ_2 be S-observable systems, I_1, I_2 their OLST-algebras and $I_1{}^c$, $I_2{}^c$ as defined in the previous theorem.

Then I_1 and I_2 are isomorphic $\Leftrightarrow$ $I_1{}^c$ and $I_2{}^c$ are isomorphic.

Proof

a) I_1 and I_2 are isomorphic $\Rightarrow$ $I_1{}^c$ and $I_2{}^c$ are isomorphic. Obvious.

b) The implication ($I_1{}^c$ and $I_2{}^c$ are isomorphic $\Rightarrow$ I_1 and I_2 are isomorphic) is easily proved on the basis of Theorem 2; in fact, the relation $\rightarrow$ is derived from the relation $\rightarrow^c$ by using difference and union which are preserved by isomorphism.

Remark

As it is shown in the following example, the previous Theorem does not hold for S-labelled systems which are not S-observable.

<u>Example 7</u>

Let us consider the systems Σ_{30} and Σ_{31} given in Figure 23 and their related algebras I_{30}, I_{31} and $I_{30}{}^c$, $I_{31}{}^c$. We can see that Σ_{30} is S-observable, while Σ_{31} is not S-observable; $I_{30}{}^c$ and $I_{31}{}^c$ are isomorphic, while I_{30} and I_{31} are <u>not</u> isomorphic, in fact, in I_{30} we have the relation $b \rightarrow_{30} c$ which has <u>no</u> correspondent in I_{31} since <u>not</u>($y \rightarrow_{31} v$).

In [DDPS88] was introduced the Exhibited Functionality equivalence (EF-equivalence) on S-labelled systems, which is formulated in a slightly different way w.r.t. ST-equivalence, but could be formulated in a way similar to ST-equivalence by requiring the isomorphism between the OLST-algebras in which the relation $\rightarrow$ is restricted to $C_{oss} \times C_{oss}$, i.e. by requiring the isomorphism between the algebraic structures I^C.

From this consideration and the previous Theorem it follows that EF-equivalence and ST-equivalence coincide in the case of S-observable systems, while in the case of S-labelled systems ST-equivalence distinguishes more than EF-equivalence, i.e.: ST-equivalence $\subset$ EF-equivalence.

(The coincidence, in the case of S-observable systems, of EF-equivalence, given in its original formulation as in [DDPS88], and ST-equivalence has been proved in [PS89a].)

In [DDPS88] it is shown that, in the case of S-observable systems, it is possible to construct a unique (up to isomorphism) canonical representative of each EF-equivalence class. Then this also holds for ST-equivalence classes. The canonical representatives are simple, pure, contact-free EN-systems without dead transitions and in which any place is observable. Such class of EN systems is of particular interest since its properties are the basic ones a well designed system has to satisfy [RT86], [Pet89].

We give now the construction of such representatives.

Construction

Given a S-observable system and its related OLST-algebra, the canonical representative of the equivalence class to which it belongs is constructed by associating a condition to each element belonging to I_{min} and an event to each equivalence class of local state transformations, where two local state transformations are equivalent iff they transform exactly the same local states. The flow relation connects a condition s to an event t if s corresponds to an elemennt of I_{min} contained in the precondition of a local state transformation corresponding to t, and an event to a condition in a similar way. The initial case is the set of conditions corresponding to the elements of I_{min} constituting the initial case of the given system; the observable cases are all the cases reachable from the initial one.

Formally, let $\Sigma = (S,T,F, c_{in}; C_{oss})$ be a S-labelled EN system and $I_\Sigma = \langle C_{oss}, c_{in}, I, \cap, -, \cup; \rightarrow \rangle$ be its OLST-algebra, then the canonical representative of the equivalence class of Σ is the EN system $CR(\Sigma) = (S',T',F', c'_{in}; C'_{oss})$ where:

- $S' = I_{min}$;
- $T' = \{t = \langle pre(t), post(t) \rangle \mid \exists x,y \in I: x \rightarrow y$ <u>and</u> $pre(t) = x-y$ <u>and</u> $post(t) = y-x\}$;
- $F' = \{(s,t) \mid s \in I_{min}$ <u>and</u> $t \in T'$ <u>and</u> $s \subseteq pre(t)\} \cup \{(t,s) \mid s \in I_{min}$ <u>and</u> $t \in T'$ <u>and</u> $s \subseteq post(t)\}$;

- $c'_{in} = \{s \in S \mid s \in I_{min}$ and $s \in c_{in}\}$;
- $C'_{oss} = C'$

end of construction

Example 8

Through the above construction the S-observable system Σ_{22} of Figure 18 can be reduced to the S-observable system Σ_{23} of Figure 19.

Even if the previous construction is formulated in a slightly different way than the one given in [DDPS88], starting from the same S-observable system the two constructions generate isomorphic systems. The properties proved in [DDPS88] on the reduced system are therefore satisfied also by the system obtained by means of the here presented construction; in particular:

a) $CR(\Sigma)$ is a S-observable system;

b) $CR(\Sigma)$ and Σ are EF-equivalent and than, since $CR(\Sigma)$ and Σ are both S-observable systems, they are ST-equivalent;

c) $CR(\Sigma)$ is minimal w.r.t. the set of places and the set of transitions in its EF-equivalence (ST-equivalence) class;

d) $CR(\Sigma)$ is a minimal contact-free EN system, which is simple, pure and such that each transition is not dead under the initial case;

c) any EF-equivalence (ST-equivalence) class of S-observable systems contains one and only one minimal contact-free EN system (up to isomorphism).

The previous construction could be applied to S-labelled systems too: in this case purity of the canonical representative is no more guaranteed since to a sequence of transitions having concession in the given system could be associated a dead transition in the canonical representative because of side conditions.

The proof of ST-equivalence between two S-observable systems can be carried on by reducing them to their canonical representatives and then verifying if they are isomorphic. The implementation of the reduction algorithm for the construction of the canonical representatives is under development as the basis for an (interactive) tool for the verification of the $\subseteq^{ST}$ and $\approx^{ST}$ relations between systems.

Let us define now the degree of concurrency of a system in canonical form as the maximal number of conditions constituting a reachable case (i.e., Degree of Concurrency(Σ) = $Max\{n \,/\, n=|c| \ \forall c \in [c_{in}>\}$). This notion can be easily extended to S-observable systems by considering the number of elements of I_{min} constituting each reachable observable case.

Since two equivalent S-observable systems have isomorphic OLST-algebras, they necessarily show the same degree of concurrency on the observable states, otherwise their canonical representatives cannot be isomorphic. Equivalent S-observable systems can have different degree of concurrency only on the unobservable states.

Then we can deduce that it is meaningless to define a notions of functional equivalence based on OLST-algebra by distinguishing between interleaving or partial order semantics (i.e., by using traces, posets, etc. instead of sequences). The OLST-algebra allows the distinction between systems having sequential non-deteministic behaviours from systems having concurrent behaviours (e.g., there is no system having a sequential non-deterministic behaviour which is ST-equivalent to the system Σ_{17} of Figure 13).

6. STATE OBSERVABILITY IN SYSTEM DESIGN

The class of S-observable systems with ST-preorder and ST-equivalence defined on it provides the concurrent system designer with useful tools in the stepwise development of a concurrent system. The different possible steps in the development process can be depicted by the grid of systems shown in Figure 24. CR_k are the canonical representatives of the classes in increasing order; $\Sigma_{r,s}$ is the generic system belonging to the rth class and at the sth level of detail, m being the level the designer possibly chooses as the final step in the refinement. The designer can move inside this grid along whatever path, at each step either changing the equivalence class in which he operates, i.e. , the structure of observable system states, in the case he moves along the $\subseteq^{ST}$ path, or adding more unobservable details inside the same equivalence class, in the case he moves along the $\approx^{ST}$paths.

In particular, along the $\subseteq^{ST}$ path the designer can either change the level of atomicity in state transformation by means of a system expansion, or can enrich the structure of observable state incrementing the system functionality by means of system extension.

Among the others, one path can be associated to the sequence of two classic activities in the system development process, namely system specification and implementation. When the designer moves along the paths of canonical representatives he can be considered inside the specification step, in which only the essentials, i.e., the observable states, are considered and their causal relatioships are stated. Once the canonical representative satisfying all the requirements is found (i.e., the representative is the specification of the system), then the implementation step can start. In fact, ST-equivalence (preserved by moving along the $\approx^{ST}$paths) disregards any unobservable system state structure, which can depend on some implementation constraints, and only requires to maintain the observable states

$$
\begin{array}{ccccccccccccc}
\ldots \subseteq^{ST} & CR_1 & \subseteq^{ST} \ldots \subseteq^{ST} & CR_i & \subseteq^{ST} \ldots \subseteq^{ST} & CR_n & \subseteq^{ST} \ldots \\
& \approx^{ST} & & \approx^{ST} & & \approx^{ST} & \\
\ldots & & \ldots & & \ldots & & \ldots \\
& \approx^{ST} & & \approx^{ST} & & \approx^{ST} & \\
\ldots \subseteq^{ST} & \Sigma_{1,j} & \subseteq^{ST} \ldots \subseteq^{ST} & \Sigma_{i,j} & \subseteq^{ST} \ldots \subseteq^{ST} & \Sigma_{n,j} & \subseteq^{ST} \ldots \\
& \approx^{ST} & & \approx^{ST} & & \approx^{ST} & \\
\ldots & & \ldots & & \ldots & & \ldots \\
& \approx^{ST} & & \approx^{ST} & & \approx^{ST} & \\
\ldots \subseteq^{ST} & \Sigma_{1,m} & \subseteq^{ST} \ldots \subseteq^{ST} & \Sigma_{i,m} & \subseteq^{ST} \ldots \subseteq^{ST} & \Sigma_{n,m} & \subseteq^{ST} \ldots
\end{array}
$$

Figure 24

structure, guaranteeing in this way the fulfilment of the specification itself.

All the other paths inside the grid correspond to system development modalities in which the specification and implementation steps are in some way interleaved. These modalities are by far the more used in practice and can find in the above mentioned grid a support to a controlled system development. In fact, whatever path is followed, the obtained system results related by ST-preorder to each intermediate system model which is generated in the development process: the morphism defining the correspondence between the OLST-algebras of the two systems is obtained by composition of the morphisms in the paths connecting them.

As an example of such a combination of the two modalities see the one presented in the introduction, it is easy to show that the first system is less w.r.t. ST-preorder than the last one, then we can say that the state transformations specified by the first one are consistently realized by the last one.

7. CONCLUSIONS

The approach presented in this paper can be improved in different directions.

In [PS89b] EN systems and their properties have been characterized in terms of Local State Transformation algebras. Furtheremore it is shown how to derive the algebra from the system and conversely the system from the algebra, and it is proved that the class of contact-free EN systems (the ST-canonical representatives) together with ST-preorder is a complete partial order.

What remains to be done in order to support the stepwise development of concurrent systems with effective design tools based on state observation is the introduction of suitable composition operations of EN systems defined on LST-algebras and the study of the conditions under which ST-preorder and ST-equivalence are preserved by such operations.

The subsequent step is the one of combining the approach based on state observation with the one based on action observation. This can be done by considering which are the mutual constraints on the observability of both actions and states such that the two refinement/abstraction notions can be interrelated in such a way that they can be consistently used in an interleaved way. This corresponds to individuate the conditions under which the following diagram commutes, where $\sim^{O}$ is a suitably chosen equivalence based on action observation.

$$\begin{array}{ccc} \Sigma_1 & \sim^{O} & \Sigma_2 \\ \approx^{ST} & & \approx^{ST} \\ \Sigma_4 & \sim^{O} & \Sigma_3 \end{array}$$

This combination of the two approaches was first motivated in [DDS87].

In the following we briefly discuss the relationships of some aspects of the here proposed approach with other works in the literature.

For what concern morphisms between net systems, the ones proposed in the literature are not related to state observability as is the case of the notion here proposed, moreover, the notion introduced by C.A. Petri [Pet73] is more flexible then the one here proposed but disregards dynamical properties; morphisms introduced by G. Winskel [Win84] require to preserve initial cases and pre-set and post-set of events, then they correspond to a special kind of system "extension" while they do not allow system "expansion". Other notions of morphisms between Place/Transition systems have been introduced by B.J. Meseguer and U. Montanari [MM88] using a categorical approach. In the case of contact-free EN-systems (the ST-canonical representatives) the morphisms here presented are in relation with their (MCatPetri) morphisms since also these latter allow one "to map a transition t to a computation with possibly many sequential and parallel steps". For what concerns the cases, (MCatPetri) morphisms require that the cases be preserved while our morphisms require that the image of a case be contained in a case.

Inside net theory, works in some ways implicitely related are: the notion of Interface Equivalence introduced by K. Voss [Vos87] which is based both on local states and on event observability and which results to be disjoint from ST-equivalence as it is shown in [DDPS88]; the notion of refinement defined by R. Valette [Val79], which substitutes for a transition predefined structures of subnet; the reduction rules defined by G. Berthelot [Ber86], which consider both structural and dynamic aspects by preserving system behaviour but are oriented more towards system analysis than system development.

The relationships we are also interested in investigating are the ones between the notion of 'implementation' informally introduced in section 6 with the notion of 'implementation' introduced by L. Lamport in [Lam86].

This research has ben conducted under the financial support of the Italian Ministero della Pubblica Istruzione and, partially, of the Esprit-BRA DEMON (3148).

8. REFERENCES

LNCS stands for Lecture Notes in Computer Sciences, Springer Verlag, Berlin

[Abr87]
S. Abramsky, Observation Equivalence as a Testing Equivalence, Theor.Comp. Science 53, pp. 225-241, 1987

[Ber86]
G. Berthelot, Checking Properties of Nets Using Transformations,LNCS 222, pp. 19-40, 1986.

[BDKP89]
E. Best, R. Devillers, A. Kiehn, L. Pomello, Fully Concurrent Bisimulation, submitted paper 1989.

[Bra87]
W. Brauer, W. Reisig, G. Rozenberg (eds.), Petri Nets: Central Models and Their Properties, LNCS 254, 1987.

[BHR84]
S.D. Brookes, C.A.R. Hoare, A.W. Roscoe, A Theory of Communicating Sequential Processes, J. ACM 31, N.3, July '84, 1984.

[CDP87]
L. Castellano, G. De Michelis, L. Pomello, Concurrency vs Interleaving: an instructive example, EATCS Bull., N. 31, pp. 12-15, 1987.

[DDM87]
P. Degano, R. De Nicola, U. Montanari, Observational equivalences for concurrency models, in 'Formal description of Programming Concepts III' (M.Virsing ed.), North Holland, 1987.

[DDS87]
F. De Cindio, G. De Michelis, C. Simone, GAMERU: a language for the analysis and design of human communication pragmatics, in G. Rozemberg (ed) "Advances in Petri Nets 86' ", LNCS 266, 1987.

[DDPS85]
F. De Cindio, G. De Michelis, L. Pomello, C. Simone, Exhibited-Behaviour Equivalence and Organizational Abstraction in Concurrent System Design, Proc. 5th International Conference on Distributed Computing, IEEE, Denver,1985.

[DDPS88]
F. De Cindio, G. De Michelis, L. Pomello, C. Simone, A State Transformation Equivalence for Concurent Systems: Exhibited Functionality Equivalence, in F.H. Vogt (ed) "CONCURRENCY 88", LNCS 335, 1988.

[DH84]
R. De Nicola, M. Hennessy, Testing equivalences for processes, TCS 34, 83-134, 1984.

[GG89]
R. van Glabbeek, U. Goltz, Refinement of actions in causality based models, in this volume, 1989.

[Hen88]
M. Hennessy, Algebraic Theory of Processes, The MIT Press, 1988.

[Jif89]
He Jifeng, Various Refinements and Simulations, in this volume, 1989.
[Lam86]
L. Lamport, On Interprocess Communication, Part 1: Basic Formalism, Distributed Computing, Vol. 1, pp. 77-85, 1986.
[Lar89]
K. Larsen, An Operational Semantics of Context, in this volume, 1989.
[MM88]
B.J. Meseguer, U. Montanari, Petri Nets are Monoids, SRI-CSL-88-3, january 1988.
[Mil80]
R. Milner, A Calculus for Communicating Systems, LNCS 92, 1980.
[Par81]
D. Park, Concurrency and Automata on Infinite Sequences, Proc. 5th GI Conference, LNCS 104, pp. 167-183, 1981.
[Pet73]
C.A. Petri, Concepts in Net Theory, Mathematical Foundations of Computer Science: Proc. of Symposium and Summer School, High Tatras, sept. 1973, Math. Inst. of the Slovak Acad. of Sciences, pp.137-146, 1973.
[Pet89]
C.A. Petri, Perfect Nets, Invited talk at the X Int. Conf. On Application and Theory of Petri Nets, Bonn, june 1989.
[Pom86]
L. Pomello, Some Equivalence Notions for Concurrent Systems: An Overview, in "Advances in Petri Nets 1985" (G.Rozenberg ed.), LNCS 222, pp. 381-400, 1986.
[PS89a]
L. Pomello, C. Simone, A State Transformation Preorder over a class of EN-systems, Proc X Int. Conf. On Application and Theory of Petri Nets, Bonn, pp. 247-271, june 1989.
[PS89b]
L. Pomello, C. Simone, Concurrent Systems as Local State Transformation Algebras: the case of Elementary Net Systems, in "Proc. 3rd Italian Conference on Theoretical Computer Science, Mantova, Nov.89, eds. Bertoni, Bohem, Miglioli, World Scientific Publ. Co., 1989.
[RT86]
G. Rozenberg, P.S. Thiagarajan, Petri Nets: basic notions, structure, behaviour, in "Current trends in Concurrency" ed. J.W. de Bakker, W.P. de Rover and G. Rozenberg, LNCS 224, pp. 585-668, 1986.
[Thi87]
P.S. Thiagarajan, Elementary Net Systems, in [Bra87], pp. 26-59, 1987.
[Val79]
R. Valette, Analysis of Petri Nets by Stewise Refinements, J. of Computer and System Science, vol.18-1, 1979.
[Voss87]
K. Voss, Interface as a Basic Concept for Systems Specification and Verification, in "Concurrency and Nets" (eds) K. Voss, H.J. Genrich, G. Rozenberg, Springer Verlag, Berlin, pp.585-604,1987.
[Win84]
G. Winskel, A New Definition of Morphism on Petri Nets, in LNCS 166, pp.140-150, 1984.

Construction of Network Protocols by Stepwise Refinement*

A. Udaya Shankar
Department of Computer Science and
Institute for Advanced Computer Studies
University of Maryland
College Park, Maryland 20742

Simon S. Lam
Department of Computer Sciences
The University of Texas at Austin
Austin, Texas 78712

Abstract. We present a heuristic to derive specifications of distributed systems by stepwise refinement. The heuristic is based upon a *conditional refinement* relation between specifications. It is applied to construct four sliding window protocols that provide reliable data transfer over unreliable communication channels. The protocols use modulo-N sequence numbers. They are less restrictive and easier to implement than sliding window protocols previously studied in the protocol verification literature.

Key words: Specification, refinement, sliding window protocols, transport protocols, distributed systems.

CONTENTS

1. Introduction
   1.1. Construction examples
   1.2. Organization of this report
2. Stepwise Refinement Heuristic
3. Sliding Window Protocol Construction: Initial Phase
   3.1. Initial system and requirements
   3.2. The sliding window mechanism
   3.3. Correct interpretation of data messages
   3.4. Correct interpretation of acknowledgement messages
   3.5. Progress requirement marking
4. Completing the Construction for Loss-only Channels
5. Completing the Construction for Loss, Reordering, and Duplication Channels
   5.1. Real-time system model
   5.2. A time constraint that enforces A_7
   5.3. A time constraint that enforces A_{10}
   5.4. Protocol I: implementation with 2N timers
   5.5. Protocol II: implementation with N timers
   5.6. Protocol III: implementation with one timer
6. Discussions
Tables 1-5
References

*The work of A. Udaya Shankar was supported by National Science Foundation under grant no. ECS-8502113 and grant no. NCR-8904590. The work of Simon S. Lam was supported by National Science Foundation under grant no. NCR-8613338 and by a grant from the Texas Advanced Research Program. This paper is an abbreviated version of [18].

1. Introduction

There are many ways to specify a distributed system. We advocate the following approach. Initially, a system is specified by a set of requirements, namely, desirable safety and progress properties that are expressed in some language. Subsequently, a specification of an implementation of the system is obtained in the form of a state transition system together with a set of fairness assumptions.[1] In general, it is quite difficult to derive the implementation specification from the requirements specification in one step. It is preferable to go through a succession of intermediate specifications, $\alpha_1, \alpha_2, \cdots, \alpha_n$, where each intermediate specification consists of a state transition system, a set of requirements and some fairness assumptions. In this paper, we present a stepwise refinement heuristic for constructing these specifications. The heuristic is based upon a weaker form of the refinement relation in [14], called *conditional refinement,* with the following property: α_{i+1} is a refinement of α_i if the heuristic terminates successfully.

At any point during a construction, we have a state transition system, a set of requirements, and a Marking. There are three types of requirements: *invariant requirements*, *event requirements* and *progress requirements*. The invariant and event requirements represent the safety properties desired of the system, and are specified by state formulas. Each event requirement is associated with a particular system event. The progress requirements are specified using *leads−to* assertions and fairness assumptions [14]. The Marking indicates the extent to which we have established that the requirements are satisfied by the specification.

We begin a construction with a set of state variables that provide just enough resolution in the system state space to *specify* the desired safety and progress properties of the distributed system. The desired safety properties are specified by invariant and event requirements. The desired progress properties are specified by progress requirements. None of the requirements are marked initially.

A succession of state transition systems is derived by applications of some *system refinement steps*. These steps increase the resolution of the system state space by adding new state variables, adding new messages, and refining a message into a set of messages. They change the set of state transitions by refining existing events and adding new events. We also apply some *requirement refinement steps* which can be used to strengthen the requirements. The objective of each refinement step is to increase the set of requirements that are marked. (Some of these refinement steps are illustrated in our construction of the sliding window protocols in Sections 3-5. A presentation of specific refinement steps is given in [18].)

The construction terminates successfully when all requirements are marked, and the nonauxiliary state variables and events satisfy the topology of the distributed system. The construction terminates unsuccessfully when a requirement is generated that is inconsistent with other requirements or with the initial condition of the system.

---

[1]If the state transition system is given in the relational notation, we refer to this as a *relational specification* [14].

1.1. Construction examples

Our heuristic is illustrated by a rigorous exercise in constructing four sliding window protocols that provide reliable data transfer between a producer and a consumer connected by unreliable channels. All protocols use modulo-N sequence numbers.[2] The desired property that sequence numbers in data messages and acknowledgement messages are interpreted correctly is stated as invariant requirements. We first construct a basic protocol that satisfies these *correct interpretation requirements* for channels that can only lose messages in transit. This basic protocol is then refined to be used for channels that can lose, duplicate and reorder messages arbitrarily. To satisfy the correct interpretation requirements for such channels, it is necessary that message lifetimes are bounded so that certain time constraints can be enforced in producing data blocks. We present three different ways of enforcing these time constraints, resulting in three protocols. The first and second of these protocols use $2N$ and N timers respectively. The third protocol uses a single timer to enforce a minimum time interval between producing successive data blocks. The minimum time interval is a function of N, the receive window size, and the maximum message lifetimes. To construct these three protocols, we use the system model developed in [16,17] in which real-time constraints can be specified and verified as safety properties.

To our knowledge, this is the first verified construction of sliding window protocols that use modulo-N sequence numbers where N is arbitrary. Our first and second protocols for loss, duplication and reordering channels appear to be novel. Our third protocol is best compared with the original Stenning's protocol [20]. Stenning verified certain safety properties assuming unbounded sequence numbers. He then informally argued that modulo-N sequence numbers can be used provided N satisfies a bound. His bound is similar to ours but not as tight as ours. Also, his protocol has several unnecessary requirements. (A detailed comparison is in Section 5.6.)

Knuth [11] has analyzed a sliding window protocol that uses modulo-N sequence numbers. He gives the minimum value of N that ensures correct data transfer for a special kind of channels, i.e., channels that can lose messages and allow messages to overtake a limited number of previously sent messages. Because of this restriction on the reordering of messages, his protocol does not require timers and the assumption of bounded message lifetimes.

In [19], we have extended the protocol for loss-only channels and the third protocol for loss, duplication and reordering channels to include the use of selective acknowledgement messages as well as variable windows for flow control.

1.2. Organization of this report

In Section 2, we give a brief description of our construction heuristic, including the conditional refinement relation between specifications. In Section 3, we derive the basic protocol and show that for channels that can lose, duplicate and reorder messages arbitrarily, its requirements are almost completely marked; only two invariant requirements concerning sequence numbers in channels

[2] In a real protocol, sequence numbers in data messages and acknowledgement messages are encoded by a small number of bits.

remain unmarked. In Section 4, we show that, for channels that can only lose messages, the basic protocol in fact satisfies all the requirements. In Section 5, we refine the basic protocol to obtain three different protocols that satisfy all the requirements for channels that can lose, duplicate and reorder messages arbitrarily. In Section 6, we discuss related work.

2. Stepwise Refinement Heuristic

The reader is assumed to be familiar with [14], which appears in these proceedings. We use the relational notation (for specifying state transition systems), the distributed systems model, and the proof rules that are presented therein. In this paper, when we say that an event has fairness, we mean "weak fairness." We also need the channel progress assumption in [14] for unreliable channels.

At any point during a construction, we have the following:

- A state transition system defined by a set of state variables $\mathbf{v} = \{v_1, v_2, \cdots\}$, a set of events $e_1, e_2, \cdots$, and an initial condition specified by the state formula *Initial*.
- A set of invariant requirements specified by state formulas $A_0, A_1, \cdots$. We use A to denote the conjunction of all the state formulas that are in the set of invariant requirements. $Initial \Rightarrow A$ holds. (We want A to be invariant.)
- A set of event requirements specified by state formulas $S_0, S_1, \cdots$. Each requirement is associated with an event. We use S_e to denote the conjunction of all the S_i's that are associated with event e. (We want S_e to hold prior to any occurrence of e.)
- A set of progress requirements $L_0, L_1, \cdots$, which are *leads-to* assertions. (To satisfy these requirements, the specification may include additional fairness assumptions for events.)
- A *Marking* consisting of (1) event requirements that are marked, (2) (A_i, e) pairs that are marked, (3) progress requirements that are marked with tags (described below), and (4) an ordering of the L_i's (to avoid circular reasoning).

We require that the Marking satisfies the following **consistency constraints**:

C1. An event requirement S_i associated with event e is marked only if $A \wedge enabled(e) \Rightarrow S_i$ holds.

C2. A pair (A_i, e) is marked only if $A \wedge S_e \wedge e \Rightarrow A_i'$ holds.

C3. A progress requirement P leads-to Q is marked with the tag *via* e_i only if the following hold:

(i) $P \wedge A \wedge A' \wedge S_{e_i} \wedge e_i \Rightarrow Q'$,

(ii) for every event $e \neq e_i$, $P \wedge A \wedge A' \wedge S_e \wedge e \Rightarrow P' \vee Q'$, and

(iii) $P \wedge A \wedge S_{e_i} \Rightarrow enabled(e_i)$.

C4. A progress requirement $L_i \equiv P$ leads-to Q is marked with the tag *via M using* L_j only if the following hold:

(i) for every event $e_r(m)$ that receives $m \in M$, $P \wedge A \wedge A' \wedge S_{e_r} \wedge e_r(m) \Rightarrow Q'$,

(ii) for every event $e \neq e_r(m)$, $P \wedge A \wedge A' \wedge S_e \wedge e \Rightarrow P' \vee Q'$, and

(iii) $L_j \equiv P \wedge count(M) \geq k$ leads-to $Q \vee count(M) \geq k+1$, and L_j is listed after L_i in the ordering.

C5. A progress requirement $L_i \equiv P$ leads-to Q is marked with the tag *by closure using* $L_{j_1}, \cdots, L_{j_n}$ only if P leads-to Q can be derived from A and $L_{j_1}, \cdots, L_{j_n}$ using the implication, transitivity and disjunction proof rules, and each L_{j_k} is listed after L_i in the ordering.

At any point in a construction, the Marking indicates the extent to which the requirements are satisfied by the state transition system at that point. Thus, the Marking gives us the means to backtrack to some extent in applying our heuristic.

Example on Marking: Consider a state transition system defined by integer state variables x, y both initially 0, and events $e_0 \equiv x'=x+1$ and $e_1 \equiv y'=y+1$. Let there be an invariant requirement $A_0 \equiv x=y \vee x=y+1$, a progress requirement $L_0 \equiv y \neq x \wedge x=n$ leads-to $y=n$, and an event requirement $S_0 \equiv x=y$ associated with e_0. We can mark (A_0, e_0) because $S_0 \wedge e_0 \Rightarrow A_0'$. We can mark L_0 with tag *via* e_1 because $y \neq x \wedge x=n \wedge A_0 \wedge e_1 \Rightarrow y'=n$, $y \neq x \wedge x=n \wedge S_0 \wedge e_0 \Rightarrow$ *false* (that is, e_0 is disabled), and *enabled*(e_1) is *true*. (A_0, e_1) and S_0 remain to be marked.

The heuristic terminates successfully when

(a) every S_j is marked,

(b) every (A_j, e) pair is marked, and

(c) every L_j is marked.

Condition (a) implies that $A \wedge e \Rightarrow S_e$ holds for every event e, which together with condition (b) imply that $A \wedge e \Rightarrow A'$ holds. At any point in a construction, we have *Initial* $\Rightarrow A$. Thus, A satisfies the invariance rule. The invariance of A and condition (c) imply that each progress assertion L_j holds according to the rule indicated in its tag (*via event, via M*, or *closure*). There is no circular reasoning in the proof of the L_k's, because there is a serial order of the L_k's such that if L_j appears in the tag of L_i then L_j follows L_i in the ordering. Note that every event e, such that there is a progress requirement marked *via* e, must be implemented with weak fairness.

At any point in the construction, conditions (a) and (b) imply that the system satisfies the safety requirements. Condition (c) alone implies that the system satisfies the progress requirements, *assuming* that the safety requirements hold.

The construction terminates unsuccessfully whenever we have an event requirement S_i of an event e that is inconsistent with the invariant requirements or with the other event requirements of e; i.e., $S_i \Rightarrow \neg A \vee \neg S_e$ holds. The only way to mark such an S_i will be to remove the event e.

To describe the heuristic, we need to distinguish between the name of an event and the formula that specifies it. We will use e_i's to refer to event names. At different points in the construction, an event named e_i can be specified by different formulas.

Suppose a sequence of state transition systems is constructed using the heuristic. Let β and α be two successive systems in the sequence. The system refinement steps used to derive α from β

may cause some requirements that are marked for β to become unmarked for α. To minimize the unmarking of requirements, we require β and α to satisfy the following conditions:

- $\mathbf{v}_\beta \subseteq \mathbf{v}_\alpha$, where $\mathbf{v}_\beta$ and $\mathbf{v}_\alpha$ are the state variable sets of β and α, respectively.
- $Initial_\alpha \Rightarrow Initial_\beta$, where $Initial_\alpha$ and $Initial_\beta$ are the initial conditions of α and β, respectively.
- If $\{e_1, \cdots, e_j\}$ is the set of event names of β, then $\{e_1, \cdots, e_k\}$, where $k \geq j$, is the set of event names of α. Let every event e_i of β be specified by the formula b_i. Let every event e_i of α be specified by the formula a_i. Then the following hold:
  - $A \wedge S_{e_i} \wedge a_i \Rightarrow b_i$, for $i = 1, \cdots, j$.
  - $A \wedge S_{e_i} \wedge a_i \Rightarrow b_1 \vee \cdots \vee b_j \vee \mathbf{v}_\beta' = \mathbf{v}_\beta$, for $i = j+1, \cdots, k$.

If the above conditions are satisfied, we say that α is a **conditional refinement** of β, that is, a refinement of β given that the invariant and event requirements of α hold. The Marking of β is preserved for α, except in the following two cases: (1) An event requirement S_j of e_i that is marked for β becomes unmarked if and only if $A \wedge enabled(a_i) \Rightarrow S_j$ does not hold for α. (2) A progress requirement P leads-to Q that was marked *via* e_i for β becomes unmarked if and only if $P \wedge A \wedge S_{e_i} \Rightarrow enabled(a_i)$ does not hold for α.

We state a few more definitions to be used in our heuristic. Consider state formulas P and Q, and an event e. We say that P is a *weakest precondition* of Q with respect to e iff it is logically equivalent to $[\forall \mathbf{v}': e \Rightarrow Q']$. Note that P is *false* at a state iff e is enabled at the state and its occurrence can cause Q to be falsified.[3] We say that P is a *sufficient precondition* iff it implies the weakest precondition; that is, it satisfies $[\forall \mathbf{v}': P \wedge e \Rightarrow Q']$. We say that P is a *necessary precondition* iff it is implied by the weakest precondition; that is, it satisfies $\neg P \Rightarrow [\exists \mathbf{v}': e \wedge \neg Q']$.

3. Sliding Window Protocol Construction: Initial Phase

Consider the distributed system topology of Figure 1. There is a producer of data blocks at entity 1, and a consumer of data blocks at entity 2. The channels may lose, duplicate, or reorder messages in transit; these are the only errors in the channels. We want data blocks to be consumed in the same order as they were produced, and within a finite time of being produced. We will construct a sliding window protocol that uses modulo-N sequence numbers to achieve this objective.

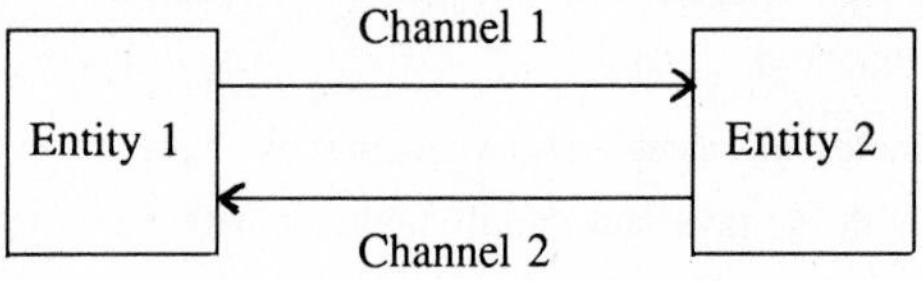

Figure 1. The network topology

---

[3]This corresponds to Dijkstra's weakest liberal precondition [5].

Notation: If B is a set of values, then *sequence of* B denotes the set of finite sequences whose elements are in B, and *sequence* $(0 \cdot\cdot M-1)$ *of* B denotes the set of M-length sequences whose elements are in B. For any sequence y, let $|y|$ denote the length of y, and $y(i)$ denote the ith element in y, with the 0th element at the left. Thus, $y = (y(0), \cdots, y(|y|-1))$. We use $y(i \cdot\cdot j)$ to denote $(y(i), y(i+1), \cdots, y(j))$ where $i, j<|y|$; it is null if $i>j$. We say "y prefix-of z" to mean $|y| \leq |z|$ and $y = z(0 \cdot\cdot |y|-1)$. We define the function $Tail(y, i)$ to return $y(i \cdot\cdot |y|-1)$ for any i, $0 \leq i < |y|$. Lastly, we use "wrt" as an abbreviation for "with respect to".

3.1. Initial system and requirements

The initial system and requirements specify the services to be offered to the producer and consumer. Let *DATA* denote the set of data blocks that can be sent in this protocol. We use a Pascal-like notation to define state variables and their domains.

At entity 1, we have the following state variable and event:

produced: sequence of *DATA*. Initially null.	
$Produce(data) \equiv$	$produced' = produced\ @\ data$

At entity 2, we have the following state variable and event:

consumed: sequence of *DATA*. Initially null.	
$Consume(data) \equiv$	$consumed' = consumed\ @\ data$

The state variables *produced* and *consumed* record the sequences of data blocks produced and consumed. In the sliding window protocols to be constructed, they will be auxiliary variables. The events *Produce* and *Consume* have a parameter *data* whose domain is *DATA*.

We have one invariant requirement and two progress requirements:

A_0	$\equiv$	*consumed* prefix-of *produced*
L_0	$\equiv$	$|produced| \geq n$ leads-to $|consumed| \geq n$
L_1	$\equiv$	$|produced| \geq n$ leads-to $|produced| \geq n+1$

A_0 specifies that data blocks are consumed in the order that they are produced. It holds initially. L_0 states that if a data block is produced, then it is eventually consumed. L_1 states that at any time another data block will eventually be produced.

3.2. The sliding window mechanism

We want to refine the initial state transition system to a sliding window protocol. Let us review the basic features found in all sliding window protocols. (See Figure 2.) At any time at entity 1, the data blocks in $produced(0 \cdot\cdot a-1)$ have been sent and acknowledged, while data blocks in $produced(a \cdot\cdot s-1)$ are unacknowledged, where $|produced|=s$. At any time at entity 2, data blocks in $produced(0 \cdot\cdot r-1)$ have been received and consumed in sequence, while data blocks in *produced*$(r \cdot\cdot r{+}RW{-}1)$ may have been received (perhaps out of sequence) and are temporarily buffered. The numbers r to $r{+}RW{-}1$ constitute the *receive window*; RW is its constant size.

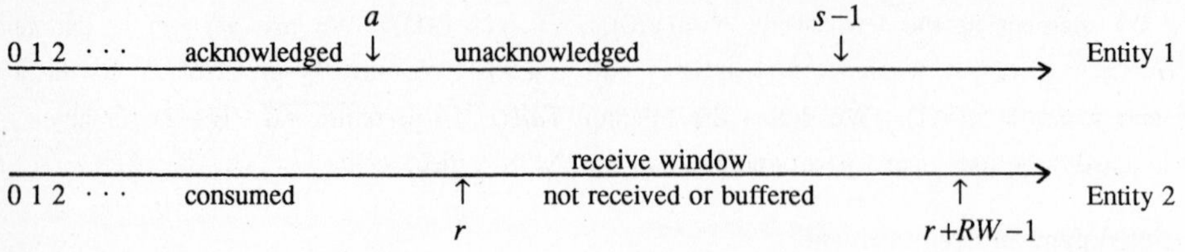

Figure 2. Relationship between a, s, r

A sliding window protocol uses modulo-N sequence numbers to identify data blocks, where $N \geq 2$. We use $\bar{n}$ to denote n mod N for any integer value n.

Entity 1 sends *produced*(n) accompanied by sequence number $\bar{n}$. When entity 2 receives a data block with sequence number $\bar{n}$, if there is a number i in the receive window such that $\bar{i}=\bar{n}$, then the received data block is interpreted as *produced*(i). Entity 2 sends acknowledgement messages containing $\bar{n}$, where n is the current value of r. When entity 1 receives the sequence number $\bar{n}$, if there is a number i in the range $a{+}1$ to s such that $\bar{i}=\bar{n}$, then it is interpreted as an acknowledgement to data blocks a to $i{-}1$, and a is updated to i. Entity 1 increments s when a data block is produced. Entity 2 increments r when a data block is consumed.

Observe that each cyclic sequence number $\bar{n}$ corresponds to an *unbounded sequence number* n. When a cyclic sequence number is received at an entity, we require the entity to correctly interpret the value of the corresponding unbounded sequence number (which is not available in the message); that is, we require $i=n$ in the preceding paragraph.

Refinement of state transition system and requirements

We now incorporate the above protocol features into the state transition system. Let the messages sent by entity 1 be of type $(D, data, cn, n)$, where D is a constant that indicates the type of the message, *data* is a data block, *cn* is a cyclic sequence number, and n is the corresponding unbounded sequence number. Let the acknowledgement messages sent by entity 2 be of type (ACK, cn, n), where ACK is a constant that indicates the type of the message, *cn* is a cyclic sequence number, and n is the corresponding unbounded sequence number. In both message types, n is an auxiliary field that will be used to reason about correct interpretation only. Its value can never be used to update a nonauxiliary state variable. We have the following invariant requirements, each of which holds initially:

A_1	$\equiv$	$(D, data, cn, n) \in \mathbf{z}_1 \Rightarrow data = produced(n) \wedge cn = \bar{n}$
A_2	$\equiv$	$(ACK, cn, n) \in \mathbf{z}_2 \Rightarrow cn = \bar{n}$

At entity 1, we add the following state variables:

$s: 0 \cdots \infty$. Initially 0.
$a: 0 \cdots \infty$. Initially 0.
sendbuff: sequence of *DATA*. Initially null.

s and a are as defined above. We will ensure below that *sendbuff* always equals $produced(a \cdots s-1)$, the unacknowledged data blocks. Recall that entity 1 must retransmit these until they are acknowledged.

For brevity in specifying events, we use the notation $P \rightarrow q$ to denote an action that does q if P holds and does nothing if $\neg P$ holds. Formally, $P \rightarrow q$ means $(P \wedge q) \vee (\neg P \wedge \mathbf{x}=\mathbf{x}')$, where $\mathbf{x}$ denotes those state variables updated in q. Similarly, $[\exists i: P \rightarrow q]$ means $[\exists i: P \wedge q] \vee (\neg[\exists i: P] \wedge \mathbf{x}=\mathbf{x}')$.

At entity 1, we refine *Produce* to appropriately update *sendbuff* and s. We also add two events, one for sending data messages and one for receiving ack messages.

$Produce(data)$	$\equiv$	$produced'=produced \,@\, data$ $\wedge\, sendbuff'=sendbuff \,@\, data \;\wedge\; s'=s+1$
$SendD(i)$	$\equiv$	$i \in [0 \cdots s-a-1]$ $\wedge\, Send_1(D, sendbuff(i), \overline{a+i}, a+i)$
$RecACK(cn, n)$	$\equiv$	$Rec_2(ACK, cn, n)$ $\wedge\, [\exists i \in [1 \cdots s-a]: \overline{a+i}=cn$ $\rightarrow (a'=a+i \wedge sendbuff'=Tail(sendbuff, i))]$

At entity 2, we add the following state variables, where *empty* is a constant not in *DATA*:

$r: 0 \cdots \infty$. Initially 0.
recbuff: sequence $(0 \cdots RW-1)$ of $DATA \cup \{empty\}$. Initially $recbuff(n)=empty$ for all n.

$r=|consumed|$ is as defined above. *recbuff* represents the buffers of the receive window. We will ensure that at any time, $recbuff(i)$ equals either *empty* or $produced(r+i)$.

At entity 2, we refine *Consume* so that it passes $recbuff(0)$ only when the latter is not empty. We also add two events, one for sending ack messages and one for receiving data messages.

$Consume(data)$	$\equiv$	$recbuff(0) \neq empty$ $\wedge\, data=recbuff(0)$ $\wedge\, recbuff'=Tail(recbuff, 1) \,@\, empty \;\wedge\; r'=r+1$ $\wedge\, consumed'=consumed \,@\, data$
$SendACK$	$\equiv$	$Send_2(ACK, \overline{r}, r)$
$RecD(data, cn, n)$	$\equiv$	$Rec_1(D, data, cn, n)$ $\wedge\, [\exists i \in [0 \cdots RW-1]: \overline{r+i}=cn \rightarrow recbuff(i)'=data]$

We add the following invariant requirements; each is a desired property mentioned in the discussion above:

A_3	$\equiv$	$\lvert produced \rvert = s \ \wedge\ \lvert consumed \rvert = r$
A_4	$\equiv$	$0 \le a \le r \le s$
A_5	$\equiv$	$sendbuff = produced(a \cdot\cdot s-1)$
A_6	$\equiv$	$i \in [0 \cdot\cdot RW-1] \Rightarrow recbuff(i) = empty \vee recbuff(i) = produced(r+i)$

Marking

For the time being, we concentrate on marking the (A_i, e) pairs. We represent the Marking by a table that has a row for each A_i and a column for each e. If (A_i, e) is unmarked, its entry in the table is blank. If (A_i, e) is marked, its entry identifies a subset J of the A_j's and S_j's of e such that $J \wedge e \Rightarrow A_i'$ holds. Thus, the reader can easily check the validity of the Marking. Also, an (A_i, e) entry in the table contains *na* to indicate that e does *not affect* any of the state variables of A_i; thus $A_i \wedge e \Rightarrow A_i'$ holds trivially. We use $A_{i,j}$ to denote $A_i \wedge A_j$, and A_{i-j} to denote $A_i \wedge A_{i+1} \wedge \cdots A_j$. The *LRD* column is for the loss, reordering, and duplication events in the channels.

	Produce	*SendD*	*RecACK*	*Consume*	*SendACK*	*RecD*	*LRD*
A_0	A_0	*na*	*na*	$A_{6,3,0}$	*na*	*na*	*na*
A_1	*na*	$A_{1,5}$	*na*	*na*	*na*	A_1	A_1
A_2	*na*	*na*	A_2	*na*	A_2	*na*	A_2
A_3	A_3	*na*	*na*	A_3	*na*	*na*	*na*
A_4	A_4	*na*		$A_{6,3,4}$	*na*	*na*	*na*
A_5	$A_{5,3,4}$	*na*	A_5	*na*	*na*	*na*	*na*
A_6	$A_{6,3,4}$	*na*	*na*	A_6	*na*		*na*

The Marking can be easily checked as follows. As an example, consider the entry for $(A_4, Consume)$, which indicates that $A_{6,3,4} \wedge Consume \Rightarrow A_4'$ holds. The details are as follows: *Consume* occurs only if $recbuff(0) \neq empty$. This and A_6 imply $recbuff(0) = produced(r)$, which together with A_3 imply $r \le s-1$. This and A_4 imply $a \le r \le s-1$. *Consume* does the update $r' = r+1$ and does not affect a or s. Thus A_4' holds. In the above proof, we used A_6 first, then A_3, and then A_4. To facilitate checking of the Marking, we have indicated this in the order of the subscripts in $A_{6,3,4}$.

Observe that the only (A_i, e) pairs that are unmarked are $(A_6, RecD)$ and $(A_4, RecACK)$. We can mark $(A_6, RecD)$ if we can ensure that *RecD* correctly interprets the cyclic sequence numbers in received data messages. Similarly, we can mark $(A_4, RecACK)$ if we can ensure that *RecACK* correctly interprets the cyclic sequence numbers in received acknowledgement messages. In the next two subsections, we will generate invariant requirements on the sequence numbers that ensure correct interpretation.

3.3. Correct interpretation of data messages

In this section, we concentrate on marking $(A_6, RecD)$. Our general approach to marking an (A_i, e) pair is as follows: Obtain a weakest precondition P of A_i with respect to e; if $A \wedge S_e \Rightarrow P$

does not hold, then introduce P as a new event requirement of e; mark (A_i, e). Sometimes we simplify the expression for P to either a sufficient or a necessary precondition. In the latter case, (A_i, e) remains unmarked. Alternatively, if $Initial \Rightarrow P$ holds, we can introduce P as an invariant requirement.

The following is a weakest precondition of A_6 wrt $RecD$:

$$W \equiv Head(\mathbf{z}_1)=(D, data, cn, n) \wedge i \in [0 \cdot\cdot RW-1] \wedge \overline{r+i}=\overline{n} \Rightarrow data=produced(r+i)$$

Instead of introducing W as an event requirement, we will strengthen it to obtain a simpler sufficient precondition. From A_1, we have $cn=\overline{n}$ and $data=produced(n)$. Thus, the consequent of W is equivalent to $produced(n)=produced(r+i)$. Let us strengthen this consequent to $n=r+i$. We do not expect this to lead to unsuccessful termination. Indeed, it appears necessary in order for $produced(n)$ and $produced(r+i)$ to be arbitrary entries from $DATA$, and for the size of $DATA$ not to be limited. Next, let us weaken the antecedent of W by replacing $Head(\mathbf{z}_1)=(D, data, cn, n)$ by $(D, data, cn, n) \in \mathbf{z}_1$. In fact, this is necessary given that channel 1 can lose messages arbitrarily. Thus, we arrive at the following sufficient precondition:

$$X \equiv (D, data, cn, n) \in \mathbf{z}_1 \wedge i \in [0 \cdot\cdot RW-1] \wedge \overline{r+i}=\overline{n} \Rightarrow n=r+i$$

We decide that X will be an invariant requirement, rather than just an event requirement of $RecD$. We proceed to generate further refinements from it.

Because $produced(r)$ is the data block to be next consumed, it is reasonable to expect that $(D, data, \overline{r}, r) \in \mathbf{z}_1$ holds at any time. This would violate X with $i=N$ unless $RW \leq N$. We also know that $RW \geq 1$, otherwise entity 2 will never accept any data block and the progress requirement L_0 will never hold. Thus, we have the following condition:

$$\boxed{1 \leq RW \leq N}$$

Observe that $i \in [0 \cdot\cdot RW-1] \wedge \overline{r+i}=\overline{n}$ iff $i \in [0 \cdot\cdot RW-1] \wedge \overline{i}=\overline{n-r}$ iff $\overline{n-r} \in [0 \cdot\cdot RW-1] \wedge i=\overline{n-r}$, where we used $RW \leq N \Rightarrow i=\overline{i}$ to establish the last "iff". Thus, we can refine $RecD$ to the following, where we have also used the modulo arithmetic property $(n-r) \bmod N = (\overline{n}-r) \bmod N$:

$$\boxed{\begin{array}{lll} RecD(data, cn, n) & \equiv & Rec_1(D, data, cn, n) \\ & & \wedge\, [\overline{cn-r} \in [0 \cdot\cdot RW-1] \rightarrow recbuff(\overline{cn-r})'=data] \end{array}}$$

We can now refine X to the following invariant requirement:

$$Y \equiv (D, data, cn, n) \in \mathbf{z}_1 \wedge \overline{n-r} \in [0 \cdot\cdot RW-1] \Rightarrow n=r+\overline{n-r}$$

Y is satisfied nonvacuously by $n-r \in [0 \cdot\cdot RW-1]$, and satisfied vacuously by $n-r \in [RW+kN \cdot\cdot N-1+kN]$ for any integer k. We want every unbounded sequence number n in channel 1 to be in the union of these intervals. Suppose that n_1 and n_2 are in channel 1; let us assume that channel 1 may contain any n between n_1 and n_2. We expect that an n equal to r may always be in channel 1. The largest contiguous union of intervals containing r is $[r+RW-N \cdot\cdot r+N-1]$, which is the union of $[r \cdot\cdot r+RW-1]$ and $[r+RW+kN \cdot\cdot r+N-1+kN]$ for $k=0$

and −1. Thus, we strengthen Y to the following invariant requirement:

$$A_7 \quad \equiv \quad (D, data, cn, n) \in \mathbf{z}_1 \Rightarrow n \in [r-N+RW \cdot\cdot r+N-1]$$

We now proceed to mark $(A_7, SendD)$. A weakest precondition of A_7 wrt *SendD* is $a \geq r-N+RW$. We will make it an invariant requirement because we want *SendD* to be always enabled to send outstanding data. Because $r \leq s$ (and we expect $r=s$ to be possible at any time), we strengthen it to the following invariant requirement:

$$A_8 \quad \equiv \quad s-a \leq N-RW$$

Because A_8 only involves variables of entity 1, it can be enforced by refining *Produce* as follows:

$$\begin{aligned} Produce(data) \quad \equiv \quad & s-a \leq N-RW-1 \\ & \wedge produced' = produced @ data \\ & \wedge sendbuff' = sendbuff @ data \ \wedge \ s' = s+1 \end{aligned}$$

In order for *Produce* not to be permanently disabled (needed for L_1), we now require the following:

$$1 \leq RW \leq N-1$$

Observe that the upper bound in A_7's consequent is implied by $n \leq s-1$ (from $A_{1,3}$), A_4, and A_8. There is no need for A_7 to repeat this constraint. Thus, we can rewrite A_7 as follows:

$$A_7 \quad \equiv \quad (D, data, cn, n) \in \mathbf{z}_1 \Rightarrow n \geq r-N+RW$$

We can extend the previous Marking to the following, where * is used to indicate an old entry, and old A_i's marked wrt every event have been aggregated into one row:

	Produce	*SendD*	*RecACK*	*Consume*	*SendACK*	*RecD*	*LRD*
$A_{0-3,5}$	*	*	*	*	*	*	*
A_4	*	*		*	*	*	*
A_6	*	*	*	*	*	$A_{7,1}$	*
A_7	*na*	$A_{8,4}$	*na*		*na*	A_7	A_7
A_8	A_8	*na*	A_8	*na*	*na*	*na*	*na*

3.4. Correct interpretation of acknowledgement messages

In this section, we concentrate on marking $(A_4, RecACK)$. The treatment is similar to the case of data messages above, and we shall omit the details. We can obtain the following invariant requirements:

A_9	$\equiv$	$(ACK,\ cn,\ n) \in \mathbf{z}_2 \Rightarrow n \le r$
A_{10}	$\equiv$	$(ACK,\ cn,\ n) \in \mathbf{z}_2 \Rightarrow n \ge s - N + 1$

We can refine *RecACK* to the following:

$$RecACK(cn,\ n) \equiv Rec_2(ACK,\ cn,\ n) \wedge [\overline{cn - a} \in [1 \cdot\cdot s - a] \rightarrow (a' = a + \overline{cn - a} \wedge sendbuff' = Tail(sendbuff,\ \overline{cn - a}))]$$

We have the following Marking:

	Produce	*SendD*	*RecACK*	*Consume*	*SendACK*	*RecD*	*LRD*
$A_{0-3,5,6,8}$	*	*	*	*	*	*	*
A_4	*	*	A_{8-10}	*	*	*	*
A_7	*	*	*		*	*	*
A_9	*na*	*na*	A_9	A_9	A_9	*na*	A_9
A_{10}		*na*	A_{10}	*na*	$A_{10,8,4}$	*na*	A_{10}

The invariant requirements and system at this point are specified in Tables 1 and 2. Note that the only unmarked pairs are $(A_7,\ Consume)$ and $(A_{10},\ Produce)$.

3.5. Progress requirement marking

We now try to mark L_0 and L_1. We assume that *SendD* (0) and *SendACK* have weak fairness. For the current system, we prove that L_0 holds if *Consume* has weak fairness, and that L_1 holds if *Produce* and *Consume* have weak fairness. We then show that these properties continue to hold if entity 2 sends an ack only in response to a received data message. For the progress markings in this section, we consider the L_i's to be ordered according to increasing subscripts. Hence, L_j is used in the tag of L_i only if $j > i$.

The following progress requirements imply L_0 and L_1:

L_2	$\equiv$	$s > a = n$ leads-to $a \ge n+1$
L_3	$\equiv$	$s = a = n$ leads-to $s = n+1$

We have the following Marking, where the tag also indicates the invariant requirements used to mark: L_0 by closure using L_2 and $A_{3,4}$. L_3 via *Produce*. L_1 by closure using L_2, L_3, and $A_{3,4}$ as follows: from L_2 and A_4, we have $s \ge n > a$ leads-to $s \ge a \ge n$; from this, L_3 and A_4, we get $s \ge n$ leads-to $s > n$, which is L_1 (because of A_3). At this point, only L_2 is unmarked. L_2 follows from the closure of the following progress requirements:

L_4	$\equiv$	$s>r=a=n$ leads-to $s\geq r>a=n$
L_5	$\equiv$	$s\geq r>a=n$ leads-to $a>n$

L_4 and L_5 are implied by the following progress requirements, which hold for the current system. Here, $(ACK, >n)$ denotes the message set $\{(ACK, j): j>n\}$, and (D, n) denotes the message set $\{(D, data, cn, n)\}$:

$L_6 \equiv$	$s>r=a=n$ leads-to $s\geq r>a=n \vee (recbuff(0)\neq empty \wedge s>r=a=n)$
$L_7 \equiv$	$recbuff(0)\neq empty \wedge s>r=a=n$ leads-to $s\geq r>a=n$
$L_8 \equiv$	$s>a=n \wedge count(D, n)\geq k$ leads-to $a>n \vee count(D, n)\geq k+1$
$L_9 \equiv$	$s\geq r>a=n \wedge count(ACK, >n)\geq k$ leads-to $a>n \vee count(ACK, >n)\geq k+1$

The details are summarized in the following progress Marking: L_0 by closure using $L_2, A_{3,4}$. L_1 by closure using $L_2, L_3, A_{3,4}$. L_2 by closure using L_4, L_5, A_4. L_3 via *Produce*. L_4 by closure using L_6, L_7. L_5 via $(ACK, >n)$ using $L_9, A_{4,8,10}$. L_6 via (D, n) using $L_8, A_{4,1,8}$. L_7 via *Consume* using A_4. L_8 via *SendD* (0) using $A_{3\text{–}5}$. L_9 via *SendACK* using A_4.

Weaker acknowledgement policy

Suppose entity 2 sends an ack message only if it has received a data message following the last ack sent. We can model this by adding a boolean variable *drecd* initially *false*, refining *RecD* by adding the conjunct *drecd'*, and refining *SendACK* to $drecd \wedge Send_2(ACK, \bar{r}, r) \wedge \neg drecd'$. The only effect of this refinement on the Marking is to unmark progress requirement L_9, which was marked *via SendACK*. However L_9 still holds because entity 1 retransmits (D, n) as long as $s\geq r>a=n$ holds. To prove this, we introduce the following progress requirements:

$L_{10} \equiv$	$drecd \wedge r>n \wedge count(ACK, >n)\geq k$ leads-to $count(ACK, >n)\geq k+1$
$L_{11} \equiv$	$s\geq r>a=n \wedge count(ACK, >n)\geq k$ leads-to $a>n \vee (drecd \wedge s\geq r>a=n \wedge count(ACK, >n)\geq k)$
$L_{12} \equiv$	$s\geq r>a=n \wedge count(ACK, >n)\geq k \wedge count(D, n)\geq l$ leads-to $a>n \vee (drecd \wedge s\geq r>a=n \wedge count(ACK, >n)\geq k) \vee count(D, n)\geq l+1$

We have a complete Marking by replacing "L_9 via *SendACK* using A_4" in the above Marking with the following: L_9 by closure using L_{10}, L_{11}. L_{10} via *SendACK*. L_{11} via (D, n) using L_{12}. L_{12} via *SendD* (0).

4. Completing the Construction for Loss-only Channels

At this point, we have obtained a system with entities as specified in Table 2. For channels that can lose, reorder, and duplicate messages, the construction is incomplete because $(A_{10}, Produce)$ and $(A_7, Consume)$ are not yet marked. We now show that if the channels can only lose messages, then these pairs can be marked for the current system.

We start by considering $(A_7, Consume)$. The following is a weakest precondition of A_7 wrt *Consume*:

$$(D, data, cn, n) \in z_1 \wedge recbuff(0) \neq empty \Rightarrow n \geq r + RW - N + 1$$

If instead of a single occurrence of *Consume*, we consider $k+1$ occurrences, then we obtain the following weakest precondition:

$$(D, data, cn, n) \in z_1 \wedge [\forall i \in [0 \cdot\cdot k]: recbuff(i) \neq empty] \Rightarrow n \geq r + RW - N + k + 1$$

Now if there have been no channel errors for a while, then $[\forall i \in [0 \cdot\cdot k]: recbuff(i) \neq empty]$ will hold when $recbuff(k) \neq empty$ holds. Thus, it is reasonable to strengthen the above weakest precondition to the following invariant requirement:

B_0	$\equiv$	$(D, data, cn, n) \in z_1 \wedge recbuff(k) \neq empty \Rightarrow n \geq r + k + RW - N + 1$

The following is a weakest precondition of B_0 wrt *RecD*:

B_1	$\equiv$	$(D, d_1, cn_1, n_1) @ (D, d_2, cn_2, n_2)$ subseq $z_1 \Rightarrow n_2 \geq n_1 + RW - N + 1$

We can see that B_0 is preserved by *SendD* as follows. $recbuff(k) \neq empty$ implies $s > r + k$, which together with $a \geq s - N + RW$ (A_8) implies $a > r + k - N + RW$. Thus *SendD* preserves B_0, because it sends only $produced(n)$ where $n \geq a$. The argument that *SendD* preserves B_1 is similar. $(D, d_1, cn_1, n_1) \in z_1$ implies $s > n_1$, which implies $a > n_1 - N + RW$.

We now consider marking $(A_{10}, Produce)$. Because entity 2 sends nondecreasing n and channel 2 does not reorder messages, we expect the following to be invariant:

B_2	$\equiv$	$(ACK, cn, n) \in z_2 \Rightarrow n \geq a$

B_2 implies A_{10} because $n \geq s - N + 1$ if $n \geq a$ (from A_8). Thus marking $(B_2, Produce)$ allows us to mark $(A_{10}, Produce)$. The following is a weakest precondition of B_2 wrt *RecACK*, and is introduced as an invariant requirement:

B_3	$\equiv$	$(ACK, cn_1, n_1) @ (ACK, cn_2, n_2)$ subseq $z_2 \Rightarrow n_1 \leq n_2$

At this point, we have the following complete Marking:

	Produce	*SendD*	*RecACK*	*Consume*	*SendACK*	*RecD*	*Loss*
$A_{0-6,8,9}$	*	*	*	*	*	*	*
A_7	*	*	*	B_0	*	*	*
A_{10}	B_2, A_8	*	*	*	*	*	*
B_0	*na*	$B_0, A_{8,6,3}$	*na*	B_0	*na*	$B_{0,1}$	B_0
B_1	*na*	$B_1, A_{8,1,3}$	*na*	*na*	*na*	B_1	B_1
B_2	*na*	*na*	B_3	*na*	B_2, A_4	*na*	B_2
B_3	*na*	*na*	B_3	*na*	$A_{9,4}$	*na*	B_3

5. Completing the Construction for Loss, Reordering, and Duplication Channels

For loss, reordering, and duplication channels, we resume the protocol construction from the end of Section 3, i.e., from the requirements and system shown in Tables 1 and 2, respectively. Recall that only the pairs (A_7, *Consume*) and (A_{10}, *Produce*) are unmarked.

Clearly, if the channels can reorder and duplicate arbitrarily, then A_7 and A_{10} cannot be enforced unless the channels impose an upper bound on the lifetimes of messages in transit. Therefore, we assume that a message cannot stay in channel i for longer than a specified $MAXLIFE_i$ time units. Given this, we show that A_7 and A_{10} are enforced if entity 1 produces a data block for $produced(n)$ only after (1) $MAXLIFE_1$ time units have elapsed since $produced(n-N+RW)$ was last sent, and (2) $MAXLIFE_2$ time units have elapsed since $produced(n-N+1)$ was first acknowledged. We then provide three ways to implement these two time constraints, using $2N$ timers, N timers, and 1 timer, respectively

5.1. Real-time system model

For this construction, we require a system model in which real-time constraints can be formally specified and verified. Such a real-time model has been presented in [17]. We now give a summary description of that model, adequate for our purposes here.

The system model presented is augmented with special state variables, referred to as *timers*, and with *time events* to age the timers. A timer takes values from the domain $\{OFF, 0, 1, 2, \cdots\}$. Define the function *next* on this domain by $next(OFF)=OFF$ and $next(i)=i+1$ for $i \neq OFF$. A timer can also have a maximum capacity M, for some positive integer M; in this case, $next(M)=OFF$.

There are two types of timers: *local timers* and *ideal timers*. Local timers correspond to the timers and clocks implemented within entities of a distributed system. They need not be auxiliary. For each entity, there is a *local time event* (corresponding to a clock tick) whose occurrence updates every local timer within that entity to its *next* value. No other timer in the system is affected. Thus, local timers in different entities are decoupled. We assume that the error in the ticking rate of the local time event of entity entity i is upper bounded by a specified constant ε_i; e.g., $\varepsilon_i \approx 10^{-6}$ for a crystal oscillator driven clock.

Ideal timers are auxiliary variables that record the actual time elapsed. There is an *ideal time event* whose occurrence updates every ideal timer in the system. The ideal time event is a hypothetical event that is assumed to occur at a *constant* rate. Ideal timers are used to measure the error in the rate of local time event occurrences. They are also convenient for relating elapsed times across different entities and channels.

A timer of an entity can be incremented by its time event. It can also be updated to either 0 or *OFF* by an event of that entity. Updating to the value 0 is referred to as *starting* the timer. Updating to the value *OFF* is referred to as *stopping* the timer. Thus, a timer that is started by an event occurrence measures the time elapsed since that event occurrence.

Given an ideal timer u and a local timer v of entity i, we define the predicate $started\text{-}together(u, v)$ to mean that at some instant in the past u and v were simultaneously started, and after that instant neither u nor v has been started or stopped. The maximum error in the rate of entity i's local time event occurrences is modeled by assuming the following condition, which we shall refer to as the *accuracy axiom*:

Accuracy axiom. $started\text{-}together(u, v) \Rightarrow |u-v| \le \max(1, \varepsilon_i u)$

An invariant requirement A_i can include *started-together* predicates. To mark (A_i, e), i.e., to derive $e \wedge A \Rightarrow A_i'$, we use the following rules. Rules (i) and (ii) are used if e is not a time event, and rule (iii) is used if e is a time event:

(i) $u'=0 \wedge v'=0$ implies $started\text{-}together(u, v)'$.

(ii) $u'=u \wedge v'=v \wedge started\text{-}together(u, v)$ implies $started\text{-}together(u, v)'$.

(iii) $u' \ne OFF \wedge v' \ne OFF \wedge started\text{-}together(u, v)$ implies $started\text{-}together(u, v)'$.

With timers and time events, time constraints between event occurrences can be specified by safety assertions. For example, let e_1 and e_2 be two events, and let v be a timer that is started by e_1 and stopped by e_2. The time constraint that e_2 *does not occur within* T time units of e_1's occurrence can be specified by the invariant requirement $enabled(e_2) \Rightarrow v \ge T$. The time constraint that e_2 *must occur within* T time units of e_1's occurrence can be specified by the invariant requirement $v \le T$. Note that to establish the invariance of an A_i involving timers, we have to show that it is preserved by the time events also.

Specification of finite message lifetime: To every message in a channel, we add an auxiliary ideal timer field, denoted by *age*, that indicates the ideal time elapsed since the message was sent. The *age* field is started at 0 when the message is sent (this update is specified in the send primitive). The following are *assumed* to be invariant:

TA_1	$\equiv$	$(D, data, \bar{n}, n, age) \in \mathbf{z}_1 \Rightarrow MAXLIFE_1 \ge age \ge 0$
TA_2	$\equiv$	$(ACK, \bar{n}, n, age) \in \mathbf{z}_2 \Rightarrow MAXLIFE_2 \ge age \ge 0$

5.2. A time constraint that enforces A_7

In this section, we concentrate on marking $(A_7, Consume)$. We show that A_7 is enforced if entity 1 produces $produced(n)$ only after $MAXLIFE_1$ ideal time units have elapsed since $produced(n-N+RW)$ was last sent.

Due to buffered data blocks, it is always possible for successive occurrences of *Consume* to increase r so that it equals s. Unlike in the case of loss-only channels, this does not allow us to infer constraints on the sequence numbers in channel 1. Thus to enforce A_7, we require the following stronger invariant requirement to hold:

C_0	$\equiv$	$(D, data, cn, n) \in \mathbf{z}_1 \Rightarrow n \ge s-N+RW$

Taking the weakest precondition of C_0 wrt *Produce*, we get the following event requirements of *Produce*:

S_0	$\equiv$	$(D, data, cn, n) \in \mathbf{z}_1 \Rightarrow n \geq s-N+RW+1$

Note that this is the first precondition in this construction that we have left as an event requirement. This is because S_0 has exactly the same form as the invariant requirement C_0 from which it was derived, with N being replaced by $N-1$. Therefore, transforming S_0 into an invariant requirement would merely lead us to repeat the step with a smaller N. Repeated reductions like this would eventually lead to $N=RW$, at which point we would have a "dead" protocol because of A_8.

S_0 can be enforced by enabling *Produce* only after $MAXLIFE_1$ time units have elapsed since the last send of any data block in $produced(0 \cdot\cdot s-N+RW)$. With this motivation, we add ideal timers $t_D(n)$, $n \geq 0$, at entity 1 to record the ideal time elapsed since $produced(n)$ was last sent. We also refine *SendD* and introduce an invariant requirement as follows:

t_D: sequence $(0 \cdot\cdot \infty)$ of ideal timer. Initially $t_D(n)=OFF$ for every n.	
$SendD(i) \equiv$	$i \in [0 \cdot\cdot s-a-1] \wedge Send_1(D, sendbuff(i), \overline{a+i}, a+i) \wedge t_D(a+i)'=0$
$C_1 \equiv$	$(D, data, cn, n, age) \in \mathbf{z}_1 \Rightarrow age \geq t_D(n) \geq 0$

We can enforce S_0 by having $X \equiv n \in [0 \cdot\cdot s-N+RW] \Rightarrow t_D(n) > MAXLIFE_1 \vee t_D(n)=OFF$ as an event requirement of *Produce*. This would make the following invariant:

C_2	$\equiv$	$n \in [0 \cdot\cdot s-N+RW-1] \Rightarrow t_D(n) > MAXLIFE_1 \vee t_D(n)=OFF$

C_2 is preserved by *SendD* because $a > s-N+RW-1$, and by *Produce* because of X. Because C_2 is an invariant requirement, we can enforce X by enforcing the following event requirement of *Produce*:

S_1	$\equiv$	$n=s-N+RW \geq 0 \Rightarrow t_D(n) > MAXLIFE_1 \vee t_D(n)=OFF$

The above discussion is formalized in the the following Marking, which now includes event requirements, and where *Ite* denotes the *Ideal time event*:

	Produce	*SendD*	*RecACK*	*Consume*	*SendACK*	*RecD*	*LRD*	*Ite*
$A_{0-6,8,9}$	*	*	*	*	*	*	*	*na*
A_7	*	*	*	C_0, A_4	*	*	*	*na*
A_{10}		*	*	*	*	*	*	*na*
C_0	S_0	A_8	*na*	*na*	*na*	C_0	C_0	*na*
C_1	*na*	C_1	*na*	*na*	*na*	C_1	C_1	TA_1
C_2	S_1, C_2	*na*	*na*	*na*	*na*	*na*	*na*	C_2

S_0 marked using S_1, $C_{1,2}$, TA_1	S_1 not marked

To enforce S_1, it is sufficient for entity 1 to keep track of the ideal timers in $t_D(s-N+RW \cdots s-1)$. This can be done with a bounded number of local timers, each of bounded capacity.

5.3. A time constraint that enforces A_{10}

In this section, we concentrate on marking (A_{10}, *Produce*). We show that A_{10} is enforced if entity 1 produces a data block for *produced*(n) only after $MAXLIFE_2$ ideal time units have elapsed since *produced*$(n-N+1)$ was acknowledged.

Taking the weakest precondition of A_{10} wrt *Produce*, we get the following event requirement of *Produce* (which, as in the case of S_0, should not be transformed into an invariant requirement):

$$S_2 \quad \equiv \quad (ACK,\ cn,\ n) \in z_2 \Rightarrow n \geq s-N+2$$

S_2 can be enforced only by ensuring that more than $MAXLIFE_2$ time units have elapsed since $(ACK, \bar{n}, n)$ was last sent, for any $n \in [0 \cdots s-N+1]$. Unlike the previous case involving data messages, entity 1 does *not* have access to the time elapsed since $(ACK, \bar{n}, n)$ was last sent. This is because *ACK* messages are sent by entity 2 and not by entity 1. However, entity 1 can obtain a lower bound on this elapsed time because of the following considerations: $(ACK, \bar{n}, n)$ is not sent once r exceeds n; a exceeds n only after r exceeds n; a and r are nondecreasing quantities. Thus, the time elapsed since a exceeded n is a lower bound on the ages of all $(ACK, \bar{n}, n)$ in channel 2. Furthermore, this elapsed time *can* be measured by entity 1.

With this motivation, we add ideal timers $t_R(n)$, $n \geq 0$, at entity 2 to record the ideal time elapsed since r first exceeded n, and refine *Consume* appropriately (for brevity, we only indicate the addition to the previous definition given in Table 2):

t_R : sequence $(0 \cdots \infty)$ of ideal timer. Initially $t_R(n) = OFF$ for every n.

Consume(*data*) $\quad\equiv\quad$ <definition in Table 2> $\wedge\ t_R(r)' = 0$

At entity 1, we add ideal timers $t_A(n)$, $n \geq 0$, to record the ideal time elapsed since a first exceeded n, and refine *RecACK* appropriately:

t_A : sequence $(0 \cdots \infty)$ of ideal timer. Initially $t_A(n) = OFF$ for every n.

$$\begin{aligned} RecACK(cn,\ n) \quad \equiv \quad & Rec_2(ACK,\ cn,\ n) \\ & \wedge [\overline{cn-a} \in [1 \cdots s-a] \\ & \quad \rightarrow (a' = a + \overline{cn-a} \wedge sendbuff' = Tail(sendbuff,\ \overline{cn-a}) \\ & \qquad \wedge [\forall i \in [a \cdots a'-1]:\ t_A(i)' = 0])] \end{aligned}$$

We have the following invariant requirements:

C_3	$\equiv$	$t_R(0) \geq t_R(1) \geq \cdots \geq t_R(r-1) \geq 0 \ \wedge \ t_R(r \cdot\cdot \infty) = OFF$
C_4	$\equiv$	$(ACK, \bar{n}, n, age) \in \mathbf{z}_2 \wedge n < r \Rightarrow age \geq t_R(n) \geq 0$
C_5	$\equiv$	$t_A(0) \geq t_A(1) \geq \cdots \geq t_A(a-1) \geq 0 \ \wedge \ t_A(a \cdot\cdot \infty) = OFF$
C_6	$\equiv$	$n \in [0 \cdot\cdot a-1] \Rightarrow t_A(n) \leq t_R(n)$

From A_8, $C_{4\text{-}6}$, and TA_2, and $1 \leq RW \leq N-1$, we see that the following implies S_2:

S_3	$\equiv$	$n = s-N+1 \geq 0 \Rightarrow t_A(n) > MAXLIFE_2$

We have the following Marking. (Using $A_4{}'$ to mark some entries is acceptable because A_4 has been proven invariant; equivalently, we can replace $A_4{}'$ with its tag $A_{8\text{-}10}$):

	Produce	*SendD*	*RecACK*	*Consume*	*SendACK*	*RecD*	*LRD*	*Ite*
$A_{0\text{-}9}$, $C_{0\text{-}2}$	*	*	*	*	*	*	*	*
A_{10}	S_2	*	*	*	*	*	*	*
C_3	*na*	*na*	*na*	C_3	*na*	*na*	*na*	C_3
C_4	*na*	*na*	C_4	C_4, TA_2	C_4	*na*	C_4	C_4
C_5	*na*	*na*	C_5	*na*	*na*	*na*	*na*	C_5
C_6	*na*	*na*	C_6, $A_4{}'$, C_3	C_6, A_4	*na*	*na*	*na*	C_6

S_0 marked using S_1, $C_{2,1}$, TA_1	S_1 unmarked	S_2 marked using S_3, A_8, $C_{4\text{-}6}$, TA_2	S_3 unmarked

5.4. Protocol I: implementation with 2N timers

The only unmarked requirements are S_1 and S_3. In Table 3, we provide a system specification in which entity 1 enforces S_1 and S_3 using two circular arrays of N local timers, namely $timer_D$ and $timer_A$. (It is possible for $timer_D$ to be of size $N-RW$ and $timer_A$ to be of size $N-1$. But it involves notation for modulo $N-RW$ and $N-1$ arithmetic.)

Given an ideal timer u and a local timer v of entity 1 which are started together, from the accuracy axiom it is clear that $u > T$ holds if $v \geq 1+(1+\varepsilon_1)T$, or equivalently if v is a timer of capacity $(1+\varepsilon_1)T$ and is *OFF*. With this motivation, define $MLIFE_i = (1+\varepsilon_1)MAXLIFE_i$ for $i = 1$ and 2.

$timer_D$ is an array $(0 \cdot\cdot N-1)$ of local timers, each of capacity $MLIFE_1$. For $n \in [\max(0, s-N+RW) \cdot\cdot s-1]$, $timer_D(\bar{n})$ tracks $t_D(n)$ up to $MLIFE_1$ local time units with an accuracy of ε_1. Thus, S_1 is enforced by including $timer_D(\overline{s-N+RW}) = OFF$, or equivalently $timer_D(\overline{s+RW}) = OFF$, in the enabling condition of *Produce*, as shown in Table 3.

$timer_A$ is an array $(0 \cdot\cdot N-1)$ of local timers, each of capacity $MLIFE_2$. For $n \in [\max(0, s-N+1) \cdot\cdot a-1]$, $timer_A(\bar{n})$ tracks $t_A(n)$ up to $MLIFE_2$ local time units with an accuracy of ε_1. Thus, S_3 is enforced by including $timer_A(\overline{s-N+1}) = OFF$, or equivalently $timer_A(\overline{s+1}) = OFF$, in the enabling condition of *Produce*, as shown in Table 3.

For brevity, we omit a formal proof that this protocol satisfies the event requirements S_1 and S_3. (It is contained in [18].)

The previous Marking of the progress requirements holds with a few minor changes. The current system is a refinement of the basic protocol, and the only event whose enabling condition has changed is *Produce*. Thus the only effect on the previous Marking is to unmark L_3, which was marked *via Produce*. The previous marking of L_2 is still valid because it did not use L_3. While L_3 does not follow immediately via *Produce*, it still holds. It is sufficient to show that the two constraints involving timers in the enabling condition of *Produce* eventually become true when $s=a$. But this holds because the time events can never deadlock [17]. Therefore, any bounded timer that is not *OFF* will eventually become *OFF*.

5.5. Protocol II: implementation with N timers

In Table 4, we provide an implementation in which both S_1 and S_3 are enforced by the N local timers in $timer_A$. Unlike in the previous implementation with $timer_D$, the enforcement of S_1 is not tight, i.e., entity 1 takes more than the minimum time to detect that S_1 holds.

Because $produced(n)$ is not sent after it is acknowledged, we have $t_D(n) \geq t_A(n)$ for all $n \in [0 \cdot\cdot a-1]$. The proof of this is trivial and is omitted. Thus, an alternative way to enforce S_1 is to enforce the following:

$$S_4 \quad \equiv \quad n=s-N-RW \geq 0 \Rightarrow t_A(n) > MAXLIFE_1$$

S_4 is analogous to S_3 and can be enforced by including $timer_A(\overline{s+RW}) > MLIFE_1$ in the enabling condition of *Produce*. We have to combine this with the other condition $timer_A(\overline{s+1}) > MLIFE_2$ needed to enforce S_3, as shown in Table 4. The Marking of the progress requirements is as in protocol I.

5.6. Protocol III: implementation with one timer

In Table 5, we provide an implementation that enforces S_3 and S_4 by using a single local timer. The timer, denoted by $timer_S$, imposes a minimum time interval δ between successive occurrences of *Produce*. We also require that $s-a$ does not exceed a constant, SW, which must be less than $N-RW$. The following inequalities must be satisfied by δ and SW:

$$1 \leq SW \leq N-RW-1$$
$$\delta \geq \max\left[\frac{MAXLIFE_1}{N-RW-SW}, \frac{MAXLIFE_2}{N-1-SW}\right]$$

For the typical case of $MAXLIFE_1 = MAXLIFE_2 = MAXLIFE$ the above constraint on δ simplifies to $\delta \geq \frac{MAXLIFE}{N-SW-RW}$. If in addition, N is very large compared to SW or RW (e.g. in TCP, $N=2^{32}$ while $SW, RW \leq 2^{16}$), then the bound simplifies to $\delta \geq \frac{MAXLIFE}{N}$.

Stenning [20] considered the case of $MAXLIFE_1 = MAXLIFE_2 = MAXLIFE$ and obtained the bound $N \geq SW + \max(M + RW, SW)$, where $M = \frac{MAXLIFE}{\delta}$. We get $N \geq SW + RW + M$, which is a tighter bound. Stenning's protocol also has several unnecessary requirements, as follows. Whenever the producer retransmits a data block with sequence number *i*, it also resends every outstanding data block with a sequence number larger than *i*. Whenever the consumer receives a data message, it must send an acknowledgement message.

Observe that the above time constraint on δ corresponds to specifying a maximum rate of data transmission, if we assume that *Produce* also transmits the accepted data block. (There is no loss of generality here; entity 1 need merely save in another buffer data blocks that are produced and not yet sent.) Note that if δ is sufficiently small, e.g. the hardware clock period, then there is no need for entity 1 to explicitly use a local timer. This would correspond to the situation in TCP [10] and the original Stenning's protocol [20].

6. Discussions

Our stepwise refinement heuristic is influenced by Dijkstra's work on the derivation of programs by using weakest preconditions [5], and by his development of distributed programs by incrementally adding invariants and actions to preserve the invariants [6,7,8,9].

There are differences and similarities between our approach and the approach of Chandy and Misra [3,4] to derive distributed programs by stepwise refinement. In both approaches, a distributed system is modeled by a set of state variables and events. Invariant and progress requirements are maintained throughout the construction. In the approach of Chandy and Misra, most of the effort is spent on refining the set of requirements; the distributed program is not shown until very detailed requirements have been obtained. In our approach, most of the effort is spent on refining the state transition system; the detailed requirements are derived in order to satisfy our various conditions for one state transition system to be a refinement of another state transition system.

In many of the examples of Chandy and Misra, the topology of the network of processes is refined by breaking up an event into several events, which are subsequently associated with different processes. This type of refinement step has also been used by other authors [1,2,15]. We have not found use for such a refinement step in our examples, which are from the area of communication protocols.

In summary, event requirements, a Marking, and the conditional refinement relation between specifications are unique features of our approach. Event requirements allow us to state safety requirements that cannot yet be made invariant without causing unsuccessful termination. The Marking provides a useful representation of the extent to which the requirements are satisfied by the current state transition system and fairness assumptions. The conditional refinement relation gives us some flexibility in generating new state transition systems, while keeping any decrease in the Marking to a minimum.

We find the relational notation to be very convenient for expressing event refinement, and for reasoning about the effect of an action on invariant requirements. However, our construction heuristic does not require it; events can be specified by guarded multiple-assignment statements as in [3].

Table 1: Invariant requirements for the basic protocol

Properties relating state variables at the entities

		$1 \leq RW \leq N-1$
A_0	$\equiv$	*consumed* prefix-of *produced*
A_3	$\equiv$	$\lvert produced \rvert = s \;\wedge\; \lvert consumed \rvert = r$
A_4	$\equiv$	$0 \leq a \leq r \leq s$
A_5	$\equiv$	$sendbuff = produced(a \cdot\cdot s-1)$
A_6	$\equiv$	$i \in [0 \cdot\cdot RW-1] \Rightarrow recbuff(i) = empty \vee recbuff(i) = produced(r+i)$
A_8	$\equiv$	$s-a \leq N-RW$

Properties of D messages

A_1	$\equiv$	$(D, data, cn, n) \in z_1 \Rightarrow data = produced(n) \wedge cn = \bar{n}$
A_7	$\equiv$	$(D, data, cn, n) \in z_1 \Rightarrow n \geq r-N+RW$

Properties of ACK messages

A_2	$\equiv$	$(ACK, cn, n) \in z_2 \Rightarrow cn = \bar{n}$
A_9	$\equiv$	$(ACK, cn, n) \in z_2 \Rightarrow n \leq r$
A_{10}	$\equiv$	$(ACK, cn, n) \in z_2 \Rightarrow n \geq s-N+1$

Table 2: System specification for the basic protocol

Entity 1

produced: sequence of *DATA*. Initially null.
$s : 0 \cdot\cdot \infty$. Initially 0.
$a : 0 \cdot\cdot \infty$. Initially 0.
sendbuff: sequence of *DATA*. Initially null.

$Produce(data)$	$\equiv$	$s-a \le N-RW-1$ $\wedge\, sendbuff' = sendbuff \,@\, data \;\wedge\; s' = s+1$ $\wedge\, produced' = produced \,@\, data$
$SendD(i)$	$\equiv$	$i \in [0 \cdot\cdot s-a-1] \;\wedge\, Send_1(D,\, sendbuff(i),\, \overline{a+i},\, a+i)$
$RecACK(cn, n)$	$\equiv$	$Rec_2(ACK, cn, n)$ $\wedge\, [\overline{cn-a} \in [1 \cdot\cdot s-a]$ $\rightarrow (a' = a + \overline{cn-a} \;\wedge\, sendbuff' = Tail(sendbuff, \overline{cn-a}))]$

Entity 2

consumed: sequence of *DATA*. Initially null.
$r : 0 \cdot\cdot \infty$. Initially 0.
recbuff: sequence $(0 \cdot\cdot RW-1)$ of $DATA \cup \{empty\}$. Initially $recbuff = empty$.

$Consume(data)$	$\equiv$	$recbuff(0) \ne empty$ $\wedge\, data = recbuff(0)$ $\wedge\, recbuff' = Tail(recbuff, 1) \,@\, empty \;\wedge\; r' = r+1$ $\wedge\, consumed' = consumed \,@\, data$
$SendACK$	$\equiv$	$Send_2(ACK, \overline{r}, r)$
$RecD(data, cn, n)$	$\equiv$	$Rec_1(D, data, cn, n)$ $\wedge\, [\overline{cn-r} \in [0 \cdot\cdot RW-1] \rightarrow recbuff(\overline{cn-r})' = data]$

Table 3: System specification for protocol I

Entity 1

produced, s, a, *sendbuff* defined as in Table 2.
t_D, t_A : sequence $(0 \cdot\cdot \infty)$ of ideal timer. Initially $t_D = t_A = OFF$.
$timer_D$: sequence $(0 \cdot\cdot N-1)$ of local timer of capacity $MLIFE_1$. Initially $timer_D = OFF$.
$timer_A$: sequence $(0 \cdot\cdot N-1)$ of local timer of capacity $MLIFE_2$. Initially $timer_A = OFF$.

Produce (*data*)	≡	$timer_D(\overline{s+RW}) = OFF \wedge timer_A(\overline{s+1}) = OFF$ $\wedge$ <definition in Table 2>
SendD (i)	≡	<definition in Table 2> $\wedge\ timer_D(\overline{a+i})' = 0 \wedge t_D(a+i)' = 0$
RecACK (cn, n)	≡	$Rec_2(ACK, cn, n)$ $\wedge [\overline{cn-a} \in [1 \cdot\cdot s-a]$ $\quad \rightarrow (a' = a + \overline{cn-a} \wedge sendbuff' = Tail(sendbuff, \overline{cn-a})$ $\qquad \wedge [\forall i \in [a \cdot\cdot a'-1]: t_A(i)' = timer_A(\overline{i})' = 0])]$

Entity 2

consumed, r, *recbuff* defined as in Table 2.
t_R : sequence $(0 \cdot\cdot \infty)$ of ideal timer. Initially $t_R = OFF$.

Consume (*data*)	≡	<definition in Table 2> $\wedge\ t_R(r)' = 0$
SendACK	≡	<definition in Table 2>
RecD (*data*, cn, n)	≡	<definition in Table 2>

Table 4: System specification for protocol II

Entity 1

produced, s, a, *sendbuff*, t_D, t_A defined as in Table 3.
$timer_A$: sequence $(0 \cdots N-1)$ of local timer of capacity $\max(MLIFE_1, MLIFE_2)$. Initially $timer_A = OFF$

$Produce(data) \equiv$ <definition in Table 2> $\wedge\ timer_A(\overline{s+RW}) = OFF$ if $MLIFE_1 \geq MLIFE_2$

$Produce(data) \equiv$ <definition in Table 2> $\wedge\ timer_A(\overline{s+1}) = OFF$ $\wedge\ (timer_A(\overline{s+RW}) = OFF \vee timer_A(\overline{s+RW}) > MLIFE_1)$ if $MLIFE_1 < MLIFE_2$

$SendD(i) \equiv$ <definition in Table 2> $\wedge\ t_D(a+i)' = 0$

$RecACK(cn, n) \equiv$ <definition in Table 3>

Entity 2 defined as in Table 3.

Table 5: System specification for protocol III

Entity 1

produced, s, a, *sendbuff*, t_D, t_A defined as in Table 3.
$timer_S$: local timer of capacity $(1+\varepsilon_1)\delta$. Initially $timer_S = OFF$.

$$Produce(data) \equiv s-a \leq SW-1 \wedge timer_S = OFF \wedge timer_S' = 0 \wedge sendbuff' = sendbuff @ data \wedge s' = s+1 \wedge produced' = produced @ data$$

$SendD(i) \equiv$ <definition in Table 4>

$$RecACK(cn, n) \equiv Rec_2(ACK, cn, n) \wedge [\overline{cn-a} \in [1 \cdots s-a] \rightarrow (a' = a + \overline{cn-a} \wedge sendbuff' = Tail(sendbuff, \overline{cn-a}) \wedge [\forall i \in [a \cdots a'-1]: t_A(i)' = 0])]$$

Entity 2 defined as in Table 3.

References

[1] R.J.R. Back and R. Kurki-Suonio, "Decentralization of process nets with a centralized control," *Second ACM SIGACT-SIGCOPS Symp. on Prin. of Distr. Comput.*, Montreal, Aug. 1983, pp. 131-142.

[2] R.J.R. Back and R. Kurki-Suonio, "A case study in constructing distributed algorithms: Distributed exchange sort," *Proc. of Winter School on Theoretical Computer Science*, Lammi, Finland, Jan. 1984, Finnish Soc. of Inf. Proc. Sc., pp. 1-33.

[3] K.M. Chandy and J. Misra, "An example of stepwise refinement of distributed programs: Quiescence detection," *ACM Trans. on Prog. Lang. and Syst.*, Vol. 8, No. 3, July 1986, pp. 326-343.

[4] K.M. Chandy and J. Misra, *Parallel Program Design: A Foundation*, Addison-Wesley, Reading, MA, 1988.

[5] E.W. Dijkstra, *A Discipline of Programming*, Prentice-Hall, Englewood Cliffs, N.J., 1976.

[6] E.W. Dijkstra, L. Lamport, A.J. Martin, C.S. Scholten, "On-the-fly garbage collection: An exercise in cooperation," *Commun. ACM*, Vol. 21, No. 11, November 1978, pp. 966-975.

[7] E.W. Dijkstra, C.S. Scholten, "Termination detection for diffusing computations," *Inform. Proc. Letters*, Vol. 11, No. 1, August 1980, pp. 1-4.

[8] E.W. Dijkstra, "Derivation of a termination detection algorithm for distributed computations," Tech. Report, EWD-840.

[9] E.W. Dijkstra, "The distributed snapshot of K.M. Chandy and L. Lamport," Tech. Report, EWD-864, November 1983.

[10] *Transmission Control Protocol*, DDN Protocol Handbook: DoD Military Standard Protocols, DDN Network Information Center, SRI, MILSTD1778, Aug 1983.

[11] D.E. Knuth, "Verification of link-level protocols," *BIT*, Vol. 21, pp. 31-36, 1981.

[12] S.S. Lam and A.U. Shankar, "Protocol verification via projections," *IEEE Trans. on Software Engineering*, Vol. SE-10, No. 4, July 1984, pp. 325-342.

[13] S.S. Lam and A.U. Shankar, "Specifying implementations to satisfy interfaces: A state transition system approach," presented at the 26th Annual Lake Arrowhead Workshop on *How will we specify concurrent systems in the year 2000?*, September 1987; full version available as Technical Report TR-88-30, Department of Computer Sciences, University of Texas at Austin, August 1988 (revised June 1989).

[14] S.S. Lam and A.U. Shankar, "A relational notation for state transition systems," Technical Report TR-88-21, Department of Computer Sciences, University of Texas at Austin, May 1988 (revised August 1989); an abbreviated version appears in these proceedings of the REX Workshop on Refinement of Distributed Systems under the title "Refinement and projection of relational specifications."

[15] K. Sere, "Stepwise removal of virtual channels in distributed algorithms," *Second Int. Workshop on Dist. Alg.*, Amsterdam, 1987.

[16] A.U. Shankar and S.S. Lam, "Time-dependent communication protocols," *Tutorial: Principles of Communication and Networking Protocols*, S. S. Lam (ed.), IEEE Computer Society, 1984.

[17] A.U. Shankar and S.S. Lam, "Time-dependent distributed systems: proving safety, liveness and real-time properties," *Distributed Computing*, Vol. 2, No. 2, pp. 61-79, 1987.

[18] A.U. Shankar and S.S. Lam, "A stepwise refinement heuristic for protocol construction," Technical Report CS-TR-1812, Department of Computer Science, University of Maryland, March 1987 (revised March 1989).

[19] A.U. Shankar, "Verified data transfer protocols with variable flow control," *ACM Transactions on Computer Systems*, Vol. 7, No. 3, August 1989; an abbreviated version appears in *Proc. ACM SIGCOMM '86 Symposium*, Aug 1986, under the title "A verified sliding window protocol with variable flow control."

[20] N.V. Stenning, "A data transfer protocol," *Computer Networks*, Vol. 1, pp. 99-110, September 1976.

A derivation of a broadcasting protocol using sequentially phased reasoning

F.A. Stomp
University of Nijmegen
Department of Computer Science
Toernooiveld, 6525 ED Nijmegen, The Netherlands
E-mail address: frank@cs.kun.nl

Contents

1 Introduction

2 Preliminaries

3 The principle for sequentially phased reasoning

3.1 Notation

3.2 Correctness formulae

3.3 The formulation of the principle

4 Problem specification

5 A derivation of a broadcasting protocol

5.1 An initial sequential solution

5.2 Refinement of the initial solution

5.3 Solving the first subtask

5.4 Solving the second subtask

5.5 Combining the programs

6 Conclusion

Abstract: In [SR89a, SR89b, SR89c] a principle has been formulated for designing, hence verifying, distributed algorithms from a particular class. This class consists of algorithms in which processes in a network perform a certain *task* which can be decomposed into a number of *subtasks* as if they are performed *sequentially* from a *logical* point of view, although from an *operational* point of view they are performed *concurrently* (cf. [GHS83, Hu83, MS79, Se82, Se83, ZS80]).
Till now the above-mentioned principle has been applied as a *verification principle* in [SR89b] to a correctness proof of a broadcasting protocol, the PIF-protocol, due to Segall [Se83], and in [SR89c] to a correctness proof of the distributed minimum-weight spanning tree algorithms of Gallager, Humblet, Spira [GHS83]. As shown in the present paper this principle can also be applied for *deriving* distributed algorithms. In particular, this is demonstrated by *deriving* a broadcasting protocol, essentially Segall's PIF-protocol. We remark that a *similar derivation* also applies for *deriving* other more complex distributed algorithms, such as those described in [Hu83, MS79, Se82, Se83, ZS80] as well as the distributed minimum-weight spanning tree algorithm of Gallager, Humblet, and Spira [GHS83].
The derivation presented in this paper shows that invariants can be generated during the development of programs, and illustrates a generalization of Back's refinement calculus [B88].

1 Introduction

Recently Stomp and de Roever [SR89a, SR89b, SR89c] have formulated a principle for designing, hence verifying, distributed algorithms from a particular class. This class consists of algorithms in which processes in a network perform a certain *task* which can be decomposed into a number of *subtasks* as if they are performed *sequentially* from a *logical* point of view, although from an *operational* point of view, i.e., in reality, they are performed *concurrently* (cf. [GHS83, Hu83, MS79, Se82, Se83, ZS80]).

The above-mentioned principle, called the *principle for sequentially phased reasoning* (*about concurrently performed subtasks*), formulated in [SR89a] for the first time, has been applied as a *verification principle* in [SR89b] to a correctness proof of a broadcasting protocol, the PIF-protocol, due to Segall [Se83], and in [SR89c] to a correctness proof of the distributed minimum-weight spanning tree algorithms of Gallager, Humblet, Spira [GHS83]. The present paper shows that this principle can also be applied for *deriving* distributed algorithms. We demonstrate this by *deriv-*

ing a broadcasting protocol, essentially Segall's PIF-protocol, and remark that a *similar derivation* also applies for *deriving* other more complex distributed algorithms, such as those described in [GHS83, Hu83, MS79, Se82, Se83, ZS80].

How does one apply this principle, which has been applied so far to posteriori-verification, to verification *during* a distributed program's derivation?

In order to answer this question, we distinguish *three stages* in the derivation process of such a program. At the *first stage* one derives, starting with some formal specification, a sequential composition of sequential programs. At the *second stage* each of these sequential programs is refined into a distributed program (using techniques of, e.g., Back and Sere [BS89], or Chandy and Misra [CM88]). At the *third stage* the sequential composition of these distributed programs (obtained in the second stage) is transformed into *one* distributed program, which is the parallel composition of processes' programs (and which is not the sequential composition of programs anymore). It is here where the principle for sequentially phased reasoning is applied. The last stage is (to the best of our knowledge) one of the new elements of this paper.

How does one accomplish the transformation at the third stage above? I.e., how does one transform the sequential composition of distributed programs (obtained in the second stage of the derivation) into a parallel composition of processes' programs?

Essentially, this is the heart of the principle for sequentially phased reasoning. This principle generalizes Elrad and Francez' principle of communication closed layers [EF82], Chou and Gafni's principle of stratified decompositions [CG88], a principle due to Back and Sere [BS89], and a principle recently proposed by Fix and Francez [FF89]. The reason that the principle of sequentially phased reasoning generalizes those principles is that it is not syntax-directed (in contrast with the principle of communication closed layers), that it allows for interference of actions of a certain process with invariants of another process, cf. Owicki and Gries' interference freedom test, (in contrast with Chou and Gafni's principle), and that it applies to dynamically changing clusters of collaborating processes' programs –one the the characteristics of the class of algorithms considered here.

Returning to the question:

(1) The distributed programs obtained in the second stage above can be represented as the parallel composition of loops whose branches consists of guards guarding atomic actions (as in Back's action calculus, see his two contributions to this volume), essentially by encoding the flow of control (cf. [SR89b]).

(2) For each process a new loop is constructed whose set of branches consists of the union of branches occurring in the (smaller) loops that are executed by that process. Of course, this transformation can be applied only, if taking the union of all branches when constructing

the big loop does not disturb the sequential structure of the first two stages above when the processes' (big) loops are placed in parallel. This obvious observation lies at the basis of the principle for sequentially phased reasoning. The technical formulation of this principle is, essentially, a translation of the observation that the sequential structure of the first and second stage above is not disturbed into (formal) verification conditions.

How is this principle formulated?

For each distributed program occurring in the sequential composition obtained in the second stage of the derivation, we prove a specification which consists of, for each process j in the network, a precondition p_j, a postcondition q_j, an invariant I_j, and a termination condition T_j. I_j has been incorporated in the specification in order to cope with the interferences of the kind discussed above, which occur, e.g., in the distributed distributed minimum-weight spanning tree of Gallager, Humblet, and Spira [GHS83]. One then requires that each process can execute actions of one of own programs at a time, and that the order in which it executes actions of distinct (own) programs agrees with the order prescribed by the sequential composition of the distributed programs. These conditions can be formulated in Manna and Pnueli's Linear Time Temporal Logic [MP83] as done in [SR89b], or in Katz and Peled's Interleaving Set Temporal Logic [KP87] as done in [SR88].

Why is this principle sound?

Its justification lies in considering computation sequences in a specific form in which all actions associated with one distributed program (obtained during the second stage) are performed consecutively. Although it might not be the case at all that each computation sequence of the distributed program obtained after applying the principle is in this specific form, *reasoning about computation sequences in this specific form is correct*, since any computation sequence of the latter program turns out to be *equivalent* to one in that form. In order to define this notion of equivalence (see [L85]), the notion of an *event* is needed: an event is the occurrence of the execution of some atomic action. Now each computation sequence induces a natural partial ordering of its events. This partial order is a causal relation in which all events generated by a single process are ordered according to their temporal order in this sequence. Additionally, in an asynchronous model of computation the event of sending a message precedes the event of receiving it; in a synchronous modes they are identical. Two computation sequences are *equivalent* if their first states coincide and if they induce the same partial order of events. In essence, equivalent computation sequences differ only in the way events generated by different processes are interleaved (w.r.t. the partial order induced by these sequences). Now, if a computation sequences is finite and equivalent to another one then the latter one is finite, too, and their last states coincide. This observation forms the basis of the soundness proof of the above-mentioned principle. (Cf. also [SR89b] and [St89] for a soundness proof of the principle in case of a synchronous model of communication).

A characteristic of the kind of network algorithms considered here is that although one unique program is executed locally by every process in the network, this execution displays a certain overall dynamic pattern: that of clusters of collaborating processes' programs which reconfigure from time to time, as in e.g., [GHS83]. In its full generality, the principle of sequentially phased reasoning can cope with this phenomenon, see [SR89c]. The full generality of this principle is not shown in this paper. Here, we derive (using this principle) a simple (distributed) broadcasting protocol, essentially Segall's PIF-protocol, from its specification following the three stages mentioned above. In this work a specification of a program consists of a precondition, a postcondition, and an invariant.

In general, the invariants required for a sound application of the principle for sequentially phased reasoning are quite complex. One contribution of this paper is the illustration that invariants of a program *can be generated* and *structured* during the first two stages of the derivation of that program. Invariants of a program as used in the principle characterize the processes' contributions to the program's computations, and may suggest directions for further refinements. In our derivation, invariants are carried along with programs derived so far. At each step of the derivation invariants are strengthened. This agrees with the intuition that when a program is refined into a more concrete one more information is available about the processes' contributions to the program's computation. A calculus in which invariants are actually strengthened at each step of a derivation is not given in this paper. It is envisaged that Back's refinement calculus [B88] could serve as a basis for such a calculus, by allowing apart from pre- and postconditions also invariants in specifications of programs. In this view the formal setting of this work would be a generalization of Back's refinement calculus.

This paper is organized as follows: In the next section we introduce some basic notions and notations used in the remainder of this paper. In section 3, the formal description of the principle for sequentially phased reasoning is presented. The problem specification, the starting point of our derivation of a broadcasting protocol, is presented in section 4. Section 5 contains the derivation of a distributed program which meets this specification. Finally, section 6 contains some conclusions.

2 Preliminaries

The (distributed) algorithms considered in this paper are performed by processes in a fixed, finite, undirected, and connected network which will be represented by a graph (V, E). Each process and each channel in the network is identified by some node and by some edge in the graph respectively. Adjacent nodes communicate by means of messages. Since edges are undirected each node can both send and receive messages along any of its adjacent edges. Communication is *asynchronous*, i.e., messages transmitted by some node along one of its adjacent edges arrive within an unpredictable time frame at the other end of that edge. Communication is assumed to be *perfect*, i.e., messages transmitted by some node along any of its adjacent edges *always* arrive in sequence, error-free, without loss, and without duplication at the other end of that edge.

In the sequel E_i will denote the set of all edges adjacent to node i; $E_{i,j}$ will denote the set of all edges adjacent to both nodes i and j, i.e., $E_{i,j}=E_i \cap E_j$ holds.

The distance between two nodes i and j in the graph (V, E) will be denoted by $dist(i, j)$, i.e., $dist(i, j)$ denotes the number of all edges on the shortest path connecting the nodes i and j. Observe that for all nodes i and j, $dist(i, j)$ has a well-defined value, since the graph (V, E) is finite and connected.

We shall use Dijkstra's language of guarded commands [D76] embedded in some self-explanatory algol-like language as a programming language. A substantial part of the derivation presented here takes place on a level of sequential programming. For two sequential programs S and S', S *is refined by* S' if the following is satisfied, see [B88]: for each postcondition Q in which programming variables occur of program S only, $wp(S, Q)$ implies $wp(S', Q)$, where wp denotes the weakest precondition [D76]. (The reason for restricting the postconditions Q to S's programming variables is explained in [B88].) Consequently, if program S is refined by program S' and if S is totally correct w.r.t. precondition P and postcondition Q (Q as above), then S' is also totally correct w.r.t. P and Q.
In our derivation, programs are always executed in an initial state satisfying some given precondition. Therefore, we introduce the notion of a refinement of program S by program S' w.r.t. some precondition P: S is refined by S' w.r.t. P, if $(P \wedge wp(S, Q)) \Rightarrow wp(S', Q)$ holds, where Q satisfies the above restriction. In this case, if the programs S and S' are both executed in an initial state satisfying precondition P, then the following holds: If every computation sequence of S is finite and ends in a state satisfying Q, then every computation sequence of S' is finite, too, and the final state satisfies Q.

In the sequel, for an unguarded statement S, $<S>$ denotes that S is executed atomically. In case of a guarded statement of the form $b \rightarrow a$, where a denotes some action and b denotes a's guard, $<b \rightarrow a>$ denotes that action a is executed atomically provided that guard b has been passed (cf. definition 3.1 below).

For convenience, we shall sometimes use the statement ℓ: $<S>$. Here ℓ denotes some label of $<S>$. Executing ℓ: $<S>$ has the same effect as executing $<S>$. In ℓ: $<S>$, ℓ is merely used to refer to $<S>$ by the name ℓ.

3 The principle for sequentially phased reasoning

In this section the design principle for reasoning *sequentially* about *concurrently* performed (sub)tasks, cf. section 1, is presented. This principle has originally been formulated in [SR89a] for a *synchronous* model of computation. Recently, however, an error has been discovered in the formulation of the principle there. It has been corrected and proved to be sound in [St89]. The principle in the context of an *asynchronous* model of computation is formulated in section 3.3, cf. also [SR89b] and [SR89c].

3.1 Notation

In order to describe our design principle in a few words, we represent a distributed algorithm by a tuple $< \{p_i \mid i \in V'\}, V', Act >$. Here p_i (node i's precondition) is a state assertion characterizing the initial values of node i's variables and the initial contents of node i's adjacent edges; V' denotes the set of nodes containing all those nodes that actually execute the algorithm; Act is a collection of (atomic) actions containing all those actions which can occur in any computation sequence of the algorithm (cf. definition 3.1 below). Each action a in the set Act has some guard associated with it. Such a guard consists of a boolean expression or of a receive-statement (cf. [Ho78]). Moreover, the set Act can be partitioned into sets Act_i such that each Act_i consists of all actions which can be executed by node i ($i \in V'$). Each action a in the set Act is either an *internal action*, i.e., one not involving any communication, a *send-action*, i.e., one guarded by a boolean expression and involving the transmission of a certain message, or a *receive-action*, i.e., one guarded by a receive-statement and which otherwise does not perform any communication. (Messages can be removed by a certain node from one of its adjacent edges at any time after the arrival of that message along that edge.)

By allowing the second component V' in the tuple above to be a proper subset of V, i.e., the set of all nodes in the network, the principle for sequentially phased reasoning (formulated in section 3.3) is also applicable to distributed algorithms in which dynamically changing set of nodes repeatedly perform certain subtasks. This can be discerned, e.g., in the distributed algorithm of Gallager, Humblet, and Spira [GHS83], cf. also [SR89c].

We conclude this subsection with the following:

Definition 3.1 A computation sequence of an algorithm as above is a maximal sequence $s_0 \xrightarrow{a_0} s_1 \xrightarrow{a_1} s_2 \xrightarrow{a_2} \cdots$ such that for all $n \geq 0$ the following is satisfied: s_n is some state, in the initial state s_0 the preconditions p_j hold for all nodes j in V', a_n is an action occurring in the set Act, action a_n is enabled in state s_n, i.e., a_n's guard can be passed in s_n, and s_{n+1} is the state resulting when action a_n is executed in state s_n.

3.2 Correctness formulae

In this section correctness formulae are introduced. These formulae enable a simple and convenient formulation of the principle for sequentially phased reasoning. Let $\mathcal{A}$=< $\{p_i \mid i \in V'\}$, V', *Act* > be an algorithm. Node j's computation can be characterized by an invariant I_j ($j \in V'$). In general, one can be more precise about node j's behavior: If node j has completed its participation at a certain point in some computation sequence of the algorithm $\mathcal{A}$, then j cannot perform any action from that point onwards. The states in which node j cannot perform any action anymore are characterized by a state assertion T_j, called j's termination condition for $\mathcal{A}$ ($j \in V'$).

We now introduce correctness formulae of the form
$\mathcal{A}$ **sat** < $\{I_j \mid j \in V'\}$, $\{T_j \mid j \in V'\}$, $\{q_j \mid j \in V'\}$ > for an algorithm $\mathcal{A}$= < $\{p_i \mid i \in V'\}$, V', *Act* >, and for state assertions I_j, T_j, q_j ($j \in V'$). Such a formula is valid iff the following holds for every computation sequence of algorithm $\mathcal{A}$ (started in a state satisfying each of the preconditions p_j, $j \in V'$):

- For all $j \in V'$, I_j is continuously holds,
- For all $j \in V'$, T_j holds iff node j will not execute any action in *Act* anymore, and
- For all $j \in V'$, q_j (node j's postcondition) holds when and if j has terminated its participation in $\mathcal{A}$.

As a preparation for the technical formulation of these connectness formulae we introduce, as in [SS84], *auxiliary proof variables* $\sigma_j(e)$ and $\rho_j(e)$ (for nodes $j \in V'$ and for edges $e \in E_j$). They are used for reasoning about communication; $\sigma_j(e)$ records the sequence of all messages transmitted by node j along edge e; $\rho_j(e)$ records the sequence of all messages received by node j along edge e. For nodes i and j and for edges $e \in E_{i,j}$, the property $\rho_j(e) \preceq \sigma_i(e)$ is preserved by any action, see [SS84]. That is, if edge e connects the nodes i and j , then the sequence of all messages received by node j along edge e is a prefix of all messages transmitted by node i along edge e. These auxiliary proof variables are changed when a node transmits or receives a message; they are not changed during the execution of an internal action.

A correctness formula as above can be formulated formally in Manna and Pnueli's Linear Time Temporal Logic [MP83]. More precisely, $\mathcal{A}$ **sat** < $\{I_j \mid j \in V'\}$, $\{T_j \mid j \in V'\}$, $\{q_j \mid j \in V'\}$ > is an abbreviation of the conjunction of the conditions (a) through (f) below. These conditions are interpreted over all computation sequences of $\mathcal{A}$. Below, $\Box$ denotes the *always*-operator and U denotes the *weak until*-operator from temporal logic, cf. [MP83].

As a preparation of the technical formulation of the conditions (a) through (f), we first introduce some notation.

Let $Int_j \subseteq Act_j$ denote the set of node j's internal actions. Let $Rec_j(e) \subseteq Act_j$ denote the set of node j's actions which involve the receipt of a message along edge $e \in E_j$. Let $Sen_j(e) \subseteq Act_j$ denote the set of node j's actions which involve the transmission of a message along edge $e \in E_j$. Hereafter IS_j will denote the set of node j's internal actions and those actions which involve the transmission of a message, i.e., $IS_j = Int_j \cup \bigcup_{e \in E_j} Sen_j(e)$. Note that $IS_j \cup \bigcup_{e \in E_j} Rec_j(e) = Act_j$ holds. Of course, for any action $a \in IS_j$, a's guard can be passed in a certain state if $en(a)$ is satisfied in that state, where $en(a)$ denotes action a's (boolean) guard.

(a) $\forall j \in V'.(p_j \Rightarrow I_j) \wedge \forall j,k \in V'.\forall e \in E_{j,k}.(p_j \Rightarrow \rho_j(e) \preceq \sigma_k(e))$ holds. That is, initially the assertion I_j holds for all nodes j in V'. Furthermore, the sequence of all messages received by a certain node along any of its adjacent edges is a prefix of the sequence of all messages transmitted by the node at the other end of that edge is satisfied initially. (From the discussion above it follows that the property $\forall j,k \in V'.\forall e \in E_{i,j}.\rho_j(e) \preceq \sigma_k(e)$ invariantly holds during execution of algorithm $\mathcal{A}$.)

(b) $\forall j \in V'.\Box((I_j \wedge \neg T_j) U (I_j \wedge T_j))$ holds. We thus have that I_j is an invariant and for all computation sequences of $\mathcal{A}$, "node j participates in the algorithm until it has completed this participation" holds for all $j \in V'$.

(c) $\forall j \in V'.\forall a \in IS_j.\Box((I_j \wedge T_j) \Rightarrow \neg en(a)) \wedge$
$\forall j,k \in V'.\forall e \in E_{j,k}.\Box((I_j \wedge T_j) \Rightarrow \rho_j(e) = \sigma_k(e))$. (For actions $a \in IS_j$ $(j \in V')$, $en(a)$ has been defined above.) I.e., if a certain node has completed its participation in algorithm $\mathcal{A}$, then it cannot perform any action associated with $\mathcal{A}$ anymore.

(d) $\forall j \in V'.\Box((I_j \wedge T_j) \Rightarrow \Box(I_j \wedge T_j))$ holds. That is, once a node has completed its participation in $\mathcal{A}$, then it will never participate in the algorithm anymore.

(e) $\forall j \in V'.\Box\Big((I_j \wedge \neg T_j) \Rightarrow \big((\exists k \in V'.\exists a \in IS_k.en(a)) \vee (\exists k,m \in V'.\exists e \in E_{k,m}.\rho_k(e) \prec \sigma_m(e))\big)\Big)$ holds. Here, for sequences t and u, $t \prec u$ denotes that t is a proper prefix of u. This condition expresses the following: if a certain node has not completed its participation in $\mathcal{A}$, then $\mathcal{A}$ cannot be completed, i.e., at least one action of $\mathcal{A}$ is enabled.

(f) $\forall j \in V'.\Box((I_j \wedge T_j) \Rightarrow q_j)$ holds. I.e., if a certain node has completed its participation in algorithm $\mathcal{A}$, then the node's postcondition is established.

3.3 The formulation of the principle

Now, suppose that we have designed two algorithms $\mathcal{A} = < \{p_i \mid i \in V'\}, V', Act^{\mathcal{A}} >$ and $\mathcal{B} = < \{r_i \mid i \in V'\}, V', Act^{\mathcal{B}} >$ which solve two subtasks of a certain task, as if they are performed one after the other. Furthermore, suppose that the whole task can be described as if the subtask solved by algorithm $\mathcal{A}$ is performed before the one solved by algorithm $\mathcal{B}$. We now describe how the two algorithms can be combined into one that solves the whole task.

First find assertions $I_j^{\mathcal{A}}$, $I_j^{\mathcal{B}}$, $T_j^{\mathcal{A}}$, $T_j^{\mathcal{B}}$, and q_j for each node j in V' such that the correctness formulae

(1) $\mathcal{A}$ **sat** $< \{I_j^{\mathcal{A}} \mid j \in V'\}, \{T_j^{\mathcal{A}} \mid j \in V'\}, \{r_j \mid j \in V'\} >$ and

(2) $\mathcal{B}$ **sat** $< \{I_j^{\mathcal{B}} \mid j \in V'\}, \{T_j^{\mathcal{B}} \mid j \in V'\}, \{q_j \mid j \in V'\} >$ are both satisfied.

Prove that the verification conditions (3) through (6) below are all satisfied. Then one is entitled to conclude that

$< \{p_i \mid i \in V'\}, V', Act^{\mathcal{A}} \cup Act^{\mathcal{B}} >$ **sat** $< \{I_j^{\mathcal{A}} \vee I_j^{\mathcal{B}} \mid j \in V'\}, \{I_j^{\mathcal{B}} \wedge T_j^{\mathcal{B}} \mid j \in V'\}, \{q_j \mid j \in V'\} >$

holds, i.e., the algorithm consisting of all actions of algorithm $\mathcal{A}$ and algorithm $\mathcal{B}$ is partially correct w.r.t. the precondition $\bigwedge_{j \in V'} p_j$ and postcondition $\bigwedge_{j \in V'} q_j$. Furthermore, for all computation sequences of the combined algorithm started in a state satisfying p_j for all j in V' the following is satisfied: $I_j^{\mathcal{A}} \vee I_j^{\mathcal{B}}$ continuously holds and node j completes its participation in the whole task iff $I_j^{\mathcal{B}} \wedge T_j^{\mathcal{B}}$ holds ($j \in V'$).

In the technical formulation of the verification conditions below, we have used the auxiliary predicate *disabled*(P, AC) for some state assertion P and for a certain set of actions AC. It expresses that if P holds, then all actions in AC are disabled. A formal definition of this predicate in Linear Temporal Logic is straightforward and therefore omitted.

The first condition below expresses that all assertions attached to a certain node j may not refer to variables which can be changed directly as a consequence of the execution of actions of other nodes.

(3) Each programming variable occurring in the assertions p_j, r_j, q_j, $I_j^{\mathcal{A}}$, $I_j^{\mathcal{B}}$, $T_j^{\mathcal{A}}$, and $T_j^{\mathcal{B}}$ is node j's own variable. In addition, if some proof variable $\rho_\ell(e)$ or $\sigma_\ell(e)$ occurs in any of these assertions, then $\ell = j$ and $e \in E_j$ hold.

The next two conditions, (4) and (5) below, express the following: if a certain node has not completed its participation in algorithm $\mathcal{A}$ or in algorithm $\mathcal{B}$, then it cannot perform any of its actions associated with $\mathcal{B}$ or $\mathcal{A}$, respectively.

(4) $\forall j \in V'.disabled(I_j^{\mathcal{A}} \wedge \neg T_j^{\mathcal{A}}, IS_j^{\mathcal{B}}) \wedge \forall j,k \in V'.\forall e \in E_{j,k}.disabled(I_j^{\mathcal{A}} \wedge \neg T_j^{\mathcal{A}}, Sen_k^{\mathcal{B}}(e))$

holds for all computation sequences of $\mathcal{A}$.

This condition states that if a certain node has not completed its participation in algorithm $\mathcal{A}$, then it can perform neither an internal action nor a send-action occurring in algorithm $\mathcal{B}$

(the first conjunct), and it cannot receive a message associated with algorithm $\mathcal{B}$ (the second conjunct). The latter is satisfied because if the node participates in algorithm $\mathcal{A}$, then it is required that none of its neighbors can send such messages.

Of course, we also require the mirror image of (g):

(5) $\forall j \in V'.disabled(I_j^{\mathcal{B}} \wedge \neg T_j^{\mathcal{B}}, IS_j^{\mathcal{A}}) \wedge \forall j,k \in V'.\forall e \in E_{j,k}.disabled(I_j^{\mathcal{B}} \wedge \neg T_j^{\mathcal{B}}, Sen_k^{\mathcal{A}}(e))$ holds for all computation sequences of $\mathcal{B}$.

We then require that each node which participates in both subtasks participates in the first subtask, i.e., the one solved by algorithm $\mathcal{A}$, before it participates in the second subtask, i.e., the one solved by algorithm $\mathcal{B}$. In order to ensure the latter condition we require that no node can participate in algorithm $\mathcal{A}$ when it has completed its participation in algorithm $\mathcal{B}$:

(6) $\forall j \in V'.disabled(I_j^{\mathcal{B}} \wedge T_j^{\mathcal{B}}, IS_j^{\mathcal{A}}) \wedge \forall j,k \in V'.\forall e \in E_{j,k}.disabled(I_j^{\mathcal{B}} \wedge T_j^{\mathcal{B}}, Sen_k^{\mathcal{A}}(e))$ holds for all computation sequences of $\mathcal{B}$.

If, in addition, one wants to prove that the algorithm solving the whole task always terminates, then it suffices to prove that both the algorithms $\mathcal{A}$ and $\mathcal{B}$ always terminate.

An algorithm $\mathcal{C} \in \{\mathcal{A}, \mathcal{B}\}$ as above terminates iff for all $j \in V'$, $\diamond(I_j^{\mathcal{C}} \wedge T_j^{\mathcal{C}})$ holds for all computation sequences of $\mathcal{C}$ started in a state satisfying $\mathcal{C}$'s precondition. Here, $\diamond$ denotes the eventual-operator from temporal logic.

4 Problem specification

We are interested in deriving by means of (formal) correctness preserving transformations a simple (distributed) broadcasting algorithm which satisfies the following requirement:

> Some value w initially recorded by a certain node $k \in V$ has to be supplied to all other nodes in V. Moreover, node k must be informed that each node in V different from k has received the value w and that all nodes have recorded this value.

For ease of exposition it is assumed that the network (V, E) constitutes a tree. In the sequel $Tree(V, E)$ will denote that (V, E) is a finite and undirected tree.

The (informal) requirement above is formalized by means of a precondition, a postcondition, and an invariant. In order to do so we introduce the following:

- Mutually distinct program variables val_j, $j \in V$. Variable val_j will be used by node j for recording the value w.

- A program variable $done_k$. This variable will be used by node k to record whether all nodes in the network have recorded the value w indeed.
- Mutually distinct program variables $queue_j$, $j \in V$. The variable $queue_j$ denotes node j's own message queue. It is used to buffer all received messages together with an identification of the edge along which the message has been received.
- Mutually distinct proof variables $\sigma_j(e)$ and $\rho_j(e)$ for nodes j in V and edges e in E_j. The variable $\sigma_j(e)$ records the sequence of all messages which have been transmitted by node j along edge e; the variable $\rho_j(e)$ records the sequence of all messages which have been received by node j along edge e, cf. section 3.

Initially, node k has recorded the value w, i.e., $val_k=w$ holds, whereas the initial values of the variables val_j for nodes j different from k are irrelevant. Furthermore, $\neg done_k$ holds initially, i.e., in the initial state node k has not recorded that all nodes in V have recorded the value w. In addition, we require that in the initial state all message queues are empty and that no node has sent nor received any messages along any of its adjacent edges. Denoting by ε both the empty message queue and the empty sequence of messages we, thus, require that initially $\forall j \in V.queue_j=\varepsilon \wedge \wedge$ $\forall j \in V.\forall e \in E_j.\big(\sigma_j(e)=\rho_j(e)=\varepsilon\big)$ is satisfied.

Altogether, the following *precondition* p is required:

$$Tree(V, E) \wedge k \in V \wedge val_k=w \wedge \neg done_k \wedge$$
$$\wedge \forall j \in V.queue_j = \varepsilon \wedge \forall j \in V.\forall e \in E_j.\big(\sigma_j(e) = \rho_j(e) = \varepsilon\big).$$

In any final state of the algorithm – still to be designed – all message queues should be empty. Also, all edges should be empty, i.e., in any final state the sequence of all messages transmitted by a certain node along any of its adjacent edges is the same as the sequence of all messages received by the node at the other end of that edge. In addition, each node j in V should have recorded the value w in its variable val_j and node k should have been informed that this has indeed occurred. This leads to the following *postcondition* q:

$$\forall j \in V.val_j=w \wedge done_k \wedge \forall j \in V.queue_j = \varepsilon \wedge \forall i,j \in V.\forall e \in E_{i,j}.\sigma_j(e) = \rho_i(e).$$

Furthermore, we require that whenever node k has concluded that all nodes in V have recorded the value w it is the case indeed that all these nodes have recorded this value. (This condition is, in fact, implicit in the above informal requirement.) The latter condition cannot be formulated in terms of a pre- and a postcondition, because it refers to *all possible states which can be reached during any execution of the algorithm* provided that such an execution is started in an initial state satisfying the precondition p defined above. Since, by assumption, we consider a *fixed* network (V, E), it follows that during execution of the algorithm $Tree(V, E)$ continuously holds. We therefore require that the following assertion I (an *invariant*) continuously holds during any execution of the algorithm started in a state satisfying p:

$$Tree(V, E) \wedge (done_k \Rightarrow \forall j \in V.val_j{=}w).$$

5 A derivation of a broadcasting protocol

In this section we derive by means of stepwise refinement a (distributed) algorithm which meets the requirement formulated in section 4. The main part of this derivation takes places on a level of sequential programming (cf. [BS89] and [CM88]).

5.1 An initial sequential solution

Ignoring the communication aspects occurring in the formal requirement formulated in section 4, it is quite straightforward to obtain, by means of a single global assignment, an algorithm for which the following holds:

Whenever execution is started in an initial state satisfying

$$p_0 \equiv Tree(V, E) \;\wedge\; k \in V \;\wedge\; val_k{=}w \;\wedge\; \neg done_k$$

then this execution is finite and every final state of the execution satisfies

$$q_0 \equiv \forall j \in V.val_j{=}w \;\wedge\; done_k.$$

Furthermore, during execution,

$$I_0 \equiv Tree(V, E) \wedge (done_k \;\Rightarrow\; \forall j \in V.val_j{=}w)$$

continuously holds.

Observe that the above requirement (slightly) differs from the one given in section 4: whereas the invariants I_0 and I (see section 4) are identical, the assertions p_0 and q_0 defined above are implied only by the assertions p and q (defined in section 4) respectively. Apart from the conditions imposed on the message queues and the sequence of transmitted and received messages, which can change only when communication occurs, the same requirements are described, however, by the assertions p_0 and p, and by the assertions q_0 and q.

One possible algorithm which is correct w.r.t. precondition p_0, postcondition q_0, and invariant I_0 consists of one atomic action assigning the values w to all variables val_j, $j \neq k$, and updating the variable $done_k$. Observe that there is no need to assign the value w to the variable val_k, since $val_k{=}w$ already holds in the initial state. The program describing this algorithm is shown below.

$$S_0 \equiv a : < \textbf{for all } j \in V\backslash\{k\} \textbf{ do } val_j \;:=\; w \textbf{ od}; done_k \;:=\; \textbf{true} > .$$

Lemma 5.1 The program S_0 is totally correct w.r.t. precondition p_0 and postcondition q_0. For every computation sequence of program S_0 the assertion I_0 continuously holds. (The program S_0 and the assertions p_0, q_0, and I_0 have been defined above.)

5.2 Refinement of the initial solution

The program S_0 is now refined into a program S_1 which consists of two atomic actions. The first action in S_1 assigns the value w to all variables val_j for nodes j different from k; the second action updates the variable $done_k$. More precisely, let the program S_1 be defined as follows:

$$S_1 \equiv a_1 : < \textbf{for all } j \in V \backslash \{k\} \textbf{ do } val_j := w \textbf{ od} >;$$
$$a_2 : < done_k := \textbf{true} >.$$

Then the following is satisfied:

Lemma 5.2 The program S_1 is a refinement of the program S_0 w.r.t. precondition p_0. For every computation sequence of program S_1 the assertion I_0 continuously holds. (The programs S_0 and S_1, and the assertions p_0 and I_0 have been defined above.)

As a consequence of lemma 5.2, the program S_1 satisfies the requirement formulated in section 5.1. The program S_1 solves the task described by the precondition p_0 and the postcondition q_0 in two stages: at the first stage the *first subtask* consisting of assigning the values w to the variables val_j for nodes j different from k is solved; thereafter the *second subtask* consisting of informing node k that all nodes in V have recorded the value w is solved. In the subsections 5.3 and 5.4 the first subtask and the second subtask are resolved respectively. The (distributed) algorithms thus obtained are combined into a single algorithm by applying the principle for sequentially phased reasoning described in section 3. This is the subject of section 5.5. The resulting algorithm satisfies the requirement formulated in section 5.1. One final step is then made to obtain an algorithm which satisfies the requirement formulated in section 4.
The program

$$S_2 \equiv \{p_0\}\ a_1 : < \textbf{for all } j \in V \backslash \{k\} \textbf{ do } val_j := w \textbf{ od} >;$$
$$\{p_1\}\ a_2 : < done_k := \textbf{true} >$$
$$\{q_0\},$$

where $p_1 \equiv Tree(V, E) \wedge k \in V \wedge \forall j \in V.val_j = w \wedge \neg done_k$ holds, is also (totally) correct w.r.t. precondition p_0 and postcondition q_0. Moreover, for every computation sequence of program S_2, I_0 continuously holds. (Observe that this is merely a consequence of the fact that the program S_2 has been obtained from the program S_1 by introducing context-information [LRG79], cf. also [B88].) Consequently, it follows that the program

$$a_1 : < \textbf{for all } j \in V \backslash \{k\} \textbf{ do } val_j := w \textbf{ od} >$$

is correct w.r.t. precondition p_0 and postcondition p_1. Since during execution of action a_1, apart from the assertion I_0, $\neg done_k$ continuously holds, provided that this execution is started in a state satisfying p_0, it is even the case that the assertion $Inv_0 \equiv Tree(V, E) \wedge k \in V \wedge \neg done_k$ is continuously satisfied for any execution of a_1 started in a state satisfying p_0.

5.3 Solving the first subtask

The action a_1 occurring in the program S_2 solves the first subtask consisting of supplying all nodes in V with the value w, cf. section 5.2, by assigning a single value, viz., w, *simultaneously* to all variables val_j for nodes j different from k. In this subsection this action will be operationalized.

As argued in the previous subsection we shall refine this action within the context of

precondition $p_0 \equiv Tree(V, E) \wedge k \in V \wedge val_k = w \wedge \neg done_k$,

postcondition $p_1 \equiv Tree(V, E) \wedge k \in V \wedge \forall j \in V.val_j = w \wedge \neg done_k$, and

invariant $Inv_0 \equiv Tree(V, E) \wedge k \in V \wedge \neg done_k$.

In order to obtain a more operational solution of action a_1 (cf. program S_2 above), a_1 will be refined by a program $\mathcal{A}_1$ in which the value w flows downwards the tree (V, E), when this tree is considered to be rooted at node k. This program is shown below. In that program the value w is first assigned to variables val_j for all neighbors j of node k. Thereafter, w is assigned to variables val_j for all nodes j at distance 2 from k. This process is continued until each node j in the network has recorded the value w in its variable val_j. Note that this process eventually terminates, since the tree (V, E) is finite.

In the program below, we have introduced fresh and mutually distinct boolean variables $start_j$ for nodes j in V. The variable $start_k$ is initialized to **true**, whereas the variables $start_j$, for all nodes $j \neq k$, are initialized to **false**. In general, the variable $start_j$, $j \in V$, is assigned the value **true** if node j has recorded the value w and it has not yet propagated w; otherwise, i.e., if node j has not recorded the value w or if j has recorded and propagated w to all nodes ℓ, $\ell \in V$, satisfying $dist(k,\ell) = dist(k,j)+1$, then $start_j$ is **false**. (Recall that $dist(i, j)$ denotes the distance between the nodes i and j, see section 2.) The refinement of action a_1 is the following:

$\mathcal{A}_1 \equiv <start_k := \mathbf{true}>; <\mathbf{for\ all}\ \ell \in V\backslash\{k\}\ \mathbf{do}\ start_\ell := \mathbf{false\ od}>;$
$\quad {}^*[\ \underset{j \in V}{\Box} <start_j \rightarrow \mathbf{for\ all}\ \ell \in V$ such that $dist(k,\ell) = dist(k,j)\ \mathbf{do}\ start_\ell := \mathbf{false}\ \mathbf{od};$
$\qquad \mathbf{for\ all}\ \ell \in V$ such that $dist(k,\ell) = dist(k,j)+1\ \mathbf{do}\ val_\ell := w;$
$\qquad\qquad start_\ell := \mathbf{true\ od}>].$

Lemma 5.3 Program $\mathcal{A}_1$ is a refinement of the action a_1 w.r.t. precondition p_0. For every computation sequence of $\mathcal{A}_1$ the assertion Inv_0 continuously holds. (Here the programs $\mathcal{A}_1$ and a_1, and the assertions p_0 and Inv_0 have been defined above.)

It follows from lemma 5.3 that the program $\mathcal{A}_1$ is totally correct w.r.t. precondition p_0 and postcondition p_1.

Observe that in any final state of the program $\mathcal{A}_1$, apart from the postcondition p_1, $\neg start_j$ holds for each node j in V, provided that execution of $\mathcal{A}_1$ is started in a state satisfying p_0. Also, observe that for every such computation sequence of program $\mathcal{A}_1$, apart from Inv_0, the following continuously holds: $val_k = w$.

Define $p_2 \equiv p_1 \wedge \forall j \in V. \neg start_j$, and define

$$Inv_1 \equiv Inv_0 \wedge val_k = w.$$

From the discussion above it then follows that the following is true:

Lemma 5.4 The program $\mathcal{A}_1$ is totally correct w.r.t. precondition p_0 and postcondition p_2. Moreover, for any computation sequence of the program $\mathcal{A}_1$ started in an state satisfying precondition p_0, Inv_1 continuously holds. ($\mathcal{A}_1$, p_0, p_2, and Inv_1 have been defined above.)

In each iteration of the loop occurring in the program $\mathcal{A}_1$ above the value w is assigned, by means of one atomic action, to variables val_j of nodes j all having the same distance from k. This implies that $\mathcal{A}_1$ is a rather deterministic program. In order to supply all nodes with the value w, observe that there is no need at all that nodes at the same distance from k record the value w simultaneously. In fact, it suffices that after recording the value w, each node supplies its neighbors downwards the tree with the value w, independently of nodes at the same distance from k as itself. Now, for each node j in V, node ℓ is some neighbor of j downwards the tree iff the following is satisfied: $dist(k,\ell) = dist(k,j)+1$ and there exists some edge adjacent to both ℓ and j. These ideas lead to the following program:

$$\begin{array}{l}\mathcal{A}_2 \equiv <start_k := \textbf{true}>; <\textbf{for all } \ell \in V \backslash \{k\} \textbf{ do } start_\ell := \textbf{false od}>; \\ \quad *[\underset{j \in V}{\Box} <start_j \rightarrow start_j := \textbf{false}; \\ \qquad\qquad \textbf{for all } \ell \in V \text{ such that } \exists e \in E_{\ell,j}.dist(k,\ell)=dist(k,j)+1 \\ \qquad\qquad \textbf{do } val_\ell := w;\ start_\ell := \textbf{true od}>].\end{array}$$

Lemma 5.5 Program $\mathcal{A}_2$ is a refinement of program $\mathcal{A}_1$ w.r.t. precondition p_0. For every computation sequence of the program $\mathcal{A}_2$, Inv_1 continuously holds. ($\mathcal{A}_2$, $\mathcal{A}_1$, p_0, and Inv_1 have been defined above.)

In the program $\mathcal{A}_2$ two distinct nodes at the same distance to k propagate the value independently of each other to their children. Two children of the same node, however, always record w simultaneously. This restriction is, obviously, not necessary at all: in order to solve the subtask considered here it is relevant only that the children of the same node *eventually* record the value w.

This observation is incorporated in the program $\mathcal{A}_3$ below, which refines program $\mathcal{A}_2$ w.r.t. precondition p_0. In $\mathcal{A}_3$ we have, in order to incorporate this observation and with an ultimate distributed program in mind which solves the subtask considered here, used:

(a) "messages" $info(val_j)$ for propagating the value identified by the variable val_j, and

(b) fresh and mutually distinct variables $\sigma_j(e)$, $\rho_j(e)$, and $queue_j$ for nodes j in V and edges $e \in E_j$.

The variables introduced in (b) above all record sequences of elements, see below, and are initialized in program $\mathcal{A}_3$ to the empty sequence.

- For $j \in V$ and $e \in E_j$, $\sigma_j(e)$ is the sequence of all "messages" (or pieces of information) that have been propagated by node j to the node at the other end of edge e from node j's point of view. (In the ultimate distributed solution of the subtask considered here variable $\sigma_j(e)$ records the sequence of all messages transmitted by node j along edge e, cf. also section 3. It will then play a role only as an auxiliary (proof) variable.)
- For $j \in V$ and $e \in E_j$, $\rho_j(e)$ is the sequence of all "messages" that have been propagated by the node at the other end of edge e to j from node j's point of view. (In the distributed solution of the subtask considered here variable $\rho_j(e)$ records the sequence of all messages received by node j along edge e, cf. also section 3. Analogous to the variable $\sigma_j(e)$, $\rho_j(e)$ will then play a role only as an auxiliary (proof) variable.)
- For $j \in V$, $queue_j$ records the sequence of all "messages" that have been propagated by some node i to node j which have not been processed yet by j together with an identification of the edge $e \in E_{i,j}$. (In the distributed solution of the subtask considered here, $queue_j$ will play the role of node j's message queue consisting of all messages received but not yet processed by j.)

The program $\mathcal{A}_3$ can now be described as follows: after initializing the variables $\rho_j(e)$, $\sigma_j(e)$, and $queue_j$ to the empty sequence for all nodes $j \in V$ and edges $e \in E_j$, node k propagates the value w, recorded by the variable val_k, to all its neighbors. This is achieved by appending the element $info(val_k)$ to the sequences identified by the variables $\sigma_k(e)$ for all edges $e \in E_k$. For nodes j different from k, j checks whether a message has been supplied by one of its neighbors. If this is the case, then for some node i and a certain edge $e \in E_{i,j}$, the sequence identified by $\rho_j(e)$ is a proper prefix of the sequence recorded by $\sigma_i(e)$. Below this is denoted by $\rho_j(e) \prec \sigma_i(e)$. Node j then appends the first element occurring in $\sigma_i(e)$ that has not yet been recorded by node j to the sequence identified by $\rho_j(e)$. Thereafter j records this element together with this element together with the identification of edge e in its queue $queue_j$. If node j's queue is non-empty, then the argument of the message at the front of the queue is recorded and the front element is removed from the queue. The value received is then recorded by node j and j propagates this value to all nodes downwards the tree by appending $info(val_j)$ to all sequences identified by $\sigma_j(e)$ for edges e which connect j with nodes downwards the tree.

Program $\mathcal{A}_3$ is shown below. Except for notation already introduced we use:

- $first(queue_j)$ to denote the first element of $queue_j$, provided $queue_j$ is non-empty,
- $rest(queue_j)$ to denote the remainder of $queue_j$ after removing the first element from $queue_j$, provided $queue_j$ is non-empty,
- $|s|$ to denote the length of sequence s, i.e., the number of all elements constituting s,
- $s[n]$ to denote the nth element in the sequence s, provided $1 \leq n \leq |s|$ holds, and
- $s\hat{\ }x$ to denote the result of appending element x to the end of the sequence s.

Elements in $queue_j$, $j \in V$, are tuples $<t(arg), e>$, see above, where e denotes an identification of a certain edge adjacent to node j, and where $t(arg)$ is some message consisting of an argument $arg = argpart(<t(arg), e>)$ and of a message-type $t = type(<t(arg), e>)$. (The type of any message in the program $\mathcal{A}_3$ is always the same as *info*. In section 5.4 we will see another kind of message-type.) Concluding the list of notation, we have also used $D_j(e)$, $j \in V$, $e \in E_j$, to denote the distance from node k to the node which differs from j and which is adjacent to edge e. Thus, $D_j(e) = n$ holds iff there exists some node $i \neq j$ such that $e \in E_{i,j}$ and $dist(k, i) = n$ are satisfied (for natural numbers n).

$$
\begin{array}{l}
\mathcal{A}_3 \equiv <\textbf{for all } \ell \in V, e \in E_\ell \textbf{ do } \sigma_\ell(e) := \varepsilon;\ \rho_\ell(e) := \varepsilon \textbf{ od}>;\ <\textbf{for all } \ell \in V \textbf{ do } queue_\ell := \varepsilon>; \\
\quad <start_k := \textbf{true}>;\ <\textbf{for all } \ell \in V \backslash \{k\} \textbf{ do } start_\ell := \textbf{false od}>; \\
\quad *[\ \square_{j \in V} <start_j \rightarrow start_j := \textbf{false}; \\
\qquad\qquad \textbf{for all } e \in E_j \text{ such that } D_j(e) = dist(k,j)+1 \textbf{ do } \sigma_j(e) := \sigma_j(e)\hat{\ }info(val_j) \textbf{ od}> \\
\quad\ \square_{i,j \in V, e \in E_{i,j}} <\rho_j(e) \prec \sigma_i(e) \rightarrow \rho_j(e) := \rho_j(e)\hat{\ }(\sigma_i(e)[|\rho_j(e)|+1]); \\
\qquad\qquad\qquad queue_j := queue_j\hat{\ }(\rho_j(e)[|\rho_j(e)|], e)> \\
\quad\ \square_{j \in V} < queue_j \neq \varepsilon \wedge type\big(first(queue_j)\big) = info \rightarrow val_j := argpart\big(first(queue_j)\big); \\
\qquad\qquad\qquad\qquad queue_j := rest(queue_j); \\
\qquad\qquad\qquad\qquad start_j := \textbf{true}> \\
\quad].
\end{array}
$$

We have the following:

Lemma 5.6 The program $\mathcal{A}_3$ is a refinement of the program $\mathcal{A}_2$ w.r.t. precondition p_0. Furthermore, the assertion Inv_1 continuously holds for every computation sequence of program $\mathcal{A}_3$. (The programs $\mathcal{A}_3$ and $\mathcal{A}_2$, and the assertions p_0 and Inv_1 have been defined above.)

From lemma 5.6 we conclude that the program $\mathcal{A}_3$ is totally correct w.r.t. precondition p_0, postcondition p_2. (The assertion p_2 has been defined above.)

We can even strengthen the postcondition p_2 of the program $\mathcal{A}_3$ above. This is the subject of the following:

Lemma 5.7 Define the assertion p_3 as the conjunction of

- p_2 (defined above),
- $\forall j \in V.queue_j = \varepsilon$ (all message queues are empty),
- $\forall e \in E_k.\sigma_k(e) = <(info(w)>$ (node k has transmitted exactly one message $info(w)$ along each of its adjacent edges),
- $\forall e \in E_k.\rho_k(e) = \varepsilon$ (node k has not received any message along each of its adjacent edges),
- $\forall j \in V\backslash\{k\}.\forall e \in E_j.\big(D_j(e) = dist(k,j)-1 \Rightarrow (\rho_j(e) = <info(w)> \wedge \sigma_j(e) = \varepsilon)\big)$ (for nodes j different from k, j has received a message $info(w)$ along the edge connecting j with its father, whereas j has not sent any messages along this edge), and
- $\forall j \in V\backslash\{k\}.\forall e \in E_j.\big(D_j(e) \neq dist(k,j)-1 \Rightarrow (\rho_j(e) = \varepsilon \wedge \sigma_j(e) = info(w))\big)$ (for nodes j different from k, j has not received any messages from nodes downwards the tree, whereas it has sent a message $info(w)$ to all such nodes).

Then the program $\mathcal{A}_3$ above is totally correct w.r.t. precondition p_0 and postcondition p_3.

The program $\mathcal{A}_3$ above cannot be represented immediately by a distributed program, since this would imply that the nodes in V would have global knowledge about the tree's topology in order to determine along which edges the *info*-message has to be transmitted. Such messages are always transmitted by a certain node in V along its adjacent edges which lead to nodes downwards the tree.

In order to solve this problem, observe that all node k's adjacent edges lead to nodes downwards the tree. Also observe that whenever a node different from k transmits the *info*-messages to nodes downwards the tree it has received such a message from its father. In order to record the edge along which this node has received the message, we have introduced in the program below fresh and mutually distinct variables $inbranch_j$ for nodes j different from k. In addition, we have also introduced boolean variables $N_j(e)$, again fresh and mutually distinct, for nodes $j \in V$ and edges $e \in E_j$. Variable $N_j(e)$ is used by node j for recording whether it has received any message along edge e. More precisely, if $N_j(e)$ holds then node j has recorded that it has received some message along the edge identified by e. The latter variables could have been omitted at this stage of the development; their relevance will become clear in section 5.4.

The program $\mathcal{A}_4$ in which the above ideas have been incorporated is shown below. Recall that elements recorded in the queue $queue_j$ are tuples of the form $(t(arg), e)$, where e is some identification of a certain edge adjacent to node j. In the program below, $chan(t(arg), e)$ denotes the edge-identification of the element $(t(arg), e)$, i.e., $chan(t(arg), e)=e$ holds.

$\mathcal{A}_4 \equiv$

$$\left.\begin{array}{l} <\textbf{for all } \ell \in V, e \in E_\ell \textbf{ do } \sigma_\ell(e) := \varepsilon;\ \rho_\ell(e) := \varepsilon \textbf{ od} >; <\textbf{for all } \ell \in V \textbf{ do } queue_\ell := \varepsilon >; \\ < start_k := \textbf{true} >; <\textbf{for all } \ell \in V\backslash\{k\} \textbf{ do } start_\ell := \textbf{false od} >; \\ <\textbf{for all } \ell \in V, e \in E_\ell \textbf{ do } N_\ell(e) := \textbf{false od} >; \end{array}\right\} Init$$

$$\begin{array}{l} *[\square < start_k \rightarrow start_k := \textbf{false};\ \textbf{for all } e \in E_k \textbf{ do } \sigma_k(e) := \sigma_k(e)\hat{\ } info(val_k) \textbf{ od}>; \\ \underset{j \in V\backslash\{k\}}{\square} <start_j \rightarrow start_j := \textbf{false}; \\ \qquad\qquad \textbf{for all } e \in E_j \text{ such that } e \neq inbranch_j \textbf{ do } \sigma_j(e) := \sigma_j(e)\hat{\ } info(val_j) \textbf{ od}> \\ \underset{j \in V\backslash\{k\}, i \in V, e \in E_{i,j}}{\square} <\rho_j(e) \prec \sigma_i(e) \rightarrow \rho_j(e) := \rho_j(e)\hat{\ }(\sigma_i(e)[|\rho_j(e)|+1]); \\ \qquad\qquad queue_j := queue_j\hat{\ }(\rho_j(e)[|\rho_j(e)|], e)> \\ \underset{j \in V\backslash\{k\}}{\square} < queue_j \neq \varepsilon \wedge type(first(queue_j)) = info \rightarrow val_j := argpart(first(queue_j)); \\ \qquad\qquad inbranch_j := chan(first(queue_j)); \\ \qquad\qquad N_j(inbranch_j) := \textbf{true}; \\ \qquad\qquad queue_j := rest(queue_j); \\ \qquad\qquad start_j := \textbf{true}> \\ ]. \end{array}$$

Lemma 5.8 The program $\mathcal{A}_4$ is a refinement of the program $\mathcal{A}_3$ w.r.t precondition p_0. For every computation sequence of program $\mathcal{A}_4$, the assertion Inv_1 continuously holds. (The programs $\mathcal{A}_4$ and $\mathcal{A}_3$, and the assertions p_0 and Inv_1 have been defined above.)

It follows from lemma 5.8 that the program $\mathcal{A}_4$ is totally correct w.r.t. precondition p_0 and postcondition p_3.

Note the the program segment labeled *Init* in the program $\mathcal{A}_4$ merely assigns an initial value to the variables $\sigma_j(e)$, $\rho_j(e)$, $queue_j$, $N_j(e)$ (for all nodes $j \in V$ and edges $e \in E_j$), and variables $start_j$ for nodes j in V. Also note that during the execution of the program $\mathcal{A}_4$ each of the actions occurring in the segment *Init* is performed exactly once. Instead of initializing these variables during the execution of the program $\mathcal{A}_4$, one can eliminate this initialization segment and include the effect of this segment in the (resulting) program's precondition. The underlying transformation principle is a consequence of repeated application of the following: Let $\overline{x} := \overline{a}$ denote the multiple assignment of a vector of values $\overline{a}$ to a vector of variables $\overline{x}$. If the program $\overline{x} := \overline{a}; S$ is totally correct w.r.t. precondition *pre* and postcondition *post*, and if the assertion *pre* does not refer to any of the variables occurring in the vector $\overline{x}$, then the program P_2 is totally correct w.r.t. precondition $pre \wedge \overline{x} = \overline{a}$ and postcondition *post*.

Now, eliminating the program segment labeled *Init* from program $\mathcal{A}_4$ above yields program $\mathcal{A}_5$ defined below:

$$
\begin{aligned}
\mathcal{A}_5 \equiv *[\Box\ & \langle start_k \rightarrow start_k := \mathbf{false};\ \mathbf{for\ all}\ e \in E_k\ \mathbf{do}\ \sigma_k(e) := \sigma_k(e)\hat{\ } info(val_k)\ \mathbf{od} \rangle \\
\underset{j \in V \setminus \{k\}}{\Box}\ & \langle start_j \rightarrow start_j := \mathbf{false}; \\
& \quad \mathbf{for\ all}\ e \in E_j\ \text{such that}\ e \neq inbranch_j\ \mathbf{do}\ \sigma_j(e) := \sigma_j(e)\hat{\ } info(val_j)\ \mathbf{od} \rangle \\
\underset{j \in V \setminus \{k\}, i \in V, e \in E_{i,j}}{\Box}\ & \langle \rho_j(e) \prec \sigma_i(e) \rightarrow \rho_j(e) := \rho_j(e)\hat{\ }(\sigma_i(e)[|\rho_j(e)|+1]); \\
& \quad queue_j := queue_j\hat{\ }(\rho_j(e)[|\rho_j(e)|], e) \rangle \\
\underset{j \in V}{\Box}\ & \langle queue_j \neq \varepsilon \wedge type(first(queue_j)) = info \rightarrow val_j := argpart(first(queue_j)); \\
& \quad inbranch_j := chan(first(queue_j)); \\
& \quad N_j(inbranch_j) := \mathbf{true}; \\
& \quad queue_j := rest(queue_j); \\
& \quad start_j := \mathbf{true} \rangle \\
].
\end{aligned}
$$

Define the assertion pre_4 to be the conjunction of program $\mathcal{A}_4$'s precondition p_0, defined above, and the result of executing the program segment labeled *Init* in $prog_4$. More precisely, let pre_4 be the conjunction of

- p_0
- $\forall j \in V. \forall e \in E_j. \big(\sigma_j(e) = \rho_j(e) = \varepsilon\big)$ (no node in V has transmitted nor received any messages along any of its adjacent edges),
- $\forall j \in V \forall e \in E_j. \neg N_j(e)$ (no node in V has recorded that it has received some message along any of its adjacent edges),
- $\forall j \in V. queue_j = \varepsilon$ (all message queues are empty), and
- $start_k \wedge \forall j \in V \setminus \{k\}. \neg start_j$.

By application of the above-mentioned transformation principle, it follows that the following is true:

Lemma 5.9 Program $\mathcal{A}_5$ is totally correct w.r.t. precondition pre_4 and postcondition p_3. For every computation sequence of $\mathcal{A}_5$ started in a state satisfying the precondition pre_4, the assertion Inv_1 continuously holds. ($\mathcal{A}_5$, pre_4, p_3, and Inv_1 have been defined above.)

We can be even more precise about the invariant which holds during execution of the program $\mathcal{A}_5$ when this execution is started in a state satisfying the precondition pre_4. This is the subject of

Lemma 5.10 Define the assertion Inv_2 to be the conjunction of

- Inv_1 (see above),
- $queue_k = \varepsilon$ (node k's queue is empty),
- $\forall e \in E_k. \big(\rho_k(e) = \varepsilon \wedge \neg N_k(e)\big)$ (node k does not receive any messages),

- $\forall j \in V\backslash\{k\}.\forall e \in E_j.\big((D_j(e)=dist(k,j)-1 \Rightarrow \sigma_j(e)=\varepsilon) \wedge (D_j(e)=dist(k,j)+1 \Rightarrow \rho_j(e)=\varepsilon)\big)$ (Each node j different from k will not transmit any messages to nodes upwards the tree and j will not receive any messages from nodes downwards the tree),

- $\forall j \in V\backslash\{k\}.$
$\big(queue_j = \varepsilon \vee \exists e \in E_j.(queue_j = <info(w), e> \wedge \rho_j(e)=<info(w)> \wedge D_j(e)=dist(k,j)-1)\big)$
(node j's queue, $j \neq k$, is empty or it contains a message $info(w)$ that has been received along a certain edge adjacent to j and adjacent to some node upwards the tree),

- the disjunction of
  - $start_k \wedge \forall e \in E_k.\sigma_k(e) = \varepsilon$ ($start_k$ holds and node k has not transmitted any messages) and
  - $\neg start_k \wedge \forall e \in E_k.\sigma_k(e) = <info(w)>$ ($\neg start_k$ holds and node k has transmitted a message $info(w)$ along each of its adjacent edges), and

- the disjunction of, for each node j different from k,
  - $\forall e \in E_j.(\sigma_j(e)=\rho_j(e)=\varepsilon) \wedge \forall e \in E_j.\neg N_j(e) \wedge \neg start_j \wedge queue_j=\varepsilon$ (satisfied initially),
  - $\exists e \in E_j.(\rho_j(e)=<info(w)> \wedge D_j(e)=dist(k,j)-1 \wedge queue_j=<info(w), e>) \wedge$
    $\wedge \forall e \in E_j.\sigma_j(e) = \varepsilon \wedge \forall e \in E_j.\neg N_j(e) \wedge \neg start_j$ (satisfied after node j has received an *info*-message),
  - $\exists e \in E_j.(\rho_j(e)=<info(w)> \wedge D_j(e)=dist(k,j)-1 \wedge N_j(e) \wedge inbranch_j = e) \wedge$
    $\wedge \forall e \in E_j.\sigma_j(e) = \varepsilon \wedge \forall e \in E_j.(e \neq inbranch_j \Rightarrow \neg N_j(e))\wedge$
    $\wedge\ start_j \wedge val_j=w \wedge queue_j = \varepsilon$ (satisfied after node j has removed the *info*-message from its queue),
  - $\exists e \in E_j.(\rho_j(e)=<info(w)> \wedge D_j(e)=dist(k,j)-1 \wedge N_j(e) \wedge inbranch_j = e) \wedge$
    $\wedge \forall e \in E_j.(e \neq inbranch_j \Rightarrow \sigma_j(e) = <info(w)>) \wedge$
    $\wedge \forall e \in E_j.(e \neq inbranch_j \Rightarrow \neg N_j(e)) \wedge$
    $\wedge \neg start_j \wedge val_j=w \wedge queue_j = \varepsilon$ (satisfied after node j has propagated the *info*-message to all nodes downwards the tree).

Then the assertion Inv_2 continuously holds during execution of program $\mathcal{A}_5$ provided that this execution is started in an initial state satisfying the precondition pre_4.

The sequential program $\mathcal{A}_5$ above can now be represented by a distributed program. In order to do so, we *first* introduce do-loops for each node j in V consisting of all those actions in the sequential program whose execution can change j's variables only. As such, node k will then execute the loop $*[<start_k \rightarrow start_k :=$**false**; **for all** $e \in E_j$ **do** $\sigma_k(e) := \sigma_k(e)\hat{\ }info(val_k)>]$, whereas each node j different from k will execute the loop

$*[\Box <start_j \rightarrow start_j := \mathbf{false};$

$\quad \mathbf{for\ all}\ e \in E_j$ such that $e \neq inbranch_j\ \mathbf{do}\ \sigma_j(e) := \sigma_j(e)\hat{\ }info(val_j)\ \mathbf{od}>$

$\Box_{i \in V, e \in E_{i,j}} <\rho_j(e) \prec \sigma_i(e) \rightarrow \rho_j(e) := \rho_j(e)\hat{\ }(\sigma_i(e)[|\rho_j(e)|+1]);$

$\quad queue_j := queue_j\hat{\ }(\rho_j(e)[|\rho_j(e)|], e)>$

$\Box < queue_j \neq \varepsilon \wedge type(first(queue_j)) = info \rightarrow val_j := argpart(first(queue_j));$

$\quad inbranch_j := chan(first(queue_j));$

$\quad N_j(inbranch_j) := \mathbf{true};$

$\quad queue_j := rest(queue_j);$

$\quad start_j := \mathbf{true}>$

].

Thereafter, in the loop associated with node j each occurrence of the assignment $\sigma_j(e) := \sigma_j(e)\hat{\ }info(val_j)$ is replaced by the action **send** $info(val_j)$ along **edge** e. This is done for each node j in V. The motivation behind this transformation is that, from a verification's point of view, see [SS84], the effect of these two actions (performed by node j) is the same. By a similar kind of reasoning this also motivates the replacement performed *next*: for each node j in V, replace in the loop executed by j the action of receiving a message and buffering this message in node j's queue, which is guarded by the test $\rho_j(e) \prec \sigma_i(e)$ for some node i, i.e., the action $<\rho_j(e) \prec \sigma_i(e) \rightarrow \rho_j(e) := \rho_j(e)\hat{\ }(\sigma_i(e)[|\rho_j(e)|+1]);\ queue_j := queue_j\hat{\ }(\rho_j(e)[|\rho_j(e)|])>$, by the action $<$**receive** M_j along **edge** $e \rightarrow queue_j := queue_j\hat{\ }(M_j, e)>$. Here i denotes some node in V and M_j denotes some fresh variable for recording the received messages (by node j).

Finally, the parallel compositions of all the do-loops thus obtained is the distributed counterpart of the sequential program. Hereafter, $\mathcal{A}$ will denote this parallel composition. For node k, this loop is the following: $*[<start_k \rightarrow start_k := \mathbf{false};$ **for all** $e \in E_j$ **do send** $info(val_k)$ along **edge** $e>]$. The loop executed by a certain node j different from k is the following:

$*[\Box <start_j \rightarrow start_j := \mathbf{false};$

$\quad \mathbf{for\ all}\ e \in E_j$ such that $e \neq inbranch_j$ **do send** $info(val_j)$ along edge e **od**$>$;

$\Box_{e \in E_j} <$**receive** M_j along **edge** $e \rightarrow queue_j := queue_j\hat{\ }(M_j, e)>$

$\Box < queue_j \neq \varepsilon \wedge type(first(queue_j)) = info \rightarrow val_j := argpart(first(queue_j));$

$\quad inbranch_j := chan(first(queue_j));$

$\quad N_j(inbranch_j) := \mathbf{true};$

$\quad queue_j := rest(queue_j);$

$\quad start_j := \mathbf{true}>$

].

We have

Lemma 5.11 The distributed program $\mathcal{A}$ consisting of the loops defined above is totally correct w.r.t. precondition pre_4 and postcondition p_3. Furthermore, for every computation sequence of this program the assertion Inv_2 continuously holds. (The assertions pre_4, p_3, and Inv_2 have been defined above.

Note that the precondition pre_4 differs from the assertion p defined in section 2, because pre_4 restricts the variables $start_j$ for nodes j in V, whereas p does not refer to these variables at all. We do not consider this problem at this stage. Finding a program which is correct w.r.t. the specification in section 4 is postponed to section 5.5.

From lemma 5.11, it follows that the distributed program $\mathcal{A}$ is totally correct w.r.t. precondition pre_4 and postcondition p_3. Furthermore, the assertions $I_j^{\mathcal{A}}$, $j \in V$, defined in the lemma below continuously hold for each computation sequence of this program provided that this computation is started in a state satisfying the precondition p. The assertions $I_j^{\mathcal{A}}$, $j \in V$, are obtained from the assertion Inv_2. In order to be complete, cf. section 3, we have also described each node's own precondition p_j and postcondition r_j. They are both obtained by "distributing" the assertions pre_4 and p_3 amongst all nodes in V.

Lemma 5.12 Let p_k be defined by $Tree(V, E) \wedge k \in V \wedge val_k{=}w \wedge \neg done_k \wedge start_k \wedge$ $\wedge\ queue_k{=}\varepsilon \wedge \forall e \in E_k.(\sigma_k(e){=}\rho_k(e){=}\varepsilon) \wedge \forall e \in E_k.\neg N_k(e)$. Define for nodes j different from k, $p_j \equiv Tree(V, E) \wedge queue_j{=}\varepsilon \wedge \forall e \in E_j.(\sigma_j(e){=}\rho_j(e){=}\varepsilon) \wedge \neg start_j \wedge \forall e \in E_j.\neg N_j(e)$.

The assertion $I_k^{\mathcal{A}}$ is the conjunction of

- $Tree(V, E) \wedge k \in V \wedge val_k{=}w \wedge \neg done_k \wedge queue_k{=}\varepsilon \wedge \forall e \in E_k.(\rho_k(e){=}\varepsilon) \wedge$ $\wedge\ \forall e \in E_k.\neg N_k(e)$
- and the disjunction of
  - $start_k \wedge \forall e \in E_k.\sigma_k(e) = \varepsilon$ and
  - $\neg start_k \wedge \forall e \in E_k.\sigma_k(e){=}{<}info(w){>}$.

The assertion $T_k^{\mathcal{A}}$, nodes termination condition for the first subtask, is defined by $T_k^{\mathcal{A}} \equiv \neg start_k$. It holds after node k has broadcasted the *info*-message to all its neighbors.

For nodes j different from k, the assertion $I_j^{\mathcal{A}}$ is the conjunction of

- $Tree(V, E)$,
- $\forall e \in E_j.\big((D_j(e){=}dist(k,j){-}1 \Rightarrow \sigma_j(e){=}\varepsilon) \wedge (D_j(e){=}dist(k,j){+}1 \Rightarrow \rho_j(e){=}\varepsilon)\big)$,
- $queue_j = \varepsilon\ \vee$ $\vee\ \exists e \in E_j.(queue_j = {<}info(w), e{>} \wedge \rho_j(e){=}{<}info(w){>} \wedge D_j(e){=}dist(k,j){-}1)$,
- the disjunction of
  - $\forall e \in E_j.(\sigma_j(e){=}\rho_j(e){=}\varepsilon) \wedge \forall e \in E_j.\neg N_j(e) \wedge \neg start_j \wedge queue_j{=}\varepsilon$,
  - $\exists e \in E_j.(\rho_j(e){=}{<}info(w){>} \wedge D_j(e){=}dist(k,j){-}1 \wedge queue_j{=}{<}info(w), e{>}) \wedge$ $\wedge\ \forall e \in E_j.\sigma_j(e) = \varepsilon \wedge \forall e \in E_j.\neg N_j(e) \wedge \neg start_j$,

- $\exists e \in E_j.(\rho_j(e)=<info(w)> \wedge D_j(e)=dist(k,j)-1 \wedge N_j(e) \wedge inbranch_j = e) \wedge$
  $\wedge \forall e \in E_j.\sigma_j(e) = \varepsilon \wedge \forall e \in E_j.(e \neq inbranch_j \Rightarrow \neg N_j(e)) \wedge$
  $\wedge\ start_j \wedge val_j=w \wedge queue_j = \varepsilon,$
- $\exists e \in E_j.(\rho_j(e)=<info(w)> \wedge D_j(e)=dist(k,j)-1 \wedge N_j(e) \wedge inbranch_j = e) \wedge$
  $\wedge \forall e \in E_j.(e \neq inbranch_j \Rightarrow \sigma_j(e) =<info(w)>) \wedge$
  $\wedge \forall e \in E_j.(e \neq inbranch_j \Rightarrow \neg N_j(e)) \wedge$
  $\wedge \neg start_j \wedge val_j=w \wedge queue_j = \varepsilon.$

The assertion $T_j^{\mathcal{A}}$, node j's termination condition for the first subtask, for nodes j different from k, is defined by $T_j^{\mathcal{A}} \equiv \neg start_j \wedge queue_j=\varepsilon \wedge \exists e \in E_j.\rho_j(e) \neq \varepsilon$, which holds after node j has sent *info*-messages to all nodes downwards the tree.

The postconditions r_j for nodes j in V is defined as follows:

$r_k \equiv Tree(V, E) \wedge k \in V \wedge val_k=w \wedge \neg done_k \wedge \neg start_k \wedge queue_k = \varepsilon$
$\wedge \forall e \in E_k.\neg N_k(e)$, and the disjunction of
$\wedge \forall e \in E_k.(\rho_k(e)=\varepsilon) \wedge$
$\wedge \forall e \in E_k.\sigma_k(e)=<info(w)>$, and for nodes j different from node k
$r_j \equiv Tree(V, E) \wedge val_j=w \wedge \neg start_j \wedge queue_j = \varepsilon \wedge$
$\wedge \exists e \in E_j.(\sigma_j(e)=\varepsilon \wedge \rho_j(e)=<info(w)> \wedge D_j(e)=dist(k,j)-1 \wedge e=inbranch_j \wedge N_j(e)) \wedge$
$\wedge \forall e \in E_j.(e \neq inbranch_j \Rightarrow (\rho_j(e)=\varepsilon \wedge \neg N_j(e) \wedge \sigma_j(e)=<info(w)>)).$

For the program $\mathcal{A}$ above, if it is always executed in an initial state satisfying each of the preconditions p_j above, $j \in V$,
$\mathcal{A}$ **sat** $<\{I_j^{\mathcal{A}} \mid j \in V\}, \{T_j^{\mathcal{A}} \mid j \in V\}, \{r_j^{\mathcal{A}} \mid j \in V\}>$ holds.

Proof: We have to show that the conditions (a) through (f) formulated in section 3 all hold for program $\mathcal{A}$. Verifying these conditions is straightforward and can be accomplished, e.g., by the techniques described in [MP83] and [SS84].

As an example of how one could prove the conditions (a) through (f), we shall show that condition (e) is satisfied, i.e., we show that

$$\forall j \in V.\Box((I_j^{\mathcal{A}} \wedge \neg T_j^{\mathcal{A}}) \Rightarrow (\exists j' \in V.\exists a \in IS_{j'}.en(a)) \vee$$
$$\vee (\exists j', j'' \in V.\exists e \in E_{j',j''}.\ \rho_{j'}(e) \prec \sigma_{j''}(e)))$$

holds for program $\mathcal{A}$. That is, it is shown that whenever a certain node in V has not yet completed its participation in the first subtask, then at least one node in V can perform an action associated with this subtask.

In the proof below it is assumed that the conditions (a) and (b), see section 3 have already been proved to hold for program $\mathcal{A}$. That is,

- initially the assertions $I_j^{\mathcal{A}}$ hold for all nodes in V, and the sequence of all messages received by a certain node along one of its adjacent edges is a prefix of the sequence of all messages transmitted by the node at the other end of that edge, and
- for each node j, $I_j^{\mathcal{A}} \wedge \neg T_j^{\mathcal{A}}$ until $I_j^{\mathcal{A}} \wedge T_j^{\mathcal{A}}$ holds.

In order to establish condition (e), we must prove the following:

(*) If $I_j^{\mathcal{A}} \wedge \neg T_j^{\mathcal{A}}$ holds for a certain node j in V, then there exists some node j' for which at least one action is enabled.

We shall show, by induction on $dist(k,j)$, $j \in V$, that the following is satisfied:

(**) If $I_j^{\mathcal{A}} \wedge \neg T_j^{\mathcal{A}}$ holds for a certain node j in V, then there exists some node j' satisfying $dist(k,j') \leq dist(k,j)$ for which at least one action in the program $\mathcal{A}$ is enabled.

This, obviously, proves property (*), because (**) implies (*).

Basis of induction: $dist(k,j)=0$ holds. Thus, $k=j$ holds, too. Obviously, property (**) is satisfied in this case.

Induction hypothesis; for all nodes j, if $I_j^{\mathcal{A}} \wedge \neg T_j^{\mathcal{A}}$ holds and $dist(k,j)=n$ is satisfied for a certain natural number n, then there exists some node j' satisfying $dist(k,j') \leq n$ for which at least one action in the program $\mathcal{A}$ is enabled.

Induction step: Assume that j is some node for which $dist(k,j)=n+1$ holds ($n \geq 0$). Consequently, $j \neq k$ holds, too. Assume, furthermore, that $I_j^{\mathcal{A}} \wedge \neg T_j^{\mathcal{A}}$ is satisfied. Recall that $T_j^{\mathcal{A}}$ has been defined as $T_j^{\mathcal{A}} \equiv \neg start_j \wedge queue_j = \varepsilon \wedge \exists e \in E_j . \rho_j(e) \neq \varepsilon$. Therefore, $I_j^{\mathcal{A}} \wedge \neg T_j^{\mathcal{A}}$ implies that one of the following is satisfied:

- $start_j$, in which case node j can obviously one of its own actions,
- $queue_j = \varepsilon$, in which case the invariant $I_j^{\mathcal{A}}$ implies that node j's message queue contains an *info*-message, and that node j can perform the action of removing this message from its queue, or
- for all $e \in E_j$, $\rho_j(e) = \varepsilon$. In this case we reason as follows: There exists some node $\ell \in V$ adjacent to node j such that ℓ is upwards the tree. More precisely, there exist some node ℓ and an edge $e' \in E_{j,\ell}$ such that $D_j(e') = dist(k,j) - 1$ holds. Since $\rho_j(e') \preceq \sigma_\ell(e')$ is an invariant for the program $\mathcal{A}$, it follows that $\sigma_\ell(e') = \varepsilon \vee \sigma_\ell(e') = \langle info(w) \rangle$ is satisfied. Therefore, node j can perform the action of receiving a message or $\sigma_\ell(e') = \varepsilon$ holds. From the invariant $I_\ell^{\mathcal{A}}$ we then obtain that $\neg T_j^{\mathcal{A}}$ holds. (**) above now follows from the induction hypothesis and the fact that $dist(k,\ell) < dist(k,j)$ is satisfied. This proves property (e).

5.4 Solving the second subtask

In this subsection the second subtask (cf. section 5.2), consisting of reporting that all nodes in the network have recorded the value w, is solved by means of a distributed program.
This amounts to deriving a distributed program in which node k assigns the value **true** to its own variable $done_k$ after k has been informed that all nodes in V have recorded the value w indeed. Now, the formal derivation of such a program can be established in essentially the same way as program $\mathcal{A}$ has been derived in the previous subsection. Therefore, we omit this derivation and merely discuss the result, i.e., we discuss the distributed program that solves the subtask considered here and that could have been obtained by means of transformations. This program is totally correct w.r.t. a precondition which is the postcondition of the program solving the first subtask (cf. lemma 5.12) and the postcondition of the whole task (cf. section 4).

The description of the above-mentioned program is the subject of the following: A node j different from k which has recorded that it has received messages along any of its adjacent edges informs its father in the tree that j itself has recorded the value w. In order to do so, node j sends a message *ack* to the node upwards the tree. As such, *ack*-messages propagates upwards the tree. A node receiving such a message along a certain edge may conclude that its son adjacent to this edge and all the nodes in this son's subtree have recorded the value w indeed. At this stage, the relevance of the variables $N_j(e)$, for nodes $j \in V$ and edges $e \in E_j$, introduced in section 5.3 becomes clear: the are used by node j to record whether a message, either of type *info* or of type *ack*, has been received along edge e. (Cf. the program below).
After node k has received a message along each of its adjacent edges, it records that all other nodes in V have received and recorded the value w. This is true because each node j different from k has transmitted an *ack*-message upwards the tree to inform other nodes that it has recorded the value w.

Formally, the program $\mathcal{B}$ which solves the subtask considered here is the parallel composition of the loops shown below:

Node k executes the loop

$*[<\neg start_k \wedge \neg done_k \wedge \forall e \in E_k.N_k(e) \rightarrow done_k := \mathbf{true}>$

$\quad \underset{e \in E_k}{\Box} <\mathbf{receive}\ M_k \text{ along } \mathbf{edge}\ e \rightarrow queue_k := queue_k\hat{\ }(M_k, e)>$

$\quad \Box <queue_k \neq \varepsilon \wedge type(first(queue_k)) = ack \rightarrow N_k(chan(first(queue_k))) := \mathbf{true};$
$\qquad queue_k := rest(queue_k) >].$

Node j different from k executes the loop

$*[< \neg start_j \wedge \forall e \in E_j.N_j(e) \rightarrow \mathbf{for\ all\ edges}\ e \in E_j\ \mathbf{do}\ N_j(e) := \mathbf{false\ od};$

$$\begin{aligned}
&\qquad\qquad\textbf{send } ack \textbf{ along edge } inbranch_j>\\
&\mathop{\Box}_{e \in E_j} <\textbf{receive } M_j \textbf{ along edge } e \rightarrow queue_j := queue_j\hat{\ }(M_j, e)>\\
&\Box <queue_j \neq \varepsilon \wedge type(first(queue_j))=ack \rightarrow N_j\big(chan(first(queue_k))\big) := \textbf{true};\\
&\qquad\qquad\qquad\qquad\qquad\qquad queue_j := rest(queue_j) >].
\end{aligned}$$

The assertion $I_k^{\mathcal{B}}$ is the conjunction of

- $Tree(V, E) \wedge k \in V \wedge val_k{=}w \wedge \neg start_k$,
- $\forall e \in E_k.\sigma_k(e) = <info(w)>$ (node k has transmitted an *info*-message along any of its adjacent edges),
- $\forall e \in E_k.\rho_k(e) \preceq <ack>$ (node k can receive at most one *ack*-message along any of its adjacent edges),
- $\forall e \in E_k.\big(N_k(e) \Rightarrow \rho_k(e){=}<info>\big)$ (if node k has recorded that it has received a message along one of its adjacent edges, then k has received an *ack*-message along that edge),
- $\forall n.\big(1{\leq}n{\leq}|queue_k| \Rightarrow \exists e \in E_k.(queue_k[n]{=}<ack, e> \wedge \rho_k(e){=}<ack> \wedge \neg N_k(e))\big)$ (only *ack*-messages, together with an identification of an edge, can be in node k's queue. Such a message has been received along one of node k's adjacent edges, say e, and $\neg N_j(e)$ holds),
- $\forall n, m.\big(1{\leq}n{<}m{\leq}|queue_k| \Rightarrow queue[n] \neq queue[m]\big)$ (all elements in node k's queue are different from each other),
- $\exists e \in E_k.\big(N_k(e) \Rightarrow \forall n.(1{\leq}n{\leq}|queue_k| \Rightarrow queue_k[n] \neq <ack, e>)\big)$ (if node k has recorded that it has received a message along a certain edge, then $queue_k$ cannot contain any messages received along that edge), and
- $done_k \Rightarrow \big(\forall e \in E_k.N_k(e) \wedge queue_k{=}\varepsilon\big)$ (if node k has recorded that all nodes in V have received the *info*-message, then it has recorded that it has received messages along each of its adjacent edges and node k's queue is empty).

Define $q_k \equiv val_k{=}w \wedge done_k \wedge queue_k{=}\varepsilon \wedge$

$$\wedge\ \forall e \in E_k.\sigma_k(e){=}<info(w)> \wedge$$

$$\wedge\ \forall e \in E_k.\rho_k(e){=}<ack>.$$

The assertion $T_k^{\mathcal{B}}$, node k's termination condition for the second subtask, is defined by $T_k^{\mathcal{B}} \equiv done_k$. It holds after node k has performed the assignment $done_k := \textbf{true}$.

The assertion $I_j^{\mathcal{B}}$ for nodes j different from k is defined to be the conjunction of

- $Tree(V, E) \wedge val_j{=}w \wedge \neg start_j$,

- $\exists e \in E_j.(e{=}inbranch_j \wedge D_j(e){=}dist(k,j){-}1)$ (node j's variable $inbranch_j$ has a defined value and it identifies one edge connecting j with a certain node upwards the tree),

- $\rho_j(inbranch_j){=}{<}info(w){>}$ (node j has received a message $info(w)$ along the edge identified by the variable $inbranch_j$),

- $\sigma_j(inbranch_j){\preceq}{<}ack{>}$ (node j can send at most one *ack*-message along the edge identified by the variable $inbranch_j$),

- $\forall e \in E_j.(e{\neq}inbranch_j \Rightarrow (\rho_j(e){\preceq}{<}ack{>} \wedge \sigma_j(e){=}{<}info(w){>}))$ (for all edges $e \in E_j$ different from the one identified by the variable $inbranch_j$, node j has transmitted a message $info(w)$ along that edge and it has received at most one *ack*-message along that edge),

- $\forall e \in E_j.(N_j(e) \Rightarrow \rho_j(e){\neq}\varepsilon)$ (if node j has recorded that it has received a message along one of its adjacent edges, then this has occurred indeed),

- $\forall n.(1{\leq}n{\leq}|queue_j| \Rightarrow \exists e \in E_j.(queue_j[n]{=}{<}ack, e{>} \wedge \rho_j(e){=}{<}ack{>} \wedge \neg N_j(e)))$ (cf. the assertion $I_k^{\mathcal{B}}$ above),

- $\forall n,m.(1{\leq}n{<}m{\leq}|queue_j|{\neq}queue_j[m])$ (cf. the assertion $I_k^{\mathcal{B}}$ above),

- $\forall e \in E_j.(\sigma_j(e){=}{<}ack{>} \Rightarrow e{=}inbranch_j \wedge \forall e' \in E_j.(\rho_j(e'){\neq}\varepsilon \wedge \neg N_j(e')))$ (if node j has transmitted an *ack*-message, then it has sent this message along the edge identified by the variable $inbranch_j$, j has received at least one message along each of its adjacent edges, and all variables $N_j(e')$, $e' \in E_j$, has been set to **false** again.

Define $q_j \equiv val_j{=}w \wedge queue_k{=}\varepsilon \wedge$

$$\begin{aligned}&\wedge \forall e \in E_j.((e{=}inbranch_j \wedge \sigma_j(e){=}{<}ack{>} \wedge \rho_j(e){=}{<}info(w){>}) \vee \\ &\qquad\qquad \vee(e \neq inbranch_j \wedge \sigma_j(e){=}{<}info(w) \wedge \rho_j(e){=}{<}ack{>} \wedge)) \\ &\wedge D_j(inbranch_j){=}dist(k,j){-}1.\end{aligned}$$

The assertion $T_j^{\mathcal{B}}$, node j's termination condition for the second subtask, is defined by $T_j^{\mathcal{B}} \equiv \sigma_j(inbranch_j){=}{<}ack{>}$. It holds after j has transmitted an *ack*-message along the edge identified by variable $inbranch_j$.

Lemma 5.13 $\mathcal{A}$ **sat** $\{r_j \mid j \in V,\{I_j^{\mathcal{B}} \mid j \in V\},\{q_j \mid j \in V\}{>}$ holds.

5.5 Combining the programs

In this subsection the design principle for sequentially phased reasoning formulated in section 3 is applied in order to obtain from the programs $\mathcal{A}$ and $\mathcal{B}$ (see the sections 5.3 and 5.4) a distributed program which solves the whole task. According to the technical formulation of the above-mentioned principle it suffices, in view of the lemmata 5.12 and 5.13, to prove that the conditions (3) through (6), see section 3, all hold. This is the subject of the following:

Lemma 5.14 The verification conditions (3),$\cdots$,(6) of the principle formulated in section 3 are satisfied for the programs $\mathcal{A}$ and $\mathcal{B}$, and assertions p_j, r_j, q_j, $I_j^{\mathcal{A}}$, $I_j^{\mathcal{B}}$, $T_j^{\mathcal{A}}$, and $T_j^{\mathcal{B}}$ as defined above.

Proof

Establishing each of the verification conditions is straightforward. Obviously, condition (3) is true. As an example of how to prove the other conditions, we shall concentrate ourselves to the condition (5).

Condition (5): It must be shown that for all nodes j in V, $disabled(I_j^{\mathcal{B}} \wedge \neg T_j^{\mathcal{B}}, IS_j^{\mathcal{B}}) \wedge$ $\wedge\ \forall j' \in V \forall e \in E_{j,j'}.disabled(I_j^{\mathcal{B}} \wedge \neg T_j^{\mathcal{B}}, Sen_{j'}^{\mathcal{A}}(e))$ holds for all computation sequences of the program $\mathcal{B}$. I.e., if a node $\jmath$ is participating in the program $\mathcal{B}$, then it cannot perform any internal or send-actions occurring in the program $\mathcal{A}$, and all actions associated with sending a message by a certain node participating in $\mathcal{A}$ to node j are disabled.

Assume that for a certain node j in V, $I_j^{\mathcal{B}} \wedge \neg T_j^{\mathcal{B}}$ holds. In order to show that condition (5) holds, we distinguish two cases:

(A) $j{=}k$ is satisfied.

The assertion $I_k^{\mathcal{B}} \wedge \neg T_k^{\mathcal{B}}$ implies that $\neg start_k$ holds. Consequently, node k's action in program $\mathcal{A}$ cannot be executed. (Note that node k's loop associated with $\mathcal{A}$ consists of one guarded action).

Now, suppose that a certain node $j' {\neq} k$ sends a message associated with the first subtask to node k (, when $I_k^{\mathcal{B}} \wedge \neg T_k^{\mathcal{B}}$ holds). Then j' sends an *info*-message along all edges e different from the one identified by the variable $inbranch_{j'}$. For every computation sequence of program $\mathcal{B}$, $D_{j'}(e){=}dist(k,j'){+}1$ holds for such edges e (cf. the assertion $I_{j'}^{\mathcal{B}}$). Consequently, node k cannot receive any such *info*-message.

(B) $j \neq k$ is satisfied.

The assertion $I_j^{\mathcal{B}} \wedge \neg T_j^{\mathcal{B}}$ implies that $\neg start_j \wedge \forall n.1{\leq}n{\leq}|queue_j|.\ type(first(queue_j[n])){\neq}info$ holds. Consequently, node j cannot execute an internal action nor can it execute a send-action associated with the first subtask.

Analogous to case (A) one can prove that node j cannot receive messages associated with the first subtask when it is participating in the second subtask.

Since its verification conditions are all satisfied, the principle for sequentially phased reasoning may be applied. We then obtain program $\mathcal{C}$ which is the parallel composition of the loops shown below. Node k executes the loop:

*[<$start_k \rightarrow start_k$:=**false**; **for all** $e \in E_j$ **do send** $info(val_k)$ along **edge** e>
□ <$\neg start_k \wedge \neg done_k \wedge \forall e \in E_k.N_k(e) \rightarrow done_k$:=**true**>
$\square_{e \in E_k}$ <**receive** M_k along **edge** $e \rightarrow queue_k := queue_k\hat{}(M_k, e)$>
□ <$queue_k \neq \varepsilon \wedge type(first(queue_k))=ack \rightarrow N_k\big(chan(first(queue_k))\big)$:=**true**;
$queue_k := rest(queue_k)$ >].

Each node j different from k executes the loop:

*[□ <$start_j \rightarrow start_j$:=**false**;
for all $e \in E_j$ such that $e \neq inbranch_j$ **do send** $info(val_j)$ along edge e **od**>;
$\square_{e \in E_j}$ <**receive** M_j along **edge** $e \rightarrow queue_j := queue_j\hat{}(M_j, e)$>
□ < $queue_j \neq \varepsilon \wedge type(first(queue_j))=info \rightarrow val_j := argpart(first(queue_j))$;
$inbranch_j := chan(first(queue_j))$;
$N_j(inbranch_j)$:=**true**;
$queue_j := rest(queue_j)$;
$start_j$:=**true**>
□ < $\neg start_j \wedge \forall e \in E_j.N_j(e) \rightarrow$ **for all edges** $e \in E_j$ **do** $N_j(e)$:=**false od**;
send ack **along edge** $inbranch_j$>
$\square_{e \in E_j}$ <**receive** M_j along **edge** $e \rightarrow queue_j := queue_j\hat{}(M_j, e)$>
□ <$queue_j \neq \varepsilon \wedge type(first(queue_j))=ack \rightarrow N_j\big(chan(first(queue_k))\big)$:=**true**;
$queue_j := rest(queue_j)$ >].

As a consequence of lemma 5.13, program $\mathcal{C}$ is totally correct w.r.t. the precondition $\bigwedge_{j\in V} p_j$ and the postcondition $\bigwedge_{j\in V} q_j$ (termination of the programs $\mathcal{A}$ and $\mathcal{B}$ is obvious). Since $\bigwedge_{j\in V} q_j$ implies the postcondition q defined in section 4, it follows that program $\mathcal{C}$ is totally correct w.r.t. precondition $\bigwedge_{j\in V} p_j$ and the postcondition q. Since $I_k^{\mathcal{A}} \vee I_k^{\mathcal{B}}$ continuously holds during execution of program $\mathcal{C}$, it follows from a simple proof that the assertion I defined in section 4, i.e., $\neg done_k \Rightarrow \forall j \in V.val_j = w$ continuously holds, too.

One problem remains to be solved. The assertions p_j above refer to variables $start_j$, $j \in V$, whereas the precondition p does not refer to these variables at all. In order to obtain a program which is correct w.r.t. the precondition p and the postcondition q we apply one more transformation step: The variable $start_j$, $j \in V$, is initialized by node j itself to the value prescribed by the assertion p_j prior to the actual execution of its own do-loop.

This observation leads to the following loops whose parallel composition satisfies the specification formulated in section 4.

Node k executes the loop:

```
<start_k :=true>;
*[<start_k→start_k :=false; for all e ∈ E_j do send info(val_k) along edge e>
 □ <¬start_k ∧ ¬done_k ∧ ∀e ∈ E_k.N_k(e) → done_k :=true>
  □     <receive M_k along edge e → queue_k := queue_k^(M_k, e)>
e ∈ E_k
 □ <queue_k ≠ ε ∧type(first(queue_k))=ack → N_k(chan(first(queue_k))) :=true;
                                                   queue_k := rest(queue_k) >].
```

Each node j different from k executes the loop:

```
<start_j :=false>;
[□ <start_j→start_j :=false;
            for all e ∈ E_j such that e ≠ inbranch_j do send info(val_j) along edge e od>;
  □     <receive M_j along edge e →queue_j :=queue_j^(M_j, e)>
e ∈ E_j
 □ < queue_j ≠ ε ∧ type(first(queue_j))=info →val_j :=argpart(first(queue_j));
                                              inbranch_j :=chan(first(queue_j));
                                              N_j(inbranch_j) :=true;
                                              queue_j :=rest(queue_j);
                                              start_j :=true>
 □ < ¬start_j ∧ ∀e ∈ E_j.N_j(e) → for all edges e ∈ E_j do N_j(e) :=false od;
                                  send ack along edge inbranch_j>
  □     <receive M_j along edge e → queue_j := queue_j^(M_j, e)>
e ∈ E_j
 □ <queue_j ≠ ε ∧type(first(queue_j))=ack → N_j(chan(first(queue_k))) :=true;
                                              queue_j := rest(queue_j) >].
```

6 Conclusion

A formal derivation of a broadcasting protocol, essentially Segall's PIF-protocol [Se83], has been derived. This derivation has illustrated that the principle of sequentially phased reasoning, formulated in [SR89a] for the first time and applied in [SR89b, SR89c] as a *verification principle*, can be used for deriving distributed algorithms. We are convinced that essentially the same derivation can be applied to other more complex distributed algorithms, such as those described in [GHS83, Hu83, MS79, Se82, Se83, ZS80].

During the derivation, we have generated and structured the invariants required for a sound application of the principle for sequentially phased reasoning. How to achieve this has not been described by means of a (formal) calculus. In the future, research will be carried out in order to develop a calculus, which generalizes Back's refinement calculus [B88], in which invariants of a program are generated and structured during that program's development process.

Currently, research is carried out by the author to formulate a principle to reason (formally) about fail-safe algorithms

Acknowledgement: The principle for sequentially phased reasoning has been developed together with W.P. de Roever. I would like to thank him for his stimulations and for the remarks he made about one of the last versions of this paper.

References

[B88] Back R.J.R., A calculus of refinements for program derivations, Acta Informatica, 25 (1988).

[BS89] Back R.J.R. and Sere K., Stepwise refinement of action systems, Proc. of Math. of Program Construction (LNCS 375), (1989).

[CG88] Chou C.T. and Gafni E., Understanding and verifying distributed algorithms using stratified decomposition, Proc. of the ACM Symp. on Principles of Distr. Comp. (1988).

[CM88] Chandy K.M. and Misra J., Parallel program design: a foundation, Addison-Wesley Publishing Company, Inc. (1988).

[D76] Dijkstra E.W., A discipline of programming. Englewood Cliffs: Prentice Hall (1976)

[EF82] Elrad T. and Francez N., Decomposition of distributed programs into communication closed layers, Science of Computer programming, 2 (1982).

[FF89] Fix L. and Francez N., Semantics-driven decompositions for the verification of distributed programs, manuscript (1989).

[GHS83] Gallager R.T., Humblet P.A., and Spira P.M., A distributed algorithm for minimum-weight spanning trees, ACM TOPLAS, 5-1 (1983).

[Ho78] Hoare C.A.R., Sequential Communication Processes, Comm. ACM, 21-8 (1978).

[Hu83] Humblet P.A., A distributed algorithm for minimum-weight directed spanning trees, IEEE Trans. on Comm., 31-6 (1983).

[KP87] Katz S. and Peled D., Interleaving set temporal logic, Proc. of the ACM Symp. on Principles of Distr. Comp. (1987).

[L85] Lamport L., Paradigms for distributed programs: computing global states. LNCS-190 (1985).

[LRG79] Lee S., de Roever W.P., and Gerhart S.L., The evolution of list copying algorithms and the need for structured program verification, Proc. of the ACM Symp. on Princ. of Prog. Lang. (1979).

[MP83] Manna Z. and Pnueli A., Verification of concurrent programs: A temporal proof system, Foundations of computer science IV, part 2, MC-tracts 159 (1983).

[MS79] Merlin P.M. and Segall A., A failsafe distributed routing protocol, IEEE Trans. on Comm., 27-9 (1979).

[Se82] Segall A., Decentralized maximum-flow algorithms, Networks 12 (1982).

[Se83] Segall A., Distributed network protocols, IEEE Trans. on Inf. Theory. IT29-1 (1983).

[SR88] Stomp F.A. and de Roever W.P., A formalization of sequentially phased intuition in network protocols, Unpublished Internal Report 88-15, University of Nijmegen (1988).

[SR89a] Stomp F.A. and de Roever W.P., Designing distributed algorithms by means of formal sequentially phased reasoning (extended abstract), Proc. of the 3rd International Workshop on Distributed algorithms (LCNS 392) (1989)

[SR89b] Stomp F.A. and de Roever W.P., Designing distributed algorithms by means of formal sequentially phased reasoning (full paper), submitted for publication in Distributed Computing.

[SR89c] Stomp F.A. and de Roever W.P., A detailed analysis of Gallager, Humblet, and Spira's distributed minimum-weight spanning tree algorithm –An example of sequentially phased reasoning–, submitted for publication.

[St89] Stomp F.A., Design an verification of distributed network algorithms, Ph. D. thesis, Eindhoven University of Eindhoven (1989).

[SS84] Schlichting R.D. and Schneider F.B., Using message passing for distributed programming, Proof rules and disciplines, ACM TOPLAS 6-3 (1984).

[ZS80] Zerbib F.B.M. and Segall A., A distributed shortest path protocol, Internal Report EE-395, Technion-Israel Institute of Technology, Haifa, Israel (1980).

Verifying Atomic Data Types

Jeannette M. Wing

School of Computer Science
Carnegie Mellon University
Pittsburgh, Pennsylvania 15213-3890
U.S.A.

Abstract: Atomic transactions are a widely-accepted technique for organizing computation in fault-tolerant distributed systems. In most languages and systems based on transactions, atomicity is implemented through atomic objects, typed data objects that provide their own synchronization and recovery. Hence, *atomicity* is the key correctness condition required of a data type implementation. This paper presents a technique for verifying the correctness of implementations of atomic data types. The novel aspect of this technique is the extension of Hoare's abstraction function to map to a set of sequences of abstract operations, not just to a single abstract value. We give an example of a proof for an atomic queue implemented in a real programming language, Avalon/C++.

Keywords: Atomicity, program verification, fault-tolerance, transactions, distributed systems, abstract data types

Table of Contents

1. Introduction
2. Model for Transaction-Based Distributed Systems
- **2.1. Histories**
- **2.2. Legality of Sequential Histories**
- **2.3. Atomicity = Serializability + Recoverability**
  - **2.3.1. Local Atomicity**
  - **2.3.2. On-line Atomicity**

3. Verification Method
4. Implementing Atomic Objects
- **4.1. Transaction Identifiers**
- **4.2. Ensuring Serializability and Recoverability**

5. An Example: A Highly Concurrent FIFO Queue
- **5.1. The Implementation**
  - **5.1.1. The Representation**
  - **5.1.2. The Operations**
- **5.2. Application of Verification Method**
  - **5.2.1. Representation Invariant**
  - **5.2.2. Abstraction Function**
  - **5.2.3. Type-Specific Correctness Condition**
- **5.3. Verifying the Implementation**
  - **5.3.1. Proof Sketch**
  - **5.3.2. Formal Proof for Enqueue and Dequeue**

6. Discussion and Related Work
- **6.1. Hybrid Atomicity Revisited**
- **6.2. Abstraction Functions Revisited**
- **6.3. Other Models for Transactions**

7. Current and Future Work
8. Acknowledgments
References

1. Introduction

A *distributed system* consists of multiple computers (called nodes) that communicate through a network. Programs written for distributed systems, such as airline reservations, electronic banking, or process control, must be designed to cope with failures and concurrency. Concurrency arises because each process executes simultaneously with other processes on the local node and processes on remote nodes, while failures arise because distributed systems consist of many independently-failing components. Typical failures include node crashes, network partitions, and lost messages.

A widely-accepted technique for preserving consistency in the presence of failures and concurrency is to organize computations as sequential processes called *transactions*. Transactions are *atomic*, that is, serializable and recoverable. Informally, *serializability* [32] means that concurrent transactions appear to execute sequentially, and *recoverability* means that a transaction either succeeds completely or has no effect. A transaction's effects become permanent when it *commits*, its effects are discarded if it *aborts*, and a transaction that has neither committed or aborted is *active*.

In most languages and systems based on transactions, atomicity is implemented through *atomic objects*, which are typed data objects that provide their own synchronization and recovery. Languages such as Argus [24], Avalon [18], and Aeolus [39] provide a collection of primitive atomic data types, together with constructs allowing programmers to define their own atomic types. The most straightforward way to define a new atomic type is to use an existing atomic data type as a representation, but objects constructed in this way often support inadequate levels of concurrency [37]. Instead, one could implement new atomic objects by carefully combining atomic and non-atomic components and exploiting the semantics of the data type to provide more concurrency. This degree of freedom comes with a price: the programmer is now responsible for proving that the implementation of the user-defined data type is indeed atomic.

In this paper, we formulate proof techniques that allow programmers to verify the correctness of atomic objects. Although language and system constructs for implementing atomic objects have received considerable attention in the distributed systems community, the problem of verifying the correctness of programs that use those constructs has received surprisingly little attention. To our knowledge, the Avalon Project conducted at Carnegie Mellon University is the only language project to address this particular program verification problem.

Techniques for reasoning about concurrent programs are well-known [2, 19, 22, 31], but are not adequate for reasoning about atomicity. They typically address issues such as mutual exclusion or the atomicity of individual operations; they do not address the more difficult problems of ensuring the serializability of arbitrary sequences of operations, nor do they address recoverability. Reasoning about atomicity is inherently more difficult than reasoning about concurrency alone.

Our work distinguishes us from most other formal specification and verification research in concurrent and distributed systems since we address the presence of failures as seriously as the presence of concurrency and distribution. Our particular approach also distinguishes our work from many others: we focus on the behavior and correctness of objects in a system and not on the processes (transactions) that manipulate them. We base the proof of correctness of the entire system on a local property of the objects in the system; if the property holds for each object, the correctness of the entire system is guaranteed. Thus, we transform the problem of proving an entire distributed system correct into the more manageable problem of proving each of the objects in the system correct.

This paper is organized as follows. In Section 2 we present our model and basic definitions, and illustrate most of them through simple examples. In Section 3 we describe three pieces in our verification technique, the most important of which is an extension of Hoare's abstraction function for data implementations. In Section 4, we introduce and motivate relevant Avalon/C++ programming language primitives. We give in Section 5 an extended example using these primitives and a correctness proof following the technique outlined in Section 3. Section 6 discusses related work, in particular contrasting the particular correctness condition we use with another more conventional one and contrasting our extended abstraction function with other kinds of mappings. Finally, we close in Section 7 with a summary of relevant current and future work.

2. Model for Transaction-Based Distributed Systems

A distributed system is composed of a set of transactions and a set of objects. A *transaction* corresponds to a sequential process. We disallow concurrency within a transaction, but allow for multiple transactions to execute concurrently. *Objects* contain the state of the system. Each object has a *type*, which defines a set of possible *values* and a set of *operations* that provide the only means to create and manipulate objects of that type. A transaction can either complete successfully, in which case it *commits*, or unsuccessfully, in which case it *aborts*. We use the term *termination* for the end of the execution of an operation and *completion* for the end of the execution of a transaction.

Typically, a transaction executes by invoking an operation on an object, receiving results when the operation terminates, then invoking another operation on a possibly different object, receiving results when it terminates, etc. It then commits or aborts.

Although Avalon permits transactions to be nested [29, 33], the model presented here and our subsequent discussion consider only single-level transactions. Nested transactions provide a means to obtain concurrency within a transaction; Lynch and Merritt [26] present a formal model of nested transactions based on I/O automata. Our model of transactions borrows heavily from Weihl's, first described in his 1984 Ph.D. thesis [36] and more recently, in [38].

2.1. Histories

We model a computation as a *history*, which is a finite sequence of *events*. There are four kinds of events: invocations, responses, commits, and aborts. An *invocation* event is written as *x op(args*) A*, where *x* is an object name, *op* an operation name, *args** a sequence of arguments, and *A* a transaction name. A *response* event is written as *x term(res*) A*, where *term* is a termination condition, and *res** is a sequence of results. We use "Ok" for normal termination. A *commit* or *abort* event is written *x Commit A* or *x Abort A*, and it indicates that the object *x* has learned that transaction *A* has committed or aborted.

A response *matches* an earlier invocation if their object names agree and their transaction names agree. An invocation is *pending* if it has no matching response. An *operation* in a history is a pair consisting of matching invocation and response events. An operation op_0 *lies within* op_1 in *H* if the invocation event for op_1 precedes that of op_0 in *H*, and the response event for op_1 follows that of op_0. For histories, we use "•" to denote concatenation, and "Λ" the empty history.

For a history *H*, we define *committed(H)* to be the set of transactions in *H* that commit in *H*, and *aborted(H)* to be the set of transactions that abort in *H*. We define *completed(H)* to be *committed(H)* ∪ *aborted(H)*, and *active(H)* to be the set of transactions in *H* not in *completed(H)*. Note that we can model a failure event (e.g,. node crash) with abort events.

Example

The following history, H_1, involves two queue objects *p* and *q*, and four transactions *A*, *B*, *C*, and *D*:

p	Enq(1)	A
p	Enq(2)	B
p	Ok()	B
q	Enq(4)	B
p	Ok()	A
q	Ok()	B
p	Commit	B
q	Commit	B
p	Enq(3)	A
p	Ok()	A
p	Abort	A
p	Deq()	C
p	Ok(2)	C
q	Enq(5)	D
p	Enq(6)	C
p	Ok()	C

The first event in H_1 is the invocation of the Enq operation on object *p* by transaction *A*. The fifth event is the matching response event. The seventh and eighth events indicate that *p* and *q* respectively have learned that *B* has committed; the eleventh indicates that *p* has learned that *A* has aborted. The Enq operation of 2 by *B* lies within the Enq of 1 by *A*.

A and *B* execute concurrently and both eventually complete, *A* unsucessfully and *B* successfully. *C* and *D* execute concurrently and are both active (have neither committed nor aborted) at the end of H_1. Hence, $committed(H_1) = \{B\}$, $aborted(H_1) = \{A\}$, $completed(H_1) = \{A, B\}$, and $active(H_1) = \{C, D\}$. When *C* dequeues from *p*, it receives a 2. *D*'s invocation of Enq on *q* is pending since there is no matching response event.

H_1 shows an example of an atomic (to be formally defined) or intuitively "correct" history. H_1 is correct because there is some ordering on nonaborted transactions that is "equivalent" to a "sequential" version of H_1 and because *A*'s effects are ignored. It would have been incorrect for *C* to dequeue 1 from *p* since *A* aborts. If *A* were to commit instead, then it would be correct either to have *C* dequeue 1, by ordering *A* before *B*, or to have *C* dequeue a 2, by ordering *B* before *A*. Notice that a transaction can perform more than one operation, possibly on different objects. *A* performs two Enq's on *p* and *B* performs one each on *p* and *q*. The intuition we would like to capture in our formal definitions is as follows: At the end of H_1 (1) *p*'s first and only element is either 2 (*C* aborts) or 6 (*C* commits); and (2) *q*'s first and only element is 4 (*q* does not have 5 in it because *D*'s invocation is pending, yet it definitely has a 4 in it because *B*'s commit precedes *D*'s invocation).

End example

A *transaction subhistory*, $H \mid A$ (H at A), of a history H is the subsequence of events in H whose transaction names are A. $H \mid S$ and $H \mid x$ are defined similarly, where S is a set of transactions and x is an object. Informally, two histories H and G are equivalent if for each transaction A, ignoring pending invocations, A performs the same events in the same order in H as in G.

Definition 1: Let $terminated(H)$ denote the longest subhistory of H such that every invocation has a matching response. Histories H and G are *equivalent* if $terminated(H) \mid A = terminated(G) \mid A$ for all transactions A.

If H and G are equivalent, then for all objects x the state of x after H should be the same as that of x after G; the converse is not true.

Definition 2: A history H is *well-formed* if it satisfies the following conditions for all transactions A:

1. The first event of $H \mid A$ is an invocation.
2. Each invocation in $H \mid A$, except possibly the last, is immediately followed by a matching response or by an abort event.
3. Each response in $H \mid A$ is immediately preceded by a matching invocation, or by an abort event.
4. If $H \mid A$ includes a commit event, no invocation or response event may follow it.
5. A transaction can either commit or abort, but not both, i.e., $committed(H) \cap aborted(H) = \emptyset$.

These constraints capture the requirement that each transaction performs a sequence of operations. It cannot invoke one operation on an object *x* and then another on *x* (or any other object) without first receiving a response from its first invocation. If a transaction commits, it cannot have any pending invocations; if it aborts, it may be in the middle of executing an operation, and thus have at most one pending invocation. Once a transaction commits, it cannot perform further operations.

Definition 3: A well-formed history *H* is *sequential* if:

1. Transactions are not interleaved. That is, if any event of transaction *A* precedes any event of *B*, then all events of *A* precede all events of *B*.
2. All transactions, except possibly the last, have committed.

Examples

H_1 is well-formed. $H_1 \mid B$ is the transaction subhistory:

p	Enq(2)	B
p	Ok()	B
q	Enq(4)	B
q	Ok()	B
p	Commit	B
q	Commit	B

and $H_1 \mid p$ is the object subhistory:

p	Enq(1)	A
p	Enq(2)	B
p	Ok()	B
p	Ok()	A
p	Commit	B
p	Enq(3)	A
p	Ok()	A
p	Abort	A
p	Deq()	C
p	Ok(2)	C
p	Enq(6)	C
p	Ok()	C

The following well-formed subhistory of H_1 is sequential:

p	Enq(2)	B
p	Ok()	B
q	Enq(4)	B
q	Ok()	B
p	Commit	B
q	Commit	B
p	Deq()	C
p	Ok(2)	C
p	Enq(6)	C
p	Ok()	C

End examples

2.2. Legality of Sequential Histories

Each object has a *sequential specification* that defines a set of *legal* sequential histories for that object. To be concrete in this paper, we use the Larch specification approach [16] to write sequential specifications for objects. Other axiomatic approaches (e.g., Iota [30], Clear [7], or OBJ [14]), or other specification methods, such as operational (e.g., VDM [6]) or state-machine oriented (e.g., I/O automata [27]) methods, would be just as appropriate.

Larch interface specifications describe the behavior of an object's operations. Interface specifications for the Enq and Deq operations for FIFO sequential queues are shown in Figure 2-1. A **requires** clause states the precondition that must hold when an operation is invoked. An **ensures** clause states the postcondition that the operation must establish upon termination. An unprimed argument formal, e.g., q, in a predicate stands for the value of the object in which the operation begins. A return formal or a primed argument formal, e.g., q', stands for the value of the object at the end of the operation. The specification for Deq is *partial* since Deq is undefined for the empty queue.

Enq(e)/Ok()
  requires true
  ensures q' = ins(q, e)

Deq()/Ok(e)
  requires ¬ isEmp(q)
  ensures q' = rest(q) ∧ e = first(q)

Figure 2-1: Interfaces for Queue Operations

QVals: **trait**
 introduces
  emp: → Q
  ins: Q, E → Q
  first: Q → E
  rest: Q → Q
  isEmp: Q → Bool
 asserts
  Q **generated by** (emp, ins)
  for all (q: Q, e: E)
   first(ins(q, e)) == **if** isEmp(q) **then** e **else** first(q)
   rest(ins(q, e)) == **if** isEmp(q) **then** emp **else** ins(rest(q), e)
   isEmp(emp) == true
   isEmp(ins(q, e)) == false

Figure 2-2: Trait for Queue Values

The assertion language for the pre- and postconditions is based on *traits* written in the *Larch Shared Language* as in Figure 2-2. A trait is akin to an algebraic specification and is used to describe the set of values of a typed object. The set of operators and their signatures following **introduces** defines a vocabulary of terms to denote values. For example, *emp* and *ins(emp, 5)* denote two different queue values. The set of equations following the **asserts** clause defines a meaning for the terms, more precisely, an equivalence relation on the terms, and hence on the values they denote. For example, from QVals, we could prove that *rest(ins(ins(emp, 3), 5))) = ins(emp, 5)*.

The **generated by** clause of QVals asserts that *emp* and *ins* are sufficient operators to generate all values of queues. Formally, it introduces an inductive rule of inference that allows one to prove properties of all terms of sort *Q*. We use the vocabulary of traits to write the assertions in the pre- and postconditions of a type's operations; we use the meaning of equality to reason about its values.

Definition 4: Given a sequential specification of an object, a sequential object history is *legal* if the state of the object before each invocation event satisfies the pre-condition of the object's invoked operation and the state of the object before each matching response satisfies the corresponding postcondition.

A sequential history *H* involving multiple objects is *legal* if it is legal at each object, i.e., each subhistory $H \mid x$ is legal with respect to the sequential specification for *x*.

2.3. Atomicity = Serializability + Recoverability

We are interested in defining when a history is atomic, i.e., serializable and recoverable. We first define when a history is serializable and then when it is atomic, by adding the recoverability property.

Definition 5: If *H* is a history and *T* is a total order on transactions, *Seq(H, T)* is the sequential history equivalent to *H* in which transactions appear in the order *T*.

For example, if $A_1, ..., A_n$ are transactions in *H* in the order *T*, then $Seq(H, T) = H \mid A_1 \bullet ... \bullet H \mid A_n$.

Serializability picks off only those equivalent sequential histories that are legal.

Definition 6: Let $S = committed(H) \cup active(H)$ in a history *H*. *H* is *serializable* if there exists some total order *T* on the transactions in *S* such that $Seq(H \mid S, T)$ is legal.

S is the set of transactions in *H* that have committed or are still active, and thus, does not include aborted transactions. Unrolling the above two definitions, serializability requires only that we find some total order *T* on nonaborted transactions in *H* that yields a legal sequential equivalent history.

Example

H_1 is serializable because ordering the transaction *B* before *C* is equivalent to the sequential history,

p	Enq(2)	B
p	Ok()	B
q	Enq(4)	B
q	Ok()	B
p	Commit	B
q	Commit	B
p	Deq()	C
p	Ok(2)	C
p	Enq(6)	C
p	Ok()	C

which is legal because *C* correctly dequeues 2, placed at the head of the queue by *B*. Notice that "equivalence" lets us ignore *D* because it has only a pending invocation in H_1 and "serializable" lets us ignore *A* because it aborts in H_1. Thus, we need only order *B* and *C*.

End example

Atomicity requires not only serializability, but recoverability as well. To define when a history is atomic, we simply restrict *S* to be just the set of committed transactions in *H*.

Definition 7: *H* is *atomic* if $H \mid committed(H)$ is serializable.

Recoverability lets us ignore noncommmitted (i.e., aborted and active) transactions; we require that the resulting history be serializable. H_1 is atomic because it is equivalent to the sequential history that contains just the events of the one committed transaction (*B*) in H_1.

2.3.1. Local Atomicity

The only practical way to ensure atomicity in a decentralized distributed system is to have each object perform its own synchronization and recovery. In other words, we want to be able to verify the atomicity of a system composed of multiple objects by verifying the atomicity of individual objects.

However, atomicity as defined so far is too weak a property to let us perform such local reasoning. That is, *H* is not necessarily atomic just because *H* | *x* is atomic for each object *x*. For example, suppose *s* and *t* are set objects. The following history H_2 is not atomic, even though H_2 | *s* and H_2 | *t* both are:

s	Ins(1)	A
s	Ok()	A
t	Mem(2)	A
t	Ok(true)	A
s	Mem(1)	B
s	Ok(true)	B
t	Ins(2)	B
t	Ok()	B
s	Commit	A
s	Commit	B
t	Commit	A
t	Commit	B

H_2 | *s* is serializable in the order in which A precedes B and H_2 | *t* is serializable in the order in which B precedes A, but H_2 clearly cannot be serializable in an order consistent with both.

To ensure that all objects choose compatible serialization orders, it is necessary to impose certain additional restrictions on the behavior of atomic objects. These restrictions let us reason about atomicity locally. Thus, if each object is guaranteed to satisfy a local atomicity property, the entire system will be globally atomic. Avalon/C++ uses a local atomicity property that Weihl calls *hybrid atomicity* [36]. Informally, a history *H* is *hybrid atomic* if it is serializable in the order in which the transactions in *H* commit.

To capture formally the restriction that transactions must be serializable in commit-time order, we make the following adjustments to our model. When a transaction commits, it is assigned a logical timestamp [21], which appears as an argument to that transaction's commit events. These timestamps determine the transactions' serialization order. Commit timestamps are subject to the following well-formedness constraint, which reflects the behavior of logical clocks: if *B* executes a response event after *A* commits, then *B* must receive a later commit timestamp. For a given history *H*, let *TS(H)* be the partial order such that $(A, B) \in TS(H)$ if *A* and *B* commit in *H* and the timestamp for *A* is less than the timestamp for *B*. *TS(H)* defines a total order on *committed(H)*.

Definition 8: A history *H* is *hybrid atomic* if *H* | *committed(H)* is serializable in the order *TS(H)*.

Serializability requires only that there exists some total order on transactions in *H*; atomicity implies we need order only the committed transactions; finally, hybrid atomicity picks an order (commit-time order) for which there must be a legal sequential equivalent. Weihl shows that hybrid atomicity is an *optimal* local atomicity property: no strictly weaker local property suffices to ensure global atomicity [36].

Objects may learn of the commitment of transactions in an order different from the actual commit-time order. This behavior reflects real distributed systems where long delays or unreliable transmission of messages may cause objects not to have the most up-to-date view of the entire system. An object may not know that a committed transaction *A* has committed, and hence believe *A* is still active. The following history,

s	Ins(1)	A
s	Ins(2)	B
s	Ok()	B
s	Ok()	A
s	Mem(2)	A
s	Ok(false)	A
s	Commit(1:15)	B
s	Commit(1:00)	A

is hybrid atomic since it is serializable in the order in which *A* precedes *B*. Here, *s* learns about the commitment of *A* after it learns about the commitment of *B*, even though *A* commits before *B*.

Though all hybrid atomic histories are atomic, not all atomic histories are hybrid atomic [36]. Ignoring the timestamp arguments to the commit events, the following history,

s	Ins(1)	A
s	Ok()	A
s	Mem(1)	B
s	Ok(false)	B
s	Commit(1:00)	A
s	Commit(1:15)	B

is atomic, but not hybrid atomic. It is serializable in the order in which *B* precedes *A*, but not in which *A* precedes *B*.

Since hybrid atomicity is local, we henceforth need only consider object subhistories.

2.3.2. On-line Atomicity

Since an object may hear about the commitment of transactions out-of-order, it may be difficult for it to choose an appropriate response to a pending invocation of an active transaction. Thus, we focus on "pessimistic" atomicity, where an active transaction with no pending invocation is always allowed to commit. Using this stronger property, called *on-line hybrid atomicity*, gives us the additional advantage that we can perform inductive reasoning over events in a history, which is not possible using simple hybrid atomicity.

> **Definition 9:** *H* is *on-line atomic* if every well-formed history *H'* constructed by appending well-formed commit events to *H* is atomic. We call any sequential history equivalent to *H'* | *committed(H')* a *serialization* of *H*.

This definition implies that *H* is on-line atomic if every one of its serializations is legal. We will typically work with serializations of *H*, letting us tack on zero, one, or more commit events to *H*. On-line atomicity allows us to choose to complete any number of active transactions, and thereby introduces inherent nondeterminism into our correctness condition.

Examples

The following history,

q	Enq(1)	A
q	Enq(2)	B
q	Ok()	B
q	Ok()	A
q	Commit(1:30)	A
q	Commit(1:15)	B
q	Deq()	C
q	Ok(2)	C

is on-line (hybrid) atomic. It has two serializations: one in which *B* precedes *A*, and one in which *B* precedes *A* and *A* precedes *C*, and it is easily verified that both are legal.

However, the following history, H_3,

q	Enq(1)	A
q	Enq(2)	B
q	Ok()	B
q	Ok()	A
q	Commit(1:15)	B
q	Deq()	C
q	Ok(2)	C

is hybrid atomic but not on-line hybrid atomic, since the history $H'_3 = H_3 \bullet q\ Commit(1{:}00)\ A \bullet q\ Commit(1{:}30)\ C$ is not serializable in the order in which *A* precedes *C*.

End examples

In summary, we henceforth consider a history to be atomic if its transactions are serializable in commit- time order, and to be on-line atomic if the result of appending commit events with well-formed commit timestamps is atomic.

3. Verification Method

We first define our notion of correctness based on the atomicity property presented in the previous section. We then give a verification method for proving the correctness of implementations of atomic objects.

An *implementation* is a set of histories in which events of two objects, a *representation* object *r* of type *Rep* and an *abstract* object *a* of type *Abs*, are interleaved in a constrained way: for each history *H* in the implementation, (1) the subhistories $H \mid r$ and $H \mid a$ satisfy the usual well-formedness conditions; and (2) for each transaction *A*, each representation operation in $H \mid A$ lies within an abstract operation. Informally, an abstract operation is implemented by the sequence of representation operations that occur within it.

Our correctness criterion for the implementation of an atomic object is as follows: An object *a* is atomic if for every history in its implementation, $H \mid a$ is atomic. We typically do not require $H \mid r$ to be atomic.

To show the correctness of an atomic object implementation, we must generalize techniques from the sequential domain. We use three "tools" in our method: (1) a representation invariant, (2) an abstraction function, and (3) the object's sequential specification. The representation invariant defines the domain of the abstraction function. The abstraction function maps a representation value to a set of sequences of abstract operations. The sequential specification determines which of those sequences are legal. The only unusual aspect of any of these tools is the range of the abstraction function: it is not a set of abstract values, but a powerset of sequences of abstract operations.

Let *Rep* be the implementation object's set of values, *Abs* be the set of values of the (sequential) data type being implemented, and *OP* be the sequential object's set of operations. The subset of *Rep* values that are legal values is characterized by a predicate called the *representation invariant*, $I: Rep \rightarrow bool$. The meaning of a legal representation is given by an *abstraction function*, $\mathcal{A}: Rep \rightarrow 2^{OP^*}$, defined only for values that satisfy the invariant. Unlike Hoare's abstraction functions for sequential objects [20] that map a representation value to a single abstract value, our abstraction functions map a representation value to a set of sequential histories of abstract operations.

Our basic verification method is to show inductively over events in a history that the following properties are invariant. Let *r* be the representation state of the abstract object *a* after accepting the history *H*, and let *Ser(H)* denote the set of serializations of H / a.

1. $\forall S \in \boldsymbol{A}(r)$, S is a legal sequential history, and
2. $Ser(H) \subseteq \boldsymbol{A}(r)$.

These two properties ensure that *every* serialization of H is a legal sequential history, and hence that H is on-line atomic. We use the object's sequential specification to help establish the first property. Note that if we were to replace the second property with the stronger requirement that $Ser(H) = \boldsymbol{A}(r)$, then we could not verify certain correct implementations that keep track of equivalence classes of serializations. In the inductive step of our proof technique, we show the invariance of these two properties across a history's events, e.g., as encoded as statements in program text.

4. Implementing Atomic Objects

Given that atomicity is the fundamental correctness condition for objects in a transaction-based distributed system, how does one actually implement atomic objects? In this section we discuss some of the programming language support needed for constructing atomic objects. We have built this support in a programming language called Avalon/C++ [8], which is a set of extensions to C++ [35].

Essentially, Avalon/C++ provides ways to enable programmers to define abstract atomic types. For example, if we want to define an `atomic_array` type, we define a new class, `atomic_array`, which perhaps provides `fetch` and `store` operations. (Syntactically, a *class* is a collection of *members*, which are the components of the object's representation, and a collection of operation implementations.) The intuitive difference between a conventional `array` type and an `atomic_array` type is that objects of `array` type will not in general ensure serializability and recoverability of the transactions that access them whereas objects of `atomic_array` type will. However, the programmer who defines the abstract atomic type is still responsible for proving that the new type is correct, i.e., that all objects of the newly defined type are atomic. By providing language support for constructing atomic objects, we gain the advantage that this proof is done only once per class definition, not each time a new object is created. The verification method used for proving that an atomic type definition is correct is the heart of this paper.

Avalon/C++ has two built-in classes that together let programmers build atomic objects. The `trans_id` class provides operations that let programmers test the serialization order (i.e., commit-time order) of transactions at runtime. The `subatomic` class provides operations that let programmers ensure transaction serializability and recoverability.

4.1. Transaction Identifiers

The Avalon/C++ `trans_id` (transaction identifier) class provides ways for an object to determine the status of transactions at runtime, and thus synchronize the transactions that attempt to access it. `Trans_id`'s are a partially ordered set of unique values. Here is the `trans_id` class definition:

```
class trans_id {
    // ... internal representation omitted ....
public:
    trans_id();                            // constructor
    ~trans_id();                           // destructor
    trans_id&=(trans_id&)                  // assignment
    bool operator==(trans_id&);            // equality
    bool operator<(trans_id&);             // serialized before?
    bool operator>(trans_id&);             // serialized after?
    bool done(trans_id&);                  // committed to top level?
    friend bool descendant(trans_id&, trans_id&);
                        // is the first a descendant of the second?
};
```

The three operations provided by `trans_id`'s relevant to this paper are the creation operation, the comparison operation, and the `descendant` predicate.

The *creation* operation, called as follows:

```
trans_id t = trans_id();
```

creates a new dummy subtransaction, commits it, and returns the subtransaction's `trans_id` to the parent transaction. Each call to the creation operation is guaranteed to return a unique `trans_id`. A `trans_id` is typically used as a tag on an operation. Calling the `trans_id` constructor allows a transaction to generate multiple `trans_id`'s ordered in the serialization order of the operations that created them.

The *comparison* operation, used in the following expression,

```
t1 < t2
```

returns information about the order in which its arguments were created. If the comparison evaluates to `true`, then (1) every serialization that includes the creation of `t2` will also include the creation of `t1`, and (2) the creation of `t1` precedes the creation of `t2`. If `t1` and `t2` were created by distinct transactions *T1* and *T2*, then a successful comparison implies that *T1* is committed and serialized before *T2*, while if `t1` and `t2` were created by the same transaction, then `t1` was created first. If the comparison evaluates to `false`, then the `trans_id`'s may have the reverse ordering, or their ordering may be unknown.

Comparison induces a partial order on `trans_id`'s that "strengthens" over time: if `t1` and `t2` are created by concurrent active transactions, they will remain incomparable until one or more of their creators commits. If a transaction aborts, its `trans_id`'s will not become comparable to any new `trans_id`'s. Hence, "<" is capturing the commit-time order, i.e., serialization order, for committed transactions.

Finally, we use the `descendant` operation to compare whether a `trans_id t'` is a child of another. If the expression

```
descendant(t',t)
```

evaluates to true, then `t'` was created by the transaction `t`. Typically `t` is the `trans_id` of a committing or aborting transaction; the predicate lets us identify all its children.

Avalon/C++ maintains a logically global `trans_id` tree that provides the information on the relationship among `trans_id`'s and the status of each transaction associated with a `trans_id`.

4.2. Ensuring Serializability and Recoverability

An atomic object in Avalon is defined by a C++ class that inherits from the Avalon built-in class `subatomic`. Here is the `subatomic` class definition:

```
class subatomic : public recoverable {
 protected:
   void seize();          // Gains short-term lock.
   void release();        // Releases short-term lock.
   void pause();          // Temporarily releases short-term lock.
 public:
 //... inherits two other operations from recoverable ...
   virtual void commit(trans_id& t);  // Called after transaction commit.
   virtual void abort(trans_id& t);   // Called after transaction abort.
};
```

A programmer defining a new atomic data type derives from class `subatomic`, gaining access to all the above operations. The details of each of these operations are not important to this paper. Roughly speaking, the first three operations permit the *implementation* of each of the operations of the user-defined atomic data type to be executed "indivisibly." This property is conventionally called "atomic," where atomicity is at the level of an individual operation (i.e., "all-or-nothing" of a single operation), as opposed to atomicity at the level of a transaction (i.e., "all-or-nothing" of a sequence of operations). The last two operations allow implementors control over the clean-up processing done by an object when it learns that a transaction has committed or aborted.

With occasional minor variations, the implementation of each operation, op, of an atomic data type, atomic_T, which inherits from class subatomic, has the following form:

```
atomic_T::op(...) {
  trans_id t = trans_id();
  when(TEST)
      BODY;
}
```

As previously explained, the call to the creation operation of trans_id generates a new trans_id which is used to "tag" the current call to op. The when statement is a conditional critical region: BODY is executed only when TEST evaluates to true. Avalon/C++ implements the when statement in terms of the seize, release, and pause operations of subatomic and guarantees mutual exclusion at the operation level by associating a short-term lock with the object. TEST is typically an expression comparing (using trans_id's "<" operation) op's newly created trans_id t with other trans_id's embedded in the object's representation. BODY typically computes a result and updates the object's state.

By inheriting from the subatomic class, the implementor can define new classes like atomic_T, and use the operations, in particular those encoded in the when statement, provided by subatomic to implement atomic_T's operations. Since most operations follow the above template, the cleverness required in implementing operations of a new atomic type is in figuring out what the synchronization conditions on atomic_T's operations are and then encoding a test for these conditions in each of the operation's TEST in order to maintain the commit-time order of transactions. Proving correctness of the implementation focuses on showing that the synchronization conditions permit for only atomic object histories.

Objects defined in a class that inherits from subatomic can also provide commit and abort operations that are called by the system as transactions commit or abort. A user-defined commit typically discards recovery information for the committing transaction, and a user-defined abort typically discards the tentative changes made by the aborting transaction. Intuitively, commit and abort operations in Avalon/C++ are expected to affect liveness, but not safety. For example, delaying a commit or abort operation may delay other transactions (e.g., by failing to release locks) or reduce efficiency (e.g., by failing to discard unneeded recovery information), but it should never cause a transaction to observe an erroneous state. We do not address liveness properties in this paper, though certain ones are clearly of great interest. We would need to rely on the extensive work on temporal logic, e.g., [28], for reasoning about liveness.

5. An Example: A Highly Concurrent FIFO Queue

In this section, we illustrate our verification technique by applying it to a highly concurrent atomic FIFO queue implementation. Our implementation is interesting for two reasons. First, it supports more concurrency than commutativity-based concurrency control schemes such as two-phase locking. For example, it permits concurrent enqueuing transactions, even though enqueuing operations do not commute. Second, it supports more concurrency than any locking-based protocol, because it takes advantage of state information. For example, it permits concurrent enqueuing and dequeuing transactions while the queue is non-empty.

We first give the Avalon/C++ implementation of the queue, then define the verification tools needed to prove its correctness, and then give a correctness proof.

5.1. The Implementation

As in the implementation of any abstract type, we present first the representation of the abstract type and then the implementations of each of the operations.

5.1.1. The Representation

We record information about `enq` operations in the following `struct`:

```
struct enq_rec {
  int item;                           // Item enqueued.
  trans_id enqr;                      // Who enqueued it.
  enq_rec(int i, trans_id& en)        // Constructor.
   {item = i; enqr = en;}
};
```

The `item` component is the enqueued item. The `enqr` component is a `trans_id` generated by the enqueuing transaction. The last component defines a constructor operation for initializing the `struct`.

We record information about `deq` operations similarly, where the `deqr` component is a `trans_id` generated by the dequeuing transaction:

```
struct deq_rec {
  int item;                          // Item dequeued.
  trans_id enqr;                     // Who enqueued it.
  trans_id deqr;                     // Who dequeued it.
  deq_rec(int i, trans_id& en, trans_id& de);  // Constructor.
   {item = i;
    enqr = en;
    deqr = de;
   }
};
```

We represent the queue as follows:

```
class atomic_queue : public subatomic {
  deq_stack deqd;                   // Stack of dequeued items.
  enq_heap enqd;                    // Heap of enqueued items.
 public:
  atomic_queue() {};                // Create empty queue.
  void enq(int item);               // Enqueue an item.
  int deq();                        // Dequeue an item.
  void commit(trans_id& t);         // Called on commit.
  void abort(trans_id& t);          // Called on abort.
};
```

The `deqd` component is a stack of `deq_rec`'s used to undo aborted `deq` operations. The `enqd` component is a partially ordered heap of `enq_rec`'s, ordered by their `enqr` fields. A partially ordered heap provides operations to enqueue an `enq_rec`, to test whether there exists a unique oldest `enq_rec`, to dequeue it if it exists, and to discard all `enq_rec`'s inserted by (aborted) transactions.

A typical scenario is that when an `enq` operation occurs, a new `trans_id` is generated and stored in a new `enq_rec`, along with the item being enqueued; the `enq_rec` is inserted in the heap. When a `deq` operation occurs, a new `trans_id` is generated and stored in a new `deq_rec`, along with the information contained in the unique oldest `enq_rec` removed from the heap; this `deq_rec` is pushed on the stack.

5.1.2. The Operations

If *B* is an active transaction, then we say *A* is *committed with respect to B* if *A* is committed, or if *A* and *B* are the same transaction. `Enq` and `deq` must satisfy the following synchronization constraints to ensure atomicity. Transaction *A* may dequeue an item if (1) the most recent transaction to have executed a `deq` is committed with respect to *A*, and (2) there exists a unique oldest element in the queue whose enqueuing transaction is committed with respect to *A*. The first condition ensures that A will not have dequeued the wrong item if the earlier dequeuer aborts, and the second condition ensures that there is something for A to dequeue. Similarly, A may enqueue an item if the last item dequeued was enqueued by a transaction committed with respect to A.

Given these conditions, here is the code for `enq`:

```
void atomic_queue::enq(int item) {
  trans_id tid = trans_id();
  when (deqd.is_empty() || (deqd.top()->enqr < tid))
    enqd.insert(item, tid);              // Record enqueue.
}
```

`Enq` checks whether the item most recently dequeued was enqueued by a transaction committed with respect to the caller. If so, the current `trans_id` and the new item are inserted in `enqd`. Otherwise, the transaction releases the short-term lock and tries again later (guaranteed by the implementation of the `when` statement). The somewhat complicated synchronization condition for `enq` is needed because transactions can perform multiple operations which must be ordered in the sequence in which they were called. (As an aside, the condition is also necessary and sufficient for nested transactions.) Consider the situation depicted in Figure 5-1.

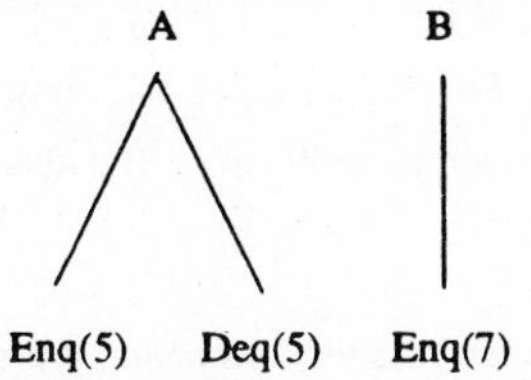

Figure 5-1: An Example of Why an Enqueuer (B) Must Wait

A and *B* are two transactions where *A* performs two operations. Suppose *A* is still active. *B* must wait for *A* to commit because if *B* commits at an earlier time than *A* the second operation of *A* will have dequeued the wrong item (7, not 5, would be at the head of the queue).

Here is the code for `deq`:

```
int atomic_queue::deq() {
  trans_id tid = trans_id();
  when ( (deqd.is_empty() || deqd.top()->deqr < tid)
       && enqd.min_exists() && (enqd.get_min()->enqr < tid)) {
    enq_rec* min_er = enqd.delete_min();
    deq_rec dr(*min_er, tid);   // Move from enqueued heap...
    deqd.push(dr);              // to dequeued stack.
    return min_er->item;
  }
}
```

`Deq` tests whether the most recent dequeuing transaction has committed with respect to the caller, and whether `enqd` has a unique oldest item. If the transaction that enqueued this item has committed with respect to the caller, it removes the item from `enqd` and records it in `deqd`. Otherwise, the caller releases the short-term lock, suspends execution, and tries again later. It is easy to see why a dequeuing transaction *B* must wait for the dequeuer *A* of the last dequeued item to be committed with respect to *B*. If *B* proceeds to dequeue without waiting for *A* to complete, then it will have dequeued the wrong item if *A* aborts. Consider the situation in Figure 5-2 where 5 and 7 are the first and second elements in the queue. If *A* aborts then *B* should get a 5.

Note that an enqueuer does not have to wait for the dequeuer of the last dequeued item to commit. Consider the situation in Figure 5-3.

Suppose A has committed, but B has not. *C* can proceed to enqueue a 7 even though *B* has not yet completed. If *B* commits, it does not matter whether it commits before or after *C*. *B* will correctly see 5 at the head of the

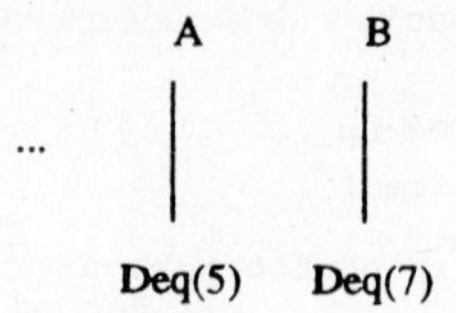

Figure 5-2: An Example of Why a Dequeuer (B) Must Wait

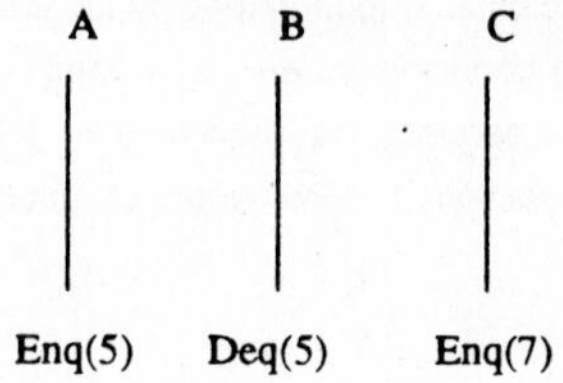

Figure 5-3: An Example of When an Enqueuer (C) Need Not Wait

queue either way and *C* will correctly place 7 as the new head. If *B* aborts, then *C* will correctly place 7 after 5, which remains at the head of the queue. Thus, *C* can proceed without waiting for *B* to complete because there is no way *C* can be serialized before *A* and it does not matter in which order *B* and *C* are serialized.

In addition to the `enq` and `deq` operations, the `atomic_queue` provides `commit` and `abort` operations that are applied to the queue as transactions commit or abort. The `commit` operation looks like:

```
void atomic_queue::commit(trans_id& committer) {
  when (TRUE)                   // Always ok to commit.
    if (!deqd.is_empty() && descendant(deqd.top()->deqr, committer)) {
      deqd.clear();             // Discard all dequeue records.
    }
}
```

When a transaction commits, it discards `deq_rec`'s no longer needed for recovery. The implementation ensures that all `deq_rec`'s below the top are also superfluous, and can be discarded. We state this property formally when giving the representation invariant in Section 5.2.1.

The `abort` operation looks like:

```
void atomic_queue::abort(trans_id& aborter) {
  when (TRUE) {                 // Always ok to abort.
    while (!deqd.is_empty()     // Undo aborted dequeue by...
      && descendant(deqd.top()->deqr, aborter)) { // aborting transaction.
      deq_rec* d = deqd.pop(); // Undo aborted dequeue.
      enqd.insert(d->item, d->enqr);   // Put it back.
    }
    enqd.discard(aborter);      // Undo aborted enqueues.
  }
}
```

`Abort` undoes every operation executed by a transaction that is a descendant of the aborting transaction. It interprets `deqd` as an undo log, popping records for aborted operations, and inserting the items back in `enqd` heap. `Abort` then flushes all items enqueued by the aborted transaction and its descendants.

5.2. Application of Verification Method

As outlined in Section 3, we need to provide a representation invariant, abstraction function, and sequential specification in order to apply our verification method.

5.2.1. Representation Invariant

The queue operations preserve the following representation invariant. For brevity, we assume items in the queue are distinct, an assumption that could easily be relaxed by tagging each item in the queue with a timestamp. For all representation values *r*:

1. No item is present in both the `deqd` and `enqd` components:

   $(\forall$ d: deq_rec$)$ $(\forall$ e: enq_rec$)$ $(d \in r.\text{deqd} \wedge e \in r.\text{enqd} \Rightarrow e.\text{item} \neq d.\text{item})$

2. Items are ordered in `deqd` by their enqueuing and dequeuing `trans_id`'s:

   $(\forall$ d1, d2: deq_rec$)$ $d1 <_d d2 \Rightarrow (d1.\text{enqr} < d2.\text{enqr} \wedge d1.\text{deqr} < d2.\text{deqr})$

   where $<_d$ is the total ordering on `deq_rec`'s imposed by the `deqd` stack.

3. Any dequeued item must previously have been enqueued:

   $(\forall$ d: deq_rec$)$ $d \in r.\text{deqd} \Rightarrow d.\text{enqr} < d.\text{deqr}$.

Thus, given an arbitrary state of the queue representation as in Figure 5-4, where the stack grows upward:

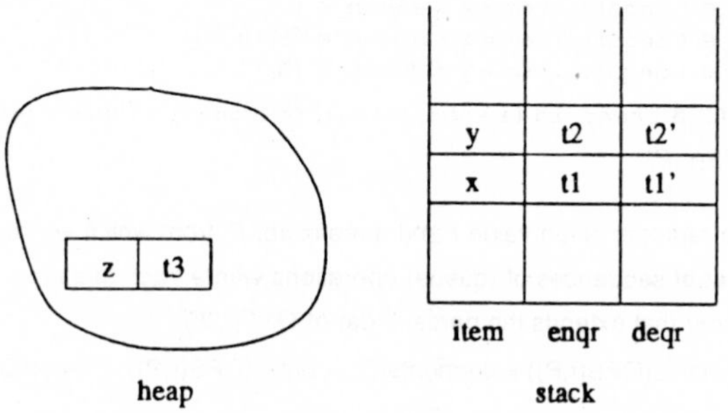

Figure 5-4: An Example Queue Representation State

The first part of the representation invariant implies that *x* (and *y*) cannot be in any `enq_rec` in the heap. The second implies that $t1 < t2$ and $t1' < t2'$. The third implies that $t1 < t1'$ (and $t2 < t2'$).

Our proof technique requires that we show the representation invariant is preserved across the implementation of each abstract operation. We conjoin it to the pre- and postconditions of each of the operations' specifications.

5.2.2. Abstraction Function

Intuitively, the abstract value of the queue is defined in terms of what has been enqueued by committing transactions and may possibly be enqueued by active transactions (what is in the heap) and what has been and may possibly be dequeued (what is on the stack). On-line atomicity requires that we allow for the possibility of active transactions to commit. For each, we pretend that it commits and reflect its effects—tentative enqueues and dequeues saved in the heap and stack—in the image of the abstraction function for a given representation value. When an active transaction actually does commit or the object finally finds out about the transaction's commitment, we know that we have already permitted for its effects to have taken place. Notice that both `commit` and `abort` do *not* change the abstract view of the queue, but only the representation.

To define the abstraction function, we need some auxiliary definitions. Let *Q* be a sequential queue history (not

Similarly, suppose the object completes an operation Deq(x) with `trans_id` *t*, carrying the representation *r* to *r'*. Let $Q = Q_1 \bullet Q_2 \in \mathbf{A}(r)$ and $Q' = Q_1 \bullet \text{Deq}(x) \bullet Q_2 \in \mathbf{A}(r')$. The representation invariant and the first conjunct of the `when` condition for Deq ensure that *x* is not an element of *DEQ(Q)*, and the second conjunct then ensures that *x* is the first element of *ENQ(Q) − DEQ(Q)*. Together, they imply that *DEQ(Q') = DEQ(Q)* • *x* is a prefix of *ENQ(Q') = ENQ(Q)*, hence that *Q* is legal by Lemma 11.

If a Commit or Abort event carries the accepted history *H* to *H'*, and the corresponding `commit` or `abort` operation carries *r* to *r'*, we must show that (1) $\mathbf{A}(r') \subseteq \mathbf{A}(r)$, and (2) that no history in $\mathbf{A}(r) - \mathbf{A}(r')$ is in *Ser(H')*. Property 1 ensures that every sequential history in $\mathbf{A}(r')$ is legal, and Property 2 ensures that no valid serializations are "thrown away." For Commit, we check that every discarded history is missing an operation of a committed transaction, and for Abort, we check that every discarded history includes an operation of an aborted transaction; either condition ensures that the discarded history is not an element of *Ser(H')*.

Naturally, this verification relies on properties of sequential queues. To verify an implementation of another data type, one would have to rely on a different set of properties, but the arguments would follow a similar pattern. The basic synchronization conditions are captured by a type-specific analog to Lemma 11, characterizing the conditions under which an operation can be inserted in the middle of a sequential history. The representation invariant and abstraction function define how the set of possible serializations is encoded in the representation, and an inductive argument is used to show that no operation, commit, or abort event can violate atomicity.

5.3.2. Formal Proof for Enqueue and Dequeue

In this section we will use induction to show the prefix property of Lemma 11. More specifically, if the prefix property holds of all serializations $h \in \mathbf{A}(r)$ at the invocation of the enqueue or dequeue operation, it holds of all serializations $h' \in \mathbf{A}(r')$ at the point of return. In the following, for $H \in \mathbf{A}(r)$, $H' \in \mathbf{A}(r')$, let $H = H_1 \bullet H_2$ and $H' = H_1 \bullet op \bullet H_2$ such that $\forall\, p \in H_1\ \neg(\texttt{tid} < trans\_id(p)) \wedge \forall\, p \in H_2\ \neg(trans\_id(p) < \texttt{tid})$, where *op* is the enqueue or dequeue operation (as the case may be) with `trans_id tid`, and *trans_id(p)* is the `trans_id` of operation *p*.

Enqueue

We decorate the `enq` operation with two assertions, one after the `when` condition, and one at the point of return.

```
void atomic_queue::enq(int item) {
  trans_id tid = trans_id();
  when (deqd.is_empty() || (deqd.top()->enqr < tid))
      WHEN: {∀y y ∈ elements(DEQ(h)) ⇒ trans_id(Enq(y)) < tid}
    enqd.insert(item, tid);
      POST: {DEQ(h') = DEQ(h)}
}
```

Proof: Case 1: The queue is empty. Trivial since the antecedent of WHEN is false.

Case 2: The queue is nonempty. Then let *y* be an item dequeued in *H*, which implies that the trans_id of the enqueue operation of *y* is ordered before `tid` by the WHEN assertion. The enqueue operation must be in H_1 since (1) the trans_id's of all enqueue operations of dequeued items are all ordered before that of deqd.top().enqr (by the representation invariant), which is ordered before `tid` (by the **when** condition); and (2) `tid` is not ordered before any operation in H_1 (by the definition of $H = H_1 \bullet H_2$). Since the enqueue operations of all dequeued items are in H_1,

DEQ(*H*) *prefix* ENQ(H_1) (*)

At the point of return, let e = Enq(x). From POST we have that:

DEQ(*H'*) = DEQ(*H*), which by (*)
⇒ DEQ(*H'*) *prefix* ENQ(H_1)
⇒ DEQ(*H'*) *prefix* ENQ($H_1 \bullet e \bullet H_2$)
⇒ DEQ(*H'*) *prefix* of ENQ(*H'*).

Dequeue

Here is the annotated `deq` operation:

```
int atomic_queue::deq() {
  trans_id tid = trans_id();
  when ((deqd.is_empty() || deqd.top()->deqr < tid)
        && enqd.min_exists() && (enqd.get_min()->enqr < tid)) {
```

{WHEN: $\forall$ *Deq operations d in h (trans_id(d)* < `tid` $\Rightarrow$ *d in H_1)}*

```
    enq_rec* min_er = enqd.delete_min(); // Transfer from enqueued heap...
    deq_rec dr(*min_er, tid);
    deqd.push(dr);                       // to dequeued stack.
    return min_er->item;
  }
```

{POST: DEQ(h') = DEQ(h) • x $\wedge$ *ENQ(h') = ENQ(H_1) • ENQ(H_2)}*

```
}
```

and the proof:

Proof: From the first conjunct of the `when` condition and the second clause of the representation invariant, we know that DEQ(H) = DEQ(H_1). The second conjunct implies that there exists some x = *first*(ENQ(H) − DEQ(H)), the first item in the sequence of enqueued items that have not yet been dequeued. The third conjunct implies that this item, x, is in H_1. Thus, by properties on sequences, there exists some x = *first*(ENQ(H_1) − DEQ(H_1)).

At the point of return, let d = Deq(x). POST implies that

DEQ(H_1 • d) *prefix* ENQ(H_1 • d)
$\Rightarrow$ DEQ(H') *prefix* ENQ(H_1 • d)
$\Rightarrow$ DEQ(H') *prefix* ENQ(H_1 • d • H_2)
$\Rightarrow$ DEQ(H') *prefix* ENQ(H').

6. Discussion and Related Work

6.1. Hybrid Atomicity Revisited

Atomicity has long been recognized as a basic correctness property within the database community [3]. More recently, several research projects have chosen atomicity as a useful foundation for general-purpose distributed systems, including Avalon [18], Argus [24], Aeolus [39], Camelot [34], EXODUS [11] and Arjuna [9]. EXODUS and Arjuna, like Avalon, extend C++ to support recoverability, but neither gives programmers fine control over serializability. Of all these projects only Avalon and Argus provide linguistic support for programmers to design and implement user-defined atomic data types, which Weihl and Liskov argue is necessary for building large, realistic systems [37].

One way to ensure atomicity of a set of concurrent transactions is to associate read and write locks with each object and to use a strict two-phase locking protocol to ensure serializability [10]. A transaction A obtains a read lock on an object x if A needs only to observe x's value. It obtains a write lock if it needs to update x's value. Each transaction first acquires all the locks it needs, then performs its operations on all objects for which it has obtained the appropriate locks, and then when it commits or aborts, releases all of its locks. Locks are held for the duration of a transaction, not individual operations; thus, two transactions that need to perform updates on the same object cannot proceed concurrently.

The two-phase read-write locking protocol is known to guarantee atomicity. However, since operations are naively divided into readers and writers, the amount of concurrency that can be obtained is restricted because the type semantics of objects are ignored. For example, consider the following two transactions that each perform two enqueue operations:

q	Enq(1)	A		q	Enq(2)	B
q	Ok()	A		q	Ok()	B
q	Enq(3)	A		q	Enq(4)	B
q	Ok()	A		q	Ok()	B

Following a read-write locking protocol would prevent *A* and *B* from executing concurrently. Suppose *A* has the write lock on *q*, then *B* would not be able to obtain it, and hence has to wait for *A* to commit or abort before proceeding. Assuming both *A* and *B* commit, the only two permissible histories would both be sequential, where either all of *A*'s operations precede all of *B*'s or vice versa, i.e., *A*'s and *B*'s operations would not be interleaved. However, it should be possible to permit for the following history in which *A* and *B* are executing concurrently:

q	Enq(1)	A
q	Ok()	A
q	Enq(2)	B
q	Ok()	B
q	Enq(3)	A
q	Ok()	A
q	Enq(4)	B
q	Ok()	B

Our correctness condition (hybrid atomicity) certainly permits this history since any extension of it with appended commit events for *A* and/or *B* is serializable.

Moreover, in the case when the queue is non-empty, we can permit a dequeuing transaction to proceed concurrently with an enqueuing one. Consider this example, which is a variation of the example drawn in Figure 5-3:

q	Enq(1)	A
q	Ok()	A
q	Enq(3)	A
q	Ok()	A
q	Commit(1:00)	A
q	Enq(2)	B
q	Deq()	C
q	Ok(1)	C
q	Ok()	B
q	Enq(4)	B
q	Ok()	B

The queue can permit *C* to perform a Deq operation and even return an element to *C* because it knows that *A* has committed and thus it knows what its first element is. Whether *B* commits or not, *C* still receives the correct element. Were two-phase read-write locking used, *B* and *C* would not be allowed to proceed concurrently because the Enq and Deq operations would both be classified as writers.

The use of commit-time serialization distinguishes Avalon from other transaction-based languages and systems, which are typically based on some form of strict two-phase locking. We chose to support commit-time serialization because it permits more concurrency than two-phase locking [36], as well as better availability for replicated data [17]. Because commit-time serialization is compatible with strict two-phase locking, applications that use locking can still be implemented in Avalon/C++. In fact, we optimize for this more traditional case: As an alternative way to build atomic data types, programmers can inherit from another built-in Avalon/C++ called `atomic`, which provides access to read and write locks.

To summarize the results of this discussion and that in Section 2, the Venn diagram in Figure 6-1 shows the relationship between atomic, hybrid atomic, and "two-phase-locking" atomic histories. Every "two-phase locking" history is hybrid atomic, but not conversely; every hybrid atomic history is atomic, but not conversely. The key point of this section is that hybrid atomicity provides more concurrency than "two-phase locking." The key point with respect to this paper, however, is that hybrid atomity is local, whereas atomicity is not.

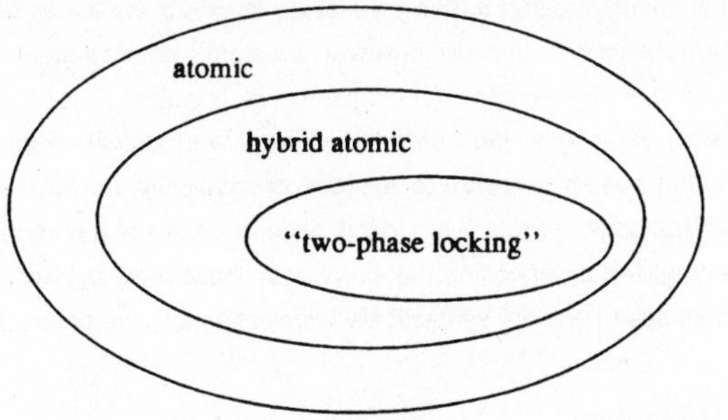

Figure 6-1: Relationships Among Atomicity Properties

6.2. Abstraction Functions Revisited

The main contribution of this paper is the verification method used for showing the correctness of the implementation of an atomic data type. This method hinges on defining an abstraction function between a low-level view of an object and an abstract view. In the sequential domain, the signature of the abstraction function is:

$\mathbf{A}: Rep \rightarrow Abs$

Because of the on-line property of our correctness condition, in particular the inherent nondeterminism, we need to map to a set of values. A first attempt at extending the abstraction function would be to extend the range as follows:

$\mathbf{A}: Rep \rightarrow 2^{Abs}$

This extension is similar to Lynch and Tuttle's use of multi-valued *possibilities mappings*, where each "concrete state" maps to a set of "abstract states" [27]. Lynch and her colleagues have used possibilities mappings to prove a wide range of distributed algorithms correct, including transaction-based locking and timestamp protocols. This abstraction function extension is also similar to what Herlihy and Wing needed to use in order to prove the correctness of *linearizable* objects [19], again because of the inherent nondeterminism in the definition of the correctness condition.

However, even mapping to the powerset of abstract values is insufficient for the on-line hybrid atomic correctness condition we require. We need to keep track of sequences of operations because we need to permit for reordering of operations. In fact, we need to be able to insert not just single operations into the middle of a history, but sequences of operations since a transaction may perform more than one operation. Hence, we finally extend the abstraction function's range to be:

$\mathbf{A}: Rep \rightarrow 2^{OP^*}$

In either extension, the standard trick of using auxiliary variables (Abadi and Lamport classify these into *history* and *prophecy* variables [1]) would also work. These variables can be included in the domain of the abstraction function (encoded as part of the representation state) and used (1) to keep track of the set of possible abstract values; (2) to log the history of abstract operations performed on the object so far; and (3) to keep track of implicit global data like the `trans_id` tree. Hence our abstraction functions can be turned into Abadi and Lamport's *refinement mappings*, where the extended domain of the representation state maps to a single abstract state.

In our initial approach to verification we tried to stick to a purely axiomatic approach in our verification method where we relied on Hoare-like axioms to reason about program statements, invariant assertions to reason about local state changes and global invariants, and auxiliary variables to record the states (e.g., program counters) of concurrent processes. In the transactional domain, however, an atomic object's state must be given by a set of possible serializations, and each new operation (or sequence of operations) is inserted somewhere "in the middle" of certain serializations. This distinction between physical and logical ordering is easily expressed in terms of reordering histories, but seems awkward to express axiomatically, i.e., using assertions expressed in terms of program text alone. Though the proofs given in this paper fall short of a pure syntax-directed verification, they could be completely axiomatized by encoding the set of serializations as auxiliary data. Even so, we have found that the resulting invariant assertions are syntactically intimidating and the proofs unintuitive and unnatural.

6.3. Other Models for Transactions

Best and Randell [4], and Lynch and Merritt [26] have proposed formal models for transactions and atomic objects. Best and Randell use *occurrence graphs* to define the notion of atomicity, to characterize interference freedom, and to model error recovery. Their model does not exploit the semantics of data, focusing instead on event dependencies. Lynch and Merritt model nested transactions and atomic objects in terms of *I/O automata*, which have been used to prove correctness of general algorithms for synchronization and recovery [12, 25]. None of these models were intended for reasoning about individual programs. Moreover, none are suitable for reasoning about high-level programming language constructs that include support for user-defined abstract data types.

7. Current and Future Work

We have applied our verification method to a *directory* atomic data type, whose behavior is much more complex than a queue's. A directory stores key-item pairs and provides operations to insert, remove, alter, and lookup items given a key. Synchronization is done per key so transactions operating on different keys can execute concurrently. Moreover, we use an operation's arguments and results to permit, in some cases, operations on the same key to proceed concurrently. For example, an "unsuccessful" insertion operation, i.e., *Ins(k, x)/Ok(false)*, does not modify *k*'s binding, so it does not conflict with a "successful" lookup operation, i.e., *Lookup(k)/Ok(y)*. Our proof of correctness relies on inductively showing a type-specific correctness condition, analogous to the "prefix" property for the queue. Informally stated, this condition says that it is legal to perform a successful remove, alter, lookup or unsuccessful lookup or insert on a key *k* as long as a key-item pair has already been successfully inserted for *k* and not yet successfully removed. This condition should hint to the reader that, in general, we need to keep track of the exact operations (including their arguments and results) and the order they have occurred already in a history to know which permutations are legal. We implemented the directory example in Avalon/C++.

In line with our philosophy of performing syntax-directed verification, we have used machine aids to verify the queue example. In particular, we used the Larch Shared Language to specify completely the queue representation, the set of queue abstract values (in terms of sequences of queue operations), the representation invariant, and the abstraction function. We used the Larch Prover [13] to prove the representation invariant holds of the representation and to perform the inductive reasoning we carried out in our verification method. We describe this work in more detail in [15].

Our work on specifying and verifying atomic data types and more recently, our work on using machine aids, has led us to explore extensions to our specification language. Two kinds of extensions seem necessary. First, we need a way to specify precisely and formally the synchronization conditions placed on each operation of an atomic object. We propose using a **when** clause analogous to the `when` statement found in Avalon/C++ or the

WHEN assertion found in our proofs. Birrell et al. use informally a **when** clause in the Larch interface specification of Modula/2+'s synchronization primitives [5] and Lerner uses it to specify the queue example [23]. Second, we would like to extend the assertion language of the Larch interface specifications. The Larch Shared Language and the input language of the Larch Prover are both restricted to a subset of first-order logic. The assertions we write, however, in both the PRE/WHEN/POST conditions in our proofs and the **requires/when/ensures** clauses in our Larch interfaces, refer to operations, histories, sets of histories, and transactions directly, thereby requiring a richer and more expressive language than that which either the Larch Shared Language or the Larch Prover supports.

8. Acknowledgments

I would like to thank Maurice Herlihy specifically for his close collaboration on the Avalon/C++ design and implementation, for his ideas about verifying atomicity, and for co-authoring a paper that presents a preliminary version of some of the ideas in this paper. I thank Bill Weihl for the original definitions of his model of transactions and atomicity properties.

I thank the participants of the 1989 REX Workshop on Stepwise Refinement of Distributed Systems: Models, Formalism, Correctness that took place in Plasmolen, The Netherlands. I especially thank Willem P. de Roever, Jr. who has been supportive and encouraging throughout my attempts at explaining this material.

Finally, I thank the following members of the Avalon Project for reading drafts of this paper: Chun Gong, David Detlefs, Karen Kietzke, Linda Leibengood, Rick Lerner, and Scott Nettles. Gong and Dave have been particularly helpful with some of the technical points. Dave and Karen have been instrumental in turning the design of Avalon/C++ into a working implementation.

This research was sponsored by the Defense Advanced Research Projects Agency (DOD), ARPA Order No. 4976, monitored by the Air Force Avionics Laboratory Under Contract F33615-87-C-1499. Additional support was provided in part by the National Science Foundation under grant CCR-8620027. The views and conclusions contained in this document are those of the author and should not be interpreted as representing the official policies, either expressed or implied, of the Defense Advanced Research Projects Agency or the US Government.

References

[1] M. Abadi and L. Lamport.
The Existence of Refinement Mappings.
Technical Report 29, DEC Systems Research Center, August, 1988.

[2] K.R. Apt, N. Francez, and W.P. DeRoever.
A Proof System for Communicating Sequential Processes.
ACM Transactions on Programming Languages and Systems 2(3):359-385, July, 1980.

[3] P.A. Bernstein and N. Goodman.
A survey of techniques for synchronization and recovery in decentralized computer systems.
ACM Computing Surveys 13(2):185-222, June, 1981.

[4] E. Best and B. Randell.
A Formal Model of Atomicity in Asynchronous Systems.
Acta Informatica 16(1):93-124, 1981.

[5] A. Birrell, J. Guttag, J. Horning, R. Levin.
Synchronization Primitives for a Multiprocessor: A Formal Specification.
In *Proceedings of the Eleventh ACM Symposium on Operating Systems Principles*, pages 94-102. ACM/SIGOPS, 1987.

[6] D. Bjorner and C.G. Jones (Eds.).
Lecture Notes in Computer Science. Volume 61: *The Vienna Development Method: the Meta-language.*
Springer-Verlag, Berlin-Heidelberg-New York, 1978.

[7] R.M. Burstall and J.A. Goguen.
An Informal Introduction to Specifications Using CLEAR.
In Boyer and Moore (editors), *The Correctness Problem in Computer Science.* Academic Press, 1981.

[8] D. L. Detlefs, M. P. Herlihy, and J. M. Wing.
Inheritance of Synchronization and Recovery Properties in Avalon/C++.
IEEE Computer :57-69, December, 1988.

[9] G. Dixon and S.K. Shrivastava.
Exploiting Type Inheritance Facilities to Implement Recoverability in Object Based Systems.
In *Proceedings of the 6th Symposium in Reliability in Distributed Software and Database Systems.* March, 1987.

[10] K.P. Eswaran, J.N. Gray, R.A. Lorie, and I.L. Traiger.
The Notion of Consistency and Predicate Locks in a Database System.
Communications ACM 19(11):624-633, November, 1976.

[11] J.E. Richardson and M.J. Carey.
Programming Constructs for Database System Implementation in EXODUS.
In *ACM SIGMOD 1987 Annual Conference*, pages 208-219. May, 1987.

[12] M.P. Herlihy, N.A. Lynch, M. Merritt, and W.E. Weihl.
On the correctness of orphan elimination algorithms.
In *17th Symposium on Fault-Tolerant Computer Systems.* July, 1987.
Abbreviated version of MIT/LCS/TM-329.

[13] S.J. Garland and J.V. Guttag.
Inductive Methods for Reasoning about Abstract Data Types.
In *Proceedings of the 15th Symposium on Principles of Programming Languages*, pages 219-228. January, 1988.

[14] J.A. Goguen and J.J. Tardo.
An Introduction to OBJ: A Language for Writing and Testing Formal Algebraic Program Specifications.
In *Proceedings of the Conference on Specifications of Reliable Software*, pages 170-189. Boston, MA, 1979.

[15] C. Gong and J.M. Wing.
Machine-Assisted Proofs of Atomicity.
1989.
in preparation.

[16] J.V. Guttag, J.J. Horning, and J.M. Wing.
The Larch Family of Specification Languages.
IEEE Software 2(5):24-36, September, 1985.

[17] M.P. Herlihy.
A quorum-consensus replication method for abstract data types.
ACM Transactions on Computer Systems 4(1), February, 1986.

[18] M.P. Herlihy and J.M. Wing.
Avalon: Language Support for Reliable Distributed Systems.
In *The Seventeenth International Symposium on Fault-Tolerant Computing*, pages 89-94. July, 1987.
Also available as CMU-CS-TR-86-167.

[19] M.P. Herlihy and J.M. Wing.
Axioms for concurrent objects.
In *Fourteenth ACM Symposium on Principles of Programming Languages*, pages 13-26. January, 1987.

[20] C.A.R. Hoare.
Proof of Correctness of Data Representations.
Acta Informatica 1(1):271-281, 1972.

[21] L. Lamport.
Time, clocks, and the ordering of events in a distributed system.
Communications of the ACM 21(7):558-565, July, 1978.

[22] L. Lamport.
Specifying Concurrent Program Modules.
ACM Transactions on Programming Languages and Systems 5(2):190-222, April, 1983.

[23] R.A. Lerner.
Specifying Concurrent Programs.
1989.
Thesis Proposal.

[24] B.H. Liskov, and R. Scheifler.
Guardians and actions: linguistic support for robust, distributed programs.
Transactions on Programming Languages and Systems 5(3):381-404, July, 1983.

[25] N. Lynch.
A Concurrency Control For Resilient Nested Transactions.
Technical Report MIT/LCS/TR-285, Laboratory for Computer Science, 1985.

[26] N. Lynch and M. Merritt.
Introduction to the Theory of Nested Transactions.
In *Proceedings of the International Conference on Database Theory.* Rome, Italy, September, 1986.
Sponsored by EATCS and IEEE.

[27] N. Lynch and M. Tuttle.
Hierarchical Correctness Proofs for Distributed Algorithms.
Technical Report MIT/LCS/TR-387, Laboratory for Computer Science, 1987, 1987.

[28] Z. Manna and A. Pnueli.
Verification of concurrent Programs, Part I: The Temporal Framework.
Technical Report STAN-CS-81-836, Dept. of Computer Science, Stanford University, June, 1981.

[29] J.E.B. Moss.
Nested Transactions: An Approach to Reliable Distributed Computing.
Technical Report MIT/LCS/TR-260, Laboratory for Computer Science, April, 1981.

[30] R. Nakajima, M. Honda, and H. Nakahara.
Hierarchical Program Specification and Verification-- A Many-sorted Logical Approach.
Acta Informatica 14:135-155, 1980.

[31] S. Owicki and D. Gries.
Verifying Properties of Parallel Programs: An Axiomatic Approach.
Communications of the ACM 19(5):279-285, May, 1976.

[32] C.H. Papadimitriou.
The serializability of concurrent database updates.
Journal of the ACM 26(4):631-653, October, 1979.

[33] D.P. Reed.
Implementing atomic actions on decentralized data.
ACM Transactions on Computer Systems 1(1):3-23, February, 1983.

[34] A.Z. Spector, J.J. Bloch, D.S. Daniels, R.P. Draves, D. Duchamp, J.L. Eppinger, S.G. Menees, D.S. Thompson.
The Camelot Project.
Database Engineering 9(4), December, 1986.
Also available as Technical Report CMU-CS-86-166, Carnegie Mellon University, November 1986.

[35] B. Stroustrup.
The C++ Programming Language.
Addison Wesley, 1986.

[36] W.E. Weihl.
Specification and implementation of atomic data types.
Technical Report TR-314, MIT Laboratory for Computer Science, March, 1984.

[37] W.E. Weihl, and B.H. Liskov.
Implementation of resilient, atomic data types.
ACM Transactions on Programming Languages and Systems 7(2):244-270, April, 1985.

[38] W.E. Weihl.
Local Atomicity Properties: Modular Concurrency Control for Abstract Data Types.
Transactions on Programming Languages and Systems 11(2):249-283, April, 1989.

[39] C.T. Wilkes and R.J. LeBlanc.
Rationale for the design of Aeolus: a systems programming language for an action/object system.
Technical Report GIT-ICS-86/12, Georgia Inst. of Tech. School of Information and Computer Science, Dec, 1986.

Predicates, Predicate Transformers and Refinement

Job Zwiers
University of Twente [1]
P.O. Box 217, 7500 AE Enschede, The Netherlands

Abstract

Data reification is generalized, allowing "abstract" data to be implemented by parallel processes. He Jifeng and Hoare's [He Jifeng] approach to integrate theories for "programs as predicates" and "programs as predicate transformers", is generalized to parallel processes and is used to formulate syntactic verification conditions to check the correctness of reification by means of processes.

Contents

Section 1: Introduction.
Section 2: The basic mathematical formalism.
Section 3: Processes and joint action semantics.
Section 4: Data refinement by processes.

1 Introduction

The diversity of methods in the field of construction, derivation and verification of concurrent systems is only partly due to the variety in models of parallelism. A more compelling reason for this diversity is formed by differences in specification methodologies. *Should programs be specified as predicates or as predicate transformers?* Both approaches have their strong and their weak points, as we argue, *in complementary fashion.*

1.1 "Programs are Predicates" and refinement

The basic idea for "programs as predicates" ($\mathcal{PP}$) starts out with the idea that "a program can be identified with the strongest predicate describing every relevant observation that can be made of the behaviour of the system during execution of the program", cfr. Hoare's Royal Society address [Hoare]. A process P meets its specification S iff the implication $P \Rightarrow S$ holds. This is denoted by P *sat* S, and we shall use the term "sat style" instead of "following the $\mathcal{PP}$ approach". Typical examples of observables are: the initial and final states in sequential programming, sequences of communication actions, possibly in combination with expectation sets [FLP] or failure sets [BHR], for CSP and (finite and infinite) sequences of program states, often used for system specification based on Temporal Logic. [MP]

We now explain a case, concerning the style of program refinement that we discuss in section 4, where $\mathcal{PP}$ in isolation is not satisfactory. We generalize the well known reification technique for data refinement [Jones2] to a program transformation technique where "abstract" data is refined by means of *processes* executing in parallel and communicating with the "user" process of that data. Within the $\mathcal{PP}$ approach a succinct formulation can be given of process refinement: Some "concrete" system C is said to refine "abstract" system A with respect to a, possibly multivalued, abstraction function ρ if ρ maps every possible observation σ for C to abstract observations $\rho(\sigma)$ that are possible for A. In sat style, this is expressed as:

$$\rho(C)\ sat\ A \qquad (*)$$

Verifying $(*)$ for large systems is feasible only when applying *compositional* [2] *methods*, that allow one to exploit the modular structure of A and C. If *op* is some process composition operator and

[1] Part of the work has been supported by ESPRIT project 432 (METEOR).

[2] The compositionality principle requires that a specification for a composed program can be inferred from specifications of its constituent parts, without reference to the internal structure of these parts [de Roever].

A and C are decomposable as $A \equiv op(A_1, A_2)$, and $C \equiv op(C_1, C_2)$, then (*) could be reduced to verifying that $\rho(C_1)$ *sat* A_1 and $\rho(C_2)$ *sat* A_2, provided that the following conditions are met:

(1) Operation *op* has to be monotone with respect to the *sat* relation:

   if P *sat* P' and Q *sat* Q' then $op(P, Q)$ *sat* $op(P', Q')$, and

(2) *op* should be ***subdistributive*** [HHS] with respect to ρ:

   $\rho(op(C_1, C_2))$ *sat* $op(\rho(C_1), \rho(C_2))$.

The first condition is satisfied by any reasonable process operation, and for a number of operations, including parallel composition, the subdistributivity property holds true too, at least for the kind of functions ρ that we need for reification. However, we get into troubles with the $\mathcal{PP}$ approach in combination with ***sequential composition.*** Subdistributivity for this operation means that:

$\rho(C_1 ; C_2)$ *sat* $\rho(C_1) ; \rho(C_2)$. (**)

And this latter property *does not hold,* neither for arbitrary functions ρ in general, nor for the particular class of abstraction functions that we are interested in. Our notion of abstraction function is a generalization of the VDM style "retrieve functions" [Jones]. Rather than mapping concrete states to abstract states, we now map *complete computational histories*, in the form of labeled state sequences, to abstract states. The intuitive reason for this is that *values* of abstract data variables at some moment during execution of A are represented at the implementation level by the *sequence of communications* between the main process and the processes representing those abstract variables. For example, in the last section we deal with a so called *priority queue*, where the (abstract) queue value at some moment of time is determined by the sequence of (concrete) communication actions that implement (abstract) insertions and deletions actions. This sequence of communications is not determined by the current *state* of the implementing process, but it *is* present within the computational history that has been reached up to that moment. Now it becomes clear why (**) fails: the abstract state represented during execution of the second component, C_2, cannot be computed from the communication history of C_2 alone. The communications of C_1, or better, the abstract value that they represent, should be taken into account too.

1.2 The "Programs are Predicate Transformers" approach

The remark ending the previous section gives a clue how to solve the problem that has been sketched above. Rather than specifying processes within the $\mathcal{PP}$ style, we ressort to a "Programs as Predicate Transformers" ($\mathcal{PT}$) approach, where we use a ***generalized form of Hoare's logic.*** This logic employs pre- and postconditions in the form of predicates on *computational histories* rather than on single states. Then, for the process $C_1 ; C_2$ as above, the precondition part from the specification of the C_2 component can make appropriate assumptions concerning the (abstract value represented by) the sequence of communications performed by C_1. Within this predicate transformer framework we give a compositional treatment of data reification by means of processes. The outer form of the syntactic verification conditions for reification resembles closely that of the verification conditions for "classical' data reification as in [Jones2] and [Hoare3]. In short, if some abstract operation, acting on an abstract data variable a, is specified by (Hoare style) pre- and postconditions $pre(a)$ and $post(a)$, then the implementing operation should satisfy a similar specification of the form $pre(retr(h|\alpha))$, $post(retr(h|\alpha))$. Here, $h|\alpha$ denotes the sequence of communications along the channels connected to the data process implementing variable a, and *retr* is the *retrieve function* mapping this sequence of communications to the corresponding abstract value stored in a.

The idea of mapping complete concrete computations to abstract ones occurs also in [AL] and [HW], where computations are coded into the (concrete) state by means of (auxiliary) history and prophecy variables. This auxiliary variable technique, however, does not clarify the relationship with the $\mathcal{PP}$ style, nor does it allow for a natural integration with the latter approach.

1.3 "Programs are Predicates" and Sequential Composition

One might think that that the problem that we have raised here is rather specific for our particular reification technique. Such is not the case; essentially the same problem shows up in compositional verification systems following the $\mathcal{PP}$ approach. In general, formalizing "programs as predicates" leads to simple axiom systems, where, for instance, Gorelick's [Gorelick] rather unnatural substitution rules for Hoare's logic can be dispensed with. (Applications of these substitution rules are in the $\mathcal{PP}$ approach replaced by applications of laws of predicate logic and the rule of consequence.) This simplicity gets lost, however, when dealing with sequential composition and iteration. Then these systems are no match for formal systems based on "programs as predicate transformers" such as weakest precondition calculi, dynamic logic, or Hoare logics, which characterize ";" and "*" essentially by

$$\frac{\{pre\}\ P_1\ \{r\} \quad , \quad \{r\}\ P_2\ \{post\}}{\{pre\}\ P_1; P_2\ \{post\}} \quad \text{and} \quad \frac{\{pre\}\ P\ \{pre\}}{\{pre\}\ P^*\ \{pre\}},$$

one of the reasons why these logics are so successful! This drawback of the $\mathcal{PP}$ approach is probably a reason why sequential composition is often watered down to prefixing by an atomic action, as in Milner's CCS [Mil], or Hoare's CSP [Hoare2]. However, derivation of concurrent systems from their specifications calls for full sequential composition, and compositionality when refining subsystems or implementing atomic actions. According to these yardsticks, the treatment of (full) sequential composition in the sat style logic of [Hoare2] is not satisfactory. The axioms presented there enable one only to eliminate sequential composition of the form $P; Q$ by rewriting the P component. Clearly P is not treated as a "black box", as required by the compositionality principle.

Other indications for this drawback of the $\mathcal{PP}$ approach are contained in Barringer, Kuiper & Pnueli's [BKP] compositional formulation of Temporal logic. Barringer, Kuiper and Pnueli had to add the cumbersome chop and chop* operations to TL to handle ";" and "*" within a compositional verification system. A similar problem besets VDM, as can be seen from its complicated rules for these operations [Jones], [Jones2]. (Although at first glance VDM specifications appear to follow the pre/postcondition style of Hoare's logic, VDM really follows the $\mathcal{PP}$ approach, since VDM style postconditions are predicates on both initial and final states.)

Since sequential composition and iteration are problematic within $\mathcal{PP}$ whereas $\mathcal{PT}$ deals nicely with those constructs, we are lead to the following conclusion: It is important to construct *hybrid* verifications systems which, due to the complementary nature of the $\mathcal{PP}$ and $\mathcal{PT}$ approaches, combine their advantages while eliminating their disadvantages. This is the subject of the next section.

1.4 Integrating $\mathcal{PP}$ and $\mathcal{PT}$

The paper starts with indicating how to unify the $\mathcal{PP}$ and $\mathcal{PT}$ approaches within a single simple algebraic framework for predicates by introducing a weakest precondition operator, thus mapping $\mathcal{PP}$ on $\mathcal{PT}$, and the less familiar "leads to" operator expressing how a pre- and a postcondition characterize a program as a single predicate, mapping $\mathcal{PT}$ on $\mathcal{PP}$. (This operator was introduced in sequential setting in [Schwarz] and extended to concurrency in [Zwiers89]). But instead of introducing two different compositional frameworks for concurrency with transformations between them as worked out in [Zwiers89], we adapt an idea of He Jifeng & Hoare's [He Jifeng] *identifying* the denotations of pre/postconditions and programs, thus obtaining two different styles of reasoning within a single setting.

The basic idea is that we start with some appropriate sat style formalism, and then add a corresponding Hoare logic on top of it, by means of abbreviations. What is important here is that the resulting logic does satisfy the nice verification rules for sequential composition and iteration presented above.

This opens up the possibility of using development strategies based on loop invariants for instance, *within what is basically a sat style approach!*

The step to Hoare logic is made intuitively by *specifying processes within a given sequential context,* as follows. Process Q is specified by a pair of processes P and R, called pre- and postcondition, by requiring that the following *sat* relation holds:

$P; Q \ sat \ R$

The rôle of a precondition P is to describe the allowed initial computations that have been observed already when Q starts executing. The resulting (composed) computation is then required to satisfy postcondition R. We use the following notation, similar to that of Hoare's logic:

$(P)\, Q\, (R)$ abbreviates $P; Q \ sat \ R$.

Within this setting a weakest precondition operator $wp(Q, R)$ can be defined (implicitly) by the equivalence:

For all X, $X \ sat \ wp(Q, R)$ iff $(X)\, Q\, (R)$.

(Technically, this classifies the weakest precondition and sequential composition as *adjoints.*) For the case of binary relations (where $P \ sat \ R$ means $P \subseteq R$) this characterization of weakest preconditions is due to [He Jifeng], where $wp(Q, R)$ is called *weakest prespecification.*

The other direction, going from a Hoare formula $(P)\, Q\, (R)$ to an equivalent *sat* formula of the form $Q \ sat \ S$ uses the "leads to" operator $\leadsto$. In [He Jifeng] this operator, called weakest postspecification, is defined using complementation and inverses of relations. Now for arbitrary *sat* systems, and in particular for the sat systems that we use for our data reification, no such notion of inverse is available. Fortunately, $\leadsto$ can also be characterized as an adjoint, i.e., without relying on program inversion:

For all X, $X \ sat \ (P \leadsto Q)$ iff $(P)\, X\, (Q)$.

These new notions extending wp and $\leadsto$ to a general concurrent setting are consistent with the classical notions of these operators in that their characterizing properties remain valid and in case of restriction to sequential programming they coincide with those notions. This is due to the fact that the exact *nature* of observations does not matter, except that for the definition of predicate transformers to make sense one assumes that processes can be sequentially composed.

Finally a remark concerning possible future extensions. For the reification technique of this paper we need to specify processes within a *left* sequential context, determining the past behaviour. This corresponds to the use of auxiliary *history* variables in [AL]. However, in [AL] and in [HW] one also needs so called (auxiliary) *prophecy variables*, determining to some extent the *future* behaviour of the system. An interesting question is whether something similar can be done by specifying processes within a *right sequential context.* Instead of using the weakest precondition, one would use the leadsto operator, with a different rôle attached to the operands however: For Hoare style logic the term $P \leadsto Q$ corresponds to the weakest *process* determined by *pre- and postcondition* P and Q. For specification within right context, however, we have a *process* P and *postcondition* Q, and the term $P \leadsto Q$ now corresponds to the weakest "continuation" that can be executed after P such that the complete computation still satisfies Q.

1.5 The joint action model for processes

The technical framework that we use in this paper is a mathematical specification language MCL related to, but even simpler than, Olderog's calculus of mixed terms [Olderog], which allows for a top-down development strategy in which assertions are gradually transformed into processes. MCL must be seen as a Mathematical Core Language containing only those operations which form the foundation of many existing (specification) languages for sequential, concurrent and reactive systems. It can be best understood as a mutually recursive definition of two languages, one for processes and one for assertions, folded into a single language. As mentioned above, MCL has no fixed interpretation; only a few weak assumptions about the underlying computational models are made.

MCL can be specialized to a particular computational model, such as the failures model of [BHR], or P. Aczel's [Aczel] compositional model for shared variable concurrency in [BKP], by fixing the semantic domains, and adding a few model dependent operations. This paper illustrates the approach for a state based model where processes communicate via *joint actions* on shared variables.

2 The basic mathematical formalism

In formalized specification methods one encounters several at least conceptually different languages:

- A *programming* or *process language*, to denote (executable) programs or processes.
- An *assertion language*, to formulate pre- and postconditions or sat predicates.
- A language of *correctness formulae*, to formulate program specifications such as Hoare formulae or sat style formulae.

For several reasons it is often necessary to treat these as sublanguages of a common unified language. For instance, an integration of processes and assertions into one language, resulting in what is now commonly called "mixed terms" cf. [Olderog], allows for a top-down development strategy in which assertions are gradually transformed into processes. We present such a mixed term language together with a class of (sat style) correctness formulae. Thereafter we discuss a unification of these two languages into what we call the mathematical core language MCL . Since our aim is to have a mathematical framework that can be applied to many different models of concurrency, the domain of interpretation for processes and the interpretation of operations such as sequential composition is not fixed. However, assuming that processes and process specifications denote *sets* of objects called observations, it is clear that we can include set theoretic operations in our language. As a consequence, part of MCL does have a fixed interpretation. In fact it is this fixed part that allows us to formulate predicate transformers for MCL . The language of correctness formulae includes quantification over typed variables where, in the syntax below, τ indicates a type. In applications we introduce types corresponding to data, a type for sequences of communications, a type for time values etc. For MCL , we leave open what types there are, except for the type of *processes,* that is always present. For process variables X, taken from a given set $\mathcal{P}var$, we have introduced a separate quantification construct where (explicit) typing has been omitted.

We give the syntax of mixed terms and (correctness) formulae. $F = \{F_1, \cdots, F_m\}$ is a set of (uninterpreted) operations where F_i has arity n_i (possibly 0).

$(P \in) Mix,$

$$P ::= \emptyset \mid Id \mid P;Q \mid P \cup Q \mid P \cap Q$$
$$\mid \overline{P} \mid F_i(P_1, \cdots, P_{n_i}) \mid X \mid \bigcap X : f$$

$(f \in) Form,$

$$f ::= \textbf{false} \mid P\ sat\ Q \mid f_1 \wedge f_2 \mid f_1 \rightarrow f_2$$
$$\mid \forall x : \tau . f \mid \forall X . f$$

The interpretation of mixed terms is defined rigorously below. First we give some intuition and motivation for the constructs that appear in the two languages above. As many of the more usual language constructs are missing, we indicate how they reappear here in the form of abbreviations.

A remark concerning terminology: we use "computation" as a generic term for those objects that are the elements of the underlying semantic domain for both processes and specifications. In fact, a process or specification denotes a *set* of such "computations". No inclination to a particular model of computation is intended here; Computations can take the form of traces, of functions or whatever else is considered appropriate as a mathematical model of the observables of processes.

Informally, $\emptyset$ denotes the empty set of computations, and $P \cup Q$, $P \cap Q$ and $\overline{P}$ denote union, intersection and complementation of sets. The formula P *sat* Q, stating that one process P is included as subset in another process Q classifies as a *correctness formula*. We use $P = Q$ as an abbreviation for $P \; sat \; Q \wedge Q \; sat \; P$.

Like sequential composition $P; Q$, the process Id has not a fixed set theoretical interpretation, but we require that Id acts as the identity element for sequential composition.

Process variables X can occur free in mixed terms and formulae. Such variables range over sets of computations. On occasion we use $\lambda X \, . \, P$ or $P(X)$ to suggest that P might contain free occurrences of X, and in this case $P(Q)$ and $(\lambda X \, . \, P) \, Q$ are understood to abbreviate $P[Q/X]$, i.e., the term P where Q has been substituted for the free occurrences of X. Apart from by applying quantification, free process variables X occurring in a correctness formula f can also be bound by a *generalized intersection.* This is a construct of the form $\bigcap X : f$, denoting the intersection of all sets X such that f holds for X. The generalized intersection construct serves to define recursive processes as well as predicate transformers, as we will indicate now. Mixed terms P with only positive occurrences of X (i.e. occurrences within the scope of an even number of negations and complementations) denote monotone functions on the complete lattice of sets of computations and thus have both a least and greatest fixed point [Tarski], defined as:

$$\mu X.P \stackrel{\text{def}}{=} \bigcap X : (P \; sat \; X)$$

$$\nu X.P \stackrel{\text{def}}{=} \bigcup X : (X \; sat \; P)$$

Here $\bigcup X : f(X)$ abbreviates $\overline{\bigcap X : f(\overline{X})}$.

An important special case that we can use in MCL as an abbreviation is iteration:

$$P^* \stackrel{\text{def}}{=} \mu X.(Id \cup P; X).$$

Closely related to fixed points are *adjoints* that in turn are used to define our predicate transformers. For mixed term $\lambda X \, . \, P$ we introduce the *right adjoint* $\mathcal{R}X \, . \, P$ as an operation on mixed terms . We define it (implicitly) by the characterization:

$$P(Q) \; sat \; S \quad \text{iff} \quad Q \; sat \; (\mathcal{R}X \, . \, P)(S).$$

Here S should not contain X free. If it is clear from context which variable X of P is meant we write P^R instead of $\mathcal{R}X.P$. If $\lambda X \, . \, P$ is completely additive , in the sense that it distributes through arbirary unions of processes, then the right adjoint P^R is guaranteed to exist and can be characterized as a generalized union:

$$P^R(S) \; = \; \bigcup X : (P \; sat \; S).$$

We use this fact to define two predicate transformers as adjoints of sequential composition. To guarantee their existence, we assume that sequential composition is completely additive in both its arguments. (As we indicate below, this assumption is satisfied for almost any reasonable definition of sequential composition.)

- The weakest precondition operator $\lambda X \, . \, [P]$ for mixed term P, where P must not contain X free itself, is defined as:

  $$\lambda X \, . \, [P] \stackrel{\text{def}}{=} \mathcal{R}X \, . \, (X; P)$$

  It is characterized by the equivalence

  $$Q; P \; sat \; S \quad \text{iff} \quad Q \; sat \; [P]S.$$

- Similarly, the leads to operator $\lambda X \, . \, P \leadsto X$ is defined as right adjoint of sequential composition for its second argument:

$$\lambda X . P \rightsquigarrow X \stackrel{\text{def}}{=} \mathcal{R}X.(P;X),$$

and is characterized by:

$$P;Q \ sat \ S \quad \text{iff} \quad Q \ sat \ P \rightsquigarrow S.$$

We note that a strongest postcondition can be defined along these lines too. However, it turns out that it coincides with the sequential composition operator!

Before presenting an integration of mixed terms and correctness formulae, we investigate how sequential composition of processes could defined. We have argued above that the domain of process denotations consists of sets of computations. So this domain must be (a subset of) some powerset $\mathcal{P}(Comp)$, where *Comp* is some appropriate domain of computations. Any reasonable definition of sequential composition of *processes*, i.e. composition of *sets* of computations, starts with an appropriate definition for the composition $\sigma_1;\sigma_2$ of single computations σ_1 and σ_2. That is, we assume that there is some given operation ";" from *Comp* $\times$ *Comp* to *Comp*.

If for example *Comp* is the set of all finite state sequences over some set of states *State*, then the composition $\sigma_0;\sigma_1$ of sequences $\sigma_0 \stackrel{\text{def}}{=} (s_0, s_1, \ldots, s_n)$ and $\sigma_1 \stackrel{\text{def}}{=} (s'_0, s'_1, \ldots s'_m)$ is defined only if the final state s_n of σ_0 equals the initial state s'_0 of σ_1. In that case, their *fusion* $\sigma_0;\sigma_1$ is $(s_0, s_1, \ldots, s_n, s'_1, \ldots s'_m)$.

This example makes clear that in general the given composition ";" on *Comp* is a *partial* operation. In this context we say that σ_0 and σ_1 are *composable* iff their composition $\sigma_0;\sigma_1$ is *defined.*

Now for sets of computations $\rho_1, \rho_2 \in \mathcal{P}(Comp)$ we define sequential composition by means of pointwise extension:

$$\rho_1;\rho_2 \ = \ \{ \sigma_1;\sigma_2 \ \mid \ \sigma_1 \in \rho_1,\ \sigma_2 \in \rho_2, \sigma_1 \text{ and } \sigma_2 \text{ composable } \}.$$

This definition yields a sequential composition operation that is *completely additive.*

For the example of state sequences above, the one element sequences (s) have the special property that for any sequence σ if $(s);\sigma$ is defined then $(s);\sigma = \sigma$. Similarly, $\sigma;(s) = \sigma$ if σ and (s) are composable. In general, we call some computation ϵ an *identity element* if it has the property that $\sigma;\epsilon = \sigma$ and $\epsilon;\sigma' = \sigma'$ for all σ, σ' such that the relevant compositions are defined. In this situation we call ϵ the left identity for σ and the right identity for σ'. We define the subset $\hat{Id}$ of *Comp* as the set of all such identities elements. Usually it is the case that for each computation $\sigma \in Comp$ there exist both a left and right identity in *Comp*. It is easily seen that in that case the set $\hat{Id}$ acts as the identity element on the level of composition of *processes*. ($\hat{Id};\rho = \rho;\hat{Id} = \rho$ for all $\rho \in \mathcal{P}(Comp)$.)

Finally we present our mathematical core language MCL . It is a straightforward unification of mixed terms and correctness formulae. One point of view is to regard MCL terms as formulae, i.e. denoting a truthvalue, where correctness formulae are distinguished by the property that their truthvalue depends only on the values of free process variables but not on the computation. (The truthvalue of general MCL terms depends on both). An attractive alternative (equivalent) view, closer to the semantics of mixed terms, is to interpret MCL terms as sets of computations viz. the set of all computations that satisfy the term in question seen as a formula. Then correctness formulae denote, depending on the free variables, either the empty set or the set *Comp* of all computations.

Syntax of MCL :

$(P \in)$ MCL ,

$$P \ ::= \ \textbf{false} \ \mid \ Id \ \mid \ P;Q \ \mid \ P \vee Q \ \mid \ P \wedge Q$$
$$\mid \ P \rightarrow Q \ \mid \ F_i(P_1, \cdots, P_{n_i}) \ \mid \ \forall x : \tau . P$$
$$\mid \ X \ \mid \ \forall X.P \ \mid \ \boldsymbol{\forall} P.$$

The set theoretical operators on mixed terms have been replaced by logical operators, but of course the interpretation *as sets* treats, for instance, $P \vee Q$ as the mixed term $P \cup Q$. Correctness formulae of the form $Q \ sat \ R$ have been replaced by a new quantification construct of the form $\boldsymbol{\forall} P$, which denotes universal quantification for the computation. The intuition here is that specifications of behaviour have, implicitly, the computation as a kind of "free variable". For instance in *trace logic*, a special variable h, denoting the computation, occurs syntactically free in the usual sense. In this case the construct $\forall P$ can be reduced to an explicit quantification of the form $\forall h : Trace . P(h)$. For other formalisms, such as temporal logic, there is no such possibility to denote the computation in a *direct* way. Nevertheless, what counts here is the *semantics,* and for a temporal formula the latter depends on a sequence σ which we regard as an implicit variable of the formula. In this case, "$\forall P$" is essential to express what is usually called "validity" of specification P.

In the alternative set theoretical view, $\forall P$ denotes either the set $\mathcal{C}omp$ or the empty set, depending on whether P denotes $\mathcal{C}omp$ or some other set. (So $\forall P$ is classified as a correctness formula). Within this context we can reintroduce P *sat* Q as an abbreviating $\forall(P \rightarrow Q)$.

Finally we note that the mixed term $\bigcap X : f$ reappears here also as an abbreviation $\bigcap X : P$ for MCL terms P ($= P(X)$). The term $(\forall P) \rightarrow X$ is true if $P(X)$ does *not* hold, and it reduces to X if it does. In the interpretation as sets we see that $(\forall P) \rightarrow X$ denotes either $\mathcal{C}omp$ or X depending on the validity of $P(X)$. Since universal quantification is interpreted as a generalized intersection for this interpretation, one sees that we can define the process $\bigcap X : P$ as follows.

$$\bigcap X : P \stackrel{\text{def}}{=} \forall X.\big((\forall P) \rightarrow X\big).$$

For the interpretation of MCL we introduce some semantic domains:

- Above we already assumed the existence of a domain of computations $\mathcal{C}omp$ and defined the domain of process denotations $\mathcal{P}(\mathcal{C}omp)$.
- Operation symbols F of arity n, do not have a *fixed* interpretation for MCL . However, we assume that (for each *specialization of MCL*), operation F is interpreted as a n-ary function $\hat{F}_i$:

  $$\hat{F} : \mathcal{P}(\mathcal{C}omp)^n \rightarrow \mathcal{P}(\mathcal{C}omp).$$

  For dealing with recursion it is convenient that the operations $\hat{F}$ are *continuous*. All operations that we actually use in this paper are defined by means of pointwise extension of some operation $f : \mathcal{C}omp^n \rightarrow \mathcal{C}omp$, or, slightly more liberal, $f : \mathcal{C}omp^n \rightarrow \mathcal{P}(\mathcal{C}omp)$. Such operations are not only continuous but even completely additive. The definition of the $\mathcal{T}$ function below has been formulated for this last case, that is, we assume that

  $$\hat{F}_i(\rho_1, \ldots, \rho_{n_i}) = \bigcup\{f_i(\sigma_1, \ldots, \sigma_{n_i}) \mid \sigma_1 \in \rho_1, \ldots, \sigma_{n_i} \in \rho_{n_i}\}.$$

- The domain Env of process variable environments is defined as the function space $\mathcal{P}var \rightarrow \mathcal{P}(\mathcal{C}omp)$, where $\mathcal{P}var$ is the set of all process variables.
- For free variables of type τ, other than process variables, we introduce a corresponding domain of environments Γ. The exact structure of Γ depends on the particular application of MCL ; we assume that a free variable x of type τ is interpreted as $\gamma(x)$, where $\gamma \in \Gamma$.

The semantics of MCL is now defined by means of the function $\mathcal{T}$, with functionality:

$$\mathcal{T} : \text{MCL} \rightarrow (Env \rightarrow (\Gamma \rightarrow (\mathcal{C}omp \rightarrow \{true, false\}))),$$

For the (equivalent) interpretation by means of *sets*, we introduce the function $\mathcal{O}bs$:

$$\mathcal{O}bs : \text{MCL} \rightarrow (Env \rightarrow (\Gamma \rightarrow \mathcal{P}(\mathcal{C}omp))).$$

The intention is that $\mathcal{O}bs(P)\eta$ is the set of all computations that satisfy predicate P, where the interpretation of free process variables X is determined by the environment η. $\mathcal{T}$ and $\mathcal{O}bs$ can be defined in terms of each other as follows:

$$\mathcal{T}(P)\eta\gamma\sigma = true \text{ iff } \sigma \in \mathcal{O}bs(P)\eta\gamma.$$

For convenience we list the definitions of both $\mathcal{O}bs$ and $\mathcal{T}$.

$\mathcal{O}bs[\![\mathbf{false}]\!]\eta\gamma = \emptyset$

$\mathcal{O}bs[\![Id]\!]\eta\gamma = \hat{Id}$

$\mathcal{O}bs[\![P;Q]\!]\eta\gamma = \mathcal{O}bs[\![P]\!]\eta\gamma \,;\, \mathcal{O}bs[\![Q]\!]\eta\gamma$

$\mathcal{O}bs[\![P \vee Q]\!]\eta\gamma = \mathcal{O}bs[\![P]\!]\eta\gamma \cup \mathcal{O}bs[\![Q]\!]\eta\gamma$

$\mathcal{O}bs[\![P \wedge Q]\!]\eta\gamma = \mathcal{O}bs[\![P]\!]\eta\gamma \cap \mathcal{O}bs[\![Q]\!]\eta\gamma$

$\mathcal{O}bs[\![P \rightarrow Q]\!]\eta\gamma = (\mathcal{C}omp - \mathcal{O}bs[\![P]\!]\eta\gamma) \cup \mathcal{O}bs[\![Q]\!]\eta\gamma$

$\mathcal{O}bs[\![F_i(P_1, \cdot\cdot, P_{n_i})]\!]\eta\gamma = \hat{F}_i(\mathcal{O}bs[\![P_1]\!]\eta\gamma, \cdot\cdot, \mathcal{O}bs[\![P_{n_i}]\!]\eta\gamma)$

$\mathcal{O}bs[\![X]\!]\eta\gamma = \eta(X)$

$\mathcal{O}bs[\![\forall X.P]\!]\eta\gamma = \bigcap\{\mathcal{O}bs[\![P]\!](\eta[\rho/X]) \mid \rho \in \mathcal{P}(\mathcal{C}omp)\}$

$\mathcal{O}bs[\![\mathbf{\forall} P]\!]\eta\gamma = \mathcal{C}omp$ if $\mathcal{O}bs[\![P]\!]\eta\gamma = \mathcal{C}omp$, else $\emptyset$

The last two clauses are simpler understood in terms of the truth function $\mathcal{T}$. For the definition of this semantic function we make here the (non essential) assumption that $\hat{F}_i$ and sequential composition are defined by means of pointwise extension, as discussed above.

$\mathcal{T}[\![\mathbf{false}]\!]\eta\gamma\sigma = \mathit{false}$

$\mathcal{T}[\![Id]\!]\eta\gamma\sigma$ iff $\sigma \in \hat{Id}$

$\mathcal{T}[\![P;Q]\!]\eta\gamma\sigma$ iff for some $\sigma_0, \sigma_1 \in \mathcal{C}omp$, $\sigma = \sigma_0;\sigma_1$
and $\mathcal{T}[\![P]\!]\eta\gamma\sigma_0$ and $\mathcal{T}[\![Q]\!]\eta\gamma\sigma_1$

$\mathcal{T}[\![P \vee Q]\!]\eta\gamma\sigma$ iff $\mathcal{T}[\![P]\!]\eta\gamma\sigma$ or $\mathcal{T}[\![Q]\!]\eta\gamma\sigma$

$\mathcal{T}[\![P \wedge Q]\!]\eta\gamma\sigma$ iff $\mathcal{T}[\![P]\!]\eta\gamma\sigma$ and $\mathcal{T}[\![Q]\!]\eta\gamma\sigma$

$\mathcal{T}[\![P \rightarrow Q]\!]\eta\gamma\sigma$ iff $\mathcal{T}[\![P]\!]\eta\gamma\sigma$ implies $\mathcal{T}[\![Q]\!]\eta\gamma\sigma$

$\mathcal{T}[\![F_i(P_1, \cdot\cdot, P_{n_i})]\!]\eta\gamma\sigma$ iff there are $\sigma_1, \ldots, \sigma_{n_i} \in \mathcal{C}omp$
such that $\sigma \in f_i(\sigma_1, .., \sigma_{n_i})$
and $\mathcal{T}[\![P_1]\!]\eta\gamma\sigma_1, \cdot\cdot, \mathcal{T}[\![P_{n_i}]\!]\eta\gamma\sigma_{n_i}$

$\mathcal{T}[\![X]\!]\eta\gamma\sigma$ iff $\sigma \in \eta(X)$

$\mathcal{T}[\![\forall X.P]\!]\eta\gamma\sigma$ iff $\forall\rho \in \mathcal{P}(\mathcal{C}omp) \,.\, \mathcal{T}[\![P]\!](\eta[\rho/X])(\gamma)(\sigma)$

$\mathcal{T}[\![\mathbf{\forall} P]\!]\eta\gamma\sigma$ iff $\forall\sigma' \in \mathcal{C}omp \,.\, \mathcal{T}[\![P]\!]\eta\gamma\sigma'$.

3 Processes and joint action semantics

The aim of this section is to construct a specification and verification method for a simple language of state based processes, communicating by means of *joint actions.* Both process language and assertion language are specializations of MCL . The language that we want to describe is as follows. We assume that $\mathcal{V}ar$ is some given set of variable names x. *Alphabets* α are subsets of $\mathcal{V}ar$. Expressions e are built up from variables by applying functions f_i. (Nullary functions denote constants.) Variables, functions and expressions should be thought of as *typed*, but we ignore the details here.

$(e \in)$ *Expr*,

$e ::= x \mid f_i(e_1, \ldots, e_{n_i})$

$(P \in)$ *Proc*,

$P ::= x!e \mid x? \mid \mathbf{skip} \mid P;Q \mid P \,\mathbf{or}\, Q \mid P \parallel Q \mid P\backslash\alpha \mid P^* \mid X \mid \mathbf{rec}X.P$

To describe the communication mechanism we have the notion of alphabet $\alpha(P)$ of a process P. To this end we assume that process variables X are *typed* in the sense that for each such variable $\alpha(X)$ is determined. Then $\alpha(P)$ is defined by the following table:

P	$\alpha(P)$
$x!e$	$\{x\} \cup \alpha(e)$
$x?$	$\{x\}$
skip	$\emptyset$
$P;Q$	$\alpha(P) \cup \alpha(Q)$
P **or** Q	$\alpha(P) \cup \alpha(Q)$
$P \parallel Q$	$\alpha(P) \cup \alpha(Q)$
$P \backslash \alpha'$	$\alpha(P) - \alpha'$
P^*	$\alpha(P)$
X	$\alpha(X)$
rec$X.P$	$\alpha(X)$

(For process **rec**$X.P$ we require that $\alpha(P) = \alpha(X)$.)

Processes $x!e$ denote an *assignment operation,* assigning the value of the (state dependent) expression e to variable x. Similarly $x?$ denotes a *random assignment* to x. Such assignments are executed as *joint actions*, that is, synchronized with similar assignments to the same variable in other processes executing in parallel. The *reading* of variables, as it occurs when evaluating an expression e, is not synchronized. Processes that are ready to perform an assignment must wait until all partners that should cooperate are ready to perform the assignment. Like the CSP style communication mechanism this waiting might end up in a deadlocked situation. Not *all* assignments are synchronized; for parallel composition $P \parallel Q$, (only) assignments to variables x in the common alphabet $\alpha(P) \cap \alpha(Q)$ are synchronized. Composing $P \parallel Q$ in parallel with a third process R can even introduce joint actions that are executed simultaneously by all three processes, in case some variable x occurs in the intersection of the alphabets of P, Q and R. Assignments to variables in alphabet α can be executed autonomously by process P, and in fact become invisible, as soon as they are *hidden* by means of the hiding operator $\backslash\alpha$.

Note that hiding can be applied to any process, including purely sequential ones, and note also that for x to be hidden in $P \parallel Q$ it need not occur in the common alphabet of P and Q. This implies that certain variables can be regarded as "local" variables for which assignments are effectivly executed as usual for sequential programming languages, i.e. not as a joint action with other processes.

The other operations on processes are fairly standard: P **or** Q makes a nondeterministic choice between P and Q, not influenced by other processes executing in parallel. $P;Q$ denotes sequential composition of processes, with **skip** as the "identity" element for this operation.

The construct **rec**$X.P$ denotes a recursive process, where the process variable X can occur free in the body P. The simpler case of iteration (zero or more times) is denoted by P^*.

We treat this process language as a specialized form of MCL . The semantics that we chose here describes the *finite observations* that one can make in the form of *finite, labeled sequences of states.*

A *state* s is treated here as a function from $\mathcal{V}ar$ to some given domain $\mathcal{V}al$ of values. So we define:

$$\mathcal{S}tate = (\mathcal{V}ar \to \mathcal{V}al).$$

For state s we denote by $s[v/x]$ the variant state that is identical to s except for argument x on which it is defined as $(s[v/x])(x) = v$.

Computations σ are finite sequences of states, where the "transition" from a state s_i to the next state s_{i+1} is labeled by the name of some variable x. The two states s_i and s_{i+1} can differ only for the value of x, that is, $s_i(y) = s_{i+1}(y)$ for all variables y other than the transition label x. So a typical computation σ has the form:

$(s_0 \xrightarrow{x_1} s_1 \xrightarrow{x_2} \cdots \xrightarrow{x_n} s_n)$. $\quad (*)$

We distinguish between so called *finished*, i.e. *terminated* computations, and *unfinished* ones. The latter should not be confused with diverging computations; the need for unfinished computations arises only because we describe the semantics of processes as *prefixed closed* sets of computations. This means that if $(*)$ is a possible observation for process P, than any prefix $(s_0 \xrightarrow{x_1} \cdots s_m)$, where $m \leq n$, is a possible observation too. For a proper definition of sequential composition these prefixes must be marked as being unfinished. To this end we extend our domain *Comp* of computations to allow elements of the form:

$(s_0 \xrightarrow{x_1} s_1 \xrightarrow{x_2} \cdots \xrightarrow{x_n} s_m \bot)$. $\quad (**)$

Now we can define the semantics of random assignments $x?$ as follows:

$$[\![x?]\!] \stackrel{\text{def}}{=} \{(s\bot), (s \xrightarrow{x} s[v/x]) \mid s \in \mathit{State}, v \in \mathit{Val}\}.$$

Assuming some given interpretation $[\![f_i]\!]$ for the function symbols f_i we can define the semantics $\mathcal{E}[\![e]\!]s$ of expressions e in state s, and the semantics of assignments $x!e$:

$$\mathcal{E}[\![x]\!]s = s(x),$$

$$\mathcal{E}[\![f_i(e_1, \ldots, e_{n_i})]\!]s = [\![f_i]\!](\mathcal{E}[\![e_1]\!]s, \ldots \mathcal{E}[\![e_{n_i}]\!]s).$$

$$[\![x!e]\!] = \{(s\bot), (s \xrightarrow{x} s[(\mathcal{E}[\![e]\!]s)/x]) \mid s \in \mathit{State}\}.$$

Two computations σ_0 and σ_1 are not (sequentially) composable if either σ_0 ends with the bottom symbol, denoting that σ_0 is unfinished, or if the final state of σ_0 is not equal to the initial state of σ_1. Otherwise their sequential composition $\sigma_0; \sigma_1$ is defined as the *fusion* of the two sequences. That is:

$$(s_0 \cdots \xrightarrow{x_n} s_n) \,;\, (s_n \xrightarrow{x_{n+1}} \cdots s_m) = (s_0 \cdots \xrightarrow{x_n} s_n \xrightarrow{x_{n+1}} \cdots s_m),$$

and similarly for σ_1 ending with a bottom symbol. Sequential composition of *sets* of computations U and V is as follows:

$$U; V \stackrel{\text{def}}{=} \{\sigma \in U \mid \sigma \text{ unfinished }\} \cup \{\sigma_0; \sigma_1 \mid \sigma_0 \in U, \sigma_1 \in V, \sigma_0 \text{ and } \sigma_1 \text{ composable .}\}$$

We define the semantics of the MCL identity process Id as:

$$[\![Id]\!] = \{(s) \mid s \in \mathit{State}\}.$$

Note that this is not a prefixed closed set, so the MCL identity process is not a suitable candidate for the semantics of **skip**. Fortunately we can define the semantics of the **skip** process as the prefix closure of that of the Id process:

$$[\![\textbf{skip}]\!] = \{(s\bot), (s) \mid s \in \mathit{State}\}.$$

Note that *on the restricted domain of prefix closed sets,* the **skip** process does act as identity element for sequential composition, although this is no longer the case for arbitrary sets of computations.

The projection operation can be described for single computations as follows. For computation $\sigma = (s_0 \xrightarrow{x_1} \cdots \xrightarrow{x_n} s_n)$ the projection $\sigma|\{y_0, \ldots y_m\}$ is obtained as follows:

- first omit all those transition labels x_i and corresponding states s_i for which x_i is not in $\{y_0, \ldots, y_m\}$,
- second, change each remaining state s_j into $s_0[s_j(y_0)/y_0, \ldots, s_j(y_m)/y_m]$.

That is, transitions corresponding to assignment to variables outside the projection alphabet $\{y_0, \ldots, y_m\}$ are omitted and the effects of such assignments on the state are undone. The definition for computations ending with a bottom symbol is similar. For sets of computations we define projection by means of pointwise extension of the projection operation on computations. In MCL this automatically introduces the right adjoint $P|^R\alpha$ of projection. $P|^R\alpha$ consists of all those computations that can be obtained by inserting some arbitrary transitions of the form "$\xrightarrow{x} s$", where x is not in α, at some arbitrary places in computations of P. Of course the resulting sequence must satisfy the property that neighbour states differ at mosts for the variable labeling the corresponding transition, so the states following such an inserted transition must be adapted, according to the value assigned to x. We call this adjoint the chaotic closure with respect to α. Chaotic closures are used to define parallelism as a derived operation. The idea is to define the semantics of $P \parallel Q$ as the *intersection* of two processes P' and Q' where P' is obtained from P by allowing interfering actions performed by Q without cooperation with P, and vice versa for Q'. Since independent actions from Q cannot be predicted from the semantics of P, the P' term makes arbitrary (i.e. non deterministic) guesses about such actions; the intersection $P' \wedge Q'$ then filters out the "right" ones.

So we define:

$$P \parallel Q \stackrel{\text{def}}{=} P|^{R}\alpha_p|\alpha_{pq} \wedge Q|^{R}\alpha_q|\alpha_{pq}, \quad \text{where } \alpha_p = \alpha(P),\ \alpha_q = \alpha(Q), \text{ and } \alpha_{pq} = \alpha_p \cup \alpha_q.$$

The other operations are easy: nondeterministic choice P **or** Q can be modeled here as $P \vee Q$, and finally, hiding $P \backslash \alpha$ is $P|(\mathcal{V}ar - \alpha)$.

We define *recursion* **rec**$X.P$ as abbreviating the (MCL) term $\mu X.(P \vee \textbf{skip})$. The inclusion of the term **skip** is motivated by the desired semantics for recursive terms like:

$\textbf{rec}X.(x!1; X)$.

The meaning of $\mu X.(x!1;X)$, i.e., the least fixed point of the equation $X = (x!1;X)$, is the *empty* set of traces. This is not the intended semantics of $\textbf{rec}X.(x!1;X)$. With the definition as given, we obtain as meaning for $\textbf{rec}X.(x!1;X)$ the set consisting of all sequences $(s \xrightarrow{x} s' \xrightarrow{x} s' \cdots \xrightarrow{x} s'\bot)$ of arbitary length, where $s' = s[1/x]$.

It is clear that we can define P^* as usual, that is, as abbreviating $\textbf{rec}X.(P;X)$ $(= \mu X.((P;X) \vee$ **skip**)), where X is some variable not occurring free in P.

The next step is to define an appropriate *assertion* language. To this end we define a class of *atomic* assertions. This involves the definition of expressions of several types.

- ($te \in$) *texp* — *Trace expressions.*

  $te ::= h \mid t \mid (te|\alpha)$

- ($ie \in$) *iexp* — *Integer expressions.*

  $ie ::= 0 \mid 1 \mid i \mid ie_1 + ie_2 \mid ie_1 \cdot ie_2 \mid |te|$

- ($ce \in$) *cexpr* — *Communication expressions,* function symbols f_i are the same as for expressions e occurring in programs.

  $ce ::= te(x)(ie) \mid v \mid f_i(ce_1, \ldots, ce_{n_i})$

- ($\chi \in$) $\mathcal{A}ssn$ — *Atomic Assertions.*

  $\chi ::= ie_0 = ie_1 \mid ce_0 = ce_1 \mid\ !te(x)(ie) \mid te_0 = te_1$

Trace expressions denote elements of the domain of computations. There is one distinguished variable h denoting the computation σ of a MCL term. The other trace variables t are called *logical variables*; they are interpreted as $\gamma(t)$, where γ is the environment funtion for the semantics of MCL . The operation of *projection onto a set of variables* α is included in the assertion language.

Integer expressions ie serve as *indices* for trace expressions. The expression $|te|$ denotes the *length* of trace te.

Communication expressions ce are similar to expressions used in programs, except that variables v are taken from a different set than the set $\mathcal{V}ar$ of program variables. Also, the value of program variable x, relative to some trace te, at index ie is denotable by $te(x)(ie)$.

There is no type of expression corresponding to *transition labels*. Rather there is the type of *atomic assertions* of the form $!te(x)(ie)$, defined to be true iff the transition label with index ie exists and equals x.

The equality relation applied to expressions of equal type forms another type of atomic assertions. Equality is interpreted *strictly*, that is, $exp_0 = exp_1$ is false if exp_0 or exp_1 is not defined.

Since in MCL the propositional logical connectives are present, we can combine atomic assertions into larger specifications. Also, we have quantification available for all types of variables that can occur free in assertions. For a more detailed account of a similar assertion language we refer to [Zwiers89].

4 Data refinement by processes

We start with a reformulation of the well known VDM style data reification technique, adapted to the process model of the previous section. Thereafter we describe an extension of reification that allows for the refinement of abstract variables by means of *processes* rather than by concrete variables. Abstract *operations* are refined into *communications* via joint actions with the implementing process. What is interesting here is that the VDM notion of "retrieve function", essentially mapping concrete states to abstract states, has to be generalized in that retrieve functions now map complete concrete histories in the form of labeled state sequences, to abstract histories. To be able to formulate *VDM style verification conditions* for reification in this generalized setting, it turns out that generalized Hoare's logic should be used here.

We simplify matters technically by concentrating on the *safety* aspects of refinement only. (The semantics that we gave in the previous section also describes "safety" properties of the observable behaviour of processes only, ignoring phenomena like divergence etc.)

Essentially, classical data reification is a program transformation technique, where "abstract" variables and operations of a high-level design are represented by more "concrete" ones on a lower level design. In its simplest form it proceeds as follows. We have available an abstract program A of the form $A'\backslash\{a\}$, where a is a variable used in the program body A', containing values from some "abstract" data type T_a. The idea is to refine A into a program C of the form $C'\backslash\{c\}$, where c is a variable containg values of an implementing "concrete" data type T_c, and where C' is like A' except that operations f_a acting on a have been replaced by suitable concrete operations f_c, acting on c. It should be verified that C has the same observable behaviour as A or, in case of nondeterminism, that the set of possible computations for C is *contained* in the corresponding set for A. To this end a so called retrieve function $retr$ is defined, relating abstract and concrete data by mapping T_c values to T_a values. This retrieve function induces a function on states, that we treat here as a relation ρ on $\mathit{State}_c \times \mathit{State}_a$. It is defined as as follows. Let the alphabet of A be the disjoint union of α and $\{a\}$, and so, the alphabet of C the disjoint union of α and $\{c\}$.

$$\rho = \{(s,t) \in \mathit{State}_c \times \mathit{State}_a \mid t(x) = s(x) \text{ for } x \in \alpha, \text{ and } t(a) = retr(s(c))\}.$$

We extend ρ to a function on computations in the form of labeled state sequences, as defined in the previous section, by applying ρ pointwise to states, labels and the bottom symbol, where we define ρ on labels and the bottom symbol as follows:

$\rho(x) = x$ for variables x other than c,

$\rho(c) = a$,

$\rho(\perp) = \perp$.

Abstract and concrete operations f_a and f_c denote relations F_a and F_c on State_a^2 and State_c^2. (*Relations* rather than *functions* to deal with nondeterministic operations.) The verification conditions for each abstract operation f_a and corresponding concrete operation f_c can now (semantically) be formulated as follows:

$$F_c ; \rho \text{ } sat \text{ } \rho ; F_a. \qquad (1)$$

Here, $F_c\,;\rho$ denotes composition of relations ("ρ after F_c"), and *sat* denotes inclusion of relations. It is easily seen that, if these verification conditions do hold, then for any possible computation σ of C', the sequence $\rho(\sigma)$ is a possible computation for A'. Moreover, from the definition of ρ it follows that $\sigma\backslash\{c\}$ *equals* $(\rho(\sigma))\backslash\{a\}$, implying that any computation of C $(= C'\backslash\{c\})$ is also a possible computation of A $(= A'\backslash\{a\})$.

An important aspect of reification is that the *semantic* characterization (1) above has a simple *syntactic* counterpart when operations are specified by means of Hoare style pre/postconditions. (In Hoare's logic, both pre- and postconditions are conditions on single states, whereas in the case of VDM style specifications the postcondition is a relational predicate on both initial and final state.)

In particular, if abstract operation f_a is specified by:

$$\{pre_a\}\ f_a\ \{post_a\},$$

then the corresponding concrete operation f_c should satisfy

$$\{pre_a[retr(c)/a]\}\ f_c\ \{post_a[retr(c)/a]\}.$$

(For a similar syntactic formulation in the case of VDM see [Jones2].)

So far for the "classical" reification technique. We now discuss an extension of it, where an abstract program as above is transformed into a parallel process. For convenience we assume that A can be decomposed as $A \equiv (a!a_0; A')\backslash\{a\}$, where $a!a_0$ initializes a to some given value a_0. As implementing process we take:

$$(C' \parallel D)\backslash\{op_1, \ldots, op_n\}.$$

Here D is a process implementing the a variable. It has $\{op_1, \ldots, op_n\}$ as its alphabet, containing one communication "port" "op", in the form of a shared variable, for each abstract operation f_a. The process C' is like A' except that operations f_a have been replaced by joint actions for the corresponding "port".

In general one would refine a single abstract operations f_a into a concrete (sub) process. Here we want to avoid the extra complexity introduced by such action refinements, and require that each atomic abstract operation is replaced by a single concrete action in the form of a joint action with the D process. This can be achieved provided we make a few (weak) assumptions about the form of abstract operations acting on a. Such operations should either be assigments to a of the form $a!e(x,a)$, where expression $e(x,a)$ contains at most variable a and a single other variable x free, or else is a "read" action of the form $y!e(a)$, in which case we will assume that all possible other assignments to y in A' are *identical* to this one. The last assumption is not a real restriction, for one can replace actions $y!e(a)$ by $z!e(a); y!z$, where z is some fresh variable. By first applying such simple local transformations, one can always obtain an abstract program A' that does satisfy our requirement.

Now assuming that the requirements on abstract actions as above are satisfied, we proceed as follows. For each assignment to a of the form $a!e(x,a)$ process D has a distinguished port op, and the action is replaced by $op!x$ in C'. For each read action of the form $y!e(a)$, process D has a distinguished port y, and the abstract operation is replaced by $y?$ in C'.

Example

A' is some program acting on a set of ordered elements V. The (abstract) operations on V are:

- $V!empty$, assigning the empty set to V,
- $V!insert(e,V)$, inserting the result of evaluating e into V, where we may assume that the new element is not already present in the set,
- $min!delete(V)$, deleting the minimum element of V and assigning it to min provided V is nonempty.

As initial value for V we take the empty set. (The book by J. Reynolds [Reynolds] contains an example of a graph algorithm that uses these particular operations on sets.)

For "classical" reification, one could represent V by a sorted sequence L of elements, where the empty set is represented by the empty sequence, $insert(e, V)$ is implemented by inserting the value of e on the appropriate place in L, and where $min!delete(V)$ is implemented by removing the "head" element of L and assigning it to y. The retrieve function, mapping sequences to sets, is straightforward.

In our case we implement V as a so called "priority queue" process Q. The implementation of this process itself need not concern us at the moment; one can easily imagine implementations in the form of a process that keep a list L as above as *internal* data structure. For more interesting implementations where a priority queue containing n elements is implemented as a chain of n parallel processes, each containing a single element, see for instance [Zwiers89] or [Barringer].

Here we treat the priority queue process Q as a black box, with an alphabet consisting of the variables $empty, enq$ and min. Resetting V to the empty set is implemented by a $empty?$ action. (The value assigned to "*empty*" is ignored.) The insert operation $V!insert(e, V)$ is implemented as an "enqueueing" action $enq!e$. The retrieval and deletion of the current minimum, $min!delete(V)$, is replaced by $min?$.

Note that from the *visible* state of $C' \parallel Q$, it is impossible to retrieve the value of the abstract set variable V. For the (visible) state of Q consists of the values of enq and min, and these contain only the last values inserted and deleted in V. However, by examining complete *histories* of states in the form of labeled state sequences $(s_0 \xrightarrow{x_1} s_1, \ldots, \xrightarrow{x_n} s_n)$, one can calculate the contents of V as follows.

Let bag_in denote the "bag", i.e. multiset, of values of those transitions in the trace denoted by $h|\{enq, empty\}$, that are not followed by a transition labeled $empty$. Similarly, define bag_out as the bag of values associated with "*min*" transitions, not followed by an "*empty*" transition in the sequence $h|\{min, empty\}$. Then the represented set is $cont_V \stackrel{\text{def}}{=} bag\_in \ominus bag\_out$, where $\ominus$ denotes the difference of two bags. (Relying on the assumption that no element is inserted twice in V, it can be shown that $cont_V$ denotes a *set*, rather than a *multiset*.)

End example

As has become clear from the example, it is possible to define "retrieve functions" mapping *complete concrete computations* of an implementation $C' \parallel D$ to abstract states of program A' but, unlike the classical situation, it is not possible to define such retrieve functions on *single concrete states*. As a consequence, it is not possible to give simple syntactic verification conditions for operations specified by means of pre/postconditions *on states*. Here we turn to *generalized* Hoare's logic, which admits pre/postconditions on complete computations. Within this framework we can formulate the analogon of the verification condition for classical reification:

Verification conditions for generalized reification

Assume that abstract variable a of type T_a, with initial value a_0 and operations $f_1, \ldots, f_n$, is implemented by process D with alphabet $\{op_1, \ldots, op_n\}$, where port op_i corresponds to operation f_i. Assume that a retrieve function $retr$ has been given mapping sequences of $op_1, \ldots, op_n$ actions to T_a values. This function should map the *empty* sequence ε to the value a_0. Moreover, if abstract operation f_a ($\in \{f_1, \ldots, f_n\}$) is specified by:

$$(pre_a)\ f_a\ (post_a),$$

then the implementing concrete operation f_c should verify:

$$D \rightarrow (pre_a[retr(h|\{op_1, \ldots, op_n\})/a])\ f_c\ (post_a[retr(h|\{op_1, \ldots, op_n\})/a]).$$

Theorem

When a retrieve function exists with properties as indicated, then the observable behaviour of the implementing process $(C' \parallel D)\backslash\{op_1, \ldots, op_n\}$ satisfies that of the abstract process $(a!a_0; A')\backslash\{a\}$.

□

(Sketch of) Proof

The retrieve function *retr* induces a corresponding abstraction function ρ on computations, as follows. For (concrete) computation $(s_0 \xrightarrow{x_1} \cdots s_n)$ define $\rho((s_0 \xrightarrow{x_1} \cdots x_n)) = (t_0 \xrightarrow{z_1} \cdots t_n)$ by the following conditions:

- If label x_i is one of the channels op_j, corresponding to abstract operations of the form $a!e(x,a)$, then z_i is a, else z_i equals x_i.
- State t_i is like s_i except that $t_i(a)$ is the value of $retr(h|\{op_1,\ldots,op_n\})$ interpreted over the prefix $(s_0 \xrightarrow{x_1} \cdots s_i)$ of the concrete computation.

It can be seen that an assertion of the form $\Phi[retr(h|\{op_1,\ldots,op_n\})/a]$ is (semantically) identical to $\rho^R(p)$, that is, syntactic substitution in assertions Φ amounts to the same as taking the right adjoint of ρ applied to Φ. Thus we see that the concrete operation f_c actually satisfies:

$$D \rightarrow (\rho^R(pre_a))\ f_c\ (\rho^R(post_a)).$$

Let $A'' \equiv a!a_0; A'$. From the definition of our Hoare formulae it is immediately clear that

$$(a!a_0)\ A'\ (A'')\quad (*).$$

From completeness results as for instance in [Zwiers89] it then follows that there also exists a (Hoare style) *proof* of that fact. Now, exploiting the structural resemblance between A' and C', and using specifications for the f_c operations as above, one can transform the proof of $(*)$ into a proof of

$$D \rightarrow (\rho^R(a!a_0))\ C'\ (\rho^R(A'')).$$

From the premisse requiring that $retr(\varepsilon) = a_0$ it follows that $\rho^R(a!a_0) = Id$, where Id is the MCL identity for sequential composition. But then we have shown that

$$D \rightarrow C'\ sat\ \rho^R(A''),$$

so using well known proof methods for parallelism, see for instance [Zwiers89], we see that

$$C' \parallel D\ sat\ \rho^R(A'').$$

By the definition of (right) adjoints this is equivalent to:

$$\rho(C' \parallel D)\ sat\ A''.$$

From the definition of ρ it now follows that

$$(C' \parallel D)\backslash\{op_1,\ldots,op_n\}\ sat\ A''\backslash\{a\}.$$

(As was to be shown.) □

Example

We consider again the priority queue example. Assume that the abstract set operations insert and delete are qspecified as follows.

$$(V = V_0)\ V!insert(e)\ (V = V_0 \cup \{e\}),$$

$$(V = V_0 \cup \{m\}\ \wedge\ m = min(V))\ min!delete(V)\ (V = V_0\ \wedge\ min = m).$$

The retrieve function $cont_V$ defined above should map the empty sequence of *enq*, *min* and *empty* communications to the empty set, a fact which is easily verified. Moreover, the derived specifications for the implementing concrete operations are:

$$Q \rightarrow (cont_V = V_0)\ enq!e\ (cont_V = V_0 \cup \{e\}),$$

$$Q \rightarrow (cont_V = V_0 \cup \{m\}\ \wedge\ m = min(cont_V))\ min?\ (cont_V = V_0\ \wedge\ min = m).$$

Note how the pre- and postconditions are formulated in terms of the expression $cont_V$. The value of this expression depends on the computational history h; not on a single state thereof. This is exactly what is possible in generalized Hoare's logic, in contrast to classical Hoare's logic. As far as reification is concerned we can stop at this point. For an implementation and verification of a priority process satisfying a specification similar to the last two formulae, see [Zwiers89].

□

5 Conclusion

Incorporation of predicate transformers into a "Programs are Predicates" approach is feasible for a broad class of systems. Such integrated systems combine the advantages of the $\mathcal{PP}$ approach with the superior proofrules for sequential composition and iteration of Hoare's logic. Moreover, program transformation by means of refining data into parallel processes can be treated very similar to more classical data reification within these systems.

References

[AL] M. Abadi, L. Lamport – The existence of refinement mappings. Technical Report 29, DEC Systems Research Center, 1988.

[Aczel] P. Aczel, Semantics for a proof rule by C.B. Jones – Unpublished note, University of Manchester, 1983.

[Barringer] H. Barringer – A survey of verification techniques for parallel programs. Springer LNCS 191, 1985.

[BKP] H. Barringer, R. Kuiper and A. Pnueli, – Now you may compose temporal logic specifications. Proc. of 16th ACM Symposium on Theory of Computing, Washington, 1984, pp. 51-63.

[BHR] S.D. Brookes, C.A.R. Hoare, A.W. Roscoe – A theory of Communicating Sequential Processes. JACM 31(7), 1984, pp. 560-599.

[FLP] N. Francez, D.Lehman, and A. Pnueli – A linear History Semantics for Distributed languages. Proc. 21st IEEE Symposium on Foundations of Computer Science, Syracuse, N.Y. 1980. Also: TCS 32, 1984, pp .25-46.

[Gorelick] G.A. Gorelick – A complete axiomatic system for proving assertions about recursive and non-recursive programs. Technical Report 75, University of Toronto, 1975.

[Harel] D. Harel – First-order dynamic logic. LNCS 68, Springer-Verlag, 1979.

[Hehner] E.C.R. Hehner – Predicative programming, part I and II. Comm. ACM 27 (1984) 134-151.

[He Jifeng] C.A.R. Hoare, and He, Jifeng – The weakest prespecification, IPL, 1987.

[HHS] He, Jifeng, C.A.R. Hoare, J.W. Sanders – Data Refinement Refined, Oxford University, 1985.

[HW] M.P. Herlihy, J.M. Wing – Axioms for Concurrent Objects. in Fourteenth ACM Symposium on Principles of Programming Languages (1987) 13-26.

[Hoare] C.A.R. Hoare – Programs are predicates, in Mathematical Logic and Programming Languages, Hoare and Shepherdson(eds), Prentice-Hall, 1985.

[Hoare2] C.A.R. Hoare – Communicating Sequential Processes, Prentice-Hall, 1985.

[Hoare3] C.A.R. Hoare – Proofs of Correctness of Data Representations, Acta Informatica 1, (1972) 271-281.

[Jones] C.B. Jones – Software development, A rigorous approach. Prentice-Hall, 1980.

[Jones2] C.B. Jones – Systematic software development using VDM. Prentice-Hall, 1986.

[MP] The anchored version of the temporal framework – Proc. of School/Workshop "Linear Time, Branching Time and Partial Order in Logics and Models for Concurrency", LNCS 354, Springer-Verlag 1989.

[Mil] R. Milner – A calculus of Communicating Sytems. LNCS 92, Springer-Verlag 1980.

[Mil2] R. Milner – Communication and Concurrency. Prentice-Hall, 1989.

[Olderog] E.-R. Olderog – Process Theory: Semantics, Specification and Verification. ESPRIT/LPC Advanced School on Current Trends in Concurrency, Springer LNCS 224, 1986.

[Reynolds] J. Reynolds – The craft of programming. Prentice-Hall

[Roever] W.P. de Roever – The quest for compositionality - A survey of proof systems for concurrency, Part I. Proc. of IFIP working group "The role of abstract models in Computer Science", ed. E.J. Neuhold, North-Holland, Amsterdam, 1985.

[Schwarz] J. Schwarz – Generic commands - A tool for partial correctness formulae The Computer Journal 20 (1977) 151-155

[Tarski] A. Tarski – A lattice-theoretical fixedpoint theorem and its applications, Pacific Journal of Mathematics, 1955.

[Zwiers89] J. Zwiers – Compositionality, Concurrency and Partial Correctness, Springer LNCS 321, 1989.

[Zwiers] J. Zwiers, W.P. de Roever – Predicates are predicate transformers:
a unified compositional theory for concurrency. To appear in the proc. of Principles of Distributed Computing '89.

Foundations of Compositional Program Refinement
— safety properties —
(first version)

Rob Gerth*
Eindhoven University of Technology†

Abstract

The aim of this paper is twofold: first is to formulate a foundation for refinement of parallel programs that may synchronously communicate and/or share variables; *programs rendered as 1st order transition systems.* The second aim is to bring closer and to show the relevance of the algebraic theory of parallel processes to that of the refinement of such 1st order systems. We do this by first developing a notion of refinement and a complete verification criteria for it for algebraic, uninterpreted transition systems—basing ourselves on already existing theory. Then we show how 1st order transition systems can be translated—while preserving those aspects of their semantics that we are interested in—into uninterpreted transition systems. Since this translation is canonical, it is used to lift the algebraic refinement and verification criteria to the level of 1st order systems. Specifically, we show that they yield *assertional methods* for refinement of such systems that resemble the methods used in Z. Manna and A. Pnueli's temporal logic proof system.

Keywords: refinement, implementation, concurrency, compositionality, algebraic process theory, transition system, simulation, assertional methods, communication, shared variables, completeness, (pre-)congruence, behavior, full abstractness.

Contents

1 Introduction
2 Uninterpreted transition systems
3 A refinement notion: failure refinement
4 A verification criterion: failure simulation
5 First Order Transition Systems
6 Verifying First Order Refinement
7 Conclusions

---

*The author is currently working in and partially supported by ESPRIT project P3096: "Formal Methods and Tools for the Development of Distributed and Real-Time Systems (SPEC)".

†Department of Computing Science, Eindhoven University of Technology, P.O. Box 513, 5600 MB Eindhoven, The Netherlands. Email: wsdcrobg@heitue5.BITNET or wsinrobg@win.tue.nl.

1 Introduction

There are a number of reasons to use transition systems as a specification tool. One is their ease of use and their intuitiveness. Many of the existing refinement and verification theories are based on transition systems. Also, it seems hard to argue against the principle that the prime characteristics of any discrete system are the states it can be in and the way the state evolves through the actions (transitions) that the system executes or participates in; at least this seems true when one is interested in implementing such systems. Transition systems concentrate on just these aspects of systems. They are the standard tools for specifying and analyzing communication protocols [LS84] and have been used to specify and develop distributed algorithms [FLS87, SdeR87, Sto89] and real-time controllers [JM88, Lyn90]. The idea generated Harel's statecharts [Har87] and Berry's Esterel [BC85]. Also, it is the motivation for algebraic process calculi such as CCS [Mil80, Mil89], CSP [Hoa85] and ACP [BK84]

Dijkstra's stepwise development paradigm [Dij76] resurfaces in this area as program-refinement. It has been used, e.g., in [WLL88] on some quite complicated algorithms and of course by Chandy and Misra in UNITY [CM88, GP89]. The most forceful and convincing proponent for its use in system specification undoubtedly has been L. Lamport, who in a series of papers [Lam83, Lam86, AL88, AL90] has turned the use of transition systems and of refinement into a practical specification method.

One important aspect of system design *is* missing in transition systems and that is the idea of *composition* of systems. For this reason, we introduce combinators with which (transition) systems, $\pi^0$and π^1, can be composed; the most important one being parallel composition: $\pi^0 \parallel \pi^1$.

Most of the existing research and methods — algebraic process calculi excepted — use a notion of refinement that is based on *trace semantics*, and use a verification criterion that is based on *Milner-simulation* [Mil71]; cf. *refinement-mapping* in [AL88], *possibility-function* in [LT87] and *multi-valued possibility mapping* in [Lyn90]. To us, the decision whether to use refinement based on trace semantics or not cannot be made arbitrarily but, rather, should follow from an analysis of what properties refinement should satisfy. Likewise, whether or not to use (a variant of) Milner simulation as a verification criterion should depend on its suitability for the chosen notion of refinement.

At this point, the most vital question is

Exactly what should it mean that a system P refines another system Q: $P \sqsubseteq Q$?

To us, this question has two aspects. The first concerns the system properties that are of interest to us, sometimes called the *observable behavior*, and that we want preserved. The second aspect concerns the (meta) properties, such as *transitivity*, that we want refinement, $\sqsubseteq$, to satisfy. These questions we shall discuss now.

System properties. There is consensus among researchers that $P \sqsubseteq Q$ at least should entail that the computations of P are all allowed (i.e., also occur) in Q:

$$P \sqsubseteq Q \quad \Longrightarrow \quad -\!\!\circ P \circ\!\!- \subseteq -\!\!\circ Q \circ\!\!- \,, \tag{1}$$

where $-\!\!\circ P \circ\!\!-$ denotes the set of computations or the *observable behavior* of P. Of course, there is still room for different decisions as to what such behaviors make visible about a system's execution. Is it only the start and terminal states of an execution that one can see or can one also observe intermediate states? Even if so, maybe one should only be able to observe the values of the shared variables of the system. Then again, shouldn't one be able to observe the actions that a system participates in; or at least its communication actions?

There are no clearcut answers to these questions and rather than making a decision in these matters—a decision that will have to be arbitrary—in this paper, on the one hand, we allow the complete state to be visible at any point during execution as well as every action that the system executes but, on the other hand, we also introduce operators that allow parts of states and actions to be 'hidden'; i.e., to be made unobservable. Finally, we allow the fact that a system has terminated or is diverging to be observed.

Systems having infinitary behavior raise an additional issue. This is illustrated by the program $P \equiv b := \mathit{true}; x := 0; \star[b \rightarrow x := x + 1 \;\square\; b \rightarrow b := \mathit{false}]$, where $\square$ denotes non-deterministic choice between the branches and $\star[\cdots]$ iterates until the guards of both branches is false. Obviously, P admits an infinite computation; namely, the one in which the second branch is never selected. Let P^{fair} be the program with the same text as P but with the additional assumption that the choice between the branches should be 'fair' in the intuitive sense in which the infinite computation in P is not (i.e., the second branch can always be chosen but never is). Should P be considered a refinement of P^{fair}? The answer seems obvious: no. Yet, this paper takes the opposite view. The reason is the difference in techniques and methods between those that deal with program properties that are determined by the finitary behavior of programs—the so-called *safety* properties—and those such as fairness that do not—the so-called *liveness* properties. In Leslie Lamport's intuitive characterization, safety properties state that along every computation path a 'bad' thing does not happen whereas liveness properties state that along every computation path some 'good' thing does happen. This description suggests invariants to describe safety properties ('a bad thing has not happened yet') and well-foundedness arguments to deal with liveness properties ('it takes less than that many more steps until the good thing happens').

For this reason and for the fact that liveness arguments usually depend on safety properties of the system, this paper restricts itself to refinement w.r.t. safety properties and ignores liveness.

Intuitively, the only difference between P and P^{fair} is the liveness property that every computation of P^{fair} terminates (i.e., along every computation the good thing 'termination' happens). The 'bad' thing of non-termination does not happen along *every* computation path of P. Hence, we shall have $P \sqsubseteq P^{fair}$.

Technically speaking, safety properties can be characterized as those properties for which, given that they hold for every finite, initial part of a computation, they also hold for the whole, possibly infinite, computation; see also [AS86]. When we define the *observable behavior* of systems, we shall also include such 'limits' of finite computations. The effect is that $-\!\!\circ P^{fair} \circ\!\!- = -\!\!\circ P \circ\!\!-$. Left to right inclusion is obvious. Because, all initial parts of the infinite computation of P are in $-\!\!\circ P^{fair} \circ\!\!-$, the infinite 'limit' computation is included, too.

Meta properties. Next, what meta properties should $\sqsubseteq$ satisfy? It seems obvious that $\sqsubseteq$ should at least be transitive: if P_0 refines P_1 and P_1 refines P_2 then clearly P_0 should refine P_2. As it seems quite unreasonable not to allow a system to be a refinement of itself, this makes $\sqsubseteq$ a *pre order*:

$$\begin{array}{c} P_0 \sqsubseteq P_1 \ , \ P_1 \sqsubseteq P_2 \quad \Rightarrow \quad P_0 \sqsubseteq P_2 \\ P \sqsubseteq P \end{array} \tag{2}$$

One should not expect $\sqsubseteq$ to be a partial order: obviously, even if both P_0 refines P_1 and P_1 refines P_0, it does not follow that P_0 and P_1 are (syntactically) identical.

A second desirable meta property concerns the composition of systems. The advantage of system composition is that one has the option to develop parts of a system independently and of integrating them in a later stage. As refinement is the formalization of system development (at least in this paper) this advantage implicitly constrains the notion of refinement that one uses: *whenever parts of a system are refined then if the refined parts are put together again, the resulting system should be a refinement of the original one.* If ones refinement notion does not satisfy this constraint, then one can only develop a system as a monolithic whole. Let $C[\cdot]$ stand for a system with a 'hole' in it (a *context*), into which another system, P, can be plugged: $C[P]$. Then the above constraint is written as follows:

$$\textit{for every context } C[\cdot]: \quad P \sqsubseteq Q \quad \Rightarrow \quad C[P] \sqsubseteq C[Q] \tag{3}$$

This makes $\sqsubseteq$ a *pre congruence* w.r.t. the program combinators; i.e., it makes $\sqsubseteq \cap \sqsupseteq$ a congruence. In the absence of other equally obvious requirements on a refinement relation, we let $\sqsubseteq$ be *determined* by the above properties (1), (2) and (3).

Perhaps this whole discussion seems a bit trite. After all, these principles and constraints all are rather obvious. Still, it is worth stressing these points, since they very much constrain adequate notions of refinement which often forces one to consider aspects of system behavior that, a priori, one was not interested in. For example, in this paper it will force us to consider the precise deadlock behavior of systems [Hen88]. Had we allowed communication action to time out—which we have not—even more detailed behavior would have had to be known [GB87].

The point of view embodied in the above discussion is not common in the area of program refinement. On the other hand, it is the point of departure in algebraic process theory [Mil80, Hen88, Hoa85, BK84]. There one starts with a (context free) programming language (or term algebra) and one looks for programming equivalences or pre orders satisfying some properties that are congruences or pre congruences and that are, if possible, *fully abstract*. A (pre) congruence is fully abstract w.r.t. some properties precisely if it is the coarsest one satisfying these properties. Our stipulating that $\sqsubseteq$ be determined by equations (1), (2) and (3), makes $\sqsubseteq$ fully abstract w.r.t. inclusion of observable behavior; in fact, it is equivalent with it.

Languages that allow synchronization have been investigated intensively in this area [Dar82, NH84, BHR84, BKO86]; for an overview of various proposed congruences see [Nic87]. One conclusion of this research is that *if the observable behavior of a program allows the state of terminated (or maximal) computations to be observed as such, then any (pre) congruence for such a language should be sensitive to the precise way in which systems may deadlock.* The standard example illustrating this (using a CSP-like language) compares P :: $[true \rightarrow R!1 \;\Box\; true \rightarrow S!1]$ and Q :: $[R!1 \rightarrow skip \;\Box\; S!1 \rightarrow skip]$. Here, $R!1$ is a send command that waits until process R wants to receive a value and then sends the value 1. In process Q send commands appear in the guards of the (I/O) guarded command. This means that process A will suspend until *either R or S is ready to receive a value* and then will execute the appropriate send command. Although, intuitively, the computations of both programs are the same, there is a context, namely $C \equiv (Q :: x := 0;\ ?x) \parallel [\cdot]$, such that if we run P and Q within C, we *do* observe a difference (; $?x$ is the program that waits until it receives a value and then assigns it to x): *$C[Q]$ does not have a maximal computation that ends in a state in which $x = 0$ holds, whereas $C[P]$ does; namely the one in which P chooses the second branch and subsequently deadlocks.*

The same research indicates that a (pre-)congruence should not be 'sensitive' to more than the computations of a program and its deadlock possibilities during execution. This is the *testing pre-order* of [NH84], the *failure set semantics* of [BHR84] and the *fully observable congruence* of [Dar82]. The refinement preorder that we develop in Section 3 will be based on this. In contrast with most researchers in this area, we shall use (uninterpreted) transition systems (with parallel composition and renaming of actions) as programming language instead if CCS or TCSP. In this sense, our set up is closer in spirit to that of [BKO86]: their process graphs correspond to our uninterpreted transition systems.

Once the notion of refinement is elucidated (in Section 3), the next question is how to prove it. Now, a transition system is specified in terms of vertices, edges and actions (associated with the edges). Hence, a usable verification criterion should be cauched in terms of these primitives. In Section 4 we develop such a criterion, called *failure simulation* and written as $\hookrightarrow$, by generalizing the notion of Milner-simulation [Mil71]. This criterion is then proven sound and complete; i.e. we prove that

$$\pi^0 \sqsubseteq \pi^1 \iff \pi^0 \hookrightarrow \pi^1 \ .$$

There are some connections here with [Dar82].

Upto this point we have looked at algebraic, uninterpreted transition systems. The rest of the paper concentrates on 1st order transition systems. If we want to use the results of the first part, we need a correspondence between such 1st order systems and the uninterpreted ones. Section 5 defines such a correspondence and also shows how various operators, such as parallel composition and the hiding of variables, can be defined in terms of uninterpreted systems. This correspondence is, in fact, quite simple

and can be illustrated with the system $\pi \equiv$ 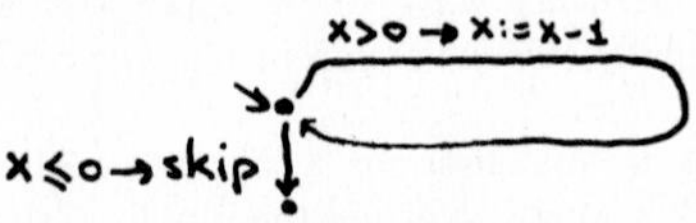

; that corresponds to

the program **while** $x > 0$ **do** $x := x - 1$ **od**. Now, π, implicitly depends on a notion of *state* and on the *meaning* of the 'labels' on the transitions. The translation makes these dependencies explicit. If we assume that x is the only variable, then we may represent a state as just a value; namely, the value of x.

Let us take the intuitive meaning of π and let us assume that the system always starts in the state 3 (i.e., in the state in which x has the value 3). Then π's translation would be

${}^t\pi \equiv$ 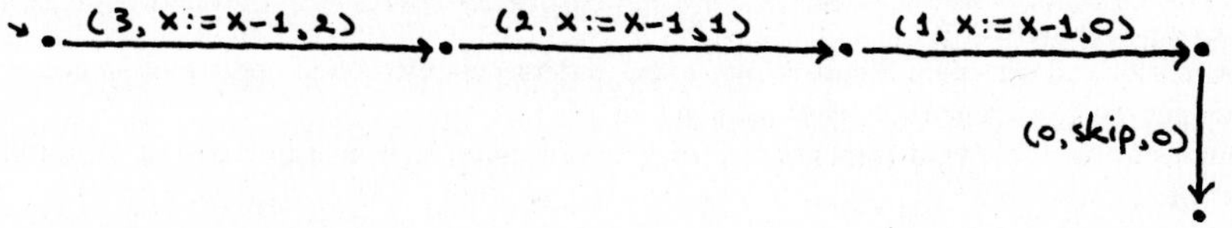

,

where now the labels on the edges record a state, an action and another state; each pair of states is in the input-output relation of the corresponding action; and ${}^t\pi$ contains a vertex for every vertex-state pair that can occur during an execution of π. Note that the labels in ${}^t\pi$ are just that: labels; no further interpretation of them is necessary. The translation also unfolds the loop but this does not happen in general: the translated system contains a cycle whenever it is possible to arrive more than once in the same vertex with the same state.

Section 6 develops on the basis of this translation a verification criterion for 1st order systems. First we *define* for 1st order systems, π^0 and π^1 that $\pi^0 \sqsubseteq \pi^1$ means that ${}^t\pi^0 \sqsubseteq {}^t\pi^1$; i.e. a system refines another if its translation refines the other one's. If one accepts the translation as reasonable in the sense that it preserves the meaning of a system, then this is the correct notion of refinement.

Now, suppose that $\pi^0 \sqsubseteq \pi^1$ where π^0 and π^1 are 1st order systems. Then we know that ${}^t\pi^0 \hookrightarrow {}^t\pi^1$, by completeness of the criterion of Section 4. So, "all" that has to be done is to find some conditions on π^0 and π^1 that imply that ${}^t\pi^0 \hookrightarrow {}^t\pi^1$. This we do, using techniques from Floyd's inductive assertion method [Flo67].

We end the introduction with establishing some notation.

Notation.

Functions, f, unless stated otherwise, are partial and have domain, $dom(f)$, and range, $ran(f)$. Functions are sometimes defined as lists, like in $[1 \mapsto 2, 2 \mapsto 3]$ which is the (partial) function, f, such that $f(1) = 2$ and $f(2) = 3$. In general, any function f is pointwise extended to $2^{dom(f)}$: if $V \subseteq 2^{dom(f)}$ then $f(V) = \bigcup\{f(v) \mid v \in V\}$. The restriction of f to V, $f\lceil V$ is the function with $dom(f\lceil V) = dom(f) \cap V$ and $(f\lceil V)(v) = f(v)$ for $v \in dom(f\lceil V)$. Finally, $f^{-1}(w) = \{v \mid f(v) = w\}$.

Relations over some set A are usually denoted by letters $\mathsf{R}, \mathsf{M}, \ldots \subseteq A \times A$. Instead of $(a, b) \in \mathsf{R}$ we often write $a\ \mathsf{R}\ b$. Also, the *post image of a under* R, $a\,\mathsf{R} = \{b \mid a\ \mathsf{R}\ b\}$ and the *pre image of b under* R, $\mathsf{R}\,b = \{a \mid a\ \mathsf{R}\ b\}$. This extends to the post image and pre image of sets. Instead of $a\,\mathsf{R}$ we occasionally write $\mathsf{R}(a)$.

The class of ordinals is Ord. Letters α, β,... range over the ordinals; letters n, m,... range over the finite ordinals (i.e., the natural numbers). As usual, ω denotes the first transfinite ordinal.

If A is some set of symbols, then $A^\star$ is the set of finite sequences over A and A^ω the set of infinite such sequences; then $A^\dagger = A^\star \cup A^\omega$. Sequences in $A^\dagger$ are denoted by s, t,...; the elements of such an s are s_i for $i < |s|$, the length of s (if $s \in A^\omega$ then $|s| = \omega$); hence, s_0 is the first element of s. As alternative sequence notation, there is $s = (s_i)_{i<|s|}$. Write $s \prec t$ if $|s| < |t|$ and $s = (t_i)_{i<|s|}$. Any function $h: A \mapsto A$ extends to $A^\dagger$ by having it act pointwise on sequences: $h(s) = (h(s_i))_{i<|s|}$. Write $\mathcal{A}(s)$ for the set of symbols in s: $\mathcal{A}(s) = \bigcup\{s_i \mid i < |s|\}$.

There is a denumerable, well-ordered set of variables Var. If Σ is some signature or similarity type, then $Tm(\Sigma)$ and $L(\Sigma)$ denote the set of terms and first order formulae over Σ (and Var). Elements of $L(\Sigma)$ are usually denoted by letters p, q, r; terms by e, t and variables by u, v, x, y, z. As usual, $p[e/x]$ ($t[e/x]$) stands for the formula (term) obtained by substituting the term or expression e for every free occurrence of x in p (t). The set of free variables of a formula or term ϕ is denoted by $FV(\phi)$.

Σ-structures or Σ-algebra's, $\mathbf{A}$, are defined as usual and give interpretations of the symbols in Σ. Given a Σ-structure $\mathbf{A}$, states σ, τ, ν are *total* functions from Var into $|\mathbf{A}|$, the universe of $\mathbf{A}$. Let $\mathcal{S}$ be the set of states. For a state σ, $\sigma\{a/x\}$ ($a \in |\mathbf{A}|$) denotes the state σ' such that for $y \not\equiv x$ $\sigma'(y) = \sigma(y)$ and $\sigma'(x) = a$.

The value of a term t in a state σ, $\sigma(t)$, and the truth-value or satisfaction of a formula p in a state σ, $\sigma \models p$ or $\mathbf{A}, \sigma \models p$, are defined as usual. Write $\mathbf{A} \models p$ if $p \in L(\Sigma)$ is valid in $\mathbf{A}$, i.e., if $\mathbf{A}, \sigma \models p$ holds for every state σ; write $\sigma \models p$ if $\mathbf{A}, \sigma \models p$ and $\mathbf{A}$ is clear from the context; and $\models p$ if p is valid, i.e., if $\mathbf{A} \models p$ holds for every Σ-structure $\mathbf{A}$.

By convention, all super- and subscripts, bars, underscores etc. of composite objects are inherited by the components: e.g., if $K = (a, b)$ then ${}^r\widehat{K}_1 = ({}^r\widehat{a}_1, {}^r\widehat{b}_1)$.

As usual, any variable that appears free in some formula, lives in the scope of an implicit universal quantification.

2 Uninterpreted transition systems

In this section, the basic framework of uninterpreted transition systems is defined and the basic notation established.

- There is some alphabet, $\mathcal{A}$ of *actions*, which is partitioned into a set of *local* actions, $\mathcal{A}^l$, and a set of *global* actions, $\mathcal{A}^g$. The intention is that local actions never synchronize with actions in other systems, whereas global action may do so.

  There are two special 'actions': δ and $\uparrow$, which are not in $\mathcal{A}$. The first one, δ, denotes the *undoable* action; the second one, $\uparrow$, signifies *divergence*. Intuitively, $\uparrow$ means that the system is engaged in an infinite, internal or hidden computation that does not yield any visible behavior. As a matter of notation, $\mathcal{A}_{xyz\ldots}$ will stand for the set $\mathcal{A} \cup \{x, y, z, \ldots\}$.

- A *directed graph* is an object $(\partial_s, \partial_t \colon \mathcal{E} \mapsto \mathcal{V})$, where
  - $\mathcal{V}$ is a set of *vertices*,
  - $\mathcal{E}$ is a set of *edges*, and
  - ∂_s, respectively, ∂_t is the function that associates each edge with a *source*, respectively, *target* vertex. In the sequel we shall often write ${}^\bullet e$ instead of $\partial_s(e)$ or $\partial_s e$, and $e^\bullet$ instead of $\partial_t(e)$ or $\partial_t e$. Moreover this notation dualizes and we write ${}^\bullet v$ for the *set* $\{e \in \mathcal{E} \mid {}^\bullet e = v\}$ and $v^\bullet$ for the set $\{e \in \mathcal{E} \mid e^\bullet = v\}$.

- An *uninterpreted transition system* (uts) *over alphabet* $\mathcal{A}$, π, is an object

$$(\partial_s, \partial_t \colon \mathcal{E} \mapsto \mathcal{V}, I, \mathcal{L} \colon \mathcal{E} \mapsto \mathcal{A}_{\delta\uparrow}) \ ,$$

  where
  - $(\partial_s, \partial_t \colon \mathcal{E} \mapsto \mathcal{V})$ is a directed graph,
  - $I \subseteq \mathcal{V}$ is the set of *initial* vertices with $I \neq \emptyset$, and
  - $\mathcal{L}$ is a *labelling function* that associates actions with the edges

  The class of uts over an alphabet $\mathcal{A}$ is $\mathsf{UTS}_{\mathcal{A}}$ or just UTS[1].

  Notice that an uts can express the occurrence of divergence and that it may have disabled actions that will never occur. Also note that any uts has at least one initial vertex and that there are no cardinality constraints on the vertex and edge sets.

  Some notation: the canonical uts is denoted by π and has components $(\partial_s, \partial_t \colon \mathcal{E} \mapsto \mathcal{V}, I, \mathcal{L} \colon \mathcal{E} \mapsto \mathcal{A}_{\delta\uparrow})$. The alphabet, $\mathcal{A}(\pi)$, of π is the set of labels appearing on its edges: $\mathcal{A}(\pi) = ran(\mathcal{L})$. If $V \subseteq \mathcal{V}$ then $V;\pi$ is the uts $(\partial_s, \partial_t \colon \mathcal{E} \mapsto \mathcal{V}, V, \mathcal{L} \colon \mathcal{E} \mapsto \mathcal{A}_{\delta\uparrow})$, with initial vertices in V. Finally, $\mathcal{L}_g(\cdot)$ is the function $\mathcal{L}(\cdot) \cap \mathcal{A}^g$.

[1] To be pedantic, it is the isomorphism class generated by uts that is of interest rather than the uts itself. Isomorphism, here, means graph isomorphism that maintains the edge labelling and initial vertices.

- The set of *sequences* of π is

$$Seq(\pi) = \{\ (v,\ (e_i)_{i<\alpha})\ \big|\ \alpha \leq \omega,\ v \in I,\ \alpha > 0 \Rightarrow v = {}^\bullet e_0,\ \forall 0 < i < \alpha\ e^\bullet_{i-1} = {}^\bullet e_i\ \}$$

Hence, a sequence is a possibly infinite path in the underlying directed graph of π that starts in an initial vertex.

- The *behavior* or *computations* of an uts, π, $-\!\!\diamond\pi\diamond\!\!-^{o}$, consists of the maximal sequences of actions that π can perform together with an indication, $\uparrow$ or $\downarrow$, whether the system may diverge at that point or is stable. The letter ρ ranges over $\{\downarrow, \uparrow\}$.

First define for any $v \in \mathcal{V}$:

$$\uparrow(v) \iff \uparrow \in \mathcal{L}({}^\bullet v) \quad \text{and} \quad \downarrow(v) \iff \mathcal{L}({}^\bullet v) \cap \mathcal{A}_\uparrow = \emptyset\ .$$

So, $\uparrow(v)$ holds if v has an outgoing edge labelled with $\uparrow$—i.e., if v may diverge—and $\downarrow(v)$ holds if v can neither diverge nor perform an action (in $\mathcal{A}$). Then

$$-\!\!\diamond\pi\diamond\!\!-^{o} = \left\{\ s\rho\ \left|\ \begin{array}{l} \exists(v,\ (e_i)_{i<\alpha}) \in Seq(\pi),\ \alpha \leq \omega,\ s = (\mathcal{L}(e_i))_{i<\alpha} \in \mathcal{A}^\dagger,\ \rho \in \{\uparrow, \downarrow\}, \\ \alpha = \omega \Rightarrow \rho = \downarrow,\ \alpha = 0 \Rightarrow \rho(v),\ 0 < \alpha < \omega \Rightarrow \rho(e^\bullet_{\alpha-1}) \end{array}\right.\right\}.$$

If $s\rho \in -\!\!\diamond\pi\diamond\!\!-^{o}$ then any $\overline{s} \in \mathcal{A}^\star$ with $\overline{s} \prec s$ is called a *partial computation*.

There is an alternative way to define the computations of an uts. Namely, by defining for every $a \in \mathcal{A}_\uparrow$ a *transition relation*, $\xrightarrow{a} \in \mathsf{UTS} \times \mathsf{UTS}$:

$$\pi \xrightarrow{a} \overline{\pi} \iff \exists e \in {}^\bullet I\ \mathcal{L}(e) = a\ \&\ \overline{\pi} = e^\bullet; \pi\ .$$

So, each uts defines, through its initial vertices, a set of actions that it can perform; namely those actions that appear as label on an edge starting in an initial state: $\mathcal{L}({}^\bullet I)$. Performing such an action transforms the uts, π, by changing its set of initial vertices to the target vertex of the corresponding edge. This generalizes and, for $s \in \mathcal{A}^\star$ we write:

$$\pi \xrightarrow{s} \overline{\pi} \iff \forall i < |s|\ \exists \pi^i \in \mathsf{UTS}\ \pi^0 = \pi,\ \pi^{|s|-1} = \overline{\pi},\ \forall 0 < i < |s|\ \pi^{i-1} \xrightarrow{s_i} \pi^i\ .$$

Also, write $\pi \xrightarrow{s}$ if there is a $\overline{\pi}$ such that $\pi \xrightarrow{s} \overline{\pi}$; if $s \in \mathcal{A}^\omega$, $\pi \xrightarrow{s}$ has the obvious meaning. Finally, $\pi \stackrel{s}{\not\longrightarrow} \overline{\pi}$ and $\pi \stackrel{s}{\not\longrightarrow}$ stand for the negations of the above relations; $\pi \not\longrightarrow$ means $\pi \stackrel{a}{\not\longrightarrow}$, $\forall a \in \mathcal{A}$.

In this setup, the behavior of a $\pi \in \mathsf{UTS}$ can be described by

$$-\!\!\diamond\pi\diamond\!\!-^{o} = \{\ s\rho\ |\ s \in \mathcal{A}^\star,\ \exists \overline{\pi}\ \pi \xrightarrow{s} \overline{\pi},\ \exists v \in \overline{I}\ \rho(v)\ \} \bigcup \{\ s\downarrow\ |\ s \in \mathcal{A}^\omega,\ \pi \xrightarrow{s}\ \}$$

The *observable behavior* of π can now be defined by

$$-\!\!\diamond\pi\diamond\!\!- = -\!\!\diamond\pi\diamond\!\!-^{o} \cup \{\ s\downarrow\ |\ s \in \mathcal{A}^\omega,\ \forall i < \omega\ \exists s_i \in \mathcal{A}^\star\ \pi \xrightarrow{s_i}\ \&\ \forall 0 < i < \omega\ s_{i-1} \prec s_i\ \}\ ,$$

in accordance with the discussion of liveness in the introduction.

As a final piece of notation, define π after s ($s \in \mathcal{A}^\star$) by

$$\pi\ \mathsf{after}\ s = V; \pi,\ \text{ where } V = \{v \mid \pi \xrightarrow{s} v; \pi\}\ .$$

We shall often write expressions such as $v \in \pi$ after s instead of the formally correct statement that π after $s = V; \pi$ and $v \in V$.

Next, the two operators to compose uts's are defined: the *parallel composition* operator, $\cdot \parallel_\gamma \cdot$, and the *renaming* operator, $h(\cdot)$.

- The set of *communication functions*, $\mathcal{G}$, is

$$\{\ \gamma\colon \mathcal{A}^g \times \mathcal{A}^g \mapsto \mathcal{A} \mid \gamma(a,b) = \gamma(b,a)\ \}\ .$$

Communication functions describe which *global* actions may synchronize during a parallel execution in $\pi^0 \parallel_\gamma \pi^1$. Synchronization occurs between exactly two global actions and the results is a local or global action. The commutativity condition ensures that the parallel composition itself is commutative (see below). Any $\gamma \in \mathcal{G}$ is identified with its extension to $\mathcal{A}_{\delta\uparrow} \times \mathcal{A}_{\delta\uparrow}$ defined by mapping pairs of actions that are *not* in $dom(\gamma)$ to δ.

- Let τ be some symbol not in $\mathcal{A}_{\delta\uparrow}$. Its meaning is explained below. The set of *homomorphisms*, $\mathcal{H}$, is

$$\{\ h\colon \mathcal{A} \mapsto \mathcal{A}_{\delta\tau} \mid ran(h \restriction \mathcal{A}^l) \subseteq \mathcal{A}^l_\tau\ \}\ .$$

Any $h \in \mathcal{H}$ is extended to a total function on $\mathcal{A}_{\delta\uparrow}$ by having $h(a) = a$ for any $a \notin dom(h)$. Homomorphisms *rename* actions; except that local actions never rename to global actions and that δ and $\uparrow$ rename to themselves. If $h(a) = \delta$ this means that the actions a can no longer occur in $h(\pi)$. If $h(a) = \tau$ this means that although a can still occur it is no longer possible to *observe* this—the action is *hidden*. As expected, h acts pointwise on sequences of actions, when τ is interpreted as the empty sequence, ε.

- For any $\pi^0, \pi^1 \in \mathsf{UTS}$ and $\gamma \in \mathcal{G}$, the parallel composition

$$\pi^0 \parallel_\gamma \pi^1 = \pi \in \mathsf{UTS}$$

is the product of π^0 and π^1 with the 'diagonals' filled in according to γ. Formally, it is defined by[2]

  - $\mathcal{V} = \mathcal{V}^0 \times \mathcal{V}^1$,
  - $\mathcal{E} = \mathcal{E}^0 \times \mathcal{V}^1 + \mathcal{E}^1 \times \mathcal{V}^0 + \mathcal{E}^0 \times \mathcal{E}^1$ (+ denotes disjoint union),
  - $I = I^0 \times I^1$,
  - for $(e,v) \in \mathcal{E}^i \times \mathcal{V}^{2-i}$ $\quad \partial_s(e,v) = (\partial^i_s(e), v),\ \partial_t(e,v) = (\partial^i_t(e), v)$
    $\mathcal{L}(e,v) = \mathcal{L}^i(e)\quad (i < 2)$ and
    for $(e^0,e^1) \in \mathcal{E}^0 \times \mathcal{E}^1$ $\quad \partial_s(e^0,e^1) = (\partial^0_s(e^0), \partial^1_s(e^1)),\ \partial_t(e^0,e^1) = (\partial^0_t(e^0), \partial^1_t(e^1))$
    $\mathcal{L}(e^0,e^1) = \gamma(\mathcal{L}^0(e^0), \mathcal{L}^1(e^1))\ .$

2–1 EXAMPLE. *If* $\pi^0 =$ 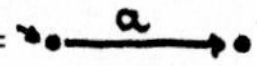

, $\pi^1 =$ 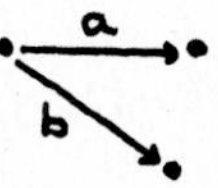

and $\gamma = [(a,a) \mapsto c]$ *then*

$\pi^0 \parallel_\gamma \pi^1 =$ 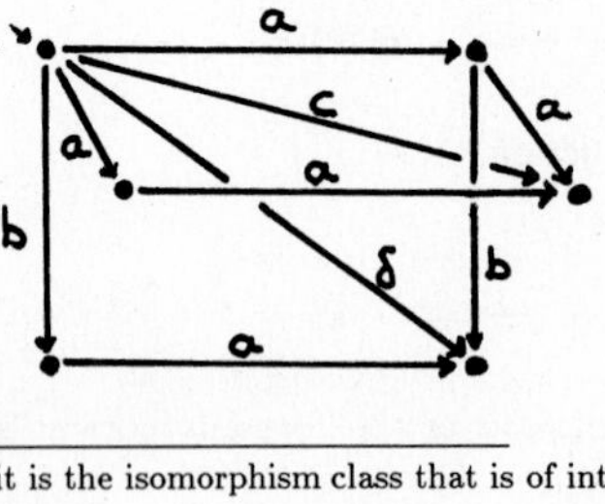

[2] Remember, it is the isomorphism class that is of interest.

Theorem 3–3 below characterizes the behavior of $\pi^0 \parallel_\gamma \pi^1$ in terms of the behaviors of π^0 and π^1. In terms of transition relations, one has

$$\pi^0 \parallel_\gamma \pi^1 \xrightarrow{a} \overline{\pi}^0 \parallel_\gamma \pi^1 \quad \text{if} \quad \pi^0 \xrightarrow{a} \overline{\pi}^0 ,$$

$$\pi^0 \parallel_\gamma \pi^1 \xrightarrow{a} \pi^0 \parallel_\gamma \overline{\pi}^1 \quad \text{if} \quad \pi^1 \xrightarrow{a} \overline{\pi}^1 \text{ and}$$

$$\pi^0 \parallel_\gamma \pi^1 \xrightarrow{a} \overline{\pi}^0 \parallel_\gamma \overline{\pi}^1 \quad \text{if} \quad \pi^i \xrightarrow{a^i} \overline{\pi}^i \ (i < 2) \text{ and } a = \gamma(a^0, a^1) .$$

The three clauses correspond to the edges in $\mathcal{E}^0 \times \mathcal{V}^1$, $\mathcal{E}^1 \times \mathcal{V}^0$ and $\mathcal{E}^0 \times \mathcal{E}^1$.

- For $\overline{\pi} \in \mathsf{UTS}$ and $h \in \mathcal{H}$, the *renamed* system

$$h(\overline{\pi}) = \pi \in \mathsf{UTS}$$

is obtained by redefining the set of edges and of initial vertices: an edge in $h(\overline{\pi})$ is any finite path in $\overline{\pi}$ on which precisely one non-erased action occurs or those infinite paths on which every action is erased. The initial vertices are the original ones, together with those vertices that can be reached from an initial vertex by a finite number of erased actions. Formally, it is defined by

- $\mathcal{V} = \overline{\mathcal{V}}$,
- $$\mathcal{E} = \left\{ (\overline{e}_i)_{i<\alpha} \;\middle|\; \begin{array}{l} 0 < \alpha \leq \omega,\ \forall 0 < i < \alpha\ \overline{\partial}_t(\overline{e}_{i-1}) = \overline{\partial}_s(\overline{e}_i), \\ \alpha < \omega \Rightarrow h((\overline{\mathcal{L}}(\overline{e}_i))_{i<\alpha}) \in \mathcal{A}_{\delta\uparrow} \\ \alpha = \omega \Rightarrow h((\overline{\mathcal{L}}(\overline{e}_i))_{i<\alpha}) = \varepsilon \end{array} \right\} ,$$
- $\partial_s((\overline{e}_i)_{i\leq n}) = \overline{\partial}_s(\overline{e}_0),\ \partial_t((\overline{e}_i)_{i\leq n}) = \overline{\partial}_t(\overline{e}_n),$
  $\partial_s((\overline{e}_i)_{i<\omega}) = \overline{\partial}_s(\overline{e}_0),\ \partial_t((\overline{e}_i)_{i<\omega}) = \overline{\partial}_t(\overline{e}_0)$ (sic),
- $I = \overline{I} \cup \{\ \partial_t((\overline{e}_i)_{i\leq n}) \mid \exists v \in \overline{I}\ (v, (e_i)_{i\leq n}) \in Seq(\overline{\pi}),\ h((\overline{\mathcal{L}}(e_i))_{i\leq n}) = \varepsilon\ \}$,
- if $e = (\overline{e}_i)_{i\leq n}$ then $\mathcal{L}(e) = h((\overline{\mathcal{L}}(e_i))_{i\leq n})$ and
  if $e = (\overline{e}_i)_{i<\omega}$ then $\mathcal{L}(e) = \uparrow$.

2–2 EXAMPLE. *If* $\pi =$

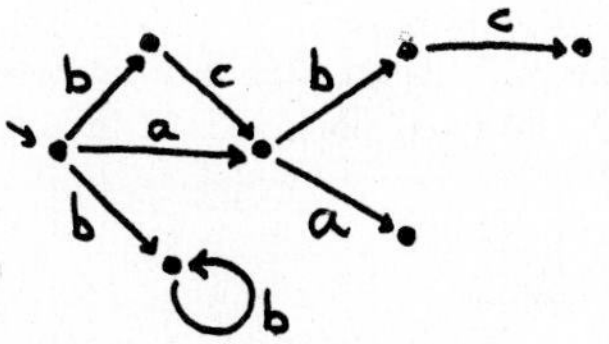

and $h = [b \mapsto \tau]$

then $h(\pi) =$

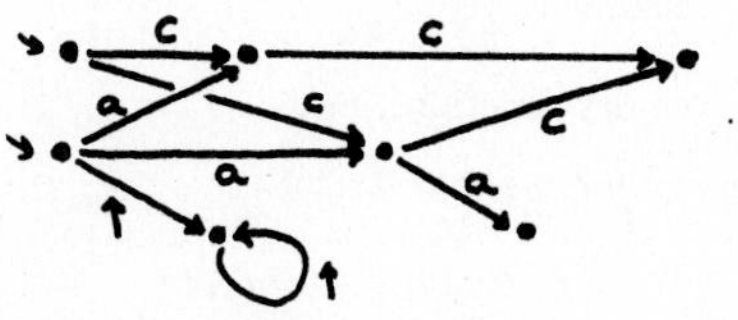

.

Although the construction of $h(\pi)$ may seem overly complicated, it induces the following simple and intuitive correspondence between the transitions in π and those in $h(\pi)$:

$$h(\pi) \xrightarrow{a} h(\overline{\pi}) \quad \text{if} \quad \exists s \in \mathcal{A}^{\star}_{\delta\uparrow}\ \pi \xrightarrow{s} \overline{\pi}\ \&\ h(s) = a \in \mathcal{A}_{\delta\uparrow} \text{ and}$$

$$h(\pi) \xrightarrow{\uparrow} h(\overline{\pi}) \quad \text{if} \quad \exists s \in \mathcal{A}^{\omega}\ \pi \xrightarrow{s}\ \&\ h(s) = \varepsilon\ \&\ \pi \xrightarrow{s_0} \overline{\pi}\ .$$

For future use, the set of *environments* or *contexts*, $\mathcal{C}$, with typical element $C[\cdot]$, is defined as the smallest set such that

- $[\cdot] \in \mathcal{C}$,
- $h \in \mathcal{H},\ \gamma \in \mathcal{G},\ \pi \in \mathsf{UTS},\ C[\cdot] \in \mathcal{C} \quad \Longrightarrow \quad h(C[\cdot]),\ \pi \parallel_\gamma C[\cdot],\ C[\cdot] \parallel_\gamma \pi \in \mathcal{C}$.

Hence, a context $C[\cdot]$ is a system with a 'hole' in it. Then, $C[\pi]$ is the system with π plugged into the hole so that $C[\pi] \in \mathsf{UTS}$. Obviously,

$$C[\cdot],\ \overline{C}[\cdot] \in \mathcal{C} \quad \Longrightarrow \quad C[\overline{C}[\cdot]] \in \mathcal{C}\ .$$

I.e., contexts compose.

3 A refinement notion: failure refinement

As argued in the introduction, the pre order, $\sqsubseteq$, should be determined by

$$\begin{array}{c} \llbracket \pi^0 \rrbracket \subseteq \llbracket \pi^1 \rrbracket \text{ and} \\ \forall C[\cdot] \in \mathcal{C}\ C[\pi^0] \sqsubseteq C[\pi^1]\ . \end{array} \tag{4}$$

The second part of this condition implies that $\sqsubseteq$ is a pre congruence w.r.t. the combinators with which contexts can be constructed. The rest of the section develops an explicit characterization of $\sqsubseteq$.

Based on (4), $\sqsubseteq$ can be defined as a greatest fixed point: first let $\mathcal{R} = \mathcal{P}(\mathsf{UTS} \times \mathsf{UTS})$—the set of relations over UTS. Define a functional $\mathcal{F}: \mathcal{R} \mapsto \mathcal{R}$ by

$$\mathcal{F}(\mathsf{R}) = \{\ (\pi^0, \pi^1) \in \mathsf{R} \mid \llbracket \pi^0 \rrbracket \subseteq \llbracket \pi^1 \rrbracket,\ \forall C[\cdot] \in \mathcal{C}\ (C[\pi^0], C[\pi^1]) \in \mathsf{R}\ \}\ .$$

Then, we have

$$\pi^0 \sqsubseteq \pi^1 \iff \exists \mathsf{R} \in \mathcal{R}\ (\pi^0, \pi^1) \in \mathsf{R}\ \&\ \mathsf{R} \subseteq \mathcal{F}(\mathsf{R})\ ,$$

whence

$$\sqsubseteq\, = \bigcup\{\mathsf{R} \in \mathcal{R} \mid \mathsf{R} \subseteq \mathcal{F}(\mathsf{R})\}\ .$$

This characterizes $\sqsubseteq$ as the greatest fixed point, $\nu\mathcal{F}$, in the standard lattice of relations (over UTS). Obviously, $\mathcal{F}$ is monotonic in this lattice so that the fixed point exists, indeed. Standard theory also implies that

$$\sqsubseteq\, = \bigcap_{\alpha \in \mathsf{Ord}} \mathcal{F}^{\alpha}(\mathcal{R})\ ,$$

where the approximants, $\mathcal{F}^{\alpha}$, to the function $\mathcal{F}$ are defined by

$$\begin{array}{rcl} \mathcal{F}^0 & = & \lambda x.x \quad \text{(i.e., the identity function) and} \\ \mathcal{F}^{\alpha} & = & \lambda x.\mathcal{F}\Big(\bigcap_{\beta<\alpha} \mathcal{F}^{\beta}(x)\Big) \quad \text{for } \alpha > 0\ . \end{array}$$

We compute the first few approximants to $\sqsubseteq$, $\mathcal{F}^{\alpha}(\mathcal{R})$:

$$\mathcal{F}^0(\mathcal{R}) = \mathcal{R};\quad \mathcal{F}^1(\mathcal{R}) = \mathcal{F}(\mathcal{F}^0(\mathcal{R})) = \{(\pi^0, \pi^1) \mid \llbracket \pi^0 \rrbracket \subseteq \llbracket \pi^1 \rrbracket\}\ ;$$

and

$$\mathcal{F}^2(\mathcal{R}) = \mathcal{F}(\mathcal{F}^1(\mathcal{R})) = \left\{ (\pi^0,\pi^1) \in \mathcal{F}^1(\mathcal{R}) \;\middle|\; \begin{array}{l} \multimap\pi^0\multimapinv \subseteq \multimap\pi^1\multimapinv, \\ \forall C[\cdot] \in \mathcal{C}\ (C[\pi^0], C[\pi^1]) \in \mathcal{F}^1(\mathcal{R}) \end{array} \right\}$$
$$= \{(\pi^0,\pi^1) \mid \multimap\pi^0\multimapinv \subseteq \multimap\pi^1\multimapinv,\ \forall C[\cdot] \in \mathcal{C}\ \multimap C[\pi^0]\multimapinv \subseteq \multimap C[\pi^1]\multimapinv\}$$
$$= \{(\pi^0,\pi^1) \mid \forall C[\cdot] \in \mathcal{C}\ \multimap C[\pi^0]\multimapinv \subseteq \multimap C[\pi^1]\multimapinv\}\ ,$$

since $[\cdot] \in \mathcal{C}$ and $[\pi] = \pi$. Finally, $\mathcal{F}^3(\mathcal{R}) = \mathcal{F}^2(\mathcal{R})$ because contexts can be composed.

From this we obtain a new characterization of $\sqsubseteq$:

$$\pi^0 \sqsubseteq \pi^1 \iff \forall C[\cdot] \in \mathcal{C}\ \multimap C[\pi^0]\multimapinv \subseteq \multimap C[\pi^1]\multimapinv\ . \tag{5}$$

This shows that whether or not $\pi^0 \sqsubseteq \pi^1$ holds, depends not only on the observable behavior of the components, π^0 and π^1, themselves but also on what a system in which they are embedded can 'sense' about them.

The following is the standard example showing some of the nature of $\sqsubseteq$ as defined by (5):

Let $\pi^0 =$ 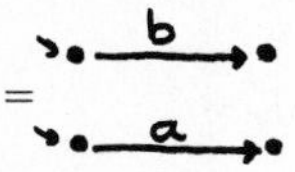

and $\pi^1 =$ 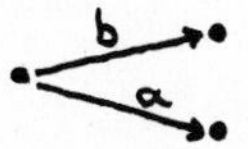

$(a, b \in \mathcal{A}^g)$. Clearly, $\multimap\pi^0\multimapinv \subseteq \multimap\pi^1\multimapinv$. We claim that $\pi^0 \not\sqsubseteq \pi^1$. For this we must construct a context, $C[\cdot]$ such that $\multimap C[\pi^0]\multimapinv \not\subseteq \multimap C[\pi^1]\multimapinv$: take $C[\cdot] = h(\pi \parallel_\gamma [\cdot])$ with $\pi =$ 

, $\gamma = [(a,a) \mapsto c]$ and $h = [a \mapsto \delta,\ b \mapsto \delta]$.

Then $\pi \parallel_\gamma \pi^0 =$ 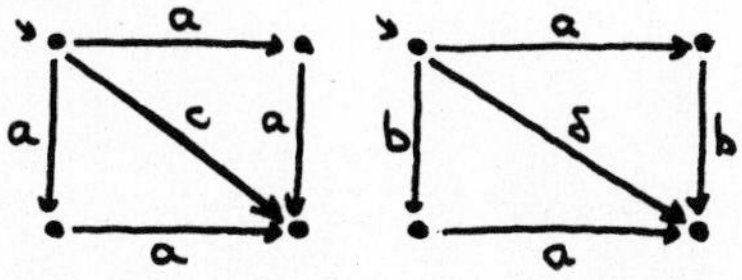

and $\pi \parallel_\gamma \pi^1 =$ 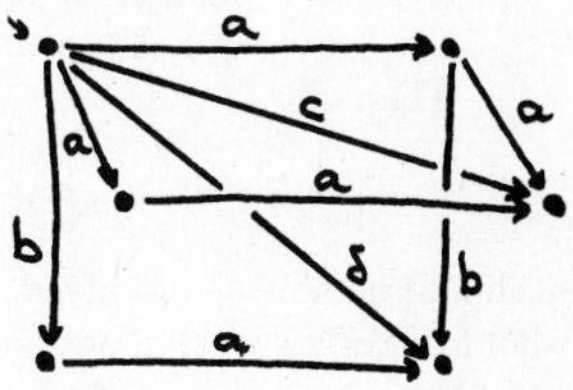

which implies that $\varepsilon\!\downarrow\ \in \multimap C[\pi^0]\multimapinv$ but $\varepsilon\!\downarrow\ \notin \multimap C[\pi^1]\multimapinv$.

Thus we see that $\sqsubseteq$ depends on the actions that a system may *refuse* to do at some point in a computation. A context tests this by offering synchronization and disabling the (non-synchronized) actions. This construction is canonical and, granting this, it implies impossibility of such a test in case the tested system can still do a *local* action—as these do not synchronize—or the system can diverge—as this cannot be prevented.

Before offering an explicit characterization of $\sqsubseteq$ we need some definitions.

3–1 Definition. *Let $\pi \in \mathsf{UTS}$, $v \in \mathcal{V}$ and $F \subseteq \mathcal{A}^g$. Then*

- *stable*$(v) \iff \mathcal{L}(^\bullet v) \subseteq \mathcal{A}^g_\delta$,
- π fails $F \iff \exists v \in I\ \mathit{stable}(v)\ \&\ F \cap \mathcal{L}(^\bullet v) = \emptyset$.

So, a node, v, in π is stable if it cannot diverge and there are no transitions with a *local* action out of it. It means that a suitable context can *control* the behavior of π if it is "at" v. In particular, π can be caused to deadlock and, more precisely, can be caused to *fail* certain global actions; namely, any set of actions F that satisfies π fails F.

Now we can state

3–2 Theorem. *Define the relation* $\underset{\sim}{\sqsubset} \subseteq \mathsf{UTS} \times \mathsf{UTS}$ *by*

$$\pi^0 \underset{\sim}{\sqsubset} \pi^1 \iff \multimap\pi^0\circ\!\!- \subseteq \multimap\pi^1\circ\!\!- \ \& $$
$$\forall s \in \mathcal{A}^\star,\ F \subseteq \mathcal{A}^g\ \pi^0 \text{ after } s \text{ fails } F \Rightarrow \pi^1 \text{ after } s \text{ fails } F\ .$$

Then $\sqsubseteq = \underset{\sim}{\sqsubset}$.

The proof, which we shall not give here in detail, is by showing two-sided inclusion. The case $\sqsubseteq \subseteq \underset{\sim}{\sqsubset}$ is proved by assuming that $\pi^0 \not\underset{\sim}{\sqsubset} \pi^1$ and then constructing a context, $C[\cdot] \in \mathcal{C}$, that makes this explicit: $\multimap C[\pi^0]\circ\!\!- \not\subseteq \multimap C[\pi^1]\circ\!\!-$ (whence $\pi^0 \not\sqsubseteq \pi^1$). The case $\multimap\pi^0\circ\!\!- \not\subseteq \multimap\pi^1\circ\!\!-$ is trivial. Otherwise, for some $s \in \mathcal{A}^\star$ and $F \subseteq \mathcal{A}^g$, we have π^0 after s fails F but not π^1 after s fails F. Construct a context $C[\cdot] = h(\rightarrow\bullet\xrightarrow{a}\bullet \parallel_\gamma [\cdot])$, with $h = [a \mapsto \delta,\ a \in F]$ and $\gamma = [(a,b) \mapsto x,\ a \in F]$, where $b \in \mathcal{A}^g$ and $x \notin \mathcal{A}(\pi^i)$ $(i \leq 1)$. We have $s{\downarrow} \in \multimap C[\pi^1]\circ\!\!-$ but $s{\downarrow} \notin \multimap C[\pi^0]\circ\!\!-$.

The proof of the other direction, $\underset{\sim}{\sqsubset} \subseteq \sqsubseteq$, uses induction on the structure of contexts and is based on two lemma's that express the behavior of $\pi^0 \parallel_\gamma \pi^1$ and $h(\pi)$ (almost) in terms of the behavior of, respectively, π^0 and π^0 and π:

3–3 Lemma.

- $\multimap\pi^0 \parallel_\gamma \pi^1\circ\!\!-^o = \{s\rho \mid \exists s^i\rho^i \in \multimap\pi^i\circ\!\!-^o\ (i \leq 1)\ s \in s^0 \parallel_\gamma s^1,\ \rho = \rho^0 \parallel \rho^1\}$, *where*
  - $\rho^0 \parallel \rho^1 = \begin{cases} \downarrow, & \text{if } \rho^0 = \rho^1 = \downarrow \\ \uparrow, & \text{otherwise} \end{cases}$,
  - $s^0 \parallel_\gamma s^1$ *is defined as follows:*
    Let $\overline{\gamma} = \gamma \circ [(a,X) \mapsto a,\ a \in \mathcal{A}^l]$ *with* $X \notin \mathcal{A}(s^0) \cup \mathcal{A}(s^1)$*; let* $e \in \mathcal{H}$ *be given by* $e(X) = \tau$.
    Then

$$s \in s^0 \parallel_\gamma s^1 \iff \exists \overline{s}^0, \overline{s}^1 \in \mathcal{A}_X^\dagger\ s^j = e(\overline{s}^j)\ (j \leq 1)\ \&\ s = \overline{\gamma}(\overline{s}^0, \overline{s}^1) \in (\mathcal{A} \setminus \{X\})^\dagger\ .$$

So, we should be able to modify s^0 and s^1 into $\overline{s}^0$ and $\overline{s}^1$ by inserting X-actions ($s^j = e(\overline{s}^j)$). An X-action in s^0 should signify a local action in s^1 and vice versa, which is ensured by having $s = \overline{\gamma}(\overline{s}_i^0, \overline{s}_i^1) \in (\mathcal{A}\setminus\{X\})^\dagger$ so that s does not contain any X-action.

3–4 Lemma.

- $$\multimap h(\pi)\circ\!\!-^o = \begin{array}{l} \{h(s)\rho \mid s\rho \in \multimap\pi\circ\!\!-^o\} \cup \\ \{h(s)\uparrow \mid s{\downarrow} \in \multimap\pi\circ\!\!-^o,\ s \in \mathcal{A}^\omega,\ h(s) \in \mathcal{A}^\star\} \cup \\ \{h(s){\downarrow} \mid \exists\overline{\pi}\ \pi \xrightarrow{s} \overline{\pi},\ stable(\overline{I}),\ h(\mathcal{L}(\overline{I})) = \{\delta\}\}\ . \end{array}$$

So, $h(\pi)$ acquires additional divergence possibilities whenever an infinite sequence is renamed to a finite one; it acquires additional (maximal) computations in case all successor actions of a stable vertex are disabled.

The proofs of these lemma's are tedious but not really difficult. They follow from the construction of $\pi^0 \parallel_\gamma \pi^1$ and of $h(\pi)$.

4 A verification criterion: failure simulation

For refinement of 1st order transition systems—usually taken to be inclusion of behaviors—the paradigm of a verification criterion is that of *Milner simulation* [Mil71].

The idea behind this is that in order to prove that $\multimap\pi^0\circ\!\!- \subseteq \multimap\pi^1\circ\!\!-$ one sets up a relation between the nodes of π^0 and π^1, such that every initial node of π^0 is related to an initial node of π^1. Such a relation should be *inductive* in the sense that if any two nodes v_0 and v_1 are related ($v^i \in \mathcal{V}^i$) then for every possible transition out of v_0 there must be a corresponding one out of v_1 (i.e., having the same effect) such that both reach nodes that again are related:

A *Milner simulation from* π^0 *to* π^1 (both in UTS) is a relation $\mathsf{M} \subseteq \mathcal{V}^0 \times \mathcal{V}^1$ satisfying for every $V_0 \in \mathcal{V}^0$, $v_1 \in \mathcal{V}^1$, $e_0 \in \mathcal{E}^0$, $a \in \mathcal{A}$:

1. $I^0 \subseteq dom(\mathsf{M});\quad v_0 \in I^0 \quad\Longrightarrow\quad \exists v_1 \in I^1\ v_0\ \mathsf{M}\ v_1,$
2. $^\bullet e_0\ \mathsf{M}\ v_1,\ \mathcal{L}^0(e_0) = a \quad\Longrightarrow\quad \exists e_1 \in {}^\bullet v_1\ e_0^\bullet\ \mathsf{M}\ e_1^\bullet\ \&\ \mathcal{L}^1(e_1) = a,$
3. $v_0\ \mathsf{M}\ v_1 \quad\Longrightarrow\quad \uparrow(v_0) \Rightarrow \uparrow(v_1)\ \&\ \downarrow(v_0) \Rightarrow \downarrow(v_1)\ .$

Clause (3) is not part of the usual definition of Milner simulation but is needed by our particular choice of behavior. The second clause is illustrated in the following picture:

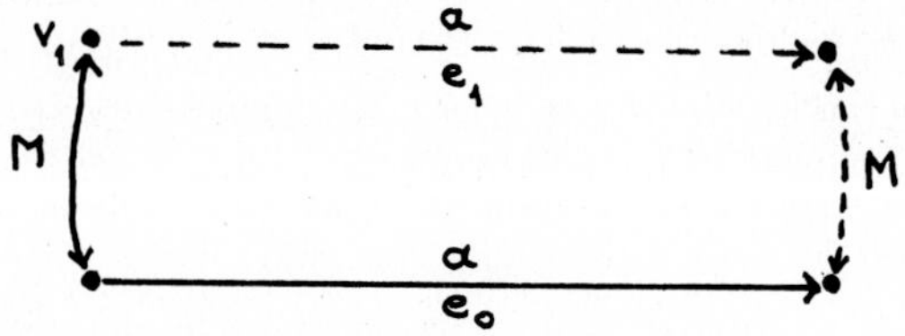

where the dotted parts are the things that have to be found.

If such a simulation can be set up, then this allows one to construct with every behavior of π^0 a corresponding one in π^1—this is the essence of the inductiveness condition. In other words, the criterion is *sound*.

Even if $-\!\!\circ\,\pi^0\circ\!\!- \subseteq -\!\!\circ\,\pi^1\circ\!\!-$, this is not always possible. The standard example is $\pi^0 =$ 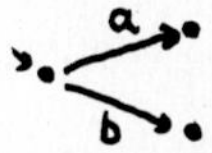

and $\pi^1 =$ 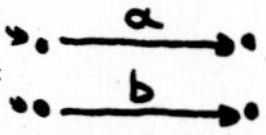

, for which there is no Milner simulation from π^0 to π^1: whatever initial vertices are related, either the a or the b-transition of π^0 cannot be mirrored. In other words, the criterion is *incomplete*.

This is well-known; as is well-known that if π^1 is *deterministic*, there is always a Milner simulation between π^0 and π^1. The so-called *subset construction* is the classical way to turn a uts π into a deterministic one, ${}^d\pi$, such that $-\!\!\circ\,\pi\circ\!\!- = -\!\!\circ\,{}^d\pi\circ\!\!-$: vertices of ${}^d\pi$ are the subsets of π's vertices; ${}^d\pi$'s initial state is I; and two sets are related by an edge in ${}^d\pi$, labelled a, if the second set comprises all the states that can be reached via an a-labelled transition in π from some state in the first set [Eil74].

The idea behind failure simulation, which will turn out to be a sound and complete criterion for failure refinement, is to combine the idea of Milner simulation with the above subset construction to render the uts (sufficiently) deterministic. First we define a special case of failure simulation (which, incidently, already is complete):

4–1 DEFINITION. *Let* $\pi^0, \pi^1 \in$ UTS. *A* simple failure simulation from π^0 to π^1 *is a relation,* $\mathsf{R} \in \mathcal{V}^0 \times 2^{\mathcal{V}^1}$ *such that for every* $e_0 \in \mathcal{E}^0$, $v_0 \in \mathcal{V}^0$, $V_1 \subseteq \mathcal{V}^1$, $a \in \mathcal{A}$:

1. $I^0 \subseteq dom(\mathsf{R});\quad v_0 \in I^0 \quad\Longrightarrow\quad \exists V_1 \subseteq I^1\ v_0\ \mathsf{R}\ V_1,$
2. $^\bullet e_0\ \mathsf{R}\ V_1,\ \mathcal{L}^0(e_0) = a \quad\Longrightarrow\quad \exists E_1 \subseteq {}^\bullet V_1\ e_0^\bullet\ \mathsf{R}\ E_1^\bullet\ \&\ \mathcal{L}^1(E_1) = \{a\},$
3. $v_0\ \mathsf{R}\ V_1 \quad\Longrightarrow\quad \exists v_1 \in V_1\ \uparrow(v_0) \Rightarrow \uparrow(v_1)\ \&\ \downarrow(v_0) \Rightarrow \downarrow(v_1)\ \&$
   $stable(v_0) \Rightarrow \big(stable(v_1)\ \&\ \mathcal{L}_g^1({}^\bullet v_1) \subseteq \mathcal{L}_g^0({}^\bullet v_0)\big) \qquad$ (hence $V_1 \neq \emptyset$) .

The second clause can be illustrated thus:

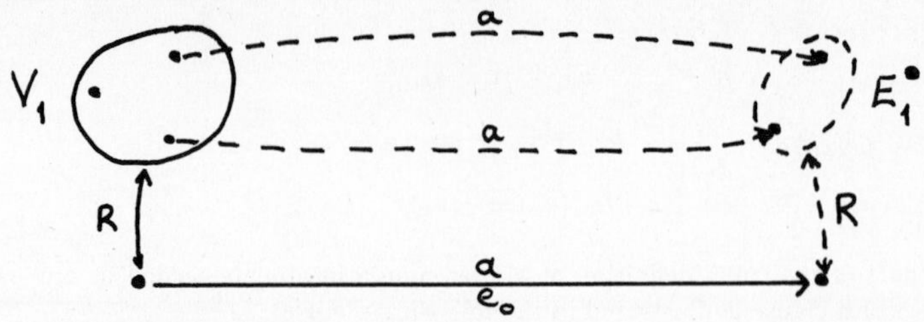

The third clause checks, in addition, that the deadlock possibilities "at" v_0 are allowed at some node $v_1 \in \mathcal{V}^1$: $\mathcal{L}_g^1({}^\bullet v_1) \subseteq \mathcal{L}_g^0({}^\bullet v_0)$; in accordance with Theorem 3–2.

This notion of simulation can be weakened without losing completeness which has the advantage of offering more layway in proving refinement. It can also be made symmetrical, relating subset to subset of nodes. This we will define now and it is what we will use in the rest of the paper.

4–2 DEFINITION. *Let* $\pi^0, \pi^1 \in \mathsf{UTS}$.

- *A failure simulation from* π^0 *to* π^1 *is a relation,* $\mathsf{R} \in 2^{\mathcal{V}^0} \times 2^{\mathcal{V}^1}$ *such that for every* $E_0 \subseteq \mathcal{E}^0$, $V_0 \subseteq \mathcal{V}^0$, $V_1 \subseteq \mathcal{V}^1$, $a \in \mathcal{A}$:

  1. $\exists (V_i^0)_{i<\alpha} \subseteq dom(\mathsf{R})\ I^0 = \bigcup_{i<\alpha} V_i^0\ \&\ \forall i < \alpha\ \exists V_i^1 \subseteq I^1\ \ V_i^0\ \mathsf{R}\ V_i^1$,
  2. ${}^\bullet E_0\ \mathsf{R}\ V_1,\ \emptyset \neq \overline{E}_0 \subseteq E_0 \cap \mathcal{L}^{0\ -1}(a),\ \overline{E}_0^\bullet \in dom(\mathsf{R}) \quad \Longrightarrow \quad \exists \overline{E}_1 \subseteq {}^\bullet V_1\ \overline{E}_0^\bullet\ \mathsf{R}\ \overline{E}_1^\bullet\ \&$ $\mathcal{L}^0(\overline{E}_0) = \mathcal{L}^1(\overline{E}_1)$,
  3. $V_0\ \mathsf{R}\ V_1 \quad \Longrightarrow \quad \forall v_0 \in V_0\ \exists v_1 \in V_1\ \uparrow\!(v_0) \Rightarrow \uparrow\!(v_1)\ \&\ \downarrow\!(v_0) \Rightarrow \downarrow\!(v_1)\ \&$ $stable(v_0) \Rightarrow \big(stable(v_1)\ \&\ \mathcal{L}_g^1({}^\bullet v_1) \subseteq \mathcal{L}_g^0({}^\bullet v_0)\big)$,
  4. ${}^\bullet E_0 \in dom(\mathsf{R}) \quad \Longrightarrow \quad \exists V_0 \dots V_n \in dom(\mathsf{R})\ (E_0 \cap \mathcal{L}^{0\ -1}(a))^\bullet = V_0 \cup \dots \cup V_n$.

- *write* $\pi^0 \hookrightarrow_{\mathsf{R}} \pi^1$ *if* R *is a failure simulation from* π^0 *to* π^1,

- *write* $\pi^0 \hookrightarrow \pi^1$ *if* $\exists \mathsf{R} \subseteq 2^{\mathcal{V}^0} \times 2^{\mathcal{V}^1}\ \pi^0 \hookrightarrow_{\mathsf{R}} \pi^1$.

Clause (1) says that every initial vertex of π^0 should occur in some set of initial vertices and that every such set is related to a set of initial vertices. Clause (2) is a direct generalization of the corresponding one in Definition 4–1: instead of a simple vertex, ${}^\bullet e_0 \in dom(\mathsf{R})$, there is a set of vertices, ${}^\bullet E_0 \in dom(\mathsf{R})$, and a set of edges, $\overline{E}_0 \subseteq E_0$, out of it, every edge in $\overline{E}_0$ labelled with a, $\overline{E}_0 \subseteq \mathcal{L}^{0\ -1}(a)$, and $\overline{E}_0^\bullet \in dom(\mathsf{R})$. This is pictured as follows:

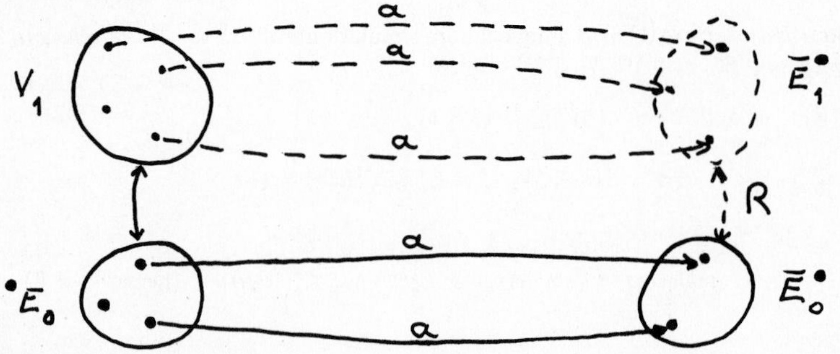

The additional clause (4) ensures that for every $a \in \mathcal{A}$ the vertices reachable by an a-labelled edge from

$^\bullet E_0$ are covered by sets in $dom(\mathsf{R})$. This is vital since we must construct an equivalent computation in π^1 for every one in π^0.

The rest of the section gives the soundness and completeness proofs to show that $\sqsubseteq = \hookrightarrow$. Fix some $\pi^0, \pi^1 \in \mathsf{UTS}$ and let $\mathsf{R} \subseteq 2^{\mathcal{V}^0} \times 2^{\mathcal{V}^1}$.

4.1 Soundness

The proof is based on the following auxiliary

4–3 Lemma. *Suppose* $\pi^0 \hookrightarrow_{\mathsf{R}} \pi^1$. *Then, for any* $s \in \mathcal{A}^\star$ *and* $v_0 \in \pi^0$ after s *there are* $V_0 \subseteq \pi^0$ after s, $V_1 \subseteq \pi^1$ after s *such that* $v_0 \in V_0$ *and* $V_0 \mathrel{\mathsf{R}} V_1$.

Proof. Induction on the length of s.

$s = \varepsilon$) π^0 after $\varepsilon = I^0$, hence clause (1) in the definition of failure simulation supplies a $V_0 \subseteq I^0$ with $v_0 \in V_0$ and $V_1 \subseteq I^1$ such that $V_0 \mathrel{\mathsf{R}} V_1$.

$s = \overline{s}a$) $v_0 \in \pi^0$ after s implies there is a $\overline{v}_0 \in \mathcal{V}^0$ such that $\overline{v}_0 \in \pi^0$ after $\overline{s}$ and $\overline{v}_0; \pi^0 \xrightarrow{a} v_0; \pi^0$. Induction gives a $\overline{V}_0 \subseteq \mathcal{V}^0$ and $\overline{V}_1 \subseteq \mathcal{V}^1$ with $\overline{v}_0 \in \overline{V}_0$ and $\overline{V}_0 \mathrel{\mathsf{R}} \overline{V}_1$. Let $E_0 \in {}^\bullet\overline{V}_0$ and $\widetilde{E}_0 = E_0 \cap \mathcal{L}^{0\,-1}(a)$. By assumption, $E_0 \neq \emptyset$ and so $\widetilde{E}_0 \neq \emptyset$. Since $^\bullet E_0 \in dom(\mathsf{R})$, clause (4) gives a $V_0 \in dom(\mathsf{R})$ and $v_0 \in V_0 \subseteq \widetilde{E}_0^\bullet$. Let $\overline{E}_0 = \widetilde{E}_0 \cap V_0^\bullet$. Clause (2) implies existence of a set $\overline{E}_1 \subseteq {}^\bullet\overline{V}_1$ such that $\overline{E}_0^\bullet \mathrel{\mathsf{R}} \overline{E}_1^\bullet$ and $\mathcal{L}^1(\overline{E}_1) = \{a\}$. So, define $V_0 = \overline{E}_0^\bullet$ and $V_1 = \overline{E}_1^\bullet$. Then $v_0 \in V_0 \subseteq \pi^0$ after s, $V_1 \subseteq \pi^1$ after s and $V_0 \mathrel{\mathsf{R}} V_1$. □

4–4 Theorem (Soundness). $\hookrightarrow \subseteq \sqsubseteq$.

Proof. Choose $\pi^0 \hookrightarrow_{\mathsf{R}} \pi^1$. First take some $s\rho \in \dot{\multimap}\pi^0\!\!\multimap$. If $s \in \mathcal{A}^\star$, then there is some $v_0 \in \mathcal{V}^0$ and $\pi^0 \xrightarrow{s} v_0; \pi^0$ with $\rho(v_0)$ true. By Lemma 4–3, there are $V^i \subseteq \pi^i$ after s ($i \leq 1$) with $v_0 \in V_0$ and $V_0 \mathrel{\mathsf{R}} V_1$. By clause (3) of the definition of failure simulation, $\rho(v_1)$ holds for some $v_1 \in V_1$; whence $s\rho \in \multimap\pi^1\!\!\multimap^o$. If $s \in \mathcal{A}^\omega$ then for every $\overline{s} \prec s$ (by definition $\overline{s} \in \mathcal{A}^\star$) there is a $\overline{v}_0 \in \pi^0$ after $\overline{s}$ and again by the previous Lemma, π^1 after $\overline{s} \neq \emptyset$. Hence, $s{\downarrow} \in \multimap\pi^1\!\!\multimap$.

Next, let $s \in \mathcal{A}^\star$ and $F \subseteq \mathcal{A}^g$. Assume that π^0 after s fails F holds. This implies a $v_0 \in \pi^0$ after s such that $stable(v_0)$ holds and $F \cap \mathcal{L}^0_g({}^\bullet v_0) = \emptyset$. The same argument as above gives a $v_1 \in \pi^1$ after s, also with $stable(v_1)$ being true and $F \cap \mathcal{L}^1_g({}^\bullet v_1) = \emptyset$. I.e., π^1 after s fails F holds, too. □

4–5 Corollary. *If there is a simple failure relation from* π^0 *to* π^1, *then* $\pi^0 \sqsubseteq \pi^1$.

Proof. If R is such a simple failure relation, then $\pi^0 \hookrightarrow_{\widehat{\mathsf{R}}} \pi^1$ with

$$\widehat{\mathsf{R}} = \{(\{v_0\}, V_1) \mid (v_0, V_1) \in \mathsf{R}\}\ .$$

□

4.2 Completeness

4–6 Theorem (Completeness). $\sqsubseteq \subseteq \hookrightarrow$.

PROOF. Let $\pi^0 \sqsubseteq \pi^1$ and define $\mathsf{R} \subseteq 2^{\mathcal{V}^0} \times 2^{\mathcal{V}^1}$ by

$$\mathsf{R} = \{(\{v_0\}, V_1) \mid \exists s \in \mathcal{A}^\star\ \pi^0 \xrightarrow{s} v_0; \pi^0\ \&\ \pi^1\ \mathsf{after}\ s = V_1; \pi^1\}\ .$$

We show that $\pi^0 \hookrightarrow_{\mathsf{R}} \pi^1$ holds:

1. By taking $s = \varepsilon$ we immediately obtain that $\{v_0\} \in dom(\mathsf{R})$ and $\{v_0\}\ \mathsf{R}\ I^1$ for all $v_0 \in I^0$.

2. Let ${}^\bullet E_0\ \mathsf{R}\ V_1$, $\overline{E}_0 \subseteq E_0 \cap \mathcal{L}^{0\ -1}(a)$ and $\overline{E}_0^\bullet \in dom(\mathsf{R})$. By definition of R, we must have $\overline{E}_0 = E_0 = \{e_0\}$ and $\mathcal{L}^0(e_0) = a$. Also, $\pi^0 \xrightarrow{s} {}^\bullet e_0; \pi^0 \xrightarrow{a} e_0^\bullet; \pi^0$; whence, if $\overline{E}_1 = {}^\bullet V_1 \cap \mathcal{L}^{1\ -1}(a)$, $\overline{E}_0^\bullet\ \mathsf{R}\ \overline{E}_1^\bullet$ and $\mathcal{L}^0(\overline{E}_0) = \mathcal{L}^1(\overline{E}_1)$.

3. $V_0\ \mathsf{R}\ V_1$ implies $V_0 = \{v_0\}$. Choose an $s \in \mathcal{A}^\star$ such that $\pi^0 \xrightarrow{s} v_0; \pi^0$ and $\pi^1\ \mathsf{after}\ s = V_1; \pi^1$.
If $\rho(v_0)$ is true then $s\rho \in \multimap\pi^0\circ\!\!-$; whence, by assumption $s\rho \in \multimap\pi^1\circ\!\!-$, which in its turn implies that $\rho(v_1)$ holds for some $v_1 \in V_1$ (because $\pi^1 \xrightarrow{s} v_1; \pi^1 \Rightarrow v_1 \in V_1$).
Next, if $stable(v_1)$ holds and $F \cap \mathcal{L}_g^0({}^\bullet v_0) = \emptyset$ for some $F \subseteq \mathcal{A}^g$ then $\pi^0\ \mathsf{after}\ s\ \mathsf{fails}\ F$ is true and, again by assumption, so is $\pi^1\ \mathsf{after}\ s\ \mathsf{fails}\ F$. From this conclude that $stable(v_1)$ holds and $F \cap \mathcal{L}_g^1({}^\bullet v_1) = \emptyset$ for some $v_1 \in V_1$.

4. Let ${}^\bullet E_0 \in dom(\mathsf{R})$ and $\emptyset \neq \overline{E}_0 = E_0 \cap \mathcal{L}^{0\ -1}(a)$. Hence, $E_0 = \{e_0\}$, $\mathcal{L}^0(e_0) = a$ and for some $s \in \mathcal{A}^\star$: $\pi^0 \xrightarrow{s} {}^\bullet e_0; \pi^0 \xrightarrow{a} e_0^\bullet; \pi^0$. This implies that $\{e_0^\bullet\} \in dom(\mathsf{R})$. □

4–7 COROLLARY. *If $\pi^0 \sqsubseteq \pi^1$ then there is a simple failure simulation from π^0 to π^1.*

PROOF. If R is the relation as defined in the proof of the completeness theorem, then

$$\overline{\mathsf{R}} = \{(v_0, V_1) \mid (\{v_0\}, V_1) \in \mathsf{R}\}$$

is a simple failure relation from π^0 to π^1. □

So, both failure simulation and simple failure simulation are sound and complete verification criteria for proving failure refinement. Note that if in clause (3) of either definition we ignore the part concerning stability and the next possible moves, the resulting simulations are sound and complete criteria for *trace refinement*: $\multimap\pi^0\circ\!\!- \subseteq \multimap\pi^1\circ\!\!-$. This is an easy consequence of the above soundness and completeness proofs.

5 First Order Transition Systems

In a first order transition system, there is an implicit notion of state and edge labels now denote tests and actions that depend on, respectively, update the state.

• Given a signature Σ, let $\mathcal{A}ct(\Sigma) = \mathcal{G}act(\Sigma) \cup \mathcal{L}act(\Sigma)$ be some set of action over Σ partitioned into $\mathcal{G}act(\Sigma)$—the global actions—and $\mathcal{L}act(\Sigma)$—the local actions. The 'actions' δ and $\uparrow$ do not appear in $\mathcal{A}ct(\Sigma)$. The precise form of these actions does not matter at this moment. We do need that given a Σ-structure, $\mathbf{A}$, there is a function, $[\![\cdot]\!]^{\mathbf{A}}: \mathcal{A}ct(\Sigma)_\uparrow \mapsto 2^{\mathcal{S}\times\mathcal{S}}$ that gives the input-output behavior of the actions. We (arbitrarily) assume that $[\![\uparrow]\!]^{\mathbf{A}} = Id_{\mathcal{S}}$. For the rest of the section, fix some Σ-structure, $\mathbf{A}$.

- The class of *1st order transition systems over* $\mathcal{A}ct(\Sigma)$ is $\mathsf{TS}_{\mathcal{A}ct(\Sigma)}$ (TS_Σ or just TS) and is defined as

$$\{\ (\partial_s, \partial_t : \mathcal{E} \mapsto \mathcal{V}, I, \mathcal{L} : \mathcal{E} \mapsto L(\Sigma) \times \mathcal{A}ct(\Sigma)_{\delta\uparrow}) \mid |\mathcal{E}| \text{ and } |\mathcal{V}| \text{ are finite } \}\ .$$

So, a 1st order transition system (ts), also denoted by π, is a transition system whose underlying graph is finite and each of whose edges is labelled with a *test* from $L(\Sigma)$ and an *action* from $\mathcal{A}ct(\Sigma)$. Write $\mathcal{L}^t(e)$, respectively, $\mathcal{L}^a(e)$ for the test, respectively, action associated with e.

- As for the meaning of a $\pi \in \mathsf{TS}$, we can define, like for uts's, transition relations, $\xrightarrow{a}$, for $a \in \mathcal{A}ct(\Sigma)$; this time as relations over $\mathsf{TS} \times \mathcal{S}$:

$$\pi, \sigma \xrightarrow{a} \overline{\pi}, \overline{\sigma} \iff \exists e \in {}^\bullet I\ \mathbf{A}, \sigma \models \mathcal{L}^t(e),\ (\sigma, \overline{\sigma}) \in [\![\mathcal{L}^a(e)]\!]^{\mathbf{A}},\ \overline{\pi} = e^\bullet; \pi\ .$$

These relations fix the behavior of a 1st order system, as they do for uts's.

- The next step is to associate with every $\pi \in \mathsf{TS}$ an uts ${}^t\pi$ which has the same behavior as π.

The transition relation defined above gives the general idea: the vertex set of ${}^t\pi$ will also record the state; an edge label in ${}^t\pi$ will also include the state-transformation.

Given $\pi \in \mathsf{TS}_{\mathcal{A}ct(\Sigma)}$, define ${}^t\pi \in \mathsf{UTS}_{\mathcal{S} \times \mathcal{A}ct(\Sigma) \times \mathcal{S}}$ by

- ${}^t\mathcal{V} = \mathcal{V} \times \mathcal{S}$,
- ${}^t\mathcal{E} = \mathcal{S} \times \mathcal{E} \times \mathcal{S}$,
- ${}^t\partial_s(\sigma, e, \overline{\sigma}) = ({}^\bullet e, \sigma)$ and ${}^t\partial_t(\sigma, e, \overline{\sigma}) = (e^\bullet, \overline{\sigma})$ iff $\mathbf{A}, \sigma \models \mathcal{L}^t(e)$ and $(\sigma, \overline{\sigma}) \in [\![\mathcal{L}^a(e)]\!]^{\mathbf{A}}$,
- ${}^tI = I \times \mathcal{S}$, and
- ${}^t\mathcal{L}(\sigma, e, \overline{\sigma}) = (\sigma, \mathcal{L}^a(e), \overline{\sigma})$.

- The following easy to prove correspondence holds between π and ${}^t\pi$:

$$\pi, \sigma \xrightarrow{a} \overline{\pi}, \overline{\sigma} \iff {}^t\pi \xrightarrow{(\sigma, a, \overline{\sigma})} {}^t\overline{\pi}\ .$$

So, ${}^t\pi$ indeed is the 'correct' translation of π. With this correspondence, we can have $⊸\pi⟜ = ⊸{}^t\pi⟜$ for $\pi \in \mathsf{TS}$. Also, we can *define* refinement for first order systems simply by

$$\pi^0 \sqsubseteq \pi^1 \iff {}^t\pi^0 \sqsubseteq {}^t\pi^1 \quad (\pi^0, \pi^1 \in \mathsf{TS})\ . \tag{6}$$

It would be better to write $\mathbf{A} \models \pi^0 \sqsubseteq \pi^1$ instead of $\pi^0 \sqsubseteq \pi^1$ so as to stress the dependence of the definition on the structure $\mathbf{A}$.

This canonical translation, ${}^t.: \mathsf{TS} \mapsto \mathsf{UTS}$, can be used to formulate a notion of simulation that is defined in terms of the vertices and edges of first order systems. This is the subject of the next section.

The above gives a general, abstract set-up to deal with (refinement of) first order systems. The key step is the translation ${}^t.$. This allows the principles developed for uts's to be 'lifted' to first order systems. The definition embodied in (6), which is based on it, implies that for any program combinator on ts's that can be defined using ${}^t.$, $h(\cdot)$ and $\cdot \parallel_\gamma \cdot$, $\sqsubseteq$ will be a pre-congruence.

The remainder of the section gives some examples. We instantiate $\mathcal{A}ct(\Sigma)$ so as to have assignments to local and shared variables and to have synchronous communication actions. We then define a *parallel composition*, $\cdot \parallel \cdot$, an *encapsulation*, $Enc(\cdot, enc)$, and a hiding operator, $Hide(\cdot, V)$, for such ts's. Encapsulation turns shared variables into local ones as specified by the function $enc\colon Svar \mapsto Pvar$; hiding makes the values of the private variables in $V \subseteq Pvar$ unobservable.

So, first partition *Var* into *Pvar* and *Svar*. *Pvar* is the set of *private* variables that can be accessed by at most one process; *Svar* is the set of *shared* variables. Also introduce a set, *Chan*, of *channel names*: communication will occur along channels between exactly two transition systems. Then, we define $\mathcal{L}act(\Sigma)$ and $\mathcal{G}act(\Sigma)$ by

$$\begin{aligned}
\mathcal{L}act(\Sigma) &= \{x := e \mid x \in Pvar,\ e \in Tm(\Sigma)\} \bigcup \\
&\quad \{C : x := e \mid x \in Pvar,\ e \in Tm(\Sigma),\ C \in Chan\}\ , \\
\mathcal{G}act(\Sigma) &= \{C!e \mid C \in Chan,\ e \in Tm(\Sigma)\} \bigcup \\
&\quad \{C?x \mid C \in Chan,\ x \in Pvar\} \bigcup \\
&\quad \{W : x := e \mid W \in \{E, S\},\ x \in Svar,\ e \in Tm(\Sigma)\}\ .
\end{aligned}$$

We shall also use *Pvar*, *Svar* and *Chan* as functions: $Pvar(\pi) \subseteq Pvar$ is the set of private variables that appear in π, etc. .

The intention is that $x := e$ is an ordinary assignment to a private variable; $C : x := e$ denotes a communication along channel C, causing x to be obtain the value of e; $C!e$, respectively, $C?x$ denotes the action of sending the value of e along channel C, respectively, receiving a value along channel C and assigning it to the variable x; and $W : x := e$ is an assignment to a shared variable where W indicates whether the assignment originated in the system, $W \equiv S$, or whether the system's environment is responsible for it, $W \equiv E$. The latter type of action needs some elaboration.

As a comparison, first look at communication between processes. If C is a channel between two processes π^0 and π^1 then π^0 should only be able to perform a $C?x$-transition if π^1 simultaneously executes a $C!e$-transition and vice versa. Hence, $\pi^0 \parallel \pi^1$ will be defined as $h({}^t\pi^0 \parallel_\gamma {}^t\pi^1)$, where the communication function γ, among other things, maps pairs $C?x$, $C!e$ onto $C : x := e$, denoting a successful communication, while the renaming function h, among other things, renames $C?x$ and $C!e$ to δ to enforce synchronous communication.

Now, if we look at assignments to a shared variable, $x \in Svar$, occurring in π^0 then, in principle, π^0 does not control when its environment assigns to x. Yet, in a program $Enc(\pi^0 \parallel \pi^1, [x \mapsto y])$, in which x has been made a private variable (y) of $\pi^0 \parallel \pi^1$, we must make sure that every assignment to x originates in either π^0 or π^1. The way this is solved here is by explicitly indicating from where an assignment to a shared variable originates: in the system, S, or in its environment, E. In the definition of $\pi^0 \parallel \pi^1$, $h({}^t\pi^0 \parallel_\gamma {}^t\pi^1)$, γ in combination with h will also map pairs $S : x := e$, $E : x := e$ into $S : x := e$ and pairs $E : x := e$, $E : x := e$ into $E : x := e$. The former pair indicates that an update by π^is ($i \leq 1$) environment is in fact performed by π^{1-i}; the latter pair indicates that the update originates in the environment of both π^0 and π^1. Also, h maps any "unmatched" $S : x; = e$ and $E : x; = e$ into δ to enforce consistency. With this set-up, encapsulating x in $\pi^0 \parallel \pi^1$ then means, among other things, that actions $E : x := e$ are renamed to δ, since π^0 and π^1 are the only processes that can assign to x.

- Next, we must define the semantics of the actions. This is straightforward:

$$\begin{aligned}
&[\![x := e]\!]^{\mathbf{A}} = [\![W : x := e]\!]^{\mathbf{A}} = \{(\sigma, \overline{\sigma}) \mid \overline{\sigma} = \sigma\{\sigma(e)/x\}\}, \quad W \in \{C, S, E\}, \\
&[\![C!e]\!]^{\mathbf{A}} = Id_{\mathcal{S}}, \\
&[\![C?x]\!]^{\mathbf{A}} = \{(\sigma, \sigma\{v/x\}) \mid v \in |\mathbf{A}|\}\ .
\end{aligned}$$

Now we are ready to define the program combinators. The strategy will be to first define the required behavior by transition relations and then constructing a translation that will generate this behavior. We shall not give proofs of our claims below.

- **Parallel composition.** Given $\pi^0, \pi^1 \in \mathsf{TS}$, $\pi^0 \parallel \pi^1$ is defined if $Pvar(\pi^i) \cap Var(\pi^{1-i}) = \emptyset$ for $i \leq 1$. We want $\pi^0 \parallel \pi^1$ to behave as follows:

- $\pi^0,\sigma \xrightarrow{a} \overline{\pi}^0,\overline{\sigma} \quad\Rightarrow\quad \pi^0 \parallel \pi^1,\sigma \xrightarrow{a} \overline{\pi}^0 \parallel \pi^1,\overline{\sigma}$ if $a \in \mathcal{L}act(\Sigma)$,

- $\begin{array}{l} \pi^0,\sigma \xrightarrow{C!e} \overline{\pi}^0,\sigma \\ \pi^1,\sigma \xrightarrow{C?x} \overline{\pi}^1,\overline{\sigma} \end{array} \quad\Rightarrow\quad \pi^0 \parallel \pi^1,\sigma \xrightarrow{C\,:\,x:=e} \overline{\pi}^0 \parallel \overline{\pi}^1,\overline{\sigma}$ if $\overline{\sigma}(x) = \sigma(e)$,

- $\begin{array}{l} \pi^0,\sigma \xrightarrow{E\,:\,x:=e} \overline{\pi}^0,\overline{\sigma} \\ \pi^1,\sigma \xrightarrow{W\,:\,x:=e} \overline{\pi}^1,\overline{\sigma} \end{array} \quad\Rightarrow\quad \pi^0 \parallel \pi^1,\sigma \xrightarrow{W\,:\,x:=e} \overline{\pi}^0 \parallel \overline{\pi}^1,\overline{\sigma}$ for $W \in \{S,E\}$,

- $\cdot \parallel \cdot$ is commutative.

So, in particular one sees that an update of a shared variable must be allowed by all components. Apart from obtaining a simple transition relation, this has the additional advantage of giving a program some control over access to a shared variable. E.g., a program $\to\bullet \xrightarrow{S:\,x:=1} \bullet$ ($x \in Svar$) effectively says that it has exclusive access to x because it does not include any environment steps. One should not interpret this as a system specifying its environment, but rather as a system that makes certain assumptions about how its environment behaves.

In order to construct ${}^t(\pi^0 \parallel \pi^1)$ so that

$$\pi^0 \parallel \pi^1,\sigma \xrightarrow{a} \overline{\pi}^0 \parallel \overline{\pi}^1,\overline{\sigma} \iff {}^t(\pi^0 \parallel \pi^1) \xrightarrow{(\sigma,a,\overline{\sigma})} {}^t(\overline{\pi}^0 \parallel \overline{\pi}^1)$$

we first define for $\sigma^0,\sigma^1 \in \mathcal{S}$ such that $\sigma^0 \lceil V = \sigma^1 \lceil V$ where $V = (Var(\pi^0) \cap Var(\pi^1)) \cup \mathcal{V} \setminus Var(\pi^0 \parallel \pi^1)$[3]:
$(\sigma^0 + \sigma^1)(x) = \begin{cases} \sigma^0(x), & \text{if } x \in Var(\pi^0) \\ \sigma^1(x), & \text{otherwise} \end{cases}$.
Also, for $a, b \in \mathcal{G}act(\Sigma)$: $a + b = \begin{cases} \overline{W} : x := e, & \text{if } a \equiv E : x := e,\ b \equiv W : x := e \text{ and } W \in \{E,S\} \\ C : x := e, & \text{if } \{a,b\}=\{C!e, C?x\} \end{cases}$.

Now we set ${}^t(\pi^0 \parallel \pi^1) = h({}^t\pi^0 \parallel_\gamma {}^t\pi^1)$ where

- $\gamma((\sigma^0, a, \overline{\sigma}^0), (\sigma^1, b, \overline{\sigma}^1)) = (\sigma^0 + \sigma^1, a + b, \overline{\sigma}^0 + \overline{\sigma}^1)$ and
- $h((\sigma, \overline{W} : x := e, \overline{\sigma})) = (\sigma, W : x := e, \overline{\sigma})$ for $W \in \{S,E\}$,
  $h((\sigma, W : x := e, \overline{\sigma})) = \delta$ for $W \in \{S,E\}$,
  $h((\sigma, C?x, \overline{\sigma})) = h((\sigma, C!e, \overline{\sigma})) = \delta$ if $C \in Chan(\pi^0) \cap Chan(\pi^1)$.

It is not difficult to see that ${}^t(\pi^0 \parallel \pi^1)$ behaves as suggested.

- **Encapsulation**. Given $\pi \in \mathsf{TS}$ and enc: $Svar \mapsto Pvar$, in the system $Enc(\pi, enc)$ the variables in $dom(enc)$ are no longer shared with π's environment and are renamed to private variables. Obviously, $Enc(\pi, enc)$ is only defined if enc is injective and $ran(enc) \cap Pvar(\pi) = \emptyset$.

For an action a let $enc(a)$ be the action obtained by renaming the variables (if any) according to enc. Also, for a state σ let $enc(\sigma)$ be the state $\overline{\sigma}$ such that: $\overline{\sigma}(x) = \begin{cases} \sigma(inc^{-1}(x)), & \text{if } x \in dom(enc) \\ \sigma(x), & \text{otherwise} \end{cases}$.

Then, $Enc(\pi, enc)$ should behave as follows:

- $\pi,\sigma \xrightarrow{a} \overline{\pi},\overline{\sigma} \quad\Rightarrow\quad Enc(\pi, enc), enc(\sigma) \xrightarrow{enc(a)} Enc(\overline{\pi}, enc), \widetilde{\sigma}$

  if $a \equiv E : x := e \Rightarrow FV(x := e) \cap dom(enc) = \emptyset$, where $\widetilde{\sigma}(x) = \begin{cases} enc(\sigma)(x), & \text{if } x \in dom(enc) \\ \sigma(x), & \text{otherwise} \end{cases}$.

[3] Formally, we should define what $Var(\pi^0 \parallel \pi^1)$ means. Such extensions of $Var(\cdot)$ and the other syntactic functions, however, should be clear.

The translation, ${}^{t}Enc(\pi, enc)$, is given by $h({}^{t}\pi)$ where

- $h((\sigma, a, \overline{\sigma})) = \begin{cases} \delta & \text{if } a \equiv E : x := e \text{ and } FV(x := e) \cap dom(enc) \neq \emptyset \\ (enc(\sigma), h(a), \widetilde{\sigma}) & \text{otherwise} \end{cases}$,
  where $\widetilde{\sigma}$ is defined as above.

Again we have

$$Enc(\pi, enc), \sigma \xrightarrow{a} Enc(\overline{\pi}, enc), \overline{\sigma} \iff {}^{t}Enc(\pi, enc) \xrightarrow{(\sigma, a, \overline{\sigma})} {}^{t}Enc(\overline{\pi}, enc) \ .$$

- **Hiding.** Given $\pi \in \mathsf{TS}$ and $V \subseteq Pvar$, $Hide(\pi, V)$, makes the private variables in V unobservable. We want $Hide(\pi, V)$ to behave as follows:

- $\pi, \sigma \xrightarrow{a} \overline{\pi}, \overline{\sigma} \Rightarrow Hide(\pi, V), \sigma \xrightarrow{a} Hide(\pi, V), \widetilde{\sigma}$, where $\widetilde{\sigma}(x) = \begin{cases} \sigma(x) & \text{if } x \in V \\ \overline{\sigma}(x) & \text{otherwise} \end{cases}$.

Then ${}^{t}Hide(\pi, V) = h({}^{t}\pi)$, with

- $h((\sigma, a, \overline{\sigma})) = (\sigma, a, \widetilde{\sigma})$, where $\widetilde{\sigma}$ is defined as above.

It is straightforward to prove that

$$Hide(\pi, V), \sigma \xrightarrow{a} Hide(\overline{\pi}, V), \overline{\sigma} \iff {}^{t}Hide(\pi, V) \xrightarrow{\sigma, a, \overline{\sigma})} {}^{t}Hide(\pi, V)$$

As we already stated, these are only examples of composition operators for 1st order systems. One can also define a hiding operator to hide actions or channels. As with encapsulation and hiding of variables, here too, this is a question of defining the appropriate renaming operator. We stress that our notion of (1st order) refinement by definition is a congruence for all such operators.

6 Verifying First Order Refinement

The intent, here, is not to find any old translation of failure simulation to first order systems, but rather to formulate it in terms of more or less standard assertional methods for transition systems: Floyd's inductive assertion method [Flo67]. For the remainder of the section, fix some $\pi^0, \pi^1 \in \mathsf{TS}_{\mathcal{A}ct(\Sigma)}$ with $\pi^0 \sqsubseteq \pi^1$ and a Σ-structure $\mathbf{A}$.

We need to define $\hookrightarrow_{\mathsf{R}} \subseteq \mathsf{TS}_{\mathcal{A}ct(\Sigma)} \times \mathsf{TS}_{\mathcal{A}ct(\Sigma)}$ and conditions on $\hookrightarrow_{\mathsf{R}}$ so that $\pi^0 \hookrightarrow_{\mathsf{R}} \pi^1$ iff ${}^{t}\pi^0 \hookrightarrow_{{}^{t}\mathsf{R}} {}^{t}\pi^1$ for an appropriate 'translation' of R. The first thing is to decide how to represent a failure simulation, R, in terms of assertions. Obviously, R, too, will relate sets of states with each other and ${}^{t}\mathsf{R}$ will be a relation over $2^{\mathcal{V}^0 \times \mathcal{S}} \times 2^{\mathcal{V}^1 \times \mathcal{S}}$, since $\mathcal{V}^i \times \mathcal{S}$ is the vertex set of ${}^{t}\pi^i$. Now, in an inductive assertion proof, the assertion associated with a vertex intends to describe the states with which the system can reach that vertex. *This suggests to associate assertions with* sets of vertices *and to relate such sets if the corresponding assertions allow both sets to be reached with the same state.* We also know from the completeness proof that which sets are related is also based on the (partial) computations. Hence, we use an assertion language, As, in which *history variables* may occur that have (partial) computations as value; i.e., that are of type $\mathcal{H}is = (\mathcal{S} \times \mathcal{A}ct(\Sigma) \times \mathcal{S})^{\star}$. Note that these history variables are additions to the assertion language and, hence, differ from what some researchers [AL88] call history variables. These are auxiliary variables that are added to a program and to which one assigns values so as to encode information about the computation history. There are some further conditions on As that we shall need later on: As will be a (weak monadic) second order language in which we allow quantification over sets of vertices and allow membership tests for vertices, edges and actions (which means that there are variables of the respective types: V, v, e and a). Also, the signature of As includes functions ${}^{\bullet}.$, $.^{\bullet}$, $\mathcal{L}^{t}(\cdot)$ and $\mathcal{L}^{a}(\cdot)$ with the obvious interpretation. Since we need to relate two ts's with each other, sub and superscripts are used in As to keep them apart:

i.e., $\exists V_0 \forall e_0 \in {}^{\bullet}V_0\ \mathcal{L}^{0\ a}(e_0) \in \mathcal{L}act(\Sigma)$ expresses the existence of a set vertices in π^0 such that the outgoing edges of any vertex in this set is labelled with a local action. Any quantification over vertices, edges, and vertex sets is implicitly restricted by the ts to which these items belong. Since, these ts's are finite, such quantifications can always be replaced by finite con- and disjunctions.

Assume that assertions all use the history variable, h. Its value is neither changed by an action in $\mathcal{A}ct(\Sigma)$ nor does an action depend on the value; also, h does not appear in any test in the label of any transition in any ta π: $\forall a \in \mathcal{A}ct(\Sigma),\ s \in \mathcal{H}is\ \ (\sigma, \overline{\sigma}) \in [\![a]\!]^{\mathbf{A}} \Rightarrow \sigma(h) = \overline{\sigma}(h)\ \&\ (\sigma\{s/h\}, \overline{\sigma}\{s/h\}) \in [\![a]\!]^{\mathbf{A}}$ and $\forall \phi \in \mathcal{L}^t(\mathcal{E})\ h \notin FV(\phi)$.

6–1 Definition. *Let $\pi, \pi^0, \pi^1 \in$ TS.*

- *A set labelling of π is a (partial) function $\lambda: 2^{\mathcal{V}} \mapsto$ As; by convention, let $\sigma \not\models \lambda(V)$ for every $\sigma \in \mathcal{S}$ if $V \notin dom(\lambda)$,*
- *Given set labellings λ^0 and λ^1 of π^0 and π^1, the relation $[\lambda^0, \lambda^1] \subseteq 2^{\mathcal{V}^0} \times 2^{\mathcal{V}^1}$ is defined by*

$$[\lambda^0, \lambda^1] = \bigcup_{\sigma \in \mathcal{S}} [\lambda^0, \lambda^1]_\sigma$$

$$[\lambda^0, \lambda^1]_\sigma = \{(V_0, V_1) \mid \exists s \in \mathcal{H}is\ \sigma\{s/h\} \models \lambda^0(V_0) \wedge \lambda^1(V_1)\}\ ,$$

- *Given a relation $[\lambda^0, \lambda^1]$, define its translation by*

$$^t[\lambda^0, \lambda^1] = \bigcup_{\sigma \in \mathcal{S}} \{(V_0 \times \{\sigma\}, V_1 \times \{\sigma\}) \mid (V_0, V_1) \in [\lambda^0, \lambda^1]_\sigma\}\ .$$

The intention is that λ^0 and λ^1 describe the states and histories with which the vertex sets in their domains can be reached.

Now we ask: *what conditions should be imposed on $[\lambda^0, \lambda^1]$ so that $^t[\lambda^0, \lambda^1]$ is a failure simulation from $^t\pi^0$ to $^t\pi^1$?*

In tackling this, we first concentrate on clause (2) of Definition 4–2, formulated below for $^t\pi^0$ and $^t\pi^1$ where R stands for $[\lambda^0, \lambda^1]$:

$$^{\bullet t}E_0\ {}^t\mathsf{R}\ {}^tV_1,\ \emptyset \neq {}^t\overline{E}_0 \subseteq {}^tE_0 \cap \mathcal{L}^{0\ -1}(a),\ {}^t\overline{E}_0^{\bullet} \in dom({}^t\mathsf{R}) \quad \Rightarrow \quad \exists^t\overline{E}_1 \subseteq {}^{\bullet t}V_1\ {}^t\overline{E}_0^{\bullet}\ {}^t\mathsf{R}\ {}^t\overline{E}_1^{\bullet}\ \& \quad (7)$$
$$^t\mathcal{L}^0({}^t\overline{E}_0) = {}^t\mathcal{L}^1({}^t\overline{E}_1)\ ,$$

Let $^{\bullet t}E_0 = {}^tV_0$[4]. Now, $^tV_0\ {}^t\mathsf{R}\ {}^tV_1$ implies there are $V_0 \subseteq \mathcal{V}^0$, $V_1 \subseteq \mathcal{V}^1$ and a $\sigma \in \mathcal{S}$ such that $^tV_i = V_i \times \{\sigma\}$ and $V_0\ \mathsf{R}_\sigma\ V_1$. The action, a, is of the form $(\sigma, \overline{a}, \overline{\sigma})$ for some $\overline{a} \in Act(\Sigma)$ and $\overline{\sigma} \in \mathcal{S}$. By assumption, there is a set of edges $^t\overline{E}_0 \subseteq {}^tE_0$, all labelled with a. So, $^t\overline{E}_0^{\bullet} = \overline{V}_0 \times \{\overline{\sigma}\}$ for some $\overline{V}_0 \in dom(\mathsf{R}_{\overline{\sigma}})$.

We need to find a set of edges $^t\overline{E}_1$, also labelled with a and such that $^t\overline{E}_1 \subseteq {}^{\bullet t}V_1$ and $^t\overline{E}_0^{\bullet}\ {}^t\mathsf{R}\ {}^t\overline{E}_1^{\bullet}$. If we have such a set, there is a $\overline{V}_1 \in ran(\mathsf{R}_{\overline{\sigma}})$ such that $^t\overline{E}_1^{\bullet} = \overline{V}_1 \times \{\overline{\sigma}\}$. The following figure sketches the situation:

[4] Note that $^{\bullet t}E_0 = {}^{t\bullet}E_0$

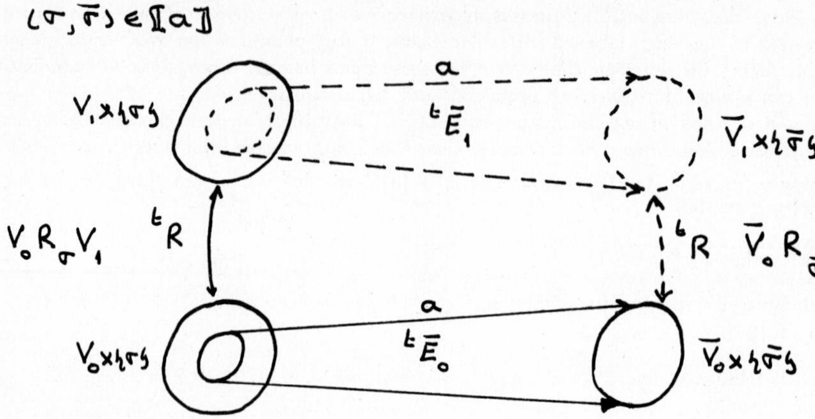

Again, the dotted parts have to be constructed.

Now, $V_0 \in dom(\mathsf{R}_\sigma)$ means that $\sigma\{s/h\} \models \lambda^0(V_0)$ for some $s \in \mathcal{H}is$. Likewise, $\overline{V}_0 \in dom(\mathsf{R}_{\overline{\sigma}})$ is equivalent with $\overline{\sigma}\{\overline{s}/h\} \models \lambda^0(\overline{V}_0)$ for an $\overline{s} \in \mathcal{H}is$. One would expect $\overline{s} = sa$ but this does not follow from the definition of R. This expectation is based on the implicit assumption that if some set of vertices V_0 is reachable by some history s and state σ, then actually $\sigma\{s/h\} \models \lambda^0(V_0)$ should hold. Not unreasonable and we define

6–2 DEFINITION (safe labelling). *Given $\pi \in \mathsf{TS}$ and a set labelling λ if π.*

- *The labelling λ* is safe for π *if for any $V \in dom(\lambda)$, $s \in \mathcal{H}is$, $\sigma \in \mathcal{S}$:*

$$V \times \{\sigma\} \subseteq {}^t\pi \text{ after } s \quad \Rightarrow \quad \sigma\{s/h\} \models \lambda(V)\ .$$

So, let us assume now that

$$\lambda^0 \text{ is a safe set labelling for } \pi^0\ . \tag{8}$$

Also, assume w.l.o.g. that $V_0 \times \{\sigma\} \subseteq {}^t\pi^0$ after s. Now we have $\overline{V}_0 \times \{\overline{\sigma}\} \subseteq {}^t\pi^0$ after sa and, hence, $\overline{\sigma}\{sa/h\} \models \lambda^0(\overline{V}_0)$. Next, consider the ${}^t\overline{V}_1$ that we need to construct. We must have $\overline{V}_0\ \mathsf{R}_{\overline{\sigma}}\ \overline{V}_1$ and, therefore, $\overline{\sigma}\{sa/h\} \models \lambda^1(\overline{V}_1)$. Well, not exactly: we know that there has to be a common computation with which both ${}^t\overline{V}_0$ and ${}^t\overline{V}_1$ are reachable but we do not know that sa is the one. Still, this too is a reasonable assumption and we demand that

$$\mathbf{A} \models \lambda^0(V_0) \to \exists V_1\ \lambda^1(V_1)\ . \tag{9}$$

Now, we can take a $\overline{V}_1$ such that $\overline{\sigma}\{sa/h\} \models \lambda^1(\overline{V}_1)$. If we can show that $\overline{V}_1^{\bullet} \subseteq {}^\bullet V_1 \cap \mathcal{L}^{1\ -1}(a)$ we are done. Why should this be? Well, basically from the idea that since $\overline{V}_1 \times \{\overline{\sigma}\}$ is reachable in ${}^t\pi^1$ via a computation sa, it has to pass through $V_1 \times \{\sigma\}$ since that set is reachable via s. Again, two implicit assumptions have been made here: the first is that because $\overline{\sigma}\{sa/h\} \models \lambda^1(\overline{V}_1)$, these vertexes are in fact reachable via sa; the second assumption is that therefore the computations have to pass through $V_1 \times \{\sigma\}$.

Let us define

6–3 DEFINITION (sure and history determined (hd) labelling). *Given $\pi \in \mathsf{TS}$ and a set labelling λ if π.*

- *The labelling λ* is sure for π *if for any $V \in dom(\lambda)$, $s \in \mathcal{H}is$, $\sigma \in \mathcal{S}$:*

$$\sigma\{s/h\} \models \lambda(V) \quad \Rightarrow \quad V \times \{\sigma\} \subseteq {}^t\pi \text{ after } s$$

- *The labelling* λ is history determined (hd) *if for any* $\overline{V} \in dom(\lambda)$ *and* $sa \in \mathcal{H}is$ *with* $a = (\sigma, \overline{a}, \overline{\sigma})$:

$$\overline{\sigma}\{sa/h\} \models \lambda(\overline{V}) \quad \Longrightarrow \quad \text{there is a unique } V \in dom(\lambda) \text{ sucht that } \sigma\{s/h\} \models \lambda(V)$$
$$\text{and } ({}^{\bullet}(V \times \{\sigma\}) \cap \mathcal{L}^{a\ -1}(a))^{\bullet} = \overline{V} \times \{\overline{\sigma}\}\ .$$

We demand that

$$\lambda^1 \textit{ is a sure set labelling for } \pi^1 \textit{ and is hd }. \tag{10}$$

Then, because λ^1 is sure, $\overline{\sigma}\{sa/h\} \models \lambda^1(\overline{V}_1)$ implies that $\overline{V}_1 \times \{\overline{\sigma}\} \subseteq {}^t\pi^1 \,\mathsf{after}\, sa$ (and so $\mathcal{L}^1(\overline{V}_1^{\bullet}) = \{\overline{a}\}$). We also have, by assumption, that $\sigma\{s/h\} \models \lambda^1(V_1)$. Hence, history determinedness of λ^1 gives that $\overline{V}_1^{\bullet} \subseteq {}^{\bullet}V_1$.

We have shown that if λ^0 *and* λ^1 *satisfy conditions (8), (9) and (10), then* ${}^t[\lambda^0, \lambda^1]$ *satisfies (7).* This derivation clearly show the different roles played by the set labellings of π^0 and of π^1. As π^0 is the implementation, we must make sure that every computation of it is also a computation of π^1. If computations are characterized using assertions, then it is essential that such assertions hold along every computation of π^0. Otherwise, not every computation of π^0 is mapped onto one of π^1. So, such assertions may 'err' on the safe side by being satisfied along computations that are not generated by π^0. Of course we may not be able to prove refinement because of this, but that is a different issue. By the same token, assertions characterizing computations in π^1, the system that is to be implemented, must be sure in the sense that they should never hold on computations that do not occur in π^1. Otherwise, some computation of π^0 might be mapped onto a computation that does not occur in π^1. Hence, these assertions may 'err' on the sure side by being invalid along certain computations of π^1.

The other conditions of failure simulation are easier to satisfy. Clause (1) reads

$$\exists ({}^tV_i^0)_{i<\alpha} \subseteq dom({}^t\mathsf{R})\ {}^tI^0 = \bigcup_{i<\alpha} {}^tV_i^0 \ \&\ \forall i < \alpha\ \exists^t V_i^1 \subseteq {}^tI^1\ \ {}^tV_i^0\, {}^t\mathsf{R}\, {}^tV_i^1\ . \tag{11}$$

We have ${}^tI^0 = I^0 \times \mathcal{S}$ and it seems natural to find a covering $V_0^0, \ldots, V_n^0$ of I^0 and to have $V_i^0 \times \{\sigma\} \in dom({}^t\mathsf{R})$ for any $\sigma \in \mathcal{S}$ and $i \leq n$ (; remember that $\pi^0 \in \mathsf{TS}$ so that I^0 is finite). Similarly for the V_i^1. So, let us demand that

$$\begin{array}{c}\exists V_0^0 \ldots V_n^0 \in dom(\lambda^0)\ I^0 = V_0^0 \cup \cdots \cup V_n^0 \ \&\ \exists V_1 \in dom(\lambda^1)\ V_1 \subseteq I^1 \ \& \\ \forall V_1 \in dom(\lambda^1)\ \ V_1 \subseteq I^1 \Rightarrow \mathbf{A} \models h = \langle\rangle \rightarrow \lambda^1(V_1)\end{array}\ , \tag{12}$$

where $\langle\rangle$ stands for the empty sequence; i.e., $\sigma\{\varepsilon/h\} \models h = \langle\rangle$.

Choose a $\sigma \in \mathcal{S}$ and consider $V_i^0 \times \{\sigma\}$ for any $i \leq n$. As $V_i^0 \subseteq I^0$, we have that $V_i^0 \times \{\sigma\} \subseteq {}^t\pi^0 \,\mathsf{after}\, \varepsilon$ and so by safeness of λ^0 that $\sigma\{\varepsilon/h\} \models \lambda^0(V_i^0)$. There is a $V_1 \in dom(\lambda^1)$ such that $V_1 \subseteq I^1$ and (hence) $\sigma\{\varepsilon/h\} \models \lambda^1(V_1)$. This means that $V_i^0 \in dom(\mathsf{R}_\sigma)$ and that $V_i^0\ \mathsf{R}_\sigma\ V_1$. Hence,

$$\begin{array}{c}{}^tI^0 = \bigcup\{V_i^0 \times \{\sigma\} \mid i \leq n,\ \sigma \in \mathcal{S}\} \text{ and} \\ \forall i \leq n, \sigma \in \mathcal{S}\ \ V_1 \times \{\sigma\} \subseteq {}^tI^1 \ \&\ V_i^0 \times \{\sigma\}\, {}^t\mathsf{R}\, V_1 \times \{\sigma\}\ ,\end{array}$$

so that (11) holds.

Next, clause (3):

$$\begin{array}{ll}{}^tV_0\, {}^t\mathsf{R}\, {}^tV_1 \ \Longrightarrow & \forall^t v_0 \in {}^tV_0\ \exists^t v_1 \in {}^tV_1\ \uparrow({}^tv_0) \Rightarrow \uparrow({}^tv_1)\ \&\ \downarrow({}^tv_0) \Rightarrow \downarrow({}^tv_1)\ \& \\ & \quad stable({}^tv_0) \Rightarrow \big(stable({}^tv_1)\ \&\ {}^t\mathcal{L}_g^1({}^{\bullet t}v_1) \subseteq {}^t\mathcal{L}_g^0({}^{\bullet t}v_0)\big)\ .\end{array}$$

We want to check $\uparrow(\cdot)$, etc. on the level of the first order systems. So we define them as auxiliary predicates in As:

6–4 DEFINITION. *Let $\pi \in \mathsf{TS}$, $v \in \mathcal{V}$ and $\sigma \in \mathcal{S}$.*

- $\sigma \models \uparrow(v)$ *iff* $\sigma \models \exists e \in {}^\bullet v\ \mathcal{L}^t(e) \wedge \mathcal{L}^a(e) = \uparrow$,
- $\sigma \models \downarrow(v)$ *iff* $\sigma \models \forall e \in {}^\bullet v\ \mathcal{L}^t(e) \rightarrow \mathcal{L}^a(e) = \delta$,
- $\sigma \models \mathit{stable}(v)$ *iff* $\sigma \models \forall e \in {}^\bullet v\ \mathcal{L}^t(e) \rightarrow \mathcal{L}^a(e) \in \mathcal{G}act(\Sigma)_\delta$,
- $\sigma \models \mathit{enabled}(v) = E$ *iff* $\sigma \models \forall e \in \mathcal{E}\ \ e \in E \leftrightarrow ({}^\bullet e = v \wedge \mathcal{L}^t(e))$.

There is a straightforward correspondence between these predicates in As and their informal counterparts for ${}^t\pi$. For $\pi \in \mathsf{TS}$ and $v \in \mathcal{V}$ we have '$\sigma \models \rho(v)$ iff $\rho((v,\sigma))$ (in ${}^t\pi$)' for $\rho \in \{\downarrow, \uparrow\}$ and '$\sigma \models \mathit{stable}(v)$ iff $\mathit{stable}((v,\sigma))$ (in ${}^t\pi$)'. For the function $\mathit{enabled}(\cdot)$ we have that '$\sigma \models \mathit{enabled}(v) = E$ iff ${}^\bullet(v,\sigma) \subseteq \{\sigma\} \times E \times \mathcal{S}$'. This, too, follows directly from the construction of ${}^t\pi$.

Hence, we demand that the following holds:

$$\begin{array}{r}\mathbf{A} \models \lambda^0(V_0) \wedge \lambda^1(V_1) \rightarrow (\forall v_0 \in V_0\ \exists v_1 \in V_1\ \uparrow(v_0) \rightarrow \uparrow(v_1) \wedge \downarrow(v_0) \rightarrow \downarrow(v_1) \wedge \\ \mathit{stable}(v_0) \rightarrow (\mathit{stable}(v_1) \wedge \mathcal{L}_g^1(\mathit{enabled}(v_1)) \subseteq \mathcal{L}_g^0(\mathit{enabled}(v_0))))\end{array} . \qquad (13)$$

The only moot point concerns the test $\mathcal{L}_g^1(\mathit{enabled}(v_1)) \subseteq \mathcal{L}_g^0(\mathit{enabled}(v_0))$. Choose some σ with $\sigma \models \lambda^0(V_0) \wedge \lambda^1(V_1)$; take some $v_0 \in V_0$ and let v_1 be the picked vertex in V_1; let $\sigma \models \mathit{stable}(v_0)$. We must prove that ${}^t\mathcal{L}_g^1({}^\bullet(v_1,\sigma)) \subseteq {}^t\mathcal{L}_g^0({}^\bullet(v_0,\sigma))$ holds. Let $\sigma \models \mathit{enabled}(v_i) = E_i$ $(i = 0,1)$. Then, by the construction of ${}^t\pi$:

$$\begin{array}{rcl} {}^\bullet(v_i,\sigma) & = & \{(\sigma, e_i, \overline{\sigma}) \mid e_i \in E_i,\ (\sigma,\overline{\sigma}) \in [\![a]\!]^{\mathbf{A}}\} \quad \text{and} \\ e_i \in E_i & \Longrightarrow & (\sigma, e_i, \overline{\sigma}) \in {}^\bullet(v_i,\sigma) \text{ for any } \overline{\sigma} \in [\![a]\!]^{\mathbf{A}}(\sigma) . \end{array}$$

Now, take an edge ${}^te_1 = (\sigma, e_1, \overline{\sigma}) \in {}^\bullet(v_1,\sigma)$ with $\mathcal{L}^1(e_1) = a$. Then, ${}^t\mathcal{L}^1({}^te_1) = (\sigma, a, \overline{\sigma})$ and $(\sigma,\overline{\sigma}) \in [\![a]\!]^{\mathbf{A}}$. As $e_1 \in E_1$, there is an edge $e_0 \in E_0$ with $\mathcal{L}^0(e_0) = a$, whence ${}^te_0 = (\sigma, e_0, \overline{\sigma}) \in {}^\bullet(v_0,\sigma)$ and ${}^t\mathcal{L}^0({}^te_0) = (\sigma, a, \overline{\sigma})$.

Finally, clause (4):

$$\exists {}^{\bullet t}E_0 \in \mathit{dom}({}^t\mathsf{R}) \quad \Longrightarrow \quad \exists {}^tV_0 \ldots {}^tV_n \in \mathit{dom}({}^t\mathsf{R})\ ({}^tE_0 \cap {}^t\mathcal{L}^{0\ -1}(a))^\bullet = {}^tV_0 \cup \cdots \cup {}^tV_n . \qquad (14)$$

We define

6–5 DEFINITION (cover). *Let λ be a set labeling for π.*

- λ covers π *if for any $V \in \mathit{dom}(\lambda)$, $\overline{a} \in \mathcal{A}ct(\Sigma)$ and $\sigma \in \mathcal{S}$:*

$$\begin{array}{rcl} \sigma \models \lambda(V) & \Longrightarrow & \exists V_0, \ldots, V_n \in \mathit{dom}(\lambda)\ \forall \overline{\sigma} \in [\![\overline{a}]\!]^{\mathbf{A}}(\sigma)\ \overline{\sigma}\{s/h\} \models \bigwedge_{i \leq n} \lambda(V_i)\ \& \\ & & \sigma \models v \in \bigcup_{i \leq n} V_i \leftrightarrow \exists e \in {}^\bullet V \cap v^\bullet\ \mathcal{L}^t(e) \wedge \mathcal{L}^a(e) = a , \end{array}$$

where $s = \sigma(h)^\frown(\sigma, \overline{a}, \overline{\sigma})$.

Assume that

$$\lambda^0 \text{ covers } \pi^0 .$$

Take some ${}^{\bullet t}E_0 = {}^tV_0 \in \mathit{dom}({}^t\mathsf{R})$; let ${}^t\overline{V}_0 = ({}^tE_0 \cap {}^t\mathcal{L}^{0\ -1}(a))^\bullet$, ${}^tV_0 = V_0 \times \{\sigma\}$ and ${}^t\overline{V}_0 = \overline{V}_0 \times \{\overline{\sigma}\}$. Hence, $a = (\sigma, \overline{a}, \overline{\sigma})$ for some $\overline{a} \in \mathcal{A}ct(\Sigma)$ and $(\sigma,\overline{\sigma}) \in [\![\overline{a}]\!]^{\mathbf{A}}$. Then we have $\sigma \models \lambda^0(V_0)$. Because λ^0 covers π^0, there are $V_0^0, \ldots, V_n^0 \in \mathit{dom}(\lambda^0)$ such that

$$\begin{array}{l} \overline{\sigma}\{\sigma(h)a/h\} \models \bigwedge_{i \leq n} \lambda^0(V_i^0) \\ \sigma \models v \in \bigcup_{i \leq n} V_i^0 \leftrightarrow \exists e_0 \in E_0\ \mathcal{L}^{0\ t}(e_0) \wedge \mathcal{L}^{0\ a}(e_0) = \overline{a} . \end{array}$$

Let ${}^tV_i^0 = V_i^0 \times \{\overline{\sigma}\}$ $(i \leq n)$. Then ${}^tV_0^0 \ldots {}^tV_n^0 \in dom({}^t\mathsf{R})$ since $V_0^0 \ldots V_n^0 \in dom(\mathsf{R}_{\overline{\sigma}})$. Finally, $({}^tE_0 \cap {}^t\mathcal{L}^{0\,-1}(a))^\bullet = \{(e_0^\bullet, \overline{\sigma}) \mid e_0 \in E_0,\ \sigma \models \mathcal{L}^{0\,t}(e_0),\ \mathcal{L}^{0\,a}(e_0) = \overline{a}\}$ and (14) follows.

We have derived a *proof rule* to establish refinement of first order transition systems. Note that below we have split up clause (12) among the premisses of the rule:

FO – REF

Given π^0, $\pi^1 \in \mathsf{TS}$ with set labellings λ^0 and λ^1:

1. λ^0 is safe for π^0 and covers π^0, $\exists V_0^0 \ldots V_n^0 \in dom(\lambda^0)\ I^0 = V_0^0 \cup \cdots \cup V_n^0$,
2. λ^1 is sure for π^1 and is hd, $\exists V_1 \in dom(\lambda^1)\ V_1 \subseteq I^1$,
   $\forall V_1 \in dom(\lambda^1)\ \ V_1 \subseteq I^1 \Rightarrow \mathbf{A} \models h = <> \rightarrow \lambda^1(V_1)$,
3. $\mathbf{A} \models \lambda^0(V_0) \rightarrow \exists V_1\ \lambda^1(V_1)$,
4. $\mathbf{A} \models \lambda^0(V_0) \wedge \lambda^1(V_1) \rightarrow (\forall v_0 \in V_0\ \exists v_1 \in V_1\ \uparrow(v_0) \rightarrow \uparrow(v_1) \wedge \downarrow(v_0) \rightarrow \downarrow(v_1) \wedge$
   $stable(v_0) \rightarrow (stable(v_1) \wedge \mathcal{L}_g^1(enabled(v_1)) \subseteq \mathcal{L}_g^0(enabled(v_0))))$

$$\frac{}{\mathbf{A} \models \pi^0 \sqsubseteq \pi^1}$$

Write $\vdash_{\mathsf{FO-REF}} \pi^0 \sqsubseteq \pi^1$ if $\mathbf{A} \models \pi^0 \sqsubseteq \pi^1$ can be derived using the rule.

The derivation of the rule establishes soundness. Completeness depends—as usual—on the expressiveness of the assertion language. Specifically, we make the following assumption:

For any $\pi \in \mathsf{TS}$ *and* $V \subseteq \mathcal{V}$, *there is a formula* $COMP(\pi, V) \in \mathsf{As}$, *such that for any* $\sigma \in \mathcal{S}$ *and* $s \in \mathcal{H}is$

$$\sigma\{s/h\} \models COMP(\pi, V) \iff V \times \{\sigma\} = {}^t\pi \text{ after } s\ .$$

Note that π and V are *not* parameters of the formula. I.e., we do not need a formula *uniformly* in π and V. Existence of such formulae means that the semantics of the actions should be definable in As and that it must be possible to describe the ith record (in $\mathcal{S} \times \mathcal{A}ct(\Sigma) \times \mathcal{S}$) of a sequence for any i.

Now, define set labellings for π^0 and π^1 as follows:

$$\begin{aligned} \lambda^0 &= \left[\{v_0\} \mapsto \bigvee\{COMP(\pi^0, V_0) \mid v_0 \in V_0 \subseteq \mathcal{V}^0\},\ v_0 \in I^0\right], \\ \lambda^1 &= [V_0 \mapsto COMP(\pi^1, V_1),\ V_1 \subseteq \mathcal{V}^1]\ . \end{aligned}$$

Observe that

$$[\lambda^0, \lambda^1]_\sigma = \left\{ (\{v_0, V_1\}) \;\middle|\; \exists s \in \mathcal{H}is\ {}^t\pi^0 \xrightarrow{s} (v_0, \sigma); {}^t\pi^0,\ \ {}^t\pi^1 \text{ after } s = V_1 \times \{\sigma\} \right\}.$$

Hence, $[\lambda^0, \lambda^1]$ is precisely the failure simulation (from ${}^t\pi^0$ to ${}^t\pi^1$) used in the proof of the completeness theorem 4–6.

We show that λ^0 and λ^1 satisfy the premisses of FO – REF, in case $\pi^0 \sqsubseteq \pi^1$ holds.

By definition, λ^0 and λ^1 are both safe and sure.

To establish that λ^0 covers π^0, take some $v_0 \in \mathcal{V}^0$, $a \in \mathcal{A}ct(\Sigma)$ and $\sigma \in \mathcal{S}$ with $\sigma \models \lambda^0(v_0)$. Define

$$\{v_0^0, \ldots, v_n^0\} = \{e_0^\bullet \mid e_0 \in {}^\bullet v_0,\ \sigma \models \mathcal{L}^{0\,t}(e_0) \wedge \mathcal{L}^{0\,a}(e_0) = a\}$$

and let $\overline{\sigma} \in [\![\overline{a}]\!]^{\mathbf{A}}(\sigma)$. By definition of λ^0 we have $\overline{\sigma}\{s/h\} \models \bigwedge_{i \leq n} \lambda^0(v_i^0)$ where $s = \sigma(h)(\sigma, \overline{a}, \overline{\sigma})$. The second part of the definition of covering, (6–5), immediately follows from the definition of $\{v_0^0, \ldots, v_n^0\}$.

For history determinedness of λ^1, take some $\overline{V}_1 \in dom(\lambda^1)$ such that $\overline{\sigma}\{sa/h\} \models \lambda^1(\overline{V}_1)$ with $s \in \mathcal{H}is$ and $a = (\sigma, \overline{a}, \overline{\sigma})$. By definition of λ^1, this means that $\overline{V}_1 \times \{\overline{\sigma}\} = {}^t\pi^1$ after sa. Let $V_1 \times \{\sigma\} = {}^t\pi^1$ after s. Then $\sigma\{s/h\} \models \lambda^1(V_1)$ holds and V_1 is the unique set with that property. Moreover, $({}^\bullet(V_1 \times \{\sigma\}) \cap \mathcal{L}^{a\ -1}(a))^\bullet = \overline{V}_1 \times \{\sigma\}$

If $I^1 = \{v_0^0, \ldots, v_n^0\}$, then $\{v_i^0\} \in dom(\lambda^0)$ for $i \leq n$. Also, $I^1 \in dom(\lambda^1)$ and $\mathbf{A} \models h =<>\rightarrow \lambda^1(I^1)$ by definition of λ^1. Finally, note that $V_1 \in dom(\lambda^1)$ and $V_1 \subseteq I^1$ implies that $V_1 = I^1$.

To show the third premiss, take some $\sigma\{s/h\} \models \lambda^0(v_0)$. This means that $V_0 \times \{\sigma\} \subseteq {}^t\pi^0$ after s and, since $\multimap{}^t\pi^0\!\multimapinv \subseteq \multimap{}^t\pi^1\!\multimapinv$, that $\sigma\{s/h\} \models \lambda^1(V_1)$ with ${}^t\pi^1$ after $s = V_1 \times \{\sigma\}$.

Finally, the fourth premiss. Take a $\sigma \in \mathcal{S}$, $s \in \mathcal{H}is$ and assume that $\sigma\{s/h\} \models \lambda^0(v_0) \wedge \lambda^1(V_1)$ for some $v_0 \in \mathcal{V}^0$ and $V_1 \subseteq \mathcal{V}^1$. Hence, $(v_0, \sigma) \in {}^t\pi^0$ after s and $V_1 \times \{\sigma\} \in {}^t\pi^1$ after s. As ${}^t\pi^0 \sqsubseteq {}^t\pi^1$ there is a $v_1 \in V_1$ such that $\rho((v_0, \sigma)) \Rightarrow \rho((v_1, \sigma))$ for $\rho \in \{\delta, \uparrow\}$ and such that $stable((v_0, \sigma)) \Rightarrow (stable((v_1, \sigma))\ \&\ {}^t\mathcal{L}_g^1({}^\bullet(v_1, \sigma)) \subseteq {}^t\mathcal{L}_g^0({}^\bullet(v_0, \sigma)))$. This immediately implies that

$$\sigma \models stable(v_0) \Rightarrow (stable(v_1)\ \&\ {}^t\mathcal{L}_g^1({}^\bullet v_1) \subseteq {}^t\mathcal{L}_g^0({}^\bullet v_0))\ .$$

We have obtained the following

6–6 Theorem (Soundness and completeness of FO – REF). *Let $\pi^0, \pi^1 \in$ TS, then*

$$\mathbf{A} \models \pi^0 \sqsubseteq \pi^1 \quad \text{iff} \quad \vdash_{\mathsf{FO-REF}} \pi^0 \sqsubseteq \pi^1\ .$$

We get a sound and complete rule for trace refinement of 1st order systems if the fourth premiss of FO – REF is dropped.

It remains to show how to prove safeness, sureness, covering and history determinedness of labellings. The next two subsections address, respectively, verifying safeness+covering and sureness+history determinedness of labellings. The intention is to show how the proof of these properties can be reduced to verifying properties of (sets of) transitions. As such, these proof principles are formulated on a level analogous to that of Floyd's inductive assertion method and Manna and Pnueli's temporal logic proof rules [MP81, MP84].

6.1 Proving safeness and covering

Proving safeness is a straightforward generalization of proving so-called *local correctness* of a (Floyd) labelling in an inductive assertion proof. A Floyd labelling, ϕ, associates assertions, $\phi(v)$ to the vertices, v, of a transition system $\pi \in$ TS. Local correctness of a labelling entails (in our notation) that $(v, \sigma) \subseteq {}^t\pi$ after $s \Rightarrow \sigma \models \phi(v)$ for all $s \in \mathcal{H}is$ and $\sigma \in \mathcal{S}$. It is proved by showing that

$$1.\ v \in I \Rightarrow \mathbf{A} \models \phi(v) \quad \& \quad 2.\ \forall e \in \mathcal{E}\ \sigma \models \phi(e^\bullet)\ \&\ \overline{\sigma} \in [\![\mathcal{L}^a(e)]\!]^{\mathbf{A}}(\sigma) \Rightarrow \overline{\sigma} \models \phi({}^\bullet e)\ .$$

Property (2) is also called "*a leads from $\phi({}^\bullet e)$ to $\phi(e^\bullet)$*" and is written $\phi({}^\bullet e) \overset{a}{\rightsquigarrow} \phi(e^\bullet)$ (if $a = \mathcal{L}(e)$).

Our case is more complicated because we deal with set labellings and we have history variables; however, the principle is the same. By convention, bold face letters, $\mathbf{V}$,... will stand for sets of sets of vertices.

6–7 Definition (leads to). *Let $\pi \in$ TS and let λ be a set labelling for π. Take some $V \in dom(\lambda)$ and $\mathbf{V}_0, \ldots, \mathbf{V}_n \subseteq dom(\lambda)$. Assume that $\emptyset \neq E = {}^\bullet V \cap \mathcal{L}^{a\ -1}(a)$ and $E^\bullet = \bigcup\bigcup_{i \leq n} \mathbf{V}_i$.*

- $V \overset{a}{\rightsquigarrow} \mathbf{V}_0, \ldots, \mathbf{V}_n$ *(a leads from V to $\mathbf{V}_0, \ldots, \mathbf{V}_n$) if for all $(\sigma, \overline{\sigma}) \in [\![a]\!]^{\mathbf{A}}$, $s \in \mathcal{H}is$:*

$$\sigma\{s/h\} \models \lambda(V) \wedge \bigvee\{\mathcal{L}^t(e) \mid e \in E\} \quad \Longrightarrow$$

$$\exists i \leq n \quad \sigma\{s/h\} \models v \in \bigcup \mathbf{V}_i \leftrightarrow \exists e \in E\ v = e^\bullet \wedge \mathcal{L}^t(e)\ \&\ \overline{\sigma}\{s(\sigma, a, \overline{\sigma})/h\} \models \bigwedge\{\lambda(\overline{V}) \mid \overline{V} \in \mathbf{V}_i\}\ .$$

As a convention, $V \overset{a}{\rightsquigarrow} \mathbf{V}_0, \ldots, \mathbf{V}_n$ holds vacuously if either $V \notin dom(\lambda)$, or $\mathbf{V}_i \not\subseteq dom(\lambda)$ for some $i \leq n$, or $E = \emptyset$, or $E^\bullet \neq \bigcup\bigcup_{i \leq n} \mathbf{V}_i$.

We have the following proof principle:

SACO

Given $\pi \in \mathsf{TS}$ and a set labelling λ for it:

$$\frac{\begin{array}{l}\forall V \in dom(\lambda)\ V \subseteq I \Rightarrow \mathbf{A} \models h = \langle\rangle \rightarrow \lambda(V), \\ \forall a \in \mathcal{A}ct(\Sigma),\ V \in dom(\lambda)\ \exists \mathbf{V}_0, \ldots, \mathbf{V}_n \subseteq dom(\lambda)\ (V \cap \mathcal{L}^{a\,-1}(a))^\bullet = \bigcup\bigcup_{i \leq n} \mathbf{V}_i\ \& \\ \qquad\qquad\qquad\qquad \forall \mathbf{V}_0, \ldots, \mathbf{V}_n \subseteq \mathcal{V}\ V \overset{a}{\rightsquigarrow} \mathbf{V}_0, \ldots, \mathbf{V}_n\end{array}}{\lambda \text{ is safe for } \pi \text{ and covers } \pi}$$

The proof rule needs one assumption concerning the vertex sets with which assertions are associated in order to be sound:

$$\forall a \in \mathcal{A}ct(\Sigma)\ \forall \overline{V} \in dom(\lambda) : \quad \forall \overline{v} \in \overline{V}\ a \in \mathcal{L}^a({}^\bullet\overline{v}) \Rightarrow \exists V \in dom(\lambda)\ \left({}^\bullet V \cap \mathcal{L}^{a\,-1}(a)\right)^\bullet = \overline{V}\,. \qquad (15)$$

So, if some set of vertices in $dom(\lambda)$ is reachable by a-transitions, then there must be another set in $dom(\lambda)$ from which every vertex in the former set is reachable by an a-transition.

Now we can prove

6–8 THEOREM. SACO *is complete. Also, if* $\exists V_0, \ldots, V_n \in dom(\lambda)\ I = V_0 \cup \cdots \cup V_n$ *and* λ *satisfies (15), then* SACO *is sound.*

PROOF.

Completeness Take some $V \in dom(\lambda)$ and $a \in \mathcal{A}ct(\Sigma)$. If $V \subseteq I$ then safeness gives $\mathbf{A} \models \lambda(V)$ since $V \times \{\sigma\} \subseteq {}^t\pi$ **after** ε holds for every $\sigma \in \mathcal{S}$. Next, let $E = {}^\bullet V \cap \mathcal{L}^{a\,-1}(\overline{a})$. Because λ covers π, there are $V_0, \ldots, V_m \in dom(\lambda)$ for every $\sigma \in \mathcal{S}$ and $v \in \bigcup_{i \leq m} V_i$ iff for some $e \in {}^\bullet v \cap E$ we have $\sigma \models \mathcal{L}^t(e)$. Since, π is finite, there are only a *finite* number of such coverings. Let $\mathbf{V}_0, \ldots, \mathbf{V}_n$ be these coverings. Clearly, $E^\bullet = \bigcup\bigcup_{i \leq n} \mathbf{V}_i$ and $\mathbf{V}_i \subseteq dom(\lambda)$ for $i \leq n$. Now, take some $(\sigma, \overline{\sigma}) \in [\![\overline{a}]\!]$ with $\sigma\{s/h\} \models \lambda(V) \wedge \bigvee\{\mathcal{L}^t(e) \mid e \in E\}$. By construction there is an $i \leq n$ such that $\sigma \models v \in \bigcup \mathbf{V}_i \leftrightarrow \exists e \in {}^\bullet V \cap v^\bullet\ \mathcal{L}^t(e)$. As $h \notin FV(\pi)$ this formula is also valid in $\sigma\{s/h\}$. By the same token, $\overline{\sigma}\{\sigma(h)(\sigma, \overline{a}, \overline{\sigma})/h\} \models \bigwedge\{\lambda(\overline{V}) \mid \overline{V} \in \mathbf{V}_i\}$. Hence, $V \overset{a}{\rightsquigarrow} \mathbf{V}_0, \ldots, \mathbf{V}_n$.

Soundness That λ covers π is clear. Safeness of λ is proven with induction on the length of the computation, s.

$s = \varepsilon$) Since $V \times \{\sigma\} \subseteq {}^t\pi$ **after** $\varepsilon \Rightarrow V \subseteq I$, this case is covered by the first premiss.

$s = \widehat{s}a$) Let $a = (\sigma, \overline{a}, \overline{\sigma})$ and let $\overline{V} \times \{\overline{\sigma}\} \subseteq {}^t\pi$ **after** s with $\overline{V} \in dom(\lambda)$ (and hence $\overline{V} \neq \emptyset$). By (15), there is a $V \in dom(\lambda)$ such that ${}^\bullet V \cap \mathcal{L}^{a\,-1}(\overline{a}) = \overline{V}^\bullet$. By definition, $V \times \{\sigma\} \subseteq {}^t\pi$ **after** $\widehat{s}$, whence $\sigma\{\widehat{s}/h\} \models \lambda(V)$ by induction. Let $E = {}^\bullet V \cap \mathcal{L}^{a\,-1}(a)$. Then, the second premiss gives $\mathbf{V}_0, \ldots, \mathbf{V}_n \subseteq dom(\lambda)$ such that $E^\bullet = \bigcup\bigcup_{i \leq n} \mathbf{V}_i$ and $\sigma\{\widehat{s}/h\} \models \bigvee\{\mathcal{L}^t(e) \mid e \in E\}$. Hence, there is an $i \leq n$ such that $\sigma\{\widehat{s}/h\} \models v \in \bigcup \mathbf{V}_i \leftrightarrow \exists e \in E\ v = e^\bullet \wedge \mathcal{L}^t(e)$. W.l.o.g. we may assume that $\overline{V} \in \mathbf{V}_i$. Hence, we obtain that $\overline{\sigma}\{s/h\} \models \lambda(\overline{V})$. □

Note that the condition in Theorem 6–8 is one of the premisses of FO – REF. Assumption (15) is satisfied by the set labelling λ^0 used in the completeness proof.

As we know that the existence of a simple failure simulation, too, is necessary for failure refinement, the rule can be simplified (by requiring that the labelling is a Floyd labelling). Thus, covering would not need to be checked. We mention without proof, that for Floyd-type labellings (i.e., labellings whose domain only contain singleton sets) the above proof rule simplifies to

Given $\pi \in \mathsf{TS}$ and a Floyd labelling ϕ for it:

$$\forall v \in I: \quad \mathbf{A} \models h = <> \rightarrow \phi(\{v\}),$$
$$\forall e \in \mathcal{E},\ (\sigma,\overline{\sigma}) \in [\![\mathcal{L}^t(e)]\!]^{\mathbf{A}},\ h \in \mathcal{H}is: \quad \sigma\{s/h\} \models \phi(\{{}^\bullet e\}) \wedge \mathcal{L}^t(e) \Rightarrow \overline{\sigma}\{s(\sigma,\mathcal{L}^t(e),\overline{\sigma})/h\} \models \phi(\{e^\bullet\})$$

ϕ is safe for π and covers π

I.e., one just proves local correctness!

6.2 Proving sureness and history determinedness

The property of sureness is dual to that of safeness. Therefore it should not come as a surprise that the proof rule below is based on a notion "*comes from*" (the dual of "leads to").

6–9 DEFINITION (comes from). *Let $\pi \in \mathsf{TS}$ and let λ be a set labelling for π. Take some $\overline{V} \in dom(\lambda)$ and $\mathbf{V} \subseteq dom(\lambda)$. Assume that $\emptyset \neq E = {}^\bullet\overline{V} \cap \mathcal{L}^{a\ -1}(a)$ and ${}^\bullet E = \bigcup \mathbf{V}$.*

- $\overline{V} \overset{a}{\leftarrow\!\!\sim} \mathbf{V}$ *(a comes from $\mathcal{V}$ to $\overline{V}$) if for all $(\sigma,\overline{\sigma}) \in [\![a]\!]^{\mathbf{A}}$ and $s \in \mathcal{H}is$*

$$\overline{\sigma}\{s(\sigma,\overline{a},\overline{\sigma})/h\} \models \lambda(\overline{V}) \Rightarrow \exists! V \in \mathbf{V}\ \sigma\{s/a\} \models \lambda(V) \wedge (\forall e\ e \in \overline{V}^\bullet \leftrightarrow \exists v \in V\ {}^\bullet e = v \wedge \mathcal{L}^t(e))\ .$$

Here, $\exists!$ means "there is a unique...". As a convention, $V \overset{a}{\leftarrow\!\!\sim} \mathbf{V}$ holds vacuously if either $E = \emptyset$ or ${}^\bullet E \neq \bigcup \mathbf{V}$.

We have the following proof principle:

SUHD

Let $\pi \in \mathsf{TS}$ and let λ be a set labelling for it:

$$\forall V \in dom(\lambda): \quad \sigma\{\varepsilon/h\} \models \lambda(V) \Rightarrow V \subseteq I,$$
$$\forall a \in Act(\Sigma),\ \overline{V} \in dom(\lambda): \quad \overline{V} \not\subseteq I\ \&\ {}^\bullet\overline{V} \cap \mathcal{L}^{a\ -1}(a) \neq \emptyset \Rightarrow \exists! \mathbf{V} \subseteq dom(\lambda)\ \overline{V} \overset{a}{\leftarrow\!\!\sim} \mathbf{V}$$

λ is sure for π and is hd

6–10 THEOREM. SUHD *is sound and complete.*

PROOF.

Soundness History determinedness is obvious. Sureness is proved by an induction on the length of the computation sequence, s.

$s = \varepsilon$) This case follows from the first premiss.

$s = \widehat{s}a$) Let $a = (\sigma,\overline{a},\overline{\sigma})$ and take some $\overline{V} \in dom(\lambda)$. Suppose that $\overline{\sigma}\{s\} \models \lambda(\overline{V})$. By the second premiss of the rule, there is a (unique) set $\mathbf{V} \subseteq dom(\lambda)$ and a (unique) set $V \in \mathbf{V}$ such that $\sigma\{\widehat{s}/h\} \models \lambda(V)$. By induction this means that $V \times \{\sigma\} \subseteq {}^t\pi$ after $\widehat{s}$. We also have that $\sigma \models e \in \overline{V}^\bullet \leftrightarrow \exists v \in V\ v = {}^\bullet e \wedge \mathcal{L}^t(e)$ because h does not appear in any test in π. This immediately implies that $\overline{V} \times \{\overline{\sigma}\} \subseteq {}^t\pi$ after s.

Completeness The first premiss directly follows from sureness of λ. For the second premiss, take an $a \in \mathcal{A}ct(\Sigma)$ and some $\overline{V} \in dom(\lambda)$ such that $\overline{V} \subseteq I$ and $\emptyset \neq {}^\bullet\overline{V} \cap \mathcal{L}^{a\ -1}(a)$. As λ is history determined, for every $s \in \mathcal{H}is$ and $(\sigma, \overline{\sigma}) \in [\![a]\!]^{\mathbf{A}}$ such that $\overline{\sigma}\{s(\sigma, a, \overline{\sigma}/h\} \models \lambda(\overline{V})$ there is a unique $V \in dom(\lambda)$ with $\sigma\{s/h\} \models \lambda(V)$ and $\left({}^\bullet(V \times \{\sigma\}) \cap \mathcal{L}^{a\ -1}((\sigma, a, \overline{\sigma}))\right)^\bullet = \overline{V} \times \{\overline{\sigma}\}$. Because $\mathcal{V}$ is finite there are only finitely many such $V \in dom(\lambda)$. Collect them in the set $\mathbf{V}$. By construction $\mathbf{V}$ is unique. We claim that $\overline{V} \overset{a}{\leftarrow\!\sim} \mathbf{V}$. So, take some $(\sigma, \overline{\sigma}) \in [\![a]\!]^{\mathbf{A}}$ and $s \in \mathcal{H}is$ such that $\overline{\sigma}\{s(\sigma, \overline{a}, \overline{\sigma})/h\} \models \lambda(\overline{V})$. By construction there is a unique $V \in \mathbf{V}$ such that $\sigma\{s/h\} \models \lambda(V)$. Finally, $\left({}^\bullet(V \times \{\sigma\}) \cap \mathcal{L}^{a\ -1}((\sigma, a, \overline{\sigma}))\right)^\bullet = \overline{V} \times \{\overline{\sigma}\}$ is equivalent with $\sigma\{s/h\} \models \forall e\ e \in \overline{V}^\bullet \leftrightarrow \exists v \in V\ {}^\bullet e = v \wedge \mathcal{L}^t(e)$ (; remember that h does not appear free in π). □

In this section we have lifted failure refinement to 1st order systems by first defining a way to describe a failure simulation in terms of (set) labellings: $[\lambda^0, \lambda^1]$. Then we translated the conditions of failure simulation in Definition 4–2 to that of conditions on the 1st order systems, using the translation, $^t.$, defined in Section 5. The resulting rule FO − REF was formulated in terms of a number of primitive notions: safeness, sureness, covers and hd. The last two subsections developed proof principles to prove these properties.

7 Conclusions

We have developed a theory of refinement for 1st order programs that is grounded in algebraic process theory. This allowed us to make use of existing results and—by virtue of a canonical embedding of 1st order transition systems into uninterpreted ones—then lift these results to 1st order systems. In the formulation of the 1st order verification criteria, we have tried to stay close to the spirit of the inductive assertion method.

This paper has laid some foundations, but there remains a lot to be done. The existing framework falls short of a refinement calculus. E.g., it is not possible to directly prove that $\mathbf{A} \models \pi^0 \parallel \pi^1 \sqsubseteq \pi$, with $\pi^0, \pi^1, \pi \in \mathsf{TS}$, because π is not a parallel composition. This would require a special proof rule that basically expresses how $\pi^0 \parallel \pi^1$ can be seen as a 1st order transition system; e.g., a location in $\pi^0 \parallel \pi^1$ would be given by a *pair* of vertices, one in π^0 and one in π^1.

One would also want a larger set of program combinators so that any system can be constructed starting from basic transition systems , $a \in \mathcal{A}ct(\Sigma)$. Luckily, existing theory tells us that this need not change the refinement notion and its verification criterion.

The 1st order systems that we introduced are still one step away from a usable specification language. Instead of explicitly describing the underlying directed (control) graph, one would like to specify the behavior of the actions and have these specifications implicitly define the control graph. This is the approach taken by Lamport [Lam83, Lam86].

This brings us to another issue: the comparison with other verification techniques for program refinement. For example, in [AL88, Mer90] it is shown how Milner simulation becomes a complete criterion for trace refinement if one allows programs to be augmented with various types of auxiliary variables. It should be investigated how these ideas relate to the methods of this paper.

Finally, the paper provides a solid basis to investigate the refinement of liveness properties, using ω-automata [Eil74].

Acknowledgments

I thank Willem P. de Roever for his comments on previous versions of the paper and also the participants of the EUT-Weizmann DESCARTES seminar for their indulgence of my strive for perfect obfuscation.

References

[AL88] M. ABADI, L. LAMPORT (1988), "The Existence of Refinement Mappings", Proc. 3d IEEE Conf. on Logic in Computer Science (LICS), pp. 165–175.

[AL90] M. ABADI, L. LAMPORT (1990), "Composing Specifications", this volume.

[AS86] B. ALPERN, F.B. SCHNEIDER (1986), "Recognizing Safety and Liveness", Technical Report TR86-727, Dept. of Computer Science, Cornell University.

[BC85] G. BERRY, L. COSSERAT (1985), The Synchronous Programming Language ESTEREL and its Mathematical Semantics, LNCS **197**, pp. 389–449, Springer Verlag.

[BHR84] S. BROOKES, C.A.R. HOARE, A. ROSCOE (1984), A Theory of Communicating Sequential Processes, *Journal of the ACM*, Vol. **31**, No. **7**, pp. 560–599.

[BK84] J. BERGSTRA, J.W. KLOP (1984), Process Algebra for Synchronous Communication, *Information and Computation*, Vol. **60**, pp. 109–137.

[BKO86] J.BERGSTRA, J.W. KLOP, E.-R. OLDEROG (1986), "Failure semantics with fair abstraction", Report CS-R8609, Center for Mathematics and Computer Science (CWI), Amsterdam.

[CM88] K.M. CHANDY, J. MISRA (1988), **Parallel Program Design**, Addison-Wesley.

[Dar82] PH. DARONDEAU (1982), "An Enlarged Definition and Complete Axiomatization of Observational Congruence of Finite Processes", LNCS **137**, pp. 47–62, Springer Verlag.

[Dij76] E.W. DIJKSTRA (1976), **A Discipline of Programming**, Prentice-Hall.

[Eil74] S. EILENBERG (1974), **Automata, Languages and Machines, Volume A**, Academic Press.

[FLS87] A. FEKETE, N. LYNCH, L. SHRIRA (1987), "A Modular Proof of Correctness for a Network Synchronizer", Proc. 2nd International Workshop on Distributed Algorithms, LNCS **312**, Springer Verlag.

[GB87] R. GERTH, A. BOUCHER (1987), "A Timed Failures Model for Extended Communicating Processes", Proc. 14th ICALP, LNCS **267**, pp. 95–115, Springer Verlag.

[GP89] R. GERTH, A. PNUELI (1989), "Rooting UNITY", Proc. 5th IEEE International Workshop on Software Specification and Design, pp. 11–19.

[Flo67] R. FLOYD (1967), "Assigning Meaning to Programs", Proc. Sympos. in Appl. Math. **19**, pp.19–32, American Mathematical Society.

[Har87] D. HAREL (1987), Statecharts: a visual approach to complex systems, *Science of Computer Programming*, Vol. **8**, No. **3**.

[Hen88] M. HENNESY (1988), **Algebraic Theory of Processes**, The MIT press.

[Hoa85] C.A.R. HOARE (1985), **Communicating Sequential Processes**, Prentice-Hall.

[JM88] F. JAHANIAN, A. MOK (1988), Modecharts: a specification language for real-time systems, *IEEE Transactions on Software Engineering*, to appear.

[Lam83] L. LAMPORT (1983), Specifying concurrent program modules, *ACM Transactions on Programming Languages and Systems*, Vol. **5**, No. **2**, pp. 190-222.

[Lam86] L. LAMPORT (1986), "Specification Simplified", Technical Report, DEC Systems Research Center, Alamaden.

[Lyn90] N. LYNCH (1990), "Multivalued Possibilities Mappings", this volume.

[LS84] S.S. LAM, A.U. SHANKAR (1984), Protocol verification via projection, *IEEE Transactions on Software Engineering*, Vol. **10**, No. **4**, pp. 325–342.

[LT87] N. LYNCH, M. TUTTLE (1987), "Hierarchical correctness proofs for distributed algorithms", Proc. 6th ACM Sympos. Principles of Distributed Computing (PODC), pp. 137–151, ACM.

[Mer90] M. MERRIT (1990), "Completeness Theorems for Automata", this volume.

[Mil71] R. MILNER (1971), "An algebraic definition of simulation between programs", Proc. 2nd Joint Confer. on Artificial Intelligence, BCS, pp. 481–489.

[Mil80] R. MILNER (1980), **A Calculus of Communicating Systems**, LNCS **94**, Springer-Verlag, New York.

[Mil83] R. MILNER (1983), Calculi for Synchrony and Asynchrony, *Theoretical Computer Science*, Vol. **25**, pp. 267–310.

[Mil89] R. MILNER (1989), **Communication and Concurrency**, Prentice Hall.

[MP81] Z. MANNA, A. PNUELI (1981), "Verification of Concurrent Programs: The Temporal Framework", *The Correctness Problem in Computer Science* (R. S. Boyer, J. S. Moore, eds.), pp. 215–274, Academic Press.

[MP84] Z. MANNA, A. PNUELI (1984), Adequate Proof Principles for Invariance and Liveness Properties of Concurrent Programs, *Science of Computer Programming*, Vol. **4**, pp. 257–289.

[Nic87] R. DE NICOLA (1987), Extensional Equivalences for Transition Systems, *Acta Informatica*, Vol. **24**, pp. 211–237.

[NH84] R. DE NICOLA, M. HENNESSY (1984), Testing Equivalences for Processes, *Theoretical Computer Science*, Vol. **34**, pp. 83–133.

[SdeR87] F. STOMP, W.P. DE ROEVER (1987), "A correctness proof of a distributed minimum-weight spanning tree algorithm", Proc. 7th IEEE International Conference on Distributed Computer Systems (ICDCS), pp. 440–448.

[Sto89] F. STOMP (1989), Design and Verification of Distributed Network Algorithms: Foundations and Applications, Ph.D. thesis, Eindhoven University of Technology.

[WLL88] J. WELCH, L. LAMPORT, N. LYNCH (1988), "A lattice-structured proof of a minimum spanning tree algorithm", Proc. ACM Symposium on Principles of Distributed Computing (PODC).

Index of notation

$dom(\cdot)$ 781
$ran(\cdot)$ 781
$A^\star$ 781
A^ω 781
$A^\dagger$ 781
$\cdot \prec \cdot$ 781
$\mathcal{A}(\cdot)$ 781, 782
Var 781
Σ 781
$Tm(\Sigma)$ 781
$L(\Sigma)$ 781
$p[e/x])$ 781
$FV(\cdot)$ 781
$\mathbf{A}$ 781
$\mathcal{S}$ 781
$\sigma\{a/x\}$ 781
$\mathcal{A}$ 782
$\mathcal{A}^l$ 782
$\mathcal{A}^g$ 782
δ 782
$\uparrow$ 782
$\mathcal{A}_{xyz\ldots}$ 782
$\mathcal{V}$ 782
$\mathcal{E}$ 782
$\partial_s(\cdot)$ 782
$\partial_t(\cdot)$ 782
$^\bullet.$ 782, 796
$.^\bullet$ 782, 796
I 782
$\mathcal{L}$ 782
UTS 782
π 782, 792
$V;\pi$ 782
$\mathcal{L}_g(\cdot)$ 782
$Seq(\cdot)$ 782
behavior 782
computation 782
ρ 782
$\uparrow(\cdot)$ 783, 799
$\downarrow(\cdot)$ 783, 799
$\multimap \cdot \multimapinv^{o}$ 783
partial computation 783
$\xrightarrow{a}$ 783, 792
$\multimap \cdot \multimapinv$ 783
$\cdot$ after $\cdot$ 783
$\mathcal{G}$ 783
τ 784
$\mathcal{H}$ 784
$\cdot \|_\gamma \cdot$ 784
$h(\cdot)$ 784
$\mathcal{C}$ 785
$\sqsubseteq$ 786, 792
$stable(\cdot)$ 787, 799
$\cdot$ fails $\cdot$ 787
$\sqsubsetsim$ 787
$\hookrightarrow_{\mathsf{R}}$ 789
$\hookrightarrow$ 789
$\mathcal{A}ct(\Sigma)$ 792
$\mathcal{G}act(\Sigma)$ 792, 793
$\mathcal{L}act(\Sigma)$ 792, 793
$[\![\cdot]\!]^{\mathbf{A}}$ 792
TS 792
$\mathcal{L}^t(\cdot)$ 792, 796
$\mathcal{L}^a(\cdot)$ 792, 796
$^t.$ 792
$\mathbf{A} \models \pi^0 \sqsubseteq \pi^1$ 792
$Pvar$ 793
$Svar$ 793
$Chan$ 793
$\pi^0 \parallel \pi^1$ 794
$Enc(\cdot, enc)$ 795
$Hide(\cdot, V)$ 795
As 796
$\mathcal{H}is$ 796
h 796
set labelling 796
λ 796
$[\lambda^0, \lambda^1]$ 796
$[\lambda^0, \lambda^1]_\sigma$ 796
$^t[\lambda^0, \lambda^1]$ 796
safe 797
sure 797
history determined 797
$enabled(\cdot)$ 799
cover 799
FO − REF 800
$\vdash_{\mathsf{FO-REF}}$ 800
local correctness 801
leads to 801
SACO 802
comes from 803
SUHD 803